Psychopathology and Life

A Dimensional Approach

Christopher A. Kearney
University of Nevada, Las Vegas

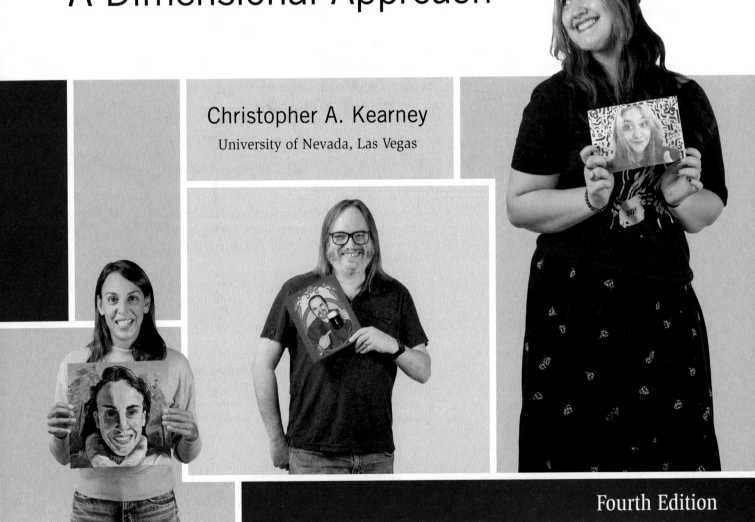

Fourth Edition

Cengage

Australia • Brazil • Canada • Mexico • Singapore • United Kingdom • United States

***Psychopathology and Life: A Dimensional Approach*, 4th edition**
Christopher A. Kearney

SVP, Product: Erin Joyner

VP, Product: Thais Alencar

Portfolio Product Director: Laura Ross

Portfolio Product Manager: Marta Healey-Gerth

Product Assistant: Fantasia Mejia

Learning Designer: Natasha Allen

Senior Content Manager: Tangelique Williams-Grayer

Digital Project Manager: Scott Diggins

Director, Product Marketing: Neena Bali

Product Marketing Manager: Chris Walz

Content Acquisition Analyst: Deanna Ettinger

Production Service: MPS Limited

Designer: Sara Greenwood

Cover Image Source: Metroland Photo/ © Cengage

Interior image Source: Metroland Photo/ © Cengage

Library of Congress Control Number: 2022914778

ISBN: 978-0-357-79784-6

Loose-leaf Edition:
ISBN: 978-0-357-79785-3

Cengage
200 Pier 4 Boulevard
Boston, MA 02210
USA

Cengage is a leading provider of customized learning solutions.
Our employees reside in nearly 40 different countries and serve digital learners in 165 countries around the world. Find your local representative at **www.cengage.com.**

To learn more about Cengage platforms and services, register or access your online learning solution, or purchase materials for your course, visit **www.cengage.com.**

Printed in the United States of America
Print Number: 01 Print Year: 2023

To my wife, Kimberlie, and my children, Derek and Claire, for their great patience and support.

—Christopher A. Kearney

About the Author

Courtesy of Christopher Kearney

Christopher A. Kearney, Ph.D., is Distinguished Professor of Psychology at the University of Nevada, Las Vegas. He is a Fellow of the American Psychological Association, a licensed clinical psychologist, and the author of numerous journal articles, book chapters, and books. He has also published a work on general child psychopathology, *Casebook in Child Behavior Disorders* (Cengage). Dr. Kearney has received several awards for his research, teaching, and mentoring, including the Harry Reid Silver State Research Award among others. In addition to his clinical and research endeavors, Dr. Kearney works closely with school districts and mental health agencies.

Brief Contents

Contents

6 Somatic Symptom and Dissociative Disorders 145

7 Depressive and Bipolar Disorders and Suicide 177

Special Features

8 Eating Disorders 217

Special Features

12 Schizophrenia and Other Psychotic Disorders 349

13 Developmental and Disruptive Behavior Disorders 381

Special Features

14 Neurocognitive Disorders 421

Preface

The goal of this text was to create something different for students. The text is designed to appeal to students by helping them understand that symptoms of psychological problems occur in many people in different ways. The text avoids characterizing mental disorders from a "yes–no" or "us–them" perspective and focuses instead on how such problems affect many people to varying degrees in their everyday lives. In essence, the text illustrates how psychopathology is really about the struggles that all of us face in our lives to some extent. This approach is represented in the title: *Psychopathology and Life.*

Psychopathology is one of the most popular courses on college campuses. Students are eager to learn about unusual behavior and how such behavior can be explained. Many students who take a psychopathology course crave a scientific perspective that can help prepare them well for graduate school and beyond. Other students take a psychopathology course because they are curious about themselves or people they know and thus seek application and relevance of the course information to their daily lives. This text is designed to appeal to both types of students. The material in the text not only reflects state-of-the-art thinking and research regarding mental disorders but also emphasizes several key themes that increase personal relevance. These themes include a dimensional and integrative perspective, a consumer-oriented perspective, and emphases on prevention and cultural diversity. Personal relevance is also achieved by providing information to reduce the stigma of mental disorder; by illustrating comprehensive models of mental disorder that include biological, psychological, and other risk factors; and by employing various pedagogical aids, visually appealing material, and technological utilities.

A Dimensional and Integrative Perspective

A focus on how psychopathology is a key part of life comes about in this text in different ways. One main way is a focus on a *dimensional perspective toward mental disorder*. Thoughts, feelings, and behaviors associated with mental disorders are present, to some degree, in all of us. Everyone experiences some level of anxiety, sadness, odd physical symptoms, worry about sexual behavior, and memory problems from time to time, for example. The chapters of this text vividly illustrate how different mental disorders can be seen along a continuum of normal, mild, moderate, severe, and very severe emotions, thoughts, and behaviors. Examples along this continuum are also provided that parallel common scenarios people face, such as interactions with others and job interviews.

The dimensional perspective is discussed within the context of an integrative perspective that includes an extensive discussion of risk and protective factors for various mental disorders. Such factors include biological (e.g., genetic, neurochemical, brain changes), personality, psychological (e.g., cognitive, learning, trauma), interpersonal, family, cultural, evolutionary, and other domains. The text emphasizes a diathesis-stress model and provides sections that integrate risk factors to present comprehensive models of various mental disorders. The appendix of medical conditions with contributing psychological factors includes a biopsychosocial perspective to explain the interplay of physical symptoms with stress and other key contributing variables. Students should note that some material in the text could trigger strong emotions.

A Consumer-Oriented Perspective

This text is also designed to recognize the fact that today's student is very *consumer oriented*. Students expect texts to be relevant to their own lives and to deliver information about diagnostic criteria, epidemiological data, brain changes, and assessment instruments in visually appealing and technologically sophisticated ways. This text adopts a consumer approach in several ways. The chapters contain suggestions for those who are concerned that they or someone they know may have symptoms of a specific mental disorder. These suggestions also come with key questions one could ask to determine whether a problem may be evident. In addition, much of the material is geared toward a consumer approach. In the discussion of neurocognitive disorders such as Alzheimer's disease, for example, questions are provided that one could ask when considering placing a parent in long-term care.

The consumer orientation of this text is also prominent in the last chapter that covers topics such as becoming a mental health professional, becoming a client in therapy, treatments available at the community level such as self-help groups, and how to judge a research article, among other topics. Throughout the chapters, special attention is also focused on issues of gender, ethnicity, law and ethics, and violence in separate boxes. In addition, separate sections specifically address symptoms of mental disorder in college students. Visually appealing examples are offered of a dimensional model for each major mental disorder, brain figures, and engaging tables and charts to more easily convey important information. The text is also linked to many online resources and contains 15 chapters, which fits nicely into a typical 15-week semester.

Several pedagogical aids are also included to assist students during their learning process. The chapters are organized in a similar fashion throughout, beginning with initial sections on normal and unusual behavior and followed by discussions of features and epidemiology, stigma, causes and prevention, assessment, treatment, and prognosis. The chapters contain section summaries and review questions at periodic intervals to help students check their understanding of what they just learned. Bold key terms are placed throughout the chapters and corresponding definitions are placed in the margin. *What Do You Think?* questions appear after the chapter-opening case study, which help students focus on important aspects of the case. Final comments are also provided at the end of each chapter to link material to previous and future chapters. Broad-based thought questions are also at the end of each chapter to challenge students to apply what they have learned to their daily lives. The writing style of the text is designed to be easy to follow and to succinctly convey key information.

Prevention

Another important theme of this text is *prevention*. Most college students function well in their environment, but everyone has some level of risk for psychological dysfunction or distress. Research-based ways to prevent the onset of psychological problems are thus emphasized throughout this text. Specific sections are offered on prevention that provide a detailed discussion of risk factors for mental disorder and how these risk factors could be minimized. A discussion of protective factors and strategies is also provided that could be nurtured during one's life to prevent psychological problems. Examples include anxiety and stress management, emotional regulation, appropriate coping, healthy diet, and adaptive parenting.

Much of the discussion in this area focuses on primary and secondary prevention, which has great appeal for students. Many prevention programs target those who have not developed a mental disorder or who may be at risk due to individual or environmental factors. A focus on prevention helps students understand what they could do to avert problematic symptoms or to seek help before such symptoms become more severe. Prevention material in the text also focuses on tertiary prevention and relapse prevention, so students can understand what steps people can take to continue healthy functioning even after the occurrence of a potentially severe mental disorder. The prevention material in this text thus has broad appeal, relevance, and utility for students.

Cultural Diversity

Mental health professionals have made a more concerted effort to achieve greater cultural diversity in their research, to apply findings in laboratory settings to greater numbers of people, and to shine a spotlight on those who are traditionally underserved. These greater efforts are emphasized in this text. In addition to the special boxes on diversity, detailed information is provided about cultural syndromes; how symptoms and epidemiology may differ across cultural groups; how certain cultural factors may serve as risk and protective factors for various disorders; how diagnostic, assessment, and treatment strategies may need to be modified for different cultural groups; and how cultural groups may seek treatment or cope differently with symptoms of mental disorder.

The discussion of cultural diversity applies to various ethnic and racial groups, but diversity across individuals is represented in many other ways as well. This includes gender differences, sexual orientation, sociocultural factors, migrant populations, and changes in symptoms as people age from childhood to adolescence to adulthood to late adulthood. The emphasis on cultural and other types of diversity is consistent with a life-based approach for the text: Symptoms of mental disorder can occur in many people in many different ways in many life stages.

Stigma

A focus on a dimensional approach to mental disorder helps advance another key theme of this text, which is to *reduce stigma*. Stigma refers to socially discrediting people because of certain behaviors or attributes that may lead to them being seen as undesirable in some way. People with schizophrenia, for example, are often stigmatized as people who cannot function or who may even be dangerous. Adopting a dimensional perspective to mental disorder helps reduce inaccurate stereotypes and the stigma associated with many of these problems. You will also see throughout this text that people are emphasized first and a mental disorder second to reduce stigma. You will not encounter words or phrases such as *schizophrenics* or *bulimics* or *the learning disabled.* Instead, you will encounter phrases such as *people with schizophrenia, those with bulimia,* or *children with learning disorder.* Special sections on stigma are also provided throughout the chapters as well as boxes that contain information to dispel common myths about people with mental disorders that likely lead to negative stereotyping.

Clinical Cases and Narratives

The dimensional perspective and a drive to reduce stigma are enhanced as well by extensive use of clinical cases and personal narratives throughout the text. Clinical cases are presented in chapters that describe a particular mental disorder and are often geared toward cases to which most college students can relate. These cases then reappear throughout that chapter during discussions of features of that disorder as well as assessment and treatment strategies. Personal narratives are also included from people who have a mental disorder and who can discuss its symptoms and other features from direct experience. All of these cases reinforce the idea that symptoms of mental disorder are present to some degree in many people, perhaps including those easily recognized by a student as someone in their life.

The fourth edition contains many new and exciting changes. Ongoing research has adapted to the most recent edition of the *Diagnostic and Statistical Manual of Mental Disorders* (*DSM*), the *DSM-5-TR*. State-of-the-art research and citations are thus presented. The chapters remain aligned as they were previously to enhance teaching in a typical semester and to reflect empirical work that has been done for each set of disorders. *DSM-5-TR* criteria and other information are presented to help illuminate symptoms of mental disorders for students and to convey various dimensional aspects as well. Examples include continua based on severity, number of symptoms or behavioral episodes, body mass index, and personality traits, among many others.

The fourth edition also contains many boxes devoted to gender, diversity, violence, and law and ethics. In addition, separate sections involve how symptoms of mental disorders often manifest themselves in college students. Updated sections on stigma also illustrate a commitment to this important topic and present fascinating research with respect to others' views of someone with a mental disorder and treatment and other strategies that have been developed to reduce stigma toward those with mental disorder.

An important process as well has been a thorough review of the material to ensure that students continue to be presented with state-of-the-art research and most current thinking regarding mental disorders, including epidemiology. Many sections of the text have thus been redone or reworked to reflect new data, and hundreds of new citations have been added, most of which are very current. One thing that has not changed, however, is a deep devotion and commitment to this work and to students and their instructors.

A brief summary of key changes and additions for each chapter in the fourth edition is provided here. This is not an exhaustive list but provides some general guidance for those familiar with previous editions.

Chapter 1: Psychopathology and Life

- Revamped sections to reflect more contemporary examples
- Updated information on college students

Chapter 2: Perspectives on Psychopathology

- Updated citations and enhanced clarification of certain sections
- Enhanced boxes on violence, law and ethics, and gender

Chapter 3: Risk and Prevention of Mental Disorders

- Updated information on epidemiology
- Revamped sections on demographic risk factors and updated information on prevention

Chapter 4: Diagnosis, Assessment, and Study of Mental Disorders

- Updated information on all assessment information
- Updated information on culture and clinical assessment

Chapter 5: Anxiety, Obsessive-Compulsive, and Trauma-Related Disorders

- Updated and enhanced information regarding epidemiology and etiology
- Updated assessment and treatment information on college students

Chapter 6: Somatic Symptom and Dissociative Disorders

- Updated information regarding risk factors, assessment, and treatment
- Updated boxes on college students

Chapter 7: Depressive and Bipolar Disorders and Suicide

- Updated information, including features and epidemiology, on mood disorders
- Revamped sections on suicide, genetics, stigma, and prevention, among other sections

Chapter 8: Eating Disorders

- Updated information, including features and epidemiology, on eating disorders
- Revamped stigma and family sections and updates on college students

Chapter 9: Substance-Related Disorders

- Updated information throughout and especially with respect to tabular data
- Revamped sections on biological risk factors, stigma, and prevention

Chapter 10: Personality Disorders

- Updated information, including features and epidemiology, on personality disorders
- Revamped content on stigma, assessment, and long-term outcome of personality disorders, among other sections

Chapter 11: Sexual Dysfunctions, Paraphilic Disorders, and Gender Dysphoria

- Updated information, including features and epidemiology, on sexual dysfunctions, paraphilic disorders, and gender dysphoria
- Revamped sections on gender dysphoria to reflect contemporary thought.

Chapter 12: Schizophrenia and Other Psychotic Disorders

- Updated information, including features and epidemiology, on psychotic disorders
- Revamped sections on biological risk factors and long-term outcome of psychotic disorders, among other sections

Chapter 13: Developmental and Disruptive Behavior Disorders

- Updated information, including features and epidemiology, on developmental and disruptive behavior disorders
- Revamped sections on stigma, genetics, and other sections regarding developmental and disruptive behavior disorders

Chapter 14: Neurocognitive Disorders

- Updated information, including features and epidemiology, on neurocognitive disorders
- Revamped sections on genetics, medications, and long-term outcome for people with neurocognitive disorders

Chapter 15: Consumer Guide to Psychopathology

- Updated information on types of psychologists, process variables, treatment manuals, and lack of access to treatment
- Revamped sections on use of assessment and research, among other sections

Appendix: Stress-Related Problems

- New prevalence information and updates regarding risk factors
- Revised section on stressful events among college students

MindTap for Kearney's *Psychopathology and Life: A Dimensional Approach*, 4th edition

Today's leading online learning platform, MindTap for Kearney, *Psychopathology and Life,* 4th edition, gives you complete control of your course to craft a personalized, engaging learning experience that challenges students, builds confidence and elevates performance.

MindTap introduces students to core concepts from the beginning of your course using a simplified learning path that progresses from understanding to application and delivers access to eTextbooks, study tools, interactive media, auto-graded assessments and performance analytics.

Use MindTap for Kearney, *Psychopathology and Life,* 4e as-is, or personalize it to meet your specific course needs. You can also easily integrate MindTap into your Learning Management System (LMS).

Infuse for Kearney's *Psychopathology and Life: A Dimensional Approach*, 4th edition

Many instructors struggle with moving their courses online quickly and easily. Whether it's for a last-minute class or total change in course delivery, the ease with which you can organize your class and get yourself and your students acquainted with the materials is key. That's why Cengage built Infuse, the first and only embedded course kit that lives inside your Learning Management System (LMS). Cengage Infuse embeds your eTextbook, simple auto-graded comprehension checks, and end-of-chapter quizzes right in your LMS—no need to learn a new technology. As an instructor, you can customize the content and personalize student feedback, or use it as is to complement your existing course materials. From course setup to course management and tracking student progress, you and your students never have to leave your LMS to access high-quality, pre-organized publisher content. Cengage Infuse helps you get your course online in 15 minutes or less—and provides you with everything you need and nothing you don't—all within the LMS you already use: Blackboard, Canvas, Brightspace by D2L or Moodle. Learn more: https://www.cengage.com/cengage-infuse.

Supplements

Instructor resources for this product are available online. Instructor assets include an Instructor's Manual, Educator's Guide, PowerPoint® slides, and a test bank powered by Cognero®. Sign up or sign in at www.cengage.com to search for and access this product and its online resources.

Acknowledgments

Producing this text required the joint efforts of Cengage Learning and MPS Limited. Special thanks to Product Managers Colin Grover and Marta Healey-Gerth, and Content Manager Tangelique Williams-Grayer. Thanks as well to Lori Hazzard at MPS Limited for management of the text's production. Gratitude is also expressed for Fantasia Mejia, Product Assistant; Scott Diggins, Digital Product Manager; and Sara Greenwood, Creative Studios Designer. The work of Chris Walz, Product Marketing Manager, is much appreciated.

All of us thank those who agreed to contribute their personal stories for this text. Their narratives were essential to this text and helped bring the material to life.

In addition, all of us thank those who helped us create the supplements for this text, including the Instructor's Manual, Test Bank, and PowerPoint.

Finally, all of us thank the instructors who use this text, as well as the students who take their courses. As always, the team welcomes your comments and suggestions regarding the text.

Thank you!

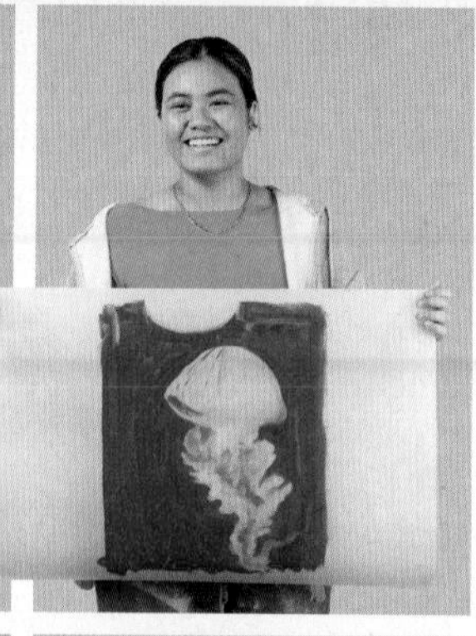
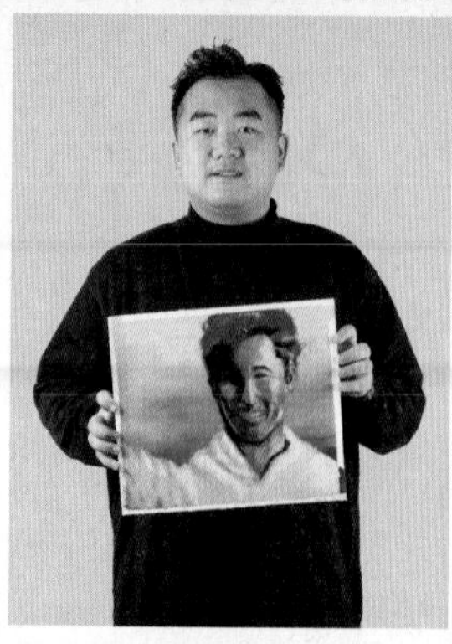

A special thank you to the artists, models, and Suffolk University for helping to turn our creative vision into a reality.

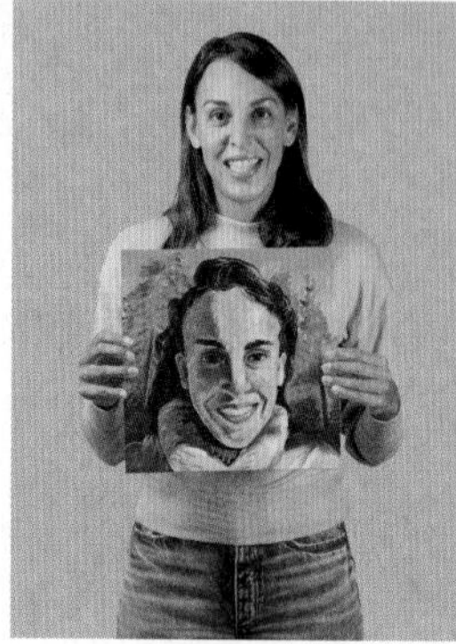

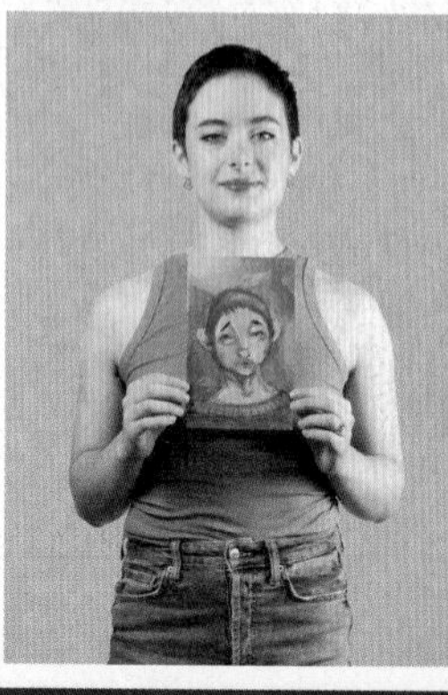

Psychopathology and Life 1

Learning Objectives

LO 1.1 Explain the importance of the terms psychopathology and mental disorder.

LO 1.2 Evaluate the strengths and limitations of deviance from the norm, difficulties in adaptation, and personal distress, and the combination of these factors in defining psychopathology.

LO 1.3 Justify the dimensional approach to understanding and explaining psychopathology.

LO 1.4 Create a timeline illustrating approaches to psychopathology from ancient times through the modern era.

LO 1.5 Compare and contrast key perspectives on psychopathology including dimensional, prevention, consumer, and multicultural.

LO 1.6 Discuss stigma associated with psychopathology including its origins and impact and how to fight it.

Case Travis

Travis is a 21-year-old college junior who has been struggling recently. He and his longtime girlfriend broke up two months ago, and he took this very hard. Travis and his girlfriend had been together for 17 months, and she was his first serious romantic relationship. However, the couple eventually became emotionally distant from one another and mutually decided to split following several arguments. Travis initially seemed fine after the breakup but then became a bit sullen and withdrawn about a week later. He began to miss a few classes and spent more time in his dorm room and on his computer.

Since the breakup several weeks ago, Travis seems to be getting worse each day. He rarely eats, has trouble sleeping, and stays in bed much of the day. He "zones out" by playing video games, watching television, or staring out the window for hours per day. Travis has lost about 10 pounds in recent weeks and looks tired and pale. He has also been drinking alcohol more in recent days. In addition, his classroom attendance has declined significantly, and he is in danger of failing his courses this semester.

Travis says little about the breakup or his feelings. His friends have tried everything they can think of to help him feel better, with no success. Travis generally declines their offers to go out, attend parties, or meet other women. He is not mean-spirited in his refusals to go out but rather just shakes his head. Travis's friends have become worried that Travis might hurt himself, but they cannot be with him all the time. They have decided that Travis should speak with someone at the psychological services center on campus and plan on escorting him there today.

Kiselev Andrey Valerevich/Shutterstock.com

What Do You Think?

1. Which of Travis's emotional or behavioral problems concern you the most? Why?
2. What do you think Travis should do?
3. What would you do if you had a friend who was experiencing difficulties like Travis?
4. What emotional or behavioral problems have you encountered in yourself or in others over the past year?
5. Are you surprised when people you know experience emotional or behavioral problems? Why or why not?

Introduction to Psychopathology

LO 1.1 Explain the importance of the terms psychopathology and mental disorder.

You and your classmates chose to take this course for many reasons. The course might be required, or perhaps you thought learning about deviant or unusual (psychopathological) behavior was intriguing. Or you might be interested in becoming a mental health professional and thought this course could help prepare you for such a career. Whatever the reason, you have likely known or will eventually know someone with a **mental disorder**. A mental disorder is a group of emotional (feelings), cognitive (thinking), or behavioral symptoms that cause distress or significant problems. About 29.2 percent of adults worldwide have had a mental disorder in their lifetime (Steel et al., 2014). Students often say that they know at least one person with a mental disorder. These students frequently say that they or an immediate family member—such as a parent, sibling, or child—had a disorder. A commonly reported disorder is depression, a problem that Travis seemed to be experiencing.

Psychopathology involves the scientific study of problematic feelings, thoughts, and behaviors associated with mental disorders. The term "psychopathology" replaces the terms "abnormal" and "abnormal psychology" to be less stigmatizing (refer to the later section on stigma) of people with mental disorders. This area of science is designed to evaluate, understand, predict, and prevent mental disorders and help those who are in distress. Psychopathology has implications for all of us. Everyone has feelings, thoughts, and behaviors, and occasionally these become a problem for us or for someone we know. Travis's situation at the beginning of the chapter represents some daily experiences people have with mental disorders. Some of us may also be asked to help a friend or sibling struggling with symptoms of a mental disorder. In addition, all of us are interested in knowing how to improve our mental health and how to prevent mental disorders so we can help family members and friends.

Psychopathology and Life provides information to help you recognize mental problems and understand how they develop. Methods used by professionals to prevent and treat mental distress and disorder are also explored. Knowing this material will not make you an expert, but it could make you a valuable resource.

Indeed, you will be better able to make informed decisions and direct yourself and others to appropriate sources of support and help. Information in Chapters 5 and 7, for example, describes how anxiety and depression affect health and behavior in yourself and others as well as ways of dealing with these common problems.

What Is a Mental Disorder?

LO 1.2 Evaluate the strengths and limitations of deviance from the norm, difficulties in adaptation, and personal distress, and the combination of these factors in defining psychopathology.

As mentioned earlier, a mental disorder is a group of emotional (feelings), cognitive (thinking), or behavioral symptoms that cause distress or significant problems. Psychopathology involves the scientific study of problematic feelings, thoughts, and behaviors associated with mental disorders. At first glance, defining problematic or psychopathological behavior seems fairly straightforward: Isn't problematic or psychopathological behavior simply behavior that is not normal? In a way, yes, but then we first must know what "normal" behavior is. We often refer to normal behavior as that which characterizes most people. One normal behavior for most people is to leave home in the morning to go to school or work and to interact with others. If a person was so afraid of leaving home that they stayed inside for many weeks or months, this might be considered psychopathological—the behavior differs from what most people do.

But what do we mean by *most* people? How many people must engage in a certain behavior for the behavior to be considered normal? And which group of people should we use to decide what is normal—women, men, people of a certain ethnicity, everyone? Clearly, defining normal and psychopathological behavior is more complicated than it might appear. Consider the case of Treva Throneberry.

Case Treva Throneberry

Treva Throneberry was born in Texas. Her sisters describe their family as a peaceful and loving one, but Treva paints a different picture. At 15 years old, Treva accused her father of sexual molestation. She later recanted her accusation but was removed from her parents' home and placed in foster care. At 17 years old, Treva ran away from her foster home and was found wandering alone by a roadside before spending time in a mental hospital. A year later, Treva moved into an apartment but soon vanished from town. Years later, she was charged by Vancouver police with fraud and forgery. Her fingerprints matched those of Treva Throneberry, who was born 30 years before, but Treva said she was an 18-year-old named Brianna Stewart. She had been attending Evergreen High School in Vancouver for the past two years, where everyone knew her as Brianna Stewart. This was the basis for the fraud and forgery charges.

Since her disappearance from Texas, Treva had been known by many other names in places across the country. In each town, she initially presented herself as a runaway 15- or 16-year-old in need of shelter who then left suddenly before her new identity turned 18 years old. She would then move to another town and start again as a 15- or 16-year-old. Her foster care mother said Treva could not envision living beyond age 18.

Treva was examined by a psychiatrist and found competent to stand trial. At her trial, Treva represented herself. She would not plea-bargain because she insisted she was Brianna Stewart and not Treva Throneberry. She argued in court that she was not insane and did not have a mental disorder that caused her to distort reality or her identity. Despite her claims, however, Treva was convicted of fraud and sentenced to a three-year jail term. She continues to insist she is Brianna Stewart.

You may think Treva's behavior is psychopathological, but why? To address this question, consider one of three criteria commonly used to determine whether an emotion, thought, or behavior is psychopathological: (1) *deviance from the norm*, (2) *difficulties adapting to life's demands* or difficulties functioning effectively (including dangerous behavior), and (3) *experience of personal distress*.

Deviance from the Norm

Treva's actions are certainly not typical of most teenagers or young adults. Because Treva's behavior is so different from others—*so different from the norm*—her behavior would be considered psychopathological. Defining psychopathological behavior based on its difference or deviance from the norm is common and has some mass appeal; most people would agree Treva's behaviors are psychopathological. Do you? Mental health professionals also rely on deviance from the norm to define psychopathological behavior, but they often do so *statistically* by measuring how frequently a behavior occurs among people. Less frequent or less probable behaviors are considered to be psychopathological or statistically deviant. Suddenly disappearing from home and assuming a new identity, as Treva did, is an infrequent behavior that is statistically far from normal behavior.

An objective, statistical method of defining psychopathological behavior involves determining the probability of a behavior for a population. Note the graph in **Figure 1.1**. This graph shows the level of physical activity (rating of 0–100) among 10-year-olds during a

Figure 1.1 A Statistical Method of Defining Psychopathology.

Extremely low and extremely high levels of activity are considered psychopathological from a statistical perspective.

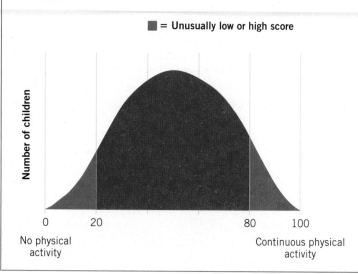

■ = Unusually low or high score

Number of children

0 20 80 100

No physical activity

Continuous physical activity

30-minute recess period. In this graph, 0 = no physical activity and 100 = continuous physical activity. The left axis of the graph shows how many children received a certain activity score: almost all children received scores in the 20 to 80 range. Based on this distribution of scores, we might statistically define and label the physical activity of children scoring 0 to 19 or 81 to 100 as unusual or "psychopathological." Note that extremely low *and* extremely high scores are considered unusual or "psychopathological." Some physical activity is the norm, but too little or too much is not. A mental health professional might thus focus on underactive and overactive children in her scientific studies.

Statistical deviance from the norm is attractive to researchers because it offers clear guidelines for identifying emotions, thoughts, or behaviors as normal or psychopathological. However, this approach has some disadvantages. One major disadvantage is that people who differ significantly from an average score are technically "psychopathological" or "disordered." But does this make sense for all behaviors or characteristics? Think about intelligence. Using a deviance-from-the-norm criterion, people who score extremely high on an intelligence test would be considered psychopathological! But high intelligence is certainly not a disorder. In fact, high intelligence is valued in our society and often associated with success instead of failure. A deviance approach to defining psychopathology is thus easy to apply but may fall short for determining what is psychopathological.

Library of Congress Prints and Photographs Division [LC-DIG-hec-28667]

Using a statistical definition of deviance, Albert Einstein would be considered "psychopathological" because of his high intelligence.

Another disadvantage of the deviance-from-the-norm criterion is that cultures differ in how they define what is normal. One culture might consider an extended rest period during the workday to be normal, and another culture might not. Likewise, symptoms of mental disorders differ from culture to culture. We often consider self-critical comments and expressions of sadness to be indicators of depression, but such behaviors are not always viewed the same way in East Asia (refer to **Focus On Diversity: Emotion and Culture**). This is important for mental health professionals to consider when treating someone. Mental health professionals must recognize their cultural biases and refrain from applying these views inappropriately to someone from another culture. Mental health professionals must also understand that deviance within a culture can change over time—what was considered deviant or unusual 50 years ago may be acceptable today.

A final problem with the deviance-from-the-norm criterion is that deciding the statistical point at which a behavior is psychopathological can be arbitrary and subject to criticism. The method does not tell us what the correct cutoff should be. Refer again to Figure 1.1. If a child has an activity score of 81, she might be considered psychopathological. Realistically, however, is a score of 80 (normal) much different from a score of 81 (psychopathological)? Where should the cutoff be, and how do we know if that cutoff point is meaningful?

Difficulties Adapting to Life Demands

Because several problems exist with the deviance-from-the-norm criterion, other judgments are sometimes made to define psychopathological behavior. One key judgment often made by mental health professionals is whether a behavior interferes with a person's ability to function effectively. One could argue that Treva's behaviors greatly interfered with her ability to function effectively. She continued to behave in ways that prevented her from adopting an adult role and that eventually landed her in jail. In the case of Travis presented at the beginning of the chapter, his depression kept him from interacting with others and could even lead to self-harm. Indeed, *dangerous behavior* toward oneself or others clearly interferes with an ability to function effectively.

Everyone occasionally has feelings of sadness and discouragement, especially after a tough event such as a breakup. Most people, however, are eventually able to focus better on school, work, or home regardless of these feelings. For people like Travis, however, feelings of sadness or discouragement become maladaptive. A **maladaptive behavior** is one that interferes with a person's life, including ability to care for oneself, have good relationships with others, and function well at school or at work. Feelings of sadness and discouragement, which at first can be normal, can lead to maladaptive behaviors such as trouble getting out of bed, concentrating, or thinking.

Think about Sasha, who has been worried since her mother was diagnosed with breast cancer last year. Her mother is currently doing well, and the cancer seems to be in remission, but Sasha cannot stop worrying that her mother's cancer will return. These worries cause Sasha to be so anxious and upset that she cannot concentrate on her schoolwork, and she finds herself irritable and unable to spend much time with her friends. Sasha's worries and behavior, which were understandable at first, have become maladaptive. According to the difficulties-adapting-to-life-demands criterion, Sasha's behaviors might be considered psychopathological. Her continual thoughts about her mother's health, coupled with irritability and trouble concentrating, prevent her from functioning well as a family member, student, and friend. In fact, Sasha may benefit from some professional intervention at this point. In this case, the focus is not on deviance or norms but on the extent to which her behavior interferes with daily functioning.

One advantage of this functioning approach is that problems in daily living—as in school, work, or relationships—often prompt people to seek treatment. Unfortunately, the difference between good functioning and maladaptive behavior is not always easy to measure. In addition, the difference between good functioning and maladaptive behavior differs from person to person. Another problem with this criterion is that different people may view a certain behavior differently. Sasha's family members might perceive her behaviors as caring and thoughtful, but one of her professors might perceive her behavior as laziness. Mental health professionals often struggle with how to determine whether a person's behavior is maladaptive or truly interferes with a person's daily functioning.

Focus On Diversity

Emotion and Culture

Emotional experience and expression are clearly influenced by culture (Lagattuta, 2014). Self-worth is promoted in the United States, an individualist culture, through praise, encouragement, and awards for personal accomplishments. As a result, Americans may be more self-focused and individual-achievement oriented. In contrast, non-Western collectivist cultures, such as in East Asia, prioritize modesty, social obligations, and interpersonal harmony. People are expected to fit in with others and avoid behaviors that bring individual attention or that create group conflict. An American student asked to present a top-notch paper to her class may quickly accept this invitation and invite friends to her presentation. A Japanese student, however, may be less receptive to such a prospect. The American student came from a culture that promotes individual achievement and recognition, whereas the Japanese student came from a culture that promotes group belongingness and not individual recognition.

Guang Niu/Getty Images News/Getty Images

Public expressions of anger are less common, and more likely to be seen as deviant, in certain cultures.

Consider another example. Expression of self-criticism is more typical of East Asian culture and does not necessarily indicate a mental disorder. In addition, expressions of depression are more likely labeled psychopathological by Americans, but anger is more likely labeled psychopathological by East Asians. Expressions of anxiety—especially about fitting in with a group—may be more common or normal in East Asians, but expressions of anger—especially when asserting one's individual rights—may be more common or normal in Americans. If deviance from the norm is used to define psychopathology, then cultural identity must be considered. An American psychologist should not, for example, apply her norms regarding emotional expression to someone from East Asia.

Another problem with the criterion of difficulties adapting to life demands is that people may engage in odd behaviors but experience little interference in daily functioning. Consider Henry, a telemarketer living alone. He never leaves home because of fear of contamination by airborne radioactivity and bacterial spores released by a government agency. Henry does not consider himself dysfunctional because he works at home, gets things delivered to him, and communicates to friends or family via telephone and email. Most would agree Henry limits his options by not leaving home and that his thinking is quite peculiar and unrealistic. But is Henry experiencing interference in daily functioning if he is happy the way things are for him? Hasn't he adapted well to his environment? Does he truly need treatment?

Experience of Personal Distress

Maladaptive behavior is not always a source of concern for people like Henry, so they may not seek treatment. Therefore, another criterion used by mental health professionals to define psychopathological behavior is experience of personal distress. Consider Margarette, who has unrealistic fears of entering tunnels or bridges while traveling by car or bus. She is extremely distressed by this and recognizes that these fears are baseless. Unfortunately, Margarette must travel through tunnels or bridges because of where she lives. She is desperate for treatment of these unrealistic fears because they cause her so much distress. In Margarette's case, extreme levels of distress created by a behavior such as fear may be important for defining her behavior as psychopathological. In other cases, a behavior could cause great distress for others, which may prompt them to initiate treatment for a person. A child with highly disruptive behavior in school may not be particularly distressed about his actions but may be referred to treatment by his parents.

A personal-distress definition of psychopathology has strengths and weaknesses. Personal distress is a hallmark feature of many mental disorders and often prompts people to seek treatment. In addition, most people can accurately assess whether they experience significant emotional and behavioral problems and can share this information when asked. However, some people (like Henry, mentioned earlier) do not report much personal distress even when exhibiting unusual behavior. And, even if a person *is* distressed, no clear guidelines exist for establishing a cutoff point that indicates a psychopathological behavior. How much personal distress is too much personal distress?

Defining Psychopathology

These three approaches to defining psychopathology have several advantages and limitations. A successful approach to defining psychopathology has thus been to combine the perspectives to merge their advantages and minimize their limitations (refer to **Table 1.1**). At least one of three characteristics must be present for psychopathology to be defined as such. Emotions, thoughts, or behaviors may be psychopathological when they

- violate social norms or are statistically deviant (like Treva's unusual behavior, insisting she was another person),
- interfere with functioning (like Sasha's worries that kept her from performing well at school), or
- cause great personal distress (like Margarette's fears of tunnels and bridges).

Agreeing on a definition of "mental disorder" is important to **psychopathologists**, who study mental

Table 1.1 Definitions of Psychopathology

Definition	Advantages	Limitations
Deviance from the norm	• We use our own judgment or gut feeling. • Once statistical or objective cutoff scores are established, they are easy to apply.	• Different cultures have different ideas about what normal behavior is. • "Statistically deviant" behaviors may be valued (e.g., high intelligence). • Arbitrary cutoffs (e.g., a score of 80 may not be much different than a score of 81).
Difficulties adapting to life's demands	• Typically easy to observe if someone is having difficulty. • Often prompts people to seek psychological treatment.	• Unclear who determines impairment or whether a consensus about impairment is required. • Thresholds for impairment not always clear.
Experience of personal distress	• Hallmark of many forms of mental disorder. • Individuals may be able to accurately report this.	• Some psychological problems are not associated with distress. • Thresholds or cutoffs for distress are not always clear.

problems to understand how disorders develop and continue and how they can be prevented or treated. A lack of consensus on a definition of psychopathology can have adverse consequences. Consider intimate partner violence (IPV), a significant problem in the United States. Much research has been conducted by psychologists and other mental health professionals to identify causes of IPV so effective treatments can be designed. Some researchers, however, define IPV as physical violence, whereas others work from a broader definition that includes physical, emotional, or sexual violence against an intimate partner. A standard or consistent definition of IPV is important because individuals who are physically violent against a partner may differ from those who are emotionally or sexually violent. Likewise, individuals using one form of violence may differ from those using multiple forms of violence against intimate partners. If so, treatments that are effective for one type of perpetrator may not be effective for other types of perpetrators. Varying definitions of a problem can thus impede our understanding of psychopathology.

Michael Blann/Digital Vision/Jupiter Images

This man has not left his home in two years, but he functions fairly normally and is not distressed. Is his behavior psychopathological?

Dimensions Underlying Mental Disorders Are Relevant to Everyone

LO 1.3 Justify the dimensional approach to understanding and explaining psychopathology.

The discussion to this point might suggest a person's behavior is either psychopathological or not, but this is not really so. Many experts view the psychopathology of emotions, thoughts, or behaviors as a matter of degree, not of kind. In other words, *emotions, thoughts, and behaviors associated with mental disorders are present, to some degree, in all of us*. This statement may seem strange or even shocking to you at first, but let's explore it a little more. Psychopathological behaviors are not simply present or absent but exist along a *continuum* in everyone to some degree. Think about motor coordination, anxiety, or sadness. Each characteristic is present to some degree in everyone at different times. We all have some degree of coordination, and we all become anxious or sad at times. These characteristics may also change over time—it's likely you are more coordinated now than you were at age 5! Different people also show different levels of these characteristics—you may know people who tend to be more anxious or sad than others.

Deciding whether a behavior is different or deviant from the norm is a matter of degree. Consider the earlier example about children's activity level—children may be underactive, overactive, and even hyperactive. Deciding whether a behavior is maladaptive also is a matter of degree. Some students concerned about their parents' health cope better than others. Even personal distress is displayed in different degrees. Some people are much more distressed about driving through tunnels than others. All these differences make us unique in some way, which is a good thing. The important thing to remember is that anxiety, sadness, anger, and other emotions and behaviors can be best described along a dimension or continuum from extremely low to extremely high levels. Sometimes we do make pronouncements about people who are "anxious" or "depressed," but this is just a convention of language. These features—like all emotions, thoughts, and behaviors—exist on a continuum. The **Continuum of Emotions, Cognitions, and Behaviors** is an example of the full range of emotions, thoughts, and behaviors that might follow from problems in college. Think about where Travis might be on this continuum.

The idea that emotions, thoughts, and behaviors exist in varying degrees on a continuum in people has important implications. When a mental health professional evaluates an individual for symptoms of mental disorder, these three dimensions—emotion, thought, and behavior—figure prominently. Various forms of mental disorder comprise emotions such as anxious or depressed mood, thoughts such as excessive worry, and behaviors such as avoidance of others or hyperactivity.

Continuum of Emotions, Cognitions, and Behaviors

	Normal	Mild
Emotions	Good alertness and positive emotional state.	Feeling sad or down temporarily, but not for long.
Cognitions	"I'm not getting the grades I want this semester, but I'll keep trying to do my best."	"I'm struggling at school this semester. I wish I could study better, or I'll fail."
Behaviors	Going to classes and studying for the next round of tests. Talking to professors.	Going to classes with some trouble studying. Less contact with others.

To explore this continuum idea more deeply, consider **Figure 1.2**. Ricardo started a job as a financial analyst six months ago and has been feeling anxious, worried, and overwhelmed for the past three weeks. His overall mood, or *emotional state*, has been highly anxious—he has great difficulty eating, sleeping, and interacting with friends. His *cognitive style* can be characterized by intense worry—almost all of his thoughts involve what he is doing wrong at his new job and fear that his coworkers and friends will discover the difficult time he is having at work. Because of his anxiety and worry, Ricardo has started to avoid coworkers and friends. This avoidance *behavior* is causing problems for Ricardo, however, because he must meet with clients almost every day.

Consider Yoko as well. Yoko is a young adult with many symptoms related to anxiety. After college, she was hired as a writer for a large software company. Yoko has dealt with bouts of anxious mood for most of her life—she almost always feels "on edge" and sometimes has physical symptoms that suggest her body is "on high alert," such as rapid heartbeat, muscle tension, and sweating. These anxiety symptoms worry Yoko, and she often wonders if something is physically wrong with her. Because of her job, however, Yoko can work at home and spends most days without much human contact. This suits Yoko fine because she has never felt completely comfortable around other people and prefers to be alone. Her job requires her to meet with her boss only at the beginning and end of each project. Yoko can tolerate this relatively infrequent contact without much difficulty. Her preference and choice to be alone most of the time therefore does not cause major problems for her.

The combination of psychological symptoms exhibited by Ricardo characterizes social anxiety disorder, which is discussed in Chapter 5. Clearly, though, the emotions, thoughts, and behaviors associated with this disorder exist on a continuum. As this example illustrates, mental disorders include characteristics found among most, if not all, people. Only when levels of these characteristics cross a threshold—when they are statistically deviant, associated with maladaptiveness, or cause great distress—are they considered psychopathological. At one time or another, you have certainly felt anxious, had worrisome thoughts, or had the desire to be alone—similar emotions and thoughts, and their accompanying behaviors, are present to some degree in all of us. In Ricardo's case, however, the degree to which these features have been present over the past three weeks hinders his daily life.

The **Continuum of Emotions, Cognitions, and Behaviors** visually depicts this dimensional perspective and focuses on several important features of psychopathology. Each dimension of psychopathology is shown along a continuum, be it *emotional* (e.g., anxious mood),

Moderate	Mental Disorder—less severe	Mental Disorder—more severe
Feeling sad, but a strong positive experience such as a good grade could lift mood.	Intense sadness most of the day with some trouble concentrating and some loss of appetite.	Extreme sadness all the time with great trouble concentrating and complete loss of appetite.
"These bad grades really hurt. This may set me back for a while. I'm really worried."	"I'm so worried about these grades that my stomach hurts. I don't know what to do.	"These bad grades just show what a failure I am at everything. There's no hope; I'm not doing anything today."
Skipping a few classes and feeling somewhat unmotivated to study. Avoiding contact with professors and classmates.	Skipping most classes and unable to maintain eye contact with others. Strong lack of motivation.	Unable to get out of bed, eat, or leave home. Lack of energy and frequent crying.

cognitive (e.g., worry intensity), or *behavioral* (e.g., avoidance of others) features. Other factors associated with psychopathology can be understood from a dimensional perspective as well. The degree to which one is distressed or experiences interference in daily functioning, for example, can be represented on a continuum. As Figure 1.2 shows, Ricardo and Yoko show similar levels of anxious mood, worry intensity, and avoidance behavior. On a scale of 0 (none) to 100 (extremely high), their anxious mood can be rated 85 (very high), their worry intensity can be rated 50 (moderate), and their avoidance can be rated 70 (high). In Yoko's case, however, these symptoms are associated with *lower levels of distress* (rating = 45) and *impairment* (rating = 50). Ricardo's level of dysfunction is severe enough to warrant a diagnosis of *social anxiety disorder*, a mental disorder that is characterized by avoidance of social situations, intense anxiety, and clinically significant impairment in functioning. Yoko, however, does not warrant this or any other anxiety diagnosis because her symptoms are not associated with significant impairment in daily functioning. Indeed, she copes with her symptoms so they do not cause her great personal distress.

You might be wondering whether the literature and research on anxiety disorders is relevant to Ricardo, Yoko, and even people with much lower levels of anxious symptoms. The answer is, yes, absolutely! Features of mental disorder, personal distress, and impairment are all dimensional or continuous in nature. In fact, research suggests that the same causal factors are responsible for these anxiety-related symptoms whether the symptoms are mild, moderate, or severe. Because everyone will experience some of the symptoms discussed in this textbook or know someone who has experienced or will experience these symptoms, psychopathology is relevant to all of us. Psychopathology is a part of life.

As you read this textbook and understand more that psychopathology is a part of life, you will identify with some of the symptoms and disorders that are discussed. This does *not* mean, however, that you or someone you know has a mental disorder. Some people, for example, are extremely neat and tidy and do not like things to be disorderly. In fact, they may feel uncomfortable when things are not lined up and organized. If this applies to you or someone you know, you may be tempted to believe you or the person has obsessive-compulsive disorder (Chapter 5). You might share an interest in neatness with someone who has obsessive-compulsive disorder, but you are probably able to tolerate this need for neatness and order and can function even if you were prevented from keeping everything organized. People with very high levels of a characteristic, like a need for neatness, are indeed at risk for developing a condition such as obsessive-compulsive disorder, especially under conditions of

Figure 1.2 Ricardo and Yoko.

Ricardo and Yoko have similar levels of anxious mood, worry intensity, and avoidance behavior. However, they differ on amount of distress experienced and levels of impairment created by their symptoms.

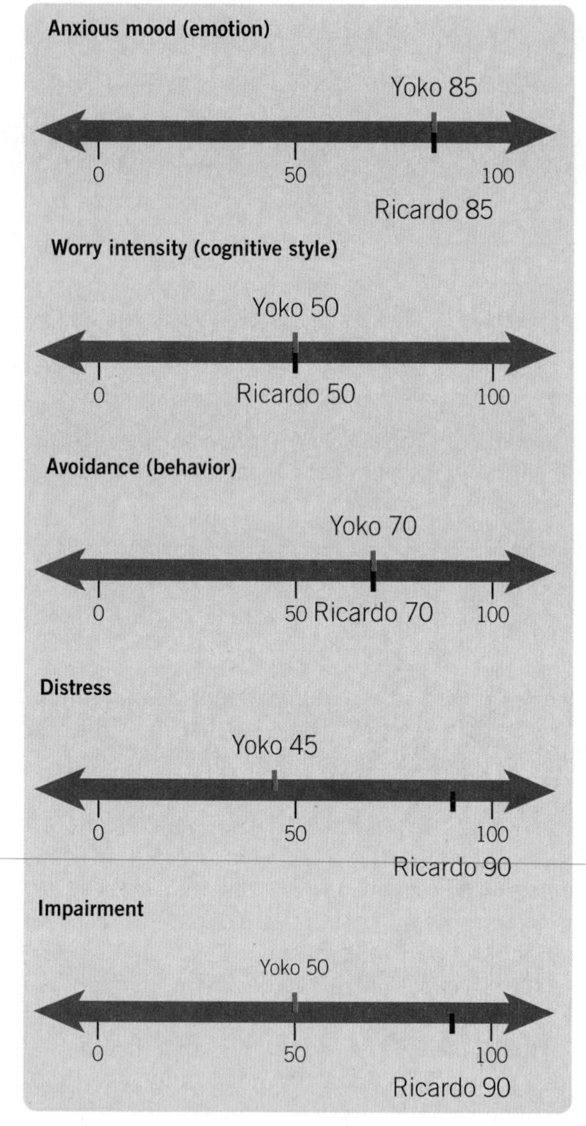

high stress. You will become more aware of who is vulnerable for a mental disorder and what can be done to maximize mental health. In doing so, the *prevention* of mental disorder, or how people can lower the probability of developing mental disorders, is also emphasized in this textbook.

Section Summary

- A mental disorder is a group of emotional (feelings), cognitive (thinking), or behavioral symptoms that cause distress or significant problems.

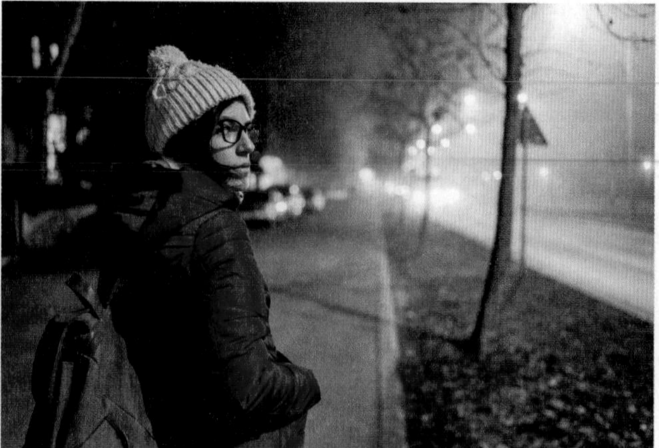

If a person remains highly fearful and distressed during a safe daily task, then their fear may be psychopathological.

- About one of four adults worldwide has had a mental disorder in their lifetime.
- Psychopathology is the scientific study of troublesome emotions, thoughts, and behaviors associated with mental disorders.
- Emotions, thoughts, and behaviors are considered psychopathological when they deviate greatly from the norm, interfere with daily functioning, or cause substantial personal distress.
- Psychopathologists study mental problems to consider how disorders develop and continue and how they can be prevented or alleviated.
- Psychopathological behaviors and characteristics are not necessarily only present or absent but actually occur to some degree in all of us.

Review Questions

1. Think about Treva. Using each of the three features that characterize psychopathological behavior, evaluate whether Treva's behavior would be considered psychopathological.
2. What are advantages and disadvantages of each characteristic of psychopathological behavior?
3. How might one merge these three characteristics into one definition?
4. What is meant by a dimension of psychopathology, and what are implications of this perspective?

History of Psychopathology

LO 1.4 Create a timeline illustrating approaches to psychopathology from ancient times through the modern era.

Knowing a little about the history of psychopathology will help you better understand some of the ideas and forces that have shaped how we view and treat mental

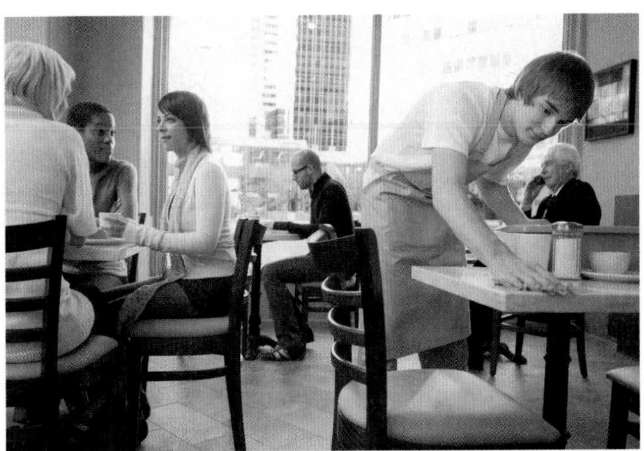
Fancy/Jupiter Images

Many adults worldwide experience a mental disorder every year. In addition, features of mental disorders are present, to some degree, in all of us.

disorders. The model a society uses to understand mental disorder will influence how that disorder is treated. Historically, not much emphasis was placed on research and the scientific method to understand mental health or well-being. In addition, ideas about mental health and disorders were often shaped by social, political, and economic forces. During times of political conservatism or economic hardship, for example, people sometimes emphasized individual and physical causes of psychopathology as well as biological treatments such as psychosurgery and medication. During times of political liberalism or economic strength, people sometimes emphasized environmental causes of psychopathology as well as psychological treatments or sociocultural approaches (Horwitz, 2020). In the next few sections, the development of psychopathology over time is examined, which helps us understand modern-day attitudes and conceptualizations of psychopathology as well as treatments.

Early Perspectives

Early writings of the Egyptians, Chinese, Greeks, and Hebrews identified patterns of, and concerns about, treating psychopathological behavior. Early theoreticians frequently attributed psychopathological behavior to supernatural causes such as possession by demons or evil spirits. The behavior was viewed spiritually, so the primary form of treatment was **exorcism**, or an attempt to cast out a spirit possessing an individual. Various exorcism techniques were used, including magic, noisemaking, incantations, prayer, flogging, starvation, and medicinal techniques or potions. These techniques were designed to make a person an unpleasant, uncomfortable, or painful host for the spirit or demon. Another ancient technique, called **trephination**, involved cutting a hole in a person's skull to help release a harmful spirit.

Early Greek and Roman Thought

The development of medicine and medical concepts among Egyptians and Greeks helped replace ancient supernatural theories with natural ones. Natural theories reject supernatural forces and instead look to things that can be observed, known, and measured as potential causes of events. Particularly influential in moving forward the field of psychopathology was Hippocrates (460–377 B.C.), a Greek physician known as the father of modern medicine. Hippocrates rejected demons and evil spirits as causes of psychopathological behavior. He believed the brain was the central organ of the body and that psychopathological behavior resulted from brain disorders or dysfunctions.

Hippocrates recommended treatments for psychopathological behavior that would restore brain functioning, including special diets, rest, abstinence from alcohol, regular exercise, and celibacy. Hippocrates's work had great impact on later Greek and Roman physicians. Throughout Greece and Rome, physicians emphasized a scientific approach to learning about causes of psychopathological behavior. Because of limited knowledge about human anatomy and biology—experimentation on humans and dissection of human cadavers was illegal—questionable practices such as bleeding and purging were employed. However, treatment of psychopathological behavior focused primarily on creating therapeutic environments that included healthy diets, regular exercise, massage, and education. These treatments remain good ideas even today.

Middle Ages

The scientific aspects and advances of Greek medicine continued in the Middle East. However, the fall of the Roman Empire brought a return to supernatural theories in Europe. Demon possession again became a prominent explanation of psychopathological behavior, and treatment focused on prayer, holy objects or relics, pilgrimages to holy places, confinement, and exorcism. A dramatic emergence of **mass madness** in Europe also appeared during the last half of the Middle Ages. Groups of individuals would be afflicted at the same time with the same disorder or psychopathological behaviors.

An example of mass madness was a dancing mania in Italy known as *tarantism*. In tarantism, individuals became victims of a tarantula's "spirit" after being bitten. The possession led to raving, jumping, dancing, and convulsions. *Lycanthropy* also developed in some groups; this is a belief that a person has been transformed into a demonic animal such as a werewolf. Another form of mass madness, *St. Vitus's dance*, or rapid, uncoordinated jerking movements, spread to

Album/Alamy Stock Photo

Early treatments for mental disorder attempted to make a person an unpleasant, uncomfortable, or painful host for a possessive spirit or demon.

North Wind Picture Archives/Alamy Stock Photo

Philippe Pinel advocated more humane treatment of persons with mental problems.

Germany and other parts of Europe. What caused these and other instances of mass hysteria remains unclear. One possibility is that people in highly emotional states tend to be suggestible. High levels of fear and panic may have led some to believe they had been "taken over" by an outside force or spirit and that these odd behaviors were contagious. Another possibility is that people inadvertently ate substances such as fungi on food that led to odd beliefs and visions.

Renaissance

A rebirth of natural and scientific approaches to health and human behavior occurred at the end of the Middle Ages and beginning of the Renaissance. Once again, physicians focused on bodily functioning and medical treatments. In addition, Paracelsus (1493–1541), a Swiss physician, introduced the notion of psychic or mental causes for psychopathological behavior and proposed a treatment initially referred to as bodily magnetism and later called hypnosis. Another new approach to treating mental disorders during the Renaissance involved special institutions known as **asylums**. Asylums were places set aside for people with mental disorder. Unfortunately, asylums were originally created simply to remove people with mental disorder from the general population because they were not able to care for themselves. As such, early asylums did not provide much treatment, and living conditions for residents were usually poor.

Reform Movement

The conditions of asylums or mental hospitals in Europe and America were generally deplorable and in need of great change. A key leader of change was Philippe Pinel (1745–1826), who was in charge of a Paris mental hospital called La Bicêtre. Shocked by the living conditions of the patients, Pinel introduced a revolutionary, experimental, and more humane treatment. He unchained patients, placed them in sunny rooms, allowed them to exercise, and required staff to treat them with kindness. These changes produced dramatic results in that patients' mental states generally improved, and order and peace was restored to the hospital.

Pinel's reforms in France soon spread to other places. William Tuke (1732–1822) created the York Retreat in England, and Benjamin Rush (1745–1813) encouraged humane treatment of people with mental disorder in the United States. Dorothea Dix (1802–1887) is credited with making the most significant changes in treating those with mental disorder and in changing public attitudes about these conditions in America. She raised awareness, funds, and political support and established more than 30 hospitals. The humane type of care emphasized during the reform movement period, sometimes referred to as **moral treatment**, paved the way for the modern approach to mental disorders.

Modern Era

The modern approach to psychopathology includes accepting those with mental disorder as people who need professional attention; scientific, biomedical, and psychological methods are used to understand and treat mental disorder. Of special note in this regard was the **mental hygiene movement** that emerged from Clifford Beers's 1908 book, *A Mind That Found Itself*. In the book, Beers described his own experiences with mental disorder and his subsequent treatment in an institution. His description of maltreatment while hospitalized sparked a mental health reform movement in the United States and later across the world. After his recovery, Beers founded the Connecticut Society for Mental Hygiene in 1908 and the National Committee for Mental Hygiene in 1909. These groups were designed to improve quality of care for those with mental disorder, help prevent mental disorder, and disseminate information to the public about mental disorder. These goals are just as relevant and important today as they were more than a century ago.

Activist Dorothea Dix is credited with helping to reform treatment of persons with mental disorder in the United States.

Clifford Beers's autobiography recounted his experiences as a patient in a mental institution and helped launch the mental hygiene movement in the United States.

Several theoretical perspectives were developed during the late 19th century and throughout the 20th century to guide work on understanding and treating mental disorders. These perspectives include biological, psychodynamic, cognitive, behavioral, sociocultural, and other theories of psychopathology. Each perspective has important applications for determining causes and appropriate treatments of mental disorder. These perspectives are *somatogenic* (emphasizing physical, bodily causes of behavior) and *psychogenic* (emphasizing psychological or mind-related causes of behavior). Major perspectives of psychopathological behavior are presented in Chapter 2 in more detail.

Section Summary

- Early theoreticians attributed psychopathological behavior to supernatural causes such as demon possession. Exorcism and trephination were primary forms of treatment.
- The development of medicine among Egyptians and Greeks helped replace ancient supernatural theories with natural ones. Treating psychopathological behavior focused on creating therapeutic environments via healthy diets, exercise, massage, and education.
- The fall of the Roman Empire led a return to supernatural theories of psychopathological behavior such as demon possession. Treatment thus focused on prayer, holy objects or relics, pilgrimages to holy places, confinement, and exorcism.
- During the end of the Middle Ages and beginning of the Renaissance, natural and scientific approaches to health and human behavior reemerged. Asylums were built for those with mental disorder but generally provided poor care and treatment.
- The Reform Movement introduced significant changes to treating mental disorder and led to the modern approach, which includes accepting those with mental disorder as individuals needing treatment and applying biomedical and psychological methods.

Review Questions

1. Give two examples of how society and culture influence ideas about the cause and treatment of mental disorder.
2. What events were responsible for rejecting supernatural explanations of mental disorder?
3. Consider Treva. What different treatments for her problems would have been used during the Middle Ages, Renaissance, and Modern Era?

Psychopathology and Life: Themes

LO 1.5 Compare and contrast key perspectives on psychopathology including dimensional, prevention, consumer, and multicultural.

LO 1.6 Discuss stigma associated with psychopathology including its origins and impact and how to fight it.

A main focus of this textbook is how psychopathology applies to your daily life. You will notice in the following chapters that the personal relevance of the textbook material is maximized. Several other themes for this book are also highlighted here, including a focus on dimensions of psychopathology as well as prevention. Please keep these themes in mind as you read, think about, and apply material that is presented in later chapters.

Dimensional Perspective

Recall the earlier discussion of dimensions, or a continuum, of emotions, thoughts, and behaviors that characterize mental disorder. This theme is worth highlighting again because it is a core principle that guides this text. An important implication of a dimensional perspective is that research on emotions, thoughts, and behavior is relevant to all of us. Everyone, you may recall, feels anxious or sad at times; this is normal. When these normal emotions or thoughts become frequent or severe, however, a mental disorder may be present. Many people are sometimes nervous about driving, especially in a new place. If a person is so anxious when driving that they cannot go to school, however, then the anxiety might be considered psychopathological. A dimensional perspective thus involves the notion that people differ only in their *degree* of symptoms.

Prevention Perspective

The average college student functions pretty well, but many students may be at some risk for mental dysfunction or distress. Therefore, *prevention* of mental disorder is emphasized throughout this textbook. Prevention stems from the concept of *mental hygiene*, or the science of promoting mental health and thwarting mental disorder through education, early treatment, and public health measures. You may recall this approach was developed and promoted by Clifford Beers more than a century ago. Prevention and mental hygiene have greatly influenced modern approaches to understanding and treating mental disorders.

This emphasis on prevention will help you recognize symptoms of mental disorder, become aware of early warning signs or risks for these problems, and take steps to prevent psychological distress in yourself or others. Risk and protective factors associated with specific mental disorders will be identified in later chapters. Strategies are also presented for responding to, or coping with, these risk factors.

A prevention approach is consistent with a **public health model** that focuses on promoting good health and good health practices to avert disease. This model applies well to psychopathology. Different aspects of our lifestyles contribute greatly to physical and mental health problems and even death. Examples include poor diet and insufficient exercise, social isolation, and unhealthy interpersonal relationships. In addition, mental disorders discussed in this textbook have been linked to declines in physical health. Public health practitioners and researchers are thus motivated to address psychological health and functioning to improve overall quality of life.

The important topic of prevention and how this concept applies to mental health is discussed further in Chapter 3. Next, however, is a brief discussion of how prevention interfaces with the study of psychopathology. Historically, emphasis has been placed on treating mental disorder once it developed, and certainly this is an important focus. However, the field of psychopathology has advanced enough to allow the identification of *risk factors* that help produce many mental disorders. This textbook presents what is currently known in this regard. Information about risk factors can also inform us about what makes someone vulnerable to psychological problems, what can be done to prevent symptoms of mental disorder, and what methods can be used to ameliorate these symptoms if they do develop.

Focus On College Students

College Students and Stigma

As you will learn throughout this textbook, college students are often at risk for various mental health problems. Unfortunately, college students also experience substantial levels of perceived stigma and self-stigma and thus often do not seek treatment or other help for these problems. This may apply especially to students with disabilities, racial and ethnic minorities, and those with career-related distress (Guaneri et al., 2019). Both education and personal contact strategies help to reduce stigma in college students; examples include film screenings, mental health days, social media, and increased empathy by listening to others' stories (Withers et al., 2021).

What can you do to reduce stigma regarding mental health problems and help-seeking in yourself and others? Be aware of campus resources such as counseling centers and available digital technologies that provide assistance to those with mental health challenges. Educate yourself about mental health problems that are common to college students, such as anxiety and depression. Understand the myths and misconceptions about mental problems that are often perpetuated on social media and other outlets. Most of all, talk to a mental health professional if you are feeling distressed or overwhelmed or are struggling in different areas of your life (Chapter 15).

Types of Prevention

Three types of prevention are commonly considered within psychopathology. **Primary prevention** involves targeting large groups of people, sometimes the entire public, who have not yet developed a mental disorder. Health promotion efforts to reduce excessive substance use are one example. Other primary prevention examples include programs to reduce job discrimination, enhance school curricula, improve housing, teach parenting skills, and provide educational assistance to children.

Secondary prevention involves addressing emerging problems while they are still manageable and before they become resistant to intervention. A good example of secondary prevention is early detection and treatment of college students with potentially damaging drinking problems. In this case, people at risk for a particular problem are addressed to prevent a full-blown disorder.

Finally, **tertiary prevention** involves reducing the severity, duration, and negative effects of a mental disorder after it has occurred. Tertiary prevention differs from primary and secondary prevention in that its aim is to lessen the effects of an *already* diagnosed disorder. Examples include various medical and psychological treatments for mental disorders. Throughout this textbook, an emphasis is made on primary and secondary prevention in addition to treatments for already existing mental disorders.

Consumer Perspective

Another major theme of this book is a *consumer perspective*. You will become a more informed consumer of scientific information on mental health that is often presented in the popular press. For example, certain antidepressant medications may actually *increase* suicidal thoughts and behaviors in some children and adolescents. Material presented in Chapter 7 will inform you about features of depression, how these features vary across age groups, and how these features can be treated using research-supported biological and psychological methods. In this way, you will hopefully understand media distortions and comprehend the true nature of various disorders and their treatment.

Another goal of this textbook is to show how you can apply research-based information to your own life. You will find strategies for improving emotional regulation, intimate relationships, and coping abilities. Doing so is also consistent with the prevention theme discussed earlier. This textbook also presents information on how mental disorders specifically relate to college students. In addition, some of you may have enrolled in this course because you are interested in certain mental health professions. Once you have learned about different mental disorders, Chapter 15 will help you navigate the field of mental health professions. Consistent with the consumer theme, material in Chapter 15 also involves seeking a therapist should you ever decide to do so.

Diversity

Diversity involves differences across genders, people of assorted racial or ethnic backgrounds, and those with various sexual identities or orientations, disabilities, religious beliefs, and socioeconomic and immigrant statuses, among other groups. Great progress has been made in recent years with respect to understanding how mental disorders vary across these groups. For example, depression tends to be more common among women than men (Chapter 7) and certain immigrant populations of ethnic minority status are at increased risk for psychotic disorder (Chapter 12). **Multicultural psychology** refers to examining the effect of culture on the way people think, feel, and act (Pedrotti & Isom, 2021). Multicultural psychology is important, among other reasons, for understanding what causes mental disorders and how to better and more specifically assess and treat mental disorders.

Diversity and multicultural psychology are important parts of this textbook. For each major mental disorder, group differences reported by researchers are discussed. In addition, special "focus on diversity" and "focus on gender" boxes occur throughout the textbook that further highlight cultural and gender differences. This textbook also includes detailed sections on culture and the sociocultural model of mental disorder (Chapter 2), gender and race and culture as risk factors for mental disorder (Chapter 3), and culture and clinical assessment (Chapter 4). A main goal is to help you understand how cultural, gender, and other group variations influence the presentation, assessment, and treatment of mental disorders.

Stigma

Another important aspect of this textbook, and one related to a dimensional perspective of psychopathology, is stigma. **Stigma** is a characterization by others of disgrace or reproach based on an individual characteristic. People with certain medical disorders are sometimes shunned or rejected by others even though their illness is no fault of their own. Such stigma can also apply to mental disorders. Children with a learning disorder are sometimes treated differently by teachers, and adults with social anxiety disorder are sometimes ridiculed by coworkers. Indeed, stigma is often associated with ableism or discrimination and prejudice against people with disabilities. Stigma is also a major reason why people do not seek treatment for mental distress (Byrow et al., 2020). This is so alarming that public health programs are often designed to reduce the stigma associated with seeking treatment for psychological problems (Mascayano et al., 2020). Specific sections throughout the textbook discuss what may lead to stigma, the effects of stigma, and ways to combat stigma associated with particular mental disorders.

Stigma and mental disorder are aligned for various reasons. Stigma likely arises from a stereotype that people with a mental disorder are unpredictable, dangerous, violent, incompetent, or responsible for their own fate (Shah et al., 2022). As you read this textbook, however, you will find that these stereotypes are inaccurate and often based on infrequent and isolated events. The vast majority of people with a mental disorder are not much different from you or your classmates, as a dimensional approach to mental disorder suggests. People with mental disorder generally are not violent, unpredictable, incompetent, or to blame for their disorder.

Stigma also occurs when government or other institutional policies negatively affect opportunities for people who may be seen as threatening, dangerous, or less deserving of support. One example of this *structural stigma* can be seen in state laws that limit health insurance coverage for mental health problems. Stereotypes and public misperceptions about mental disorder also come from social media, news stories and editorials, television reports and shows, and movies (Waqas et al., 2020). The media's focus on negative aspects and consequences of mental disorder, whether accurate or not, promotes prejudice and discrimination. Conversely, media messages that emphasize favorable portrayals and empathy can help reduce stigma (Hecht et al., 2021).

Effects of Stigma

Stigma affects people in different ways (refer to **Figure 1.3**). One type of stigma is **public stigma**, which refers to the general disgrace the public confers on people with mental disorder that can result in prejudice, stereotyping, and discrimination. People with mental disorder, for example, may experience difficulty securing employment, housing, and health care coverage. Public stigma can also hinder treatment of mental disorders by restricting opportunities for care and by limiting insurance benefits. Think about neighborhood

Figure 1.3 Public Stigma and Self-Stigma.

Public stigma may lead some people to avoid the label of mental disorder by not seeking services that might be helpful. Self-stigma may lead people with mental disorder to feel incompetent and unworthy of help.

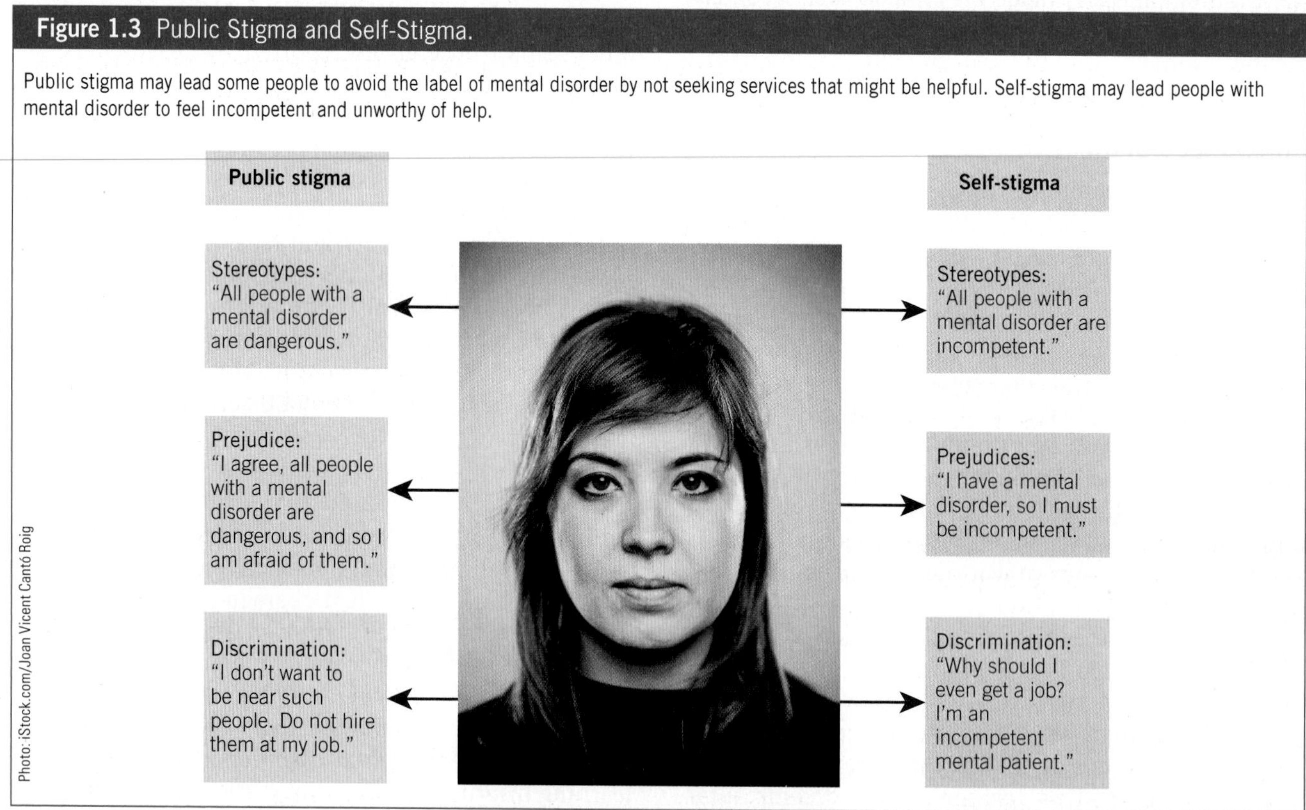
Public stigma
Self-stigma
Stereotypes: "All people with a mental disorder are dangerous."
Prejudice: "I agree, all people with a mental disorder are dangerous, and so I am afraid of them."
Discrimination: "I don't want to be near such people. Do not hire them at my job."
Stereotypes: "All people with a mental disorder are incompetent."
Prejudices: "I have a mental disorder, so I must be incompetent."
Discrimination: "Why should I even get a job? I'm an incompetent mental patient."
Photo: iStock.com/Joan Vicent Cantó Roig

From Corrigan, P. How stigma interferes with mental health care. American Psychologist, 59, 614–625, Figure 1. Copyright © 2004 by the American Psychological Association. Reprinted by permission.

complaints that arise when an agency wants to build a group home for people with intellectual developmental disorder (Chapter 13). In a sense, public stigma is a type of social injustice (Corrigan, 2015).

Another way stigma can affect people is **self-stigma**, which refers to disgrace people assign themselves because of public stigma or ableism (Shah et al., 2022). Some people adopt the public notion that a mental disorder is something to be ashamed of; this can affect self-esteem or cause an individual to deny a problem exists. Self-stigma can lead as well to damaging behaviors such as reluctance to seek treatment. You can imagine that self-stigma is especially pertinent to children. Imagine a child who is told they have a learning disorder—how might this knowledge affect the child's motivation to work in the classroom? Substantial personal stigma often prevents college students from seeking help for mental health issues as well (Bird et al., 2020).

Fighting Stigma

Stigma can be fought in two key ways: *education* and *promoting personal contact.* Educational efforts to combat stigma range from distributing materials that present factual information about mental disorder to online and direct courses regarding the truth about mental disorder (Dobson & Stuart, 2021). Educational efforts to combat stigma do have short-term effects on participants' attitudes, although less support is available for long-term effects (Waqas et al., 2020).

Promoting personal contact involves increased contact with someone with a mental disorder to dispel myths and stereotypes. Methods of promoting personal contact include encouraging volunteer activities in mental health settings and providing classroom experiences in which individuals whose lives are touched by mental disorder present their stories. These encounters have significant effects on attitudes about mental disorder (Peter et al., 2021). Indirect contact with mental health consumers via video has also been shown to reduce stigma and is part of the reason that many video case studies of persons with mental disorder were developed in conjunction with this textbook (Amsalem et al., 2021).

This textbook strives to fight stigma in several ways. First, by providing factual information about mental disorders, myths can be dispelled about the disorders. Second, emphasis is placed on the idea that symptoms of mental disorders are present to some degree in all of us. Indeed, material in this textbook is likely to be personally relevant to your life or the lives of people you know because mental disorders are so prevalent. Third, this textbook emphasizes people first and mental disorders second. References are made to people with schizophrenia (not "schizophrenics"), children with a learning disorder (not "the learning disabled"), and individuals with mental disorder (not "the mentally ill"). After all, if someone you know has cancer, you would not call that person a "cancer"! However, keep in mind as well that identity-first or person-first language is a highly personal choice.

Finally, a unique feature of this textbook is use of *narratives* (like Alison Malmon's narrative presented in this chapter). These features are first-person accounts of people who experience and deal with symptoms of mental disorder in themselves or family members. Common themes throughout these narratives are that stigma directed toward those with mental disorder is inappropriate and that we all have a vested interest in advocating for those with mental disorder. These accounts are informative, make these conditions more personally relevant, and inspire all of us to advocate for the rights and needs of those with mental disorder.

Section Summary

- Emotions, thoughts, and behaviors associated with psychopathology and mental disorder are present, to some degree, in all of us.
- Mental hygiene refers to the science of promoting mental health and preventing mental disorder through education, early treatment, and public health measures.
- Primary prevention targets groups of people who have not developed a disorder to decrease overall rates of a given problem.
- Secondary prevention addresses problems while they are still manageable and before they become resistant to intervention.
- Tertiary prevention reduces duration and negative effects of a mental disorder after it occurs or is diagnosed in an individual.
- Stigma associated with mental disorder can result in discrimination, social avoidance, and failure to seek treatment.
- Stigma can be fought via education and by promoting personal contact with those with a mental disorder.

Review Questions

1. How might Treva Throneberry's behavior be considered dimensional in nature?
2. What are implications of a dimensional viewpoint?
3. What are different types of prevention, and how might each be used to address a problem like depression?
4. How is psychopathology relevant to your life? What instances of stigma have you seen?

Personal Narrative

Alison Malmon

I was 18 years old when my world crumbled. Shortly after spring break in my first year of college, I got a call from my mother that forever changed our lives. "Ali, Brian shot himself," she said. "He's dead." Brian was my only sibling. Born four years and four days before me, he was an extraordinary child. He rose to the top of our high school, taking all Advanced Placement classes. He was captain of the debate team, soloist in the annual Rock and Roll Revival show, announcer for school football games, and a columnist for our local paper. He had friends, was smart and funny, and was my role model.

There was no question in Brian's mind that he wanted to go to college in New York City—he had fallen in love with the city a few years earlier and was determined to one day own one of its infamous tall black buildings. So as I entered high school, Brian was on his way to Columbia University. Four years later, he had stormed Columbia just as he did in high school: He had joined an a cappella group and become president. He was also a columnist for, and sports editor of, the Columbia daily newspaper and the star of the school's Varsity Music and Comedy show. In addition, he was on the Dean's List every semester, pursuing a political science degree with a strong focus on journalism, with plans to go on to law school.

So when Brian came home for a weekend in November of his senior year to "de-stress," I wasn't too surprised. But that weekend quickly turned into a week, a week into a month, and a month into the rest of the semester. Before I knew it, Brian was home for basically my entire senior year of high school. He began seeing a psychiatrist, and only then did we discover Brian was suffering from schizoaffective disorder (Chapter 12) and had been since February of his first year at Columbia. He had been hearing voices typical of schizophrenia and experiencing depressive episodes for almost three years. He had been walking the streets at night, and packing up his dorm room in boxes, because voices told him to. He had been sleeping days at a time and hated to leave his dorm room because he was so depressed. But he never told anyone. In retrospect, his friends at school remember that he "sometimes went into a funk," but no one ever confronted him about it.

Matthew Worden

Alison Malmom

By the time he sought help and came home, Brian had already lost hope. He suffered through what was supposed to be the best time of his life in pain, fear, and complete isolation; no matter how much therapy and medications he tried once he came home, the pain was too much to bear. During my first year at the University of Pennsylvania, Brian took his own life. He was just 22.

Final Comments

The goal of this chapter has been to introduce the field of psychopathology and important relevant concepts. Major definitions of psychopathology have advantages and disadvantages, and no gold standard exists to define what is psychopathological. However, each of these definitions taps an important facet of psychopathology that "rings true" to some extent. In addition, emotions, thoughts, behaviors, distress, and impairment from psychopathological behavior are dimensional and thus present to some degree in all of us. This textbook advocates the public health model as a viable and effective way to conceptualize, prevent, and treat mental disorders. Throughout this book, emphasis is placed on themes of dimensionality of psychopathology, prevention of mental disorders, a consumer perspective, diversity, and stigma. The hope is that you find the material engaging and useful not just today but throughout your lifetime.

I can't even try to describe what it was, and continues to be, like since Brian's death. I lost my big brother, my other half; I am now an only child. My family has been torn apart and our entire fabric has had to be rewoven as well as we know how. A loss to suicide is truly something only other suicide survivors can understand. I live every day with the "what ifs?"—the guilt, and the devastation. The unbearable pain has lessened and I am able to get through each day a little easier, but my life will never be the same. Brian was such a promising young man with so much of his life ahead of him. I simply feel sad for anyone whose life he did not have the chance to touch.

When Brian first died, one of the most salient emotions I felt was fear. I became scared thinking that, had I been in his situation and began suffering from a mental disorder in college, I probably would have done exactly what Brian had. I would have felt responsible, kept my symptoms to myself, and suffered in silence. Nobody was talking about mental health issues on my campus; no one was educating students about signs and symptoms of various disorders, where they could get help, and that they could get better. The stigma surrounding the issues was causing too many people to suffer in shame and isolation. And I knew that if I would have kept quiet like Brian did, too many of my peers were also suffering in silence.

So I formed a campus group called Active Minds (www.activeminds.org) to educate my peers about these issues and get people talking. With more young adults talking, sharing what they and their family and friends had gone through, we would break down walls of silence and more of my peers might feel comfortable getting help they deserved. We were the ones suffering. We were the ones watching our friends suffer. It was time for young adults to be engaged in and educated about mental health issues and to tell each other: "This can happen to you. I know, because it happened to me. But you can get help for what you're going through, and you can feel better."

This idea of education and discussion to reduce stigma was extremely well supported at my school and within the mental health community. Just 18 months after starting that group at Penn, I formed my own nonprofit organization with the goal to introduce this concept to young adults nationwide. I now work full time as the executive director of the organization Active Minds, Inc., developing and supporting chapters of Active Minds at high schools and colleges around the country, and helping to give a voice to young adults in this field. Every time a young person shares her story, or concentrates his energy to combat stigma he has encountered, our voice is strengthened.

I would give anything to have my brother Brian back with me today. But since I can't, I will do everything in my power to ensure no other young adult has to suffer in silence like he did, and no other sister has to lose her big brother to suicide.

Source: Used with permission.

Key Terms

mental disorder 4
psychopathology 4
maladaptive behavior 7
psychopathologists 8
exorcism 13
trephination 13
mass madness 13
asylums 14
moral treatment 14
mental hygiene movement 14
public health model 16
primary prevention 17
secondary prevention 17
tertiary prevention 17
multicultural psychology 17
stigma 17
public stigma 18
self-stigma 19

Z.

Perspectives on Psychopathology 2

Learning Objectives

LO 2.1 Explain the role of models in understanding psychopathology.

LO 2.2 Characterize the biological model of psychopathology, including its assumptions, strengths, limitations, clinical implications, and empirical support.

LO 2.3 Outline the psychodynamic model of psychopathology, including its history, assumptions, strengths, limitations, clinical implications, and empirical support.

LO 2.4 Describe the humanistic model of psychopathology, including its assumptions, strengths, limitations, clinical implications, and empirical support.

LO 2.5 Characterize the cognitive-behavioral model of psychopathology, including its assumptions, strengths, limitations, clinical implications, and empirical support.

LO 2.6 Describe the sociocultural model of psychopathology, including its assumptions, strengths, limitations, clinical implications, and empirical support.

Case Mariella

Mariella, a 19-year-old college freshman, has been repeatedly asking herself, "What's going on?" and "What should I do?" Something was not right. Mariella was outgoing, bright, and cheery in high school but was now fatigued, blue, and pessimistic in college. She was starting her second semester and thought the tough college adjustment period her friends and family talked about should be over by now. Were her feelings of fatigue and discontent just a temporary "funk," or was something seriously wrong?

Mariella's fatigue and discontent began early in her first semester and worsened toward finals week. She enrolled in five courses and was soon overwhelmed by extensive reading assignments, large classes, and fast-approaching deadlines. She struggled to finish her work, often seemed isolated from others, and felt unimportant in the huge academic setting. Mariella believed no one cared whether she was in class, and she longed for days in high school when she interacted with a close-knit group of teachers and friends. Her college professors seemed to treat her like a number and not a student, and her classmates always seemed to be rushing about with little time to talk.

Mariella was an "A" student in high school but was now struggling to get Cs in her college classes. She had great trouble concentrating on what she read, which led to low test scores. Mariella did talk to her friends and family members back home about her troubles, but no one truly understood what she was going through. Instead, they thought Mariella was experiencing simple, normal homesickness that would soon end.

iStock.com/Prostock-Studio

Mariella began spending more time alone as her first semester approached mid-November. She often slept, engaged in marathon watching of programs, listened to music, and went online. She no longer found much enjoyment doing things that used to appeal to her, such as going to parties and playing the guitar. Mariella declined invitations from others to go out, and her roommate noticed that Mariella seemed sad and lonely. Unfortunately, no one took the time to ask Mariella if something serious might be wrong.

Mariella also lost significant weight her first semester. When she went home for Thanksgiving, her family members were surprised at how she looked. Mariella had noticed no major change except for occasional hunger, but in fact she had lost 10 pounds from her 120-pound frame. Unfortunately, she received flattering comments on how she looked, so the larger problem of her sad mood went undetected. Her concentration and eating problems continued when she returned to school to finish her first semester, and Mariella struggled to finish her final examinations and receive passing grades.

Mariella was happy to return home for the winter break and hoped her feelings of fatigue and discontent were simply related to school. Unfortunately, she remained sad, did not regain lost weight from the previous semester, and continued to sleep much of the day. She dreaded returning to school but felt pressure from others to do so. Mariella became quite despondent when she returned to school in mid-January. She knew something would have to change to endure this second semester, but she felt confused and unsure. Once again she was asking, "What's going on?" and "What should I do?"

What Do You Think?

1. Why do you think Mariella feels the way she does?
2. What should Mariella do? What would you do if in her situation?
3. Which aspects of Mariella's story concern you most?
4. Do you know people who have had similar experiences? What did they do?
5. What should Mariella's friends and family do to help?

Introduction

LO 2.1 Explain the role of models in understanding psychopathology.

If Mariella had lived centuries ago, demonic possession might have been a common explanation for her problems. Scientists and mental health professionals today, however, focus on a person's biology, environment, and other factors to help people like Mariella. Scientists and mental health professionals develop perspectives or **models**—ways of looking at things—to piece together why someone like Mariella has problems.

Perspectives or models are systematic ways of viewing and explaining what we observe in the world. When you try to explain high prices for an item, you might think about the economic model of *supply and demand*

Figure 2.1 The Use of Models.

Models or perspectives affect the way we think about causes of mental disorder, our methods of assessment, and our methods of prevention and treatment.

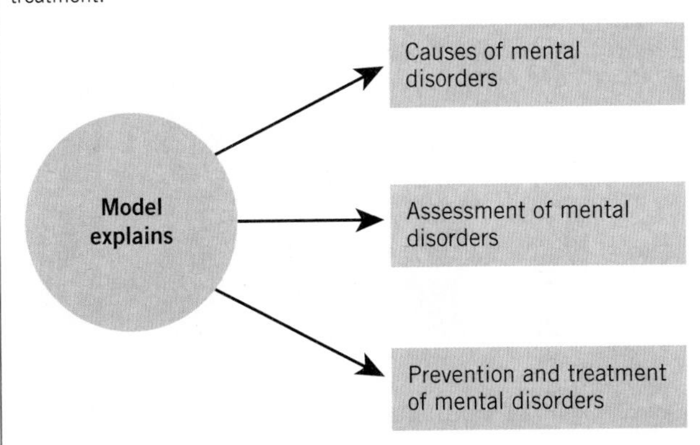

to conclude everyone wants the item but supplies are limited. Or if a friend of yours is ill you might think about the disease model of *germ theory* to ask whether they were around a sick person or if they ate spoiled food. Mental health professionals use models to help explain unusual behavior or mental disorders in people like Mariella. Five main models to explain mental disorders are described in this chapter:

- The *biological model* focuses on genetics, neurotransmitters, brain changes, and other physical factors.
- The *psychodynamic model* focuses on internal personality characteristics.
- The *humanistic model* focuses on personal growth, choice, and responsibility.
- The *cognitive-behavioral model* focuses on specific thoughts and learning experiences.
- The *sociocultural model* focuses on external environmental events and includes the family systems perspective.

These models dominate the mental health profession today and influence the way we think about, assess, and treat mental disorders (refer to **Figure 2.1**). Each model has strengths and weaknesses, but each provides mental health professionals with ways of understanding what is happening to someone like Mariella. This chapter shows how each model could be used to explain Mariella's problems and help her. Many mental health professionals also integrate these models to study and explain mental disorders.

Interfoto/Alamy Stock Photo

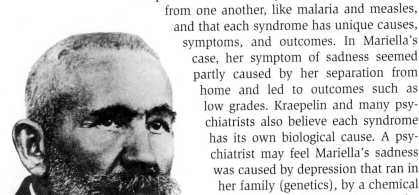

Emil Kraepelin is considered by many to be the father of psychiatric classification and a key contributor to the biological model.

The Biological Model

LO 2.2 Characterize the biological model of psychopathology, including its assumptions, strengths, limitations, clinical implications, and empirical support.

The **biological model** rests on the assumption that mental states, emotions, and behaviors arise from brain function and other physical processes. This model has been in use for centuries and is stronger than ever today. Read news reports, watch television, or go online—countless articles and advertisements are available about medications and other substances to treat depression, anxiety, sexual dysfunction, and other conditions. Despite the incessant advertising, however, the biological model of mental disorder, including the use of medications, is supported by scientific research that links genetics, neurochemistry, and brain changes to various psychological problems.

The biological model of mental disorder was pioneered by *Emil Kraepelin* (1856–1926), who noticed various **syndromes** or clusters of symptoms in people. Mariella had a cluster of symptoms that included concentration problems, oversleeping, sadness, and weight loss. Her symptoms are commonly described within the syndrome of *depression* (Chapter 7). Kraepelin believed, as do many psychiatrists and other mental health professionals today, that syndromes and symptoms have biological causes. Kraepelin proposed two major types of mental disorders, each with different biological causes: *dementia praecox* (similar to schizophrenia, discussed in Chapter 12) and *manic-depressive psychosis* (similar to bipolar disorder, discussed in Chapter 7).

Kraepelin also believed syndromes to be separate from one another, like malaria and measles, and that each syndrome has unique causes, symptoms, and outcomes. In Mariella's case, her symptom of sadness seemed partly caused by her separation from home and led to outcomes such as low grades. Kraepelin and many psychiatrists also believe each syndrome has its own biological cause. A psychiatrist may feel Mariella's sadness was caused by depression that ran in her family (genetics), by a chemical (neurotransmitter) imbalance, or by some brain change. These biological causes are discussed next.

Genetics

Do you think Mariella's sadness may have also been present in some of her family members? Many mental disorders such as depression do seem to run in families. Genetic material may be involved when symptoms of a mental disorder are passed from parents to children. Genetic material refers to molecular "codes" contained in the nucleus of every human cell (Scott & Ritchie, 2022). *Genes* are the smallest units of inheritance that carry information about how a person will appear and behave. Genes carry information about hair and eye color, weight and height, and even vulnerability to diseases such as lung cancer or mental disorders such as depression. Human genes are located on 46 *chromosomes* or threadlike structures arranged in 23 pairs. A person's chromosomes come half from the biological mother and half from the biological father.

The genetic composition of a person is known as a **genotype** and is fixed at birth. Genotypes produce characteristics such as eye color that do not change over time. An observable characteristic of a person is known as a **phenotype**, which *can* change over time. Observable characteristics can include intelligence, as well as symptoms of a mental disorder such as difficulty concentrating. Phenotypes can change because they result from genetic *and* environmental influences. Your intelligence is partly determined by genetics from your parents but also by the type of education you received as a child. Scientists are interested in knowing which genetic and environmental influences impact the development of emotions, cognitions, and behavior. This research specialty is known as **behavior genetics** (Simmel & Fuller, 2021).

Behavior geneticists are interested in the degree to which a mental disorder is determined by genetics. *Heritability* refers to the amount of variation in a phenotype attributed to genetic factors, often expressed as a number ranging from 0 to 1. Some mental disorders such as anxiety-related disorders have modest heritability, but many major mental disorders have more substantial genetic influences in their development (refer to **Figure 2.2**). Disorders with particularly high heritability include bipolar disorder and schizophrenia (Baselmans et al., 2021).

Behavior geneticists also focus on what *specific* genes are inherited and how these genes help produce a mental disorder. Researchers in the field of **molecular genetics** analyze *deoxyribonucleic acid* (DNA)—the molecular basis of genes—to identify associations between specific genes and mental disorders. Molecular genetics is quite challenging for several reasons. First, most mental disorders are influenced by multiple genes, not just one. When you hear a media report that researchers found a gene for Alzheimer's disease, keep in mind they likely found only one of many genes. Second, the same symptoms of a mental disorder may be caused by different genes in different people. Third, humans have an estimated 20,000 to 25,000 protein-coding genes, so finding specific ones related to a certain disorder is like finding a needle in a haystack. Despite these challenges, advances in molecular genetics will likely lead to findings that help scientists determine how and if disorders are genetically distinct from one another. Knowledge of specific genes can also help researchers determine how genes influence physical changes in the body, discussed next.

Figure 2.2 Heritability of Major Mental Disorders.

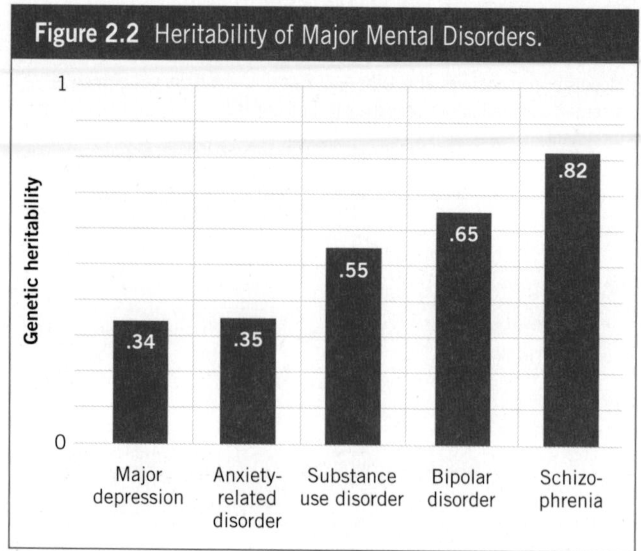

Adapted from Merikangas, K. R., & Risch, N. (2005). Will the genomics revolution revolutionize psychiatry? In N.C. Andreasen (Ed.), Research advances in genetics and genomics: Implications for psychiatry (pp. 37–61). Washington, DC: American Psychiatric Publishing; Kendler, K. S., Chen, X., Dick, D., Maes, H., Gillespie, N., Neale, M. C., & Riley, B. (2012). Recent advances in the genetic epidemiology and molecular genetics of substance use disorders. *Nature Neuroscience,* 15, 181–189.

Nervous Systems and Neurons

Physical structures in our body are affected by genetics, and this can contribute to mental disorder. The **central nervous system** includes the brain and spinal cord and is responsible for processing information from our sensory organs such as eyes and ears and prompting our body into action. The **peripheral nervous system** helps control muscles and voluntary movement, regulates the cardiovascular and endocrine (hormone) systems, assists with digestion, and adjusts body temperature. The nervous systems are composed of billions of **neurons**, or nerve cells, that have four major components: cell body, dendrites, axon, and terminal buttons (refer to **Figure 2.3**).

A small gap called the **synapse** exists between neurons. Neurons communicate with each other using **neurotransmitters**, or chemical messengers that allow information to cross the synapse. Not all neurotransmitters released into the synapse are used, so an unused neurotransmitter is reabsorbed and recycled in a process called **reuptake**. Medications influence neurotransmitter systems to treat mental disorders. Medications may *block synapses* to decrease

Figure 2.3 Basic Parts of a Neuron.

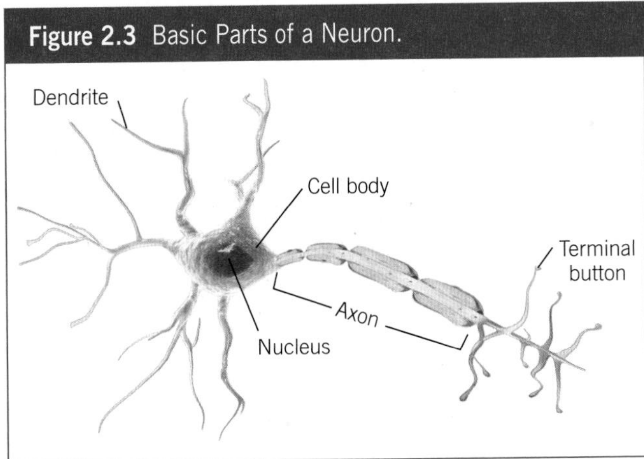

Adapted from Josephine F. Wilson, Biological foundations of human behavior, Fig. 2.6, p. 30. Reprinted by permission of the author.

neurotransmitter levels or *block reuptake* to increase neurotransmitter levels. People with depression often take drugs such as Prozac or Paxil to increase availability of certain neurotransmitters for improved energy and mood. Six major neurotransmitters are discussed throughout this textbook: serotonin, norepinephrine, dopamine, gamma-aminobutyric acid (GABA), acetylcholine, and glutamate. **Table 2.1** lists functions associated with each.

Brain

The brain is our most complex and important organ and comprises about *86 billion* neurons (Herculano-Houzel, 2020). The brain consists of two cerebral hemispheres that are mirror images of each other. The *right hemisphere* controls movement for the left side of the body, influences spatial relations and patterns, and affects emotion and intuition. The *left hemisphere* controls movement for the right side of the body, influences analytical thinking, and affects grammar and vocabulary. The two hemispheres do communicate with each other, however. Complex behaviors such as playing a piano or using language are influenced by both hemispheres.

The **cerebral cortex** covers much of each hemisphere and is largely responsible for consciousness, memory, attention, and other higher-order areas of human functioning. The brain itself is divided into four main lobes (refer to left side of **Figure 2.4**). The **frontal lobe** is in the front portion of the brain and has many important functions such as movement, planning and organization, inhibiting behavior or responses, and decision making. The frontal lobe is thus a central focus of many mental health researchers. The **parietal lobe** is behind the frontal lobe and is associated with touch. The **temporal lobe** is at the base of the brain and is associated with hearing and memory. The **occipital lobe** is behind the parietal and temporal lobes and is associated with vision.

The brain may also be organized along the *forebrain, midbrain,* and *hindbrain.* The forebrain contains the **limbic system** (refer to right side of Figure 2.4), which regulates emotions and impulses and controls thirst, sex, and aggression. The limbic system is important for several mental disorders and is composed of the hippocampus, cingulate gyrus, septum, and amygdala. Farther down the forebrain, the **basal ganglia** help control posture and motor activity. The **thalamus** and **hypothalamus** are at the crossroads of the forebrain and midbrain and relay information between the forebrain and lower brain areas. The midbrain also contains the *reticular activating system,* which is involved in arousal and stress or tension. The hindbrain includes the *medulla, pons,* and *cerebellum*. These structures are involved in breathing, heartbeat, digestion, and motor coordination.

Biological Assessment and Treatment

How can knowledge about genetics, neurotransmitters, and brain changes be used to evaluate and treat

Table 2.1 Major Neurotransmitter Systems Associated with Mental Disorders

Neurotransmitter system	Functions
Serotonin	Processing of information; regulation of mood, behavior, and thought processes
Norepinephrine	Regulation of arousal, mood, behavior, and sleep
Dopamine	Influences novelty-seeking, sociability, pleasure, motivation, coordination, and motor movement
Gamma-aminobutyric acid	Regulation of mood, especially anxiety, arousal, and behavior
Acetylcholine	Important in motor behavior, arousal, reward, attention, learning, and memory
Glutamate	Influences learning and memory

Figure 2.4 Major Features of the Human Brain.

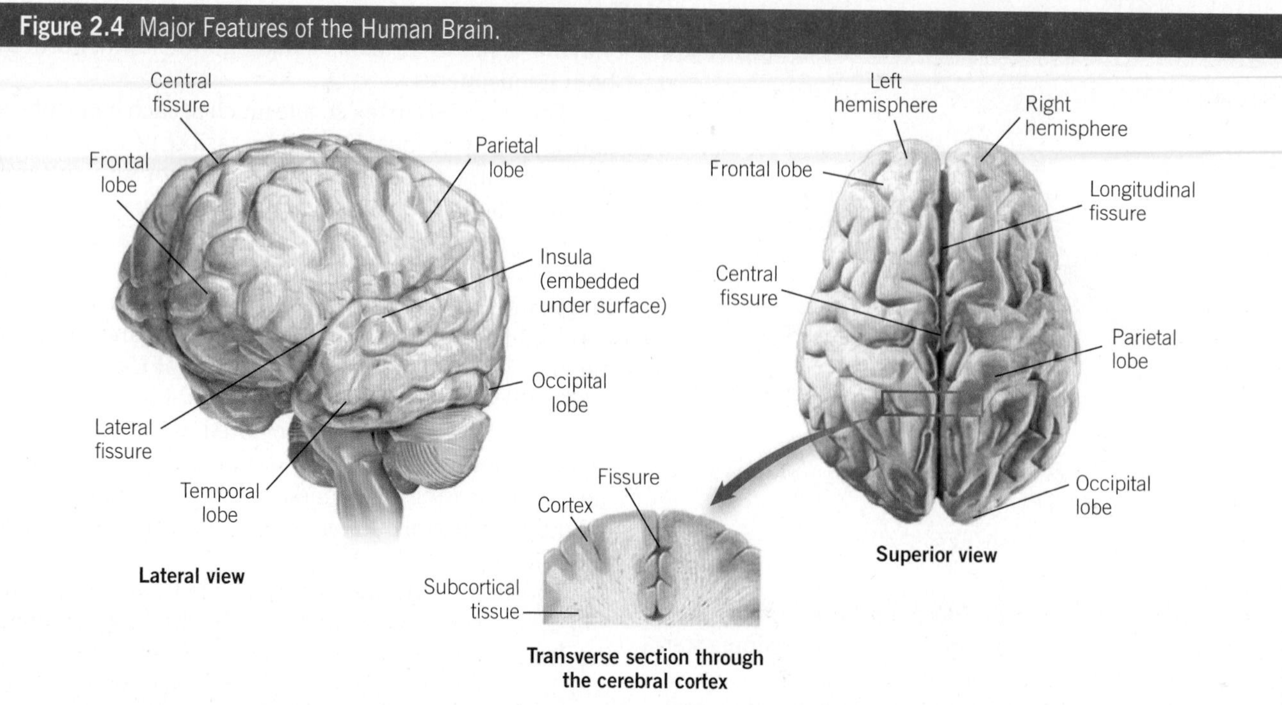

Structure	Location and Description
Central fissure	Deep valley in the cerebral cortex that divides the frontal lobe from the rest of the brain
Cerebellum	Located within the hindbrain; coordinates muscle movement and balance
Cerebral cortex	Outer-most layer of the brain; covers almost all of each hemisphere of the brain; referred to as the grey matter of the brain (named after its characteristic coloring)
Frontal lobe	Located in the front of the brain (in front of the central fissure); is the seat of a number of very important functions, including controlling movement, planning, organizing, inhibiting behavior or responses, and decision-making
Hemisphere (left)	Controls the right half of the body; is typically responsible for analytic thinking, and is responsible for speech
Hemisphere (right)	Controls the left side of the body; is involved in the determination of spatial relations and patterns, and is involved in emotion and intuition
Lateral fissure	Deep valley in the cerebral cortex that is above the temporal lobe
Longitudinal fissure	Deep valley in the cerebral cortex that divides the left and right hemispheres of the brain
Occipital lobe	Located behind the parietal and temporal lobes of the brain; associated with vision
Parietal lobe	Located behind the frontal lobe of the brain and above the lateral fissure; associated with the sensation of touch
Prefrontal cortex	Controls attention and impulse control; used in problem solving and critical thinking
Subcortical tissue	Brain tissue immediately below the cerebral cortex
Temporal lobe	Located below the lateral fissure of the brain; associated with auditory discrimination

people with mental disorders? A biologically oriented mental health professional such as a psychiatrist might first give a diagnostic interview (Chapter 4) to better understand a person's problems. Biologically oriented health professionals also use assessment methods to obtain images of brain structure and functioning. *Magnetic resonance imaging* (MRI) provides high-quality brain images to reveal tumors, blood clots, and other

Figure 2.4 Continued

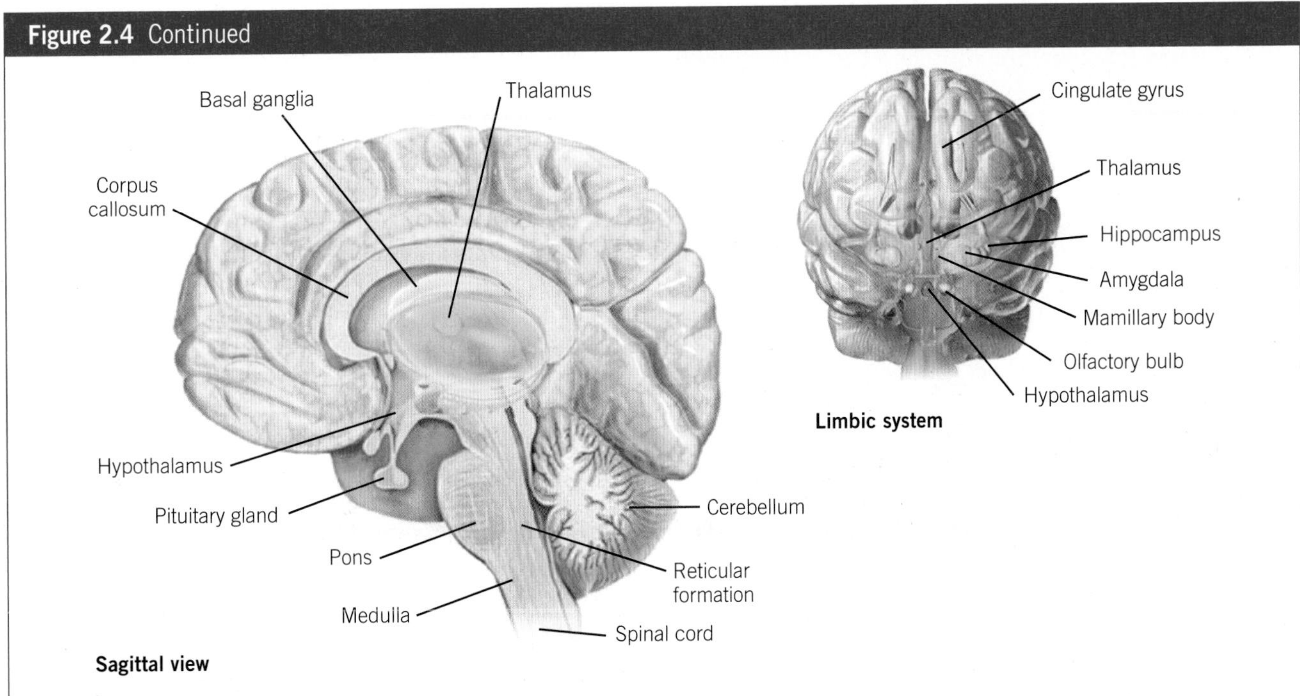

Structure	Location and Description
Amygdala	Structure in the limbic system that is involved in emotion and in aggression
Basal ganglia	Brain structures that control posture, motor activity, and anxiety level
Corpus callosum	A band of nerve fibers that connects the two hemispheres of the brain, allowing for communication between the right and left sides of the brain
Hindbrain	Most posterior part of the brain; includes the medulla, pons, and cerebellum; these structures are involved in important "automatic" activities of the body like breathing, heartbeat, and digestion; in addition, the cerebellum controls motor coordination
Hippocampus	Part of the limbic system involved in memory and learning
Hypothalamus	Regulates basic biological needs like hunger, thirst, and body temperature
Limbic system	Regulates emotions and impulses; responsible for basic drives like thirst, sex, and aggression; consists of several structures that are implicated in psychological disorders: the hippocampus, cingulate gyrus, septum, and amygdala
Medulla	Located in the hindbrain; involved in regulating breathing and blood circulation
Pituitary gland	Regulates other endocrine glands and controls growth; sometimes called the "master gland."
Pons	Located in the hindbrain; involved in sleep and arousal
Reticular formation	Internal structures within the midbrain that are involved in arousal and stress or tension
Spinal cord	Transmits information between the brain and the rest of the body; controls simple reflexes
Thalamus	Relays signals to and from the cerebral cortex to other brain structures

structural differences. **Figure 2.5** compares MRI images of a youth with autism to a youth without autism. Other methods for brain imaging are described in Chapter 4.

Biologically oriented mental health professionals decide on treatment once a comprehensive evaluation is complete. Psychiatric medications are commonly used to treat mental disorders by affecting neurotransmitter systems. Medications that decrease *dopamine* generally have antipsychotic effects to ease symptoms of schizophrenia. Medications that increase *norepinephrine* or *serotonin* often have antidepressant effects. Medications that increase *GABA* often have antianxiety effects.

Figure 2.5 MRI Scans from the Cerebellar Areas of a 16-Year-Old Boy with Autism (A) and a 16-Year-Old Boy without Autism (B).

Note the somewhat smaller cerebellar area in the youth with autism, which may contribute to unusual motor movements and cognitive impairments often observed in people with autism.

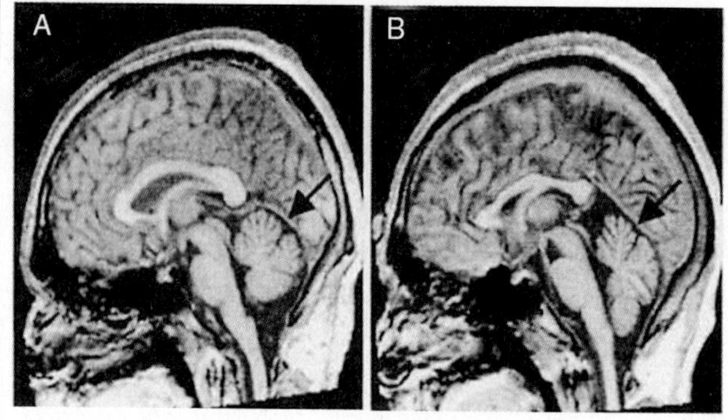

From Palmen, J. M. C., van Engeland, H., Hof, P. R., & Schmitz, C. (2004). Neuropathological findings in autism. *Brain, 127,* 2572–2583. Copyright ©2004. Used with permission of Oxford University Press. Permission conveyed through Copyright Clearance Center, Inc.

Evaluating the Biological Model

The biological model is respected because genetics, neurotransmitters, and brain areas clearly influence problems such as anxiety (Chapter 5), depression and bipolar disorder (Chapter 7), schizophrenia (Chapter 12), intellectual developmental disorder and autism (Chapter 13), and Alzheimer's disease (Chapter 14). Findings from this model have led to better knowledge about which genes are inherited, how neurotransmitter effects and medications can help treat mental disorder, and how brain changes over time lead to psychopathology. The biological perspective comprises much of the material in this textbook.

The biological perspective also has some limitations. First, biological factors do not provide a full account of *any* form of mental disorder. Some disorders have substantial genetic contributions, such as schizophrenia or bipolar disorder, but environmental or nonbiological factors are clearly influential as well. An exclusive focus on biological factors would also deny crucial information about cultural, family, stress, and other factors that influence all of us. Second, we do not know yet exactly how biological factors *cause* mental disorder. We can only say biological changes appear to be significant risk factors for mental disorder. Biological risk factors also clearly interact with environmental risk factors, as is discussed throughout this textbook.

Section Summary

- The biological model assumes that mental states, emotions, and behaviors arise largely from physical processes.
- A genetic approach to mental disorder focuses on heritability and molecular genetics.
- Neurons are the basic unit of the nervous systems and communicate using chemical messengers or neurotransmitters.
- The brain is composed of billions of neurons, as well as several lobes and other structures important for basic functioning.
- The biological model is important for understanding many components of major mental disorders, but it cannot explain all aspects of the disorders.

Review Questions

1. How might the biological model explain Mariella's problems?
2. Explain the concepts of behavior genetics, heritability, and molecular genetics.
3. Identify some major neurotransmitter systems implicated in mental disorders.
4. What are major structures of the brain, and which ones might be most important for Mariella's condition?
5. What might a biologically oriented mental health professional recommend as treatment for Mariella?

The Psychodynamic Model

LO 2.3 Outline the psychodynamic model of psychopathology, including its history, assumptions, strengths, limitations, clinical implications, and empirical support.

The biological model focuses on internal physical structures related to mental disorder. The **psychodynamic model** also focuses on internal structures but mental ones rather than physical. The psychodynamic model comes from *Freudian theory* that assumes mental states and behaviors arise from motives and conflicts within a person. The term *intrapsychic* refers to psychological dynamics that occur within a person's mind, so this term is often used to describe the psychodynamic model. The psychodynamic model represents one of the most sweeping contributions to the mental health field and its influence permeates our culture. Psychodynamically oriented words or phrases such as *ego, unconscious,* and *Freudian slip* have become part of our common vernacular. You may have even encountered aspects of Freudian thought in art, literature, films, and textbooks.

Several basic principles comprise the psychodynamic perspective (Berzoff et al., 2022). One basic principle is that *childhood experiences shape adult personality*. The belief that childhood development influences adult behavior is almost universally accepted. You can likely identify certain childhood experiences that shaped who you are today. You are a product of your biology, youthful experiences, and events happening now. Ignoring any of these factors means we lose much information

Focus On Violence

A More Complex Approach

Violence and aggression are complex behaviors that cannot necessarily be explained by single models such as a biological one. Instead, a more complex and developmental approach is often needed. One example is aggression in adolescents with delinquent behavior or conduct disorder (Chapter 13). Some youth have certain biological qualities that may predispose them to conduct problems such as aggression, although not all youth with these qualities necessarily become aggressive. Those who are more likely to become aggressive tend to experience harsh parental discipline, emotional neglect, and conflicts with aggressive peers. These experiences then interact with academic and social problems, which can lead to association with deviant peers in middle or high school. If parents' supervision declines during this time, then the child may not develop adequate social skills to control anger and aggression. In this scenario, many contributing factors are involved, including biological, psychological, and social factors (Frick & Kemp, 2021).

A more in-depth approach may be necessary to explain forms of violence in adulthood as well. Intimate partner violence is a significant problem among college students but one that cannot be fully explained just by learning or sociocultural factors. One group of researchers examined college students in dating relationships who recorded daily instances of interpersonal violence and other behaviors. Students were much more likely to engage in physical or psychological interpersonal violence on days they were drinking alcohol, using marijuana, or were more angry, hostile, or irritable (negative affect). The study also revealed that multiple factors can interact in various ways to influence different kinds of violence. For example, number of alcoholic drinks consumed in addition to negative affect was most closely related to physical violence (Shorey et al., 2014).

about your personality and history with others. Imagine if we focused only on Mariella's problems for the past few months—we would lose other information, such as her high school experiences that may influence her current symptoms.

A second key principle of the psychodynamic perspective is that *causes and purposes of human behavior are not always obvious but partly unconscious*. Unconscious means the part of the mind where mental activity occurs but of which a person is unaware. Scientists in disciplines such as neuroscience have found that certain mental and behavioral processes do not appear to be under cognitive control (di Giannantonio et al., 2020). The implication is that realms of emotion, cognition, and behavior exist of which we are not consciously aware. These hidden realms of emotion, thought, and behavior may also affect motives that drive us to act in certain ways. This is known as **unconscious motivation**. Healthy behavior is considered behavior for which a person understands the motivation (do you know why you are doing what you are doing?). Unhealthy behavior results when we do not fully understand the unconscious causes of our behavior. The goal of psychodynamic therapy is thus to make the unconscious more conscious.

A third key principle of the psychodynamic perspective is that *people use defense mechanisms to control anxiety or stress*. **Defense mechanisms** are strategies to cope with anxiety or stressors such as conflict with others. Psychodynamic theorists believe most humans can adapt to challenges and stressors by using healthy defense mechanisms. Some people with a mental disorder over-rely on less effective defense mechanisms, or defense mechanisms do not work well for them and they become quite stressed.

A fourth key principle of the psychodynamic model is that *everything we do has meaning and purpose and is goal-directed*. This is known as **psychic determinism**. Mundane and bizarre behavior, dreams, and slips of the tongue all have significant meaning in the psychodynamic model. Behaviors may in fact have different meanings. Think about Mariella's weight loss: Was her behavior motivated by a simple desire to lose weight, or was it a signal to others that she needed help?

Brief Overview of the Psychodynamic Model

An overview of the major concepts of the psychodynamic model is next. This includes a description of the structure of the mind, as well as an explanation of psychosexual stages and defense mechanisms.

Structure of the Mind

A major component of the psychodynamic model of personality and mental disorders is *structure of the mind*. According to Freud and other psychodynamic theorists, the mind (and hence personality) is composed of three basic structures in the unconscious: *id*, *ego*, and *superego* (refer to **Figure 2.6**). The **id** is the portion of the personality that is present at birth. The purpose of the id is to seek immediate gratification and discharge tension as soon as possible. This process is the **pleasure principle**. The id propels us to meet demands of hunger, thirst, aggression, or sexual or physical pleasure as soon as possible. The id is thus hedonistic and without values, ethics, or logic. Think about a baby who cries when they want something and does not want to wait for it. Babies, and maybe even some adults you know, have "id-oriented" personalities.

Figure 2.6 Freud's Structure of the Mind.

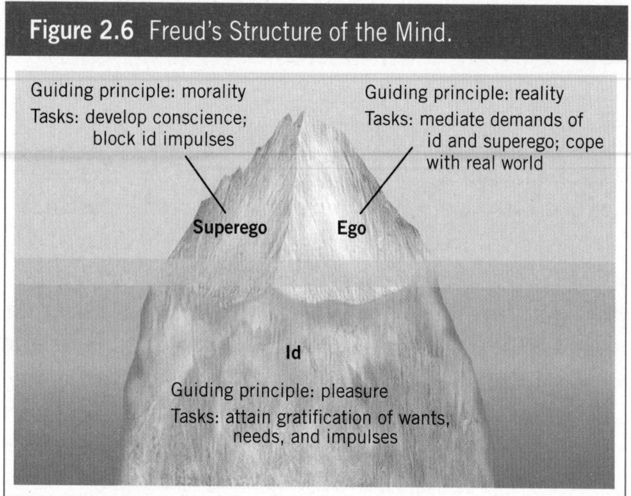

Adapted from Rathus, *Psychology: Concepts and Connections*, 9th ed., Fig. 11.1, p. 402. Copyright © 2005 Wadsworth, a part of Cengage Learning. Reproduced by permission. www.cengage.com/permissions.

The id uses a **primary process** form of thinking if gratification is not immediate—this involves manufacturing a fantasy or mental image of whatever lessens the tension. You might want to date someone but are convinced they will reject your invitation, so you simply fantasize about being with that person. Or you might think about food when you are hungry. Dreaming is also a form of primary process. Primary processes cannot provide real gratification such as a date or food, however, so we must develop a second personality structure to help us address real-life demands—the ego.

The **ego** is an organized, rational system that uses higher-order thinking processes to obtain gratification. The ego is the executive of the personality and operates along the **reality principle**, or need to delay gratification of impulses to meet environmental demands. If you badly want a laptop computer, then your id might urge you to steal one. This would land you in trouble, however, so the ego tries to mediate demands of the id and demands of the environment. The ego uses **secondary process** to do this. Secondary process involves learning, perception, memory, planning, judgment, and other higher-order thinking processes to plan a workable strategy. The ego might plan to schedule some overtime shifts at work so you can earn extra money to buy the laptop. The id thus receives what it wants eventually but in a socially acceptable way. A strong ego is often considered by psychodynamic theorists to be the hallmark of mental health.

The roots of the psychodynamic model can be traced back to the life and times of Sigmund Freud (1856–1939).

The third component of the personality is the **superego**. The superego develops in early childhood and represents societal ideals and values conveyed by parents through rewards and punishments. The superego is essentially one's sense of right and wrong. Punished behavior becomes part of one's *conscience*, and rewarded behavior becomes a part of one's *ego ideal*. The conscience punishes individuals by making them feel guilty or worthless for doing something wrong, whereas the ego ideal rewards individuals by making them feel proud and worthy for doing something right. The role of the superego is to block unacceptable id impulses, pressure the ego to pursue morality rather than expediency, and generate strivings toward perfection. Your superego might punish you by using guilt, shame, and worry if you decide to steal a laptop.

Freud's Psychosexual Stages

Not all psychodynamic theorists adhere strictly to Freudian principles, but they do agree childhood is extremely important in shaping a person's character and personality. Freud himself proposed that each person progresses through **psychosexual stages of development**. These stages occur early in life and are marked by *erogenous zones*, or areas of the body through which hedonistic id impulses are expressed. **Table 2.2** provides a description of each stage.

Severe difficulties experienced by a child at a psychosexual stage may be expressed later in life as symptoms of mental disorders. These difficulties are marked by excessive frustration or overindulgence at a psychosexual stage and can result in **fixation**, or delayed psychosexual development. The particular stage at which such frustration or overindulgence is encountered will determine the nature of later symptoms. A child neglected or deprived during the oral stage of development may compensate in adulthood by engaging in excess oral behaviors such as smoking, talkativeness, or drinking too much alcohol. A child overindulged by parents during toilet training in the anal stage may compensate in adulthood by being overly neat or compulsive.

A psychodynamic theorist might say Mariella's basic needs of nurturance and safety were unsatisfied during her oral stage of development, and so she remained fixated at this stage. Her depression may thus be a signal to others that she craves social attention and comfort.

Defense Mechanisms

The ego experiences *anxiety* when the id urges it to seek impulsive gratification or when the superego imposes shame and guilt. Anxiety is a painful emotion that warns the ego to quell the threat and protect the organism. The ego uses secondary processes of memory, judgment, and learning to solve problems and stave off external threats. But these measures are less useful when internal threats arise from the id or superego. What then? The ego has at its disposal various tactics called defense mechanisms, which are unconscious mental processes used to fend off conflict or anxiety.

We all use defense mechanisms, such as when we claim we did not really want to date someone who just turned down our invitation. Use of defense mechanisms becomes a problem, however, when we use them excessively or when we use a select few defense mechanisms exclusively. If we constantly deny reality and continue to ask out people who are likely to reject us, then we may get depressed. Moderation and variety are important for mental health, including use of defense mechanisms.

Table 2.3 lists many defense mechanisms proposed by psychodynamic theorists. Let's discuss some of the primary ones. **Repression** is a basic ego defense that occurs when a person banishes from consciousness threatening feelings, thoughts, or impulses, like a strong sexual desire for a stranger. **Regression** involves returning to a stage that previously gave a person much gratification—think of a middle-aged man under stress who begins to act as if he were a teenager. **Reaction formation** occurs when an unconscious impulse is consciously expressed by its behavioral opposite. "I love you" is thus expressed as "I hate you," a phenomenon common among tweens who like someone but who are afraid of rejection. **Projection** occurs when unconscious feelings are attributed to another person. Someone who feels guilty about cheating on a partner may accuse the partner of infidelity.

Psychodynamic Assessment and Treatment

Psychodynamic theorists believe symptoms of mental disorders are caused by unresolved conflicts. A psychodynamically oriented therapist treating Mariella's depression might explore a history of loss, such as loss of important relationships. Mariella's relationships with friends and family at home were indeed affected by attending college. Psychodynamic theorists also believe we unconsciously harbor anger and resentment toward those we love. Mariella may have been unconsciously jealous of, and angry at, her friends and family members who did not move far away and who did not fully appreciate her problems in college. Perhaps she internalized feelings of resentment by directing the feelings toward herself—anger turned inward. This may have led to symptoms of depression such as low self-esteem and sadness. Mariella's depression may have been caused by this unconscious conflict of emotions.

How does a psychodynamic theorist know what unconscious material exists for a client? A psychodynamic mental health professional often assesses unconscious motivations and conflicts using *projective techniques.* Projective techniques are based on the **projective hypothesis**, or an assumption that people project unconscious needs and conflicts onto ambiguous stimuli such as inkblots. People *impose their own structure* on unstructured stimuli and thus reveal something of themselves. Unconscious material is thus uncovered. In Chapter 4, two major projective tests are discussed that are used to access unconscious material—the *Rorschach* and the *Thematic Apperception Test* (TAT). However, an overview of projective assessment within the context of Mariella's case is presented next.

A psychodynamic theorist might expect a depressed client like Mariella to respond to projective tests in ways that indicate underlying anger and hostility. Such findings would support the psychodynamic explanation of depression as "anger turned inward" in response to loss. Mariella might be given an inkblot from the Rorschach and asked, "What might this be?" or asked to develop a story about characters depicted in the TAT. Mariella could reveal unconscious material about herself because she must impose some structure, organization,

Table 2.2 Freud's Psychosexual Stages of Development

Stage	Age	Focus
Oral stage	0–6 months	Mouth is the main focus of satisfaction.
Anal stage	6 months–3 years	Attention becomes centered on defecation and urination.
Phallic stage	3–6 years	Sexual organs become the prime source of gratification.
Latency stage	6–12 years	Lack of overt sexual activity or interest.
Genital stage	12 years to adulthood	Mature expression of sexuality.

Table 2.3 Examples of Defense Mechanisms

Defense mechanism	Description
Denial	Refusing to accept or acknowledge reality
Displacement	Expressing one's unacceptable feelings onto a different object or person than the one that is truly the target of the feelings
Fantasy	Imagining some unattainable desire
Identification	Modeling another person's behavior or preferences to be more like them
Intellectualization	Providing an in-depth intellectual analysis of a traumatic or other situation to distance oneself from its emotional content
Overcompensation	Emphasizing strength in one area to balance a perceived limitation in another area
Projection	Attributing one's own unacceptable motives or impulses to another person
Rationalization	Developing a specific reason for an action, such as justifying why one did not purchase a particular car
Reaction formation	Expressing an unconscious impulse by engaging in its behavioral opposite
Regression	Returning to an earlier psychosexual stage that provided substantial gratification
Repression	Keeping highly threatening sexual or aggressive material from consciousness
Sublimation	Transforming emotions or sexual or aggressive material into more acceptable forms such as dancing or athletic or creative activity
Undoing	Reversing an unacceptable behavior or thought using extreme means

and interpretation onto ambiguous materials. She may respond to an inkblot by saying it represents "two bears fighting with each other" or develop a story from a TAT card about a woman who is mad at a friend. A psychodynamic theorist might conclude from these responses that Mariella is "projecting" her anger and hostility onto the neutral stimulus of an inkblot or TAT card. This "projected" anger and hostility is considered to be unconscious material.

Psychodynamic theorists also use other techniques to access unconscious material. **Free association** means asking a client to say whatever comes to mind during the session, without exercising censorship or restraint. This is not easy (try it) because the client must stop censoring or screening thoughts that may seem ridiculous, aggressive, embarrassing, or sexual. A psychodynamic therapist is looking for slips of the tongue, or Freudian slips, that reveal quick glimpses of unconscious material. Mariella could be speaking during free association and "accidentally" say she has always resented her mother for pushing her to do things outside the home.

A related technique is **dream analysis**. Dreams are thought to reveal unconscious material because ego defenses are lowered during sleep. The **manifest content** of a dream is what actually happens during the dream. The manifest content of a dream may be, for example, that the dreamer is confronted with two large, delicious-looking ice cream cones. The **latent content** of a dream, however, is its symbolic or unconscious meaning. Dreaming about ice cream cones may symbolically represent a longing to return to the mother's breast.

How might psychodynamic theorists use information from projective tests, free association, and dreams to treat Mariella? A key goal of psychodynamic treatment is to help clients gain *insight* into their current problems. **Insight** means understanding the unconscious determinants of irrational emotions, thoughts, or behaviors that create problems or distress. The need for defense mechanisms and psychological symptoms should disappear once these unconscious reasons are fully confronted and understood. A psychodynamic theorist believes Mariella can improve by understanding the true, underlying reasons for her depression, including feelings of anger turned inward.

Psychodynamic theorists interpret past experiences and information from projective assessments to help accomplish insight. **Interpretation** is a cornerstone of psychodynamic therapy and the method by which unconscious meanings of emotions, thoughts, and behavior are revealed. A mental health professional will "translate" for a client what may be causing current symptoms involving emotions, thoughts, or behaviors. Significant insight or behavioral change rarely comes from a single interpretation but rather through a slow process in which meaning behind certain emotions, thoughts, and behaviors is repeatedly identified in one context after another. A psychodynamic therapist might point out Mariella's various child, adolescent, and adult experiences, as well as projective assessment responses to illustrate a history of becoming angry with others but bottling up such anger and becoming depressed. Certain dreams and Freudian slips would be instructive as well.

A client's behavior with a therapist can also illuminate the unconscious and reveal conflicts with others. **Transference** is a key phenomenon in psychodynamic therapy that occurs when a client reacts to a therapist as if the latter is an important figure from childhood. Positive and negative feelings can be transferred. Conflicts and problems that originated in childhood are thus reinstated in the therapy room. Mariella might one day yell at her therapist to reflect anger toward her mother.

Client–therapist interactions provide important clues about the nature of a client's problems but are also an opportunity for the therapist to carefully and supportively interpret transference in an immediate and vital situation. A client will, ideally, then recognize the irrational nature and origins of transference feelings and cope with these in more rational ways. The client can begin to control such reactions in real-world settings and to use them as a basis for further interpretation and analysis.

Evaluating the Psychodynamic Model

As mentioned, the most influential principle of the psychodynamic perspective may be that childhood experiences greatly affect adult functioning. The influence of this principle is evident in popular media as well as in psychology and psychiatry. Think about how we value the health, welfare, and education of children. We also emphasize the negative consequences of child maltreatment, ineffective parenting, and inadequate education. Children are not little adults who can easily avoid the stress of a dysfunctional family or dangerous home or neighborhood. Psychodynamic theory has certainly helped us focus on providing better environments for our children. The psychodynamic theory of defense mechanisms also makes intuitive sense. Many of us use defenses to ward off anxiety and cope with psychological threats in our environment.

A strict view of the psychodynamic perspective does reveal some limitations, however. Perhaps the biggest limitation is that little empirical support exists for many of the major propositions of the perspective. Psychodynamic theory was mostly formed from anecdotal evidence, and many concepts such as the id are abstract and difficult to measure. If we cannot measure an important variable reliably and with confidence, then its usefulness is questionable. Psychodynamic theory thus lost much of its broad, mainstream appeal, but a short-term therapy approach based on the theory remains popular among some mental health professionals (Driessen et al., 2020).

Section Summary

- The psychodynamic model rests on the assumption that mental states and behaviors arise from unconscious motives and intrapsychic conflicts.
- Two major assumptions of this perspective are psychic determinism and unconscious motivation.
- According to psychodynamic theorists, the id, ego, and superego comprise the mind.
- Psychosexual stages are developmental stages that influence personality and psychopathology.
- Defense mechanisms are used to cope with life demands and intrapsychic conflict.
- Problems occur when we use defense mechanisms exclusively or excessively.
- Strengths of the psychodynamic perspective include defense mechanisms and an emphasis on how childhood experiences influence adult personality.
- A limitation of the psychodynamic perspective is the relative lack of research support for its major assumptions.

Review Questions

1. How might the psychodynamic model explain Mariella's problems?
2. How might a psychodynamically oriented therapist assess and treat Mariella?
3. Describe the following features of the psychodynamic perspective and how they can help us understand Mariella's symptoms: psychic determinism, unconscious motivation, structure of the mind, psychosexual stages, defense mechanisms.
4. Review the list of defense mechanisms in Table 2.3. Which have you used, and which do you use the most?
5. What are strengths and limitations of the psychodynamic perspective?

The Humanistic Model

LO 2.4 Describe the humanistic model of psychopathology, including its assumptions, strengths, limitations, clinical implications, and empirical support.

Biological and psychodynamic perspectives focus primarily on internal factors such as genetics and unconscious conflicts. Some theorists have reacted to these models with disdain because the models do not emphasize personal growth, free will, or responsibility. Biological and psychodynamic theorists concentrate heavily on how factors such as genetics and unconscious conflicts automatically shape human behavior. Other theorists, however, focus more on how people can make choices

Focus On Law and Ethics

Dangerousness and Commitment

Determining whether someone is dangerous to oneself or others is extremely difficult. Behaviors such as suspiciousness, excitability, uncooperativeness, and tension are not good predictors of dangerousness. Making the task more difficult is that a large majority of people with mental disorders are *not* dangerous (Whiting et al., 2021). A psychologist's ability to predict dangerous behavior may be better in the short term than the long term, although errors still occur. Some variables may help predict dangerousness, including psychopathy (Chapter 10), school and work maladjustment, excessive substance use, violent criminal history, early age of onset of violent behaviors, injury to victims, and psychotic symptoms (Chapter 12) (Ogloff & Davis, 2020).

The issue of predicting dangerousness relates to committing someone to a mental hospital against their will. The conflict between individual rights to be free versus societal rights to be protected from dangerous people has been an issue for centuries. Detaining and separating people perceived as dangerous to the general population has become an accepted practice. **Civil commitment** refers to involuntary hospitalization of people at serious risk of harming themselves or others or people who cannot care for themselves (Lamb & Weinberger, 2020). Commitment in this regard can occur on an *emergency* basis for a few days or more *formally* for extended periods by court order.

Criminal commitment refers to involuntary hospitalization of people charged with a crime. A person may be hospitalized to determine their competency to stand trial or after acquittal by reason of insanity. **Competency to stand trial** refers to whether a person can participate meaningfully in their own defense and can understand and appreciate the legal process (Cochrane et al., 2021). Such competency is often questioned for people who commit crimes while experiencing intellectual developmental disorder, psychotic disorders, dementia, or substance use problems.

Insanity is a legal term that refers to mental incapacity at the time of a crime, perhaps because a person did not understand right from wrong or because the person was unable to control personal actions at the time of the crime. A person judged to be insane is not held criminally responsible for an act but may be committed as a dangerous person, sometimes for extensive periods of time. The insanity defense has always been controversial, but very few defendants (about 1 percent) actually use this defense. This may be complicated, however, by the number of people with intellectual problems in the criminal justice system (Long & Ebert, 2022).

---

that influence their environment and how they can take responsibility for their actions.

One group of theorists that emphasize human growth, choice, and responsibility adopt a **humanistic model** of psychology. A main assumption of the humanistic model is that people are naturally good and strive for personal growth and fulfillment. Humanistic theorists believe we seek to be creative and meaningful in our lives and that, when thwarted in this goal, become alienated from others and possibly develop a mental disorder. A second key assumption of the model is that humans have choices and are responsible for their own fates. A person with a mental disorder may thus enhance their recovery by taking greater responsibility for their actions.

Humanistic theorists adopt a **phenomenological approach**, which is an assumption that one's behavior is determined by perceptions of oneself and others. Humanistic theorists believe in a subjective human experience that includes individual awareness of how we behave in the context of our environment and other people. To fully understand another person, therefore, you must understand the world as they understand it and not as you understand it. We all have different views of the world that affect our behavior. Humanistic theory was shaped greatly by the works of Abraham Maslow, Carl Rogers, and Rollo May. These theorists are explored next to expand on a discussion of the humanistic model.

Abraham Maslow

Abraham Maslow (1908–1970) believed humans have basic and higher-order needs they strive to satisfy during their lifetime (refer to **Figure 2.7**). The most basic needs are physiological and include air, food, water,

Figure 2.7 Maslow's Hierarchy of Needs.

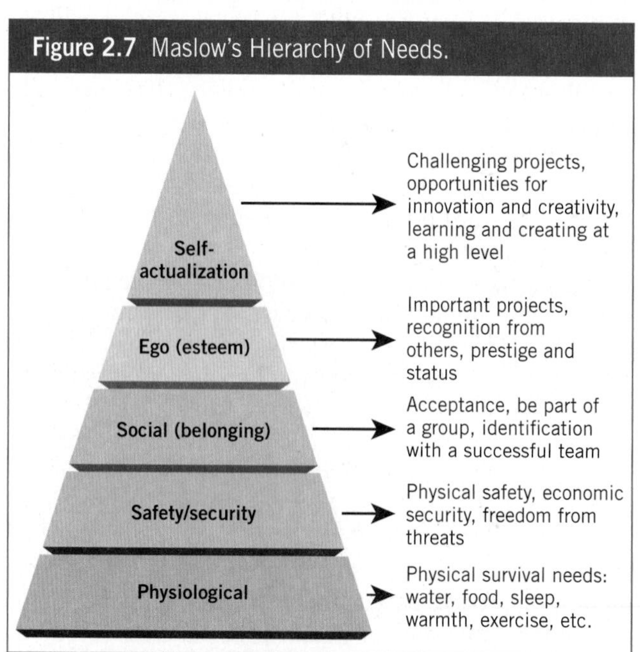

sex, sleep, and other factors that promote *homeostasis,* or maintenance of the body's internal environment. We feel anxious or irritable when these needs are not met but feel a sense of well-being when the needs are met and when we have achieved homeostasis. These needs must be largely fulfilled before a person can meet other needs. *Safety needs* include shelter, basic health, employment, and family and financial security. *Love and belongingness needs* include intimacy with others and close friendships—a strong social support network. *Esteem needs* include confidence in oneself, self-esteem, achievement at work or another important area, and respect from others. These needs are thought to apply to everyone and may even be adapted to the care of intensive care and dying patients (Reed, 2020).

The highest level of need is **self-actualization**, defined as striving to be the best one can be. Maslow believed humans naturally strive to learn as much as they can about their environment, seek beauty and absorb nature, create, feel close to others, and accomplish as much as possible. Self-actualized people are also thought to be moral beings who understand reality and can view things objectively. Pursuit of self-actualization normally occurs after other basic needs have been met, although some people may value other needs such as respect from others more highly than self-actualization.

Maslow believed healthy people are motivated toward self-actualization and become mature in accepting others, solving problems, seeking autonomy, and developing deep-seated feelings of compassion and empathy for others. Unhealthy people, however, experience personal or other obstacles to self-actualization and may develop mental problems as a result. Compare Rachel, who takes whatever classes she wants and excitedly pursues her degree, with Colby, who is pressured by his parents toward a career in which he has no interest. Colby is more likely to experience frustration in his goal toward personal self-actualization and become depressed. Recall as well that Mariella felt considerable pressure from family members to return to college for her second semester. Her feelings of sadness may have been related to diversion from more desired life goals.

Carl Rogers

Carl Rogers (1902–1987) expanded on Maslow's work to become one of the leading proponents of the humanistic model of psychology. Rogers also believed humans strive for self-actualization and that frustration toward this goal could lead to mental problems such as depression. Rogers believed people raised in the right environment could work toward self-actualization and a strong *self-concept* in which one feels differentiated from others in a positive way. Think of someone who is rightfully proud to be the first in their family to graduate from college.

What is the right environment for self-actualization? Rogers presented the concepts of conditional and unconditional positive regard. **Conditional positive regard** refers to an environment in which others set the conditions or standards for one's life. Think about someone like Colby whose major life decisions are made by parents, teachers, or other influential people. People like Colby may feel a sense of loss of control over events and thus feel helpless to change anything. Their drive toward self-actualization and psychological health is thus thwarted. People who feel a sense of loss of control over life events do indeed seem to be at risk for anxiety disorders (Chapter 5).

Unconditional positive regard refers to an environment in which a person is fully accepted as they are and allowed to pursue their own desires and goals. Someone like Rachel who is given freedom to choose her own way in life is more predisposed toward self-actualization and psychological health than Colby. Mariella might also have felt less sad if her family members recognized her signs of depression and offered different ideas about what she could do in her life.

Rogers developed **client-centered therapy** that relies heavily on unconditional positive regard and *empathy.* A client-centered therapist establishes a therapeutic environment in which a client is completely accepted and unjudged. Unconditional positive regard in therapy refers to respecting a client's feelings, thoughts, and actions and providing a sympathetic understanding of the client's statements. Many client-centered therapists allow clients to speak freely without assigning blame, criticism, or even feedback about what to do. The therapist instead concentrates on trying to understand the world as the client understands it and often reflects a client's statements so the client can develop their own solution to a problem. Consider the following exchange between a client-centered therapist and Colby:

Colby: I've been feeling so down lately, I get so tired of my life.

Therapist: It sounds as though things are upsetting you.

Colby: Yeah, my parents are always on my case to be a lawyer because my dad and grandfather were lawyers.

Therapist: That sounds like a lot of pressure.

Colby: It is a lot of pressure. Sometimes I just want to tell them to leave me alone so I can do whatever I want.

Therapist: I can understand that. Tell me more about that.

Colby: I think I need to have a heart-to-heart talk with my dad. I just can't take this anymore.

The client-centered therapist in this exchange did not tell Colby what to do but instead displayed empathy and allowed Colby to speak freely without worrying about being judged. The therapist also reflected Colby's feelings and statements so he could arrive at his own solution. Client-centered therapists believe many mental problems result from *other-centeredness,* or oversensitivity to demands, criticisms, and judgments of others. Colby's therapist treated him as a responsible adult who needed to become more *person-centered* and find his way back to a path of self-actualization (Längle & Klaassen, 2021). Client-centered therapists believe clients are their own best experts of their problems and that healthy functioning requires more autonomous decision making.

Rollo May

Rollo May (1909–1994) adopted a similar approach to humanistic psychology. May's *existential psychology* is heavily based on the concept of *authenticity,* or how closely one adheres to one's personality. Someone who is authentic is true to their nature and honest in their interactions with others. Someone who is not authentic may develop a façade and act like someone else in social situations. Perhaps you know someone who tries to be extroverted when really they are introverted or someone who conforms to the "in" crowd so they will be liked. People who are not authentic are thought to be at risk for alienation from others. Several personality disorders discussed in Chapter 10 involve odd behaviors that often result in social isolation.

Existential theorists believe people are alone in the world and may therefore develop a sense of *meaninglessness.* People who feel meaningless in their world and who are not authentic may be at risk for anxiety and other problems. Existential therapists help their clients discover reasons for their anxiety, manage their anxiety in healthier ways, seek social support from others, develop strong moral values, and act more honestly with others (Balogh et al., 2021). Someone who is introverted could acknowledge that they are less willing to talk in social situations and develop friendships through good listening and other nonverbal support.

Humanistic Assessment and Treatment

Humanistic theorists believe in a *qualitative* model of assessment. Qualitative assessment focuses on unique characteristics of an individual and often includes general questions about one's perceptions of the world. Humanistic theorists do not group people together to identify common characteristics and often shun formal psychological testing (Chapter 4; Bland, 2022). A client-centered therapist interviewing Colby would focus on how Colby perceives his world and might thus ask certain questions such as "How might you speak to your father about your concerns?" Specific questions for Colby would not likely be used for Mariella, however, because Mariella's way of viewing the world is completely different from Colby's.

Treatment from a humanistic perspective is *nondirective,* meaning the therapist does not adopt a paternalistic or commanding tone for therapy. A psychiatrist might tell you what medication to take, and a psychodynamic therapist might tell you what your dream means, but a nondirective therapist does not impose their worldview or opinions onto their client. The therapist instead engages in reflective listening so a client can develop solutions, relieve tension, and resume a path toward self-actualization. Nondirective treatments are sometimes considered to be *pretherapy,* or actions taken first in treatment to develop a good relationship with a client (Gregory, 2020). Nondirective treatments thus fit well with most other kinds of therapy.

Evaluating the Humanistic Model

The humanistic model has several strengths, particularly its focus on human choice and growth. The humanistic model is optimistic and tied to contemporary *positive psychology,* which refers to the study of what factors allow people to thrive in their environments. The humanistic model also emphasizes responsibility. Biological theorists focus on disease models of mental disorder, so treatment usually involves medication or some external agent of behavior change. Psychodynamic theorists focus on personality models of mental disorder, so treatment usually involves better insight with the help of a therapist. Humanistic theorists, however, emphasize that clients themselves must take responsibility for their recovery. Such an approach would seem useful for people with disorders such as anxiety, depression, and substance use. People who actively participate in treatment often have better outcomes than those who participate less (Huber et al., 2021).

Rogers's client-centered approach has also contributed greatly to the way therapists approach their clients in session. Many therapists, especially in the first few sessions of therapy, develop a warm, supportive environment for their clients to enhance self-disclosure. Different *process variables* that contribute to treatment success are discussed in Chapter 15. Process variables are factors common to all treatments that seem to help clients. One particularly helpful process variable is a therapeutic environment based on *respect, empathy,* and *full acceptance* of client expressions. A client must feel free to communicate private thoughts without fear of rejection or ridicule. Humanistic therapies may thus be helpful for people who need to express grief or discuss difficult personal issues (Pinheiro et al., 2021). Nondirective treatment may also be useful for clients highly mistrustful of, or hostile toward, a therapist.

The humanistic perspective is partly represented in ethical guidelines that psychologists adhere to when treating clients (Trachsel et al., 2021). Psychologists are expected to refrain from biases from possible prejudices toward people of a different culture, sexual orientation, age, gender, or political affiliation, among other factors. Psychologists are expected to respect a client's dignity and rights, including the right to self-determination. If a psychologist feels they cannot be unbiased with a client and this interferes with their ability to conduct therapy, then a referral to another therapist should be made.

The humanistic approach has several limitations as well. The theory lacks strong empirical support in part because concepts such as self-actualization are difficult to define and test. Many factors other than human perceptions of the world also influence behavior and mental disorder. In addition, client-centered therapy may be more effective for people who are more verbal, social, intelligent, and willing to talk. The therapy may thus apply less to people with a severe mental disorder such as schizophrenia or intellectual developmental disorder, to children, or to those who are suicidal (Elliot et al., 2021).

Section Summary

- The humanistic model focuses on how humans can make choices that influence their environment and how they can take responsibility for their actions.
- The phenomenological approach is based on the assumption that one's behavior is determined by perceptions of oneself and others.
- Abraham Maslow outlined a series of human needs; the highest level is self-actualization, or pursuit of one's full potential.
- Carl Rogers developed client-centered therapy, which focuses on unconditional positive regard, or complete acceptance of a client, and empathy.
- Rollo May's existential approach emphasized authenticity, or how closely one adheres to one's personality, as well as anxiety about alienation from others.
- The humanistic perspective relies on qualitative assessment of an individual's perceptions of himself and the world as well as nondirective therapy.
- Strengths of the humanistic perspective include its emphasis on personal responsibility for recovery and process variables important for treatment.
- Limitations of the humanistic perspective include relative lack of strong research support and less utility for certain groups of people.

Review Questions

1. How might the humanistic model explain Mariella's problems?
2. How might a client-centered therapist assess and treat Mariella?
3. Describe the following features of the humanistic perspective and how they can help us understand Mariella's symptoms: phenomenological approach, self-actualization, conditional positive regard, authenticity.
4. What are strengths and limitations of the humanistic perspective?

The Cognitive-Behavioral Model

LO 2.5 Characterize the cognitive-behavioral model of psychopathology, including its assumptions, strengths, limitations, clinical implications, and empirical support.

The psychodynamic and humanistic perspectives covered so far focus specifically on internal variables, have less empirical support, or seem not to apply well to many people with a mental disorder. Another perspective of mental disorders focuses on external as well as internal factors, has good empirical support, and is relevant to many people with a mental disorder. The *behavioral perspective* focuses on external acts, and the *cognitive perspective* focuses on internal thoughts. Some theorists discuss these perspectives separately, but many contemporary researchers and therapists understand the limitations of working within just one model. Many mental health professionals now combine these perspectives into a singular *cognitive-behavioral model.* These perspectives are first discussed separately and then together to show how combining the perspectives provide a good explanation for mental disorders and treatment.

Behavioral Perspective

The **behavioral perspective** developed partly in reaction to psychodynamic theory. Many psychologists were concerned that variables such as id and unconscious were difficult to measure and less important to mental health outcomes. The behavioral perspective instead focuses on environmental stimuli and behavioral responses—variables that can be directly observed and measured. The behavioral perspective is based on the assumption that all behavior—normal or psychopathological—is learned. The behavioral model became prominent in psychology because learning principles received much empirical support and applied to many topics of psychological research. Treatment approaches from a behavioral perspective were also found to be quite effective for many problems such as anxiety and intellectual developmental disorders. The behavioral perspective is based heavily on a learning approach, so a discussion of key learning principles is important.

Learning Principles

Two learning principles are critical to the behavioral perspective: classical conditioning and operant conditioning. *Classical conditioning* essentially refers to learning by association and was studied initially by

Ivan Pavlov (1849–1936), a Russian physiologist. Pavlov was interested in the digestive system but made some interesting observations during his experiments with dogs. Pavlov gave meat powder repeatedly to dogs to produce salivation, and he found the dogs often salivated *beforehand*, such as when hearing approaching footsteps! Pavlov was intrigued and explored the nature of this reaction. He rang a bell immediately before a dog received meat powder. This was repeated several times and resulted in dogs salivating after the bell but *before* the meat powder. The dogs learned to salivate to a stimulus, in this case a ringing bell that should not by itself cause salivation. The dogs had learned by association: the bell meant food.

This important experiment led ultimately to **classical conditioning** theory ("conditioning" means learning). Learning occurs when a *conditioned stimulus* (CS; bell) is paired with an *unconditioned stimulus* (UCS; meat powder) so future presentations of the CS (bell) result in a conditioned response (CR; salivation). Classical conditioning theory also suggests that problems such as trauma-based disorders might develop because classical conditioning once took place. Posttraumatic stress disorder (Chapter 5) partly involves avoiding situations or people that remind someone of a traumatic experience. Sexual assault victims with this disorder may avoid certain parts of an area associated with the assault, or may feel anxious when they encounter someone who reminds them of their attacker. These behavioral and emotional reactions might be understood via classical conditioning: a location or physical feature (CS) was paired with an assault (UCS), and now the CS produces the classically conditioned response (CR) of intense fear and avoidance (refer to **Figure 2.8**).

Figure 2.8 Principles of Classical Conditioning.

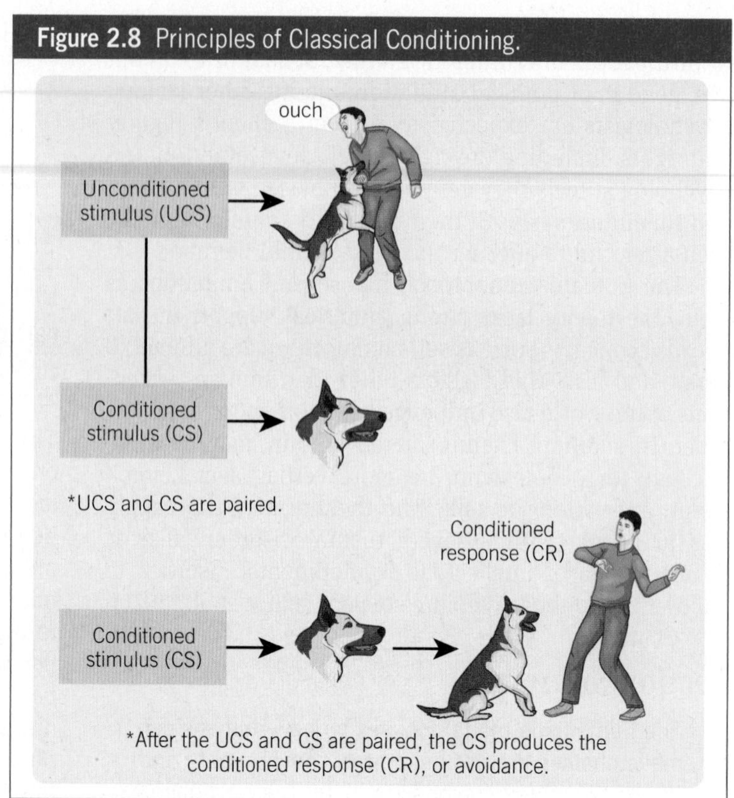

Operant conditioning is based on the principle that behavior followed by positive or pleasurable consequences will likely be repeated, but behavior followed by negative consequences, such as punishment, will not likely be repeated. Reinforcement is thus an important aspect of operant conditioning. **Positive reinforcement** involves giving a pleasant event or consequence after a behavior. A child praised or rewarded for cleaning their room is likely to repeat the behavior in the future. Positive reinforcement can also maintain maladaptive behavior, as when someone with depression receives sympathy from others or when parents allow a child to miss school and play video games.

Negative reinforcement involves removing an aversive event following a behavior, which also increases the future likelihood of the behavior. Why do you wear deodorant? You likely do not do so for all the wonderful compliments you get during the day but rather to avoid negative comments about body odor! Negative reinforcement can also explain why some fears are maintained over time. Someone afraid of spiders may avoid closets because spiders like to live in dark places. Such avoidance is reinforced because spiders are not encountered and so the aversive event of fear is removed. Such avoidance is also likely to continue in the future (refer to **Figure 2.9**).

Behavior can also be "shaped" through reinforcement. Students might shape a professor's teaching style by rewarding more interesting lectures. Students might provide strong reinforcement by maintaining eye contact, asking questions, or saying, "That is really interesting!" when a professor provides multiple examples or case illustrations. You can guess where this is headed. When students reinforce successive approximations of this lively lecture style, they have the power to make the class more engaging, fresh, and interesting. If you try this on your professors, please do not let them know the source of the idea, and please do not keep them completely under your control!

Cognitive Perspective

The **cognitive perspective** arose from the behavioral perspective because people often behave in ways that have little to do with reinforcement. How did Tony develop an intense fear of heights when he never had a traumatic experience involving heights? An understanding of thoughts, perceptions, and emotions may better

Figure 2.9 Principles of Operant Conditioning.

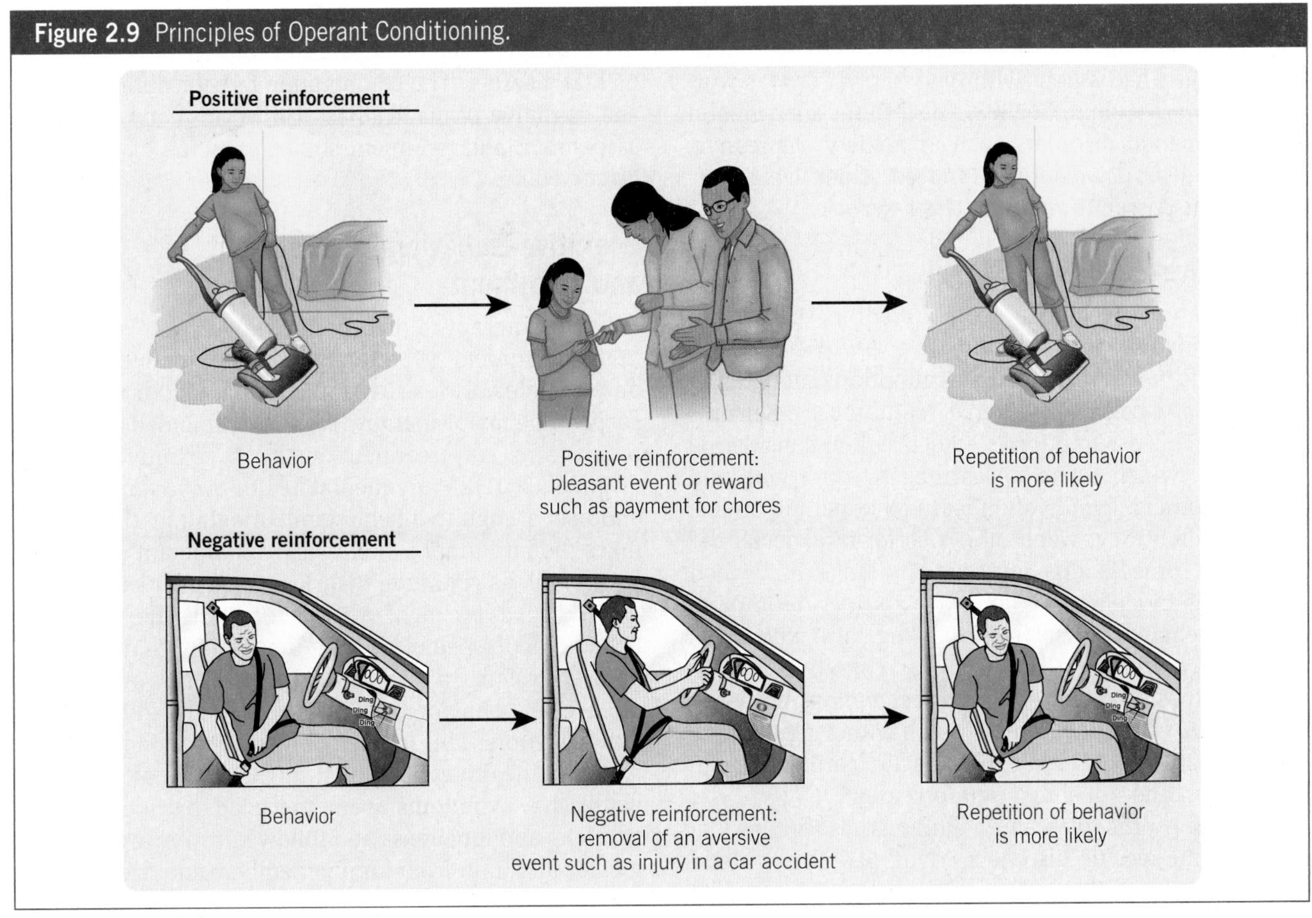
Positive reinforcement
Behavior
Positive reinforcement: pleasant event or reward such as payment for chores
Repetition of behavior is more likely
Negative reinforcement
Behavior
Negative reinforcement: removal of an aversive event such as injury in a car accident
Repetition of behavior is more likely

account for Tony's fear and avoidance. Not everything can be explained by simple principles of classical and operant conditioning. The cognitive perspective instead suggests that emotions and behavior are influenced by how we perceive and think about our present and past experiences. Learning principles help comprise the behavioral perspective, but other principles comprise the cognitive perspective. These are discussed next.

Cognitive Principles

Each of us actively processes and interprets our experiences. Such processing and interpretation is influenced by **cognitive schemas**, or beliefs or expectations that represent a network of accumulated knowledge. We enter many situations with some expectation of what may happen. Think about the unwritten script that occurs when you enter a restaurant. You wait to be seated, place your order, eat, pay, and leave. If a restaurant conducted this script in a different order, you might be a little confused. Our schemas or expectations about events affect our behavior and emotional experiences. College students told they are drinking a beverage with alcohol—when in fact they are drinking a nonalcoholic beverage—often report feeling intoxicated. They talk loudly or become silly as though they are intoxicated. Their *expectancies* of what they are like when intoxicated influence their behavior, even when not drinking alcohol!

Cognitive distortions are another important principle of the cognitive perspective and refer to unrealistic, inaccurate thoughts people have about environmental events. Cognitive theory (Beck et al., 2021) holds that mental disorder may result if one has negative views of oneself ("I'm not good at anything"), other people in the world ("No one cares about anyone except themself"), and the future ("Things will never get easier for me").

Cognitive distortions often come in the form of *arbitrary inference*, which means reaching a conclusion based on little evidence. A professor may notice that 2 out of 50 students fell asleep during one lecture and assume they are a bad teacher. The professor ignored the greater evidence that most people did pay attention and instead focused on the two who did not. Professors also see students who agonize over one or two mistakes at the expense of understanding the greater value of their examination or project.

Another common cognitive distortion is *personalization*, or erroneously blaming oneself for events. If a coworker refused to speak to you one day, you might personalize the event by wondering what offense you committed. You are ignoring other, more reasonable explanations for what happened—perhaps your coworker just had a fight with their partner or was worried about a sick child. Cognitive distortions are common to many mental disorders such as anxiety, depressive, eating, and sexual disorders. Indeed, cognitive distortions are discussed throughout this textbook.

A Cognitive-Behavioral Model

Contemporary psychologists often combine behavioral and cognitive approaches into a *cognitive-behavioral model.* This model rests on the assumption that learning principles *and* cognitions interact to influence a person's behavior. This assumption is evident when considering **modeling**, which refers to learning by observing and imitating others. People often learn by watching others, such as when they watch others perform a specialized skill. We process this information, judge how good someone is modeling the behavior, and decide to practice the behavior ourselves. Modeling, also known as *vicarious conditioning,* implies that cognitive mechanisms such as thoughts, beliefs, or perceptions influence learning. A combined cognitive-behavioral perspective helps explain why certain behaviors are learned through observation and not simple reinforcement.

Learning principles and cognitions also interact to help explain specific disorders. Many people are afraid of airplanes even though airplanes are not typically dangerous or threatening. Classical and operant conditioning may help explain why fear in these situations is maintained, but why do people *start* avoiding harmless objects or situations in the first place? People who avoid a harmless stimulus internalized something that *now motivates or drives subsequent avoidance behavior.* A type of learning called **avoidance conditioning** is thus often proposed. Avoidance conditioning combines classical and operant conditioning and accommodates an internal state like fear as a *motivating or driving factor* that influences behavior. This internal state is the cognitive aspect of phobia development.

Consider Shawn's flying phobia (refer to **Figure 2.10**). A neutral stimulus such as flying on an airplane becomes paired with an unpleasant unconditioned stimulus such as nausea—classical conditioning. Shawn later avoids flying because internalized *fear* of experiencing nausea drives him to do so. The internalized state that drives Shawn's future avoidance could not be explained by simple classical or operant conditioning. The internalized state or cognitive component instead provides a more complete account of why Shawn's phobia continued over time.

Contemporary models of mental disorders often include a combination of learning principles and cognitive influences such as expectancies and motivations. Substantial research also supports the idea that cognitive schemas and distortions influence forms of mental disorder. The combination of behavioral/learning and cognitive principles has also led to many important assessment and treatment strategies, some of which are discussed next.

Cognitive-Behavioral Assessment and Treatment

Behavior therapy represented a novel way of treating mental disorders and initially included treatments based on principles of classical and operant conditioning. The scope of behavior therapy has since expanded to include other forms of treatment such as cognitive therapy (Wenzel, 2021). Many mental health professionals today endorse a cognitive-behavioral orientation that recognizes the importance of classical and operant conditioning as well as cognitive theories of mental disorders.

A key assessment approach within the cognitive-behavioral perspective is **functional analysis**. Functional analysis refers to evaluating antecedents and consequences of behavior, or what preceded and followed certain behaviors. This is often done by observing a person. A mental health professional might note that Mariella's depressive symptoms were preceded by school-based stressors and loneliness and followed by rewards such as greater attention from family members and friends.

Cognitive variables must also be considered during assessment. Mariella may have certain cognitive distortions, such as believing her troubles in school were related to lack of ability, that others did not care about her, and that things would not improve in the future.

Figure 2.10 Avoidant Conditioning.

Shawn is conditioned to avoid flying.

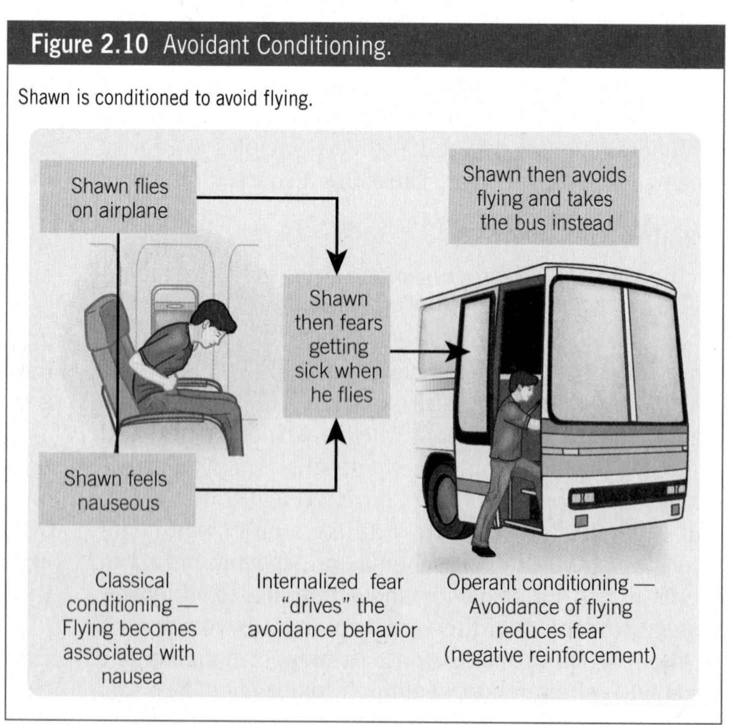

Shawn flies on airplane
Shawn then avoids flying and takes the bus instead
Shawn then fears getting sick when he flies
Shawn feels nauseous
Classical conditioning — Flying becomes associated with nausea
Internalized fear "drives" the avoidance behavior
Operant conditioning — Avoidance of flying reduces fear (negative reinforcement)

Her symptoms may have been at least partly caused by these kinds of cognitive schemas or beliefs that are linked to depression. A therapist would assess for these cognitive processes as well during a functional analysis.

How might a cognitive-behavioral therapist treat Mariella's symptoms? **Cognitive-behavioral therapy** refers to a large collection of treatment techniques to change patterns of thinking and behaving that contribute to a person's problems. These techniques have much empirical support and are among the most effective forms of therapy (Van Dis et al., 2020). Many therapists now use cognitive and behavioral techniques for their clients. The following techniques might be used to treat Mariella's depression:

1. Scheduling activities to counteract her inactivity and her focus on depressive feelings. Mariella might be given "homework assignments" to go to the movies with friends or play the guitar before others.
2. Mariella might be asked to imagine successive steps leading to completion of an important task, such as attending an exercise class, so potential barriers or impediments can be identified, anticipated, and addressed. This is called *cognitive rehearsal.*
3. Mariella might engage in assertiveness training and role-playing to improve her social and conversational skills.
4. Mariella might be asked to identify thoughts such as "I can't do anything right" that occur before or during feelings of depression.
5. The reality or accuracy of Mariella's thoughts might be examined by gently challenging their validity ("What kinds of things *do* you do well?").
6. Mariella might be taught to avoid personalizing events for which she is not to blame. She may be shown that her classmates' busy behaviors reflect their own hectic lives and not attempts to rebuff Mariella.
7. Mariella could be helped to find alternative solutions to her problems instead of giving up.

A common therapeutic technique from this perspective is **cognitive restructuring**, or helping someone think more realistically in a given situation. How might cognitive restructuring help Mariella? Recall that Mariella was distancing herself from family, friends, and enjoyable activities. She felt her friends did not understand her or care about her. A therapist using cognitive restructuring might help Mariella think about the situation more realistically. The therapist might help her understand her friends are not avoiding her, but rather she is avoiding them. Mariella is not giving her friends the opportunity to support and care for her because Mariella is isolating herself. A therapist using cognitive restructuring will be quite direct with Mariella, using discussions and making arguments that Mariella is viewing her situation unrealistically. Unrealistic beliefs such as "My friends don't care about me" are unfounded and lead to depression. The therapist may also try to teach Mariella to "modify her internal sentences." Mariella might be taught when feeling depressed to pause and ask herself what her immediate thoughts are. The therapist would then ask Mariella to objectively evaluate these thoughts and make corrections. The therapist might thus have her imagine particular problem situations and ask her to think more realistically in these situations.

Other cognitive-behavioral techniques are used to treat mental disorders as well. **Systematic desensitization** is an approach used to treat fear-related concerns. A client is first taught to relax, typically via progressive muscle relaxation techniques. The therapist and client then construct a hierarchy of situations or objects related to the feared stimulus. Items at the bottom of the hierarchy arouse fear at low levels; for a person afraid of dogs, this might mean watching a dog in a film. More fear-provoking items are further along the hierarchy. Contact with an actual feared situation, such as petting a dog, is at the top of the hierarchy. Clients reach a state of relaxation and progressively encounter each object or situation on the hierarchy. If a client becomes too fearful, the procedure is halted so the client can once again become relaxed. Progression along the hierarchy is then restarted. A person is thus desensitized to the previously feared stimulus or situation. From a classical conditioning perspective, the client has learned to respond to a previously feared stimulus with relaxation instead of excessive arousal.

A key element of systematic desensitization is **exposure treatment**, which involves directly confronting a feared stimulus. This can be done gradually or, in the case of *flooding*, the client does not relax in advance but is instead exposed immediately to a feared stimulus. Exposure treatment can be done by having clients imagine the presence of a feared stimulus or by facing the feared stimulus or situation in real life. Clients are understandably fearful in these situations, but if they continue to stay in the presence of the stimulus, fear diminishes. A nonfearful response becomes associated with a previously feared stimulus or situation through repeated exposure sessions.

Systematic desensitization and exposure treatment are based on classical conditioning, but other behavior therapy techniques are based on operant conditioning, which emphasizes reinforcement. A relatively simple application is when a mental health professional stops reinforcing a problematic behavior and reinforces more adaptive and acceptable behavior. Or a therapist might help parents manage consequences for their children to increase positive behavior such as completing homework and decrease negative behavior such as aggression.

Operant conditioning principles are also apparent in token economies to modify behaviors of those sometimes present in institutional settings such as people with intellectual developmental disorder or schizophrenia. A **token economy** is a reinforcement system for certain behaviors in which tokens or points are given for positive behaviors and exchanged later for tangible rewards. Someone with schizophrenia on an inpatient hospital unit may earn points for positive behaviors such as attending group therapy sessions and showering. These points could later be exchanged for privileges such as day passes from the hospital. Token economies are also used to improve social and academic skills and other behaviors in children.

Evaluating the Cognitive-Behavioral Model

The cognitive-behavioral perspective has contributed greatly to our understanding and treatment of mental disorders. The behavioral approach and its emphasis on learning principles revolutionized the study and treatment of mental disorders following psychodynamic theory. The model has been broadened to include thought processes, expectancies, and other internal states. A combined cognitive-behavioral model is among the most influential for conceptualizing the development and maintenance of problematic behavior. The perspective also offers a broad array of treatment choices for many mental disorders. These cognitive-behavioral treatments often have been shown to be effective and efficient, often requiring fewer than 20 sessions.

Limitations of the cognitive-behavioral model should be noted, however. Most problematic might be the model's concept of how mental disorders first develop. Some cognitive-behavior theorists reduce complex behaviors such as depression to simple learning history or cognitive schemas, but this may not be plausible. Many biological, personality, and social factors also contribute to depression and other disorders. The "chicken and egg" problem is also relevant to cognitive-behaviorism: Did problematic thoughts, beliefs, or expectancies *cause* Mariella's depression, or did these cognitive patterns *result* from her depression?

The cognitive-behavioral perspective appears less able to provide clear and comprehensive historical accounts of how problematic behavior developed in the first place. The cognitive-behavioral perspective seems best suited to explain and address *current* functioning and highlight targets of change that can be used in treatment. The perspective is particularly good for identifying specific symptoms that need change, such as Mariella's isolated behavior and cognitive distortions.

Section Summary

- The behavioral perspective on mental disorders is based on the assumption that behavior is learned.
- Two major learning principles underlie the behavioral approach: classical conditioning and operant conditioning.
- The cognitive perspective suggests that problematic symptoms and behavior develop from the way we perceive and think about our present and past experiences.
- Key principles of the cognitive perspective include schemas and cognitive distortions.
- Behavioral and cognitive perspectives have been combined to form the cognitive-behavioral model.
- Major cognitive-behavioral treatment approaches include cognitive restructuring, systematic desensitization, exposure, and token economy.
- Strengths of a cognitive-behavioral model include its broad array of effective treatments.
- A key limitation of the cognitive-behavioral model is accounting for how mental problems originally develop.

Review Questions

1. How might the cognitive-behavioral model explain Mariella's problems?
2. What treatments might a cognitive-behavioral therapist use to treat Mariella's problems?
3. Describe the following learning principles and how they might help us understand Mariella's symptoms: classical conditioning, operant conditioning, modeling.
4. What are strengths and limitations of a cognitive-behavioral perspective on mental disorders?

The Sociocultural Model

LO 2.6 Describe the sociocultural model of psychopathology, including its assumptions, strengths, limitations, clinical implications, and empirical support.

The models of mental disorder discussed so far in this chapter—biological, psychodynamic, humanistic, and cognitive-behavioral—focus primarily on individuals and their personal characteristics. We do not live in a vacuum, however—many outside factors affect how we feel, think, and behave. Biological, psychodynamic, humanistic, and cognitive-behavioral perspectives do acknowledge some environmental role in psychological problems. The **sociocultural perspective** differs from these models in its greater emphasis on environmental factors; its core assumption is that outside influences play a *major* role in a person's psychological problems. The sociocultural perspective focuses on influences that social institutions and other people have on a person's mental health.

Many sociocultural factors potentially influence the development, symptom expression, assessment, and treatment of mental disorders. Several prominent

Focus On Gender

A More Complex Approach

Different models are useful for understanding symptoms, causes, and treatment of mental disorder. The use of a single model to describe a mental disorder can be a problem, however, when gender differences arise. For example, a well-established finding is that female and male children experience similar rates of depression but female adults experience depression at twice the rate of male adults. To explain this finding using just a psychodynamic or cognitive-behavioral model would be difficult. Instead, researchers generally develop integrative models to help explain gender differences. Some have proposed models that focus on negative life events as well as biological, cognitive, and emotional factors (Hyde & Mezulis, 2020). For example, a girl may experience sexual maltreatment as a child, develop a negative cognitive style, experience increased biological arousal, and display emotional difficulties into adulthood that include depression. These factors may pertain more to girls than to boys, which may help explain gender differences in adult depression.

Another problem that differs by gender is excessive alcohol use, which is much more common in boys than girls by late adolescence. Single models such as the humanistic or sociocultural perspective cannot fully account for this difference. Instead, an integrative model may be best. Early in life, certain biological and psychological factors that predispose alcohol use appear to be similar for boys and girls. During adolescence, however, some important changes may take place. Boys may become more impulsive and sensation seeking, experience later brain maturation, and be more sensitive to peer influences than girls (White, 2020). These factors may predispose boys to disruptive drinking more than girls.

examples of sociocultural influences on mental health are highlighted here. This is not an exhaustive list, but these examples best highlight this perspective and current areas of investigation. This section begins with more global influences, such as culture and gender and neighborhoods, and finishes with a topic closer to home—family.

Culture

Culture refers to the unique behavior and lifestyle shared by a group of people. Culture is composed of viewpoints, beliefs, values, and preferences that are evident in rituals, food, customs, laws, art, music, and religion. Culture is not innate but external, learned, and transmitted to others. Culture is not the same as **ethnicity**, which refers to clusters of people who share cultural traits and who use those traits to distinguish themselves from others. Culture is also different from **race**, which refers to a category typically based on physical characteristics (Atkin et al., 2022).

One difference between ethnicity and race is that ethnic groups identify themselves as such. The concept of race, however, evolved from early attempts to categorize people based on physical characteristics such as skin color, hair texture, and facial features. However, analyses of genetic material (DNA) actually reveal more differences *within* racial groups than *between* racial groups (Lorusso & Winther, 2022). This reinforces the idea that race is not biologically based but rather socially defined. Culture includes but is not limited to concepts of ethnicity and race, and culture is learned from others and passed to succeeding generations.

Culture can influence mental disorder in several ways. Culture might serve as a distant but *direct cause* of mental disorders. Culturally shared beliefs and ideas can lead to particular forms of stress that, in turn, lead to a specific problem called a **cultural syndrome** (American Psychiatric Association [APA], 2022). *Dhat syndrome* is an anxiety-related belief observed in Indian men that one is "losing" semen through nocturnal emissions, masturbation, or urination. The cultural belief driving the fear is that excessive semen loss results in illness (Kar et al., 2021). Culture can also *influence the way individuals cope with stressful situations. Amok* is a condition in South Asian and Pacific Islander cultures in which a person attacks others. Cultures in which this condition is observed are often characterized by nonconfrontation, so amok may be a failure to cope with extreme stress (Imai et al., 2019).

Culture can also influence mental disorders by *shaping the content of symptoms. Anthrophobia* is a phobia of interpersonal relations in Japanese culture that involves fears of one's body odor, flushing or blushing, and eye contact. These symptoms reflect hypersensitivity to

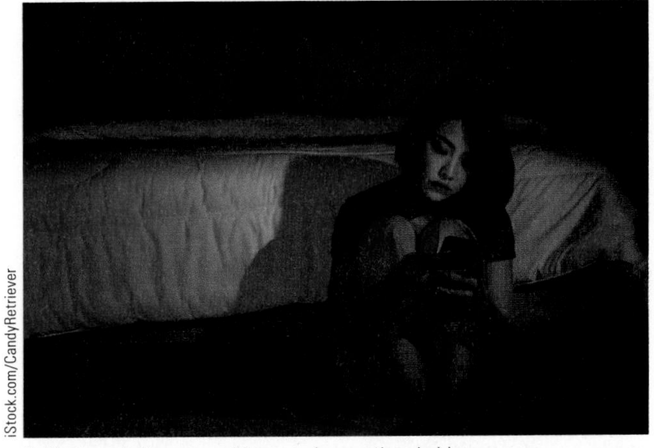

iStock.com/CandyRetriever

Culture can influence problems such as anthrophobia.

Table 2.4 How Does Culture Contribute to Mental Disorders?

Methods	Examples
Direct cause: culturally shared belief leads to stress, and then to symptoms of mental disorder	Dhat syndrome
Influences the way individuals cope with stress	Amok
Shapes the content of the symptoms or the symptoms themselves	Anthrophobia Anorexia nervosa

being looked at or looking at others as well as concern about how one's own behavior is viewed by others. Disorders found primarily in Western societies also contain unique symptoms and features. *Anorexia nervosa* (Chapter 8) involves excessive concern about being overweight and severe weight loss that threatens one's health. This condition is often observed in American and European cultures but is less common in Samoa and the Pacific Islands, where certain foods are less available or where being overweight is more accepted. A sociocultural theory stipulates that anorexia nervosa is more prevalent in processed food-abundant societies that stress an "ideal body" as thin (Rymarczyk, 2021). Culture thus affects the development of psychological problems in various ways (refer to **Table 2.4**).

Gender

Mental disorders affect people of different genders but some problems seem more common in one gender than another. Men are more likely to have antisocial personality and substance use disorder, but women are more likely to have anxiety-related and depressive disorders (APA, 2022). Gender differences may be explained by differences in biology, gender identity, socialization, and social situations in which women and men find themselves (Merikangas & Almasy, 2020). Biological differences in sex hormones may help explain why more men than women have sexual disorders (Chapter 11).

Gender identity refers to one's awareness of being male or female or perceived degree of masculinity or femininity. Gender identity can be influenced by parenting style and interactions with others, among other factors, and can be related to mental health. People who are androgynous in their personality, as opposed to strictly masculine or feminine, tend to have better cognitive flexibility and mental health (Luo & Sahakian, 2022).

Men are also less likely to find themselves in certain situations compared with women, especially as victims of domestic violence and sexual assault. This may help explain why men have fewer anxiety-related disorders than women (Chapter 5). Our *expectations of men and of women*, or socialization differences, also play a role in mental health. We generally expect men to be less emotionally expressive. Men who are anxious and depressed may thus be more likely to use alcohol and other drugs to self-medicate their symptoms, whereas women may be more likely to talk to friends or a therapist.

Gender differences are most evident for depression, where women have much higher rates than men, and social support seems to be a key factor. Women generally have more social support than men with respect to number of close relationships and level of intimacy of these relationships. If social support declines, however, then women may be more susceptible to depression because they rely more on social support for their well-being (Richardson & Barkham, 2020). Recall that Mariella's separation from family members and friends near home was related to her sadness.

Women may be more likely than men to respond to stress by "tending-and-befriending" (Hlay et al., 2022). Women often respond to stress by nurturing and protecting offspring (tend) and by affiliating with others to reduce risk of harm (befriend). Doing so may have an evolutionary component. When a threat existed, quieting offspring and blending into the environment was adaptive because one was not perceived as a threat. Affiliating with a social group following a threat also increased the chance one would be protected. This tending and befriending pattern has also been linked to neurobiological systems that characterize attachment to others and caregiving. This theory and related findings illustrate that understanding gender differences can help us explain mental disorders and develop treatments. Mariella could volunteer to help others to help reduce her social isolation and depression.

Neighborhoods and Communities

Another influence on mental well-being involves surrounding neighborhoods and communities. Several

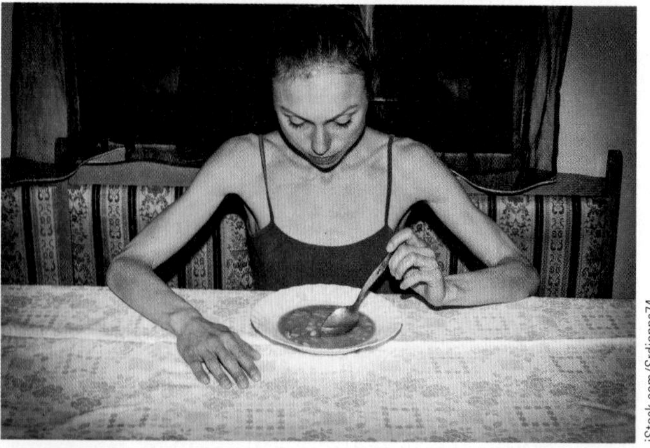
iStock.com/Srdjanns74

According to a sociocultural model, anorexia nervosa may be a condition that occurs more in processed food-abundant societies that stress a thin ideal.

neighborhood characteristics are associated with poorer mental health (Baranyi et al., 2021). Examples include discrimination, unemployment, food and housing insecurity, inadequate transportation, overcrowding, violence, substance use, and excessive noise and pollution. These variables, or *social determinants*, are often associated with elevated rates of mental health challenges such as anxiety, depression, and self-harm and suicide (Alegría et al., 2018).

Why do certain neighborhood characteristics relate to poorer mental health? A common theme appears to be stress. Certain neighborhoods generate many stressful life events. People from these neighborhoods also have fewer resources available to them to handle these stressors, so their ability to cope is taxed. Individual differences exist, however, with respect to how able and how well one can cope with such stressors. Some people are "resilient" to such stressors, and psychologists have focused more on features and mechanisms of this resilience (Ungar & Theron, 2020). Knowledge about resilience can help psychologists prevent negative mental health outcomes even for people who live under adverse conditions. Resilience is discussed in more detail in Chapter 3 within the context of risk and prevention.

Family

Many theorists believe that positive family relationships decrease risk for psychological problems but that family conflict can increase risk. A **family systems perspective** assumes that each family has its own rules and organizational structure, or hierarchy of authority and decision making. When family members keep to their rules and organization, a sense of homeostasis or stability is created. Dysfunctional families, however, experience problems and distress because the rules and structure are not optimal (Davies et al., 2021). Some problematic family relationships and environmental variables are discussed next.

Problematic Family Relationships

Inflexible families are overly rigid and do not adapt well to changes within or outside the family. This can lead to substantial conflict, especially as a child reaches adolescence and wants more independence. *Enmeshed* families are characterized by family members who are overly involved in the private lives of other family members. This can lead to overdependence of family members on one another and feelings of being controlled by others. A family systems theory of anorexia nervosa suggests some individuals try to regain control over their lives by refusing to eat in reaction to parents' excessive involvement and control.

Disengaged families are characterized by family members who operate independently of one another with little parental supervision. This family structure might predispose children to develop conduct problems or get into legal trouble. Families can also be characterized by *triangular relationships,* or situations in which parents avoid talking to each other and address marital conflicts by keeping their children involved in all conversations and activities.

Problematic Family Environment

Family environment refers to features or dimensions of family functioning. One feature of family environment is *family affect,* or the degree to which a family is cohesive, organized, and free of conflict. Another feature is *family activity,* or the degree to which families engage in cultural, recreational, and religious activities together. *Family control* is the degree to which a family is rigid or flexible when adapting to new situations or challenges (Bush et al., 2020).

Family environment does seem to influence the mental health of individual family members. For example, **expressed emotion** is the degree to which family interactions are marked by emotional overinvolvement, hostility, and criticism. A parent in a family with high expressed emotion might say to their son: "You never get out of the house. You are never going to amount to anything if you keep it up." Communications like this, although perhaps intended to motivate the son, likely lead to stress and negative feelings of self-worth. People with schizophrenia living in families with high expressed emotion, especially criticism, are at greater risk for relapse compared with people living in families with low expressed emotion (Ma et al., 2021). Interventions have thus been developed to help family members understand how their actions can negatively affect someone who has, or who is at risk for, a mental disorder.

Sociocultural Assessment and Treatment

Socioculturalists believe psychological problems largely develop because of the impact of social institutions and other people. What sociocultural factors may have affected Mariella, who was Latina? Mariella's culture is typically *collectivist,* meaning less emphasis on the self and more emphasis on interdependence with others such as friends and family members. Social support is thus likely quite important for Mariella, and her isolation at school may have influenced her sadness and pessimism. The importance of Mariella's academic achievement from a cultural and family perspective is also important to consider. Mariella may have experienced intense pressure to do well at college, which in turn led to added stress. Her family's dismissive reaction to her depressive symptoms when she was home may have led to further pessimism and self-criticism as well. Overall, many potential cultural, gender, and familial issues may have influenced the development and maintenance of Mariella's depressive symptoms.

Clinicians should thus conduct a thorough assessment of an individual's culture. A cultural assessment does not simply include race but also a person's self-defined ethnicity, sources of social support, affiliations and interactions with social institutions, and larger worldview factors such as religious preference. A person's gender role within a cultural context as well as important neighborhood and community factors should also be assessed. A thorough evaluation of family structure, dynamics, and environment is necessary for understanding a person's mental health as well.

Sociocultural assessment methods are less advanced than those of other models of mental disorder. Measures are available for social stressors, social support, and family environment, but fewer measures are available for features of culture, gender role, and neighborhood or community variables. A mental health professional, therefore, may be limited to using an unstructured interview when conducting these assessments (unstructured interviews are problematic assessment tools; Chapter 4).

Treatment from a sociocultural perspective focuses on addressing a person's difficulties at global and individual levels. Globally, sociocultural interventions focus on decreasing or preventing stress created for people through sexism, racism, or age or religious discrimination. Consider discrimination based on race or ethnicity, which places additional burden and stress on people and may lead to economic hardship and limited resources for education, health care, and employment. People who experience discrimination because of lack of economic resources are also likely to live in stressful neighborhoods or communities—neighborhoods with higher rates of unemployment, poverty, crime, and substance use problems. Unremitting stress from these circumstances can have a significant negative impact on a person's mental health. Racial and ethnic disparities also exist with respect to access to physical and mental health care (Mongelli et al., 2020).

A comprehensive program is clearly needed to address the influence of racial and ethnic discrimination on mental health and access to services. This would include programs to make community members aware of the discrimination, public policy and laws to prevent such discrimination, and efforts to decrease disparities in employment, housing, and economic well-being. Another priority is to increase the diversity of mental health professionals because finding such a professional from one's background is important to many people.

Treatment from a sociocultural perspective also focuses on addressing a person's difficulties at *individual* levels. *Family therapy* or *couples therapy*—in which multiple family members meet with a therapist at the same time—are used by various kinds of mental health professionals (Capuzzi & Stauffer, 2021). These therapies allow for better assessment of a family's problems and provide the opportunity to intervene with all members. Many family and couples therapists directly coach individuals on what to say to other family members and provide feedback about their interactions in order to improve communication. Therapists may focus less on family or dyad members and more on particular relationship issues or communication patterns. One family member might be exhibiting more emotional distress or behavioral problems than others, but this is thought to reflect problems within a family or couple. All family members must thus engage in treatment and change the way they interact with other family members.

Evaluating the Sociocultural Model

The sociocultural perspective has much strength for understanding mental disorders. First, the perspective highlights the importance of social influences on emotions, cognitions, and behaviors. Humans are indeed social beings and so our mental health is clearly influenced by people and institutions around us. Second, the sociocultural perspective provides a good understanding of different sources of stress that have an impact on a person and how that person copes with stress. Sources of stress may occur at global and individual levels. Finally, the sociocultural perspective emphasizes the critical role that family members have in influencing mental health.

Limitations of the sociocultural model should be noted, however. First, evidence linking social, cultural, or environmental factors to mental health is largely correlational. Whether these factors *cause* symptoms of mental disorders is unclear. Second, we do not yet know why people exposed to adverse influences have various outcomes: Some will develop psychological problems, and some will not. Why does one child living in an unsafe neighborhood with a dysfunctional family become depressed but their sibling has few psychological effects? The sociocultural perspective has great strength, but its account of how psychological problems develop remains incomplete.

Family therapy is a commonly used treatment in the sociocultural model of mental disorder.

Personal Narrative

An Integrative Psychologist: Dr. John C. Norcross

In the early days of psychotherapy, an ideological cold war reigned as clinicians were separated into rival schools—biological, psychodynamic, cognitive-behavioral, humanistic, sociocultural, and so on. Clinicians traditionally operated from within their own theoretical frameworks, often to the point of not considering alternative conceptualizations and potentially superior treatments.

As the field of psychotherapy has matured, integration has emerged as a clinical reality and the most popular approach. Clinicians now acknowledge the inadequacies of any one theoretical school and the potential value of many perspectives. Rival therapy systems are increasingly viewed not as adversaries but as partners; not as contradictory but as complementary.

My practice and research is devoted to *integration:* a dissatisfaction with single-school approaches and a concomitant desire to look across school boundaries to understand how patients can benefit from other ways of conducting treatment. The goal is to enhance the effectiveness and applicability of psychotherapy by tailoring it to the singular needs of each client. Clients frequently require an eclectic mix or hybrid of different perspectives.

Applying identical treatments to all patients is now recognized as inappropriate and probably unethical. Imagine if a physician delivered the same treatment—say, neurosurgery or an antibiotic—to every single patient and disorder. Different folks require different strokes. That's the mandate for integration.

How do we select treatment methods and relationship stances that fit? On the basis of research evidence, clinical experience, and patient preferences. A client who denies the existence of an obvious problem (the precontemplation stage), for example, will profit from a different relationship and treatment than a client who is committed to changing their behavior right now (the action stage). Or a client who seeks more insight into the early childhood antecedents of a problem, for another example, will probably secure better results in psychodynamic therapy than one who seeks psychoactive medication (biological therapy) or specific skills in restructuring thoughts (cognitive therapy). And a client who responds negatively to external guidance and direct advice (high reactance) will surely require a different treatment than one who enjoys them (low reactance). Decades of research can now direct us in making better marriages between some treatments and certain disorders and client characteristics.

The integrative psychotherapist leads by following the client. An empathic therapist works toward an optimal relationship that enhances collaboration and results in treatment success. That optimal relationship is determined by both patient preferences and the therapist's knowledge of the client's personality and preferences. If a client frequently resists, for example, then the therapist considers whether they are pushing something that the client finds incompatible (preferences), or the client is not ready to make changes (stage of change), or is uncomfortable with a directive style (reactance).

Integration refers typically to the synthesis of diverse systems of psychotherapy, but we need not stop there. We can combine therapy formats—individual, couples, family, and group. We frequently integrate medication and psychotherapy, also known as combined treatment. Integration gets us beyond either/or to both/and.

In practice, integrative psychologists are committed to the synthesis of practically all effective, ethical change methods. These include integrating self-help and psychotherapy, integrating Western and Eastern perspectives, integrating social advocacy with psychotherapy, integrating spirituality into psychotherapy, and so on. When asked about my doctrine, I reply with the words of the Buddha: "Anything that can help to alleviate human suffering."

As a university professor teaching psychopathology and clinical psychology, I find that my students naturally favor integration. Theoretical purity, they remind me, is for textbooks, not people. And as a clinical psychologist in part-time independent practice, I find my clients overwhelmingly require an integrative or eclectic approach. Rigid therapy, they teach me, is bad therapy.

Integrative therapy brings evidence-based flexibility and empathic responsiveness to each clinical encounter. Integrative therapy offers the research evidence and clinician flexibility to meet the unique needs of individual patients and their unique contexts. For these reasons, integration will assuredly be a therapeutic mainstay of the 21st century. Come join us!

—By Dr. John C. Norcross

Courtesy of Dr. John C. Norcross

Source: Reprinted by permission of the author.

Section Summary

- A sociocultural perspective focuses on how other people, social institutions, and social forces influence a person's mental health.
- Culture is the unique behavior and lifestyle shared by a group of people.
- Gender differences, including our expectations of different genders, may affect certain mental disorders.
- Various aspects of neighborhoods and communities are associated with changes in mental health.
- Family structure and functioning can impact the psychological well-being of individuals.
- A strength of the sociocultural perspective is its focus on social and environmental factors and family on mental health.
- A limitation of the sociocultural perspective is the lack of evidence that adverse environments cause mental disorders.

Review Questions

1. How can the sociocultural model help explain Mariella's problems?
2. Describe what is meant by "culture." How might culture influence the development of Mariella's problems?
3. Discuss how gender roles may influence Mariella's mental health.
4. What aspects of neighborhoods and communities are associated with stress and mental health?
5. How might family structure, functioning, and environment be associated with Mariella's problems?
6. What socioculturally based treatment might a mental health professional use to help Mariella?
7. What are strengths and limitations of the sociocultural perspective?

Final Comments

You might wonder which major perspective of psychopathology is the best one, especially when each one provides such a different view of mental disorder (**Table 2.5**). Each perspective has its own strengths and limitations and none provides a complete and comprehensive account of all psychological problems. Many mental health professionals thus adopt the notion of a *biopsychosocial model* to mental disorder. A biopsychosocial model stipulates that mental disorder can be attributed to many biological (e.g., genetic, brain changes), psychological (thought, emotional changes), and social (family, societal) variables. These variables work in tandem to produce healthy or unhealthy behavior.

A general theoretical model that resembles the biopsychosocial model, the *diathesis-stress model,* is presented in Chapter 3 and addresses the issue of how mental health problems develop. This model incorporates notions of *diathesis,* or predisposition or vulnerability to mental disorder, and *stress,* which can be environmental, interpersonal, or psychological. This model, because of its flexible, wide-ranging definition of diathesis and stress, can accommodate the

Table 2.5 Perspectives to Explain Mental Disorder

Biological
Mental disorder is related to brain or neurochemical changes or genetics.
Psychodynamic
Mental disorder is related to internal mental structures and childhood experiences.
Humanistic
Mental disorder is related to choices people make in their environment and how satisfied they are with their real self.
Cognitive-Behavioral
Mental disorder is a learned behavior and is influenced by how people perceive and think about their environment.
Sociocultural
Mental disorder is related to outside influences such as social institutions or family members.
Biopsychosocial
Mental disorder is related to a variety of biological, individual, and social environmental risk factors that interact with one another.

five perspectives covered in this chapter as well as combinations of these perspectives. The diathesis-stress model is perhaps the best way to think about mental health issues. Chapter 3 begins with a detailed description of this model and its implications for studying, treating, and preventing psychological problems.

Key Terms

models 24
biological model 25
syndromes 25
genotype 26
phenotype 26
behavior genetics 26
molecular genetics 26
central nervous system 26
peripheral nervous system 26
neurons 26
synapse 26
neurotransmitters 26
reuptake 26
cerebral cortex 27
frontal lobe 27
parietal lobe 27
temporal lobe 27
occipital lobe 27
limbic system 27
basal ganglia 27
thalamus 27
hypothalamus 27
psychodynamic model 30
unconscious motivation 31
defense mechanisms 31
psychic determinism 31
id 31
pleasure principle 31
primary process 32
ego 32
reality principle 32
secondary process 32
superego 32
psychosexual stages of development 32
fixation 32
repression 33
regression 33
reaction formation 33
projection 34
projective hypothesis 34
free association 34
dream analysis 34
manifest content 34
latent content 34
insight 34
interpretation 34
transference 35
civil commitment 36
criminal commitment 36
competency to stand trial 36
insanity 36
humanistic model 36
phenomenological approach 36
self-actualization 37
conditional positive regard 37
unconditional positive regard 37
client-centered therapy 37
behavioral perspective 39
classical conditioning 40
operant conditioning 40
positive reinforcement 40
negative reinforcement 40
cognitive perspective 40
cognitive schemas 41
cognitive distortions 41
modeling 42
avoidance conditioning 42
functional analysis 42
cognitive-behavioral therapy 43
cognitive restructuring 43
systematic desensitization 43
exposure treatment 43
token economy 44
sociocultural perspective 44
culture 45
ethnicity 45
race 45
cultural syndrome 45
family systems perspective 47
expressed emotion 47

Risk and Prevention of Mental Disorders

3

Learning Objectives

LO 3.1 Explain the occurrence of mental disorders using the diathesis-stress model.

LO 3.2 Describe the contributions of epidemiology to understanding mental disorders.

LO 3.3 Characterize risk and protective factors for mental disorders and the impact of resilience.

LO 3.4 Discuss the assumptions, activities, and effectiveness of programs intended to prevent mental disorders.

Case Kevin

Kevin is a 21-year-old business major who has been attending a large public university for three years. Kevin was initially anxious about attending college because no one else in his family had done so. He thought the transition to college was going to be tough and unlike anything he had experienced previously. His actual transition to college was a "mixed blessing." On the one hand, Kevin was invigorated by his classes and by meeting so many new people. He liked interacting with his professors and looked forward to graduating with an eye toward an MBA.

On the other hand, Kevin had never been to so many parties. His experience was far beyond his expectations about the party scene at college. His experience began during his first semester when Kevin was invited to a party at the dorm room of a new acquaintance. The beverage that night was "trash-can punch" that tasted good and had plenty of alcohol. Kevin thus felt poorly the next day when he woke up around noon, but he could not turn down an invitation for another party later that evening. Kevin kept telling himself he would eventually slow down, but that was three years ago. Kevin did not drink every night but seemed to attend a party at least four nights a week—every sporting and campus event and weekend was an opportunity for someone to throw a big party.

iStock.com/StuartDuncanSmith, iStock.com/James McQuillan

Kevin met hundreds of people at these parties in three years, but there was a clear downside. Kevin's drinking increased over the years to the point where he could get tipsy only after 6 to 10 drinks. Of course, Kevin did not usually stop at 6 to 10 drinks and so felt miserable the next day. Over time he tried to schedule his classes in the late afternoon or early evening to accommodate his "social" activities, but even these classes he often skipped because they conflicted with "Happy Hour." Kevin's studying suffered tremendously, and he almost failed school his first semester, first year, and two semesters since then. He accumulated only three semesters worth of credits during his three years at school.

Kevin's parents were unhappy about their son's progress. He did his best to hide his grades, but his parents became aware of his poor academic performance. Kevin's parents could not understand why their son was doing so poorly in college because he had been a straight-A student in high school. They did not know about the parties, however, and Kevin was certainly not going to tell them about his social life. Kevin thus rarely went home on weekends—too many parties to miss, and who wants to get "grilled" by their parents?—but promised his parents via text and e-mail that he would concentrate better and improve his grades.

Kevin felt he had things under control until he looked in his rearview mirror one night to see flashing lights. He had been drinking heavily and was weaving across lanes. He was a bit confused and even wondered if he had accidentally hurt someone. He was processed at the police station, and Kevin knew he faced his greatest challenge. What was he going to tell his parents about this "driving under the influence" charge? He had trouble believing what was happening but resigned himself to the possibility that his college days might be over.

What Do You Think?

1. Do you think Kevin has a problem with alcohol? Why or why not?
2. Why do you think Kevin is drinking so much?
3. What should Kevin do? Should he tell his parents? To whom should he turn for help?
4. Do you know people who have had similar experiences? What did they do?
5. Do you think Kevin's situation could have been prevented? If so, how?

The Diathesis-Stress Model

LO 3.1 Explain the occurrence of mental disorders using the diathesis-stress model.

Why do some college students like Kevin develop problems with alcohol use but others do not? College is stressful for most students, but not everyone develops a drinking problem. Did Kevin have a certain genetic structure, an oral fixation, or a maladaptive cognitive schema that led to his drinking problems? Or was some combination of these factors within a stressful college environment responsible?

Different models of mental disorder were discussed in Chapter 2 that have various strengths and limitations. The *diathesis-stress model* was also introduced as a way of integrating these models to explain mental disorders. The diathesis-stress model not only integrates perspectives but is consistent with a continuum of mental health and mental disorder. This chapter thus begins by examining the diathesis-stress model in detail and discussing its implications for studying, treating, and preventing mental disorders.

Diathesis, Stress, and Mental Health

A **diathesis** is a biological or psychological predisposition to disorder. Diatheses are often genetic or biological, but some diatheses are psychological. Some people expect alcohol use to make them more sociable and fun to be around. These people are more likely than others to drink alcohol. This expectancy is thus a psychological predisposition to use alcohol excessively. Kevin expected that drinking would make him more sociable, so he may be more likely to drink and use alcohol excessively.

Another psychological predisposition is *impulsivity,* or acting too quickly without thinking of the consequences. Impulsive people may predispose themselves to dangerous situations such as drinking too much and then driving. Cognitive schemas can also be considered psychological diatheses or predispositions. Recall Mariella from Chapter 2. Her negative views or schemas about herself, the world, and the future can be viewed as a diathesis or predisposition for her depression.

Figure 3.1 A Diathesis-Stress Model of Alcohol Use.

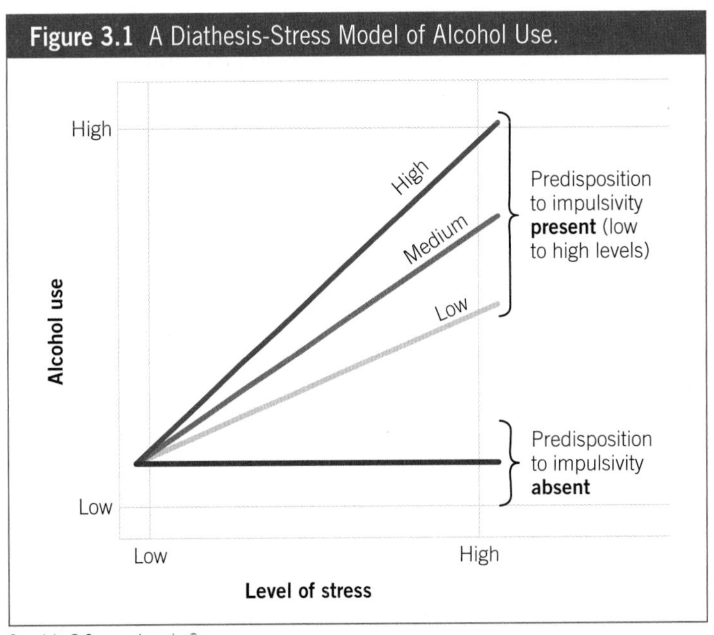

Biological or psychological diatheses *do not guarantee* one will develop problems such as excessive alcohol use or depression. A diathesis is a *vulnerability*—you can be vulnerable to a certain problem or mental disorder, but this does not mean you will necessarily develop it. Many people have a genetic predisposition for lung cancer but never develop the disease because they were not exposed to tobacco smoke. Kevin's expectancies about alcohol or Mariella's cognitive style may predispose them toward certain disorders but do not guarantee these disorders will occur. Something must *trigger* these predispositions, such as exposure to tobacco smoke or the stress of college life. Traumatic experiences such as assault are another stressor linked to many of the mental disorders discussed in this textbook.

A *combination* of predisposition *and* stress can impact the development of psychological problems according to the diathesis-stress model. Stress can be environmental, interpersonal, or psychological, but it must *interact* with a predisposition for a disorder to occur. Predispositions and stressors also occur on a continuum from weak to strong (or low to high). This is consistent with current research and this textbook's dimensional approach to mental health. We need to examine the diathesis-stress model in general (the big picture) and more specifically (the little picture) to understand it better.

Diathesis-Stress: The Big Picture

Let's examine the big picture of the diathesis-stress model using Kevin as an example. **Figure 3.1** illustrates predisposition, stress, and a potential psychological problem involving alcohol use on a continuum. This model shows the interaction of a predisposition (impulsivity) with stress along a continuum as they contribute to levels of alcohol use. Predisposition to be impulsive is on a continuum because people are impulsive to *varying degrees.* Some people may even have no impulsivity traits (labeled *Predisposition to impulsivity absent* in Figure 3.1). One of Kevin's friends, Kira, is quite conscientious about her life and always considers decisions carefully. Kira is not impulsive and would likely not use alcohol excessively even when faced with substantial stress.

Most people have *some* degree of diathesis or predisposition or vulnerability, whether low or high. Most of us are impulsive to *some* extent, and this is illustrated in Figure 3.1 as multiple lines bracketed by *Predisposition to impulsivity present*. Each line represents a different impulsivity level. Higher levels of a predisposition—impulsivity in this case—even with smaller amounts of stress result in more alcohol use. Lower levels of impulsivity, even with high stress, result in less alcohol use. *However, the combination of strong predisposition and high stress results in the most alcohol use.*

This model helps us understand why two people exposed to the same level of stress do or do not develop a certain mental disorder. Kevin and Kira's college stress is likely similar, but their predispositions for high alcohol use are quite different. Many soldiers in wartime develop posttraumatic stress disorder (Chapter 5), but many do not. Why? Because soldiers (and people in general) differ considerably with respect to their vulnerability to posttraumatic stress disorder.

Diatheses such as impulsivity are clearly important but interact with stressors that can also be viewed along a continuum (Figure 3.1). Two people with the same level of impulsivity may show different outcomes based on level of stress. Mariella may have been troubled because significant college stress triggered her predisposition for depression. Her friend Gisela, however, who had the same type of predisposition but who stayed home after high school, showed no symptoms of depression.

Diathesis-Stress: The Little Picture

Let's also examine the little picture of the diathesis-stress model by showing how diatheses and stressors can interact in subtle ways. One example is that a diathesis or predisposition can *influence a person's perception of stress.* Stress is subjective, and so one event can be perceived and experienced as much more stressful by one person than another who has a different level of diathesis or vulnerability. Mariella's cognitive predisposition for depression—viewing the world as disappointing, unsympathetic, and unforgiving—could impact her internal definition of a stressful event and her experience of the event as stressful. Mariella's rejection or lack of support from friends is more likely to be perceived as stressful and lead to depression than someone without such a worldview. We therefore must recognize that stress varies from person to person and can depend in part on level and type of diathesis or predisposition.

Our predispositions also *influence our life course and choice of experiences.* Someone predisposed toward a shy temperament may choose over time to have fewer friends and engage in more solitary activities. The person's choice of life experiences is guided, at least in part, by their diathesis. Our predispositions can affect the preferences we have and the decisions we make. The type of friends or romantic partners we choose, the experiences we seek, the jobs we take, and the places we choose to live are likely influenced by diatheses. These choices and experiences also influence the people, places, and events we encounter in life and thus affect our life course. A diathesis will partly determine the range and varieties of life events we experience, and some of these may be perceived as stressful. A shy person who surrounds himself with only a few close friends may be more likely than others to feel deliberately alienated at work.

Kevin's impulsivity may have predisposed him to quickly attending parties and drinking as well as a preference for encountering new people and exciting environments. These preferences helped expose him to certain environments and experiences where excessive alcohol use is more likely to occur. Some of these experiences may also have created stress from low grades and nagging parents, which may have led to more drinking to cope with the stress. The diathesis of high impulsivity affects a person's life choices and life course. The opposite is also true—less impulsive people may be less likely to seek these experiences and less exposed to some of these stressors.

Implications of the Diathesis-Stress Model

The diathesis-stress model has many implications for studying, treating, and preventing psychological problems. A key implication is that we must study certain diatheses or vulnerabilities to mental disorder to fully understand why and how these disorders develop. We must understand the **etiology**, or cause, of mental disorders. A diathesis-stress model does so by including aspects of all theoretical models discussed in Chapter 2. All possible diatheses are considered, such as genetics, neurochemical and brain changes, unconscious processes, learning experiences, thought patterns, and cultural and family factors. Knowing these diatheses is also important for treating mental disorders when they occur and for preventing mental disorders before they begin.

Diatheses or vulnerabilities are *risk factors* for mental disorders. Risk factors are discussed later in this chapter and all chapters describing mental disorders. Researchers study risk factors by comparing people with many symptoms of a disorder to people with few or no symptoms of a disorder. Differences between these groups may represent risk factors or vulnerabilities for the disorder. People like Kevin with excessive alcohol use can be compared to people like Kira with less alcohol use. We may find key differences such as genetic structure, impulsivity, and stress, and some of these differences could be useful for treatment and prevention. College freshmen found to be impulsive and stressed could undergo an awareness program to decrease excessive alcohol use. The search for risk factors intersects with the study of patterns of mental disorder in the general population, a topic discussed next.

Section Summary

- A diathesis is a biological or psychological predisposition or vulnerability to disorder.
- A combination or interaction of diathesis and stress may impact the development of a mental disorder.
- A diathesis can influence perception and experience of stress as well as life course and choice of experiences.
- A diathesis-stress model integrates theoretical perspectives of mental disorder and provides information about etiology (cause), treatment, and prevention.

Review Questions

1. What is a diathesis, and how does a diathesis affect the way we view and experience stressful events?
2. Why might two people exposed to the same traumatic event act differently afterward?
3. How is a diathesis-stress model consistent with a dimensional or continuum approach to mental disorder?
4. How might a diathesis-stress model help us understand mental disorders?

Epidemiology: How Common Are Mental Disorders?

LO 3.2 Describe the contributions of epidemiology to understanding mental disorders.

Epidemiology is the study of patterns of disease or disorder in the general population. Epidemiology can involve any physical or mental condition related to poor health or mortality among children and adults. **Epidemiologists** are scientists who investigate the extent of a public health problem such as a mental disorder by making observations, surveying people, and using other methods. **Personal Narrative/John Snow: A Pioneer in Epidemiology and Prevention** presents a famous example of epidemiology: John Snow's discovery of the cause of a cholera outbreak and subsequent prevention of new disease cases. Prevention is an important application of information gathered from epidemiological research.

Epidemiologists often focus on incidence and prevalence of mental disorder. **Incidence** refers to *new* cases of a mental disorder within a specific time period such as a month or year. A *one-year incidence* of a mental disorder is the percentage of people who, for the first time, developed that disorder in the previous 12 months. **Prevalence** refers to *all* cases of a mental disorder, including new and existing cases, within a specific time period such as a month or year. A *one-year prevalence* of depression includes all cases of existing depression during the previous 12 months, regardless of when the disorder began.

Epidemiologists also provide **lifetime prevalence** estimates of mental disorders. Lifetime prevalence refers to the proportion of those who have had a certain mental disorder *at any time in their life* up to the point they were assessed. Lifetime prevalence indicates risk for certain disorders over the entire life span, whereas smaller prevalence times such as a year provide a snapshot of whether people have recently been diagnosed with a specific disorder. Both prevalence types help us understand the likelihood of mental disorder and are discussed in more detail next and throughout this textbook.

Personal Narrative

John Snow: A Pioneer in Epidemiology and Prevention

John Snow (1813–1858) is often referred to as the "Father of Epidemiology." His investigation of a catastrophe is considered classic among epidemiologists, and his simple intervention is a fine example of prevention. An outbreak of cholera occurred in 1854 in London primarily among people living near Cambridge and Broad Streets; 500 deaths were reported in this area over a 10-day period. Snow thought people were contracting cholera from a contaminated water source, so he obtained information on cholera deaths from the General Register Office. He used this information and surveyed the scene of the deaths to determine that nearly all deaths occurred a short distance from the Broad Street pump (a water source for this area). He went to each address of the deceased and calculated the distance to the nearest water pump, which was usually the Broad Street pump. He also determined that some of the deceased recently drank from this pump. These data supported his theory of the spread of cholera through water, and he concluded that the water source for the Broad Street pump was contaminated. Snow presented his findings to local authorities, the handle to the pump was removed, and the local cholera outbreak ended. This is a great example of epidemiological findings leading to a preventive intervention—one that saved untold lives.

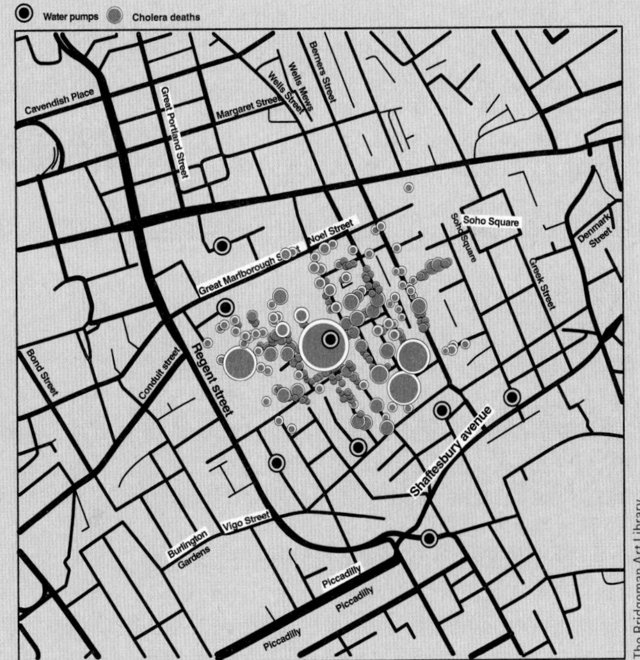

The Bridgeman Art Library

Map showing the distribution of deaths from cholera in an area of London.

The map featured here shows the distribution of cholera deaths in a London area. The circles represent the way the deaths were concentrated in one region, leading John Snow to question whether the source of the outbreak originated there.

Prevalence of Mental Disorders

Epidemiologists help determine the prevalence of mental disorders. A major epidemiological survey of Americans, the *National Comorbidity Survey-Replication* (NCS-R), was a representative, community-based survey of about 10,000 people aged 18 years and older. The survey included structured interviews to assess people for major mental disorders and serves as the basis for the next several sections.

Overall Prevalence and Severity

NCS-R data revealed that 46.4 percent of Americans experience a mental disorder at some point in their life, a figure somewhat higher than the global number of about one in three persons (Christensen et al., 2020; Kessler, Berglund et al., 2005; Kessler, Chiu, et al., 2005). This percentage may seem high, but keep two key points in mind. First, not everyone who meets criteria for a mental disorder is in treatment. Many people who experience psychological symptoms, including college students, do not seek a mental health professional or do not have access to mental health care (Oswalt et al., 2020). Common barriers to care include cost, stigma, transportation vulnerability, lack of insurance, excessive wait times, and few available care providers in a given area (Carbonell et al., 2020).

Second, mental disorders differ with respect to severity and many people show only mild symptoms. This point reinforces a major theme of this textbook: Symptoms of mental disorders are present to some extent in all of us and can be represented along a continuum. People with certain symptoms or diagnoses are not qualitatively different from those without. Mariella's symptoms of depression are something we all feel from time to time. Her symptoms may be more severe than ours at the moment, but the symptoms are something with which we can identify.

NCS-R data included serious, moderate, and mild levels of severity. Each level was defined by certain features associated with a disorder. For example, *serious severity* was defined by features such as suicide attempt with lethal intent, occupational disability, psychotic symptoms, or intense violence. **Figure 3.2** illustrates percentage of severity levels for some major mental disorders. Mental disorder was generally classified as serious (22.3 percent), moderate (37.3 percent), or mild (40.4 percent) in severity. Serious severity was most evident with respect to mood (i.e., depressive and bipolar) disorders (45.0 percent).

Specific Prevalence Rates

Prevalence information for specific disorders is crucial so we know where to assign treatment and prevention resources. **Figure 3.3** outlines lifetime and 12-month prevalence rates for some major mental disorders.

Figure 3.2 Severity of 12-Month Major Mental Disorders.

Rates indicates the proportion of people in the United States with the mental disorder at each level of severity (serious, moderate, mild).

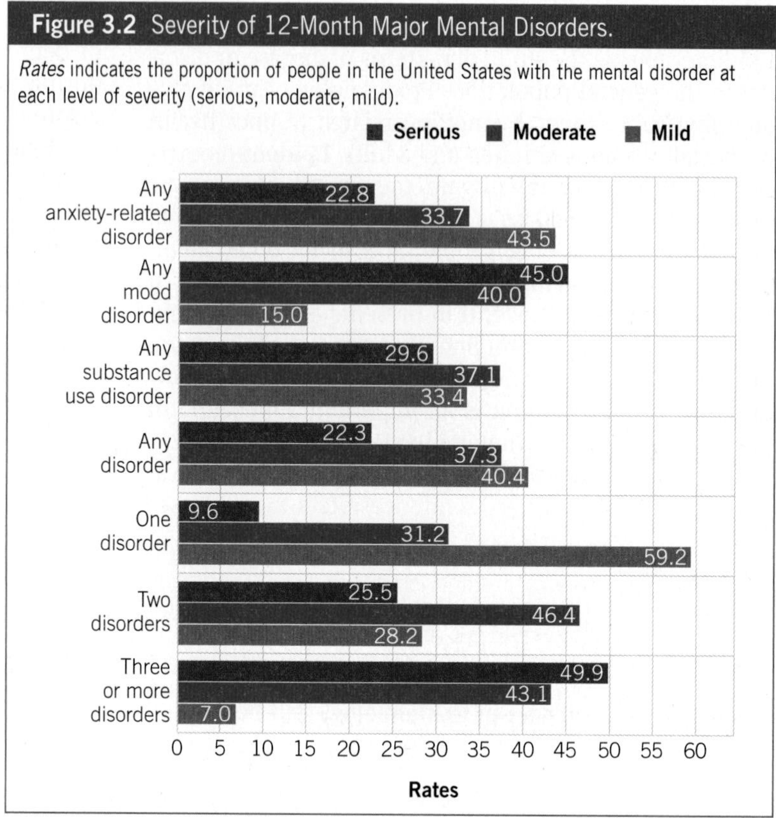

Adapted from Kessler, Chiu, et al. (2005).

Figure 3.3 Lifetime and 12-Month Prevalence of Major Mental Disorders.

Lifetime and *12-month* rates represent the proportion of U.S. residents with the mental disorder.

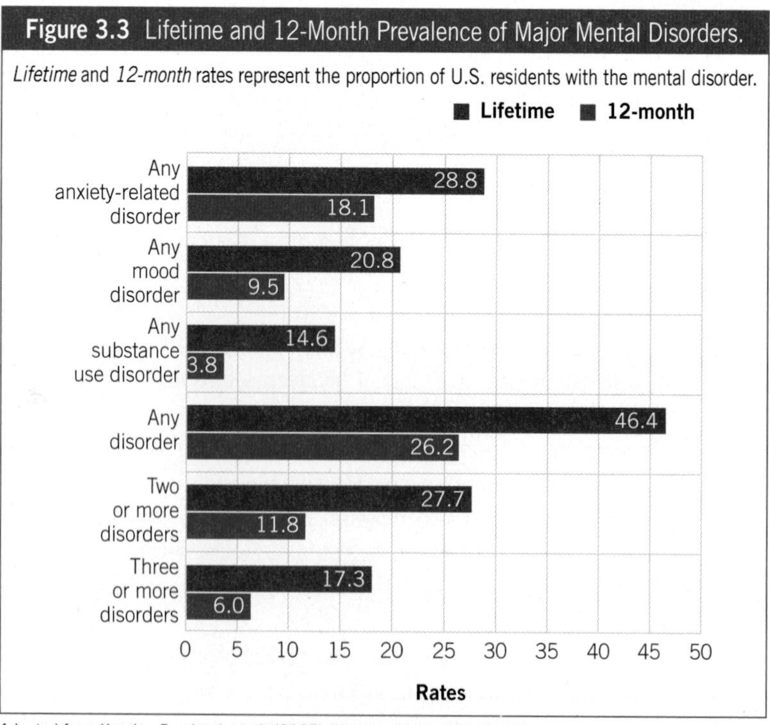

Adapted from Kessler, Berglund, et al. (2005); Kessler, Chiu, et al. (2005).

Lifetime prevalence rates for anxiety-related disorders (28.8 percent), including specific phobia (12.5 percent) and social anxiety disorder (12.1 percent), are substantial. Mood disorders (20.8 percent) are also relatively common. Lifetime prevalence for substance use disorders in general was 14.6 percent and for alcohol use disorder in particular was 13.2 percent.

The NCS-R also provided *12-month prevalence rates,* which are lower than lifetime prevalence rates because of the shorter time frame. Researchers found that more than one-fourth of Americans (26.2 percent) had one or more mental disorders over the previous year. Anxiety-related (18.1 percent), mood (9.5 percent), and substance use (3.8 percent) disorders were quite common (Figure 3.3).

Comorbidity

Comorbidity refers to the presence of two or more disorders in a person and is a significant concern for mental health professionals. This is so because recovery among people with two or more mental disorders is less likely than among people with one mental disorder. According to the NCS-R, 27.7 percent of Americans will have more than one mental disorder in their lifetime, and 11.8 percent will have had more than one mental disorder in the past year. A significant percentage of Americans thus experience more than one mental disorder. Comorbidity is also clearly related to severity of mental disorder. Data from Figure 3.2 indicate that a much higher percentage of those with three or more disorders (49.9 percent) were classified as serious severity than those with only one disorder (9.6 percent).

Age of Onset

A unique aspect of the NCS-R was that questions were asked about the *onset* of mental disorder. People who received a diagnosis for a mental disorder at some point in their lives were asked if they could remember when their symptoms started and how their symptoms progressed. Several interesting findings emerged (refer to **Figure 3.4**). First, the median age of onset for a mental disorder is 14 years. Second, *anxiety-related* disorders have an earlier onset (age 11 years) than *substance use* (age 20 years) or *mood* (age 30 years) disorders. Not everyone diagnosed with these disorders has these exact ages of onset, of course, but these estimates do indicate that many mental disorders first appear in adolescence or young adulthood.

Cohort Effects and Children

Cohort effects are significant differences in disorder expression depending on demographic features such as age or gender. Younger Americans may be more likely to develop substance use disorders compared with older Americans. Why? One possible reason is that alcohol was less available to adolescents decades ago than today. Our views on underage college drinking have also changed over the years, and the behavior may be more tolerated now than in the past. Attention-deficit/hyperactivity disorder and online gambling problems are also identified more now than in the past.

Figure 3.5 presents NCS-R data on mental disorders by age. People aged 18 to 59 years have higher lifetime

Figure 3.4 Median Age of Onset of Major Mental Disorders.

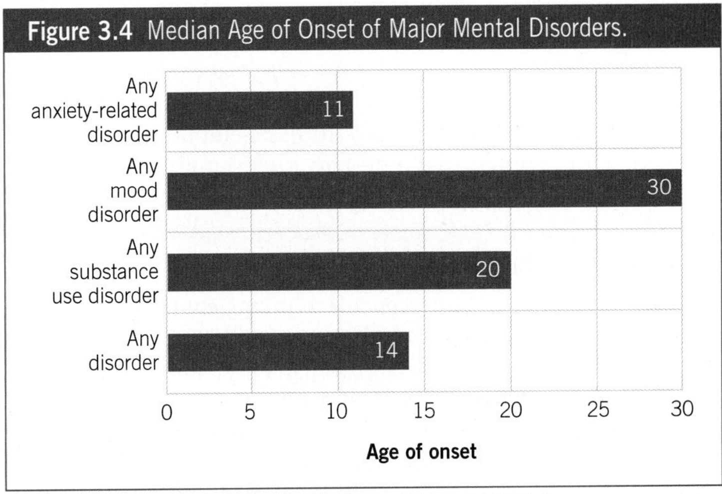

Adapted from Kessler, Berglund, et al. (2005); Kessler, Chiu, et al. (2005).

Figure 3.5 Lifetime Prevalence of Mental Disorders By Age.

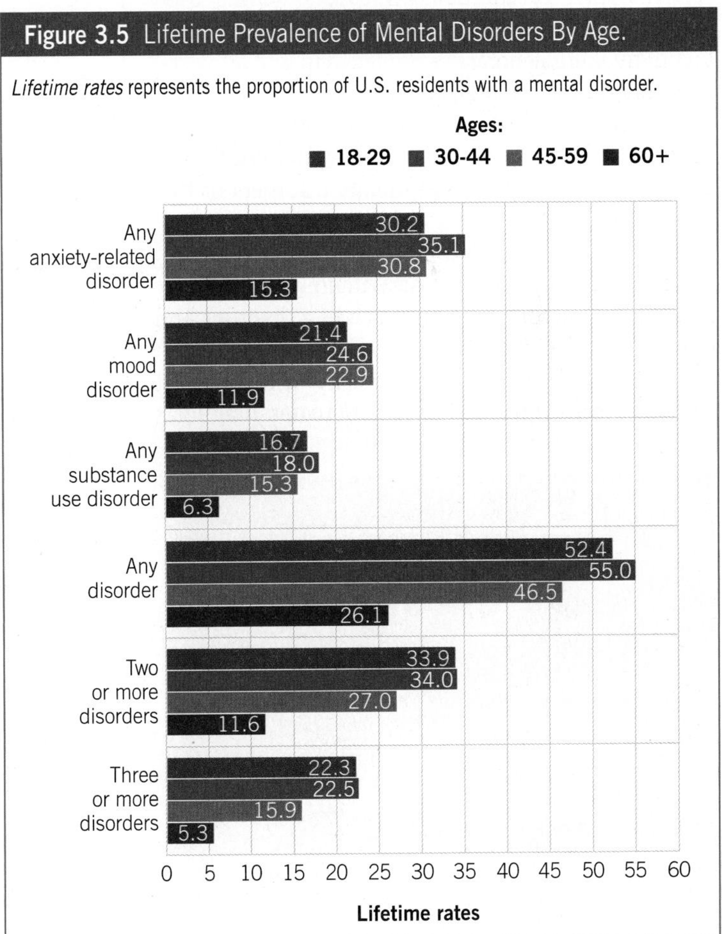

Adapted from Kessler, Berglund, et al. (2005).

rates of some major (anxiety-related, mood, substance use) mental disorders than people aged 60 years or older. Why these age differences exist is unclear. Higher lifetime prevalence rates for younger people may be due to greater willingness to admit psychological problems, or adults may underreport or forget symptoms as they get older and further from their disorder onset.

What about youth? Epidemiologists estimate that about 20.1 percent of young children and 25.0–31.0 percent of adolescents have a mental disorder. Children and adolescents are most likely to be diagnosed with anxiety-related, disruptive, mood, and substance use problems (Silva et al., 2020; Vasileva et al., 2021). Many children are also reported by their parents to have emotional or behavioral difficulties that interfere with family, academic, and social functioning (Gruber et al., 2021).

Treatment Seeking

The NCS-R researchers asked people with anxiety-related, mood, or substance use disorders about their use of treatment services in the previous year (Green et al., 2020; Wang et al., 2005). Many (41.1 percent) used services, including 21.7 percent who used mental health services, 22.8 percent who used general medical services, and 13.2 percent who used non–health care services such as alternative medicine (some used two or more types of service). People who sought treatment were generally younger than age 60 years, female, from a non-Hispanic White racial background, previously married, more affluent, and living in urban areas. People who sought treatment also tended to have more severe mental disorders or two or more mental disorders.

Many people with a mental disorder do eventually seek treatment. Unfortunately, a lengthy delay often occurs between onset of a disorder and first treatment contact. Less than half of those with a mental disorder seek treatment within the first year of onset. The typical delay between diagnosis and treatment for many disorders was *10 years or more*. Less delay was evident for mood disorders but greater delay was evident for anxiety-related disorders.

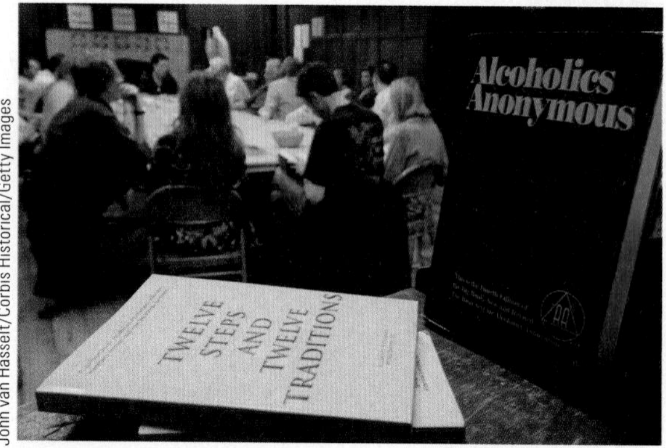

John van Hasselt/Corbis Historical/Getty Images

Epidemiological studies show that some mental disorders, such as alcohol use disorder, are most prevalent among young adults. Most people eventually seek treatment for their psychological problems but only after a delay of many years.

Treatment Cost

Many people seek treatment for mental disorders, but the price of such care can be steep. The annual cost for mental health treatment is in the hundreds of billions of dollars when considering conditions that require long-term care (McDaid et al., 2019). Mental health and substance use services thus represent a significant proportion of the overall healthcare economy. Other, indirect costs compound this issue and include lost productivity at work, home, and school due to disability and impairment or premature death. Mental and substance use disorders account for substantial years of life lost due to premature mortality and years lived with disability (Rehm & Shield, 2019). This rate of disability far exceeds that of cardiovascular disease, respiratory disease, and cancer (refer to **Figure 3.6**).

Figure 3.6 Mental Disorders Are the Leading Cause of Disability.

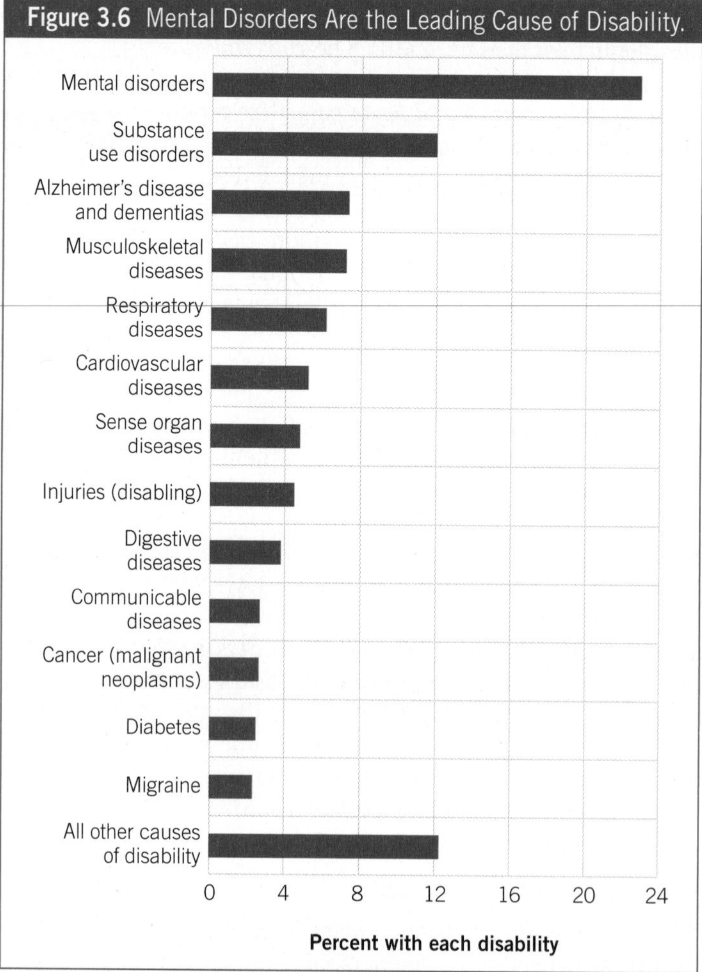

Adapted from President's New Freedom Commission on Mental Health (2003). Achieving the promise: Transforming mental health care in America. Rockville, MD: U.S. Department of Health and Human Services, Substance Abuse and Mental Health Services Administration, Center for Mental Health Services, National Institutes of Health, National Institute of Mental Health.

Section Summary

- Epidemiology is the study of patterns of disease or disorder in the general population.
- Incidence refers to number of new cases of a mental disorder within a specific time period, and prevalence refers to all cases present during a specific time period.
- Lifetime prevalence refers to proportion of those who have had a certain mental disorder at any time in their life up to the point they were assessed.
- About half of American adults have a diagnosable mental disorder, although many are not in treatment or have mild symptoms.
- Anxiety-related, mood, and substance use disorders are especially common.
- Comorbidity refers to the presence of two or more disorders in a person and is related to greater severity of mental disorder.
- Most mental disorders first appear in adolescence or early adulthood.
- Cohort effects refer to significant differences in expression of mental disorder depending on demographic features such as age and gender.
- Mental disorders are more common among youth and younger adults than older adults, although underreporting in older adults may be a factor.
- Many people eventually seek treatment for a mental disorder, but many others delay treatment for several years.
- The cost of mental health care is prohibitive because mental disorder is a leading cause of disability worldwide.

Review Questions

1. What is epidemiology, and how do epidemiologists help us understand mental disorders?
2. What is the difference between incidence and prevalence?
3. What do we know about the prevalence of mental disorders among Americans?
4. What factors are associated with treatment seeking?
5. Describe the financial and disability costs of mental disorders.

Risk, Protective Factors, and Resilience

LO 3.3 Characterize risk and protective factors for mental disorders and the impact of resilience.

How do mental health professionals understand problems like Jana's? A diathesis-stress model helps us understand factors involved in the development of mental disorder. Some factors are *diatheses* or *vulnerabilities*: features or attributes within a person. Other factors comprise the "stress" part of the model and are typically portrayed as "environmental": outside a person and perhaps more transient in nature. Diatheses and stressors may be *risk* factors for a mental disorder, but, as mentioned, not everyone with a predisposition for a mental disorder necessarily develops one. Something must therefore *protect* some people from developing a mental disorder. The concepts of *risk* and *protective factors* are discussed next.

Risk Factors

A **risk factor** is an individual or environmental characteristic that precedes a mental disorder and is correlated with that disorder. Risk factors can be biological, psychological, or social. Jana's severe childhood sexual maltreatment is a risk factor for problems she experienced in adulthood. Risk factors are associated with an increased probability a disorder will develop, but they do not imply cause. Jana has a mental disorder called *borderline personality disorder* (Chapter 10). A childhood history of severe sexual maltreatment is more common in people with borderline personality disorder than those without the disorder. Recall that risk factors are often identified by comparing prevalence of the risk factor in those with and without a certain disorder. Factors more common in people with a mental disorder may be the ones that place them "at risk" for developing the disorder.

Case Jana

Jana is a 22-year-old college student with a long history of psychological problems. Jana often feels depressed and anxious, has trouble controlling her moods, and can lash out at others for no reason. This has affected her relationships because many people are afraid they might "set her off." Jana has frequently cut herself with razor blades when under stress or when she is angry at herself. Jana has wanted to die many times and has made several suicide attempts over the past 10 years. She tends to make bad decisions and does so impulsively, which has landed her in legal trouble for shoplifting and other offenses. Jana has also struggled with excessive alcohol and other drug use for years. Her friends say Jana often "zones out" for 30 minutes or so when she gets upset, as though she is not really there. Jana has visited many mental health professionals over the years. When they ask what may have caused her problems, Jana points to her childhood, when an uncle maltreated her sexually.

Some risk factors are more "fixed," such as gender at birth or family history of a disorder. Other risk factors are more dynamic and can change over time, such as social support. Risk factors can also vary across age, gender, or culture. Risk factors for excessive alcohol use in a 21-year-old African American man are not the same as those for a 45-year-old European American woman. Many risk factors also exist for a particular mental disorder and may interact with each other in complex ways to influence the development of the disorder.

Risk factors must *precede* the development of a condition, so the mental disorder itself cannot cause its risk factors. We would not consider Kevin's college struggles to be a risk factor for his excessive alcohol use. Excessive alcohol use instead led to skipping classes and low grades. For someone else, however, low grades could trigger stress that then leads to excessive alcohol use. For this person, low grades are a risk factor.

Identifying risk factors can lead to better treatment and prevention (refer to **Focus on College Students: Suicide**). Childhood sexual maltreatment is a risk factor for borderline personality disorder, as with Jana, so those seeking to prevent borderline personality disorder might focus on preventing such maltreatment. This might be accomplished by educating parents and children about appropriate and inappropriate intimacy and by informing parents and children about resources available to them if problems occur (such as a state Department of Family and Protective Services). How identifying risk factors can lead to prevention efforts is discussed later in this chapter. Several key risk factors identified for various mental disorders are discussed next.

iStock.com/Liubomyr Vorona

Women are at greater risk for developing anxiety-related and depressive disorders. Men are at greater risk for developing antisocial personality disorder and substance use disorders.

Gender

Risk of mental disorder is different for men and women. A consistent finding is that men are more likely than women to have substance use, antisocial personality, sexual, and developmental disorders (Chapters 9, 10, 11, and 13, respectively). Women are at greater risk for anxiety-related disorders and depression (Chapters 5 and 7, respectively). They are also more likely to have neurocognitive disorders such as Alzheimer's disease because they generally live longer than men (Chapter 14). Women are also more likely than men to have more than one mental disorder at any point in time (Green et al., 2019).

Age

Age is also a significant risk factor for mental disorders, especially during the period from adolescence to early adulthood (Figure 3.5). The percentages of people with onset of any mental disorder before ages 14, 18, and 25 years are 34.6 percent, 48.4 percent, and 62.5 percent, respectively (Solmi et al., 2021). Unfortunately, earlier onset of a disorder can be related to lower chance for recovery. Other disorders, however, such as dementia, tend to occur at later ages (Hassen et al., 2022).

Focus On College Students

Suicide

One of the leading causes of death among young adults is suicide, especially those in college (Centers for Disease Control and Prevention, 2021). One explanation may be the stress of college, combined with negative life events. Such stress may come from leaving family and peers, facing new academic demands, or even sexual assault. These stressors may create new psychological difficulties or exacerbate existing ones. Significant risk factors for college student suicide include having an existing mental disorder such as depression, alcohol or other drug use, history of trauma, major physical illness, lack of social support and access to care, stigma associated with seeking help, and identification as LGBTQ+. Conversely, however, protective factors include resilience, access to appropriate care, family and community support, good problem-solving and conflict resolution skills, positive beliefs about the future, and cultural and religious beliefs that discourage suicide (Li et al., 2020). Research regarding risk and protective factors is important for developing good assessment strategies and for targeting prevention and treatment efforts.

Race and Ethnicity

The extent to which race and ethnicity are risk factors for mental disorder has been difficult to establish. European Americans have been found in general to have higher lifetime prevalence rates for mental disorders than African Americans, Asians, and Latinos (Alvarez et al., 2019). Most studies of race and ethnicity focus on more nuanced aspects of mental disorder, however. For example, rates of posttraumatic stress disorder tend to be higher among African Americans who may have greater exposure to certain traumatic events (Sibrava et al., 2019). In addition, mood disorders tend to be higher among Hispanic adolescents than non-Hispanic Whites (Avenevoli et al., 2015). Substance use disorders are most frequent among American Indian peoples (Skewes & Blume, 2019). Some specific differences may be evident, but we cannot yet conclude that race and ethnicity are general risk factors for mental disorder. Specific racial and ethnic differences are discussed in greater detail for each disorder throughout this textbook.

Education, Socioeconomic Status, and Marital Status

Less education, low socioeconomic status, and poverty are well-established risk factors for mental disorder (Ridley et al., 2020). Marital status is a significant and consistent risk factor for mental disorder as well. Entry into marriage is generally associated with enhanced psychological well-being and less distress, whereas divorce and widowhood are generally associated with mental health challenges (Mina, 2019). Marital disruption is most strongly associated with a higher risk for anxiety-related, mood, and substance use disorders, as well as suicide (Kessler, Berglund, et al., 2005). A summary of major risk factors for mental disorder is in **Table 3.1**.

Other Risk Factors

Other risk factors seem to represent more general vulnerabilities to mental disorder. *Individual risk factors* include genetic predisposition, low birth weight and premature birth, neuropsychological deficits, language disabilities, chronic physical illness, and history of child maltreatment. *Family risk factors* include severe marital discord, overcrowding or large family size, paternal criminality, maternal mental disorder, and admission to foster care. *Community* or *social risk factors* include violence, poverty, less access to resources and accommodations, community disorganization, inadequate schools, and racism, sexism, and discrimination (Ridley et al., 2020). Many other risk factors were also covered in Chapter 2 when discussing biological, psychodynamic, humanistic, cognitive-behavioral, and sociocultural models of mental disorder. Understanding these many risk factors is important for developing effective treatments and preventing mental disorders before they start. This is also true for protective factors, which are discussed next.

Protective Factors

We must identify risk factors to determine who is vulnerable to mental disorder, but we must also identify **protective factors** associated with *lower risk* of mental disorder. Protective factors are the flip side of risk factors. Less social support is a risk factor for depression, therefore greater social support can be

Table 3.1 Summary of Major Risk Factors for Mental Disorders

Risk factor	Findings
Age	The highest rates of mental disorders are in adolescence and early adulthood.
Education	Individuals who do not complete high school are significantly more likely to be diagnosed with a mental disorder, especially substance use disorders, than those who complete or go beyond high school.
Employment	Individuals who are unemployed are more likely to develop psychological problems than those who are employed.
Gender	Men are at greater risk for antisocial personality disorder and substance use disorders. Women are at greater risk for anxiety-related and depressive disorders. Women are more likely than men to be diagnosed with more than one mental disorder at any point in time.
Marital status	Marital disruption (divorce or separation) is associated with mental disorders in general and with anxiety-related, mood, and substance use disorders in particular.
Race and ethnicity	Research has demonstrated mixed results in general, with some specific differences.

Social support may serve as a protective factor against psychological problems.

thought of as a protective factor. Those with strong social support from friends and family are *less likely* to develop depression than those with limited social support. Perhaps you have been thanked by a friend for being caring and supportive during a difficult period in their life. Your support, and the support of others, may have protected them from becoming severely depressed.

Research on protective factors has not been as extensive as that for risk factors, but **Table 3.2** provides some examples. Like risk factors, protective factors can be biological, psychological, or social and can operate at individual, family, or community levels. Happily married people have the lowest lifetime and 1-year prevalence rates of mental disorder. Social support or contact with friends and others, and level of satisfaction with these social contacts, are important protective factors as well (Li et al., 2021). Personality and psychological factors such as self-efficacy, problem-solving skills, hopefulness, and a focus on positive events also help protect people against mental disorder (Waters et al., 2022).

Table 3.2 Protective Factors Against Mental Disorders and Problems

Individual	Positive temperament Social competence Spirituality or religion
Family	Supportive relationships with parents Good sibling relationships Adequate monitoring and rule-setting by caregivers
Community or social	Commitment to schools Availability of health and social services Social cohesion

Resilience

Recall from Chapter 2 that some people function well even in adverse circumstances such as poverty and maltreatment. Some people adapt well in these circumstances because of **resilience**, or the ability to withstand and rise above extreme adversity (Ungar & Theron, 2020). Psychologists have become increasingly interested in studying factors associated with resilience, especially among children at risk for negative outcomes due to unfavorable environments such as war, domestic violence, or poverty (refer to **Figure 3.7**).

Resilience was originally studied among children of parents with schizophrenia (Chapter 12). A child with a biological parent with schizophrenia is at genetic and environmental risk for schizophrenia, but many children with these risk factors do not develop the disorder and actually adapt quite well (Wambua et al., 2020). The study of resilience has since expanded to include traumatic events or adverse environmental or social situations. Many people exposed to these circumstances develop posttraumatic disorder but many others do not. What characterizes people who adapt well under these circumstances? What are their resiliency factors?

Key resiliency factors among children include good social and academic competence and effectiveness in work and play situations. Key resiliency factors among adults include supportive families and communities

Figure 3.7 Typical Patterns of Disruption in Normal Functioning Across Time After a Traumatic Event.

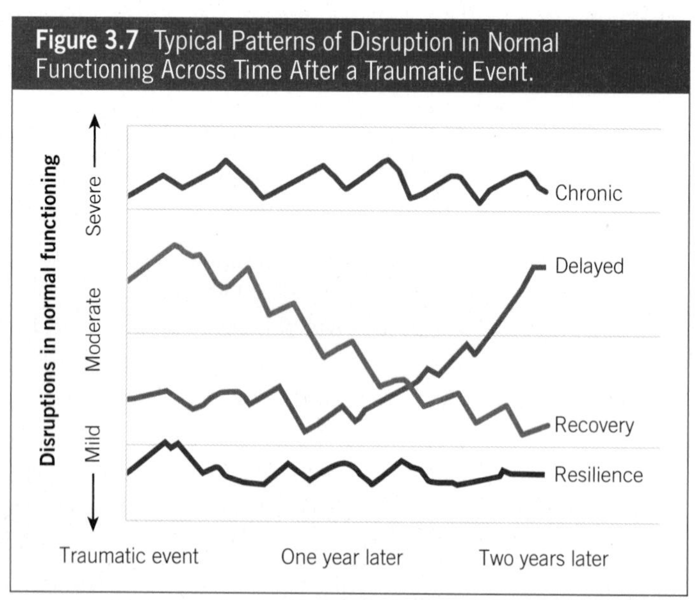

Adapted from G.A. Bonanno, *American Psychologist, 59*, Fig. 1, p. 21. Copyright © 2004 by the American Psychological Association. Used with permission.

Rawpixel.com/Shutterstock.com

Spirituality and religion can serve as protective factors against psychological problems.

as well as spirituality and religion. Spirituality and religion are also linked to greater life satisfaction and well-being (Schwalm et al., 2022). African Americans report higher levels of religiosity than other racial or ethnic groups, and religiosity seems to protect against higher rates of psychological problems. But how does religiosity or spirituality provide an advantage? Perhaps people with strong religiosity or spirituality adhere to healthier lifestyles (such as not smoking or drinking alcohol), provide and receive higher levels of social support (such as a church community), or promote positive, optimistic beliefs related to faith (Manning et al., 2019).

Resiliency factors are associated with good outcome, but whether they *cause* good outcome remains unclear. Still, strong attachments or bonds with family members and the community, as well as good problem-solving and coping skills, seem to buffer people against adverse circumstances. Studies of resilience and competence also help mental health professionals in several practical ways. These studies guide the development of interventions to prevent or eliminate risk factors, build resources, enhance relationships, and improve self-efficacy and self-regulation (Ungar & Thereon, 2020).

Section Summary

- A risk factor is an individual or environmental characteristic that precedes a mental disorder and is correlated with that disorder.
- Men are at greater risk for substance use, antisocial personality, sexual, and developmental disorders; women are at greater risk for anxiety-related and depressive disorders.
- Mental disorder appears more prevalent among younger than older adults.
- The extent to which race and ethnicity are risk factors for mental disorder has been difficult to establish, but some specific differences have been reported.
- Lower educational and socioeconomic levels, as well as divorce or separation from a partner, are general risk factors for mental disorder.
- Other risk factors include individual, family, and community or social factors.
- Protective factors are associated with lower rates of mental disorder.
- Resilience refers to the ability to withstand and rise above extreme adversity and may protect people from developing mental disorder.
- Resiliency and protective factors vary across age, gender, race, and ethnicity.

Review Questions

1. What is the difference between risk factors and protective factors?
2. What are major risk factors for mental disorders?
3. What features do protective factors and resiliency factors have in common?
4. Why is it important to identify risk, protective, and resiliency factors?

Prevention

LO 3.4 Discuss the assumptions, activities, and effectiveness of programs intended to prevent mental disorders.

A discussion of risk factors and protective factors such as resilience leads naturally to a focus on one of the main themes of this textbook—prevention. **Prevention** refers to thwarting the development of later problems and may be more efficient and effective than individual treatment after a mental disorder occurs. Those engaging in prevention often use risk and protective factors to identify people who need more help before major problems develop. Prevention is therefore a guiding principle of many public health programs.

Many prevention programs aim to reduce risk and increase protective factors regarding mental disorder. Child maltreatment, such as that Jana experienced, is a key risk factor for several mental disorders. Many prevention programs therefore try to reduce the prevalence of childhood maltreatment. Prevention programs may also aim to *enhance protective factors.* Protective factors for children include good social and academic competence and growing up in a positive home environment. Prevention programs could thus be designed to help kids make friends and do well in school and educate parents about proper child-rearing methods. Prevention programs often focus on children and families who are "at risk" for certain disorders based on these kinds of characteristics.

Focus On Violence

Prevention of Femicide

Femicide, the murder of women, is a leading cause of premature death among females. Approximately 38.6 percent of all homicides against women worldwide are committed by an intimate partner (Garcia-Vergara et al., 2022). Several risk factors connected to femicide include abuse during pregnancy, estrangement, forced sex, gun access, nonfatal strangulation, perpetrator mental disorder and/or substance use, prior domestic violence, stalking, stepchild in the home, and threats to kill and threats with a weapon (Caicedo–Roa et al., 2020). In addition, many victims of femicide tend to be more hidden, especially LGBTQ+, older, and/or disabled persons (Cullen et al., 2021). Identifying risk factors for femicide in abusive relationships may help us understand what foundation is needed for prevention efforts.

Prevention can include broader efforts to change social and cultural conditions that reinforce a patriarchal and proprietary approach to gender relations (Daher-Nashif, 2022). Prevention can also include specific actions at individual and community levels. At an individual level, this can include various safety strategies, domestic violence resources, and police escorts when leaving a relationship. An important tactic is to inform and involve trusted others. At a community level, this can include early childhood home visitations, family engagement and housing programs, parenting skills, strong legal protections, and treatment and support for survivors (Centers for Disease Control and Prevention, 2022).

Table 3.3 presents various techniques to prevent child maltreatment in children in high-risk families. This particular approach emphasizes different aspects of parenting and caring for a child that may serve to "protect" against maltreatment. The approach covers basic education and training in positive parenting, problem-solving skills, and anger management. The hope is that a successful approach such as this one will lead to less maltreatment.

Prevention on a Continuum

The basis of *prevention* is to build mental health and limit the scope of problems, including mental health problems, before they occur or worsen. Individuals do benefit from prevention and treatment programs along a continuum of intervention for mental disorders (Fusar-Poli et al., 2020). This continuum is represented in the following way: *prevention* occurs before a disorder develops, *treatment* occurs after a disorder develops (or as a disorder is developing), and *maintenance* occurs long after a disorder has developed for people whose symptoms require ongoing attention (refer to **Figure 3.8**).

Three Types of Prevention

Mental health professionals have adopted three major approaches to prevention. These approaches were introduced in Chapter 1 and are discussed in more detail next.

Primary and Universal Prevention

The purest form of prevention is **primary prevention**, where an intervention is given to people with no signs of a disorder. Primary prevention practices are administered to prevent *new cases* of a disorder. This type of prevention is a departure from traditional ways of addressing mental disorder in which interventions are given *after* significant problems develop. **Universal prevention** is similar to primary prevention in that large groups of people not affected by a particular problem are targeted to reduce new cases of a disorder (Figure 3.8). Advertisements to educate the public about the dangers of excessive drug use are an example. Universal prevention interventions target everyone, however, so they can be costly.

Other examples of primary or universal prevention are also available. Newborn children are regularly screened for phenylketonuria (PKU), a disorder that can result in intellectual developmental disorder (Chapter 13). Children with PKU can be placed on a special diet that prevents intellectual developmental disorder from occurring. Other examples of primary prevention include mandatory car seats for preschoolers to prevent accident fatalities as well as parenting classes to prevent child maltreatment (Table 3.3). Primary prevention also includes programs to reduce job discrimination, enhance school curricula, improve housing, and help children in single-parent homes. Some primary prevention programs work fairly well, such as school-based programs for bullying (Kennedy, 2020). Other primary prevention programs work less well, however, such as for sexual violence perpetration (Schneider & Hirsch, 2020).

Secondary and Selective Prevention

Secondary prevention refers to addressing problems while they are manageable and before they are more resistant to treatment. Secondary prevention is designed to "nip a problem in the bud" before it progresses to a full-blown disorder. Secondary prevention programs promote the early identification of mental health problems as well as treatment at an early stage so mental disorders do not develop.

A secondary prevention approach suggests that many people will be screened for early signs of mental health problems. These people are not necessarily seeking help and may not even appear to be at risk. Such screening

Table 3.3 A Sample Approach for Preventing Child Maltreatment in High-Risk Families

Basic problem-solving training	Learn to recognize and define typical life problems
Positive parenting: enjoying the child	• Gain education on the child's development and how to enjoy the child's unfolding abilities • See the world through the child's eyes • Learn activities for parent and child together: child-led play and mutual reinforcement
Parenting skills	Learn general skills such as how to: • *Define behaviors and goals* • *Recognize developmentally appropriate goals* • *Identify antecedents and consequences* • *Identify rewards* • *Identify a reasonable level of control*
	Learn request skills such as how to: • *Make requests to ensure compliance (alpha commands)* • *Make reasonable requests*
	Learn how to reduce the frequency of undesirable behaviors: • *Ignore* • *Reward the absence of negative behaviors* • *Implement time-out* • *Get past the "testing the limits" phase*
	Learn how to increase desirable behaviors: • *Use praise* • *Use explicit rewards: appropriate rewards, token economy*
Extending parenting	Learn about child safety, especially the following: • *Discipline and maltreatment—how discipline can slip into maltreatment, outcomes of maltreatment* • *Responsibility for selecting safe care agents* • *Other kinds of injury, "child proofing"* • *Supervision* • *Child as precious to parent: work to protect*
Anger management	Learn how to see oneself through the child's eyes: • *Recall one's own parents and parental anger* • *Characterize how being the focus of anger feels*
	Learn to control your own emotions: • *See your anger as a feeling, color, or state*
	Learn behavioral treatments: • *Power to alter your state* • *Relaxation* • *Becoming aware of anger triggers* • *Safety valves* • *Self-esteem*
	Learn to see successful parenting as anger reducing

Adapted from "Integrating Child Injury and Abuse-Neglect Research: Common Histories, Etiologies, and Solutions" by L. Peterson and D. Brown, 1994, *Psychological Bulletin, 116,* 293-315.

Figure 3.8 Prevention Exists on a Continuum of Intervention for Mental Health Problems.

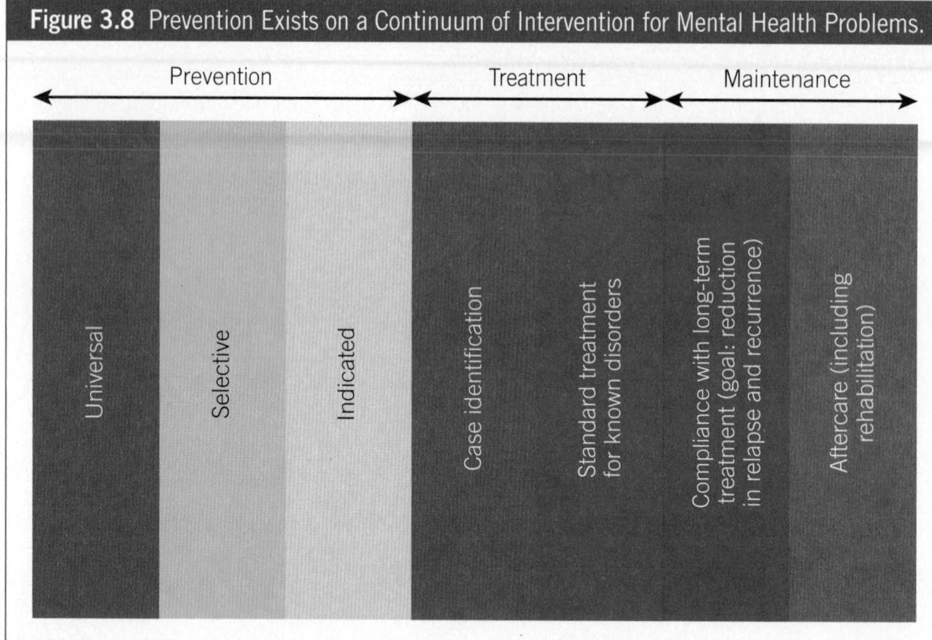

Source: Adapted from Institute of Medicine, Summary: Reducing risks for mental disorders: Frontiers for preventive intervention research, Fig. 2.1, p. 8. Washington, DC: National Academy Press.

may be conducted by community-service personnel such as psychologists, physicians, teachers, clergy, police, court officials, social workers, or others. May 1 of each year is set aside as National Anxiety Disorders Screening Day, which helps provide quick assessment for those who may be struggling with initial panic or other anxiety symptoms. Early identification of problems is followed, of course, by appropriate referrals for treatment.

Selective prevention is similar to secondary prevention in that people at risk for a particular problem are targeted (Figure 3.8). Selective prevention practices target individuals or subgroups of the population who are more likely than the general population to develop a particular mental disorder. Targeted individuals are identified on the basis of biological, psychological, or social risk factors associated with the onset of a disorder. A program to find and help youth genetically predisposed to schizophrenia would be an example of selective prevention. Selective prevention has been recommended especially for high-risk problems such as depression and suicide (Large, 2022).

Tertiary and Indicated Prevention

Tertiary prevention refers to reducing the duration and additional negative effects of a mental disorder *after onset.* Tertiary prevention differs from primary and secondary prevention in that new cases of mental disorder are not reduced. Instead, the goal is to stabilize symptoms, provide rehabilitation, prevent relapse, improve a person's quality of life, and lessen effects of an *existing* mental disorder. Tertiary prevention programs often focus on (1) educating peers and family members to reduce stigmatization, (2) providing job training to increase competence, and (3) teaching independent living skills to help someone be more self-reliant. A person recovering from an episode of schizophrenia might need help in these areas to avoid rehospitalization (Woods et al., 2021).

A key goal of tertiary prevention is to prevent additional problems from occurring. Tertiary prevention programs are not much different from traditional treatment of individuals with mental disorders. The focus remains, however, on preventing *other* problems; thus, tertiary prevention does share something in common with primary and secondary prevention. The goal of each type of prevention is to reduce problems associated with mental disorder on a community- or population-wide basis.

Indicated prevention targets individuals (not groups) who are at very high risk for developing extensive problems in the future (Figure 3.8). These "high-risk" individuals are identified as having many risk factors and few protective factors for a certain mental disorder. Unlike tertiary prevention, indicated prevention focuses on people who have not yet developed a full-blown mental disorder.

Prevention Programs for Mental Disorders

Prevention programs have been quite successful or promising in areas such as school adjustment, learning and health problems, injuries from accidents, and child maltreatment. Areas of limited success include prevention of complex problems such as excessive substance use and delinquency in adolescents (Welsh et al., 2020). A key advantage of prevention is that enormous resources can be saved that otherwise would go toward future treatment, hospitalization, and/or incarceration of people with mental disorder. Specific examples of prevention programs to address problems commonly experienced by young adults are presented next.

Primary/Universal Prevention of Alcohol Use Disorders on College Campuses

Kevin's problems at college come as little surprise given that excessive alcohol use is widespread on college campuses today. Kevin often engaged in what is known as *binge drinking,* which means consuming five or more drinks on one occasion for men and four or more drinks on one occasion for women. Binge drinking is associated with worse academic performance, risk for violence or physical injury, risky sexual behavior, and health problems. About one-third of college students engaged in binge drinking in the past month (National Institute on Alcohol Abuse and Alcoholism, 2021). Because binge drinking among college students is a major problem, efforts to prevent it are a top priority.

Many college campuses have prevention programs to curb excessive or binge drinking. These programs can be thought of as *primary* or *universal* prevention programs because all students, not just those at risk for alcohol use disorder, are exposed to these efforts. These programs include general education during freshman orientation, special events during the academic year such as "Alcohol Awareness Week," and peer education programs in which students themselves support their peers' healthy attitudes and lifestyle choices regarding alcohol use.

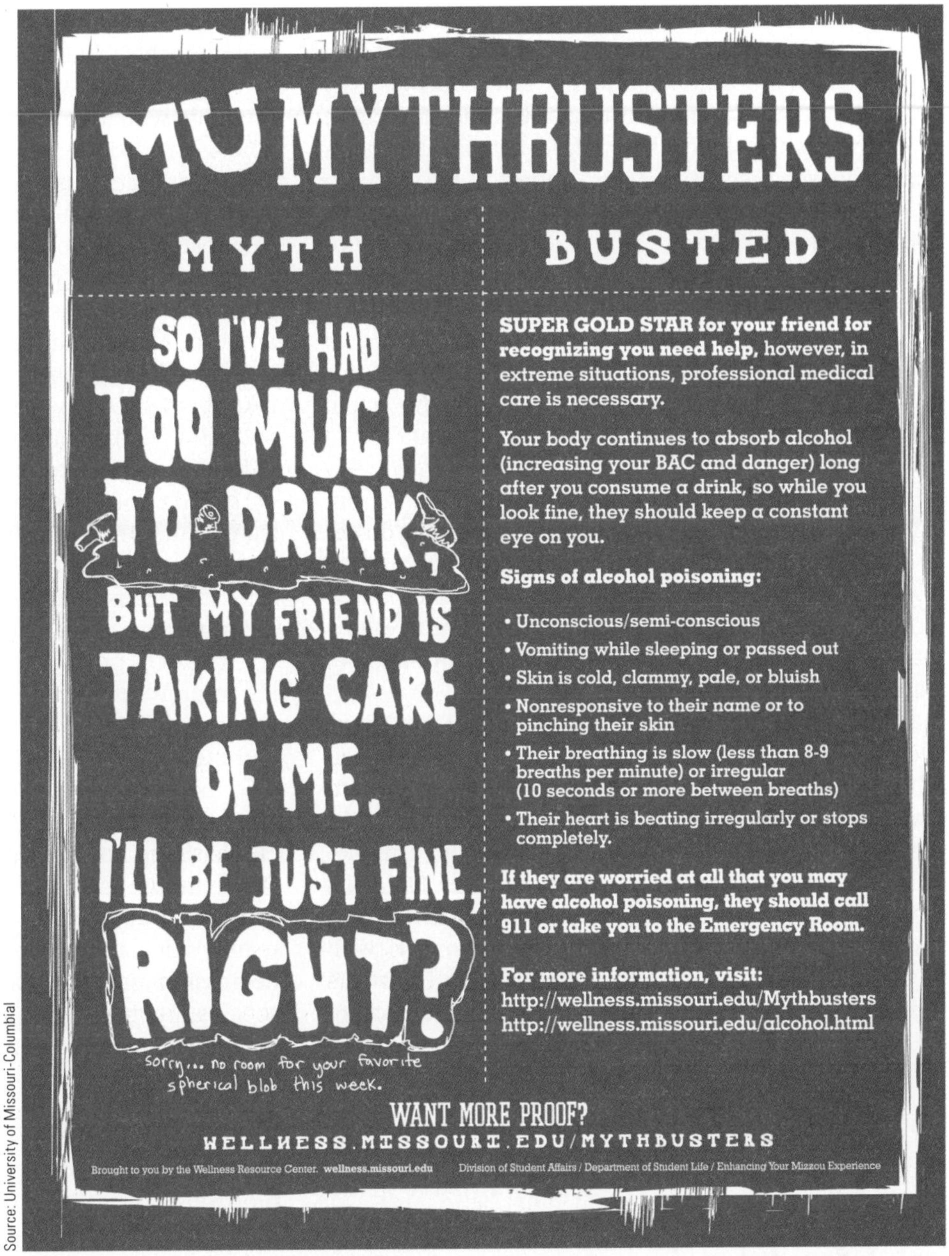

MU MYTHBUSTERS

MYTH

SO I'VE HAD TOO MUCH TO DRINK, BUT MY FRIEND IS TAKING CARE OF ME. I'LL BE JUST FINE, RIGHT?

sorry... no room for your favorite spherical blob this week.

BUSTED

SUPER GOLD STAR for your friend for recognizing you need help, however, in extreme situations, professional medical care is necessary.

Your body continues to absorb alcohol (increasing your BAC and danger) long after you consume a drink, so while you look fine, they should keep a constant eye on you.

Signs of alcohol poisoning:

- Unconscious/semi-conscious
- Vomiting while sleeping or passed out
- Skin is cold, clammy, pale, or bluish
- Nonresponsive to their name or to pinching their skin
- Their breathing is slow (less than 8-9 breaths per minute) or irregular (10 seconds or more between breaths)
- Their heart is beating irregularly or stops completely.

If they are worried at all that you may have alcohol poisoning, they should call 911 or take you to the Emergency Room.

For more information, visit:
http://wellness.missouri.edu/Mythbusters
http://wellness.missouri.edu/alcohol.html

WANT MORE PROOF?
WELLNESS.MISSOURI.EDU/MYTHBUSTERS

Brought to you by the Wellness Resource Center. wellness.missouri.edu

Division of Student Affairs / Department of Student Life / Enhancing Your Mizzou Experience

Source: University of Missouri-Columbia

This screenshot from the University of Missouri Wellness Resource Center illustrates attempts to educate students about the facts regarding college drinking.

The *Wellness Resource Center (WRC)* at the University of Missouri sponsors a prevention program targeting excessive alcohol use. Major components of the program include promoting responsible decision making and providing accurate information about how much alcohol is consumed by college students (called *social norming*). Peers provide much of the information about drinking and its related problems to fellow students. The WRC's responsible decision-making program is administered by trained peer educators who visit residence halls, fraternity and sorority houses, classrooms, and junior high and high schools to speak about alcohol and other drug issues and making healthy lifestyle choices about eating, exercising, and smoking.

For example, one peer presentation introduces participants to the Virtual Bar, an interactive computer program that demonstrates the effect of alcohol on the body. Participants decide whether the character sips, drinks, or slams a range of alcoholic drinks to understand how this affects blood alcohol content. In addition, participants learn to consider time, alcohol content, gender, and weight when making decisions about alcohol use. Another presentation focuses on the practice of having 21 drinks on one's 21st birthday. The program emphasizes the danger of such a practice (alcohol poisoning and death), and promotes safe, responsible drinking. Finally, START (Student Alcohol Responsibility Training) is an online training program that educates participants in planning and hosting a fun and safe party. Topics covered include party safety, alcohol consumption by guests, preventing MIPs (minors in possession), and legal responsibilities. *Social norming* is an important component of many substance use prevention programs. This approach is based on the assumption that students often overestimate how much other students drink and that students drink in amounts they perceive others to drink. Programs like the WRC correct this misperception by educating students about the actual amount of alcohol their peers drink. Survey data reveal that Missouri students believed 60 percent of their peers drink three times a week or more, but actual data from students themselves reveal that only 33 percent do so. The WRC corrects students' norms for drinking by placing weekly ads in the student newspaper, distributing written materials across campus, giving away bookmarks, and placing mouse pads with this information in student computer labs.

The WRC also sponsors prevention organizations such as PARTY (Promoting Awareness and Responsibility Through You), a peer education organization that promotes responsible decision making; GAMMA (Greeks Advocating the Mature Management of Alcohol), an organization of fraternity/sorority students who promote responsible alcohol use; and CHEERS, a statewide program of student volunteers who work with local bars and restaurants to provide designated drivers with free soft drinks. Note how this prevention program is quite comprehensive and extensive.

Courtesy of Screenings for Mental Health, Inc.

The Signs of Suicide (SOS) prevention program helps prevent suicide attempts and increase knowledge about depression.

Primary/Universal Prevention of Suicidal Behavior in High School Students

Recall the case of Jana, a 22-year-old college student, who had been suicidal many times over the past few years. Suicide is one of the leading causes of death among 15- to 24-year-olds. In addition, 6 percent of undergraduates and 4 percent of graduate students have seriously considered suicide in the past 12 months (King et al., 2015). The need for early and effective suicide prevention programs is thus clear. These programs may help people like Jana who struggle with thoughts of suicide and self-harm.

Signs of Suicide (SOS) is a school-based prevention program with two main components (Schilling et al., 2014). An educational component involves the review of a video and a discussion guide. These materials highlight the link between suicide and depression, show that suicidal behavior is not a normal reaction to emotional distress, and provide guidelines for recognizing signs and symptoms of depression in oneself and others. Students are also taught what to do (ACT) if signs of depression are present in a peer: *acknowledge* (A) the signs and take them seriously, let the person know you *care* (C), and *tell* (T) a responsible adult about the situation. The video has interviews of people who have been touched by suicide and provides ways of reacting if a peer has signs of depression or suicide. The second component involves a self-screening: Individuals evaluate themselves for signs of depression and suicidal thoughts and are prompted to seek help if necessary.

The SOS program appears to be successful at helping to prevent suicidal behavior. SOS participants show fewer suicide attempts, greater knowledge of depression, and more adaptive attitudes about depression and suicide than nonparticipants. This program has also been adapted for graduating seniors who are college-bound, emphasizing how to access resources on campus and in the community. A program like SOS might have helped Jana learn about her signs of depression and distress, realize suicidal behavior is not a good way to cope with depression or stress, and develop a plan for getting social support when she felt overwhelmed. These skills may have reduced Jana's suicidal behaviors.

Secondary/Selective Prevention of Eating Disorder Symptoms

Researchers have also evaluated secondary prevention programs for college students. Stice and colleagues (2012) conducted such a program to prevent eating disorder symptoms and unhealthy weight gain in female college students. *Healthy Weight* is a selective prevention program that focuses on healthy dietary intake and appropriate physical activity in women with body image concerns. Body image refers to beliefs about one's appearance, how one feels about their body, and one's sense of control over their body. Concerns about body image may be a risk factor for eating disorders (Chapter 8). Recall that secondary or selective prevention targets people who do not currently have a certain mental disorder but who may be at risk for developing additional symptoms of the disorder. Students targeted by the researchers thus appeared to be at risk for developing an eating disorder.

Healthy Weight is a four-session program that begins with education about how participants can make small but lasting healthy changes to diet and physical activity to ensure that their energy intake and output are balanced. Participants are encouraged to pursue a healthy ideal, not a thin ideal, by using adaptive choices such as starting meals with high-fiber foods, reducing portion sizes, and not having unhealthy foods at home. Scheduled and creative exercise routines are discussed as well. Participants keep eating and exercise diaries to maintain motivation toward a healthy body weight. They are also encouraged to discuss possible future obstacles in this regard and develop ways of overcoming barriers to healthy behavior change.

Most students (67 percent) attended all four sessions (four hours total) of the *Healthy Weight* program. Compared with controls, students in the *Healthy Weight* intervention displayed fewer eating disorder symptoms, increased exercise, less dieting, and less body dissatisfaction. Intermittent dieting is often considered a risk factor for eating disorders, so the program helped reduce behaviors that may have led to a full-blown diagnosis. Intervention effects were strongest for students who had more eating disorder symptoms and who felt more pressure to be thin. The results suggested that a brief group intervention can be a powerful preventative strategy. Prevention programs can thus successfully "buffer" young people from developing psychological problems. Many examples of primary, secondary, and tertiary prevention of mental disorders are presented throughout this textbook.

Section Summary

- Prevention refers to thwarting the development of later problems and guides many mental health programs.
- Prevention can be viewed along a continuum with treatment and maintenance.
- Primary prevention refers to providing intervention to people with no signs of a particular disorder.
- Universal prevention targets large groups of people without a particular problem to reduce new cases of a disorder.
- Secondary prevention refers to addressing manageable problems before they become more resistant to treatment.
- Selective prevention targets people at risk for a particular problem.
- Tertiary prevention refers to reducing the duration and negative effects of a mental disorder after its onset.
- Indicated prevention targets individuals at very high risk for developing extensive problems in the future.
- Many prevention programs target children, adolescents, and young adults.

Review Questions

1. What is prevention? What prevention programs are on your college campus?
2. How might prevention be viewed along a continuum? What are advantages in doing so?
3. Describe a primary, secondary, and tertiary prevention program for alcohol use disorder in college students. Who would these programs target?
4. What are important features of prevention for mental disorders in college students?

Focus On Law and Ethics

Constructs Related to Insanity

Recall from Chapter 2 that *insanity* is a legal term that refers to mental incapacity at the time of a crime. The concept of insanity has been shaped by some key historical standards. One standard is the *M'Naghten rule,* which refers to the idea that a criminal defendant is not guilty by reason of insanity if, at the time of the crime, they did not know the nature or quality of their actions or did not know the difference between right and wrong. The M'Naghten rule means that defendants must have the cognitive ability to know right from wrong. If a defendant did not know the difference, such as someone experiencing a psychotic episode (Chapter 12) or someone with severe intellectual developmental disorder (Chapter 13), then this could be the basis for an insanity defense.

Another important historical standard is the *irresistible impulse* or *control* rule. In this situation, one could argue for an insanity defense if a person had a mental disorder that did not allow him to control their actions during a crime. A person may have known the difference between right and wrong but still could not exercise behavioral control. In addition, the *Durham rule* refers to the idea that a person may not be responsible for a criminal act if the act was due to a "mental disease or defect." Both of these standards, however, have been criticized as being too broad (Kolla & Brodie, 2012).

The *American Law Institute* (ALI) attempted to address this concern by blending the M'Naghten and irresistible impulse concepts. The ALI recommended that a person could use an insanity defense if a mental disorder prevented them from knowing right from wrong or prevented them from being able to control their actions. The *American Psychiatric Association* (APA) later recommended paring the ALI definition to include only the first part (i.e., to the M'Naghten rule). Many states and the federal government use the APA distinction today, although some states have eliminated the insanity defense altogether.

Personal Narrative

Kim Dude and the Wellness Resource Center

I began my student affairs career in residential life where my role was to encourage students to be successful by helping them make healthy, safe, and responsible decisions in all aspects of their lives. I wrote a grant to the U.S. Department of Education to create an alcohol and drug abuse office and became the Director of ADAPT (Alcohol and Drug Abuse Prevention Team). The mission of ADAPT later expanded, and it became the Wellness Resource Center (WRC).

The students and staff of the Wellness Resource Center realize that one single approach or one single event is not sufficient in helping college students make responsible decisions concerning alcohol or other aspects of their health. Four theoretical models guide the WRC's prevention efforts: (1) responsible decision making, (2) social norming, (3) harm reduction, and (4) environmental management. It takes a comprehensive yearlong effort to have an impact on student behavior.

The responsible decision-making approach is used through peer educator presentations and major campus-wide events such as Alcohol Responsibility Month, Safe Spring Break, Safe Holiday Break, and Wellness Month. The WRC challenges students to make informed, responsible decisions regarding all aspects of their health, and presents between 150 and 200 outreach programs per year.

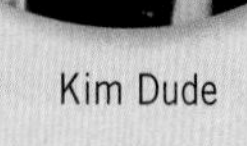

Courtesy of Kim Dude

Kim Dude

The WRC implements a social norms approach. Social norms theory suggests that students' misperceptions and overestimations of their peers' alcohol and drug use increase problem behaviors and decrease healthy behaviors because students are acting in accordance with what they think is "normal." Our research on University of Missouri students indicates a significant difference between student perceptions and the reality of peer alcohol and other drug use. By correcting misperceptions of the norm, the WRC has decreased problem behavior and seen an increase in healthy behavior. The WRC's social norming efforts are comprehensive and incorporate not only an extensive marketing campaign but also educational outreach programs and training.

A harm reduction approach accepts that students sometimes make risky choices and that it is important to create safety nets to keep them from hurting themselves or someone else. The WRC created and supports Project CHEERS, a designated-driver program in which more than 50 bars in Columbia give free soda to designated drivers. Additionally, the WRC provides an educational intervention called BASICS (Brief Alcohol Screening Intervention for College Students) for students caught in violation of the alcohol and drug policies of the university and/or for students who are concerned about their use. The program is composed of a two-hour interactive workshop and a one-hour individual follow-up session led by two PhD-level counseling psychology graduate students.

The WRC also takes an environmental management approach by actively working to influence the campus and community

Final Comments

The diathesis-stress model is a useful way of thinking about various influences on mental disorders. Diatheses (predispositions) and stressors can be thought of as risk factors for mental disorders. Most mental disorders begin in adolescence or early adulthood when the burden of mental disorder is high. This highlights the need for early prevention efforts to address risk factors and thwart disorder development. Prevention programs are more efficient and cost-effective in the long run than traditional treatment because enormous costs related to disability and tertiary care can be lessened. Throughout this textbook, not only effective treatments but also contemporary and personal approaches for preventing various psychological problems are discussed. Examples include suggestions for reducing anxiety and sadness (Chapters 5 and 7), enhancing prenatal care to prevent intellectual problems (Chapter 13), and improving memory to limit cognitive decline (Chapter 14). Next, Chapter 4 covers methods used by mental health professionals to assess, diagnose, classify, and study mental disorders. This discussion will further provide the foundation for understanding the mental disorders discussed in Chapters 5 through 14.

environment through the campus and community coalition called the Access to Alcohol Action Team. The Columbia Tobacco Prevention Initiative works with all three high schools in Columbia as well as Columbia College and Stephens College on the tobacco control issues. The WRC has also created two statewide coalitions called Missouri Partners In Prevention and Partners In Environmental Change, composed of the 13 state colleges and universities in Missouri. Both PIP and PIEC provide technical assistance, training, and programmatic support for the campus, and are funded by the Missouri Division of Alcohol and Drug Abuse.

My professional journey has been filled with many challenges. Our society glamorizes the misuse and abuse of alcohol through the media, movies, television, music, magazines, and even campus traditions. We have faced a long list of obstacles including the lack of power to make significant change, strong campus organizations that revolve around alcohol, territory issues with other professionals, and the opinions that student alcohol abuse is simply a rite of passage. Additionally, because the WRC is more than 80 percent grant funded, securing and maintaining funding has been one of the biggest obstacles we have faced.

Another great challenge is trying to change the environment. The WRC cannot do this alone. As the saying states, "It takes a village to raise a child." Everyone in the community needs to be part of the solution: parents, law enforcement, community leaders, educators, business owners, etc. I was taught that if you are not part of the solution, you are part of the problem. We all need to be part of the solution and help change laws, policies, and practices so that we have an environment that supports and encourages good decision making.

I am proud to say that the WRC has been successful over the years despite its obstacles and has been recognized as one of the top prevention programs in the country. So much of our survival and our success is the result of a positive attitude and the desire to never give up. I want to share a story that I love. A woman was walking down a street in a large city past a construction site. She came across three construction workers and asked them each a simple question. "Excuse me sir, what are you doing?" The first man said he was laying bricks, the second man said he was building a wall, and the third man stated proudly that he was building a great cathedral. All three men were doing the same task and yet each viewed it differently. Ultimately, we are all playing a part in building a great cathedral. Some days we may feel like we are just laying bricks, but we are part of a much bigger picture. We are taking part in the great task of building a community that encourages and supports good decision making by all. My philosophy in life is embodied in this quote from Leon Joseph Cardinal Suenens: "Happy are those who dream dreams and are ready to pay the price to make them come true."

Kim Dude was recognized by the U.S. Department of Education's Network: Addressing Collegiate Alcohol and Other Drug Issues as the recipient of the Outstanding Contribution to the Field award in 2003. Kim has also been honored by the Phoenix Programs in Columbia, Missouri, with the Buck Buchanan Lifetime Service Award for her prevention efforts.

Source: Used with permission.

Key Terms

diathesis 55
etiology 56
epidemiology 57
epidemiologists 57
incidence 57
prevalence 57
lifetime prevalence 57
comorbidity 58
cohort effects 59
risk factor 62
protective factors 63
resilience 64
prevention 65
primary prevention 66
universal prevention 66
secondary prevention 66
selective prevention 68
tertiary prevention 68
indicated prevention 68

Diagnosis, Assessment, and Study of Mental Disorders

4

Learning Objectives

LO 4.1 Characterize the dimensional and categorical approaches to defining mental disorders, including their assumptions, strengths, and limitations.

LO 4.2 Discuss the restrictions and advantages of diagnosis.

LO 4.3 Explain the approach of the *Diagnostic and Statistical Manual of Mental Disorders* to the diagnosis of mental disorders.

LO 4.4 Characterize the process of clinical assessment, including its purpose and the criteria for assessment instruments.

LO 4.5 Describe the major assessment categories including the tests and instruments associated with each and their strengths and limitations.

LO 4.6 Demonstrate the importance of considering culture in clinical assessment.

LO 4.7 Define the key components of the scientific method.

LO 4.8 Describe the important approaches to the scientific study of psychopathology, including experimental, quasi-experimental, nonexperimental, and developmental designs and case studies, including the methods, strengths, and limitations of each.

Case Professor Smith

Forty-five-year-old **Professor Smith** could not understand what had been happening to him over the past six months. He had been experiencing strange sensations throughout his body, including chest pains and headaches. He felt short of breath, light-headed, shaky, and hot throughout his chest and arms during these episodes. These symptoms came on abruptly, sometimes even during sleep, but ended within 15 minutes. Professor Smith had a number of recent setbacks, including denial for promotion to full professor, so this was the last thing he needed.

What could be wrong? Professor Smith had several medical tests to rule out heart problems, a brain tumor, and other maladies. His physician reassured him nothing was medically wrong, but the symptoms persisted. Professor Smith found it harder to concentrate on his work and his career seemed to be on hold. Despite looming deadlines, he struggled to read books and journals and could not concentrate long enough to write a paragraph. His teaching was suffering as well, and he canceled several classes because of his physical symptoms.

Professor Smith felt he needed to know what was happening but had no clear answer. Even worse, these symptoms and problems at work were creating a strain on his family and friendships. Those who cared about him wanted to help but had trouble doing so because Professor Smith became more isolated, frustrated, and depressed. This depression seemed to worsen recently as he had trouble sleeping, felt fatigued much of the day, and lost 20 pounds. Finally, he agreed to visit a clinical psychologist after constant pleas from his wife and at the suggestion of his physician. He was skeptical, but what harm could it do at this point?

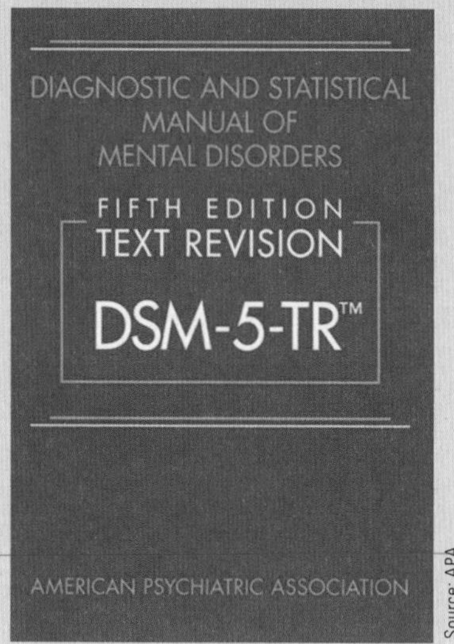

Source: APA

What Do You Think?

1. Is Professor Smith's behavior psychopathological? Do you think he has a mental disorder?
2. Do you know anyone with problems like Professor Smith's?
3. What other information about his condition would be useful to know?
4. What do you think would be the best way to find out more about his problems? Do you think interviews, psychological evaluations, or other medical tests would help?
5. What kind of treatment might give Professor Smith some relief?

American Psychiatric Association. (2022). *Diagnostic and statistical manual of mental disorders* (5th ed., text rev.). Arlington, VA: American Psychiatric Association.

Defining Psychopathology and Mental Disorder

LO 4.1 Characterize the dimensional and categorical approaches to defining mental disorders, including their assumptions, strengths, and limitations.

LO 4.2 Discuss the restrictions and advantages of diagnosis.

Professor Smith's case illustrates how certain symptoms can limit someone's ability to live comfortably, maintain a career, and even talk to others. These symptoms are indeed quite distressing to him and seem out of the ordinary. Professor Smith has consulted a psychologist to find out what is wrong and what can be done to help. What do mental health professionals do when they address people with mental disorder? Mental health professionals define, classify, assess, and study mental disorders. These endeavors are discussed in this chapter, starting with definition.

Dimensions and Categories

Mental health professionals often focus on **dimensions** and **categories** to define psychopathology and mental disorder. A *dimensional approach* refers to defining psychopathology along a continuum or spectrum. Recall three definitions of psychopathological behavior from Chapter 1: (1) behavior that deviates from the norm, (2) behavior associated with difficulty adapting to life's demands, and (3) behavior accompanied by personal distress. Each definition lies on a continuum. Some behaviors deviate a little from the norm and involve slight adaptation problems or distress, and some behaviors deviate substantially from the norm and involve significant adaptation problems and distress. Recall from Chapter 2 how Mariella's symptoms of depression reflected to some extent a normal reaction to being separated from family and friends but also that some of her depressive symptoms seemed problematic. Recall from Chapter 3 the discussion of mild, moderate, and severe intensity of symptoms. These examples show psychopathological behavior on a continuum or from a dimensional perspective.

One way to think about psychopathological behavior from a dimensional perspective is to consider its many forms. Psychopathological behavior actually consists of *emotional states, cognitive styles* or ways of thinking, and *physical behavior.* Each form can be viewed along a continuum or dimensional perspective. Professor Smith experiences *emotional* sadness, *cognitive* worry, and *behavioral* avoidance. His symptoms are severe, but all of us become sad and worrisome and avoid things from time to time. We show emotions, thoughts, and behaviors along a spectrum of intensity or oddity.

A different way of defining psychopathological behavior or mental disorder is a *categorical approach.* A category is a large class of frequently observed syndromes (mental disorders) composed of psychopathological behaviors or features that occur in a person. Many chapters in this book represent broad categories of mental disorder, such as anxiety, depressive, psychotic, personality, developmental, and neurocognitive disorders.

Depression is a widely recognized syndrome or mental disorder that often includes sad mood, sleep and appetite disturbance, and suicidal thoughts. A certain number of symptoms must be present from a categorical perspective before a person's behavior can be considered psychopathological—for depression, five of nine main symptoms must be present. Someone with only three or four symptoms of depression would not be considered to have a mental disorder. A **diagnosis** from a categorical perspective is defined by rules that outline how many and what features of a mental disorder must be present.

The categorical approach can be thought of as a "yes–no" approach: One either has or does not have a mental disorder. The approach is derived from a medical model that makes sense when you consider a disease such as measles. You either have measles right now or you do not (pick one!). A "yes–no" approach works well for many physical disorders but perhaps less well for mental disorders. Imagine if someone visited a psychologist and complained of sad mood, trouble sleeping, suicidal thoughts, and no other symptoms. This person has *no mental disorder* from a strict categorical perspective because not enough symptoms of depression are evident. But doesn't the person have a problem that should be treated?

We can best view psychopathological behavior along a continuum. Still, many mental health professionals adopt a common categorical approach to classifying mental disorder, and this approach is described next. The approach used throughout this textbook will be to organize mental disorders by general categories but explain the dimensional aspects of each category in detail.

DSM

A categorical approach to mental disorder commonly used in the United States and much of the world is the *Diagnostic and Statistical Manual of Mental Disorders (DSM*; American Psychiatric Association [APA], 2022). General features of **mental disorder** according to the *DSM* include the following:

- A group of cognitive, emotional, or behavioral disturbances or symptoms called a **syndrome**.
- These symptoms are usually associated with emotional distress or disability (impairment) in life activities.
- The syndrome is not simply an expected or culturally approved response to a specific event, such as grief and sadness following death of a loved one.
- The symptoms are considered to reflect dysfunction in psychological, biological, or developmental processes.

A syndrome (or mental disorder or diagnosis) includes a group of psychopathological behaviors or number of symptoms *associated with* distress, significant work or interpersonal problems, or likelihood of future problems. Recall Ricardo and Yoko from Chapter 1 who had symptoms of anxiety. Ricardo qualified for a *DSM* diagnosis of social anxiety disorder because his symptoms interfered with daily functioning. Yoko's anxiety symptoms, however, were not accompanied by significant impairment in daily functioning, and so she did not qualify for a diagnosis.

This description of syndrome or mental disorder incorporates definitions of psychopathological behavior from Chapter 1 and this chapter. The description focuses on behavior that deviates from the norm, behavior associated with difficulty adapting to life's demands, and behavior accompanied by distress. The *DSM* definition of mental disorder is restrictive because it focuses on *clusters* of psychopathological behaviors associated with distress or disability. Several psychopathological behaviors must be present at the same time *and* cause significant problems for someone to qualify for a diagnosis of a mental disorder.

Advantages of Diagnosis

Several advantages do exist regarding diagnoses. A primary advantage of diagnosis is *communication*—a wealth of information can be conveyed in a single term. Imagine if a person with a diagnosis of schizophrenia was referred to a mental health professional. A symptom pattern might immediately come to the professional's mind even though nothing was known about the person: delusions, hallucinations, severe social/occupational dysfunction, and continuous symptoms for at least six months. You can think of a diagnosis as "verbal shorthand" for describing features of a mental disorder. We do not have to ask so many questions about a person's symptoms when we know their diagnosis.

A second advantage of diagnosis is that standard rules are provided for defining mental disorders and for seeking the cause of these disorders. We must group people based on symptoms they share to study the cause of a mental disorder. Important comparisons between groups can then be made about developmental characteristics, personality features, performance on different tasks, or other variables that could shed light on risk factors and cause. Recall from Chapter 3 that childhood sexual maltreatment is a risk factor for borderline personality disorder. A reliable and systematic way of defining borderline personality disorder was necessary first, however, to even reach this conclusion. Use of diagnoses assists this process.

A third advantage of diagnosis is that, because everyone uses the same system, clinicians can find useful assessment strategies, such as questionnaires for depression, and researchers can examine prevalence rates of a certain mental disorder at local, state, and national levels. Managed care agencies also rely on diagnostic codes to reimburse people for mental health services. Diagnoses are most important because *they may suggest which treatment is most effective*. A diagnosis of schizophrenia, for example, suggests that antipsychotic medication is likely to be more effective than psychodynamic therapy. More than one treatment is often effective for mental disorders, however.

Diagnoses thus serve many useful functions, and researchers and practitioners commonly use them to understand mental disorder. Laypeople also use diagnoses to understand what is wrong. If you were diagnosed with a particular disease, you would likely "Google" it to get more information. Diagnoses also ease the sense of uniqueness or loneliness people feel when something is wrong. Professor Smith learned his condition was called "panic disorder" and that the problem can be successfully treated. How do you think he felt once he learned this?

Section Summary

- Mental health professionals often focus on dimensions and categories to define psychopathological behavior and mental disorder.
- A dimensional approach refers to defining psychopathological behavior along a continuum.
- A category is a large class of frequently observed syndromes or mental disorders.
- A diagnosis is defined by rules that outline how many and what features of a mental disorder must be present.
- Mental disorder from the *DSM* categorical approach involves a group of psychopathological behaviors associated with distress or disability.
- Advantages of diagnosis include enhanced communication, improved definition and understanding of mental disorder, coordinated research, and ideas about which treatment may be most effective for a given disorder.

Review Questions

1. What is it about Professor Smith's behavior and symptoms that led his therapist to diagnose him with a mental disorder?
2. Which general features of the *DSM* definition of mental disorder are highlighted in Professor Smith's case?
3. Why do you think the *DSM* definition of mental disorder requires the presence of significant distress or disability?
4. How might diagnosis allow mental health professionals to communicate about Professor Smith's problems, study what caused his problems, and determine what treatment might be effective for him?

Classifying Psychopathological Behavior and Mental Disorder

LO 4.3 Explain the approach of the *Diagnostic and Statistical Manual of Mental Disorders* to the diagnosis of mental disorders.

Recall that mental health professionals define, classify, assess, and study mental disorders. Definition was discussed in the previous section. **Classification** is next and refers to arranging mental disorders into broad categories or classes based on similar features. The *DSM* is a primary method of classification with criteria and research-based information about mental disorders listed in the manual (*DSM-5-TR*; APA, 2022).

Some of the diagnostic categories discussed in this textbook may be familiar to you because of their prevalence and media coverage. You may have heard a lot about anxiety, depression, attention-deficit/hyperactivity disorder (ADHD), Alzheimer's disease, alcohol use disorder, and anorexia nervosa. Other diagnoses may be less familiar to you, such as somatic symptom disorder and paraphilic disorders. Researchers have studied these disorders in one form or another for decades and the disorders are often the focus of clinical attention because of their prevalence and severity.

The *DSM* relies on categories to organize mental disorder but also encourages clinicians to use dimensional assessments in addition to diagnoses. Recall that "dimensional" means viewing behavior or symptoms along a continuum. One type of dimensional assessment might include ratings of a person's symptoms as mild, moderate, or severe in intensity. Another dimensional assessment could involve a person's degree of insight into, or recognition of, their mental condition. Dimensional assessments allow clinicians to consider fluctuations in symptoms, to track a client's progress in therapy, and to evaluate all of a client's symptoms, not simply those that are part of an assigned diagnosis. Other types of dimensional assessments are discussed throughout the textbook.

How might such a categorical and dimensional approach work for Professor Smith? Professor Smith's therapist assigned two diagnoses based on his symptoms. The primary diagnosis (initial focus of treatment) was panic disorder. Professor Smith's "episodes" suggest he has periodic panic attacks with chest pain, shaking, breathlessness, hot flashes, and light-headedness (Chapter 5). These attacks are recurrent and unexpected, and Professor Smith has been concerned about additional attacks and their implications ("Am I having a heart attack?"). Professor Smith also received a diagnosis of major depressive disorder (Chapter 7). He has had sad mood, insomnia, difficulty concentrating, fatigue, weight loss, and poor appetite for more than two weeks. These symptoms characterize depression.

Professor Smith's therapist also used dimensional assessments. One type of dimensional assessment involved symptom intensity ratings along a continuum (i.e., mild, moderate, severe). For example, some of Professor Smith's anxiety and depressive symptoms were mild to moderate in nature. These included his headaches and sad mood. In contrast, some of his anxiety and depressive symptoms were severe in nature. These included his shortness of breath, light-headedness, trouble sleeping, and fatigue.

Another dimensional assessment involved the impact of Professor Smith's symptoms on different areas of his life. Professor Smith's symptoms such as his inability to concentrate or finish projects had the greatest negative impact on his career. His symptoms also had some impact on his marriage, but his wife was supportive of him during this difficult time. These dimensional assessments allowed the therapist to concentrate treatment first on those symptoms that caused Professor Smith the most amount of distress and that seemed most urgent. A dimensional approach thus adds substantial information to a simple diagnosis. A dimensional approach is emphasized when discussing mental disorders throughout this textbook.

Assessing Psychopathological Behavior and Mental Disorder

LO 4.4 Characterize the process of clinical assessment, including its purpose and the criteria for assessment instruments.

LO 4.5 Describe the major assessment categories including the tests and instruments associated with each and their strengths and limitations.

Defining and classifying mental disorder are important tasks that involve detailed clinical assessment. **Clinical assessment** involves evaluating a person's strengths and weaknesses and understanding the problem at hand to develop a treatment. This may include providing a diagnosis for the person. This next section describes assessment procedures implemented in clinics, hospitals, and offices of mental health professionals.

The clinical assessment process often begins with a *referral*. Someone—perhaps a parent, teacher, partner, friend, judge, or a person themself—asks a question: "Why is Samantha struggling at her job?" "Why are my child's moods so unstable?" "Why do I feel anxious all the time?" "Why does Professor Smith keep canceling his classes?" People may then be referred to a therapist who might provide a *DSM* diagnosis but who will also examine emotional, cognitive, personality, and biological issues that must be addressed. Mental health professionals try to understand precisely what a client seeks or needs and use a wide array of procedures and measures to do so (refer to **Focus on Diversity: Culture and Diagnosis**).

Reliability, Validity, and Standardization

An important expectation of mental health professionals is that they use assessment measures that are strong psychometrically. This means the measures should be reliable, valid, and standardized. Each of these concepts is discussed separately.

Reliability

Reliability refers to consistency of scores or responses. Three main ways of evaluating reliability include *test–retest, interrater,* and *internal consistency reliability* (refer to **Table 4.1**). Each type of reliability is used to examine consistency of assessment data. **Test–retest reliability** is the extent to which a person provides

Table 4.1 Types of Reliability for Psychological Tests and Structured Interviews

Type of reliability	Definition
Test–retest reliability	Consistency of test scores or diagnoses across some period of time
Interrater reliability	Agreement between two or more raters or judges about level of a trait or presence/absence of a feature or diagnosis
Internal consistency reliability	Relationship among test items that measure the same variable

Focus On Diversity

Culture and Diagnosis

Culture has an impact on our thoughts, personal perspectives and worldviews, emotional expression, and behavior. Culture must be considered when a person is evaluated for psychological problems, and mental health professionals must be aware of their own biases when they evaluate people of other cultures. What may be considered unusual in one culture may not be in another culture. Consider Joey, a 10-year-old boy of Chinese descent who moved to the United States with his parents four years earlier (Fang et al., 2013). Joey was referred to a mental health clinic by his pediatrician after reports of seeing ghosts at bedtime on a daily basis for the past two years. Joey stated that he actually sees ghosts (does not dream about them), they appear to be teenagers, and they intend to hurt his family. Joey goes to bed each night with a stick and a flashlight ready to defend himself and his family if necessary. However, over time, he has become less scared of the ghosts and simply watches them but does not interact with them. Joey reports that he has no trouble falling asleep, and he is functioning well at school and at home. Joey's parents began to wonder if Joey might possess some special powers to connect to the spiritual world, which according to some Chinese customs naturally interact with humans. Those with this gift are considered to be more vulnerable to "spirit attack."

Joey's experiences and beliefs may seem quite unusual or even evidence of a serious mental disorder like schizophrenia. However, cultural explanations may account, at least partially, for his experience. One possible Chinese Indigenous explanation is a form of sleep paralysis called "ghost oppression" (*guai ya chun*; "ghost presses bed"). However, this does not seem to fit Joey's report in that he did not report an inability to move while awakening. However, seeing ghosts is not an uncommon experience among Chinese people, and thus does not necessarily indicate psychotic symptoms like hallucinations or delusions. But why did Joey feel that the ghosts might hurt him or his family? Clinicians that evaluated Joey and his family attributed these feelings to the stress of immigration for both Joey and his family. Treatment focused on supporting Joey and his family in their adjustment to life in the United States as well as encouraging the family to spend more time together to strengthen their bond. Over time, Joey's primary symptoms of seeing ghosts at bedtime improved and the family reported better functioning.

Joey's case highlights the importance of considering culture when evaluating psychological symptoms. The *DSM* includes a Cultural Formulation Interview to help mental health professionals gain information about how a person's culture may affect their symptoms and treatment (APA, 2022). Questions surround how a person understands and explains their condition, what social stressors and supports they may have, whether their cultural background or identity affects their symptoms, what cultural factors may influence their ability to cope and to seek help, and concerns about their therapist or the mental health setting. Mental health professionals are also encouraged to be aware of how a person's culture can influence risk factors and the course of a disorder.

---

similar answers to the same test items across time. If Karl provides different scores on the same anxiety questionnaire on two consecutive Mondays, then the data may not be very useful. If we interview someone and find that their diagnosis changes from week to week, this demonstrates limited test–retest reliability for the interview (refer to **Personal Narrative: Anonymous**). Recall that Professor Smith received a primary diagnosis of panic disorder. If he came back the next week for a follow-up interview and no longer met criteria for panic disorder, how useful would this interview be? Panic disorder does not come and go this rapidly.

Test–retest reliability is important, but the consistency of scores or diagnoses will naturally diminish as time between test and retest grows longer. This may reflect actual change. Professor Smith may not meet criteria for panic disorder two years from now, but this may reflect the fact that he received treatment and no longer shows symptoms of the disorder.

Interrater reliability is the extent to which two raters or observers agree about their ratings or judgments of a person's behavior. Interrater reliability is often used to examine the usefulness of a diagnostic interview. Two mental health professionals may give Professor Smith the same diagnostic interview on the same day and arrive at the same diagnosis. This would reflect good interrater reliability.

Internal consistency reliability refers to whether items on a test appear to be measuring the same thing. You would expect items on a test of anxiety to generally relate to one another. If they do not, then the items may not be measuring the same thing or may be measuring something else. Some measures of anxiety are sometimes criticized for measuring depression more than anxiety. For us to consider them useful, test items should have high internal consistency reliability.

Validity

Validity is the extent to which an assessment technique measures what it is supposed to measure. Key types of validity include *content, predictive, concurrent,* and *construct validity* (refer to **Table 4.2**). **Content validity** is the degree to which test or interview items actually cover aspects of the variable or diagnosis under study. If a test of depression contained items only about sad mood, the test would not have high content validity because depression also involves problematic thinking patterns and withdrawn behavior.

Table 4.2 Common Types of Validity

Type of validity	Definition
Content validity	How well test or interview items adequately measure aspects of a variable, construct, or diagnosis
Predictive validity	How well test scores or diagnoses predict and correlate with behavior or test scores that are observed or obtained at some future point
Concurrent validity	How well test scores or diagnoses correlate with a related but independent set of test scores or behaviors
Construct validity	How well test scores or diagnoses correlate with other measures or behaviors in a logical and theoretically consistent way

Predictive validity refers to whether test or interview results accurately predict some *future* behavior or event. A test of school success has good predictive validity if current scores relate to children's school achievement two years from now. **Concurrent validity** refers to whether current test or interview results relate to an important *present* feature or characteristic. A child's diagnosis of conduct disorder should reflect their current level of problematic behavior.

Construct validity refers to whether test or interview results relate to other measures or behaviors in a logical, theoretically expected fashion. Recall Kevin's impulsivity and alcohol problems from Chapter 3. A valid test of impulsivity might be expected to correlate with a diagnosis of alcohol use disorder, school or work problems, and lower levels of the neurotransmitter serotonin. If this test does so, then we can be more confident in its construct validity. If people with problems similar to Kevin's scored high on this test of impulsivity, this would also support the test's construct validity.

Standardization

Standardization refers to administering or conducting assessment measures in the same way for everyone. If you took the SAT or ACT, you may have noticed all the rules and guidelines for administering, scoring, and interpreting the test. Proctors gave the test in a standardized or similar way for all high school students in the country.

Assessment measures can be standardized in several ways. First, the same test items and testing procedures, such as time limits or item order, can be used for everyone. Second, the way the test is scored can be the same for everyone. Everyone's SAT verbal scores are based on the same scoring system. Third, our interpretation of test scores can be standardized by collecting normative data from large groups of people across age, gender, and race. Test scores can thus be compared among members of these groups. Scores obtained by a 25-year-old Latina student, for example, can be compared with typical scores obtained by Latina students in this age range. We can then interpret these scores by seeing whether they are higher or lower than average scores obtained by members of the appropriate normative group.

Reliability, validity, and standardization are important for developing and refining clinical assessment techniques. Different methods of clinical assessment are explored next. This section begins with a discussion of *interviews,* which mental health professionals use to gather information about a person's concerns, symptoms, and history.

Interview

The interview is the most common assessment technique and is used to solicit a wide range of information about mental disorders. Interviewers often ask questions about the frequency and nature of symptoms of different mental disorders. Interview questions also focus on events or experiences that preceded symptom onset, such as child maltreatment or death of a parent. Interviews have a range of applications and can be easily adapted to match a person's situation.

Interviews differ in two key ways. First, interviews differ with respect to *purpose*. The purpose of one interview may be to evaluate the history and concerns of a person seeking psychological help for the first time, but another interview might focus solely on *DSM* diagnoses. Second, interviews may be *unstructured* or *structured.* **Unstructured interviews** allow an interviewer to ask any question that comes to mind in any order. This type of interview is often unreliable because two clinicians evaluating the same person may arrive at different ideas of what is happening. **Structured interviews** require an interviewer to ask standardized questions in a specified sequence. Interviewers ask people the same questions, so two clinicians who evaluate the same person are more likely to arrive at the same diagnosis or conclusion.

The clinical interview is the most commonly used assessment technique.

Personal Narrative

Anonymous

I glanced at the clock on the opposite wall, taking a break from staring at a worn patch in the carpet near my feet. It was nearly 5 PM; the last time I looked up was about 1 PM. My only motivation was to determine where we were in the rhythm of the day, to see how much longer I had to bear before I could retreat to my room. There, my eyes heavy from sleeping pills and emotional exhaustion, I could succumb to the only thing that brought relief from my depression: sleep. It had not taken me long to discover that the most time-consuming activity on psychiatric units was doing nothing other than waiting for something to happen. Waiting to see your psychiatrist. Your social worker. Your nurse. Waiting for a therapy group. For art therapy. Pet therapy (if you're lucky). Waiting for a shower. To brush your teeth. Waiting for morning meds. Afternoon meds. Evening meds. Night meds. Breakfast. Lunch. Dinner. How did I get here?

My depression during my sophomore year in college was not my first episode. I had gone through periods of depression twice during high school, received antidepressant treatment and counseling, and recovered. I took having a depressive disorder seriously and was diligent about seeking and getting help. I did not share my condition with other people, but I did not feel stigmatized. Depression seemed common in society. A little like having mild asthma or high blood pressure. I never thought of myself as someone who was truly "sick"—I saved that term for people with schizophrenia or bipolar disorder, people I assumed spent most of their lives in secluded state institutions, receiving antipsychotics and getting "shock therapy." If someone suggested I would know someday what it's like to be in a hospital, to take a plethora of drugs, and to be considered severely and chronically disordered, I would have found the notion bizarre and comical, if not impossible. That was not me.

Near the end of my sophomore year, I noticed some familiar feelings that, in the past, heralded depression. Over the course of a few weeks, I lost my appetite. Things I normally found engaging—reading, being with friends, participating in groups on campus—had no allure. I lacked the concentration to read more than a page or two or even follow a conversation. As my mood sunk, family and friends became concerned. I became increasingly depressed and despondent over a matter of weeks, and even though I recognized the symptoms and was educated about treatments, I did not want to admit that I was experiencing a relapse of the disorder I thought had ended with my adolescence.

Ultimately, a close friend realized what was happening. Fearing for my safety, he made an urgent appointment with a local psychiatrist; I did not have the energy to protest. The psychiatrist spoke with me about my history, my current symptoms and thoughts of suicide, and determined that I needed to be hospitalized. My recollections of this decision, my admission, and the first few days in the hospital are foggy. My primary emotional response was shock and bewilderment, tempered only by the deadening apathy that engulfed my mood. I couldn't quite get my head around how things had gotten "this far." I was on a locked unit with severely disordered men and women, many acutely psychotic. I was watched constantly by an aide, denied access to my shoelaces, and allowed to make calls only from a phone in the "day room." But despite the indignities and trauma of this experience, I can say now it saved my life. I was discharged after a few weeks, not completely over my depression but on the way to feeling well again. I had started treatment and begun to feel optimistic about my future. Within a month of getting back to school, I truly felt all this sadness and

Several structured diagnostic interviews are available. The *Structured Clinical Interview for DSM-5* (SCID-5; First et al., 2015) is a popular structured diagnostic interview for major mental disorders. The SCID-5 gives clear instructions to the interviewer about what questions to ask and in what order to ask them. Structured interviews like the SCID-5 standardize questions to be asked and help interviewers obtain relevant information. Structured interviews are available for various mental disorders as well as many psychological and other variables such as personality and family history of mental disorder.

Diagnoses and ratings from structured diagnostic interviews are generally reliable across raters and have high content validity because they are based on specific criteria. Many structured interviews appear to have high construct validity as well. Structured interview diagnoses or ratings usually relate to scores and ratings from other psychological, behavioral, or biological tests in expected ways.

A disadvantage of structured diagnostic interviews is the time necessary to administer and score them. These interviews are comprehensive and can take several hours to conduct. In many clinical settings, clients are seen for only an hour at a time and often for only a few sessions, so these interviews may be less attractive as assessment devices. Structured diagnostic interviews are thus particularly common to research settings.

strife was behind me, and I never imagined that things could become even more challenging and complicated.

Right before my junior year I experienced symptoms that, unlike those during my depressions, I did not find troubling. I was always someone who needed a good nine hours of sleep to feel well rested, but I started getting by on dramatically less. Some nights I would not touch the bed (if I was even home), other nights I would fall asleep for two or three hours and then jolt awake, energized and ready to go. My waking hours became filled with frenzied activity—I never felt smarter, more able, or more confident. My thinking was swift and sharp and seemed to reach near superhuman perfection. These feelings continued, but the ecstasy soon devolved into agitation. Every annoyance seemed like a concerted, even conspiratorial, effort to thwart my plans. When my psychiatrist saw me in his office, he knew immediately what was wrong. I was experiencing a manic episode. An ambulance was called and I was brought to the hospital. I was enraged and scared at the same time, but eventually acquiesced to treatment. New medications—antipsychotics and mood stabilizers this time—were used to control my mood. Most of my symptoms abated within a few weeks, but the medications left me sedated and feeling somewhat dull. New medications for a new diagnosis: bipolar I disorder.

I came away from this traumatic experience dismayed and disheartened, my self-image shattered. I had already come to terms with being a "psychiatric patient" and acknowledged that my first hospitalization was necessary (although at the time I had no doubt it would be my last). But during my first manic episode, I was "publicly" sick in a way I hadn't been before. I was embarrassed and humiliated. Being told I had a disorder only "other people" got—"other people" being unfortunates who lived their lives in drug-induced stupors in institutions or group homes—compounded my feelings of defeat.

As I recovered, I reevaluated some of these feelings and saw things more realistically. I also met other young adults, through a support group, who struggled with the same disorder. It was enlightening and heartening to hear many of their stories, and they provided invaluable advice and support. My ideas as to what it meant to have a mental disorder shifted largely as a result of these conversations, allowing me to approach my own situation with more hope and strength. I began to see medications and therapy as my toolbox for maintaining a stable life in which I could achieve my goals. This involved tinkering to find the best combination of medicines and trade-offs in terms of putting up with some side effects if my overall health was good.

Coming to terms with having bipolar disorder and learning how to effectively take care of myself has been a process of peaks and valleys. After three years of feeling well, I relapsed and experienced episodes of mania and depression. Both required hospitalization and medication changes. Experiencing relapse after a few years of feeling great was a wake-up call. I secretly felt I was somehow "past" that sort of thing. Since then I've tried to be optimistic while still recognizing I have a chronic disorder, and the chance of having more episodes in the future is very high. Thankfully, when I am stable, I have no lingering symptoms. My goal is no longer to avoid getting sick again but to keep myself stable and healthy for as long a stretch as possible. Despite my disorder, I've graduated college and entered graduate school. I've had lasting and meaningful relationships. I live on my own and have traveled widely. My disorder hasn't defined my life, and despite the inevitable challenges ahead, I don't believe it ever will.

Source: Used with permission.

Intelligence Tests

Intelligence tests are probably the most common form of clinical assessment after the interview. Intelligence tests assess cognitive functioning and provide estimates of a person's intellectual ability. Mental health professionals are interested in assessing cognitive processes such as memory, language, comprehension, reasoning, and speed with which we process and interpret information. Many people associate intelligence tests with assessment of learning disorder and brain dysfunction, but information provided by these tests can also be used to understand symptoms of mental disorders such as schizophrenia or depression.

Most intelligence tests include multiple *subscales* or *subtests* to measure specific aspects of cognitive functioning such as memory, arithmetic, mastery of general information, or visual-perceptual organization. Some subtests require a person to answer direct questions, but other subtests require people to complete tasks or solve problems. Scores on these subtests are typically combined and compared with normative data from people of similar age and gender. This form of standardization allows an individual's scores to be interpreted as low, average, or high.

The *Wechsler Adult Intelligence Scale—Fourth Edition* (WAIS-IV; Wechsler, 2008) is one of the most popular intelligence tests. Items regarding a particular domain such as arithmetic are placed in one section (subtest) and arranged in order of increasing difficulty. Item scores from each subtest are converted to *scaled scores,* which represent standardized scores within an age group. Scaled scores are added to derive *intelligence quotients* (IQs), which are general measures of intellectual functioning. Several WAIS-IV subtests are described in **Table 4.3** and a simulated WAIS-IV item is illustrated in **Figure 4.1**.

Table 4.3 Simulated Examples of Wechsler Adult Intelligence Scale Subtests

Vocabulary	The examinee must define words. For example, "What does the word *impede* mean?"
Similarities	The examinee must explain how two objects are alike. For example, "How are a *wheel* and *ski* alike?"
Digit span	Two lists of digits are read aloud by the examiner. For the first list, the examinee must repeat the digits in the order they were read. For example, "*2-8-3-9-6.*" For the second list, the digits must be repeated backward.

Source: Wechsler (2008).

Figure 4.1 Simulated Item from the WAIS-IV Picture Completion Subtest.

Can you find what's missing in this picture? Simulated items similar to those found in the Wechsler Adult Intelligence Scale, Fourth Edition (WAIS-IV).

Source: Copyright © 2008 NCS Pearson, Inc. Reproduced with permission. All rights reserved. "Wechsler Adult Intelligence Scale" and "WAIS" are trademarks, in the United States and/or other countries, of Pearson Education, Inc. or its affiliates.

Intelligence quotients often include *full-scale, verbal,* and *performance* IQs. The full-scale IQ may be most familiar to you; it gives an estimate of overall intellectual ability. Verbal IQ specifically represents use and comprehension of language, and performance IQ specifically represents spatial reasoning. Individual IQs are calculated in relation to normative data. The score of a 20-year-old man, for example, is compared with the scores of other 20-year-old men. To make scores easier to interpret, the mean for each age group is 100; this makes the IQ scale consistent across age groups.

Intelligence test scores can give mental health professionals a sense of a person's strengths and weaknesses. This information is important for diagnosing, assessing, and treating psychological problems. Some disorders, such as Alzheimer's disease, are defined primarily by cognitive deficits that may be assessed by intelligence tests. Other disorders have cognitive and behavioral features that intelligence tests can at least tap. Intelligence tests are therefore administered to many clients in clinical and research settings.

Intelligence test scores must be interpreted with caution. IQ scores do not indicate how smart a person is but rather how well they are likely to do in future academic work. Most intelligence tests focus on verbal and spatial ability but do not measure other forms of competence such as social skill, creativity, and mechanical ability. Intelligence tests have also been criticized for bias because people across cultures think differently. A test that is completely "culture-free" has not been developed. Instead, "culture-relevant" tests more specific to the skills or stored information of a particular group may be preferable (Sternberg, 2020).

Personality Assessment

A clinical assessment measure that may be more familiar to you is personality assessment. **Personality assessment** refers to instruments that measure different traits or aspects of our character. Most of us could name or describe at least one personality or psychological test based on what we have read or seen on television shows or films. Many of us have read or seen media that portrayed the "inkblot test" as a measure of personality. Many other personality assessment measures are also available, however. These can be divided into objective and projective tests.

Objective Personality Measures

Objective personality measures involve administering a standard set of questions or statements to which a person responds using set options. Objective tests often use a *true/false* or *yes/no* response format, but others provide a *dimensional scale* such as 0 = *strongly disagree,* 1 = *disagree,* 2 = *neutral,* 3 = *agree,* and 4 = *strongly agree.* Self-report, paper-and-pencil questionnaires are popular objective tests of general or limited aspects of personality, and many types are discussed throughout this textbook. Examples include the *Social Phobia and Anxiety Inventory* (Chapter 5) and *Beck Depression Inventory* (Chapter 7). These questionnaires are economical, impartial, simple to administer and score, and more reliable and standardized than other assessment methods.

The *Minnesota Multiphasic Personality Inventory—3* (MMPI-3), which clinicians have used in some form for decades and which is still a widely used general personality questionnaire, is briefly illustrated here (Ben-Porath & Tellegen, 2020). Thousands of studies using the MMPI in its different versions have been published (e.g., Bopp et al., 2022), and scores from the scale have been used to measure everything from psychosis to marriage suitability.

The developers of the original MMPI believed the content of a test item mattered less than whether people with the same mental disorder endorsed the same items. Do people with depression endorse the item "I like mechanics magazines" more so than people without depression? If so, then the item might appear on a scale of depression. An item that does not appear on the surface to be related to depression may thus become an item on the depression scale. The MMPI-3 includes 335 items to which a person answers "True" or "False."

A potential problem with questionnaires such as the MMPI-3 is susceptibility to distortion. Some people might wish to place themselves in a favorable light, and others may try to "fake bad" to receive compensation. Other people tend to agree with almost any item regardless of content. If a mental health professional is unaware of these response styles in a given client, then the test could be misinterpreted. The **MMPI-3** thus has several **validity scales** to detect people who are trying to look a certain way or who are defensive or careless when taking the test. Validity scales help us understand someone's motives and test-taking attitudes. A mental health professional might disregard the test results if these scales indicate that the results are not valid. Scores on **MMPI-3 clinical scales** are also calculated (**Table 4.4**). Scores from these and other MMPI-3 scales can suggest diagnoses as well as various problematic behaviors and personality styles. How does a mental health professional interpret MMPI-3 profiles? Think about Professor Smith, who agreed to consult with a clinical psychologist after struggling with panic attacks and depression for many months. The clinical psychologist asked Professor Smith to complete the MMPI-3 before their first session, and this information was used with a clinical interview. The following excerpt is from a report based on Professor Smith's MMPI-3 profile:

> Professor Smith approached testing in a frank manner, and his responses suggest a valid MMPI-3 profile. His scores indicate concern about his present mental state and a willingness to receive help to overcome his problems. The MMPI-3 clinical profile highlights several problems and symptoms Professor Smith experienced during initial treatment. His responses suggest he is anxious, nervous, tense, and high-strung. He worries excessively and expects more problems to occur in the future. Professor Smith also has concerns about his health and body. He may complain of feeling fatigued, exhausted, and pained. Professor Smith appears depressed, pessimistic, and discouraged about his current situation and may feel lonely and insecure. He has great difficulty concentrating on his work and is likely to be indecisive. Professor Smith may blame himself for his current problems and feel guilty or disappointing to others. His responses also indicate little zest for life and preoccupation with inability to accomplish personal goals.

The MMPI-3 interpretation does not rely on a single score but rather a profile of a client based on all scores. Profiles like Professor Smith's can then be interpreted using certain guidelines. These guidelines outline frequently obtained profiles and descriptions of typical symptoms, complaints, and characteristics of those who produce these profiles. These guidelines help mental health professionals standardize the interpretation of the MMPI-3.

Projective Personality Measures

Not all personality tests emphasize standardized administration, scoring, and interpretation as the MMPI-3 does. Some tests require mental health professionals to use their skill and judgment to interpret an individual's responses. **Projective tests** are based on the assumption that people faced with an ambiguous stimulus such as an inkblot will "project" their own needs, personality, and conflicts. One person looking at a particular inkblot might see a monster's face, but another person might

Table 4.4 MMPI-3 Clinical Scales and Description

1. Demoralization: unhappiness and dissatisfaction
2. Somatic Complaints: physical health complaints
3. Low Positive Emotions: lack of positive emotional responses
4. Antisocial Behavior: rule breaking and irresponsible behavior
5. Ideas of Persecution: beliefs that others are a threat
6. Dysfunctional Negative Emotions: maladaptive anxiety, anger, irritability
7. Aberrant Experiences: unusual perceptions or thoughts
8. Hypomanic Activation: overactivation, aggression, impulsivity, grandiosity

Source: MMPI®-3 (Minnesota Multiphasic Personality Inventory®-3) Manual for Administration, Scoring, and Interpretation. Copyright © 2020

see two children playing near a stream. Projective techniques differ drastically from objective questionnaires like the MMPI-3 because responses are not linked to certain scales and because responses are interpreted as individual characteristics such as one's unconscious processes. Projective tests can include *sentence completion tasks,* in which people complete a series of unfinished sentences, and *drawing tests,* in which people are asked to draw a figure such as a house or their family. Two other popular projective tests are discussed next: the Rorschach and the Thematic Apperception Test.

Rorschach. Hermann Rorschach was a Swiss psychiatrist who experimented with inkblots as a way to identify psychological problems. The *Rorschach* test consists of 10 inkblot cards that are symmetrical from right to left. Five cards are black and white (with shades of gray) and five are colored. A simulated Rorschach card is in **Figure 4.2**.

The Rorschach can be administered in different ways, but many clinicians give a client the first card and say, "Tell me what you see—what it looks like to you." All cards are shown to a client in order, and the clinician writes down every word the client says. The clinician then moves to an *inquiry* phase: They remind the client of each previous response and ask what prompted each response. The client also indicates the exact location of various responses for each card and may elaborate or clarify responses. Many clinicians focus on these major aspects of responses:

- *Location* refers to area of the card to which the client responded; examples include the whole blot, a large detail, a small detail, or white space.
- *Content* refers to nature of the object seen, such as an animal, person, rock, or fog.
- *Determinants* refer to aspects of the card that prompted a client's response, such as the inkblot's form, color, texture, apparent movement, and shading.

Scoring the Rorschach involves computing the ratio of certain responses, such as responses to colored parts of the inkblots, to total number of responses. Clinicians may also compute the ratio of one set of responses to another, such as number of responses describing human movement to number of color responses. However, the reliability and validity of Rorschach scores have been questioned for decades (Viglione et al., 2022). Many mental health professionals do not formally score the Rorschach but rely instead on their clinical impressions of a client's responses.

Figure 4.2 Inkblot Similar to Rorschach Inkblots.

From Timothy Trull, *Clinical Psychology* (7th ed.), Fig. 8.2. (Copyright © 2005 Wadsworth, a part of Cengage Learning. Reproduced with permission. www.cengage.com/permissions)

Thematic Apperception Test. Another popular projective test to assess motivations and interpersonal style is the *Thematic Apperception Test* (TAT). The TAT is a series of pictures like the ones in **Figure 4.3**. Most TAT cards depict people in various situations, but some cards contain only objects. Clinicians typically select 6 to 12 cards to give to a client. Clients are asked to say what is happening in the picture now and in the future. Instructions vary from clinician to clinician, but many say something such as, "I want you to make up a story about each of these pictures. Tell me who the people are, what they are doing, what they are thinking or feeling, what led up to the scene, and how it will turn out." The client's stories are then transcribed word-for-word by the clinician.

A mental health professional can learn about a client's personality from these stories. One person might say a picture in Figure 4.3 shows a mother worried about her daughter who is leaving home, but another might say a woman is constantly fighting with her mother and now refuses to talk to her. These different stories help us understand how a client relates to others. The TAT is not generally used to derive specific diagnoses but rather to make judgments about personality themes such as hostility, defensiveness, jealousy, and rebelliousness. The reliability and validity of this test may be enhanced by using certain coding and rating techniques (Stein et al., 2020).

Figure 4.3 Thematic Apperception Test (TAT) Cards.

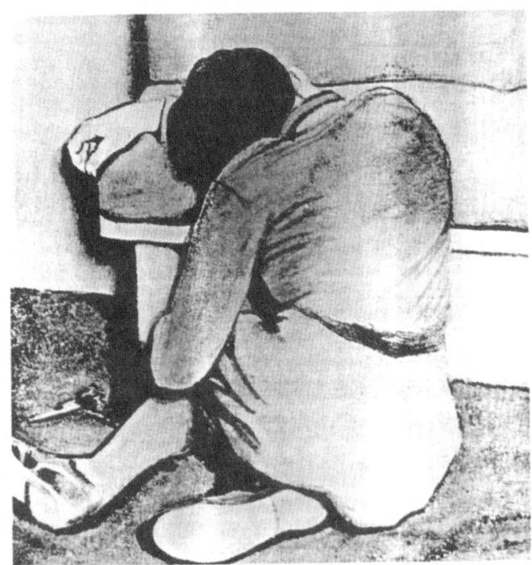

Behavioral Assessment

The purpose of **behavioral assessment** is to measure overt behaviors or responses shown by a person (Piazza et al., 2021). Instead of relying only on Professor Smith's report of how fearful and anxious he is when lecturing in class, a behavioral assessor might also observe Professor Smith in this situation. Behavioral assessment provides a snapshot of an actual problem behavior. Traditional assessments such as intelligence or personality tests rely on responses as indirect indicators of underlying traits or characteristics. Behavioral assessment relies on as little interpretation or inference as possible—the behavior observed is the main interest.

Behavioral assessment often involves a **functional analysis** of behavior. This involves understanding **antecedents**, or what precedes a behavior, and **consequences**, or what follows a behavior. A functional analysis for Professor Smith might reveal that certain student questions (antecedents) led to stress and panic attacks and that letting class out early (consequences) helped ease these anxious feelings, which is reinforcing. Consequences are often reinforcers of problematic behavior.

Careful and precise description of antecedents, behavior, and consequences is crucial to functional analysis. Important antecedents that you could easily measure and observe include student questions, time spent lecturing, and class attendance. You would also have to specify behaviors of interest, such as frequency and length of Professor Smith's chest pains. Important consequences that you could easily measure and observe include the number of minutes Professor Smith let class out early and the number of times he excused himself from class. You would also have to obtain similar level of detail for other situations in which Professor Smith had a panic attack because antecedents and consequences of behavior often differ from situation to situation.

Behavioral therapists often broaden functional analysis to include organismic variables. **Organismic variables** include a person's physiological or cognitive characteristics that may help the therapist understand a problem and determine treatment. A major organismic variable for Professor Smith is worry about future panic attacks and fear that certain physical sensations indicate an impending attack. Organismic variables such as worries and cognitions are also sometimes assessed via self-report questionnaires.

Naturalistic Observation

Behavioral assessors often use observation to conduct a functional analysis. One form is **naturalistic observation**, in which a client is directly observed in their natural environment. A naturalistic observation might involve observing Professor Smith in his office, classroom, and home for a week. It is clear, though, that naturalistic observation can be impractical, difficult, time-intensive, and expensive. Observers also cannot know for sure the problem behavior will even occur, so they sometimes must be present for long periods to capture a certain behavior.

Controlled Observation

Controlled observation is a more practical and less expensive form of observation and involves analogue tests; these tests involve tasks that approximate situations people face in real life and that may elicit a certain problem behavior (Piazza et al., 2021). A person anxious about public speaking could be asked to give a short presentation before others in a psychologist's office. Or a troubled married couple might be asked to solve a hypothetical problem. A person's responses are observed and analyzed in each case. This information helps us understand precise mistakes the person makes when speaking before others or the couple makes when solving a problem. These observations can then lead to a treatment plan that might include relaxation and interpersonal skills training for the anxious public speaker and problem-solving and communication skills training for the troubled couple.

Self-monitoring

Controlled observations are more practical than naturalistic observations but can be difficult to arrange. Many behavior assessors thus rely on **self-monitoring**, where a person observes and records their own emotions, thoughts, and behaviors. Professor Smith could be asked to complete a daily diary to record the frequency, intensity, and duration of his panic attacks, related thoughts and emotions, and antecedents and consequences of his panic attacks. Self-monitoring can be informal or more structured like a *dysfunctional thought record* (**Figure 4.4**). Dysfunctional thought records help identify and monitor situations, thoughts, responses, and outcomes associated with problems such as depression. A therapist and client can thus better understand what precedes and follows these problems. Technological advances also mean clients can record their emotions, thoughts, and behaviors

Figure 4.4 An Example of a Dysfunctional Thought Record.

The dysfunctional thought record is a type of self-monitoring diary or log used to identify what may prompt and what may follow negative emotions.

Directions: When you notice your mood getting worse, ask yourself, "What's going through my mind right now?" and as soon as possible jot down the thought or mental image in the Automatic Thought(s) column.

Date/time	Situation	Automatic thought(s)	Emotion(s)	Adaptive response	Outcome
	1. What actual event or stream of thoughts, or daydreams or recollection led to the unpleasant emotion? 2. What (if any) distressing physical sensations did you have?	1. What thought(s) and/or image(s) went through your mind? 2. How much did you believe each one at the time?	1. What emotion(s) (sad/anxious/angry/etc.) did you feel at the time? 2. How intense (0–100%) was the emotion?	1. (optional) What cognitive distortion did you make? 2. Use questions at bottom to compose an adaptive response to the automatic thought(s). 3. How much do you believe each response?	1. How much do you now believe each automatic thought? 2. What emotion(s) do you feel now? How intense (0–100%) is the emotion? 3. What will you do (or did you do)?
Friday 2/23 10 AM	Talking on the phone with Donna.	She must not like me anymore. 90%	Sad 80%	Maybe she's upset about something else. 60%	A little bit/Less sad (50%)/I will ask Donna if she is upset with me.
Tuesday 2/27 12 PM	Studying for my exam.	I'll never learn this. 100%	Sad 95%	Maybe I can't learn all of this, but I can learn some of this. 50%	Somewhat/More motivated (60%)/I will study as hard as I can and ask someone to help me.
Thursday 2/29 5 PM	Thinking about my economics class tomorrow.	I might get called on and I won't give a good answer. 80%	Anxious 80%	Doing my best is all I can do. 70%	To some extent/A little better (70%)/I'll just give the best answer I can.
	Noticing my heart beating fast and my trouble concentrating	What's wrong with me? 70%	Anxious 80%	I'm just nervous; I'm not having a heart attack. 90%	Less so/More calm (80%)/Relax and steady my breathing.

Questions to help compose an adaptive response: (1) What is the evidence that the automatic thought is true? Not true? (2) Is there an alternative explanation? (3) What's the worst that could happen? Could I live through it? What's the best that could happen? What's the most realistic outcome? (4) What's the effect of my believing the automatic thought? What could be the effect of my changing my thinking? (5) What should I do about it? (6) If_____[friend's name] was in the situation and had this thought, what would I tell him/her?

Source: Adapted from J. S. Beck, Cognitive Therapy: Basics and Beyond, New York: Guilford, 1995.

during their everyday lives. Tablets, smartphones, and laptops have been used to collect self-monitoring data (Melbye et al., 2020).

Biological Assessment

Recall from Chapter 2 that mental disorders often involve changes in brain structure or function. Many medical tests are available for examining general central nervous system dysfunction, such as from a stroke, but technological advances have led to amazing assessment techniques that can measure very specific central nervous system changes. Brain imaging techniques now provide detailed and precise evaluations of brain structure and function. An overview is provided next of neuroimaging and other biological tests used to assess psychopathology, although these tests are typically used in research settings or in cases involving clear brain dysfunction from problems such as stroke.

Neuroimaging

Brain images can be derived in several ways. **Computerized axial tomography (CAT scan)** assesses *structural differences* of the brain. A CAT scan can detect brain tumors and other structural differences such as enlarged ventricles or hollow spaces in the brain sometimes seen in people with schizophrenia or other mental disorders. The CAT scan is essentially an X-ray of a cross-section of the brain. X-ray dye (iodine) is injected into the person, and the CAT scan assesses brain tissue density by detecting the amount of radioactivity from a moving beam of X-rays that penetrates the tissue. A computer then interprets this information to provide a two-dimensional picture of that cross-section of the brain.

Magnetic resonance imaging (MRI) produces higher-quality brain images without radiation. MRI is costly but is better than CAT scans in detecting brain tumors, blood clots, and other structural differences. A person lies in a large cylindrical magnet, and radio waves are beamed through the magnetic field. Sensors read the signals, and a computer integrates the information to produce a high-resolution brain image. **Functional MRI (fMRI)** goes a step further in that pictures are taken rapidly to assess metabolic changes in the brain; fMRI thus assesses how the brain is *working*. This can have important implications for understanding risk factors of mental disorder. If fMRI results reveal a person's frontal lobes to be poorly activated during a decision-making task, then frontal lobe dysfunction may be associated with a learning or thought disorder.

Positron emission tomography (PET scan) is an invasive procedure to evaluate brain structure *and* function. Radioactive molecules are injected into the bloodstream and emit a particle called a positron. Positrons collide with electrons, and light particles emit from the skull and are detected by the PET scanner. A computer uses this information to construct a picture of how the brain is functioning. PET scans can identify seizure activity and even brain sites activated by psychoactive drugs (refer to **Figure 4.5**).

iStock.com/PeopleImages

Cell phones, laptops, and tablets can be used to monitor emotions, thoughts, and behaviors as they occur.

Neurochemical Assessment

Neurochemical assessment is a biological assessment of dysfunctions in specific *neurotransmitter* systems. Recall from Chapter 2 that neurotransmitters are brain chemicals that can activate or inhibit neurons and are often part of several main systems such as: *serotonin, norepinephrine, gamma-aminobutyric acid* (GABA), and *dopamine*. Many symptoms of mental disorder are influenced by dysfunction of one or more of these neurotransmitter systems in certain regions of the brain.

No technology allows us to *directly* assess how much neurotransmitter is in a specific brain region, but we can *indirectly* assess this by focusing on neurotransmitter **metabolites**. Metabolites are byproducts of neurotransmitters that can be detected in urine, blood, and cerebral spinal fluid. Low levels of a metabolite suggest a low level of the associated neurotransmitter and vice versa. Later sections of this textbook will cover how scientists have used this methodology to evaluate neurochemical theories of depression (low levels of serotonin) and schizophrenia (high levels of dopamine).

Psychophysiological Assessment

Psychophysiological assessment involves evaluating bodily changes possibly associated with certain mental conditions. We experience certain bodily changes when we are highly anxious, such as increased heart rate or sweating (yes, measures exist for sweating!). These kinds of bodily changes could be examined in someone

Figure 4.5 Examples of Brain Imaging Techniques.

Several brain imaging techniques are used in biological assessment. Here are some examples: (top left) a CAT scan; (top right) an MRI scan; (bottom left) an fMRI scan; and (bottom right) a PET scan.

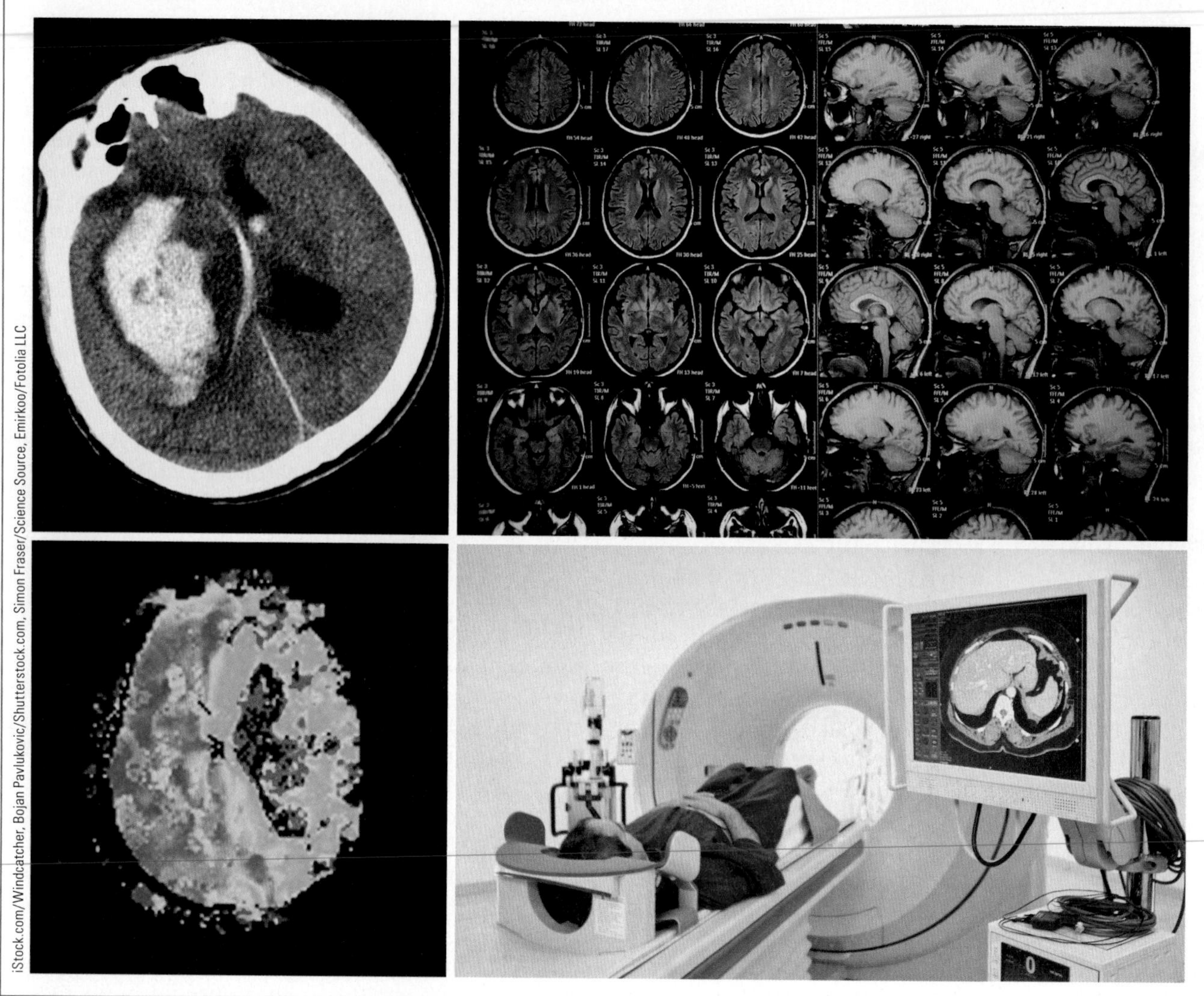

iStock.com/Windcatcher, Bojan Pavlukovic/Shutterstock.com, Simon Fraser/Science Source, Emirkoo/Fotolia LLC

like Professor Smith who is seeking treatment for an anxiety disorder.

A common type of psychophysiological assessment is an **electrocardiogram**, which measures heart rate. Electrodes are placed on a person's chest, and the electrical impulse produced by the heartbeat and detected by each electrode is fed to an instrument that measures and integrates this information. Heart rate has been used to assess various emotional states and risk factors. Those with anxiety disorders (Chapter 5), for example, are at greater risk of cardiovascular disease (Zhang et al., 2021). We might also expect Professor Smith's heart rate to be elevated, even when he is not experiencing a panic attack, because his fear of future attacks makes him anxious most of the time.

Galvanic skin conductance is another index of emotional state. Some emotional states increase sweat gland activity and thus electrical conductance of the skin (electricity moves faster through skin when a person sweats). This is especially true for people with anxiety. Some people, however, may display *lower* levels of skin conductance. This is true for some people with antisocial personality disorder who manipulate and harm others without guilt (Chapter 10; De Looff et al., 2021). People with antisocial personality disorder often have lower anxiety and fear about negative consequences to their behavior.

The **electroencephalogram (EEG)** is a measure of brain activity. Electrodes are placed at various locations on the scalp so electrical activity in various brain areas can be assessed. Unusual activity may indicate a lesion or tumor in that area or even seizure activity or epilepsy. Observation of possible unusual brain wave activity might be followed by additional testing such as MRI.

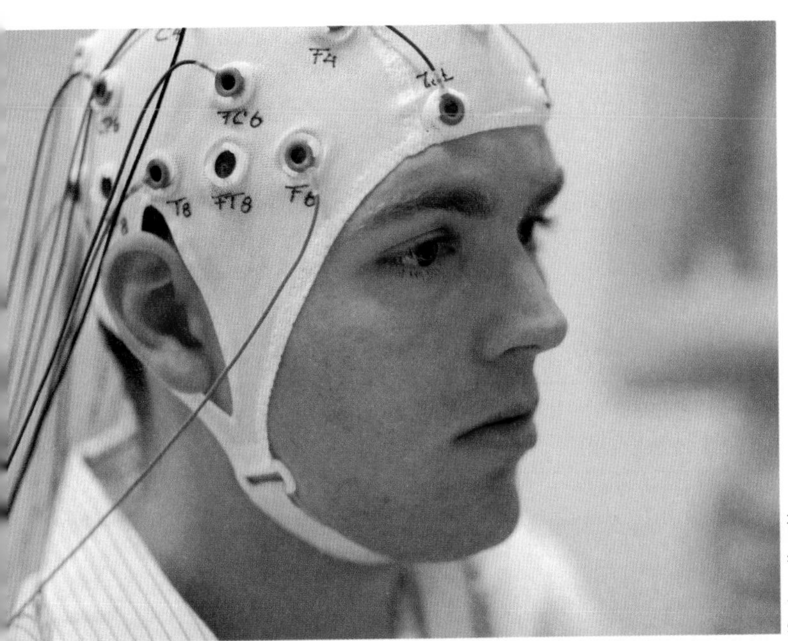

One form of psychophysiological assessment is the electroencephalogram (EEG).

Neuropsychological Assessment

Methods of biological assessment are *direct* measures of brain and physical function. Methods of **neuropsychological assessment**, however, are *indirect* measures of brain and physical function. Neuropsychological assessment is a noninvasive method of evaluating brain functioning via one's performance on standardized tests and tasks that indicate brain–behavior relationships (Donders, 2020). Many mental disorders involve some cognitive impairment, so neuropsychological tests can help identify or rule out physical problems. Biological assessment methods are invasive and expensive, so neuropsychological tests are often used as first-line screening measures. If problems are noted from these tests, then biological assessment may follow.

Neuropsychological tests typically assess abstract reasoning, memory, visual-perceptual processing, language functioning, and motor skills. Two general approaches are used for neuropsychological testing. One approach is to employ commonly used neuropsychological batteries such as the *Halstead-Reitan Battery.* These batteries involve various subtests that tap many cognitive and behavioral functions. The following descriptions of two Halstead-Reitan subtests provide good examples:

- *Tactual performance test*: The examinee is blindfolded and asked to place 10 variously shaped blocks into proper slots on a board using touch only. This is done once for each hand (dominant and nondominant) and once with both hands. The blindfold is then removed, and the examinee draws the board and located blocks from memory. This subtest assesses damage to the brain's right parietal lobe and tactile and spatial memory.
- *Seashore rhythm test*: The examinee hears 30 pairs of rhythmic acoustic patterns and states whether the patterns are the same or different. This subtest assesses damage to the brain's anterior temporal lobes and nonverbal auditory perception.

A second approach to neuropsychological testing is to administer one or more standardized tests to evaluate a specific area of brain functioning. This is known as *focal testing.* Suppose a neuropsychologist is primarily concerned with a person's memory functioning. The neuropsychologist might administer the *Benton Visual Retention Test,* which measures memory for designs (refer to **Figure 4.6**). Ten cards are presented for 10 seconds each. After each presentation, the examinee draws the design from memory, and the examiner looks at number and type of errors in the drawings. A related test is the *Bender Visual-Motor Gestalt Test,* which contains 14 stimulus cards and may be used for anyone aged four years or older (South & Palilla, 2021). These tests assess immediate memory, spatial perception, and perceptual-motor coordination.

Figure 4.6 Examples from the Benton Visual Retention Test.

Two cards from the Benton Visual Retention Test that assesses memory for designs.

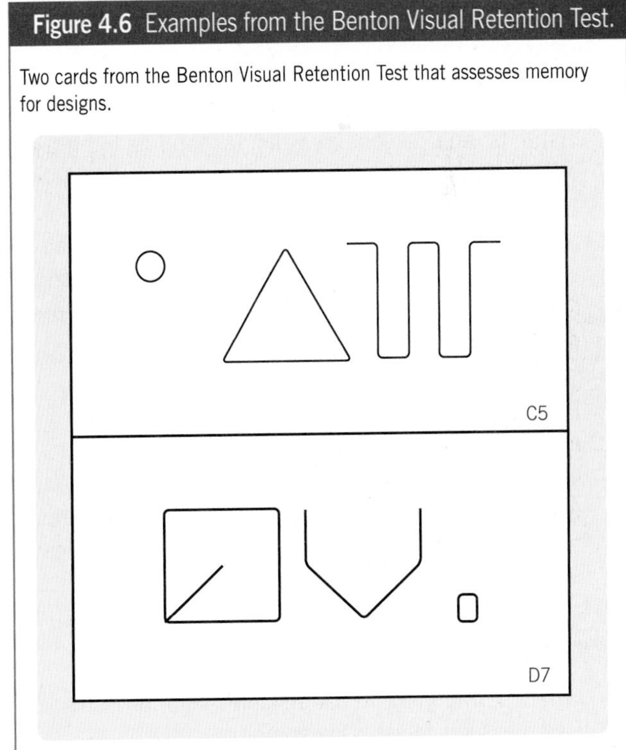

Adapted from M.D. Lezak, D.B. Howieson, E.D., Bigler, D. Tranel. (2012). Neuropsychological Assessment (5th ed.), New York: Oxford University Press.

Section Summary

- Classification refers to arranging mental disorders into broad categories or classes based on similar features.
- The *DSM* is a main system of classification that includes diagnoses but also allows for dimensional assessments.
- Clinical assessment involves evaluating a person's strengths and challenges as well as understanding a problem to develop treatment.
- Reliability refers to consistency of scores or responses and includes test–retest, interrater, and internal consistency reliability.
- Validity is the extent to which an assessment technique measures what it is supposed to measure and includes content, predictive, concurrent, and construct validity.
- Standardization refers to administering and conducting clinical assessment measures in the same way for everyone.
- Structured and unstructured interviews are the most common type of assessment.
- Intelligence tests are commonly used to assess cognitive aspects of mental disorders but must be viewed with caution, especially when comparing scores across cultures.
- Objective personality measures involve administering a standard set of questions or statements to which a person responds using set options.
- Objective personality measures such as the MMPI-3 are economical, relatively simple to administer and score, and reliable.
- Projective tests such as the Rorschach and TAT rely on the assumption that people project their needs, conflicts, and personality when responding to ambiguous stimuli.
- Behavioral assessment measures overt behaviors or responses and is often conducted via functional analysis of antecedents and consequences of behavior.
- Observational methods used in behavioral assessment include naturalistic and controlled observation and self-monitoring.
- Biological assessment includes neuroimaging techniques as well as procedures for assessing neurochemistry and body physiology.
- Neuropsychological assessment indirectly evaluates brain function via performance on standardized tests and tasks that indicate brain–behavior relationships.

Review Questions

1. Why is it important to use reliable, valid, and standardized measures to assess people?
2. What can intelligence tests tell us about clients like Professor Smith?
3. Compare and contrast information you might obtain about Professor Smith from objective and projective personality tests.
4. How does behavioral assessment differ from other forms of assessment?
5. What information from a biological assessment of Professor Smith might complement that obtained from interviews, personality tests, and behavioral assessment?

Culture and Clinical Assessment

LO 4.6 Demonstrate the importance of considering culture in clinical assessment.

Recall from Chapter 2 the sociocultural perspective of mental disorder, which focuses on influences that social institutions and other people have on one's mental health. The important topic of cultural considerations when assessing mental disorder is addressed next, beginning with how culture might influence the development of psychological problems.

Culture and the Development of Mental Disorders

Recall from Chapter 2 that culture refers to unique behaviors and lifestyles that distinguish groups of people. Culture represents a unique worldview and is reflected in customs, laws, art, and music. Culture can also influence the development of mental disorders in several ways.

1. *Culture may influence stress and psychological problems.* Culturally shared beliefs or ideas may lead to extreme stress and symptoms of mental disorders. A form of mental disorder may be unique to a culture because of specific ideas or beliefs that are part of that culture. *Ataque de nervios* is a syndrome common to Latino/as (APA, 2022). A person with this syndrome may sense losing control, shout uncontrollably, experience attacks of crying and trembling, and faint or feel suicidal. These symptoms typically result from a stressful family event. Latino/a culture emphasizes family well-being and stability, so a family crisis can be extremely stressful and produce *ataque de nervios.*
2. *Culture may influence a person's reaction to stress.* Certain cultures may disapprove of certain reactions to stressful events, such as becoming depressed. Some people may thus be expected to react to stress in only limited ways. A Japanese businessman's financial failure might lead to suicide because the disgrace and shame of publicly acknowledging bankruptcy would be too painful.
3. *Culture may influence which symptoms of a disorder are expressed and the content of the symptoms.* Symptoms of depression differ among people of various cultures. Societies or cultures that do not emphasize the concept of "guilt," as in Indonesia, are less likely to have depressed clients who feel guilty. The content of

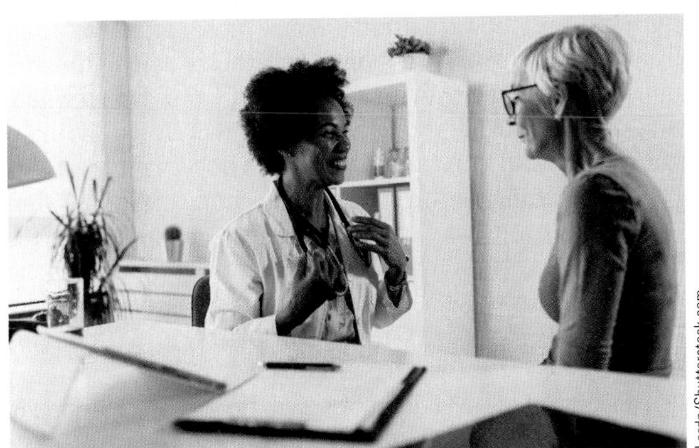

Culture can influence the development of psychological problems, and mental health professionals and medical doctors must consider cultural influences when conducting a clinical assessment or physical examination.

phobias or delusions can also depend on culture. People from less developed countries may be less likely to fear airplanes or believe their mind is controlled by satellites.

4. *Culture may reinforce certain forms of mental disorder.* The prevalence of certain mental disorders varies as a function of culture. General lifestyle patterns and attitudes, as well as acceptance of a disorder by the culture, likely influence prevalence. Anorexia nervosa is more prevalent in societies that emphasize and reward thinness (Chapter 8).

Culture and Clinical Assessment

Culture clearly influences the development and presentation of mental disorders, so culture must influence clinical assessment as well. This is important not only for assessing people from other countries but also for assessing diverse groups within the United States. This presents unique challenges to many clinicians, however. Four main areas should be considered during assessment (Tseng, 2015).

1. *Clinicians must overcome a language barrier if one exists.* An interpreter with a background in mental health should be used if necessary. This is not the best option because people may feel uncomfortable disclosing certain information to more than one person. The interpreter could also misinterpret or mistranslate information. This points to the need for culturally responsive clinicians, especially ones that come from the culture or are fluent in the language of the client if an interpreter is not available.
2. *Clinicians must obtain information about the cultural background of a client.* This might involve reading clinical books on diversity or consulting with cultural experts. A mental health professional must also distinguish behavior collectively shared by a culture and a client's responses or behaviors. A helpful question to a client or family members thus might be, "How do your friends and other members of your community typically react in similar situations?" In addition, this would involve hiring and adequately supporting clinicians who are culturally competent and share backgrounds with their clients.
3. *Clinicians must be culturally sensitive.* Mental health professionals must be aware that culture influences emotions, thoughts, and behavior. Psychological problems should also be understood and interpreted from a cultural perspective. Many people from East Asian cultures are more reserved and soft-spoken than people from the West. A mental health professional must be careful not to misinterpret this style as evidence of an interpersonal problem or depression.
4. *Clinicians must be knowledgeable about cultural variations in psychological problems.* Mental health professionals must find assessment and other materials that consider cultural variations in mental disorder. The DSM presents general categories of information relevant to cultural considerations. First, for many mental disorders, a description of culture-related diagnostic issues is included: how cultural background may influence the cause or presentation of symptoms, preferred terms for distress, and/or prevalence of the disorder. Second, cultural syndromes are discussed; these are covered throughout this textbook. Third, an outline is presented for cultural formulation of presenting problems (**Table 4.5**).

Table 4.5

DSM Cultural Formulation

The *DSM* (APA, 2022) suggests that a mental health professional should supplement traditional diagnostic formulations with a cultural formulation of presenting symptoms of clients whose cultural background differs from the treating mental health professional. Information is obtained to address the following topics:

- **Cultural identity of the client:** Note the client's ethnic or cultural reference groups as well as language abilities and preferences.
- **Cultural ideas of distress:** Note how the identified cultural group might explain the present symptoms and how these symptoms compare with those experienced by those in the cultural reference group.
- **Cultural factors related to the social environment:** Note how the cultural reference group might interpret social stressors, as well as availability of social supports and other resources that may aid treatment.
- **Cultural influences on the relationship between the client and the mental health professional:** Indicate differences in cultural and social status between the client and mental health professional that might influence diagnosis and treatment.
- **Overall cultural assessment:** Summarize how cultural factors and considerations are likely to influence the assessment and treatment of the client.

Adapted from American Psychiatric Association. (2022). *Diagnostic and statistical manual of mental disorders* (5th ed. text revision). Arlington, VA: American Psychiatric Association.

Section Summary

- Culture may influence stress and psychological problems.
- Culture may influence a person's reaction to stress.
- Culture may influence which symptoms of a disorder are expressed and the content of the symptoms.
- Culture may reinforce certain forms of mental disorder.
- Mental health professionals must overcome a language barrier if one exists, obtain information about a client's culture, be culturally sensitive, and be aware of cultural variations in psychological problems.

Review Questions

1. How might culture influence the development of psychological problems?
2. What considerations regarding culture are important for clinical assessment?
3. Consider the assessment methods and instruments discussed earlier in this chapter. How might cultural considerations affect the use of these?

Studying Psychopathology and Mental Disorder

LO 4.7 Define the key components of the scientific method.

LO 4.8 Describe important approaches to the scientific study of psychopathology, including experimental, quasi-experimental, nonexperimental, and developmental designs and case studies, including the methods, strengths, and limitations of each.

Classification, assessment, and cultural considerations have so far been discussed regarding mental disorder. Mental health professionals also rely on the scientific method to study, describe, explain, predict, and treat disorders. The **scientific method** has three basic steps: generating a hypothesis, developing a research design, and analyzing and interpreting data to test the hypothesis. The most powerful scientific method is presented first: the *experiment.*

Experiment

An **experiment** is a research design that allows us to draw cause-and-effect conclusions about particular variables or events. Researchers generally follow a specific path to draw such conclusions, beginning with a hypothesis.

Hypothesis

A **hypothesis** is a statement about the cause of an event or about the relationship between two events. We might hypothesize that treatment A is more effective than treatment B for depression. Hypotheses are educated guesses based on previous studies but must be *testable* and *refutable.* This means hypotheses must contain constructs that can be measured or observed so others can try to replicate the study. Recall from Chapter 2 that one criticism of the psychodynamic perspective was that constructs such as id and unconscious cannot be directly or accurately measured, and so a cause–effect relationship between these constructs and behavior cannot be established.

If we develop a testable and refutable hypothesis regarding treatment for depression, then we must specify how we define depression and exactly what comprises treatments A and B. We might define depression as scores on a questionnaire or number of hours a person sleeps during the day. We might define treatment A as a specific drug such as Prozac given at 60 milligrams (mg)/day and define treatment B as Prozac given at 20 mg/day. Our hypothesis is now *testable:* We can measure or observe depression and provide specific doses of a medication. Our hypothesis is also *refutable:* Other people can clearly understand what we did, and they can try to replicate these results. We may also find no differences between our two groups, which refutes or contradicts our hypothesis.

Research Design

The next step in the scientific experimental method is to develop a *research design* that allows us to test the hypothesis, or in this case, tell us whether treatment A is indeed more effective than treatment B. Research designs comprise dependent and independent variables. **Dependent variables** are those that measure a certain outcome the researcher is trying to explain or predict. Dependent variables in our experiment might include scores on a depression questionnaire or number of hours a person sleeps during the day. An **independent variable** is a manipulated variable that researchers hypothesize to be the cause of the outcome. The independent variable in our experiment is *treatment:* Some people will receive treatment A, and some people will receive treatment B.

Once we develop a testable and refutable hypothesis with dependent and independent variables, we must then test the hypothesis. We can do so by choosing people with depression from the general population and randomly assigning them to an experimental group and a control group. **Randomization** means assigning people to groups so each person has the same chance of being assigned to any group. The goal of randomization is to make sure our groups represent the general population with respect to age, gender, cultural background, income level, or other variables that could influence the dependent variable. If we examined only Hispanic men in our study, then our results would probably not be too useful to everyone.

The **experimental group** is one that receives the active independent variable, in this case medication at two levels. We actually need two experimental groups for our study: one receiving medication at 60 mg/day and one receiving medication at 20 mg/day. The **control group** is one that does not receive the active independent variable. We may thus include people who are on a wait list for medication and monitor them over time to note if changes occur. They will receive no medication for a certain period of time, so we will learn if changes in the experimental group are significantly different than changes in the control group. If our hypothesis is correct, then manipulation of the independent variable in the experimental group will lead to less depression, but this change will not occur in the control group.

We will assign 50 people (participants) with depression to treatment A (experimental group 1; 60 mg/day), 50 people with depression to treatment B (experimental group 2; 20 mg/day), and 50 people with depression to the control group (0 mg/day) for our experiment. Some control groups in an experiment such as this one receive a **placebo** or a substance or treatment that has no actual therapeutic effect. In this example, control group participants could receive a pill with no active treatment ingredient. Experimenters use placebos to control for *bias* or the possibility that a person receiving a medication will show improved symptoms simply because they expect to improve. Some experiments also use **double-blind designs**, meaning that neither the experimenter nor the participants know who received a placebo or an active treatment. In this case, perhaps only an independent pharmacist knows who received a placebo or active treatment. **Triple-blind designs** are experiments in which participants, experimenters, independent raters of outcome, and even data managers are unaware of who received a placebo or active treatment. Blinded designs are meant to control for as much bias from different people as possible (refer to **Focus on Law and Ethics: Who Should Be Studied in Mental Health Research?**).

In our experiment, we will then monitor our participants over several weeks by examining their scores on a depression measure and tracking the number of hours they sleep during the day. We may find after three months that people in experimental group 1 experienced a substantial drop in depression, people in experimental group 2 experienced a slight drop in depression, and people in the control group experienced no change in depression. This is done by analyzing and interpreting data, the third step in the scientific method. We could then conclude our hypothesis was correct: treatment A (60 mg/day) was indeed more effective than treatment B (20 mg/day). We could also conclude treatment is better than no treatment under these conditions.

Results such as these are a powerful testament to the causal role of treatment for reducing symptoms of depression. The groups were similar at the beginning of the experiment with respect to depression. The only difference between the groups was level of medication given. Differences in depression at the conclusion of the experiment can thus be attributed confidently to the manipulation differences between the groups—those receiving higher amounts of antidepressant medication experienced greater improvement.

Results such as these can be contaminated by variables other than the independent variable, however. If differences existed between the experimental and control groups, then we would have trouble concluding our treatment was effective. Imagine if the experimental group was mostly male African Americans and the control group was mostly female European Americans. How confident could we be in our results? Factors such as this affect the **external validity** of a study, or the extent to which results can be generalized to the whole population.

Focus On Law and Ethics

Who Should Be Studied in Mental Health Research?

Much concern has been expressed over the relative lack of women and diverse participants in mental health research. Some feel that many studies use samples composed predominantly of male European Americans. This is a problem because results about causes and treatment of mental disorders in male European Americans may not generalize to others. Important biological differences exist between genders (like hormones) that may affect the development and expression of psychological problems. Diverse ethnic groups are also subject to different types and degrees of environmental stressors, and these differences may influence mental health as well. Conclusions about psychological problems and their treatment in male European Americans may not be valid for other genders or people of color.

These concerns have heightened clinical psychologists' awareness of these issues, and more formal requirements for studies supported by the U.S. government are now in place. The National Institutes of Health (NIH) has a policy about including women and members of minority groups in studies of human participants. These groups must be represented in NIH-supported projects unless some clear and compelling rationale exists for not doing so. Researchers must also provide a detailed and specific plan for the outreach and recruitment of women and minority participants in their study. Researchers can thus address whether general conclusions for men or European Americans also hold for women and diverse groups.

If the experimental group experienced something other than the manipulation, or treatment, then our conclusions would also be affected. Imagine if some members of the experimental group were attending therapy sessions in addition to their medication but members of the control group were not. How confident could we then be that medication was the major cause of improved symptoms? Factors such as this can decrease the **internal validity** of an experiment, or the extent to which a researcher can be confident that changes in the dependent variable (depression symptoms) truly resulted from manipulation of the independent variable (medication).

The experiment remains the best strategy for testing hypotheses about mental disorder. Unfortunately, researchers are not able to use this strategy as much as they would like. Experiments are costly in time and resources and require many people to study. Experiments are sometimes criticized for being unethical as well. Making people wait in the control group for medication that could help their depression sooner might raise some questions. If we wanted to study the effects of alcohol use on women and their unborn children, we would not want to deliberately introduce alcohol consumption to their diets. Because experiments can be costly and difficult to conduct, researchers often use correlational studies.

Correlational Studies

A correlation is an association or relationship between two variables. **Correlational studies** allow researchers to make statements about the association or relationship between variables based on the extent to which they change together in a predictable way. A dependent variable and an independent variable may be related to each other such that high scores on one are associated with high scores on the other and vice versa. You would expect number of hours spent studying for a psychology test to be associated with higher grades. Height and weight in people are also closely associated. These examples indicate **positive correlations** where two variables are highly related to one another—as one goes up, the other does as well.

Dependent and independent variables may also be related to each other such that low scores on one are associated with high scores on the other and vice versa. You might expect greater dosage of medication to be related to lower scores on a depression measure. This would indicate a **negative correlation** in which two variables are also highly related to one another—as one goes up, the other goes down.

Correlations or associations between two variables are represented by a *correlation coefficient*, which is a number from +1.00 to −1.00. The sign of the coefficient, + or −, refers to type of association between variables. A positive sign indicates a positive correlation, and a negative sign indicates a negative correlation. The *absolute value* of the correlation coefficient, how high the number is regardless of its sign, refers to the *strength* of the association between the two variables.

The closer a correlation is to +1.00 or −1.00, the stronger the association. A correlation coefficient of exactly +1.00 or −1.00 means two variables are perfectly related: As one variable changes, the other variable always changes as well. Knowing someone's score on the independent variable thus allows us to predict a person's score on the dependent variable with 100 percent accuracy. A correlation coefficient of 0.00 means no relationship exists between the two variables: Knowing someone's score on the independent variable allows no prediction about a score on the dependent variable.

Correlations of +1.00 or −1.00 are rare. Correlation coefficients of +0.50 to +0.99 or −0.50 to −0.99 reflect strong association between two variables. Correlation coefficients of +0.30 to +0.49 or −0.30 to −0.49 reflect moderate association between two variables. Correlation coefficients of +0.01 to +0.29 or −0.01 to −0.29 reflect weak association between two variables. Examples of correlation coefficients are in **Figure 4.7**.

A correlation between two variables does not mean one variable *causes* another. *Correlation does not imply causation.* A problem with correlational methods is that we cannot rule out other explanations for the relationship between two variables because correlation does not control for the influence of third variables. This is the *third variable problem.* A strong correlation might exist in a growing city between number of churches built and number of violent crimes: The more churches built, the more violent crimes occur. Can we conclude church building *caused* more violent crime? Of course not. A *third variable* explains this effect: massive population growth. As more people move into a city, more churches and more crimes are to be expected.

Another problem with correlation methods is *directionality.* We know a correlation exists between marital conflict and adolescent delinquency. This effect might at first seem easy to explain—frequent parental fighting increases family stress, models violence as a way to solve problems, and reduces child supervision. But the *opposite direction* is also possible: Some children get into trouble in their teenage years and cause their parents to fight about how best to handle this situation. We may have a strong correlation but we cannot know for sure which variable is the cause and which is the effect. We would have to conduct an experiment to know for sure.

Quasi-Experimental Methods

An alternative approach to experiments and correlations is **quasi-experimental methods** or mixed designs. Mixed designs do not randomly assign people to experimental and control groups like a true experiment does. An experimenter instead examines groups that already

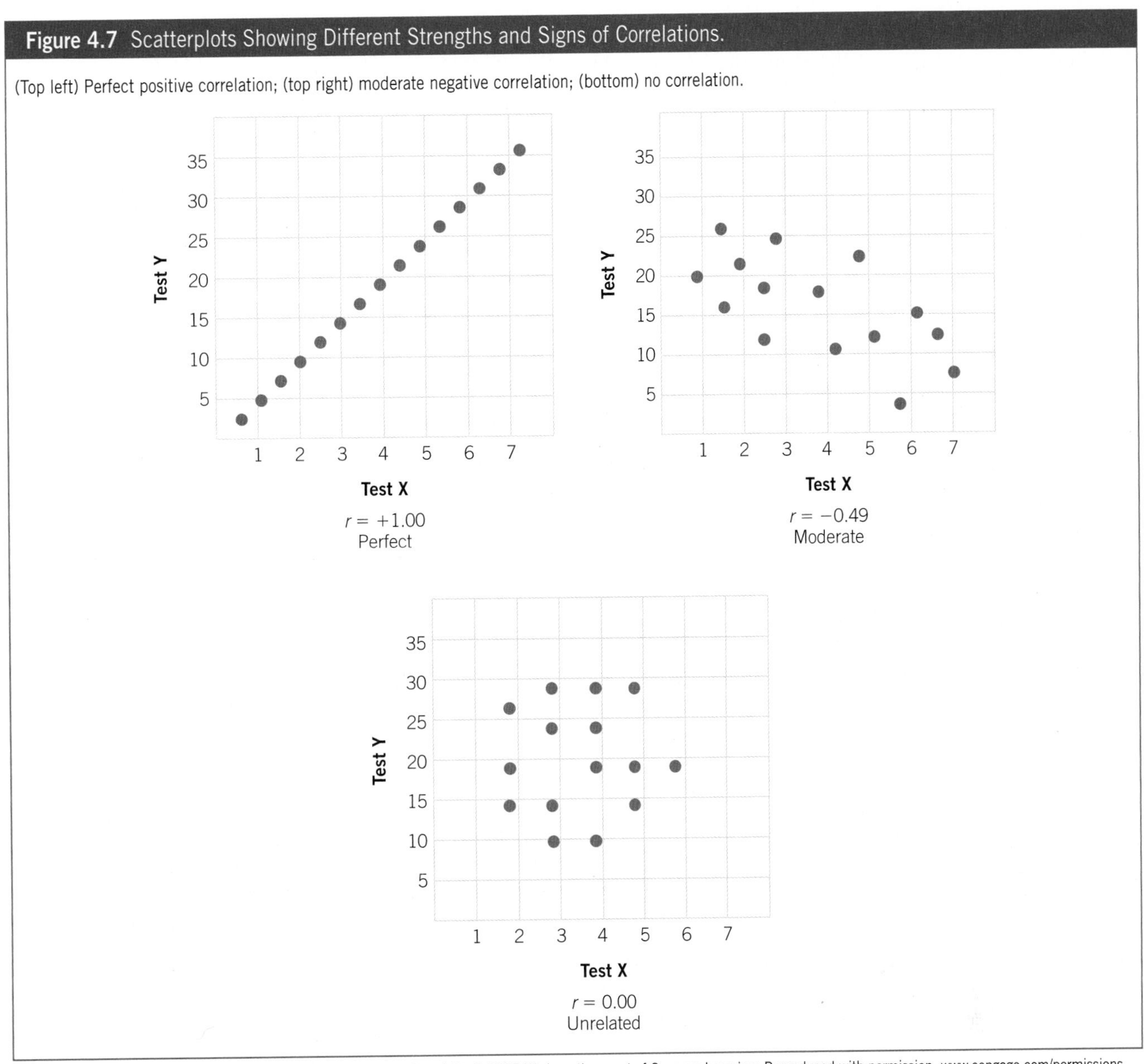

Figure 4.7 Scatterplots Showing Different Strengths and Signs of Correlations.

(Top left) Perfect positive correlation; (top right) moderate negative correlation; (bottom) no correlation.

exist. People already diagnosed with depression might be compared to people without depression. We could compare these groups along different variables such as family history of depression and stressful life events. We could even examine subgroups within the depressed group to learn what medications they are taking and whether any effects can be seen. We could also calculate correlations between level of depression and many other variables such as age, income level, and family size.

Quasi-experiments involve no randomization, so researchers who use quasi-experiments must minimize confounds in their investigation. **Confounds** are factors that may account for group differences on a dependent variable. If we examine people with and without depression regarding stressful life events, then we should be aware of these other factors. People with depression may have more stressful life events than people without depression, but people with depression may simply be more likely to *remember* stressful life events than people without depression. Confounds such as this impact the internal validity of results.

Researchers often try to *match* people in their groups on many variables to guard against these kinds of problems. They may try to ensure their groups are similar with respect to gender, age, race, income level, and symptoms of a specific disorder such as depression. Unfortunately, researchers cannot identify every variable necessary to match groups and protect internal validity. Experimental and control groups may still differ along important dimensions even after matching.

Other Alternative Experimental Designs

Other designs also serve as alternatives to a large-scale true experiment. A **natural experiment** is an observational study in which nature itself helps assign groups. Recall John Snow from Chapter 3 who found that some residents getting sick from tainted drinking water were accessing a particular pump, whereas other residents not getting sick were accessing a different pump. The "natural" independent variable in this case was the source of drinking water. Natural experiments also commonly occur following disasters such as tsunamis or hurricanes. Many natural experiments were conducted during the early part of the COVID-19 pandemic, such as between groups using and not using masks (e.g., Lyu & Wehby, 2020).

Another alternative experimental design is an **analogue experiment** that involves simulating a real-life situation under controlled conditions. Often this simulation is done because recreating certain events or conditions is not ethical. Researchers may be interested in examining trauma-related imagery and memories but obviously subjecting participants to an actual trauma is out of the question. Instead, the researchers may conduct an analogue experiment in which participants watch a distressing video and then are monitored afterward (Meyer & Morina, 2022). Such a study could provide valuable information about different kinds of coping strategies that might be relevant to posttraumatic stress disorder (Chapter 5).

Researchers also use **single-subject experimental designs** that involve one person or a small group of persons who are examined under certain conditions. Single-subject designs still have experimental and control conditions to observe and measure behavior but do so in innovative ways. One type of single-subject experimental design is an *ABAB* or *reversal* design. In this case, "A" may represent a control condition, and "B" may represent a treatment condition. If a research participant consistently benefits from the "B" condition but not the "A" condition, then we have some evidence that a treatment is working. Such a design is sometimes used for unusual behaviors where obtaining large groups would be difficult. Reversal designs are commonly used to examine treatments of such behaviors in persons with severe developmental disorders (Chan, 2021).

Developmental Designs

Researchers also use developmental designs to examine new participants or already-existing groups to learn how a certain problem or mental disorder unfolds over time. Developmental designs consist of longitudinal, cross-sectional, and sequential studies. **Longitudinal studies** involve examining the same group of people over a long period of time. Researchers sometimes follow youth whose parents had schizophrenia during childhood and adolescence to learn what risk factors eventually lead to the mental disorder.

Longitudinal studies are important for examining behavior change and development, but a major drawback is the time needed to complete the study. Some longitudinal studies last 20 years or more. Longitudinal studies also run the risk of *attrition,* which means some participants will drop out of the study over time or can no longer be contacted by the researcher. If 100 children begin a study but only 15 are left at the end of adolescence, how useful would the results be?

An alternative approach to longitudinal studies is a **cross-sectional study**, which involves examining different groups of people at one point in time. If a researcher were interested in examining children of parents of schizophrenia, then they might find children at different ages—say, 2, 7, 12, and 17 years—and study them right now. Cross-sectional studies are highly useful but suffer from *cohort effects.* This means children at different ages are being raised in different eras, which may affect their functioning. Think about the fast-paced changes in technology that occur in our society today. A two-year-old child will likely have access to different kinds of experiences than a 17-year-old did. These differences will be reflected in their behavior to some extent.

Some researchers thus blend aspects of longitudinal and cross-sectional studies into a **sequential design**. A sequential design begins as a cross-sectional study, but the groups are examined over a short time frame. From the example above, 2-, 7-, 12-, and 17-year-old children whose parents had schizophrenia may be examined now *and* over a five-year period. Cross-sectional *and* longitudinal changes can thus be examined.

Case Study

The research designs discussed so far are useful but not always practical. A researcher using the **case study method** makes careful observations of one person over time. The researcher may describe in great detail types of symptoms, assessment, and treatment relevant to that case. Substantial data are made available about one person, but no experimental manipulation occurs and no internal validity is present. We also cannot generalize results from one person to the overall population, so no external validity is present.

Case studies are useful for several reasons, especially for describing rare phenomena. People with multiple personalities, for example, are too few to allow for a large experiment. Or a person may have an unusual presentation of symptoms and family background. Case studies are also useful for testing new treatments on a few people to judge their effect and safety. Data from these "pilot studies" can then be used to justify further studies with more people.

Researchers use many methods to study mental disorders and each method has its advantages and limitations. Information derived from each of these methods is presented throughout this textbook. Please keep in mind each method's strengths and drawbacks.

Consuming the Media's Research

Many types of research can be conducted, and some types (e.g., experiments) allow for stronger conclusions than others (e.g., case studies). This is important to remember when reading a media report about a research finding regarding a mental disorder. Media outlets often focus on sensational aspects of a research study, especially differences found between genders. When you read these reports, pay close attention to the study that is cited and whether the study is an experiment or something less rigorous. Take the extra step of reading the original research paper to get a sense of what the researchers truly found and what drawbacks exist for the study. Don't just fall for the headline—be a wise consumer of media reports on psychological research.

Section Summary

- The scientific method involves generating a hypothesis, designing a research plan, and analyzing data to test the hypothesis.
- An experiment allows a researcher to draw cause-and-effect conclusions about variables.
- A hypothesis is a statement about the cause of an event or about the relationship between two events.
- Dependent variables are those measuring a certain outcome, and independent variables are those manipulated by a researcher to test a hypothesis.
- Experimental and control groups are key to an experiment, which must include randomization of participants.
- Internal validity and external validity are important components of an experiment that allow researchers to be confident about their results and generalize their results to the overall population.
- Experimenters use certain procedures to control for bias such as placebos and blinded designs.
- Correlational studies allow researchers to examine associations between variables and often include evaluating positive and negative correlations.
- Correlation does not imply causation because of third variable and directionality problems.
- Quasi-experiments involve examining groups that already exist along an independent variable.
- Other alternative experimental designs include natural experiments, analogue experiments, and single-subject research designs.
- Researchers often examine the development of mental disorders via longitudinal, cross-sectional, and sequential designs.
- Researchers use the case study method to make careful observations of one person.

Review Questions

1. Describe three major steps used in the scientific method.
2. Discuss various steps and components of an experiment.
3. Describe the correlational approach to research and its problems.
4. Describe the main characteristics of natural experiments, analogue experiments, and single-subject research designs.
5. Describe developmental designs and their advantages and disadvantages.
6. What is a case study, and why would a researcher conduct one?

Final Comments

Mental health professionals take seriously the precise definition, classification, assessment, and study of psychological problems. This is done to better understand, treat, and prevent mental disorders. If we have a well-defined mental disorder that can be more easily assessed, then we can actively work to identify risk factors for the disorder that allow for early detection and prevention of symptoms. We have now reached the point in the book where major mental disorders will be described at length. Each of the following chapters covers important information about features, epidemiology (including diversity), stigma, risk factors, prevention, assessment, and treatment of these disorders. Keep in mind that the behaviors described can be considered along a continuum or spectrum. We all have many aspects of these problems to some extent at some point in our lives. Some of the most common forms of mental disorder are discussed first, the anxiety, obsessive-compulsive, and trauma-related disorders.

Key Terms

dimensions 76
categories 76
diagnosis 77
mental disorder 77
syndrome 77
classification 78
clinical assessment 79
reliability 79
test–retest reliability 79
interrater reliability 80
internal consistency reliability 80
validity 80
content validity 80
predictive validity 81
concurrent validity 81
construct validity 81
standardization 81
unstructured interviews 81
structured interviews 81
intelligence tests 83
personality assessment 84
objective personality measures 84
MMPI-3 validity scales 85
MMPI-3 clinical scales 85
projective tests 85
behavioral assessment 87
functional analysis 87
antecedents 87
consequences 87
organismic variables 87
naturalistic observation 87
controlled observation 87
self-monitoring 88
computerized axial tomography (CAT scan) 89
magnetic resonance imaging (MRI) 89
functional MRI (fMRI) 89
positron emission tomography (PET scan) 89
neurochemical assessment 89
metabolites 89
psychophysiological assessment 89
electrocardiogram 89
galvanic skin conductance 90
electroencephalogram (EEG) 90
neuropsychological assessment 91
scientific method 94
experiment 94
hypothesis 94
dependent variable 94
independent variable 94
randomization 94
experimental group 95
control group 95
placebo 95
double-blind design 95
triple-blind design 95
external validity 95
internal validity 96
correlational studies 96
positive correlation 96
negative correlation 96
quasi-experimental methods 96
confounds 97
natural experiment 98
analogue experiment 98
single-subject experimental design 98
longitudinal studies 98
cross-sectional study 98
sequential design 98
case study method 98

Anxiety, Obsessive-Compulsive, and Trauma-Related Disorders

5

Learning Objectives

LO 5.1 Distinguish between worry, anxiety, and fear.

LO 5.2 Differentiate between anxiety disorders based on their diagnostic criteria and clinical presentations.

LO 5.3 Differentiate between obsessive-compulsive and related disorders based on their diagnostic criteria and clinical presentations.

LO 5.4 Differentiate between trauma-related disorders based on their diagnostic criteria and clinical presentations.

LO 5.5 Discuss the epidemiology of anxiety, obsessive-compulsive, and trauma-related disorders.

LO 5.6 Describe the stigmatizing beliefs associated with anxiety, obsessive-compulsive, and trauma-related disorders and the impact of those beliefs on individuals with the disorders.

LO 5.7 Identify risk factors for anxiety, obsessive-compulsive, and trauma-related disorders.

LO 5.8 Discuss efforts to prevent anxiety, obsessive-compulsive, and trauma-related disorders.

LO 5.9 Characterize the assessment of individuals with anxiety, obsessive-compulsive, and trauma-related disorders.

LO 5.10 Evaluate approaches to the treatment of individuals with anxiety, obsessive-compulsive, and trauma-related disorders.

Case Angelina

Angelina was 25 years old when she was referred to a specialized outpatient clinic for people with anxiety-related disorders. She came to the clinic after a scary episode in which she nearly had a car accident. Angelina said she was driving across a high bridge when she suddenly felt her heart start to race, her breath become short, and her vision become blurry. These feelings were so intense she thought she might wreck the car and hurt herself or others. She was able to pull the car off to the shoulder of the bridge as she struggled with her symptoms. The symptoms seemed to ease a bit after a few minutes. Angelina then waited another 20 minutes, still shaken from the experience, before driving straight home to where she felt safe.

The therapist who spoke to Angelina asked if such an episode had happened before. Angelina said the experience had occurred several times, usually when she was driving or surrounded by many people. Angelina generally felt she could handle her symptoms during these episodes. This last episode, though, and two more that followed, were much more intense than what she had felt before. She recently saw an emergency room doctor and a cardiologist to determine any potential medical causes for her symptoms, but none were found. Angelina was then referred for outpatient psychological treatment.

The therapist asked more about Angelina's history with these symptoms. Angelina said she had always been "the nervous and worried type" and that her anxiety worsened as she attended college. She had particular trouble driving to school and walking into class where other people were sitting and possibly looking at her. Angelina usually sat in the back of the class in case she had to exit quickly to calm herself. The therapist asked Angelina if she worried something bad might happen. Angelina said she was most concerned about the professor looking at her or being asked a question for which she did not have an answer. She was also concerned other people would notice her physical symptoms of anxiety.

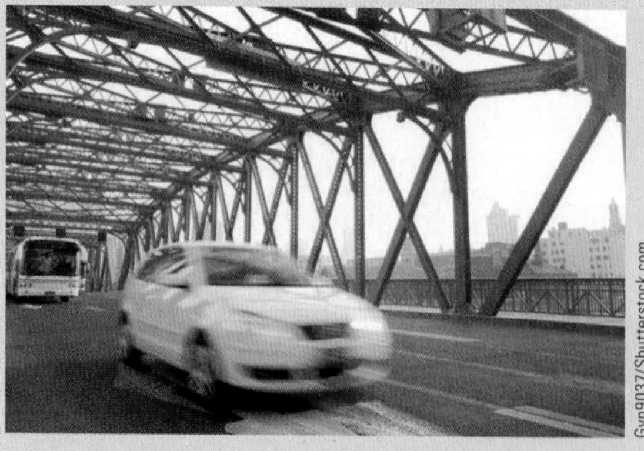

Gyn9037/Shutterstock.com

Angelina's nervousness escalated a year earlier when she began to experience specific episodes of intense anxiety. Angelina said her first "anxiety attack" happened as she walked into class to take a midterm examination. Her heart began racing, and she was short of breath. When the professor handed her the test, she was shaking and having much trouble concentrating. Angelina said she felt she "wasn't even there" and that "everything was moving in slow motion." Worse, she felt she could not concentrate well enough to take the test. She did complete the test, however, and received a "B-minus" (she was normally an "A/B" student). Other "anxiety attacks" after that point tended to occur when she was going to school or about to enter a classroom. These attacks happened about once a week but not typically on weekends or when she was not in school.

Over the past few months, Angelina's "attacks" became more frequent and affected other, similar situations. Angelina would sometimes have trouble driving to a place and shopping among a crowd of people. She was also reluctant to date because she might "seize up" and look foolish. Her greater concern, however, was that she might have to drop out of college even though she was near graduation. This belief arose from the fact that on her way to her first day of class, Angelina had driven across the bridge that led to her worst anxiety attack. The two other attacks that followed also caused her to miss so many classes, she felt she had to drop all of them. Angelina was thus sad and tearful, feeling she would not be able to return to college and finish her degree.

Angelina now spent her days at home, and her mother had driven her to the therapist's office. She had trouble going to the supermarket or restaurants and preferred to avoid them altogether. Even speaking to the therapist now led Angelina to report an anxiety rating of 8 on a 0 to 10 scale. The therapist asked her what she would like to be different in her life, and Angelina said she wanted to be like her old self—someone who went to school, saw her friends, dated, and enjoyed life. The therapist asked her if she could commit to a full-scale assessment and treatment program, and Angelina agreed to do so.

What Do You Think?

1. Which of Angelina's symptoms seem typical of someone in college, and which seem very different?
2. What external events and internal factors might be responsible for Angelina's feelings?
3. What are you curious about regarding Angelina?
4. Does Angelina remind you in any way of yourself or someone you know? How so?
5. How might Angelina's anxiety affect her life in the future?

Worry, Anxiety, Fear; and Anxiety, Obsessive-Compulsive, and Trauma-Related Disorders: What Are They?

LO 5.1 Distinguish between worry, anxiety, and fear.

Have you ever been *concerned* that something bad will happen? Have you ever been *nervous* about an upcoming event? Have you ever been *afraid* of something, like Angelina was? Some people worry a lot about what could happen in the future. Other people become nervous or anxious at the thought of going on a date, speaking in public, or taking a test. For others, the sight of a snake or an airplane causes intense and immediate fear. For people like Angelina, worry, anxiety, and fear can spiral into an uncontrollable state that makes them want to avoid many things such as school. But what are worry, anxiety, and fear, and what are the differences among them?

Worry is a largely cognitive or "thinking" concept that refers to concerns about possible future threat. People who worry tend to think about the future and about what painful things might happen. A person might worry about paying bills on time or experiencing a violent attack. Worry is not necessarily a bad thing because it helps people prepare for future events and solve problems. If you have a test next week and have not prepared for it, you may feel a sense of dread and then develop a study schedule. Worry is thus normal and even adaptive. Worry is often a gradual process that starts slowly for a distant event (oh, yeah, that test is coming) but becomes more intense as the event draws closer (uh-oh, better get studying). If the event draws closer and seems even more threatening, as when a test draws nearer and one is still not prepared, then *anxiety* may occur.

Anxiety is an emotional state that occurs as a threatening event draws close. Worry is more cognitive in nature, but anxiety has three key parts: *physical feelings, thoughts,* and *behaviors*. Physical feelings may include heart racing, sweating, dry mouth, shaking, dizziness, and other unpleasant symptoms. Thoughts may include beliefs that one will be harmed or will lose control of a situation. Behaviors may include avoiding certain situations or constantly asking others for reassurance. If you have a test tomorrow, and have not studied, then you may feel muscle tension (physical feeling), believe you will not do well (thought), and skip the test (behavior). Think about Angelina—what were her major physical feelings, thoughts, and behaviors? Anxiety, like worry, is a normal human emotion that tells us something is wrong or needs to change.

Fear is an intense emotional state that occurs as a threat is imminent or actually occurring. Fear is a *specific* reaction that is clear and immediate: fright, increased arousal, and an overwhelming urge to get away. A fear reaction is usually toward something well defined. If you take a test you have not studied for, you may experience severe physical arousal and distress and leave the situation quickly. Many

Sritanya/Shutterstock.com

Tero Vesalainen/Shutterstock.com

Bruce Laurance/The Image Bank/Getty Images

Anxiety is an emotional state that involves a sense of apprehension that something bad might happen. Worry is thinking about possible future threats. People worry about daily events such as school or job-related tasks and finances. Fear is an intense emotional state that occurs when some threat is imminent.

Continuum of Worry, Anxiety, and Fear

Worry	Anxiety	Fear
Potential threat	Approaching threat	Imminent threat
Little arousal (physical feelings)	Moderate arousal	Severe arousal
Heavily cognitive	Moderately cognitive	Scarcely cognitive
Little avoidance	Moderate avoidance	Severe avoidance
General and slow reaction (caution)	More focused and quicker reaction (apprehensiveness)	Very focused and fast reaction (fight or flight)

people are afraid of snakes. If someone places a cobra nearby, you may immediately become frightful and physically aroused, and run away as quickly as possible. Fear is an ancient human feeling that tells us we are in danger and that we may have to fight whatever is before us or flee the situation as quickly as possible (fight or flight). Fear is thus normal and protects us from potential harm. Fear that is particularly intense and severe is *panic*.

Differences among worry, anxiety, and fear can be illustrated along a continuum or dimension (refer to **Continuum of Worry, Anxiety, and Fear**). Worry occurs in reaction to *potential* threat, anxiety occurs in reaction to *approaching* threat, and fear occurs in reaction to *imminent* threat. Worry is a largely cognitive concept that involves fewer physical feelings (arousal) and less avoidance than anxiety or fear. Anxiety and fear involve more physical feelings and greater desire to avoid or escape as a threatening event comes closer in time and distance. Worry also tends to be a general and slow reaction that is cautionary. Anxiety is a more specific reaction that often spurs a person into action. Fear involves an immediate and focused reaction so a person can confront or flee a certain situation.

Worry, anxiety, and fear can also be viewed along a dimension of *severity*. Worry, anxiety, and fear are normal human emotions, so all of us experience them to some extent. We worry about the safety of our children, become anxious when about to perform or

Continuum of Anxiety and Anxiety-Related Disorders

	Normal	Mild
Emotions	Slight physical arousal but good alertness.	Mild physical arousal, perhaps feeling a bit tingly, but with good alertness.
Cognitions	"I'm going on a job interview today. I hope they like me. I'm going to show them what I've got!"	"I'm going on a job interview today. I wonder if they will think badly of me. I hope my voice doesn't shake."
Behaviors	Going to the job interview and performing well.	Going to the job interview but fidgeting a bit.

interview before others, and are frightened when an airplane experiences severe turbulence. These experiences are a common part of life, and many people learn to cope with them successfully. Many people go on first dates even when nervous, and they eventually relax and have a good time. Worry, anxiety, or fear may become more intense, however, to the point where a person finds it difficult to concentrate, finish a task, or relax (refer to **Continuum of Anxiety and Anxiety-Related Disorders**).

Worry, anxiety, and fear may even become *severe* and create enormous trouble for a person—this could be an *anxiety, obsessive-compulsive, or trauma-related disorder* (these are sometimes collectively referred to as **anxiety-related disorders** in this chapter). People like Angelina with these kind of disorders have persistent episodes of severe worry, anxiety, or fear that keep them from doing things they would normally like to do, such as shop, drive, attend school, or get a new job. An anxiety-related disorder can be *less severe,* as when a person worries so much about getting into a car accident that driving is difficult. Or an anxiety-related disorder can be *more severe,* as when a person is so fearful of germs that they never leave the house. People with anxiety-related disorders generally experience worry, anxiety, or fear that is severe, that lasts for long periods of time, and that interferes with daily living. The major anxiety-related disorders that cause many people like Angelina so much distress are covered next.

Anxiety, Obsessive-Compulsive, and Trauma-Related Disorders: Features and Epidemiology

LO 5.2 Differentiate between anxiety disorders based on their diagnostic criteria and clinical presentations.

LO 5.3 Differentiate between obsessive-compulsive and related disorders based on their diagnostic criteria and clinical presentations.

LO 5.4 Differentiate between trauma-related disorders based on their diagnostic criteria and clinical presentations.

LO 5.5 Discuss the epidemiology of anxiety, obsessive-compulsive, and trauma-related disorders.

The following sections summarize the major features and characteristics of the most commonly diagnosed anxiety-related disorders. Many of the disorders in this chapter have anxiety as a key component and were historically studied as one diagnostic group. The disorders are often separated now into smaller diagnostic groups labeled anxiety, obsessive-compulsive, and trauma- and stressor-related disorders (this latter label is shortened in this chapter). The concept of a panic attack is discussed first, which serves as a key part of several anxiety-related disorders.

Panic Attack

Have you ever felt scared for no reason? Perhaps you were just sitting or standing and suddenly felt intense fear out

Moderate	Anxiety-Related Disorder—less severe	Anxiety-Related Disorder—more severe
Moderate physical arousal, including shaking and trembling, with a little more difficulty concentrating.	Intense physical arousal, including shaking, dizziness, and restlessness, with trouble concentrating.	Extreme physical arousal with dizziness, heart palpitations, shaking, and sweating with great trouble concentrating.
"Wow, I feel so nervous about the interview today. I bet I don't get the job. I wonder if I should just forget about it?"	"Oh, no that interview is today. I feel sick. I just don't think I can do this. They will think I'm a terrible fit!"	"No way can I do this. I'm a total loser. I can't get that job. Why even bother? I don't want to look foolish!"
Drafting two e-mails to cancel the interview but not sending them. Going to the interview but appearing physically nervous.	Postponing the interview twice before finally going. Appearing quite agitated during the interview and unable to maintain eye contact.	Canceling the interview and staying home all day.

of the blue. If so, you may have experienced a panic attack similar to the ones Angelina reported. A **panic attack** involves a period of time, usually several minutes, in which a person experiences intense feelings of fear, apprehension that something terrible will happen, and physical symptoms. A panic attack is not a diagnosis but an event that commonly occurs in people with anxiety disorders. Features of a panic attack are in **Table 5.1** (APA, 2022).

Common physical symptoms include accelerated heart rate, shortness of breath, chest pain or discomfort, dizziness, and feelings of choking. People having a panic attack also often worry about dying, going "crazy," or losing control and doing something terrible. Angelina's panic attack in her car led her to think she might crash. Panic attacks may also involve feelings that surrounding events are not real (*derealization*) or that a person is watching themself go through the situation (*depersonalization*). Recall Angelina's feeling of detachment when taking her test.

Panic attacks that occur out of the blue, or without warning or predictability, are *unexpected panic attacks.* This can make panic attacks quite scary. Some people even have panic attacks during sleep (Smith et al., 2022). Over time, a person with panic attacks may be able to predict when these attacks are more likely to occur. Angelina said her panic attacks tended to occur when she was driving or among crowds. An *expected panic attack* has a specific trigger; for example, a person may experience severe panic symptoms when speaking in public. Panic attacks thus involve many troubling physical symptoms and thoughts, two components of anxiety described earlier.

Table 5.1 DSM-5-TR

Panic Attack

Note: Symptoms are presented for the purpose of identifying a panic attack; however, panic attack is not a mental disorder and cannot be coded. Panic attacks can occur in the context of any anxiety disorder as well as other mental disorders (e.g., depressive disorders, posttraumatic stress disorder, substance use disorders) and some medical conditions (e.g., cardiac, respiratory, vestibular, gastrointestinal). When the presence of a panic attack is identified, it should be noted as a specifier (e.g., "posttraumatic stress disorder with panic attacks"). For panic disorder, the presence of panic attack is contained within the criteria for the disorder and panic attack is not used as a specifier.

An abrupt surge of intense fear or intense discomfort that reaches a peak within minutes, and during which time four (or more) of the following symptoms occur:

Note: The abrupt surge can occur from a calm state or an anxious state.

1. Palpitations, pounding heart, or accelerated heart rate.
2. Sweating.
3. Trembling or shaking.
4. Sensations of shortness of breath or smothering.
5. Feelings of choking.
6. Chest pain or discomfort.
7. Nausea or abdominal distress.
8. Feeling dizzy, unsteady, light-headed, or faint.
9. Chills or heat sensations.
10. Paresthesias (numbness or tingling sensations).
11. Derealization (feelings of unreality) or depersonalization (being detached from oneself).
12. Fear of losing control or "going crazy."
13. Fear of dying.

Note: Culture specific symptoms should not count as one of the four required symptoms.

American Psychiatric Association. (2022). *Diagnostic and statistical manual of mental disorders* (5th ed., text rev.). Arlington, VA: American Psychiatric Association.

Table 5.2 DSM-5-TR

Panic Disorder

A. Recurrent unexpected panic attacks. A panic attack is an abrupt surge of intense fear or intense discomfort that reaches a peak within minutes, and during which time four (or more) of the following symptoms occur:

Note: The abrupt surge can occur from a calm state or an anxious state.

1. Palpitations, pounding heart, or accelerated heart rate.
2. Sweating.
3. Trembling or shaking.
4. Sensations of shortness of breath or smothering.
5. Feelings or choking.
6. Chest pain or discomfort.
7. Nausea or abdominal distress.
8. Feeling dizzy, unsteady, light-headed, or faint.
9. Chills or heat sensations.
10. Paresthesias (numbness or tingling sensations).
11. Derealization (feelings of unreality) or depersonalization (being detached from oneself).
12. Fear of losing control or "going crazy."
13. Fear of dying.

Note: Culture-specific symptoms should not count as one of the four required symptoms.

B. At least one of the attacks has been followed by one month (or more) of one or both of the following:

1. Persistent concern or worry about additional panic attacks or their consequences.
2. A significant maladaptive change in behavior related to the attacks.

C. The disturbance is not attributable to the physiological effects of a substance or another medical condition.

D. The disturbance is not better explained by another mental disorder.

American Psychiatric Association. (2022). *Diagnostic and statistical manual of mental disorders* (5th ed., text rev.). Arlington, VA: American Psychiatric Association.

Panic Disorder

People who regularly experience *unexpected* panic attacks have **panic disorder**, a diagnosis involving the criteria in **Table 5.2** (APA, 2022). At least one of these attacks must be followed by a month or more of concern about having another attack, worry about what the panic attack might mean, or a change in behavior. Angelina did indeed worry about having more attacks and wondered if she might have to drop out of school because of her attacks. Her driving behavior also changed drastically. Panic attacks and panic disorder must not be a result of substance use or a medical condition. Panic disorder is different from other anxiety disorders (refer to following sections) in which panic attacks are more closely linked to specific (or expected) situations such as public speaking.

Panic disorder is a frightening condition for several reasons. First, a person often has little idea when a panic attack might happen. Panic attacks can occur frequently during the day or be spaced out across several days. Imagine going places and always wondering if a panic attack might strike. Second, panic attacks are not harmful, but many people with panic disorder become terrified of their own internal sensations of dizziness, heart palpitations, or other panic attack symptoms. Some people with panic disorder may believe their symptoms indicate something serious such as a terminal heart condition or illness. People with panic disorder thus fear the onset of more panic attacks.

People with panic disorder, like Angelina or Professor Smith from Chapter 4, might avoid situations in which they may have panic symptoms. Recall that behavioral avoidance is a main component of anxiety. Some people with panic disorder may thus be diagnosed with agoraphobia. **Agoraphobia** refers to anxiety about being in places where panic symptoms may occur, especially places where escape might be difficult. Agoraphobia also refers to *avoiding* those places or enduring them with great anxiety or dread (refer to **Table 5.3**; APA, 2022). About half of those with panic disorder have agoraphobia, though agoraphobia appears more common among people with severe or chronic panic disorder (Shin et al., 2020).

Social Anxiety Disorder

Social anxiety disorder, also called *social phobia*, is marked by intense and ongoing fear of potentially embarrassing social or performance situations. A diagnosis of social anxiety disorder involves the criteria in **Table 5.4** (APA, 2022). Social situations include interactions with others, such as dating, having conversations, or attending parties. Performance situations include some evaluation from others, such as taking a test, giving an oral presentation, or playing a musical instrument at a recital. If someone with social anxiety disorder fears only speaking or performing in public, then the disorder is specified as *performance only.*

People with social anxiety disorder are extremely fearful they will act in a way that causes great personal embarrassment or humiliation in these situations. Many people with the disorder believe they will do something "dumb" or "crazy" to make them appear foolish before others. They may fear stuttering, fainting, freezing, or shaking around other people. People with social anxiety disorder

Table 5.3 DSM-5-TR

Agoraphobia
A. Marked fear or anxiety about two (or more) of the following five situations: 1. Using public transportation. 2. Being in open spaces. 3. Being in enclosed places. 4. Standing in line or being in a crowd. 5. Being outside of the home alone.
B. The individual fears or avoids these situations because of thoughts that escape might be difficult or help might not be available in the event of developing panic-like symptoms or other incapacitating or embarrassing symptoms.
C. The agoraphobic situations almost always provoke fear or anxiety.
D. The agoraphobic situations are actively avoided, require the presence of a companion, or are endured with intense fear or anxiety.
E. The fear or anxiety is out of proportion to the actual danger posed by the agoraphobic situations and to the sociocultural context.
F. The fear, anxiety, or avoidance is persistent, typically lasting for 6 months or more.
G. The fear, anxiety, or avoidance causes clinically significant distress or impairment in social, occupational, or other important areas of functioning.
H. If another medical condition is present, the fear, anxiety, or avoidance is clearly excessive.
I. The fear, anxiety, or avoidance is not better explained by the symptoms of another mental disorder—for example, the symptoms are not confined to specific phobia, situational type; do not involve only social situations (as in social anxiety disorder); and are not related exclusively to obsessions (as in obsessive-compulsive disorder), perceived defects or flaws in physical appearance (as in body dysmorphic disorder), reminders of traumatic events (as in posttraumatic stress disorder), or fear or separation (as in separation anxiety disorder). Note: Agoraphobia is diagnosed irrespective of the presence of panic disorder. If an individual's presentation meets criteria for panic disorder and agoraphobia, both diagnoses should be assigned.

American Psychiatric Association. (2022). *Diagnostic and statistical manual of mental disorders* (5th ed., text rev.). Arlington, VA: American Psychiatric Association.

may have *expected panic attacks* in social and performance settings and avoid these settings. Or they endure the settings with great anxiety or dread. Angelina had trouble dating, answering questions in class, and shopping and eating in front of others. These are all situations where she could be negatively evaluated. Social avoidance can obviously interfere with one's ability to live their daily life. People with social anxiety disorder may find it difficult to attend school, take high-profile jobs, and make and keep friends.

Specific Phobia

Most people are leery of snakes, so this kind of fear is normal. For other people, though, fear of something is so strong and pervasive that it interferes with daily functioning. Think about a fear of snakes so strong a person cannot walk in a yard or go to the park. Such is the case for some people with **specific phobia**. A specific phobia is an excessive, unreasonable fear of a particular object or situation. A diagnosis of specific phobia involves the criteria in **Table 5.5** (APA, 2022). People with specific phobia may have expected panic attacks when they encounter a dog, airplane, clown, or whatever they fear. Specific phobias are arranged into five types:

- *Animal phobias* involve fears of—you guessed it, animals—especially dogs, rodents, insects, and snakes or other reptiles.
- *Natural environment phobias* involve fears of surrounding phenomena such as heights, water, and weather events such as thunderstorms.
- *Blood-injection-injury phobias* involve fears of needles, medical procedures, and harm to self.
- *Situational phobias* involve fears of specific areas such as enclosed spaces in airplanes and elevators.
- *Other phobias* involve any other intense fear of a specific object. Examples include more common ones such as *iophobia* (fear of poison) but also unusual ones such as *levophobia* (fear of things to one's left), *arachibutyrophobia* (fear of peanut butter sticking to the roof of the mouth), and *hippopotomonstrosesquippedaliophobia* (you guessed it—fear of long words).

Table 5.4 DSM-5-TR

Social Anxiety Disorder
A. Marked fear or anxiety about one or more social situations in which the individual is exposed to possible scrutiny by others. Note: In children, the anxiety must occur in peer settings and not just during interactions with adults.
B. The individual fears that he or she will act in a way or show anxiety symptoms that will be negatively evaluated (i.e., will be humiliating or embarrassing; will lead to rejection or offend others).
C. The social situations almost always provoke fear or anxiety. Note: In children, the fear or anxiety may be expressed by crying, tantrums, freezing, clinging, shrinking, or failing to speak in social situations.
D. The social situations are avoided or endured with intense fear or anxiety.
E. The fear or anxiety is out of proportion to the actual threat posed by the social situation and to the sociocultural context.
F. The fear, anxiety, or avoidance is persistent, typically lasting for six months or more.
G. The fear, anxiety, or avoidance causes clinically significant distress or impairment in social, occupational, or other important areas of functioning.
H. The fear, anxiety, or avoidance is not attributable to the physiological effects of a substance or another medical condition.
I. The fear, anxiety, or avoidance is not better explained by the symptoms of another mental disorder, such as panic disorder, body dysmorphic disorder, or autism spectrum disorder.
J. If another medical condition is present, the fear, anxiety, or avoidance is clearly unrelated or is excessive.

American Psychiatric Association. (2022). *Diagnostic and statistical manual of mental disorders* (5th ed., text rev.). Arlington, VA: American Psychiatric Association.

Table 5.5 DSM-5-TR

Specific Phobia
A. Marked fear or anxiety about a specific object or situation. Note: In children, the fear or anxiety may be expressed by crying, tantrums, freezing, or clinging.
B. The phobic object or situation almost always provokes immediate fear or anxiety.
C. The phobic object or situation is actively avoided or endured with intense fear or anxiety.
D. The fear or anxiety is out of proportion to the actual danger posed by the specific object or situation and to the sociocultural context.
E. The fear, anxiety, or avoidance is persistent, typically lasting for 6 months or more.
F. The fear, anxiety, or avoidance causes clinically significant distress or impairment in social, occupational, or other important areas of functioning.
G. The disturbance is not better explained by the symptoms of another mental disorder.

American Psychiatric Association. (2022). *Diagnostic and statistical manual of mental disorders* (5th ed., text rev.). Arlington, VA: American Psychiatric Association.

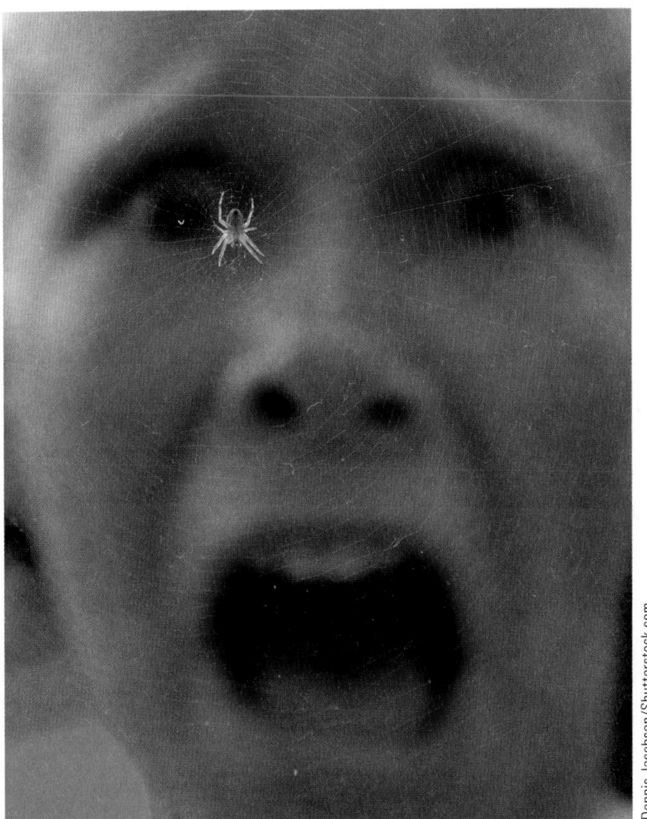

Dennis Jacobsen/Shutterstock.com

Many people are afraid of spiders, but a phobia of spiders, known as arachnophobia, involves a more intense and irrational fear.

Generalized Anxiety Disorder

Many people experience some level of worry, but people with **generalized anxiety disorder** experience strong, persistent, and extreme levels of worry about various events or activities. A diagnosis of generalized anxiety disorder involves the criteria in **Table 5.6** (APA, 2022). People with generalized anxiety disorder have trouble controlling their worry and thus often have trouble concentrating, sleeping, or resting. Those with generalized anxiety disorder often worry excessively about routine things such as paying bills or picking up their children on time. Such worry is *not in proportion* to actual risk or problems. Many people worry about paying bills when their homes are near foreclosure, but people with generalized anxiety disorder might worry about paying bills when no financial problems exist. Other common worries of those with generalized anxiety disorder include health issues, work-related tasks, and competence in different activities.

You may have noticed from Table 5.6 that people with generalized anxiety disorder do not usually experience panic attacks but rather have muscle tension or trouble sleeping and concentrating. Generalized anxiety disorder and worry are largely *cognitive* concepts, so physical and behavioral symptoms are less prominent than what is seen in panic disorder and social and specific phobias. People with generalized anxiety disorder do not focus on internal symptoms of panic but more on potential external threats (Aktar et al., 2022). They also believe these threats to be dangerous or full of dire consequences. One might worry excessively that not paying a bill 15 days *early* will result in a damaged credit rating and inability to buy a new car.

The key aspect of generalized anxiety disorder, worry, is reported by many people to be a lifelong problem. Recall Angelina said she was always the "nervous and worried type." Generalized anxiety disorder that develops early in life is not usually associated with a specific life event, or trigger, but later-onset generalized anxiety disorder often *is* related to a particular stressor such as bankruptcy. Generalized anxiety disorder is perhaps the least reliably diagnosed of the major anxiety disorders. Uncontrollable and excessive worry, muscle tension, and scanning the environment for threats, however, are key symptoms that separate generalized anxiety disorder from other anxiety disorders (Crocq, 2022).

Table 5.6 DSM-5-TR

Generalized Anxiety Disorder
A. Excessive anxiety and worry (apprehensive expectation), occurring more days than not for at least six months, about a number of events or activities.
B. The individual finds it difficult to control the worry.
C. The anxiety and worry are associated with three (or more) of the following six symptoms (with at least some symptoms having been present for more days than not for the past six months): Note: Only one item is required in children. 1. Restlessness or feeling keyed up or on edge. 2. Being easily fatigued. 3. Difficulty concentrating or mind going blank. 4. Irritability. 5. Muscle tension. 6. Sleep disturbance.
D. The anxiety, worry, or physical symptoms cause clinically significant distress or impairment in social, occupational, or other important areas of functioning.
E. The disturbance is not attributable to the physiological effects of a substance or another medical condition (e.g., hyperthyroidism).
F. The disturbance is not better explained by another mental disorder (e.g., anxiety or worry about having panic attacks in panic disorder).

American Psychiatric Association. (2022). *Diagnostic and statistical manual of mental disorders* (5th ed., text rev.). Arlington, VA: American Psychiatric Association.

Case Jonathan

Jonathan was a 33-year-old man in therapy for behaviors that recently cost him his job and that were threatening his marriage. Jonathan said he had overwhelming urges to check things to determine if they were in place and to order things if they were not. Jonathan said he would go to work and spend the first three hours organizing his desk, office, email messages, and computer files. He would also check other offices to deermine if things were grossly out of place, such as plants, wastebaskets, and keyboards. He did this so often his coworkers complained that Jonathan spent more time with them than in his own office. Jonathan did get some work done, but he usually could not concentrate for more than three hours per day. He was fired for his lack of productivity.

Jonathan said he often had troubling thoughts about things being out of order. He told his therapist he worried that disorganization would lead him to forget important pieces of information such as what bills needed to be paid and what reports were due. He spent so much time organizing items at work and home, however, that he could accomplish little else. His wife recently threatened to leave if Jonathan did not seek professional help. Jonathan also said he felt depressed and wished he "could think like a normal person."

Obsessive-Compulsive Disorder

Many of us have little rituals or habits, or **compulsions**, we do every day to keep order or check on things, but not to the extent Jonathan does. Keeping things in place has its advantages in a competitive workplace or if you want to find something at home. Checking the windows and doors at night before going to bed can also protect against harm. For other people, however, rituals or compulsions are associated with painful thoughts, or **obsessions**, and become overly time-consuming, distressing, and destructive. Obsessions can also come in the form of constant ideas, impulses, or even images.

Obsessive-compulsive disorder involves obsessions, or troublesome thoughts, impulses, or images; and/or compulsions, or ritualistic acts done repeatedly to reduce anxiety from the obsessions. A diagnosis of obsessive-compulsive disorder involves the criteria in **Table 5.7** (APA, 2022). Obsessions occur spontaneously, frequently, and intrusively, meaning they are unwanted by the person but uncontrollable. Obsessions may also be quite strange—one might have images or thoughts of massive bacteria on doorknobs or credit cards. This is a *contamination* obsession. Other common obsessions include the following:

Table 5.7 DSM-5-TR

Obsessive-Compulsive Disorder

A. Presence of obsessions, compulsions, or both:

Obsessions are defined by (1) and (2):

1. Recurrent and persistent thoughts, urges, or images that are experienced, at some time during the disturbance, as intrusive and unwanted, and that in most individuals cause marked anxiety or distress.
2. The individual attempts to ignore or suppress such thoughts, urges, or images, or to neutralize them with some other thought or action (i.e., by performing a compulsion).

Compulsions are defined by (1) and (2):

1. Repetitive behaviors (e.g., hand washing) or mental acts (e.g., repeating words silently) that the individual feels driven to perform in response to an obsession or according to rules that must be applied rigidly.
2. The behaviors or mental acts are aimed at preventing or reducing anxiety or distress, or preventing some dreaded event or situation; however, these behaviors or mental acts are not connected in a realistic way with what they are designed to neutralize or prevent, or are clearly excessive.

Note: Young children may not be able to articulate the aims of these behaviors or mental acts.

B. The obsessions or compulsions are time-consuming or cause clinically significant distress or impairment in social, occupational, or other important areas of functioning.

C. The obsessive-compulsive symptoms are not attributable to the physiological effects of a substance or another medical condition.

D. The disturbance is not better explained by the symptoms of another mental disorder (e.g., excessive worries, as in generalized anxiety disorder).

American Psychiatric Association. (2022). *Diagnostic and statistical manual of mental disorders* (5th ed., text rev.). Arlington, VA: American Psychiatric Association.

- *Doubt,* such as concern about leaving the front door open
- *Need for order,* such as need to have food organized by expiration date
- *Impulses toward aggression,* such as intolerable thoughts about harming an infant
- *Sexual imagery,* such as recurrent mental pictures of pornography

Compulsions are motor behaviors or mental acts performed in response to an obsession. Someone who obsesses about the front door being open will keep checking the door to make sure it is closed and locked. This may continue so many times in a row that the person misses school or work that day.

Many people with obsessive-compulsive disorder will perform certain rituals more often than usual, such as this woman, who trims her grass with a pair of scissors several hours every day.

Compulsions may take place at least *one hour per day,* but often last much longer. Compulsions other than checking include hand washing, ordering, counting, silently repeating words or phrases, and seeking reassurance from others. Hand washing usually occurs in response to a contamination obsession—a person may obsess about bacteria on their hand and then wash vigorously and often to compensate. Obsessions and compulsions occur nearly every day, are extremely distressing, and interfere with a person's ability to concentrate or work.

Obsessive-Compulsive-Related Disorders

Other mental disorders include those related to obsessive-compulsive disorder. *Hoarding disorder* refers to people who have persistent difficulty parting with possessions, who feel they need to save items, and who experience cluttered living areas. Other related disorders include people who continually pull out their own hair (*trichotillomania*) or pick their skin (*excoriation disorder*).

Another disorder in this section, **body dysmorphic disorder**, was once grouped with somatic symptom disorders (Chapter 6) but is now thought to be more closely related to obsessive-compulsive behavior. A diagnosis of body dysmorphic disorder involves the criteria in **Table 5.8** (APA, 2022). People with body dysmorphic disorder are preoccupied with an imaginary or slight "defect" in their appearance. Many people with this disorder worry excessively about minor alterations in facial features, hair, wrinkles, skin spots, and size of body parts like noses or ears. Many of us are concerned with our appearance, but people with body dysmorphic disorder are so preoccupied they may spend hours per day checking and grooming themselves or they may visit cosmetic surgeons and undergo several surgeries to correct imagined or minor flaws. People with body dysmorphic disorder may be unable to date or work because of deep embarrassment about some perceived body flaw.

Posttraumatic Stress Disorder and Acute Stress Disorder

The disorders discussed so far are often linked to *regularly* occurring events like public speaking. Other disorders—posttraumatic stress and acute stress disorder—follow a *specific traumatic event.* These disorders are referred to as *trauma- and stressor-related disorders*. Think about people victimized by violence or natural disasters as well as soldiers who faced constant danger in wartime. Some people can eventually deal with these stressors as they fade in memory over time. Other people like Marcus, however, find recovery from trauma to be a long and painful process.

Table 5.8 DSM-5-TR

Body Dysmorphic Disorder
A. Preoccupation with one or more perceived defects or flaws in physical appearance that are not observable or appear slight to others.
B. At some point during the course of the disorder, the individual has performed repetitive behaviors (e.g., mirror checking, excessive grooming, skin picking, reassurance seeking) or mental acts (e.g., comparing his or her appearance with that of others) in response to the appearance concerns.
C. The preoccupation causes clinically significant distress or impairment in social, occupational, or other important areas of functioning.
D. The appearance preoccupation is not better explained by concerns with body fat or weight in an individual whose symptoms meet diagnostic criteria for an eating disorder.

American Psychiatric Association. (2022). *Diagnostic and statistical manual of mental disorders* (5th ed., text rev.). Arlington, VA: American Psychiatric Association.

Case Marcus

Marcus was a 27-year-old man in therapy for symptoms following a traumatic event. Marcus was about to enter a shopping center at night two months ago when two men threatened him with a gun and demanded his wallet. Marcus was initially shocked the event was occurring and thus hesitated, which prompted one of the men to strike him in the face. Marcus then gave his wallet to the men, who fled. A shaken Marcus called police to report the incident and was taken to the hospital for treatment. The two assailants had not yet been caught at the time of Marcus's therapy.

Marcus said he had been having trouble sleeping at home and concentrating at work. The latter was especially problematic because he was an accountant. He also felt he was living his life in a "slow motion fog" and that people seemed very distant from him. He increasingly spent time at home and avoided major shopping areas and large parking lots, especially at night. Marcus also feared the gunmen would find and rob him again because they had his driver's license. Most distressing, however, were Marcus's recurring images of the event; he said, "I just can't get the whole scene out of my mind." He thus tried to block thoughts about the trauma as much as possible, with little success.

Posttraumatic stress disorder is marked by frequent reexperiencing of a traumatic event through images, memories, nightmares, flashbacks, or other ways. A diagnosis of posttraumatic stress disorder (PTSD) involves the criteria in **Table 5.9** (APA, 2022). Marcus's images of his trauma constantly entered his mind. He also became upset at reminders of the trauma, such as walking through a large parking lot at night, and avoided many discussions of the event. People with posttraumatic stress disorder may also feel detached from others, have fewer positive emotional responses than before the event, and expect additional harm or negative consequences. A person may also experience substantial physical arousal and have problems sleeping, concentrating, or completing everyday tasks. PTSD symptoms must last at least one month but some symptoms may be delayed more than six months from time of trauma, and this refers to *delayed expression.* Separate PTSD criteria exist for children younger than age seven years (Table 5.9). Young children with PTSD may display reexperiencing symptoms through play, for example.

What about people with problems immediately after a trauma? **Acute stress disorder** refers to distressing memories and dreams, negative mood, dissociation (feelings of detachment from reality or disconnectedness from others), avoidance, and arousal that last between three days and one month after the trauma. A diagnosis of acute stress disorder involves the criteria in **Table 5.10** (APA, 2022). People with acute stress disorder may be eventually diagnosed with PTSD if symptoms continue longer than one month. Acute stress disorder is a good predictor of PTSD (Ramos-Lima et al., 2020).

What traumas might lead to acute stress disorder or posttraumatic stress disorder? Key traumas include sexual or other physical assault, war, natural disasters, robbery, home invasion, or witnessing horrifying events. More common events such as a car accident, learning of a trauma to a close friend or relative, or experiences of first responders (e.g., police, fire personnel) can also result in either disorder. Not everyone who experiences a traumatic event necessarily develops acute stress disorder or posttraumatic stress disorder, however (Lowe et al., 2021).

Separation Anxiety Disorder

Some anxiety-related disorders are more common in youth. **Separation anxiety disorder** is marked by substantial distress when separation from a major attachment figure occurs or is expected to occur. This distress must last at least four weeks in children, so initial distress about going to school is excluded. The separation anxiety must also be developmentally inappropriate. This means a child is at an age, perhaps in elementary school, where separation should not be a problem but is. A diagnosis of separation anxiety disorder involves the criteria in **Table 5.11** (APA, 2022). A child with separation anxiety disorder will often have trouble going to school or sleeping alone, throw a tantrum when a parent wants to go someplace without them, and have physical complaints such as a stomachache when away from a parent.

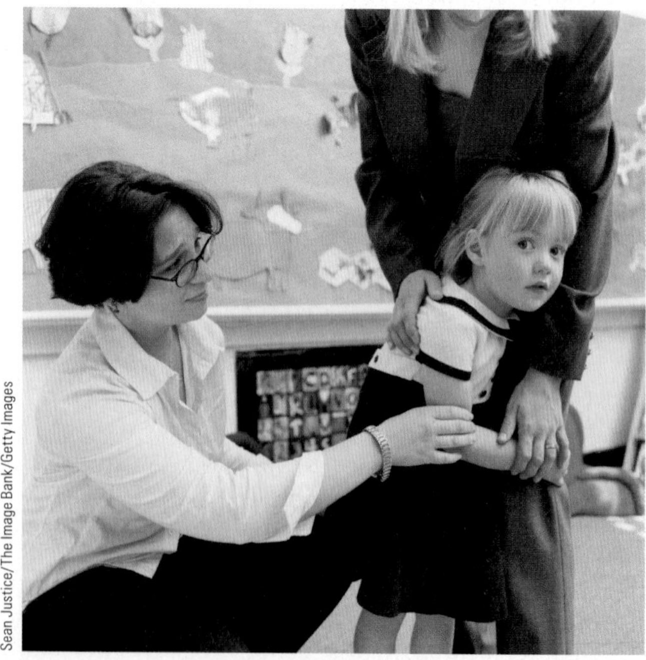

Sean Justice/The Image Bank/Getty Images

Many children have separation anxiety when they are younger, but some continue to have the problem even during school-age years.

Table 5.9 **DSM-5-TR**

Posttraumatic Stress Disorder

Note: The following criteria apply to adults, adolescents, and children older than 6 years. For children 6 years and younger, see corresponding criteria below.

A. Exposure to actual or threatened death, serious injury, or sexual violence in one (or more) of the following ways:

1. Directly experiencing the traumatic event(s).
2. Witnessing, in person, the event(s) as it occurred to others.
3. Learning that the traumatic event(s) occurred to a close family member or close friend. In cases of actual or threatened death of a family member or friend, the event(s) must have been violent or accidental.
4. Experiencing repeated or extreme exposure to aversive details of the traumatic event(s) (e.g., first responders collecting human remains; police officers repeatedly exposed to details of child abuse).

   Note: Criterion A4 does not apply to exposure through electronic media, television, movies, or pictures, unless this exposure is work related.

B. Presence of one (or more) of the following intrusion symptoms associated with the traumatic event(s), beginning after the traumatic event(s) occurred:

1. Recurrent, involuntary, and intrusive distressing memories of the traumatic event(s).

   Note: In children older than 6 years, repetitive play may occur in which themes or aspects of the traumatic event(s) are expressed.
2. Recurrent distressing dreams in which the content and/or affect of the dream are related to the traumatic event(s).

   Note: In children, there may be frightening dreams without recognizable content.
3. Dissociative reactions (e.g., flashbacks) in which the individual feels or acts as if the traumatic event(s) were recurring. (Such reactions may occur on a continuum, with the most extreme expression being a complete loss of awareness of present surroundings.)

   Note: In children, trauma-specific reenactment may occur in play.
4. Intense or prolonged psychological distress at exposure to internal or external cues that symbolize or resemble an aspect of the traumatic event(s).
5. Marked physiological reactions to internal or external cues that symbolize or resemble an aspect of the traumatic event(s).

C. Persistent avoidance of stimuli associated with the traumatic event(s), beginning after the traumatic event(s) occurred, as evidenced by one or both of the following:

1. Avoidance of or efforts to avoid distressing memories, thoughts, or feelings about or closely associated with the traumatic event(s).
2. Avoidance of or efforts to avoid external reminders (people, places, conversations, activities, objects, situations) that arouse distressing memories, thoughts, or feelings about or closely associated with the traumatic event(s).

D. Negative alterations in cognitions and mood associated with the traumatic event(s), beginning or worsening after the traumatic event(s) occurred, as evidenced by two (or more) of the following:

1. Inability to remember an important aspect of the traumatic event(s) (typically due to dissociative amnesia and not to other factors such as head injury, alcohol, or drugs).
2. Persistent and exaggerated negative beliefs or expectations about oneself, others, or the world (e.g., "I am bad," "No one can be trusted," "The world is completely dangerous," "My whole nervous system is permanently ruined").
3. Persistent, distorted cognitions about the cause or consequences of the traumatic event(s) that lead the individual to blame himself/herself or others.
4. Persistent negative emotional state (e.g., fear, horror, anger, guilt, or shame).
5. Markedly diminished interest or participation in significant activities.
6. Feelings of detachment or estrangement from others.
7. Persistent inability to experience positive emotions (e.g., inability to experience happiness, satisfaction, or loving feelings).

E. Marked alterations in arousal and reactivity associated with the traumatic event(s), beginning or worsening after the traumatic event(s) occurred, as evidenced by two (or more) of the following:

1. Irritable behavior and angry outbursts (with little or no provocation) typically expressed as verbal or physical aggression toward people or objects.
2. Reckless or self-destructive behavior.
3. Hypervigilance.
4. Exaggerated startle response.
5. Problems with concentration.
6. Sleep disturbance (e.g., difficulty falling or staying asleep or restless sleep).

continued

Table 5.9 DSM-5-TR—cont'd

F. Duration of the disturbance (Criteria B, C, D, and E) is more than one month.

G. The disturbance causes clinically significant distress or impairment in social, occupational, or other important areas of functioning.

H. The disturbance is not attributable to the physiological effects of a substance (e.g., medication, alcohol) or another medical condition.

Specify whether:

With dissociative symptoms: The individual's symptoms meet the criteria for posttraumatic stress disorder, and in addition, in response to the stressor, the individual experiences persistent or recurrent symptoms of either of the following:

1. **Depersonalization:** Persistent or recurrent experiences of feeling detached from, and as if one were an outside observer of, one's mental processes or body (e.g., feeling as though one were in a dream; feeling a sense of unreality of self or body or of time moving slowly).
2. **Derealization:** Persistent or recurrent experiences of unreality of surroundings (e.g., the world around the individual is experienced as unreal, dreamlike, distant, or distorted).

   Note: To use this subtype, the dissociative symptoms must not be attributable to the physiological effects of a substance (e.g., blackouts, behavior during alcohol intoxication) or another medical condition (e.g., complex partial seizures).

Specify if:

With delayed expression: If the full diagnostic criteria are not met until at least six months after the event (although the onset and expression of some symptoms may be immediate).

Posttraumatic Stress Disorder for Children 6 Years and Younger

A. In children 6 years and younger, exposure to actual or threatened death, serious injury, or sexual violence in one (or more) of the following ways:

1. Directly experiencing the traumatic events(s).
2. Witnessing, in person, the event(s) as it occurred to others, especially primary caregivers.

   Note: Witnessing does not include events that are witnesses only in electronic media, television, movies, or pictures.
3. Learning that the traumatic event(s) occurred to a parent or caregiving figure.

B. Presence of one (or more) of the following intrusion symptoms associated with the traumatic event(s), beginning after the traumatic event(s) occurred:

1. Recurrent, involuntary, and intrusive distressing memories of the traumatic event(s).

   Note: Spontaneous and intrusive memories may not necessarily appear distressing and may be expressed as play reenactment.
2. Recurrent distressing dreams in which the content and/or affect of the dream are related to the traumatic event(s).

   Note: It may not be possible to ascertain that the frightening content is related to the traumatic event.
3. Dissociative reactions (e.g., flashbacks) in which the child feels or acts as if the traumatic event(s) were recurring. (Such reactions may occur on a continuum, with the most extreme expression being a complete loss of awareness of present surroundings.) Such trauma-specific reenactment may occur in play.
4. Intense or prolonged psychological distress at exposure to internal or external cues that symbolize or resemble an aspect of the traumatic event(s).
5. Marked physiological reactions to reminders of the traumatic event(s).

C. One (or more) of the following symptoms, representing either persistent avoidance of stimuli associated with the traumatic event(s), or negative alterations in cognitions and mood associated with the traumatic event(s), must be present, beginning after the event(s) or worsening after the event(s):

Persistent Avoidance of Stimuli

1. Avoidance of or efforts to avoid activities, places, or physical reminders that arouse recollections of the traumatic event(s).
2. Avoidance of or efforts to avoid people, conversations, or interpersonal situations that arouse recollections of the traumatic event(s).

Negative Alterations in Cognitions

3. Substantially increased frequency of negative emotional states (e.g., fear, guilt, sadness, shame, confusion).
4. Markedly diminished interest or participation in significant activities, including constriction of play.
5. Socially withdrawn behavior.
6. Persistent reduction in expression of positive emotions.

continued

Table 5.9 DSM-5-TR—cont'd

D. Alterations in arousal and reactivity associated with the traumatic event(s), beginning or worsening after the traumatic event(s) occurred, as evidenced by two (or more) of the following:

1. Irritable behavior and angry outbursts (with little or no provocation) typically expressed as verbal or physical aggression toward people or objects (including extreme temper tantrums).
2. Hypervigilance.
3. Exaggerated startle response.
4. Problems with concentration.
5. Sleep disturbance (e.g., difficulty falling or staying asleep or restless sleep).

E. The duration of the disturbance is more than one month.

F. The disturbance causes clinically significant distress or impairment in relationships with parents, siblings, peers, or other caregivers or with school behavior.

G. The disturbance is not attributable to the physiological effects of a substance (e.g., medication or alcohol) or another medical condition.

Specify whether:

With dissociative symptoms: The individual's symptoms meet the criteria for posttraumatic stress disorder, and the individual experiences persistent or recurrent symptoms of either of the following:

1. **Depersonalization:** Persistent or recurrent experiences of feeling detached from, and as if one were an outside observer of, one's mental processes or body (e.g., feeling as though one were in dream; feeling a sense of unreality of self or body or of time moving slowly).
2. **Derealization:** Persistent or recurrent experiences of unreality of surroundings (e.g., the world around the individual is experienced as unreal, dreamlike, distant, or distorted).
   Note: To use this subtype, the dissociative symptoms must not be attributable to the physiological effects or a substance (e.g., blackouts) or another medical condition (e.g., complex partial seizures).

Specify if:

With delayed expression: If the full diagnostic criteria are not met until at least six months after the event (although the onset and expression of some symptoms may be immediate).

American Psychiatric Association. (2022). *Diagnostic and statistical manual of mental disorders* (5th ed., text rev.). Arlington, VA: American Psychiatric Association.

Epidemiology of Anxiety, Obsessive-Compulsive, and Trauma-Related Disorders

Anxiety-related disorders are commonly found in the general population, affecting 28.8 percent of Americans at some point in their lives and 18.1 percent in the past 12 months. Lifetime and 12-month prevalence rates for the major anxiety-related disorders are in **Figure 5.1**. Social anxiety disorder and specific phobia are especially common, affecting about one in eight people. Common phobias include snakes and other animals, heights, flying in airplanes, enclosed spaces, illness or injury, blood, water, death, bad weather, medical procedures, and being alone (Coelho et al., 2020).

Keep in mind, however, that many more people experience *symptoms* of anxiety-related disorders without receiving a formal diagnosis. Some, for example, including college students, experience a traumatic life event and display various symptoms as a result (refer to **Focus On College Students: Trauma and PTSD**). In addition, many people delay treatment for anxiety-related problems. People with panic disorder often visit medical before mental health professionals because of their physical symptoms, and people with social or performance anxiety are also generally shy and may not believe their condition to be serious (Curcio & Corboy, 2020; Wittchen et al., 2022). People with specific phobia often do not seek treatment until the fear keeps them from doing something important like going to work (de Vries et al., 2021).

Anxiety-related disorders are generally more common among women than men (Merikangas & Almasy, 2020). Several reasons that may account for this difference are outlined in **Focus On Gender: Are There True Gender Differences in Anxiety-Related Disorders?** Anxiety-related disorders tend to be fairly equal among young boys and girls. During adolescence and early adulthood, however, as these disorders become more common, women show greater prevalence than men. Anxiety-related disorders generally begin at age 19 to 31 years, although somewhat earlier for social anxiety disorder (median age of onset, 13 years) and separation anxiety disorder (median age of onset, 7 years; Kessler, Berglund, et al., 2005; Solmi et al., 2022).

Table 5.10 DSM-5-TR

Acute Stress Disorder

A. Exposure to actual or threatened death, serious injury, or sexual violation in one (or more) or the following ways:

1. Directly experiencing the traumatic event(s).
2. Witnessing, in person, the event(s) as it occurred to others.
3. Learning that the event(s) occurred to a close family member or close friend. Note: In case of actual or threatened death of a family member or friend, the event(s) must have been violent or accidental.
4. Experiencing repeated or extreme exposure to aversive details of the traumatic event(s) (e.g., first responders collecting human remains, police officers repeatedly exposed to details of child abuse).
   Note: This does not apply to exposure through electronic media, television, movies, or pictures, unless this exposure is work related.

B. Presence of nine (or more) of the following symptoms from any of the five categories of intrusion, negative mood, dissociation, avoidance, and arousal, beginning or worsening after the traumatic event(s) occurred:

Intrusion Symptoms

1. Recurrent, involuntary, and intrusive distressing memories of the traumatic event(s). Note: In children, repetitive play may occur in which themes or aspects of the traumatic event(s) are expressed.
2. Recurrent distressing dreams in which the content and/or affect of the dream are related to the event(s). Note: In children, there may be frightening dreams without recognizable content.
3. Dissociative reactions (e.g., flashbacks) in which the individual feels or acts as if the traumatic event(s) were recurring. (Such reactions may occur on a continuum, with the most extreme expression being a complete loss of awareness of present surroundings.) Note: In children, trauma-specific reenactment may occur in play.
4. Intense or prolonged psychological distress or marked physiological reactions in response to internal or external cues that symbolize or resemble an aspect of the traumatic event(s).

Negative Mood

5. Persistent inability to experience positive emotions.

Dissociative Symptoms

6. An altered sense of the reality of one's surroundings or oneself.
7. Inability to remember an important aspect of the traumatic event(s) (typically due to dissociative amnesia and not to other factors such as head injury, alcohol, or drugs).

Avoidance Symptoms

8. Efforts to avoid distressing memories, thoughts, or feelings about or closely associated with the traumatic event(s).
9. Efforts to avoid external reminders (people, places, conversations, activities, objects, situations) that arouse distressing memories, thoughts, or feelings about or closely associated with the traumatic event(s).

Arousal Symptoms

10. Sleep disturbance.
11. Irritable behavior and angry outbursts (with little or no provocation), typically expressed as verbal or physical aggression toward people or objects.
12. Hypervigilance.
13. Problems with concentration.
14. Exaggerated startle response.

C. Duration of the disturbance (symptoms in Criterion B) is three days to one month after trauma exposure.
Note: Symptoms typically begin immediately after the trauma, but persistence for at least three days and up to a month is needed to meet disorder criteria.

D. The disturbance causes clinically significant distress or impairment in social, occupational, or other important areas of functioning.

E. The disturbance is not attributable to the physiological effects of a substance or another medical condition and is not better explained by brief psychotic disorder.

American Psychiatric Association. (2022). *Diagnostic and statistical manual of mental disorders* (5th ed., text rev.). Arlington, VA: American Psychiatric Association.

Few racial differences have been found with respect to anxiety-related disorders within the United States. Rates of anxiety disorders among racial/ethnic minorities may be lower than for Whites (Vilsaint et al., 2019). African Americans and Latinos may experience higher rates of PTSD compared to other groups, however (Asnaani & Hall-Clark, 2017). Anxiety-related disorders are generally more common in Euro/Anglo cultures (10.4 percent) than in African cultures (5.3 percent; Baxter et al., 2013). People of one culture, however, may fear certain stimuli more so than people of another culture because of environmental experiences. A person living in a dense forest may be more afraid of animals than a person living in a large urban setting. The nature of how anxiety-related disorders are expressed can also differ from culture to culture. The following are examples of anxiety-related disorders across the globe (refer to **Focus On Diversity: Anxiety-Related Disorders and Sociocultural Factors**):

- *Koro:* intense fear of one's penis or nipples retracting into the body or shrinking in size (South and East Asia)
- *Taijin kyofusho:* intense fear of offending other people, perhaps through one's own body odor, inept conversation, or physical difference (Japan)
- *Dhat:* anxiety about loss of semen (India, Sri Lanka, China)
- *Pa-leng:* intense fear of cold that may lead to wearing layers of clothes even in hot weather (Asia)
- *Ataques de nervios:* a panic-like condition of uncontrollable episodes of shouting, crying, and trembling as well as feelings of heat rising to the head and aggression (Puerto Rico)
- *Latah:* an exaggerated startle response mixed with shouting obscenities (Malaysia)

Anxiety-related disorders are highly comorbid, or associated with, other mental disorders. People with one anxiety-related disorder often have another

Table 5.11 DSM-5-TR

Separation Anxiety Disorder

A. Developmentally inappropriate and excessive fear or anxiety concerning separation from those to whom the individual is attached, as evidenced by at least three of the following:

1. Recurrent excessive distress when anticipating or experiencing separation from home or from major attachment figures.
2. Persistent and excessive worry about losing major attachment figures or about possible harm to them, such as illness, injury, disasters, or death.
3. Persistent and excessive worry about experiencing an untoward event (e.g., getting lost) that causes separation from a major attachment figure.
4. Persistent reluctance or refusal to go out, away from home, to school, to work, or elsewhere because of fear of separation.
5. Persistent and excessive fear of or reluctance about being alone or without major attachment figures at home or in other settings.
6. Persistent reluctance or refusal to sleep away from home or to go to sleep without being near a major attachment figure.
7. Repeated nightmares involving the theme of separation.
8. Repeated complaints of physical symptoms when separation from major attachment figures occurs or is anticipated.

B. The fear, anxiety, or avoidance is persistent, lasting at least four weeks in children and adolescents and typically six months or more in adults.

C. The disturbance causes clinically significant distress or impairment in social, academic, occupational, or other important areas of functioning.

D. The disturbance is not better explained by another mental disorder.

American Psychiatric Association. (2022). *Diagnostic and statistical manual of mental disorders* (5th ed., text rev.). Arlington, VA: American Psychiatric Association.

Figure 5.1 Lifetime and 12-Month Prevalence Rates for the Anxiety-Related Disorders.

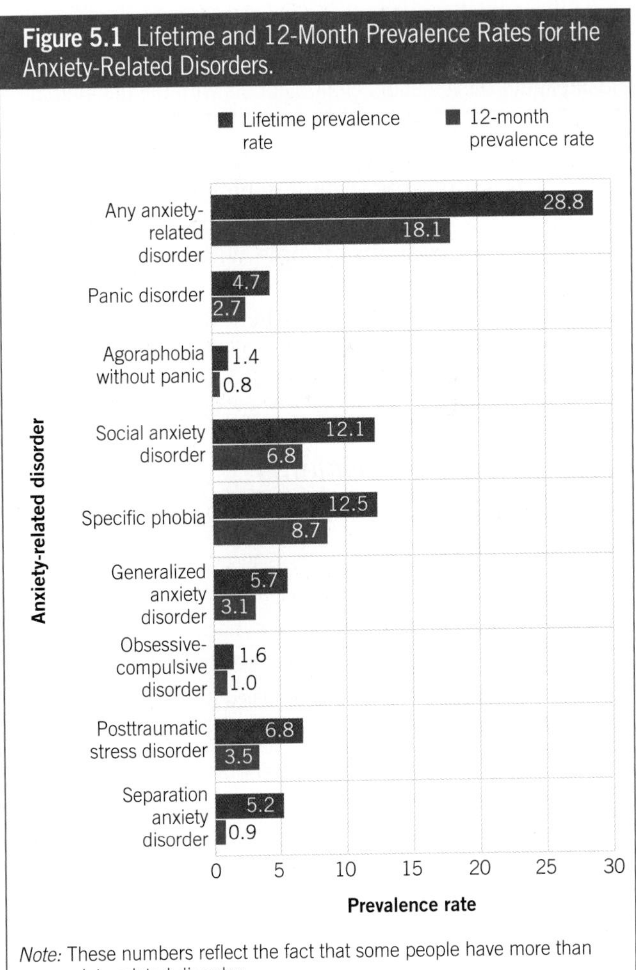

Note: These numbers reflect the fact that some people have more than one anxiety-related disorder.

Adapted from Kessler, Chiu, Demler, & Walters (2005) and Kessler, Berglund, et al. (2005).

anxiety-related disorder. Anxiety-related disorders and depression are also commonly seen in the same individual because the disorders share many features such as irritability, restlessness, and withdrawal (Saha et al., 2021). Anxiety-related disorders and substance use disorder may be comorbid as well because some people self-medicate or ease their anxiety symptoms by using alcohol or other drugs (Garey et al., 2020). Anxiety-related disorders are also associated with eating disorders and avoidant, obsessive-compulsive, and dependent personality disorders (Chapters 8 and 10; Schaumberg et al., 2021). As mentioned, obsessive-compulsive disorder is sometimes associated with hoarding and with trichotillomania, or a compulsion to pull out one's hair, eyelashes, eyebrows, and other body hair (Grant et al., 2020).

Stigma Associated with Anxiety, Obsessive-Compulsive, and Trauma-Related Disorders

LO 5.6 Describe the stigmatizing beliefs associated with anxiety, obsessive-compulsive, and trauma-related disorders and the impact of those beliefs on individuals with the disorders.

Recall from Chapter 1 that an important aspect of this textbook is addressing *stigma,* which refers to characterizing others with disgrace or reproach based on an individual characteristic. People with anxiety-related disorders may feel stigma or negative judgment when nervously speaking before others or when having trouble boarding an airplane. Researchers have indeed found that people sometimes have negative attitudes toward those with an anxiety disorder. These attitudes include viewing people with an anxiety disorder as weak, dangerous, self-centered, or lazy. Such attitudes often prevent people with an anxiety disorder from seeking treatment (Curcio & Corboy, 2020). Reluctance to seek help may be especially evident among military personnel who often avoid treatment for PTSD because of self-stigma (Correll et al., 2021). Researchers have tried to address this issue by developing peer-based interventions that encourage military personnel to enter treatment and then monitor adherence to treatment. A key aspect of these programs is to convey the idea that seeking treatment is a sign of strength and to remove military cultural barriers such as stigma that prevent seeking treatment.

Section Summary

- Anxiety is composed of three parts: physical feelings, thoughts, and behaviors.
- Anxiety-related disorders often involve excessive worry, anxiety, or fear.
- Panic attacks involve intense physical feelings such as heart racing, sweating, and dizziness; and thoughts that one will lose control or die. Panic attacks may be expected or unexpected.
- Panic disorder refers to regular unexpected panic attacks and worry about the consequences of these attacks.
- People with panic disorder may also have agoraphobia, or avoidance of situations in which a panic attack might occur.
- Social anxiety disorder refers to intense and ongoing fear of potentially embarrassing situations in the form of expected panic attacks.

Focus On College Students

Trauma and PTSD

Trauma and trauma-related disorders may be particularly common among college students. One group of researchers asked incoming college students to complete items from a widely used trauma questionnaire to assess how many had experienced trauma and how many were currently experiencing symptoms related to posttraumatic stress disorder (PTSD). Two-thirds (66 percent) reported a traumatic life event, and 25 percent reported three or more events; 9 percent met criteria for PTSD. Most common traumas were life-threatening illness (35 percent), sudden death of a loved one (34 percent), accident/natural disaster (26 percent), physical violence (24 percent), sexual assault (7 percent), and combat (1 percent). Trauma exposure was more common for female students (Read et al., 2011). Such traumas can lead to substantial risk for excessive alcohol and other drug use, depression, and withdrawal from college, among other problems.

Mental health professionals often note that, because many incoming freshman experience psychological problems related to trauma, university outreach efforts should involve several components. First, incoming students should be educated about the substantial prevalence of existing traumas and the concept of PTSD. Second, campus resources that are available to assist students with these problems should be widely publicized. Third, information about trauma types and number of traumas experienced should be collected anonymously by university counseling centers, in part to help identify students who may be at most risk for PTSD. Finally, treatments for trauma and PTSD among college students should be developed with an eye toward the special academic and other challenges that many of these students face.

- Specific phobia refers to excessive, unreasonable fear of an object or situation.
- Generalized anxiety disorder refers to extreme levels of persistent, uncontrollable worry.
- Obsessive-compulsive disorder refers to the presence of obsessions, or troublesome and recurring thoughts, and compulsions, or physical or mental acts performed in response to an obsession to lessen distress.
- Posttraumatic stress disorder refers to constant reexperiencing of a traumatic event through images, memories, nightmares, flashbacks, or other ways.
- Acute stress disorder refers to short-term anxiety and dissociative symptoms following a trauma.
- Separation anxiety disorder refers to children with excessive worry about being away from home or from close family members.
- Anxiety-related disorders are common to the general population, often develop in later adolescence and early adulthood, and are associated with other anxiety, mood, and substance use disorders.
- People with anxiety-related disorders may feel stigma from others and thus may be less likely to seek treatment.

Review Questions

1. How do Angelina's symptoms differ from normal worry, anxiety, or fear?
2. Identify different kinds of panic attacks and the main features of panic disorder.
3. Describe anxiety-related disorders that involve severe social anxiety, fear of a specific object, worry, bizarre ideas and behaviors, and symptoms following a trauma.
4. Which anxiety-related disorder applies mostly to children?
5. Describe the epidemiology of anxiety-related disorders, including issues of gender and culture.

Anxiety, Obsessive-Compulsive, and Trauma-Related Disorders: Causes and Prevention

LO 5.7 Identify risk factors for anxiety, obsessive-compulsive, and trauma-related disorders.

LO 5.8 Discuss the efforts to prevent anxiety, obsessive-compulsive, and trauma-related disorders.

Attention is turned next to factors that may help cause anxiety-related disorders and how knowing about these factors might help us prevent these disorders.

Biological Risk Factors for Anxiety, Obsessive-Compulsive, and Trauma-Related Disorders

Why do people have such intense physical feelings, unpleasant thoughts, and urges to avoid situations? Recall from Chapter 3 that mental disorders are often viewed from a diathesis-stress model, which attributes causes to a combination of biological and environmental variables. Many people have a genetic or biological predisposition toward certain personality characteristics and mental conditions. These biological predispositions are sometimes strong and sometimes weak, but they are almost always influenced or triggered to some degree by

Focus On Gender

Are There True Gender Differences in Anxiety-Related Disorders?

Females have more anxiety-related disorders than males. This is often reported in studies that assume a gender binary, but is it actually true, and why? Are women just more nervous than men? Or are women more likely to report anxiety and more willing to seek therapy than men, who may prefer to keep their anxiety private or self-medicate their anxiety using alcohol or other drugs? These are common explanations for one gender difference in anxiety-related disorders.

A closer look at this gender difference reveals more intricate explanations. Women experience more physical and sexual trauma than men; about 30 percent of women experience physical or sexual violence in their lifetime (World Health Organization, 2021). Women are more likely to be sexually assaulted and may thus be predisposed to develop acute or posttraumatic stress, agoraphobia, or other anxiety-related disorders.

Women also tend to ruminate in a brooding and worrisome way more than men, but men tend to engage in anger rumination more than women (Ando et al., 2020). Women report more social and work-related fears than men, but men report more fears of dating than women (Asher & Aderka, 2018). Women also have more cleaning and contamination obsessions, but men have more sexual and symmetry-related obsessions (Hallion et al., 2015). Therapist bias may also be a contributing factor. Therapists may be more likely to assign an anxiety-related diagnosis to a female based on misguided expectations or assumptions about that gender (Ali et al., 2010). Controversy about a true gender difference in anxiety-related disorder is not likely to end anytime soon because many plausible explanations are supported by research.

life events. We thus must consider biological predispositions *and* environmental events when discussing risk factors for anxiety-related disorders. Biological predispositions in people with anxiety-related disorders may include genetics, brain features, neurochemical features, behavioral inhibition, and evolutionary influences.

Genetics

Genetic researchers often rely on *family studies,* in which a certain disorder is examined in people and their close relatives. If many more close, or *first-degree,* relatives have the disorder compared with the general population, the disorder is said to "run in the family" and perhaps have a genetic basis. First-degree relatives include parents, siblings, and children. Researchers also conduct *twin studies,* in which identical twins and nonidentical, or fraternal, twins are compared. Identical (monozygotic) twins share much more genetic material with each other than fraternal/nonidentical (dizygotic) twins. Family and twin studies are often used to determine heritability rates (Chapter 2).

Anxiety-related disorders do have some moderate genetic basis. First-degree relatives of people with *panic disorder* are 6 to 17 times more likely than control participants to have panic disorder. The heritability of panic disorder has been estimated to be 0.48 (Tretiakov et al., 2020). Studies also reveal social anxiety disorder to be more common in close family relatives compared with controls. The heritability of social anxiety disorder has been estimated to be 0.50 (Bas-Hoogendam et al., 2018). Generalized anxiety disorder also seems to run in families, especially for those with comorbid depression. The heritability of generalized anxiety disorder has been estimated to be 0.32 (Gottschalk & Domschke, 2022).

Specific phobia also seems to run in families: 31 percent of first-degree relatives of people with phobia report having a phobia themselves, compared with 9 percent of control participants (Perez et al., 2013). The heritability of specific phobia has been estimated to be 0.30 for animal, situational, and blood-illness phobias (Eaton et al., 2018). Family members often share the same type of phobia as well. A family member with an animal or blood-injection-injury phobia may be more likely than controls to have relatives with that phobia type (Van Houtem et al., 2013). Family data indicate obsessive-compulsive disorder to be more common among first-degree relatives of people with the disorder (8.2 percent) compared with control participants (2.0 percent). Children with obsessive-compulsive disorder are also more likely than control participants to have parents with the disorder (Mahjani et al., 2021; Perez et al., 2013). Twin data also indicate moderately higher concordance for obsessive-compulsive disorder among identical than fraternal twins. The heritability of obsessive-compulsive symptoms ranges from 0.29–0.58 (Strom et al., 2021). Genetic influences for symptoms of posttraumatic stress disorder appear to be modest but higher for people like Marcus exposed to assault or combat compared with people exposed to nonassault trauma such as car accidents or natural disasters. The heritability of posttraumatic stress disorder ranges from 0.30–0.40 (Wang et al., 2022).

What can thus be said about these different genetic studies? Anxiety-related disorders do tend to run in families, and some people appear to be more genetically predisposed toward certain anxiety-related disorders. The contribution of genetics to the cause of anxiety-related disorders is less than other major mental disorders such as schizophrenia, however (Chapter 12). No single gene or set of genes leads *directly* to an anxiety-related disorder. Genetics may instead help produce brain or neurochemical features or temperaments that help lead to an anxiety-related disorder or otherwise interact with environmental events to predispose someone to develop an anxiety-related disorder. Potential brain features that are associated with anxiety-related disorders are discussed next.

Focus On Diversity

Anxiety-Related Disorders and Sociocultural Factors

Anxiety-related disorders are experienced differently across cultures, and sociocultural factors certainly influence why some people experience different kinds of anxiety symptoms. Some examples are described here. One thing that does not change across cultures, though, is the amount of distress these problems bring to people's lives.

Recall that *koro* represents an intense fear of one's penis or nipples shrinking into one's body. One sociocultural factor that may influence this phenomenon is strong religious or Taoist beliefs about the need for sexual restraint and the harm that frequent semen ejaculation can bring. Because semen is seen as a source of energy or strength, any perceived threat to this, such as genital shrinkage, may provoke anxiety. Such beliefs may also affect *dhat,* or fear of loss of semen (Aneja et al., 2015).

Taijin kyofusho represents a fear of offending others, which is a bit different from the Western form of social anxiety in which a person fears looking foolish before others. *Taijin kyofusho* may be heavily influenced by Japanese emphases on the importance of appropriately presenting oneself to others and concern for others' well-being (Lin et al., 2020). Many cultures, including Hispanic ones, also place great emphasis on physical symptoms to express distress or anxiety. Such a phenomenon may help to explain the concept of *ataques de nervios,* a panic-like state that partially involves anguish and loss of sensation (Felix et al., 2015).

Brain Features

Recall from Chapter 2 that several areas of the brain are important for certain kinds of behavior. Particularly important brain areas for increased physical arousal and anxiety-related disorders include the amygdala and the septal-hippocampal system (refer to **Figure 5.2**). The *amygdala* is a brain area long associated with fearful responses. The amygdala can be activated by a scary face or an imminent threat such as a nearby snake, and helps produce physical symptoms such as fast heart rate and sweating and emotional states of anxious apprehension and fear (refer to **Figure 5.3**; Kenwood et al., 2022). This helps a person cope with threat.

Key changes in the amygdala might be related to overarousal and excessive startle responses in people with different anxiety-related disorders (Brehl et al., 2020). Such changes may thus be closely associated with specific phobia or social anxiety disorder. People with obsessive-compulsive disorder or posttraumatic stress disorder also show significant activity in the amygdala when exposed to reminders of their trauma or other anxiety-provoking stimuli (Bystritsky et al., 2021). Changes in the amygdala may be influenced by certain genes but more research in this area is needed.

Connections from the amygdala to other key areas of the brain seem even more pertinent to anxiety-related disorders. One such area is the *septal-hippocampal system*, which may help a person respond to threats and remember and learn about highly anxiety-provoking situations (Besnard & Leroy, 2022). Unfortunately, this area may remain activated even when no threat exists, so a person with an anxiety-related disorder could be worried or anxious or fearful of something not threatening or, as with Marcus, could continue to vividly remember aspects of trauma. This area may be particularly affected by antianxiety drugs (Fernández-Teruel & Tobeña, 2020). The amygdala and the septal-hippocampal system connect as well to the *prefrontal cortex* and *bed nucleus of the stria terminalis*, brain structures also heavily involved in behavioral and emotional aspects of anxiety (Bystritsky et al., 2021).

Other brain features seem very specific to certain disorders. People with obsessive-compulsive disorder can have altered functioning of the *orbitofrontal cortex, basal ganglia, caudate nucleus, anterior cingulate,* and *thalamus*. People with this disorder may experience increased or decreased volume (size) or activity in these areas. Such changes may result in intrusive thoughts, repetitive motor behaviors, depression, and disruptions in information processing (Haber et al., 2021). Panic attacks and disorder have been specifically linked to changes in the *locus coeruleus,* which is a main norepinephrine center in the brain (refer to next section; Ross & Van Bockstaele, 2021). These brain areas interact with various neurotransmitters, which are discussed next.

Figure 5.2 Key Brain Areas Implicated in the Anxiety-Related Disorders.

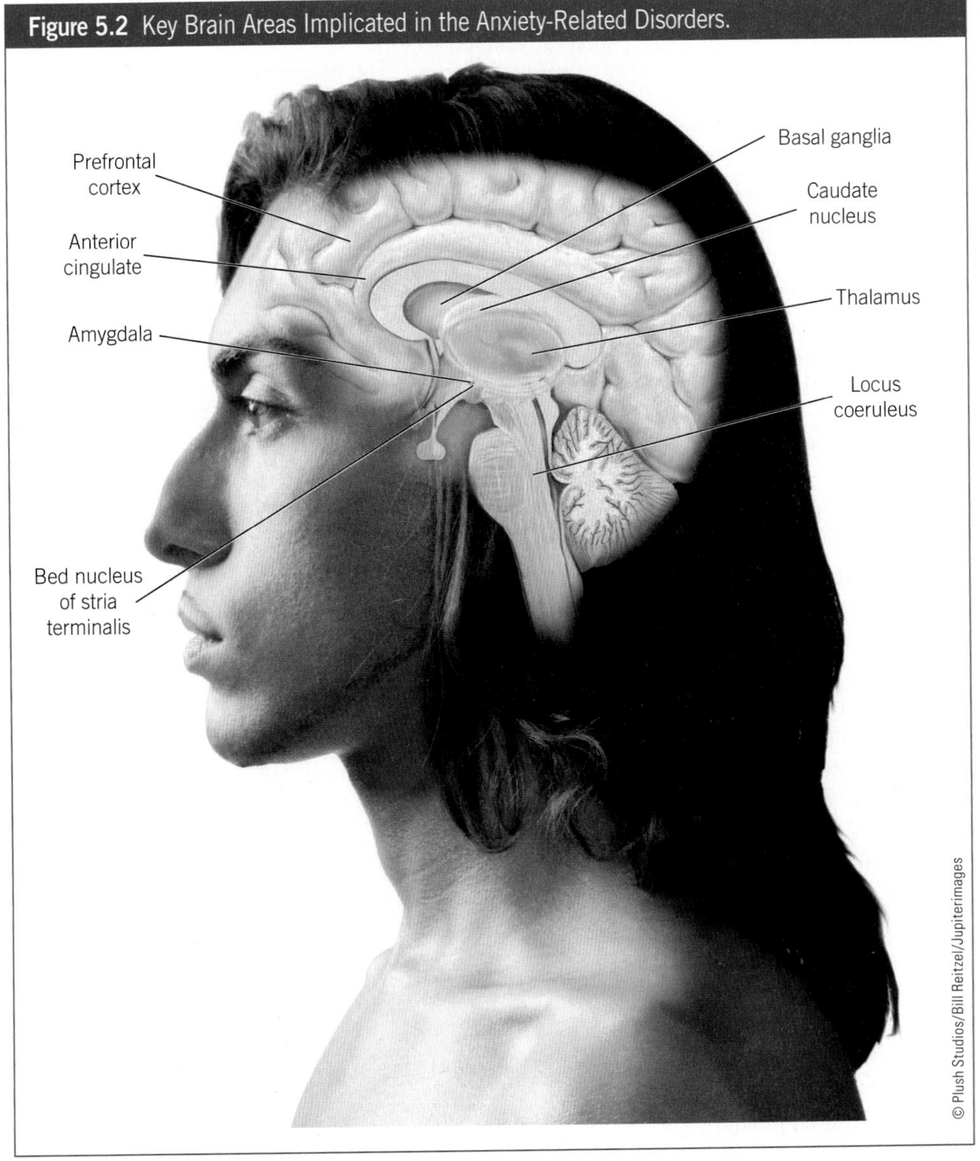

Figure 5.3 Fear can be Expressed as a Facial Image (Left) and as a Brain Image (Right).

In this functional magnetic resonance image (fMRI; right) of a person experiencing fear, the amygdala is active.

Theprint/iStock/Getty Images

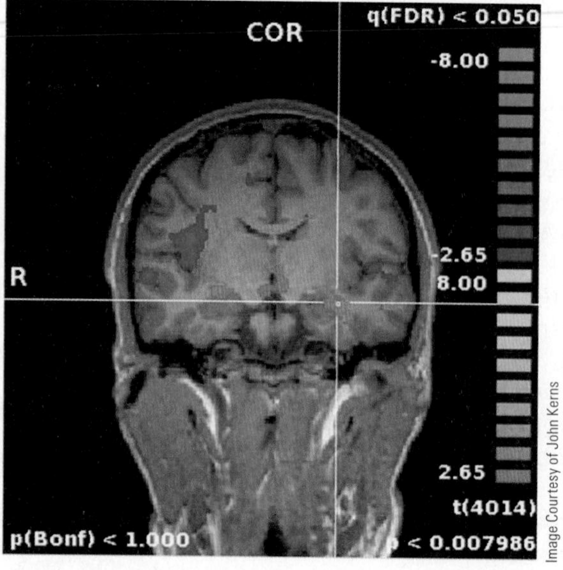

Image Courtesy of John Kerns

Neurochemical Features

Recall from Chapter 2 that neurotransmitters affect a person's mood and behavior, so it makes sense that people with anxiety-related disorders may have significant neurochemical changes. Neurotransmitters most closely linked to anxiety-related disorders include serotonin, norepinephrine, and gamma-aminobutyric acid (GABA; Garakani et al., 2021). Changes in these neurotransmitter and related systems, as with the brain features just discussed, may be partly the result of genetic influences.

Serotonin is closely related to mood and motor behavior. Changes in serotonin have been found in people with many anxiety-related disorders, especially panic, obsessive-compulsive, and generalized anxiety disorders (refer to **Figure 5.4**). Serotonin receptors may be particularly sensitive in people with these disorders, creating hyperactivity in different parts of the brain. Medications effective for people with anxiety-related disorders often help normalize serotonin activity in the brain to produce calm (Gosmann et al., 2021). Serotonin is also related to depression (Chapter 7), so changes in this neurotransmitter may help explain the high comorbidity between anxiety and depression.

Norepinephrine is related to excessive physical symptoms of anxiety, partly because the locus coeruleus is concentrated with norepinephrine receptors. This is especially pertinent to people with panic, phobic, and posttraumatic stress disorders. Some people with anxiety-related disorders may have poor regulation of norepinephrine, which can lead to sporadic bursts of activity and related physical symptoms, as in panic attacks. *GABA* helps inhibit nerve cells related to anxiety. This neurotransmitter may be deficient in people with anxiety-related disorders and thus contribute to excessive worry and panic symptoms (Masdrakis & Baldwin, 2021).

Figure 5.4 Serotonin Pathways of the Brain.

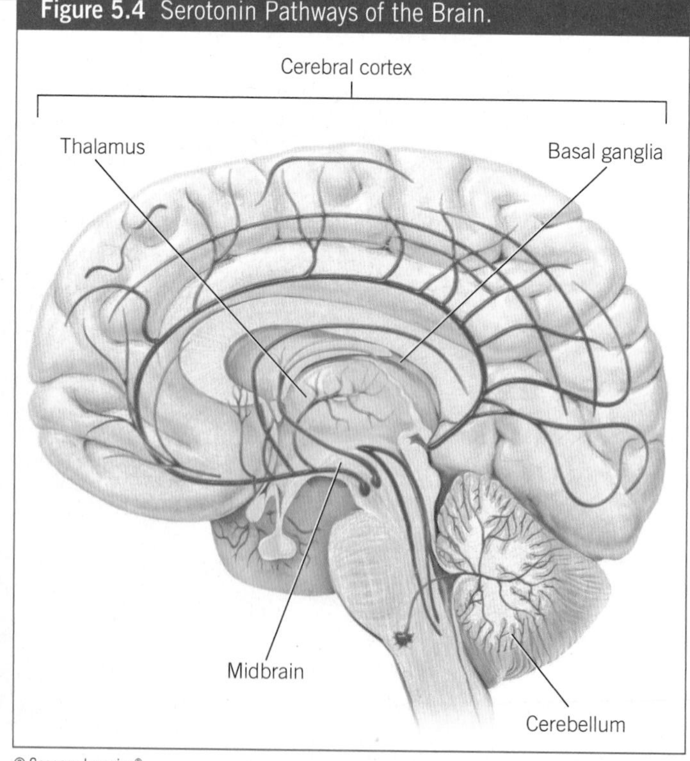

Another important neurochemical change in people with anxiety-related disorders involves the *hypothalamic-pituitary-adrenal* (HPA) system and a substance called *cortisol* (Chestnut et al., 2021). The HPA system is responsible for helping a person respond to stressful situations by releasing substances allowing the body to confront or flee a threatening stimulus (fight or flight). One such substance is cortisol, levels of which elevate when a person is faced with threat but that diminish over time as the threat fades. Your professor may administer a pop quiz causing you to become quite physically aroused as your cortisol level increases. Your cortisol level drops, however, as you become more calm and focus.

In some people with excess arousal and anxiety-related disorders, cortisol levels remain high *even when threat subsides*. They may thus be agitated, watchful of threat, or physically anxious for little reason (Harrewijn et al., 2020). This is not always the case, however; some people with posttraumatic stress disorder have *suppressed* levels of cortisol (Almeida et al., 2021). Research work continues to investigate exactly what role cortisol plays with respect to the cause of these disorders.

Behavioral Inhibition

Genetic contributions or brain features could also predispose someone for certain personality patterns, or temperaments, that have an impact on anxiety-related disorders. One such pattern is **behavioral inhibition**, or withdrawal from unfamiliar or new stimuli (Sandstrom et al., 2020). Perhaps 10 to 15 percent of people are born with behavioral inhibition, which comes in the form of irritability, shyness, fearfulness, overcautiousness, and physical feelings of anxiety. Toddlers and children with behavioral inhibition are subdued and react fearfully to new people or situations, often preferring to be close to their parents. Such behavior is normal for many young children, who eventually outgrow early shyness or fearfulness of new things, but behavioral inhibition in some youth is more stable across the lifespan (Tang et al., 2020).

People with behavioral inhibition seem to be at risk for anxiety-related disorders, which makes sense because many people with these disorders avoid new situations, stay close to home (like Angelina), or become nervous or worry about unfamiliar circumstances. Long-term studies reveal children with behavioral inhibition to be more likely than control participants to develop anxiety-related disorders, especially social anxiety disorder (Buzzell et al., 2021). However, not all people with anxiety-related disorders show behavioral inhibition. Factors such as a supportive family and social network likely protect some people from developing an anxiety-related disorder (Zimmermann et al., 2020). Other personality characteristics may also interact with behavioral inhibition to contribute to anxiety-related disorders, such as neuroticism or general distress, desire to avoid harm, and anxiety sensitivity (refer to later section; Barlow et al., 2021).

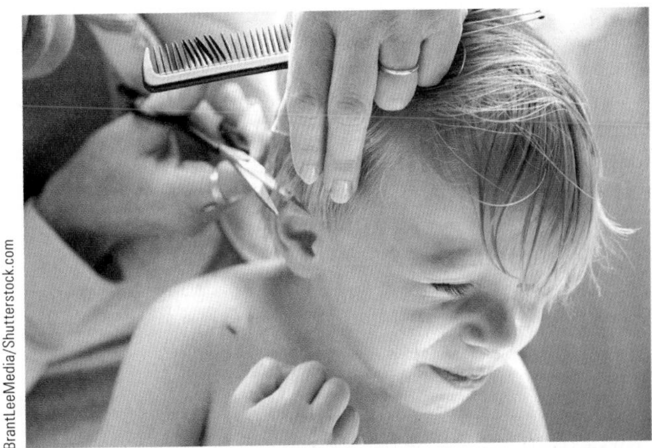

BrantLeeMedia/Shutterstock.com

Some children are naturally hesitant or even fearful in new situations, such as getting one's first haircut.

Evolutionary Influences

Evolutionary influences may also contribute to anxiety-related disorders. *Preparedness* is the idea that humans are biologically prepared to fear certain stimuli more than others. People of all cultures seem particularly afraid of snakes and spiders but rarely of trees and flowers. We may have realized as we evolved that snakes and spiders represent true threats to be avoided but that trees and flowers are rarely threatening. People today are thus more likely, or prepared, to develop a phobia of snakes or spiders than a phobia of trees or flowers (Frynta et al., 2021).

Evolutionary theories have also been proposed for other anxiety-related disorders. Social anxiety may help preserve social order by inducing people to conform to social standards, form clear hierarchies, and avoid conflict (Karasewich & Kuhlmeier, 2020). Compulsive behaviors such as checking, hoarding, or washing may have been historically adaptive when hunting and gathering food (Rajkumar, 2020). Fainting after a skin injury such as a needle injection may be an adaptive response to inescapable threat (Amoroso et al., 2020).

Environmental Risk Factors for Anxiety, Obsessive-Compulsive, and Trauma-Related Disorders

Environmental risk factors for anxiety-related disorders that may develop over a person's lifetime are discussed next. These include cognitive factors, anxiety sensitivity, family factors, learning experiences, and cultural factors.

Cognitive Factors

An environmental risk factor closely related to anxiety-related disorders is negative thought patterns, or **cognitive distortions**. People with anxiety-related disorders often have *ongoing* thoughts about potential or actual threat from external events. Recall that people with generalized anxiety disorder often scan their environment looking for threats or things to worry about. They generally perceive events in a *negative light* or look first at how they might be harmed. Angelina's concern that her professor might look at her was based on an assumption she would be called on, not know the answer to a question, and look foolish. Others with anxiety disorders experience *intolerance of uncertainty*, that is, fear of the unknown and a belief that uncertainty is threatening (Moriss et al., 2021).

Common cognitive distortions in people with anxiety-related disorders include jumping to conclusions, catastrophizing, and emotional reasoning (Mercan et al., 2021). Someone who *jumps to conclusions* assumes something bad will happen or has happened despite lack of evidence to support this assumption. A person may wrongly assume that speaking before a small group will result in a poor performance. Similarly, someone may assume terrible but incorrect consequences will result from an event—this is **catastrophizing**. A person who makes mistakes in a speech may thus wrongly assume they will lose their job. A person may also assume their physical feelings reflect how things truly are—this is **emotional reasoning**. People who are nervous speaking before others, and who have strong physical feelings of anxiety, may wrongly assume everyone can tell how nervous they are.

People with anxiety-related disorders also make errors in judgment about their skill. Many underestimate their level of social skill, believing they are less competent than others even when it is not true. People with anxiety-related disorders also tend to view social events negatively, believe their anxiety symptoms to be highly visible to others, and pay close attention to their own errors when interacting with others. A person at a party may feel they are being judged harshly by others, that others can easily perceive their nervousness or trembling, and that they are constantly making minor slips of the tongue. Most people dismiss minor errors when speaking to others, but people with anxiety-related disorders can perceive these errors as serious and self-defeating (Gilboa-Schechtman et al., 2020).

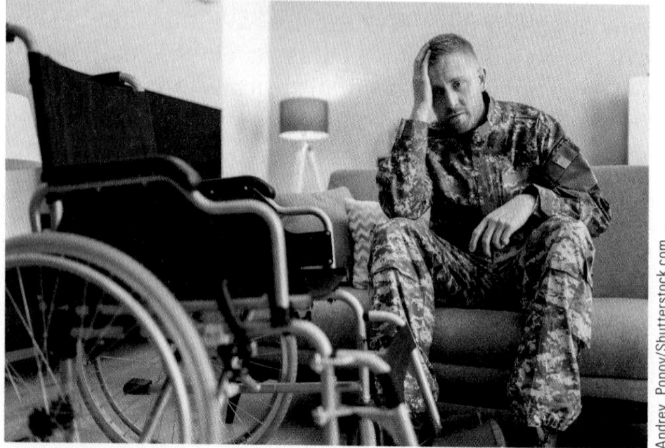

Trauma from events such as war or terrorism can cause posttraumatic stress disorder. PTSD makes it difficult to process traumatic events, even when threats of violence or harm are no longer present.

Andrey_Popov/Shutterstock.com

Many people with anxiety-related disorders think negatively and then avoid anxious situations. They subsequently feel better after avoiding these situations because their physical arousal goes away. This rewards their negative way of thinking and avoidance. People with generalized anxiety disorder may believe worrying helps prevent bad things from happening. Anxiety-related disorders are thus maintained over time. Angelina assumed terrible things would happen if she had a panic attack, avoided situations where a panic attack might occur, and felt relieved when those terrible things did not happen. Patterns like this keep many people from seeking treatment, and they kept Angelina from shopping, dating, and attending school.

People with obsessive-compulsive disorder have catastrophic beliefs about their own thoughts. Jonathan and others with obsessive-compulsive disorder are greatly troubled by their intrusive and spontaneous thoughts, feeling guilty or blaming themselves for having them. This may be tied to **thought–action fusion**, in which one believes thinking about something, such as hurting a baby, means they are a terrible person or that the terrible thing is more likely to happen (Lee et al., 2020). Many people with obsessive-compulsive disorder also view their thoughts as dangerous, and this increases physical arousal and triggers even more obsessions. People with the disorder also try to suppress their thoughts, but this only leads to more obsessions (Heapy et al., 2022). Try *not* to think about "blue dogs" for the next minute. What happens?

Cognitive theories of anxiety-related disorders also focus on **emotional processing**, or a person's ability to think about a past anxiety-provoking event without significant anxiety (McTeague et al., 2020). Think about a person once trapped in an elevator and intensely fearful. Good emotional processing means the person can later talk about the story, listen to others' accounts of being trapped in an elevator, or even ride elevators without anxiety. People with anxiety-related disorders, however, often have trouble processing difficult events. Poor emotional processing helps explain why many forms of anxiety are maintained for long periods of time even when no threat is present. This is especially relevant to people like Marcus with posttraumatic stress disorder. Marcus continued to experience reminders of the event in the form of nightmares and intrusive thoughts. He had not yet reached the point where he had fully processed or absorbed what had happened and was therefore still unable to function well on a daily basis.

Anxiety Sensitivity

Related to cognitive distortions is the erroneous belief that internal physical sensations are dangerous. Many of us are naturally concerned about our health, but some people become extremely worried about even minor physical changes. **Anxiety sensitivity** is a fear of the potential dangerousness of internal sensations (Warren et al., 2021). A person may experience a minor change in heart rate and excessively worry they are having a heart attack. Recall that Angelina went to an emergency room doctor and a cardiologist because she felt her symptoms were dangerous. Symptoms of panic are not actually dangerous, but many people wrongly think the symptoms mean a serious medical condition, insanity, loss of control, or imminent death.

Children and adults with anxiety symptoms and anxiety-related disorders, especially those with panic attacks and panic disorder, often show high levels of anxiety sensitivity (Zahler et al., 2020). This makes sense when you consider that people with panic attacks often fear another panic attack and thus more negative physical symptoms and consequences. Anxiety sensitivity may be a characteristic learned over time, or it might be a type of temperament that is present early in life and related to certain biological predispositions.

Family Factors

Family-based contributions to anxiety-related disorders are also important. Parents of anxious children may be overcontrolling, affectionless, overprotective, rejecting, and demanding. Rejecting parents could trigger a child's worry about being left alone or anxiety about handling threats from others without help. Overprotective or controlling parents may restrict a child's access to friends or other social situations or prematurely rescue a child from an anxious situation, thus rewarding anxiety. Parents of anxious children may also encourage avoidance in their children and discourage prosocial behaviors ("OK, you don't have to go to that birthday party"). Such parents also tend to avoid or withdraw from various situations themselves (Creswell et al., 2020).

Parents of anxious children may also overemphasize opinions of, and negative evaluations from, others. Families of anxious children tend to be isolated or unstable and avoid many social situations. Parents may also serve as a model for their child's anxiety (Wang et al., 2020). A parent with panic disorder may avoid anxious situations, appear physically nervous, attend closely to internal sensations, or withdraw from chores after having an attack. Some children may view these behaviors as ways of coping with anxious situations and do the same. Another important family variable involves insecure or anxious attachment patterns, which commonly occur in children with anxiety-related disorders (Elling et al., 2022). Childhood maltreatment is another key risk factor for anxiety-related disorders and especially for posttraumatic stress disorder (Sistad et al., 2021).

How might these parent/family experiences interact to produce an anxiety-related disorder? Parental practices, modeling, and insecure attachment could lead to reduced opportunities for a child to practice anxiety management skills in different social and evaluative situations. A child's demands for close physical proximity to a parent may be frequently rewarded, and a child and parent may have an overdependent relationship that prevents effective separation. Factors such as maltreatment can cause physical brain changes that lead to an anxiety-related disorder as well.

Learning Experiences

Excessive fear can also be a learned response. Modeling parent behavior is one learned pathway, but children can also become fearful through *direct learning* or *information transfer* (Meulders, 2020). Direct learning may involve *classical conditioning* and *operant conditioning*. Classical conditioning is derived from Ivan Pavlov's famous experiment in which he saw dogs instinctively salivate at the sight and smell of food (refer to **Figure 5.5**). Food is an *unconditioned stimulus*, and salivation is an *unconditioned response* because no learning occurs—the salivation is automatic. Pavlov then associated the

Figure 5.5 Classical Conditioning Model of Fear.

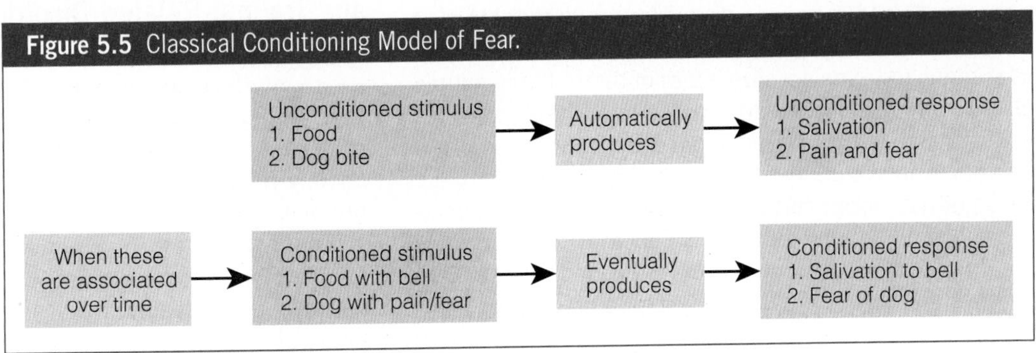

food/unconditioned stimulus with a ringing bell and conditioned his dogs to eventually salivate to the bell. The food/unconditioned stimulus became associated with the bell, a *conditioned* (or learned) *stimulus*. Repeated pairings or associations of the food and bell then produced a situation where the conditioned stimulus (bell) produced a *conditioned response,* in this case salivation.

Such a process can also occur for the development of fears. Think about someone who walks through a park and is bitten by a vicious dog. The bite is an unconditioned stimulus because it immediately causes pain and fear or an unconditioned response—no learning is necessary. If negative experiences with a dog happened repeatedly, then any exposure to a dog (now a conditioned stimulus) would result in fear of that dog (now a conditioned response). This fear may then become *generalized,* as when a person becomes afraid of many dogs, even those that have not bitten them. Such a model is often used to explain phobias, but many intense panic attacks also occur following stressful life events (Scheer et al., 2020).

Direct learning of fears may also involve operant conditioning, or subsequent rewards for fearful behavior. Parents often reinforce certain apprehensions in their children, such as wariness around strangers. Too much reinforcement in this area could lead to a situation in which a child rarely interacts with other peers or adults and then does not develop good social or communication skills. Social anxiety may thus result when the child later tries to interact with others but does so in an awkward way that leads to social rejection and further social anxiety (Chiu et al., 2021).

Fears are also reinforced by avoidance. If you are nervous about an upcoming dental appointment, then you might cancel it. The feeling of relief you then experience is quite rewarding and may motivate you to cancel more appointments in the future. Some fears develop from classical *and* operant conditioning. A person bitten by a dog may associate dogs with pain and fear and then avoid dogs for the rest of their life. The fear thus remains even though no additional trauma is taking place (Fullana et al., 2020).

Another factor in fear development is information transfer. A child may hear stories from other children or adults about the dangerousness of certain stimuli such as spiders and thus develop a fear of them. Many people also seem predisposed to fear certain things such as spiders, snakes, strangers, separation from loved ones, heights, and water. We may have developed an innate sense of fear about certain things that could harm us as we evolved. This is sometimes called a *nonassociative theory of fear* because no trauma is needed for someone to show the fear (Burdakov & Peleg-Raibstein, 2020).

Learning experiences may also lead a person to develop a sense of *lack of control* over, or sense of *unpredictability* about, life events (Kan et al., 2021). Difficulties at school and subsequent avoidance of evaluative situations there could lead a person to excessively worry about their competence and place in the surrounding world. Children maltreated by their parents have difficulty knowing who they can trust and may develop a sense of lack of control about their environment. Marcus experienced a severe threat to his safety and later felt a sense of unpredictability regarding future threats.

Cultural Factors

Recall that many anxiety-related disorders are present worldwide and often come in different forms across cultures. Still, ethnic groups may be more susceptible to certain kinds of anxiety-related disorders because of where they live and because of difficult conditions they experience. African Americans, for example, tend to have higher rates of posttraumatic stress disorder than other groups, which may be related to negative life events associated with overpolicing and community violence (Lewis & Wu, 2021). In addition, Hispanic college students who experience racial/ethnic discrimination are at risk for posttraumatic stress symptoms and maladaptive alcohol use (López et al., 2022).

Posttraumatic stress and other anxiety-related disorders in people around the world have also been linked to mass trauma. People exposed to earthquakes, volcanic eruptions, typhoons, and other natural disasters commonly develop symptoms of posttraumatic stress and depression (Bountress et al., 2020). Other examples include soldiers in wartime, refugees, and torture survivors. Many people with anxiety-related disorders in various cultures also show different kinds of anxiety symptoms, often in the form of physical symptoms. Cambodian refugees have common panic-like symptoms that include feelings of paralysis during and after sleep and images of a being approaching them in the night (Hinton et al., 2020). These findings confirm that clinicians must be sensitive to cultural issues when conducting assessment and treatment.

Causes of Anxiety, Obsessive-Compulsive, and Trauma-Related Disorders

How might the many risk factors discussed here interact to produce an anxiety-related disorder? Researchers emphasize integrative, diathesis-stress models or pathways to help explain the cause of different anxiety-related disorders (Mumper et al., 2020). These theorists believe certain people are born with *biological vulnerabilities* to experience high anxiety. Some people have genetic predispositions or various brain or neurochemical features that cause them to feel highly physically aroused and upset when negative life events occur. Others may have certain temperaments, such as behavioral inhibition, that predispose them to anxiety-related disorders as well.

People also develop a *psychological vulnerability* toward anxiety-related disorders. Some people continue to have anxiety-provoking thoughts, family experiences that reinforce anxious behavior, and anxiety-related learning experiences. Some people may also feel they lack control over many situations in their lives. Still others could experience anxiety-provoking trauma in the form of maltreatment, surrounding threats, or exposure to violent attacks or natural disasters.

One possible developmental pathway to social anxiety disorder in youth is illustrated in **Figure 5.6**. Some youth are clearly born with predispositions toward overarousal and behavioral inhibition, demonstrating fear and excitability, particularly in new situations. These predispositions may be the result of genetics and key brain and neurochemical features. These youngsters may be raised by parents who are themselves predisposed toward anxious and avoidant behavior. The early child–parent relationship could thus be marked by poor attachment and problematic social interactions. Toddlers may isolate themselves from others by playing alone or be subject to social isolation from nervous parents. Parents may be unwilling to expose the child to birthday parties, play dates, or preschool.

If a toddler remains socially isolated and if their social interactions with parents are problematic, this could set the stage for later difficulties. The child may imitate the parents' behaviors of avoiding or withdrawing from different situations; this leaves the child with few opportunities to build social skills and receive appropriate feedback from others. The child will also fail to control social anxiety or develop good coping skills in different situations. Children not in preschool or surrounded by peers, or those neglected or otherwise maltreated, might be more at risk for such outcomes.

As these children age and enter elementary and middle school, many academic, athletic, and social demands are placed on them. Youth are expected to cooperate with others on school projects, play on teams, and develop friendships. Unfortunately, children already predisposed to social anxiety and who have had early isolation and poor skill development may experience rejection from others. Such rejection could lead to other consequences such as increased anxiety in social and evaluative situations, thoughts that interactions with others and anxiety symptoms are dangerous, increased avoidance of others, limited social skill development, and worry about future social and evaluative situations. As these youth enter high school, their patterns of social anxiety and avoidance may become ingrained, and they may meet diagnostic criteria for social anxiety disorder.

Other anxiety-related disorders also likely involve a blend of biological and psychological vulnerabilities. Some people with panic disorder have naturally elevated physical arousal and easily get upset or worried about stressful life events like starting school (biological vulnerability). This stress may lead to an unexpected panic attack, as it did for Angelina. Most people who have a panic attack dismiss the event as merely unpleasant but some, like Angelina, feel the panic attack is uncontrollable and will cause terrible things like a car accident (psychological vulnerability). They then fear another panic attack and avoid situations in which attacks may occur. A person might also monitor their internal sensations such as heart rate to determine if a panic attack is about to happen. Of course, doing so will increase physical arousal, likely trigger another panic attack, and increase worry that even more will occur. The person is thus always

Figure 5.6 Sample Developmental Pathway of Social Anxiety Disorder.

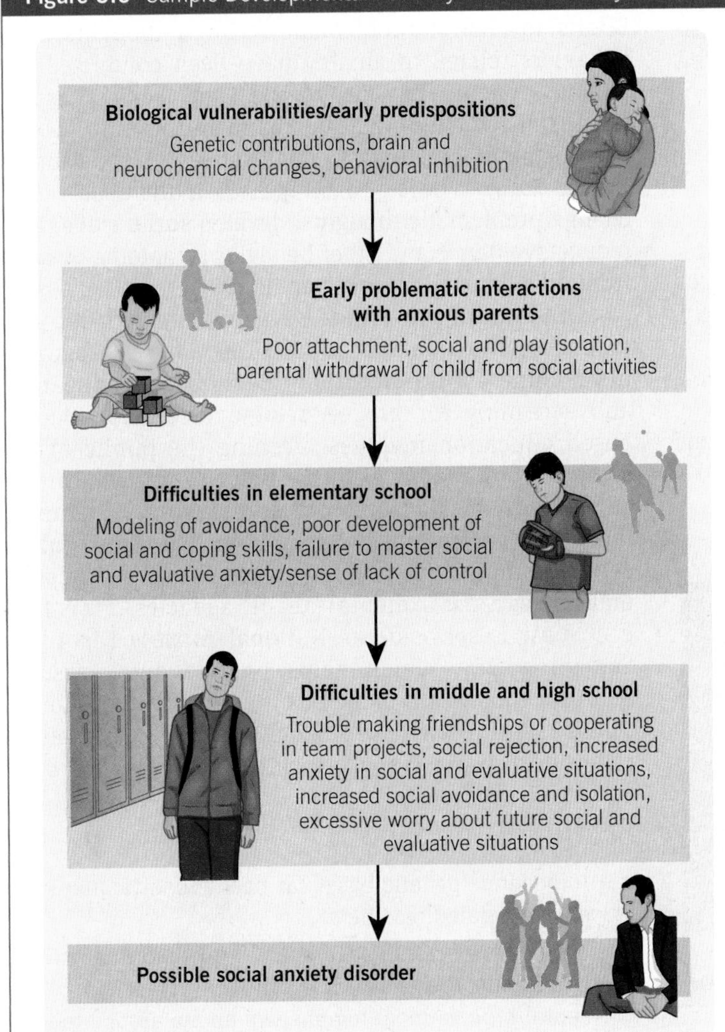

worrying about having a panic attack or actually *having* a panic attack. Such was the case for Angelina.

Other anxiety-related disorders involve more specific causal factors. People with specific phobias may have had a direct traumatic experience, such as a dog bite, that caused intense fear. People with posttraumatic stress disorder must, by definition, have experienced a traumatic event for the disorder to occur. The presence of trauma and later recollections of the trauma likely converge with one's belief that these events are uncontrollable. The person may continue to experience high levels of physical arousal (just like during the trauma) and scan the environment looking for threats or reminders of the trauma. Unwanted thoughts about the trauma can also continue.

People with generalized anxiety disorder, a largely cognitive condition, may believe negative life events will happen frequently, suddenly, and uncontrollably. A person may even look for threats when they are not there. Worry about minor life events may be reinforced because it lowers physical arousal and keeps someone from thinking about more serious emotional or fearful issues. A person with obsessive-compulsive disorder may also believe their thoughts are dangerous. All anxiety-related disorders, however, involve an intricate combination of different biological and psychological vulnerabilities.

Prevention of Anxiety, Obsessive-Compulsive, and Trauma-Related Disorders

Given what we know about risk factors and cause of anxiety-related disorders, what could be done to prevent them? Many fears and anxiety-related disorders begin in adolescence or early adulthood, so thinking of prevention during childhood and adolescence makes sense. Researchers have identified several goals that might be important for prevention. These goals center on building a child's ability to control situations that might lead to anxiety.

Photo and Co/The Image Bank/Getty Images

Children have to be taught the difference between dangerous and nondangerous situations. This mother is showing her children how to safely cross a street.

Children could be taught the difference between dangerous and nondangerous situations and learn which situations should definitely be avoided, such as being in the middle of the street. Children could also be taught strategies to address potentially threatening situations such as bullies, busy roads, and swimming pools. Rules about safety, talking to a teacher, and being with friends could be covered. Children could also be taught social and coping skills necessary when unfortunate events do occur. Youth may be taught how to cope with being turned down for a date, failing a test, or being cut from a team. The general idea is to teach children to successfully handle stressful situations and not resort to avoidance or feelings of loss of control. Other aspects of prevention that might be important include changing negative thoughts, having parents model good ways of handling stress, improving parent attitudes toward their children, reducing parent anxiety, curtailing actual harmful situations, and identifying and providing therapy for children with anxious parents (Hugh-Jones et al., 2021).

Anxiety prevention strategies also apply to adults. Efforts to change problematic feelings, thoughts, and behaviors related to anxiety have been conducted for anxious college students, physical and sexual assault victims, those with public-speaking anxiety, and people with agoraphobia or stressful lifestyles (Mendelson & Eaton, 2018). These programs help individuals relax, change problematic thoughts, develop social skills, and reduce avoidance and other behavior symptoms by confronting whatever provokes anxiety.

Other adult prevention programs are broader and focus on the general population. These programs have come in the form of media-based education and screening for anxiety-related disorders. Media-based education involves teaching the public about symptoms of anxiety and that these symptoms can be successfully treated before they get worse. Examples include telephone information lines, websites, public service announcements, printed materials, and cooperation with local mental health agencies. May 1 of each year is set aside as National Anxiety Disorders Screening Day, which helps provide quick assessment for those with panic or other anxiety symptoms. Those identified with problematic anxiety can then be referred for professional treatment.

Section Summary

- A moderate genetic basis has been found for many anxiety-related disorders.
- Several brain areas have been implicated in anxiety-related disorders, especially the amygdala and septal-hippocampal regions, which are associated with physical arousal, emotion, and memories surrounding fearful and anxiety-provoking stimuli.

- Other brain areas are specific to certain anxiety-related disorders, such as the anterior cingulate in obsessive-compulsive disorder and the locus coeruleus in panic disorder.
- Neurotransmitters most implicated in anxiety-related disorders include serotonin, norepinephrine, and gamma-aminobutyric acid (GABA).
- People with behavioral inhibition—a temperamental pattern of irritability, shyness, fearfulness, overcautiousness, and physical feelings of anxiety—seem predisposed to disorders such as social anxiety disorder.
- Anxiety may be influenced by evolutionary processes in that some avoidance behaviors seem adaptive in certain contexts.
- Cognitive risk factors include distorted thinking about the dangerousness of various stimuli as well as assumptions that something bad will happen or that others can easily notice one's anxiety.
- Anxiety sensitivity refers to fear of the potential dangerousness of one's own internal sensations such as dizziness and increased heart rate.
- Family factors may contribute to anxiety-related disorders, especially overcontrolling, affectionless, overprotective, rejecting, and demanding parents.
- People can learn aspects of fear and anxiety through direct experience, information transfer, or reinforcement for fear of strangers or other stimuli.
- Cultural factors influence the development of anxiety-related disorders, particularly in people more commonly exposed to traumas.
- Biological and environmental risk factors can make a person vulnerable to anxiety-related disorder.
- Preventing an anxiety-related disorder involves building ability to control situations that might lead to anxiety, education about dangerous and nondangerous situations, changing negative thoughts, coping better with stress, and practicing skills in real-life situations.

Review Questions

1. Describe data that support a genetic contribution to anxiety-related disorders.
2. What key brain and neurochemical features may be related to anxiety-related disorders? What temperamental characteristic occurs early in life and may predict anxiety-related disorders? How so?
3. What are some cognitive distortions associated with anxiety-related disorders, and what is anxiety sensitivity?
4. How might family factors, learning experiences, and cultural backgrounds help cause anxiety-related disorders?
5. Describe an overall causal model for anxiety-related disorders.
6. What factors might be important for a program to prevent anxiety-related disorders?

Anxiety, Obsessive-Compulsive, and Trauma-Related Disorders: Assessment and Treatment

LO 5.9 Characterize the assessment of individuals with anxiety, obsessive-compulsive, and trauma-related disorders.

LO 5.10 Evaluate approaches to the treatment of individuals with anxiety, obsessive-compulsive, and trauma-related disorders.

Assessment and treatment methods most relevant to people with anxiety-related disorders are covered next. Assessment and treatment methods are discussed in general because most of these strategies apply to each anxiety-related disorder. However, tables are also provided that contain treatment information specific to each major anxiety-related disorder. The assessment and treatment methods discussed next are extremely important for people with overwhelming anxiety (refer to **Personal Narrative: Anonymous**) as well as other problems discussed in this textbook.

Assessment of Anxiety, Obsessive-Compulsive, and Trauma-Related Disorders

Recall from Chapter 4 that mental health professionals use various methods to evaluate people. The primary methods to evaluate or assess people with anxiety-related disorders include interviews, self-report questionnaires, self-monitoring and observations from others, and psychophysiological assessment.

Interviews

What would you be curious to know about Angelina, Jonathan, and Marcus? Mental health professionals who treat people with anxiety-related disorders are often curious about thoughts and physical feelings, daily activities and avoidance, targets of anxiety and fear, and long-term goals. This information is important for knowing how to treat someone with an anxiety-related disorder because specific client characteristics can be identified and addressed. Angelina's therapist was able to uncover some interesting information about what exactly happens during her panic attack while driving:

Therapist: What kinds of thoughts do you have when driving?

Angelina: I think I'm going to crash the car because it keeps swerving in the lane.

Therapist: What do you usually think and do next?

Angelina: I focus a lot on my symptoms, like my heart racing or dizziness, and try to look around fast to see where I can pull the car over . . . I think I'm going to smash into someone because I'm not being too careful.

Therapist: Are you able to get the car over to the shoulder?

Angelina: Yes, I've never had an accident, but you never know, the next time could be the time I really hurt someone!

Many therapists prefer unstructured interviews, but structured interviews usually rely on diagnostic criteria and contain a list of questions a therapist asks each client with a possible mental disorder. A common interview for people with anxiety-related disorders is the *Anxiety Disorders Interview Schedule* (ADIS-5; Brown & Barlow, 2013). This interview is primarily useful for evaluating anxiety disorders, but other disorders can be assessed as well.

Self-Report Questionnaires

Anxiety-related disorders consist of many internal symptoms such as increased heart rate or negative

Personal Narrative

Anonymous

From as far back as I can remember, my life had been disrupted by mental disorder. As a child and through adolescence, obsessions and compulsions wreaked havoc on my brain and my life. I used to have irrational fears of catching fatal illnesses or getting abducted by aliens.

The obsessions could be best described as chaos occurring in my head. Any thought I had was accompanied with that current obsession. There was no complete joy in any activity, because at no point was my day free from anxiety. I became a prisoner of my own brain. Furthermore, I would complete certain rituals, such as adding numbers in my head, or placing items in my pockets in the exact same order every day; if I didn't do this, I feared something bad would happen.

As time went on, these obsessions and compulsions occurred periodically in my life, lasting for a few weeks or a few months at a time. During my last few years of high school and freshmen year of college, the obsessions subsided and were at worst mild and short-lived. However, they reared their ugly head my sophomore year in college, and it was at this point that I knew I had a mental disorder; I realized a neurotypical brain wouldn't function this way. I knew these fears and thoughts were completely irrational, but I couldn't help them.

I began to seek help during the summer; by that time the obsessions had ceased, but a horrible feeling came over me as I drove to school for that fall semester. That feeling I felt, which progressively got worse throughout the semester, was depression. It's a feeling that sucks the life out of you.

I finally saw a psychiatrist in the fall, and he prescribed me psychotropic medication. The depression began to ease for a while, but when the winter came, depression reclaimed my entire body. I spent months in the dark cloud of depression. I couldn't sleep, couldn't eat and after a while, questioned how I could live like this much longer. I saw my doctor more frequently during this time period, and after a while, we were able to work out the proper medications that were able to completely alleviate my symptoms.

From that moment on, every day has been a gift to be alive. Now to say that every day from then on has been the best day of my life would be a lie. However, I was almost dead; I now have a new lease on life and I appreciate all things in life to a greater degree.

Besides my new lease on life, this experience also had another powerful effect on me. From then on I decided to be an advocate for mental health. I had formed a chapter of the National Alliance on Mental Illness (NAMI) at my school. In overcoming this past experience, I felt as if I had been to the gates of hell and back, and now it was time to use my experience to make sure no one goes to those gates, at least not alone.

In my eyes I've always viewed it as an obligation to speak about my disorder and help others. God blessed me with numerous gifts to help me become a successful student and person. I knew that if I told others I dealt with depression and anxiety, they would be completely shocked. I was also pretty certain that the people who knew me wouldn't view me any differently. Therefore, I felt that I wouldn't face much stigma. It still wasn't the easiest step to take. I want to assure people they can be successful and break down the stigma every chance I get, and most importantly making sure no one feels as I did on those desolate earlier days.

The stigma of mental disorder causes problems in many aspects of society. People don't want to receive treatment due to the perceived notion of being embarrassed, or fear of the unknown. This hurts the economy, the health care system, education, and, most importantly, people's individual lives. To eliminate this stigma, those in the mental health field must work tirelessly against this prejudice. Those with a mental disorder should not be ashamed of their disorder; some of the smartest and most creative people in the world had a mental disorder. As more people step out of the seclusion caused by stigma, the stigma itself will disappear. People will realize how commonplace mental disorder is in this society, how real of a medical condition it is, and how to treat it effectively.

Source: Used with permission.

thoughts, so clients are often asked to rate symptoms on questionnaires. The *Anxiety Sensitivity Index—3* evaluates fear of the dangerousness of one's internal sensations, a key aspect of panic disorder. Selected items from this scale are in **Table 5.12** (Ebesutani et al., 2014; Taylor et al., 2007). Other commonly used questionnaires for people with anxiety-related disorders are in **Table 5.13**.

Self-Monitoring and Observations from Others

People with anxiety-related disorders are often asked to monitor and keep a record of their symptoms on a daily basis (Melbye et al., 2020). This serves several purposes. First, monitoring symptoms every day cuts down on having to remember what happened the previous week, such as what happened during a certain episode of worry, and helps provide material for discussion in a therapy session. Second, monitoring increases a person's self-awareness of the frequency, intensity, and change in anxiety symptoms over time, such as panic attacks. Third, monitoring helps keep a person focused on a task such as exposure to anxiety instead of distracting or avoiding. Others who know the client well may also provide information about anxiety symptoms such as avoidance. This applies especially to parents regarding their children.

Anxious clients are usually asked to record episodes of panic attacks and/or specific physical symptoms, thoughts, and behaviors (Ebenfeld et al., 2020). Angelina's therapist asked her to track her panic attacks, list her thoughts during and after each attack, and rate her symptoms of accelerated heart rate and trouble breathing.

Behavioral avoidance tests may also be done to determine how close someone with an anxiety-related disorder can get to a feared situation or object (Hamm, 2020). Marcus's therapist accompanied him as he drove near the spot he was attacked, but Marcus did not get very far before stopping.

Psychophysiological Assessment

Psychophysiological assessment is sometimes done to measure severity of physical symptoms in people with anxiety-related disorders. Common measures include heart rate, blood pressure, and respiration, but more sophisticated measures may be used in research settings. These include skin conductance and resistance, electromyogram (for muscle tension), and measures of vasomotor activity. In *skin conductance,* electrodes are placed on a person's fingertip and wrist and a small, nonpainful electrical current is introduced to one electrode. A computer measures the time the current takes to travel from one electrode to another. An anxious person may have more active sweat glands and thus conduct the electricity faster than a nonanxious person (Gold et al., 2022). Some researchers also use *biological challenge procedures* during assessment. These procedures may involve inducing panic-like symptoms (e.g., increased heart rate) using a certain agent such as carbon dioxide to safely assess how a person typically responds to anxious symptoms (Lapidus et al., 2020). Psychophysiological assessment may reveal rich information about a client, but it is costly and time-intensive. This kind of assessment is most often seen in research or medical settings.

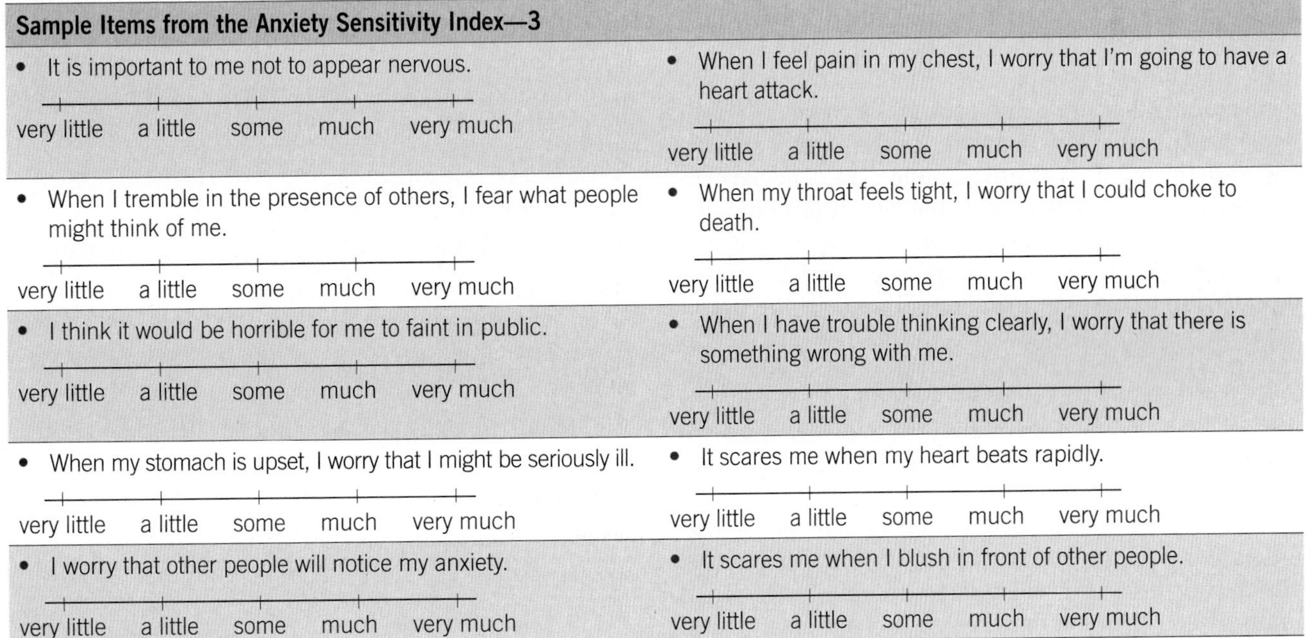

Table 5.12

Sample Items from the Anxiety Sensitivity Index—3	
• It is important to me not to appear nervous. very little — a little — some — much — very much	• When I feel pain in my chest, I worry that I'm going to have a heart attack. very little — a little — some — much — very much
• When I tremble in the presence of others, I fear what people might think of me. very little — a little — some — much — very much	• When my throat feels tight, I worry that I could choke to death. very little — a little — some — much — very much
• I think it would be horrible for me to faint in public. very little — a little — some — much — very much	• When I have trouble thinking clearly, I worry that there is something wrong with me. very little — a little — some — much — very much
• When my stomach is upset, I worry that I might be seriously ill. very little — a little — some — much — very much	• It scares me when my heart beats rapidly. very little — a little — some — much — very much
• I worry that other people will notice my anxiety. very little — a little — some — much — very much	• It scares me when I blush in front of other people. very little — a little — some — much — very much

Table 5.13 Common Questionnaires for Assessing Anxiety-Related Disorders

Questionnaire	What does it assess?
Beck Anxiety Inventory	General symptoms of anxiety
Children's Manifest Anxiety Scale	Worry, oversensitivity, concentration problems, and physical feelings of anxiety
Fear Questionnaire	Avoidance due to agoraphobia, blood injury phobia, or social anxiety disorder
Fear Survey Schedule for Children—Revised	Fears of failure and criticism, the unknown, injury and small animals, danger and death, and medical procedures
Impact of Event Scale	Hyperarousal, reexperiencing, and avoidance/numbing symptoms of posttraumatic stress disorder
Maudsley Obsessional-Compulsive Inventory	Checking, washing, doubting, and slowness/repetition
Mobility Inventory	Agoraphobia-related avoidance behavior
Multidimensional Anxiety Scale for Children—2	Harm avoidance and physical, separation, and social anxiety
Panic and Agoraphobia Scale	Severity, frequency, and duration of panic attacks and avoidance
Penn State Worry Questionnaire	Intensity and excessiveness of worry
Social Anxiety Scale for Children—Revised	Fear of negative evaluation, social avoidance and distress, and generalized social distress
Social Interaction Anxiety Scale	Anxiety about interpersonal interactions
Social Phobia and Anxiety Inventory	Physical, cognitive, and behavioral components to social anxiety
State-Trait Anxiety Inventory	Anxiety symptoms at this moment and anxiety symptoms felt much of the time
Symptom Checklist 90-R Crime-Related PTSD Scale	Symptoms of posttraumatic stress disorder

Biological Treatment of Anxiety, Obsessive-Compulsive, and Trauma-Related Disorders

Recall that anxiety consists of three components: physical feelings, thoughts, and behaviors. Treating anxiety-related disorders may thus involve biological interventions, or medications, to quell physical feelings and enhance approach behaviors. Antianxiety medication is a leading method of treating people with anxiety-related disorders. Some of the most common antianxiety medications are in **Table 5.14**. One particular class of antianxiety drug is the *benzodiazepines,* or drugs that produce a sedating effect. Recall that one risk factor for anxiety-related disorder may be excess neurochemical activity in different areas of the brain. Benzodiazepines help modify this excess activity to make a person feel more calm. These drugs may also enhance the GABA system of the brain to produce a more inhibiting effect on anxiety. Benzodiazepines are often used to treat people with panic disorder (Piccoli et al., 2021).

Another major class of drugs for anxiety-related disorders is the *antidepressants* (refer also to Chapter 7), specifically, drugs that moderate serotonin levels in the brain. Recall that serotonin levels are not always well regulated in people with anxiety-related disorders, so antidepressants sometimes help provide this regulation. Antidepressant drugs are often used to treat people with

Table 5.14 Common Medications for People with Anxiety-Related Disorders

Benzodiazepines
• Alprazolam (Xanax)
• Lorazepam (Ativan)
• Clonazepam (Klonopin)
• Diazepam (Valium)
• Chlordiazepoxide (Librium)
• Temazepam (Restoril)
• Oxazepam (Serax)
Antidepressants
• Fluoxetine (Prozac)
• Paroxetine (Paxil)
• Sertraline (Zoloft)
• Fluvoxamine (Luvox)
• Citalopram (Celexa)
• Escitalopram oxalate (Lexapro)

social and generalized anxiety and obsessive-compulsive and posttraumatic stress disorders (Van Leeuwen et al., 2021).

Drug treatment is effective for 60 to 80 percent of adults with anxiety-related disorders but less so for people with severe, long-term anxiety comorbid with other mental disorders. Relapse rates can also be high when a person stops taking the drug (Garakani et al., 2020). Medication side effects can be unpleasant as well. Possible side effects of benzodiazepines include motor and memory problems, fatigue, depression, and irritability and hostility. Possible side effects of antidepressants include nausea, drowsiness, dizziness, and sexual dysfunction (Ribeiro & Schlindwein, 2021). Antidepressants have not been found to be addictive, but their sudden discontinuation can lead to unpleasant physical symptoms. People who use benzodiazepines, however, can become dependent on the drugs (Lee et al., 2021).

Psychological Treatments of Anxiety, Obsessive-Compulsive, and Trauma-Related Disorders

Psychological interventions have also been designed to address each of the three anxiety components—physical feelings, thoughts, and behaviors. You will learn in this textbook that many of these interventions are similar to those described for other disorders. *Transdiagnostic treatments* are those that can be used for people with various problems, especially those related to anxiety and depression (Chapter 7; Carlucci et al., 2021). In addition, many of these interventions are now being conducted not just in person but via the Internet or apps as well.

Psychoeducation and Somatic Control Exercises

Many anxiety-related disorders involve uncomfortable levels of physical arousal. Such arousal can come in the form of increased heart rate, dizziness, short breath, hot flashes, and other symptoms. People with generalized anxiety disorder can also have severe muscle tension. Physical feelings of anxiety can trigger unpleasant thoughts and then avoidance, so an important first step of treatment is to educate a person about the three components of anxiety and how these components relate to them. This process is **psychoeducation**. Examples are in **Table 5.15**.

Angelina's therapist knew her client often had unpleasant and intense physical symptoms during her panic attacks. These symptoms then led to worries about harm from a panic attack and avoidance of places where an attack could occur. Teaching people with anxiety-related disorders about their symptoms and about how their physical feelings, thoughts, and behaviors influence each other is important to develop a good treatment plan, to ease concerns about the disorder, to emphasize that many people have these symptoms, and to convey that the symptoms can be successfully treated. Clients are sometimes taught **somatic control exercises** to address physical feelings of anxiety.

Table 5.15 Psychoeducation and Somatic Control Exercise Examples for People with Anxiety-Related Disorders

Disorder	Psychoeducation example	Somatic control exercise example
Panic disorder	Education about typical panic attack symptoms and a person's sequence of physical feelings to thoughts to behaviors	Correct breathing and muscle relaxation during a panic attack
Social anxiety disorder	Education about common worries and avoidance associated with social and evaluative anxiety	Muscle relaxation during a public speaking assignment
Specific phobia	Education about the irrational and excessive nature of fear and how avoidance interferes with quality of life	Correct breathing and muscle relaxation during exposure to a feared stimulus such as a dog
Generalized anxiety disorder	Education about excessive, uncontrollable worry and difficulty sleeping and other physical consequences	Muscle relaxation before bedtime to ease transition to sleep
Obsessive-compulsive disorder	Education about the nature and content of key thoughts (obsessions) and how they can lead to specific behaviors (compulsions)	Muscle relaxation following getting one's hand dirty
Posttraumatic stress disorder	Education about how one's trauma has led to symptoms of reexperiencing, physical arousal, and avoidance of certain places	Correct breathing during a trip near where the trauma occurred
Separation anxiety disorder	Education to parents and children about worries regarding harm befalling a parent or the child	Muscle relaxation upon having to enter school without parents

Somatic control exercises help clients manage physical arousal so it is less strong and threatening. Common somatic control exercises include relaxation training and breathing retraining (Table 5.15 has examples for each anxiety-related disorder).

In **relaxation training**, a person is taught to tense and release different muscle groups to diffuse tension (Bandealy et al., 2021). The therapist may ask a person to sit in a comfortable chair, close their eyes, make a fist, and hold tightly for 10 seconds. The person then releases the fist quickly and repeats the process (try it). This is done for other muscle groups as well, such as those in the shoulders, face, stomach, and legs. The therapist encourages the client to attend to the difference between a tense muscle and a relaxed one.

Another procedure to reduce physical feelings of anxiety is **breathing retraining** (Efron et al., 2021). This procedure involves having a person change their breathing during anxious times to include long, deep breaths in through the nose and out through the mouth. The person is encouraged to feel the breaths in the diaphragm (diaphragmatic breathing) by holding their fingers below their stomach. Breaths should be slow, deep, and regular (try it a few times). One advantage of this strategy is that a person can use it in public situations without drawing much attention.

Cognitive Therapy

Recall that another aspect of anxiety-related disorder is negative thoughts. Angelina was concerned a panic attack might cause extensive harm to her or others. Therapists often use **cognitive therapy** to change these negative thought patterns. Cognitive therapy involves examining negative statements a person may be making and encouraging the person to challenge the thought (Van Dis et al., 2020). Cognitive therapy helps people change their way of reasoning about the environment, think more realistically, and learn the positive side of things as well as the negative. Examples of cognitive therapy for different anxiety-related disorders are in **Table 5.16**.

Recall that many people with anxiety-related disorders engage in cognitive distortions such as catastrophizing, or incorrectly assuming terrible things will happen from a certain event. Angelina catastrophized by assuming she would lose control or harm herself or others during a panic attack. A first step in cognitive therapy is to educate the person about their cognitive distortions and ask them to keep track of the distortions during the week (Noble et al., 2021). Angelina was asked to keep a daily log of panic attacks as well as thoughts that accompanied the attacks. She was also shown how many of her thoughts led to her avoidant behaviors.

Table 5.16 Cognitive Therapy Examples for People with Anxiety-Related Disorders

Disorder	Cognitive therapy example
Panic disorder	Examine evidence whether heart palpitations truly indicate a heart attack. Discuss worst-case scenario of having a panic attack in a store and how the person could control panic symptoms without avoidance.
Social anxiety disorder	Test a client's hypothesis that if they call a coworker for information that the coworker will become irritated and hang up on them. Have the client guess the probability of this happening and then make the call to see if their prediction is accurate.
Specific phobia	Examine the worst-case scenario for what could happen if the client were exposed to something they feared, such as a snake. Explore the realistic probabilities of unlikely scenarios such as being attacked by the snake.
Generalized anxiety disorder	Examine a client's belief that worry itself has successfully stopped disaster from happening. Instead, help the client understand that worrying about some disaster does not make the disaster less likely to happen.
Obsessive-compulsive disorder	Consider a client's concern that taking risks will lead to disaster. A client may be persuaded to deliberately make mistakes and realize that disaster will not result. Or a therapist may convey that compulsions such as checking and handwashing do not necessarily guarantee safety or total cleanliness.
Posttraumatic stress disorder	Investigate a client's belief that all thoughts about the trauma must be suppressed. Teach the client that thoughts about the trauma are not harmful and that a full processing of these thoughts is necessary for recovery.
Separation anxiety disorder	An older child or adolescent may be encouraged to consider alternative explanations for a parent being late to pick them up from school. Examples include traffic congestion and unexpected errands and not necessarily a car accident, which is a low-probability occurrence.

Clients are encouraged to dispute negative thoughts by *examining the evidence* for and against a certain thought (LaFreniere & Newman, 2020). A person is encouraged to look realistically at what is happening instead of assuming the negative in a situation. Angelina was convinced panic would lead to a car accident. She was asked if she had ever had a car accident before from a panic attack, and she said no. She was also asked what she did when she did panic while driving, and she said she usually went to the side of the road. The therapist helped her examine evidence about the situation:

Therapist: You said earlier you think you will crash the car when having a panic attack. What evidence do you have this will happen?

Angelina: I'm swerving a bit and feel I have to pull over because of my symptoms.

Therapist: But earlier you said you've never been in a car accident, right? So what is the evidence against the idea you might crash?

Angelina: Well, I am a very careful driver, and especially when I feel these symptoms coming on. I drive slower and usually stay in the right lane so I can get over to the shoulder. Plus, I've never gotten a ticket for my driving.

Therapist: That sounds like a lot of evidence against crashing.

Angelina: Yes, I guess that's true, maybe I can handle the symptoms while driving better than I thought.

Clients may also engage in *hypothesis testing* or *behavioral experiments* to identify what the actual chances are that something bad will happen (Jansson-Fröjmark & Jacobsen, 2021). Angelina was asked to rate the probability she would lose control and be institutionalized for a panic attack in the upcoming week. Angelina regularly replied that the odds of this happening were 60 to 80 percent, although the therapist would give estimates closer to 1 percent. Angelina came to understand over time that the therapist's hypotheses were more accurate than hers, and her estimates of disaster decreased.

Clients are also encouraged to *decatastrophize* by thinking about the worst that could happen in a situation and thinking about whether this is really so bad (Vera et al., 2021). Angelina was terrified of shopping at the mall for fear of a panic attack. The therapist calmly asked her, "What is the worst thing that could happen if you had a panic attack at the mall?" Angelina said she would feel her physical symptoms. Again the therapist asked, "What's the worst thing about that?" Angelina said she would feel embarrassed. The therapist challenged this again by saying, "OK. Have you ever felt embarrassed before?" Angelina had, of course, and saw that being embarrassed was an uncomfortable but controllable and temporary state of mind. She came to understand over time that, even if she had a panic attack, the consequences were not severe and that she could handle them.

A key goal of cognitive therapy is to increase a person's ability to challenge negative thoughts and develop a sense of control over anxious situations. Cognitive therapy can be used to help people control fears of symptoms, negative consequences, threat, obsessions, and reexperiencing images or thoughts (Table 5.16). Many studies have shown cognitive therapy to be a useful component for treating people with anxiety-related disorders (Van Dis et al., 2020). Cognitive therapy is often combined with exposure-based practices, which are discussed next.

Exposure-Based Practices

Face your fears. Have you heard that phrase before? This is one of the most important aspects of treatment for people with anxiety-related disorders. **Exposure-based practices** are typically used by therapists to draw a person closer to whatever they are anxious or fearful about (Buchholz & Abramowitz, 2020). A person's fear tends to increase as they approach a feared object or situation. As the person continues to stay in the situation, however, they become more used to it, and fear tends to

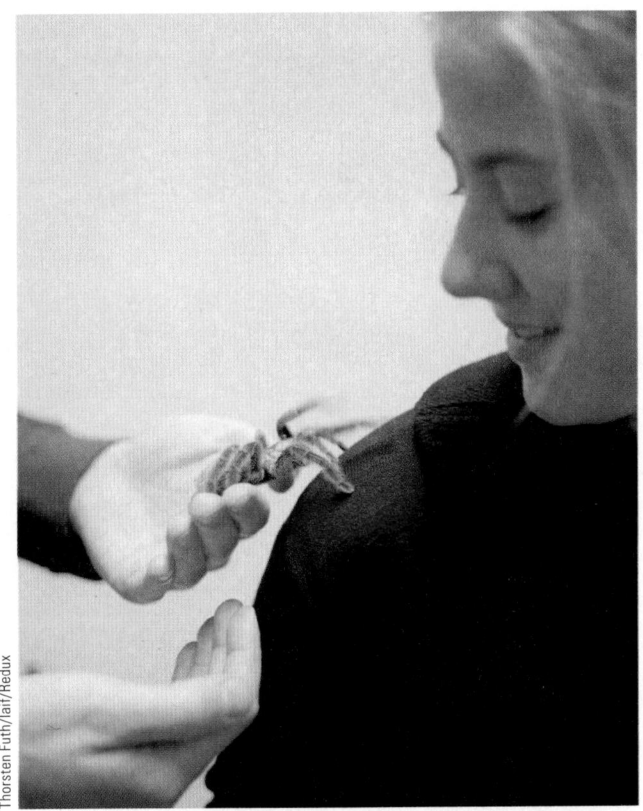
Thorsten Futh/laif/Redux

Exposure therapy for people with phobias often means actual physical contact with the feared stimulus.

Table 5.17 Exposure-Based Therapy Examples for People with Anxiety-Related Disorders

Disorder	Exposure-based therapy example
Panic disorder	Ride in a car with a client who fears panic attacks while driving. This may consist of sitting in a car, then driving in a parking lot, then driving on an empty road, then driving on a busier road, and then driving on a freeway.
Social anxiety disorder	Gradually increase the number of minutes a person is expected to stay at a social function. Have the client practice social- and performance-based tasks such as introducing oneself, maintaining a conversation, or speaking in public.
Specific phobia	Gradually approach a feared stimulus such as a dog. This may begin with watching films of dogs, then visiting a pet store, then visiting an animal shelter, then visiting a park, and then slowly approaching a friendly dog.
Generalized anxiety disorder	Ask a client to expose herself to worry instead of suppressing it but to consider alternative explanations for events. Also, practice refraining from checking, cleaning, or other "worry behaviors."
Obsessive-compulsive disorder	Ask a client to plunge their hands into a pile of dirt and not wash. Or ask them to park near a large trash bin but breathe normally, throw shoes haphazardly into a closet and refrain from ordering them, or drive to work after checking the oven just once.
Posttraumatic stress disorder	Gradually approach a setting where a trauma took place or visit a key gravesite. Engage in discussions about the traumatic event instead of suppressing reminders about the event.
Separation anxiety disorder	Require a child to attend school without their parents initially for one hour per day. On subsequent days, add an extra 15 to 30 minutes until full-time school attendance is achieved.

fade. The problem many people with anxiety-related disorders have is they avoid a situation or escape it as fear becomes severe. A person engaged in exposure-based practices is asked to stay in the situation, such as a shopping center, to experience high levels of fear and learn that the fear will eventually decrease over time and that the person can control the fear. Examples of exposure-based practices for different anxiety-related disorders are in **Table 5.17**.

Collanges/Image Point FR/BSIP/Newscom

Virtual reality therapy for people with phobias is an innovative treatment that works well for difficult cases.

Exposure can be gradual or fast-paced. Gradual or *graded* exposure occurs when a person slowly approaches a feared situation while practicing relaxation training and/or cognitive therapy (Wuthrich et al., 2021). An anxiety hierarchy is formed (refer to **Figure 5.7**) that lists items ranging from easy to hard. The person is then exposed to the easiest (bottom) item until their anxiety level is low. They are then exposed to each subsequent step on the hierarchy until they reach the final goal. Angelina's therapist accompanied her on various driving trips, excursions to the mall and restaurants, and classes at school (items in Figure 5.7). Angelina was also given homework assignments to practice these and other exposures on her own, including calling friends, going on dates, and driving across a high bridge. She was encouraged during these times to change her thoughts and note her control over her anxiety symptoms.

Real-life exposures are *in vivo* exposures, but other exposures can be *imaginal*. The latter may involve describing difficult or grotesque stories to a person to have them think about negative events. We obviously do not want to recreate a trauma for someone with posttraumatic stress disorder. Many with posttraumatic stress disorder continue to try to avoid thinking about the event, which of course triggers

Figure 5.7 Sample Anxiety Hierarchy for Angelina.

Item	Anxiety rating (0-10)	Avoidance rating (0-10)
Driving across a high bridge	9	9
Going on a date	9	9
Attending class	9	8
Shopping in a large department store	9	7
Eating in a restaurant	8	7
Driving along a flat road	7	6
Walking along campus	5	5
Going to a supermarket	4	3
Riding in the car with someone driving	3	2
Attending a therapy session	2	2

more memories and flashbacks. A person doing imaginal exposure thinks first about minor aspects of the trauma and later thinks about more detailed descriptions of the entire event. Anxiety tends to fade as a person thinks more about the event and talks about it.

Exposure for posttraumatic stress disorder can be supplemented as well with a technique known as *eye movement desensitization and reprocessing* (EMDR). EMDR involves inducing back-and-forth eye movements in people as they recall and process traumatic memories. This process is similar to rapid eye movement during sleep and may help reduce the strength of traumatic memories in the hippocampus, as well as anxiety triggered by the amygdala (Russell & Shapiro, 2022). Another type of exposure that simulates in vivo experiences is *virtual reality therapy,* which involves asking a client to wear a headset and watch computer-generated images. These images can be related to stimuli people fear, such as being on an airplane, sitting in an enclosed space, or standing in a high place. A virtual environment can also be set up for people with public speaking anxiety. Virtual reality therapy is effective for people with phobias and is particularly useful for people with unusual or difficult-to-treat phobias (Emmelkamp & Meyerbröker, 2021).

Exposure can also be fast-paced and intensive, as in **flooding** (Remmerswaal et al., 2021). Flooding involves exposing a person to fear with little preparation. A person afraid of dogs could be placed in a room with a dog (in a safe situation, of course) until intense fear subsides and they can approach the dog. Exposure can also be made to internal sensations as well as external items. This refers to **interoceptive exposure** and is most useful for those with panic attacks (Behar & Borkovec, 2020). A person undergoing interoceptive exposure is exposed to their most terrifying physical feeling and asked to endure it or engage in relaxation training. A person afraid of increased heart rate might be asked to run up and down a flight of stairs for one minute and then calm down and realize the symptom is not dangerous nor does it have to be avoided.

Exposure-based therapies are useful for all anxiety-related disorders. This is true even for obsessive-compulsive disorder, for which exposure and **response (or ritual) prevention** are often used (Reid et al., 2021). A person may be exposed to their obsession and not allowed to engage in the compulsion. A person with a contamination obsession might be asked to plunge their hands into dirt and then refrain from washing. Their anxiety will initially be high, but over time they will learn that anxiety decreases without having to wash and that the thought is not harmful. Response prevention for someone with body dysmorphic disorder might involve limiting the number of times they can check some perceived flaw or groom themselves.

A similar procedure is used for people with generalized anxiety disorder. A person is asked during **worry exposure** to concentrate on their anxious thought and then think of as many alternatives to the event as possible (Behar & Borkovec, 2020). A father worried about his teenager getting into a car accident because they are late coming home would think about this scenario and then give more believable alternatives—perhaps the teenager was caught in traffic or dropped off a friend. People with generalized anxiety disorder are also encouraged to stop their "worry behaviors" such as avoiding tasks, checking on loved ones, or cleaning their house (Malivoire, 2020). Managing time and prioritizing tasks (those to be done today, tomorrow, the next day) is also important.

Exposure-based practices are often integrated with other behavioral procedures such as *modeling* and *biofeedback*. A client during modeling watches someone else engage in an approach behavior and then practices it themself. Someone afraid of dogs could gradually approach a dog as their therapist pets the dog to model lack of fear. Clients during biofeedback are attached to a device that gives them visual feedback about heart rate, respiration rate, or brain wave activity. Clients are taught to relax and control their arousal by understanding how relaxation lowers heart and respiration rates. This process is sometimes tied to exposures. A client may be asked to perform a stressful task such as counting backward by sevens and then relax and note how heart and respiration rates decline (Rosenberg & Hamiel, 2021).

Mindfulness

Traditional cognitive-behavioral therapies work well for many people with anxiety-related disorders, but not all, particularly those with severe or complicated symptoms. Clinical researchers have thus designed another set of therapies to help people better understand and accept their anxiety symptoms. The therapist helps a client develop **mindfulness**, or greater daily awareness and acceptance of their symptoms and how the symptoms can be experienced without severe avoidance or other impairment (Maddock & Blair, 2021).

A therapist might ask Jonathan, who had severe obsessions and compulsions, how he could accept his thoughts and behavioral urges but still get work done at his job. Someone with social anxiety disorder at a party could be asked to accept the fact they are anxious but still consider what they need to say and do to interact with others. Therapists using mindfulness help people recognize they are anxious but focus on how the anxiety can be "set aside" or how to allow thoughts to "pass through their body" so they can still function socially and occupationally. Mindfulness approaches continue to gain prominence as a key treatment for anxiety-related disorders, especially among college students (Zhou et al., 2020).

What If I Have Anxiety or an Anxiety-Related Disorder?

People are often screened for anxiety-related disorders, and the answers to some basic questions may indicate whether further assessment or even treatment is warranted. Some of these questions are in **Table 5.18**.

Table 5.18 Screening Questions for Anxiety-Related Disorder

Do you find that many of the anxiety symptoms described in this chapter apply to you?
Are there many things you would like to do but can't because you feel too anxious?
Are you greatly troubled by your anxiety symptoms?
Do other people notice your anxiety or encourage you to seek help?
Does your anxiety last much of the time, even when nothing stressful is happening?
Has your work or social life or sleep suffered a lot because of anxiety or worry?
Do you get extremely upset over even little things most of the time?
Have you experienced a traumatic event that you just can't seem to put behind you?
Do you feel sad, irritable, tense, and pessimistic much of the time?
If you could improve your life, would it include feeling less anxious?

If you find yourself answering "yes" to most of these questions, then you may wish to consult a clinical psychologist, psychiatrist, or other mental health professional. Cognitive-behavioral therapy and/or medication for your anxiety may be best.

If you feel you have unpleasant anxiety but not necessarily an anxiety-related disorder, then teaching yourself to relax, changing your thoughts, and facing your fears may be best. Talk about your feelings with your family and friends or attend an anxiety screening. Further information about screening and treatment for anxiety disorders can be found at the websites of the Anxiety Disorders Association of America (www.adaa.org) and the Association for Behavioral and Cognitive Therapies (www.abct.org). Anxiety and anxiety-related disorders can be quite distressing; if they are for you, do not wait to seek more information.

Long-Term Outcome for People with Anxiety, Obsessive-Compulsive, and Trauma-Related Disorders

What is the long-term picture, or *prognosis*, for people with anxiety-related disorders? Factors that predict better treatment outcome include treatment compliance and completion, longer treatment (especially exposure), better social skills and social support, less depression and other comorbid disorders, less severe trauma and anxiety symptoms, less avoidance, less behavioral inhibition, fewer negative thinking patterns, and fewer stressful life events (Hovenkamp-Hermelink et al., 2021). Angelina's long-term prognosis was probably good because she sought treatment soon after her most severe panic attacks, was motivated and did complete treatment successfully, had supportive friends and family, and did not have other major disorders such as depression or substance use. Jonathan's prognosis might be poorer because his symptoms seem more ingrained and severe. Marcus's prognosis may depend on how well he can address the trauma he experienced.

Researchers have also looked at the long-term functioning of children with anxiety and anxiety-related disorders. Many fears and worries in childhood are temporary, such as a four-year-old's fear of monsters in the closet. Some traits related to anxiety, however, are more stable over time. These include behavioral inhibition and shyness. Disorders that stem from these characteristics, like social anxiety or generalized anxiety disorder, may be fairly chronic over time, especially if associated with depression (Hung et al., 2020). Childhood problems such as separation anxiety disorder can lead to long-term problems if left untreated. Obsessive-compulsive disorder is fairly stable for children and adolescents in severe cases as well (Bellia et al., 2021). The best approach for addressing anxiety-related disorders at any age is early and complete treatment.

Section Summary

- Interviews, self-report questionnaires, and observations are used to collect information about people with anxiety-related disorders because of the internal nature of the symptoms.
- Psychophysiological assessment of anxiety-related disorders can involve heart rate, muscle tension, sweat gland activity, and other symptoms.
- Effective treatment for anxiety-related disorders addresses unpleasant physical feelings, negative thoughts, and avoidant behaviors. Biological treatment for anxiety-related disorders includes medications such as benzodiazepines and antidepressants.
- Psychological treatments for people with anxiety-related disorders often begin with psychoeducation and somatic control exercises like relaxation training or breathing retraining.
- Cognitive therapy can involve techniques such as examining the evidence, hypothesis testing, and decatastrophizing.
- Exposure-based practices are important to help a person reduce anxious avoidance.
- Exposure may be done quickly through flooding or more gradually.
- Long-term outcome for people with anxiety-related disorders is best when they receive early and longer treatment and have less severe symptoms.

Review Questions

1. Outline the major assessment techniques for anxiety-related disorders, including interviews, self-report questionnaires, observations, and psychophysiological measurement.
2. What different methods may be used to control physical symptoms of anxiety?
3. What techniques might be used to help an anxious person change negative thoughts?
4. What strategies could a mental health professional use to help someone with anxiety eliminate avoidance?
5. What is the prognosis or long-term outcome for people with anxiety-related disorders?

Focus On Law and Ethics

The Ethics of Encouragement in Exposure-Based Practices

Imagine you are the therapist treating Angelina for her panic attacks and agoraphobia. Imagine also that one of your treatment sessions involves accompanying Angelina to a local shopping center she has not visited for several months. She greatly fears having a panic attack, but your job is to expose her to the setting so she can realize her intense anxiety will subside and she can control her panic symptoms. People with panic disorder and agoraphobia are often able to successfully complete their anxiety hierarchy. In other cases, though, fear is so intense it takes a lot of encouragement, even prodding, by the therapist.

How much prodding is too far? Don't people have a right to live their lives the way they want to, even if it means avoiding some places? On the other hand, don't therapists have an obligation to their client to end their distress, even if it means short-term fear? The ethical guidelines of the American Psychological Association stipulate that psychologists are expected to "make reasonable efforts to answer patients' questions and to avoid apparent misunderstandings about therapy." The client should thus know ahead of time what will occur in therapy, including difficult real-life exposures, and agree to it. This also involves **informed consent**, which means people entering therapy should be fully informed about all potential risks and benefits of therapy.

Angelina expressed a lot of hesitation about the exposure process, but the therapist made sure she was fully educated about what to expect—such as a possible panic attack—as well as what benefits successful therapy might bring, such as ability to return to school. In this way, no surprises awaited Angelina, and she was more accepting of the therapy process.

Final Comments

People with anxiety and anxiety-related disorders experience substantial distress from intense physical feelings, negative thoughts, and avoidance of things they normally like to do. This is important to remember the next time someone you know speaks in front of others or flies nervously in an airplane. Fear and anxiety are normal, but there can be situations in which the emotions get out of control. If they do, talking to someone about it or contacting a qualified mental health professional is a good idea.

Thought Questions

1. Think about films or other media in which you have seen anxious characters. Do you think these characters display realistic or unrealistic symptoms of anxiety? How so?
2. What situations make you most anxious? How do you feel physically, what do you think in those situations, and what do you do? Would you change anything after having read this chapter?
3. What would you now say to a friend who might be very anxious?
4. What separates "normal" anxiety from "pathological" anxiety? Do you think anxiety has more to do with personal, family, or other factors? Why?
5. What do you think could be done socially to reduce anxiety in people?

Key Terms

worry 105
anxiety 105
fear 105
anxiety-related disorders 107
panic attack 108
panic disorder 109
agoraphobia 109
social anxiety disorder 109
specific phobia 110
generalized anxiety disorder 111
compulsions 112
obsessions 112
obsessive-compulsive disorder 112
body dysmorphic disorder 113
posttraumatic stress disorder 114
acute stress disorder 114
separation anxiety disorder 114
behavioral inhibition 125
cognitive distortions 126
catastrophizing 126
emotional reasoning 126
thought–action fusion 126
emotional processing 126
anxiety sensitivity 127
behavioral avoidance tests 133
psychoeducation 135
somatic control exercises 135
relaxation training 136
breathing retraining 136
cognitive therapy 136
exposure-based practices 137
flooding 139
interoceptive exposure 139
response (or ritual) prevention 139
worry exposure 139
mindfulness 140
informed consent 141

Somatic Symptom and Dissociative Disorders

6

Learning Objectives

LO 6.1 Describe the changing conceptualizations of somatic symptom and dissociative disorders, from psychoanalysis to contemporary understandings.

LO 6.2 Characterize somatization and its progression to somatic symptom disorders.

LO 6.3 Distinguish between somatic symptom disorders using their diagnostic criteria and clinical characteristics.

LO 6.4 Summarize the epidemiology of somatic symptom disorders.

LO 6.5 Describe the stigma associated with somatic symptom disorders and its impact on those with the disorders.

Learning Objectives (continued)

LO 6.6 Discuss the risk factors for and prevention of somatic symptom disorders.

LO 6.7 Characterize the assessment and treatment of individuals with somatic symptom disorders.

LO 6.8 Describe dissociation and its progression to dissociative disorders.

LO 6.9 Distinguish between dissociative disorders using their diagnostic criteria and clinical characteristics.

LO 6.10 Summarize the epidemiology of dissociative disorders.

LO 6.11 Describe the stigma associated with dissociative disorders and its impact on those with the disorders.

LO 6.12 Discuss the risk factors for and prevention of dissociative disorders.

LO 6.13 Characterize the assessment and treatment of individuals with dissociative disorders.

Somatic Symptom and Dissociative Disorders: A Historical Introduction

LO 6.1 Describe the changing conceptualizations of somatic symptom and dissociative disorders, from psychoanalysis to contemporary understandings.

This chapter is essentially two mini-chapters: one on somatic symptom disorders and one on dissociative disorders. Somatic symptom and dissociative disorders were once thought related but are now considered distinct disorders. Somatic symptom disorders generally involve physical symptoms with great distress and impairment. Dissociative disorders involve a disturbance of consciousness, memory, or identity (American Psychiatric Association [APA], 2022).

In the past, both somatic symptom disorders and dissociative disorders were thought to be the result of psychological factors such as trauma. Psychodynamic theorists believed strange or "hysterical" behaviors resulted from unconscious conflicts related to personal trauma. An adult severely neglected as a child may relate to others with difficulty, seek attention through constant physical complaints, or channel distress into bizarre and medically unexplained sensory-motor symptoms. These symptoms may include glove anesthesia (numbness in the hand only), paralysis, and sudden blindness or deafness. Or a person may develop amnesia about traumatic events in childhood that allows them to detach or dissociate from those events.

As perspectives other than the psychodynamic one gained traction within clinical psychology, disorders related to physical symptoms and disorders related to consciousness, memory, or identity were differentiated. Researchers now study somatic symptom disorders and dissociative disorders as largely distinct entities, so the disorders are described separately here.

Somatization and Somatic Symptom Disorders: What Are They?

LO 6.2 Characterize somatization and its progression to somatic symptom disorders.

We get more aches and pains as we age. Many aches and pains result from normal wear in joints, muscles, and tendons. We also take longer to heal as we age and often cannot do what we could when we were 20 years old. We thus spend more time in doctors' offices as we age. All of this is normal. Many of us also visit health professionals for regular checkups and preventive care.

Many people also engage in **somatization**, or a tendency to communicate distress through physical symptoms and to pursue medical help for these symptoms (Macina et al., 2021). The prefix *soma* means "body"; therefore, anything "somatic" refers to the physical body. Many of us become concerned with strange symptoms that compel us to visit a physician. We may be told nothing is wrong or that the problem is minor and not to be dwelled on. We then experience relief and usually let the matter rest. Other times physicians prescribe a general remedy for a vague problem like moderate back pain, which typically addresses the problem to our satisfaction. All of these are normal occurrences.

Other people like Gisela make frequent doctor visits for physical symptoms that have no clear biological cause. Physicians are struck by the number of visits these patients request or number of surgeries they want. These patients are not relieved by constant reassurances from their physicians that no real problem exists. Hostility can thus occur between physicians and these patients, and many of the patients visit multiple doctors and hospitals for relief or to understand what is wrong with them. Many resist suggestions that their physical symptoms have some psychological basis. Gisela dismissed the psychologist's suggestion that stress or family issues caused her symptoms.

People with extreme somatization may have a **somatic symptom disorder** (refer to **Continuum of Somatization and Somatic Symptom Disorders**). A person with a somatic symptom disorder experiences physical symptoms that may or may not have a discoverable physical cause. These symptoms may resemble minor complaints such as general achiness or pain in different areas of the body. Complaints that are more moderate may include loss of sexual desire, nausea and vomiting, and bloating. The person is highly distressed by the symptoms.

Other disorders are related to somatic symptom disorder, although the term *somatic symptom disorders* is used in this chapter to refer to a collection of these disorders (APA, 2022). For example, some people are excessively preoccupied with the consequences of various physical symptoms. These people may be less concerned with general symptoms but fear they have some serious disease. In addition, other people have symptoms that are quite severe and include sudden blindness, deafness, or paralysis. These physical symptoms may be linked to anxiety and depression. Finally, other people deliberately induce symptoms in themselves.

A psychological component likely contributes to somatic symptom disorders. Such components often involve stress, conflict, isolation, or trauma. You may have heard the term *psychosomatic* to describe people with physical symptoms that seem "all in their head." A person may be constantly complaining about real physical symptoms or diseases, but the complaints seem a little exaggerated or far-fetched. Psychosomatic conditions and somatic symptom disorders are not exactly the same, but our body and mind are closely connected, so disturbances in one area can lead to problems in the other. The most commonly diagnosed somatic symptom disorders are described next.

Jose Luis Pelaez Inc/DigitalVision/Getty Images

Many people naturally worry about various health concerns as they age, but excessive worry can become a problem.

Somatic Symptom Disorders: Features and Epidemiology

LO 6.3 Distinguish between somatic symptom disorders using their diagnostic criteria and clinical characteristics.

LO 6.4 Summarize the epidemiology of somatic symptom disorders.

The next sections cover somatic symptom disorder, illness anxiety disorder, conversion disorder, and factitious disorder.

Somatic Symptom Disorder

Do you ever have strange, unexplained feelings in your body? Many people do, such as a sudden pain in the head or a twinge in the abdomen. Most of us pay little attention to these changes because they are not severe and do not last long. Other people like Gisela pay much attention to these physical symptoms and may complain about them for many years. A diagnosis of somatic symptom disorder may thus apply.

Somatic symptom disorder involves at least one physical symptom that causes a person great distress as well as impairment in daily functioning. A key part of the disorder, however, is that the person has recurrent thoughts that the symptom is serious or has great anxiety about the symptom or one's health. The person may also devote substantial time and energy to the symptom, such as visiting doctors. Gisela's symptoms caused her to experience distress, miss work, and fail to complete obligations at home. Keep in mind the symptoms the person feels are real—they are not "faked"—and the symptoms may or may not have a medical explanation. A diagnosis of somatic symptom disorder involves the criteria in **Table 6.1** (APA, 2022). Some people with somatic symptom disorder experience significant pain. Gisela reported pain in several areas of her body. People with somatic symptom disorder may complain of pain in areas of the body difficult to assess for pain. Common examples include the back, neck, face, chest, pelvic area, abdomen, sciatic nerve, urinary system, and muscles. Some people initially experience pain from a physically traumatic event but continue to report pain even when fully healed. A burn victim may continue

Case Gisela

Gisela was referred to psychological treatment by her physician. Gisela was 29 years old and had a five-year history of physical complaints that medical tests could not explain. She often complained of general abdominal and back pain but no specific physical trauma. Gisela visited her physician several times a year, typically with some variation of the same complaint, and asked for waivers and doctors' notes to help her miss work. The physician conducted a wide array of tests multiple times over several years but concluded that Gisela's constant complaints were due to stress, child rearing, marital issues, or another psychological variable.

Following two cancellations, Gisela met with a clinical psychologist who often accepted referrals from physicians. Gisela was emotional during her initial interview and said she had difficulty caring for her two small children and her husband while working full time. She said she often felt pain in her "lower gut," as well as different places in her back. Gisela could not specify an area of pain, instead saying, "It just hurts all over." The therapist asked Gisela about when or how often pain occurred, but she gave vague answers such as "all the time," "when I am at work or working at home," and "I don't know exactly." Gisela added she sometimes felt numbness in her feet, a symptom her doctors could not explain. She also had occasional nausea and vomiting.

The psychologist asked how long Gisela had been in pain, and she replied, "It feels like I've had it all my life." She also could not connect her symptoms to any physical trauma. She had not been, for example, in a car accident or the victim of a crime. The psychologist then suggested that Gisela's back pain might be due to the psychological and physical stress of caring for two small children. Gisela dismissed this notion, however, saying the pain could not be explained by simply lifting children because the pain was often sharp, severe, and debilitating. She thus felt unable to complete chores, go to work, or drive when her pain flared.

iStock.com/Fizkes

The psychologist also explored other concerns Gisela had, such as her fear that "something is really wrong with me." Gisela worried she had a serious condition such as Epstein-Barr virus, lupus, or Lyme disease. She also became defiant when the psychologist mentioned her doctor tested for these disorders multiple times with negative results. Gisela said she did not trust her doctor to care adequately for her. She also revealed she had seen other doctors in the past but complained they seemed overwhelmed by their numbers of patients and did not have time to consider all possibilities for her symptoms.

The psychologist received permission from Gisela to speak to her husband, physician, and boss. Each said Gisela was a sweet, decent person who truly loved her children and husband. Each commented, however, about Gisela's great need for attention, continual symptom complaints, and desire for reassurance. Her husband and boss described Gisela as a manipulative person who would bend the truth to get something she wanted. Her husband said Gisela sometimes embellished difficulties to avoid obligations or gain attention and volunteered that she was no longer interested in sex.

Gisela also revealed that she often evaluated herself for physical problems. She often noted her pulse rate and blood pressure, kept a diary of times when her pain flared, and concentrated on minor changes in her physical condition. These factors seemed related to a somatic symptom disorder. Gisela's psychologist suggested a treatment approach that would include physical and psychological components, although Gisela remained more interested in alleviating her physical symptoms than any psychological problem.

What Do You Think?

1. Which of Gisela's symptoms seem typical or normal for someone with family and job demands, and which seem very different?
2. What external events and internal factors might be responsible for Gisela's dramatic presentation of physical symptoms?
3. What are you curious about regarding Gisela?
4. Does Gisela remind you in any way of yourself or someone you know? How so?
5. How might Gisela's physical complaints affect her life in the future?

to report pain even when grafts and dressings are finished and when no medical explanation for pain exists. Other people undergo limb amputation and still report pain in that limb, a condition known as *phantom pain* that may have psychological and physical causes (Erlenwein et al., 2021).

Other common complaints include fatigue, shortness of breath, dizziness, and heart palpitations. People with somatic symptom disorder may also have certain personality traits or patterns—they may be attention seeking, seductive, manipulative, dependent, and/or hostile toward family, friends, and clinicians. They may show aspects of personality disorders marked by dramatic or unstable behavior (Chapter 10; Macina et al., 2021).

Somatization problems may be "functional" or "presenting." *Functional somatization* refers to what was just described—medically unexplained symptoms not part of another mental disorder. *Presenting somatization* refers to somatic symptoms usually presented as part of another mental disorder, especially anxiety or depression (Murray et al., 2016). Someone with depression may feel fatigued or have low sexual drive, but these physical symptoms are because of the depression. Overlap may occur between functional and presenting somatization. Mental conditions such as depression, health anxiety, and stress are good predictors of whether someone with chronic physical symptoms will seek help (Tu et al., 2020).

Illness Anxiety Disorder

Other people are less concerned with *symptoms* than of some overall *disease*. People with **illness anxiety disorder** (previously called hypochondriasis) are preoccupied with having some serious disease that may explain general bodily changes. Someone with illness anxiety disorder may worry about having hepatitis or AIDS based on minor changes in pulse rate, perspiration, or energy level. Recall that Gisela worried about illnesses such as Lyme disease.

A diagnosis of illness anxiety disorder involves the criteria in **Table 6.2** (APA, 2022). People with illness anxiety disorder may worry about having a particular disease even after medical tests prove otherwise. A person may receive a negative HIV test but still worry about developing AIDS. Such a preoccupation must last at least six months and cause substantial distress or impairment in daily functioning. A diagnosis of illness anxiety disorder can also involve frequent medical care such as testing, or avoidance of doctors and hospitals.

People with illness anxiety disorder may have other unique characteristics. Thoughts about having an illness are constant and may resemble those of obsessive-compulsive disorder (Chapter 5). People with illness anxiety disorder may also have significant fears of contamination and of taking prescribed medication. They are intensely aware of bodily functions,

Table 6.1 DSM-5-TR

Somatic Symptom Disorder
A. One or more somatic symptoms that are distressing or result in significant disruption of daily life.
B. Excessive thoughts, feelings, or behaviors related to the somatic symptoms or associated health concerns as manifested by at least one of the following: 1. Disproportionate and persistent thoughts about the seriousness of one's symptoms. 2. Persistently high level of anxiety about health or symptoms. 3. Excessive time and energy devoted to these symptoms or health concerns.
C. Although any one somatic symptom may not be continuously present, the state of being symptomatic is persistent (typically more than 6 months). Specify if symptoms primarily involve pain, if symptoms have a persistent course, and if severity is mild (one criterion B symptom), moderate (two criterion B symptoms), or severe (2–3 criterion B symptoms with multiple somatic complaints or one very severe somatic symptom).

American Psychiatric Association. (2022). *Diagnostic and statistical manual of mental disorders* (5th ed., text rev.). Arlington, VA: American Psychiatric Association.

Table 6.2 DSM-5-TR

Illness Anxiety Disorder
A. Preoccupation with having or acquiring a serious illness.
B. Somatic symptoms are not present or, if present, are only mild in intensity. If another medical condition is present or there is a high risk for developing a medical condition, the preoccupation is clearly excessive or disproportionate.
C. There is a high level of anxiety about health, and the individual is easily alarmed about personal health status.
D. The individual performs excessive health-related behaviors or exhibits maladaptive avoidance.
E. Illness preoccupation has been present for at least 6 months, but the specific illness that is feared may change over that period of time.
F. The illness-related preoccupation is not better explained by another mental disorder. Specify whether medical care is frequently used (care-seeking type) or medical care is rarely used (care-avoidant type).

American Psychiatric Association. (2022). *Diagnostic and statistical manual of mental disorders* (5th ed., text rev.). Arlington, VA: American Psychiatric Association.

Continuum of Somatization and Somatic Symptom Disorders

	Normal	Mild
Emotions	Optimism regarding health.	Mild physical arousal and feeling of uncertainty about certain physical symptoms.
Cognitions	No concerns about health.	Some worry about health, perhaps after reading a certain media article.
Behaviors	Attending regular, preventive checkups with a physician.	Checking physical body a bit more or scheduling one unnecessary physician visit.

and many complain about their symptoms in detail (unlike those with somatic symptom disorder). This may be because they want to help their physician find a "diagnosis" and a "cure" even though an actual disease may not exist. Many people with illness anxiety disorder fascinate themselves with medical information and have *autosuggestibility*, meaning that reading or hearing about an illness can lead to fear of having that disease (Wieder et al., 2021). This may be particularly problematic in that many websites offer self-diagnostic tools.

Conversion Disorder

People with **conversion disorder** experience motor or sensory problems that *suggest* a neurological or medical disorder, even though one has not been found. Examples include sudden blindness or deafness, paralysis of one or more areas of the body, loss of feeling or ability to experience pain in a body area, feeling of a large lump in the throat (*globus hystericus*), and **pseudoseizures**, or seizure-like activity such as twitching or loss of consciousness without electrical disruptions in the brain.

A diagnosis of conversion disorder involves the criteria in **Table 6.3** (APA, 2022). Symptoms related to the disorder are real—again, they are not "faked"—but have no medical explanation. The symptoms are also not part of a behavior or experience that is part of one's culture. Many religious and healing rituals in different cultures involve peculiar changes such as loss of consciousness, but this is not conversion disorder.

Psychological, not physical, stressors generally trigger symptoms of conversion disorder. Examples include trauma, conflict, and stress. A soldier may suddenly become paralyzed in a highly stressful wartime experience. A psychodynamic theorist might say the terror of trauma is too difficult to bear, and so distress is "converted" into a sensorimotor disability that is easier to tolerate. You might guess that these symptoms cause

Table 6.3 DSM-5-TR

Conversion Disorder (Functional Neurological Symptom Disorder)
A. One or more symptoms of altered voluntary motor or sensory function.
B. Clinical findings provide evidence of incompatibility between the symptom and recognized neurological or medical conditions.
C. The symptom or deficit is not better explained by another medical or mental disorder.
D. The symptom or deficit causes clinically significant distress or impairment in social, occupational, or other important areas of functioning or warrants medical evaluation. Specify symptom type, if symptoms are acute (less than six months) or persistent (six months or more), and if symptoms occur with or without a psychological stressor.

American Psychiatric Association. (2022). *Diagnostic and statistical manual of mental disorders* (5th ed., text rev.). Arlington, VA: American Psychiatric Association.

Moderate	Somatic Symptom Disorder—less severe	Somatic Symptom Disorder—more severe
Moderate physical arousal and greater uncertainty about one's health.	Intense physical arousal misinterpreted as a sign or symptom of some terrible physical disorder.	Extreme physical arousal with great trouble concentrating on anything other than physical state.
Strong worry about aches, pains, possible disease, or appearance. Fleeting thoughts about death or dying.	Intense worry about physical state or appearance. Intense fear that one has a serious disease. Common thoughts about death and dying.	Extreme worry about physical state. Extreme fear of having a serious potential disease. Frequent thoughts about death and dying.
Scheduling more doctor visits but generally feeling relieved after each one.	Regular doctor shopping and requests for extensive and repetitive medical tests with little or no relief. Checking body constantly for symptoms.	Avoidance of many social and work activities. Scheduling regular surgeries, attending specialized clinics, or searching for exotic diseases.

substantial distress and significantly interfere with daily functioning. However, many people with conversion disorder also experience *la belle indifference,* meaning they are relatively unconcerned about their symptoms. This seems odd because most of us, if we suddenly developed a severely disabling condition, would be distraught. A lack of concern, however, may indicate other psychological factors are at play, perhaps including dramatic or attention-seeking behavior (Chekira et al., 2020).

Factitious Disorder and Malingering

Factitious disorder refers to deliberately falsifying or producing physical or psychological symptoms (refer to **Table 6.4**; APA, 2022). A person with factitious disorder may fabricate physical complaints such as stomachaches or psychological complaints such as sadness to assume the sick role. People with factitious disorder may purposely make themselves sick by taking medications or inducing fevers. Factitious disorder is thus different from somatic symptom and illness anxiety disorders in which a person does not deliberately cause their symptoms.

Munchausen syndrome is a factitious disorder in which a person causes symptoms and claims they have a physical or mental disorder. This could involve mimicking seizures or injecting fecal bacteria into oneself. The disorder may be somewhat more common among women visiting obstetricians and gynecologists, including women who deliberately induce vaginal bleeding. Some people with Munchausen syndrome may experience stressful life events or depression or have aspects of a personality disorder (Espada et al., 2021). The prevalence of factitious disorder is 0.8 to 1 percent but higher in clinical and medical settings; Munchausen syndrome is rare. Treatments for factitious disorder are not well developed (Jafferany et al., 2018).

Munchausen syndrome by proxy (or *factitious disorder imposed on another*) refers to adults who deliberately induce illness or pain into a child and then present the child for medical care (Table 6.4). The parent is usually the perpetrator and often denies knowing the origin of the child's problem. The child generally improves once separated from the parent. Most child victims of Munchausen syndrome by proxy are younger than age four years, and most perpetrators are mothers. A main motive for these terrible acts is attention and sympathy the parent receives from others (Abdurrachid et al., 2022).

External incentives are absent in factitious disorder, but **malingering** refers to deliberate production of physical or psychological symptoms *with some external motivation.* Malingering is not a formal diagnosis like factitious disorder but rather an additional condition that may be a focus of clinical attention. A person may complain of back pain or claim they hear voices to avoid work or military service, obtain financial compensation or drugs, or dodge criminal prosecution (APA, 2022). Symptom exaggeration may occur, especially in cases involving disability or workers compensation, personal injury, criminality, and medical or psychiatric issues (Bass & Wade, 2019).

Physicians are often encouraged to note when reported symptoms do not match findings from medical tests (Rumschik et al., 2019). Mental health professionals may use

Table 6.4 DSM-5-TR

Factitious Disorder Imposed on Self
A. Falsification of physical or psychological signs or symptoms, or induction of injury or disease, associated with identified deception.
B. The individual presents himself or herself to others as ill, impaired, or injured.
C. The deceptive behavior is evident even in the absence of obvious external rewards.
D. The behavior is not better explained by another mental disorder, such as delusional disorder or another psychotic disorder.
Factitious Disorder Imposed on Another (Previously Factitious Disorder by Proxy)
A. Falsification of physical or psychological signs or symptoms, or induction of injury or disease, in another, associated with identified deception.
B. The individual presents another individual (victim) to others as ill, impaired, or injured.
C. The deceptive behavior is evident even in the absence of obvious external rewards.
D. The behavior is not better explained by another mental disorder, such as delusional disorder or another psychotic disorder. Note: The perpetrator, not the victim, receives this diagnosis.
Specify if there is a single episode or recurrent episodes of falsification of illness and/or induction of injury.

American Psychiatric Association. (2022). *Diagnostic and statistical manual of mental disorders* (5th ed., text rev.). Arlington, VA: American Psychiatric Association.

neuropsychological testing or tests such as the Minnesota Multiphasic Personality Inventory—3 (MMPI-3; Chapter 4) to identify someone with malingering (Aparcero et al., 2022). People who malinger sometimes deliberately do worse on certain tests that even grossly impaired people can do. Mental health professionals generally avoid promises of external commitments such as financial benefits and gently confront a malingering client to keep them focused on immediate and verifiable problems (Bass & Wade, 2019).

Epidemiology of Somatic Symptom Disorders

Many people with somatic symptom disorders remain in the medical system and not the mental health system, and many have vague symptoms, so data regarding epidemiology remain sparse. Complicating matters is that several known medical conditions include vague, undefined symptoms that make it difficult to tell whether a person has a true physical disorder. Examples of these conditions include fibromyalgia (widespread pain in muscles and soft tissue), chronic fatigue syndrome, lupus (an autoimmune disorder causing organ damage), and irritable bowel syndrome (Appendix).

Many people display moderate somatization and not a formal somatic symptom disorder. Medically unexplained symptoms occur in about 20 percent of new referrals to primary care physicians and 52 percent of new referrals to secondary care physicians (Jadhakhan et al., 2019). Formal somatic symptom disorders are less common, however. The prevalence of somatic symptom disorder may be 4.5 percent (Häuser et al., 2020). The prevalence rate of illness anxiety disorder in the general population may range from 0.04 to 4.5 percent, although this may rise to 8.5 percent in medical settings (Scarella et al., 2019). Conversion disorder has been less studied epidemiologically and is probably more rare. Conversion disorder may be present in only 0.3 percent of the general population, but this rate likely differs across cultures (Canna & Seligman, 2020). Somatic symptoms are also common among college students (refer to **Focus On College Students: Somatization**).

The most common medically unexplained symptoms across cultures are *gastrointestinal problems* and *strange skin sensations* such as feelings of burning, crawling, and numbness. These symptoms are reported more often among people in Africa and southern Asia than in Europe and North America. Conversely, Europeans and North Americans tend to be more preoccupied with symptoms related to heart disease and cancer compared with other regions of the world (Bouman, 2015). In addition, many

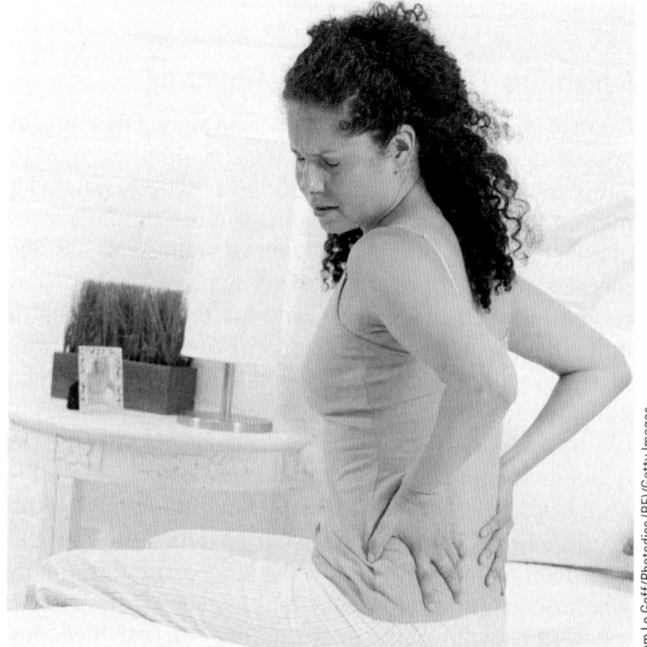

Tom Le Goff/Photodisc (RF)/Getty Images

Back pain is one of the most common complaints reported by people with somatic symptom disorder.

Focus On College Students

Somatization

Stress is obviously a big part of the college experience, and somatic symptoms can accompany exam stress in many cases. College students in one study reported a variety of somatization problems that dramatically increased during an examination period, which was defined as the day of the exam. Somatic symptoms that increased most included headache, back pain, nausea, stomach discomfort or churning, loss of appetite, and excessive tiredness. Other symptoms that increased somewhat included abdominal and joint pain, frequent diarrhea, and sexual indifference. Much of the increased somatization was due to neuroticism, or a general personality trait characterized by anxiety, worry, and moodiness (Zunhammer et al., 2013). Others have found college student somatization to relate to perfectionism, depression, loneliness, and symptoms of eating disorder (Chapter 8; Kate et al., 2020). Stress in college thus appears to exacerbate many anxiety- and mood-related problems that perhaps previously existed.

people of non-Western nations express distress (depression and anxiety) in more somatic than cognitive forms. Certain cultures may socially reinforce somatic expressions of distress (Canna & Seligman, 2020).

Somatic symptom disorders are closely related to depression and anxiety, as well as greater general impairment and health care use. Somatic symptom and illness anxiety disorders have features similar to panic, generalized anxiety, and obsessive-compulsive disorders. Somatic symptom and illness anxiety disorders also present together in 20 percent of cases (Lee et al., 2015). Overlap between somatic symptoms and personality disorders, especially personality disorders involving dramatic or erratic behavior, has also been noted (Dokucu & Cloninger, 2019).

Stigma Associated with Somatic Symptom Disorders

LO 6.5 Describe the stigma associated with somatic symptom disorders and its impact on those with the disorders.

People of different cultures may report various types of psychological symptoms depending on local norms and whether stigma is present. For example, those from Asian cultures tend to use somatic complaints to express depression because doing so is less stigmatizing than admitting emotional sadness (Kalra et al., 2020). In addition, fear of stigma may delay treatment among some people with depression and somatization. Indeed, family members, friends, and even physicians may view a person with a somatic symptom disorder as more of a nuisance than someone who needs psychological help (Stortenbeker et al., 2022).

Stigma can affect illness behaviors as well. People with unexplained medical symptoms, such as those with chronic fatigue syndrome, often face blame or dismissal from others who attribute their symptoms to emotional problems. This may affect their decision to seek treatment. People with somatization concerned about stigma may also continue to emphasize somatic and not psychological explanations for their symptoms. Such stigma concerns even affect people with severe medical conditions such as epilepsy (Chakraborty et al., 2021).

Section Summary

- Somatic symptom and dissociative disorders were once thought to be linked, but they are now examined as largely separate entities.
- Somatization is a tendency to communicate distress through physical symptoms and to pursue medical help for these symptoms.
- Somatic symptom disorder refers to medically explained or unexplained pain or other physical symptoms that cause distress and impairment.
- Illness anxiety disorder refers to excessive concern that one has a serious disease.
- Conversion disorder refers to medically unexplained neurological symptoms.
- Factitious disorder refers to deliberately inducing symptoms in oneself or others, whereas malingering refers to doing so for some external motivation.
- Somatization is common among medical patients, but formal somatic symptom disorders are less prevalent.
- Somatic symptom disorder and illness anxiety disorder are more common than conversion disorder.
- Medically unexplained symptoms differ across cultures and are closely related to depression and anxiety and personality disorders.
- Fear of stigma could delay treatment among some people with somatic symptom disorders.

Review Questions

1. What is the difference between somatization and a somatic symptom disorder?
2. Define and contrast different somatic symptom disorders.
3. How does functional somatization differ from presenting somatization?
4. How common are different somatic symptom disorders?
5. How might stigma affect somatic symptom disorders?

Somatic Symptom Disorders: Causes and Prevention

LO 6.6 Discuss the risk factors for and prevention of somatic symptom disorders.

Data regarding the cause of somatic symptom disorders have emerged slowly. Key factors related to the development of these disorders may include genetics, brain changes, illness behavior, and cognitive, cultural, evolutionary, and other factors.

Biological Risk Factors for Somatic Symptom Disorders

Genetics

Somatic symptom disorder may have a moderate genetic basis, with a heritability estimate of 0.44 (Kendler et al., 2011). Illness anxiety disorder may also have a moderate genetic basis, with a reported heritability estimate of 0.54 to 0.69 (Taylor & Asmundson, 2012). Somatic symptom disorders often cluster among family members, particularly female relatives and between parents and children (Elliott et al., 2020). Several aspects of somatic symptom disorders have a genetic basis as well, especially anxiety, anxiety sensitivity (Chapter 5), depression (Chapter 7), and alexithymia (difficulty understanding one's emotions; Eijsbouts et al., 2021).

Brain Features

Another biological risk factor for somatic symptom disorders may be brain changes, especially in areas relevant to emotion, perception, and physical feeling. Key aspects of the brain thus include the amygdala and limbic system, hypothalamus, and cingulate, prefrontal, and somatosensory cortices (refer to **Figure 6.1**; Pick et al., 2019). These areas may be overactive in some people with somatic symptom disorders (Kozlowska et al., 2020). Some people may thus perceive or "feel" bodily changes and experiences that are not actually occurring. Recall from Chapter 5 that the amygdala is associated with fearful emotional responses and physical symptoms such as increased heart rate and sweating. An overactive amygdala may thus explain why people with somatic symptom disorders experience many physical changes and concern about the changes.

Figure 6.1 Brain Areas Implicated in Somatic Symptom Disorders.

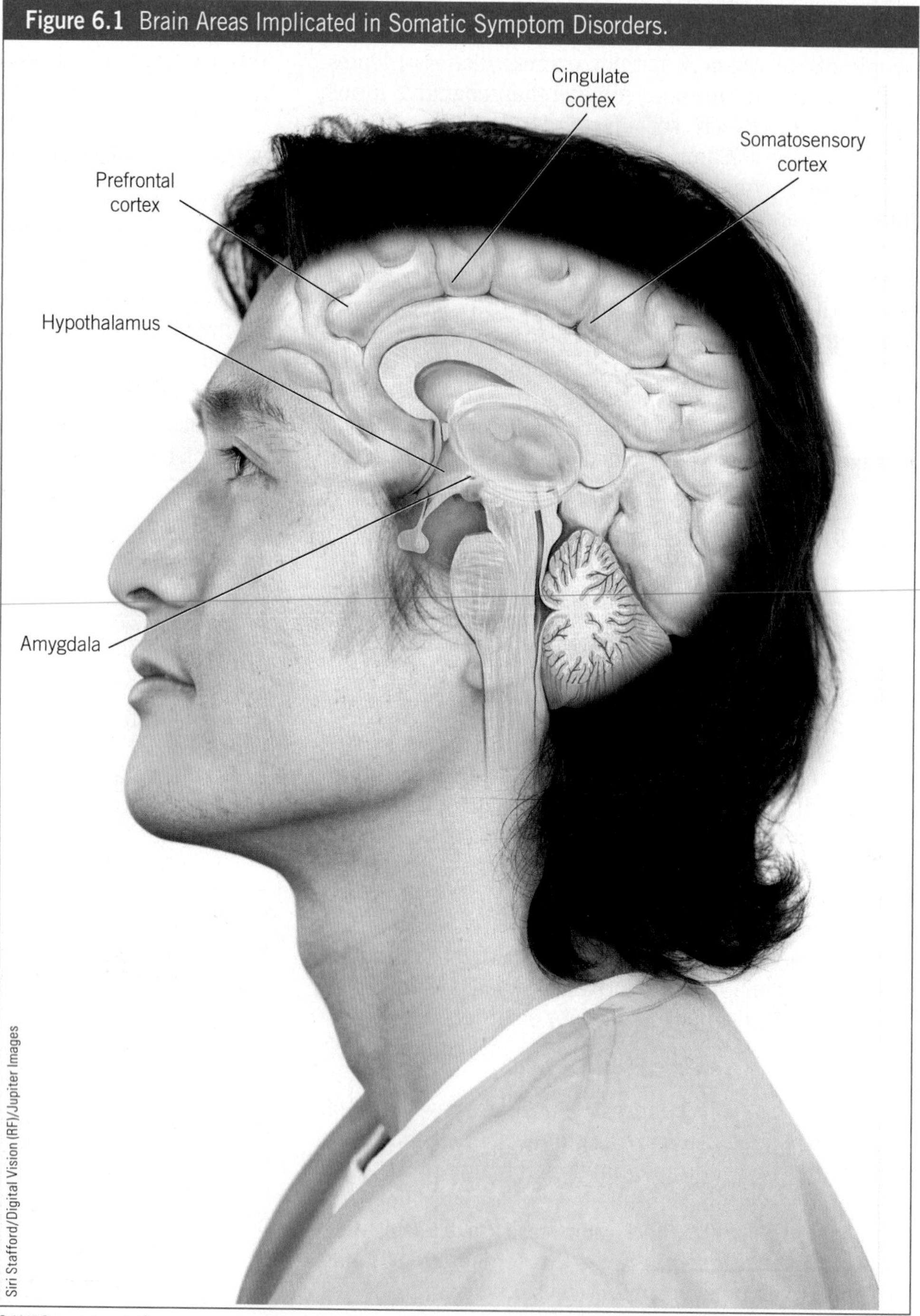

Others propose that changes in these brain areas interfere with inhibitory behavior and promote hypervigilance about symptoms, as well as increased central nervous system activity and stressful responses (Witthöft et al., 2020). Some disruption is occurring in communications between the brain and body. Some people with somatic symptom disorders may thus feel they must constantly check physical status indicators such as heart rate, blood pressure, and respiration (Toussaint et al., 2021).

Recall that some people report feeling pain in a recently amputated limb. People with phantom limb pain appear to have changes in the brain's motor and somatosensory cortices. The brain initially seems to have trouble adjusting to the missing limb because motor and somatosensory cortices must undergo a neuronal reorganization to account for the missing limb (Zheng et al., 2021). Other researchers have also noted substantial somatization among people with medical illnesses such as coronary heart disease, multiple sclerosis, diabetes, chronic obstructive pulmonary disease, cancer, or arthritis (Marek et al., 2020).

Other biological evidence also suggests that people with somatic symptom disorders have brain changes that lead to distractibility, difficulty growing accustomed to continuous stimuli such as physical sensations, and limited cognitive functioning. These brain changes may include dysfunction in the frontal lobe and right hemisphere (Su et al., 2020). Changes in the right hemisphere may help explain why many somatic complaints tend to be on the left side of the body.

Neuroimaging evidence also reveals possible changes in blood flow to key brain areas. Researchers have found changes in different areas of the cortex among people with conversion disorder (Diez et al., 2021). Decreased blood flow may occur in areas of the prefrontal cortex and other aspects of the brain related to loss of sensory and motor function as found in conversion disorder (Demartini et al., 2021; refer to **Figure 6.2**).

Figure 6.2 Brain Imaging of Decreased Blood Flow in People with Conversion Disorder.

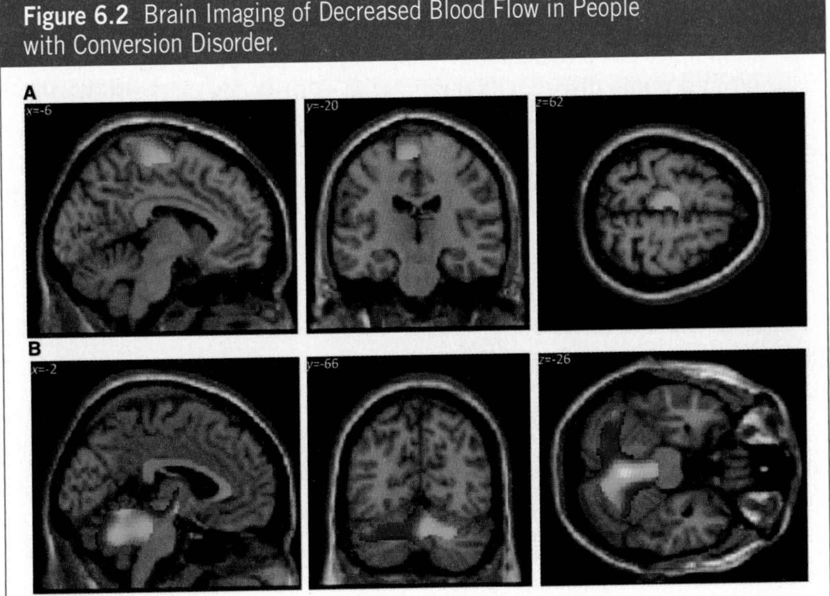

From Black, D.N., Seritan, A.L., Taber, K.H., & Hurley, R.A. (2004). Conversion hysteria: Lessons from functional imaging. *Journal of Neuropsychiatry and Clinical Neuroscience, 16*, 245–251.

Environmental Risk Factors for Somatic Symptom Disorders

Environmental risk factors are also likely for people with somatic symptom disorders, especially those preoccupied with disease. These factors include illness behavior and reinforcement, as well as cognitive, cultural, and other factors.

Illness Behavior and Reinforcement

Illness behavior is a key concept of somatic symptom disorders and refers to behaviors one does when sick (Cosci & Guidi, 2021). Examples include resting in bed, visiting a physician, and taking medication. Partners, family members, and friends may reinforce these behaviors by giving sympathy, attention, and comfort. This may help explain the phenomenon of *la belle indifference* in people with conversion disorder. We also generally accept sickness as a socially appropriate means of withdrawing from obligations, so negative reinforcement can be powerful as well. For people with somatic symptom disorders, like Gisela, social reinforcement for constant complaints or doctor visits may help explain why these disorders persist for long periods. Such demands for attention may intersect as well with someone's dramatic personality structure or disorder.

Another form of comfort relevant to this population is *reassurance.* Many of us feel reassured by medical tests and doctor reports that give us a "clean bill of health," but people with somatic symptom disorders may not. Reassurance is also an effective anxiety-reducer in the short term but not the long term. People like Gisela may thus pursue ongoing, repetitive, and lengthy medical tests and visits. Children may model parents' use of reassurance seeking as they age (O'Connor et al., 2020). Children may copy parents' frequent complaints about physical symptoms or calls to friends for sympathy.

Secondary gain sometimes refers to receiving social reinforcement for somatic complaints. Psychodynamic theorists view *primary gain* as unconscious use of physical symptoms to reduce psychological distress. People who pay close attention to minor physical symptoms thus reduce attention toward some internal or external stressor (Cretton et al., 2020). Some people may find it easier to concentrate on minor bodily changes than major life stressors such as relationship conflict, financial troubles, or academic failure.

Cognitive Factors

Related to illness behaviors are *illness beliefs* or *somatic attributions,* or perceived causes of physical symptoms. People may believe a virus, a psychological condition such as depression, or an external problem such as working too much, causes their illness or physical sensation (Hulgaard et al., 2019). People with somatic symptom disorders tend to adopt biological or illness explanations for their symptoms compared with people with other disorders who adopt psychological explanations. A person coming home from a long and difficult day at work may adopt a physical explanation for their fatigue (I am sick), whereas many of us would adopt a psychological explanation (I am stressed out).

Those with somatic symptom disorders also perceive themselves as particularly vulnerable to illness and thus engage in more illness behaviors (Keen et al., 2022). The presence of anxiety and depression, problems also related to cognitive distortions, seem closely linked to increased health anxiety and internal illness beliefs as well (Nikcevic et al., 2021).

Another cognitive factor in somatic symptom disorders is *somatosensory amplification,* or a tendency to notice and magnify physical sensations (Barends et al., 2020). This is a condition also found in those with panic disorder and refers to people who attend closely to minor bodily changes. The changes thus become magnified and seem more severe than they are. Indeed, overlap exists between illness anxiety disorder and panic disorder (Scarella et al., 2019). Try it. Concentrate intensely on your heart rate for a few minutes and note any changes or a feeling your heart is "pounding" more so than before.

Cultural Factors

Recall that people of non-Western nations tend to express feelings of depression and anxiety as physical symptoms more than people of Western nations do. Psychological conditions are highly stigmatizing in non-Western countries, so a greater emphasis on physical symptoms may be more acceptable. Many cultures have "cultural idioms of distress" to make various experiences seem more normal (Sudheer & Banerjee, 2021). Consider the Vietnamese notion of *phong tap,* which refers to general aches and pains and distress attributable to fatigue and cold. Attributing one's mental distress to external factors beyond one's control is acceptable practice. This may fit into the notion mentioned earlier that social reinforcement in a culture is important for how people express their distress.

Other Factors

Other general factors may also apply to somatic symptom disorders. Examples include poor medical attention and care, stressful life events, and general emotional arousal (Russell et al., 2022). Poor medical attention and care may include insufficient feedback by a general physician to someone worried about a particular disease as well as unnecessary treatment. Stressful life events relate closely to severity of conversion disorder symptoms (Diez et al., 2021). These general factors seemed evident for Gisela. Her life was clearly stressful because she had two small children and a full-time job, and she became overexcited quickly. Her belief that her doctors seemed overwhelmed by their numbers of patients may also have been valid. Some also point to large-scale events such as terrorism as potentially related to medically unexplained symptoms (**Focus On Violence: Terrorism and Medically Unexplained Symptoms**).

Causes of Somatic Symptom Disorders

Different factors likely cause somatic symptom disorders, but much controversy remains about exactly how these problems originate. Perhaps the best way to

Focus On Violence

Terrorism and Medically Unexplained Symptoms

Do terrorist attacks and suicide bombings create physical changes in people exposed to these events? Somatization and somatic symptom disorders are certainly related to various psychological factors and personal trauma, but some have claimed that even large-scale traumas such as terrorism may have a causal role. For example, somatization and conversion disorders are commonly found in emergency rooms following acts of terrorism or a major disaster (Burnett, 2021). Stress related to fear of attack at an unknown moment can create intense physiological changes in some people. Holman and Silver (2011) examined 2,592 adults who completed a health survey before 9/11 and an assessment of acute stress responses after the terrorist attacks. Reports of physical ailments increased 18 percent over three years following 9/11. Many people across the country were thus traumatized by the terrorist attacks and had medical symptoms as a result.

understand somatic symptom disorders is as changes in perception, control, and attention (Henningsen et al., 2018). Some people misinterpret or *misperceive* sensory experiences as real and dangerous symptoms of some serious medical problem. One might think of general gastrointestinal discomfort as stomach cancer. Someone with somatic symptom disorder may also view internal sensory experiences as *uncontrollable*, meaning the symptoms are beyond their ability to influence or treat. This makes the experiences more frightening.

The way people with somatic symptom disorders misperceive internal sensations is similar to the way some people with anxiety-related disorders, especially panic disorder, do (Chapter 5). Recall that somatic symptom and anxiety-related disorders are closely linked. One possibility for this link is that physical symptoms of anxiety, such as heart palpitations or dizziness, become part of a powerful memory later used to explain minor physical discomfort (Löwe et al., 2021). An anxious person might have chest pain and worry (wrongly) they are having a heart attack. This person may later have slightly blurred vision and worry (wrongly) they have a brain tumor.

Many people with somatic symptom disorders also *overattend* to even minor changes in their body (Witthöft et al., 2020). If you constantly and intensively concentrate on your heart or respiration rate, you may notice some changes over time. These are normal, of course. For some people with somatic symptom disorders, however, overattention amplifies the intensity of their symptoms and contributes to worries about their meaning. They may come to believe they have some serious disease. Not surprisingly, such overattention exists in people with anxiety-related and depressive disorders (Chapters 5 and 7). All of these processes—sensory misperception, feelings of uncontrollability, and overattention—can then lead to illness behaviors, social reinforcement for playing the "sick role," avoidance of daily activities, and a somatic symptom disorder (Fobian & Elliott, 2019).

Prevention of Somatic Symptom Disorders

Data are scarce regarding the prevention of somatic symptom disorders, but information about the disorders in children and adolescents may be instructive. Stressful life events, traumatic experiences such as maltreatment, history of physical disease, unnecessary medical interventions, and the presence of other mental disorders such as anxiety and depression relate to somatization in youths (Lin et al., 2020; Okur Güney et al., 2019). Others have stated as well that some youths receive substantial attention from parents for somatic complaints, and this serves as a reinforcer (Smith et al., 2020).

Given this information, strategies to prevent the development of somatic symptom disorders may include several components. Examples include educating children and parents about dangerous and nondangerous physical symptoms, attending to serious but not common bodily changes, helping youths cope with traumatic events and related mental disorders, ensuring adequate and competent health care, and practicing anxiety management (Chapter 5). Given that somatic symptom disorders may endure over time, addressing risk factors for the problems as early as possible is important.

Section Summary

- Biological risk factors for somatic symptom disorders may include genetic predispositions, as well as key brain changes in the amygdala, hypothalamus, limbic system, and cingulate, prefrontal, and somatosensory cortices.
- Environmental risk factors for somatic symptom disorders include illness behaviors, which involve medically related behaviors potentially reinforced by significant others.
- Cognitive factors are likely powerful influences in somatic symptom disorders because many people with these disorders use somatic explanations for even minor bodily changes.
- Cultural and other factors may influence somatic symptom disorders as well. Poor medical attention and care, stressful life events, and emotional arousal may be risk factors.
- A causal model of somatic symptom disorders focuses on misperception of symptoms, feelings of uncontrollability about symptoms, and overattention to minor bodily changes.
- Risk factors in children and adolescents may inform strategies for preventing somatic symptom disorders. Examples include stressful life events, traumatic experiences, and comorbid anxiety and depression.

Review Questions

1. Describe how certain brain changes may be associated with somatic symptom disorders.
2. What forms of social reinforcement relate to somatic symptom disorders?
3. What cognitive factors relate to somatic symptom disorders?
4. Describe an overall causal theory to explain Gisela's somatic symptom disorder.
5. Outline a prevention strategy for a youth at risk for medically unexplained symptoms.

Somatic Symptom Disorders: Assessment and Treatment

LO 6.7 Characterize the assessment and treatment of individuals with somatic symptom disorders.

Strategies for assessing and treating somatic symptom disorders are discussed next. Keep in mind the psychological assessment of someone with a possible somatic symptom disorder should be done in conjunction with a comprehensive medical evaluation.

Table 6.5 Guidelines for a Therapist Communicating with a Person with Possible Somatic Symptom Disorder

Acknowledge that the symptoms are real and distressing to the client.
Accept the need to address somatic complaints.
Avoid attempts to convince the client of a psychological cause for symptoms.
Continue to gently refer to the role of tension and stress.
Discuss various topics, not just symptoms.
Schedule regular visits not predicated on complaints.
Develop goals in conjunction with the client.
Discuss how symptoms limit a client's functioning instead of what might be physically wrong.
Maintain empathy with a client but set limits on behavior.

From Maynard (2003).

Assessment of Somatic Symptom Disorders

Assessing someone like Gisela with a somatic symptom disorder usually involves interviews, questionnaires, and personality assessment. Each method is discussed next.

Interviews

Interviews to gather information about people with somatic symptom disorders include structured, research-based ones such as the *Structured Clinical Interview for DSM-5, Composite International Diagnostic Interview, Somatoform Disorders Schedule,* and *International Diagnostic Checklists* (First et al., 2015; Kessler et al., 2013). These interviews cover diagnostic criteria for various somatic symptom disorders.

Questions given to someone like Gisela with a possible somatic symptom disorder should involve a detailed history of physical and psychological problems. Somatic symptom disorders can be complex and long-standing, and we know these disorders often begin in childhood and adolescence, so questions about one's history should extend far into the past. Pertinent topics include early and recent life experiences and stressors, medication and substance use history, others' reactions to somatic complaints, cognitive distortions, interference in daily functioning, and motivation for seeking and pursuing psychological treatment for what the client may believe is mostly a medical problem.

Gisela hesitated about using psychological treatment to address what she thought were simply medical problems. Interviewing a person with a somatic symptom disorder thus requires a therapist to develop good rapport with their client. Guidelines for communicating with a person with a somatic symptom disorder are in **Table 6.5**.

Questionnaires

Screening instruments also exist for possible somatic symptom disorders. Common ones include the *Screening for Somatoform Disorders (SOMS)* and *SOMS-7,* which cover diagnostic criteria and measure a person's medically unexplained physical symptoms (Zijlema et al., 2013). Psychological factors are often a part of somatic symptom disorders, so some questionnaires assess these constructs. The *Somatic Symptoms Experiences Questionnaire,* for example, assesses health worries, illness experience, difficulties in interaction with doctors, and impact of illness (Herzog et al., 2014).

Other questionnaires specific to hypochondriasis include the *Whiteley Index, Illness Behaviour Questionnaire, Illness Attitude Scales,* and *Somatosensory Amplification Scale* (SAS). These scales measure diagnostic symptoms, perceptions of illness, and awareness of internal sensations (Fava et al., 2012). Sample SAS items are in **Table 6.6**.

Personality Assessment

Recall that somatic symptom disorders and unrealistic health concerns sometimes relate to certain personality traits or disorders. Assessment for this population may thus include personality inventories. The *Minnesota Multiphasic Personality Inventory—3* (MMPI-3)

Table 6.6 Sample Items from the Somatosensory Amplification Scale

I am often aware of various things happening within my body.
When I bruise myself, it stays noticeable for a long time.
I can sometimes feel the blood flowing in my body.
I can sometimes hear my pulse or my heartbeat throbbing in my ear.
I am quick to sense the hunger contractions in my stomach.
Even something minor, like an insect bite or a splinter, really bothers me.
I have a low tolerance for pain.

Note: Items are scored on a scale from 1 to 5 reflecting how much each item characterizes a person (5 equals more so).

Barsky, A. J., Wyshak, G., & Klerman, G. L. (1990). The Somatosensory Amplification Scale and its relationship to hypochondriasis. *Journal of Psychiatric Research, 24,* 323–334. Reprinted by permission of Elsevier.

includes clinical subscales for somatic complaints and malaise or a sense of physical debilitation and poor health (Whitman et al., 2021). The MMPI is commonly used to identify people with malingering and somatoform patient conditions in forensic and legal settings (Ben-Porath et al., 2022). Others have found the scales useful for assessing coping strategies, emotional dysfunction, somatic complaints, low positive emotions, and cynicism related to psychogenic physical conditions (Modiano et al., 2021).

Biological Treatment of Somatic Symptom Disorders

People with somatic symptom disorders often experience comorbid anxiety and depression, so a key treatment approach has been medication to address these conditions. The most common medications for this population have been selective serotonergic reuptake inhibitors (Chapters 5 and 7) such as escitalopram (Lexapro), fluoxetine (Prozac), fluvoxamine (Luvox), and paroxetine (Paxil). Use of these drugs for somatic symptom and illness anxiety disorders helps improve anxiety and depression, as well as fears of disease, symptom preoccupation, and overall functioning (Tyrer, 2018). Antidepressant medication may help reduce the severity of pain as well (Roughan et al., 2021). Much work remains regarding these medications with respect to dosing, treatment duration and individualized assignment, and long-term outcome, however (Bonilla-Jaime et al., 2022).

Psychological Treatments of Somatic Symptom Disorders

Somatic symptom disorders are associated with problematic illness behaviors and significant cognitive factors, so the use of psychological treatments for these disorders can be important. Psychological treatments for somatic symptom disorders in fact resemble the treatments for anxiety-related disorders (Chapter 5). Keep in mind, however, that many people with somatic symptom disorder resist the idea of treatment from a mental health professional. Clients like Gisela might have to first recognize that their symptoms may have some psychological basis, but this is often not easy for them to do.

Cognitive Therapy

Cognitive therapy for anxiety-related disorders involves examining inaccurate statements a person may be making and encouraging the person to challenge the thought and think more realistically. This therapy works the same way for treatment of people with somatic symptom disorders. People with somatic symptom disorders should first understand the connection between their problematic thoughts and their physical symptoms. Someone who constantly worries about having a disease and who checks their body constantly for changes may amplify those changes and misperceive them as dangerous. Cognitive therapy helps a person examine evidence to challenge this thought process. A person may come to realize that minor physical sensations and changes are not dangerous because all humans have them and because the symptoms are often temporary and controllable.

A client with a somatic symptom disorder may also benefit from logically examining their thoughts about the consequences of physical symptoms. Someone like Gisela may constantly worry her physical symptoms will devastate her life. A therapist might help Gisela understand she can effectively cope with or control physical symptoms and additional stressors in her life. Biofeedback, in which a person learns to consciously control bodily functions such as heart rate, can be useful in this regard (Wagner et al., 2021; Appendix).

The various somatic symptom disorders involve problematic thought processes that can be treated with cognitive therapy. People with illness anxiety disorder fear their symptoms indicate a serious disease. A cognitive therapist may help a client with illness anxiety disorder discuss evidence for and against a disease belief, assess realistic probabilities for a certain physical symptom, and understand that a 100 percent certainty of knowing one is not ill is never possible. A person with abdominal distress should list all possible reasons and probabilities for such distress, including cancer but also gas, indigestion, and other common but harmless conditions (Ventura et al., 2021). Mindfulness-based cognitive therapy with meditation may be helpful as well (Zargar et al., 2021).

Behavior Therapy

Behavior therapy for somatic symptom disorder helps a person reduce excess behaviors such as checking symptoms and visiting doctors. Behavior therapy aims to reduce the excess attention-seeking and reassurance-seeking behaviors that many people with somatic symptom disorders engage in; these behaviors cause others to reinforce their symptoms. **Contingency management** involves educating family members and friends about a person's somatic symptom disorder and encouraging them to reinforce "well" behaviors such as going to work, finishing chores, and staying active. This seems especially important for treating conversion disorder, in which an emphasis is placed on removing medical and social attention for unusual sensory-motor conditions, administering physical therapy to restore normal movement, and helping clients cope with stress and trauma (Miller et al., 2020).

The primary behavioral treatment components for somatic symptom disorders are relaxation training, exposure, response prevention, and social skills and assertiveness training (Orzechowska et al., 2021). You may notice these treatments are similar to those mentioned in Chapter 5 for anxiety-related disorders, especially obsessive-compulsive disorder. Somatic symptom disorders often have an anxious component, so treatments aimed at anxiety may work well for this population. Relaxation training and exposure are often conducted together to help ease muscle tension, which aggravates physical symptoms, and reduce anxiety when a person confronts anxiety-provoking stimuli. Such stimuli usually include avoided situations such as social interactions, dating, and work. Gisela's therapist worked with her to establish a regular pattern of work attendance. Response prevention involves limiting the number of times a person can monitor physical symptoms or engage in some other excess behavior. Many therapists use behavioral procedures with cognitive therapy to treat people with somatic symptom disorders.

Cognitive plus behavioral therapy for people with somatic symptom disorders is quite helpful in many cases (Patel et al., 2020). Exposure, response prevention, and cognitive therapy in one study produced significant improvements in illness attitudes and behaviors as well as somatoform symptoms (Weck et al., 2015). Success rates for people with somatic symptom disorders are generally less positive, however, than for people with anxiety disorders or depression. This is because people with somatic symptom disorders often show multiple symptoms over long periods (Dunphy et al., 2019). The most useful approach for this population will likely include medication *and* comprehensive psychological treatment within medical and mental health settings.

What If I or Someone I Know Has a Somatic Symptom Disorder?

If you suspect you or someone you know might have features of a somatic symptom disorder, then seeking a full medical and psychological examination is important. You may also want to think about related problems of stress, anxiety, or depression that aggravate physical symptoms or worries about having some disease (Chapters 5 and 7). Somatic symptom disorders can be distressing and often greatly interfere with one's ability to accomplish even simple tasks. Encouraging someone who may have features of a somatic symptom disorder to continue to stay active and "work through" their symptoms is a good idea as well.

Long-Term Outcome for People with Somatic Symptom Disorders

Longitudinal studies indicate that many people (50–75 percent) with medically unexplained symptoms or somatic symptom disorder show improvement over time but that about 10 to 30 percent deteriorate. People with illness anxiety disorder often have a more chronic course, with 50 to 70 percent maintaining their symptoms over time. Predictors of more chronic course of somatic symptom disorder include greater severity of symptoms such as degree of pain or illness behavior as well as poor physical functioning. Other possible predictors include comorbid mood problems and unrealistic fears of illness (olde Hartmann et al., 2013).

How do people with somatic symptom disorders fare after treatment? People do respond to treatment for these problems, although researchers have found certain characteristics related to better long-term outcome. These characteristics include longer treatment as well as less anxiety and fewer pretreatment symptoms, comorbid conditions, cognitive distortions about bodily functioning, and hospital stays (Liu et al., 2019; Olatunji et al., 2014). As mentioned throughout this textbook, the more severe one's symptoms, the more difficult successful treatment tends to be.

Section Summary

- Therapists use interviews and questionnaires to assess people with somatic symptom disorders. These measures concentrate on diagnostic criteria, history of symptoms, illness behaviors and beliefs, personality patterns, and other relevant topics.
- Biological treatments for people with somatic symptom disorders include antidepressant medication to ease comorbid depression, fears of disease, and symptom preoccupation.
- Psychological treatments for people with somatic symptom disorders involve cognitive-behavioral strategies to reduce illness behaviors and avoidance, improve physical functioning, address trauma, and limit checking and other excessive behaviors.
- The long-term outcome of people with somatic symptom disorders is variable but may be somewhat worse for people with illness anxiety disorder. Severity of symptoms and degree of comorbid conditions are good predictors of outcome.

Review Questions

1. Describe various methods of assessing people with somatic symptom disorders.
2. What medications might be best for people with somatic symptom disorders?
3. What issues might arise when trying to get family members involved in treating someone with a somatic symptom disorder?
4. Describe psychological treatments for people with somatic symptom disorders.
5. Outline the long-term outcome for people with somatic symptom disorders.

Normal Dissociation and Dissociative Disorders: What Are They?

LO 6.8 Describe dissociation and its progression to dissociative disorders.

Have you ever been in a stressful situation where you felt "out of it"? Perhaps you were taking a test or talking before a group of people and suddenly felt as if you were watching yourself do the task or floating above yourself? These experiences, though somewhat odd, are normal and represent **dissociation**. Dissociation refers to some separation of emotions, thoughts, memories, or other inner experiences from oneself. In other words, we feel as if we have split from ourselves.

Such separation is often mild and temporary and can include things like daydreaming, being absorbed by a film, "spacing out," or highway hypnosis, in which a person drives for a distance but cannot recall how they arrived at their destination (Green et al., 2020). In other cases, separation is moderate, meaning a person may feel temporarily outside of their body or walk through hallways as if in a fog. Or a person may feel they cannot recall all details of a certain event (refer to **Continuum of Dissociation and Dissociative Disorders**).

These episodes of dissociation are normal because they are temporary and do not interfere with daily life. A person may take an important test and feel dissociated for the first few minutes. They may feel as if they are watching themself take the test and have trouble concentrating on the questions. Usually, however, this feeling dissipates quickly, and the ability to concentrate returns. We may feel we are "coming back to the test" and perceive it more clearly than before. Another person may witness a terrible accident and feel as if events are progressing in dreamlike slow motion. Everything might then suddenly snap back to "real time." Minor dissociation may help us temporarily handle stress by keeping it at arm's length. The dissociation usually dissipates as we adjust to the stressful situation, calm ourselves, and do what we need to do.

In some cases, however, separation can be severe and lead to **dissociative disorders**. Dissociative disorders involve disturbance in consciousness, memory, or identity (APA, 2022). A person may experience some form of dissociation for lengthy periods of time or in some extremely odd way. Erica may have coped with recent or past stress by forgetting information that reminded her of trauma. She may have even developed a separate personality at age seven years that "kept" traumatic memories of that time hidden so she would not have to think about them. Such extreme dissociation may be reinforced over time because it works so well—in other words, the person does not have to address a particular trauma. Unfortunately, as with Erica, long-term dissociation can cause significant social and even legal problems.

Dissociative Disorders: Features and Epidemiology

LO 6.9 Distinguish between dissociative disorders using their diagnostic criteria and clinical characteristics.

LO 6.10 Summarize the epidemiology of dissociative disorders.

Dissociative disorders include dissociative amnesia, dissociative identity disorder, and depersonalization/derealization disorder. Features of these challenging disorders are discussed next.

Dissociative Amnesia

Do you ever forget things for no reason? Of course you do! We all forget things from time to time, and forgetfulness increases with age (Chapter 14). Normal forgetfulness is nothing much to worry about because the items we forget are minor and can easily be remembered with a cue. For some people like Erica, however, forgotten items are highly *personal*—examples include childhood experiences, family members, and even identifying information like one's name. A diagnosis of **dissociative amnesia** may thus apply (refer to **Table 6.7**; APA, 2022).

Table 6.7 DSM-5-TR

Dissociative Amnesia
A. An inability to recall important autobiographical information, usually of a traumatic or stressful nature, that is inconsistent with ordinary forgetting. Note: Dissociative amnesia most often consists of localized or selective amnesia for a specific event or events; or generalized amnesia for identity and life history.
B. The symptoms cause clinically significant distress or impairment in social, occupational, or other important areas of functioning.
C. The disturbance is not attributable to the physiological effects of a substance or a neurological or other medical condition.
D. The disturbance is not better explained by dissociative identity disorder, posttraumatic stress disorder, acute stress disorder, somatic symptom disorder, or major or mild neurocognitive disorder. Specify if with dissociative fugue, or travel or wandering associated with amnesia for identity or other autobiographical information.

American Psychiatric Association. (2022). *Diagnostic and statistical manual of mental disorders* (5th ed., text rev.). Arlington, VA: American Psychiatric Association.

Dissociative amnesia involves forgetting highly personal information, typically after some traumatic event. A person may have trouble remembering their name after a car accident or assault. To be defined as dissociative amnesia, such forgetfulness is not caused by substance use or neurological or other medical disorder. The memory loss can, however, cause distress and impair one's ability to function on a daily basis. Imagine being unable to remember who you are—this would cause enormous stress and would obviously prevent you from working and even taking care of yourself.

Dissociative amnesia can come in several forms. People with dissociative amnesia may have only one severe episode of forgetfulness or several smaller or equally severe episodes. This may depend on the

Case Erica

Erica was attending outpatient therapy for depression and "strange experiences." The 25-year-old was attending therapy sessions for about three months after a breakup with her boyfriend. Her romantic relationship lasted only a few months but was conflictive and occasionally violent. Erica said her interactions with her boyfriend were "intense" because they engaged in frequent sexual contact but also constant fighting about time spent together, progression of the relationship, and failure to communicate verbally. Erica said her boyfriend hit her on more than one occasion, although hospitalization or the police were never involved. Erica and her boyfriend mutually agreed to part after a serious decline in the quality of their relationship.

Erica said she was depressed and tearful about the breakup and especially about being alone. She said she was having trouble eating and sleeping and missed several days of work to stay in bed. Erica's therapist was able, however, to help her client gradually gain control of her life and improve her mood. Erica became more active in seeing her family members and friends, resumed work on a regular basis, thought about new dating opportunities, and engaged in cognitive therapy to reduce self-blame about her past relationship.

Therapy progressed in these areas but remained stagnant in other areas. Erica often had trouble remembering things from the past week or even the day before, seemed distracted in therapy sessions, and even missed some sessions. The therapist sometimes asked Erica if anything was wrong, but Erica would only say she was having some recent memory difficulties and felt "strange." When asked for details, Erica said she would sometimes come home to find her apartment a mess even though she was a very neat person. She also received two speeding tickets in the mail but did not remember a police officer stopping her. Erica also said she sometimes forgot what day of the week it was.

Erica's therapist tried to go into detail about these experiences, but with little success. The therapist also thought it strange that Erica was generally unwilling or unable to talk about past relationships or even her childhood. When asked about these periods in her life, Erica became ashen and said she could not "really remember my birthdays or anything specific" about childhood. Following several unfruitful sessions, Erica's therapist decided a more in-depth discussion of Erica's past would help her fully understand her current depression and relationship problems.

The therapist called Erica one night at home to ask if she could delve into Erica's past in more detail. This might involve conversations with Erica's parents and others who had known her for a long time. Erica answered the telephone and listened to the therapist before excusing herself. The therapist waited about four minutes before a young voice came on the telephone. The therapist was confused because Erica lived alone and had no children. The young voice on the line told the therapist, "I can't let you talk to her about those things." The therapist, startled and alarmed, asked the voice to explain. The voice said, "We can't talk about those bad things," paused, and said, "We just can't." The therapist asked the voice to identify itself but the voice only said, "It's me," before hanging up. The therapist called back, but no one answered.

Erica came to her therapy session the next day as if nothing had happened. The therapist told her about the telephone conversation but Erica was perplexed and did not know how to respond. The therapist then asked Erica about recent days and times that she could not remember, and the previous night was one of those times. The therapist delicately explained to Erica that she may be experiencing episodes of dissociation whenever stressful events occurred and that Erica may have a separate personality structure. Erica was confused but listened intently because the description of dissociation fit her history. Erica did say, somewhat out of the blue, that the young voice her therapist heard was likely 7 years old. She did not know why she thought this to be the case. Erica's therapist believed her client was likely having symptoms of a dissociative disorder and perhaps even had multiple personalities.

What Do You Think?

1. Which of Erica's symptoms seem normal, and which seem odd for someone with intense, recent life stressors such as hers?
2. What external events and internal factors might be responsible for Erica's odd symptoms?
3. What are you curious about regarding Erica?
4. Does Erica remind you in any way of yourself or someone you know? How so?
5. How might Erica's odd symptoms affect her life in the future?

Egon Endrenyi/Hypnotic/Universal/Kobal/Shutterstock.com

Jason Bourne, Matt Damon's character in *The Bourne Identity,* has dissociative amnesia and spends much of the film attempting to discover his true identity.

degree of trauma in their life. Recollection of important personal information may return suddenly for some but more gradually in others. Oddly, a person may forget *personal information* but remember historical events or how to drive a car. Such semantic or procedural memory can be lost in some cases, however (Becquet et al., 2021). Dissociative amnesia seems common among television characters, but loss of widespread personal information is actually quite rare.

Dissociative amnesia can also include **dissociative fugue**. Some people develop amnesia about personal events and suddenly move to another part of the country or world. People with dissociative fugue cannot recall their past, and sometimes their identity, and end up living and working far away from family and friends. The person often assumes a new identity or is greatly confused about personal identity. Dissociative fugue most often occurs after a traumatic event. A person about to be publicly embarrassed in a scandal may suddenly move to another part of the country and assume a new name and job. Fugue states are characterized by dissociation, so in this case the person did not consciously plan to move. Instead, they likely had little recollection of what happened to them in the past. Fugue states can eventually disappear and a person may resume their old life, although memories of the original trauma may still be poor (Mangiulli et al., 2022).

Dissociative Identity Disorder

Other people with dissociative disorder experience *identity* problems that involve formation of different personalities. Those with **dissociative identity disorder** actually have two or more distinct personalities within themselves (this disorder was once called *multiple personality disorder*). These personalities may wrest control of a person's consciousness and for a time become the dominant personality (refer to **Table 6.8**; APA, 2022). When this happens, as it did for Erica, a person may feel as if strange events are happening around them. The person may have trouble recalling personal information and have memory gaps about childhood or recent events. To be defined as dissociative identity disorder, the development of multiple personalities must not result from substance use or a medical condition. Identity "splitting" is often due to a traumatic event or set of events such as child maltreatment (Reinders & Veltman, 2021).

What is remarkable about dissociative identity disorder is that *true* differences supposedly exist among the personalities. Each personality may have its own distinctive traits, memories, posture, clothing preferences, and even physical health (Rolls, 2015). Keep in mind a person with dissociative identity disorder is *not pretending* to be someone different, such as when someone imitates someone else. Instead, true differences exist in behavior and other characteristics that make someone unique. Some researchers, however,

Table 6.8 DSM-5-TR

Dissociative Identity Disorder
A. Disruption of identity characterized by two or more distinct personality states, which may be described in some cultures as an experience of possession. The disruption in identity involves marked discontinuity in sense of self and sense of agency, accompanied by related alterations in affect, behavior, consciousness, memory, perception, cognition, and/or sensory-motor functioning. These signs and symptoms may be observed by others or reported by the individual.
B. Recurrent gaps in the recall of everyday events, important personal information, and/or traumatic events that are inconsistent with ordinary forgetting.
C. The symptoms cause clinically significant distress or impairment in social, occupational, or other important areas of functioning.
D. The disturbance is not a normal part of a broadly accepted cultural or religious practice. Note: In children, the symptoms are not better explained by imaginary playmates or other fantasy play.
E. The disturbance is not attributable to the physiological effects of a substance (e.g., a drug of abuse, medication) or another medical condition (e.g., seizures).

American Psychiatric Association. (2022). *Diagnostic and statistical manual of mental disorders* (5th ed., text rev.). Arlington, VA: American Psychiatric Association.

Continuum of Dissociation and Dissociative Disorders

	Normal	Mild
Emotions	Feeling good connection with others and environment.	Mild physical arousal, especially when forgetting something.
Cognitions	No concerns about forgetfulness.	Slight worry about lack of concentration on an examination or about increasing forgetfulness as one ages.
Behaviors	Occasional forgetfulness but little problem remembering with a cue.	Daydreaming during class, minor "spacing out" during a boring psychology lecture, mild forgetfulness.

question the existence of multiple personalities and focus more on differences in representations of emotional states or sociocultural expectations (Lynn et al., 2022). Others maintain that dissociative identity disorder is a valid diagnosis but one that should involve a clearer definition of symptoms (Paris, 2019).

Many people with dissociative identity disorder have a *host personality* and *subpersonalities,* or alters. A host personality is the one most people observe and is likely present most of the time. A host personality is like your general personality that changes from time to time but is not dramatically different. Subpersonalities, however, are additional, distinct personalities within a person that occasionally supplant the host personality and interact with others. This may help explain memory gaps. A different personality may have temporarily dominated Erica's consciousness, trashed her apartment, and sped recklessly while driving. This would help explain some of Erica's odd experiences and her difficulty remembering recent events. Subpersonalities may also have their own set of memories, such as the 7-year-old Erica who may have been shielding memories of severe maltreatment from the host personality.

The relationships between subpersonalities and between subpersonalities and the host personality can be complex. Different relationship possibilities exist for the various personalities of the person with dissociative identity disorder, including the following:

- A *two-way amnesiac* relationship means the personalities are not aware of the existence of one other.
- A *one-way amnesiac* relationship means some personalities are aware of other personalities, but this awareness is not always reciprocated.
- A *mutually aware* relationship means the personalities are aware of all other personalities and may even communicate with one another (Marsh et al., 2021).

The Olympian/McClatchy-Tribune/MCT/Getty Images

Jeffrey Ingram (pictured with his wife) woke up on a sidewalk in downtown Denver with no memory of who he was. Doctors believed he was in a dissociative fugue state.

Moderate	Dissociative Disorder—less severe	Dissociative Disorder—more severe
Greater difficulty concentrating, feeling more alienated from others and one's environment.	Intense difficulty concentrating and feelings of estrangement from others.	Feelings of complete alienation and separation from others or one's environment.
Greater worry about minor dissociation, such as sitting in a car at the supermarket and wondering how one arrived there.	Intense worry about substantial dissociation or "gaps" in memory or little realization that something is wrong.	Potential lack of insight or thought about one's personal identity or changed living situation.
Highway hypnosis, more frequent forgetfulness, or acting as if in a fog or a dream.	Infrequent episodes of depersonalization, intense forgetfulness, or missing appointments with others.	Severe and frequent episodes of dissociation, constant amnesia or fugue, presence of multiple personalities.

Erica was clearly unaware of at least one subpersonality, but the subpersonality was aware of Erica, who was the host personality. This is common to many people with dissociative identity disorder, especially at the beginning of therapy.

Depersonalization/Derealization Disorder

Another dissociative disorder is **depersonalization/derealization disorder**, which involves persistent experiences of detachment from one's body as if in a dream state (refer to **Table 6.9**; APA, 2022). People with this disorder maintain a sense of reality but may feel they are floating above themselves, watching themselves go through the motions of an event, or feel as if they are in a movie or like a robot. Depersonalization often exists with *derealization,* or a sense that surrounding events are not real (Millman et al., 2022). Think about suddenly waking up to an odd noise—you perhaps feel disoriented or feel the surrounding environment is a bit surreal.

Depersonalization or derealization episodes can be short or long, but a person may have trouble feeling sensations or emotions. These episodes cause great distress and significantly interfere with daily functioning. The depersonalization or derealization episodes should not occur because of another mental disorder such as panic disorder, or substance use or a medical condition. However, people with panic and other anxiety-related disorders commonly report depersonalization and derealization. Brief episodes of depersonalization are common in the general population and are not a mental disorder (APA, 2022). Symptoms of depersonalization and fugue are also sometimes difficult to tease apart.

Table 6.9 DSM-5-TR

Depersonalization/Derealization Disorder
A. The presence of persistent or recurrent experiences of depersonalization, derealization, or both: 1. Depersonalization: Experiences of unreality, detachment, or being an outside observer with respect to one's thoughts, feelings, sensations, body, or actions. 2. Derealization: Experiences of unreality or detachment with respect to surroundings.
B. During the depersonalization or derealization experiences, reality testing remains intact.
C. The symptoms cause clinically significant distress or impairment in social, occupational, or other important areas of functioning.
D. The disturbance is not attributable to the physiological effects of a substance (e.g., a drug of abuse, medication) or another medical condition (e.g., seizures).
E. The disturbance is not better explained by another mental disorder.

American Psychiatric Association. (2022). *Diagnostic and statistical manual of mental disorders* (5th ed., text rev.). Arlington, VA: American Psychiatric Association.

Epidemiology of Dissociative Disorders

You can understand how researchers have a difficult task when studying people with dissociative disorders. Symptoms of these disorders are often hidden, and many people with dissociative disorders do not seek therapy. Many people who attend therapy for some *other disorder*, however, also experience symptoms of dissociation. Erica's original reason for attending therapy was symptoms of depression. Symptoms of dissociation are also common in posttraumatic stress, panic, and obsessive-compulsive disorders (Buchnik-Daniely et al., 2021). Symptoms of dissociation can also be prevalent among college students (refer to **Focus On College Students: Dissociation**). The prevalence of pathological dissociation ranges depending on the assessment method but may be up to 10 percent. Prevalence rates are less for depersonalization/derealization and dissociative identity (1–2 percent) disorders (Sar, 2017). The prevalence of dissociative amnesia, however, is highly debatable. Some researchers claim this is a rare phenomenon, but others believe the disorder is more common than previously thought. The discrepancy derives from controversy as to whether adults can suddenly recall long-forgotten events from childhood (refer to **Focus On Law and Ethics: Recovered Memories and Suggestibility**; Otgaar et al., 2022).

Pathological dissociation may be more common in younger people and is fairly equal across men and women. Men may be more likely to experience amnesia, however, and women may be more likely to experience dissociative identity disorder (Scholzman & Nonacs, 2016). Dissociative experiences may also be more common among certain cultural groups. *Pibloktoq* is an episode involving a type of dissociative fugue in which Arctic people leave home and shed their clothes in the cold weather (Teodoro et al., 2020). Others note that racial and ethnic minority young adults may be more vulnerable to dissociative symptoms in response to traumatic stress (Polanco-Roman et al., 2021) (refer to **Focus On Diversity: Dissociation and Culture**).

Aspects of dissociative disorders seem highly comorbid with other mental disorders, especially those involving trauma. Up to 30 percent of people with posttraumatic stress disorder, for example, report high levels of dissociative symptoms (Lanius et al., 2018). Dissociative behavior is also quite common among homeless and runaway youths and adolescents who have experienced trauma (Ross et al., 2020).

Stigma Associated with Dissociative Disorders

LO 6.11 Describe the stigma associated with dissociative disorders and its impact on those with the disorders.

Stigma may be an important issue in dissociative disorders. One group of researchers examined social stigma among people who were provided a description of a psychological disorder to which they had been randomly assigned: depression, dissociative identity disorder, or schizophrenia. Participants then completed a measure of prejudicial attitudes toward people with mental disorder. Social stigma was found to be lowest among those assigned with depression but higher and nearly equal among those assigned dissociative identity disorder or schizophrenia. This included social stigma beliefs such as the need to be fearful and avoidant of someone who may be dangerous, that individuals with these disorders are unpredictable, and that people with certain psychological disorders are not deserving of sympathy (Reisinger & Gleaves, 2022). The findings confirm that stigma toward people with mental disorder is strong, and may cause some people with dissociative or related disorders to be reluctant to pursue treatment.

Focus On College Students

Dissociation

Have you ever "zoned out" during a lecture or while studying? Many students experience minor dissociation and fantasizing. Other instances of dissociation, however, can be more serious. One study indicated that college students who had a history of childhood or adolescent sexual maltreatment and had a desire to dissociate also tended to engage in more binge drinking, which was defined in men as having six or more drinks in one session and in women as having four or more drinks in one session (Chapter 9). The authors speculated that some college students want to dissociate but do not always have the ability to do so and thus turn to alcohol to enhance dissociation (Klanecky et al., 2012). Dissociation has also been found to be higher among college students with a history of nonsuicidal self-injury, such as cutting oneself (Karpel & Jarram, 2015). Another study indicated that only about 38 percent of college students sought help for dissociative and other problems caused by a history of maltreatment (Sedlacek et al., 2015). If you find yourself struggling with the issues noted here, then seeking help at your student counseling center may be a good start.

Section Summary

- Normal dissociation refers to separation of emotions, thoughts, memories, or other inner experiences from oneself. Dissociation that occurs in a severe or very odd way may be a dissociative disorder.
- Dissociative amnesia refers to loss of memory for highly personal information. This may be related to dissociative fugue, which involves sudden movement away from home or work with loss of memories for personal and other information.
- Dissociative identity disorder refers to two or more distinct personality states within a person. These states may include a host personality and subpersonalities that can differ in their awareness of each other.
- Depersonalization/derealization disorder refers to persistent experiences where a person feels detached from their body as if in a dream state.
- Dissociation is common in people with mental disorders, although the prevalence of formal dissociative disorders in the general population is less common. Dissociative disorders are often associated with trauma and trauma-related mental disorders.
- Many people with dissociative symptoms feel stigmatized by others.

Review Questions

1. What is the difference between normal and psychopathological dissociation?
2. Discuss features of major dissociative disorders.
3. What is a host personality and subpersonalities?
4. What types of relationships might subpersonalities have with one another?
5. How common are dissociative experiences?

Dissociative Disorders: Causes and Prevention

LO 6.12 Discuss the risk factors for and prevention of dissociative disorders.

The cause of dissociative disorders remains unclear, but evidence is emerging that key brain changes and trauma are important risk factors. These factors likely work in tandem in diathesis-stress fashion to help produce dissociative disorders.

Biological Risk Factors for Dissociative Disorders

Brain and memory changes are key risk factors of dissociative disorders. These risk factors are discussed next.

Brain Features

A key aspect of dissociative disorders is disintegration of consciousness, memory, and identity. Brain areas responsible for integrating incoming information may thus be altered in some way. Key brain areas for integration include the amygdala, locus coeruleus, thalamus, hippocampus, anterior cingulate cortex, and frontal cortex (refer to **Figure 6.3**; Roydeva & Reinders, 2021). Some believe disintegration or dissociation in times of stress creates an arousal threshold in these brain areas. Reaching this threshold triggers increased alertness but also inhibition of strong emotional responses such as anxiety (Krause-Utz et al., 2021).

We may detach ourselves from a terrible event so we can control our responses and react adaptively. A person in a car accident may feel they are floating above the crash scene but at the same time can rescue others,

Focus On Law and Ethics

Recovered Memories and Suggestibility

Reports have appeared in the media over the years about people accused of child maltreatment or domestic violence by other individuals who have suddenly recalled these events after many years. A heated controversy in this area, however, is the topic of *recovered memories*. Recall that Erica's subpersonality seemed to have memories of severe maltreatment from childhood. In other people with dissociative disorders, memories of past maltreatment emerge as amnesia or fugue dissipates during treatment. The validity of these recovered memories remains unclear, however. This takes on greater meaning when a prosecutor decides to indict someone based on recovered memories.

This controversy stems from the fact that children, adolescents, and even adults may be susceptible to leading questions about past events. This is *suggestibility*. In one study, maltreated children were asked misleading questions about a recent play activity in a hospital. An example is the question "There wasn't a chair out there in the hallway, was there?" when in fact there was. Young children were more prone to "fall" for misleading questions than older children and adolescents (Chae et al., 2011).

Some thus recommend strict ethical guidelines for assessing people with memories of maltreatment. These guidelines include warning clients about the possibility of recovering false memories, outlining limits to confidentiality, obtaining special training for eliciting memories, making conclusions only with corroborating evidence, and always acting in the best interests of a client (Rocchio, 2020).

talk to police, and call family members. The person's alertness is increased, but excesses in emotion and physical arousal are temporarily blunted. This person may later appreciate the full weight of what happened and experience nightmares or flashbacks of the trauma. People with acute stress or posttraumatic stress disorder commonly have dissociation (Chapter 5; Lynn et al., 2022).

Dissociative disorders, especially depersonalization/derealization and perhaps amnesia/fugue, may also be due to problems in connections between various brain areas, especially between sensory systems (eyesight, hearing) and the limbic system. A possible consequence of such disruption is that a person witnesses an event, especially a strongly negative event, but "detaches" themself and experiences little emotional response. Such disconnection can also lead to blunted pain experiences and a decrease in irrelevant thoughts. Evidence indicates that people undergoing depersonalization have blunted reactions to arousing stimuli (Boulet et al., 2021).

Memory Changes

Work in the area of memory changes and dissociative disorder remains in development, but some suggest that intense negative emotions lead to *compartmentalization* and *difficulty retrieving information* (Millman et al., 2022). Exposure to a negative event and intense negative emotions may instigate a segregation or "compartmentalization" of one part of the mind from other areas. This appeared to happen with Erica—her therapist later discovered that her client's seven-year-old alter personality held memories of childhood trauma. Compartmentalization may help explain why certain memories or personalities are not "known" by the host personality.

Compartmentalization may not be complete, however. When one personality learns new information, interference in learning in another personality can occur. One personality may also retrieve information learned by another personality (Marsh et al., 2021). This provides support for the existence of mutually aware or one-way amnesiac relationships among personalities. Transfer of information across different personalities may depend, however, on emotional and personal content of the information. Difficulty retrieving information is also common in people with dissociative identity disorder and dissociative amnesia. People with these disorders may have trouble distinguishing true and false memories, especially of childhood. People with these disorders often have deficits in short-term memory and working memory, which is the ability to hold information while completing another task. Problems in these areas of memory, which may result from increased emotional arousal, may relate to irrelevant thoughts and dissociative experiences (Matsumoto & Kawaguchi, 2020).

Think about trying to remember someone's telephone number as you are driving a car (working memory). If you are extremely upset about something at this time, you may temporarily forget the telephone number because you are thinking about other things and "spacing out" a bit. People with dissociative disorders may have such

Focus On Diversity

Dissociation and Culture

Dissociation is evident across many cultures, although many other conditions seem related to the Western concept of dissociation. One such condition is *possession disorder,* in which a person believes they are possessed by some type of entity (Ventriglio et al., 2018). In Japan, animal and other spirits are commonly thought to influence people's behavior. In Thailand, *phii bob* refers to the belief that the spirit of another living person can enter a person's body and cause behavioral changes. One particular Islamic belief is that of *jinn,* or genies, that can cause harm to humans sometimes through possession (Abdul-Rahman, 2019). These phenomena underscore the importance of considering a person's cultural background when addressing a possible case of dissociative disorder.

Certain cultures may be more predisposed to dissociative experiences like depersonalization. Depersonalization experiences might be more common to people of Western countries (Kerr, 2014). This is because a person's "sense of self" in these countries tends to be highly individualistic and autonomous, and thus more susceptible to separation from one's social context. Non-Western societies tend to emphasize a more collectivist orientation involving greater social integration and interdependence. People who adopt a collectivist sense of self may thus be less predisposed to depersonalization or other dissociative experiences.

Gailan Haji/EPA-EFE/Shutterstock.com

People in a trance-like state show behaviors that resemble a dissociative disorder.

problems on a grander scale. What causes these memory changes to begin with, however, remains unclear. One possibility is that people with dissociative amnesia and identity disorder have reduced blood flow in the right frontotemporal cortex (refer to **Figure 6.4**; Roydeva & Reinders, 2021). Excessive stress and trauma may create these metabolic changes.

Environmental Risk Factors for Dissociative Disorders

Important environmental risk factors for dissociative disorders such as trauma and cultural influences are discussed next.

Trauma

Traumatic experiences and posttraumatic stress disorder are closely linked to dissociative disorders. Adult dissociation often follows a severe traumatic event such as child maltreatment (Paetzold & Rholes, 2021). Consider a four-year-old child experiencing severe physical maltreatment from a parent. The options available to this child are few: They are unlikely to run away, kill the parent, or commit suicide. An alternative coping strategy is to dissociate or detach from the trauma in a psychological way. Such dissociation may be mild in the form of thinking about something else or more severe in the form of developing amnesia or even a different personality. Perhaps this occurred in Erica's case.

Traumatic problems may follow dissociation in other cases. A good predictor of posttraumatic stress disorder is dissociation *during* a traumatic event (Serrano-Ibáñez et al., 2021). Someone who dissociates during a traumatic event may not cognitively process all relevant stimuli in that situation. Such avoidance can help produce symptoms of posttraumatic stress disorder, and exposure to reminders of the trauma is a key part of treatment for posttraumatic stress disorder (Chapter 5). A person who is assaulted may dissociate somewhat and even describe their attacker to police. They may cognitively avoid other stimuli associated with the event, however, such as the parking lot where the assault occurred. If they walk through that parking lot in the future, doing so may trigger posttraumatic stress.

Dissociation may thus be a way of temporarily coping with a terrible event. This is especially likely if the event involved intense fears of death, loss, or lack of control. Such fears are in addition to the terror of the trauma and increase the likelihood one will experience long-term emotional distress or posttraumatic stress disorder (deMello et al., 2022). Other researchers, however, refute a causal relationship between dissociation and trauma because some third variable may explain the relationship. A third variable such as intense family conflict could explain trauma *and* dissociation in an adolescent (so trauma or dissociation may not have caused the other). People with dissociative disorders also do not remember earlier traumatic events with great accuracy (Sajjadi et al., 2021).

Figure 6.3 Major Brain Areas Implicated in the Dissociative Disorders.

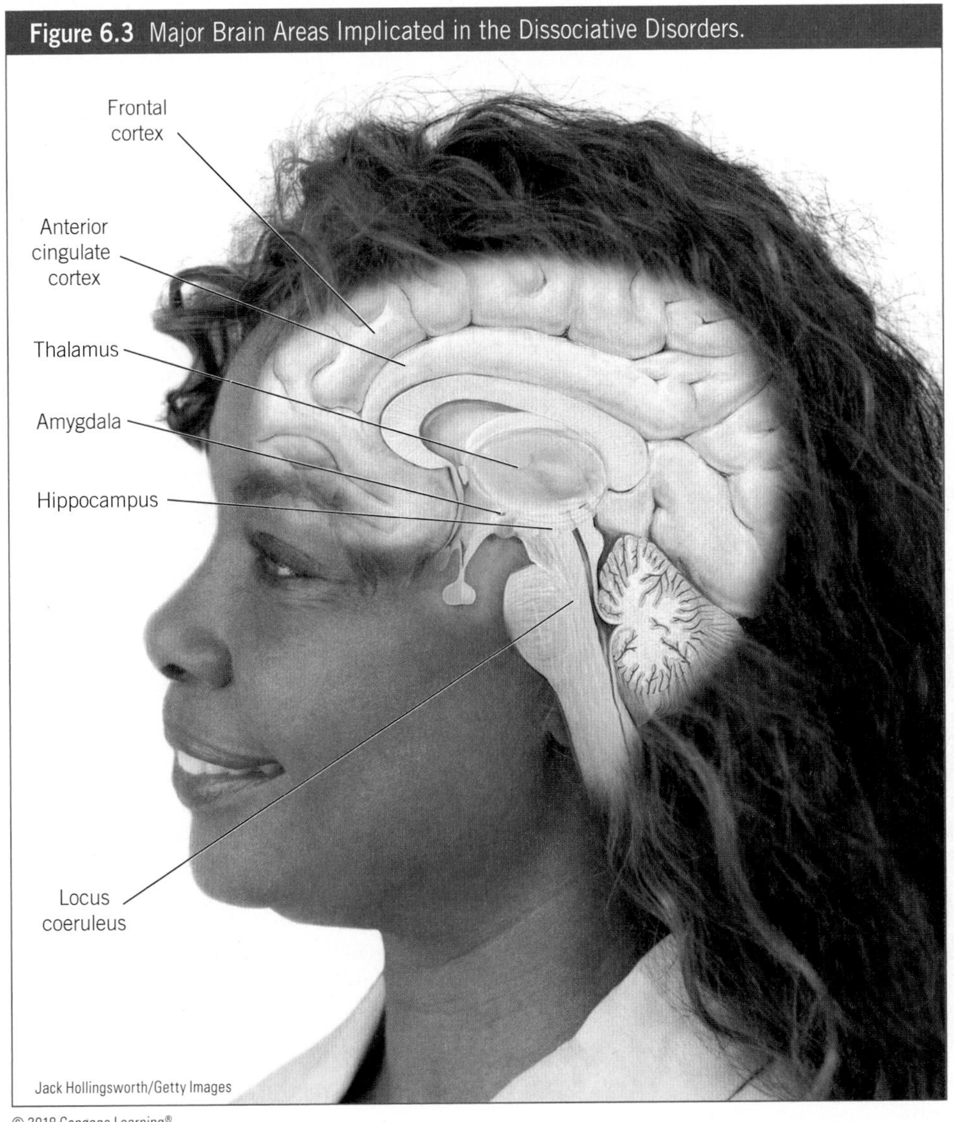

Cultural Factors

Cultural factors may also relate to dissociation because cases of dissociative identity disorder seemed to peak before 1920 and after 1970. In addition, 82 percent of cases of the disorder occur in Western countries (Boysen & VanBergen, 2013). Changes in how the concept of "self" is defined from generation to generation may affect the prevalence of dissociative identity disorder (Kihlstrom, 2022). Some people may rely on "an alternate personality" explanation to avoid personal responsibility for certain acts, even violent ones. We sometimes refer to ourselves and others in terms of Dr. Jekyll and Mr. Hyde (refer to **Focus On Violence: Dissociative Experiences and Violence Toward Others**).

Less research is available about dissociative disorders in other countries. Researchers have recognized dissociative amnesia and depersonalization in various countries and found the disorders followed traumatic circumstances as they often do in Western cultures. Dissociative fugue and dissociative identity disorder, however, may be confused with other, local concepts of dementia (Chapter 14) or *possession trance disorder* (Ventriglio et al., 2018). Possession trance disorder (or dissociative trance disorder) refers to a sense that a new identity attributable to a spirit or other entity replaces one's identity and controls a person's behavior and possibly their memory. This underscores the need to consider local contexts and beliefs before assigning a diagnosis.

Causes of Dissociative Disorders

Neurodevelopmental approaches may help explain how disparate factors such as brain and memory changes interact with trauma to help cause dissociative disorders (Reinders et al., 2018). Consider what normally happens in a positive childhood. First, children grow to develop strong and positive attachments to family members and caregivers, emotional regulation, and adaptive brain structure. Children learn to associate well with others, control excess emotions such as rage, and adapt to normal life changes.

Second, young children begin to coordinate different aspects of thinking and emotions into a consolidated *sense of self*. A youngster gains information from different situations and learns that certain rules apply and that they have some control over what will happen. A sense of self develops as children realize who they are and how the world works.

Third, loving parents accelerate this process by setting rules, providing support, and helping a child gain control of emotions and behaviors. We teach our children to listen carefully, come to us when scared, and communicate and develop self-control—"Use your words!" We also encourage them to explore different aspects of life while protecting them from harm. Many parents also develop daily routines for their children so youngsters feel safe in knowing what comes next.

A maltreated child, however, may not develop a strong and unified sense of self. The child is unsure about which rules apply, who to trust, and what happens next. An integrated sense of self and control over different life situations is thus lacking. This could lead to overarousal and development of different personalities or dissociative states. A lack of unified self may relate to changes in the orbitofrontal cortex, an area of the brain largely responsible for memory and consciousness (Raccah et al., 2021). Greater empirical data to support these ideas remain necessary, however.

Figure 6.4 Reduced Blood Flow in the Frontal Lobe of a Person with Dissociative Amnesia.

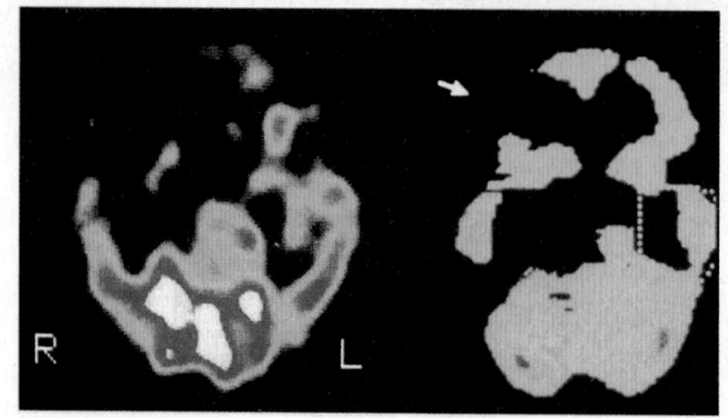

From Plate 2 of Markowitsch, H.J. (1999). Functional neuroimaging correlates of functional amnesia. *Memory, 7*, 561–583.

Prevention of Dissociative Disorders

Data are lacking regarding prevention of dissociative disorders, but preventing traumatic events that might lead to dissociative disorders may be instructive. An important traumatic event is child maltreatment. No studies have shown that reducing child maltreatment necessarily prevents dissociative disorders, but this is certainly possible. Efforts to prevent child maltreatment generally focus on the following:

- Teaching children to resist maltreatment by reporting it to others.
- Educating children about unsafe situations.
- Educating parents about normal child development and high-risk situations that often lead to maltreatment, such as family transitions and stress.
- Teaching parents appropriate disciplinary practices.
- Implementing home visitation programs staffed by nurses, physicians, social workers, paraprofessionals, or others, especially following a child's birth.
- Providing support groups for parents.
- Encouraging pediatricians, psychologists, and other health professionals to report suspected incidents of maltreatment.

Focus On Violence

Dissociative Experiences and Violence Toward Others

A key component of different dissociative disorders is that a person becomes detached from reality at one time or another. An interesting question, however, is whether people in dissociative states are particularly violent toward other people. Occasionally we see people charged with a violent crime who claim no memory of their act or that "a different part of themselves" was responsible.

One of the "Hillside Stranglers"—responsible for the rape and strangulation of several young women in California in 1977 and 1978—later claimed to have alter personalities. Films such as *Psycho* reinforce the impression as well that dissociative experiences are associated with violence. Some have also speculated that men often commit violent acts when dissociated and end up in prison, whereas women with dissociation are more likely to be less aggressive and enter therapy. Prisoners often report severe dissociative experiences (Geng et al., 2022).

Mary Evans/Universal Pictures/Ronald. Grant/Everett Collection

In the film *Psycho*, the character Norman Bates appeared to have different personalities; some were meek and some were violent.

Violence and dissociation may be linked in a couple of ways. First, a person may experience dissociative/traumatic flashbacks, believe they are in danger, and lash out at others. Second, dissociation may occur during the commission of a violent crime of passion. A man who strangles another person during an intense argument may have trouble grasping the enormity of his act and experience a sense of depersonalization. These possibilities underscore the importance of closely monitoring a person's dissociative symptoms in treatment.

Bettmann/Getty Images

"Hillside Strangler" Kenneth Bianchi at one point falsely claimed he had alter personalities responsible for his killings.

Section Summary

- Biological risk factors for dissociative disorders may include key brain changes in areas most responsible for memory and consciousness integration.
- Memory changes in people with dissociative disorders often involve compartmentalization of personal material and failure to retrieve information.
- Trauma and dissociation are linked but the causal relationship between the two remains unclear.
- Neurodevelopmental models of dissociative disorder concentrate on how young, maltreated children fail to develop a unified sense of self.
- Prevention of dissociative disorders has not received much research attention, but prevention of child maltreatment may be helpful in this regard.

Review Questions

1. What brain changes may be associated with dissociative disorders?
2. What memory changes seem central to dissociative disorders?
3. How are trauma and dissociation linked?
4. Describe a general causal theory of dissociation in early life.
5. Outline a strategy for preventing child maltreatment.

Dissociative Disorders: Assessment and Treatment

LO 6.13 Characterize the assessment and treatment of individuals with dissociative disorders.

The next sections discuss assessing and treating dissociative disorders. A full medical examination must first rule out biological conditions that may explain dissociative symptoms. Biological conditions with similar symptoms could include epilepsy, migraine headache, and brain injury or disease, among others.

Assessment of Dissociative Disorders

Assessing someone like Erica with a possible dissociative disorder may be accomplished using interviews and questionnaires.

Courtesy of Gordon M. Grant

Through interviews with her therapist, Judy Castelli, an artist, uncovered a forgotten history of psychological, physical and sexual abuse. She was subsequently diagnosed with dissociative identity disorder involving 44 personalities.

Interviews

Interviewing people with dissociative disorder can be a difficult task for several reasons. First, many people with these disorders, such as those with amnesia or fugue, do not seek therapy for dissociation. Second, recollection of memories from dissociative states is often limited. Third, accessing different personalities in someone with dissociative identity disorder can be quite challenging.

Still, interviews are available to assess for dissociative symptoms and disorders. Prominent ones include the *Clinician-Administered Dissociative States Scale* and *Structured Clinical Interview for Dissociative Disorders—Revised* (SCID-D-R; Pomeroy, 2015. The SCID-D-R is a semistructured interview for symptoms of amnesia, depersonalization, derealization, identity confusion, and identity alteration. The interview also covers severity of these symptoms and degree to which they interfere with daily functioning. Sample SCID-D-R questions include the following:

- Have you ever felt as if there were large gaps in your memory? (amnesia)
- Have you ever felt that you were watching yourself from a point outside of your body, as if you were observing yourself from a distance (or watching a movie of yourself)? (depersonalization)
- Have you ever felt as if familiar surroundings or people you knew seemed unfamiliar or unreal? (derealization)
- Have you ever felt as if there was a struggle going on inside of you? (identity confusion)
- Have you ever acted as if you were a completely different person? (identity alteration)

An interview of someone with a possible dissociative disorder should include a detailed history of trauma and symptoms of acute stress or posttraumatic stress disorder. Recall that many people with dissociative disorder have experienced recent or past traumatic events. Erica's therapist embarked on a long assessment process that included interviews of Erica and her seven-year-old personality, who named herself Erica-Bad. The therapist compiled a detailed history about severe maltreatment of Erica-Bad by her father, who was now deceased. The therapist also explored recent stressors such as Erica's breakup with her boyfriend to know why the subpersonality suddenly appeared to the therapist. The conflict and distress of Erica's relationship and breakup seemed to have triggered intense, compartmentalized memories of maltreatment in childhood.

Questionnaires

Questionnaires are also available to assess dissociative symptoms; one commonly used questionnaire is the *Dissociative Experiences Scale—Revised* (DES; Lyssenko et al., 2018). The DES covers three main categories of dissociative symptoms: dissociative amnesia, absorption and imaginative involvement, and depersonalization/derealization. Absorption and imaginative involvement refer to engaging in fantasy to such an extent that reality and fantasy are blurred.

An adolescent version of this scale (A-DES) covers dissociative amnesia, absorption and imaginative involvement, passive influence, and depersonalization and derealization. Passive influence refers to the experience of not having full control over one's body and physical sensations. The DES and A-DES are useful for identifying people with pathological levels of dissociative symptoms. Sample A-DES items are in **Table 6.10**.

Other popular scales contain items or subscales relevant to dissociative symptoms. Examples include MMPI-3 items and the dissociation scale from the *Trauma Symptom Checklist for Children* (Briere, 2012). The use of multiple measures to assess dissociation is usually recommended because dissociative symptoms are often complex, hidden, and unpredictable.

Biological Treatment of Dissociative Disorders

The biological treatment of dissociative disorders largely involves medication to ease comorbid symptoms of anxiety,

Table 6.10 Sample Items from the Adolescent Dissociative Experiences Scale

I get so wrapped up in watching TV, reading, or playing video games that I don't have any idea what's going on around me.
People tell me I do or say things that I don't remember doing or saying.
I feel like I'm in a fog or spaced out and things around me seem unreal.
I don't recognize myself in the mirror.
I find myself someplace and don't remember how I got there.

Note: Items are scored on a 0-to-10 scale where 0 = never and 10 = always.

Source: Armstrong, J. G., Putnam, F. W., Carlson, E. B., Libero, D. Z., & Smith, S. R. (1997). Development and validation of a measure of adolescent dissociation: The Adolescent Dissociative Experiences Scale. *Journal of Nervous and Mental Disease, 185,* 491–497.

posttraumatic stress, depression, and related conditions such as personality disorders. The most commonly used drugs are anxiolytics, antidepressants, and antipsychotic and anticonvulsant medications. Much of the research in this area comes from case study material, and some people with dissociative disorders do improve in their symptoms when taking these medications. Other researchers, however, report less effect (Sutar & Sahu, 2019).

One problem with using these drugs to treat dissociative disorders is that side effects of these medications, especially antipsychotic drugs, can include feelings of dissociation (Le et al., 2021). Another issue is that medications used for dissociative symptoms were designed for other mental disorders, so little information is available about the biological treatment of dissociative disorders per se (Sutar & Sahu, 2019). Medication may be an adjunct to psychological treatment for dissociation.

Psychological Treatments of Dissociative Disorders

Psychological treatments for dissociative disorders are often geared toward reducing comorbid problems of anxiety, posttraumatic stress, and depression. Many of the cognitive-behavioral approaches discussed in Chapter 5 also apply to people with dissociative disorders. The goals of these approaches are also the same: help people cope with trauma, develop skills to think rationally and realistically, and reduce avoidance of social and other activities. Cognitive-behavioral treatment of symptoms of posttraumatic stress disorder is usually essential for addressing the problems of people with dissociative disorders (Lynn et al., 2019). Additional approaches to treat the core symptoms of dissociation, especially with respect to dissociative identity disorder, are sometimes necessary as well. These approaches are discussed next.

Psychotherapy

A key goal of psychological treatment for dissociative disorders is to help a person reintegrate memories, personalities, and other aspects of consciousness. For dissociative amnesia, the goal is to help a person recall previous aspects of certain trauma or past events in a supportive and safe way and ease their transition back to a normal routine (Mangiulli et al., 2022). For depersonalization/derealization disorder, the goal is to help a person reinterpret symptoms as nonthreatening, increase safety behaviors, and decrease avoidance (Gentile et al., 2014).

For dissociative identity disorder, treatment is often complex and can last months to years. Some clinicians use a psychodynamic stage approach for this population that may resemble the following (Brand et al., 2019; Kluft, 2022):

1. Create a safe, empathic environment in therapy to build a strong therapist-client relationship that also includes all subpersonalities.
2. Enhance a person's ability to function on a daily basis, which includes communicating with and gaining cooperation from subpersonalities.
3. Gather detailed information about all subpersonalities, especially their personal histories.
4. Discuss and process traumatic events associated with each subpersonality, sometimes using hypnosis. Processing means repeated and detailed discussions of these events.
5. Encourage cooperation, empathy, and communication among all subpersonalities as these traumatic events are processed.
6. Integrate subpersonalities into one another, perhaps beginning with those sharing similar histories or personality traits. A single personality is sought, but a collection of fewer subpersonalities may be the final result.
7. Learn coping skills as an alternative to dissociation to address difficult daily events, especially in social relationships.
8. Engage in long-term follow-up to help prevent relapse toward dissociation.

Hypnosis

Hypnosis refers to a relaxed and focused state of mind in which a person is highly suggestible. People with dissociative disorders may undergo hypnosis to increase continuity of memory and identity. A person may undergo hypnosis to try to retrieve forgotten memories, access hidden personalities, or integrate different dimensions of consciousness (Kihlstrom, 2022). Some use hypnosis as well to derive more information about traumatic experiences that led to dissociative states (Weider et al., 2022). Hypnosis may be useful but data to support this approach largely involve case reports. Hypnosis may also lead to distorted memories (Lynn et al., 2020).

Other Psychological Approaches

People with dissociative identity disorder may benefit from supportive family therapy as they enter the reintegration process and address past traumas (Leiderman, 2020). Techniques are sometimes necessary to address suicidality in subpersonalities as well (Chapter 7). Dissociative experiences among youths may be associated with ongoing maltreatment, so eliminating maltreatment and providing a safe environment are obviously important (Deblinger et al., 2015). The psychological treatment of dissociative disorders generally involves helping a person develop a unified sense of self and daily cohesiveness with respect to emotions, thoughts, and behaviors.

Erica's therapist devoted two years to detailed discussions of past trauma. Erica's siblings participated in therapy to help confirm previous aspects of maltreatment and provide support. The therapist was able to establish a good working relationship with Erica-Bad, the seven-year-old subpersonality. The child personality gave important information about the past, including physical and sexual maltreatment from Erica's father and uncle. This process was a long and painful journey that required antidepressant medication and interventions to address intermittent suicidal urges.

What If I or Someone I Know Has a Dissociative Disorder?

Knowing if you or someone you know has a dissociative disorder can be difficult because the symptoms of these disorders are often murky. Pay attention to ongoing forgetfulness, odd experiences, and detachment from others, among other sudden peculiarities. If you suspect someone you know might be experiencing symptoms of a dissociative disorder, then referring them for a full medical examination and even an emergency room consultation is important. The possible consequences of being in a state of dissociation can be devastating.

Long-Term Outcome for People with Dissociative Disorders

The long-term outcome for people with dissociative disorders is variable because integration of consciousness is difficult and because the problems usually extend from childhood. Some people with dissociative amnesia or fugue are able to recover and return to their past lifestyles. Others continue to have problems with information recall and disruption in their lives. They may experience more episodes of severe memory loss as well (Mangiulli et al., 2022).

Many people with dissociative identity disorder do respond positively to biological and psychological treatment. Improvements may occur with respect to dissociation, anxiety, depression, and pain as a person addresses traumas and integrates subpersonalities (Webster et al., 2018). A person's initial degree of dissociation, other psychopathology, and trauma may be good predictors of whether full personality integration can be achieved (Nester et al., 2022).

Erica did not achieve full integration of her host personality and subpersonality (Erica-Bad). Over time and with extended treatment, however, appearances

Personal Narrative

Heather Pate

Heather Pate has dissociative identity disorder (DID). Her therapist diagnosed Pate with this rare mental disorder. "She said it's what was called multiple personality disorder," Pate remembers. "And my immediate response was, 'No I'm not Sybil.'" Pate refers to *Sybil,* a book and subsequent movie about a young woman coming to grips with the dissociative identity disorder—which was then called multiple personality disorder. Experts believe it develops from overwhelming childhood trauma. To cope, the patient's personality splits, or develops additional personalities.

Pate estimates she has more than 30 personalities. "When I think I've gotten to where I think they're all there, somebody pops up," she explains. Besides Heather, who she is most of the time, there's also a teenager called 'A' and a pair of 8-year-old twins Little One and Tommy.

DID is stigmatized—even within the mental health community. And, it's a rare mental disorder. Experts estimate that only 1 percent of all people are affected by it. Unfortunately for Pate, she knows no one else in Central Virginia with dissociative identity disorder. "Even with the voices, the personalities internally, you would think you wouldn't be alone, but it does feel very alone."

What's helped Pate manage the disorder and symptoms? She receives treatment to integrate her personalities, and she adjusted her outward appearance and habits by wearing cartoon T-shirts and keeping sugary drinks with her, to satisfy all the ages inside.

Pate has adapted to the disorder, and is considered "high-functioning." She was diagnosed but worked full-time and was married. Now, giving a face to the condition is her mission, and she hopes to become a peer counselor.

"There is a purpose and plan for my life," she says. "To be able to come alongside others is that much more healing and encouraging and helpful and a part of the wellness in and of itself."

—By Amy Lacey

Photographee.eu/Shutterstock.com

Source: Published April 13, 2016. http://wric.com/2016/04/13/faces-of-recovery-living-with-dissociative-identity-disorder-did/

by Erica-Bad became fewer and Erica herself experienced less disruption in her daily life. She also felt less depressed, began to forge good relationships with her siblings, and considered new dating opportunities.

Section Summary

- Interviews to assess people with dissociative disorders often cover recent and past stressors and the presence of amnesia, depersonalization, derealization, identity confusion, and identity alteration.
- Questionnaires screen for dissociative symptoms such as amnesia, absorption and imaginative involvement, depersonalization, and passive influence.
- The biological treatment of dissociative disorders usually includes medication for concurrent symptoms of anxiety, depression, and other problems.
- Psychotherapy for dissociation helps a person reintegrate consciousness, process traumatic events, and learn to cope with daily events without using dissociation.
- The long-term outcome of people with dissociative disorders is variable and likely depends on severity of past trauma and current degree of psychopathology.

Review Questions

1. Describe various methods to assess people with dissociative disorders, and devise an assessment strategy you think might be most helpful.
2. What medications might be best for people with dissociative disorders?
3. What aspects of psychotherapy might be best for people with dissociative disorders?
4. How might expressive and other psychological therapies help people with dissociation?
5. Describe the long-term outcome for people with dissociative disorders.

Final Comments

Somatic symptom and dissociative disorders are among the strangest but most fascinating disorders discussed in this textbook. Perhaps you noticed many of the similarities among these sets of disorders and the anxiety-related disorders in Chapter 5; related factors include apprehension, trauma, interpersonal difficulties, cognitive distortions, and avoidance of social and other situations. Treatments for these problems often overlap. The next chapter covers another set of disorders closely related to those discussed so far: the depressive and bipolar disorders.

Thought Questions

1. If you were a medical doctor, what would you say and do in response to a patient who presents with somatic symptom or illness anxiety disorder?
2. Think about people in the news who have claimed that some dissociative experience has kept them from remembering a crime or other event. Do you believe them? Why or why not?
3. What would you say to a friend who told you that their relative seems to be "spacing out" a lot in their life?
4. What separates "normal aging" from somatization and "normal forgetfulness" from dissociation? At what point does one "cross the line" from regular changes in thinking, memory, and behavior to more serious problems?
5. How might we reduce the prevalence of somatic symptom and dissociative disorders in the general population?

Key Terms

somatization 146
somatic symptom disorder 147
illness anxiety disorder 149
conversion disorder 150
pseudoseizures 150
factitious disorder 151
Munchausen syndrome 151
malingering 151
contingency management 159
dissociation 161
dissociative disorders 161
dissociative amnesia 161
dissociative fugue 163
dissociative identity disorder 163
depersonalization/derealization disorder 165

Depressive and Bipolar Disorders and Suicide

7

Learning Objectives

LO 7.1 Describe mood, including the extremes of depression and mania.

LO 7.2 Distinguish between the types of depressive disorders and among the types of bipolar disorders based on their diagnostic criteria and clinical features.

LO 7.3 Summarize the epidemiology of depressive and bipolar disorders.

LO 7.4 Describe the phenomenon of suicide, including Durkheim's types of suicide and the epidemiology of suicide.

LO 7.5 Describe the stigma associated with depressive disorders and bipolar disorders and its impact on those with the disorders.

LO 7.6 Discuss the risk factors for depressive disorders, bipolar disorders, and suicide.

LO 7.7 Evaluate programs to prevent depressive disorders, bipolar disorders, and suicide.

LO 7.8 Characterize the assessment and treatment of individuals with depressive disorders, bipolar disorders, and suicidal ideation.

Case Katey

Katey was a 30-year-old woman referred for outpatient therapy after a stay in an inpatient psychiatric unit. Katey's hospital visit came after police found her atop a tall building threatening to jump. Her behavior at the time was somewhat bizarre—the police said Katey was talking very fast and claiming she could fly. Katey was difficult to converse with, but police officers eventually convinced her to move away from the edge of the building and come with them to the psychiatric hospital.

At the hospital, Katey said she had been feeling strange over the past several weeks. She rarely slept and instead wanted to "meet new and interesting people." She frequented dance clubs and bars and fearlessly walked down alleyways to meet people. These actions led to some potentially dangerous situations and interactions, but fortunately no physical harm had come to her. She also said she needed to talk fast because "so many thoughts fly through my head." Katey had lost her job recently and much of her contact with family members. She was also in danger of losing her apartment because she had spent her savings on lavish clothes.

Katey's therapist asked what happened the night the police found her. Katey said she had been drinking at a dance club and could not remember how she arrived at the top of the building. Her memory of that night was poor, although she did recall bits and pieces of conversations. Katey received medication at the hospital and slept for most of three days, saying she felt much more "normal" and "with it" afterward.

Katey said she had always battled moodiness and substance use problems. She said her "mood swings" began in adolescence after her first breakup with a boyfriend and continued during her college and early career years. She often compensated for mood changes by drinking alcohol and working hard. Katey said she could occasionally go two or three days working with little sleep, and this intense activity seemed to alleviate some sadness. She remained haunted, however, by her often-changing mood.

Katey said she was married briefly several years ago, but the marriage ended because both partners tired of the other's "drama." Since that time, Katey continued her work as a legal assistant and received substantial raises over the years. Her work during recent months, however, was sloppy and tardy, and she was often absent. Katey's boss fired her three months ago after several warnings. Katey said her firing triggered much anxiety for her and prompted her current string of strange behaviors.

Katey also said she occasionally thought about hurting herself. These thoughts usually came when she felt unhappy but intensified recently as her unusual behavior became more stressful. Katey reluctantly admitted she once tried halfheartedly to kill herself in college. Her attempt followed a night of drinking during which she became sad and found some pills (unknown kind) in her roommate's bathroom. She took several pills but woke the next morning in a daze and with a severe headache. Katey said she had not attempted suicide from that point to the night when police found her atop the building.

Katey cried in session and felt her life was in disarray. She had no job, few friends, was barely hanging on to a place to live, and had not spoken with her family in months. Her recent emotional states seemed to propel her toward self-destruction. Katey said she desperately wanted to regain control of her moods and her life in general. Her therapist assured her that Katey's compliance with medication and therapy attendance would go a long way in helping her do so.

What Do You Think?

1. Which of Katey's symptoms seem typical of a young adult, and which seem very different?
2. What external events and internal factors might be responsible for Katey's feelings?
3. What are you curious about regarding Katey?
4. Does Katey remind you in any way of yourself or someone you know? How so?
5. How might Katey's mood changes affect her life in the future?

Normal Mood Changes and Depression and Mania: What Are They?

LO 7.1 Describe mood, including the extremes of depression and mania.

Have you ever been very sad or "down in the dumps" like Katey? Have you ever reacted badly to a stressful life event like a breakup? Have you ever felt you could not control your behavior or ever had thoughts about hurting yourself? For most people, sadness is a natural reaction to unfortunate events that happen in their lives. Many of us become sad when we receive a poor grade, have an argument with a loved one, or discover a friend is sick. Such sadness is usually mild and temporary.

Other times our sadness can be more intense and last for a longer period. We are particularly sad when a family member dies, when lengthy separation from loved ones occurs, or when overwhelmed by life's demands. This sadness lingers but eventually fades as we cope with the stressor more effectively. We often rely on our friends and family members to help us through life's "rough patches."

For people like Katey, however, sadness continues for a long time, occurs for little reason, or is so intense that interacting with others is difficult. The sadness often prevents a person from functioning effectively at school or work. A person may have trouble eating, sleeping, or concentrating; feel responsible for things beyond their control; and feel extremely fatigued. Sadness or a sense of hopelessness can become so intense that harming oneself or dying by suicide seems like the only way to stop the pain. These symptoms refer to *depression,* which is at the far end of the sadness continuum (refer to **Continuum of Sadness and Depression**).

Sadness is an emotion or mood, and its natural opposite is happiness. Many events and people make us happy, and all of us strive to be happy when we can. Most of us find happiness in the little things of life, such as coming home and hugging one's children, talking to close friends, and accomplishing significant goals at work. Sometimes we even get carried away with our happiness, such as laughing a little too loudly at a social event. Such behaviors might even cause us some embarrassment!

Other people sometimes experience an intense state of happiness called *euphoria.* Euphoria is a wonderful feeling many people sense immediately after hearing good news or after a joyous event like childbirth. Euphoria is usually a short-term feeling that fades as a person becomes accustomed to whatever experience they had—the joy of having a newborn quickly gives way to exhaustion! Euphoria is not generally harmful as long as it is temporary.

Euphoria can remain ongoing for some people, however. People with chronic euphoria often have constant feelings of being "on the go," thoughts "racing" through their head, a sense of pressure to keep talking, and chronic loss of sleep. They are also distracted and make poor personal decisions, as Katey did. One may also have a sense of *grandiosity,* or a belief that they are especially powerful or talented when this is not actually true. These symptoms can be so severe they lead to extreme irritability and self-destructive or even suicidal behavior. These symptoms refer to *mania,* which is at the far end of the happiness and euphoria continuum (refer to **Continuum of Happiness, Euphoria, and Mania**).

Depressive and Bipolar Disorders and Suicide: Features and Epidemiology

LO 7.2 Distinguish between the types of depressive disorders and among the types of bipolar disorders based on their diagnostic criteria and clinical features.

LO 7.3 Summarize the epidemiology of depressive and bipolar disorders.

LO 7.4 Describe the phenomenon of suicide, including Durkheim's types of suicide and the epidemiology of suicide.

People whose depression or mania becomes so severe it interferes with daily functioning may have a **depressive disorder** or a **bipolar disorder**. Depressive and bipolar disorders are sometimes collectively referred to as mood disorders. Someone with only depression may have a unipolar (one pole) disorder, as in *unipolar depression* or *depressive disorder*. Depression and mania can occur in the same individual, however, as they do in Katey's case. This person may have a bipolar (two pole) disorder. The next sections cover major depressive and bipolar disorders that cause people like Katey so much distress. Suicide, which is often associated with depressive and bipolar disorders, is also discussed.

Major Depressive Episode

A **major depressive episode** involves a period of time, typically at least two weeks but usually longer, in which a person experiences sad or empty moods most of the day, nearly every day (Criteria A–C in **Table 7.1**; American Psychiatric Association [APA], 2022). A major depressive episode does not refer to temporary sadness that may last a day or two or for only part of a day. Instead, the problem refers to a lengthy period in which a person is depressed during different times of the day and almost every day of the week. The sadness is usually intense, to the point that the person has trouble functioning in their daily life. Such was true for Katey.

People experiencing a major depressive episode also lose pleasure doing things they used to enjoy. A person may have always enjoyed being with friends or family, pursuing a hobby, or working at their job. After a major depressive episode, however, they may withdraw from these activities or no longer get much pleasure from them. Katey became increasingly withdrawn from her family. Recall from other chapters (on anxiety-related and somatic symptom/dissociative disorders) that people with mental disorders often avoid or withdraw from social contact. You will find throughout this textbook that many people with mental disorder often have problems interacting with others.

Major depressive episodes also may involve severe changes in appetite, weight, and sleep. People who are depressed often fail to eat or they overeat, perhaps to help compensate for sadness. People who are depressed also have trouble sleeping and may wake up very early

Cavan Images/Photonica/Getty Images

People with depression are often sad and isolated from others.

each morning, lying in bed until it is time to rise for the day (*early morning wakening*). Conversely, though, many people with depression have a heavy feeling of fatigue and loss of energy that leads to oversleeping. Such *hypersomnia* may also be a way to escape painful life events or extreme feelings of sadness.

A key characteristic of a major depressive episode is a feeling of "slowness," or trouble gathering much physical energy. A person may simply want to lie on the couch all day, passively surf websites at work, or sleep a lot. People with very severe cases of depression, or *melancholia*, may be so slowed down they do not move any muscles for hours. Although depressive episodes can resemble anxiety-related disorders in many respects (Chapter 5), this melancholic feeling of slowness is much more characteristic of depression.

People experiencing a major depressive episode tend to feel worthless and guilty about many things, including life events beyond their control. They may blame themselves for not preventing a friend's divorce. Trouble

Continuum of Sadness and Depression

	Normal	Mild
Emotions	Good mood.	Mild discomfort about the day, feeling a bit irritable or down.
Cognitions	Thoughts about what one has to do that day. Thoughts about how to plan and organize the day.	Thoughts about the difficulty of the day. Concern that something will go wrong.
Behaviors	Rising from bed, getting ready for the day, and going to school or work.	Taking a little longer than usual to rise from bed. Slightly less concentration at school or work.

Continuum of Happiness, Euphoria, and Mania

	Normal	Mild
Emotions	Feeling good.	Happiness about good events that day, such as an unexpected check in the mail. Feeling a "bounce" in one's step.
Cognitions	Thoughts about the pleasant aspects of the day.	Thoughts about the good things in life.
Behaviors	Normal daily activity.	Completing daily tasks with great vigor. Being quite social and talkative.

concentrating or making decisions is also common in this population and often leads to problems at work or school, as was true for Katey. The most serious symptom of a major depressive episode is thoughts or ideas about death or suicide, or an actual suicide attempt. Many people facing a major depressive episode, like Katey, have morbid thoughts and fantasies about dying, their own funeral, and cutting or otherwise hurting themselves. These thoughts sometimes precede actual attempts to harm oneself. Tragically, these attempts are sometimes fatal.

A major depressive episode must interfere with daily functioning and not be directly caused by a medical condition or substance. People temporarily *bereaved* after the loss of a loved one may not necessarily receive a diagnosis of a major depressive episode because grief is a normal human reaction. Feelings of sadness in children are more difficult to identify, so irritable mood can replace obvious signs of unhappiness. Failure to gain weight may also be symptomatic of a major depressive episode in youths.

Moderate	Depression—less severe	Depression—more severe
Feeling upset and sad, perhaps becoming a bit teary-eyed.	Intense sadness and frequent crying. Daily feelings of "heaviness" and emptiness.	Extreme sadness, very frequent crying, and feelings of emptiness and loss. Strong sense of hopelessness.
Dwelling on the negative aspects of the day, such as a couple of mistakes on a test or a cold shoulder from a coworker.	Thoughts about one's personal deficiencies, strong pessimism about the future, and thoughts about harming oneself (with little intent to do so).	Thoughts about suicide, funerals, and instructions to others in case of one's death. Strong intent to harm oneself.
Coming home to slump into bed without eating dinner. Tossing and turning in bed, unable to sleep. Some difficulty concentrating.	Inability to rise from bed many days, skipping classes at school, and withdrawing from contact with others.	Complete inability to interact with others or even leave home. Great changes in appetite and weight. Suicide attempt or completion.

Moderate	Mania—less severe	Mania—more severe
Sense of temporary euphoria about some grand life event such as a wedding or birth of a newborn. Feeling on "cloud nine."	Intense euphoria for a longer period. Feelings of agitation and inflated self-esteem.	Extreme euphoria for very long periods, such as months. Sense of grandiosity about oneself, such as the belief that one is a great playwright.
Thoughts racing a bit about all the changes to one's life and how wonderful life is.	Intense, racing thoughts that lead to distractibility and difficulty concentrating.	Racing thoughts almost nonstop that lead to complete inability to concentrate or speak to others coherently.
Some difficulty sleeping due to sense of elation.	Less need for sleep, pressure to talk continuously, working for hours on end.	Engaging in pleasurable activities that lead to damage, such as racing a car down a residential street or spending all of one's money.

Table 7.1 DSM-5-TR

Major Depressive Disorder
A. Five (or more) of the following symptoms have been present during the same two-week period and represent a change from previous functioning; at least one of the symptoms is either (1) depressed mood or (2) loss of interest or pleasure. Note: Do not include symptoms that are clearly attributable to another medical condition. 1. Depressed mood most of the day, nearly every day, as indicated by either subjective report (e.g., feels sad, empty, hopeless) or observation made by others (e.g., appears tearful). (Note: In children and adolescents, can be irritable mood.) 2. Markedly diminished interest or pleasure in all, or almost all, activities most of the day, nearly every day (as indicated by either subjective account or observation). 3. Significant weight loss when not dieting or weight gain (e.g., a change of more than 5% of body weight in a month), or decrease or increase in appetite nearly every day. (Note: In children, consider failure to make expected weight gain.) 4. Insomnia or hypersomnia nearly every day. 5. Psychomotor agitation or retardation nearly every day (observable by others, not merely subjective feelings of restlessness or being slowed down). 6. Fatigue or loss of energy nearly every day. 7. Feelings of worthlessness or excessive or inappropriate guilt (which may be delusional) nearly every day (not merely self-reproach or guilt about being sick). 8. Diminished ability to think or concentrate, or indecisiveness, nearly every day (either by subjective account or as observed by others). 9. Recurrent thoughts of death (not just fear or dying), recurrent suicidal ideation without a specific plan, or a suicide attempt or a specific plan for committing suicide.
B. The symptoms cause clinically significant distress or impairment in social, occupational, or other important areas of functioning.
C. The episode is not attributable to the physiological effects of a substance or to another medical condition. Note: Criteria A–C represent a major depressive episode. Note: Responses to a significant loss may include the feelings of intense sadness, rumination about the loss, insomnia, poor appetite, and weight loss noted in Criterion A, which may resemble a depressive episode. Although such symptoms may be understandable or considered appropriate to the loss, the presence of a major depressive episode in addition to the normal response to a significant loss should also be carefully considered. This decision inevitably requires the exercise of clinical judgment based on the individual's history and the cultural norms for the expression of the distress in the context of loss.
D. The occurrence of the major depressive episode is not better explained by schizoaffective disorder, schizophrenia, schizophreniform disorder, delusional disorder, or other specified and unspecified schizophrenia spectrum and other psychotic disorders.
E. There has never been a manic episode or hypomanic episode. Note: This exclusion does not apply if all of the manic-like or hypomanic-like episodes are substance-induced or are attributable to the physiological effects of another medical condition.

American Psychiatric Association. (2022). *Diagnostic and statistical manual of mental disorders* (5th ed., text rev.). Arlington, VA: American Psychiatric Association.

Major Depressive Disorder

Major depressive disorder, sometimes called *major depression* or *unipolar depression*, usually involves a longer period during which a person may experience multiple major depressive episodes (refer to **Figure 7.1**). A two-month interval of normal mood must occur for episodes to be considered separate from one another (APA, 2022). Major depressive disorder can be diagnosed, however, in someone who has only a single or first episode of depression. Major depressive disorder may be mild, moderate, or severe and may occur with or without *psychotic features* such as bizarre ideas or hearing voices that are not real (psychotic features are discussed in more detail in Chapter 12). Depressive symptoms may also be *peripartum* or *postpartum*, occurring during pregnancy or after the birth of a child (refer to **Focus On Gender: Forms of Depression Among Women**) (Liu et al., 2021). In addition, depression in some people occurs more in fall or winter months, or *seasonal depression*. People with seasonal depression often experience reduced energy, low motivation, and anxiety with depressed mood (Galima et al., 2020).

Figure 7.1 Cycle of Major Depressive Disorder.

Major depressive disorder may involve one or more major depressive episodes.

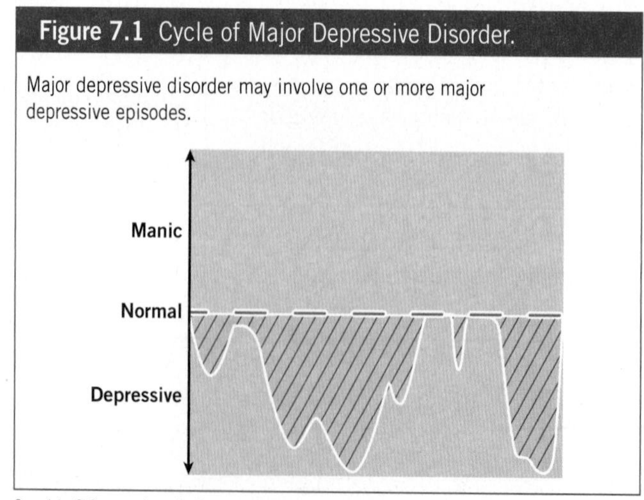

Focus On Gender

Forms of Depression Among Women

Women report more depression than men, and this difference may be due to genetic factors as well as stressful marital and other relationships. However, conditions specific to women may also help to explain this difference. Examples include premenstrual dysphoric disorder and postpartum depression.

Premenstrual dysphoric disorder is a controversial condition that refers to depressive or other symptoms during most menstrual cycles in the past year (refer to **Table 7.2**; APA, 2022). These symptoms include depressed, anxious, or angry mood; mood swings; fatigue; trouble concentrating; eating and sleeping changes; feeling out of control; and physical symptoms such as bloating or joint pain. The symptoms mainly occur in the week prior to menses and must cause distress or interfere with a woman's daily functioning. About 1 to 6 percent of women may have this condition, which may link to hormonal changes that alter serotonin levels. Treatment thus usually involves antidepressant medication (Reilly et al., 2022).

Peripartum depression or **postpartum depression** refers to symptoms of depression or a major depressive episode that occurs during pregnancy or in the weeks after childbirth (APA, 2022). Postpartum depression is not simply the "blues" that many women face after childbirth, which may be caused by hormonal changes or social isolation. Instead, postpartum depression is a severe condition that affects about 12 percent of women after they give birth. Postpartum depression is commonly associated with depression and anxiety during pregnancy (peripartum), stressful life events during pregnancy, lower social support, and previous history of depression (Shorey et al., 2018). Women with these risk factors should thus be monitored closely before and after childbirth in case suicidal ideation is present.

Persistent Depressive Disorder (Dysthymia)

Another mood disorder similar to major depression is **persistent depressive disorder**, commonly called *dysthymia*, which is a chronic feeling of depression for at least two years (refer to **Table 7.3**; APA, 2022). People with persistent depressive disorder may not have all the severe symptoms of major depression but instead have "low-grade" symptoms that persist for much of their life (refer to **Personal Narrative: Karen Gormandy**). A mixture of symptoms is often seen involving appetite and sleep changes, fatigue, low self-esteem, trouble concentrating or making decisions, and feeling hopeless (Schramm et al., 2020).

Persistent depressive disorder still involves an intense feeling of sadness most of every day, with relief from symptoms never longer than two months at a time (refer to **Figure 7.2**). Some people with dysthymia also have one or more major depressive episodes during the two-year course of their disorder. The presence of dysthymia *and* a major depressive episode at the same time is *double depression* (Ventriglio et al., 2020). Double depression may be difficult to spot unless a client has seen a therapist for some time and the therapist notices a sudden or gradual worsening of the client's symptoms.

Persistent depressive disorder must not be caused by a medical condition or substance, and the disorder must significantly interfere with daily functioning. The disorder may be classified as *early* or *late onset* depending on whether symptoms developed before age 21 years or at age 21 years or older. Persistent depressive disorder may be diagnosed in children and adolescents after a *one-year* period of depressed *or* irritable mood.

Other Depressive Disorders

Other formal depressive disorders may be diagnosed as well. *Disruptive mood dysregulation disorder* refers to youth aged 6 to 18 years with recurrent temper outbursts that are severe and well out of proportion to a given situation (refer to **Table 7.4**; APA, 2022). The outbursts occur at least three times per week, and the child is often irritable or angry. Symptoms must be present for at least one year and be evident in multiple settings. Onset is before age 10 years. The disorder was meant to address the fact that many children with these symptoms may have been diagnosed and treated for bipolar disorder (discussed later in the chapter). Another formal depressive disorder is *premenstrual dysphoric disorder* (refer to **Focus on Gender: Forms of Depression Among Women**).

Manic and Hypomanic Episodes

As mentioned, euphoria for a short time is usually not harmful. Feelings of euphoria that continue uncontrollably for long periods, however, can lead to destructive behavior.

Figure 7.2 Cycle of Persistent Depressive Disorder.

Persistent depressive disorder (dysthymia) involves low-grade symptoms of depression for at least two years.

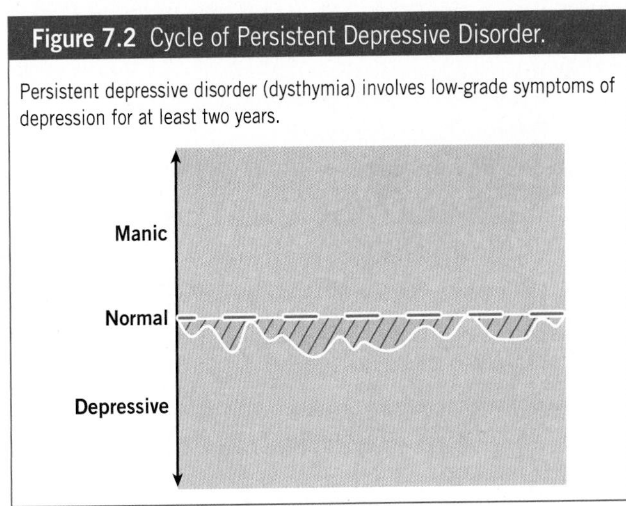

Table 7.2 DSM-5-TR

Premenstrual Dysphoric Disorder
A. In the majority of menstrual cycles, at least five symptoms must be present in the final week before the onset of menses, start to *improve* within a few days after the onset of menses, and become *minimal* or absent in the week postmenses.
B. One (or more) of the following symptoms must be present: 1. Marked affective lability. 2. Marked irritability or anger or increased interpersonal conflicts. 3. Marked depressed mood, feelings of hopelessness, or self-deprecating thoughts. 4. Marked anxiety, tension, and/or feelings of being keyed up or on edge.
C. One (or more) of the following symptoms must additionally be present, to reach a total of *five* symptoms when combined with symptoms from Criterion B above. 1. Decreased interest in usual activities. 2. Subjective difficulty in concentration. 3. Lethargy, easy fatigability, or marked lack of energy. 4. Marked changes in appetite; overeating; or specific food cravings. 5. Hypersomnia or insomnia. 6. A sense of being overwhelmed or out of control. 7. Physical symptoms such as breast tenderness or swelling, joint or muscle pain, sensation of "bloating," or weight gain. Note: The symptoms in Criteria A–C must have been met for most menstrual cycles that occurred in the preceding year.
D. The symptoms are associated with clinically significant distress or interference with work, school, usual social activities, or relationships with others.
E. The disturbance is not merely an exacerbation of the symptoms of another disorder, such as major depressive disorder, panic disorder, persistent depressive disorder (dysthymia), or a personality disorder (although it may co-occur with any of these disorders).
F. Criterion A should be confirmed by prospective daily ratings during at least two symptomatic cycles. (*Note:* The diagnosis may be made provisionally prior to this conformation.)
G. The symptoms are not attributable to the physiological effects of a substance or another medical condition.

American Psychiatric Association. (2022). *Diagnostic and statistical manual of mental disorders* (5th ed., text rev.). Arlington, VA: American Psychiatric Association.

Table 7.3 DSM-5-TR

Persistent Depressive Disorder
A. Depressed mood for most of the day, for more days than not, as indicated by either subjective account or observations by others, for at least two years. Note: In children and adolescents, mood can be irritable and duration must be at least one year.
B. Presence, while depressed, of two (or more) of the following: 1. Poor appetite or overeating. 2. Insomnia or hypersomnia. 3. Low energy or fatigue. 4. Low self-esteem. 5. Poor concentration or difficulty making decisions. 6. Feelings of hopelessness.
C. During the two-year period (one year for children or adolescents) of the disturbance, the individual has never been without the symptoms in Criteria A and B for more than two months at a time.
D. Criteria for a major depressive disorder may be continuously present for two years.
E. There has never been a manic episode or a hypomanic episode, and criteria have never been met for cyclothymic disorder.
F. The disturbance is not better explained by a persistent schizoaffective disorder, schizophrenia, delusional disorder, or other specified or unspecified schizophrenia spectrum and other psychotic disorder.
G. The symptoms are not attributable to the physiological effects of a substance (e.g., a drug of abuse, a medication) or another medical condition (e.g., hypothyroidism).
H. The symptoms cause clinically significant distress or impairment in social, occupational, or other important areas of functioning. Specify if in partial or full remission, early (before age 21 years) or late (after age 21 years), and mild, moderate, or severe.

American Psychiatric Association. (2022). *Diagnostic and statistical manual of mental disorders* (5th ed., text rev.). Arlington, VA: American Psychiatric Association.

Table 7.4 DSM-5-TR

Disruptive Mood Dysregulation Disorder
A. Severe recurrent temper outbursts manifested verbally and/or behaviorally that are grossly out of proportion in intensity or duration to the situation or provocation.
B. The temper outbursts are inconsistent with developmental level.
C. The temper outbursts occur, on average, three or more times per week.
D. The mood between temper outbursts is persistently irritable or angry most of the day, nearly every day, and is observable by others.
E. Criteria A–D have been present for 12 or more months. Throughout that time, the individual has not had a period lasting three or more consecutive months without all of the symptoms in Criteria A–D.
F. Criteria A and D are present in at least two of three settings and are severe in at least one of these.
G. The diagnosis should not be made for the first time before age 6 years or after age 18 years.
H. By history or observation, the age at onset of Criteria A–E is before 10 years.
I. There has never been a distinct period lasting more than one day during which the full symptom criteria, except duration, for a manic or hypomanic episode have been met. Note: Developmentally appropriate mood elevation, such as occurs in the context of a highly positive event or its anticipation, should not be considered as a symptom of mania or hypomania.
J. The behaviors do not occur exclusively during an episode of major depressive disorder and are not better explained by another mental disorder. Note: This diagnosis cannot coexist with oppositional defiant disorder, intermittent explosive disorder, or bipolar disorder, though it can coexist with others, including major depressive disorder, attention-deficit/hyperactivity disorder, conduct disorder, and substance use disorders. Individuals whose symptoms meet criteria for both disruptive mood dysregulation disorder and oppositional defiant disorder should only be given the diagnosis of disruptive mood dysregulation disorder. If an individual has ever experienced a manic or hypomanic episode, the diagnosis of disruptive mood dysregulation disorder should not be assigned.
K. The symptoms are not attributable to the physiological effects of a substance or to another medical or neurological condition.

American Psychiatric Association. (2022). *Diagnostic and statistical manual of mental disorders* (5th ed., text rev.). Arlington, VA: American Psychiatric Association.

Table 7.5 DSM-5-TR

Manic Episode
A. A distinct period of abnormally and persistently elevated, expansive, or irritable mood and abnormally and persistently increased goal-directed activity or energy, lasting at least one week and present most of the day, nearly every day (or any duration if hospitalization is necessary).
B. During the period of mood disturbance and increased energy or activity, three (or more) of the following symptoms (four if the mood is only irritable) are present to a significant degree and represent a noticeable change from usual behavior: 1. Inflated self-esteem or grandiosity. 2. Decreased need for sleep. 3. More talkative than usual or pressure to keep talking. 4. Flight of ideas or subjective experience that thoughts are racing. 5. Distractibility, as reported or observed. 6. Increase in goal-directed activity (either socially, at work or school, or sexually) or psychomotor agitation. 7. Excessive involvement in activities that have a high potential for painful consequences.
C. The mood disturbance is sufficiently severe to cause marked impairment in social or occupational functioning or to necessitate hospitalization to prevent harm to self or others, or there are psychotic features.
D. The episode is not attributable to the physiological effects of a substance or to another medical condition. Note: A full manic episode that emerges during antidepressant treatment (e.g., medication, electroconvulsive therapy) but persists at a fully syndromal level beyond the physiological effect of that treatment is sufficient evidence for a manic episode and, therefore, a bipolar I diagnosis.

American Psychiatric Association. (2022). *Diagnostic and statistical manual of mental disorders* (5th ed., text rev.). Arlington, VA: American Psychiatric Association.

Personal Narrative

Karen Gormandy

Falling into depression was slow and deceptively delicious. By all accounts, it should have never been. There were no signs or clues when I was very young. In fact, my childhood was a blast.

But by the time I was 12, I was someone else. Not the wild child who was dubbed the "Queen of Play" but a confused adolescent whose actions, thoughts, and desires were motivated by a desire to disengage and become numb. I'm not sure what happened or how it started, but I remember beginning to feel the inward pull when I was 12 years old, when within months of arriving to New York from Trinidad my mother moved out. No one said anything for days. She was just not there. Days later, my father called me into his bedroom and told me she was gone and he didn't know when she'd be back. I was 15 before it was full-blown, almost immobilizing depression.

I would get up, go to school, and simply sit—inattentive and spaced out in class—the teachers' voices, when I did hear them, sounded like distorted noise and incomprehensible static. It wasn't long before I wasn't doing assignments; pretty soon I was cutting classes. I would get all the way to school and stand in front of the building knowing full well I was not going to set foot in there; I would turn tail and head home.

I would take the subway as far as Lexington Avenue and without leaving the station, would catch a train back to Queens, stop off at the candy store, get a Twix bar for lunch and a monthly Harlequin, and share the last leg of my trip home on the bus with a smattering of MTA workers returning home from the graveyard shift.

Before I knew it, when my father flicked the light on for me to get me up for school, I would follow the sound of his footsteps down the carpeted stairs, listen for the front door to close and instead of getting up, I'd turn over and go back to sleep.

I don't think anyone noticed that I spent my entire sophomore year of high school in my room. I left it only when everyone else was in bed to indulge my one pleasure—the late and then the late late show.

When my mother returned to the family, I was 17 and firmly ensconced under sheets and blankets that had not been changed in weeks and surrounded by books that took me far away from anything that resembled my world. All she could think to do was sprinkle holy water in my room and pray that whatever force that was having its way with me would leave. I don't remember how I came to get up and out and back to school. It may have had something to do with a threat from the Board of Education.

My second major depressive episode didn't last quite a year. I had started college on a high note, excited and expectant. But there was a part of me that was knotted up. My husband had taken a job out of state and my teenage son, Justin, was spending more and more time with his friends. I thought my going to school would give me something to replace my lost identity as wife and my dwindling presence as mother. Displacement was not so easy. School could not cover up or replace the shock of being left by my husband and not needed as much by my son.

I lasted a year, and then my resolve started to collapse. I had studied architecture in San Francisco and at the University of Colorado, and I continued on and enrolled as an architecture major at Montana State University. After the second semester, my work was becoming more and more un-architectural and

People with depression often sleep a lot or have trouble sleeping and do not take pleasure in many activities.

A **manic episode** is a period during which a person feels highly euphoric or irritable (refer to **Table 7.5**; APA, 2022). The person has key symptoms that may lead to severe problems during this period of euphoria. They may have a sense of *grandiosity,* or a feeling they can do something unlikely or impossible (Annmella et al., 2020). Katey felt she might be able to fly. A person may also pursue pleasurable activities to such an extent that the activities become self-destructive. Examples include engaging in a shopping or sexual spree, pouring money into foolish investments, or joyriding in a car at high speeds. Severe problems in functioning at school or work can also result from extreme *distractibility* many people have during a manic episode. People experiencing a manic episode also tend to speak rapidly, as if their mind is generating so many thoughts

wilder. I drew curves and lines that had no order and created work outside the perimeters of the assignments.

By the time winter came, I was ready to jump out of my own skin. I was agitated, grumpy, and unhappy. I would get up, see Justin off to school, go to class but not do the assignments. After a few weeks, I would go to one class and skip all my other classes, work frantically to catch up on the schoolwork, and when it became too hard to catch up, I stopped going. Justin moved out at 16, and I stopped getting up in the morning.

Days went by and aside from getting out of bed to go to the bathroom, or to watch TV—my attention span lasted an hour or so before I got drowsy and went back to bed—I stayed under a cocoon of covers. When Justin dropped in, I got out of bed and pretended to be a mother. I can't remember where the time went; I hibernated and lost track of days and nights.

I started to cry. I cried a lot. I cried in front of the university bursar when he asked me why I hadn't paid the rent. Too much in shock to think of a polite answer, I just blurted out the truth: that I wasn't sure if I was married, that I wasn't sure what was happening with my son. He recommended a university therapist.

Jim Murphy was a compassionate, sensitive therapist. He had red hair and the old trick of wearing a full beard so that he wouldn't be mistaken for a student. My moods were easy to read: invisible—when I stuffed my wild hair under a baseball cap and kept my eyes trained to the ground, or defiant—I let my wooly mane loose and uncombed, glared at all the young, hopeful students (who I was furiously jealous of!) in the eye and defied them to stare back. I got brave enough to insist Justin see a doctor. The doctor said he tested positive for marijuana, but otherwise he was fine.

After four sessions, I was on Zoloft and academic probation instead of being suspended. I could reapply for financial aid and get myself back into the university's good graces.

With Jim's help, I rethought my future and changed my major from architecture to film, enrolled in art classes to begin in summer, and spent the spring alone. I went for long walks and drives, and borrowed movies and TV series and watched them again and again. I laughed again.

My fall was slow and almost sensual. My journey up and out is a daily decision. The inclination not to give up and to shut down is like fighting a powerful force of nature that is as strong and as unyielding as gravity. There are days when I am repelled by the sight of myself in the mirror and the surges of self-loathing are incapacitating.

I am in talk therapy. Therapy is a safe place to be raw and vulnerable, maybe it has something to do with just acknowledging the existence of my demons. For whatever reason, it's what I need. My moods undulate not in an up/down, happy/sad way, but more in a hanging on, keeping it together, being distracted kind of way. At this writing it's pretty horrible. The sadness seems ever present and I have to return to meds.

A place to be honest about my feelings, a few very good and empathetic friends and supportive community—such as NAMI (National Alliance on Mental Illness)—keeps me out of the hole. Sometimes I can even remember and smile at the wild child I used to be.

—By Karen Gormandy

Courtesy of Karen Gormandy

Source: Used with permission.

they cannot express them quickly enough. Such *flight of ideas* was true for Katey at times.

Those in a manic state may be highly agitated and pursue a certain goal with great enthusiasm. They may "pour themselves" into a project at work and seem to accomplish a lot, although closer examination reveals the project to be filled with mistakes. Katey worked hard, but her sloppiness cost her job. Someone in a manic episode usually requires little sleep to feel fully rested. Manic episodes last at least one week but could be much longer, perhaps lasting weeks or months. The manic episode must interfere with daily functioning and not be caused by a medical condition or substance.

Other people experience what is known as a **hypomanic episode**. Have you ever suddenly had a huge

Anton Mukhin/Shutterstock.com

People in a state of mania often do things that may be self-destructive, such as indulging in a shopping spree that they cannot afford.

burst of energy or inspiration and completely cleaned your home or finished a project at work? Many of us have felt a "rush" like this, although the experience never lasts more than a few hours or a couple of days. A hypomanic episode, however, comprises the same symptoms as a manic episode but may not cause severe impairment in daily functioning. Unlike "bursts of energy" that many of us occasionally have, hypomanic episodes last at least four days (refer to **Table 7.6**; APA, 2022).

Bipolar I Disorder

Bipolar I disorder refers to one or more manic episodes in a person. The disorder is sometimes called *manic-depression* because a person may alternate between episodes of major depression and mania or hypomania. Such was likely true for Katey. Bipolar I disorder may involve just a single manic episode, however. People with bipolar I disorder often have a major depressive episode that lasts weeks or months, followed by an interval of normal mood before another manic or hypomanic episode (refer to **Table 7.7** and **Figure 7.3a**; APA, 2022). Other people with bipolar I disorder have *mixed features,* which refers to mania with symptoms of depression that do not rise to the level of a major depressive episode.

Some people with bipolar I disorder experience *rapid cycling,* which means they frequently switch from depression to mania and back again with little or no period of normal mood. At least four cycles occur per year in these cases. Still others with the disorder, especially females and those with psychotic symptoms, experience *ultra-rapid cycling* or even *continuous (ultradian) cycling* in which sharp changes in mood toward depression or mania occur almost daily for a certain period (Strawbridge et al., 2022).

Bipolar II Disorder

Bipolar II disorder comprises episodes of hypomania that alternate with episodes of major depression. Full-blown manic episodes are not seen as they are in bipolar I disorder (refer to **Table 7.8** and **Figure 7.3b**; APA, 2022). Hypomanic episodes could worsen and become manic episodes, however, so bipolar II may become bipolar I disorder. For a diagnosis of bipolar II disorder to be made, the condition must not be caused by a medical problem or substance. Hypomanic episodes by themselves may not cause significant impairment in functioning, but hypomanic episodes with major depressive episodes (bipolar II disorder) do significantly interfere with daily functioning.

Cyclothymic Disorder

Cyclothymic disorder, sometimes called *cyclothymia,* refers to symptoms of hypomania and depression that fluctuate over at least a two-year period (refer to **Table 7.9**; APA, 2022). People with cyclothymic disorder

Table 7.6 DSM-5-TR

Hypomanic Episode
A. A distinct period of abnormally and persistently elevated, expansive, or irritable mood and abnormally and persistently increased activity or energy, lasting at least four consecutive days and present most of the day, nearly every day.
B. During the period of mood disturbance and increased energy and activity, three (or more) of the following symptoms (four if the mood is only irritable) have persisted, represent a noticeable change from usual behavior, and have been present to a significant degree: 1. Inflated self-esteem or grandiosity. 2. Decreased need for sleep. 3. More talkative than usual or pressure to keep talking. 4. Flight of ideas or subjective experience that thoughts are racing. 5. Distractibility as reported or observed. 6. Increase in goal-directed activity or psychomotor agitation. 7. Excessive involvement in activities that have a high potential for painful consequences.
C. The episode is associated with an unequivocal change in functioning that is uncharacteristic of the individual when not symptomatic.
D. The disturbance in mood and the change in functioning are observable by others.
E. The episode is not severe enough to cause marked impairment in social or occupational functioning or to necessitate hospitalization. If there are psychotic features, the episode is, by definition, manic.
F. The episode is not attributable to the physiological effects of a substance. Note: A full hypomanic episode that emerges during antidepressant treatment (e.g., medication, electroconvulsive therapy) but persists at a fully syndromal level beyond the physiological effect of that treatment is sufficient evidence for a hypomanic episode diagnosis. However, caution is indicated so that one or two symptoms (particularly increased irritability, edginess, or agitation following antidepressant use) are not taken as sufficient for diagnosis of a hypomanic episode, nor necessarily indicative of a bipolar diathesis.

American Psychiatric Association. (2022). *Diagnostic and statistical manual of mental disorders* (5th ed., text rev.). Arlington, VA: American Psychiatric Association.

do not have full-blown *episodes* of depression, mania, or hypomania. Instead, general *symptoms* of hypomania and depression cycle back and forth, perhaps with intermediate periods of normal mood (refer to **Figure 7.3c**). A diagnosis of cyclothymic disorder requires that these symptoms not be absent for more than two months. Cyclothymic symptoms may last only one year in children and adolescents. Cyclothymic disorder must not be caused by a medical condition or substance but must significantly interfere with daily functioning.

Suicide

Suicide refers to killing oneself and is commonly associated with depressive and bipolar disorders. Suicide is not a mental disorder but is the most serious aspect of depressive and bipolar disorders. Suicide also occurs in people with other mental disorders or no mental disorder. Different aspects of suicide include suicidal ideation, suicidal behavior, suicide attempt, and suicide

Table 7.7 DSM-5-TR

Bipolar I Disorder
A. Criteria have been met for at least one manic episode (Criteria A–D under "Manic Episode").
B. The occurrence of the manic and major depressive episode(s) is not better explained by schizoaffective disorder, schizophrenia, schizophreniform disorder, delusional disorder, or other specified or unspecified schizophrenia spectrum and other psychotic disorder.

American Psychiatric Association. (2022). *Diagnostic and statistical manual of mental disorders* (5th ed., text rev.). Arlington, VA: American Psychiatric Association.

Table 7.8 DSM-5-TR

Bipolar II Disorder
A. Criteria have been met for at least one hypomanic episode (Criteria A–F under "Hypomanic Episode") and at least one major depressive episode (Criteria A–C under "Major Depressive Episode").
B. There has never been a manic episode.
C. The occurrence of the hypomanic episode(s) and major depressive episode(s) is not better explained by schizoaffective disorder, schizophrenia, schizophreniform disorder, delusional disorder, or other specified or unspecified schizophrenia spectrum and other psychotic disorder.
D. The symptoms of depression or the unpredictability caused by frequent alternation between periods of depression and hypomania causes clinically significant distress or impairment in social, occupational, or other important areas of functioning.

American Psychiatric Association. (2022). *Diagnostic and statistical manual of mental disorders* (5th ed., text rev.). Arlington, VA: American Psychiatric Association.

Figure 7.3 Comparison of Cycles of Bipolar I Disorder, Bipolar II Disorder, and Cyclothymic Disorder.

(a) Bipolar I disorder may involve alternating manic and major depressive episodes. (b) Bipolar II disorder may involve alternating hypomanic and major depressive episodes. (c) Cyclothymic disorder may involve alternating symptoms of hypomania and depression.

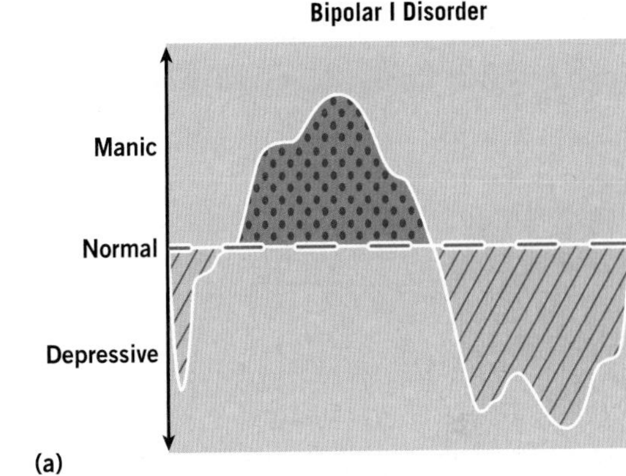

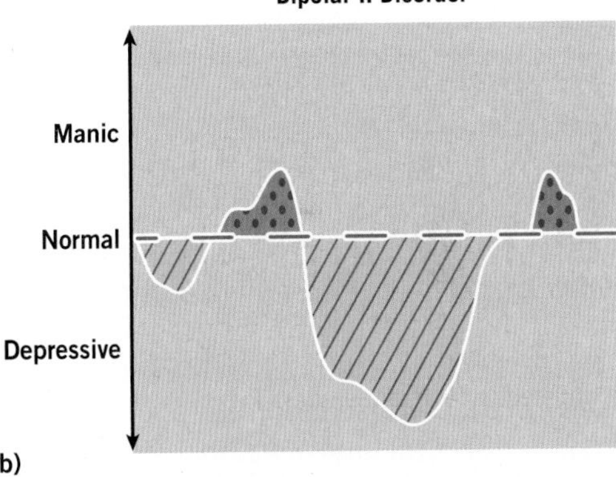

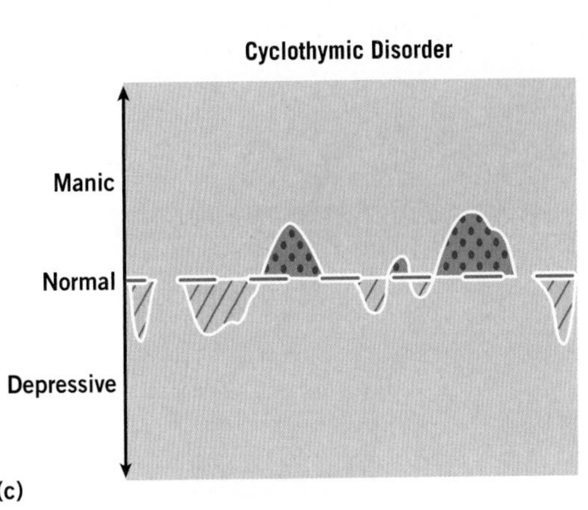

Table 7.9 DSM-5-TR

Cyclothymic Disorder
A. For at least two years (at least one year in children and adolescents) there have been numerous periods with hypomanic symptoms that do not meet criteria for a hypomanic episode and numerous periods with depressive symptoms that do not meet criteria for a major depressive episode.
B. During the above two-year period (one year in children and adolescents), the hypomanic and depressive periods have been present for at least half the time and the individual has not been without the symptoms for more than two months at a time.
C. Criteria for a major depressive, manic, or hypomanic episode have never been met.
D. The symptoms in Criterion A are not better explained by schizoaffective disorder, schizophrenia, schizophreniform disorder, delusional disorder, or other specified or unspecified schizophrenia spectrum and other psychotic disorder.
E. The symptoms are not attributable to the physiological effects of a substance or another medical condition.
F. The symptoms cause clinically significant distress or impairment in social, occupational, or other important areas of functioning.

American Psychiatric Association. (2022). *Diagnostic and statistical manual of mental disorders* (5th ed., text rev.). Arlington, VA: American Psychiatric Association.

completion (refer to **Figure 7.4**; Turton et al., 2021). *Suicidal ideation* refers to thoughts about death, killing oneself, funerals, or other morbid ideas related to one's death. Thinking about suicide does not mean a person will complete suicide, but such thoughts can be a risk factor. *Suicidal behavior,* sometimes called *parasuicidal behavior* or *deliberate self-harm,* refers to self-destructive behavior that may or may not indicate a wish to die. Examples include cutting or burning oneself.

Suicide attempt refers to severe self-destructive behavior in which a person *is* trying to kill themself. Common methods of suicide attempt include firearms, hanging, alcohol/substance/medication overdose, carbon monoxide poisoning, and jumping from a high place. A suicide attempt may or may not lead to *suicide completion,* which refers to people who do kill themselves. All aspects of suicide are commonly associated with people with depressive, bipolar, and other mental disorders.

Some theorists have proposed different types of suicide. One influential theorist was *Emile Durkheim* (1858–1917), a French sociologist who studied people and their relationship to society. Durkheim believed some people complete suicide for different reasons related to social integration. *Egoistic suicide* refers to a situation in which a person's social integration is weak, and so they believe completing suicide comes at little cost to others. Think of a teenager who believes no one cares for them—social alienation is indeed a risk factor for suicide (Moyano et al., 2020). *Anomic suicide* refers to a situation in which a person has great difficulty adapting to disrupted social order created by events such as economic crises. A surge of suicide among older adults in China relates somewhat to massive economic changes there (Cai et al., 2022).

Fatalistic suicide refers to a situation in which a person feels oppressed by society and that their only means of escape is through death. Some people may feel condemned by fate, such as a woman who cannot have children—involuntary childlessness in women can be a risk factor for suicide attempt (Payne et al., 2021). *Altruistic suicide* refers to a situation in which a person completes suicide to benefit society or others around them. Think of a soldier who sacrifices their life to save comrades (Rusch, 2022).

Epidemiology of Depressive and Bipolar Disorders

General feelings of sadness are common: Adults report having symptoms of depression that are mild (16.2 percent), moderate (5.7 percent), moderately severe (2.1 percent), or severe (0.7 percent) (Ettman et al., 2020).

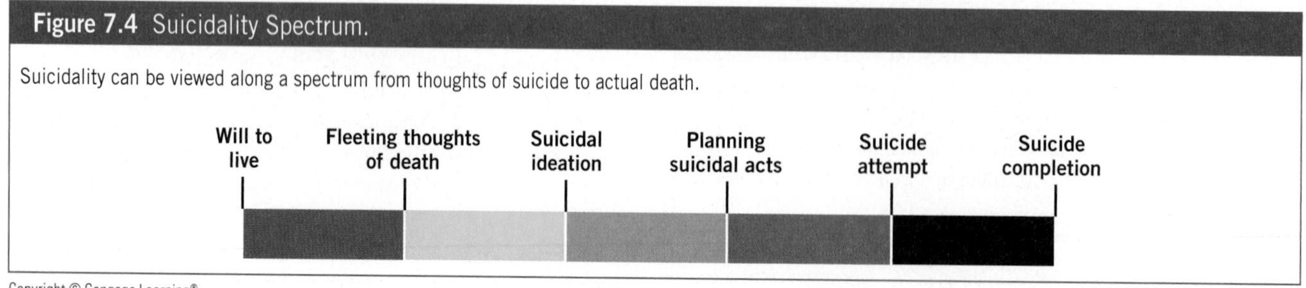

Figure 7.4 Suicidality Spectrum.

Suicidality can be viewed along a spectrum from thoughts of suicide to actual death.

Feelings of sadness can intensify and result in diagnoses of major depressive disorder or dysthymia. The prevalence of major depressive disorder worldwide is 5.0 percent among adults and 5.7 percent among adults aged 60+ years (World Health Organization, 2021). The lifetime prevalence of dysthymia is 1 to 6 percent (Schramm et al., 2020). Adolescents also experience substantial symptoms of depression (34 percent), major depressive disorder (8 percent), and dysthymia (4 percent) (Shorey et al., 2022).

Depression in women increases significantly around the beginning of adolescence, and female adolescents and adults are generally depressed at twice the rate of males. Women may be more willing to admit symptoms of depression than men, but several studies indicate women to be more likely to have a first episode of depression, longer episodes of depression, and more recurrent episodes of depression than men. This gender difference may relate to frequency of stressors and other events in the lives of women (Hyde & Mezulis, 2020). Women also become depressed during certain seasons such as winter and have anxious depression more so than men (Wirz-Justice et al., 2019).

Rates of depression differ around the world (refer to **Figures 7.5** and **7.6**). Rates of depression are elevated in higher income countries compared to lower income countries (Lim et al., 2018). Among Americans, rates of depression are higher in Whites than non-Whites but individuals from minoritized groups tend to have more persistent depression (Flores et al., 2021). Cross-cultural differences with respect to depression may relate to how people develop a sense of self, such as within an individualistic versus collectivist culture (Bartucz et al., 2022).

Severe depression and dysthymia usually begin in late adolescence or early adulthood, but they could occur at any age. Many people have the disorders

Figure 7.5 Rates of Major Depression and Dysthymia by Gender in Community Surveys.

Gender differences in rates of major depression (a) and dysthymia (b) vary in different areas of the world.

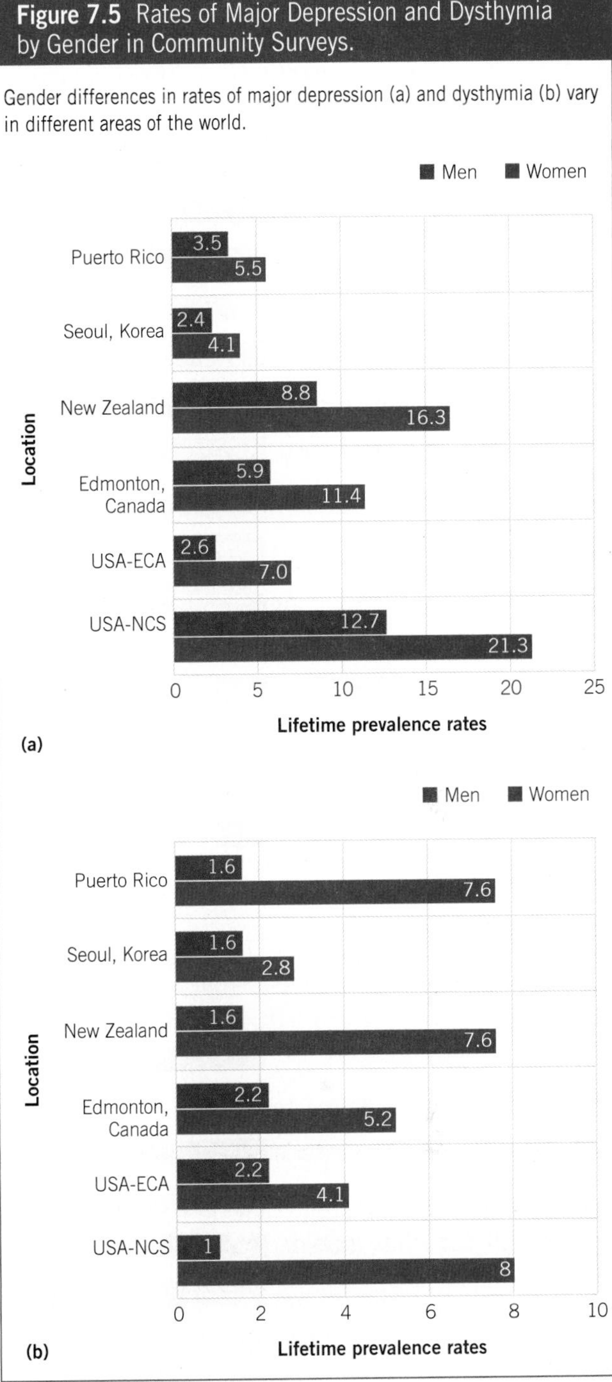

Source: ECA, Epidemiologic Catchment Area; NCS, National Comorbidity Study.

Nineteen-year-old Army Pfc. Ross McGinnis died saving the lives of four comrades in Iraq by voluntarily jumping on a grenade tossed into their military vehicle. He received the Medal of Honor for what may have been an example of altruistic suicide.

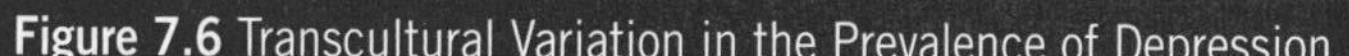

Figure 7.6 Transcultural Variation in the Prevalence of Depression.

(a) Current depression rate in selected countries. (b) Lifetime prevalence rate of depression in selected countries.

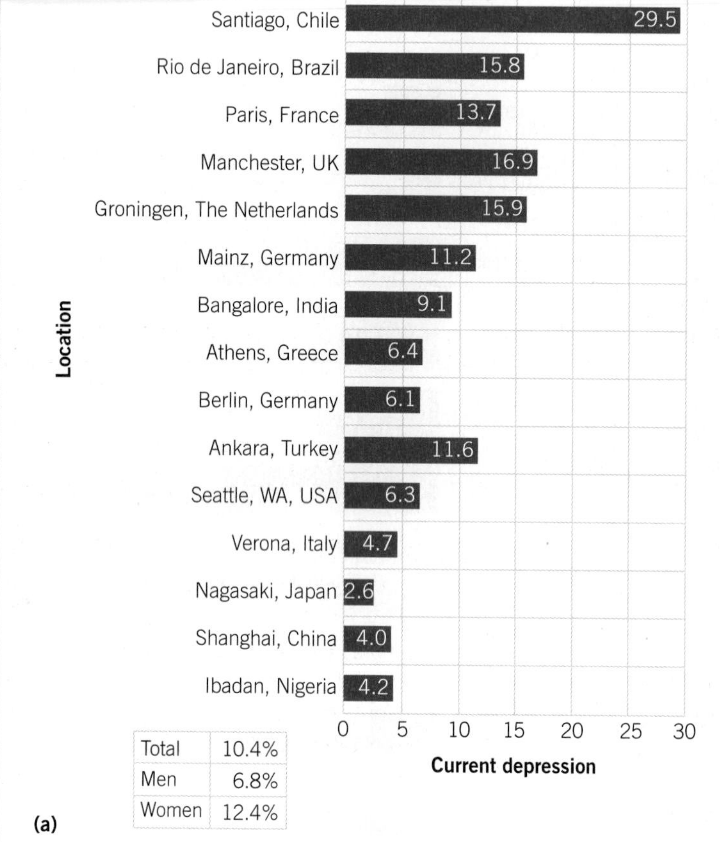

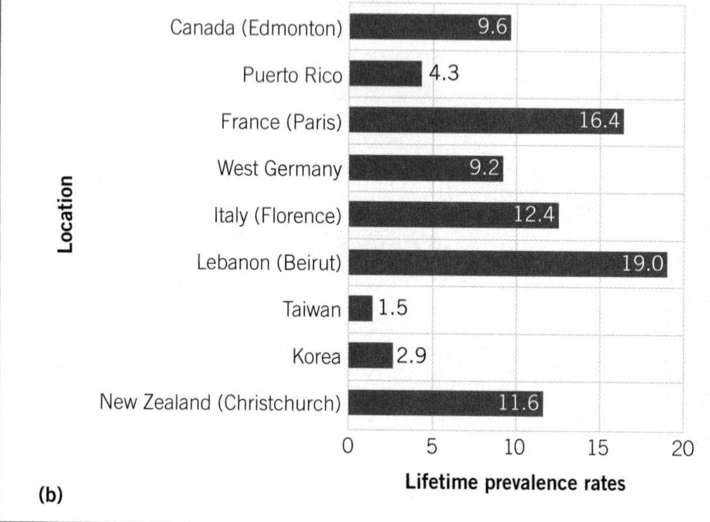

for several years before seeking treatment, and most adults are first diagnosed around age 31 years (Solmi et al., 2021). Many people with dysthymia do not seek treatment until severe depression develops. Others do not seek treatment because they assume depressive symptoms are simply part of their shy or withdrawn personality. Less than half of people with depressive or bipolar disorders sought treatment for the problem in the previous year (Call et al., 2018; Humpston et al., 2021).

Severe depression and dysthymia are highly comorbid with many other mental disorders, particularly anxiety-related and personality disorders and substance use problems. Even on its own, depression is especially harmful—many with the disorder experience work and school difficulties and problems with interpersonal and marital relationships (König et al., 2020; Virtanen et al., 2020). Does this remind you of Katey?

Bipolar disorders are less common. Worldwide prevalence rates are similar for bipolar I (0.6 to 1.0 percent) and bipolar II (0.4 to 1.1 percent) disorders (McIntyre et al., 2020). Cyclothymic disorder occurs in about 0.4 to 2.5 percent of the general population (Perugi et al., 2015). Bipolar I and cyclothymic disorders seem equally present in men and women and among people of different cultures (Buoli et al., 2019). Bipolar II disorder may be somewhat more common in women than men, perhaps because of the presence of major depressive episodes (Bayes et al., 2019). The age of onset of bipolar I, bipolar II, and cyclothymic disorders seems to be adolescence and early adulthood, although many of these youths may be diagnosed instead with disruptive behavior (Chapter 13) or depressive disorders. The increasingly frequent diagnosis of bipolar disorder in youth remains somewhat controversial because many are still learning how to regulate their emotions (Duffy et al., 2020).

People with bipolar I, bipolar II, and cyclothymic disorders often have several comorbid mental disorders, especially substance use, eating, anxiety-related, and personality disorders (McIntyre et al., 2020. Those with the disorders tend to have many recurrent depressive and manic episodes, and the disorders can lead to severe consequences with respect to daily functioning (Cirone et al., 2021).

Epidemiology of Suicide

About 700,000 lives are lost due to suicide worldwide each year (World Health Organization, 2021). Suicide is typically one of the leading causes of death in the United States, particularly among people aged 35-54 years (Garnett et al., 2022). About 4.3 percent of Americans thought about suicide, 1.3 percent made a suicide plan, and 0.6 percent attempted suicide in the past year (Ivey-Stephenson et al., 2022). Among first-year college students, many engage in suicidal ideation (17.2 percent), plans (8.8 percent), and attempts (4.3 percent) (Mortier et al., 2018). Most suicides come from firearms, suffocation, and poisoning, although many people deliberately kill themselves in cars and other "accidents" to save family members and friends from additional grief. Men are more likely than women to use particularly lethal methods of suicide such as firearms and hanging. Men thus actually complete suicide at four times the rate of women. Suicide *attempts*, however, are much more common in women than men, perhaps because women try to complete suicide in ways that take longer and have a higher chance of rescue. Examples include drug overdose and carbon monoxide poisoning (Garnett et al., 2022).

Suicide rates are highest in Eastern Europe but considerably lower in the United States, Taiwan, Korea, Japan, China, and Canada and lowest among Latin American and Muslim countries (refer to **Figure 7.7**; World Health Organization, 2021). Suicide is more common among European Americans, lower skilled workers, and sexual minorities and less common among married, socially integrated, and religiously affiliated people. Rates of adolescent suicide have increased substantially over the past several decades, and adolescent and adult Native Americans are at particular risk. African Americans, Hispanics, and Asian/Pacific Islanders tend to have lower rates of suicide (Ramchand et al., 2021).

Risk for suicide in people with bipolar disorder is 20 to 30 times greater than the general population (Miller & Black, 2020). In addition, about 15 percent of those with depression complete suicide (Orsolini et al., 2020). Many with depression have suicidal ideation (53.1 percent) or have made a suicide attempt (31.0 percent) (Cai et al., 2021). Suicidality is also associated with family history of mental disorder, hopelessness, misuse of alcohol and other drugs, and several other mental disorders, such as anxiety and schizophrenia (Sisti et al., 2020).

Stigma Associated with Depressive and Bipolar Disorders

LO 7.5 Describe the stigma associated with depressive disorders and bipolar disorders and its impact on those with the disorders.

People with depressive and bipolar disorders may experience substantial stigma given the debilitating nature of their symptoms. One group of researchers surveyed hundreds of people worldwide with depression. Most (79 percent) reported some form of discrimination in at least one domain. In addition, many said they had stopped themselves from (1) starting a close personal relationship (37 percent), (2) applying for work (25 percent), or (3) applying for education or training opportunities (20 percent). Participants also generally stated that they concealed their depression or were unwilling to disclose their depression for fear of discrimination by others (Lasalvia et al., 2013). High levels of stigma have also been found among people with bipolar disorder. Many reportedly believe that the public holds negative attitudes toward people with a mental disorder (Perich et al., 2022).

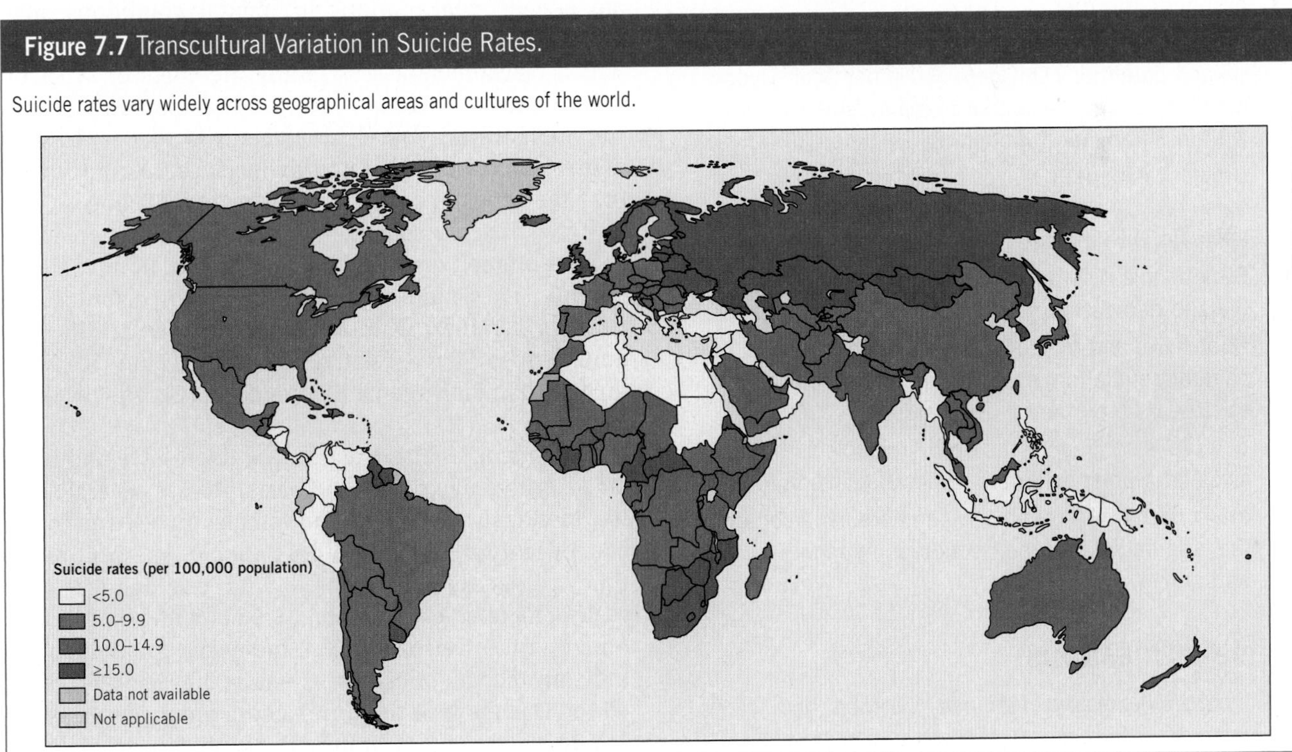

Figure 7.7 Transcultural Variation in Suicide Rates.

Suicide rates vary widely across geographical areas and cultures of the world.

Researchers have found that programs to combat stigma can be effective, especially for stigma related to depression. In one study, researchers asked people with depression to review two websites. One website included education about aspects of depression, such as symptoms, causes, sources of help, prevention, and the need to seek treatment. The site also contained short biographies of famous people with depression. A second website was devoted to cognitive behavioral methods to help people think more realistically, solve problems more effectively, and cope better with relationship difficulties or events that could trigger depressive symptoms. Perceived stigma was reduced significantly more for the website intervention group compared with control participants who did not review online materials (Griffiths et al., 2014). The study supports the assertion in Chapter 1 that education is a powerful antidote to stigma.

Section Summary

- Depressive and bipolar disorders refer to extreme emotional states of sadness or euphoria.
- A major depressive episode is a lengthy period of sad or empty mood, eating and sleeping problems, concentration difficulties, fatigue, sense of worthlessness, and suicidal thoughts or attempts. Major depressive disorder may involve several major depressive episodes.
- Persistent depressive disorder (dysthymia) is a chronic feeling of depression for at least two years.
- Other formal depressive disorders include disruptive mood dysregulation disorder and premenstrual dysphoric disorder.
- A manic episode is a period of uncontrollable euphoria and potentially self-destructive behavior. Hypomanic episodes are similar to manic episodes but with less impaired functioning.
- Bipolar I disorder involves one or more manic episodes. Bipolar II disorder refers to hypomanic episodes with major depressive episodes.
- Cyclothymic disorder refers to symptoms of hypomania and depression that fluctuate over a long time.
- Depressive and bipolar disorders are common in the general population and often occur with anxiety-related or other mental disorders.
- Suicide is commonly observed in people with depressive and bipolar disorders, especially among men.
- Many people with depressive and bipolar disorders feel stigmatized for their condition by family members and others.

Review Questions

1. What are depressive and bipolar disorders, and how do these differ from normal sadness or happiness?
2. What are characteristics of depression?
3. Describe differences between bipolar I, bipolar II, and cyclothymic disorder.
4. Describe different dimensions of suicide.
5. How common are depressive and bipolar disorders and suicide? What populations are most at risk?

Depressive and Bipolar Disorders and Suicide: Causes and Prevention

LO 7.6 Discuss the risk factors for depressive disorders, bipolar disorders, and suicide.

LO 7.7 Evaluate programs to prevent depressive disorders, bipolar disorders, and suicide.

The next sections cover factors that cause major depressive and bipolar disorders and suicide. The sections also cover how knowing about these factors might help us prevent depressive and bipolar disorders and suicide.

Biological Risk Factors for Depressive and Bipolar Disorders and Suicide

Biological risk factors in people with depressive and bipolar disorders include genetics, brain features, neurochemical and hormonal features, and sleep deficiencies.

Genetics

Researchers rely on family and twin studies to evaluate genetic contributions to mental conditions such as depressive and bipolar disorders. *Family studies,* in which researchers assess family members of a person with a mental disorder, indicate that depression does run in families. First-degree relatives of people with depression have depression themselves 2.8 times more than the general population (Levinson & Nichols, 2018). Children of depressed parents are three times more likely to have a mood disorder than children of nondepressed parents (Weissman et al., 2021). Bipolar disorder also runs in families. Relative risk for bipolar disorder among first-degree relatives is about 7 to 10 times greater than in the general population (Charney & Sklar, 2018).

Twin studies also suggest that depressive and bipolar disorders have a genetic basis. Across several studies, identical twin males and females have been found concordant for depression 40.3 and 50.0 percent of the time, respectively, compared with nonidentical twin males and females (28.0 and 33.5 percent, respectively; Strakowski & Nelson, 2015). Studies of bipolar disorder indicate that identical twins share the disorder about 40 to 70 percent of the time, a concordance rate much higher than that of fraternal twins (15–25 percent; Charney & Sklar, 2018; Strakowski, 2014). Overall, genetics account for about 37 to 50 percent of depression symptoms, but heritability for bipolar disorder is about 79 to 93 percent (Charney & Sklar, 2018; Levinson & Nichols, 2018).

Several genes for depression have been implicated, and many researchers believe depression results from a *polygenic transmission* in which a small set of genes work interactively to cause this complex mental disorder (Sealock et al., 2021). Researchers have also found that genes on different chromosomes work in a polygenic fashion to help produce bipolar disorder (Gordovez & McMahon, 2020). Some people seem genetically predisposed toward certain depressive and bipolar disorders, although no one gene or set of genes likely leads directly to the disorders. Genetics may instead help produce brain, neurochemical, hormonal, or other changes that lead to a depressive or bipolar disorder or otherwise interact with environmental events to lead to these disorders. Some of these potential biological differences are discussed next.

Figure 7.8 Images Comparing the Brain of a Control Participant (Top) with the Brain of a Clinically Depressed Person (Bottom).

Note the lower activity (less yellow coloring) of the cortex and other areas in the brain of someone who is depressed.

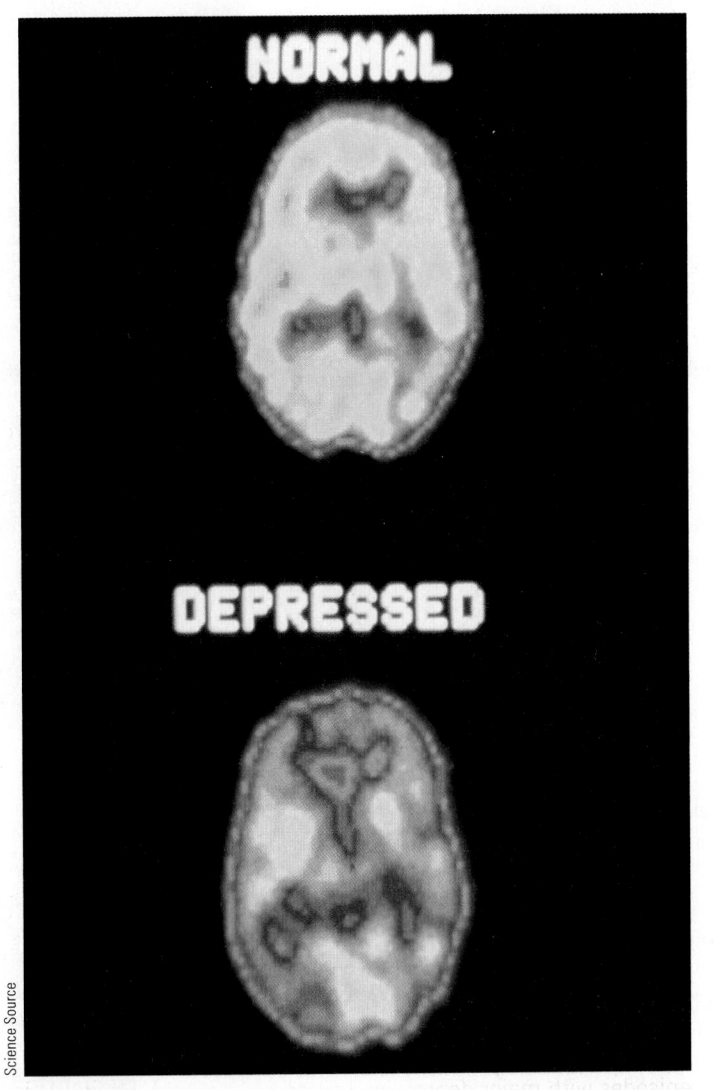

Brain Features

People with depressive and bipolar disorders may have differences in brain areas affected by genetic predispositions. People with these disorders often display reduced activity and size changes in the *prefrontal* and *other cortical areas* of the brain (refer to **Figure 7.8**; Hare & Duman, 2020). This reduced activity relates to decreased serotonin levels (refer to next section). People who have experienced strokes (Chapter 14) or other brain injuries that affect the prefrontal cortex often display depression afterward as well (Medeiros et al., 2020).

Other brain areas implicated in mood disorders include the *amygdala, hippocampus, caudate nucleus,* and *anterior cingulate cortex,* which may be smaller or damaged (refer to **Figure 7.9**; Damborská et al., 2020). This is particularly so in people who have lived a long time or those with long histories of depression, which may help explain the prevalence of depression among older people (Sherestha et al., 2020). These brain areas are involved in goal-directed behavior and inhibition of negative mood and troublesome thoughts. Someone with less activation of these areas (depression) may thus fail to pursue important work goals and have recurrent negative thoughts. Memory difficulties among people with depression might also relate to these brain changes (Nikolin et al., 2021).

Subtle damage to certain brain areas may also contribute to mood disorders in general and depression in particular, especially damage to *white matter, basal ganglia,* and the *pons* (Kieseppä et al., 2022). These brain areas may be involved in regulation of attention, motor behavior, memory, and emotions, all of which can be problematic in people with depressive or bipolar disorders.

On the other hand, *increased* activity of these key brain areas may occur in people with bipolar disorder (refer to **Figure 7.10**). Heightened activity in the anterior cingulate and increased size of the *putamen* relate to mania (Keramatian et al., 2021). These areas work with other brain structures to influence motor activity, so hyperactivity in these areas may help explain constant restlessness, movement, and goal-directed activity in people with bipolar disorder. In addition, changes in areas such as the hippocampus that affect depression do not always seem evident in people with bipolar disorder

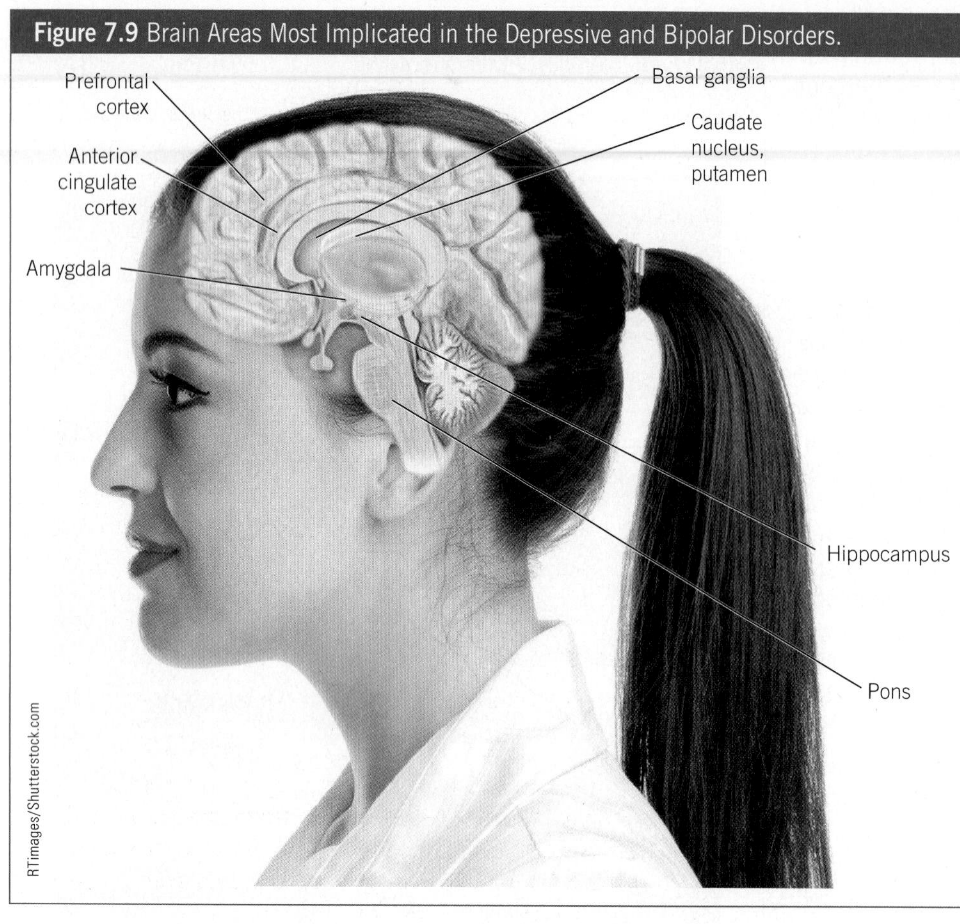

Figure 7.9 Brain Areas Most Implicated in the Depressive and Bipolar Disorders.

Brain changes affecting depressive and bipolar disorders likely intersect with neurochemical and hormonal features, which are discussed next.

Neurochemical and Hormonal Features

Recall from Chapter 3 that mental disorders such as depression involve certain neurotransmitters, especially serotonin, norepinephrine, and dopamine. These neurotransmitters closely link to limbic and other key brain systems that influence motivation level and emotional state. People with depression have lower than normal levels of these neurotransmitters, especially serotonin (refer to **Figure 7.12**; Borroto-Escuela et al., 2021). Antidepressant medications are often effective in people with mood disorders because they boost serotonin levels in the brain (later treatment section).

(Hansen et al., 2021). Instead, areas such as the amygdala and hippocampus seem intact.

Certain brain areas may be reduced in size in some people with bipolar disorder, and these changes may relate somewhat to changes found in people with schizophrenia (Chapter 12). Indeed, the two disorders have some symptoms in common (refer to **Figure 7.11**). People with bipolar disorder and people with schizophrenia may have reduced white and gray matter in the brain (Yang et al., 2022). Such changes may interfere with connections among important brain areas, which could lead to disruptive thought patterns observed in people with bipolar disorder and schizophrenia.

Brain changes for depression generally seem to involve cortical-limbic circuits, whereas brain changes for bipolar disorder generally seem to involve limbic-thalamic-cortical circuits, so some overlap is apparent (Jiang et al., 2021). These changes may come from early effects such as genetics, maternal stress during pregnancy and altered hormonal levels, reduced blood flow to the fetus, poor prenatal care, or pregnant mothers' use of antidepressant medication, among other reasons (Cattarinussi et al., 2021). Not everyone who experiences these early effects necessarily develops a mood disorder, however.

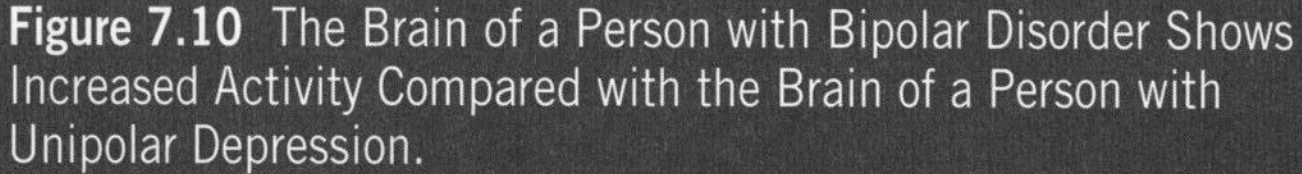

Figure 7.10 The Brain of a Person with Bipolar Disorder Shows Increased Activity Compared with the Brain of a Person with Unipolar Depression.

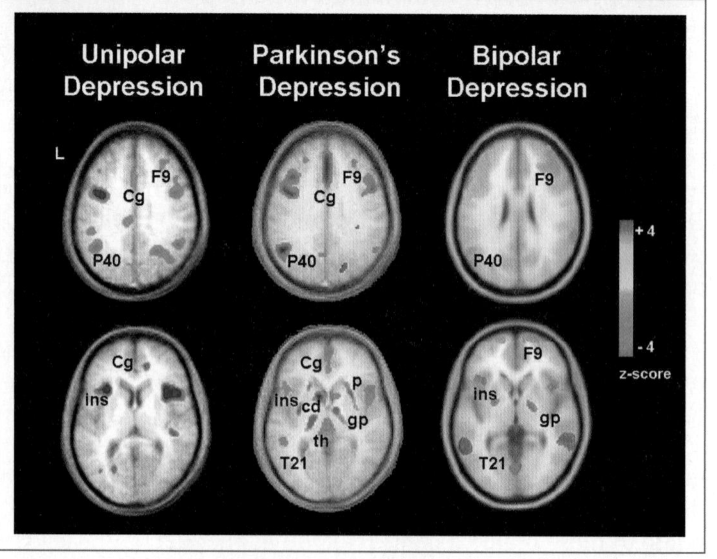

From Mayberg, H. S., Keightley, M., Mahurin, R. K., & Brannan, S. K. (2004). Neuropsychiatric aspects of mood and affective disorders. In S. C. Yudofsky & R. E. Hales (Eds.), *Essentials of neuropsychiatry and clinical neurosciences* (pp. 489–517). Washington, DC: American Psychiatric Publishing.

Figure 7.11 Symptom Overlap Between Schizophrenia and Bipolar Disorder.

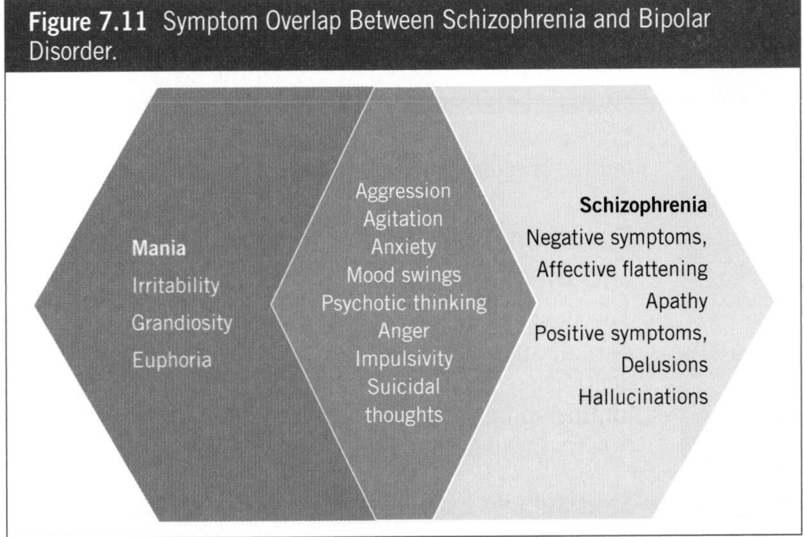

From C. Daban et al. (2006). Specificity of cognitive deficits in bipolar disorder versus schizophrenia: A systematic review. *Psychotherapy and Psychosomatics, 75,* 72–84. Reprinted by permission of S. Karger AG, Basel.

Neurochemical features of bipolar disorder are less clear, although elevations in dopamine may occur and may explain some overlap with schizophrenia. Such elevations could help create inflammation and cellular damage, especially in the prefrontal cortex (Zhu et al., 2022). Excess glutamate may relate as well to some manic symptoms. Excess glutamate also occurs in people with schizophrenia and can produce severe damage to neurons in the brain (Shen & Tomar, 2021). Medications for bipolar disorder, such as lithium, help reduce levels of dopamine and glutamate (Sato, 2021).

Key hormonal changes also occur in depressive and bipolar disorders. People with depression and cognitive deficits such as memory problems often have increased *cortisol* levels (Hakamata et al., 2022). This is especially true after experiencing a stressor. Recall from Chapter 5 that increased cortisol, as well as disruption of the hypothalamic-pituitary-adrenocortical axis, impacts the anxiety-related disorders. This may help explain why people with mood and anxiety-related disorders show similar symptoms such as agitation or restlessness. Increased cortisol may mean a person has a more biologically based depression best treated with medication (Lightman et al., 2020).

Other hormonal changes also relate to depressive and bipolar disorders. People with underactive thyroid conditions (and thus low levels of thyroid hormones) often experience symptoms of depression (Lorentzen et al., 2020). A key thyroid hormone, *triiodothyronine,* interacts significantly with serotonin and is sometimes used with antidepressants to relieve depression (Voineskos et al., 2020). Rapid cycling in bipolar disorder relates to a less active thyroid as well, so treating the latter condition is often important (Tost et al., 2020). People with depression also have suppressed levels of growth hormone and the hormones somatostatin and prolactin (Maffioletti et al., 2020). These deficiencies, along with increased cortisol, may help explain the sleep and mood changes observed in people and especially premenopausal women with depression.

Sleep Deficiencies

People with depressive and bipolar disorders often have disruptions in their normal sleep–wake cycle. Those with depression often have insomnia or hypersomnia and usually feel tired during the day. On the other hand, people with bipolar disorder in a manic state usually sleep very little. What might explain these effects?

People with depression tend to enter *rapid eye movement* (REM) sleep more quickly and display less slow-wave, or deep, sleep than normal (Riemann et al., 2020). Depression also seems related to intense but less stable REM sleep. These factors can disrupt sleep and cause fatigue. Sleep problems affect up to 90 percent of people with depression and likely relate to genetic factors and changes in hormones and neurotransmitters such as serotonin (Fang et al., 2019). A disruption in *circadian rhythms,* or one's internal sleep–wake clock, may also occur in people with early morning wakening or depression in winter months. The latter may occur because sunlight is less available to help regulate a person's internal clock (Pandi-Perumal et al., 2020).

Figure 7.12 Positron Emission Tomography (PET) Scan of Lower Serotonin Function in a Person with Major Depression (Right) Compared with a Person without Depression (Left).

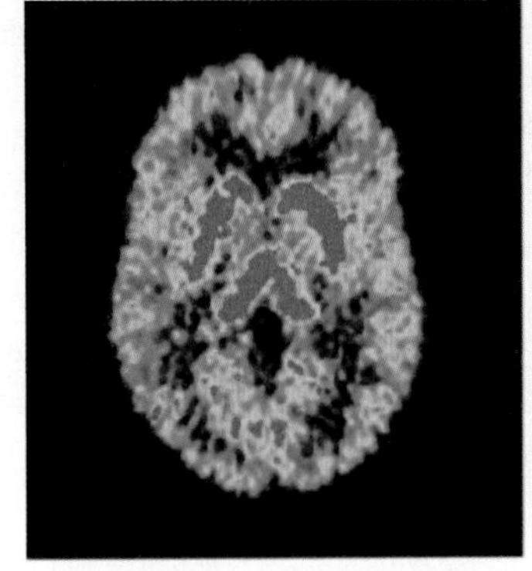
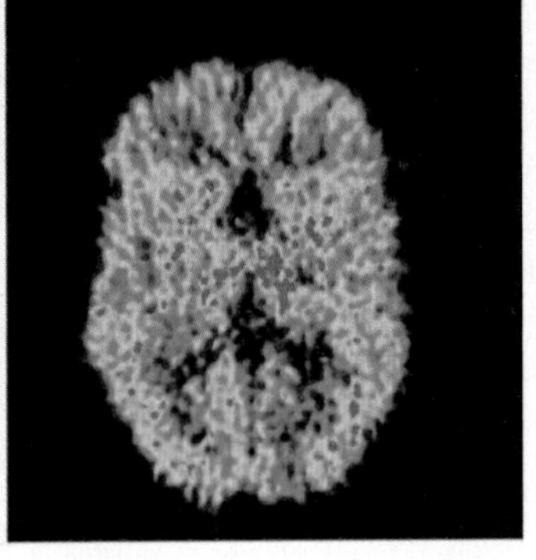

Original source unknown.

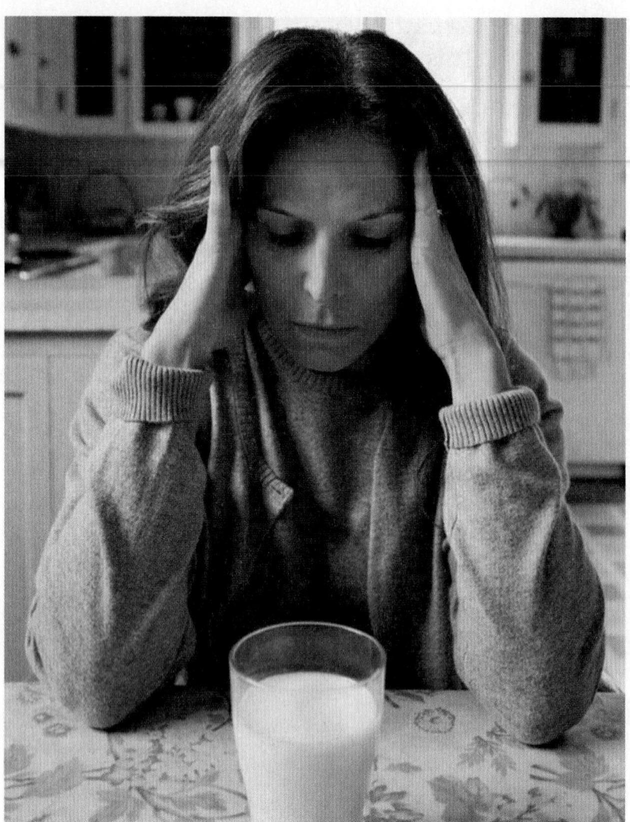

Gravity Images/The Image Bank/Getty Images

Increased cortisol levels may help explain why some people with depression are so agitated.

People with bipolar disorder may also have disrupted REM and slow-wave sleep, and some sleep deprivation may trigger manic episodes and especially rapid cycling (Meyer et al., 2020). Changes in one's social routine during the day—such as loss of a partner, travel across time zones, or birth of a newborn—may disrupt biological rhythms that surround sleep. This likely occurs more so for people predisposed to sensitive internal biological clocks or those with limited coping skills. Disruption of circadian rhythms may spiral out of control and contribute to a manic state (Walker et al., 2020). Such may have been true for Katey, whose late night attendance at clubs may have helped trigger a manic episode.

Environmental Risk Factors for Depressive and Bipolar Disorders and Suicide

The next sections cover environmental risk factors that develop over time to create depressive or bipolar disorders. These include stressful life events and cognitive, interpersonal, and family factors. Cultural and evolutionary influences are also discussed.

Stressful Life Events

We all experience negative life events that cause us to struggle, but we often "bounce back" with the help of others. For people predisposed to depression, however, stressful life events seem more frequent, painful, and difficult to cope with (refer to **Focus On College Students: Depression**). Stressful life events often precede depressive symptoms, though their relationship to *ongoing* depression is less clear. Stressful life events may help trigger manic symptoms as well, as Katey's job loss did (Sato et al., 2018).

Why do some people develop depression after a stressful life event but others do not? The *severity* and *meaning* of the stressful life event are clearly important (Hovenkamp-Hermelink et al., 2019). People who become depressed tend to experience major, uncontrollable, and undesirable events highly significant to them. Examples include death of a child or partner, job loss, marital infidelity, business failure, and serious illness. Social support and ability to cope with a negative event are also important. A person who recently

Focus On College Students

Depression

About 30.6 percent of college students experience depression, particularly among female students and students in their earlier years of study. In addition, many college students reportedly feel very sad (37.5 percent), very lonely (36.1 percent), or hopeless (25.9 percent). Most commonly reported symptoms of depression include trouble sleeping, fatigue, loss of energy, appetite changes, and self-criticism. Some college students (20 percent) report increased pessimism, guilt, and sense of failure, and many turn to excessive alcohol use to cope (Geisner et al., 2012; Ibrahim et al., 2013).

Stressful life events often help predict depression symptoms in college students and include relationship breakup, illness, and relocation to college (Zuo et al., 2020). Interethnic difficulties and conflicts as well as achievement stress also contribute to depression symptoms in Asian American, African American, and Latino/a American college students (Wei et al., 2010). College students with sleep difficulties, disconnection from others, and a sense of hopelessness are also at higher risk for suicide (Li et al., 2020). Treatments for depression in college students are largely successful and primarily include cognitive behavior therapy, behavioral activation, and interpersonal therapy. Treatment for depressed college students may be more effective for those with supportive families and healthier lifestyles (Liu et al., 2022). College students sometimes self-stigmatize regarding treatment and thus delay seeking needed help (Duffy et al., 2019). If you feel symptoms of depression or suicidality, however, then seeking help, perhaps at your school's counseling center, is strongly encouraged.

lost a loved one may be less depressed if they have a supportive partner and regular eating and sleeping patterns. Personality traits may be important as well, including dependency, rumination, conscientiousness, and self-criticism (Allen et al., 2018). The impact of stressful life events often interacts with a person's cognitive misinterpretations of these events, which are discussed next.

Orion Production/Shutterstock.com

Stressful life events such as caring for two young children while working full time can help trigger depressive or bipolar disorders.

Cognitive Factors

An environmental risk factor closely related to depressive and bipolar disorders is negative thought patterns, or **cognitive distortions**. Recall that cognitive distortions were mentioned in Chapter 5 because many people with anxiety-related disorders have unrealistic thoughts about potential or actual threat from internal sensations or external events. Examples of unrealistic thoughts include jumping to conclusions, catastrophizing, and emotional reasoning (refer to **Figure 7.13**).

People with depression may develop overly distorted, pessimistic views of themselves, the world around them, and their future. This is the **negative cognitive triad**. Some people view a certain event in a negative way and have catastrophic thoughts about the event (Beck et al., 2019). These thoughts tend to be **automatic thoughts**, meaning they constantly repeat over the course of a day.

Consider Victor, who recently failed his math test, as an example of the negative cognitive triad. After receiving his grade, Victor believed he was not too bright (oneself), thought others would perceive him as a complete failure (world), and thought he would have to drop out of school (future). Victor gave a single negative event much more weight than should be the case. Many people with depression focus their thoughts on themes of loss and personal failure, inadequacy, and worthlessness (Ferrari et al., 2018).

Figure 7.13 Negative Cognitive Triad Involving Cognitive Distortions about the Self, World, and Future.

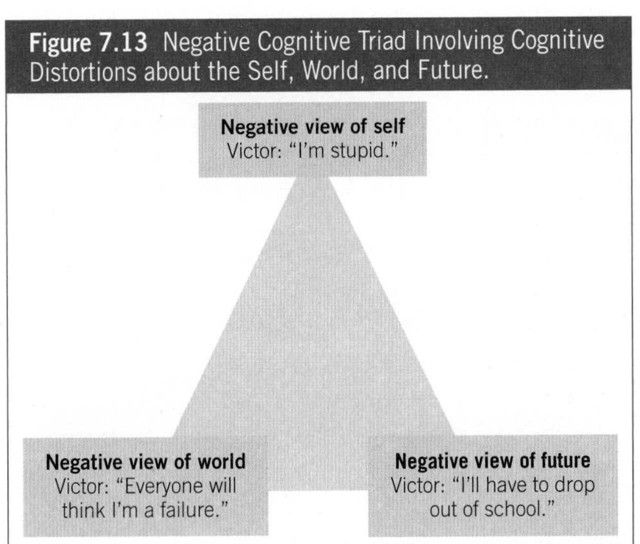

Negative view of self
Victor: "I'm stupid."
Negative view of world
Victor: "Everyone will think I'm a failure."
Negative view of future
Victor: "I'll have to drop out of school."

A similar cognitive theory of depression, **hopelessness** (or attribution) **theory**, focuses on attitudes or *attributions* people make about an event (Mullarkey & Schleider, 2020). Some people with depression may experience a negative life event, assume the event will last a long time (*stable*), and believe the event will affect most areas of their life (*global*). Victor assumed a single bad performance on a math test would doom the entire semester and would affect other courses and even his interpersonal relationships.

Hopelessness may also result from *internal* attributions because a person could excessively blame themself for a negative life event and develop low self-esteem. Hopelessness develops because a person believes that, no matter what they do, their efforts will not lead to change. A person may believe increased studying will not lead to passing grades or college graduation. This sense of **learned helplessness** might relate to excessive dependency on others (Song & Vilares, 2021). Cognitive theories of depression generally relate to mild or moderate cases of depression or what is sometimes called nonbiological, environmentally based, or *exogenous* depression.

Cognitive risk factors can also be important for bipolar disorder. Cognitive distortions in this regard often refer to beliefs that one can do something they cannot actually do (recall Katey's belief she might be able to fly) or beliefs that using medication will be harmful. These beliefs may lead people to stop using medication. People entering a manic or hypomanic episode will also adopt a more carefree attitude, underestimate risk, develop an overly optimistic outlook, emphasize immediate gratification, minimize problems, experience increased speed of thoughts, and have trouble concentrating and paying attention (Yesilyaprak et al., 2019).

Interpersonal Factors

Depression also seems linked to interpersonal difficulties such as social skill deficits, communication problems, and relationship or marital conflict. People with depression perceive themselves as socially ineffective with others. Other people who observe a person with depression may also reject the person and rate him as having poor social skills. Social skill problems may involve less eye contact, sad facial expression, head drooping, little smiling, or lack of motivation to communicate or to be expressive. Social skill deficits do predict levels of depression (Knight & Baune, 2019). Many people with depression also have flat affect or little emotion when speaking, often seek reassurance from others, and have sad facial expressions (Cowan et al., 2022).

Depression also affects many romantic and marital relationships, although such relationships can also serve as a protective factor. Marital dissatisfaction, however, relates closely to depression, especially for partners with high neuroticism, anxious attachment, lower self-esteem, and a tendency to believe a partner intentionally hurts them emotionally. Marital dissatisfaction often leads to more conflict and less communication, which can increase depression. Depression and marital problems may co-occur because one spouse becomes withdrawn or angry, sexual relations suffer, or problems are not solved well. The relationship between marriage and depression is likely complex, however (Goldfarb & Trudel, 2019).

Depression may relate to amount of social reinforcement one receives for certain behaviors (Frey et al., 2021). Some people receive attention, reassurance, comfort, and sympathy from others when depressed. Friends and family members may call or visit more, offer to help with children and chores, and listen to problems. Conversely, prosocial behavior may be ignored or taken for granted—a person may thus revert to depressive behavior to receive more attention. A social behavioral theory of depression may help explain why some depressive behaviors continue over time.

Family Factors

Children of parents with a depressive or bipolar disorder have more of these disorders themselves compared with the general population. Genetics may play a role in this connection, but problems among family members are also likely a factor. One such problem involves attachment. Impaired attachment to parents at an early age, especially anxious or ambivalent or avoidant attachment, can lead to later depression that surrounds overdependency on others, loss, fear of abandonment, poor self-worth, self-criticism, and anger toward parents and oneself (Spruit et al., 2020). Recall that Katey had little contact with her family members.

Depression in mothers can also be a strong risk factor for depression in children. Depressed mothers often display inadequate parenting, tend to disengage from their children, and show many negative and few positive behaviors toward their children. Depressed mothers may withdraw from or ignore child-rearing situations that demand supervision and discipline, and focus on criticism and not affection toward their children. Depressed fathers also tend to be withdrawn, indecisive, cynical, and irritable (Pedersen et al., 2021). Children may thus model depressive symptoms in their parents and develop overly negative views of themselves. Family stressors such as marital problems, maltreatment, and poverty also relate to child depression (LeMoult et al., 2020). Children may thus develop cognitive and attributional distortions and limited social skill with respect to communication, problem solving, and assertiveness. These problems relate to interpersonal difficulties, social withdrawal, and depression (Bird et al., 2018).

Rido/Shutterstock.com

Arsenii Palivoda/Shutterstock.com

Marital problems may be a key trigger for depression. Mothers with depression are at significant risk for having children with depression.

Children whose parents have bipolar disorder are also at high risk for developing the disorder themselves. This is especially so if a parent has other mental disorders such as a substance use or personality disorder. Marital conflict, inadequate parenting, and low parental warmth and family cohesion closely relate to childhood bipolar disorder (Stapp et al., 2020). Inadequate parenting includes substantial criticism and other negative behaviors toward a child. How such parent and family problems specifically lead to bipolar disorder remains unclear. One possibility is that unstable parent and family behaviors hinder a child's ability to control their emotions (Koenders et al., 2020).

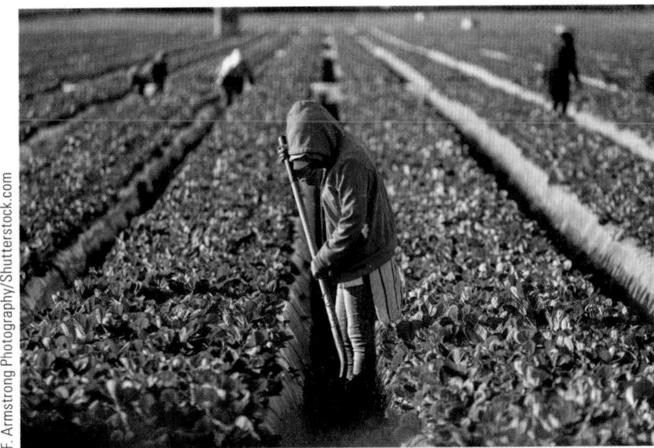

F. Armstrong Photography/Shutterstock.com

Migrant workers and immigrants have been shown to be especially susceptible to depression.

Cultural Factors

Recall that rates of depression vary across areas of the world and even among subgroups of a country like the United States. One possible explanation is that depression and other mental disorders are especially high among immigrant and migrant populations (a similar finding is discussed for schizophrenia in Chapter 12). In the United States, the Hispanic population is one of the fastest growing subgroups. Many Latinos are Mexicans who immigrate to the United States for better working conditions but who have high rates of health problems, stress, and depression (Ryan et al., 2021). High rates of depression and other mental health problems also occur among migrant workers in Europe (Urrego-Parra et al., 2022). However, those who stay close to others who share a common cultural identity may experience some protection from depression (Cornejo et al., 2020).

Bipolar disorders are observed fairly equally across cultures, but researchers have found some interesting differences when examining specific aspects of these disorders. One group of researchers found that African American mothers had a higher prevalence of bipolar disorder (2.5 percent) than Caribbean black mothers (1.2 percent; Boyd et al., 2011). In addition, Subramaniam and colleagues (2013) found bipolar disorder to be more frequent among Indians than Chinese living in Singapore. These subtle differences may be due to various risk factors, but some populations may also be less likely to seek help earlier for their symptoms. Recent immigrants, for example, tend to use fewer services than those who have lived longer in a particular country (Salami et al., 2019). Some diverse individuals may hide symptoms or seek help only when symptoms are severe, and so clinicians must be sensitive to differences in culture and ways mental disorders are expressed.

Evolutionary Influences

Evolutionary theories also exist for depressive and bipolar disorders. Some believe depressed states evolved so certain people could withdraw from social interactions. Perhaps certain people feel their value to others is low and their burden on others is high. A person may feel at risk for exclusion from the social group and thus minimize contact with the group. This might help explain depressive symptoms such as sensitivity to comments of others and low risk-seeking behavior (Rantala et al., 2018). In addition, depression may have evolved so people could ruminate over problems until a proper solution is found, because depressive behaviors signal to others the need for help, or that depression and withdrawal from difficult situations helps lower stress (Zhang et al., 2020).

Evolutionary theories of mania are sparser, although hypomanic states may help improve physical fitness, level of prestige to enhance reproductive opportunities, and energy for invading or settling a new territory (Rantala et al., 2021). In addition, cyclothymic tendencies may increase creativity and extravagance, which could assist sexual seduction and chances for leadership of a group (McIntyre et al., 2020).

Causes of Depressive and Bipolar Disorders and Suicide

Integrative models are often emphasized to explain how many risk factors can produce depressive and bipolar disorders (refer to **Figure 7.14**). Certain people are likely born with a *biological vulnerability* to experience different depressive or bipolar disorders. Some people clearly have a genetic predisposition toward depression or bipolar disorder. These genetic factors may interact with or predispose someone toward important neurochemical, hormonal, and brain changes that affect ability to control mood and related behavior.

People also develop a *psychological vulnerability* toward depressive and bipolar disorders. Some people experience stressful and life-changing events such as loss of one's mother in early childhood, come to believe they have little control over life events, and experience interpersonal and family problems that contribute to their disorder or deprive them of social support.

Think about depression. Some people are naturally predisposed, perhaps via genetics and/or low serotonin and norepinephrine levels or prefrontal brain changes, to experience depressed mood and lack of motivation or energy (*biological vulnerability*). As these people develop as children, sad mood and slow motor behavior may interact with various parental and family factors mentioned earlier. These factors include poor attachment, disengaged parenting, family dysfunction, and modeling depressive behaviors. In turn, these factors can lead to a child's difficulty controlling emotions, solving problems, and interacting with others.

During adolescence and young adulthood, more stressful life events are likely to occur. These events include family changes and conflict, alienation from peers and others, illness, or academic challenges and problems. A cognitive vulnerability may develop in which one believes they have little control over these events and develops a sense of hopelessness about changing negative experiences (*cognitive-stress psychological vulnerability*). Some may try to escape depression by marrying or having a child early in life, but this strategy is not generally effective. If a person also experiences limited social support and is overdependent on others, then depression may be even more likely.

Some people have a strong biological vulnerability to depression that requires few environmental triggers. People with biologically oriented, or *endogenous,* depression often develop sadness for little apparent reason. Other people have a weak biological predisposition toward depression but still become depressed when frequent, overwhelming, and negative life events occur. People with environmentally oriented, or *exogenous,* depression develop sadness primarily because they cope poorly with major life stressors. Exogenous or *reactive* depression often follows some major event.

Figure 7.14 Sample Developmental Pathway of Depression.

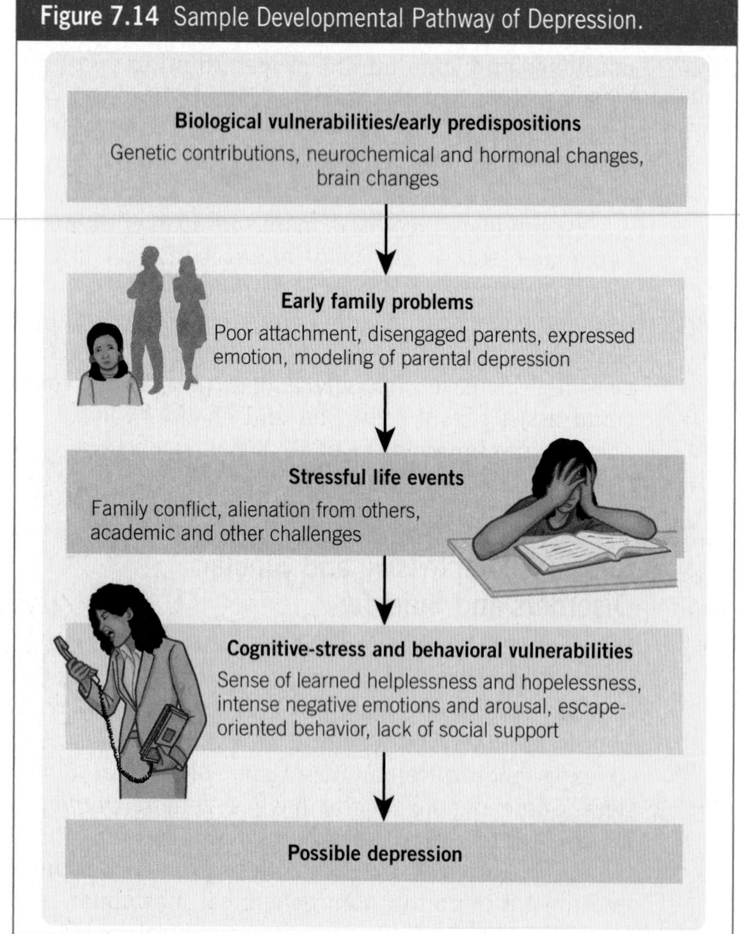

People with bipolar disorders likely have a strong biological vulnerability toward recurrent manic or hypomanic episodes. Genetic predispositions and neurochemical changes are well documented in this population. Little environmental influence may be needed to trigger the disorders. Some psychological factors relate to onset and duration of bipolar symptoms, including stressful life events, family hostility and conflict, lack of social support, cognitive distortions, and personality disturbances (Park et al., 2020). Katey's therapist discovered that Katey's mother also had symptoms of bipolar disorder and that Katey was alienated from her family.

What about suicide? Models of suicide also gravitate toward integrating various risk factors into an organized framework. Key biological variables may include tendencies to ruminate intensely about stressful life events and then to experience strong negative emotions after these events. These repetitive thinking processes and negative emotions aggravate one another over time and lead to an *emotional cascade* that is difficult for a person to tolerate and can lead to self-injury (Titus & DeShong, 2020).

These biological vulnerabilities can be aggravated by environmental factors such as limited social support and inability to cope effectively with stress as well as symptoms of depression or bipolar disorder. A person who reaches the point of suicide feels unable to escape torment and feels such pain is intolerable and will last a long time. Severe hopelessness develops such that a person has trouble thinking about problem solutions other than suicide (Pettorruso et al., 2020).

Prevention of Depressive and Bipolar Disorders and Suicide

Depressive and bipolar disorders often begin in adolescence or early adulthood, so it makes sense to think of prevention during childhood and adolescence. Several target areas might be important for prevention. These targets involve coping with stressful life events and addressing individual, cognitive, and family factors. Individual factors include social skill and interpersonal problems, medical illness, and academic difficulties, among others. Cognitive factors include low self-esteem, attributional distortions, and hopelessness, among others. Family factors include marital conflict and disengaged or hostile parents, among others (Reynolds, 2020).

Prevention programs for depressive disorders typically address (1) people without any symptoms of the disorders; (2) people at risk for developing the disorders, such as children of parents with depressive disorders; and (3) people who have a depressive disorder and wish to prevent relapse. For people without symptoms of depressive disorder, researchers have evaluated large-scale primary or universal prevention programs. One such program was developed by Ian Shochet and colleagues; its two sections are the *Resourceful Adolescent Program-Adolescents* (RAP-A) and the *Resourceful Adolescent Program-Family* (RAP-F). The RAP-A program involves teaching adolescents to:

- Declare existing strengths, such as being a good student or son/daughter
- Manage stress in difficult situations
- Modify negative thoughts to think more realistically
- Solve problems effectively
- Develop and use social support networks such as friends and other social groups
- Develop strategies to reduce family and interpersonal conflict, such as negotiating solutions and repairing relationships
- Enhance social skill and recognize other people's perspectives

The RAP-F program, which focuses on parents, involves stress management, education about normal teenager development, promotion of self-esteem, and strategies to reduce family conflict. An advantage of this program is that it is based in schools where more adolescents might have access (Shochet et al., 2022).

For people at risk for developing depressive disorders, researchers have evaluated large-scale secondary or selected/indicated prevention programs. One group of researchers evaluated a program that focused on adolescents whose parents had a history of depression. Teenagers participated in group and booster sessions to identify and challenge unrealistic thoughts, especially thoughts related to their depressed parents ("I will be just like my parents"). Parents also attended education sessions. At-risk adolescents who received the prevention program displayed less onsets of depression over time than controls, even after six years (Brent et al., 2015). An advantage of this approach is that one key intervention ingredient—cognitive restructuring—was found so effective. Cognitive restructuring, or cognitive therapy, as discussed in Chapter 5, involves examining negative statements a person may be making and encouraging the person to challenge the thought and think more realistically.

For people with a depressive disorder, researchers have evaluated relapse prevention programs (Moriarty et al., 2020). People with depression often need help identifying situations such as solitary settings that place them at risk for future depression, managing stress, coping with and resolving difficult situations such as marital conflict, and enhancing self-confidence (Zhang et al., 2018). Relapse prevention for depression also involves helping people remain on antidepressant medication and increasing mindfulness regarding their behaviors (Breedvelt et al., 2021).

Less work is available regarding prevention of bipolar disorder, although youth whose parents have the disorder are certainly at risk themselves. Prevention research in this area has concentrated on youth just beginning to show symptoms of bipolar disorder or who have a positive family history for the disorder (Post et al., 2020). For people with bipolar disorder, relapse prevention focuses on learning about one's symptoms, maintaining medication, and increasing family and social support (Miklowitz et al., 2021).

Preventing suicide must also be a priority among people with depressive and bipolar disorders. General programs to prevent suicide focus on adolescents and involve school-based suicide awareness programs, screening teenagers at risk for suicide, enhancing problem-solving and coping skills, educating peers and teachers to identify high-risk behaviors, and providing crisis intervention to those at risk. Other suicide prevention strategies include community-based crisis centers and hotlines. These programs do help reduce suicide rates among youth (Posamentier et al., 2022).

Suicide prevention programs for adults also focus on awareness and education among the public, such as helping people understand risk factors associated with suicide and reducing stigma of mental disorder. These programs also focus on primary care physicians, clergy, pharmacists, and other "first responders" to help them recognize and treat suicidal tendencies in people who come for help. Screening programs to help identify early suicidal behaviors are an avenue to get people help via medication and psychotherapy. Follow-up care after a suicide attempt is critical as well to prevent a second attempt. These programs have also been moderately successful for lowering suicide rates in specific groups (Hofstra et al., 2020).

Section Summary

- Biological risk factors for depressive and bipolar disorders include genetics, brain changes, neurochemical and hormonal differences, and sleep deficiencies.
- Environmental risk factors for depressive and bipolar disorders include stressful and uncontrollable life events, negative thought processes and misattributions, problematic interpersonal relationships, and parent and family factors. Cultural and evolutionary factors may also be influential.
- Biological and environmental risk factors can make a person vulnerable to a depressive or bipolar disorder. These risk factors inhibit one's ability to control emotions, cope with stress, solve problems, and relate to others effectively.
- Depressive and bipolar disorders may result from a combination of early biological factors with environmental factors related to ability to cope, think adaptively, and regulate intense emotions.
- Preventing depressive and bipolar disorders involves building one's ability to control situations that might lead to symptoms.

Review Questions

1. Describe data that support a genetic contribution to depressive and bipolar disorders.
2. What key brain, neurochemical, and hormonal brain changes relate to depressive and bipolar disorders, and how might sleep deficiencies contribute?
3. Describe two main cognitive theories of depression.
4. How might interpersonal and family factors help cause depressive and bipolar disorders?
5. Describe an overall causal model for depressive and bipolar disorders.
6. What factors might be important in designing a program to prevent depressive and bipolar disorders as well as suicide?

Depressive and Bipolar Disorders and Suicide: Assessment and Treatment

LO 7.8 Characterize the assessment and treatment of individuals with depressive disorders, bipolar disorders, and suicidal ideation.

Primary methods to assess people with depressive and bipolar disorders include interviews, self-report questionnaires, self-monitoring, observations from others, and physiological measurement. A full medical examination is often recommended as well. Medical conditions related to depression, for example, include neurological impairments, brain injuries, cardiovascular problems, hormonal changes, immune disorders, and terminal illnesses (refer to **Table 7.10**). Symptoms of depressive and bipolar disorders may also relate to drug intoxication, withdrawal, or side effects. If a physical condition or substance contributes to a person's depressive or bipolar symptoms, then medical treatment or expanded psychological treatment may be necessary.

Interviews

Structured interviews usually cover diagnostic criteria and contain questions a therapist asks each client. Structured interviews for people with depressive and bipolar disorders include the *Schedule for Affective Disorders and Schizophrenia* and *Structured Clinical Interview* (First et al., 2015). The *Schedule for Affective Disorders and Schizophrenia for School-Age Children* is useful for youths (Bergman et al., 2015). Other interview-format instruments determine how severe a person's symptoms are or how a person is responding to treatment. Examples include the *Brief Psychiatric Rating Scale* and *Hamilton Rating Scale for Depression* (refer to **Table 7.11**).

Therapists commonly use unstructured interviews to assess people with depressive and bipolar disorders. Important topics to cover during such an interview include:

- Past and present mood symptoms
- Risk factors such as interpersonal and cognitive factors
- Medical and treatment history
- Ongoing problems and comorbid diagnoses
- Motivation for change
- Social support
- Suicidal thoughts and behaviors

Therapists must also understand that people with depressive and bipolar disorders often speak at a different pace, bias their information in negative (depression) or positive (manic) ways, and may be uncomfortable sharing personal information. Building rapport is thus very important. Therapists can also examine nonverbal behaviors in an interview to help determine symptoms and severity of a depressive or bipolar disorder. Important nonverbal behaviors for depression, for example, include reduced facial expression, less eye contact, slow movement, muted affect, and low energy level (Altmann et al., 2021).

Self-Report Questionnaires

Depressive and bipolar disorders involve severe changes in emotions and thoughts, so clients are often asked to rate their symptoms on questionnaires. Self-report questionnaires for people with depression focus on recent depressive symptoms, problematic thoughts, and hopelessness. A common self-report measure is the *Beck Depression Inventory—II,* which addresses negative attitudes toward oneself, level of impairment due to depression, and physical symptoms. A child version of this scale is also available; selected items are in **Table 7.12** (Beck & Dozois, 2014; Kovacs, 2010). The *Beck Hopelessness Scale* assesses level of pessimism about the future and strongly relates to suicidal behavior (Spokas et al., 2012). The *Automatic Thoughts Questionnaire—Revised* assesses negative thoughts common to people with depression.

The interview remains a dominant psychological approach for assessing people with bipolar-related disorders. However, some measures assess self-reported symptoms of mania and hypomania. Examples include the *General Behavior Inventory* and *Hypomanic Personality*

Table 7.10 Disorders Associated with Depression

Neurological disorders	Systemic disorders
Focal lesions: Stroke Tumor Surgical ablation Epilepsy	**Endocrine disorders:** Hypothyroidism and hyperthyroidism Adrenal diseases (Cushing's, Addison's) Parathyroid disorders
Regional degenerative diseases: Parkinson's disease Huntington's disease Pick's disease Fahr's disease Progressive supranuclear palsy Carbon monoxide exposure Wilson's disease	**Inflammatory/infectious diseases:** Systemic lupus erythematosus Neurosyphilis AIDS Tuberculosis Mononucleosis Sjögren's syndrome Chronic fatigue syndrome
Diffuse diseases: Alzheimer's disease AIDS dementia Multiple sclerosis	**Metabolic disorders:** Uremia Porphyria Vitamin deficiencies
Miscellaneous disorders: Migraine Paraneoplastic syndromes	**Miscellaneous disorders:** Medication side effects Chronic pain syndromes Sleep apnea Cancer Heart disease

Table 7.11 Hamilton Rating Scale for Depression

Instructions: For each item, select the number that corresponds to the statement that best characterizes the patient.

1. Depressed mood (sadness, hopeless, helpless, worthless)
   0. Absent
   1. These feeling states indicated only on questioning
   2. These feeling states spontaneously reported verbally
   3. Communicates feeling states nonverbally—i.e., through facial expression, posture, voice, and tendency to weep
   4. Patient reports VIRTUALLY ONLY these feeling states in their spontaneous verbal and nonverbal communication

2. Feelings of guilt
   0. Absent
   1. Self-reproach, feels they have let people down
   2. Ideas of guilt or rumination over past errors or sinful deeds
   3. Present illness is a punishment. Delusions of guilt
   4. Hears accusatory or denunciatory voices and/or experiences threatening visual hallucinations

3. Suicide
   0. Absent
   1. Feels life is not worth living
   2. Wishes they were dead or any thoughts of possible death to self
   3. Suicidal ideas or gestures
   4. Attempts at suicide (any serious attempt rates 4)

4. Insomnia early
   0. No difficulty falling asleep
   1. Complains of occasional difficulty falling asleep—i.e., more than 1/2 hour
   2. Complains of nightly difficulty falling asleep

5. Insomnia middle
   0. No difficulty
   1. Patient complains of being restless and disturbed during the night
   2. Waking during the night—any getting out of bed rates 2 (except for purposes of voiding)

6. Insomnia late
   0. No difficulty
   1. Waking in early hours of the morning but goes back to sleep
   2. Unable to fall asleep again if they get out of bed

From Hamilton M. (1967). Development of a rating scale for primary depressive illness, *British Journal of Social & Clinical Psychology*, 6(4):278–296. Reproduced with permission from *The British Psychological Society.* Reprinted with permission from John Waterhouse and the British Psychological Society.

Table 7.12 Sample Items from the Children's Depression Inventory

Choose one: • am sad once in a while. • am sad many times. • am sad all the time.
Choose one: • do not think about killing myself. • think about killing myself, but I would not do it. • want to kill myself.
Choose one: • nobody really loves me. • am not sure if anybody loves me. • am sure that somebody loves me.

Scale (Pendergast et al., 2015; Sperry et al., 2015). Reports from significant others in a person's environment may also be useful, and these methods are discussed next.

Self-Monitoring and Observations from Others

People with depressive and bipolar disorders can monitor and log their own symptoms on a daily basis. Recall from Chapter 5 that daily self-monitoring reduces the need to recall events and increases focus and self-awareness on one's symptoms. For people with depressive and bipolar disorders, important information to record each day may include ratings of sadness or euphoria, activities with others, attendance at work or school, negative or suicidal thoughts, eating and sleeping patterns, and unpleasant physical symptoms, among other topics. Others who know a client well can also record their more obvious mood symptoms, such as grandiosity like Katey's onetime belief she could fly. This applies especially to people with bipolar disorder—Katey's therapist made sure family members and friends helped monitor Katey's mood and behavior between treatment sessions.

Laboratory Assessment

People with depressive disorders can have marked changes in hormones or neurotransmitters, so laboratory assessment techniques may apply. The *dexamethasone suppression test* (DST) involves injecting a person with dexamethasone, which is a corticosteroid. Dexamethasone is similar to cortisol and decreases the pituitary gland's release of adrenocorticotropic hormone, which in turn decreases release of cortisol from the adrenal gland. Recall that people with depression have differences in the hypothalamic-pituitary-adrenal axis. Cortisol levels from dexamethasone decline over time for most people but remain high—or not suppressed—in people with major depression (refer to **Figure 7.15**).

Some researchers have found DST results to relate closely to depression, but the results can also characterize people with other mental and medical or hormonal disorders such as Cushing's syndrome (Galm et al., 2020). Other laboratory assessments for this population include tests for neurotransmitter and hormonal or thyroid levels as well as sleep studies. Laboratory assessments are costly and require a lot of time, however, and so are more common in research than clinical settings.

Assessment of Suicide

Recall that suicidality is common in people with depression and mania, as it was for Katey. A critical area of assessing depressive and bipolar disorders, therefore, is suicidal thoughts and behaviors. Therapists usually address suicidality by asking clients if they have thoughts of harming themselves. Most people accurately answer this question. Therapists also study a person's history and current risk factors to determine the likelihood they may complete suicide. Recall that high-risk factors for suicide include being male, older, single, European American, unemployed, or socially isolated.

People at risk for suicidal behavior also tend to have a mental disorder, have experienced a recent and stressful life event, feel socially alienated or a burden to others, and are sad, agitated, or angry (Turecki et al., 2019). People who feel a strong sense of **hopelessness**, or a feeling they have no options or control over situations in their lives, are at high risk for suicide (Pettorruso et al., 2020). This was true for Katey, although she did not currently have thoughts of harming herself. Still,

Figure 7.15 Primary Bodily Functions Involved in the Dexamethasone Suppression Test (DST).

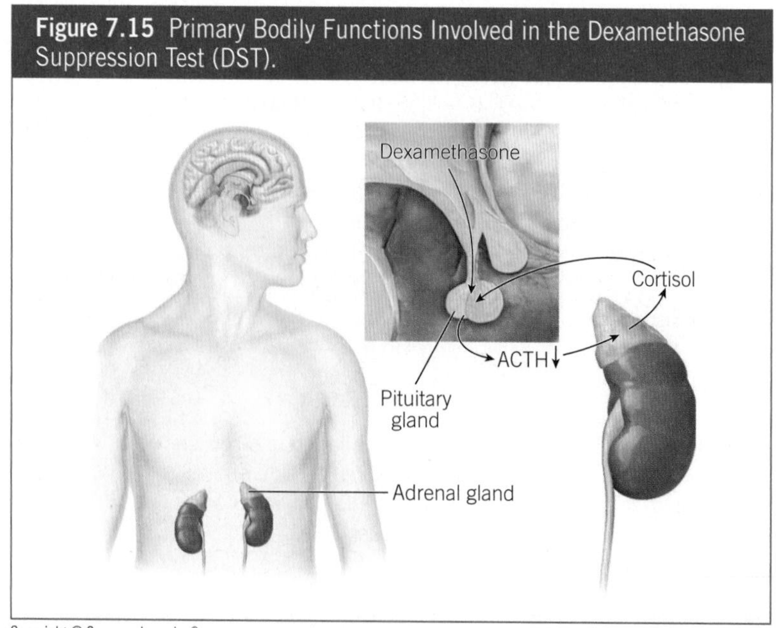

her therapist continued to assess for possible suicidality during treatment.

One system for assessing suicide is in **Figure 7.16**. Following a consideration of major risk factors, therapists are encouraged to ask about recent symptoms of depression or anxiety and substance use. Risk can then be determined even further by asking specific questions about the detail of one's plan to complete suicide. Someone who has a carefully designed plan may be at high risk for doing so. Questions should also surround access to weapons, willingness to die, psychotic symptoms such as hearing voices, previous suicide attempts, family history of suicide, and ability to resist the act of suicide (LeCloux et al., 2022). If a person is at high and imminent risk for suicide, a therapist must take drastic action to prevent the act. These clinical actions are discussed further in the later treatment section.

Researchers also use *retrospective analysis* to examine people who have attempted or completed suicide. Retrospective analysis, sometimes called a *psychological*

Figure 7.16 Schematic for Assessment of Suicidality.

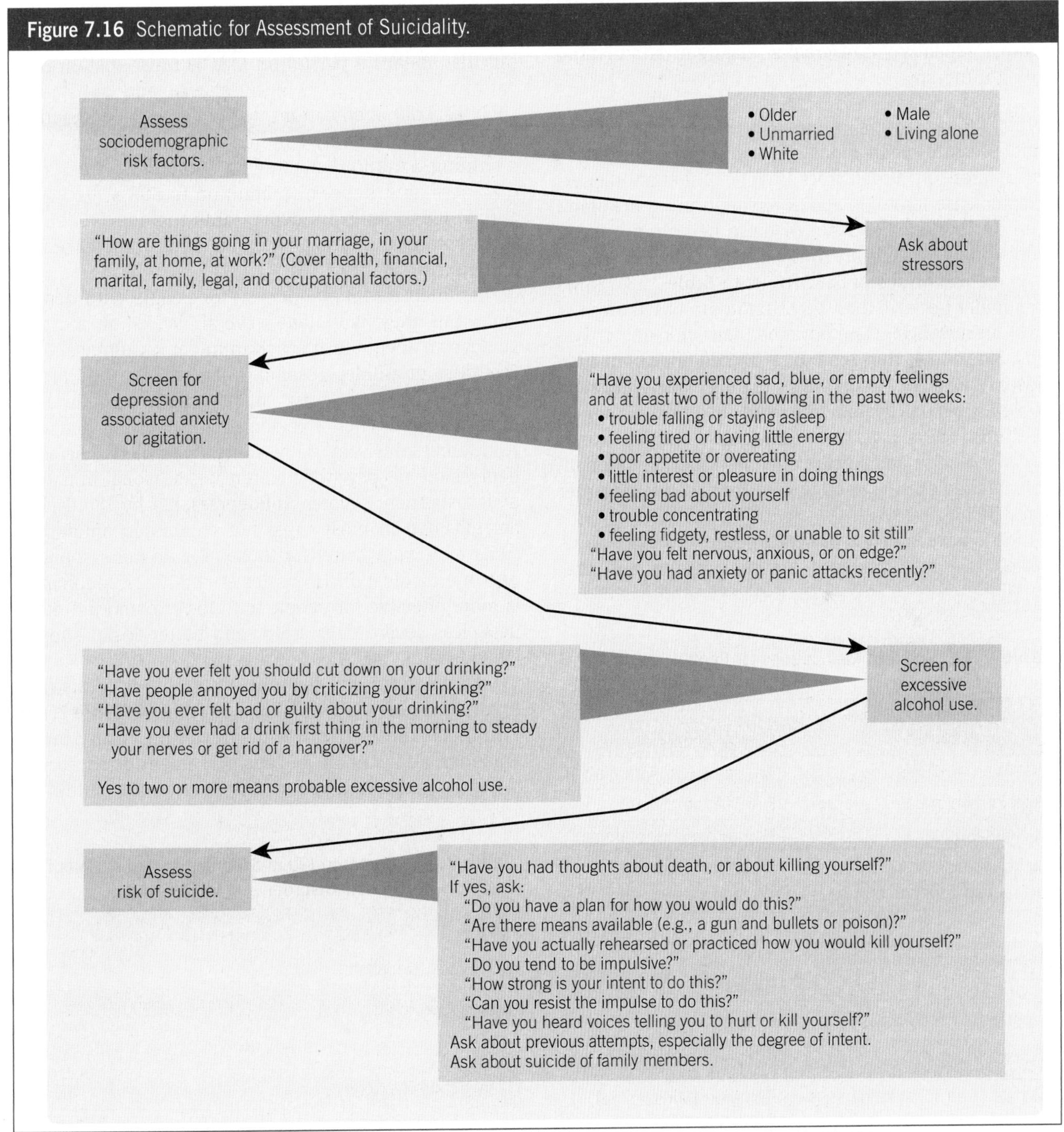

Assess sociodemographic risk factors.
• Older • Unmarried • White • Male • Living alone
"How are things going in your marriage, in your family, at home, at work?" (Cover health, financial, marital, family, legal, and occupational factors.)
Ask about stressors
Screen for depression and associated anxiety or agitation.
"Have you experienced sad, blue, or empty feelings and at least two of the following in the past two weeks:
• trouble falling or staying asleep
• feeling tired or having little energy
• poor appetite or overeating
• little interest or pleasure in doing things
• feeling bad about yourself
• trouble concentrating
• feeling fidgety, restless, or unable to sit still"
"Have you felt nervous, anxious, or on edge?"
"Have you had anxiety or panic attacks recently?"
"Have you ever felt you should cut down on your drinking?"
"Have people annoyed you by criticizing your drinking?"
"Have you ever felt bad or guilty about your drinking?"
"Have you ever had a drink first thing in the morning to steady your nerves or get rid of a hangover?"
Yes to two or more means probable excessive alcohol use.
Screen for excessive alcohol use.
Assess risk of suicide.
"Have you had thoughts about death, or about killing yourself?"
If yes, ask:
"Do you have a plan for how you would do this?"
"Are there means available (e.g., a gun and bullets or poison)?"
"Have you actually rehearsed or practiced how you would kill yourself?"
"Do you tend to be impulsive?"
"How strong is your intent to do this?"
"Can you resist the impulse to do this?"
"Have you heard voices telling you to hurt or kill yourself?"
Ask about previous attempts, especially the degree of intent.
Ask about suicide of family members.

Source: Hirschfeld, R. M., & Russell, J. M. (1997). Assessment and treatment of suicidal patients. *New England Journal of Medicine*, 337, 910–915.

autopsy, may involve interviewing family members and friends, examining suicide notes, and evaluating medical records (Mérelle et al., 2020). Retrospective studies often reveal that physical or mental disorders, interpersonal conflicts, stressful life events, or job or financial or family loss are key risk factors in suicide (Richardson et al., 2021).

Biological Treatment of Depressive and Bipolar Disorders and Suicide

Biological treatments for people with depressive and bipolar disorders include medication, electroconvulsive therapy, repetitive transcranial magnetic stimulation, and light therapy.

Medication

Antidepressant medications are often helpful for people with depression. Recall from Chapter 2 that antidepressants increase serotonin and norepinephrine in the brain, often by blocking reuptake of these neurotransmitters. Many antidepressants are thus called **selective serotonin reuptake inhibitors**, or SSRIs (refer to **Table 7.13**). SSRIs are popular because they affect serotonin-based areas of the brain specifically and not other neurotransmitter systems. Side effects thus tend to be limited but can include nausea, headache, agitation, sweating, gastrointestinal problems, sexual dysfunction, and insomnia (Wang et al., 2018). SSRIs have been associated with increased risk of self-harm and suicide attempt, especially for children and adolescents, though data are mixed (Hengarner et al., 2021).

SSRIs have largely replaced **tricyclic antidepressants** (Table 7.13) that produced the same neurotransmitter effect but had more side effects. Tricyclics affect serotonin as well as norepinephrine and other neurotransmitter systems. Side effects of tricyclics include a wide range of cardiovascular, muscular, allergic, gastrointestinal, endocrinological, and other symptoms. Tricyclics and SSRIs are both effective, but many physicians and patients prefer SSRIs because of their fewer side effects (Anagha et al., 2021). Tricyclics may be used if a person does not respond well to an SSRI.

Other antidepressants are available if SSRIs or tricyclics are not effective (refer to Table 7.13). **Monoamine oxidase inhibitors** (MAOIs) enhance tyramine to increase norepinephrine and serotonin. Unfortunately, this also means a person on MAOIs must abstain from various foods such as aged cheese and substances such as cold medications to avoid a toxic reaction. Severe side effects are common to these drugs as well, including agitation, manic-like symptoms, weakness, dizziness, and nausea. In addition to SSRIs, tricyclics, and MAOIs, other antidepressants include Wellbutrin (bupropion) and Effexor (venlafaxine) to increase norepinephrine (Table 7.13).

Antidepressants work well for people with depression, but they may take several weeks or more to achieve an adequate effect (Kornhuber & Gulbins, 2021). Overdose of antidepressants is also one method of suicide. Adding other crisis management procedures is thus indicated when a person is suicidal (later section). Antidepressants may be less effective when a person's depression has psychotic features, is seasonal in nature, or is extremely severe. Antidepressants by themselves are effective in most cases but combining antidepressants may work better for those who do not respond to just one medication (Henssler et al., 2022). Medication is more effective for people with fewer comorbid disorders, less severe depression, and better social support (Woods et al., 2021).

Medication for people with bipolar disorder involves **mood-stabilizing drugs** (refer to **Table 7.14**). Lithium is most effective for preventing future manic episodes and suicide because, as mentioned earlier, the drug reduces levels of dopamine and glutamate.

Table 7.13 Common Medications for People with Depression

Selective serotonin reuptake inhibitors (SSRIs):	**Tricyclic antidepressants:**
Citalopram (Celexa)	Anafranil (Clomipramine)
Escitalopram oxalate (Lexapro)	Elavil (Amitriptyline)
Fluoxetine (Prozac)	Norpramin (Desipramine)
Fluvoxamine (Luvox)	Sinequan (Doxepin)
Paroxetine (Paxil)	
Sertraline (Zoloft)	
Monoamine oxidase inhibitors (MAOIs):	**Others:**
Marplan (Isocarboxazid)	Effexor (Venlafaxine)
Nardil (Phenelzine)	Wellbutrin (Bupropion)
Parnate (Tranylcypromine)	Remeron (Mirtazapine) Duloxetine (Cymbalta)

Table 7.14 Common Mood-Stabilizing Medications for People with Bipolar Disorder

Carbamazepine (Tegretol)
Divalproex (Depakote)
Lamotrigine (Lamictal)
Lithium (Eskalith)
Olanzapine (Zyprexa)
Thorazine (Chlorpromazine)

The drug also affects thyroid and adrenocorticotropic hormones, which were mentioned earlier with respect to the dexamethasone suppression test (Kishi et al., 2021). Lithium can be highly toxic, so periodic blood tests are necessary. Lithium's toxicity, intense side effects, and the fact that some people with bipolar disorder want to keep their euphoria or have limited insight can make compliance to the medication problematic (Vázquez et al., 2021).

Lithium is sometimes used in combination with other medications, especially in cases of severe bipolar disorder. Divalproex, for example, is an anticonvulsant drug that increases gamma-aminobutyric acid (GABA) levels and creates a sedating effect. The drug may be especially useful for people with rapid cycling and mixed features. Lithium and divalproex are also sometimes used with another anticonvulsant such as carbamazepine or with antipsychotic medications (Chapter 12; Yatham et al., 2021). Other medications such as lamotrigine are better for treating the depressive aspect of bipolar disorder (Fountoulakis et al., 2022). People who respond best to these treatments have less severe symptoms and continue to take their medication (Consoloni et al., 2021). Katey took lithium and divalproex and did appear calmer during treatment.

Electroconvulsive Therapy

An unusual but often effective treatment for people with very severe or melancholic depression is **electroconvulsive therapy**, or ECT. Sometimes known as "shock therapy," ECT involves placing one or two electrodes on a person's head and deliberately inducing a seizure into the brain via shock for 0.5 to 2.0 seconds. The person first receives sedative medication to prevent convulsions. People with severe depressive symptoms such as difficulty moving who have not responded to medication may receive ECT in an inpatient setting. The process usually requires 6 to 12 sessions over two to four weeks, and common side effects include temporary memory loss and confusion (Porta-Casteràs et al., 2021).

ECT is generally effective for people with very severe depression, even more so than medication, especially if two electrodes and higher dosage is used. Relapse rates can be high, however (Jelovac et al., 2021). People with mania can also benefit from ECT, particularly those who do not respond to medication (Abascal-Peiró et al., 2022). How ECT works is not completely clear, but some evidence points to changes in the brain circuits and neurotransmitters involved in mood (Porta-Casteràs et al., 2021). ECT remains a common but still controversial treatment (refer to **Focus On Law and Ethics: Ethical Dilemmas in Electroconvulsive Therapy**).

Repetitive Transcranial Magnetic Stimulation

An alternative to ECT is **repetitive transcranial magnetic stimulation** (rTMS), which involves placing an electromagnetic coil on a person's scalp and introducing a pulsating, high-intensity current. The current produces a magnetic field lasting 100 to 200 microseconds, and the procedure is less invasive than ECT. rTMS may increase the brain's metabolism of glucose and blood flow to the prefrontal cortex, but the procedure remains somewhat controversial and in need of more extensive study (Nguyen et al., 2021). rTMS may be more useful for suicidal ideation and depression than mania (Cui et al., 2021).

Light Therapy

An innovative treatment for people with seasonal depression, especially those primarily depressed in

Focus On Law and Ethics

Ethical Dilemmas in Electroconvulsive Therapy

Electroconvulsive therapy (ECT) is an effective treatment for people with severe depression. Still, ECT remains controversial because many people view the procedure with alarm and because exactly how ECT works remains unclear. One researcher, Max Fink, outlined several ethical principles for therapists who consider ECT. These principles include *beneficence* (does the procedure help the person?), *nonmaleficence* (does the procedure harm the person in any way?), *respect for autonomy* (is the person fully informed of the benefits and risks of the procedure?), and *justice* (does the procedure preserve the person's dignity?).

These principles can create ethical dilemmas. Fink outlined these dilemmas in vignettes. One vignette involves an older woman with cardiovascular problems and severe depression. Even if ECT is the preferred choice of treatment in this situation, should it be used at the risk of worsening the cardiovascular symptoms? In another vignette, a person with severe depression is hospitalized after a suicide attempt and too distraught to speak with doctors. Even if ECT might work, would doing so be advisable because the person cannot give proper consent or understand the treatment? (Fink et al., 2014).

Other vignettes create additional questions. What if a person gives consent for ECT but family members adamantly oppose the treatment? What if ECT allows a person to become legally competent to stand trial for a crime? What if a person refuses ECT but continues to be suicidal? Answering these questions is difficult and requires a thorough review of several ethical principles. What would you do in these situations?

winter months, is *light therapy.* Light therapy generally consists of having a person sit before a bright light of 2,000 to 10,000 lux (a unit of illumination) for 30 to 120 minutes per day during the winter. Traditional light therapy involved large light "boxes," but modern devices include smaller towers a person can view while reading or working on a computer. The therapy is usually administered in the morning or evening and may work by enhancing photon absorption or by adjusting circadian rhythms or melatonin levels. People with seasonal depression generally respond positively to light therapy, and the procedure may also be useful for some people with nonseasonal depression (Dong et al., 2022).

Psychological Treatments for Depressive and Bipolar Disorders and Suicide

Psychological treatments for depressive and bipolar disorders and suicide are discussed next. Psychological treatments are quite effective for mild and moderate mood problems and include behavioral activation, cognitive therapy, mindfulness, interpersonal therapy, and family and marital therapy. Most of these apply best to depression but some can apply to bipolar disorder as well.

Behavioral Activation and Related Therapies

People with depression often isolate themselves from others and lose interest in previously pleasurable activities. Others may then provide sympathy and attention and socially reinforce depressed behavior. Therapists rely on *behavioral activation* to address this process. Essential components of behavioral activation include psychoeducation about depression, increasing daily activities and exercise, and rewarding progress. Specific activities a therapist may focus on include the following:

- Educational and creative activities, such as learning a musical instrument or engaging in photography
- Domestic activities, such as cleaning or cooking
- Health and appearance activities, such as going to the dentist and shopping for new clothes
- Leisure activities, such as walking in the park and increased exercise
- Religious activities such as going to church

The overall goal of behavioral activation is to get a person more involved with daily social activities that will help produce positive feelings and self-esteem (Stein et al., 2021). Behavioral activation may be combined with other behavioral approaches as well:

- *Contingency management* may involve teaching significant others to reinforce active, prosocial behavior.
- *Self-control therapy* may involve having a person reinforce themself for active, nondepressed behaviors.
- *Social skills training* may help a person, especially an adolescent with depression, improve methods of social interaction, including making eye contact, smiling more, and discussing topics other than depression.
- *Coping* or *problem-solving skills training* may be used to help people find effective solutions for problems instead of avoiding them.

Therapists often combine behavioral techniques with other psychological approaches such as reminiscence therapy (refer to **Focus On Diversity: Depression in Older People**) and cognitive therapy, which are described next.

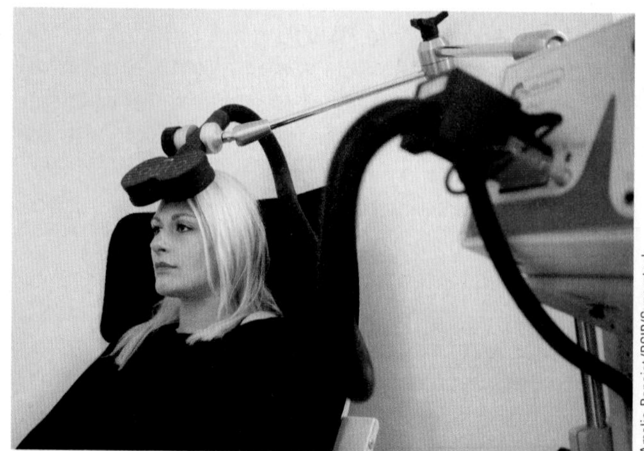

Amelie-Benoist/BSIP/Superstock

Repetitive transcranial magnetic stimulation (rTMS) is a treatment for people with depression.

Image Point Fr/Shutterstock.com

Light therapy may be especially useful for people with seasonal depression.

Focus On Diversity

Depression in Older People

Many people think of depression as a condition that largely affects adolescents and young adults, but researchers have focused on another population that has more than its share of depression: older people. About 13.3 percent of older people have major depression (Abdoli et al., 2022). In addition, the rate of suicide among people aged 85 years and older is 20.9 per 100,000 people, which is the highest among all age groups (Ehlman et al. 2022).

Depression among older people is sometimes difficult to detect for several reasons. First, many older people with depression focus on complaints of physical symptoms of their depression rather than mood. Second, symptoms of depression such as withdrawal or motivation loss may be thought of by others as a desire to relax during retirement or simply signs of "old age." Third, symptoms of sadness may be dismissed as simple bereavement over friends who begin to pass away. Fourth, symptoms of depression often mimic those found in dementia (Chapter 14), especially slowed speech and movement and difficulties in memory and concentration. What might initially appear to be Alzheimer's disease may actually be depression.

Treating depression in older people often involves cognitive and family therapy as well as medication. One treatment designed specifically for older people with depression is **reminiscence therapy**. Reminiscence therapy involves a systematic review and discussion of each phase of a person's life, from birth to present, with a particular focus on trying to resolve conflicts and regrets. The therapy seems generally effective for older people with depression, but more research is needed to determine what types of people might benefit most (Li et al., 2020).

Cognitive Therapy

Cognitive therapy is a main staple of treatment for people with depressive and bipolar disorders. Recall from Chapters 5 and 6 that cognitive therapy involves examining a person's negative or unrealistic thoughts and encouraging them to challenge their thoughts. Cognitive therapy helps people change their ways of reasoning about the environment and find the positive and realistic side of things as well as the negative. A person also learns about the relationship between thoughts, emotion, and behavior. One may believe they will fail a test, become sullen and withdrawn from others, and fail to study or prepare for the test. Becoming aware of these kinds of sequences and using cognitive techniques will help them refrain from such catastrophic thinking and problematic behaviors.

Cognitive therapy for depression entails examining evidence for and against a certain thought, hypothesis testing to determine the actual chances something bad will happen, and decatastrophizing worst-case scenarios. The main goals of cognitive therapy for depression are to increase a person's ability to challenge negative thoughts and develop a sense of control over life events that seem unpredictable and overwhelming. Cognitive therapy helps a person who believes they will fail an upcoming test to learn how to realistically appraise whether failure will *actually* happen and how to properly study so failure is less likely to happen.

Cognitive therapy for depression is certainly better than no treatment and appears to be as effective as medication. Cognitive therapy may produce better, longer term results than medication because clients have learned specific skills to combat depressive thoughts. Cognitive therapy with medication is a standard treatment for depression in many clinical settings, but the therapy may be less effective for people with severe depression or those who are actively suicidal (Furukawa et al., 2021).

Cognitive therapy can also be effective for bipolar disorder (Miklowitz et al., 2021). One main goal of this approach, as with depression, is to challenge and change unrealistic beliefs. Many people with bipolar disorder mistakenly believe that euphoria will improve their quality of life when in fact it often leads to self-destructive behavior. Cognitive therapy for bipolar disorder also concentrates on improving problem-solving skills, organization, memory, social support, and safety behaviors; avoiding high-risk behaviors such as substance use; and recognizing early warning signs of mania. This may also involve daily thought records, consultations with friends and family members, and strategies to delay impulsive behaviors (Tsapekos et al., 2020). Cognitive therapy for bipolar disorder also aims to enhance medication compliance.

Mindfulness

Recall from Chapter 5 that mindfulness aims to help people understand and accept their symptoms but still live a normal life. Recall how mindfulness for anxiety-related disorder involves greater awareness and acceptance of symptoms and how symptoms can be experienced without severe avoidance or other impairment. Therapists also apply mindfulness to people with depression and focus on helping people experience the present rather than dwell on past failures or negative expectations about the future. A therapist encourages a client to be aware of their body and movement in the here and now and to use meditation and other practices to enhance this awareness (Johannsen et al., 2022).

Some of the most problematic aspects of depression are troublesome emotions, thoughts, and physical behaviors. A therapist engaging in mindfulness thus encourages a client to view sad mood, thoughts, and physical feelings as events that pass through the mind and not as indicators of reality. Clients are encouraged to disengage from habitual thoughts and focus on "being" in the moment. Therapists often combine mindfulness with cognitive therapy for individuals or groups. Mindfulness is effective for treating depression and may be especially helpful for preventing relapse (McCartney et al., 2021).

Interpersonal Therapy

Another psychological approach to treating depressive and bipolar disorders is *interpersonal therapy,* or IPT. The basis of IPT is that a person's attachment or relationships with others are key to mental health. IPT focuses on repairing problematic relationships or coping with loss of close relationships (Weissman, 2020). IPT concentrates on four main categories of relationship difficulty:

- *Grief* due to the loss of a loved one
- *Role disputes* with others such as a spouse, partner, parent, coworker, or friend
- *Role transitions* or major changes in a person's life, such as ending a relationship, starting a new job, coping with an illness, or retiring from one's career
- *Interpersonal deficits* such as lack of social skill and trouble maintaining relationships with others

Interpersonal therapy is an *eclectic* approach, or one that uses techniques from different theoretical orientations such as psychodynamic, cognitive, behavioral, and family systems approaches. Therapists who use IPT for depression concentrate on exploring a person's unrealistic expectations of others, solving interpersonal problems effectively, finding new friends, and improving methods of good communication. IPT is especially useful if a person's depression stems from problematic relationships with others, but it is useful as well as part of an overall treatment plan with cognitive therapy and medication (Lemmens et al., 2020). IPT may also be useful for people with bipolar disorder, especially when therapists link the approach to scheduling regular patterns of sleep (Morton & Murray, 2020).

Prostock-studio/Shutterstock.com

Marital therapy is an effective treatment for depression, especially in women.

Family and Marital Therapy

Family and marital therapy for depressive and bipolar disorders may be conducted within the context of IPT or separately. Family therapy is especially helpful for families marked by high **expressed emotion**, or excessive hostility, criticism, and overinvolvement. Family therapy is particularly useful for adolescents with depression. Family therapists focus on improving communication and problem-solving skills among family members. Contingency management, in which a person with depression is encouraged to be active and associate with others, is a common ingredient of family therapy as well. Parents who show withdrawn behavior may also receive treatment for their depression or counseling regarding their child-rearing practices. Family therapy regarding depression is generally effective for parents and children (Carr, 2019).

Katey's treatment did include family members who provided social and financial support and who helped her remain on medication. Katey's mother also had symptoms of bipolar disorder, so family members learned about the condition and what symptoms to monitor. Katey eventually moved in with her parents to help stabilize her condition, so therapy also involved reducing role conflicts and improving communication among family members. Family therapy for bipolar disorder is often important to prevent relapse, as was true for Katey (Wittenborn et al., 2022).

Marital therapy is also commonly used to treat depression, especially in women. A marital therapist will try to improve communication and problem-solving skills and increase mutually pleasurable and prosocial behavior such as scheduling activities that *each* partner likes to do. Cognitive-behavioral components for treating depression are used as well. Marital therapy can be an effective treatment for depression, especially when marital issues are a main reason for depression (Alder et al., 2018). Intervention that includes partners may be useful as well for helping people with bipolar disorder remain on their medication (Wittenborn et al., 2022).

Psychological treatments for depression are quite effective by themselves but are commonly supplemented by medication. Psychological treatments for bipolar disorder, however, are *almost always* supplemented with medication, as was true for Katey. In severe cases of depressive or bipolar disorder, biological treatments are often used first and may be much more effective than psychological treatments.

Treatment of Suicidality

What should a therapist do if someone is suicidal? Therapists usually determine if risk of suicide is imminent, meaning the person is likely to complete suicide if left alone. In cases of suicidality, ethical issues of therapist–client confidentiality are not as important as client safety, so a therapist must do what is necessary to protect a client's life. If suicide seems imminent, as was true for Katey, then a therapist typically arranges hospitalization in an inpatient psychiatric unit. If a person calls a therapist and threatens suicide, the therapist may call for emergency services to have the person transferred to a hospital. Often this also involves informing people close to the person, such as a partner, and working closely with hospital staff to help the person cope with their current crisis. Medication, group therapy, and constant supervision are strategies to address people in hospital settings who are suicidal (Webb et al., 2020).

If a person is not at imminent risk for suicide but might be so in coming hours or days, therapists may draft a *no-suicide contract*. This is an agreement, often signed by a therapist and client, in which the client agrees to contact and speak with the therapist before any self-destructive act. Contracts are not a perfect intervention, but clients may adhere to the contracts and refrain from impulsive behavior. Others argue that a client's *commitment to a treatment statement* is more effective than a no-suicide contract. A commitment to treatment statement represents an agreement between a therapist and client that the client will adhere to the treatment process and to living, openly communicate about suicidal thoughts and urges, and access emergency care when needed (Bryan & Rudd, 2018).

A therapist will also contact the person frequently during the week and encourage significant others, with the client's permission, to closely supervise the client and remove potentially lethal items such as firearms and medications from the home. Issues related to thoughts of suicide, such as a recent stressful life event or substance use, are addressed as well (Swift et al., 2021).

What If I Am Sad or Have a Depressive or Bipolar Disorder?

The answers to some basic questions (refer to **Table 7.15**) may help you decide if you wish further assessment or even treatment for a possible depressive or bipolar disorder. If you find the answer to most of these questions is yes, then you may wish to consult a clinical psychologist, psychiatrist, or other mental health professional (Chapter 15). Additional professional information is available from the Association for Behavioral and Cognitive Therapies (www.abct.org) and the National Alliance for Research on Schizophrenia and Depression (www.narsad.org).

Table 7.15 Screening Questions for Depressive and Bipolar Disorder

Do you find any of the mood symptoms described in this chapter apply to you much more so than most people your age?
Are there many things you would like to do but cannot because you feel too sad?
Are you greatly troubled by your mood symptoms?
Do other people notice your sadness or euphoria or encourage you to seek help?
Does your sadness or euphoria last much of the time, even when nothing stressful is happening?
Has your work or social life or sleep deteriorated because of sadness or euphoria?
Do you get extremely upset over even little things most of the time?
Have you experienced a stressful life event that you just cannot seem to put behind you?
Do you feel sad, irritable, tense, and pessimistic much of the time?
If you could make your life better, would it include feeling less sad?

If you think you have a depressive or bipolar disorder, consult with a mental health professional that specializes in this problem. Do not diagnose yourself. If you think you have sadness or euphoria but not necessarily a depressive or bipolar disorder, then becoming more socially active, changing your thoughts, and resolving interpersonal conflicts may be best. Talk about your feelings with family and friends, or attend a depression screening in your community. If you think you have severe symptoms, however, then be sure to seek consultation from a qualified therapist.

Long-Term Outcome for People with Depressive and Bipolar Disorders and Suicide

What is the long-term picture, or prognosis, for people with depressive and bipolar disorders like Katey? Factors that predict good treatment outcome for depression include better treatment compliance and completion, longer and more complex treatment, early recovery from depression, and fewer past episodes of major depression and residual symptoms. Other factors related to good outcome include fewer stressful life events and comorbid diagnoses, less rumination, more positive self-image, high self-esteem, good family and marital relationships, and older age of onset (Kraus et al., 2019).

Major depressive episodes last an average of 20 to 30 weeks. Most people (50–70 percent) experiencing a major depressive episode recover within one year, but about 14 to 35 percent continue to experience depressive episodes, and 6 to 15 percent experience chronic depression over many years. Even after recovery, up to 30 percent of those experiencing one major depressive episode will experience a second one. Those with dysthymic disorder often recover (74 percent), but time to recovery is lengthy. People with depression are also more likely to die from cardiovascular and other problems than people without depression (Klein, 2016; Lichtman et al., 2014). Recurring depression is related to younger age and younger age of onset, number of previous episodes, severity of the previous episode, suicidality, and continued impairment (Bartova et al., 2019).

For those in treatment for bipolar disorder, similar prognostic factors are evident. People with bipolar disorder who respond well to treatment tend to have more classic forms of the disorder, with less rapid cycling. Good treatment outcome is related to medication compliance and effectiveness (especially *early* in the disorder), better cognitive functioning, fewer comorbid diagnoses, less expressed emotion in families, ongoing contact with mental health professionals, and good occupational status (Arvilommi et al., 2014; Ellis et al., 2014; Hui et al., 2019).

Depressive episodes in bipolar disorder tend to last 2.8 to 4.3 months, and manic episodes in bipolar disorder tend to last two to four months. Length of these episodes generally decreases, or gets faster, with each successive episode. About 50 percent of people with a first episode of bipolar disorder recover completely, but the remainder experience recurrent episodes. Recurring bipolar disorder is related to younger age of onset, more severe depressive or psychotic symptoms, treatment delays, and cognitive deficits. Better long-term outcome relates to employment and ability to live independently (Hulvershorn & Nurnberger, 2014; Merikangas et al., 2016).

What about people released from a hospital after suicidal behavior? Within two years after discharge in one study, about 67 percent engaged in additional suicidal behavior, 38 percent engaged in suicidal behavior with certain suicide attempt, and 6 percent completed suicide. Future suicidal behavior was predicted by younger age, number of past suicidal behaviors, childhood maltreatment, poor physical health, and comorbid diagnoses. Younger age and hopelessness predicted suicide attempt (Hayashi et al., 2012). Others have found as well that ongoing suicidal behavior over several years relates closely to low socioeconomic status, poor adjustment, family history of suicide, and lack of outpatient treatment before hospitalization (Isometsa et al., 2014; Soloff & Chiappetta, 2012). Repeated follow-up contacts with people after discharge appears to lower the risk of suicidal behavior (Luxton et al., 2015).

Katey's long-term prognosis remains unclear. On the plus side, she was currently in treatment and sticking with it, and seemed to have good family support. On the minus side, her mental condition lasted for years without adequate treatment, she used alcohol and had suicidal behaviors, and she lost her life savings and job. Good outcome will likely have to include ongoing and intense medication and psychological treatment as well as strong support from significant others.

Section Summary

- Assessing people with depressive and bipolar disorders often includes structured and unstructured interviews and self-report questionnaires.
- Observations and information from therapists, partners, children, parents, and others are important for assessing depressive and bipolar disorders.
- Laboratory assessments for depression include the dexamethasone test.
- Assessing risk of suicide is critical in depressive and bipolar disorders and often focuses on detail of suicide plan, access to weapons, and support from others.
- Biological treatment of depressive and bipolar disorders includes selective serotonin reuptake inhibitors (SSRIs), tricyclics, monoamine oxidase inhibitors (MAOIs), and mood-stabilizing drugs.
- Electroconvulsive therapy (ECT) involves deliberately inducing a brain seizure to improve very severe depression. Repetitive transcranial magnetic stimulation (rTMS) involves placing an electromagnetic coil on a person's scalp and introducing a current to relieve depressive symptoms.
- Light therapy is often used for people with seasonal depression.
- Psychological treatment of depressive and bipolar disorders includes behavioral approaches to increase activity and reinforcement from others for prosocial behavior. Cognitive therapy is also a main staple for depressive and bipolar disorders and may be linked to mindfulness.
- Interpersonal and marital and family therapists concentrate on improving a person's relationships with others to alleviate symptoms of depressive and bipolar disorders.
- Addressing suicidal behavior, sometimes via hospitalization, is a critical aspect of treating people with depressive and bipolar disorders.
- Long-term outcome for people with depressive and bipolar disorders is best when they receive early treatment, remain on medication, have fewer comorbid diagnoses, and experience good support from others.

Review Questions

1. Outline major assessment techniques for depressive and bipolar disorders, including interviews, self-report questionnaires, observations, and laboratory assessment.
2. What medications help control symptoms of depressive and bipolar disorders? How do they work?
3. Describe electroconvulsive, repetitive transcranial magnetic, and light therapies.
4. What psychological treatment strategies could a mental health professional use to help someone improve interpersonal functioning and mood? How so?
5. What is the prognosis or long-term outcome for people with depressive and bipolar disorders?

Final Comments

People with depressive and bipolar disorders experience tremendous distress from swings of emotion, hopelessness, troubling thoughts, and self-destructive behavior. This is important to remember if you or someone you know feels sad or withdrawn from others. Occasional feelings of sadness and euphoria are normal, but they can sometimes linger and get out of control. If they do, then talking to someone about it or contacting a qualified mental health professional is a good idea. You can observe how symptoms of depression and anxiety cause so much distress for people, and these symptoms occur together in people with eating disorders, which are discussed in the next chapter.

Thought Questions

1. Think about television shows or films you have seen that have characters with mood problems. Do you think these characters display realistic or unrealistic symptoms of mood changes? How so?
2. Think about situations that make you most sad, such as illness of a loved one or breakup of a relationship. Think about situations that make you most euphoric, such as a great test grade or a new baby relative. How do you feel physically, what do you think in those situations, and what do you do? Having read the chapter, would you change anything?
3. What would you say to a friend who might be very sad or euphoric and who might be considering suicide?
4. What separates "normal" from "psychopathological" mood? Do you think depressive and bipolar disorders have more to do with personal, family, or other factors? Why?
5. What do you think family members and friends could do to reduce severe mood changes in people they know?

Key Terms

depressive disorder 179
bipolar disorder 179
major depressive episode 179
major depressive disorder 182
premenstrual dysphoric disorder 183
peripartum depression 183
postpartum depression 183
persistent depressive disorder (dysthymia) 183
manic episode 186
hypomanic episode 187
bipolar I disorder 188
bipolar II disorder 188
cyclothymic disorder 188
suicide 189
cognitive distortions 199
negative cognitive triad 199
automatic thoughts 199
hopelessness (attribution) theory 199
learned helplessness 199
hopelessness 206
selective serotonin reuptake inhibitors (SSRIs) 208
tricyclic antidepressants 208
monoamine oxidase inhibitors (MAOI) 208
mood-stabilizing drugs 208
electroconvulsive therapy (ECT) 209
repetitive transcranial magnetic stimulation (rTMS) 209
reminiscence therapy 211
expressed emotion 212

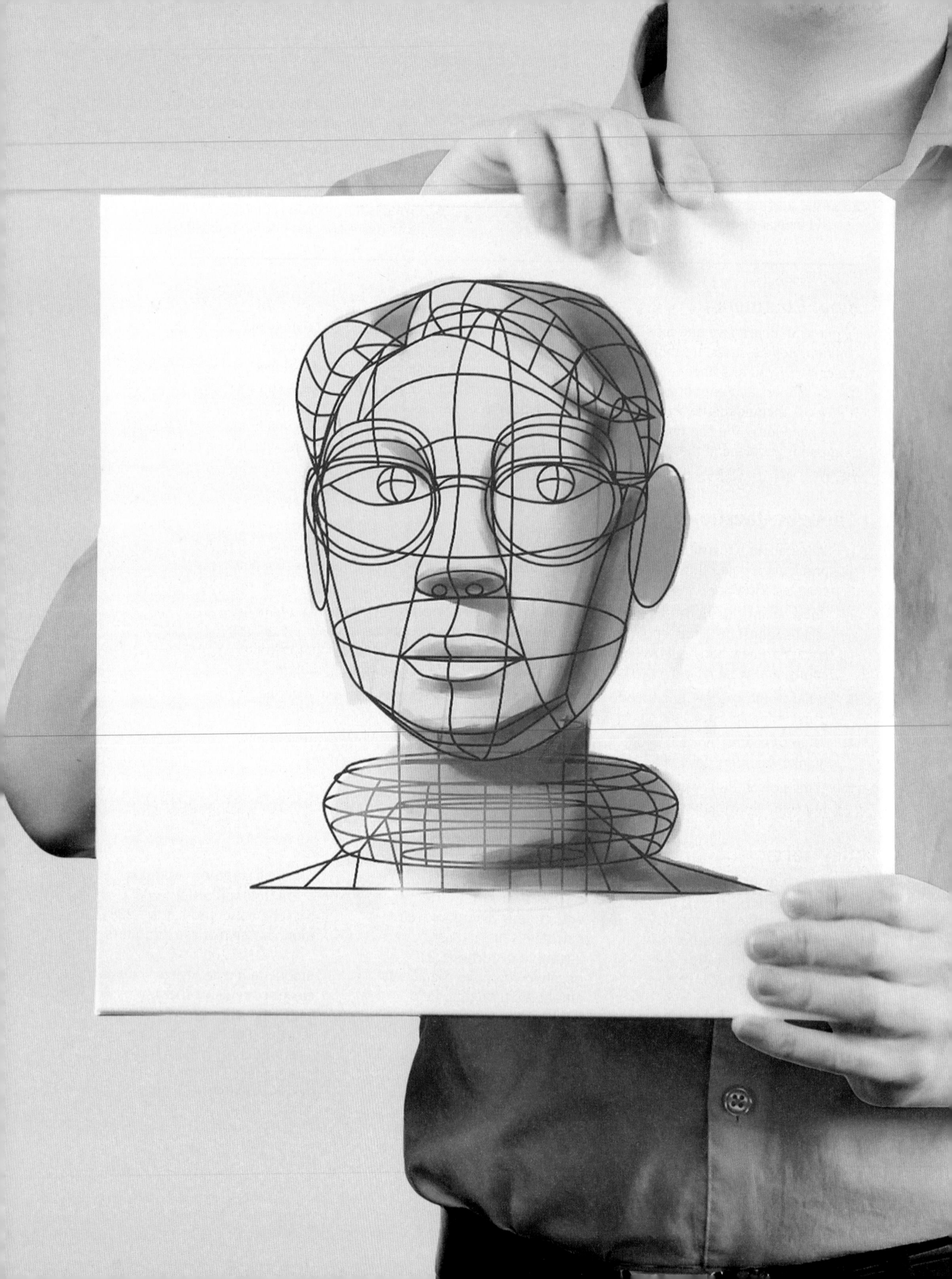

Eating Disorders 8

Learning Objectives

LO 8.1 Describe the continuum of concerns about weight, body shape, and eating, from common thoughts and behaviors to eating disorders.

LO 8.2 Distinguish among the types of eating disorders based on diagnostic criteria and clinical characteristics.

LO 8.3 Summarize the epidemiology of eating disorders.

LO 8.4 Describe the stigma associated with eating disorders and its impact on those with the disorders.

LO 8.5 Discuss the risk factors for eating disorders.

LO 8.6 Evaluate programs to prevent eating disorders.

LO 8.7 Characterize the assessment and treatment of individuals with eating disorders.

Case Sooki

Sooki is a 19-year-old Asian American college student who is 5 feet 4 inches tall and weighs 90.4 pounds. Friends have not noticed that Sooki has lost so much weight over the past year (25 pounds!) because she wears baggy clothes. About a year ago, Sooki became extremely afraid of becoming fat. She was convinced that weight gain would be the worst thing possible and that her college life would be ruined. Sooki began skipping meals and, when she did eat once or twice a day, consumed only a "salad" or other small items. Her salad consists of four lettuce leaves, part of a carrot, an apple slice, and no dressing. Sooki is preoccupied with food and calories. Every bite of food she eats is carefully considered, and she carries charts that list calories per serving of many foods. She drinks only water and diet soda.

Sooki is obsessed with how much she weighs and how she looks. She owns two scales: one is near her bed, and one is in her bathroom. She weighs herself 10 or more times a day. Sooki has told others her butt is too big and her stomach is "poochy." Sooki is markedly underweight but frequently checks her body in the mirror to make sure she is not becoming fat. Her self-esteem depends heavily on her body weight. When Sooki weighs more than 90.0 pounds, she feels bad about herself; when she weighs less than 90.0 pounds, she is perkier. Sooki views weight loss as an impressive achievement in self-discipline. Family members have noticed her weight change and have told Sooki she is underweight. Still, Sooki does not perceive her eating and low weight as a problem. She hopes to lose more weight by eliminating "fattening" foods from her diet such as apple slices and diet soda. Sooki has kept to herself recently and leaves her room only to attend class.

Cameramannz/Shutterstock.com

What Do You Think?

1. Which of Sooki's symptoms seem typical for a college student, and which seem very different?
2. What external events and internal factors might be responsible for Sooki's problems?
3. What are you curious about regarding Sooki?
4. Does Sooki remind you in any way of yourself or someone you know? How so?
5. How might Sooki's eating problems affect her life in the future?

Weight Concerns, Body Dissatisfaction, and Eating Disorders: What Are They?

LO 8.1 Describe the continuum of concerns about weight, body shape, and eating, from common thoughts and behaviors to eating disorders.

Have you ever looked in the mirror and worried you were overweight? Have you ever been concerned about how much you eat? These questions are common for many people, especially with greater awareness about the dangers of obesity. Concern about weight is normal and can be adaptive. Achieving and maintaining normal weight is important for reducing risk of heart disease, diabetes, stroke, and other potentially fatal conditions. Regular exercise and good eating habits also improve our mood and reduce stress. Most of us weigh ourselves every so often to check where we are, and this is normal.

Other people take concern about weight to a higher level. People with **weight concerns** feel overweight much of the time, even when they are not, and view their weight negatively. Perhaps you know someone with a thin physique who thinks a lot about weight and exercises vigorously. People with weight concerns focus on how much they weigh during different times of the day and often have a *drive for thinness*. People with weight concerns focus intently on certain areas of their body they would like to tone or decrease in size. Weight concerns are not a problem if a person is not distressed, remains in a normal weight range, and avoids physical damage from overexercising.

Some people with weight concerns adopt a negative self-evaluation of what their body looks like. **Body dissatisfaction** refers to dissatisfaction or distress with one's appearance, an overinvestment in the way one appears, and avoidance of certain situations or things because they elicit body concerns (Allen & Robson, 2020). People with body dissatisfaction are more than just concerned about their weight. They are constantly unhappy about their weight and think about what could be different with their appearance. They spend substantial money on exercise equipment and gym memberships and avoid social and other situations in which people might judge their weight negatively. Sooki eventually avoided most situations other than class.

Weight concerns and body dissatisfaction are dimensional constructs, meaning we all have these characteristics to some degree. Some people have *intense* weight concerns and body dissatisfaction that escalate toward an **eating disorder**. People with eating disorders have great worry and distress about their weight and body. Sooki was quite *fearful* of gaining weight. Weight concerns and body dissatisfaction are two of the three key components of an eating disorder. The third major component is **eating problems**, which involve restricted eating or excessive dieting and lack of control of eating.

Restricted eating, or **dieting**, refers to deliberate attempts to limit food intake or change types of foods that are eaten. People with eating disorders focus intently on foods that result in weight gain or loss. Such focus is driven by weight concerns or body dissatisfaction. Sooki rarely ate, and maintained very low calorie meals because she believed she was too fat.

Lack of control over eating involves inability to keep oneself from eating large amounts of food. People who lack control over eating consume excessive quantities of food. This feature thus has cognitive (believing one has lost control) and behavioral (eating too much) components. People who lack control over eating can gain substantial weight and be considered overweight for someone of their height, age, and gender. Some people may develop *obesity* as a result, but obesity is not considered an eating disorder.

Weight concerns, body dissatisfaction, and eating problems occur along a continuum (refer to **Continuum of Body Dissatisfaction, Weight Concerns, and Eating Disorder**). Most of us have occasional weight concerns or body dissatisfaction that we address or can cope with. Intense weight concerns or body dissatisfaction cause some people, however, to go to extremes to control their weight. These extremes include severely restricted eating, excessive exercise, or taking medicine or laxatives that lead to weight loss. These people are highly distressed, limit their social activities, and experience significant emotional, behavioral, and even medical consequences. People with these characteristics, like Sooki, have an eating disorder.

Eating disorders can be less severe, as when people are highly bothered by their weight and appearance but still eat occasionally. Eating disorders can also be more severe, however, when a person stops eating and essentially starves themself to death. Severe eating disorders also involve intense distress and sadness. This chapter covers the major eating disorders that affect many people like Sooki.

Eating Disorders: Features and Epidemiology

LO 8.2 Distinguish among the types of eating disorders based on diagnostic criteria and clinical characteristics.

LO 8.3 Summarize the epidemiology of eating disorders.

This section summarizes the major features and other characteristics of the most common eating disorders: anorexia nervosa, bulimia nervosa, and binge-eating disorder.

Image Source/Alamy Stock Photo

A drive for thinness can lead to eating problems or an eating disorder.

Anorexia Nervosa

People with **anorexia nervosa** refuse to maintain a minimum, normal body weight, have an intense fear of gaining weight, and show disturbance in the way they view their body shape and weight (refer to **Table 8.1**; American Psychiatric Association [APA], 2022). Sooki likely met diagnostic criteria for anorexia nervosa because of her low body weight, intense fear of being fat, and disturbed body image. Severity of anorexia nervosa is based partly on body mass index (Table 8.1).

You might think people with anorexia nervosa have no appetite, but they do. In fact, people with

Table 8.1 DSM-5-TR

Anorexia Nervosa
A. Restriction of energy intake relative to requirements, leading to a significantly low body weight in the context of age, sex, developmental trajectory, and physical health. *Significantly low weight* is defined as a weight that is less than minimally normal or, for children and adolescents, less than that minimally expected.
B. Intense fear of gaining weight or of becoming fat, or persistent behavior that interferes with weight gain, even though at a significantly low weight.
C. Disturbance in the way in which one's body weight or shape is experienced, undue influence of body weight or shape on self-evaluation, or persistent lack of recognition of the seriousness of the current low body weight. Specify if restricting or binge-eating/purging type, partial or full remission, and current severity as mild (BMI ≥17 kg/m²), moderate (BMI 16–16.99 kg/m²), severe (BMI 15–15.99 kg/m²), or extreme (BMI <15 kg/m²).

American Psychiatric Association. (2022). *Diagnostic and statistical manual of mental disorders* (5th ed., text rev.). Arlington, VA: American Psychiatric Association.

Continuum of Body Dissatisfaction, Weight Concerns, and Eating Disorder

	Normal	Mild
Emotions	Positive feelings about oneself.	Some anxiety about one's body shape and weight.
Cognitions	"I feel pretty good about my body and about my weight."	"I wish I were more fit and weighed a little less. Maybe I could cut back a bit on my eating."
Behaviors	Eating without concerns.	Tries to eat less at meals and may skip a meal every now and then.

anorexia nervosa often think about food, as Sooki did, and even prepare elaborate meals for others. Unfortunately, people with anorexia nervosa have an intense dissatisfaction with their bodies and thus fear gaining weight. They are driven to thinness and often look for ways to reduce weight.

People with anorexia nervosa lose weight mainly by eating less and exercising excessively. If they do eat, they avoid foods with the most calories. Many people with anorexia nervosa initially lose weight by eliminating soft drinks or fattening foods such as desserts from their diets. Over time, however, they eliminate more and more foods and increasingly skip meals. These **restricting behaviors** form the basis for one subtype of anorexia nervosa (Table 8.1). Sooki is a member of this restricting subtype.

Others with anorexia nervosa lose weight by binge eating (refer to later section) and purging. **Purging** refers to ridding oneself of food or bodily fluids (and thus weight) by self-induced vomiting, misusing laxatives or diuretics, or performing enemas. Binge eating and purging form the basis for a second subtype of anorexia nervosa (Table 8.1).

A particularly fascinating feature of anorexia nervosa is a person's belief they are fat despite overwhelming evidence to the contrary. Sooki lost 25 pounds, nearly 20 percent of her body weight, but still saw her buttocks as large and her stomach as "poochy." People with anorexia nervosa have extreme misperceptions about how they look, feeling fat even when clearly emaciated. A good analogy would be the accentuation and distortion of body size and shape that happens to a reflection in a fun house mirror.

People with anorexia nervosa may not appreciate the serious physical and medical consequences of their very low weight. Individuals with anorexia nervosa become emaciated, dehydrated, and hypotensive (low blood pressure). Anemia, kidney dysfunction, cardiovascular problems, dental problems, electrolyte imbalance, and osteoporosis may result as well. Some people with anorexia nervosa eventually die by self-starvation or suicide (refer to **Personal Narrative: Kitty Westin [Anna's Mother]**).

Bulimia Nervosa

Have you ever eaten so much your stomach hurt? How about feeling guilty after a huge meal? Most of us have overindulged at a buffet or felt self-conscious about eating too many sweets, and this is normal. We are usually concerned about how much we eat and what the consequences might be if we eat too much. Most of us can control our eating and understand that overeating occasionally happens. For others like Lisa, however, episodes of overeating are frequent and cause many problems.

Bulimia nervosa is marked by binge eating, inappropriate methods to prevent weight gain, and self-evaluation greatly influenced by body shape and weight

Moderate	Eating Disorder—less severe	Eating Disorder—more severe
Moderately anxious and feels down about body shape and weight.	Intense anxiety and sadness over apparent inability to lose enough weight.	Severe anxiety and depression over one's body shape and weight.
"Wow, I feel fat. I need to start cutting back on eating. If I don't cut back, I'm going to get even fatter."	"I feel fat all the time, and I wish my body were thinner. I've got to get rid of all these awful calories in my body!"	"I'm extremely fat, and I hate my body! I have to stop eating now! No one understands."
Regularly skips meals and eats low calorie foods only. Starts exercising more to lose weight.	Eats one meal a day, usually a salad with no dressing. May purge after meals or take laxatives.	Eats only rarely and when forced to do so; exercises excessively and purges frequently to lose more weight.

(refer to **Table 8.2**; APA, 2022). **Binge eating** means eating an amount of food in a limited time—such as two hours or less—that is much larger than most people

Case Lisa

Lisa is a 25-year-old woman in therapy for an eating disorder. She has been overconcerned about her body for many years and said she never felt good about school, friends, or herself if she thought she was overweight. Lisa was never skinny but was not overweight either—it just seemed to her that she was overweight. Lisa was constantly trying to limit her eating and weight by dieting. Unfortunately, her appetite would build over time and erupt into an eating feast. Lisa stocked her house with foods like whole cakes, quarts of ice cream, and packages of cookies and ate these foods voraciously during her binges. Lisa felt panicked and out of control of her eating when this happened.

Lisa's episodes of overeating became more frequent in the past year, occurring about five times a week. This made Lisa even more fearful of gaining weight. She was also embarrassed by the way she dealt with her overeating, which involved vomiting after each binge. She hid her vomiting from others, but her teeth were soon eroding as a result. Lisa's binging and purging continued until one day when she noticed a substantial amount of blood in her vomit. She realized she needed help.

Table 8.2 DSM-5-TR

Bulimia Nervosa
A. Recurrent episodes of binge eating. An episode of binge eating is characterized by both of the following: 1. Eating, in a discrete period of time, an amount of food that is definitely larger than what most individuals would eat in a similar period of time under similar circumstances. 2. A sense of lack of control over eating during the episode.
B. Recurrent inappropriate compensatory behaviors in order to prevent weight gain, such as self-induced vomiting; misuse of laxatives, diuretics, or other medications; fasting; or excessive exercise.
C. The binge eating and inappropriate compensatory behaviors both occur, on average, at least once a week for 3 months.
D. Self-evaluation is unduly influenced by body shape and weight.
E. The disturbance does not occur exclusively during episodes of anorexia nervosa. Specify if partial or full remission and severity as mild (1–3 episodes of inappropriate compensatory behaviors per week), moderate (4–7 episodes of inappropriate compensatory behaviors per week), severe (8–13 episodes of inappropriate compensatory behaviors per week), or extreme (14+ episodes of inappropriate compensatory behaviors per week).

American Psychiatric Association. (2022). *Diagnostic and statistical manual of mental disorders* (5th ed., text rev.). Arlington, VA: American Psychiatric Association.

Oleg Elkov/Shutterstock.com

Obesity, while not physically healthy, is not considered an eating disorder.

would eat in that circumstance. Binge eating typically occurs in private and may be triggered by depression, stress, or low self-esteem. Binge eating is also accompanied by lack of control over eating. Many people who binge are ashamed of their eating problem and hide their symptoms.

People with bulimia nervosa use inappropriate behaviors, or **compensatory behaviors**, to prevent weight gain (refer to **Table 8.3**). Lisa induced vomiting after a binge, and this method is used by 80 to 90 percent of those who seek treatment for bulimia nervosa. Vomiting is negatively reinforcing (Chapter 2) because it reduces stomach discomfort as well as fear of weight gain. *Purging* compensatory behaviors include vomiting, misuse of laxatives or diuretics, or enemas. *Nonpurging* compensatory behaviors include fasting for several days or exercising excessively (Table 8.3). Compensatory behaviors can lead to serious physical and medical complications. Excessive vomiting can lead to dental problems, swelling of salivary glands, or esophageal problems. Overusing laxatives and diuretics can lead to chronic diarrhea or bowel problems.

People with bulimia nervosa, like those with anorexia nervosa, emphasize body shape and weight to evaluate themselves. The major difference between the disorders is that people with anorexia nervosa are characterized by excessively low weight, whereas people with bulimia nervosa may be normal weight or overweight. Severity of bulimia nervosa is based partly on number of episodes of compensatory behavior per week (Table 8.2).

Table 8.3 Compensatory Behaviors

Compensatory behaviors to prevent weight gain after binge eating include the following:
• Misuse of laxatives
• Misuse of enemas
• Excessive exercise
• Misuse of diuretics
• Fasting
• Self-induced vomiting

Binge-Eating Disorder

Some people have recurrent episodes of binge eating but *without* compensatory behaviors like purging, excessive exercise, or fasting. People with **binge-eating disorder** experience lack of control over eating during a certain period that leads to discomfort (refer to **Table 8.4**; APA, 2022). To be diagnosed as such, binge eating must occur, on average, once a week for at least three months. Other features of binge eating episodes include eating more rapidly than normal, eating despite feeling uncomfortably full, eating large amounts even when not hungry,

Table 8.4 DSM-5-TR

Binge-Eating Disorder

A. Recurrent episodes of binge eating. An episode of binge eating is characterized by both of the following:

1. Eating, in a discrete period of time, an amount of food that is definitely larger than what most people would eat in a similar period of time under similar circumstances.
2. A sense of lack of control over eating during the episode.

B. The binge-eating episodes are associated with three (or more) of the following:

1. Eating much more rapidly than normal.
2. Eating until feeling uncomfortable full.
3. Eating large amounts of food when not feeling physically hungry.
4. Eating alone because of feeling embarrassed by how much one is eating.
5. Feeling disgusted with oneself, depressed, or very guilty afterward

C. Marked distress regarding binge eating is present.

D. The binge eating occurs, on average, at least once a week for 3 months.

E. The binge eating is not associated with the recurrent use of inappropriate compensatory behavior as in bulimia nervosa and does not occur exclusively during the course of bulimia or anorexia nervosa.

Specify if partial or full remission and severity as mild (1–3 binge-eating episodes per week), moderate (4–7 binge-eating episodes per week), severe (8–13 binge-eating episodes per week), or extreme (14+ binge-eating episodes per week).

American Psychiatric Association. (2022). *Diagnostic and statistical manual of mental disorders* (5th ed., text rev.). Arlington, VA: American Psychiatric Association.

eating alone because of embarrassment over quantity of food consumed, and feeling disgusted, depressed, or guilty after overeating. Individuals with binge-eating disorder are greatly distressed about their behavior. They typically have varying degrees of obesity and may have enrolled in weight control programs.

Binge-eating disorder is similar to bulimia nervosa except people with bulimia nervosa regularly engage in compensatory behaviors to prevent weight gain (Hübel et al., 2021). People with binge-eating disorder also binge over a much longer period of time and their binging may be less frantic than those with bulimia nervosa. Severity of binge-eating disorder is based partly on number of binge eating episodes per week (Table 8.4).

Epidemiology of Eating Disorders

Eating disorders are not as common as the anxiety and depressive disorders discussed in previous chapters, but they do occur frequently enough to be of great concern to mental health professionals. Lifetime prevalence rates have been reported for anorexia (0.2 percent), bulimia (0.6 percent), and binge-eating disorder (1.5 percent) (Qian et al., 2022). Symptoms of eating disorders are also common among adolescents and young adults with other mental disorders. The medical complications of eating disorders can also be quite severe, so researchers have paid great attention to these problems.

Peak age of onset for anorexia nervosa is during adolescent years, and the disorder may be more common in industrialized societies (van Eeden et al., 2021). Mortality is significantly associated with anorexia nervosa in many countries, and eating disorder has the highest death rate of any major mental disorder. These deaths may be the result of complications from the eating disorder but also include elevated suicide rates (Shahnaz & Klonsky, 2021). Peak age of onset for bulimia nervosa and for binge-eating disorder is 15 to 20 years (Favaro et al., 2019).

Prevalence rates for eating disorders may seem low but consider other related facts. Many people have *symptoms* of eating disorder that do not rise to the level of a formal diagnosis, including college students (refer to **Focus On College Students: Eating Disorders**). Many people also do not seek treatment for their eating disorder. Only 13.0 to 35.6 percent of those with an eating disorder seek mental health care (Ali et al., 2020). People may shun treatment for eating disorders because they feel embarrassed or stigmatized. Many people with eating disorders are secretive about their symptoms and feel they do not have a problem. Sooki viewed restricted food intake and weight loss as a virtue and not a problem to be acknowledged and treated.

Eating disorders are much more common among women (2.6 percent) than men (0.7 percent) (Qian et al., 2022). Several reasons may account for this gender difference (refer to **Focus On Gender: Why Is There a Gender Difference in Eating Disorders?**). A sociocultural role might contribute to eating disorder symptoms in girls and women. Some theorists focus on "objectification" of women, media models of thinness for women, stress from maltreatment and sexual harassment, less recognition of achievements, and excessive attention to beauty and body shape (Bardone-Cone et al., 2020). Self-objectification, self-surveillance, and disordered eating are more common, for example, among ballet dancers (Doria & Numer, 2022). Symptoms of eating disorder have also been linked to actresses, models, and elite female athletes in sports requiring thinness (Chapa et al., 2022).

Focus On College Students

Eating Disorders

Symptoms of eating disorders are prominent among young adults and especially among college students. One study of thousands of college students revealed that 13.5 percent of women and 3.6 percent of men screened positive for an eating disorder. In particular, women and men endorsed items such as, "Do you believe yourself to be fat when others say you are thin?" (33.8 and 9.2 percent, respectively), "Do you worry you have lost control over how much you eat?" (26.4 and 8.4 percent, respectively), "Would you say that food dominates your life?" (16.8 and 7.1 percent, respectively), and "Do you make yourself sick because you feel uncomfortably full?" (13.7 and 4.3 percent, respectively). Of those who screened positive for an eating disorder, many reported recent binge drinking (54.1 percent), major or other depression (23.9 percent), recent nonsuicidal self-injury (13.1 percent), and suicidal thoughts (4.0 percent). Unfortunately, only 20 percent of those who screened positive for an eating disorder sought treatment (Eisenberg et al., 2011).

Recall from Chapter 2 a selective prevention program that was designed to address eating problems in undergraduate students. Other researchers have also outlined procedures for college students with eating problems that parallel the treatment techniques described in this chapter. This includes screening students for low and high risk of eating problems. Low-risk students could receive online eating prevention programs and education about healthy avenues to stabilize and lose weight and prevent obesity. High-risk students, especially those at particular risk for anorexia nervosa, could be referred to on-campus services for cognitive-behavioral or interpersonal therapy to address problematic eating restraint patterns, body mass index, eating attitudes, body image concerns, social support, emotional regulation, and binge eating (Wilfley et al., 2013). If you feel you are at high risk for an eating disorder, seeking consultation at a counseling center may be a good idea.

Personal Narrative

Kitty Westin (Anna's Mother)

Photo courtesy of Kitty Westin, The Anna Westin Foundation

Anna Westin

I remember Anna Selina Westin's birthday like it was yesterday. She was a beautiful, healthy baby with bright blue eyes, curly blond hair, and a "rose bud" mouth. She grew and developed into a young woman full of life and love, and she had hopes, dreams, and a future full of promise until she became ill with a deadly disorder that affects millions: anorexia. When Anna was 16 years old, she was first diagnosed with anorexia. She committed suicide after struggling with the disorder for five years and was only 21 years old when she died.

I write about my experience with Anna hoping that people reading our story will better understand the seriousness of the disorder and how it affects the family. But before I go on, I would like to say that my husband and I are very proud of Anna and the effort she put into fighting her disorder. We feel no shame that she had the disorder or that she committed suicide. We both understand that anorexia is a disorder, not a choice. By telling our story honestly and openly we hope to dispel the stigma and shame often associated with an eating disorder and suicide. Since we made the decision to talk honestly about Anna's life and death, we have opened ourselves up to questions—frequently asked questions are *What were Anna's symptoms?* and *When did you first notice them?*

In retrospect, Anna most likely showed signs of developing an eating disorder long before we recognized them. When Anna was a young girl, she was perfectionistic and high achieving and needed to get everything "just right." She was dissatisfied with herself when she had difficulties and was intolerant of her own perceived imperfections. She showed signs of anxiety and had periods of depression from a young age.

Anna was petite, and I remember that she began talking about her size and shape when she was about 15 years old. I recall the day she came home from school very upset because an acquaintance had made a remark about the size of her thighs. This may have been the start of her obsession with being thin. Soon after that incident, she announced she had decided to become a vegetarian. At the time I was not concerned about this (although I was confused). I questioned her commitment to this "lifestyle," and she assured me that she would eat a healthy and balanced diet. I did not know at the time that this behavior was the beginning of restricting and that within a few months Anna would restrict almost all foods. It seemed that almost overnight Anna went from being a personable, caring, and spirited adolescent to being hostile, angry, withdrawn, and uncommunicative. Her weight dropped noticeably, and she avoided all situations with the family that involved food, including family meals.

Anna continually denied that she had any problems eating or issues with her size, but it became apparent that she was ill and getting sicker by the day. We brought her to our family physician for a checkup. The doctor referred her for an evaluation for an eating disorder. Anna was diagnosed with anorexia nervosa. Like most families suddenly faced with the trauma of caring for a seriously ill member, we were not prepared and woefully ignorant when we learned our daughter's diagnosis. Unlike so many other problems like diabetes, cancer, and heart disease, there was little information and support available to help us understand anorexia. We did not know where to turn for education, support, and guidance. We were often confused, always afraid, and sometimes angry.

Anna was first diagnosed and treated for anorexia when she was 16 years old. She was treated successfully in an outpatient program and seemed to recover fully. At that time

Men with eating disorders are not as well studied as women, but some interesting findings have emerged. Eating disorders appear to be on the rise among male athletes, especially in sports in which leanness may lead to a competitive advantage. Examples include wrestling, rowing, and running (Satterfield & Stutts, 2021). Men with eating disorders often display depression, self-injury, substance use disorder, and anxiety (Barnes et al., 2020; Eskander et al., 2020).

Similar rates of eating disorder are present for Asian, Black, Latina, and White women in the United States, though symptoms sometimes differ (Acle et al., 2021). Rates of risk factors for eating disorders—such as pressure to be thin, body dissatisfaction, and dieting—are also similar among these groups. Prevalence of anorexia nervosa may be lower in Hispanic than White individuals, and prevalence of anorexia with binge-eating disorder may be lower in non-Hispanic Black than White individuals (Egbert et al., 2022).

Eating disorders have been described as *cultural syndromes*, or problems that appear only in certain cultures and Western, industrialized nations.

I did not understand that the relapse rate for eating disorders is high and that we should remain vigilant for a number of years. I wish that someone had told me that the average time between diagnosis and recovery is seven years; that may have alerted me to the dangers of relapse and we may have done some things differently.

Anna seemed to do well after completing her first treatment for anorexia and she graduated from high school and went on to college. During the ensuing years, she had bouts of depression and anxiety, especially when under stress, but overall she reported feeling healthy and happy. Her anorexia returned, however, and this time she was gravely ill by the time we were able to get her the care she needed. We have tried to determine what triggered her relapse, and nothing has stood out, so we conclude that her biochemistry must have been the primary factor. We were able to get Anna admitted to a specialized eating disorders treatment program, and because she had responded so well the first time, we were not overly concerned and had no reason to doubt that she would fully recover.

Anna was a "typical" eating-disordered patient: resistant, angry, and in denial. However, once she was in the program getting the support she needed and restoring her health, she realized the seriousness of her disorder and the importance of the treatment and she became much more cooperative and receptive. Anna was getting the best care available and the program she was in used a multidisciplinary approach that included medical doctors, psychologists, psychiatrists, social workers, registered nurses, dietitians, tutors, physical and occupational therapists, and care managers. In addition to Anna's individual and group therapy, we were involved in family therapy and education groups. We finally felt like we were learning what we needed to know to help Anna. However, the effects anorexia was having on the family were enormous. My husband and I argued over many things including how best to deal with Anna, and our anger and frustration was often directed toward each other. Our younger daughters struggled to understand the disorder and found it difficult to accept that their sister was ill and could possibly die. We all walked on eggshells fearing that if we did or said the wrong thing, we would upset Anna and exacerbate the situation. It was hard to know when we should back off and when to get involved. We were advised not to watch Anna eat, but you tell me how we could do this when we were afraid that our child would die unless she ate? After all, food was the "medicine," and aren't parents supposed to make sure their child takes the medicine required to treat a disorder?

In spite of these things, treatment seemed to be going well. We were able to maintain confidence that Anna was on the road to recovery. Then suddenly we ran into a roadblock we did not expect and it changed everything. The roadblock was our insurance company. They refused to pay for most of the care Anna's medical team recommended, stating it was not medically necessary. Our family was forced to guarantee payment to keep her in the hospital. When Anna heard this, she felt guilty and like she was a burden on our family. We assured her that she needed to concentrate and put her energy into healing and we would worry about the money, but I don't think she was able to hear this. Anna committed suicide a few months later. I don't "blame" the insurance company for her death; I know that anorexia killed her. However, insurance did contribute to her death because they added to her feelings of worthlessness and hopelessness.

There are no adequate words to describe the grief and loss our family felt and continues to feel since Anna died. However, we have been able to transform some of these powerful emotions into something positive by starting a foundation in Anna's name and joining the fight against eating disorders.

Source: Used with permission.

A deeper look, however, reveals a more nuanced finding. Anorexia nervosa is reported in most countries around the world and cannot be solely attributed to the influence of Western ideals favoring thinness. Rates of anorexia nervosa differ little in Western and non-Western countries. Cases of bulimia nervosa in non-Western countries, however, are linked to Western ideals, and prevalence rates of bulimia are lower in non-Western than Western countries. Bulimia nervosa may be a cultural syndrome (Keel & Forney, 2015).

Eating disorders are highly comorbid with other mental disorders, including other eating disorders and symptoms of another eating disorder (Momen et al., 2022). Eating disorders are also comorbid with depression, body dysmorphic disorder, emotional dysregulation, self-injurious behavior, and suicide (Grave et al., 2021). People with anorexia nervosa like Sooki are often socially isolated, sad, and less interested in sexual activity. They often report problems getting close to others and experience shame and guilt. People with binge-eating disorder report their overeating often occurs during a depressed

Focus On Gender

Why Is There a Gender Difference in Eating Disorders?

Women have more eating disorders than men—but why? A prominent explanation for gender differences in eating disorders concerns gender roles. Our society values a female gender role that involves a woman who can do everything—a great career, happy marriage and family, active social life, and good looks. This gender role emphasizes thinness, perfectionistic striving, and some autonomy from the family because of career. Striving for thinness, perfectionism, and loneliness or isolation are also correlates of eating disorders, so this role model may influence some women to develop symptoms of eating disorders (Goel et al., 2021).

The everything ideal intersects as well with how "ideal" women are portrayed in the media—thin—and this can affect how girls and women evaluate themselves. Women's bodies are also more likely to be "objectified" by being looked at, evaluated, and sexualized. This reinforces the culture of thinness, leads to more maltreatment and sexual harassment, and may keep women from achieving as much as men in their careers (Allison et al., 2021; Bödicker et al., 2021).

Biological factors almost certainly contribute to eating disorders, but whether these factors contribute to the difference in eating disorder prevalence rates among the genders remains unclear. Certain biological vulnerabilities may be expressed differently in women and men. Dieting to reduce weight may lower serotonin functioning more in women than men (Smolak & Levine, 2015). Reduced serotonin is associated with overeating and carbohydrate craving. Another possible reason involves natural physical development. As boys and girls enter puberty, boys become more muscular and closer to the "ideal" for men, but girls obtain increased body fat and curves and move away from the "ideal" for women.

Peter Dazeley/Photographer's Choice/Getty Images

Are we teaching young girls that thin is the way to be? Barbie embodies the tall, thin, glamorous look.

state and precedes guilt and shame. About 63.5 percent of those with binge-eating disorder are overweight or obese (Agüera et al., 2021). People with eating disorders often exhibit symptoms of anxiety-related disorders as well. Anorexia nervosa is often present with obsessions about food and body shape and compulsive behavior such as hoarding food. Anxiety disorder symptoms prominent in bulimia nervosa include fears of social situations and being evaluated by others (Schaumberg et al., 2021).

Leonard Zhukovsky/Shutterstock.com

Eating disorders could be more common in sports where leanness offers an advantage.

Personality and substance use disorders are also common in people with bulimia nervosa and binge-eating disorder. These disorders likely overlap because they share the symptoms of emotional dysregulation and impulse-control problems. People with bulimia nervosa have relatively higher rates of borderline personality disorder, a condition characterized by high levels of impulsivity (Chapter 10). Those with bulimia nervosa also experience higher rates of excessive alcohol and stimulant use. Use of stimulants may begin as a way to control weight and appetite but then becomes an addiction (Gibson et al., 2021).

Stigma Associated with Eating Disorders

LO 8.4 Describe the stigma associated with eating disorders and its impact on those with the disorders.

Attitudes about people with an eating disorder or related conditions can be quite harsh. One group of researchers asked hundreds of participants to read a vignette about someone with anorexia, bulimia, binge-eating disorder, obesity, or major depression and complete a stigma questionnaire (refer to **Table 8.5**). Those described in the vignettes as having an eating disorder were blamed for their condition much more than those described as having depression. Those described as having obesity were held more responsible for their condition than the others. In particular, raters attributed lack of self-discipline more to obesity and binge-eating disorder. Only those with depression were rated as significantly impaired (Ebneter & Latner, 2013). People often view eating disorders as "self-inflicted" and related to will-power. Recall from Chapter 1 that attitudes such as these result in viewing others as weak in character and "different" from the rest of us.

These results were mirrored in a survey of people with an eating disorder. Those with anorexia, bulimia, or related symptoms were asked about stigmatizing attitudes and beliefs and their effect on personal well-being. Participants conveyed that two beliefs were particularly common and damaging: "I should be able to just pull myself together" and "I am personally responsible for my condition." Those with bulimia more often believed that they had no self-control, and male participants often believed they were "less of a man." Those with more symptoms, those who had an eating disorder longer, those with lower self-esteem, and those who were more reluctant to seek help were more likely to endorse some form of stigmatization (Griffiths et al., 2014). The study indicates the powerful nature of self-stigma in preventing people from seeking help for a potentially life-threatening condition.

Table 8.5 Stigma Statements

1. Blame/personal responsibility
____ is to blame for their condition
People with a problem like ____'s could snap out of it if they wanted
A problem like ____'s is a sign of personal weakness
____ could pull themself together if they wanted to
____'s problem is not a real medical illness
2. Impairment/distrust
People with a problem like ____'s are dangerous
I would not employ someone if I knew they had had a problem like ____'s
I would not vote for a politician if I knew they had had a problem like ____'s
____ is hard to talk to
People with a problem like ____'s are unpredictable
____ is less competent than peers

Source: Ebneter & Latner, 2013.

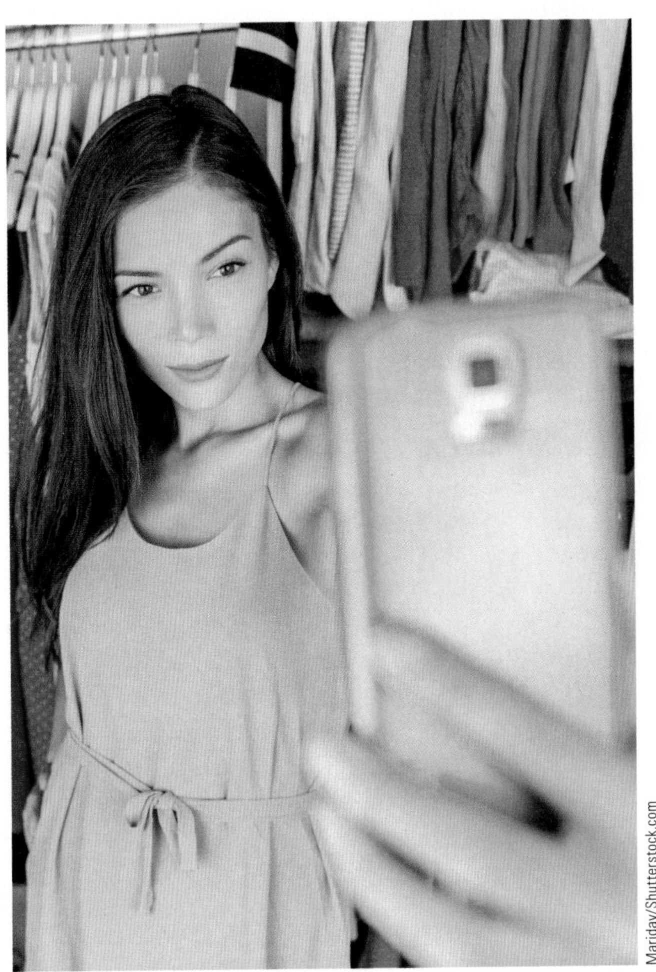

Maridav/Shutterstock.com

Selfie culture may relate to changes in eating behavior.

Section Summary

- Major features of eating disorders include weight concerns, body dissatisfaction, and eating problems. Eating problems include restricted eating or dieting and lack of control over eating.
- Eating disorders include anorexia nervosa, bulimia nervosa, and binge-eating disorder.
- Women are much more likely to have anorexia nervosa or bulimia nervosa than men, and many people with an eating disorder do not seek treatment.
- Similar rates of eating disorder symptoms are found among many major racial and ethnic groups in the United States, though some specific differences may exist.
- Anorexia nervosa has been observed in countries around the world and does not appear to be a cultural syndrome; bulimia nervosa is primarily found in Western cultures and may be a cultural syndrome.
- People often view those with eating disorders as responsible for their behavior, which may stigmatize this population.

Review Questions

1. How do Sooki's symptoms differ from normal concern about body shape or weight?
2. Identify main features of, and major differences between, anorexia nervosa, bulimia nervosa, and binge-eating disorder.
3. Describe the epidemiology of eating disorders, including issues of gender and culture.
4. How might people with eating disorder be stigmatized by others?

Eating Disorders: Causes and Prevention

LO 8.5 Discuss the risk factors for eating disorders.

LO 8.6 Evaluate programs to prevent eating disorders.

The next sections cover factors that cause eating disorders as well as how knowing about these factors might help us prevent these conditions.

Biological Risk Factors for Eating Disorders

Recall from previous chapters that mental disorders are often viewed from a *diathesis-stress model*, or a combination of biological and environmental variables. Many people are born with a genetic or biological predisposition toward certain neurological features or personality characteristics. Environmental conditions or life events often influence or trigger these biological predispositions. Biological predispositions in people with eating disorders include genetics, brain features, neurochemical features, and personality traits such as perfectionism and impulsivity.

Genetics

Eating disorders do run in families. Heritability is moderate for anorexia (0.28 to 0.74), bulimia (0.60), and binge-eating disorder (0.39 to 0.45). In addition, female relatives of those with anorexia are 11 times more likely to have anorexia themselves than relatives of those without anorexia. Higher family relative risk also occurs for bulimia (Bulik et al., 2019). Genes on multiple chromosomes appear to contribute to these predispositions (Watson et al., 2021). Genetic influences may be stronger for certain subtypes of eating disorder, especially the restricting subtype of anorexia nervosa, and specifically for areas surrounding appetite, energy regulation, and drive for thinness (Kennedy et al., 2022). No one gene or set of genes leads *directly* to an eating disorder, however. Genetics likely set the stage for brain or neurochemical features or temperaments that help lead to eating disorders or interact with environmental events to trigger eating disorders. The next section covers some brain features found in those with eating disorders.

Brain Features

Recall from Chapter 2 that the *hypothalamus* is the brain structure that regulates hunger and eating and is involved in appetite (refer to **Figure 8.1**). Eating disorder researchers thus focus on this structure. Damage to the lateral hypothalamus leads to weight and appetite changes in animals. Others have focused on the connection of the lateral hypothalamus to the *amygdala*. This connection seems related to learned cues that surround eating. These cues override feelings of fullness and thus promote more eating (Li et al., 2021).

The nucleus accumbens has also been implicated in eating disorders because this brain structure is linked to the lateral hypothalamus as well as sensory pleasure from food. Other brain regions such as the prefrontal, orbitofrontal, and somatosensory cortexes are associated with the rewarding aspects of food and may play a part in eating disorders (Vidal et al., 2021). In addition, the thalamus is potentially involved in excess food intake (Mele et al., 2020).

Animal models of brain structures and eating disorder may not completely relate to humans, however. Recall that people with anorexia nervosa *do have an appetite*—they just choose not to eat. An animal model also does not explain body image disturbance or fear of becoming fat in anorexia nervosa or bulimia nervosa. The hypothalamus and amygdala and other key brain areas (Figure 8.1) are likely involved

AberCPC/Alamy Stock Photo

Is it biological makeup or bad habits that lead to obesity?

Figure 8.1 Brain Areas Implicated in Eating Disorders.

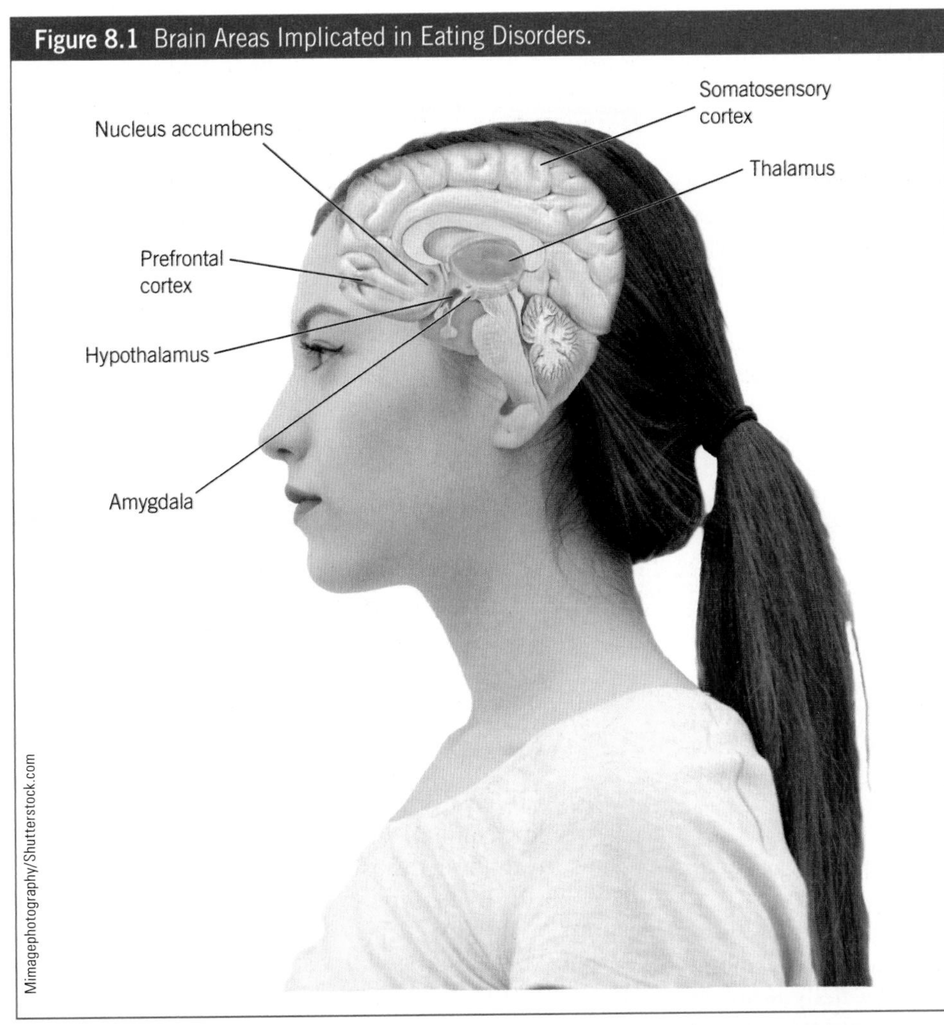

in eating disorders, but structural or functional problems with these brain structures cannot completely account for symptoms of these disorders.

Neurochemical Features

The neurotransmitter most closely linked to eating disorders is *serotonin* (Karth et al., 2022). Serotonin influences mood regulation, obsessive thinking, impulsivity, and eating behavior. Serotonin is also responsible for **satiety**, or feeling full from eating. People with anorexia nervosa who engage in food restriction may disrupt their serotonin functioning. People with bulimia nervosa and binge-eating disorder may have low levels of serotonin, which can cause malfunction in the body's satiety feedback mechanism, leading to binges.

Anorexia nervosa and bulimia nervosa are characterized by reduced serotonin activity, and people with anorexia nervosa and bulimia nervosa also show limited responsivity to serotonin-stimulating medications (Himmerich et al., 2021). Serotonin dysfunction is also associated with features common to anorexia nervosa or bulimia nervosa, including self-destructive behavior, impulsivity, compulsivity, obsessive thinking, and depression. Recall from Chapter 7 how serotonin closely relates to depression, and some research indicates a shared genetic risk between anorexia nervosa and major depression (Zsigo et al., 2022).

Dopamine may also play a role in eating disorders. Dopamine is linked to pleasurable aspects of food as well as motivation to obtain food (Manfredi et al., 2021). Dysfunction in the dopamine system might lead those with anorexia nervosa to have less motivation to obtain food, whereas the opposite would be true for those with bulimia nervosa and binge-eating disorder. One might thus expect differences in dopamine functioning between those with anorexia nervosa and those with other forms of eating disorders characterized by binging.

Endogenous opioids are bodily chemicals that reduce pain, enhance positive mood, and suppress appetite. These chemicals are released during starvation and after intense exercise, so they may have an impact on eating disorders. Endogenous opioid release is rewarding, so this may reinforce self-starvation and excessive exercise in anorexia nervosa. Low levels of endogenous opioids promote *craving of food* and thus may characterize bulimia. Craving food may lead to binges and then stress relief or euphoria, so binging is reinforced (Valbrun & Zvonarev, 2020). The next section covers more observable factors that may be influenced by neurochemical substances and that contribute to the development and maintenance of eating disorders.

Personality Traits

Perfectionism is often cited as a risk factor for eating disorders, especially among people with an obsessive drive for thinness. People with anorexia nervosa have fixed or rigid thoughts of ideal body type, compensatory and almost ritualistic behavior to lose weight, and strict adherence to certain patterns of eating (or not eating). People with bulimia nervosa also have an ideal body type in mind and perfectionism often drives dieting that perpetuates the binge–purge cycle. Perfectionism appears to be associated with, but not necessarily a cause of, eating disorder (Robinson & Wade, 2021).

Impulsivity is another personality feature cited as a risk factor for bulimia nervosa. Binge eating is often characterized by a desperate, urgent quality. Those who binge describe these episodes as driven and uncontrollable. Recall that substance use and personality disorders are comorbid with eating disorders and especially bulimia nervosa. These substance use and personality disorders are characterized by high levels of impulsivity. Impulsivity does not likely lead directly to an eating disorder but does seem to predispose some people to symptoms of bulimia or to binge-eating disorder (Carr et al., 2021).

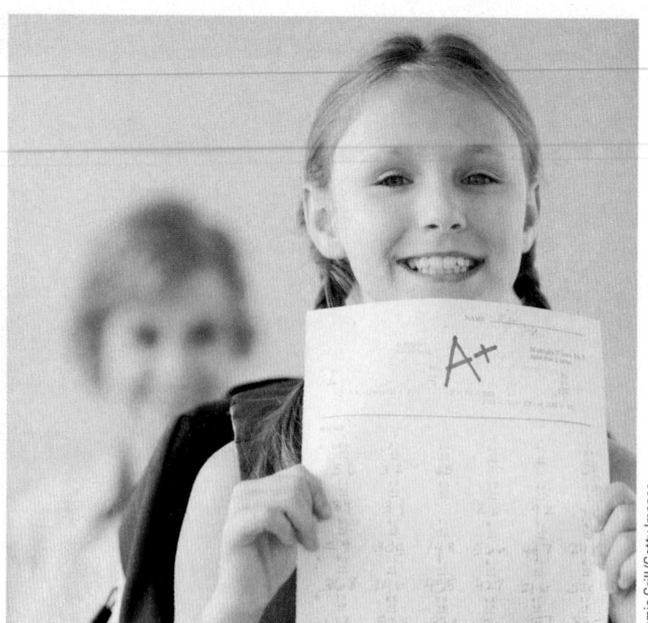

Jamie Grill/Getty Images

Perfectionism appears to be associated with, but not necessarily a cause of, eating disorder.

Environmental Risk Factors for Eating Disorders

The next sections cover environmental risk factors that develop over a person's lifetime. These include family factors, media exposure to the "thin ideal," and cognitive and cultural factors.

Family Factors

A leading set of risk factors for eating disorders is various transitions and dynamics that can occur among families. Several family transitions, especially if linked to less support, may be related to the onset of eating disorders. These transitions include death of a family member, illness or hospitalization, and substantial changes involving school, relationships, home, and job (Steiger & Booij, 2020). Eating disorder in a parent, especially a mother, has also been found to predict body dissatisfaction and weight and shape concerns in adolescent girls (Martini et al., 2020). In addition, mothers with an eating disorder often have restrictive eating patterns that can translate into eating problems in children (Ferreira et al., 2021).

Another factor in eating disorder is substantial reinforcement given by family members to a person who has lost significant weight. An eating disorder may thus become accommodated and enabled by family members. Conversely, families of people with eating disorders are sometimes described as intrusive, controlling, hostile, disorganized, and unsupportive. Family dysfunction and conflict often mark this population as well (Anderson et al., 2021). Family members of people with eating disorders also make frequent and negative comments about body shape and weight (Grogan et al., 2020).

Other family factors contribute to eating disorders *and* to many other major mental disorders described in this textbook. *Expressed emotion*, a concept involving hostility, conflict, and overinvolvement (Chapter 7), relates to families of those with eating disorder (Martini et al., 2020). In addition, insecure attachment relates to depression and can be associated with eating disorders as well. Many people with eating disorders also report family history of childhood trauma such as neglect or emotional, physical, or sexual maltreatment. Child maltreatment is not necessarily a risk factor specific to eating disorders, however. You will find throughout this textbook that many people with mental disorders report high rates of childhood maltreatment.

Media Exposure to the "Thin Ideal"

Another risk factor for eating disorder, especially in Western society, is media promotion of the "thin ideal." American beauty queens, models, and Playboy bunnies became increasingly thin over several decades (refer to **Figure 8.2**). Young people, especially young girls, are influenced by the media's depiction of attractiveness and ideal body type. Body types for many celebrities and athletes seem to set a standard, but many of these "models" are severely underweight and thin. Women on television and in other media are generally much thinner than most American women.

This media ideal clashes with the fact that size and weight of the average woman have increased over the years. The media provides few examples of non-thin women comfortable with their weight and appearance. An adolescent girl thus perceives a big difference

Figure 8.2 Playboy Centerfolds and Miss America Contestants Became Thinner and Farther below the Norm over Time.

Percentage of expected weight refers to the ratio of actual weight to what is typical for women of a particular height and age.

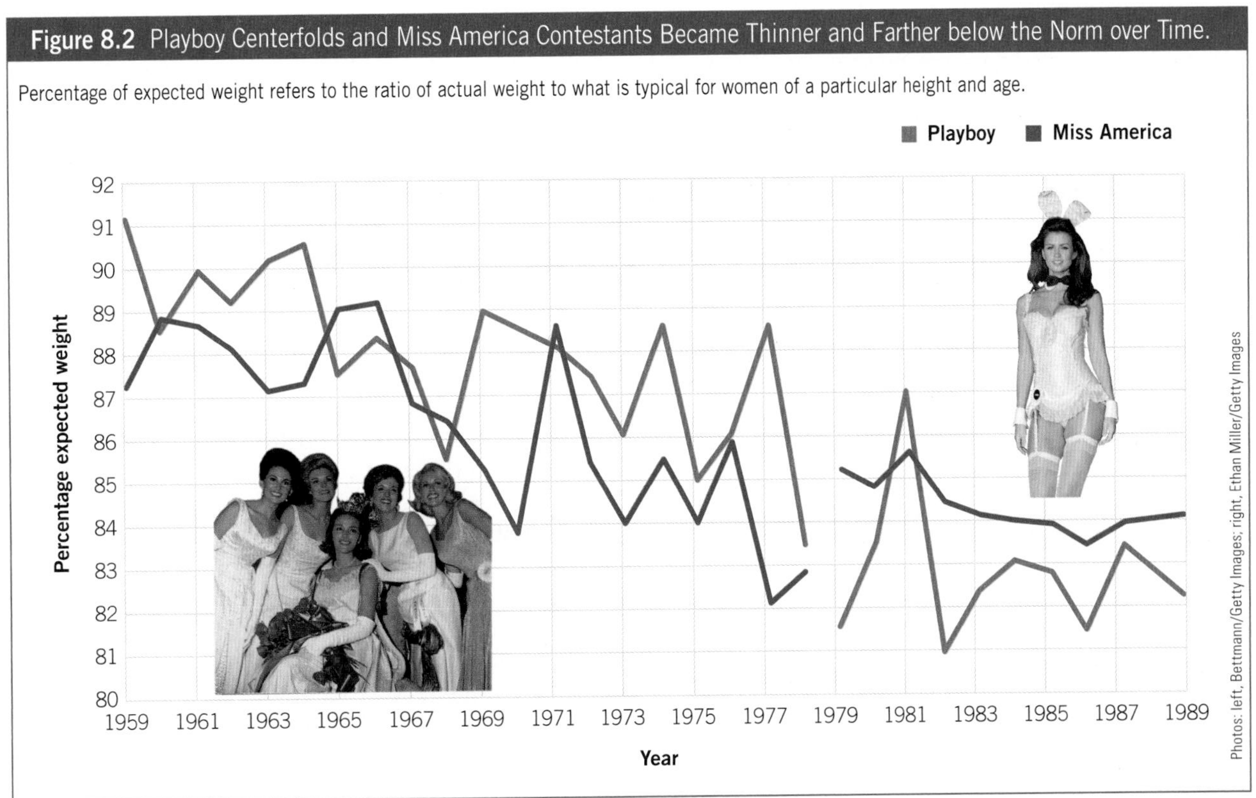

Photos: left, Bettmann/Getty Images; right, Ethan Miller/Getty Images

between what is portrayed in the media and what she observes in the mirror. Some of these girls (and boys) try to achieve the media ideal but find they can only do so via severely restricted eating, excessive exercise, or purging. Media depictions do influence body dissatisfaction and eating disorder symptoms in youth (Jiotsa et al., 2021).

Cognitive Factors

Major cognitive risk factors for eating disorder include *body dissatisfaction* and *body image disturbance.* Recall that family and media influences can affect body dissatisfaction. For some people, a discrepancy occurs between actual body size and weight and a perceived "ideal" body size and weight equated with attractiveness. Body dissatisfaction is a risk factor as well as a maintenance factor for eating disorders. Body image disturbance refers to faulty self-evaluation of one's body weight and shape despite contradictory evidence (Dahlenburg et al., 2020). Sooki thought she was fat even though others told her she was underweight. Distorted self-evaluation often leads to restricting diet and food consumption, as was true for Sooki.

Mike Kemp/Corbis News/Getty Images

Real or perceived pressure from others to look a certain way could spur excessive dieting and even an eating disorder.

Cultural Factors

Recall that eating disorders are present worldwide and that bulimia nervosa may be found more in Western cultures. Anorexia nervosa may also be less common in certain countries where certain foods are more scarce or where being overweight is more valued. A mental disorder involving distorted body image and self-starvation is less likely in these countries. Research into cultural factors of eating disorder is thus most prevalent in the United States.

As noted earlier, few racial or ethnic differences in America have been found for eating disorder. European American women do not differ from Latinas or Asian American women with respect to body dissatisfaction. European American women do, however, report higher levels of body dissatisfaction than African American women. This may reflect greater acceptance of body weight and shape among African American women (Awad et al., 2020).

Causes of Eating Disorders

Recall from earlier chapters how a diathesis-stress model could be used to integrate various risk factors to explain mental disorder, and the same model can apply to eating disorders (refer to **Figure 8.3**). Biological diatheses, or vulnerabilities, include genetics or brain or neurochemical features that lead some people to have trouble regulating mood or behavior and to react strongly when upset or stressed. Psychological vulnerabilities include low self-esteem, perfectionism, impulsivity, body dissatisfaction, and a distorted body image. Environmental stressors such as child maltreatment, family conflict, and social or media-based pressures to be thin also play a role.

Figure 8.3 shows how biological vulnerabilities, psychological vulnerabilities, and stressors or sociocultural factors could interact to cause severely restricted eating. Two different paths then emerge—one leads to anorexia nervosa and one leads to bulimia nervosa. Two subtypes of anorexia nervosa are characterized by restricted eating and by binging and purging. Both subtypes, however, involve *excessive weight loss.* Binging and purging are also evident in bulimia nervosa but normal or above normal weight is maintained. Eating disorders thus involve interplay between diatheses and stressors.

Prevention of Eating Disorders

Many risk factors for eating disorder occur at an early age, so prevention of these problems usually begins in

Gregorio T. Binuya/Everett Collection

How much do media images influence body image?

Peter Dazeley/Getty Images

Even young children can be influenced by media depictions of the thin ideal.

Figure 8.3 Sample Causal Model of Eating Disorders.

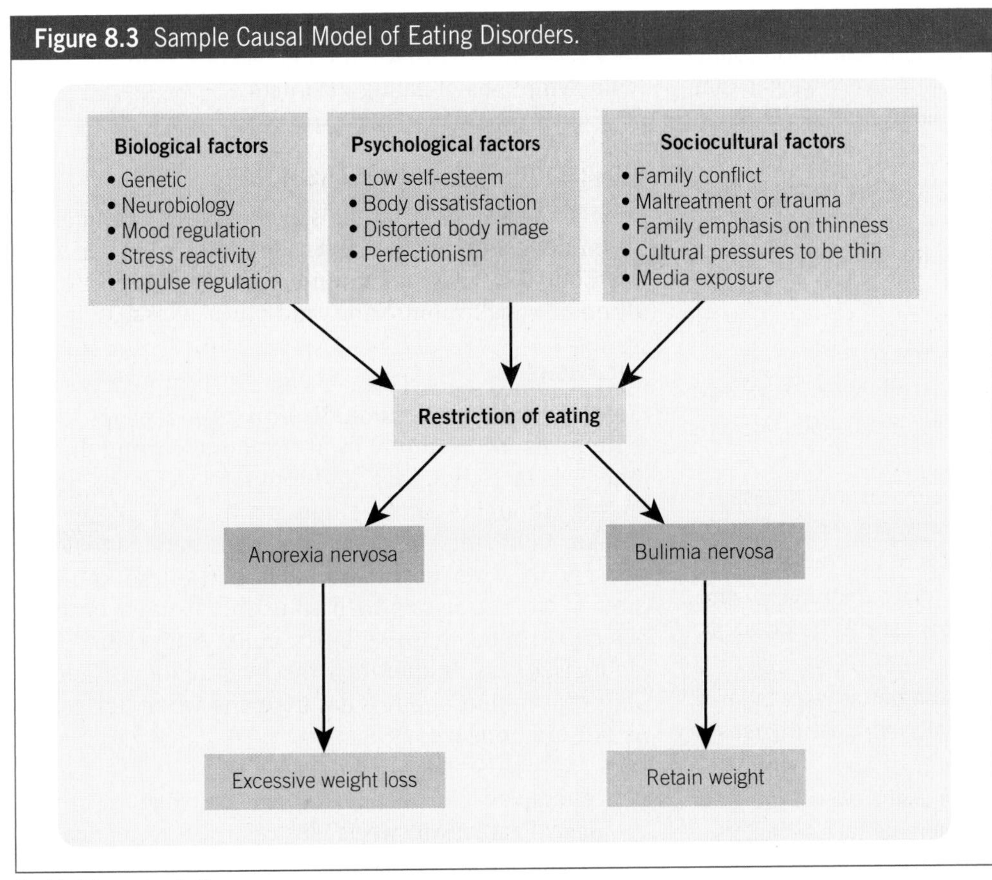

childhood or adolescence. Preventing eating disorder is important for two key reasons. First, eating disorders are associated with significant impairment, inpatient hospitalization, suicide attempts, and mortality. Second, less than one third of people with eating disorders receive treatment, and treatment is not effective for all those with eating disorders.

Eating disorder prevention programs emphasize education about eating disorders and consequences, resisting sociocultural pressures for thinness, healthy weight-control behaviors, and interactive exercises to address risk factors such as body dissatisfaction. *National Eating Disorders Awareness Week* involves a media campaign to educate people about eating disorder and quick screening assessments in selected clinics for those struggling with eating problems. People with problematic eating patterns or concerns can then be referred for professional treatment. Prevention efforts for eating problems have generally shown modest effects. Prevention programs tend to be more effective if high-risk individuals are targeted, if body dissatisfaction is a key focus, if multiple sessions are conducted, and if the efforts are interactive in nature (Stice et al., 2021).

"Student Bodies" is an eight-week program administered via the Internet (Jones et al., 2015). The program combines a structured cognitive-behavioral curriculum with a discussion group. People are screened for risk factors and then invited to participate. Primary goals are to reduce excessive weight concerns and body dissatisfaction. Participants log onto a website with updated content each week. The program involves reading the content, completing assignments, and participating in a moderated online discussion group. Participants also self-monitor and write entries in a Personal Journal of Body Image. College women report that this program does reduce weight concerns (Grammar et al., 2020). The program also reduced onset of eating disorders

NPS Photo/Alamy Stock Photo

In some cultures, being heavier is more desirable than being thinner.

Artem Varnitsin/Shutterstock.com

American women of certain ethnicities may be more susceptible to the thin ideal than others.

among people with an elevated body mass index (refer to Assessment of Eating Disorders section) and among some who use compensatory behaviors to prevent weight gain. Prevention programs like this one hold promise for reducing the incidence of eating disorder symptoms.

Section Summary

- Eating disorders have some genetic basis, but environmental risk factors are also important in the development of these disorders.
- Brain structures likely involved in eating problems are the hypothalamus and amygdala. Neurochemicals such as serotonin, dopamine, and endogenous opioids are also influential.
- Perfectionism and impulsivity are personality-based risk factors for eating disorders, as are certain family characteristics and media exposure to the thin ideal.
- Body dissatisfaction and body image disturbance are cognitive features that put people at risk for developing eating disorders.
- Cultural factors affect eating disorder as well; bulimia nervosa appears to be a cultural syndrome, whereas anorexia nervosa does not.
- The diathesis-stress model is a useful way of integrating various biological and environmental risk factors for eating disorders.
- Eating disorder prevention programs target one or more risk factors and are modestly successful at reducing risk for eating disorders.

Review Questions

1. Describe data that support a genetic contribution to eating disorders.
2. What key brain and neurochemical features relate to eating disorders? What personality characteristics are associated with eating disorders?
3. What cognitive features are considered risk factors for eating disorders? Why?
4. How might family factors, media influences, and cultural backgrounds help cause eating disorders?
5. What topics are typically addressed in programs to prevent eating disorders?

Eating Disorders: Assessment and Treatment

LO 8.7 Characterize the assessment and treatment of individuals with eating disorders.

The next sections cover different methods of assessing and treating eating disorders. These methods are important for people like Sooki, Lisa, and Rachel (refer to **Personal Narrative: Rachel Webb**) who struggled with symptoms of eating disorders.

Assessment of Eating Disorders

Mental health professionals use various methods to examine people with eating disorders. The primary methods they use include interviews, self-report questionnaires, self-monitoring, and physical assessment.

Interviews

Mental health professionals who assess people with eating disorders often inquire about current height and weight, thoughts and physical feelings about eating, thoughts and feelings about body shape and image, behaviors to prevent weight gain, and long-term goals. This information is important for knowing how to treat someone with an eating disorder because specific client characteristics can be identified and addressed. Lisa's therapist discovered some interesting information about what happens when her eating is out of control:

Therapist: What happens when you binge?

Lisa: I eat lots of sweets, like cake, ice cream, cookies, and candy bars.

Therapist: What are you usually thinking about during a binge, and what happens next?

Lisa: While I'm eating, I just don't feel I can stop. I get mad at myself for not being able to stop my eating, and I feel depressed. The only thing I can do right after the binge to make myself feel better is to throw up. It's embarrassing to admit throwing up so much, but it does make me feel better.

Therapist: What usually happens after you vomit?

Lisa: Well, later, I start feeling guilty and thinking I'll never get any better. That's when the depression kicks in again.

Many therapists prefer unstructured interviews, but structured interviews usually rely on diagnostic criteria and contain set questions a therapist asks each client with a possible mental disorder (Chapter 4). A common structured interview for eating disorders and one used in treatment outcome studies is the *Eating Disorders Examination* (EDE 16.0D; Fairburn et al., 2015). The EDE provides eating disorder diagnoses as well as scores on four subscales relevant to eating disorder problems: restraint, eating concern, shape concern, and weight concern. Other interviews focused on general disorders have sections for eating disorder symptoms. The *Structured Clinical Interview* (First et al., 2015) has questions about anorexia nervosa and bulimia nervosa symptoms. Binge-eating disorder can also be assessed with this interview.

Personal Narrative

Rachel Webb

Ana and Mia are nicknames for anorexia nervosa and bulimia nervosa.

Photo courtesy of Rachel Webb

Rachel Webb

Dear Mia,

We've come a long way together, but I'm afraid I'm going to have to ask you to leave. You have become that last drunken guest at the party that is my life. I'm not sure who invited you, but every time I've almost pushed you out the door you come crashing back in.

You arrived early, long before I was conscious of your presence. You waited in the corner, through years of taunting and abuse until my deeply buried self-hatred could no longer be ignored. That's when you decided we needed each other.

I needed a way to deal with my world; a way to silently punish myself for my many shortcomings in a way no one else would perceive. You needed someone you could seduce and brainwash. You needed someone who would believe the things you whispered in her ear.

"You're defective."

"You're ugly."

"You're stupid."

"You're worthless."

Funny how the things you were telling me were the same things I heard every day at school. It must have been most convenient for you that I already believed those things about myself.

You convinced me that despite the rosy suburban childhood my parents tried to give me, I was miserable. Despite my loving family and supportive adult friends, I was unlovable. Despite my wall full of swimming medals and writing awards, I was talentless. Despite my ability to build a career, I was a failure.

Through all of that, you stayed. You were waiting for me to crash diet before I tried on bridal gowns for the wedding I would call off. You were waiting for my boyfriend to dump me. Waiting for me to have a bad day, or just to be tired and bored. The day my parents told me I was fat fully announced your arrival.

But our time is over. For all of our time together, I have realized that I am stronger than you.

The beginning of the end came two years ago, on that morning when I was semiconscious on my bathroom floor, covered in my own vomit. That's when you went too far. The shadows in the corner parted, and I saw you for what you really are.

I decided then and there that you had to leave. But no matter how hard I try (cleaning up the dirty glasses, vacuuming the floor, saying how early I have to get up in the morning), you refuse to leave and your presence is still puzzling.

All I know is you helped me start a war with my body. You prevented me from enjoying myself and my family and my friends. From being able to eat meals like a normal person. From experiencing the normal cycle of being hungry, eating, and stopping when I felt full.

I'm not sure what I could have done to prevent our relationship. It really all goes back to fifth grade, doesn't it? When I couldn't get through a day at school without being ostracized or punched. You followed me through my teenage years, and we flirted and played until you lucked out. When I was in college, I dated a jerk, and all of the things I learned about myself in fifth grade were confirmed.

Once we were well acquainted, you disintegrated my muscle tone until I couldn't carry a bag of groceries, change the tank on my office water cooler, or walk more than a block or two without needing to sit down. You've given me an irregular heartbeat and low blood pressure that causes me to faint if I stand still for too long. I'm certain you've given me cavities, but I'm too afraid to go to the dentist. Time will only tell as to whether you've given me osteoporosis.

Somehow, after all this time, I have grown stronger than you. I have regained my muscle and am prepared to throw you out with an imprint of a combat-booted foot planted squarely in your backside. At this point, you need a willing host, and I am no longer willing.

So please, take your tingling fingertips and bruised knuckles. Take your sunken eyes and your cracked lips. Take your perpetually sore throat and your raging headaches. Take the self-doubt and self-loathing that you brought with you.

And whatever you do, don't come back. Because I am stronger than you are, and I know how much you hate that.

Source: Used with permission.

Self-Report Questionnaires

Self-report questionnaires are often used to screen for eating problems. The *Eating Disorder Diagnostic Scale* provides diagnostic information for eating disorders. Scores can be calculated for key components of eating disorders like body dissatisfaction and binge eating. Selected items from this scale are in **Table 8.6**. A list of other questionnaires that mental health professionals use when assessing people with eating disorders is in **Table 8.7**.

Self-Monitoring

People with eating disorders can monitor and record their daily symptoms and behaviors. Daily recording is likely more accurate than a retrospective report of the past week. A person can also focus on what happened immediately before or after a symptom or behavior. The act of self-monitoring itself can lead to fewer symptoms and behaviors—we generally do an excess behavior less if we record each time it happens. We become more aware of our behaviors and gain better control over them.

Table 8.6 Sample Items from the Eating Disorder Diagnostic Scale

Body dissatisfaction/fear of gaining weight
Over the past three months . . .
• Have you felt fat?
• Have you had a definite fear that you might gain weight or become fat?
• Has your weight influenced how you think about (judge) yourself as a person?
• Has your shape influenced how you think about (judge) yourself as a person?
Note: Each of these items is rated as 0 ("not at all"), 1, 2 ("slightly"), 3, 4 ("moderately"), or 5 or 6 ("extremely").
Binge eating
During these episodes of overeating and loss of control did you . . .
• Eat much more rapidly than normal?
• Eat until you felt uncomfortably full?
• Eat large amounts of food when you didn't feel physically hungry?
• Eat alone because you were embarrassed by how much you were eating?
• Feel disgusted with yourself, depressed, or very guilty after overeating?
• Feel very upset about your uncontrollable overeating or resulting weight gain?
Note: These questions are answered yes or no.

Source: Stice, E., Telch, C. F., & Rizvi, S. L. (2000). Development and validation of the Eating Disorder Diagnostic Scale: A brief self-report measure of anorexia, bulimia, and binge-eating disorder. *Psychological Assessment*, 12, 123–131. Reprinted by permission of the authors.

Table 8.7 Common Questionnaires for Assessing Eating Disorders

General diagnosis of eating disorders
• *Eating Disorders Inventory—2* (EDI-2)
• *Kids Eating Disorders Survey* (KEDS)
Body dissatisfaction/body image disturbance
• *Body Shape Questionnaire* (BSQ)
• *Body Image Avoidance Questionnaire*
Dietary restraint
• *Dutch Eating Behavior Questionnaire* (DEBQ)
• *Three-Factor Eating Questionnaire* (TFEQ-R)
Binge eating
• *The Binge Eating Scale*

Source: Pike, K.M. (2005).

Self-monitoring can be accomplished using a written diary to indicate frequency of behaviors such as binge eating, purging, or excessive exercise; emotions and thoughts that preceded these behaviors; and consequences after the behavior such as stress relief, comfort, or guilt. Diaries can also be used to track and record meals eaten and calories consumed. This information can be extremely helpful for understanding one's eating problem and for planning treatment.

A high-tech version of self-monitoring involves using **electronic diaries** via smartphone applications to record behavior. Sooki might be asked to carry an electronic diary to document meals, thoughts about her body, and fear of becoming fat. She could also indicate her mood state before and after restricting her eating as well as events before and after skipping meals. People with anorexia nervosa who use electronic diaries show many changes in mood throughout the day. They also endorse many eating disorder symptoms and rituals such as skipping meals, checking joints and bones for fat, and consuming fluids to curb appetite. Electronic diaries can thus provide rich data for mental health professionals who plan treatment (Wasil et al., 2021).

Physical Assessment

People with eating disorders should always have a thorough medical examination. Many eating disorder symptoms are physical, such as low weight, and eating disorders can result in serious medical symptoms and life-threatening outcomes. A physical examination can focus on height and weight to determine body mass index (BMI; refer to **Table 8.8**), heart rate and rhythm, and muscle tone and strength. Physical assessment can also help physicians and mental health professionals decide the first step of treatment. Someone with anorexia nervosa found to be severely malnourished may require

Table 8.8 Body Mass Index (BMI) Chart

BMI (kg/m²) Height (in.)	19	20	21	22	23	24	25	26	27	28	29	30	35	40
	Weight (lb.)													
58	91	96	100	105	110	115	119	124	129	134	138	143	167	191
59	94	99	104	109	114	119	124	128	133	138	143	148	173	198
60	97	102	107	112	118	123	128	133	138	143	148	153	179	204
61	100	106	111	116	122	127	132	137	143	148	153	158	185	211
62	104	109	115	120	126	131	136	142	147	153	158	164	191	218
63	107	113	118	124	130	135	141	146	152	158	163	169	197	225
64	110	116	122	128	134	140	145	151	157	163	169	174	204	232
65	114	120	126	132	138	144	150	156	162	168	174	180	210	240
66	118	124	130	136	142	148	155	161	167	173	179	186	216	247
67	121	127	134	140	146	153	159	166	172	178	185	191	223	255
68	125	131	138	144	151	158	164	171	177	184	190	197	230	262
69	128	135	142	149	155	162	169	176	182	189	196	203	236	270
70	132	139	146	153	160	167	174	181	188	195	202	207	243	278
71	136	143	150	157	165	172	179	186	193	200	208	215	250	286
72	140	147	154	162	169	177	184	191	199	206	213	221	258	294
73	144	151	159	166	174	182	189	197	204	212	219	227	265	302
74	148	155	163	171	179	186	194	202	210	218	225	233	272	311
75	152	160	168	176	184	192	200	208	216	224	232	240	279	319
76	156	164	172	180	189	197	205	213	221	230	238	246	287	328

Body weight in pounds according to height and body mass index

BMI	Weight class
18.5 or less	Underweight
18.5–24.9	Normal
25.0–29.9	Overweight
30.0–34.9	Obese
35.0–39.9	More obese
40 or greater	Extremely obese

inpatient hospitalization to insert and maintain a nasogastric tube for feeding. Common laboratory tests to assess people with eating disorders include the following:

- Metabolic panel to assess for electrolyte imbalance due to poor nutrition
- Blood count to check for anemia
- Enzyme tests to rule out severe malnutrition
- Serum amylase tests to suggest purging behavior
- Bone scans to rule out calcium deficiency or bone mass loss

Treatment of Eating Disorders

Recall that eating disorders have symptoms involving emotional, physical, cognitive, and behavioral features. The general aims of biological and psychological treatment for eating disorder are thus to (Kotilahti et al., 2020):

- Return the person to a healthy weight
- Treat physical complications
- Increase motivation to restore healthy eating patterns
- Educate the person about healthy eating patterns
- Help the person recognize and change core problematic feelings, thoughts, and behaviors about the eating disorder
- Enlist family support for change
- Prevent relapse

Biological Treatments of Eating Disorders

Biological treatments for eating disorders involve controlled weight gain and medication.

Controlled Weight Gain

Many people with anorexia nervosa lose so much weight that their condition becomes life-threatening. People with severe anorexia nervosa who seek treatment are often first admitted to inpatient care involving *controlled weight gain* and nutrition guidance (Kolar et al., 2022). Controlled weight gain can include a nighttime nasogastric tube to increase basic nourishment, improve vital functioning, and provide a minimal amount of energy. Those with anorexia may also be given regular snacks and small meals under staff supervision as well as praise for their eating (Garber et al., 2020).

Controlled weight gain is often conducted in conjunction with a nutritionist who educates a person about healthy food choices. Physicians and mental health professionals should expect only small gains in weight per week and focus more intently on body mass index than weight (Redgrave et al., 2021). People with anorexia who start to gain weight may become increasingly anxious, depressed, or irritable as they do so, so these mood states must also be managed. Controlled weight gain is thus often used in conjunction with the medications described next.

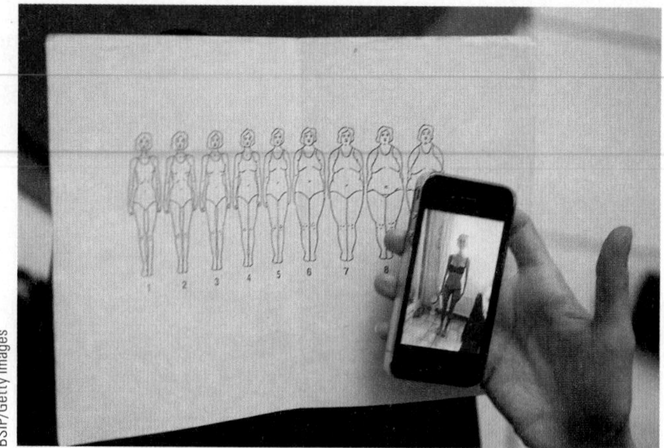

BSIP/Getty Images

Some assessments for eating disorders can be administered electronically.

Medication

Recall that serotonin changes contribute to eating disorders and that depression, which is associated with low serotonin, is highly comorbid with eating disorders. Medication for eating disorders has thus primarily involved *selective serotonin reuptake inhibitors* (SSRIs) (Chapter 7). These medications are not overly helpful with people with anorexia nervosa because the drugs do not necessarily increase weight (Frank, 2020). SSRIs are helpful, however, for treating comorbid depression, anxiety, obsessional thinking, and purging (if present). Antipsychotic medications (Chapter 12) may also be used for cases involving severe obsessional thinking or delusional body image disturbances. Research regarding antipsychotics for eating disorders has produced mixed results, though the use of olanzapine seems to help increase body mass index (Muratore & Attia, 2022).

SSRIs and psychological treatment (discussed in the next section) do significantly reduce binge eating and purging and help ease impulse control problems reported by many people with bulimia nervosa and binge-eating disorder (Monteleone et al., 2022). Appetite suppressants are sometimes used to help with weight loss in these groups as well. The drugs reduce eating but mental health professionals must ensure that clients on these drugs monitor heart rate and blood pressure (Schneider et al., 2021).

Psychological Treatments of Eating Disorders

Psychological treatments for eating disorders involve family therapy and cognitive-behavioral therapy.

Family Therapy

Family therapy is useful for many people with eating disorders but is particularly helpful for adolescents with anorexia nervosa. A popular form of therapy for those with anorexia nervosa is a family systems approach. This approach initially focuses on obtaining cooperation from all family members, examining family patterns of eating and attitudes toward a client's symptoms, and improving eating and weight gain (Fleming et al., 2021). Family therapy can begin as early as the controlled weight gain program in an inpatient setting. Family members can praise an adolescent for gaining weight and refraining from pressures to stay thin.

Family therapy after a person has left the hospital may focus on reducing conflict among family members and ensuring everyone can maintain appropriate patterns of food preparation and consumption. Family therapists also address expressed emotion to ease overinvolvement, criticism, and hostility among family members (Stewart et al., 2021). Parents are initially encouraged to take control of what their adolescent eats, but over time this responsibility shifts to the teen. Family therapy generally lasts 6 to 12 months and tends to work better in the short term than the long term (Baudinet et al., 2021). Family therapy may be more effective if combined with medication or the cognitive-behavioral approaches discussed next.

Figure 8.4 A Binge-Purge Cycle in Bulimia Nervosa.

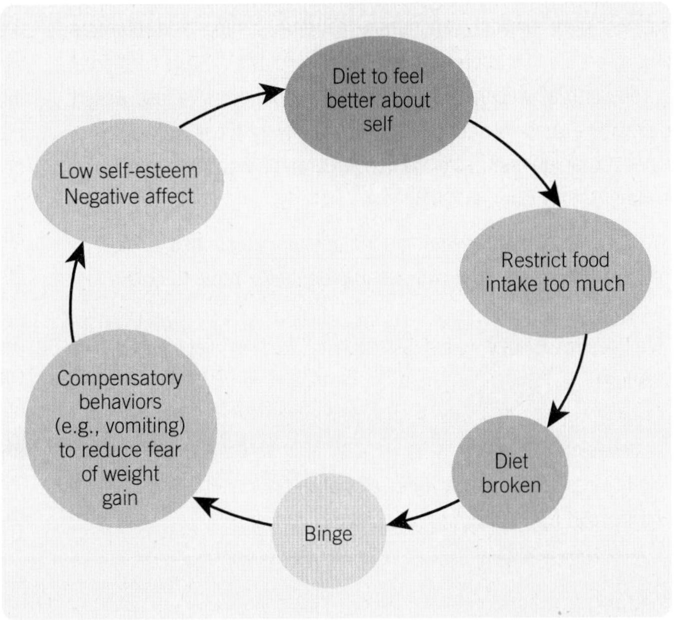

Cognitive-Behavioral Therapy

Therapists who treat eating disorders often combine cognitive and behavioral therapies into a singular approach described here. Cognitive-behavioral therapy (CBT) is a dominant approach for treating many different eating disorders and especially bulimia nervosa and binge-eating disorder (Atwood & Friedman, 2020). CBT often focuses on binging and purging cycles as well as cognitive aspects of body dissatisfaction, overconcern with weight and shape, and perfectionism. The therapy is often conducted in conjunction with a nutrition and medication program and possibly family therapy.

CBT for bulimia nervosa rests on cognitive and behavioral factors that influence development and maintenance of symptoms (refer to **Figure 8.4**; Solmi et al., 2021). People with bulimia nervosa have a rigid idea of an ideal body shape and weight, which leads them to overly restrict food intake to increase self-esteem. This rigid stance makes a person psychologically and physiologically vulnerable to periodically lose control over their eating (binge). These episodes are negatively reinforced because they reduce distress and negative feelings from restrictive dieting. People then feel compelled to purge (vomit) to prevent weight gain after a binge. Purging is also negatively reinforced because anxiety after the binge is reduced. Unfortunately, those with bulimia often feel guilty and depressed after a binge–purge cycle, which leads again to low self-esteem. This cycle thus brings them back to the initial situation—excessive dieting to improve self-esteem.

We can observe this cycle develop with Lisa. Lisa was preoccupied with her weight and often limited her eating and weight by dieting. Dieting made her feel good about herself in the short term, but pressures of daily life and continued worry about her weight led to high stress. Lisa reduced her stress by eating, which in her case led to loss of control and overeating. Lisa felt better after a binge but then panicked and felt deep shame about her excess behavior. She then vomited to reduce her distress. Unfortunately, her usual stressors and worries about weight awaited her the next day and the cycle began again.

Cognitive-behavioral therapists try to interrupt this cycle by questioning social standards for physical attractiveness; challenging beliefs that encourage severe food restriction; and developing normal eating patterns and habits. Several strategies are thus used, including the following:

- Self-monitoring eating, thoughts, urges, and behaviors
- Education about the model for bulimia nervosa and need for change
- Weekly weighing
- Education about body weight regulation, adverse effects of dieting, and consequences of purging
- Problem solving
- Changing rigid dieting
- Cognitive restructuring to address concerns about eating, body weight, and body shape
- Exposure methods to increase acceptance of body weight and shape
- Relapse prevention training

Cognitive-behavioral treatment for bulimia nervosa, often enhanced to specifically focus on an individual's eating habits and concerns, lasts about 20 weeks

Focus On Law and Ethics

How Ethical Are Pro-Ana (Pro-Anorexia) Websites?

Some websites explicitly encourage extreme dieting and promote eating disorders like anorexia nervosa as a lifestyle. These "pro-ana" or "pro-anorexia" websites offer information about how to lose weight and provide a sense of support and community for those with anorexia nervosa. Common features or content on pro-ana websites include the following (Ging & Garvey, 2018):

- Visual images/memes that can include thin celebrities, motivation quotes, and writings to promote extreme thinness as a lifestyle
- Methods to facilitate weight loss such as laxatives, diet pills, and fasting
- Creative writings and expressions from those who aspire to be underweight
- Body mass and metabolic rate calculations
- A message board or forum or social media posts

Most would agree this seems like a disturbing trend, especially given what we know about influences on the development of anorexia nervosa in young girls. But what effect do these websites have on adults? Can harm actually be done? Some have found that those who view a pro-ana website, but not other websites, show decreased self-esteem and perceived attractiveness and appearance, as well as increased negative affect and perceptions of being overweight. Others have found no effect on body dissatisfaction, however (Delforterie et al., 2014). Still, a survey of adult pro–eating disorder website users revealed that 70 percent had purged, binged, or used laxatives to control their weight. In addition, 24.8 percent were underweight, 20.9 percent were overweight or obese, and only 12.9 percent were in treatment. Level of website usage was found to be related to more severe symptoms of eating disorder (Peebles et al., 2012). The impact of pro-ana websites may thus be negative and possibly lead to enhanced risk for eating disorders.

(Fairburn et al., 2015). In *Stage 1*, the therapist explains the cognitive-behavioral model of bulimia nervosa, begins weekly weighing, and teaches the client to self-monitor eating, drinking, the contexts in which these occur, and associated thoughts and feelings. A typical monitoring sheet is in **Figure 8.5**. A therapist will review these monitoring sheets and other homework assignments in subsequent sessions. The therapist also provides education about the nature of bulimia nervosa and gives feedback about eating as well as how to limit purging or vomiting. Lisa was taught to delay the time between a binge and her purging to observe that her distress level would drop by itself without having to vomit.

Stage 2 of cognitive-behavioral treatment addresses all forms of dieting, concerns about weight and shape, perfectionism, low self-esteem, and problem-solving skills. Lisa was taught to prepare healthy foods, limit types of food she brought into the house, discuss what she valued about herself other than weight, and how to avoid times and places that put her at risk for binging. She also enlisted the help of friends who helped monitor her eating behavior. The aim of *Stage 3* is to prevent relapse.

Individualized maintenance plans, like that outlined in **Figure 8.6**, can be developed so a client can anticipate and plan for future eating problems and setbacks.

Figure 8.5 A Monitoring Sheet Used in Cognitive-Behavioral Treatment for Bulimia Nervosa.

Day__________ Date __________

Time	Food and liquid consumed	Place	Context
7:35	1 grapefruit 1 cup black coffee	Kitchen	Feel really fat.
11:10	1 apple	Work	
3:15	2 Twix 1 bread roll a fruit cake	High St. " Market	Everyone looked at me in the market. I'm out of control. I hate myself. I can't stop crying.
3:30	2 chocolate eggs 2 bread rolls 1/2 pint of milk	" Kitchen "	
5:10	1 bowl of cereal 1 bowl of cereal 1 pita bread with cottage cheese 1 glass water	" " " "	
6:00	a baked potato 1 can diet soda	Outside "	Weighed myself lost 8 lbs - too heavy
9:00	1 cup soup	Kitchen	Feel fat and ugly.
9:20	1 ice cube	"	
10:00	1 cup coffee	"	Why do I do this? I want to be thin. I can't help it
11:20	1 coffee (black)	Sitting room	
	1 coffee (black) 6 shortbread biscuits 4 pieces of chocolate 2 pieces of toast 2 glasses of water	Kitchen " " " "	Weighed myself lost 7 lbs - fat Took a laxative.

Figure 8.6 A Maintenance Plan Following Cognitive-Behavioral Treatment for Bulimia Nervosa.

Eating problems may recur at times of stress. You should regard your eating problem as an Achilles' heel: It is the way you are prone to react at times of difficulty. You discovered during treatment that certain techniques helped you regain control over eating. The techniques that you found most helpful are listed below. These should be reinstituted under two sets of circumstances:

1. If your eating problem is getting worse
2. If you sense you are at risk of relapse

At such times there will often be some underlying problem. You must therefore examine what is happening in your life and look for any events or difficulties that might be of relevance. If any problems seem relevant, you should consider all possible solutions in order to construct a plan of action. In addition, you should use one or more of the following strategies to address your eating:

1. Set some time aside so that you can reflect on the current situation. You need to devise a plan of action. Reckon on formally reevaluating your progress every day or so. Some strategies may have worked; some may not.
2. Restart monitoring everything you eat, when you eat it.
3. Confine your eating to three planned meals each day, plus two planned snacks.
4. Plan your days ahead. Avoid both long periods of unstructured time and overbooking. If you are feeling at risk of losing control, plan your meals in detail so that you know exactly what and when you will be eating. In general, you should try to keep one step ahead of the problem.
5. Identify the times at which you are most likely to overeat (from recent experience and the evidence provided by your monitoring sheets) and plan alternative activities that are not compatible with eating, such as meeting friends, exercising, or taking a bath or shower.
6. If you are thinking too much about your weight, make sure that you are weighing yourself no more than once a week. If necessary, stop weighing altogether. If you want to reduce weight, do so by cutting down the quantities that you eat at each meal rather than by skipping meals or avoiding certain foods. Remember, you should accept a weight range, and gradual changes in weight are best.
7. If you are thinking too much about your shape, this may be because you are anxious or depressed. You tend to feel fat when things are not going well. You should try problem solving in order to see whether you can identify any current problems and do something positive to solve, or at least minimize, them.
8. If possible, confide in someone. Talk through your problem. A trouble shared is a trouble halved. Remember, you would not mind any friend of yours sharing his or her problems with you.
9. Set yourself limited realistic goals. Work from hour to hour. One failure does not justify a succession of failures. Note down any progress, however modest, on your monitoring sheets.

From Fairburn, C. G., Marcus, M. D., & Wilson, G. T. (1993). Cognitive behaviour therapy for binge eating and bulimia nervosa: A comprehensive treatment manual. In C. G. Fairburn & G. T. Wilson (Eds.), Binge eating: Nature, assessment, and treatment (pp. 361–404). New York: Guilford.

Nutritionists can also help with structured meal plans and exercise regimens to address weight control issues during these stages. Evidence supports the effectiveness of cognitive-behavioral treatment for binge eating but less so for weight control (Palavras et al., 2021).

What If I Have Weight Concerns or an Eating Disorder?

People are often screened for eating disorders, and the answers to some basic questions may indicate whether further assessment or even treatment is warranted. Some of these questions are in **Table 8.9**. If you find yourself answering "yes" to most of these questions, then you may wish to consult a clinical psychologist, psychiatrist, or other mental health professional (Chapter 15). Cognitive-behavioral therapy and/or medication may be best.

If you feel you have eating concerns but not necessarily an eating disorder, then teaching yourself to gain better control over your eating patterns and change your thoughts about your body may be best. Talk about your concerns with family members and friends or attend an eating disorders screening. Further information about screening and treatment for eating disorders can be found at the websites of the National Eating Disorders Association (www.nationaleatingdisorders.org) or the National Association of Anorexia Nervosa and Associated Eating Disorders (www.anad.org).

Table 8.9 Screening Questions for Eating Disorders

• Are you constantly thinking about your weight and food?
• Are you dieting strictly and/or have you lost a lot of weight?
• Are you more than 10 percent below your healthy weight?
• Are people concerned about your weight?
• Is your energy level down?
• Do you constantly feel cold?
• Are you overeating and feeling out of control?
• Are you vomiting, using laxatives or water pills, herbal agents, or trying to fast as a way to control your weight?
• Are you overexercising or do others consider your exercise excessive?
• Does your weight drastically fluctuate?
• Do any of the above interfere with your enjoyment of life, relationships, or everyday functioning?

Note: These questions are not intended to diagnose an eating disorder. They are simply designed to indicate that a person may be thinking too much about food, weight, etc., or engaging in potentially eating-disordered behaviors. Yes answers to more than five of these questions could indicate a problem that should be evaluated by a professional. For a list of mental health professionals and support groups in your area, visit the National Association of Anorexia Nervosa and Associated Eating Disorders at www.anad.org.

Source: National Association of Anorexia Nervosa and Associated Eating Disorders (www.anad.org).

Long-Term Outcome for People with Eating Disorders

What is the long-term picture, or *prognosis*, for people with eating disorders? The picture is less optimistic for those with anorexia nervosa. Anorexia nervosa has the highest mortality rate of any mental disorder, including depression—about 5 percent of those with anorexia nervosa eventually die via starvation or suicide. Factors that predict early death include excessive alcohol use, low body mass index, and poor social adjustment (Auger et al., 2021). Another 30 percent remain chronically impaired, with symptoms waxing and waning over time. The better news is that many people with anorexia nervosa show improved though not totally absent symptoms over time (Dobrescu et al., 2020). Sooki eventually sought treatment but dropped out after only a few sessions. Her prognosis over time is thus likely to be variable or poor.

Treatment outcomes for people with anorexia nervosa vary and can range from good (20–35 percent) to intermediate (45–60 percent) to poor (20 percent). About 30 percent drop out of treatment, however (Zipfel et al., 2014). People who seek treatment for anorexia nervosa generally do better if they are in treatment at a younger age, have a shorter duration of the disorder, are employed, are not taking medication, and have better social adjustment. Other factors, such as depression and frequency of binging, often affect treatment outcome as well. Many people with anorexia eventually develop bulimia nervosa or binge-eating disorder and must seek treatment for these conditions as well (Andrés-Pepiñá et al., 2020).

The picture is more optimistic for bulimia nervosa. People with bulimia nervosa can have an intermittent course involving recurring symptoms and symptom-free periods. Symptoms of bulimia nervosa often diminish over time. Other people with bulimia nervosa have a more chronic course, however, in which symptoms persist. Remission rates for bulimia range from 63 to 92 percent (Nagl et al., 2016). The course of binge-eating disorder is also variable, with symptoms sometimes lasting many years (Keski-Rahkonen, 2021). Binge-eating disorder is associated with health problems such as obesity as well as cardiovascular, metabolic, and sleep-related conditions (Agüera et al., 2021).

About 40 percent of people who seek treatment for bulimia nervosa show full recovery, but the remainder often display stable symptoms over time. Some show various improvements in dysfunctional dieting, weight loss, and body image. Cognitive-behavioral treatment is more effective than medication or other psychological treatments for bulimia nervosa, though medication is often used in conjunction with psychological treatment (Hagan & Walsh, 2021). People who seek treatment for bulimia nervosa generally do better if they respond early to treatment, have better impulse control, and show less depression and compensatory behaviors (Matherne et al., 2022). Such was the case for Lisa.

Section Summary

- Major approaches to assess eating disorders include interviews, self-report questionnaires, self-monitoring, and physical assessment.
- Treatments for eating disorders share some general aims: returning to a healthy weight; increasing motivation to restore healthy eating patterns; providing education about healthy eating; aiding recognition of problematic feelings, thoughts, and behaviors; enlisting support from others; and preventing relapse.
- Controlled weight gain and medication are prominent biological approaches to treating eating disorders.
- Family and cognitive behavioral therapies are the most effective psychological treatments for eating disorders.
- Of the eating disorders, the prognosis, course, and treatment outcome for bulimia nervosa is most favorable, followed by binge-eating disorder and anorexia nervosa.

Review Questions

1. Describe major assessment techniques for eating disorders, including interviews, self-report questionnaires, self-monitoring, and physical assessment.
2. What different methods may be used to treat anorexia nervosa?
3. What different methods may be used to treat bulimia nervosa?
4. What strategies could a mental health professional use to help someone with binge-eating disorder?
5. What is the long-term outcome for people with eating disorders?

Final Comments

Eating disorders are not as prevalent as other disorders discussed in this textbook, but they are serious conditions with many adverse physical outcomes. These disorders are especially relevant to college-age, young adults. Eating problems lie on a continuum, so many people likely share eating concerns and symptoms with those who meet criteria for an eating disorder. Help is available, so if you or someone you know has concerns about body weight and shape or eating behaviors, talking to someone about it or contacting a qualified mental health professional is a good idea.

Thought Questions

1. Think about models or television or film stars that seem markedly underweight or overweight. Do you think they have symptoms of an eating disorder? Which disorders, and why?
2. Have you ever been concerned about your body shape or weight? How about your own eating behavior? What factors may have influenced this? What information in this chapter seems most relevant to you?
3. What would you now say to a friend who might have concerns about their body weight or shape or about their eating behaviors?
4. What separates "normal" eating or weight concerns from "psychopathological" eating or weight concerns?
5. Do you think eating disorders have more to do with biological, family, cultural, or other factors? Why?

Key Terms

weight concerns 218
body dissatisfaction 218
eating disorder 219
eating problems 219
restricted eating 219
dieting 219
lack of control over eating 219
anorexia nervosa 219
restricting behaviors 220
purging 220
bulimia nervosa 220
binge eating 221
compensatory behaviors 222
binge-eating disorder 222
satiety 229
endogenous opioids 229
electronic diaries 236

Substance-Related Disorders 9

Learning Objectives

LO 9.1 Characterize the continuum from substance use to substance-related disorders.

LO 9.2 Distinguish among substance-related disorders using their diagnostic criteria and clinical characteristics.

LO 9.3 Summarize the epidemiology of substance-related disorders.

LO 9.4 Describe the stigma associated with substance-related disorders and its impact on those with the disorders.

LO 9.5 Discuss the risk factors for and prevention of substance-related disorders.

LO 9.6 Characterize the assessment and treatment of individuals with substance-related disorders.

Case Elon

Elon was a student at a large public college who enjoyed the party scene even more than his friend Kevin (Chapter 3). Kevin entered college with an eye toward academics, but Elon entered college with an eye toward socializing and having as much fun as possible. Elon had achieved good grades in high school and received an academic scholarship for the first two years of college. Elon's good performance in high school courses was due more to his intellectual talent than hard work. He was therefore able to enter college, but he found himself overwhelmed by professors' demands for extensive writing projects, reading assignments, and oral presentations.

Elon was somewhat impulsive but also extroverted and gregarious. He blended into parties, made friends, and found sexual partners with ease. Elon drank alcohol excessively at these parties, as he had sometimes done in high school, and smoked marijuana on occasion. Using these drugs eased his concern about the demands of school and satisfied his personal need for attention and companionship. Unfortunately, Elon failed all but one course his first semester.

Elon received academic probation and vowed to improve his reading and studying during his second semester. This strategy worked for the first two weeks, but Elon became bored with the course material and again started to attend campus parties. He also became bored with his usual social and party scene and began to experiment with creative sexual practices and different drugs. Elon began using cocaine to boost effects of his alcohol use and used marijuana to calm himself after using too much cocaine.

Elon was soon almost out of money from buying alcohol and other drugs. He stopped attending classes and spent much of his day sleeping and playing videogames. At night, Elon found a party or sought people who could give him illicit drugs. He remained sexually active but his ability to perform was impaired. He thus sought more powerful drugs and drug combinations to satisfy his need for a "high."

Elon settled on a particular drug combination called PNP—"party and play"—that involved crystal methamphetamine and sildenafil (a drug such as Viagra or Cialis that helps men achieve penile erections). This combination allowed Elon to experience greatly enhanced mood, feelings of invulnerability, and sexual performance. The drug combination was quickly addictive and Elon eventually spent nearly all his time seeking or using the drug cocktail.

Elon continued his drug use despite an arrest for disorderly conduct and a visit to the emergency room for a seizure (a side effect of methamphetamine with sildenafil). Elon's parents searched for and eventually found their son sleeping at a place near campus. Elon had no recollection of the past few days, and his parents took him to a drug rehabilitation facility. Elon was about to undergo the painful process of drug withdrawal and the even more painful process of admitting to his parents what happened to him.

What Do You Think?

1. Which of Elon's symptoms seem typical for a college student, and which seem very different?
2. What external events and internal factors might be responsible for Elon's drug use?
3. What are you curious about regarding Elon?
4. Does Elon remind you in any way of yourself or someone you know? How so?
5. How might Elon's drug use affect his life in the future?

Normal Substance Use and Substance-Related Disorders: What Are They?

LO 9.01 Characterize the continuum from substance use to substance-related disorders.

How many people do you know regularly use some kind of drug? The number might surprise you. Many people have a glass of wine, smoke a cigarette, drink soda, or take prescribed pain or sleep medication during the day or night. Each substance contains a key drug—alcohol, nicotine, caffeine, or a morphine derivative in these cases—that affects behavior. Many people drink alcohol to unwind after a hard day, smoke cigarettes to relax, drink caffeinated beverages to boost energy, and take medication for pain. Many of us engage in **substance use** that somehow affects our behavior. Such use is normal and may not lead to significant problems if the drug is used carefully.

Other people engage in substance use a bit more frequently. You may know someone who drinks a couple of alcoholic beverages or smokes a half-pack of cigarettes every day. This is substance use on a grander scale but is not necessarily a problem if the person can stop using the drug or if they are not physically addicted to the drug. Someone going through a rough time of life may drink alcohol more frequently than before but not necessarily drive and wreck a car when drinking. Or, a person may smoke cigarettes occasionally but have no daily cravings for nicotine. No impairment occurs in daily functioning, and no substantial physical harm takes place.

Some people continue to engage in substance use and do so to a greater degree, however. You may know people whose alcohol or other drug use seems problematic for them. Daily functioning *does* seem impaired, or some physical harm *is* taking place in these cases. A person may attempt to drive while impaired, fight with family members over use of a drug, or have trouble going to work. A person may thus be engaging in substance use to a moderate or intense degree (refer to the **Continuum of Substance Use and Substance-Related Disorders**).

For people like Elon, substance use becomes so severe that many areas of life are greatly impaired. Elon's extensive and varied drug use caused his academic failure, financial ruin, and legal troubles. He was also endangering his life because of physical addiction to drugs. Elon was spending nearly all his time looking for and using legal and illegal drugs. He must have known his lifestyle was self-destructive, but he reached a point where he could not control his own drug-seeking behavior. Elon was experiencing substance use to a *severe degree*, or a **substance-related disorder**. Features of this problem are discussed next.

Substance-Related Disorders: Features and Epidemiology

LO 9.02 Distinguish among substance-related disorders using their diagnostic criteria and clinical characteristics.

LO 9.03 Summarize the epidemiology of substance-related disorders.

Substance-related disorders include substance use disorder as well as substance intoxication and withdrawal. These problems are discussed next.

Substance Use Disorder

Substance use disorder involves *repeated* use of substances to the point that recurring problems are evident. Diagnostic criteria for alcohol use disorder, for example, are in **Table 9.1** (American Psychiatric Association [APA], 2022). Severity of substance use disorder is based partly on the number of diagnostic criteria shown by a person (Table 9.1). Substance use disorders generally involve impaired control, social impairment, risky use, and tolerance and/or withdrawal.

Impaired control means the person has difficulty reducing their substance use, ingests more and more of the drug over time, spends a great amount of time looking for the drug or recovering from its use, and has intense craving for the drug. Elon tried to reduce his substance use but was unsuccessful in doing so. Elon eventually spent so much time searching for drugs (drug-seeking behavior) that he gave up many of his academic and social activities. Drug-seeking behavior sometimes relates to *psychological dependence* on a drug, meaning a person believes they need the drug to function effectively. A person may use cocaine at work because they feel they need it to present well before others or to accomplish many tasks in a short period of time.

Social impairment means the person is experiencing key problems in their life because of substance use. Such problems could include missing many work or school days, neglecting child care, driving or operating machinery while impaired, experiencing legal troubles, fighting, or arguing with partners or friends about intoxication. Elon clearly had a substance use disorder because he was missing classes, withdrawing from friends and family members, and driving while impaired.

Table 9.1 DSM-5-TR

Alcohol Use Disorder

A. A problematic pattern of alcohol use leading to clinically significant impairment or distress, as manifested by at least two of the following, occurring within a 12-month period:

1. Alcohol is often taken in larger amounts or over a longer period than was intended.
2. There is a persistent desire or unsuccessful efforts to cut down or control alcohol use.
3. A great deal of time is spent in activities necessary to obtain alcohol, use alcohol, or recover from its effects.
4. Craving, or a strong desire or urge to use alcohol.
5. Recurrent alcohol use resulting in a failure to fulfill major role obligations at work, school, or home.
6. Continued alcohol use despite having persistent or recurrent social or interpersonal problems caused or exacerbated by the effects of alcohol.
7. Important social, occupational, or recreational activities are given up or reduced because of alcohol use.
8. Recurrent alcohol use in situations in which it is physically hazardous.
9. Alcohol use is continued despite knowledge of having a persistent or recurrent physical or psychological problem that is likely to have been caused or exacerbated by alcohol.
10. Tolerance, as defined by either of the following:
    a. A need for markedly increased amounts of alcohol to achieve intoxication or desired effect.
    b. A markedly diminished effect with continued use of the same amount of alcohol.
11. Withdrawal, as manifested by either of the following:
    a. The characteristic withdrawal syndrome for alcohol.
    b. Alcohol (or a closely related substance, such as a benzodiazepine) is taken to relieve or avoid withdrawal symptoms.

Specify if in early or sustained remission and if in a controlled environment as well as mild (2–3 symptoms), moderate (4–5 symptoms), or severe (6+ symptoms).

American Psychiatric Association. (2022). *Diagnostic and statistical manual of mental disorders* (5th ed., text rev.). Arlington, VA: American Psychiatric Association.

Continuum of Substance Use and Substance-Related Disorders

	Normal	Mild
Emotions	Stable mood.	Mild discomfort about the day; feeling a bit irritable or down.
Cognitions	No concern about substance use.	Thoughts about the difficulty of the day. Worry that something will go wrong at work.
Behaviors	Occasional but appropriate alcohol use or use of medication.	Drinking a bit more than usual; relying on medication to sleep.

Risky use means that the person continues taking the drug despite the fact that it places them in hazardous situations. The person's use of the drug continues even though they may know that doing so is harmful or that it creates physical or psychological problems. Elon knew his lifestyle was destructive, but he could not stop his drug use.

Finally, people with substance use disorder often show *tolerance and/or withdrawal.* **Tolerance** refers to the need to ingest greater and greater quantities of a drug to achieve the same effect. Someone who regularly drinks three beers a day will find over time that the same physiological "high" from this amount no longer exists. The person must thus drink more beer or switch to another, more powerful drug to achieve the same effect. **Withdrawal** refers to maladaptive behavioral changes when a person stops using a drug (refer to later section).

Substance Intoxication

Have you known someone who got drunk but, when you spoke to them the next day, seemed fine despite a hangover? The person perhaps experienced **substance intoxication**, a usually reversible condition brought on by excessive use of a drug such as alcohol. Diagnostic criteria for alcohol intoxication, for example, are in **Table 9.2** (APA, 2022). A person who becomes intoxicated experiences maladaptive changes in behavior—they may become aggressive, make inappropriate sexual advances, and show impaired judgment and rapid shifts in mood. Impaired judgment may lead to a poor decision to drive, and rapid shifts in mood may lead to depression.

An intoxicated person may also have difficulty staying awake, thinking clearly, or even walking. Some people may be intoxicated for short periods, but others go on *binges* and remain intoxicated for lengthy periods. Elon later vaguely recalled to a counselor that he once

Table 9.2 DSM-5-TR

Alcohol Intoxication
A. Recent ingestion of alcohol.
B. Clinically significant problematic behavioral or psychological changes that developed during, or shortly after, alcohol ingestion.
C. One (or more) of the following signs or symptoms developing during, or shortly after, alcohol use: 1. Slurred speech. 2. Incoordination. 3. Unsteady gait. 4. Nystagmus. 5. Impairment in attention or memory. 6. Stupor or coma.
D. The signs or symptoms are not attributable to another medical condition and are not better explained by another mental disorder, including intoxication with another substance.

American Psychiatric Association. (2022). *Diagnostic and statistical manual of mental disorders* (5th ed., text rev.). Arlington, VA: American Psychiatric Association.

Moderate	Substance-Related Disorder—less severe	Substance-Related Disorder—more severe
Considerable stress and sadness (note that opposite emotions occur when drug is used).	Intense stress, sadness, and feelings of emptiness; agitation about not having access to a specific drug or drugs.	Extreme stress, sadness, and feelings of emptiness. Extreme agitation when drug is not available.
Dwelling on negative aspects of the day; worry about threats to one's job or marriage. Thoughts about ways to hide excessive substance use.	Frequent thoughts about using substances and worry about harm to personal health.	Thoughts focused almost exclusively on drug use and self-destruction of one's lifestyle.
Drinking alcohol regularly at night; occasionally missing work; heavy use of medication.	Regular intoxication such that many days are missed from work; arguments with partner about substance use; arrests for impairment.	Very frequent intoxication; loss of job or marriage; physical addiction to a drug; seeking to secure or use drugs most of the time.

used meth (methamphetamine) for six straight days. Keep in mind that intoxication is not generally considered psychopathological *without* maladaptive behavioral changes. A person who comes home after a long week at work, drinks several margaritas, and falls asleep does not have a mental disorder.

Substance Withdrawal

Substance withdrawal refers to maladaptive behavioral changes when a person stops using a drug. Diagnostic criteria for alcohol withdrawal, for example, are in **Table 9.3** (APA, 2022). When a person stops taking a drug, severe physical and behavioral changes can occur. These changes are usually the opposite of the intoxicating effect of a drug and may include nausea, vomiting, tremors, fever, seizures, hearing voices or seeing things not actually there (hallucinations), and death. Behavioral changes, such as anxiety, depression, and other mood states, may also occur. A well-known feature of alcohol withdrawal is *delirium tremens* (DTs), which involves severe confusion and autonomic overactivity in the form of sweating, heart palpitations, and trembling.

The *DSM* lists many kinds of substances or drugs that a person could experience problems with (APA, 2022). Not all of these drugs necessarily involve a substance use disorder (e.g., caffeine), intoxication (e.g., tobacco), or withdrawal (e.g., hallucinogens), however. A list of substances and relevant diagnostic categories is in **Table 9.4**. The specific characteristics of these substances are discussed next.

Table 9.3 DSM-5-TR

Alcohol Withdrawal

A. Cessation of (or reduction in) alcohol use that has been heavy and prolonged.

B. Two (or more) of the following, developing within several hours to a few days after the cessation of (or reduction in) alcohol use described in Criterion A:

1. Autonomic hyperactivity (e.g., sweating or pulse rate greater than 100 bpm).
2. Increased hand tremor.
3. Insomnia.
4. Nausea or vomiting.
5. Transient visual, tactile, or auditory hallucinations or illusions.
6. Psychomotor agitation.
7. Anxiety.
8. Generalized tonic-clonic seizures.

C. The signs or symptoms in Criterion B cause clinically significant distress or impairment in social, occupational, or other important areas of functioning.

D. The signs or symptoms are not attributable to another medical condition and are not better explained by another mental disorder, including intoxication or withdrawal from another substance.

Specify if with perceptual disturbances.

American Psychiatric Association. (2022). *Diagnostic and statistical manual of mental disorders* (5th ed., text rev.). Arlington, VA: American Psychiatric Association.

Table 9.4 DSM-5-TR

Diagnoses Associated with Substance Class

	Psychotic disorders	Bipolar disorders	Depressive disorders	Anxiety disorders	Obsessive-compulsive and related disorders
Alcohol	I/W	I/W	I/W	I/W	
Caffeine				I	
Cannabis	I			I	
Hallucinogens					
Phencyclidine	I	I	I	I	
Other hallucinogens	I*	I	I	I	
Inhalants	I		I	I	
Opioids			I/W	W	
Sedatives, hypnotics, or anxiolytics	I/W	I/W	I/W	W	
Stimulants**	I	I/W	I/W	I/W	I/W
Tobacco					
Other (or unknown)	I/W	I/W	I/W	I/W	I/W

Note: X = The category is recognized in DSM-5.
I = The specifier "with onset during intoxication" may be noted for the category.
W = The specifier "with onset during withdrawal" may be noted for the category.
I/W = Either "with onset during intoxication" or "with onset during withdrawal" may be noted for the category.
P = The disorder is persisting.
*Also hallucinogen persisting perception disorders (flashbacks).
**Includes amphetamine-type substance, cocaine, and other or unspecified stimulants.

Types of Substances

A brief description of major substances that are used excessively as well as their street names and effects is in **Table 9.5**. Drugs fall into several main categories based on effects they have on behavior. Several categories were discussed in previous chapters, such as anxiolytics in Chapter 5 and antidepressants in Chapter 7. Other categories such as neuroleptic or antipsychotic drugs (Chapter 12) are discussed in subsequent chapters. Other main categories of drugs are discussed in the next sections and include depressants, stimulants, opiates, hallucinogens, marijuana, and others.

Depressants

Depressant, or sedative, drugs are those that inhibit aspects of the central nervous system. Common depressants include alcohol, anesthetics for surgery, antiseizure medications for epilepsy, barbiturate drugs people use to calm themselves (largely replaced now by antianxiety drugs, discussed in Chapter 5), and hypnotic drugs used to aid sleep. Popular examples of the latter include zolpidem (Ambien) and eszopiclone (Lunesta).

Alcohol is the most well-known and widely used depressant drug. You might be wondering why alcohol is classified as a depressant when, after a couple of drinks, a person may feel elated or relieved. This is because alcohol initially affects a neurotransmitter system most responsible for inhibition, the gamma- aminobutyric acid (GABA) system. Recall from Chapter 5 that impairment in the GABA system may relate to excess activity that may lead to panic attacks. Alcohol is thus inhibiting a key inhibitory brain system. This process is **disinhibition**. A person may thus do things they might not do normally, such as talk a little more, dance, or make a sexual advance. They may feel a "high" or sense of well-being when actually experiencing reduced central nervous system activity.

	Sleep disorders	Sexual dysfunctions	Delirium	Neurocognitive disorders	Substance use disorders	Substance intoxication	Substance withdrawal
	I/W	I/W	I/W	I/W/P	X	X	X
	I/W					X	X
	I/W		I		X	X	X
			I		X	X	
			I		X	X	
			I	I/P	X	X	
	I/W	I/W	I/W		X	X	X
	I/W	I/W	I/W	I/W/P	X	X	X
	I/W	I	I		X	X	X
	W				X		X
	I/W	I/W	I/W	I/W/P	X	X	X

Alcohol effects closely relate to **blood alcohol level**, or concentration of alcohol in the blood. Various blood alcohol levels related to alcohol intake for men and women of different sizes are in **Table 9.6**. Common effects of alcohol use at different levels are in **Table 9.7**. People usually start feeling intoxicated at a blood alcohol level of 0.08, which is often the legal cutoff for "driving under the influence" (DUI). **Lethal dose**, or LD, is the dose of a substance (alcohol in this case) that kills a certain percentage of test animals. LD1 is the dose at which 1 percent of test animals die at a certain blood alcohol level. An LD50 kills about half and, in humans, occurs at a blood alcohol level of 0.40. This blood alcohol level is therefore extremely dangerous.

As a person drinks more alcohol past the disinhibition stage, they become more intoxicated as *excitatory* areas of the brain become depressed or inhibited. These excitatory areas of the brain include the reticular activating system, the limbic system, and the cortex. You may notice that someone who continues to drink alcohol experiences changes in behavior and personality, perhaps becoming more surly or aggressive. Reflexes and other motor behaviors also become impaired, judgment and reasoning become clouded, and attention and concentration become difficult to maintain. Note how this can be quite dangerous should the person decide to drive.

Other common effects of alcohol at this stage include increased sexual desire but poor performance, an erroneous belief that problem-solving ability is adequate as one is becoming sober, and memory impairment. You may have difficulties remembering the name of a new person you met the night before

Marcus Andreassen/Gonzales Photo/Alamy Stock Photo

Binge drinking can lead to many untoward consequences.

Table 9.5 Common Substances and Their Street Names

Drug	Street names
Acid (LSD)	Acid, blotter, and many others
Club drugs	XTC, X (MDMA); Special K, Vitamin K (ketamine); liquid ecstasy, soap (GHB); roofies (Rohypnol)
Cocaine	Coke, snow, flake, blow, and many others
Ecstasy/MDMA (methylene-dioxymethamphetamine)	XTC, X, Adam, hug, beans, love drug
Heroin	Smack, H, ska, junk, and many others
Inhalants	Whippets, poppers, snappers
Marijuana	Pot, ganga, weed, grass, and many others
Methamphetamine	Speed, meth, chalk, ice, crystal, glass
PCP/phencyclidine	Angel dust, ozone, wack, rocket fuel, and many others
Prescription medication	Commonly used opioids include oxycodone (OxyContin), propoxyphene (Darvon), hydrocodone (Vicodin), hydromorphone (Dilaudid), meperidine (Demerol), and diphenoxylate (Lomotil); common central nervous system depressants include barbiturates such as pentobarbital sodium (Nembutal), and benzodiazepines such as diazepam (Valium) and alprazolam (Xanax); stimulants include dextroamphetamine (Dexedrine) and methylphenidate (Ritalin)

Source: National Institute on Drug Abuse and National Institute on Alcohol Abuse and Alcoholism.

while drinking. People who continue drinking may also mix their alcohol with other drugs, which can lower the dose necessary for death. This is because mixing different drugs (polysubstance use) causes a *synergistic* or multiplicative, not additive, effect. Drinking three shots of whiskey and snorting three lines of cocaine does not add to six units of effect but rather multiplies to nine. Interaction effects of alcohol with other common drugs are in **Table 9.8**.

Because alcohol use intensifies and a person becomes extremely drunk, strong changes in personality and behavior occur. Many people become depressed, stupefied, or unconscious. Walking and talking become difficult, and a person may have trouble breathing. As the alcohol depresses areas of the brain necessary for involuntary actions, such as the medulla that controls breathing, a person is at risk for asphyxiation and death.

Binge drinking involves ingesting large amounts of alcohol in a short period and relates to many college student deaths and problems. A college student at Colorado State University died after binge drinking over an 11-hour period (refer to **The Sam Spady Story** at the end of this chapter). According to the National Institute of Alcoholism and Alcohol Abuse, binge drinking corresponds to five or more drinks for men and four or more drinks for women in a two-hour period. A College Alcohol Study conducted by the Harvard School of Public Health surveyed 14,941 students at 140 American colleges and universities. Some of the study's most important findings include the following:

- Within the past 30 days, 22 percent of students drank on 10 or more occasions, 45 percent binged when drinking, 29 percent were drunk three or more times, and 47 percent drank to get drunk.
- Only 19 percent of students abstained from alcohol.
- More students drank alcohol than used cocaine, marijuana, or cigarettes combined.
- The strongest predictor of binge drinking was fraternity or sorority residence or membership.
- Other risk factors for binge drinking are male gender, athletic status, European American background, and age less than 24 years.
- Frequent binge drinkers are 17 times more likely to miss a class, 10 times more likely to vandalize property, and 8 times more likely to be injured because of their drinking.
- 10 percent of female students who are frequent binge drinkers were reportedly subjected to nonconsensual sex compared with 3 percent of female non–binge drinkers.

People addicted to alcohol (alcoholism) are clearly at risk for other health problems. Withdrawal symptoms can be particularly severe and include delirium tremens, mentioned earlier. Extensive alcohol use is

Table 9.6 Relationships among Gender, Weight, Alcohol Consumption, and Blood Alcohol Level

Blood alcohol levels (mg/100 ml)								
Absolute alcohol (ounces)	**Beverage intake***	**Female (100 lb)**	**Male (100 lb)**	**Female (150 lb)**	**Male (150 lb)**	**Female (200 lb)**	**Male (200 lb)**
1/2	1 oz spirits† 1 glass wine 1 can beer	0.045	0.037	0.03	0.025	0.022	0.019
1	2 oz spirits 2 glasses wine 2 cans beer	0.090	0.075	0.06	0.050	0.045	0.037
2	4 oz spirits 4 glasses wine 4 cans beer	0.180	0.150	0.12	0.100	0.090	0.070
3	6 oz spirits 6 glasses wine 6 cans beer	0.270	0.220	0.18	0.150	0.130	0.110
4	8 oz spirits 8 glasses wine 8 cans beer	0.360	0.300	0.24	0.200	0.180	0.150
5	10 oz spirits 10 glasses wine 10 cans beer	0.450	0.370	0.30	0.250	0.220	0.180

*In 1 hour.
†100-proof spirits.

From Ray, O. (1978). Drugs, society, and human behavior (2nd ed.). St. Louis, MO: C.V. Mosby, p. 147. Reprinted by permission.

Table 9.7 Blood Alcohol Levels (BALs) and Expected Behavior

Percent BAL	Behavior
0.01	Few overt effects, slight feeling of relaxation
0.03	Relaxed with slight exhilaration, decrease in visual tracking, minimal impairment in mental functions
0.05	Feeling relaxed and warm, some release of inhibition, some impaired judgment, lowered alertness, slight decrease in fine motor skills, mild reduction in visual capability in tracking and glare recovery
0.06	Mild relaxation, slight impairment in fine motor skills, increase in reaction time, slurred speech, poor muscle control, exaggerated emotions
0.08	Legal evidence of intoxication and DUI in many jurisdictions; vision impaired, increased loss of motor functions, may stagger
0.09	Judgment now clouded, lessening of inhibitions and self-restraint, reduced visual and hearing acuity, increased difficulty in performing motor skills
0.10	Slowed reaction times, slurred speech, drowsiness, nausea, deficits in coordination, impaired motor functioning, and difficulty in focusing, judging moving targets, and glare recovery
0.15	Major impairment in physical and mental functions, difficulty in standing, walking and talking; disturbed perception, blurred vision, large increases in reaction times, falling asleep, vomiting
0.20	Marked depression of sensory and motor functions, mentally confused, gross body movements can be made only with assistance, unable to maintain an upright position, incoherent speech, needs assistance to walk, has difficulty staying awake, vomiting
0.25	Severe motor disturbance, sensory perceptions greatly impaired, staggering, as well as behaviors seen at 0.20
0.30	Stuporous but conscious, severe mental confusion, difficulty in reacting to stimuli, general suppression of sensibility, little comprehension of what is going on, respiratory depression, brain functions severely depressed, repeatedly falling down, passes out, may be in coma
0.40	Almost complete anesthesia, reflexes are depressed, breathing and heartbeat may stop, unconscious and may be dead
0.50	Completely unconscious, deep coma if not dead
0.60	Death most likely; depression of brain centers that control heart rate and breathing

From R. J. Craig, Counseling the alcohol and drug dependent client: A practical approach (p. 93) New York: Pearson, 2004. Reprinted by permission of Pearson Education, Inc.

Table 9.8 Alcohol–Other Drug Interactions

Drug	Prescribed purpose	Interaction
Anesthetics (e.g., Diprivan, Ethrane, Fluothane)	Administered before surgery to render a patient unconscious and insensitive to pain	• Increased amount of drug required to induce loss of consciousness • Increased risk of liver damage
Antibiotics	Used to treat infectious diseases	• Reduced drug effectiveness • Nausea/vomiting • Headache • Convulsions
Antidepressants (e.g., Elavil)	Used to treat depression and other forms of mental disorder	• Increased sedative effects • May decrease effectiveness of antidepressant • Potential for dangerous rise in blood pressure
Antihistamines (e.g., Benadryl)	Used to treat allergic symptoms and insomnia	• Intensified sedation • Excessive dizziness
Antiulcer medications (e.g., Tagamet, Zantac)	Used to treat ulcers and other gastrointestinal problems	• Prolonged effect of alcohol • Increased risk of side effects
Narcotic pain relievers (morphine, codeine, Darvon, Demerol)	Used to alleviate moderate to severe pain	• Intensified sedation • Increased possibility of a fatal overdose
Nonnarcotic pain relievers (aspirin, ibuprofen, acetaminophen)	Used to alleviate mild to moderate pain	• Increased risk of stomach bleeding • Increased risk of the inhibition of blood clotting • Increased effects of consumed alcohol Note: acetaminophen (Tylenol) taken during or after drinking may significantly increase one's risk of liver damage.
Sedatives and hypnotics (Valium, Dalmane, Ativan, sleeping pills)	Used to alleviate anxiety and insomnia	• Severe drowsiness • Depressed cardiac and respiratory functions • Increased risk of coma or fatality

Adapted from the National Institute on Alcohol Abuse and Alcoholism. (1995, January). Alcohol Alert (Publication No. 27 PH 355). Bethesda, MD: NIAAA.

also associated with increased risk for suicide, homicide, unprotected sexual activity, sexual assault, and traffic and other accidents (Volpicelli & Menzies, 2022). People who chronically and excessively use alcohol may also experience **cirrhosis of the liver** in which scar tissue replaces liver tissue, leading to loss of function and possibly death (Arab et al., 2022). **Korsakoff's syndrome**, a problem also discussed in Chapter 14, involves confusion, memory loss, and coordination difficulties because of thiamine deficiency from extended alcohol use (Ritz et al., 2021).

The harmful effects of alcoholism have a wide reach and include children of people with alcoholism. These children are at increased risk of neglect or other maltreatment and at risk for developing substance-related problems later in life (Sanmartin et al., 2020). Some newborns exposed to maternal alcohol use during pregnancy have **fetal alcohol syndrome**. Fetal alcohol syndrome is a condition that produces distinct facial features (refer to **Figure 9.1**), slowed physical growth, cognitive impairment, and learning problems throughout elementary school (Kruithof & Ban, 2021). Alcohol use by pregnant mothers, particularly binge drinking, can produce more general *fetal alcohol effects* as well. These effects on the child could include reduced verbal intelligence and increased delinquent behavior and learning problems (Branton et al., 2022).

Stimulants

Stimulant drugs activate or stimulate the central nervous system. Common stimulants include bronchodilators to ease breathing and treat asthma, methylphenidate to treat attention-deficit/hyperactivity disorder (Chapter 13), and drugs focused on here: caffeine, nicotine, cocaine, and amphetamines.

Caffeine is a legal drug that is commonly found in soda, coffee, tea, and chocolate. Many people use caffeine to boost energy. Caffeine helps release epinephrine and norepinephrine, so mood, alertness, and cardiovascular activity become elevated. Moderate caffeine use is not dangerous, but someone who ingests large amounts for an extended period is susceptible to withdrawal symptoms, including headaches, irritability, sleepiness, anxiety, vomiting, and muscle tension and pain (Booth et al., 2020).

Figure 9.1 Characteristic Facial Features of Youths with Fetal Alcohol Syndrome.

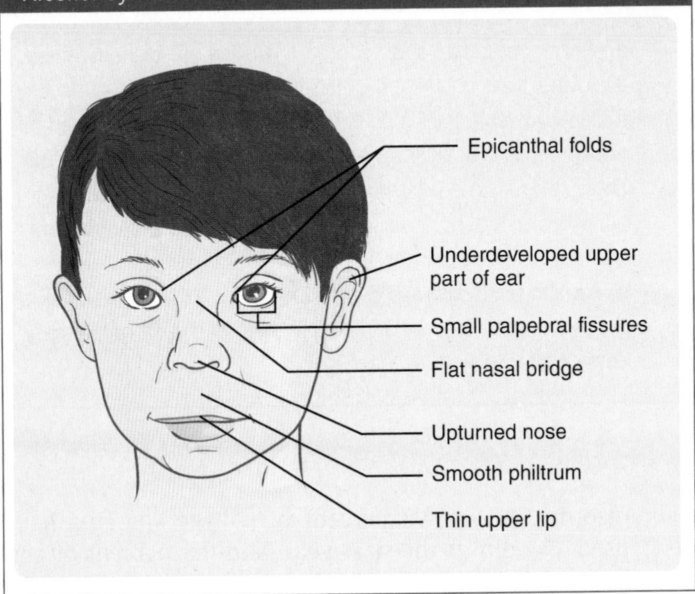

People generally ingest *nicotine* via cigarettes and other tobacco products. Most cigarettes contain about 0.5 to 2.0 mg of nicotine and about 10 percent of this is absorbed during smoking. Nicotine is an extremely deadly poison—if you ingested 30 to 60 mg of pure nicotine, you would die within minutes (Maessen et al., 2020). Nicotine's effect on the brain is similar to caffeine, and many people who smoke find increased cardiovascular activity and motor tremors but also relaxation. The relaxation may come from increased serotonin following nicotine ingestion. Nicotine is an extremely addictive substance and can produce withdrawal symptoms of restlessness, irritability, and concentration and sleep problems. About 16.6 percent of college students smoked cigarettes and 28.0 percent vaped nicotine in the past year (Patrick et al., 2022). *Cocaine* is a powerful stimulant usually ingested by sniffing or snorting crystals or smoking in the form of crack. People may mix cocaine with other drugs, such as alcohol or heroin. Cocaine stimulates dopamine, norepinephrine, and serotonin systems to produce euphoria, high energy similar to mania, and bizarre, paranoid, and occasionally violent behavior. High doses can lead to heart attacks and respiratory failure and death. Cocaine can be physically addictive, and a strong psychological dependence develops toward the drug. Withdrawal from cocaine can cause severe depression, overeating, and sleep problems. About 3.9 percent of college students have used cocaine in the past year (Patrick et al., 2022).

Cocaine is often smoked in the form of crack.

Amphetamines are also powerful stimulants that primarily increase dopamine and norepinephrine. About 90 percent of all excessive amphetamine use today involves *methamphetamine* (refer to **The Methamphetamine and Opioid Epidemics**). Methamphetamine can be snorted or smoked and results in a sudden "high" that can last hours. A person may feel empowered to do many things, as Elon did, or feel invulnerable to harm. Sexual desire may be enhanced as well. A person may become psychologically or physically addicted to methamphetamine after just a few doses. People addicted to methamphetamine sometimes experience severe decay or loss of teeth from exposure to the drug's toxic chemical composition (Alqarni et al., 2021). Withdrawal from methamphetamine can be severe; common symptoms include depression, anxiety, fatigue, paranoia, and intense cravings for the drug. About 0.3 percent of college students have used methamphetamine in the past year (Patrick et al., 2022).

Opiates

Opiates (sometimes called narcotics or *opioids*) are drugs commonly used to relieve pain or cough, such as morphine or codeine. Morphine and codeine can be used excessively, but a related opiate, heroin, is overused more. Heroin is a derivative of morphine that is typically injected. The drug produces a sudden "rush"

The Methamphetamine and Opioid Epidemics

Many drugs have been cause for concern in America's "drug war," but perhaps none are as dangerous and insidious as methamphetamine as well as opioids from prescription medications. According to the Substance Abuse and Mental Health Services Administration, over 1.5 million Americans used methamphetamine and over 2.5 million misused prescription pain relievers in the past month. Unfortunately, treatment facilities specifically for methamphetamine and prescription medication misuse are not as prevalent as for other drugs.

Why has use of these drugs become such an epidemic? The pleasurable effects of these drugs are extremely intense and include euphoria, analgesia, and reduced inhibition. Methamphetamine stimulates pleasure centers in the brain to release large amounts of dopamine and opioids activate endogenous receptors related to reward centers. Both drugs are also relatively easy to obtain. The physical downsides of using methamphetamine in particular are numerous and severe, however, and include brain and liver damage, malnutrition, skin infections, immune system problems, convulsions, stroke, and death. Many people like Elon who use methamphetamine experience such a powerful high that they completely ignore these physical effects.

of euphoria followed by alternating periods of drowsiness and wakefulness. Opiates work by stimulating different types of opiate receptors in the brain across the hippocampus, amygdala, thalamus, and locus coeruleus. Heroin is extremely addictive and can result in severe withdrawal symptoms of agitation, chills, drowsiness, cramps, vomiting, sweating, and diarrhea. About 0.1 percent of college students have used heroin in the past year (Patrick et al., 2022).

Modern-day painkillers are also related to morphine and can be highly addictive. Drugs such as OxyContin, Darvon, Vicodin, Percocet, and Percodan are narcotic-based medications that can cause addiction in only a few doses. Prescription drug use is becoming one of the fastest-growing forms of substance-related disorder. About 0.8 percent of college students have used Vicodin in the past year, and 0.3 percent of college students have used OxyContin in the past year (Patrick et al., 2022).

Hallucinogens

Hallucinogens are drugs that cause symptoms of psychosis, such as hallucinations (seeing or hearing things not actually there), disorganized thinking, odd perceptions, and delirium (a cognitive state of confusion and memory problems). Hallucinogen use can involve peyote or LSD (lysergic acid diethylamide), the latter of which seems to spur dopamine in the brain (a phenomenon also linked to psychoses such

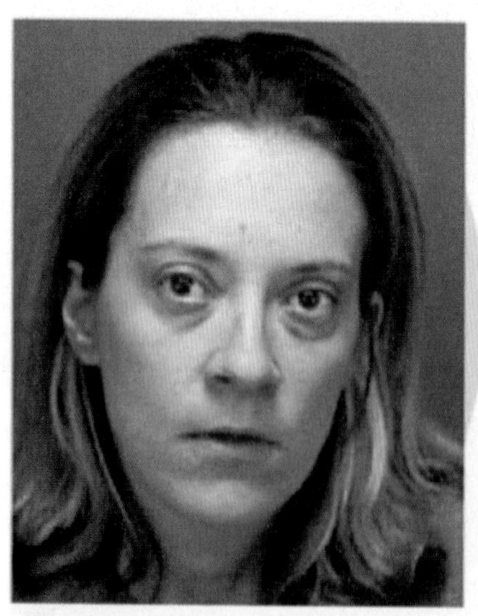

1 AGE: 33

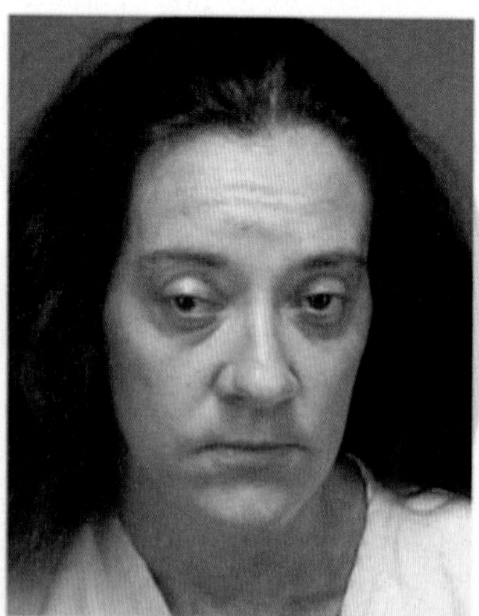

2 AGE: 37

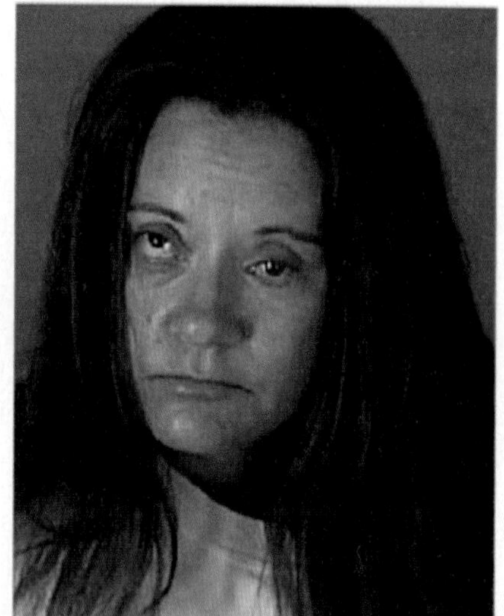

3 AGE: 39

AP Images/Rehabs.com/Rex Features

These are booking photographs of a woman arrested for methamphetamine use.

as schizophrenia). Another drug, *ecstasy* (MDMA or methylenedioxymethamphetamine), acts as both stimulant and hallucinogen. In the past year, about 6.8 percent of college students have used hallucinogens, including LSD (4.3 percent) and MDMA (1.6 percent) (Patrick et al., 2022).

Marijuana

Marijuana comes from *Cannabis sativa,* or the hemp plant, that contains an active ingredient known as THC (delta-9-tetrahydrocannabinol). Marijuana is typically smoked but can be part of edibles as well. Marijuana stimulates cannabinoid receptors throughout the brain and especially the cortex, hippocampus, basal ganglia, and hypothalamus. The drug creates feelings of joy, well-being, humor, and a dreamlike state. Time often feels distorted; attention, vigilance, and short-term memory diminish; creativity is enhanced; and motor behavior is impaired. Marijuana may not be physically addictive for everyone because tolerance is not always present, but heavy users are more at risk. Minor withdrawal symptoms, such as sleep problems, anxiety, and irritability, may occur. Marijuana is a medical treatment for glaucoma and may quell nausea, vomiting, convulsions, and pain. About 40.3 percent of college students have used marijuana in the past year (Patrick et al., 2022).

Other Drugs

Other drugs also relate to excessive substance use:

- *Designer drugs* or *club drugs* represent manmade modifications of psychoactive drugs, such as amphetamines and heroin. *Phencyclidine* (PCP) induces strong perceptual distortions and often highly violent and dangerous behavior. Club drugs may also include *date rape drugs* (refer to **Focus on Gender: Date Rape Drugs**).
- *Inhalants* are volatile liquids stored in containers that give off strong fumes; users inhale the fumes to produce feelings of euphoria and lightheadedness. Examples include glue, spray paint, cleaning agents, paint thinner, and gasoline.
- *Steroids* are synthetic substances to enhance muscle growth and secondary sexual characteristics but are sometimes used excessively by adolescents and athletes to gain a competitive edge.

Image Source/Getty Images

People who take hallucinogenic substances such as LSD can experience symptoms similar to psychosis, such as distorted perceptions.

Epidemiology of Substance-Related Disorders

Substance use is common among college students, and this is true as well for the general population. Data in this section come from the National Survey on Drug Use and Health for American adults and for use in the past month (U.S. Department of Health and Human Services, 2022). About 55.3 percent of adults used alcohol and 24.3 percent engaged in binge drinking. Recent alcohol use is more common among men (57.4 percent) than women (51.2 percent) and among European Americans (58.9 percent) than African Americans (49.0 percent), Hispanics (47.7 percent), Asian Americans (37.3 percent), and American Indians/Alaska Natives (35.3 percent). In addition, 7.2 percent of Americans had recently driven a motor vehicle under the influence of alcohol. Some (5.0 percent) pregnant women also engaged in binge drinking in the past month.

Tobacco use is also common. About 22.1 percent of American adults used some tobacco product, mostly cigarettes. This rate rises for adults aged 18 to 25 years (25.1 percent) and men (27.1 percent) compared with women (17.4 percent). Tobacco use occurs among African Americans (25.4 percent), European Americans (23.5 percent), Hispanics (16.1 percent), and Asian Americans (10.5 percent). Nicotine vaping

Focus On Gender

Date Rape Drugs

According to the National Women's Health Information Center, date rape drugs are used to induce dizziness, disorientation, and loss of inhibition and consciousness so a woman can be sexually assaulted. Other crimes, such as robbery, may be committed as well while a woman is in a drugged state. Date rape drugs generally include *ketamine* ("special K"), *rohypnol* ("roofies"), and *GHB* (gamma hydroxybutyrate or "liquid ecstasy"). These drugs are typically tasteless, odorless, and colorless and can be slipped into a person's drink. Alcohol also intensifies the effects of these drugs and can lead to serious physical problems such as slowed heart rate and blood pressure.

What can you do to protect yourself? According to the Center, open all containers yourself, do not share or accept drinks from others, do not drink from open containers such as punch bowls, always be with a nondrinking and trusted friend, and always keep your drink with you, even if using the restroom. If you have to leave a drink behind, then assume the worst and do not drink it again. If you feel you have been drugged and assaulted—possibly evidenced by memory lapses or genital or other body bruising or other signs—then contact the police or go to an emergency room as soon as possible. Provide a urine sample for a physician as soon as possible (the drugs may still be in your system) and do not urinate, bathe, or change clothes before getting help.

---

is higher among European Americans (4.5 percent) than other racial groups.

About 14.1 percent of American adults used illicit drugs in the past month. This drug use is more common for men (15.7 percent) than women (12.6 percent) and for people aged 18 to 25 years (23.9 percent) (refer to **Figure 9.2**). Recent illicit drug use occurs among African Americans (16.8 percent), American Indians/Alaska Natives (14.8 percent), European Americans (14.8 percent), Hispanics (11.6 percent), and Asian Americans (4.9 percent). Types of drug use are in **Table 9.9**. Of particular interest regarding these statistics is what type of drug people used for the first time in the past 12 months, and at what age (refer to **Figures 9.3** and **9.4**).

The prevalence of any substance use disorder is 14.5 percent for the past 12 months (alcohol, 10.2 percent; illicit drugs, 6.6 percent). Substance use disorder is more common among men (8.0 percent) than women (5.7 percent) and among people aged 18 to 25 years (24.4 percent). Substance use disorder is higher among American Indians/Alaska Natives (17.5 percent) compared with multiracial individuals (13.3 percent), European Americans (7.1 percent), African Americans (6.9 percent), Hispanics (6.0 percent), and Asian Americans (3.2 percent). People with substance use disorder are also much more likely to be unemployed than employed full-time.

Substance-related disorders are comorbid with many other mental disorders, especially anxiety-related, depressive, and personality disorders. Substance-related disorders also relate closely to severe psychological stress, especially among 18- to 25-year-olds. Many more people with a major depressive episode experience

Figure 9.2 Past Month Illicit Drug Use Among People Aged 12 Years and Older.

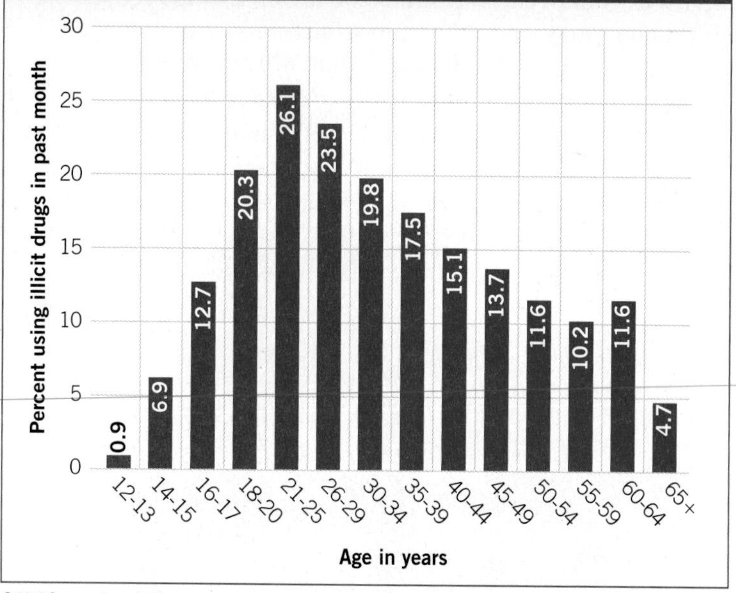

Table 9.9 Types of Drug Use in Lifetime, Past Year, and Past Month among Persons Aged 12 Years or Older: Percentages

Drug	Lifetime	Past year	Past month
Marijuana	45.7	17.9	11.8
Cocaine	14.2	1.9	0.7
Hallucinogens	15.9	2.6	0.6
Inhalants	9.7	0.9	0.3
Misuse of opioids		3.4	1.0
Misuse of prescription pain relievers		3.3	0.9
Misuse of prescription stimulants		1.8	0.5
Methamphetamine	5.6	0.9	0.6
Misuse of prescription tranquilizers or sedatives		2.2	0.8

Figure 9.3 Past Year First-Time Use of Drugs.

Drug	Numbers of first-time drug users (in thousands)
Marijuana	2839
Pain relievers	1223
Tranquilizers	950
LSD	859
Stimulants	734
Inhalants	678
Ecstasy	632
Cocaine	489
Sedatives	343
Heroin	103
PCP	52

Figure 9.4 Average Age of First Use of Drugs.

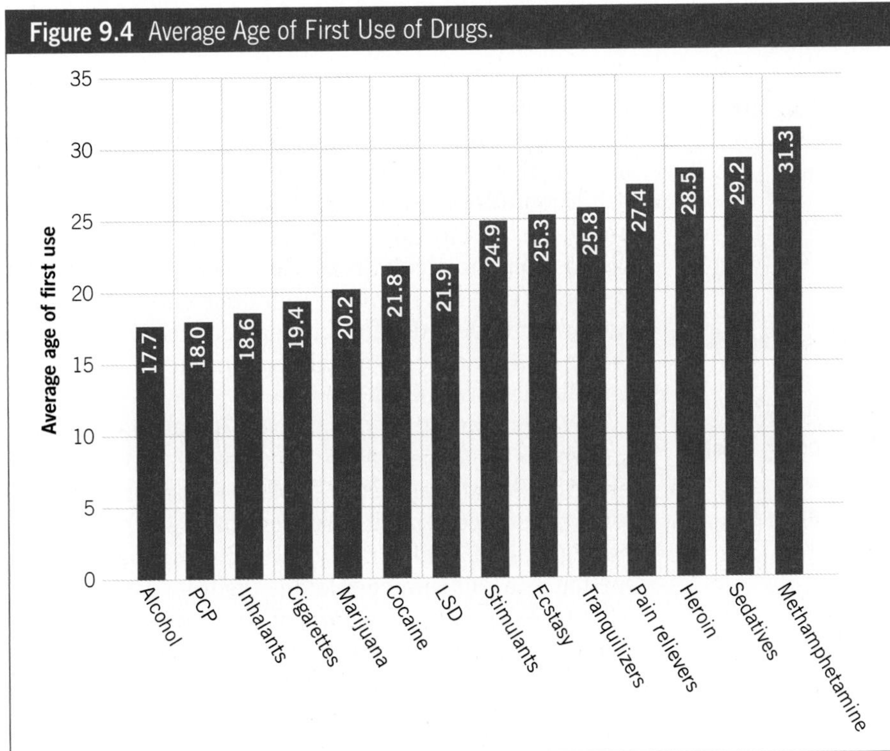

substance use disorder compared to people without a major depressive episode. People overusing one drug also commonly overuse another drug (polysubstance use). Such polysubstance use has increased substantially with respect to opioid use (Compton et al., 2021).

Stigma Associated with Substance-Related Disorders

LO 9.04 Describe the stigma associated with substance-related disorders and its impact on those with the disorders.

People with substance-related disorders often face social discrimination with respect to employment, housing, and interpersonal rejection. One survey of people with substance-related disorder revealed that many felt stigmatized. Many in the sample believed that once others knew of the person's substance problem, they treated them unfairly (60 percent) or were afraid of them (46 percent). Many in the sample also believed that some family members gave up on them (45 percent), some friends rejected them (38 percent), and employers paid them a lower wage (14 percent). Participants in the survey reported that hearing others say unfavorable or offensive things about people in treatment for substance use was a common stigmatizing experience. Others have found as well that stigma toward individuals with substance-related disorders negatively affects attempts to access treatment services (Luoma et al., 2014; van Boekel et al., 2013).

Several interventions have been designed to reduce stigma associated with substance-related disorders. These interventions often involve learning about substance-related disorders, accepting difficult feelings, emphasizing human connection and mutual acceptance, focusing more on the process of thinking (i.e., thinking about how thinking happens in the mind) rather than the content of negative thoughts, exploring goals and values in life, communicating positive stories of people with substance-related disorders, and boosting employment skills. Such interventions have been found effective for reducing self-stigma, shame, and social isolation among those with a substance-related disorder as well as improving public attitudes regarding this population (Earnshaw, 2020; Wogen & Restrepo, 2020).

Section Summary

- Substance-related disorders include substance use disorder, intoxication, and withdrawal.
- Substance use disorder refers to repeated use of substances that lead to recurring problems.
- Substance intoxication is a usually reversible condition brought on by excessive use of alcohol or another drug.
- Tolerance refers to the need to ingest greater amounts of a drug to achieve the same effect.
- Withdrawal refers to maladaptive behavioral and physiological changes when a person stops taking a drug.
- Substances may be categorized by the effect they have on people. Depressants inhibit the central nervous system, whereas stimulants activate the central nervous system.
- Opiates are drugs commonly used to relieve pain, and hallucinogens are drugs that cause psychosis-like symptoms.
- Marijuana works by stimulating cannabinoid brain receptors.
- Substance use is quite common, and substance-related disorders are among the most common mental disorders.
- People with substance-related disorders are often stigmatized via social discrimination with respect to employment, housing, and interpersonal rejection.

Review Questions

1. What is the difference between substance use and substance use disorder?
2. What is substance intoxication and withdrawal?
3. Identify major classes of drugs and their psychological effects.
4. Describe what to do if you ingest a date rape drug.
5. How common are substance-related disorders, and what populations are most at risk?

Substance-Related Disorders: Causes and Prevention

LO 9.05 Discuss the risk factors for and prevention of substance-related disorders.

Factors that cause substance-related disorders are covered next. Knowing about these factors might help us prevent substance-related disorders is also discussed.

Biological Risk Factors for Substance-Related Disorders

Biological risk factors in people with substance-related disorders include genetics, brain features, and neurochemical characteristics.

Genetics

Genetics influence substance-related disorders, especially alcoholism. The heritability estimate for alcoholism is about 0.50 (Deak & Johnson, 2021). Early family studies revealed that people whose family members overused alcohol were three to four times more likely to overuse alcohol themselves compared with people without such a family history. A problem with family studies, however, is that environmental influences could explain the effect. Children could be modeling parental misuse of alcohol instead of receiving a genetic predisposition for the problem. Genetic influences may be stronger for men than women and for severe compared with less severe cases of alcoholism. Alcoholism is likely predisposed by many genes working together (Blum et al., 2020).

Genetic models for alcoholism are modest, but variables *related to* alcoholism may have a stronger genetic effect. Genetics may affect a person's *metabolism* of alcohol—some people process alcohol faster than others and may be less susceptible to alcoholism (Sanchez-Roige et al., 2020). Genetics may also affect a person's *low response to alcohol* (Brenner et al., 2020). People with low response to alcohol must drink more to achieve the same psychological effects and may therefore be more at risk than the general population for alcoholism. Genetics may also affect the brain's neurochemistry to induce *craving* for alcohol or increase disinhibition and sensitivity to alcohol (refer to the neurochemical section later in the chapter; Biernacka et al., 2021).

What about other substances? Heritability appears strongest for dependence on cocaine, opiates, and nicotine (Maldonado et al., 2021). Relatives of people with substance-related disorders have been found to be eight times more likely than control participants to have a substance-related disorder themselves. This is especially true for cocaine. Many genes are likely responsible for this effect (Fernàndez-Castillo et al., 2022). Genes may influence receptors, such as opiate receptors, that increase responsiveness to certain drugs (Liu et al., 2021). Genes may also influence development of key brain structures implicated in substance-related disorders. These brain features are discussed next.

Brain Features

Many brain features link to substance-related disorders. Brain changes in substance-related disorders coincide with several inducements toward compulsive drug use: priming, drug cues, cravings, and stress (Fronk et al., 2020). *Priming* refers to a situation in which a single drug dose, such as a drink of alcohol or line of cocaine, leads to an uncontrollable binge. *Drug cues* refer to stimuli associated with drug use, such as friends, favorite hangouts, and other things that stimulate further drug use. *Cravings* refer to an obsessive drive for drug use, much as Elon had a consuming desire to seek and use drugs to the exclusion of almost all other activities. *Stress* is a common trigger of relapse in people with substance-related disorders. Recall that drug use is commonly associated with anxiety and depression.

Brain features related to each of these areas are primarily part of the **mesolimbic system**, a major dopamine pathway and one strongly implicated in sensations of pleasure, reward, and desire (refer to the neurochemical section later in the chapter). The mesolimbic system generally begins in the brain's *ventral tegmental area* and ends in the *nucleus accumbens* (refer to **Figure 9.5**). Drugs such as crack cocaine greatly stimulate this system and often lead to priming effects and intense cravings (Bittencourt et al., 2021). Continued drug use that stimulates the mesolimbic system can then become associated with certain cues such as a particular bar or group of friends that help perpetuate someone's addiction (Michaels et al., 2021).

The mesolimbic pathway links as well to other brain areas central to addiction (refer to **Figure 9.6**):

- *Amygdala*, which is involved in assigning a high "reward value" to stimuli, such as drugs, stress-induced pursuit of drug use, and conditioning place preferences for drug use, such as a particular area of town.

Figure 9.5 Mesolimbic Pathway in the Brain.

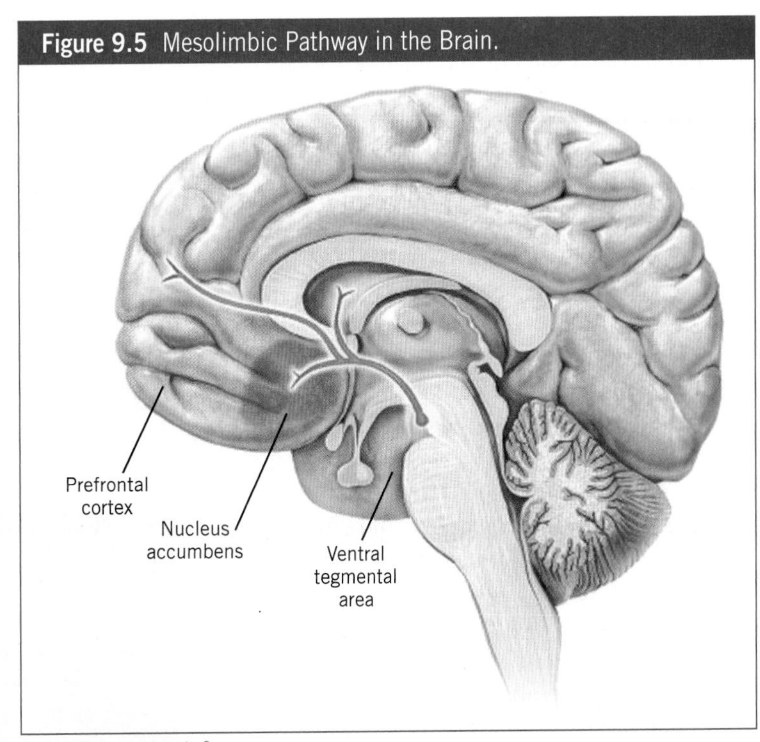

Figure 9.6 Major Brain Areas Implicated in Substance-Related Disorders.

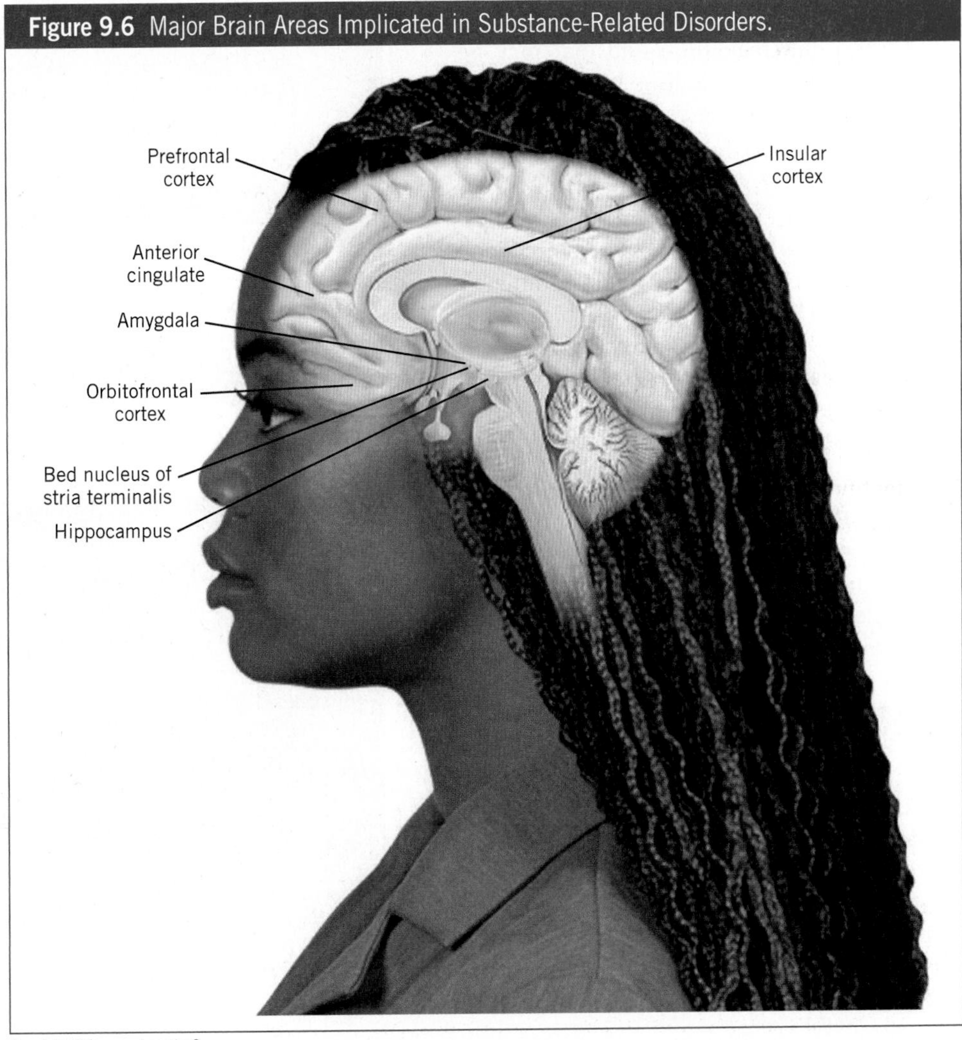

- *Anterior cingulate,* which is involved in self-control and problem solving and may be particularly relevant to emotional salience or excessive preoccupation with particular drugs.
- *Bed nucleus of the stria terminalis,* which you may recall from Chapter 5 is involved in stress reactions and may be involved in drug-seeking behavior to cope with stress. The amygdala and bed nucleus of the stria terminalis are key aspects of the hypothalamic-pituitary-adrenal axis that are implicated in anxiety-related disorders. This may help explain the high association of substance-related and anxiety-related disorders.
- *Hippocampus,* which is involved in acquiring new information and forming new memories and may be important for storing powerful memories of emotionally arousing stimuli such as drug use.
- *Insular cortex or insula,* which is involved in pain processing, and stimulation of which has been linked to drug craving.
- *Prefrontal cortex,* which is involved in upper-level cognitive processes such as control and regulation and that may be altered by drug use, thus leading to continued drug craving and use. The prefrontal cortex may also become extremely responsive to stimuli that predict drug availability.
- *Orbitofrontal cortex,* which is involved in decision making in unpredictable or uncertain situations and in which drug-induced changes could result in impulsive behavior, the latter clearly related to drug use, as described later in the section on personality (Ekhtari et al., 2021).

Neuroimaging studies support these findings. **Figure 9.7** illustrates a brain scan of a person with a history of excessive cocaine use and one with no such history. Blood flow to the prefrontal cortex, illustrated by brighter colors, diminishes in the person who uses a substance excessively. Euphoria often accompanies less activity in this area, so people may not engage in high-level thinking and reasoning while intoxicated. The prefrontal cortex does, however, become highly stimulated when surrounding stimuli predict drug availability, and this is likely due to a strong connection between the prefrontal cortex and the mesolimbic system. The result is someone who focuses intently on drug use and whose excitatory brain responses are not well controlled. Craving and drug-seeking behavior are enhanced but capability to reduce drug intake is impaired (Kang et al., 2022).

People who excessively use substances for long periods may also have reduced brain size and altered activity (refer to **Figure 9.8**; Little et al., 2021). This could lead to greater cognitive and memory decline

Figure 9.7 Brain Image of Person Who Uses Cocaine Excessively Compared with a Normal Control Participant.

Normal metabolic activity, indicated by bright red and yellow, is blunted in the person using drugs.

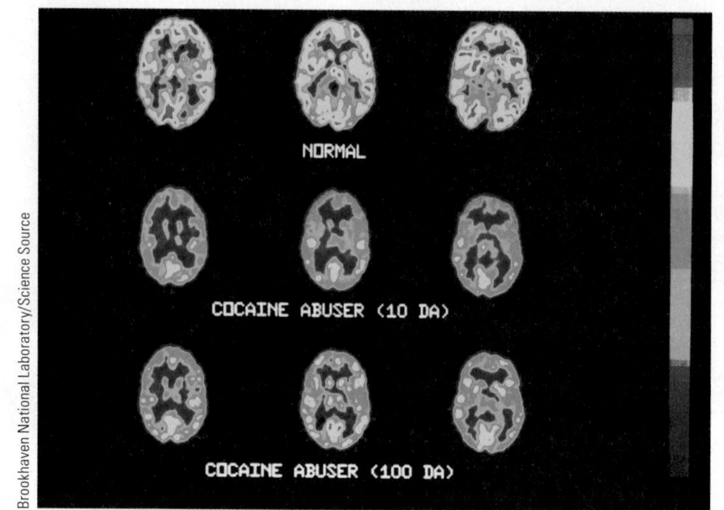

Figure 9.8 Brain Image of Person with Alcoholism Going Through Detoxification.

Alcohol is a depressant. Brain activity increases (yellow) with increasing time without alcohol.

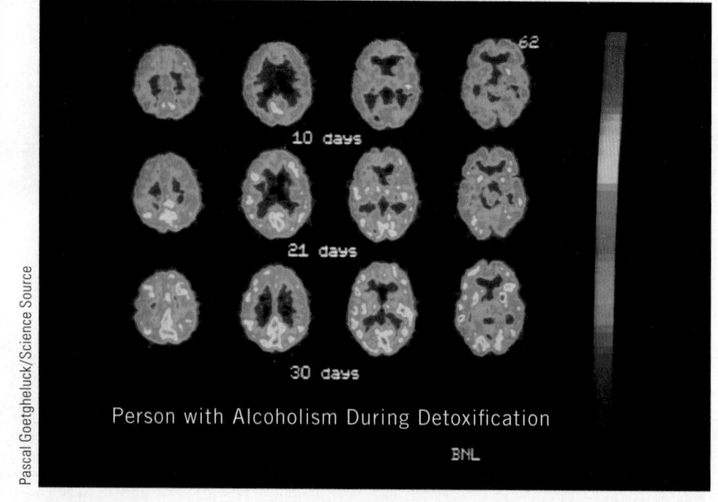

than is normal with age. Reduced brain size occurs in other heavily cognitive disorders discussed in this textbook, such as psychotic disorders (Chapter 12) and Alzheimer's disease (Chapter 14). Excessive alcohol use over time can also produce brain changes that lead to motor, visual, and speech problems.

Changes in brain function also occur in children with fetal alcohol syndrome whose mothers ingested alcohol during pregnancy. Damage to the corpus callosum, basal ganglia, and cerebellum can contribute to substantial cognitive and learning problems observed in this population (Inkelis et al., 2020). General reduction in brain size in newborns with fetal alcohol syndrome is evident as well (refer to **Figure 9.9**).

Neurochemical Features

The mesolimbic dopamine pathway appears to be the main neural base for the reinforcing effects of many drugs, especially alcohol, stimulants, opiates, and marijuana. These drugs increase dopamine release in the nucleus accumbens by stimulating *D2* (specialized dopamine) receptors or blocking reuptake of dopamine. Some people with substance-related disorders have fewer D2 receptors (Xi & Jordan, 2022). This means they may not be able to obtain much reward from everyday life events and so resort to excesses such as drug use to obtain sufficient rewards. This is known as **reward deficiency syndrome** (Blum et al., 2021).

Opiates like heroin and morphine act directly on opioid receptors in the nucleus accumbens as well as other areas of the brain and spinal cord. Excess dopamine release in the nucleus accumbens relates also to drug relapse and overwhelming drug-seeking behavior (Freels et al., 2020). Stress may activate the prefrontal cortex that, you may recall, has a strong connection to key components of the mesolimbic dopamine pathway: the ventral tegmental area and nucleus accumbens.

Other neurotransmitters influence substance-related disorders as well, but even these neural pathways affect dopamine release in the mesolimbic system. Glutamate, GABA, acetylcholine, serotonin, and norepinephrine have excitatory or inhibitory connections to the mesolimbic dopamine system (Blum et al., 2020). GABA appears to have an inhibitory effect on dopamine release in the mesolimbic system. Drugs that suppress this inhibitory effect, therefore, such as alcohol or morphine, may thus help stimulate dopamine release (Vialichko et al., 2021). Keep in mind that much of these data come from animal studies, so extrapolating results to humans may be problematic.

Dopamine release acts as a powerful reward (euphoria), thus providing an incentive to increase and maintain drug use. Dopamine release also promotes reward-related learning so a person is often seeking rewards such as drugs (Galaj & Ranaldi, 2021). Such conditioning or learning might explain Elon's extremely driven behavior toward seeking and using methamphetamine. Over time, the reward system becomes specifically attuned to availability of specific drugs. This helps explain why people abstinent from a drug for many years can quickly relapse toward excessive drug use.

Figure 9.9 Brain Damage to a Newborn with Fetal Alcohol Syndrome Compared with a Normal Control.

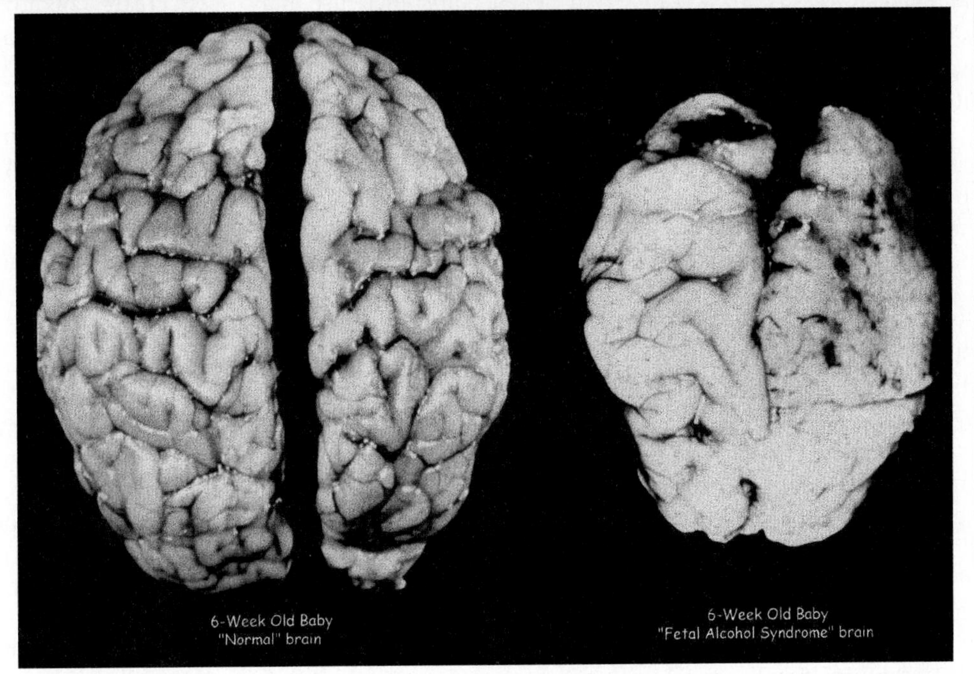

Environmental Risk Factors for Substance-Related Disorders

Environmental risk factors for substance-related disorders are covered next. These include stress, cognitive factors, learning, personality factors, and family factors. Cultural and evolutionary influences are also discussed.

Wavebreakmedia Micro/Fotolia LLC

People often engage in substance use to relieve stress and depression.

Stress

Stress is an important trigger for many of the mental disorders discussed in this textbook; for substance-related disorders, this is especially true. Stress can clearly trigger substance use, such as when people have a glass of wine to relax, smoke a cigarette to unwind, or snort a line of cocaine to enhance mood. Recall that people with anxiety and depression often engage in substance use to cope with stressors such as interacting with others and feeling miserable. Ongoing use of substances to cope with stressors can lead to a pattern of overuse. Excessive substance use is closely associated with early physical and sexual maltreatment, less parental and social support, and chronic distress (Mitchell et al., 2022).

Stress is important as well regarding relapse toward substance-related disorders, as when a person has been abstinent for some time but regresses back to old drinking or drug-using habits. **Stress-induced relapse** involves an activation of certain brain substances related to stress, such as corticotropin-releasing hormone and cortisol, that help us cope but also increase dopamine activity in the mesolimbic pathway. Stress also increases norepinephrine, which helps stimulate key components of the mesolimbic pathway: the bed nucleus of the stria terminalis, nucleus accumbens, and amygdala (Snyder & Silberman, 2021). Environmental stress thus triggers dual responses in the brain: coping and desire for reward. Stress may enhance drug relapse in other key ways as well. Increased glutamate from stress may produce a state of sadness from dopamine depletion to trigger cravings for increased dopamine by using drugs (Abdullah et al., 2022). Chronic stress may also weaken a person's ability to cope effectively with difficult situations by creating damage to the prefrontal cortex (Zhao et al., 2021). A person's ability to sustain attention, recall appropriate coping skills learned in therapy, and inhibit maladaptive responses such as drinking and driving may be impaired.

Cognitive Factors

Recall that *cognitive distortions* are erroneous beliefs one has about oneself and the surrounding world that can lead to maladjustment. Cognitive distortions can be a part of substance-related disorders. One common misperception among people with substance-related disorders is increased *positive expectancies* about effects of various substances and minimization of negative effects (Mason et al., 2020). A person may discount or dispute the addictive qualities of a drug and claim "I can stop anytime I want." Some people may also believe that using certain substances will lead to enhanced personal or social functioning. A person may falsely believe that drug use will increase social skill with others or with accomplishments at work. College students often have positive expectancies regarding alcohol use, including enhanced sociability, courage, sexuality, and calmness (Ramirez et al., 2020).

Recall from Chapter 3 that another misperception among many people with substance-related disorders, especially college students, is that other people use alcohol and other drug amounts similar or in excess to their own (Graupensperger et al., 2021). Such a misperception seemed evident for Kevin and Elon, who felt their initial drinking was in line with the typical college experience. Such misperception, however, reinforces a person's belief that their drinking or other drug use is not a problem. People with alcoholism also selectively attend to cues that indicate alcohol is nearby, such as encountering a favorite drinking buddy (Todd et al., 2022).

Cognitions affect substance use, but consider also that severe substance use may itself create cognitive changes by altering the prefrontal cortex. Alcohol and other drugs can create massive changes in the brain that affect attention, perception, judgment, memory, problem solving, decision making, and other higher cognitive processes. People with alcoholism often have *blackouts*, in which they remember nothing during a period of heavy drinking, or *grayouts*, in which they can remember events during a heavy period of drinking only when someone reminds them of what happened or if they drink heavily again (Boness et al., 2022).

Learning

Recall from Chapter 5 that classical and operant conditioning can impact anxiety disorders. These learning processes also apply to substance-related disorders. Classical conditioning essentially refers to learning by association, and many people with substance-related disorders associate certain environmental cues with drug use. If a person often uses methamphetamine with friends at a local park, they are more likely in the future to use the drug when surrounded by these cues. Treatment for substance use disorder can thus be difficult—a person may become sober but then relapse quickly when they return to places where cues for substance use are strong.

A stunning example of classical conditioning was the large-scale remission of heroin addiction by Vietnam veterans. Many Vietnam-based soldiers were thought addicted to heroin, spurring concern about what would happen when they returned to the United States. Remarkably, however, the addiction rate in these soldiers dropped considerably after they came home. One explanation is that cues surrounding heroin use—such as intense stress, completely different geography, and certain peer groups—disappeared once the soldiers returned home. However, many of these veterans continued to experience other problems such as PTSD (Blosnich et al., 2022).

Drug use can be rewarding, of course, and therefore maintained by operant conditioning. Recall that reward centers of the brain are highly stimulated by drug use and people can become particularly vulnerable to drug-conditioned stimuli. Positive reinforcers of drug use include fitting in with peers, a sense of euphoria and invulnerability, and feelings of sexual prowess, as was true for Elon. Drug use can also serve as a powerful *negative reinforcer* in that stress, pressure, depression, and withdrawal symptoms recede. Negative reinforcers serve as strong indicators of craving and relapse (Pahng & Edwards, 2021). Furthermore, the negative effects or punishers of drug use are often distant. People who smoke cigarettes enjoy the immediate sense of relief and relaxation but may worry little about far-off consequences such as lung cancer and emphysema (a lung disease marked by damage to air sacs and difficulty breathing).

Personality Factors

A personality trait closely related to substance-related disorder, one discussed in Chapter 3, is *impulsivity.* Impulsivity generally refers to risk taking, lack of planning, chaotic lifestyle, desire for immediate gratification, and explosiveness. Impulsive sensation seeking is particularly associated with heavy substance use in adolescents (Waddell et al., 2022).

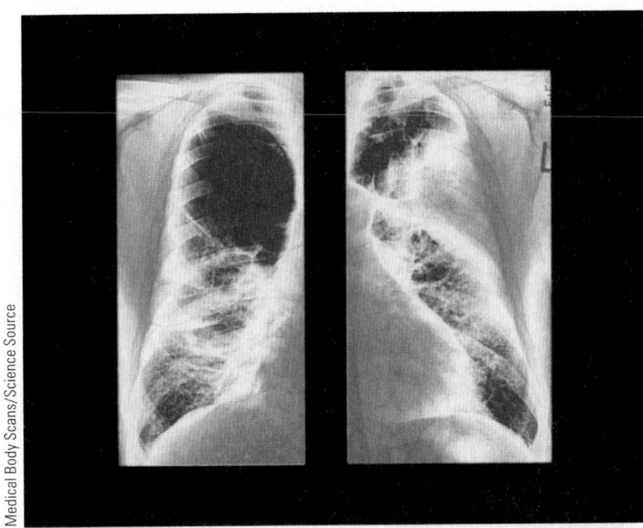

Medical Body Scans/Science Source

A long-term consequence often minimized by smokers is emphysema. Color enhanced frontal X-ray of the chest showing emphysema. The lungs are colorized blue. A large cavity (right) is infected and filled with fluid.

Researchers have also linked substance use disorder and impulsive aggression in general with domestic violence, violent crime, and suicide in particular. Knowing which comes first, however, substance use or violence, has not been clearly established (refer to **Focus On Violence: Alcohol and Violence**). *Psychopathy* also relates closely to substance-related disorders. Psychopathy refers to antisocial behavior, lack of remorse for aggressive behavior, and need for immediate gratification. People with addictions are generally less likely to inhibit their behavior and delay gratification (Yan et al., 2021). People with psychopathy or substance use disorder may also react quickly or impulsively to stressors by aggressively facing a perceived threat and/or by using drugs to cope with a threat. Certain brain changes may also be similar in both groups (da Costa Azevedo et al., 2022).

Focus On Violence

Alcohol and Violence

Alcohol and violence go hand in hand. According to the U.S. Centers for Disease Control and Prevention (CDC), approximately 40 percent of violent and nonviolent crimes were committed under the influence of alcohol, and 40 percent of people convicted of rape and sexual assault claimed they were under the influence of alcohol at the time of the crime. Furthermore, 72 percent of college campus rapes occur when victims are too intoxicated to consent to or refuse sex. Nearly 50 percent of child maltreatment cases are associated with parental drug use, and two thirds of victims of domestic violence say alcohol was involved in the violent incident. About 23 percent of suicide deaths are attributable to alcohol as well. Among assailants at an emergency room, alcohol was involved in more than half of cases.

Less information is available as to the direction of these effects. Drinking alcohol may precede domestic assault but may also follow marital or other relationship problems. Other factors are also present, such as other mental disorder, access to weapons, and stress. Still, research studies as well as media reports of extreme cases of domestic violence do point to alcohol misuse as a substantial contributing factor. In particular, the intensity of domestic violence is greater when the offender is intoxicated compared to when the offender is not (Sontate et al., 2021). Whatever the direction, the close link between alcohol use and violence clearly indicates the need for extensive education and prevention.

iStock.com/LeonidKos

Impulsivity is a key personality trait associated with substance-related disorders.

Family Factors

Family factors play an important role in the onset and maintenance of substance-related disorders. Children of parents with substance-related disorders are much more likely than the general population to use substances themselves. Having a parent who smokes is also associated with greater risk of smoking among adolescents (Zhao et al., 2021). Children raised in homes where parents smoke are also at increased risk for health problems associated with secondhand smoke, such as chronic ear infections, asthma, bronchitis, fire-related injuries, and *sudden infant death syndrome* (Bednarczuk et al., 2020).

Substance use in adolescents also increases with permissive parent attitudes about drug use, particularly cigarette smoking and alcohol use (Mehanović et al., 2022).Parent permissiveness can impact drinking among college students as well (Waldron et al., 2021). Other family factors related to increased risk include parent psychopathology and conflict (Ballester et al., 2020; Zhang et al., 2020). Conversely, protective factors include parental warmth and responsiveness as well as parental control marked by shaping acceptable behaviors, setting explicit rules, and providing adequate supervision (Trucco, 2020).

The popular media are especially enamored of one particular family factor involved in substance-related disorders: **codependency**. Codependency generally refers to dysfunctional behaviors that partners, children, and others engage in to cope with the stress of having a family member with a substance-related disorder. Codependency can involve intense care of a person with a substance-related disorder to the detriment of one's own health. Partners and children of a father with alcoholism may constantly help him to bed or call his workplace to explain his absence. Family members thus inadvertently reward—or *enable*—the behavior of the person with alcoholism. People in codependent relationships may also feel responsible for a person's substance problem and tightly control their relationships with others to avoid rejection. Codependent relationships are thus generally considered unhealthy.

Do children whose parents use drugs excessively have significant problems later in adulthood? Much of the literature has focused on children of parents with alcoholism, and the answer to this question seems to be yes, to some extent. Adult children of parents with alcoholism are at greater risk for excessive substance use, antisocial behavior such as aggression, anxiety-related disorders and distress, depression, low self-esteem, and difficult family relationships. However, these results do not apply to all adult children of parents with alcoholism—especially women—many of whom show resilience (Ossola et al., 2021). The latter findings raise questions about the validity and utility of the concept of codependency.

Cultural Factors

Recall that rates of substance use disorder are more even among various racial and ethnic groups but higher among American Indians/Alaska Natives. The reasons why some American Indians/Alaska Natives have such high rates of substance-related disorder is not completely clear. Substance use disorder in this population may be associated with higher rates of trauma and homelessness as well as less access to treatment services (Ramos et al., 2021). Members of ethnic minority communities may also be at greater risk for *severe consequences* from drug use, especially in situations involving injection, incarceration, and easier access to alcohol and other drugs (Mital et al., 2020).

Rates of alcohol consumption and alcoholism also differ around the world. Attitudes toward drinking and whether members of a culture commonly engage in heavy drinking have much to do with these differences. Some cultures integrate alcohol into daily life and meals, as occurs in Mediterranean nations. Other cultures exemplify more abstinence to alcohol and less daily consumption. One group of cultures with historically low rates of alcoholism is in Asia and, in particular, Japan, China, and Korea. Asians are more predisposed to facial flushing and other unpleasant physical reactions when drinking alcohol, which tends to suppress desire for alcohol

(Yokoyama et al., 2021). Facial flushing and sensitivity to alcohol relate to elevated levels of acetaldehyde, a metabolite of alcohol. Among Asians, genetic predispositions may cause acetaldehyde to generate quickly and remain in the body for longer periods. This process produces and prolongs unpleasant physical reactions and may thus provide greater protection from alcoholism. Others, however, have not found this to be so, and rates of alcoholism have increased in certain parts of Asia such as Taiwan (Lee et al., 2021).

Evolutionary Influences

Some have proposed evolutionary theories for substance-related disorders. One evolutionary theory is that the mesolimbic dopamine system is not strictly a reward-based system but one intricately involved in survival motivation. People who view chemical substances as threats to their reproductive ability may avoid these substances, whereas people who view chemical substances as boosting their reproductive ability may be more accepting of these substances (Laksmidewi & Soejitno, 2021). Some people such as Elon engage in alcohol and other substance use because they believe it will enhance their social desirability and attractiveness to others.

Another evolutionary view of addiction is that individuals within societies generally pursue positions of dominance and submission to maintain social order. Some advantages to submission exist, such as avoiding aggressive behavior, but such a position also causes stress because one can be excluded from group resources at any time. Coping with such stress may involve drug use. Submission may also lead to a socially dependent relationship with a dominant individual, which may cause maltreatment and subsequent feelings of depression assuaged by substance use (Giacolini et al., 2021).

Causes of Substance-Related Disorders

Substance-related disorders are quite complicated in terms of risk factors that help cause the problems. To arrange risk factors into a general model of addiction, many theorists and researchers adopt a biopsychosocial approach that incorporates aspects of the *diathesis-stress model* discussed for other disorders. Biological factors may predispose a person toward substance use, and environmental factors may trigger this predisposition to produce a substance-related disorder. We may eventually need different theories of cause because many kinds of substance-related disorders may exist.

Comprehensive models of addiction often divide biological and environmental risk factors into distal or proximal ones. **Distal factors** are background factors that indirectly affect a person and can generally contribute to a mental disorder. Biological distal factors with respect to substance-related disorders include genetic predisposition and perhaps temperaments such as an impulsive personality. Environmental distal factors include problematic family relationships, parental drug use, and early learning and drug experiences.

Proximal factors are more immediate factors that directly affect a person and more specifically contribute to a mental disorder. Biological proximal factors include activation of the mesolimbic dopamine pathway upon drug use. Environmental proximal factors include stress, depression, peer pressure, positive expectancies about substance use, and availability of substances. Proximal factors may also include consequences of drug use, both positive (e.g., enhanced mood and relief from stress) and negative (e.g., ill physical effects and occupational and legal troubles).

Some of these factors interact to propel a person toward substance use disorder (refer to **Figure 9.10**). Recall that craving for substances often involves selective attention to cues that remind a person of drug use. This selective attention also appears to have a biological basis in that dopamine is released from brain features of the mesolimbic pathway. This highly rewarding event further reinforces a person's drug-seeking behavior (Corkrum & Araque, 2021). Ongoing stress in a person's life may also lead to long-term excessive alcohol use that creates changes in the prefrontal cortex. These brain changes can then help produce even more stress as a person's memory and concentration falter and can lead to even greater focus on obtaining rewarding substances. Key neuronal and other brain changes can also make a person particularly sensitive to craving and desire for future drug use (Liu et al., 2021).

Various factors seemed to set the stage for Elon's excessive alcohol and other drug use. His distal biological risk factors included an impulsive personality and high

BananaStock/Jupiter Images

Family factors are associated with substance-related disorders.

Figure 9.10 Sample Causal Model of Substance-Related Disorder.

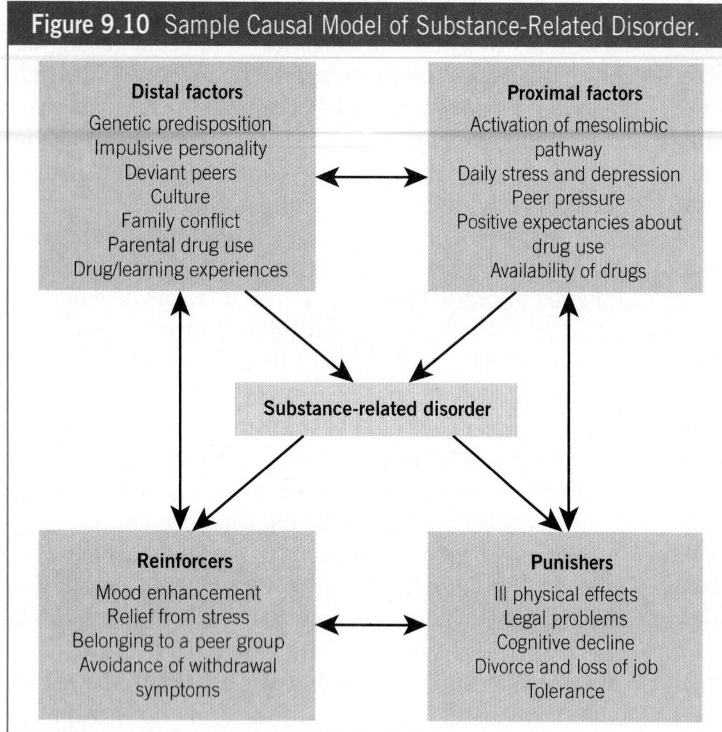

levels of arousal assuaged by alcohol use. A family history of alcoholism may have been present as well. Proximal risk factors included entry into college and substantial stress following intense academic demands. Elon also greatly enjoyed the pleasurable aspects of sex and drug use and was clearly exciting key areas of the brain such as the mesolimbic pathway. Elon later expanded and increased his drug use and engaged in drug-seeking behavior. Many people with substance-related disorders experience a phenomenon they describe as *rock-bottom*, meaning their brain function and behavior are almost singularly geared toward seeking and using drugs. Such devastating effects underscore the need for prevention, and these efforts are described next.

Prevention of Substance-Related Disorders

Given the significant personal and health-based consequences of extended drug use, prevention efforts for substance-related disorders have received much attention. Prevention efforts include those for adults as well as those for children and adolescents. Recall from Chapter 3, the discussion of a prevention program sponsored by the University of Missouri's Wellness Resource Center. Program components included promoting responsible decision making and providing accurate information about alcohol consumption by college students. Once misperceptions are corrected about the extent and acceptability of student drinking, binge and heavy drinking can decline (refer to **Focus on College Students: Substance Use**).

Prevention programs also aim to reduce alcohol and other drug intake in pregnant mothers to prevent fetal alcohol effects in newborns. These programs focus on screening for alcohol and other drug use, educating mothers about ill effects of such use, managing stress and reducing depression, increasing social support, and visiting the mother's home (Erng et al., 2020). Similar techniques help reduce excessive substance use among older people, health care professionals, hospital patients, victims and perpetrators of violence, and people with comorbid mental disorders (Afuseh et al., 2020; Grella et al., 2021). Other prevention programs target children and adolescents and often focus on:

- Reducing availability of illegal drugs
- Increasing legal consequences for drug use
- School-related media programs to educate youth and change drug-related attitudes
- Programs to increase work and leisure opportunities to deflect youths from drug-seeking opportunities
- Peer-based programs to enhance methods of declining offers to use drugs

Focus On College Students

Substance Use

Treatment for college students with drinking problems is relatively successful. Many programs use motivational interviewing, alcohol education, normative comparisons, and moderation strategies. Programs tailored to college students also include changing positive expectancies about alcohol use and increased use of designated drivers. Most studies reveal significant improvements in alcohol-related knowledge, attitudes toward drinking, normative beliefs about drinking, and intentions to reduce alcohol intake. Motivational interviewing with personalized feedback about one's drinking also seems especially effective for people who drink more heavily (Mun et al., 2022).

Treatment for problematic drinking in college students is important given the substantial negative consequences that can result. One group of researchers surveyed hundreds of college students about drinking behavior, social and physically pleasurable alcohol expectancies, and sexual victimization. Sexual victimization was generally associated with child sexual maltreatment, hooking up more often, and heavier drinking. Greater alcohol expectancies were associated with sexual victimization in women, including forced sexual contact or intercourse, and especially those in sororities. In addition, men who hooked up more often and had close friends who consumed much alcohol were more likely to drink heavily and experience sexual victimization (Tyler et al., 2015). Beliefs that alcohol will increase happiness or power, and heavy drinking subsequently, can thus lead to many damaging consequences.

Universal efforts to prevent substance use disorder often target the public. Examples include raising the minimum drinking age, lowering the legal limit for defining driving while impaired, airing antidrug commercials, banning advertisements for tobacco in some media, engaging in drug testing in the workplace, and implementing heavy taxation on alcohol and tobacco products. The general effectiveness of these policies for reducing drug use, especially for children and adolescents, has been relatively modest, however (O'Connor et al., 2020).

A controversial approach to preventing extended health problems in those addicted to drugs is to reduce needle sharing by supplying new, clean needles or syringes. *Needle exchange* or *harm reduction programs* provide unused needles and syringes to intravenous drug users, cleansing materials such as bleach or skin ointment, education about communicable diseases such as HIV, and access to mental health services. Some criticize needle exchange programs for potentially maintaining excessive drug use habits, but the programs can help reduce bloodborne diseases and risk factors associated with drug use (Taylor et al., 2021).

Relapse prevention is also a key way of reducing further drug use in someone with a substance-related disorder. Relapse prevention involves reducing exposure to alcohol and other drugs, improving motivation to continue abstinence, self-monitoring daily mood and tempting situations, recognizing and coping appropriately with drug cravings, reducing anxiety and depression, modifying unrealistic thoughts about drug use, and developing a crisis plan if alcohol or other drugs are used again (Ramadas et al., 2021). Medication to reduce the pleasurable nature of a specific drug and regular attendance at self-help group meetings may also be useful for relapse prevention (refer to the later treatment section). Relapse prevention strategies can be effective for delaying time to substance reuse, though some people with substance-related disorders require continuing care interventions (McKay, 2021).

Section Summary

- Biological risk factors for substance-related disorders include genetic contributions, especially for metabolism, low response to alcohol, and craving.
- Brain features implicated in substance-related disorders are those closely linked to the mesolimbic pathway and primarily include the amygdala, anterior cingulate, bed nucleus of the stria terminalis, and prefrontal cortex.
- Neurochemical features implicated in substance-related disorders primarily involve dopamine release from the mesolimbic pathway.
- Stress is a major environmental trigger for excessive substance use and often leads to relapse.
- Cognitive factors—especially positive expectancies about substance use—help increase substance use.
- Classical and operant conditioning are important learning processes implicated in substance-related disorders.
- Impulsive personality and related traits can predispose some people toward substance use disorder.
- Family factors such as conflict can be predictors of later substance use disorder and perhaps codependent relationships.
- Some cultural differences with respect to drug use are present, but the reasons for these differences remain unclear.
- Evolutionary theories of substance use include enhancement of reproductive fitness and easing anxiety and depression from difficult relationships.
- The cause of substance-related disorders is likely complicated and involves several proximal and distal factors and reinforcers.
- Prevention of substance-related disorder can occur at the adult level, as with relapse prevention, or at the youth level to prevent excessive drug use before it begins.

Review Questions

1. Describe data that support a genetic contribution to substance-related disorders.
2. What key brain and neurochemical changes relate to substance-related disorders?
3. Describe cognitive and learning factors associated with substance use.
4. How do personality and family factors help cause substance-related disorders?
5. Describe an overall causal model for substance-related disorders.
6. What factors might be important for preventing substance-related disorders?

Substance-Related Disorders: Assessment and Treatment

LO 9.06 Characterize the assessment and treatment of individuals with substance-related disorders.

Substance-related disorders are among the most harmful mental disorders discussed in this textbook. The disorders can devastate an entire family (refer to **Personal Narrative: One Family's Struggle with Substance-Related Disorders**). The accurate assessment and effective treatment of these disorders is therefore critical. The next sections cover key methods, such as interviews, psychological testing, observations from others, and laboratory testing, to assess substance-related disorders.

Personal Narrative

One Family's Struggle with Substance-Related Disorders

The Father

I dreamed that my daughter, Carrick, was perched on the edge of a dock on a lake. I stood behind her. As she slipped into the water, it dawned on me that she was taking a swimming test and I was the only one observing her. Her back arched and her arms plunged in a graceful butterfly stroke, but her head did not emerge. Her skin suddenly blanched, and I sensed she was in trouble. I jumped into the gray chop, landing beyond where her efforts had carried her. As I faced her, she sank feet first, her long hair swirling in the water. She was just inches away but it seemed an infinite distance. I felt responsible, as if my thinking that she might drown made it happen. I wanted to change the direction the dream was taking, but couldn't do it. I knew she would plunge faster than I could dive after her, and that I would not be able to bring her to the surface even if I managed to catch her.

I woke up. My chest felt raw and empty, as if my ribcage had been ripped open. At first I thought the dream was about my feeling that I have something to lose again. But as I've thought about it, I realize that my subconscious was confirming what I've learned the hard way. I cannot "save" my daughter. If she wants, I can only try to help her learn to swim. When it comes to addiction, that's all anybody can do.

Thom Forbes, Father

For several years, I've lived with the specter of my daughter killing herself. It haunted me whenever the phone rang at a time when it didn't normally, or if a holiday passed without our having heard from her, or when I saw or heard Deirdre, my wife, weeping. However her death happened—a heroin overdose, hypothermia, murder, suicide, AIDS—I knew I would have to find the words to express what had happened, and why.

Carrick started smoking marijuana when she was 12 years old, and worked her way to a heroin addiction by 17. She sees her drug dependencies, as do I, as the inevitable outcome of genes and other influences. We have had a trying journey. When Carrick was using drugs, she often overwhelmed Deirdre, our son Duncan, and me—individually and collectively. We all have different ways of coping. My way has been to try to find some connections to the experiences of others. And so, as part of this journey, I have been writing *The Elephant on Main Street: An Interactive Memoir of Addictions,* which became a website (www.elephantonmain.com).

Courtesy of Thom Forbes

Thanksgiving Day was the first that Carrick spent at home in five years. Four years earlier, she was in a wilderness therapy program in the high desert of Utah. Three years earlier, she was living on the streets of Philadelphia with a lost soul who called himself Chaos Destruction. Two years earlier, she was hanging with Pete, who had just been released from state prison for drug dealing. She and Pete were either incarcerated on Riker's Island or about to be—she was so strung out on heroin and cocaine that one day blended into the next.

After Thanksgiving dinner, our 15-year-old son Duncan surprised us with a box of chocolates and a greeting card. He wrote: "Mom, Dad, Carrick, Pete. I love you guys all. We stick through the hardest times as a family." That's what this small piece of the narrative is all about: sticking together through the hardest times—and telling the story.

The Mother

I have alcoholism, which has been in remission since I had my last drink. My husband, to whom I have been married almost 30 years, is in recovery and has been sober for many years. My father was a high-functioning alcoholic, and my 21-year-old daughter is in recovery, having suffered an addiction to heroin, since the age of 17. When I was 10 years sober, I developed severe treatment-resistant major depression. I took refuge in sleep, finding even routine activities too overwhelming to accomplish. There seemed no reason to continue living. Suicidal ideation filled my waking hours. Eventually I was hospitalized. After electroconvulsive therapy, a uniquely designed regimen of antidepressant medications, and talk therapy, I began down another road to recovery.

Today I feel better than I ever have about waking up in the morning and facing life's challenges and joys. I've concluded that I want to devote the remainder of my working life to battling the effect of chemical dependency, which often coexists with mental disorder, on individuals, families, and communities. I want people to know the damage addiction and mental

Courtesy of Thom Forbes

Deirdre Forbes, Mother

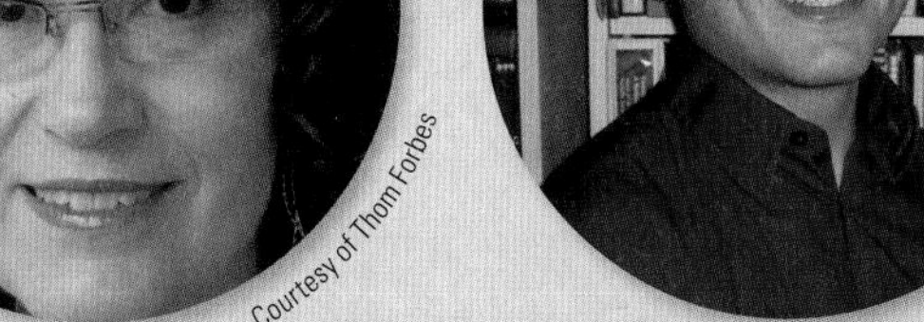

Courtesy of Thom Forbes

Duncan Forbes, Brother

disorder can do, but I also want them to see and understand that recovery works. I want people to see I am unusual only because I am part of a minority who speak out about their recovery, not because I am in recovery. Stigma and discrimination keep many in recovery from doing so.

The Child and Brother

Being the ghost child wasn't that bad in the beginning of the drama between Carrick and my parents. I had freedom really; I got to do whatever I wanted. Like a ghost, I was there but no one really saw me. But I didn't realize that why I was so free was because all of the attention was on my sister. I didn't care at all because everything was going fine for me. I didn't care . . . not yet.

There were times where my sister's problems wouldn't bother me at all, but then there would be other times where I would be in the middle of an argument and be overwhelmed with the drama and tension between my parents and my sister. All I wanted to do was just to walk away from it, let them deal with the problem because hey, it doesn't concern me, it's not my problem, it's Carrick's problem. Or so I thought. But it became my problem, too, in at least four ways:

Money. As the problem got worse, Carrick started asking me for money. Most of the time I would give it to her because I wanted to be a good little brother and I wanted to help her out. Then my parents told me she was just using the money to buy drugs. That's when I just felt like punching a wall. I felt like I should have known why she wanted the money so badly. When I stopped giving her money, she started stealing from me. Then she would deny stealing from me, and that's when Carrick's problem started becoming my problem.

Sleep. There were some nights when my sister and my parents would just argue throughout the whole night, nonstop yelling, and I couldn't sleep at all. They would argue on school nights, and I just wanted to get the hell out of there.

Communication. I could barely talk with my parents because they were always mindful of my sister. If I asked them to do something for me, they would just say things like "Well, after when Carrick comes home," or "I have to take Carrick somewhere." It was always "Carrick, Carrick, Carrick."

Random fights on small things. Sometimes fights would start about the most random things, like television shows. After the problem was resolved, I usually realized it wasn't clean Carrick who was arguing with me over television, it was the mean Carrick, who was high, fighting with me.

I didn't really understand how serious my sister's problem was until I grew older. During her downfall, I thought she was just in a little trouble that wouldn't have a giant effect on her future, and that the problem would eventually go away. As we grew up, and Carrick started controlling her problem and pushing herself to go to school, the attention started shifting toward me. They were afraid that I might head down the wrong road and might end up messing up my life. When I'd go out with my friends, they asked questions like "who, what, when, why, where?" I have to admit; I guess those antidrug commercials really do work for parents.

Overall, Carrick's problem didn't just concern her. It concerned the whole family. Anyone's actions in the family will certainly affect another person's life. A family is like a chain. If you break the chain, you break the family. We all depend on each other. We all need each other.

I also learned a lot from this problem. I'm able to help out people in my school who might have similar problems, or who might be heading down the wrong road. I think I got a lot smarter when it comes to drugs and drinking.

After seeing what drugs have done to my sister, mentally and physically, it gives me a perfect reason to say "No." I'm thankful that I don't have to learn what trouble drugs can cause by doing them. I can just look at what they did to my sister. After all I've been through, I feel like a better man who is able to make the right decisions.

I guess if it weren't for Carrick, I probably wouldn't have any reason not to try drugs or drink. But I'm thankful for my sister, because I have learned so much from her. And I realized that anyone who has a problem in a family always affects someone else in the family.

Source: Used with permission.

Interviews

Interviews are a frequent means of assessing many mental disorders. Common types of interviews for substance-related disorders include screening interviews and motivational interviews. **Screening interviews** are specifically designed to assess recent and lifetime problems with respect to substance use. One commonly used screening interview is the *Addiction Severity Index*. The *ASI* contains structured questions about medical status, employment, social support, alcohol and other drug use, and legal, family, and psychiatric status. Composite scores from the measure are good predictors of substance use disorder (Denis et al., 2013).

Motivational interviewing is an assessment and treatment strategy that involves obtaining information about a person's substance-related problem *and* providing feedback to help increase their readiness for change. An interviewer provides empathy, illustrates discrepancies between what a person is currently doing and what their long-term goals are, and helps a person believe change is possible. Clinicians who use motivational interviewing ask open-ended questions, listen and reflect information carefully, provide treatment choices, outline problems associated with current drug use, support a person's statements about wanting to change, and set specific treatment goals. A motivational interviewer actively gives advice and reinforces a person's willingness to change current behavior. Motivational interviewing is effective at reducing alcohol consumption (Santa Ana et al., 2021).

Psychological Testing

Therapists also use psychological tests to screen and assess for drug use. A well-known test is the *Minnesota Multiphasic Personality Inventory* (MMPI-3) discussed in Chapter 4. The MMPI-3 has a subscale for substance abuse that involves current and past misuse of alcohol and other drugs (Whitman et al., 2021). Another scale discussed at more length in Chapter 10 is the *Millon Clinical Multiaxial Inventory—IV*. This scale assesses personality disorders but has two subscales for alcohol use and drug use. Items on these subscales center on behaviors associated with substance use that can help predict risk for such use (Sellbom et al., 2022).

Other common screening measures include the Michigan Alcoholism Screening Test and the CAGE. These scales are particularly useful for assessing recent and severe use of alcohol. The *Michigan Alcohol Screening Test* is a 24-item measure of drinking habits, interpersonal and legal problems related to drinking, and treatment for alcoholism. The *CAGE* is a four-item measure that includes variations of the following questions. Answering yes to two or more of these questions relates to greater risk for substance use disorder (Brousse et al., 2014):

- Have you ever felt you needed to **C**ut down on your drinking?
- Have people **A**nnoyed you by criticizing your drinking?
- Have you ever felt bad or **G**uilty about your drinking?
- Have you ever felt you need a drink first thing in the morning (**E**ye-opener) to steady your nerves or get rid of a hangover?

Observations from Others

Excessive drug use is often a hidden problem, and many people do not accurately report their alcohol or other drug use. Therapists may thus conduct observations and solicit reports from others. Family members, partners, coworkers, and friends can help monitor a person's behavior and report days missed from work, time away from home, family arguments over drug use, and binges, among other things. This must be done with great care and with knowledge and consent of the person with a substance-related disorder. Observations like these are often part of family therapy for people with substance-related disorders (refer to the section on treatment later in the chapter).

Laboratory Testing

Laboratory tests involve analyzing urine, blood, breath, hair, saliva, or sweat to detect recent drug use. Potential employers and drug treatment facilities often use these measures to determine abstinence from drugs. *Urine screens* are perhaps the most common laboratory measure of recent substance use, though periods of detection differ by drug (refer to **Table 9.10**). Some drugs such as phencyclidine can be detected as much as eight days after use, but other drugs such as alcohol cannot be detected past 10 hours.

Urine screens detect presence or absence of certain drugs and are a good initial screening method. A downside of urine screens is the prevalence of wrong results, so the tests may precede other laboratory measures. Urine screens consist of the following processes:

- *Chromatography* separates chemicals into their individual components.
- *Spectrometry* identifies exact molecular structure of certain chemicals and usually follows chromatography.
- *Spectral methods* detect certain luminescence that various drugs emit under fluorescent light.
- *Immunoassays* assess for antibodies generated from a substance.

Blood tests also assess for recent drug use, especially alcohol. Blood alcohol tests are used when a person is suspected of driving under the influence of alcohol, when a person's memory or thinking ability seems impaired, for adolescents, and for people in a drug rehabilitation facility. Recall the table provided earlier of different blood alcohol levels and typical behavior associated with those levels (Table 9.7).

A quicker method of assessing recent alcohol use and blood alcohol level is via one's breath, as when a police

Table 9.10 Periods of Detection for Various Drugs by Urinalysis

Drug	Period of detection
Alcohol	6–10 hours
Amphetamine	1–2 days
Barbiturates	2–10 days
Benzodiazepines	1–6 weeks
Cocaine	1–4 days
Codeine	1–2 days
Hashish	1 day–5 weeks
Heroin	1–2 days
LSD	8 hours
Marijuana	1 day–5 weeks
MDMA (ecstasy)	1–2 days
Mescaline	2–3 days
Methadone	1 day–1 week
Methamphetamine	1–2 days
Morphine	1–2 days
Nicotine	1–2 days
Phencyclidine (PCP)	2–8 days
Tetrahydrocannabinol (THC)	1 day–5 weeks

From R. J. Craig, Counseling the alcohol and drug dependent client: A practical approach (p. 91), New York: Pearson, 2004. Reprinted by permission of Pearson Education, Inc.

officer uses a *toximeter* or *Breathalyzer test* that a person breathes into. Several handheld Breathalyzer devices are now available so a person can test oneself before driving. Blood alcohol levels will tend to rise more quickly if you are female, have drunk hard liquor, have drunk substantial amounts of alcohol (such as more than one drink per

zstock/Fotolia LLC

Handheld breathalyzers are available for self-testing one's alcohol level.

hour), weigh less, are older, have not eaten recently, are using other drugs or medications, or mix alcohol with carbonated beverages, which speeds absorption. For some people, drinking an abundance of water during and after alcohol use slows alcohol absorption and helps them avoid a severe hangover. Drinking lots of water *and* lots of alcohol, however, will still leave you impaired.

Hair analysis is becoming a preferred method of drug testing because someone can detect illicit drug use months after a person ingested a drug. Strands of hair close to the scalp are analyzed to detect drug use in the past few months (Musshoff et al., 2020). Hair analysis is popular because substances to hide drug use cannot easily contaminate results. Downsides to hair testing are that the amount of drug a person took, and when the person took the drug, cannot be clearly established. Racial bias may also be a factor (refer to **Focus on Law and Ethics: Drug Testing**). *Saliva* and *sweat* tests for drug use have also been developed. Common drugs found among drivers whose saliva was tested include alcohol, cannabis, cocaine, and methamphetamine (Alcañiz et al., 2021).

Focus On Law and Ethics

Drug Testing

Sophisticated methods of drug testing such as hair and saliva analyses are now available, so important ethical questions arise. A key ethical dilemma is one's right to privacy versus a public's right to know of potentially dangerous situations. A flashpoint in this dilemma has been drug testing of current employees for substance use. Some argue employees have a right to safeguard personal information, especially about legal drug use such as alcohol or tobacco. Drug testing may also be humiliating for a person who must urinate before someone, or the testing may be discriminatory if people are chosen because of some visible characteristic such as disability or race. A person conducting hair analysis might also show bias if the type of hair sample identifies a person as a likely ethnic minority.

Others argue that employers have a right to know if an employee is impaired on the job and might harm others. You would not want airplane pilots or truckers to be drunk when flying or driving. Others take a middle ground on this issue, claiming that drug testing is ethical under strict conditions such as establishing policies acceptable to workers *and* employers, engaging in selective but not universal drug testing, providing prior notice of testing, notifying employees of test results, and carefully maintaining confidentiality of drug testing results (Bhave et al., 2020).

Ethical questions regarding drug testing apply to other populations as well. Some claim mandatory drug testing of high school athletes is coercive, lacks informed consent and confidentiality, and unfairly targets a specific group of people (Schneider, 2022). Many parents also disagree with professional association statements that drug test results for teenagers be completely confidential—does a parent have a right to know about their child's drug use? Finally, some express concern that drug testing on pregnant women could lead to prosecution for harm to the fetus (Cosgrove & Vaswani, 2020).

Biological Treatment of Substance-Related Disorders

You might think it odd that other substances or medications could treat substance-related disorders. Many now believe, however, that a combination of medication and psychological treatment may be best to address persistent substance-related problems. Medications for these disorders include agonists, antagonists, partial agonists, and aversives.

Agonists

Agonists are drugs that have a similar chemical composition as the excessively used drug. Agonist drug treatment thus takes advantage of **cross-tolerance**, or tolerance for a drug one has never taken. A good example of agonist drug treatment is *methadone* for people addicted to heroin or other opiates. Methadone shares a chemical composition with opiate drugs and so binds to opiate receptors in the brain as opiates do. Methadone treatment is given as a person reduces opiate use so cravings for, and withdrawal symptoms from, the opiate are less severe. Once a person is fully cleansed of the addictive drug, methadone doses are gradually reduced as well. Another drug, a methadone derivative known as *levo-alpha-acetyl-methadol* (LAAM), lasts longer in the body and may need to be taken only three times a week compared with daily doses for methadone. LAAM may thus be more effective than methadone for helping people end opiate addiction (Mahdi & Moustafa, 2020).

Agonist agents are also used for nicotine addiction. *Nicotine replacement therapy* refers to ingesting safe amounts of nicotine without smoking tobacco. The alternative ingestion comes in the form of a nicotine patch (Nicoderm), gum (Nicorette), inhaler, or nasal spray. No one form is greatly more effective than another, although the patch is the easiest to use and the inhaler the most difficult. These devices also help reduce cravings and withdrawal symptoms, and their strength can be gradually reduced until a person is no longer addicted (Mersha et al., 2020).

Antagonists

Antagonists are drugs that block the pleasurable effects of an addictive drug and thus potentially reduce cravings for the drug. A good example is *naltrexone* (Revia), which blocks opiate receptors in the brain, and specifically the nucleus accumbens, to decrease craving for alcohol and reduce its pleasurable effects. The drug is effective for reducing alcohol consumption and craving (Murphy et al., 2022). A combination of naltrexone with *acamprosate*, a drug that may also have some antagonist properties, is effective as well for preventing relapse in people with alcoholism (Guglielmo et al., 2021). A related antagonist, *naloxone* (Narcan), is used in emergency situations to treat opiate overdose (Chua et al., 2022).

Partial Agonists

Partial agonists are drugs that may act as an agonist or antagonist depending on how much of a neurotransmitter is produced. Dopamine has a close association with substance-related disorders, so a partial agonist will increase dopamine levels when this neurotransmitter is not highly produced in the brain and decrease dopamine levels when this neurotransmitter *is* highly produced in the brain. Psychotic disorders (Chapter 12) are also impacted by dopamine and so partial agonists may be useful when a person has psychosis with a substance-related disorder (Hernández-Huerta & Morillo-González, 2021).

A common partial agonist for substance-related disorders is *buprenorphine* (Subutex), which acts as an agonist at certain opiate receptors but an antagonist at other opiate receptors. The drug helps control craving for opiates by binding to key opiate receptors but has fewer side effects such as sedation than pure agonists such as methadone. Buprenorphine also appears to be nearly if not equally effective as methadone, so the drug may be given if methadone does not work well, or as a transition between methadone and abstinence (Scott et al., 2021).

Aversives

Aversive drugs are those that make ingestion of an addictive drug quite uncomfortable. A good example is *disulfiram* (Antabuse). When someone takes this drug, there are no ill effects until they drink alcohol. After alcohol intake, the person experiences nausea, vomiting, diarrhea, and blood pressure changes that may deter more alcohol use or create a learned taste aversion. Think about what happens when you eat something at a restaurant and then get sick—you do not want to go back to that restaurant for quite a while!

Disulfiram is an aldehyde dehydrogenase inhibitor, meaning that high levels of acetaldehyde build up quickly. Recall from the cultural factors section that high levels of acetaldehyde may cause several unpleasant symptoms and deter certain people from using alcohol. A person with alcoholism does not take disulfiram every day, but may take the drug during "high-risk" times such as going on vacation or during a holiday season. Disulfiram is also effective for treating cocaine use (Brandt et al., 2021). A related drug, *calcium carbimide* (Temposil), has similar but milder effects than disulfiram.

Another aversive drug is *silver acetate,* a substance placed in gum, lozenges, or mouthwash (Gómez-Coronado et al., 2018). Silver acetate has no major side effects when used alone. When mixed with nicotine, however, as when a person smokes a cigarette after using the mouthwash, mucous membranes are irritated and a foul taste occurs in the person's mouth. Deterring the response (smoking) or creating a learned taste aversion is thus key. Disulfiram and silver acetate only work if a person is sufficiently motivated to use the substances to limit alcohol and tobacco use.

Psychological Treatment of Substance-Related Disorders

Psychological treatment of substance-related disorders generally involves inpatient and residential treatment, brief interventions, cognitive-behavioral therapy, family and marital therapy, group therapy, and self-help groups.

Inpatient and Residential Treatment

Elon eventually entered a drug rehabilitation facility after substantial drug use and dangerous behavior. People who are intoxicated or dependent on a particular substance often must first undergo *inpatient* or *residential treatment* in which the major focus is detoxification and rehabilitation. **Detoxification** involves withdrawing from a drug under medical supervision, which may include medications mentioned previously. A person may be gradually withdrawn from heroin use by using methadone and sedatives to quell intense withdrawal symptoms. Detoxification also involves providing good nutrition, rest, exercise, and a stress-free environment to cleanse the body of addicted drugs. Elon was asked to replace vitamins and minerals missing from his diet in the past few months, drink plenty of water, and adhere to a normal routine with set times for sleeping and waking.

Rehabilitation from drug use is the next phase of inpatient or residential treatment. Many rehabilitation treatment programs focus on abstinence, education about substance-related disorder and its consequences, effects of addiction on family members, and cognitive-behavioral techniques to prevent relapse (discussed in a later section). Individuals with substance-related disorders often share their experiences with professionals and other residents and confront problems currently facing them. Elon eventually realized the full consequences of his actions, such as expulsion from college, and how much pain he caused his parents. Residential treatment programs tend to be more effective for people with severe substance-related disorders, comorbid mental disorders, and fewer social resources (de Andrade et al., 2019).

Brief Interventions

Brief interventions for substance-related disorders include short-term strategies to change behavior as much as possible in a limited time. Brief interventions include the motivational interviewing technique discussed earlier, which includes providing feedback about one's excessive substance use and negotiating and setting a goal for change. A therapist may encourage a client to commit to drinking only on weekends or allow a family member or trusted coworker to monitor their alcohol use at home or work. Brief interventions can be as short as 5 to 15 minutes in length.

Brief interventions also focus on identifying high-risk situations for excessive substance use, especially when a person is stressed, lonely, bored, or depressed. Exploring the pros and cons of substance use, providing information about substance use and its negative consequences, and bolstering social support are important as well. The goal of brief interventions is not necessarily to achieve complete abstinence but to stabilize or reduce a person's substance use enough so they can pursue the more thorough types of therapy discussed next. Brief interventions are often used in primary care medical settings but may be less effective for those with severe substance use problems (Ghosh et al., 2022).

Cognitive-Behavioral Therapy

Various aspects of cognitive-behavioral therapy have been discussed for anxiety-related, somatic symptom, depressive, bipolar, and eating disorders. *Cognitive therapy* essentially refers to challenging and changing unrealistic thoughts about a given situation. Recall that one cognitive mistake commonly made by people who engage in heavy drinking, especially college students, is that others drink as much or more than they do. Correcting this misperception is thus important. Cognitive therapy may also involve modifying cognitive distortions discussed in Chapters 5 and 7, especially those related to catastrophizing. A person with substance use disorder may mistakenly believe if they do not take a certain drug such as cocaine, their performance on a work task will be subpar. Cognitive therapy is thus important for addressing psychological dependence and is usually incorporated into behavior therapy techniques.

Behavior therapy refers to changing learning patterns and other maladaptive behaviors associated with a given disorder. **Skills training** is a key behavioral treatment for substance-related disorders. Skills training involves helping a person understand antecedents and consequences of drug use (recall functional analysis from Chapter 4) and recognizing what situations represent a high risk for return to drug use. The stress of school was a strong trigger or antecedent of Elon's drug use, and elation and sexual prowess were potent consequences. He also came to understand that certain situations were quite risky for him, especially association with drinking buddies and college parties.

Following this step, a person is encouraged to avoid high-risk situations or cope with them effectively (*stimulus control*). In a high-risk situation, a person may be taught how to appropriately decline offers for alcohol or other drugs, understand one's limit and adhere strictly to it, leave a situation (party) after a certain time, bring a friend to help monitor alcohol or other drug use, or think about negative consequences to drug use. People can also learn to plan for emergencies, such as who to contact when tempted by drug use, and control physical arousal and strong emotions tied to cravings for drugs. People with substance-related disorders must also understand that even small events, such as taking a wrong turn when driving and encountering a liquor store, can produce strong cravings that require an adaptive response like calling a friend (Roos et al., 2020).

Skills training may also involve **self-monitoring** in which a person constantly records the amount of drug taken or various situations and emotions that lead to urges for drug use. The idea here is to make a person as aware as possible of antecedents to drug use as well as actual drug use—the more we are aware of our excess behaviors, the less we tend to engage in them. Therapists may combine skills training with **cue exposure therapy** in which a person is exposed to cues such as the sight and smell of alcohol or a cigarette and then uses skills such as relaxation or discussion to successfully decline drug use. Therapists use skills training to prevent relapse to excessive drug use and may combine the training with other approaches such as mindfulness (Vinci et al., 2021).

A key aspect of behavior therapy for substance-related disorders is **contingency management**, or rewarding positive behaviors via praise and other reinforcers from family members, friends, and close associates. Elon's parents verified and rewarded their son's abstinence after regular drug screens. Contingency management may also involve incentives after drug-free urine or other screening. Contingency management has modest effects for treatment attendance and for abstinence, though effects may diminish if rewards do not continue (Pfund et al., 2021).

A **community reinforcement approach** to substance-related disorders is similar to contingency management. A person with substance use disorder is not only rewarded by others for abstinence but also encouraged to change conditions in their environment—such as those at work, home, and recreationally—to make them more rewarding than substance use. Therapists often combine this approach with family therapy, medication, and ongoing drug testing. The approach helps boost abstinence and engagement in the treatment process (Archer et al., 2020).

Family and Marital Therapy

Substance-related disorders involve great harm to significant others, and better treatment outcomes for people with these disorders usually involve good family and partner/marital relationships. Family and marital therapies are thus important components of treatment. These treatments involve family members or the spouse or partner of a person with a substance-related disorder to help motivate a person to seek treatment, increase positive communications within the family, solve problems effectively, and monitor a person's substance use. The general goal of these techniques is to foster a living environment that helps prevent relapse to excessive alcohol or other drug use and that reduces the "enabling" behaviors discussed earlier (Ariss & Fairburn, 2020).

Clinicians often use family therapy to treat adolescents with substance use problems, and **multidimensional family therapy** is a popular form. Multidimensional family therapy consists of a 12-week program that focuses on developing a strong adolescent–parent bond, enhancing good negotiation and family problem-solving skills, improving supervision of the adolescent, and correcting learning and school-based problems. The therapy has been shown to be as or more effective than cognitive-behavioral therapy for improving family cohesion and peer relations and for reducing future arrests and excessive substance use. Establishing a strong adolescent-parent alliance appears to be crucial for family members to remain in treatment and complete the program successfully (Bonnaire et al., 2020).

Group Therapy

Group therapy has always been a popular form of treatment for people with substance-related disorders. The group meets together with a therapist with the goal of helping to reduce alcohol and other drug use. Group therapy approaches can differ widely based on the orientation of the therapist, but common practices include providing education about the consequences of excessive drug use, encouraging commitment to change, enhancing social support, recognizing cues that lead to excessive substance use, restructuring destructive lifestyles and relationships, and identifying alternative ways of coping with stress. The effectiveness of group therapy is not necessarily better than individual treatment but may improve if comorbid psychological problems such as anxiety or depression are addressed (Korecki et al., 2020).

Self-Help Groups

Self-help groups are similar to group therapy in that several people with a substance-related disorder meet to support one another and encourage abstinence. Self-help groups are thus a cost-effective means of assisting people with substance-related disorders. Most self-help groups are led not by a professional therapist but by people with a particular substance use problem. Perhaps the most well-known self-help group is *Alcoholics Anonymous*, which relies on a Twelve Step and Twelve Tradition program that (hopefully) leads one to abstinence under the guidance of a sponsor or senior member (refer to **Table 9.11**). The general philosophy of Alcoholics Anonymous is that alcoholism is a disease controlled only by complete abstinence. Therapists can also use the Twelve Step approach with clients. The approach is useful for helping people maintain continuous abstinence and helps reduce intensity of drinking as well as consequences of alcohol addiction (Kelly et al., 2020). Related Twelve Step groups include Narcotics Anonymous as well as groups for family members of people with alcoholism or other substance-related disorders, including Al-Anon/Alateen and Nar-Anon. Other groups, such as Double Trouble in Recovery, address people with substance-related disorders and other mental disorders such as depression.

What If I or Someone I Know Has a Substance-Related Problem or Disorder?

If you or someone you know wants to reduce drinking or smoking, then working with family members to monitor substance use, consulting self-help guides, and

Table 9.11 The Twelve Steps and Traditions of Alcoholics Anonymous

The Twelve Steps of Alcoholics Anonymous	The Twelve Traditions of Alcoholics Anonymous
We admitted we were powerless over alcohol—that our lives had become unmanageable.	Our common welfare should come first; personal recovery depends upon A.A. unity.
Came to believe that a Power greater than ourselves could restore us to sanity.	For our group purpose, there is but one ultimate authority—a loving God as He may express Himself in our group conscience. Our leaders are but trusted servants; they do not govern.
Made a decision to turn our will and our lives over to the care of God *as we understood Him.*	The only requirement for A.A. membership is a desire to stop drinking.
Made a searching and fearless moral inventory of ourselves.	Each group should be autonomous except in matters affecting other groups or A.A. as a whole.
Admitted to God, to ourselves and to another human being the exact nature of our wrongs.	Each group has but one primary purpose—to carry its message to the alcoholic who still suffers.
Were entirely ready to have God remove all these defects of character.	An A.A. group ought never endorse, finance, or lend the A.A. name to any related facility or outside enterprise, lest problems of money, property, and prestige divert us from our primary purpose.
Humbly asked Him to remove our shortcomings.	Every A.A. group ought to be fully self-supporting, declining outside contributions.
Made a list of all persons we had harmed, and became willing to make amends to them all.	Alcoholics Anonymous should remain forever non-professional, but our service centers may employ special workers.
Made direct amends to such people whenever possible, except when to do so would injure them or others.	A.A., as such, ought never be organized; but we may create service boards or committees directly responsible to those they serve.
Continued to take personal inventory and when we were wrong promptly admitted it.	Alcoholics Anonymous has no opinion on outside issues; hence the A.A. name ought never be drawn into public controversy.
Sought through prayer and meditation to improve our conscious contact with God, *as we understood Him,* praying only for knowledge of His will for us and the power to carry that out.	Our public relations policy is based on attraction rather than promotion; we need always maintain personal anonymity at the level of press, radio, and films.
Having had a spiritual awakening as the result of these steps, we tried to carry this message to alcoholics, and to practice these principles in all our affairs.	Anonymity is the spiritual foundation of all our traditions, ever reminding us to place principles before personalities.

Source: The Twelve Steps are reprinted with permission of Alcoholics Anonymous World Services, Inc. ("AAWS"). Permission to reprint the Twelve Steps does not mean that AAWS has reviewed or approved the contents of this publication, or that AAWS necessarily agrees with the views expressed herein. A.A. is a program of recovery from alcoholism only—use of the Twelve Steps in connection with programs and activities which are patterned after A.A., but which address other problems, or in any other non-A.A. context, does not imply otherwise.

discovering healthier ways to cope with stress and other triggers may be sufficient. Substance-related problems can be devastating, however, and can easily lead to severe consequences such as a car accident, arrest, or job loss. If you or someone you know has a serious substance-related problem, then seeking medical and psychological help as soon as possible is very important. Consulting a qualified professional who specializes in substance use treatment is recommended.

Long-Term Outcome for People with Substance-Related Disorders

Treating people with substance-related disorders can be complicated and involves many pharmacological and psychological components. Treatment outcomes for people with substance-related disorders are better with combined pharmacological and behavioral interventions than either type alone (Blondino et al., 2020). About 30 percent of people drop out of treatment for substance-related disorders, however. Higher dropout rates are associated with cocaine, methamphetamine, and major stimulant use as well as with lengthier treatment programs (Lappan et al., 2020). Relapse is also common in this population and is impacted by motivation to quit substance use, resilience, social support, depression, probation status, and substance use intensity (Guliyev et al., 2021; Yamashita et al., 2021). What is the long-term outcome of people with substance-related disorders? Much of this literature has focused on people with alcoholism. Longitudinal studies indicate that remission rates for alcoholism over several decades are 27 to 69 percent. Approximately 4 to 5 percent of those with an alcohol use disorder remit each year (Timko et al., 2016). Significant illness and mortality are associated with chronic alcohol use. Long-term dependence on alcohol may relate to intense craving for alcohol, family history of alcoholism, greater alcohol intake, history of other drug use, and presence of legal and other problems related to drinking (Schuckit et al., 2021; Schuckit & Smith, 2021).

Long-term follow-up of injection drug users indicates that many enter paths involving cessation or persistent use and relapse. Outcomes can include early cessation (14 percent), early cessation with later relapse (11 percent), gradual cessation (32.2 percent), high frequency injection with later decrease (18.2 percent), and persistent high frequency injection (24.6 percent). Persistent injection use is associated with younger ages and not being in a stable relationship (Dong et al., 2019). In addition, injection pathways can be impacted by the number of close associates who do or do not inject drugs (Rudolph et al., 2021). Keep in mind as well that people who inject drugs are part of a particularly vulnerable group with often limited access to harm reduction measures, treatment programs, and hospital care (Muncan et al., 2020).

Section Summary

- Assessing people with substance-related disorders includes screening and motivational interviews as well as psychological testing and observations from others.
- Laboratory testing for substance-related disorders includes urine, blood, hair, saliva, and sweat screens for toxins.
- Biological treatment for substance-related disorders includes medications such as agonists, antagonists, partial agonists, and aversives.
- Inpatient and residential treatment for substance-related disorders focuses on short-term detoxification and rehabilitation.
- Brief interventions for substance-related disorders involve stabilizing or reducing substance use enough so more thorough forms of treatment can be applied.
- Cognitive-behavioral therapy for substance-related disorders involves modifying unrealistic cognitions about drug use and identifying and changing high-risk situations that could lead to relapse.
- Family, marital, and group therapies provide social support and reinforcement for abstinent behavior.
- Self-help groups involve meetings of people with similar substance use problems who share support and experiences to maintain abstinence.
- Many people who seek treatment for a substance-related disorder successfully control the problem, but some experience severe problems much of their life.

Review Questions

1. Outline major assessment techniques for substance-related disorders, including interviews, psychological testing, and laboratory assessment.
2. What medications help control symptoms of substance-related disorders? How do they work?
3. Describe inpatient therapy for substance-related disorder.
4. What psychological treatment strategies could a mental health professional use to help someone achieve abstinence? How so?
5. What is the long-term outcome for people with substance-related disorders?

The Sam Spady Story

An undergraduate student at Colorado State University died after binge drinking both beer and shots over an 11-hour period. The student, Samantha Spady, was a homecoming queen, cheerleading captain, and honor student in high school. She was a business major with big ambitions, but instead of fulfilling them, she became one of over 1500 college students aged 18 to 24 years who die from alcohol-related incidents each year (National Institute on Alcohol Abuse and Alcoholism, 2022). Her story is the subject of a documentary (*Death by Alcohol: The Sam Spady Story*) available via a website established to honor Samantha and educate others about the dangers of binge drinking. The website (http://www.samspadyfoundation.org) also lists key signs that someone might have alcohol poisoning after binge drinking and needs *immediate help*:

- Unconscious or semiconscious
- Breathing less than 10 times per minute or irregular (check every two minutes)
- Cold, clammy, pale, or bluish skin
- Cannot be awakened by pinching, prodding, or shouting
- Vomiting without waking up

Courtesy of Sam Spady Foundation

Final Comments

Substance use is common and accepted in our society, as demonstrated by widespread use of caffeine, alcohol, and tobacco. Some people thus "cross the line" into using more dangerous drugs or using legal drugs to a much greater extent. Many of us might have stereotypes about the kind of people that have a substance-related disorder but the reality is that such disorders impact people from all walks of life and involve many different kinds of drugs. Indeed, someone close to you or the person next to you may be experiencing problems with alcohol, marijuana, opioids, prescription medications, or other substances. This is important to think about because stigma is a powerful reason why many people do not seek treatment for a substance-related disorder.

Thought Questions

1. Think about shows or films that have characters with substance use problems. Do you think these characters display realistic or unrealistic symptoms of substance use problems? How so?
2. Think about situations where you engage in substance use. What factors propel you to do so? Why do you think people you know use legal (or illegal) drugs? Having read the chapter, would you change anything about your substance use?
3. What would you now say to a friend who might be using substances too much?
4. What separates "normal" from "psychopathological" substance use? Do you think excessive substance use has more to do with biological, personal, family, or other factors? Why?
5. What do you think family members and friends could do to reduce excessive substance use in people they know?

Key Terms

Personality Disorders

10

Learning Objectives

LO 10.1 Describe personality, the trait approach to personality, and personality disorders.

LO 10.2 Discuss the approach to personality disorders used in the current *Diagnostic and Statistical Manual of Mental Disorders.*

LO 10.3 Distinguish between the types of odd or eccentric personality disorders based on their diagnostic criteria and clinical features.

LO 10.4 Summarize the epidemiology of odd or eccentric personality disorders.

LO 10.5 Distinguish among the types of dramatic personality disorders based on their diagnostic criteria and clinical features.

LO 10.6 Summarize the epidemiology of dramatic personality disorders.

LO 10.7 Distinguish between the types of anxious/fearful personality disorders based on their diagnostic criteria and clinical features.

Learning Objectives (continued)

LO 10.8 Summarize the epidemiology of anxious/fearful personality disorders.

LO 10.9 Describe the stigma associated with personality disorders and its impact on those with the disorders.

LO 10.10 Discuss the risk factors for personality disorders.

LO 10.11 Evaluate programs to prevent personality disorders.

LO 10.12 Characterize the assessment and treatment of individuals with personality disorders.

Personality Traits, Unusual Personality, and Personality Disorder: What Are They?

LO 10.1 Describe personality, the trait approach to personality, and personality disorders.

All of us have personality traits that make up who we are. A **personality trait** can be thought of as a disposition or a readiness to act in a certain way. Think about someone with great integrity. You know this person can be trusted because they are likely to be honest and reliable in what they do. You may also know someone who is shy, meaning they are more willing to shun social contacts and pursue solitary activities. Common personality traits that everyone has to some degree include the following:

- *Openness:* active imagination and sensitivity; opposite is practicality and routine-oriented
- *Conscientiousness:* self-disciplined and achievement-oriented; opposite is less goal-oriented and more laid-back
- *Extraversion:* socially gregarious behavior; opposite is introversion
- *Agreeableness:* compassionate and cooperative; opposite is suspiciousness and antagonism
- *Neuroticism:* tendency to express negative emotional states; opposite is emotional stability

Some people show extreme levels of personality traits that cause problems. Perhaps you know people who have trouble controlling their emotions, who always fight with family members, or who are impulsive or suspicious of others. However, many people with intense personality traits still function fairly well because others tolerate their idiosyncrasies or because their behavior does not significantly interfere with their job or partnership. Intense personality traits can even be adaptive, as when someone who is overly pushy does well in a sales career.

For people like Michelle, however, personality traits are so extreme that they cause many problems. These people often have unusual, intense, and severe personality traits that appear in many situations. Michelle showed intense impulsivity, anger, and separation anxiety that prevented her from having stable relationships or going to college. People with extreme levels of personality traits that cause great impairment in functioning, especially social and occupational functioning, have a **personality disorder**. Personality disorders lie at

Table 10.1 DSM-5-TR

General Personality Disorder
A. An enduring pattern of inner experience and behavior that deviates markedly from the expectations of the individual's culture. This pattern is manifested in two (or more) of the following areas: 1. Cognition (i.e., ways of perceiving and interpreting self, other people, and events). 2. Affectivity (i.e., the range, intensity, lability, and appropriateness of emotional response). 3. Interpersonal functioning. 4. Impulse control.
B. The enduring pattern is inflexible and pervasive across a broad range of personal and social situations.
C. The enduring pattern leads to clinically significant distress or impairment in social, occupational, or other important areas of functioning.
D. The pattern is stable and of long duration, and its onset can be traced back at least to adolescence or early adulthood.
E. The enduring pattern is not better explained as a manifestation or consequence of another mental disorder.
F. The enduring pattern is not attributable to the physiological effects of a substance or another medical condition.

American Psychiatric Association. (2022). *Diagnostic and statistical manual of mental disorders* (5th ed., text rev.). Arlington, VA: American Psychiatric Association.

Case Michelle

Michelle was 23 years old when she was admitted to a psychiatric inpatient unit after her sixth suicide attempt in two years. She told her ex-boyfriend that she swallowed a bottle of aspirin, and he rushed her to the emergency room. Michelle had a five-year history of depressive symptoms that never seemed to ease. She was sad and had poor appetite, low self-esteem, difficulty concentrating, and hopelessness. Michelle's symptoms of depression were never severe enough to warrant hospitalization or treatment, however.

Michelle also had great difficulty controlling her emotions. She became intensely sad, irritable, or anxious almost at a moment's notice. These intense negative feelings were often triggered by setbacks or arguments but rarely lasted more than four to five hours. Michelle also had a long history of impulsive behaviors, such as excessive drug use, indiscriminant sexual activity, and binge eating.

Michelle's anger was also unpredictable and intense. She once used a hammer to smash a wall after receiving a bad grade on a test. Michelle's relationships with her friends, boyfriends, and parents were intense and unstable as well. People often complained that Michelle became angry with them and criticized them for no apparent reason. She also frequently expressed her fear that others (including her parents) might leave or abandon her. Michelle once aggressively clutched a friend's leg to convince her to stay for dinner. Separation was obviously difficult for Michelle. She tried to leave home and attend college four times but always returned home within a few weeks. She told her ex-boyfriend before her hospital admission, "I want to end it all" and "No one loves me."

What Do You Think?

1. Which of Michelle's behaviors seem typical of a stressed-out 23-year-old, and which seem very different?
2. What external events and internal factors might be responsible for Michelle's troubles?
3. What are you curious about regarding Michelle?
4. Does Michelle remind you in any way of yourself or someone you know? How so?
5. How might Michelle's unusual behaviors affect her life in the future?

the end of a dimensional spectrum (refer to **Continuum of Normal Personality and Personality Disorder Traits Related to Impulsivity**; DeYoung et al., 2022).

People with a personality disorder have unusual ways of thinking about themselves and others (cognitive feature), experiencing and expressing emotions (affective feature), interacting with others (interpersonal feature), and controlling impulses (impulse control; refer to **Table 10.1**). Think about someone who is overly suspicious. Suspiciousness is a personality trait with cognitive ("Other people want to hurt me"), affective (angry or hostile outbursts), and interpersonal (keeping others at "arm's length") features. A suspicious person may also show impulse control problems by sending angry, "flaming" e-mails to others at work if they feel threatened.

Personality disorders involve stable, long-standing, and inflexible traits. People like Michelle who have a personality disorder often say their traits can be traced back to childhood or adolescence. Inflexible traits are a key aspect of personality disorder. The traits are difficult for a person to change and appear across many situations. Think about someone's impulsive behavior at a party—being spontaneous and taking some risks might seem normal in this situation. Being impulsive and goofing around at a job site or during a funeral, however, would be maladaptive and inappropriate. People with a personality disorder have great difficulty changing their behavior from one situation to another and from one interpersonal context to another. Such inflexibility causes significant distress or impairment in social, occupational, or other areas of functioning.

Personality disorders involve traits that deviate significantly from the expectations of a culture. This is important to remember because what may appear to be strange or deviant from the perspective of one culture may be quite normal and adaptive in another (Choudhary & Gupta, 2020). Being "reserved" or "shy" in one culture can be perceived as "courteous" and "dignified" in another culture. Clinicians who assess people for possible personality disorder must consider someone's cultural background. The next sections cover how personality disorders are organized according to different clusters of traits.

Organization of Personality Disorders

LO 10.2 Discuss the approach to personality disorders used in the current *Diagnostic and Statistical Manual of Mental Disorders.*

The *Diagnostic and Statistical Manual of Mental Disorders* (*DSM-5-TR*) organizes personality disorders into three main clusters based on similarity of traits (refer to

Continuum of Normal Personality and Personality Disorder Traits Related to Impulsivity

	Normal	Mild
Emotions	Stable mood and low levels of impulsive urge.	Occasional mood swings and impulsive urges.
Cognitions	Occasional thoughts of spontaneity in a socially adaptive way.	Occasional thoughts of spontaneous activity such as stealing.
Behaviors	Acts different in different situations depending on the social context.	Occasionally acts inappropriately in work or social situations.

Table 10.2). The first cluster is the *odd/eccentric* group, which includes paranoid, schizoid, and schizotypal personality disorders. People with odd/eccentric personality disorders display features that seem bizarre to others. The second cluster is the *dramatic/erratic/emotional* group that includes antisocial, borderline, histrionic, and narcissistic personality disorders. People with dramatic/erratic/emotional personality disorders display features that seem exaggerated to others. The third cluster is the *anxious/fearful* group, which includes avoidant, dependent, and obsessive-compulsive personality disorders. People with anxious/fearful personality disorders display features that seem apprehensive to others. Each of these clusters are covered separately in this chapter.

Table 10.2 DSM-5-TR

Personality Disorders		
Odd/eccentric	**Dramatic/erratic/ emotional**	**Anxious/fearful**
Paranoid	Antisocial	Avoidant
Schizoid	Borderline	Dependent
Schizotypal	Histrionic	Obsessive-compulsive
	Narcissistic	

American Psychiatric Association. (2022). *Diagnostic and statistical manual of mental disorders* (5th ed., text rev.). Arlington, VA: American Psychiatric Association.

The *DSM-5-TR* also contains an alternative model of personality disorder that is based on dimensions of functioning and requires further study (Krueger & Hobbs, 2020). This dimensional model emphasizes impairments in personality functioning and traits rather than specific categories of disorder. For example, a person could have one or two personality traits that are inflexible and maladaptive. The person could show these traits across many situations and experience great impairment. Think about someone who is often impulsively aggressive toward others at work and in personal relationships.

This dimensional model involves four key elements of personality functioning that could be impaired:

- Identity (e.g., have boundaries with others and regulate one's emotions)
- Self-direction (e.g., pursue life goals or self-reflect)
- Empathy (e.g., understand others' perspectives and the effects of one's own behavior on others)
- Intimacy (e.g., be close with others and desire to be with others)

This dimensional model also involves personality traits that can be pathological:

- Negative affectivity (e.g., presence of many negative emotions)
- Detachment (e.g., avoidance of others and restricted emotions)

Moderate	Personality Disorder—less severe	Personality Disorder—more severe
Frequent mood swings and some impulsive urges but little impairment at work or with relationships.	Intense mood swings and impulsive urges with significant impairment at work or with relationships.	Extreme mood swings and impulsive or aggressive urges that lead to self-harm, arrest, or violence.
Frequent odd thoughts or thoughts of dangerous activity such as harming self or others.	Intense thoughts of suicide, paranoia, abandonment, attention from others, vengeance, or work.	Extreme and constant thoughts of suicide, paranoia, abandonment, attention from others, vengeance, or work.
Problematic personality trait such as impulsivity or emotional reactivity shown in many situations.	Problematic personality traits and dangerous behavior shown in most situations.	Problematic personality traits and dangerous behavior shown in almost all situations with intense distress and impairment.

- Antagonism (e.g., callousness toward others or self-importance)
- Disinhibition (e.g., impulsive behavior and immediate gratification)
- Psychoticism (e.g., odd behaviors and thoughts)

A dimensional model of personality disorders thus involves impairment in personality functioning *and* one or more pathological personality traits. As such, specific categories of personality disorder are emphasized less, and a continuum of personality constructs is emphasized more. The categorical approach to personality disorders remains popular among researchers and therapists, however, and thus provides the structure for the rest of the chapter.

Odd or Eccentric Personality Disorders: Features and Epidemiology

LO 10.3 Distinguish between the types of odd or eccentric personality disorders based on their diagnostic criteria and clinical features.

LO 10.4 Summarize the epidemiology of odd or eccentric personality disorders.

Odd or eccentric personality disorders include paranoid, schizoid, and schizotypal personality disorders.

Paranoid Personality Disorder

Many of us have moments when we do not trust certain people or are cautious around others because we fear harm. Moments of suspiciousness can be realistic and adaptive at times, as when a stranger suddenly approaches you. Other people, however, are constantly mistrustful and suspicious of others, even those they know well. **Paranoid personality disorder** involves a general distrust and suspiciousness of others (refer to **Table 10.3**). People with this disorder often read harmful intentions from neutral interactions or events and assume the worst. They blame others for their misfortunes and have trouble working collaboratively or closely with others. Someone with paranoid personality disorder may be rigid, controlling, critical, blaming, and jealous. This person may engage in lengthy and acrimonious legal disputes that are difficult to resolve. People with paranoid personality disorder are sometimes not good coworkers or partners because they are highly argumentative, hostile, and sarcastic.

Schizoid Personality Disorder

Many people like to be alone and seem a little awkward around others. Shyness is a personality trait generally accepted in our society as normal and tolerable. In addition, many people who are shy still desire social relationships. Other people, however, show extreme social detachment and isolation and may have **schizoid personality disorder** (refer to **Table 10.4**). People with this disorder have little interest in establishing or

Table 10.3 DSM-5-TR

Paranoid Personality Disorder
A. A pervasive distrust and suspiciousness of others such that their motives are interpreted as malevolent, beginning by early adulthood and present in a variety of contexts, as indicated by four (or more) of the following: 1. Suspects, without sufficient basis, that others are exploiting, harming, or deceiving him or her 2. Is preoccupied with unjustified doubts about the loyalty or trustworthiness of friends or associates. 3. Is reluctant to confide in others because of unwarranted fear that the information will be used maliciously against him or her. 4. Reads hidden demeaning or threatening meanings into benign remarks or events. 5. Persistently bears grudges. 6. Perceives attacks on his or her character or reputation that are not apparent to others and is quick to react angrily or to counterattack. 7. Has recurrent suspicions, without justification, regarding fidelity of spouse or sexual partner.
B. Does not occur exclusively during the course of schizophrenia, a bipolar disorder or depressive disorder with psychotic features, or another psychotic disorder and is not attributable to the physiological effects of another medical condition.

American Psychiatric Association. (2022). *Diagnostic and statistical manual of mental disorders* (5th ed., text rev.). Arlington, VA: American Psychiatric Association.

Table 10.4 DSM-5-TR

Schizoid Personality Disorder
A. A pervasive pattern of detachment from social relationships and a restricted range of expression of emotions in interpersonal settings, beginning by early adulthood and present in a variety of contexts, as indicated by four (or more) of the following: 1. Neither desires nor enjoys close relationships, including being part of a family. 2. Almost always chooses solitary activities. 3. Has little, if any, interest in having sexual experiences with another person. 4. Takes pleasure in few, if any, activities. 5. Lacks close friends or confidantes other than first-degree relatives. 6. Appears indifferent to the praise or criticism of others. 7. Shows emotional coldness, detachment, or flattened affectivity.
B. Does not occur exclusively during the course of schizophrenia, a bipolar disorder or depressive disorder with psychotic features, another psychotic disorder, or autism spectrum disorder and is not attributable to the physiological effects of another medical condition.

American Psychiatric Association. (2022). *Diagnostic and statistical manual of mental disorders* (5th ed., text rev.). Arlington, VA: American Psychiatric Association.

maintaining relationships with others and show little emotional expression. They have few, if any, friends, rarely partner with others or have sex, and often do not express joy, sadness, warmth, or intimacy. People with schizoid personality disorder generally do not show the suspiciousness or paranoid ideation of those with paranoid personality disorder but often prefer to work in isolation and may find jobs that involve minimal social contact. If they do partner with others or become parents, they show little warmth and emotional support and appear neglectful, detached, and disinterested.

Schizotypal Personality Disorder

Perhaps you know someone who is quirky and unusual in how they act or dress. The behavior of some people we meet may seem quite odd or even bizarre. This is not necessarily a problem, however, because different forms of behavior and dress are common to our society. Other people like Jackson (whose story appears shortly), however, have extremely unusual behaviors, perceptions, and thoughts that cause them significant problems. **Schizotypal personality disorder** involves interpersonal deficits, cognitive and perceptual aberrations, and behavioral eccentricities (refer to **Table 10.5**). People with schizotypal personality disorder have extreme social anxiety and perhaps paranoia. They are odd, eccentric, or peculiar in their behavior or appearance; display inappropriate or constricted affect; and have few (if any) friends or confidants outside their immediate family. Schizotypal personality disorder differs from paranoid and schizoid personality disorders in that people with schizotypal personality disorder are usually more odd or eccentric in their behavior and more often have perceptual and cognitive disturbances.

New Africa/Shutterstock.com

People with paranoid personality disorder are prone to be suspicious and may have difficulty working with others.

Table 10.5 DSM-5-TR

Schizotypal Personality Disorder
A. A pervasive pattern of social and interpersonal deficits marked by acute discomfort with, and reduced capacity for, close relationships as well as by cognitive or perceptual distortions and eccentricities of behavior, beginning by early adulthood and present in a variety of contexts, as indicated by five (or more) of the following: 1. Ideas of reference (excluding delusions of reference). 2. Odd beliefs or magical thinking that influences behavior and is inconsistent with subcultural norms. 3. Unusual perceptual experiences, including bodily illusions. 4. Odd thinking and speech. 5. Suspiciousness or paranoid ideation. 6. Inappropriate or constricted affect. 7. Behavior or appearance that is odd, eccentric, or peculiar. 8. Lack of close friends or confidants other than first-degree relatives. 9. Excessive social anxiety that does not diminish with familiarity and tends to be associated with paranoid fears rather than negative judgments about self.
B. Does not occur exclusively during the course of schizophrenia, a bipolar disorder or depressive disorder with psychotic features, another psychotic disorder, or autism spectrum disorder.

American Psychiatric Association. (2022). *Diagnostic and statistical manual of mental disorders* (5th ed., text rev.). Arlington, VA: American Psychiatric Association.

Case Jackson

Jackson is a 27-year-old man who just started college after taking time off to "explore himself." Jackson entered school to study sociology, philosophy, anthropology, and psychology so he could "explain the human race." Jackson comes to class with blue spiky hair and dressed in dirty T-shirts and long pants. He often talks to classmates when his instructor is speaking and has alienated most of his peers. Jackson has few friends, poor hygiene, and odd mannerisms. He sometimes stands in class to take notes in the middle of the room, asks questions that have little to do with the class topic, and speaks in a monotone voice. Jackson's instructor was concerned when his student claimed events on the local news were about him. Jackson said stories involving fire, abduction, and a car accident mirrored what happened to him that day. He also expressed sadness because his classmates would not work on a group project with him.

Many people with schizotypal personality disorder have unusual ideas, beliefs, and communication. They misinterpret or overpersonalize events, have unusual ideas that influence their behavior (they may think it possible to communicate via telepathy, for example), and have difficulty being understood by others. They may show *ideas of reference* where they believe everyday events somehow involve them when actually they do not (Rodríguez-Testal et al., 2019). People with schizotypal personality disorder may drift toward "fringe" groups that support their unusual thinking and odd beliefs. These activities can provide structure for some people with schizotypal personality disorder but also contribute to greater deterioration if psychotic-like or dissociative experiences are encouraged.

10,000 Hours/DigitalVision/Getty Images

Schizoid personality disorder involves a strong desire to be alone.

People with schizotypal personality disorder are most likely to seek treatment for anxiety-related or depressive disorders. They may show brief or transient psychotic episodes in response to stress. These episodes are relatively short, however, lasting a few minutes to a few hours, and do not typically indicate a psychotic disorder (Chapter 12). Only a small portion of people with schizotypal personality disorder develop schizophrenia, but many develop depression. Some of those with schizotypal personality disorder remain marginally employed, withdrawn, and transient throughout much of their lives.

Epidemiology of Odd or Eccentric Personality Disorders

Personality disorders occur in about 7.8 percent of the general population, although estimates are higher among psychiatric outpatients. Personality disorders are associated with significant social and occupational dysfunction, comorbid psychopathology, lower quality of life, and suicidality (Winsper et al., 2020). Maladaptive personality traits are also present in many people with a major mental disorder (Conway et al., 2020).

Researchers estimate that odd or eccentric personality disorders occur in 3.8 percent of the general population. Specific prevalence rates have been reported for paranoid (2.3 percent), schizoid (1.1 percent), and schizotypal (0.8 percent) personality disorders (Winsper et al., 2020).

Many people with odd or eccentric personality disorders either do not seek treatment or seek treatment for other problems. These personality disorders are highly comorbid with anxiety-related, depressive, bipolar, substance use, and psychotic disorders, as well as disruptive behavior disorders such as attention-deficit/hyperactivity disorder. Findings are mixed with respect to gender differences related to odd or eccentric personality disorders (Hsu et al., 2021).

Racial and ethnic differences are not prominent in personality disorders. Race and ethnicity should be closely considered, however, when assessing a client for an odd or eccentric personality disorder. Someone who is angry, frustrated, and guarded does not necessarily have paranoid personality disorder. Consider a recent immigrant to the United States who is unfamiliar with English and American customs. This person would be understandably cautious and suspicious of others. Some people may also appear introverted, isolated, or aloof when these behaviors are a natural part of their culture. A diagnosis of schizoid personality disorder would not apply. Clinicians must also be sure not to confuse symptoms of schizotypal personality disorder with religious experiences, folk beliefs, or linguistic peculiarities shown by certain cultural groups. For example, the *ghost dance* is performed by many Native Americans who believe the ritual allows them to visit relatives or friends who have left their bodies. Such a belief should not be mistaken for evidence of a personality disorder.

Section Summary

- Personality disorders involve dysfunctional and inflexible personality traits that deviate significantly from cultural expectations and are shown across many situations.
- Personality disorders include traits that are odd or eccentric; dramatic, erratic, or emotional; and anxious or fearful.
- Odd or eccentric personality disorders include paranoid, schizoid, and schizotypal personality disorders.
- Paranoid personality disorder involves general distrust and suspiciousness of others.
- Schizoid personality disorder involves social isolation and restricted emotional experience and expression.
- Schizotypal personality disorder involves social anxiety, paranoid fears, and eccentric behavior, perceptions, and thoughts.
- Personality disorders are prevalent throughout the general population, but odd or eccentric personality disorders are more common in clinical samples.
- Odd or eccentric personality disorders are comorbid with other mental disorders such as anxiety-related and depressive disorders but are not highly linked to gender, race, or ethnicity.

Review Questions

1. What are the main features of a personality disorder?
2. What are the main clusters of personality disorder?
3. What are the main odd or eccentric personality disorders and their features?
4. How common are odd or eccentric personality disorders?
5. What mental disorders are most associated with odd or eccentric personality disorders?

Dramatic Personality Disorders: Features and Epidemiology

LO 10.5 Distinguish among the types of dramatic personality disorders based on their diagnostic criteria and clinical features.

LO 10.6 Summarize the epidemiology of dramatic personality disorders.

Recall that a second cluster of personality disorder involves dramatic, erratic, or overly emotional behavior that seems exaggerated to others. This group includes antisocial, borderline, histrionic, and narcissistic personality disorders. Consider the case of Duane for antisocial personality disorder.

Case Duane

Duane was a man in his 20s whose father had left when he was a child. Duane frequently encountered trouble as a youth that led to extended stints in reform school or prison. He earned respect from others, however, because of his fearlessness, self-confidence, and intelligence. He eventually became a pilot and businessman and was adept at construction. Duane was charming, especially to women, and helped break up several marriages among his friends and relatives. Duane was also aggressive toward others and impulsive. He once broke into a friend's safe and traded gunshots with a police officer.

Duane used his charm to become a successful businessman in construction but had little capacity for love or empathy and little interest in the truth. He exaggerated his prowess in hunting and shooting but lacked insight that others could notice his lies. Duane enjoyed being admired and respected by others, but those who knew him well understood he was a manipulator and that his good fellowship was false. Duane used his charm to swindle people out of money and often found dangerous situations such as flying through fog to be thrilling.

Source: Lykken, D. T. (1995). *The antisocial personalities.* Hillsdale, NJ: Erlbaum.

Antisocial Personality Disorder

Duane exhibits many features of **antisocial personality disorder**. Antisocial personality disorder involves a pattern of behavior that reflects an extreme disregard for and violation of the rights of others (refer to **Table 10.6**). Antisocial personality disorder involves deceitfulness, impulsivity, irritability/aggressiveness, criminal acts, and irresponsibility. Not all people with antisocial personality disorder have criminal records, however. People with the disorder often commit reckless acts that neglect the safety of others, and they lack remorse for harm they inflict. Those with antisocial personality disorder are unlikely to maintain steady employment. Some people with the disorder can obtain professional and criminal success as long as their violations and deceptions are undiscovered. Their success may unravel at some point, however, because of their impulsivity, negligence, and lack of foresight. People with antisocial personality disorder may at first appear charming, fun, and engaging, but many of their social relationships eventually fail because of poor empathy, infidelity, and lack of responsibility as well as episodes of maltreatment, exploitation, and angry hostility.

Table 10.6 DSM-5-TR

Antisocial Personality Disorder

A. A pervasive pattern of disregard for and violation of the rights of others, occurring since age 15 years, as indicated by three (or more) of the following:

1. Failure to conform to social norms with respect to lawful behaviors, as indicated by repeatedly performing acts that are grounds for arrest.
2. Deceitfulness, as indicated by repeated lying, use of aliases, or conning others for personal profit or pleasure.
3. Impulsivity or failure to plan ahead.
4. Irritability and aggressiveness, as indicated by repeated physical fights or assaults.
5. Reckless disregard for safety or self or others.
6. Consistent irresponsibility, as indicated by repeated failure to sustain consistent work behavior or honor financial obligations.
7. Lack of remorse, as indicated by being indifferent to or rationalizing having hurt, mistreated, or stolen from another.

B. The individual is at least age 18 years.

C. There is evidence of conduct disorder with onset before age 15 years.

D. The occurrence of antisocial behavior is not exclusively during the course of schizophrenia or bipolar disorder.

American Psychiatric Association. (2022). *Diagnostic and statistical manual of mental disorders* (5th ed., text rev.). Arlington, VA: American Psychiatric Association.

Antisocial personality disorder is evident in childhood in the form of conduct disorder (Chapter 13). Conduct disorder involves aggression toward people and animals, property destruction, deceitfulness or theft, and serious violations of laws and rules. Evidence of conduct disorder before age 15 years is required for a diagnosis of antisocial personality disorder. Not all children with conduct disorder will eventually meet criteria for antisocial personality disorder, although some do (North et al., 2022).

Psychopathy is a diagnostic construct related to antisocial personality disorder. Psychopathy involves little remorse or guilt, poor behavioral control, arrogance, superficial charm, exploitativeness, and lack of empathy (De Brito et al., 2021). Many people with psychopathy are intensely goal-directed toward money, sex, and status. Many people with antisocial personality disorder like Duane display psychopathy. Antisocial personality disorder and psychopathy overlap with respect to antisocial behaviors and impulsivity (Azevedo et al., 2020; refer to **Focus on Violence: Personality Disorders and Violence**).

Borderline Personality Disorder

Some people are dramatic in their behavior but still maintain good social and occupational relationships. Other people like Michelle (the first case study), however, have features of borderline personality disorder (refer to **Table 10.7**). **Borderline personality disorder** involves a pattern of impulsivity and unstable affect,

Table 10.7 DSM-5-TR

Borderline Personality Disorder

A pervasive pattern of instability of interpersonal relationships, self-image, and affects, and marked impulsivity, beginning by early adulthood and present in a variety of contexts, as indicated by five (or more) of the following:

1. Frantic efforts to avoid real or imagined abandonment.
2. A pattern of unstable and intense interpersonal relationships characterized by alternating between extremes of idealization and devaluation.
3. Identity disturbance: markedly and persistently unstable self-image or sense of self.
4. Impulsivity in at least two areas that are potentially self-damaging.
5. Recurrent suicidal behavior, gestures, or threats, or self-mutilating behavior.
6. Affective instability due to a marked reactivity of mood.
7. Chronic feelings of emptiness.
8. Inappropriate, intense anger or difficulty controlling anger.
9. Transient, stress-related paranoid ideation or severe dissociative symptoms.

American Psychiatric Association. (2022). *Diagnostic and statistical manual of mental disorders* (5th ed., text rev.). Arlington, VA: American Psychiatric Association.

interpersonal relationships, and self-image. The term "borderline" reflects a traditional view that the disorder was on the "borderline" of neurosis and psychosis. People with borderline personality disorder frequently experience strong, intense negative emotions and are prone to suicidal threats, gestures, or attempts. They are unsure of their self-image as well as their views of other people. They harbor intense abandonment fears and feelings of emptiness, as Michelle did. Stressful situations may lead to transient paranoid ideation or dissociation. Associated features include self-defeating behavior such as making a bad decision that destroys a good relationship, depressive or substance use disorder, and premature death from suicide. Approximately 5.9 percent of those with borderline personality disorder complete suicide and 46 to 92 percent attempt suicide (Temes et al., 2019; refer to **Focus on Violence: Personality Disorders and Violence**).

Self-harm is a common feature of borderline personality disorder.

Andrii Kondiuk/Shutterstock.com

Histrionic Personality Disorder

Have you ever known someone who always had to be the center of attention? Some people have quite an entertaining presence and are the life of the party. Other people, however, take attention-seeking behaviors to an extreme. People with **histrionic personality disorder** display pervasive and excessive emotionality and attention seeking (refer to **Table 10.8**). Hallmarks of histrionic personality disorder include actions that place oneself in the center of attention, provocative or inappropriately intimate behavior, fleeting and superficial emotional expression, and suggestibility. Histrionic personality disorder is different than borderline personality disorder in that the latter typically involves self-destructive behavior, feelings of deep emptiness and identity disturbance, and angry disruptions in close relationships.

People with histrionic personality disorder experience difficult romantic relationships and friendships. They have trouble balancing strong needs for attention and intimacy with the reality of a situation. They have trouble delaying gratification and tend to act impulsively. People with this disorder have an intense need to be loved, desired, and involved with others on an intimate basis and will use various means toward this end. They may use their physical appearance to draw attention to themselves and be melodramatically emotional or inappropriately seductive. They may perceive a relationship as being more intimate than it is because of their need for romantic fantasy.

Table 10.8 DSM-5-TR

Histrionic Personality Disorder
A pervasive pattern of excessive emotionality and attention seeking, beginning by early adulthood and present in a variety of contexts, as indicated by five (or more) of the following: 1. Is uncomfortable in situations in which he or she is not the center of attention. 2. Interaction with others is often characterized by inappropriate sexually seductive or provocative behavior. 3. Displays rapidly shifting and shallow expression of emotions. 4. Consistently uses physical appearance to draw attention to self. 5. Has a style of speech that is excessively impressionistic and lacking of detail. 6. Shows self-dramatization, theatricality, and exaggerated expression of emotion. 7. Is suggestible. 8. Considers relationships to be more intimate than they actually are.

American Psychiatric Association. (2022). *Diagnostic and statistical manual of mental disorders* (5th ed., text rev.). Arlington, VA: American Psychiatric Association.

Narcissistic Personality Disorder

Have you ever known someone who talked endlessly about their accomplishments? Some people who promote themselves have a healthy level of self-confidence

Those with histrionic personality disorder like to be the center of attention.

Peter Cade/Stone/Getty Images

that might be annoying but not pathological. Other people, however, have such a strong need to impress others that they experience many social problems. People with **narcissistic personality disorder** display grandiosity, need for admiration, and lack of empathy for others (refer to **Table 10.9**). People with this disorder have an exaggerated sense of self-importance and believe they are so unique they can only be understood by similarly "special" people. These views lead to distasteful interpersonal behaviors such as arrogance, exploitation, and a sense of entitlement (King et al., 2020). Narcissistic personality disorder differs from borderline and histrionic personality disorders in that those with narcissistic personality disorder have marked grandiosity but less self-destructiveness, impulsivity, or concerns about abandonment.

People with narcissistic personality disorder seem to have high self-confidence and self-esteem but are actually quite vulnerable to real or perceived threats to their status (Edershile et al., 2021). People with the disorder may express rage or become vengeful if challenged. They tend to have "serial friendships," meaning relationships end when others no longer express admiration or envy. People with the disorder cannot tolerate criticism or defeat, and this may keep them from high levels of achievement.

Table 10.9 DSM-5-TR

Narcissistic Personality Disorder

A pervasive pattern of grandiosity (in fantasy or behavior), need for admiration, and lack of empathy, beginning by early adulthood and present in a variety of contexts, as indicated by five (or more) of the following:

1. Has a grandiose sense of self-importance.
2. Is preoccupied with fantasies of unlimited success, power, brilliance, beauty, or ideal love.
3. Believes that he or she is "special" and unique and can only be understood by, or should associate with, other special or high-status people (or institutions).
4. Requires excessive admiration.
5. Has a sense of entitlement.
6. Is interpersonally exploitative.
7. Lacks empathy: is unwilling to recognize or identify with the feelings and needs of others.
8. Is often envious of others or believes that others are envious of him or her.
9. Shows arrogant, haughty behaviors or attitudes.

American Psychiatric Association. (2022). *Diagnostic and statistical manual of mental disorders* (5th ed., text rev.). Arlington, VA: American Psychiatric Association.

Epidemiology of Dramatic Personality Disorders

Researchers estimate that dramatic personality disorders occur in 2.8 percent of the general population. Specific prevalence rates have been reported for antisocial (1.4 percent) and borderline (1.8 percent) personality disorders (Winsper et al., 2020). Features of borderline personality disorder also commonly occur in college students (refer to **Focus on College Students: Personality Disorders**). Histrionic and narcissistic personality disorders may be less common. Specific prevalence rates have been reported for histrionic (0.6 percent) and narcissistic (1.9 percent) personality disorders (Winsper et al., 2020).

People with antisocial personality disorder are commonly found in substance use treatment, forensic, and prison settings (Azevedo et al., 2020). In general, antisocial personality disorder shows the strongest association with a wide range of criminal offenses, compared with other personality disorders (Nichita & Buckley, 2020). Antisocial personality disorder is more common among

Focus On College Students

Personality Disorders

A common set of problems in college students includes depression, suicidal ideation, nonsuicidal self-injury, and features of borderline personality disorder. About 15 percent of college students have substantial features of borderline personality disorder, and about 4 percent have a probable or definite diagnosis (Pistorello et al., 2012). A key predictor of symptoms of borderline personality disorder in college students is a history of child sexual maltreatment. In addition, pervasive invalidation by a primary caregiver, which may include rejection, hostility, and neglect, tends to predict features of borderline personality disorder (Hong & Lishner, 2016). Others have also found that rejection sensitivity, or the tendency to anxiously anticipate and readily perceive social rejection, helps explain why borderline features lead to less social support among some college students (Zielinski & Veilleux, 2014).

One group of researchers thus tested a dialectical treatment program for college students with nonsuicidal self-injury and features of borderline personality disorder. Treatment included individual and group therapy that focused on distress tolerance, emotional regulation, interpersonal effectiveness, and mindfulness. Those who completed treatment showed improvements in suicidality and suicidal thoughts, depression, social adjustment, and symptoms of borderline personality disorder (Pistorello et al., 2012). Briefer dialectical behavior therapy can also be successful for college students (Chugani et al., 2020). Treatment for suicidality, depression, and features of borderline personality disorder is thus effective for college students and adaptable to campus counseling centers.

men and is often associated with difficulties in social functioning, physical health, work, substance use, and relationship stability (Holzer et al., 2022).

Borderline personality disorder is the most frequently diagnosed personality disorder in inpatient and outpatient settings. Borderline personality disorder is closely associated with substance use, depression, and suicidality (Howe et al., 2021). More women than men reportedly meet criteria for borderline personality disorder but men with borderline personality disorder tend to be more aggressive, impulsive, and impaired than women with the disorder (Sher et al., 2019). Borderline personality may be misdiagnosed among adolescents who sometimes become angry and fight with family members. Many youth eventually "grow out" of these behaviors and become responsible adults. People with true borderline personality disorder, however, show chronic and pervasive maladaptive traits into adulthood.

Histrionic personality disorder is diagnosed more among women, but cultural, gender, and age norms must be considered to determine whether a certain behavior indicates this disorder (Schulte Holthausen & Habel, 2018). The diagnostic criteria for this disorder closely resemble traits that define stereotypic femininity, so clinicians may misdiagnose histrionic personality disorder in women (Boysen et al., 2014). Cultural groups also differ with respect to emotional expression (Keltner et al., 2019). Histrionic personality should be considered only if a person's emotional expression is excessive within their cultural group and causes distress or impairment (refer to **Focus On Violence: Personality Disorders and Violence**).

Narcissistic personality disorder appears to be more prevalent among men (Schulte Holthausen & Habel, 2018). The disorder is a controversial one for several reasons. First, idealism is characteristic of many adolescents and young adults and should not be mistaken for the traits and behaviors of narcissistic personality disorder. The disorder should be diagnosed only when such beliefs are extremely unrealistic and cause significant distress or impairment. Second, not all mental health professionals worldwide recognize narcissistic personality disorder. Pathological narcissism may be a manifestation of a modern, Western society that is self-centered and materialistic and less centered on familial or interpersonal bonds (Ronningstam et al., 2018).

Section Summary

- Dramatic, erratic, or emotional personality disorders include antisocial, borderline, histrionic, and narcissistic personality disorders.
- Antisocial personality disorder involves an extreme disregard for and violation of the rights of others.
- Psychopathy involves problematic interpersonal styles such as arrogance, lack of empathy, and manipulativeness.
- Borderline personality disorder involves impulsivity, unstable affect and interpersonal relationships, and suicidality.
- Histrionic personality disorder involves an excessive need for attention, superficial and fleeting emotions, and impulsivity.
- Narcissistic personality disorder involves grandiosity, need for admiration, and lack of empathy for others.
- The most common dramatic personality disorders are antisocial and borderline personality disorders, but all disorders of this group involve substantial distress and/or impairment.

Review Questions

1. What are the main features of antisocial personality disorder and psychopathy?
2. What are key features of borderline, histrionic, and narcissistic personality disorders?
3. Describe the epidemiology of the dramatic personality disorders, including issues of gender and culture.

Focus On Violence

Personality Disorders and Violence

The personality disorders most often associated with violence are the dramatic personality disorders, especially borderline personality disorder and antisocial personality disorder. These personality disorders involve high levels of impulsivity and risk taking. Violence committed by those with borderline personality disorder is typically directed toward themselves in the form of self-harm, self-mutilation, or suicidal behavior. Violence committed by those with antisocial personality disorder, however, is typically directed toward others. Antisocial behavior may be marked by psychopathy as well.

Studies of the relationship between psychopathy and violence have produced some interesting findings regarding the nature of violent acts associated with this condition. People with psychopathy, compared with nonpsychopathic criminals, are more likely to commit violence that is predatory (e.g., stalking), callous or cold-hearted, less emotionally driven, and more premeditated; in addition, psychopathy is associated with reactive (emotional) violence. However, some evidence suggests that people with prominent features of a type of psychopathy—consisting of a chronic antisocial and socially deviant lifestyle—appear more likely to commit crimes of passion and engage in reactive (emotionally driven) violence than their counterparts (Thomson et al., 2022).

Anxious/Fearful Personality Disorders: Features and Epidemiology

LO 10.7 Distinguish between the types of anxious/fearful personality disorders based on their diagnostic criteria and clinical features.

LO 10.8 Summarize the epidemiology of anxious/fearful personality disorders.

Recall that a third cluster of personality disorder involves anxious or fearful behavior that seems apprehensive to others. This group includes avoidant, dependent, and obsessive-compulsive personality disorders.

Avoidant Personality Disorder

Have you ever known someone who was shy and seemed uncomfortable at parties or other social events? Shyness is common in our society and usually tolerated well. Many people who are shy have a good self-image. Other people, however, have intense fears of inadequacy and negative evaluation. These people want relationships with others but have extreme difficulty initiating contact. **Avoidant personality disorder** involves a pervasive pattern of anxiety, feelings of inadequacy, and social hypersensitivity (refer to **Table 10.10**).

Table 10.10 DSM-5-TR

Avoidant Personality Disorder

A pervasive pattern of social inhibition, feelings of inadequacy, and hypersensitivity to negative evaluation, beginning by early adulthood and present in a variety of contexts, as indicated by four (or more) of the following:

1. Avoids occupational activities that involve significant interpersonal contact because of fears of criticism, disapproval, or rejection.
2. Is unwilling to get involved with people unless certain of being liked.
3. Shows restraint within intimate relationships because of the fear of being shamed or ridiculed.
4. Is preoccupied with being criticized or rejected in social situations.
5. Is inhibited in new interpersonal situations because of feelings of inadequacy.
6. Views self as socially inept, personally unappealing, or inferior to others.
7. Is unusually reluctant to take personal risks or to engage in any new activities because they may prove embarrassing.

American Psychiatric Association. (2022). *Diagnostic and statistical manual of mental disorders* (5th ed., text rev.). Arlington, VA: American Psychiatric Association.

Case Betty

Betty is a 47-year-old woman who has been married 27 years. She has five children aged 8, 12, 16, 20, and 24 years. Her husband insisted on having children every four years in their marriage, and Betty complied. Betty has been a homemaker during her marriage, taking care of her children and husband by assuming all household chores. Her few friends describe Betty as meek, quiet, and subservient. She is not the kind of person who "rocks the boat," and she usually complies with others' requests in PTA, Scout, and church meetings. Betty rises at 5 a.m. and will not go to sleep before 11 p.m. unless all her tasks are completed. She was recently hospitalized for depression and exhaustion but left against medical advice to prepare dinner for her family at home.

People with avoidant personality disorder often avoid jobs or situations that require significant interpersonal contact; they are perceived as "shy" or "loners." People with the disorder avoid others because they perceive themselves as inept, unappealing, or inferior. They are also afraid of being embarrassed or rejected by others. People with avoidant personality disorder become involved with others only in situations in which they feel certain of acceptance. Those with the disorder want close relationships, so this aspect makes them different from people with schizoid personality disorder. Other features of avoidant personality disorder include hypervigilance in social situations and low self-esteem.

People with avoidant personality disorder often do well at their jobs as long as they can avoid public presentations or leadership. Social functioning and social skills development are usually greatly impaired, however. If a person with avoidant personality disorder does develop a close relationship, they will likely cling to the person dependently. Many people with avoidant personality disorder also have anxiety-related disorders such as social phobia as well as depression.

Dependent Personality Disorder

Have you ever known someone who was a "follower" and always seemed to conform to what others wanted to do? Many of us occasionally bend to our friend's wishes to go someplace or do something we are not thrilled about doing. At other times, however, we speak up and assert what we want. For people like Betty, however, conformity is a way of life. **Dependent personality disorder** involves a pervasive, excessive need to be cared for, leading to submissiveness, clinging behavior, and fears of separation (refer to **Table 10.11**).

People with dependent personality disorder "give their lives over" to others—they ask for advice and guidance about even the smallest of decisions, seem helpless,

Table 10.11 DSM-5-TR

Dependent Personality Disorder
A pervasive and excessive need to be taken care of that leads to submissive and clinging behavior and fears of separation, beginning by early adulthood and present in a variety of contexts, as indicated by five (or more) of the following: 1. Has difficulty making everyday decisions without an excessive amount of advice and reassurance from others. 2. Needs others to assume responsibility for most major areas of his or her life. 3. Has difficulty expressing disagreement with others because of fear of loss of support or approval. 4. Has difficulty initiating projects or doing things on his or her own (because of a lack of self-confidence in judgment or abilities rather than a lack of motivation or energy). 5. Goes to excessive lengths to obtain nurturance and support from others, to the point of volunteering to do things that are unpleasant. 6. Feels uncomfortable or helpless when alone because of exaggerated fears of being unable to care for himself or herself. 7. Urgently seeks another relationship as a source of care and support when a close relationship ends. 8. Is unrealistically preoccupied with fears of being left to take care of himself or herself.

American Psychiatric Association. (2022). *Diagnostic and statistical manual of mental disorders* (5th ed., text rev.). Arlington, VA: American Psychiatric Association.

and readily abdicate responsibility for most areas of their lives. Their fear that others may reject or leave them is so intense, they will not express disagreements with others. They may even volunteer to do unpleasant, demeaning tasks to gain nurturance and approval. People with dependent personality disorder are prone to low self-esteem, self-doubt, self-criticism, and depression and anxiety-related disorders. Their neediness and desperation often prevents them from carefully selecting a person who will protect them and be supportive. The result may be bad choices—they may choose their partners indiscriminately and become quickly attached to unreliable, uncaring, and abusive people.

Obsessive-Compulsive Personality Disorder

Have you ever known someone who was very organized and attended to all details of a task with great passion? Perhaps you have known someone with a type A personality marked by competitiveness, time-consciousness, impatience, and "workaholism." Attention to detail and organization are considered positive traits in our society, although some aspects of type A personality have been linked to heart disease in men. Other people, however, spend inordinate amounts of time on detail and organization. **Obsessive-compulsive personality disorder** involves a preoccupation with orderliness, perfectionism, and control (refer to **Table 10.12**). Despite the similarity in name, this personality disorder is different from obsessive-compulsive disorder (Chapter 5) in that those with the personality disorder do not generally have obsessions or compulsions.

People with obsessive-compulsive personality disorder are rigid, stubborn, and perfectionistic to the point that tasks never get completed. Their preoccupation with rules, details, and morality cause them trouble at work and outside of work. They are perceived as inflexible and miserly and may be described by others as controlling. Other features of this personality disorder include hoarding, indecisiveness, reluctance to delegate tasks, low affection, rumination, and anger outbursts.

Many people with obsessive-compulsive personality disorder are successful at their career. They can be excellent workers to the point of excess, sacrificing their social and leisure activities, marriage, and family for their job. People with this disorder tend to have strained relationships with their partner and children because of their tendency to be detached and uninvolved but also authoritarian and domineering. A partner may complain of little affection, tenderness, and warmth.

Table 10.12 DSM-5-TR

Obsessive-Compulsive Personality Disorder
A pervasive pattern of preoccupation with orderliness, perfectionism, and mental and interpersonal control, at the expense of flexibility, openness, and efficiency, beginning by early adulthood and present in a variety of contexts, as indicated by four (or more) of the following: 1. Is preoccupied with details, rules, lists, order, organization, or schedules to the extent that the major point of the activity is lost. 2. Shows perfectionism that interferes with task completion. 3. Is excessively devoted to work and productivity to the exclusion of leisure activities and friendships (not accounted for by obvious economic necessity). 4. Is overconscientious, scrupulous, and inflexible about matters of morality, ethics, or values (not accounted for by cultural or religious identification). 5. Is unable to discard worn-out or worthless objects even when they have no sentimental value. 6. Is reluctant to delegate tasks or to work with others unless they submit to exactly his or her way of doing things. 7. Adopts a miserly spending style toward both self and others; money is viewed as something to be hoarded for future catastrophes. 8. Shows rigidity and stubbornness.

American Psychiatric Association. (2022). *Diagnostic and statistical manual of mental disorders* (5th ed., text rev.). Arlington, VA: American Psychiatric Association.

Relationships with colleagues at work may be equally strained by excessive perfectionism, domination, indecision, worrying, and anger. Jobs that require flexibility, openness, creativity, or diplomacy may be particularly difficult for someone with obsessive-compulsive personality disorder.

People with obsessive-compulsive personality disorder may be prone to various anxiety and physical disorders because of their worrying, indecision, and stress. People with the disorder who are angry and hostile may be prone to cardiovascular disorders. Depression may not develop until a person recognizes the sacrifices that have been made by their devotion to work and productivity, which may not occur until middle age. Most people with this personality disorder experience early employment or career difficulties and even failures that may result in depression.

Epidemiology of Anxious/Fearful Personality Disorders

Researchers estimate that anxious/fearful personality disorders occur in 5.0 percent of the general population. Specific prevalence rates have been reported for avoidant (2.7 percent), dependent (0.8 percent), and obsessive-compulsive (3.2 percent) personality disorders (Winsper et al., 2020). Anxious/fearful personality disorders are often comorbid with anxiety-related, depressive, and somatic symptom disorders.

Avoidant personality disorder occurs more frequently in women (Schulte Holthausen & Habel, 2018). Religious and cultural influences may be responsible for self-effacing behaviors in some individuals (Sørensen et al., 2020). Some people may appear to "avoid" socializing with others, especially at events in which alcoholic beverages are served. One must understand the "avoidant" behavior in the context of someone's strong beliefs and prohibitions.

Dependent personality disorder is more common in women (Schulte Holthausen & Habel, 2018). The prevalence and diagnosis of dependent personality disorder may also vary across cultures, however, because many societies value dependency-related behaviors. Western societies place more emphasis and value on expressions of autonomy and self-reliance, so people in these cultures may be more prone to a diagnosis of dependent personality disorder (Winsper et al., 2020). Interpersonal connectedness and interdependency are highly valued in other cultures, so dependency may be perceived as pathological less often.

Obsessive-compulsive personality disorder occurs more frequently in men (Schulte Holthausen & Habel, 2018). Mental health professionals must be careful not to misdiagnose this disorder because many people are conscientious, devoted to their work, organized, and perfectionistic. Only when these features produce significant distress or impairment can they be considered indicators of obsessive-compulsive personality disorder.

Avid_creative/E+/iStockphoto.com

Obsessive-compulsive personality disorder is characterized by perfectionism, excessive dedication to work, and inflexibility.

Stigma Associated with Personality Disorders

LO 10.9 Describe the stigma associated with personality disorders and its impact on those with the disorders.

Many people with personality disorders have strong emotions and impulsive behavior. This kind of behavior can increase the chances of being stigmatized. Paris (2015) highlighted several reasons why those with personality disorders may be stigmatized. First, despite that fact that we all have a personality, we tend to assume those with personality problems bring it on themselves, whereas we attribute our own personality difficulties to challenging situations or events. Second, many mental health professionals (and laypeople as well) still hold the view that personality disorders are incurable, despite evidence to the contrary. Evidence indicates that some mental health professionals believe that clients with personality disorders are more difficult to manage than clients without personality disorders (Weinberg & Ronningstam, 2020). Such negative perceptions may lead some mental health professionals to withdraw or keep their emotional distance from those with powerful affective states such as anger or troublesome behaviors such as self-injury or multiple suicide attempts. Finally, Paris argued that many patients with personality disorder are misdiagnosed and often receive ineffective psychological treatment or medication. The result is often a continuation of symptoms and difficulties, leading to the individual experiencing self-stigmatizing thoughts like "I am untreatable" or "I will never get better" (refer to **Focus On Gender: Mirror Images of Personality Disorders?**).

Imagine a scenario in which negative perceptions of a client with borderline personality disorder can actually worsen symptoms. The cycle may begin when a mental health professional expects that a certain client will be difficult and manipulative. The therapist may then withdraw emotionally to avoid being manipulated and assume that the client's behavior is something the client can control but chooses not to. Unfortunately, the unresponsiveness of the therapist can actually trigger a client's tendency to be self-critical and this may lead to self-destructive behavior. This behavior may induce the therapist to withdraw even more, and the client may eventually leave treatment prematurely (Desrosiers et al., 2020). Anti-stigma interventions for mental health professionals may thus focus on greater acceptance of and commitment to clients with personality disorders as well as enhanced skills training to address difficult behaviors and reduce social distance (Carrara et al., 2021).

Section Summary

- Anxious/fearful personality disorders include avoidant, dependent, and obsessive-compulsive personality disorders.
- Avoidant personality disorder involves a pervasive pattern of anxiety, feelings of inadequacy, and social hypersensitivity.
- Dependent personality disorder involves a pervasive, excessive need to be cared for, leading to submissiveness, clinging behavior, and fears of separation.
- Obsessive-compulsive personality disorder involves a preoccupation with orderliness, perfectionism, and control.
- The most common anxious/fearful personality disorders are avoidant and obsessive-compulsive personality disorders, but all disorders of this group involve substantial distress and/or impairment.
- Strong emotions and impulsive behavior often associated with personality disorders can be a source of stigma for this population.

Review Questions

1. What are the main features of avoidant personality disorder?
2. What are key features of dependent and obsessive-compulsive personality disorders?
3. Describe the epidemiology of the anxious/fearful personality disorders, including issues of gender and culture.

Focus On Gender

Mirror Images of Personality Disorders?

A long-standing debate is whether personality disorders essentially derive from the same causes but go in different directions for men and women. Some disorders do seem more particular to men, especially paranoid, schizoid, schizotypal, antisocial, narcissistic, avoidant, and obsessive-compulsive personality disorders. Other disorders seem more particular to women, especially borderline, histrionic, and dependent personality disorders.

Are certain personality disorders "mirror images" of one another after some childhood trauma? Evaluations of people with antisocial and borderline personality disorders reveal that both groups suffered more child maltreatment than control participants. Those who eventually develop borderline personality disorder often have cognitive schemas related to detachment from others, emotional expression, need gratification, helplessness and powerlessness, and feeling worthy of punishment. Those who eventually develop antisocial personality disorder often have cognitive schemas related to attacking, bullying, and humiliating others (Kunst et al., 2020).

Certain precursors to personality disorders may also be evident in children, some of which may be more pertinent to boys or girls. Precursors to personality disorder that may be more present in boys include restricted emotion, distant relationships, exaggerated sense of self, and lack of concern for others' needs. Precursors to personality disorder that may be more present in girls include expressive emotion, overly close relationships, negative sense of self, and overconcern for others' needs. These patterns may have important ramifications for preventing and treating personality disorders (Chanen & Thompson, 2019).

Personality Disorders: Causes and Prevention

LO 10.10 Discuss the risk factors for personality disorders.

LO 10.11 Evaluate programs to prevent personality disorders.

The next sections cover risk factors and how our knowledge of these factors might help us prevent personality disorders. Researchers of personality disorders often focus on genetic, neurobiological, family environment, cognitive, and personality factors. The following discussion is organized by cluster of personality disorder; for each cluster, biological risk factors, environmental risk factors, and causes are discussed.

Biological Risk Factors for Odd or Eccentric Personality Disorders

Recall that odd or eccentric personality disorders include paranoid, schizoid, and schizotypal types. Genetics likely play a limited role in the development of odd or eccentric personality disorders, with heritability estimates of just 0.29 to 0.38 (Kendler et al., 2011). Schizotypal personality disorder may share a common genetic risk factor with schizophrenia. This is consistent with the theory that schizotypal personality disorder lies on the "schizophrenia spectrum," a continuum of schizophrenia-like syndromes and symptoms. Schizotypal personality disorder may represent a less severe and less dysfunctional form of schizophrenia (Kemp et al., 2021).

Genetics may set the stage for cognitive and perceptual problems important in odd or eccentric personality disorders, especially schizotypal personality disorder. This is known as a *psychobiological theory of personality disorders* (Komasi et al., 2022). Many people with these disorders have trouble attending to and selecting relevant stimuli in the environment (Pan et al., 2022). This results in misunderstandings, suspiciousness of others, extreme social detachment, and trouble separating what is real and what is imagined. These problems appear to be somewhat biologically based.

Twin studies of personality traits also suggest a genetic influence on the development of odd or eccentric personality disorders. The personality traits of restricted emotional expression, suspiciousness, and cognitive distortion appear to be influenced by genetic factors. These three traits are central to odd or eccentric personality disorders (Perrotta, 2020). Genetics may also influence changes in the neurotransmitter dopamine that can predispose a person to odd or eccentric behaviors (Attademo et al., 2021).

Environmental Risk Factors for Odd or Eccentric Personality Disorders

Family factors are also thought to influence the development of odd or eccentric personality disorders. Parental maltreatment, neglect, and emotional withdrawal relate closely to these personality disorders as well as other mental disorders we describe in this textbook (Memis et al., 2020). Odd or eccentric personality disorders are clearly influenced as well by cognitive distortions. Paranoid personality disorder may develop when paranoid beliefs are reinforced by a cognitive set that leads a person to focus on signs of malicious intent in others (Raihani et al., 2021). Examples of cognitive beliefs that underlie odd or eccentric personality disorders are in **Table 10.13**.

Causes of Odd or Eccentric Personality Disorders

Odd or eccentric personality disorders are likely caused by some genetic predisposition as well as stressors that emerge in a person's life (refer to **Figure 10.1**). A genetic predisposition such as a family history of schizophrenia may influence later changes that help produce an odd or eccentric personality disorder. A genetic diathesis may influence family environment—parents who are emotionally withdrawn themselves may become physically or emotionally abusive to a child. A genetic diathesis may also set the stage for dysfunction in the dopamine neurotransmitter system that leads to cognitive and perceptual deficits associated with odd or eccentric personality disorders.

Neurobiology and family environment also influence each other. Some parents may become withdrawn from a child with odd cognitions or behaviors brought about by dopamine dysfunction. Neurobiological vulnerabilities also influence the development of cognitive beliefs such as mistrust and personality traits such as suspiciousness or restricted emotion that characterize odd or eccentric personality disorders. Cognitive beliefs and personality traits influence each other as well, as when a person who believes coworkers mean them harm becomes generally paranoid and suspicious.

Table 10.13 Examples of Cognitions Associated with Odd or Eccentric Personality Disorders

1. My privacy is more important to me than is closeness to people (schizoid, schizotypal).
2. I shouldn't confide in others (schizoid, schizotypal).
3. I cannot trust other people (paranoid).
4. Other people have hidden motives (paranoid).
5. It isn't safe to confide in other people (paranoid).

Reprinted from Beck et al. (1990), pp. 359–363.

Figure 10.1 Sample Causal Model of Cluster A Personality Disorders.

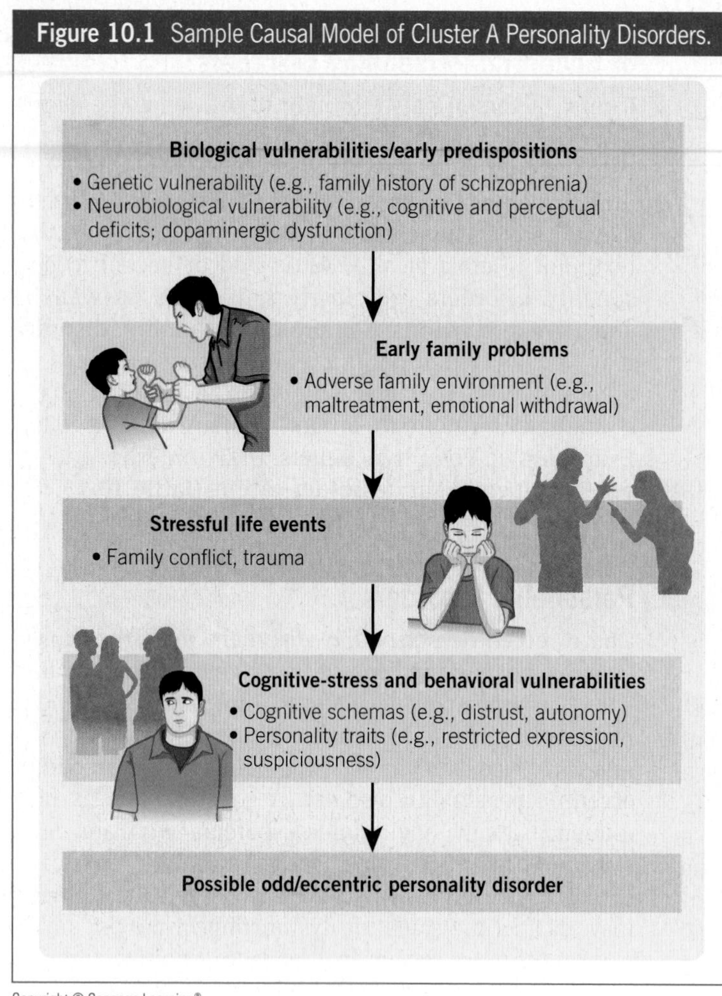

Biological vulnerabilities/early predispositions
• Genetic vulnerability (e.g., family history of schizophrenia)
• Neurobiological vulnerability (e.g., cognitive and perceptual deficits; dopaminergic dysfunction)
Early family problems
• Adverse family environment (e.g., maltreatment, emotional withdrawal)
Stressful life events
• Family conflict, trauma
Cognitive-stress and behavioral vulnerabilities
• Cognitive schemas (e.g., distrust, autonomy)
• Personality traits (e.g., restricted expression, suspiciousness)
Possible odd/eccentric personality disorder

Impulsivity in borderline personality disorder may relate as well to dysfunction of the orbitofrontal cortex (Dusi et al., 2021).

Another dimension important to dramatic personality disorders is affective instability (Reichl & Kaess, 2021). People with affective instability are prone to rapid, intense mood shifts when frustrated, criticized, or separated from others. The noradrenergic neurotransmitter system is most closely associated with these mood shifts. People given substances that release catecholamine, which operates on the noradrenergic system, show intense emotional reactivity. People with significant mood shifts may be hypersensitive to fluctuations in the noradrenergic neurotransmitter system. Affective instability in borderline personality disorder may relate as well to poor functioning in the frontal cortex and other areas important for emotion (refer to **Figure 10.2**; Sicorello & Schmahl, 2021).

Antisocial behavior and affective instability, which are large parts of the dramatic personality disorders, also appear to have significant genetic predispositions (Cupaioli et al., 2021). Antisocial behavior in particular demonstrates a strong family history (Black & Kolla, 2022). Genetic predispositions exist for many other behaviors associated with these conditions as well. These behaviors include anxiety, anhedonia (severe depression), disinhibition, and oppositionality (Chapters 5, 7, and 13).

Biological Risk Factors for Dramatic Personality Disorders

Recall that dramatic personality disorders include antisocial, borderline, histrionic, and narcissistic types. Dramatic personality disorders have moderate genetic predispositions, with heritability estimates of 0.32 to 0.50 (Kendler et al., 2011). Impulsivity/aggression is most associated with borderline and antisocial personality disorder. People high on the impulsive/aggressive dimension, such as Duane with antisocial personality disorder, have a low threshold for action and often act without deliberating. They do not anticipate well the potential negative consequences of their actions and do not profit from past experience or knowledge of negative consequences. Impulsive aggression is associated with reduced serotonin (da Cunha-Bang & Knudsen, 2021).

Psychopathy in adults and conduct disorder in boys are also associated with reduced brain size in areas that may be related to moral development. These areas include the amygdala, frontal and temporal cortexes, superior temporal gyrus, and hippocampus (Van Dongen, 2020).

Environmental Risk Factors for Dramatic Personality Disorders

Child maltreatment relates closely to dramatic personality disorders. Antisocial personality disorder may develop because of traumatic childhood experiences, such as physical or sexual maltreatment, aggressive parents, divorce, and inconsistent parental discipline (Degli Esposti et al., 2020). Borderline personality disorder relates to childhood sexual maltreatment and poor parental bonding with a child due to perceived abandonment or actual separation (Perrotta, 2020).

Various parent–child relationships likely influence histrionic personality disorder, including one in which parental love and attention depends on a child's attractiveness and sexual provocativeness (Sperry, 2015). One result might be that a daughter's self-worth depends primarily on how her father relates to her, and this pattern may repeat itself in adulthood with other men. Psychosocial theories of narcissistic personality disorder primarily focus on underlying feelings of inadequacy that drive one to seek recognition from others (Diamond & Hersh, 2020).

Figure 10.2 Brain Features Most Implicated in Borderline Personality Disorder.

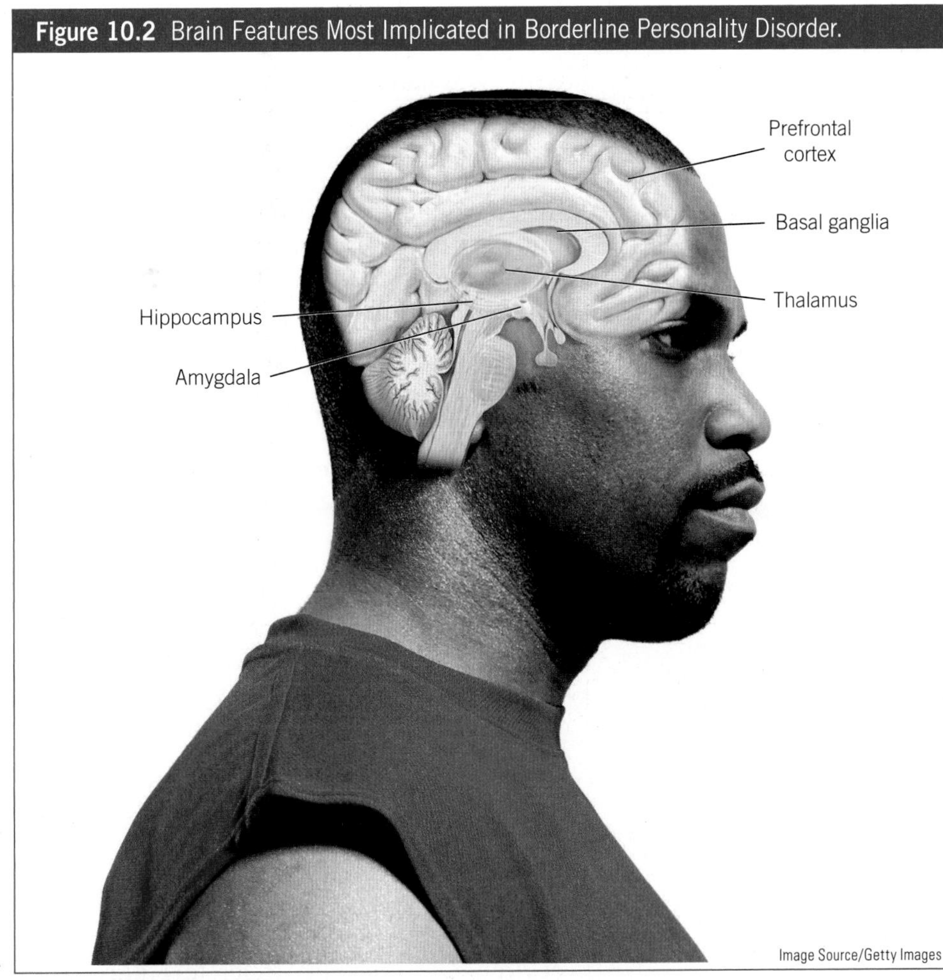

Causes of Dramatic Personality Disorders

Dramatic personality disorders may be caused by genetic predispositions and family-based stressors (refer to **Figure 10.3**). A family history of depressive, bipolar, substance use, or antisocial personality disorder likely serves as a genetic diathesis. This genetic diathesis directly influences family environmental (child maltreatment or poor parental bonding) and neurobiological (impulsive aggression, affective instability) factors related to dramatic personality disorders. Family environmental factors influence, and are influenced by, cognitive beliefs such as "I need what I want *now*" and personality traits such as emotional dysregulation that comprise dramatic personality disorders. Neurobiological factors such as noradrenergic dysfunction also influence these cognitive beliefs and personality traits.

Several cognitive beliefs also underlie symptoms of dramatic personality disorders (refer to **Table 10.14**). Some believe that deception, lying, cheating, and seductiveness are acceptable ways of securing one's needs. These beliefs can lead to aggressive or provocative interpersonal styles and problems that characterize antisocial and other dramatic personality disorders.

Table 10.14 Examples of Cognitions Associated with Dramatic Personality Disorders

1. I should be the center of attention (histrionic).
2. I cannot tolerate boredom (histrionic).
3. Other people should satisfy my needs (narcissistic).
4. Lying and cheating are okay as long as you don't get caught (antisocial).
5. If I want something, I should do whatever is necessary to get it (antisocial).

Reprinted from Beck, et al. (1990), pp. 359-363.

Biological Risk Factors for Anxious/Fearful Personality Disorders

Recall that anxious/fearful personality disorders include avoidant, dependent, and obsessive-compulsive types. Genetics play a modest role in the development of anxious/fearful personality disorders, with heritability estimates of 0.34 to 0.47 (Kendler et al., 2011). Other dimensions of anxious/fearful personality disorders that may have some genetic bases include behavioral inhibition, tendency to anticipate harm or future negative events, excessive sensitivity to negative events, heightened arousal, and a tendency to read threat or potential harm into benign events (Notaras & van den Buuse, 2020).

People with anxious/fearful personality disorders may inherit neurobiological vulnerabilities as well, especially those involving the noradrenergic and gamma-aminobutyric acid (GABA) neurotransmitter systems. These vulnerabilities lead to heightened fearfulness and sensitivity to potential threat. Inherited personality traits may also contribute to the development of these disorders. Inhibition (avoidant personality disorder), compulsivity (obsessive-compulsive personality disorder),

Figure 10.3 Sample Causal Model of Cluster B Personality Disorders.

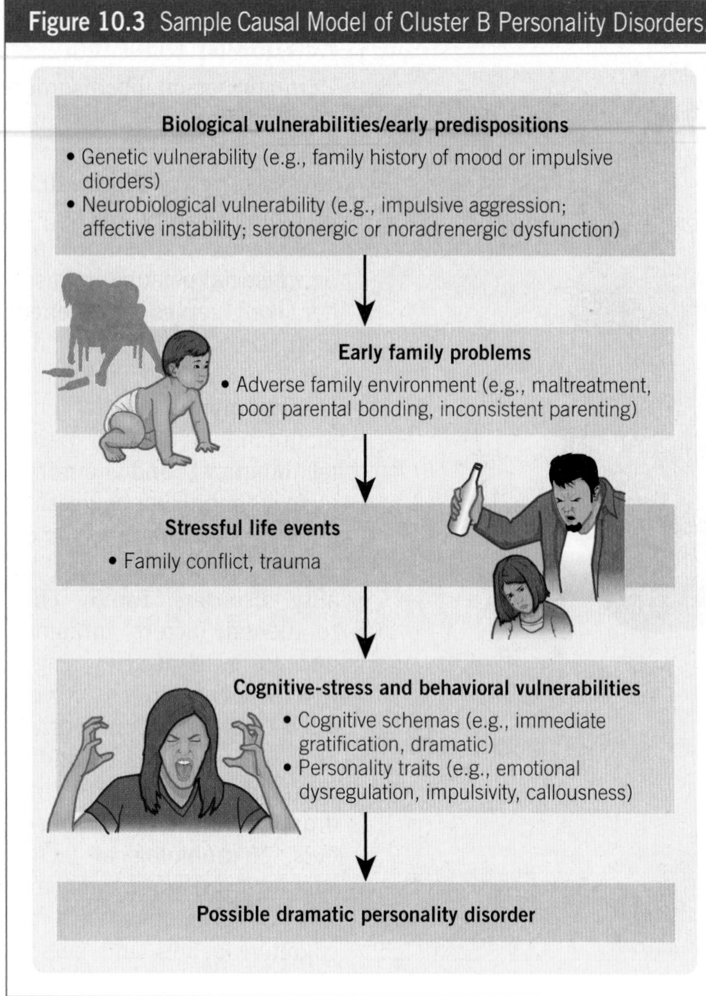

anxiousness, insecure attachment, social avoidance, and submissiveness are traits central to anxious/fearful personality disorders. These traits have a moderate to strong genetic basis (Reich & Schatzberg, 2021).

Biological vulnerabilities/early predispositions
• Genetic vulnerability (e.g., family history of mood or impulsive diorders)
• Neurobiological vulnerability (e.g., impulsive aggression; affective instability; serotonergic or noradrenergic dysfunction)
Early family problems
• Adverse family environment (e.g., maltreatment, poor parental bonding, inconsistent parenting)
Stressful life events
• Family conflict, trauma
Cognitive-stress and behavioral vulnerabilities
• Cognitive schemas (e.g., immediate gratification, dramatic)
• Personality traits (e.g., emotional dysregulation, impulsivity, callousness)
Possible dramatic personality disorder

Environmental Risk Factors for Anxious/Fearful Personality Disorders

Avoidant personality disorder may result when an anxious, introverted, and unconfident person experiences repeated episodes of embarrassment, rejection, or humiliation in childhood (Sørensen et al., 2020). Adolescence may be a particularly difficult time for these individuals because of the importance of attractiveness, popularity, and dating. The interaction of these temperamental traits and negative experiences may lead to cognitive schemas such as excessive self-consciousness or feelings of inadequacy or inferiority that comprise avoidant personality disorder (Valentino et al., 2020).

Dependent personality disorder may result from an interaction between an anxious/fearful temperament and insecure attachment to parents (Priebe et al., 2022). People with the disorder, such as Betty, rely on others for reassurance, help, and a sense of security because they perceive themselves as weak and ineffectual. They are also preoccupied with threats of abandonment, and they feel helpless. These cognitive schemas set the stage for those with dependent personality disorder to become depressed when faced with interpersonal loss or conflict (refer to **Table 10.15**).

Less is known about family or environmental influences regarding obsessive-compulsive personality disorder. Children who ultimately develop obsessive-compulsive personality disorder may have been well behaved and conscientious but perhaps overly serious and rigid (Marincowitz et al., 2021). Cognitive schemas associated with obsessive-compulsive personality disorder include hyper-responsibility for oneself and others, perfectionism, excessive attention to detail, and catastrophic thinking when faced with perceived failure or setback (Kunst et al., 2020).

Causes of Anxious/Fearful Personality Disorders

Anxious/fearful personality disorders may be caused by genetic predispositions and family environment problems (refer to **Figure 10.4**). A family history of anxiety-related disorder may serve as the genetic diathesis for anxious/fearful personality disorders and influences the development of family environment, neurobiological, cognitive, and personality risk factors. Insecure attachment to parents or rejection from parents relate to underlying neurobiological vulnerabilities of anxiety or inhibition. Family environment and neurobiological factors influence the development of cognitive beliefs such as those related to low self-esteem or catastrophizing events. These factors also influence personality

Table 10.15 Examples of Cognitions Associated with Anxious/Fearful Personality Disorders

1. I am needy and weak (dependent).
2. I am helpless when I'm left on my own (dependent).
3. I am socially inept and socially undesirable in work or social situations (avoidant).
4. It is important to do a perfect job on everything (obsessive-compulsive).
5. Any flaw or defect of performance may lead to catastrophe (obsessive-compulsive).

Reprinted from Beck, et al. (1990), pp. 359–363.

Figure 10.4 Sample Causal Model of Cluster C Personality Disorders.

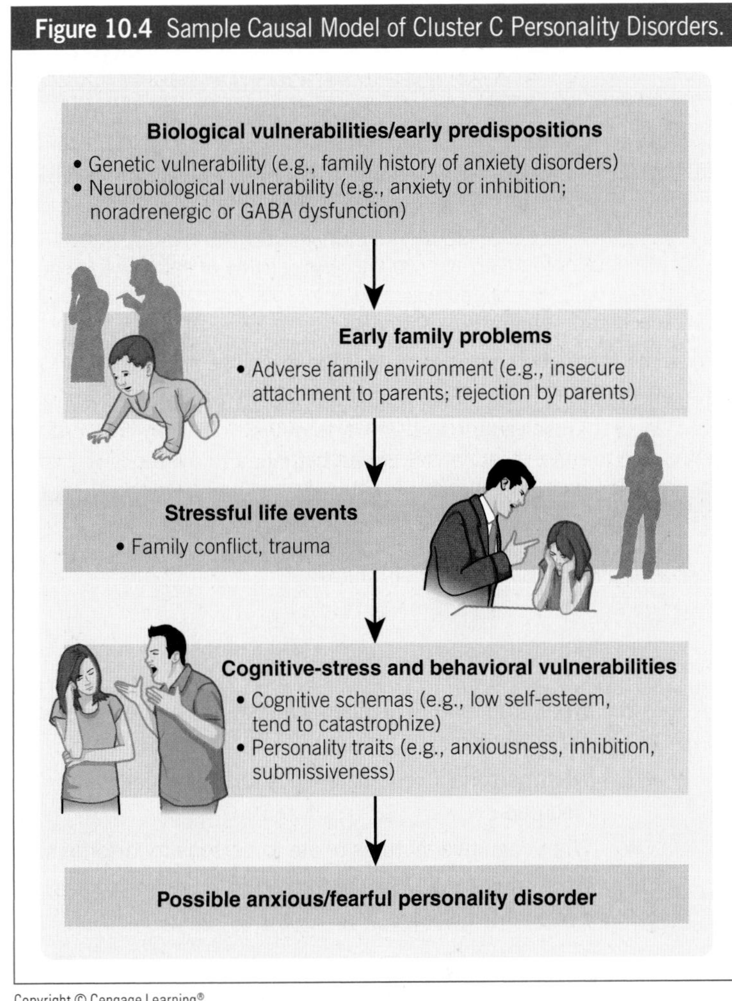

traits such as anxiousness or inhibition that underlie anxious/fearful personality disorders.

Prevention of Personality Disorders

Prevention efforts for personality disorders are rare. Researchers have focused, however, on three major risk factors of personality disorders that may be the focus of future prevention efforts in this area. One of these risk factors is child maltreatment. Efforts to prevent child maltreatment may help influence the development of personality disorders. Successful prevention of child maltreatment often involves frequent home visits, reducing maternal stress, increasing social support, and parent training (Lipscomb & Arkadie, 2020). Skills commonly taught to parents to reduce maltreatment are summarized in **Table 10.16**.

Another main risk factor for personality disorders is poor interpersonal skills. Many people with personality disorders experience great difficulty in interpersonal contexts such as family relationships, friendships, and work situations (Perrotta, 2021). Many are socially withdrawn, aggressive, impulsive, insecure, dependent, and highly attention seeking. Efforts to enhance a person's social skills may help prevent troublesome interpersonal styles that characterize personality disorder.

Interpersonal skills training is especially relevant to deficits found in avoidant personality disorder such as extreme shyness and difficulty initiating relationships. Social skills that are taught can include listening and attending, empathy, appropriate self-disclosure, and respectful assertiveness (McCloskey et al., 2021). Training in each of these skills involves educating a client about the skills, modeling appropriate social interactions, and asking the client to practice the skills.

A third major risk factor for personality disorder is *emotional dysregulation*. Problems in emotional responsiveness such as restricted affect or affective instability characterize many personality disorders. Prevention efforts help people identify, cope with, change, and control negative emotional states. Treatment procedures for borderline personality disorder (discussed in a later section) might be modified for prevention efforts (Chanen & Nicol, 2021). People can learn to describe emotional states (love, joy, anger, sadness, fear, shame), identify events or interpretations that prompt these emotions, understand how an emotion is experienced or expressed, and attend to the aftereffects of an emotion. A training plan for emotional regulation of anger is in **Table 10.17**.

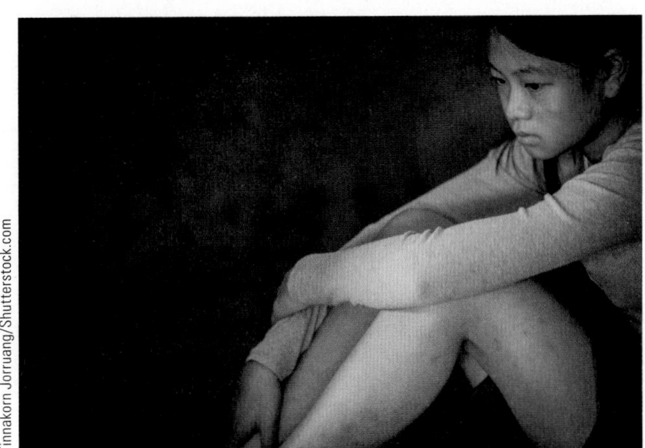

Programs designed to prevent child maltreatment may decrease the likelihood of personality disorder symptoms in these children when they grow up.

Table 10.16 Prevention of Child Maltreatment

Skills taught	
Basic problem solving	Parents are taught to recognize and define typical life problems, list a goal, develop options and plans, and evaluate the outcome.
Positive parenting: enjoying the child	Parents are taught about normative development and how to enjoy the child's unfolding abilities. In addition, parents learn to engage in child-led play and to view the world through the child's eyes.
Parenting skills	Parents are taught how to recognize developmentally appropriate goals for the child, how to make requests in a way that ensures compliance, how to decrease unwanted behaviors from the child, and how to increase desired behaviors through reward and praise.
Extending parenting	Parents are taught about child safety. Instruction includes material on discipline and maltreatment, selecting safe caregivers, childproofing to prevent injury, and supervising children.
Anger management	This module teaches parents to view themselves through the eyes of their children, to recognize and control anger, to relax, and to build in options that can be used if they feel anger is coming on (for example, distracting oneself, taking deep breaths, removing oneself from the situation).

Adapted from "Integrating Child Injury and Abuse-Neglect Research: Common Histories, Etiologies, and Solutions," by L. Peterson and D. Brown, 1994, *Psychological Bulletin, 116,* 293–315.

Section Summary

- Genetic influences may be particularly strong for schizotypal personality disorder because of its place on the schizophrenia spectrum.
- A psychobiological theory of personality disorder suggests that genetics set the stage for cognitive and perceptual problems that underlie odd or eccentric and other personality disorders.
- Parental maltreatment and withdrawal as well as cognitive distortions comprise major environmental risk factors for odd or eccentric personality disorders.
- Dramatic personality disorders have significant genetic predispositions, especially with respect to impulsive/aggressive behavior and affective instability.
- Dramatic personality disorders also relate closely to childhood traumas such as severe maltreatment as well as cognitive distortions.
- Anxious/fearful personality disorders may be caused by genetic factors that underlie anxiety and inhibition as well as difficulties in interpersonal contexts such as relationships with parents, friendships, and coworkers.
- Prevention of personality disorders might focus on reducing major risk factors such as child maltreatment, diminished interpersonal skills, and emotional dysregulation.

Review Questions

1. What aspects of personality disorders have a genetic predisposition?
2. What brain and neurochemical features relate to personality disorders?
3. What personality characteristics relate to personality disorders?
4. What cognitive features relate to personality disorders?
5. What topics might be addressed in programs to prevent personality disorders?

Personality Disorders: Assessment and Treatment

LO 10.12 Characterize the assessment and treatment of individuals with personality disorders.

The previous discussion of features and risk factors for personality disorders was divided into the three main clusters. Assessment and treatment in this area, however, often cuts across many personality disorders; therefore, this section is presented as a general overview.

Assessment of Personality Disorders

Clinicians often use self-report questionnaires, unstructured clinical interviews, semistructured clinical interviews, and informant reports to assess personality disorders.

Self-Report Questionnaires

Self-report questionnaires include items that assess symptoms of personality disorder. Personality disorder questionnaires are easy to administer and economical with respect to time and effort. Self-report instruments are generally used as screening instruments and not as

Table 10.17 Emotion Regulation Training

ANGER WORDS—examples			
anger	disgust	grumpiness	rage
aggravation	dislike	hate	resentment
agitation	envy	hostility	revulsion
annoyance	exasperation	irritation	scorn
bitterness	ferocity	jealousy	spite
contempt	frustration	loathing	torment
cruelty	fury	mean-spiritedness	vengefulness
destructiveness	grouchiness	outrage	wrath

1. Prompting events for feeling anger—examples	4. Expressing and acting on anger—examples
• Losing power or respect • Being insulted • Not having things turn out the way you expected • Experiencing physical or emotional pain • Being threatened with physical or emotional pain by someone	• Gritting or showing your teeth in an unfriendly manner • A red or flushed face • Verbally or physically attacking the cause of your anger; criticizing • Using obscenities or yelling, screaming, or shouting • Clenching your hands or fists • Making aggressive or threatening gestures • Pounding on something, throwing things, breaking things • Brooding or withdrawing from contact with others
2. Interpretations that prompt feelings of anger—examples	**5. Aftereffects of anger—examples**
• Expecting pain • Feeling that you have been treated unfairly • Believing that things should be different • Rigidly thinking "I'm right" • Judging that the situation is illegitimate, wrong, or unfair	• Narrowing of attention • Attending only to the situation making you angry and not being able to think of anything else • Remembering and ruminating about other situations that have made you angry in the past • Depersonalization, dissociative experience, numbness
3. Experiencing the emotion of anger—examples	
• Feeling out of control or extremely emotional • Feeling tightness in your body • Feeling your face flush or get hot • Teeth clamping together, mouth tightening • Crying; being unable to stop tears • Wanting to hit, bang the wall, throw something, blow up	

Adapted from Skills Training Manual for Treating Borderline Personality Disorder by Marsha Linehan. © 1993 The Guilford Press.

diagnostic measures because they do not assess level of impairment or distress. Self-report instruments also do not typically assess whether symptoms were evident since young adulthood.

A popular self-report of various personality constructs is the *Millon Clinical Multiaxial Inventory—IV* (Millon et al., 2015). The measure consists of 24 scales related to all personality disorders and other problems such as depression and excessive substance use. Child and adolescent versions are also available. Recall as well from Chapter 4 that the *Minnesota Multiphasic Personality Inventory—3* is a well-used self-report measure that can suggest diagnoses but also indicates various problematic behaviors and personality styles. Sample items from another popular personality disorder measure, the *Personality Diagnostic Questionnaire—4+*, are in **Table 10.18** (Bouvard et al., 2011).

Table 10.18 Examples of Personality Diagnostic Questionnaire—4 (PDQ-4) Items

Disorder	Example
Avoidant	Over the past several years . . . I avoid working with others who may criticize me.
Dependent	Over the past several years . . . I can't make decisions without the advice, or reassurance, of others.
Borderline	Over the past several years . . . I either love someone or hate them, with nothing in between.
Antisocial	Over the past several years . . . I do a lot of things without considering the consequences.
Paranoid	Over the past several years . . . I keep alert to figure out the real meaning of what people are saying.
Schizotypal	Over the past several years . . . I get special messages from things happening around me.

Reprinted with permission from Steven E. Hyler, M.D.

Interviews

Many clinicians use unstructured clinical interviews to assess personality disorders, although researchers prefer the structured interview. Unstructured interviews allow a mental health professional to ask any question about personality disorder symptoms. Unstructured interviews are often less reliable and more susceptible to interviewer bias than structured interviews, however. Mental health professionals who use unstructured clinical interviews or case review may not assess specific personality disorder diagnostic criteria or they may express cultural bias (Asp et al., 2020).

Structured interviews take more time but are systematic, comprehensive, replicable, and objective. Structured interviews for personality disorder provide a mental health professional with useful suggestions for inquiries about various symptoms. One example is the *Structured Clinical Interview for DSM-5 Personality Disorders* (First et al., 2016). Structured interviews may focus more on diagnostic than dimensional aspects of personality disorders, however, and so could be supplemented by other instruments that measure personality traits (Hummelen et al., 2021).

Informant Reports

A disadvantage of self-report questionnaires and interviews is their emphasis on a person's self-report. This is a problem because many people with personality disorders have distorted self-image and self-presentation that can color their answers on these measures. An alternative method of assessing personality disorder is the **informant report** (Oltmanns & Widiger, 2021).

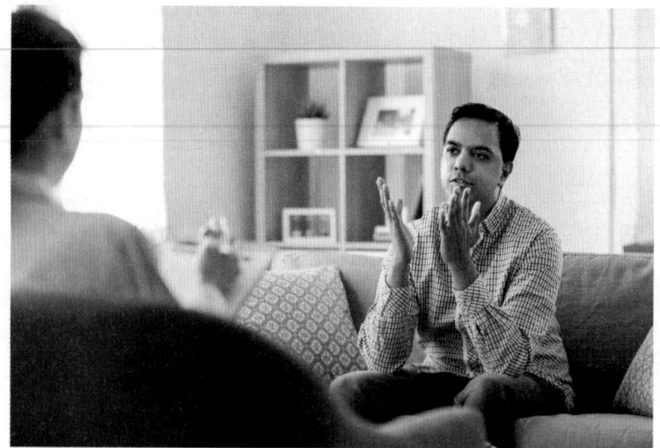

Ground Picture/Shutterstock.com

Structured interviews are the gold standard for personality disorder assessment.

Informants such as family members or close friends can provide an important historical perspective on a person's traits, especially if the informants themselves have no mental disorder.

Informant reports do have some downsides, however. These reports often conflict with self-reports, and so a clinician may be unsure which perspective is most truthful (Hutsebaut et al., 2021). Relatives and close friends will not know everything about a person that would be necessary to provide a valid description, they may be biased, and they may have false assumptions about or expectations of a person. Informant report of personality disorder features remains a promising assessment method, however (Brauer et al., 2022).

Biological Treatments of Personality Disorders

People with personality disorders appear to benefit to some degree from various medications. Medication use has been targeted primarily toward those with borderline personality disorder. Medications for this population include antidepressant, antianxiety, and antipsychotic drugs. The beneficial effects of these drugs are usually limited to one area of functioning such as impulsivity or affective instability. Not all studies indicate positive results, however, and many people drop out of medication treatment (Gartlehner et al., 2021).

Medication may be more effective for specific groups of symptoms and not an overall personality disorder. Three main symptom groups that may respond to medication include *cognitive-perceptual, affect,* and *impulsive aggression* (Stoffers-Winterling et al., 2021). Cognitive-perceptual symptoms of odd or eccentric personality disorders may be treated with antipsychotic drugs such as perphenazine, trifluoperazine, or haloperidol (Chapter 12). Affective (emotional) symptoms of dramatic personality disorders may be treated with selective serotonin reuptake inhibitors such as fluoxetine or mood stabilizers such as topiramate or lamotrigine (Chapter 7).

Impulsive aggressive problems of people with dramatic personality disorders may be treated with selective serotonin reuptake inhibitors, mood stabilizers (Chapter 7), or antipsychotic drugs.

Psychological Treatments of Personality Disorders

Personality disorders are among the most difficult mental disorders to treat because their symptoms are severe, chronic, long-standing, and associated with intense dysfunction, distress, and impairment. Clinicians in this area usually focus on maladaptive personality traits (Cheli, 2020).

Not everyone with a personality disorder seeks treatment, but some do. Some people with personality disorder, particularly those with borderline personality disorder, seek many forms of treatment such as individual, group, and family/couple therapy; day treatment; hospitalization; and medication. People with borderline personality disorder also pursue lengthy treatment (McMain et al., 2022). Many treatment studies in personality disorder thus focus on borderline personality disorder; common therapies used include short-term psychodynamic, cognitive-behavioral, and dialectical behavior therapies (refer to **Focus On Law and Ethics: Personality and Insanity**).

Short-Term Psychodynamic Therapy

Short-term psychodynamic therapy involves frequent meetings with a therapist to develop a close alliance and help clients transfer negative emotions. This therapy focuses on conflicts or themes that impede a person's life, such as abandonment, emptiness, jealousy, or aggression. A psychodynamic therapist will explore historical events in a person's life that may have led to problematic personality traits. Issues of child maltreatment or other trauma may also be discussed to help a client develop insight into their symptoms. Interpersonal conflict resolution, appropriate emotional experience, and less self-destructive behavior are key aspects of short-term psychodynamic therapy as well (Busmann et al., 2021).

Jupiter Images/Getty Images

Family members can provide useful information about someone's personality traits and problems.

Cognitive-Behavioral Therapy

Cognitive-behavioral therapy for personality disorders often focuses on easing symptoms of anxiety and depression (Chapters 5 and 7). Clinicians may use cognitive therapy to modify unrealistic thoughts, social skills training to improve interpersonal relationships, relaxation training to ease high levels of physical arousal, and behavioral activation to increase social contacts. Marital and family therapy may be used as well to improve communication and problem-solving skills (Helps & Le Coyte Grinney, 2021).

Focus On Law and Ethics

Personality and Insanity

Some people with personality disorders may be prone toward criminal acts. Could they claim a personality disorder as the basis for an insanity defense? People with antisocial personality disorder generally cannot use this condition as an insanity defense (Greenberg et al., 2020). For example, serial killers cannot claim that being a "psychopath" or "sociopath" is grounds for an insanity plea. However, aspects of a certain personality disorder could mitigate responsibility for a criminal act. Recall from Chapter 3 that a common standard for insanity is that a person was unable to distinguish right from wrong at the time of the crime. Impairments and comorbid disorders found in some personality disorders can be so severe that they lessen criminal responsibility (Campbell & Craissati, 2018). An example is someone with borderline personality disorder and a history of severe maltreatment who harmed someone but did so during symptoms of posttraumatic stress disorder and paranoid psychosis.

Gray areas such as this have thus led some states to modify the verdict a jury may give when a defendant asserts an insanity defense. One alternative verdict is **guilty but mentally ill**, which assumes that the defendant is guilty of a crime and that they should receive punishment for the crime. However, the court has discretion to order psychiatric treatment before or after incarceration. Another alternative is **diminished capacity**. This means a person did not have a mental disorder that absolves them for responsibility for a crime but did have a diminished mental capacity. Excessive alcohol use or trauma, for example, may have led a defendant to the point that they did not possess the mental state or intent relevant to the crime. Diminished capacity may mean that a person is convicted of a lesser offense (e.g., manslaughter instead of murder) or given a lighter sentence (Meixner, 2021).

Dialectical Behavior Therapy

One form of cognitive-behavioral treatment, **dialectical behavior therapy**, is quite useful for people with borderline personality disorder (Linehan, 2020). Dialectical behavior therapy addresses symptoms commonly associated with this disorder, including suicidal gestures/attempts, self-injury, and self-mutilation. Clients learn various skills to change behavioral, emotional, and thinking patterns that cause problems and extreme distress. Treatment strategies address each of the following areas:

- *Interpersonal effectiveness skills training:* Clients learn to manage interpersonal conflict, appropriately meet their desires or needs, and say no to unwanted demands from others.
- *Emotional regulation skills training:* Clients learn to identify different emotional states, understand how emotions affect them and others, engage in behavior likely to increase positive emotions, and counteract negative emotional states.
- *Distress tolerance skills training:* Clients learn to tolerate or "get through" stressful situations using distraction exercises (to ultimately gain a better perspective), self-soothing strategies such as listening to beautiful music, and techniques to improve their experience of the current moment such as imagery or relaxation.
- *Mindfulness skills training:* Clients learn to self-observe their attention and thoughts without being judgmental.

Clinicians often conduct dialectical behavior therapy in a group format, and clients often remain in treatment for several months to a year. Dialectical behavior therapy is effective for reducing suicidal behaviors, excessive substance use, number of days of psychiatric hospitalization, and treatment dropout. The therapy may also improve depression and hopelessness in some clients (Warlick et al., 2022). Michelle, the case from the beginning of the chapter, would be a good candidate for dialectical behavior therapy because of her suicidality and her feelings of sadness and hopelessness.

A good way to illustrate dialectical behavior therapy is to present portions of a transcript of an actual therapy session. The client in this scenario was a 30-year-old woman with borderline personality disorder who was hospitalized 10 times in the previous two years for suicidal ideation and self-harm in the form of drinking Clorox bleach, cutting and burning herself, and one suicide attempt. A dialectical behavior *therapist* (T) explains the program and goals to the *client* (C) in the following segment (Linehan & Kehrer, 1993, pp. 428–429):

T: Now, the most important thing to understand is that we are not a suicide-prevention program, that's not our job. But we are a life enhancement program. The way we look at it, living a miserable life is no achievement. If we decide to work together, I'm going to help you try to improve your life so that it's so good that you don't want to die or hurt yourself. You should also know that I look at suicidal behavior, including drinking Clorox, as problem-solving behavior. I think of alcoholism the same way. The only difference is that cutting, burning, unfortunately, it works. If it didn't work, nobody would do it more than once. But it only works in the short term, not the long term. So quitting cutting, trying to hurt yourself, is going to be exactly like quitting alcohol. Do you think this is going to be hard?

SeventyFour/Shutterstock.com

An important component of dialectical behavior therapy involves training in various emotional and interpersonal skills.

C: Stopping drinking wasn't all that hard.

T: Well, in my experience, giving up self-harm behavior is usually very hard. It will require both of us working, but you will have to work harder. And like I told you when we talked briefly, if you commit to this, it is for one year. Individual therapy with me once a week, and group skills training once a week. So the question is, are you willing to commit for one year?

C: I said I'm sick of this stuff. That's why I'm here.

T: So you've agreed to not drop out of therapy for a year, right?

C: Right.

T: And you do realize that if you don't drop out for a year, that really does, if you think about it, rule out suicide for a year?

C: Logically, yeah.

T: So, we need to be absolutely clear about this, because this therapy won't work if you knock yourself off. The most fundamental mood-related goal we have to work on is that, no matter what your mood is, you won't kill yourself, or try to.

C: Alright.

T: So that's what I believe to be our number one priority, not our only one, but our number one, that we will work on that. And getting you to agree, meaningfully of course, and actually following through on staying alive and not harming yourself and not attempting suicide no matter what your mood is. Now the question is whether you agree to that.

C: Yes, I agree to that.

The therapist reinforces the client for using distress tolerance skills when their request for pain medication was refused by their physician in this next segment (Linehan & Kehrer, 1993, p. 433):

T: That's good thinking. That's when you're thinking about the advantages and disadvantages of doing it. OK, so at that point the advantages of making it worse were outweighed by the disadvantages. OK. So you keep up the good fight here. Now what else did you try?

C: I tried talking about it with other patients.

T: And what did they have to say?

C: They said I should get pain medication.

T: Right. But did they say you should cut yourself or hurt yourself if you didn't get it?

C: No. And I tried to get my mind off my pain by playing music and using mindfulness. I tried to read and do crossword puzzles.

T: Um hmm. Did you ever try radical acceptance?

C: What's that?

T: It's where you sort of let go and accept the fact that you're not going to get the pain medication. And you just give yourself up to that situation. You just accept that it ain't going to happen, that you're going to have to cope in some other way.

C: Which I did yesterday. I needed a little Ativan to get me there but I got there.

T: Yesterday?

C: Yeah. I took a nap. When I woke up I basically said, "Hey, they're not going to change, so you've just got to deal with this the best that you can."

T: And did that acceptance help some?

C: I'm still quite angry about what I believe is discrimination against borderline personalities. I'm still very angry about that.

T: OK. That's fine. Did it help though, to accept?

C: Um hmm.

T: That's good. That's great. That's a great skill, a great thing to practice. When push comes to shove, when you're really at the limit, when it's the worst it can be, radical acceptance is the skill to practice.

What If I or Someone I Know Has a Personality Disorder?

People are sometimes screened for personality disorders, and the answers to some basic questions may indicate whether further assessment or even treatment is warranted. Some of these questions are in **Table 10.19**. If you find yourself answering "yes" to most of these questions, then you may wish to consult a clinical psychologist, psychiatrist, or other mental health professional (Chapter 15). Cognitive-behavioral therapy or medication may be best.

Table 10.19 Screening Questions for Personality Disorders

• Do you often have difficulty maintaining boundaries with others or managing your emotions?
• Do you often have trouble directing yourself toward your life goals or engaging in self-reflection?
• Do you have problems understanding the emotions of other people and the effects of your behavior on others?
• Are you unable to be close with others?
• Do you find yourself to be often impulsive, aggressive, detached, callous, or odd toward others?

If you feel concerned about how you relate to others, but do not necessarily have a personality disorder, then teaching yourself to gain better control over moods and impulses and communicating and relating better to others may be helpful. Discuss your concerns with family members and friends as well. Further information about screening and treatment for personality disorders is available from several websites (e.g., http://www.tara4bpd.org/dyn/index.php; http://www.borderlinepersonalitydisorder.com/).

Long-Term Outcomes for People with Personality Disorders

Personality disorders are generally best treated by cognitive-behavioral and some psychodynamic treatments that reduce symptoms and improve social functioning (Keefe et al., 2021). However, long-term changes in personality structure are much more difficult to achieve (Bozztello et al., 2019). Therapy for antisocial personality disorder in particular has not been highly effective (Bateman, 2022). In addition, almost one-third of those with personality disorders do not complete treatment (Iliakis et al., 2021). Factors that do predict treatment completion include commitment to change, good therapeutic relationship, and low impulsivity (Folmo et al., 2021).

Treatment effectiveness for personality disorders may improve if specific treatments are tailored to specific skills and behaviors. Behavioral treatments to lower social fear and improve interpersonal skills are most effective for avoidant personality disorder. Dialectical behavior therapy seems particularly effective for borderline personality disorder (Linehan, 2020). Other personality disorders may be amenable to specific treatments as well. Examples include empathy training for psychopathy, social problem-skills training for antisocial adults, and assertiveness skills training for people with dependent personality disorder (Livesley et al., 2016).

Symptoms of personality disorder often affect outcome for people with other mental disorders. People with anxiety, depressive, and substance use disorders

Personal Narrative

Anonymous

I have borderline personality disorder, and because it is often difficult for individuals who don't have a mental disorder to understand what all the intricacies are of living with such a condition, I'm hoping that the following account will shed some light on the matter. More than anything else, the most important point I wish to convey is that individuals with a mental disorder are very much like anyone else—they wish to be treated with respect and understanding and given the opportunity to share their knowledge and talents to make the world a better place.

Living with a mental disorder has probably been the most difficult, and at the same time rewarding, aspect of my life. Even though I've made great strides to learn to manage my disorder over the past several years, I would have to say that I am still at a point where much of my self-definition is determined by my mental disorder. My hopes are that someday I will move beyond this narrowed definition of who I am and be able to more adequately self-identify with aspects that do not include my disorder and that more positively identify the other competencies that I possess.

If I recall correctly, my disorder dates all the way back to the first memories I have. For some reason, I've always sort of felt biologically "off." I can remember experiencing "weird" feelings, but I still to this day cannot identify exactly what they were. I only know that as I was given the proper medication, these feelings decreased substantially. I was 17 when I saw my first psychiatrist.

My parents would now say that, all through my childhood and especially during my adolescence, something was very wrong, but they couldn't put their finger on it. I experienced a fair amount of negative affect, which often seemed to them a bad "attitude." I was never able to clarify for my parents what was wrong, and because I tended to be a rather compliant child in most ways and didn't verbalize my difficulties, they had no idea the extent of my pain.

From the very first moments of my life, it was obvious that I was a very "sensitive" child. Temperamentally, I was hurt by the smallest of things, needed help dealing with very strong emotions (especially negative), needed help in calming myself, was clingy, and felt overly stimulated by certain environments. I sensed subtleties that others did not pick up on. I hated school because teachers I had often were experienced as too harsh, and even the smallest of correction felt painful to me. My perceptions of others (like a teacher getting mad) were magnified because of my enhanced sensitivity, and the pain of even these normal childhood occurrences was too much for me.

I would not say I had any "traumatic" events happen in my life—at least not anything that many others haven't experienced. My parents divorced when I was 5, and my mother remarried when I was 11. I was not abused or neglected, although I only saw my father on weekends, and he usually was too busy with work to pay much attention to me. I had a difficult time living with my mother and stepfather, never really feeling able to adjust. I think the hardest things for me were the fact that my emotional makeup and that of my family's were very different, and I did not get very important emotional needs met that were imperative to my overall functioning. I was a very expressive child, and my parents were very much the opposite in many ways—they were more reserved, didn't feel the need to talk about feelings as much, and thought that I should be able to "control" my emotions the same way they did. Unfortunately, because of my disorder, this was not possible, and so my pain went underground and unrecognized, and my life got progressively worse.

When I finally did visit my first therapist and psychiatrist, I was given some degree of help, but ultimately was never diagnosed properly and therefore never received the appropriate treatment. My parents continued to seek help for me, took me to a plethora of therapists, and still found that no one seemed able to really do anything to help me get better. It was not until many years later (at the age of 25), after years of hospitalizations, one suicide attempt, one unsuccessful treatment of electroconvulsive therapy (ECT), and a failed marriage, that I was finally given the correct diagnosis. And it was my good fortune that, at that time, the treatment I needed was being provided by the county mental health system that I had entered.

After my divorce, I qualified for SSI and entered the county mental health system of care. I had only ever utilized private insurance, so having to go to the county mental health clinic was quite a change—they only served the most severely disturbed and economically challenged of the population. I had grown up in a very educated, middle-class environment, and for me

and symptoms of personality disorder generally have poorer long-term outcome than people without symptoms of personality disorder (Asp et al., 2020). Underlying beliefs related to personality disorders—such as those in Tables 10.13, 10.14, and 10.15—may predict negative outcome for cognitive therapy for depression (Wojnarowski et al., 2019).

The research on long-term outcome of personality disorders is primarily confined to antisocial and borderline personality disorders. Antisocial behavior

to get on SSI and receive services from the county was a hard adjustment. The ironic thing is that it wasn't until I reached this level of economic need that I finally was offered the proper treatment. None of the private insurances offered this treatment, and knew very little about the diagnosis I had and how to treat it. Unfortunately, to this day, my mental disorder still remains highly stigmatized in the therapeutic community, and many clinicians will not treat individuals like me because they feel our problems to be wearing and intractable.

As I entered the county system, I was given the diagnosis of borderline personality disorder (BPD). Past therapists I had visited had toyed with the idea that I might have this disorder, but few wanted to label me with such a seemingly harsh diagnosis. (Some therapists think that to label someone a borderline is thought to be akin to giving someone the death sentence!) Unfortunately, it was to my detriment. When I started obtaining services from the mental health system, I was told they were just starting a new program for individuals with this disorder and asked me if I would be interested. At that point I was willing to try anything, so I said yes. The treatment was called dialectical behavior therapy (DBT), and is still to this day one of the few empirically supported treatments that work for this population of individuals. I was the first of three individuals to enter this program, and I continued the treatment intensively for the next four to six to eight years.

Because behaviors exhibited by those with BPD can seem outrageous and confusing to many who witness them, analogies may prove helpful to fully understand what these individuals experience. The analogy that resonates closest with my own experience of the disorder relates to the life of a third-degree burn victim. Because burn victims obviously have virtually no skin, any movement or touch may prove excruciatingly painful—great care and sensitivity is needed in all contact. An individual with BPD is very much like a third-degree burn victim, only with no "emotional" skin. Unfortunately, because no one can "observe" the condition, the extreme sensitivity and heightened reactivity of people with BPD seem irrational to those around them. Because the smallest of things affect these individuals, our current stressful and fast-paced society is often not conducive to their particular needs.

Another helpful analogy can be described by thinking about the lens of a telescope. Because individuals with BPD constantly struggle with their perceptions of reality due to such frequent and intense emotional states, their ability to retain clarity of thought is much like constantly looking through a telescope lens that is out of focus. You may be aware that the lens is out of focus, but try as you might, those darn emotions keep wanting to run the show! So even though the reality is that "most people I meet like me," my actual perception is often very different. Most of the time I perceive myself as extremely flawed, utterly incompetent, and deserving of punishment regardless of the fact that others discount these notions of my reality on a daily basis. It's almost like I just have to accept that during periods of intense emotion (which is much of the time), life may appear hopeless, but the negative feelings will eventually pass.

Currently, I am in the process of finishing my master's degree in marriage and family therapy. I have told no one in my program about my disorder. Unfortunately, because there remains so much stigma regarding BPD, it would not be in my best interests to divulge my condition at this time. Ironically, the fact that I am entering a profession that purports to treat individuals like myself with compassion, and yet continues to berate and ridicule us doesn't seem to make much of a difference at this time. Because of the present gap in transfer of information that so often resides between the research community and the everyday experiences of the practicing clinician, I currently remain unable to come forward. However, even though prejudice runs strong right now, I don't believe this will always be so. As individuals like myself enter the field and use our own successes to help others in similar situations, I do think there will be a reduction in prejudice and a recognition that therapists and patients alike, really aren't all that different after all.

And with that, I'd like to leave a quote that significantly reflects my personal beliefs about what truly constitutes a "life worth living":

> I have learned that success is to be measured not so much by the position that one has reached in life, as by the obstacles which he has overcome while trying to succeed.
>
> —Booker T. Washington

Source: Used with permission.

develops as conduct disorder in a child and about 40 to 79 percent of male youth with conduct disorder later develop antisocial personality disorder (Black & Goldstein, 2022). People with antisocial personality disorder experience high rates of mortality, criminality, excessive substance use, unemployment, relationship difficulties, and imprisonment. Many with antisocial personality disorder show fewer symptoms in their 40s; they tend to be less impulsive and commit fewer acts that could lead to arrest or incarceration.

Some with antisocial personality disorder continue a chronic pattern even past age 40 years, however, and continue to commit criminal acts or die prematurely (Black & Kolla, 2022).

People with borderline personality disorder often show a waxing and waning course for their symptoms. Most people with borderline personality disorder improve with time but may still experience impairment in school and work situations (Álvarez-Tomás et al., 2019). Better functioning over time is related to absence of childhood sexual maltreatment, no family history of substance use disorder, and a good work history. Poorer functioning over time is related to unstable relationships, depression, and suicidal and self-injurious behavior (Winsper, 2021). Unfortunately, the suicide rate remains elevated over time in people with borderline personality disorder and especially in those who experienced sexual assault (Rodante et al., 2019). Long-term outcome for other personality disorders has been studied on a more limited basis. Some problems tend to be more stable over time than others, especially the odd/eccentric cluster of paranoid, schizoid, and schizotypal personality disorders. Less stable problems include histrionic, narcissistic, and dependent personality disorders. Personality traits related to these disorders can be particularly persistent over time, such as rigidity, detachment, mistrust of others, impulsivity, manipulativeness, self-harm, and eccentric perceptions (Skodol & Oldham, 2021). Negative temperament and neuroticism in general also appear to be quite stable over time and can predict problems such as anxiety disorders, depression, and cognitive decline (Banjongrewadee et al., 2020).

Section Summary

- Clinicians who assess symptoms of personality disorder typically use self-report questionnaires, interviews, and informant reports.
- Biological treatments for personality disorders involve medications to ease anxiety and depression, stabilize mood, and reduce comorbid psychotic symptoms.
- Psychological treatments for personality disorders include short-term psychodynamic therapy, cognitive-behavioral interventions, and dialectical behavior therapy.
- Psychological treatment for personality disorders is moderately effective but less so than for other major mental disorders. Effectiveness may improve if specific treatments are tailored to specific personality disorders.
- Personality disorders may remit over time but many people experience a chronic course marked by impairment or suicide.

Review Questions

1. Describe the major assessment techniques for personality disorders.
2. What medications are primarily used to treat personality disorders?
3. What general psychological approaches may be used to treat personality disorders?
4. What treatment approaches may be useful for specific personality disorders?
5. What is the long-term outcome for people with personality disorders?

Final Comments

Personality disorders are prevalent in clinical settings and the general population. The disorders produce great distress, social and occupational problems, and serious negative outcomes such as suicide or incarceration. Most symptoms and features of personality disorders develop by young adulthood, so they are especially relevant to young adults. The traits and features that comprise these disorders lie on a continuum, so most of us to some degree, or at least on occasion, experience problems like those with a personality disorder. Personality disorders, unlike many mental disorders discussed in this textbook, can be chronic. This makes it even more important for those with personality disorders to seek help from a mental health professional.

Thought Questions

1. Think about television or film characters that portray someone with many interpersonal problems or conflicts. Is this character a good example of a personality disorder? Which disorder, and why?
2. Have you ever been concerned about the way you interact with others? Are you too shy, outgoing, or abrasive? What factors may have influenced the way you are with other people? What information in this chapter seems most relevant to you?

3. What would you now say to friends who might have concerns about their interpersonal style, emotions, or problems with impulse control?
4. What separates "normal" personality quirks from "psychopathological" personality traits?
5. Do you think personality disorders have more to do with biological, family, cultural, or other factors? Why?

Key Terms

personality trait 282
personality disorder 282
paranoid personality disorder 285
schizoid personality disorder 285
schizotypal personality disorder 286
antisocial personality disorder 289
psychopathy 289
borderline personality disorder 289
histrionic personality disorder 290
narcissistic personality disorder 291
avoidant personality disorder 293
dependent personality disorder 293
obsessive-compulsive personality disorder 294
informant report 304
guilty but mentally ill 305
diminished capacity 305
dialectical behavior therapy 306

Sexual Dysfunctions, Paraphilic Disorders, and Gender Dysphoria 11

Learning Objectives

LO 11.1 Characterize the continuum from typical sexual behavior to sexual dysfunctions.

LO 11.2 Distinguish among sexual dysfunctions using their diagnostic criteria and clinical characteristics.

LO 11.3 Summarize the epidemiology of sexual dysfunctions.

LO 11.4 Describe the stigma associated with sexual dysfunctions and its impact on those with the disorders and their partners.

LO 11.5 Discuss the risk factors for and prevention of sexual dysfunctions.

LO 11.6 Characterize the assessment and treatment of individuals with sexual dysfunctions.

Learning Objectives (continued)

LO 11.7 Characterize the continuum from typical sexual desires to paraphilias to paraphilic disorders.

LO 11.8 Distinguish among paraphilic disorders using their diagnostic criteria and clinical characteristics.

LO 11.9 Summarize the epidemiology of paraphilic disorders.

LO 11.10 Discuss the risk factors for and prevention of paraphilic disorders.

LO 11.11 Characterize the assessment and treatment of individuals with paraphilic disorders.

LO 11.12 Discuss the diagnostic criteria for and epidemiology of gender dysphoria.

LO 11.13 Describe the risk factors for gender dysphoria.

LO 11.14 Characterize the assessment of and interventions with youth and adults with gender dysphoria.

Normal Sexual Behavior and Sexual Dysfunctions: What Are They?

LO 11.1 Characterize the continuum from typical sexual behavior to sexual dysfunctions.

One of the most basic human drives is sex. Most people desire sexual activity or fantasize about sexual activity. Most people engage in regular sexual activity with partners or others. Regular sexual activity usually means a cycle of wishing to have sex, becoming aroused during early stages of sexual intercourse, and achieving orgasm. Sexual desire and intercourse are thus natural and normal human activities.

Problems can develop during this normal sexual cycle, however. **Sexual dysfunctions** refer to problems that occur during *regular* sexual activity. Unusual sexual activities are thus not the problem. Sexual dysfunctions generally refer to problems of sexual desire, arousal, or orgasm as well as pain during intercourse (refer to **Continuum of Sexual Behavior and Sexual Dysfunctions**).

Continuum of Sexual Behavior and Sexual Dysfunctions

	Normal	Mild
Emotions	Regular arousal and desire to have regular sexual behavior.	Lessened sexual desire or arousal before or during sexual behavior.
Cognitions	Thoughts about sexual behavior.	Occasional concern about sexual desire, arousal, orgasm, or performance.
Behaviors	Engaging in regular sexual behavior.	Occasionally engaging in less sexual behavior or less satisfying sexual behavior.

Sexual dysfunctions are considered to be a problem if they cause much distress and interfere with sexual or interpersonal functioning.

Sexual Dysfunctions: Features and Epidemiology

LO 11.2 Distinguish among sexual dysfunctions using their diagnostic criteria and clinical characteristics.

LO 11.3 Summarize the epidemiology of sexual dysfunctions.

Sexual dysfunctions involve a disturbance of the normal sexual response cycle—desire, arousal, and orgasm—or pain during intercourse. Sexual dysfunctions may be *lifelong*, meaning they have been present since a person began sexual relations, or *acquired*, meaning they began after a time when a person had no problem in sexual relations. Douglas and Stacy's sexual problems began after the birth of their child. Sexual dysfunctions may generalize to almost all sexual situations or be limited to specific situations or partners. Sexual dysfunctions are organized as well by intensity, which may involve *mild*, *moderate*, or *severe symptoms*. Finally, sexual dysfunctions must be considered within the context of other factors that might be relevant to cause and treatment. These include partner, relationship, individual vulnerability (e.g., history of sexual maltreatment, depression), cultural/religious, and medical factors (APA, 2022). Features of the main psychosexual dysfunctions are described next.

Case Douglas and Stacy

Douglas and **Stacy** were referred to a therapist for marital problems that largely stemmed from lack of intimacy. The couple said their sex life declined substantially in quantity and quality since the birth of their first child several months ago. Both were exhausted from their new lifestyle of child care and work, felt little desire for sex and were now having problems when sex was attempted. Douglas reported failure to maintain an erection during foreplay and Stacy said she felt little arousal during sex. The couple was drifting apart emotionally and rarely had an extended conversation. Douglas privately admitted to the therapist that he considered having an affair but wanted to repair his marriage. Stacy felt overwhelmed by many new demands on her time and was becoming depressed about lack of support from her husband.

What Do You Think?

1. How do Douglas and Stacy's issues differ from a typical married couple with a new child? Which behaviors seem normal for their situation and which seem unusual?
2. What external events and internal factors might be responsible for Douglas and Stacy's sexual problems?
3. What are you curious about regarding Douglas and Stacy?
4. Do Douglas and Stacy remind you in any way of yourself or someone you know? How so?
5. How might Douglas and Stacy's behaviors affect their lives in the future?

Moderate	Sexual Dysfunction—less severe	Sexual Dysfunction—more severe
Substantially lessened sexual desire or arousal before or during sexual behavior.	Substantial lack of sexual desire or arousal.	Lack of any desire or arousal for sex.
Greater worry about sexual desire, arousal, orgasm, or performance.	Substantial worry about sexual desire, arousal, orgasm, or performance that causes distress.	Obsession-like worry about sexual desire, arousal, orgasm, or performance that causes great distress.
Sometimes avoiding sexual behavior due to lack of desire or arousal, or performance concerns.	Constant problems in sexual behavior due to problems in desire, arousal, or performance or pain during intercourse.	Avoiding all sexual behavior or experiencing severe pain during intercourse.

Male Hypoactive Sexual Desire Disorder

Some sexual dysfunctions involve problems with the *desire* and *arousal* phases of sexual relations. **Male hypoactive sexual desire disorder** is a lack of fantasies or desire to have sexual relations (refer to **Table 11.1**; APA, 2022). The disorder thus has cognitive and motivational components (Wang et al., 2022). If a person is not particularly distressed by this fact, a diagnosis would not apply. Clinicians are encouraged to consider several factors that might affect a person's sexual desire, such as age, living environment, cultural background, and stress level. A diagnosis would not generally be made if a person was unable to have sex or had other problems that prevented adequate sexual activity. The disorder instead refers to someone who simply does not desire to have sex, which may be problematic for the person's partner.

Female Sexual Interest/Arousal Disorder

Female sexual interest/arousal disorder involves lack of interest or arousal in most sexual encounters, which may include reduced physical sensations (refer to **Table 11.2**; APA, 2022). Female sexual interest/arousal disorder may be problematic if partner intimacy is affected. This disorder does not apply if a substance or medical condition, such as pregnancy or reduced blood flow, affects someone's level of arousal.

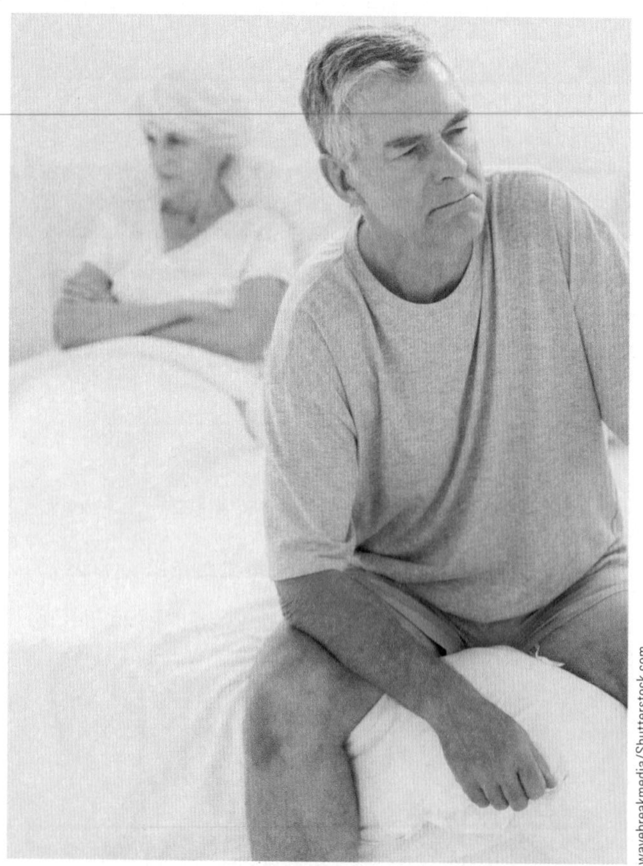

wavebreakmedia/Shutterstock.com

Sexual dysfunctions can cause great distress for a couple.

Erectile Disorder

Some men experience **erectile disorder**, or *impotence*, which refers to difficulty obtaining and maintaining an erection during sexual relations (refer to **Table 11.3**; APA, 2022). Some men cannot attain an erection at all, even during masturbation or rapid eye movement sleep, but others can attain an erection during masturbation but not with a partner (Anderson et al., 2022). Other men attain an erection for a partner but cannot maintain the erection for long or prior to penetration, and still others attain only a partial erection or cannot attain a full erection all the time (like Douglas). Erectile disorder is only diagnosed if the person is highly distressed by the condition. Erectile disorder is not diagnosed if the dysfunction is due to a substance or medical condition.

Female Orgasmic Disorder

Some sexual dysfunctions involve the *orgasmic* phase of sexual relations. **Female orgasmic disorder** refers to a delay or absence of orgasm during sexual relations (refer to **Table 11.4**; APA, 2022). The experience of orgasm is subjective, of course, meaning it cannot be directly measured. Orgasm in a woman with orgasmic disorder should generally be one less intense than what is considered typical for the average woman, and this is based largely on self-report. Female orgasmic disorder must cause considerable distress and must not be caused by a substance or medical condition. Orgasm that can be obtained periodically via intercourse or masturbation is usually enough to *exclude* a diagnosis of female orgasmic disorder unless the woman remains distressed about the situation (Marchand, 2021).

Delayed Ejaculation

Delayed ejaculation refers to delay or absence of orgasm in men during sexual activity with a partner (refer to **Table 11.5**; APA, 2022). The experience of orgasm is

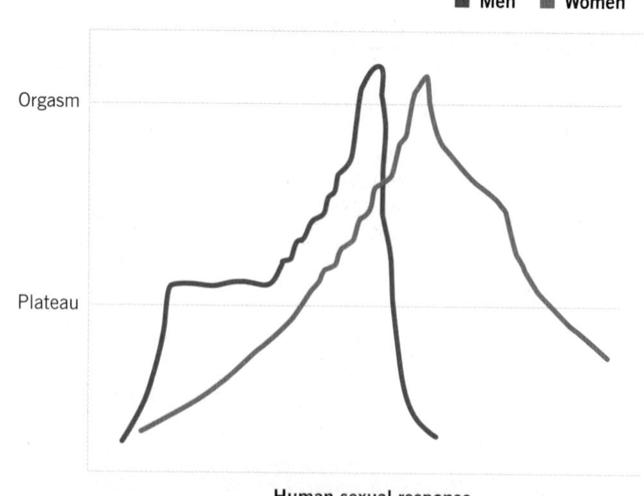

Sexual dysfunctions involve problems with the human sexual response cycle pictured here or pain during intercourse.

Table 11.1 DSM-5-TR

Male Hypoactive Sexual Desire Disorder
A. Persistently or recurrently deficient (or absent) sexual/erotic thoughts or fantasies and desire for sexual activity. The judgment of deficiency is made by the clinician, taking into account factors that affect sexual functioning, such as age and general and sociocultural contexts of the individual's life.
B. The symptoms in Criterion A have persisted for a minimum duration of approximately six months.
C. The symptoms in Criterion A cause clinically significant distress in the individual.
D. The sexual dysfunction is not better explained by a nonsexual mental disorder or as a consequence of severe relationship distress or other significant stressors and is not attributable to the effects of a substance/medication or another medical condition. Specify if lifelong or acquired, generalized or situational, and/or mild, moderate, or severe.

American Psychiatric Association. (2022). *Diagnostic and statistical manual of mental disorders* (5th ed., text rev.). Arlington, VA: American Psychiatric Association.

Table 11.2 DSM-5-TR

Female Sexual Interest/Arousal Disorder
A. Lack of, or significantly reduced, sexual interest/arousal, as manifested by at least three of the following: 1. Absent/reduced interest in sexual activity. 2. Absent/reduced sexual/erotic thoughts or fantasies. 3. No/reduced initiation of sexual activity, and typically unreceptive to a partner's attempts to initiate. 4. Absent/reduced sexual excitement/pleasure during sexual activity in almost all or all sexual encounters. 5. Absent/reduced sexual interest/arousal in response to any internal or external sexual/erotic cues. 6. Absent/reduced genital or nongenital sensations during sexual activity in almost all or all sexual encounters.
B. The symptoms in Criterion A have persisted for a minimum duration of approximately six months.
C. The symptoms in Criterion A cause clinically significant distress in the individual.
D. The sexual dysfunction is not better explained by a nonsexual mental disorder or as a consequence of severe relationship distress (e.g., partner violence) or other significant stressors and is not attributable to the effects of a substance/medication or another medical condition. Specify if lifelong or acquired, generalized or situational, and/or mild, moderate, or severe.

American Psychiatric Association. (2022). *Diagnostic and statistical manual of mental disorders* (5th ed., text rev.). Arlington, VA: American Psychiatric Association.

Table 11.3 DSM-5-TR

Erectile Disorder
A. At least one of the three following symptoms must be experienced on almost all or all occasions of sexual activity: 1. Marked difficulty in obtaining an erection during sexual activity. 2. Marked difficulty in maintaining an erection until the completion of sexual activity. 3. Marked decrease in erectile rigidity.
B. The symptoms in Criterion A have persisted for a minimum duration of approximately six months.
C. The symptoms in Criterion A cause clinically significant distress in the individual.
D. The sexual dysfunction is not better explained by a nonsexual mental disorder or as a consequence of severe relationship distress or other significant stressors and is not attributable to the effects of a substance/medication or another medical condition. Specify if lifelong or acquired, generalized or situational, and/or mild, moderate, or severe.

American Psychiatric Association. (2022). *Diagnostic and statistical manual of mental disorders* (5th ed., text rev.). Arlington, VA: American Psychiatric Association.

Table 11.4 DSM-5-TR

Female Orgasmic Disorder
A. Presence of either of the following symptoms and experienced on almost all or all occasions of sexual activity: 1. Marked delay in, marked infrequency of, or absence of orgasm. 2. Markedly reduced intensity of orgasmic sensations.
B. The symptoms in Criterion A have persisted for a minimum duration of approximately six months.
C. The symptoms in Criterion A cause clinically significant distress in the individual.
D. The sexual dysfunction is not better explained by a nonsexual mental disorder or as a consequence of severe relationship distress or other significant stressors and is not attributable to the effects of a substance/medication or another medical condition. Specify if lifelong or acquired, generalized or situational, and/or mild, moderate, or severe. Specify if never experienced an orgasm.

American Psychiatric Association. (2022). *Diagnostic and statistical manual of mental disorders* (5th ed., text rev.). Arlington, VA: American Psychiatric Association.

subjective, so one must determine if a person is under psychological stress or has other problems that interfere with orgasm. Delayed ejaculation must cause considerable distress and must not be caused by a substance or medical condition. Some men can obtain orgasm via masturbation but not with a partner, so generalized and situational subtypes are considered.

Premature (Early) Ejaculation

Men with orgasmic problems may also have **premature (early) ejaculation**, which refers to orgasm that occurs before the person wishes, such as before or very soon after penetration (refer to **Table 11.6**; APA, 2022). Premature (early) ejaculation is often diagnosed when a sexual partner is dissatisfied with the man's response (Colonnello et al., 2021). A man's environment must be considered as well as his sexual history and experience. Premature (early) ejaculation is usually not a problem during masturbation but can be common during intercourse. If the situation does not interfere with sexual relations and does not cause distress, then a diagnosis is not necessary. If the situation is a frustrating one for the man, then help may be necessary. Premature (early) ejaculation must not be due to a substance or medical condition.

Genito-Pelvic Pain/Penetration Disorder

Sexual dysfunction may also involve pain during intercourse. **Genito-pelvic pain/penetration disorder** involves pain during vaginal penetration and/or fear of pain before penetration (refer to **Table 11.7**; APA, 2022).

Table 11.5 DSM-5-TR

Delayed Ejaculation
A. Either of the following symptoms must be experienced on almost all or all occasions of partnered sexual activity, and without the individual desiring delay: 1. Marked delay in ejaculation. 2. Marked infrequency or absence of ejaculation.
B. The symptoms in Criterion A have persisted for a minimum duration of approximately six months.
C. The symptoms in Criterion A cause clinically significant distress in the individual.
D. The sexual dysfunction is not better explained by a nonsexual mental disorder or as a consequence of severe relationship distress or other significant stressors and is not attributable to the effects of a substance/medication or another medical condition. Specify if lifelong or acquired, generalized or situational, and/or mild, moderate, or severe.

American Psychiatric Association. (2022). *Diagnostic and statistical manual of mental disorders* (5th ed., text rev.). Arlington, VA: American Psychiatric Association.

Table 11.6 DSM-5-TR

Premature (Early) Ejaculation
A. A persistent or recurrent pattern of ejaculation occurring during partnered sexual activity within approximately one minute following vaginal penetration and before the individual wishes it. Note: Although the diagnosis of premature (early) ejaculation may be applied to individuals engaged in nonvaginal sexual activities, specific duration criteria have not been established for these activities.
B. The symptoms in Criterion A must have been present for at least six months and must be experienced on almost all or all occasions of sexual activity.
C. The symptoms in Criterion A cause clinically significant distress in the individual.
D. The sexual dysfunction is not better explained by a nonsexual mental disorder or as a consequence of severe relationship distress or other significant stressors and is not attributable to the effects of a substance/medication or another medical condition. Specify if lifelong or acquired, generalized or situational, and/or mild, moderate, or severe.

American Psychiatric Association. (2022). *Diagnostic and statistical manual of mental disorders* (5th ed., text rev.). Arlington, VA: American Psychiatric Association.

Table 11.7 DSM-5-TR

Genito-Pelvic Pain/Penetration Disorder
A. Persistent or recurrent difficulties with one (or more) of the following: 1. Vaginal penetration during intercourse. 2. Marked vulvovaginal or pelvic pain during vaginal intercourse or penetration attempts. 3. Marked fear or anxiety about vulvovaginal or pelvic pain in anticipation of, during, or as a result of vaginal penetration. 4. Marked tensing or tightening of the pelvic floor muscles during attempted vaginal penetration.
B. The symptoms in Criterion A have persisted for a minimum duration of approximately six months.
C. The symptoms in Criterion A cause clinically significant distress in the individual.
D. The sexual dysfunction is not better explained by a nonsexual mental disorder or as a consequence of a severe relationship distress or other significant stressors and is not attributable to the effects of a substance/medication or another medical condition. Specify if generalized or situational.

American Psychiatric Association. (2022). *Diagnostic and statistical manual of mental disorders* (5th ed., text rev.). Arlington, VA: American Psychiatric Association.

The severity of the pain can vary—some women can have sex with some discomfort, but others must refrain from sex altogether. Even the expectation or fear of penetration can cause discomfort, and many women with the condition avoid sexual relations (Banaei et al., 2021). The disorder must cause significant distress, as when a woman wants to become pregnant but cannot, and must not result from a substance or medical condition. Debate remains as to the nature of this disorder, however (refer to **Focus on Gender: Gender Biases in Sexual Dysfunctions and Paraphilic Disorders**).

Epidemiology of Sexual Dysfunctions

General sexual problems are common in women and men (Briken et al., 2020; refer to **Tables 11.8** and **11.9**). Prevalence rates for formal sexual dysfunctions, however, are difficult to obtain because of the subjective nature of the problems and because people with sexual dysfunctions are not often referred for psychological treatment unless relationship conflict or pain occurs. Many cases of erectile disorder are not referred for treatment until a couple wishes to become pregnant or seeks relationship therapy. Women with sexual pain often refer themselves to gynecologists and not mental health professionals (Carr, 2019; Wheeler & Guntupalli et al., 2020).

Prevalence rates for formal sexual dysfunctions vary considerably. In women, prevalence rates vary for problems of interest and desire (33–35 percent), arousal (21–28 percent), orgasm (16–25 percent), and pain (5–22 percent). In men, prevalence rates vary for problems of desire and interest (15–25 percent), erectile dysfunction (1–10 percent in those younger than age 40 years and then steadily increasing), ejaculation dysfunction (1–10 percent), orgasm (2–8 percent), and pain (16.8 percent; McCabe et al., 2016). Prevalence rates vary widely because of cultural variables and response rates to surveys (refer to differences worldwide in **Table 11.10**). Few racial or ethnic differences have been found in the United States for sexual dysfunctions. Racial and ethnic differences in sexual dysfunctions may be better explained by broader risk factors related to stress, trauma, and health (Parish et al., 2021).

Sexual dysfunctions tend to co-occur with one another and with anxiety-related and depressive disorders (Pyke, 2020). Making distinctions among these

Table 11.8 Prevalence of Sexual Problems by Demographic Characteristics (Women)

	Lacked interest in sex	Unable to achieve orgasm	Experienced pain during sex	Sex not pleasurable	Anxious about performance	Trouble lubricating
Age, years						
18–29	32%	26%	21%	27%	16%	19%
30–39	32%	28%	15%	24%	11%	18%
40–49	30%	22%	13%	17%	11%	21%
50–59	27%	23%	8%	17%	6%	27%
Marital status						
Currently married	29%	22%	14%	21%	9%	22%
Never married	35%	30%	17%	25%	18%	17%
Divorced, separated, or widowed	34%	32%	16%	25%	15%	19%
Education						
Less than high school	42%	34%	18%	28%	18%	15%
High school graduate	33%	29%	17%	23%	12%	20%
Some college	30%	24%	16%	23%	12%	21%
College graduate	24%	18%	10%	18%	10%	22%
Race or ethnicity						
White	29%	24%	16%	21%	11%	22%
Black	44%	32%	13%	32%	16%	15%
Hispanic	30%	22%	14%	20%	12%	12%
Other	42%	34%	19%	23%	23%	17%

Source: Data are from National Health and Social Life Survey (Laumann et al., 1999).

Table 11.9 Prevalence of Sexual Problems by Demographic Characteristics (Men)

	Lacked interest in sex	Unable to achieve orgasm	Climax too early	Sex not pleasurable	Anxious about performance	Trouble maintaining or achieving erection
Age, years						
18–29	14%	7%	30%	10%	19%	7%
30–39	13%	7%	32%	8%	17%	9%
40–49	15%	9%	28%	9%	19%	11%
50–59	17%	9%	31%	6%	14%	18%
Marital status						
Currently married	11%	7%	30%	6%	14%	9%
Never married	19%	8%	29%	11%	21%	10%
Divorced, separated, or widowed	18%	9%	32%	13%	26%	14%
Education						
Less than high school	19%	11%	38%	14%	23%	13%
High school graduate	12%	7%	35%	6%	18%	9%
Some college	16%	8%	26%	9%	19%	10%
College graduate	14%	7%	27%	6%	13%	10%
Race or ethnicity						
White	14%	7%	29%	7%	18%	10%
Black	19%	9%	34%	16%	24%	13%
Hispanic	13%	9%	27%	8%	5%	5%
Other	24%	19%	40%	9%	21%	12%

Source: Data are from National Health and Social Life Survey (Laumann et al., 1999).

disorders can be quite difficult. A person may be primarily depressed and potentially more interested in sex if their mood was better. Trauma-related experiences and posttraumatic stress disorder can also affect sexual dysfunctions (Bird et al., 2021). Distinguishing arousal, desire, and orgasmic problems can also be challenging (Zheng et al., 2020).

Sexual dysfunctions can also relate closely to physical conditions. Women may experience pain because of diminished elasticity or vaginal lubrication, scar tissue, infection, or anatomical problems or diseases (Corosa et al., 2020). Erectile disorder is often related to diabetes and hypertension (Defeudis et al., 2022). Sexual dysfunctions may link to certain substances as

Focus On Gender

Gender Biases in Sexual Dysfunctions and Paraphilic Disorders

Sexual dysfunctions and paraphilic disorders (later sections) are among the most controversial diagnoses. Part of the reason for this is that possible gender bias exists with respect to some of the disorders. Genito-pelvic pain/penetration disorder is an example. A person may blame their partner for avoiding sexual contact but genito-pelvic pain/penetration disorder may be linked to important psychological factors such as depression, anxiety, relationship problems, and past sexual trauma (Alizadeh & Farnam, 2021). For some women, the problem they experience is not just sexual and isolated to them, but rather pain-related and linked to stress in their partner relationships. Successful therapy may require active involvement of their sexual partner.

Conversely, women rarely if ever are diagnosed with transvestic disorder (later section), perhaps because women commonly wear masculine or feminine clothing in public. Men, however, may be more stigmatized for wearing feminine apparel. Think about how other paraphilias such as frotteurism, exhibitionism, and voyeurism (later sections) may have some gender bias.

Table 11.10 Prevalence of Sexual Dysfunctions by Geographical Area for Sexually Active Participants

Sexual dysfunction	Northern Europe	Southern Europe	Non-European West	Central/ South America	Middle East	East Asia	Southeast Asia	Total
Men								
Early ejaculation	10%	13%	16%	22%	8%	19%	25%	14%
Erection difficulties	8%	8%	11%	9%	8%	15%	22%	10%
Lack of interest in sex	7%	6%	9%	9%	13%	12%	20%	9%
Inability for orgasm	5%	7%	8%	8%	7%	10%	15%	7%
Sex not pleasurable	4%	5%	6%	4%	8%	7%	12%	6%
Women								
Lack of interest in sex	17%	21%	19%	20%	29%	27%	34%	21%
Inability for orgasm	10%	17%	16%	16%	17%	23%	34%	16%
Lubrication difficulties	13%	12%	19%	18%	12%	28%	28%	16%
Sex not pleasurable	10%	15%	12%	14%	22%	21%	28%	15%
Painful intercourse	5%	8%	8%	14%	14%	20%	22%	10%

Source: Lewis, R. W. (2013). A critical look at descriptive epidemiology of sexual dysfunction in Asia compared to the rest of the world-a call for evidence-based data. *Translational Andrology and Urology, 2*, 54–60.

well. Examples include low sexual arousal due to antidepressant medication and erectile dysfunction due to smoking (Bakr et al., 2022).

Stigma Associated with Sexual Dysfunctions

LO 11.4 Describe the stigma associated with sexual dysfunctions and its impact on those with the disorders and their partners.

As you might guess, stigma associated with sexual dysfunctions can be quite powerful (refer to **Focus on College Students: Sexual Dysfunctions**). Stigma associated with sexual dysfunction in men is often linked to denial of the problem and failure to seek treatment. Men are often embarrassed to discuss the issue and instead consult various websites for solutions. Researchers have thus proposed that medical professionals should initiate conversations about sexual dysfunction with their male patients, particularly those with risk factors such as medication use for diabetes or heart disease (Russo et al., 2020).

Stigma with respect to sexual dysfunction can apply to women as well. Recurrent painful intercourse is not uncommon among women. However, many women are initially confused about the source of pain, try to pursue strategies for relief that do not work, and are reluctant to seek professional help. In addition, health care providers rarely raise this topic with their patients (Dai et al., 2020). Another source of stigma comes from secondary problems that can result because of sexual pain. These problems include infertility, relationship problems, and divorce. Fertility specialists should thus consider these situations when counseling couples (Luca et al., 2021).

Section Summary

- Sexual dysfunctions involve disturbance of the sexual response cycle and may be lifelong or acquired.
- Male hypoactive sexual desire disorder and female sexual interest/arousal disorder involve lack of fantasies or desire to have sexual relations.
- Erectile disorder refers to difficulty obtaining or maintaining a full erection during sex.
- Female orgasmic disorder and delayed ejaculation refer to delay or absence of orgasm during sex.
- Premature (early) ejaculation refers to orgasm that occurs before desired.

- Genito-pelvic pain/penetration disorder involves problems of pain during intercourse.
- Sexual dysfunctions are common, increase with age, associate with one another and with anxiety and depression, and may link to many medical conditions and substances.
- Sexual dysfunctions can be highly stigmatizing and can affect people's decisions to seek treatment.

Review Questions

1. What sexual dysfunctions affect sexual desire and arousal?
2. What sexual dysfunctions affect sexual orgasm?
3. What sexual dysfunction involves pain during intercourse?
4. Discuss the epidemiology of sexual dysfunctions.
5. Discuss stigma surrounding some sexual dysfunctions.

Sexual Dysfunctions: Causes and Prevention

LO 11.5 Discuss the risk factors for and prevention of sexual dysfunctions.

Risk factors for sexual dysfunctions continue to be explored and likely include biological and environmental variables. These risk factors as well as prevention of sexual dysfunctions are discussed next.

Biological Risk Factors for Sexual Dysfunctions

Recall that biological factors such as medical conditions and substances affect sexual performance. Sexual dysfunctions must not be caused exclusively by a medical condition or a substance; however, researchers often investigate sexual problems that are related to medical conditions or substance use. Medical conditions that impair sexual performance in men include prostate cancer and subsequent treatment as well as cardiovascular problems. Medical conditions that impair sexual performance in women include cervical and other gynecological cancers as well as menopause. Some medical conditions that may affect sexual functioning could also be present in any gender, such as diabetes, general pain, renal disease, multiple sclerosis, and spinal cord injuries or paralysis (Scott et al., 2021). These medical conditions can lead to sexual pain or difficulties with arousal or orgasm.

Various substances also interfere with normal sexual functioning. Examples include alcohol, nicotine, some prescription medications, opioids, and marijuana. Alcohol use impairs male and female sexual performance (Bodnár et al., 2021). Drugs for psychiatric conditions like depression and schizophrenia can also impair sexual response (Trinchieri et al., 2021).

Psychological Risk Factors for Sexual Dysfunctions

Psychological factors also impair the sexual response cycle. One key factor is anxiety or worry during sexual performance about satisfactorily pleasing oneself and one's partner. Men may worry about obtaining an erection, ejaculating prematurely, or having enough energy to complete the act. Such was true for Douglas. Women may worry about pain during intercourse and lack of orgasm. Worry about performance may lead to failure that creates more anxiety and avoidance of sex (Pyke, 2020).

Men and women may also distract themselves during sex to monitor their own performance. The **spectator role** involves greater concern with evaluating performance than enjoying relaxed sexual activity. Sexual experience becomes less enjoyable and less

Focus On College Students

Sexual Dysfunctions

Sexual dysfunctions often increase in prevalence with age, especially for men, so younger college students may not think much about these problems. If a young adult does experience a sexual problem, substantial stigma may apply. One group of researchers surveyed college students in the United States and Sweden and found that self-stigma for a sexual problem was significantly related to less likelihood for seeking professional treatment. This was especially the case for men and religious participants. In addition, men were more likely to seek help from a family physician, whereas women were more likely to seek help from a gynecologist or urologist (Bergvall & Himelein, 2014).

Others have found that sexual dysfunctions in college students often relate to experiences of sexual victimization. One group of researchers found that college women who had experienced sexual coercion or rape reported more sexual dysfunctions related to desire, arousal, and pain than nonvictims (Turchik & Hassija, 2014). College men who had been sexually victimized also report sexual functioning difficulties. Male survivors of sexual assault are especially unlikely to disclose the event, which means they may be less likely to seek help for subsequent sexual dysfunction as well (Luetke et al., 2021).

likely to produce a satisfactory sexual response when a person is distracted from erotic thoughts by criticizing their sexual behavior. Men sometimes try to delay ejaculation by thinking of negative or positive sexual experiences or by thinking about irrelevant items, with variable success (Raveendran & Agarwal, 2021).

Difficulties during sexual performance can also result from poor interactions between partners during sex. Many couples do not speak during sex when a conversation about what a person enjoys and does not enjoy would greatly enhance the experience. One person may wish for more oral gratification and another may wish for more manual clitoral stimulation. These interests should be shared with one another, even during intercourse. Marital or relationship problems can also interfere with adequate sexual activity (Lawless et al., 2022). Problems may include conflict, stress, sexual boredom, difficulty with intimacy or fertility, or impulsive behavior.

Historical psychological variables can be important as well for determining sexual dysfunctions. Early sexual experiences for someone may have been traumatic, as when a child or adolescent is sexually maltreated, when a first sexual experience goes badly, or when fear of pregnancy is intense (Pulverman & Meston, 2020). Future sexual experiences may thus be painful physically and psychologically. Another early factor is family treatment of sex as a "dirty" or repulsive act that was not to be discussed or practiced. Strict religious practices that may lead to punishment of masturbation or other sexual activity may also be a factor (Saleh et al., 2021). These family practices could lead to ignorance about the normal sexual process and problems when sex is attempted, such as attempting intercourse too quickly.

General knowledge about sex over time is important as well, as many aging people require greater stimulation for an erection or experience less vaginal lubrication (Fisher et al., 2020). Acknowledging these normal changes and making adjustments in one's sexual activity to compensate for them is therefore important. People with mental disorders such as depression or anxiety commonly experience sexual dysfunctions as well. These disorders can help cause sexual dysfunctions and help maintain them over time (Pyke, 2020).

Cultural Factors

Sexual dysfunctions are common across various cultures. Cultural beliefs differ widely, however, with respect to whether a sexual problem is thought to be dysfunctional and whether someone will seek help (Newlands et al., 2020). Cultures differ as well with respect to emphasis on sex as important in intimate relationships, sex and procreation, verbal communication about sex, sexual satisfaction, orgasm frequency, religiosity, and multigenerational family members within a household (Armstrong, 2021). In addition, cultures that emphasize female genital mutilation or cutting are obviously responsible for elevated rates of sexual dysfunction (Pérez-López et al., 2020). Other factors relevant to certain cultures, such as violence, depression, and harsh sexual attitudes, can also affect sexual problems (Gul & Schuster, 2020).

Causes of Sexual Dysfunctions

Integrated causal models for sexual dysfunctions have been proposed, and a common one is in **Figure 11.1** (Wincze & Weisberg, 2015). People with dysfunctional sexual performance respond to sexual demands

Figure 11.1 Sample Model of Erectile Dysfunction.

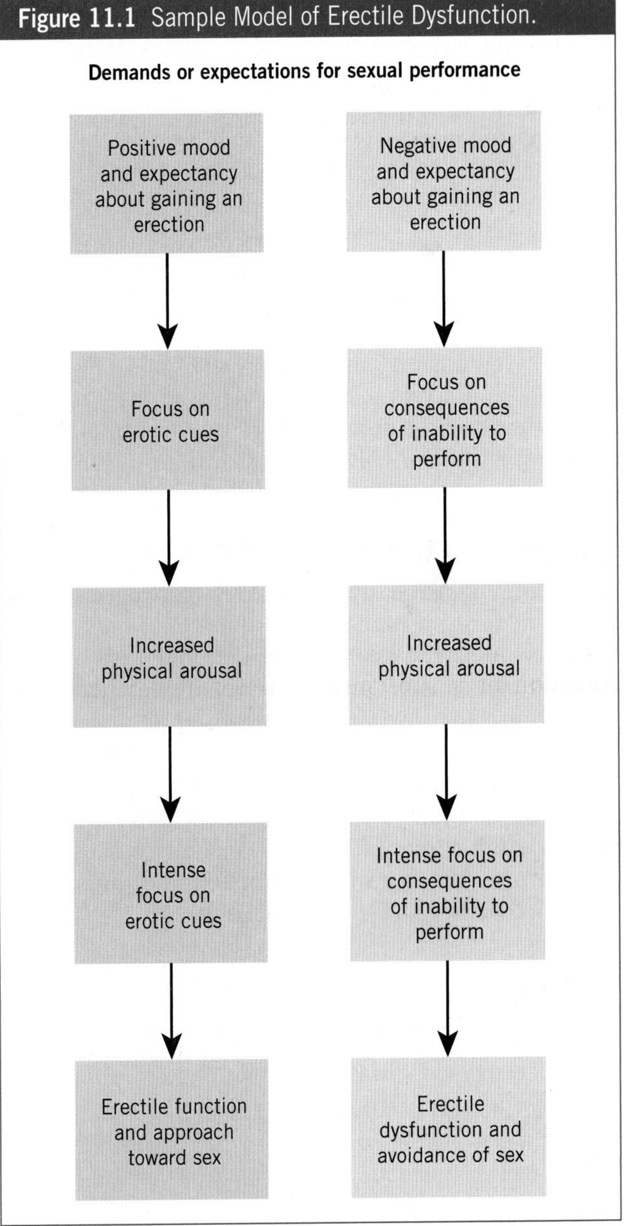

in several negative ways. A person may expect problems to happen, such as anxiety, lack of erection, or pain. The person may then focus on failure to perform rather than enjoyment of the experience, feel helpless or threatened in sexual situations, and avoid many sexual interactions. Avoiding sexual experiences may not allow a person to experience or practice positive sexual interactions. A cycle is thus created that leads to anxiety, lack of control, expectation of failure, and more avoidance.

Causal factors for sexual dysfunction have also been organized along a "balancing scale" that tilts toward successful or dysfunctional sexual performance (refer to **Figure 11.2**; Wincze & Weisberg, 2015). This model includes various biological and psychological risk factors, the presence of which can "tilt" the scale toward one end or another. A person who is depressed, who has negative interactions with a partner, who does not enjoy sexual activity, and who has certain medical conditions may have a certain sexual dysfunction. Douglas and Stacy's sexual experience became dominated by a new, uncomfortable environment that involved exhaustion from child care.

Figure 11.2 Positive and Negative Factors that Affect Sexual Functioning.

	More successful sexual functioning	Less successful sexual functioning
Psychological factors	▶ Good emotional health ▶ Attraction toward partner ▶ Positive attitude toward partner ▶ Positive sex attitude ▶ Focus on pleasure ▶ Newness ▶ Good self-esteem ▶ Comfortable environment for sex ▶ Flexible attitude toward sex	▶ Depression or PTSD ▶ Lack of partner attraction ▶ Negative attitude toward partner ▶ Negative attitude toward sex ▶ Focus on performance ▶ Routine, habit ▶ Lower self-esteem ▶ Uncomfortable environment for sex ▶ Rigid, narrow attitude toward sex
Physical factors	▶ No smoking ▶ No excess alcohol ▶ No medications that affect sex ▶ Good physical health ▶ Regular, appropriate exercise ▶ Good nutrition	▶ Smoking ▶ Too much alcohol ▶ Antihypertensive medication/drugs ▶ Poor physical health ▶ Heart and blood-flow problems ▶ Diabetes

Prevention of Sexual Dysfunctions

Prevention of sexual dysfunctions has focused primarily on *relapse prevention* with couples. Much of this involves booster sessions or other methods to help couples continue to practice psychological treatment techniques for sexual dysfunction and/or manage comorbid physical or psychological problems. Successful prevention of later problems during sex will continue to require effort from both sexual partners as well as good communication. Constant pressure from one partner is not productive and should be avoided (Fahs & Swank, 2021).

Section Summary

- Biological risk factors for sexual dysfunctions commonly include illnesses and substances.
- Psychological risk factors for sexual dysfunctions include worry during performance, relationship problems, traumatic early sexual experiences, strict family practices regarding sex, and limited sexual knowledge.
- An integrated causal approach to sexual dysfunctions likely involves a combination of biological events and expectations that negative events will occur during sex.
- Preventing sexual dysfunctions primarily involves relapse prevention after a couple completes treatment.

Review Questions

1. What biological risk factors may influence sexual dysfunctions?
2. What psychological risk factors may influence sexual dysfunctions?
3. What is the spectator role?
4. How might a "balancing scale" help us understand sexual dysfunctions?
5. How might one help a couple prevent future episodes of sexual dysfunction?

Sexual Dysfunctions: Assessment and Treatment

LO 11.6 Characterize the assessment and treatment of individuals with sexual dysfunctions.

Assessment of Sexual Dysfunctions

Sexual dysfunctions involve many psychological and medical ingredients, so a comprehensive assessment is important. A full health assessment should also precede a psychological one to rule out or medically address any physical problem.

Interviews

Interviews for people with sexual dysfunctions must be done carefully given the highly sensitive nature of the material being covered. Important areas to cover during an interview include sexual history, knowledge, beliefs, desires, and practices. Other relevant information would necessarily involve relationship issues such as marital conflict, medical history and current medications, stress, lifestyle changes, comorbid psychological problems such as depression, and goals for treatment. The interview should also help build rapport with clients who may find such discussions difficult.

Questionnaires

Self-report questionnaires with respect to sexual dysfunctions generally surround issues of sexual satisfaction, arousal, anxiety, preferences, attitudes, and knowledge. These measures are useful but should only be used in conjunction with other assessment measures because self-report may be biased. Common self-report questionnaires for sexual dysfunctions include the *Female Sexual Function Index* (refer to **Table 11.11**) and *International Index of Erectile Function* (Rosen, 2015).

Self-Monitoring

Couples may also record information about their daily sexual history. This could involve descriptions of sexual activity, degree of desire or arousal, type of affectionate behaviors, orgasm frequency and quality, satisfaction with the sexual experience, and emotional states and thoughts about the sexual experience (Tavares et al., 2020). Monitoring information from both partners is important and can be compared to identify discrepancies. Self-monitoring is obviously used instead of direct observation by others given the sensitive nature of the behavior.

Physiological Assessment

Physiological assessment of sexual dysfunctions overlaps to some degree with procedures mentioned later for paraphilic disorders, such as the *penile plethysmograph*. Physiological assessment of sexual dysfunctions remains in development, but a common strategy for assessing erectile disorder is *nocturnal penile testing* (Chaliy et al., 2021). Erections during sleep are monitored physiologically because no sexual anxiety or demands for performance are present. If a man continues to have erectile difficulties during sleep, he may be diagnosed with erectile disorder. If erections occur without difficulty during sleep, then psychological factors such as performance anxiety may need to be addressed. Nocturnal penile testing can be done at a sleep laboratory or using a portable device at home.

Table 11.11 Female Sexual Function Index

Question	Response options
Over the past four weeks, how often did you feel sexual desire or interest?	5 = Almost always or always 4 = Most times (more than half the time) 3 = Sometimes (about half the time) 2 = A few times (less than half the time) 1 = Almost never or never
Over the past four weeks, how confident were you about becoming sexually aroused during sexual activity or intercourse?	0 = No sexual activity 5 = Very high confidence 4 = High confidence 3 = Moderate confidence 2 = Low confidence 1 = Very low or no confidence
Over the past four weeks, when you had sexual stimulation or intercourse, how difficult was it for you to reach orgasm (climax)?	0 = No sexual activity 1 = Extremely difficult or impossible 2 = Very difficult 3 = Difficult 4 = Slightly difficult 5 = Not difficult
Over the past four weeks, how often did you experience discomfort or pain during vaginal penetration?	0 = Did not attempt intercourse 1 = Almost always or always 2 = Most times (more than half the time) 3 = Sometimes (about half the time) 4 = A few times (less than half the time) 5 = Almost never or never

Developed by Bayer, A. G., Zonagen, Inc. and Target Health Inc.

Biological Treatment of Sexual Dysfunctions

Medical treatment for sexual dysfunctions has concentrated most on drugs for erectile disorder. The most well known of these drugs is *sildenafil*, which helps to increase blood flow to the penis and thus to form an erection. Sildenafil—sold under the brand names Viagra, Levitra, and Cialis—comes in pill form, but other drugs may be injected directly into the penis to cause the same effect. The most common is *prostaglandin E1*, which relaxes muscles in the penis to assist an erection.

Other methods to improve erectile quality include *implants* surgically inserted into the penis. These implants may be inflatable, semirigid, or continually rigid to maintain erections, but problems include awkwardness and possible damage to the penis (Chung & Mulhall, 2021). Other surgical procedures may be done as well to correct penile blood flow problems. An alternative to surgery is a *vacuum system* in which a tube is placed around the penis, and a pump helps draw blood into the penis (Del Popolo et al., 2020). The erection is then maintained by placing an elastic band at the base of the penis. Such a device may also be used to enhance clitoral blood flow. Medications remain the primary biological intervention for erectile difficulty, but these surgical and manual methods are also effective.

Other drugs, especially antidepressants, have been used for sexual dysfunctions such as premature ejaculation (Martin-Tuite & Shindel, 2020). Vaginal lubricants and hormone replacement therapy may be useful for painful intercourse (Nappi et al., 2021). Medical problems that result in painful sexual intercourse should be resolved as well. People with low sexual desire may receive *testosterone*, *estrogen*, or *androgen* hormonal treatment (Vegunta et al., 2020). *Flibanserin*, a medication that increases dopamine and norepinephrine and reduces serotonin, has also been used for female hypoactive sexual desire disorder (Simon et al., 2022).

Psychological Treatments of Sexual Dysfunctions

Medical approaches to addressing sexual dysfunctions are often accompanied by psychological approaches, or *sex therapy*. Sex therapy involves different techniques to enhance performance during sex. A common technique for premature ejaculation is the **stop–start procedure** (Gul et al., 2022). The penis is stimulated by oneself or a partner until an erection occurs and ejaculation seems close. The top of the penis is then pinched to suppress stimulation, prevent ejaculation, and allow the erection to be maintained longer. As the person becomes more accustomed to controlling arousal, intercourse begins slowly so ejaculation can be further delayed. In this way, more lengthy intercourse can occur.

For men and women with low sexual desire, sex therapy may consist of initially banning sexual contact and rebuilding a couple's sexual repertoire. This is called **sensate focus**. A couple may be asked to refrain from sex and caress and massage each other only in nonsexual areas—avoiding breasts and genital areas. Both partners can thus become more relaxed and focused on pleasure, and the pressure to perform in intercourse eases. As therapy progresses, partners guide each other's hands to different areas of the body that give the most pleasure for that person. Verbal communication about likes and dislikes during this process is important as well.

Intercourse is gradually reintroduced to the intimacy process as a couple becomes more experienced in relaxing and giving pleasure to a partner during sex. *Fantasy training* and exposure to erotic material to increase the range of sexual fantasies a partner may have during sex may also be done with sensate focus (Seal & Meston, 2020). Douglas and Stacy were relieved by the initial ban on intercourse, and fantasy training helped start them toward a path of better sensuality.

Masturbation training may also be useful for people with orgasmic problems. A partner practices effective masturbation and stimulation so orgasm is enhanced and brought about more quickly (Marchand, 2021). Specific areas of stimulation that help produce orgasm, such as clitoral stimulation, are explored and can then be extended to intercourse with a partner to hopefully bring about orgasm at that time.

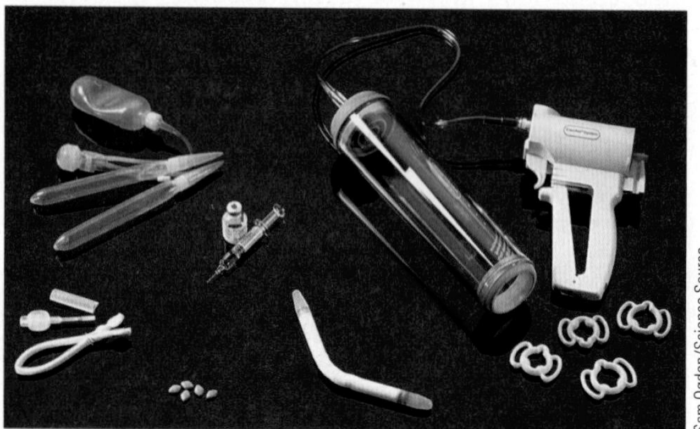

Sam Ogden/Science Source

Various treatments for erectile disorder are pictured here, including a penile vacuum (right). It stimulates blood flow into the penis, and the rings are used to keep the blood in.

Yakobchuk Viacheslav/Shutterstock.com

Sensate focus is a sex therapy technique to enhance sexual pleasure for a couple and reduce sexual dysfunction.

Pain during intercourse may be addressed in various ways as well. Psychological treatment generally focuses on initially prohibiting intercourse, gradually inserting dilators to increase vaginal size, practicing relaxation training, and using *Kegel exercises* to strengthen pelvic floor muscles (Khosravi et al., 2022). Kegel exercises may involve inserting a finger into the vagina and then systematically squeezing and releasing the vaginal muscles. Vaginal lubricants during this process may be helpful as well.

Psychological approaches for sexual problems may also target related issues such as relationship conflict, exhaustion, trauma, depression, anxiety, and excessive substance use. Sex may be scheduled at relaxing and convenient times and places, such as early in the morning or at a hotel away from the demands of children. This was especially helpful for Douglas and Stacy. Increasing sexual knowledge between partners, enhancing safe-sex practices, and reducing sexual myths and avoidance are important as well (Vaishnav et al., 2020). Couples may appreciate that either partner can initiate sex, that condom use is acceptable, and that orgasm is not always the final product of intercourse.

What If I or Someone I Know Has a Sexual Dysfunction?

If you feel you or someone you know may have a sexual dysfunction, then consulting with a physician and clinical psychologist who specializes in these problems may be best. Some screening questions are in **Table 11.12**. Sexual dysfunctions are best addressed by a comprehensive medical examination and perhaps medication as well as psychological procedures to enhance sexual performance. Relationship therapy may also be necessary before pursuing a sexual solution.

Table 11.12 Screening Questions for Sexual Dysfunction

Do you or someone you know have difficulty in sexual relations with others?
Do you or someone you know have little or no desire for sexual intercourse?
Do you or someone you know avoid sex (or conversations about sex) because of performance worries?
Do you or someone you know have trouble achieving an orgasm during intercourse?
Do you or someone you know experience pain during intercourse?

Long-Term Outcomes for People with Sexual Dysfunctions

Some sexual conditions such as erectile problems and low sexual desire often worsen over time. Other problems such as premature ejaculation may get better over time, and sexual satisfaction often improves as couples mature in their relationship. Other problems, such as sexual pain, may not change much without treatment over time. In general, men tend to experience more sexual problems with age than women (Briken et al., 2020).

Many people do, however, respond positively to medical and psychological treatment approaches for sexual dysfunctions. Some women (49.8 percent) who receive flibanserin for low sexual desire improve and some effectiveness has been found for men who receive testosterone (Reddy et al., 2022; Simon et al., 2022). Men with erectile disorder using sildenafil and related oral medications achieve a positive response in 69 to 75 percent of cases (Yuan et al., 2013). Effects of medication may be enhanced by psychological therapy (Atallah et al., 2021).

Psychological interventions tend to be more effective for some sexual dysfunctions than others. Treatment tends to work better for female hypoactive sexual desire disorder and sexual pain and moderately well for erectile dysfunction and female orgasmic disorder (Dewitte et al., 2021; Weinberger et al., 2019). Psychotherapy alone for premature ejaculation may be effective in some cases, but its combination with medication often produces better results (Saleh et al., 2021). Many people drop out of treatment for sexual dysfunctions, however. Positive outcome in sex therapy may relate to good relationship quality, high partner motivation for improvement, lack of serious comorbid disorders such as depression, physical attraction between partners, and treatment compliance (Segraves, 2015). Couples like Douglas and Stacy who work on problems together, and do so in a warm, supportive way, seem better destined for success during sex.

Section Summary

- Interviews for sexual dysfunctions cover sexual history, knowledge, beliefs, desires, and practices as well as relevant relationship issues.
- Self-report questionnaires are useful for assessing sexual dysfunctions and focus on sexual satisfaction, arousal, anxiety, preferences, attitudes, and knowledge.
- Self-monitoring is sometimes used as an assessment technique for sexual dysfunction.
- Physiological assessment of sexual dysfunctions can include nocturnal penile testing.
- Biological treatments for sexual dysfunctions include medication, implants, vaginal lubricants, and hormone therapy.

- Psychological interventions for sexual dysfunctions concentrate on sex therapy to address premature ejaculation, orgasmic problems, pain, and relationships.
- People with sexual dysfunctions generally respond well to treatment, especially if a couple communicates well and complies with treatment.

Review Questions

1. What topics might be covered when using interviews and self-report measures to assess sexual dysfunctions?
2. How can self-monitoring and physiological assessment help a clinician know more about sexual dysfunctions?
3. What medications are available to treat sexual dysfunctions?
4. Describe the start-stop procedure, sensate focus, and masturbation training.
5. What is the long-term outcome for people with sexual dysfunctions?

Normal Sexual Desires, Paraphilias, and Paraphilic Disorders: What Are They?

LO 11.7 Characterize the continuum from typical sexual desires to paraphilias to paraphilic disorders.

Many people engage in regular sexual activity with no problem but have unusual fantasies and desires during sex. These fantasies are usually harmless and do not indicate a clinical problem. Other people have odd sexual fantasies and find a consenting partner to help fulfill the fantasies. If sexual behavior is odd but consensual and legal and causes no harm or distress, then the behavior is considered normal. Many couples mutually agree to engage in sexual "games" that may involve domination, peculiar attire, tickling, videotaping, and other creative activities (refer to **Continuum of Sexual Behavior and Paraphilic Disorders**). Some of these activities can become quite frequent and fervent. **Paraphilias** are preferential, intense, and/or persistent sexual interests that may be odd but are not a mental disorder.

Other people experience unusual sexual fantasies and behaviors that consume much of their time and energy. Someone might spend hours at work on sexual websites, spend all day at an adult store, have urges to do something unusual or illegal, and constantly wonder what it would be like to have sex with different partners. These fantasies and behaviors are not necessarily pathological but do verge on becoming a problem if work, interpersonal relationships, or financial or legal standing are threatened.

For other people, sexual fantasies can become quite distressing, central to their life, or linked to illegal or harmful behaviors that interfere with work, concentration, or regular sexual relationships. **Paraphilic disorders**

Continuum of Sexual Behavior and Paraphilic Disorders

	Normal	Mild
Emotions	Regular arousal and desire to have typical sexual behavior.	Mild physical arousal when thinking about unusual sexual behavior.
Cognitions	Thoughts about typical sexual behavior.	Thoughts about unusual sexual behavior.
Behaviors	Engaging in typical sexual behavior.	Visiting websites that cater to unusual sexual behavior.

include problems arising from sexual behavior or fantasies involving highly unusual activities (APA, 2022). A person's online role-playing may not necessarily rise to the level of a mental disorder. If the person spent so much time satisfying their urges that they were arrested for an illegal activity or were distressed by obsessive fantasies, however, then the person may have a paraphilic disorder.

Paraphilic Disorders: Features and Epidemiology

LO 11.8 Distinguish among paraphilic disorders using their diagnostic criteria and clinical characteristics.

LO 11.9 Summarize the epidemiology of paraphilic disorders.

Major features of the most commonly diagnosed paraphilic disorders are summarized next. Each paraphilia has a particular focus of sexual fantasies, urges, or behaviors (refer to **Table 11.13**).

Exhibitionistic Disorder

The particular focus of **exhibitionistic disorder**, or *exhibitionism* or *flashing* or *indecent exposure,* is exposing one's genitals to strangers who do not expect the exposure (refer to **Table 11.14**; APA, 2022). Tom exposed himself to unsuspecting teenagers in the hope of getting a strong reaction. Paraphilic disorders such as exhibitionism generally involve acting on one's fantasies or having significant distress or interpersonal problems because of the fantasies. Tom acted on his fantasies *and* was quite distressed by them.

A person with exhibitionism may expose themself to others and then quickly flee the scene. Usually no actual sexual contact with others takes place. The person often leaves the scene to masturbate to fantasies that the stranger was sexually aroused by, or somehow enjoyed, the exposure. A person with exhibitionism may

Table 11.13 Major Paraphilic Disorders

Paraphilic disorder	Focus of arousal
Exhibitionistic	Exposing genitals to strangers
Fetishistic	Nonliving object or nongenital body part
Frotteuristic	Physical contact with a non-consenting person
Pedophilic	Children
Sexual Masochism and Sexual Sadism	Humiliation from or to others
Transvestic	Dressing as another gender
Voyeuristic	Secretly watching others undress or engage in sex

Moderate	Paraphilic Disorder—less severe	Paraphilic Disorder—more severe
Strong physical arousal when fantasizing about unusual sexual behavior.	Intense physical arousal when fantasizing about or engaging in unusual sexual behavior.	Extreme physical arousal when fantasizing about or engaging in unusual sexual behavior.
Sexual fantasies that lead to urges toward highly unusual sexual behaviors.	Sexual fantasies about unusual sexual behavior that become central to a person's life and create distress.	Obsession-like sexual fantasies about unusual sexual behavior that cause great distress.
Spending substantial time online or in adult stores, especially regarding unusual sexual behavior.	Inability to concentrate or have regular sexual relationships. Engaging in some unusual sexual behavior.	Engaging in or being arrested for highly unusual sexual behavior such as inappropriate contact with a child.

Table 11.14 DSM-5-TR

Exhibitionistic Disorder
A. Over a period of at least six months, recurrent and intense sexual arousal from the exposure of one's genitals to an unsuspecting person, as manifested by fantasies, urges, or behaviors.
B. The individual has acted on these sexual urges with a nonconsenting person, or the sexual urges or fantasies cause clinically significant distress or impairment in social, occupational, or other important areas of functioning. Specify if sexually aroused by exposing genitals to prepubertal children, mature individuals, or both. Specify if in a controlled environment or in full remission.

American Psychiatric Association. (2022). *Diagnostic and statistical manual of mental disorders* (5th ed., text rev.). Arlington, VA: American Psychiatric Association.

misinterpret the stranger's shock or surprise as sexual arousal (Smaniotto et al., 2021). If the person is caught, however, as Tom was, an arrest is often made. Exhibitionism may also occur with *scatalogia*, or sexual arousal via obscene electronic communications to others (Chan, 2022).

Fetishistic Disorder

The particular focus of **fetishistic disorder**, or *fetishism*, is nonliving objects or a nongenital body area to begin or enhance sexual arousal (refer to **Table 11.15**; APA, 2022). People with fetishism often need certain types of clothing or other objects nearby when masturbating or engaging in intercourse. The objects allow the person to become excited during sexual activity, such as obtaining an erection, and to achieve orgasm. Many people with fetishism prefer female underclothes, stockings, high heels or boots, lingerie, or clothing fabrics such as rubber, latex, leather, nylon, or silk. The fetish object is usually held or seen or smelled during masturbation to achieve excitement, or a partner may be asked to wear the fetish object (Harrison & Murphy, 2022). Fetishism is not a mental disorder unless a person is greatly upset by the urges or behaviors or until the behavior interferes with sexual or other areas of functioning. A nondistressed person whose partner wears high heels to bed would not be diagnosed with fetishism. If the person shoplifted certain shoes for this purpose, however, a diagnosis of fetishism might be warranted.

Frotteuristic Disorder

The particular focus of **frotteuristic disorder**, or *frotteurism*, is physical contact with someone who has not given consent (refer to **Table 11.16**; APA, 2022). Physical contact often involves rubbing against someone in a crowded place such as a bar, public transport, or entertainment event. A person with frotteurism may engage in light contact such as "accidentally" rubbing

Case Tom

Tom was 36 years old when he was court-referred for therapy after an arrest for lewd conduct. The incident had occurred two months earlier when Tom parked his car on a street near a local high school. Three female teenagers walked by Tom's car and saw him masturbating in the front seat. One teenager grabbed her cell phone and took a picture of Tom's license plate as he quickly drove away. The police were called and, based on the picture of the license plate, arrived at Tom's home to make the arrest. A plea arrangement allowed Tom to stay out of jail but with considerable community service, registration as a sex offender, and court-mandated therapy.

Tom's therapist asked him to provide a history of behavior that led up to the arrest. Tom initially said he always had "kinky" sexual ideas, even from adolescence, but had never before acted on them. He often daydreamed and fantasized about being a powerful male figure that was highly attractive to women, particularly adolescents and young women. His fantasies ventured into many different scenarios. One fantasy involved watching young women, including teenagers, undress before him or wear schoolgirl outfits that made them look young. Another fantasy involved sadomasochistic interactions with young women in which he controlled their behavior and attire. Still another key fantasy involved his exposure to young women, who would then (in his fantasy) become attracted to him and wish to spend time with him.

Tom said he had dominating women in his life, including his mother and teachers, and that his personality was actually shy and meek. He thought his fantasies compensated for a deep sense of inadequacy he often felt around women, although he appeared to be socially skilled and not easily intimidated. Tom said his sex life with his wife was normal, that he had been married eight years, that he had one child, and that neither his wife nor anyone else was aware of his secret fantasies. He reportedly had no desire to actually practice his fantasies until about four years ago.

When asked what changed four years ago, Tom said he became more involved in online chat rooms. He discovered various rooms that catered to his fantasies by allowing him to role-play and learn of others' fantasies that soon became his own. He found himself

Table 11.15 DSM-5-TR

Fetishistic Disorder
A. Over a period of at least six months, recurrent and intense sexual arousal from either the use of nonliving objects or a highly specific focus on nongenital body part(s), as manifested by fantasies, urges, or behaviors.
B. The fantasies, sexual urges, or behaviors cause clinically significant distress or impairment in social, occupational, or other important areas of functioning.
C. The fetish objects are not limited to articles of clothing used in cross-dressing (as in transvestic disorder) or devices specifically designed for the purpose of tactile genital stimulation (e.g., vibrator). Specify if in a controlled environment or in full remission. Specify if body part, nonliving object, or other.

American Psychiatric Association. (2022). *Diagnostic and statistical manual of mental disorders* (5th ed., text rev.). Arlington, VA: American Psychiatric Association.

genitals against another person, or may engage in more extensive contact such as groping someone. The person may flee the scene quickly and masturbate to a fantasy of having a long-term relationship with the victim. The person will likely not see the victim again unless they are caught at the time of the incident (Choi et al., 2020).

Tang Yan Song/Shutterstock.com

People with frotteurism often prefer crowded places.

Pedophilic Disorder

The particular focus of **pedophilic disorder**, sometimes called *pedophilia*, is sexual attraction to a child (refer to **Table 11.17**; APA, 2022). Pedophilic disorder is not necessarily the same thing as *child molestation*. Someone who molests children may not be attracted to children but may have sexual contact with them because of deficits in impulse control, social skill, empathy, and emotional regulation (Longobardi et al., 2020). Characteristics of those with pedophilic disorder do overlap to some degree with characteristics of those who molest children, however. The term *sex offender* is a legal one that partly refers to someone convicted of child sexual maltreatment, whether they have pedophilic disorder or not (Zgoba & Mitchell, 2021).

daydreaming more and more about exhibiting himself to young women, who would then be overwhelmed by his sexual prowess and become attentive to him. He role-played many versions of this scenario in Internet chat rooms, found websites largely devoted to his fantasies, subscribed to services that provided pictures related to his fantasies, and even found other people in his area who had similar fantasies and who guided him about the best places to act out his fantasies.

Tom eventually confessed about numerous occasions where he had surreptitiously exposed himself before young women. The exposure was so covert the women did not even know what Tom had done. Tom would then go to a hidden place and masturbate to a fantasy that the young woman had seen his genitals and that she longed to be with him.

Tom engaged in a much riskier exposure on the day of his arrest. He was actively seeking a reaction from one of the teenagers, after which he planned to drive home and masturbate to a fantasy that she was sexually aroused by his presence. Tom was now mortified about what happened and worried about the effect of his arrest on his marriage and career. Tom said he was deeply ashamed of what he had done and wished he could be free of his constant sexual fantasies. He sobbed and said he would do anything to make sure something like this incident would never happen again.

What Do You Think?

1. How are Tom's fantasies and behaviors different from a typical adult? Would any of his behaviors seem normal in a certain context or for someone of a certain age?
2. What external events and internal factors might be responsible for Tom's fantasies and behaviors?
3. What are you curious about regarding Tom?
4. Does Tom remind you in any way of yourself or someone you know? How so?
5. How might Tom's fantasies and behaviors affect his life in the future?

Table 11.16 DSM-5-TR

Frotteuristic Disorder
A. Over a period of at least six months, recurrent and intense sexual arousal from touching or rubbing against a nonconsenting person, as manifested by fantasies, urges, or behaviors.
B. The individual has acted on these sexual urges with a nonconsenting person, or the sexual urges or fantasies cause clinically significant distress or impairment in social, occupational, or other important areas of functioning. Specify if in a controlled environment or in full remission.

American Psychiatric Association. (2022). *Diagnostic and statistical manual of mental disorders* (5th ed., text rev.). Arlington, VA: American Psychiatric Association.

Table 11.17 DSM-5-TR

Pedophilic Disorder
A. Over a period of at least six months, recurrent, intense sexually arousing fantasies, sexual urges, or behaviors involving sexual activity with a prepubescent child or children (generally age 13 years or younger).
B. The individual has acted on these sexual urges, or the sexual urges or fantasies cause marked distress or interpersonal difficulty.
C. The individual is at least age 16 years and at least five years older than the child or children in Criterion A. Specify if exclusive to children or nonexclusive, sexually attracted to males or females or both, and limited to incest. Specify if in a controlled environment or in full remission.

American Psychiatric Association. (2022). *Diagnostic and statistical manual of mental disorders* (5th ed., text rev.). Arlington, VA: American Psychiatric Association.

Pedophilic acts involve behaviors such as observation, exposure, subtle physical contact, fondling, oral sex, and penetration. The exact age at which someone is considered to be pedophilic is controversial but is currently defined as someone at least 16 years old and at least five years older than the victim. Pedophilic disorder may not apply to someone in late adolescence who has sex with someone aged 12 to 13 years but could apply if the sexual partner is younger. This remains controversial, however, because many youths have been identified as sexual offenders (Lillard et al., 2020). Age-of-consent laws vary from state to state.

Many people with pedophilic disorder or those who molest children have a preferred target, such as girls aged 6 to 13 years who have not yet entered puberty. Many people with pedophilic disorder target boys *and* girls, however, especially if victims under

Brad Barket/Getty Images

Genarlow Wilson was convicted of aggravated child molestation at the age of 17 years for having consensual oral sex with his 15-year-old girlfriend. He served two years in prison before the Georgia Supreme Court overturned his 10-year sentence, saying his crime "does not rise to the level of adults who prey on children."

age six years are available (Blackman & Dring, 2016). Those with pedophilic disorder may rationalize their behavior by believing sexual acts somehow benefit a child educationally or sensually (Blalock & Bourke, 2022). Many people with pedophilic disorder are not distressed by their behavior and concentrate on young family members such as daughters and nieces. Those with pedophilic disorder may "groom" a child by offering extensive attention and gifts, then demanding sexual favors in return. Others may even go as far as abducting children. Children are often threatened with loss of security if they disclose maltreatment to others (Grandgenett et al., 2021). People with pedophilic disorder may be subtyped as well along certain characteristics (Fanetti et al., 2015):

- *Preferred victim* (male, female, or both)
- *Relationship to victim* (family member/incestuous or nonfamily member/nonincestuous)
- *Sexual arousal* (to children only or to people of various ages)
- *Aggressiveness* (presence or absence of cruelty during an act of pedophilic disorder)

Sexual Masochism and Sexual Sadism

The particular focus of **sexual masochism** and **sexual sadism** is a desire to be humiliated or made to suffer or to humiliate or to make suffer, respectively (refer to

Table 11.18; APA, 2022). Sexual masochism involves desire to suffer during sexual activity, often in the form of bondage, pain, treatment as an infant (infantilism), extensive humiliation such as verbal abuse, or oxygen deprivation (*hypoxyphilia* or *asphyxiophilia*). Masochistic desires can be fulfilled during masturbation in the form of self-punishment or by involving others. The physical maltreatment sought by people with masochism can be severe and quite painful. Sexual sadism involves desire to inflict suffering on someone during sexual activity, often in the same forms of maltreatment described for masochism. Sadism is often about *controlling* an individual during sexual activity, and sadistic behavior is sometimes conducted toward someone with masochism (Seto et al., 2021). Sadism and masochism can exist in one person (*sadomasochism*) who enjoys switching roles. Sadomasochistic acts can range in severity from mild slapping or tickling to moderate humiliation to severe pain or restraints to rape, mutilation, or murder.

Transvestic Disorder

The particular focus of **transvestic disorder**, or *transvestism*, is dressing as another gender (refer to **Table 11.19**; APA, 2022). This disorder is often seen in men who dress and imagine themselves as women (*autogynephilia*). Transvestism differs from simple fetishism in that certain clothes are not necessary for sexual arousal, but rather help a person engage in the fantasy of being another gender. The dressing in transvestism can be secret, such as wearing panties underneath one's clothing, or obvious, such as wearing a dress and makeup in public.

Voyeuristic Disorder

The particular focus of **voyeuristic disorder**, or *voyeurism*, is secretly watching others undress or engage in sexual activity without being noticed (refer to **Table 11.20**; APA, 2022). People with voyeurism usually do not want sexual contact with the person(s) being watched. They become sexually aroused by the fact the watched persons placed themselves in such a vulnerable position and by the fact they themselves could be caught. A person with voyeurism often masturbates when watching others or does so later to the fantasy of having sex with the watched person(s).

Paul Brown/Shutterstock.com

People with transvestism dress as another gender for sexual excitement, sometimes in public.

Table 11.18 DSM-5-TR

Sexual Masochism Disorder
A. Over a period of at least six months, recurrent and intense sexual arousal from the act of being humiliated, beaten, bound, or otherwise made to suffer, as manifested by fantasies, urges, or behaviors.
B. The fantasies, sexual urges, or behaviors cause clinically significant distress or impairment in social, occupational, or other important areas of functioning.
Sexual Sadism Disorder
A. Over a period of at least six months, recurrent and intense sexual arousal from the physical or psychological suffering of another person, as manifested by fantasies, urges, or behaviors.
B. The individual has acted on these sexual urges with a nonconsenting person, or the sexual urges or fantasies cause clinically significant distress or impairment in social, occupational, or other important areas of functioning. Specify if in a controlled environment or in full remission. Specify with asphyxiophilia.

American Psychiatric Association. (2022). *Diagnostic and statistical manual of mental disorders* (5th ed., text rev.). Arlington, VA: American Psychiatric Association.

Table 11.19 DSM-5-TR

Transvestic Disorder
A. Over a period of at least six months, recurrent and intense sexual arousal from cross-dressing, as manifested by fantasies, urges, or behaviors.
B. The fantasies, sexual urges, or behaviors cause clinically significant distress or impairment in social, occupational, or other important areas of functioning. Specify if in a controlled environment or in full remission. Specify if with fetishism or autogynephilia.

American Psychiatric Association. (2022). *Diagnostic and statistical manual of mental disorders* (5th ed., text rev.). Arlington, VA: American Psychiatric Association.

Table 11.20 DSM-5-TR

Voyeuristic Disorder
A. Over a period of at least six months, recurrent and intense sexual arousal from observing an unsuspecting person who is naked, in the process of disrobing, or engaging in sexual activity, as manifested by fantasies, urges, or behaviors.
B. The individual has acted on these sexual urges with a nonconsenting person, or the sexual urges or fantasies cause clinically significant distress or impairment in social, occupational, or other important areas of functioning.
C. The individual experiencing the arousal and/or acting on the urges is at least 18 years of age. Specify if in a controlled environment or in full remission.

American Psychiatric Association. (2022). *Diagnostic and statistical manual of mental disorders* (5th ed., text rev.). Arlington, VA: American Psychiatric Association.

Atypical Paraphilic Disorders

Paraphilic disorders may also be diagnosed as *other specified paraphilic disorder* (APA, 2022). Atypical paraphilic disorders also involve an unusual focus of arousal during sexual activity as well as distress or impairment, but are less common (Molen et al., 2021). Examples are in **Table 11.21**.

Table 11.21 Some Atypical Paraphilic Disorders

Paraphilic disorder	Focus of arousal
Acrotomophilia/ apotemnophilia	Amputees or being an amputee
Autagonistophilia	Being observed, filmed, or on stage
Autonepiophilia	Pretending to be a baby in diapers
Biastophilia	Surprise assault of another person
Gynemimetophilia	Transgender partners
Kleptophilia	Stealing from others
Klismaphilia	Enemas
Narratophilia	Erotic, "dirty" talk
Necrophilia	Contact with corpses
Olfactophilia	Odors from certain body areas
Partialism	Specific body part, such as hair
Symphorophilia	Staging an accident and then watching
Troilism	Involvement of a third person in sex
Urophilia and coprophilia	Urine and feces
Zoophilia	Animals

Epidemiology of Paraphilic Disorders

Sexual fantasies involving various themes are common in humans (refer to **Focus on College Students: Sexual Fantasies and Paraphilic Interests**). Paraphilic interests that do not rise to the level of a formal mental disorder are also prevalent in the general population, especially for voyeurism and fetishism (refer to **Table 11.22**). Rates of actual experience regarding at least one lifetime act of paraphilic behavior are also common, again primarily for voyeurism and fetishism, but also exhibitionism and frotteurism. Intense or persistent paraphilic desires or experiences occur in less than 10 percent of the general population, however (Joyal & Carpentier, 2016).

Charting the exact prevalence of formal paraphilic disorders is difficult because the behaviors are usually secret and rarely brought to a therapist's attention. Harsh societal stigma against unusual sexual practices often forces people with paraphilic disorders to online activities (Molen et al., 2022). Survey data about fantasies may not be helpful because people may answer questions in a socially desirable way and because simple fantasies are not enough to diagnose someone with a paraphilic disorder. The presence of a paraphilic disorder is thus usually determined when a person is arrested or seeks medical or psychological help (Thibaut et al., 2020).

Table 11.22 Prevalence (%) of Men and Women Who Desire to Experience Various Paraphilic Behaviors

	Men	Women
Voyeurism	60.0	34.7
Fetishism	40.4	47.9
Exhibitionism (extended)	35.0	26.9
Frotteurism	34.2	20.7
Masochism	19.2	27.8
Sadism	9.5	5.1
Transvestism	7.2	5.5
Exhibitionism (strict)	5.9	3.4
Sex with child	1.1	0.2

Source: From Table 1a of Joyal, C.C., & Carpentier, J. (2016). The prevalence of paraphilic interests and behaviors in the general population: A provincial survey. *Journal of Sex Research*, 2016, 1–11.

Paraphilic disorders are much more common in men than women. This is especially true for voyeuristic disorder (12 percent of men; 4 percent of

Focus On College Students

Sexual Fantasies and Paraphilic Interests

Sexual fantasies about typical and unusual themes (paraphilic interests) are obviously quite common in humans. One group of researchers surveyed thousands of people, including sources from universities, to glean detailed information about the kinds of sexual fantasies that people experience. Among women, common fantasies surrounded themes of exotic or public places to enjoy sex (27.2 percent), submissive behavior (18.8 percent), strangers (14.3 percent), exhibitionism (8.9 percent), homosexual activities (8.2 percent), group sex (7.8 percent), authority figure or celebrity (7.1 percent), and a sexual object (6.5 percent).

Among men, common fantasies surrounded themes of voyeurism (15.0 percent), fetishism (14.0 percent), threesome (12.6 percent), oral sex (11.7 percent), anal sex (11.7 percent), exotic or public places to enjoy sex (11.3 percent), homosexual activities (8.9 percent), sex with an acquaintance (8.5 percent), and group sex (8.1 percent). Interestingly, however, the most intense fantasies for people involved feeling romantic emotions during a sexual relationship. The authors noted that the frequency of these various fantasies indicates that they are not good indicators themselves of psychopathology (Joyal et al., 2015). Instead, as mentioned in this chapter, paraphilic disorders are diagnosed only when problems arise from sexual behavior or fantasies involving unusual activities.

---

women), exhibitionistic disorder (2–4 percent of men; rare in women), sexual masochism disorder (2.2 percent of men; 1.3 percent of women), sexual sadism disorder (2–3 percent, mostly in men), pedophilic disorder (3–5 percent in men; rarer in women), and transvestic disorder (3 percent of men; rare in women). Frotteuristic, fetishistic, and atypical paraphilic acts are likely more common among men, but the general prevalence of disorders associated with these behaviors is unclear (Beech et al., 2016). Case reports from around the globe suggest that paraphilic disorders are not culture specific. Paraphilic activity, especially among men, may be universally common (Seto et al., 2021).

Paraphilic disorders generally develop during adolescence and the early 20s and several preferences may be present in a given individual (Tozdan & Briken, 2021). Tom had exhibitionism but also fantasies about watching teenagers and young women undress before him without their knowledge. Pedophilic disorder is also comorbid with other mental disorders such as anxiety-related, depressive, substance use, and personality disorders (Abé et al., 2021). Paraphilic disorders are sometimes associated with violent behavior. Acts of child molestation and pedophilic disorder can obviously involve serious damage or death to a child. Rape can be sadistic as well, particularly if inflicting pain is sexually arousing for the perpetrator (Liu et al., 2022; refer to **Focus on Violence: Rape**).

Section Summary

- People with paraphilic disorders experience sexual urges, fantasies, and behaviors that involve unusual stimuli and cause significant distress or impairment.
- Paraphilic disorders include exhibitionism, fetishism, frotteurism, pedophilic disorder, sexual masochism and sexual sadism, transvestism, and voyeurism.
- Paraphilic disorders are more common in men and typically begin in adolescence or young adulthood.
- Paraphilic disorders can be linked to other mental disorders and violence.

Review Questions

1. What are major features of a paraphilia?
2. What are major targets of sexual arousal in people with different paraphilic disorders?
3. How might pedophilic disorder differ from child molestation?
4. What are possible subtypes of pedophilic disorder?
5. What are common demographic and clinical features of paraphilic disorders?

Paraphilic Disorders: Causes and Prevention

LO 11.10 Discuss the risk factors for and prevention of paraphilic disorders.

The exact cause of paraphilic disorders is not known, but some biological predispositions and environmental risk factors may exist. These factors are discussed next.

Biological Risk Factors for Paraphilic Disorders

Moderate to strong relationships have been found between certain paraphilic behaviors (exhibitionism,

Focus On Violence

Rape

Acts of sadism can involve severe violence such as rape. Many rapists are aroused by stimuli involving sexual force and control. Sexual perpetrators who are more sadistic tend to be socially isolated and angry and less sexually experienced (Craig & Bartels, 2021). Note that much of the work in this area has involved male perpetrators.

Rape can occur within partner or dating relationships. *Acquaintance or date rape* affects many female college students and often involves male acceptance of violence, alcohol or other drug use, and isolated situations. Drugs such as *flunitrazepam* (Rohypnol or "roofies") may also be secretly given to women to induce a near state of unconsciousness and vulnerability to rape (refer to Chapter 9). Some men who engage in this kind of coercive sexual activity may eventually assault people they do not know.

Only a fraction of all rapes are reported to police. Sometimes a woman is unsure a crime took place, as in the case of partner or date rape. Other women may take some responsibility for the attack (even though it was clearly not their fault) or be afraid of the consequences of reporting the attack. Whether a rape is reported or not, however, the psychological after-effects can include depression, posttraumatic stress and anxiety disorders, sleep difficulties, and various sexual and interpersonal problems.

masochism, sadism, and voyeurism) and sexual coercion in twins (Baur et al., 2016). In addition, genetics potentially affect the *reward deficiency syndrome* sometimes implicated in people with pedophilic disorder. Reward deficiency syndrome is a spectrum of impulsive, compulsive, or addictive behaviors such as intense sexual urges (Blum et al., 2022). Men with an extra Y chromosome may also display sexual aggression, though factors such as immaturity and interpersonal difficulties may be more influential (Maiti & Langan, 2021).

Neuropsychological problems such as dementia may also lead to less inhibited and more compulsive and unusual sexual behaviors (Chapter 14). This may be due to damage in temporal-limbic brain areas that influence sex drive and in frontal lobe brain areas that influence sexual inhibition (refer to **Figure 11.3**; Latella et al., 2021). Hormonal changes may also exist in some people with paraphilic disorders, but consistent evidence remains needed (Baltodano-Calle et al., 2022).

Phovoir/Shutterstock.com

Some researchers claim paraphilic disorders are deviations from common courtship practices.

Some personality characteristics seem common to people with paraphilic disorders. Examples include low empathy as well as poor social, intimacy, self-regulation, and problem-solving skills (especially around women). Other traits include impulsivity, psychopathy, dependency, sense of inferiority and inadequacy, anger, neuroticism, sensation-seeking, and narcissism (Craig & Bartels, 2021). Antisocial characteristics and antisocial personality disorder (Chapter 10) also characterize some people with sexual interest in children (Wittström et al., 2020). One specific personality profile does not fit most people with pedophilic disorder or other paraphilic disorders, however.

Environmental Risk Factors for Paraphilic Disorders

Environmental risk factors for paraphilic disorders may include family contributions, learning experiences, cognitive distortions, and cultural and evolutionary factors. These risk factors are discussed next.

Family Contributions

Difficult family circumstances may contribute to paraphilic disorder development. People with paraphilic disorders often describe their early home lives as emotionally abusive, unstable, or violent (Stinson et al., 2022). Such early problems could lead to less developed social, sexual, and intimacy skills because appropriate parental feedback was not given. Family factors also contribute to pedophilic disorder, and poor attachment and frequent and aggressive sexual activity within a family may predispose some toward sexual offenses (Grady et al., 2021). Indeed, having a father or brother convicted of a sexual offense increases one's risk for the same result compared to the general population (Långström et al., 2015).

Figure 11.3 Major Brain Areas Implicated in the Paraphilic Disorders.

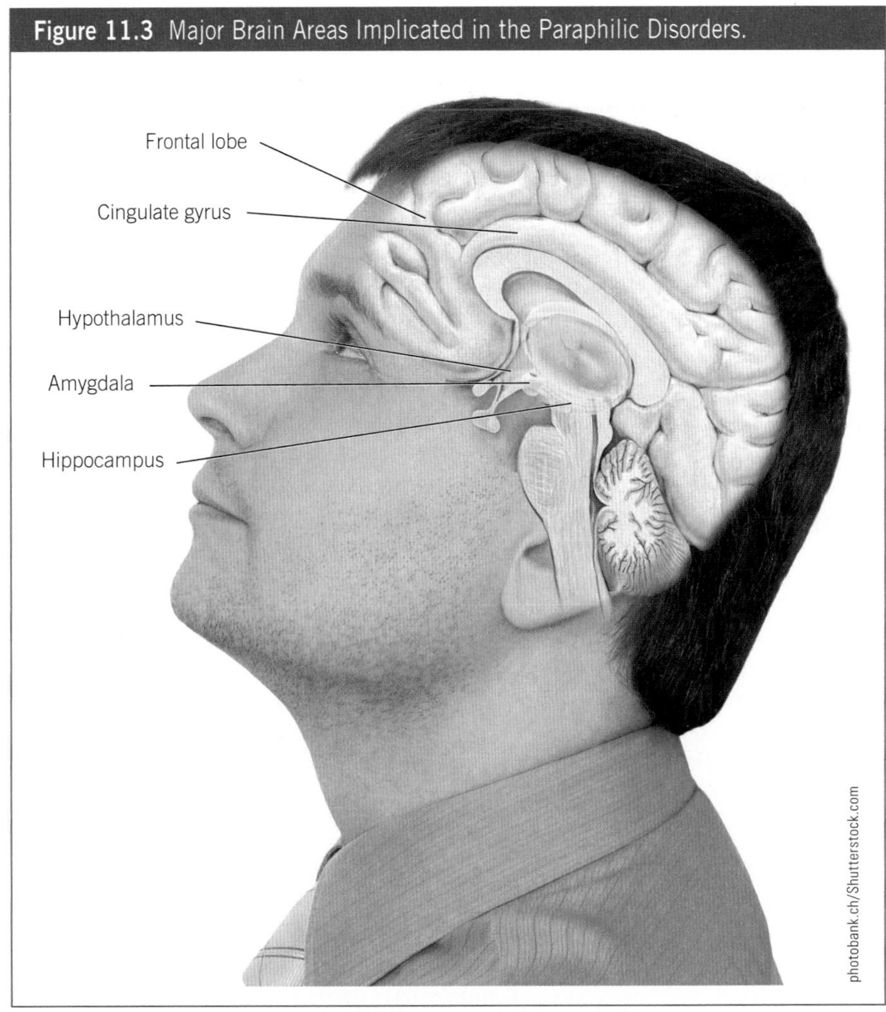

et al., 2022). Courtship among two people generally involves the following stages:

- Finding and evaluating a potential partner
- Communicating with the partner in a nonphysical way, such as smiling or talking
- Physical contact without sexual intercourse, such as kissing or petting
- Sexual intercourse

Voyeurism, exhibitionism, frotteurism, and *preferential rape* (when a person prefers rape more than a consenting partner) may link to disruptions in each of these four stages, respectively. A person with voyeurism may have difficulty finding potential sexual partners and resorts to secretive behavior. Such disruptions could be caused by faulty learning patterns or biological variables, but no definitive conclusions have been made.

Cognitive Distortions

Many people with paraphilic disorders or those who commit sexual offenses have strong cognitive distortions or irrational beliefs about their peculiar sexual behavior (Molen et al., 2021). These beliefs allow a person to justify their behavior. Tom believed the surprised reactions of others to his genital exposure represented sexual arousal on their part or a desire to be with him. People who view explicit and illegal images online often justify their actions by claiming distance from specific acts or that the images simply appeared in front of them (Winder et al., 2015). In addition, those with paraphilia sometimes rationalize their behavior by believing that no one is harmed. People with pedophilic disorder may believe that they have little control or responsibility for their acts, that sexual acts somehow benefit a child, that a child victim is more interested in sexual acts than is actually so, and that a child is a sexual being (Perrotta, 2020).

Learning Experiences

Some paraphilic disorders may begin with a learning experience in which a person associates sexual arousal or orgasm with an unusual object or situation or person. A teenager may have inadvertently and secretly noticed someone undressing and then became sexually aroused. Sexual arousal was classically conditioned with the voyeuristic act, and this association was later reinforced by masturbation and orgasm. Learning theory may help explain some paraphilic disorder development, especially because paraphilic disorders occur more in men (who masturbate more). But learning theory cannot be the sole explanation for paraphilic disorders; if it were, then most people would have paraphilic disorders. Paraphilic behaviors may also be reinforced by family members or others or the behaviors were learned as a way to reduce anxiety or escape from difficult life circumstances. Paraphilic disorders may become a problem similar to obsessive-compulsive disorder in some cases (Chapter 5; Saleh et al., 2021).

Paraphilic disorders may also result when *courtship behaviors* are not properly learned or expressed (Brown

Cultural and Evolutionary Factors

Paraphilic disorders are present in different areas of the globe, but some paraphilias may be more prevalent in certain cultures that practice greater tolerance for such behavior. Substantial cultural differences exist with respect to the age of consent for sex, age differences between brides and grooms, touching of nonconsenting women, sexualization of inanimate objects, and masochism (Zgourides, 2020). In addition, transvestism has been prominently displayed in films worldwide, suggesting some level of cultural acceptance. Sweeping generalizations regarding culture and paraphilic disorders cannot yet be made, however.

From an evolutionary standpoint, paraphilic disorders may be understood by considering parental investment in offspring. Some people may be more invested in type of offspring they bear, so they may be more discriminating in their sexual interactions. Other people, however, may be less invested in type of offspring they bear and engage in more variable sexual practices. A related evolutionary theory is that humans evolved by becoming more diverse in ways that partners try to attract mates (Craig & Bartels, 2021).

Causes of Paraphilic Disorders

Integrated causal models for general paraphilic disorders have not been highly developed, although specific models for pedophilic disorder have been presented. Some researchers focus on neurodevelopmental models of pedophilic disorder in which early risk factors set the stage for other risk factors that then lead to pedophilic disorder. One important early risk factor involves changes in cortical development that leads to sexual hyperarousal and difficulty limiting sexual arousal to adults. Other early risk factors include sexual maltreatment as a child and inadequate attachment with parents.

These early risk factors could interact with later risk factors such as limited social and sexual skill development, learning experiences leading to deviant sexual arousal toward children, and cognitive distortions and maladaptive personality patterns. The latter may include antisocial tendencies that prevent stoppage of pedophilic acts. These risk factors collectively could help produce pedophilic disorder (Abé et al., 2021).

Biological predisposition toward sexual hyperarousal and poor self-regulation may be evident in other paraphilic disorders (Kahn et al., 2021). This predisposition likely interacts with key environmental variables such as unusual sexual learning experiences, cognitive distortions, social skill deficits, paraphilic fantasies reinforced by masturbation, and attempts to suppress paraphilic fantasies, which paradoxically leads to more fantasies (refer to **Figure 11.4**). Tom was aroused by various stimuli and had several exposures without being caught. His acts were reinforced by subsequent masturbation and orgasm, and his attempts to stop his fantasies and behavior were unsuccessful. Much more research is needed regarding the development of specific paraphilic disorders like Tom's.

Prevention of Paraphilic Disorders

Information is scarce regarding prevention of paraphilic disorders despite the importance of this goal. Part of the reason for this is that people with paraphilic disorders often have multiple targets for their sexual desire and because sexual behaviors are usually secretive. Prevention programs could focus on developing appropriate social and sexual skills in childhood and adolescence (Craig & Bartels, 2021). Youth might thus be better able to engage in prosocial gender interactions, understand sexual desire and adaptive sexual activities, and avoid sexism and violence. Interventions to improve family communication and problem-solving skills might be helpful as well.

Prevention of paraphilic disorders often comes in the form of *relapse prevention* after a person has been arrested or seeks help. Relapse prevention has primarily applied to people with pedophilic disorder or sexual offenders. A key aspect of relapse prevention training is to help a person identify situations that place them at risk for committing a paraphilic act. Examples of

Figure 11.4 Sample Developmental Pathway of a Paraphilic Disorder.

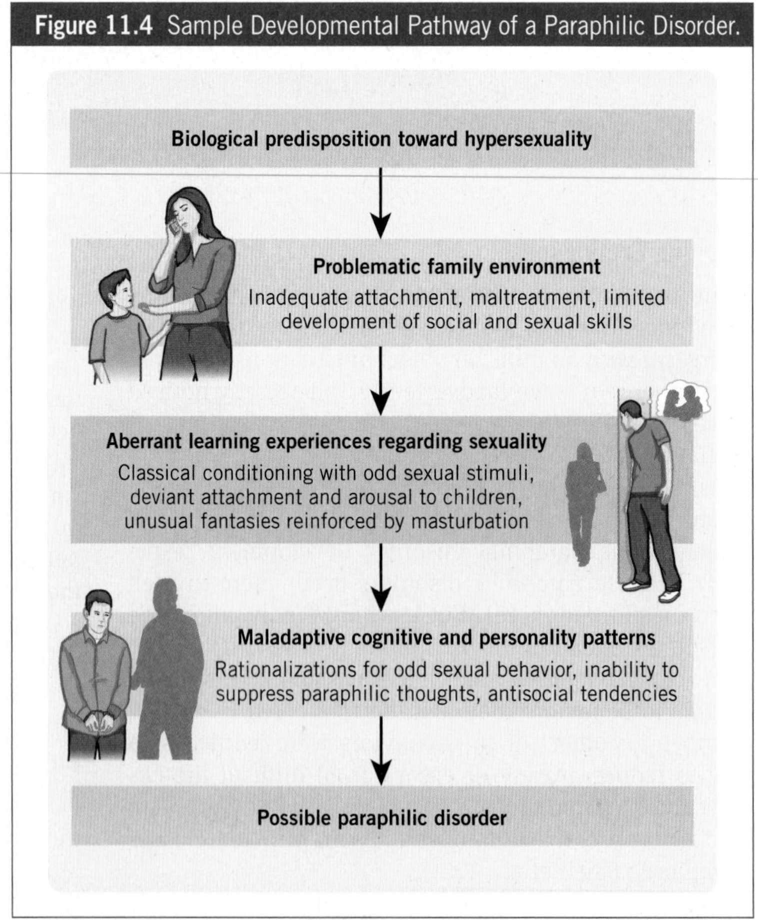

places to avoid might include schools (pedophilic disorder), dormitories (voyeurism), parking lots (exhibitionism), bars (frotteurism), and isolated settings with computers (Marhenke, 2022). Partners or police officers can also keep track of a person and remind them to stay away from or leave certain places.

Relapse prevention of paraphilic disorders can also involve identifying emotional and cognitive triggers to paraphilic acts, including anxiety, anger, depression, boredom, and intense sexual thoughts. The person is taught skills to manage these emotions and thoughts and to develop appropriate social and intimacy interactions with others. Other treatment procedures mentioned later in this chapter, such as cognitive therapy or empathy training, may be helpful during relapse prevention as well (Ramsay et al., 2020).

Section Summary

- Paraphilic disorders may relate to certain biological risk factors such as genetics, neuropsychological problems, and hormonal changes.
- Those with paraphilic disorders may have limited social and intimacy skills as well as certain personality traits.
- Family variables may contribute to paraphilic disorders, including hostile family behaviors, inadequate attachment, and aggressive sexual activity within the home.
- Paraphilic disorders may be affected as well by learning experiences and courtship problems.
- People with paraphilic disorders often have cognitive distortions to justify or rationalize their sexual behavior.
- The cause of paraphilic disorders may involve hypersexuality, deviant sexual arousal, learning experiences, social skills deficits, and other important variables.
- Preventing paraphilic disorders may involve teaching appropriate social and sexual skills as well as relapse prevention after one has been arrested or seeks treatment.

Review Questions

1. What are major biological risk factors for paraphilic disorders?
2. What personality and family characteristics are evident in people with paraphilic disorders?
3. How might learning experiences and cognitive distortions contribute to paraphilic disorders?
4. What is an integrated theory for the cause of pedophilic disorder?
5. What strategies might be used to prevent paraphilic behavior?

Paraphilic Disorders: Assessment and Treatment

LO 11.11 Characterize the assessment and treatment of individuals with paraphilic disorders.

Assessment of Paraphilic Disorders

Sexual desire and arousal can be subjective, so assessing paraphilic disorders often depends on a person's self-report as well as questionnaires that focus on sexual interests. Physiological measurement has also been used as an assessment method.

Interviews

When interviewing someone with a possible paraphilic disorder, a clinician would likely focus on past and present sexual interests and activities, paraphilic acts, legal problems or sexual offenses, interactions with sexual partners, family and medical history, and comorbid problems like anxiety, depression, and substance use. Other important issues include sense of empathy and responsibility to victims, impulsive and aggressive behavior, and level of insight about the wrongfulness of one's behavior. Interviews must be conducted with care given the delicate nature of the material being covered and the sometimes evasive nature of an interviewee who is in legal trouble, such as a sex offender. Information from interviews often needs to be supported by legal officials, partners, documentation, or polygraph testing (Jung et al., 2020).

Questionnaires

Questionnaires and screening instruments may be useful for assessing people with paraphilic disorders, but this method may be problematic if someone fears legal consequences or wants to appear socially desirable. Still, some inventories assess sexual history and unusual interests, hypersexuality, and sexually aggressive and pedophilic behavior. Examples include the *Bradford Sexual History Inventory, Clarke Sex History Questionnaire, Multidimensional Inventory of Development, Sex, and Aggression, Multiphasic Sex Inventory,* and *Sex Offender Treatment Intervention and Progress Scale* (Craig & Bartels, 2021).

Other screening instruments focus on sexual offense histories. The *Screening Scale for Pedophilic Interests* (SSPI) is based on prior pedophilic behavior. The SSPI is useful for identifying people with pedophilic disorder who are likely to harm additional children (McPhail et al., 2021). Sample items from the SSPI are in **Table 11.23**.

Physiological Assessment

Physiological assessment of paraphilic disorders is often called *phallometric testing.* A person is usually presented with visual or auditory stimuli that represent different sexual acts or activities. Subsequent arousal in men is evaluated via *penile plethysmograph* or strain gauge, a rubber ring that measures circumference of the penis. Sexual response in women is measured by examining blood volume in the vaginal area via a *vaginal photoplethysmograph* or perineal (vaginal/anal) muscle function via a *myograph* or *perineometer*. Sexual interest can also be examined by showing erotic media and measuring how long a person attends to the material (Bickle et al., 2021).

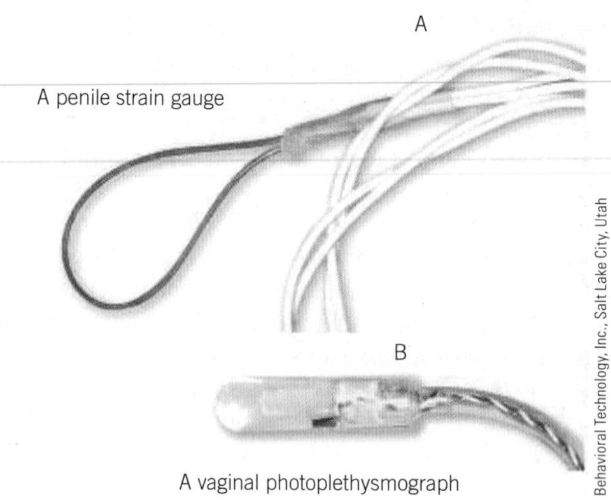

Physiological assessment devices for sexual response.

Biological Treatment of Paraphilic Disorders

A key treatment of paraphilic disorders is pharmacotherapy to reduce testosterone levels in men and, thus, sexual desire, arousal, and unusual behavior. The main drugs to do so include *medroxyprogesterone acetate* (Depo-Provera), *leuprolide acetate* (Lupron), and *cyproterone acetate* (Cyproterone). These drugs reduce unusual sexual desires or dangerous sexual activity, but side effects and noncompliance to taking the medications are common (Saleh et al., 2021).

Antidepressant medications, especially selective serotonin reuptake inhibitors (Chapter 7), may reduce sexual urges and diminish performance or relieve depression or compulsive behaviors that trigger paraphilic acts (Jannini et al., 2022). Side effects and noncompliance can be problematic. *Chemical castration* by injecting certain drugs to eliminate production of testosterone has been advocated by some to treat people with violent sexual behavior. The procedure is obviously a drastic one, however, and may not completely eliminate all unusual sexual desires and behaviors. Programs to monitor sexual predators have thus become more common (refer to **Focus on Law and Ethics: Sex Offender Notification and Incarceration**).

Table 11.23 Items from the Screening Scale for Pedophilic Interests (SSPI)

Offender has male victim (Yes = 2; No, female victims only = 0)
Offender has more than one victim (Yes = 1; No, single victim only = 0)
Offender has a victim aged 11 or younger (Yes = 1; No, child victims were 12 or 13 years old = 0)
Offender has an unrelated victim (Yes = 1; No, related victims only = 0)

Note: Higher scores indicate greater risk of harming additional children.

Source: Seto, M.C., & Lalumiere, M.L. (2001). A brief screening scale to identify pedophilic interests among child molesters. *Sexual Abuse: A Journal of Research and Treatment, 13*, 15–25.

Psychological Treatments of Paraphilic Disorders

Behavior therapy has also been explored to reduce maladaptive paraphilic activities. Early forms of behavior therapy included aversive treatments that paired sexual images with unpleasant stimuli such as foul odors, but newer therapies focus more on pairing sexual arousal with healthier fantasies and sexual behavior. **Orgasmic reconditioning** or *masturbatory reconditioning* involves initial masturbation to an unusual sexual stimulus or imagined scenes, but the person switches to more appropriate stimuli or scenes such as intercourse with a partner immediately before orgasm. The pleasurable orgasm is thus associated with appropriate sexual content. Later in therapy, the person can switch to more appropriate scenes much earlier and further away from orgasm. More complete arousal to appropriate stimuli is thus achieved. Orgasmic reconditioning may also link to *masturbatory satiation* in which a person continues to masturbate after orgasm to paraphilic stimuli. The less arousing and perhaps irritating nature of this activity is therefore associated with the paraphilic stimulus (Craig & Bartels, 2021).

Therapists may also use *cognitive therapy* to help a person with paraphilic disorder change unrealistic thoughts. A person's justifications or reasons for unusual or illicit sexual behavior can be confronted, challenged, and modified. Therapy can also involve educating a person to identify and avoid high-risk

Focus On Law and Ethics

Sex Offender Notification and Incarceration

A seven-year-old New Jersey girl, Megan Kanka, was raped and murdered in 1994 by a previously convicted sex offender who lived across the street from her family; they were unaware of his past history. After her death, several states and the federal government passed laws that "sexual predators," or those with histories of sexual crimes against children, would have to register with police (so-called Megan's laws). Many of these laws gave communities the right to be notified as to who these people were, even after they served long prison sentences. You may be able to find registered sex offenders in your location listed on a police department website. These laws raise important ethical dilemmas surrounding the conflict between an individual's right to privacy and societal rights to be protected. The laws imply that government agencies such as prisons and mental health centers have not successfully curbed pedophilic behavior, essentially leaving supervision of convicted sex offenders in the hands of community groups (Burchfield et al., 2014).

Another controversial practice regarding sexual offenders surrounds committing people to a mental hospital *after* their full prison term has expired. Several states allow authorities to transfer a convicted sexual offender to an inpatient mental health facility, even against the person's will, for an indefinite period. The sex offender is kept involuntarily in some setting (often one connected to a prison) until such time that they are determined not to be dangerous to the community. Such laws raise an important ethical dilemma—who has more rights, the person who has completed a full prison sentence for crimes or community members who wish to be protected against a potentially violent offender?

situations such as playgrounds, teaching social and other skills to control impulses and reduce anxiety and depression, and increasing empathy by having a person identify with the victim and understand the harm that was caused. These therapy components may be useful in individual and group settings and in Twelve Step programs (similar to the ones for substance-related disorders discussed in Chapter 9) for people with sexual addictions (Hallberg et al., 2020).

What If I or Someone I Know Has a Paraphilic Disorder?

If you feel you or someone you know may have a paraphilic disorder, then consulting a clinical psychologist or other mental health professional who understands these problems may be best. Some screening questions are in **Table 11.24**. Paraphilic disorders are best addressed by cognitive-behavioral procedures to enhance appropriate behavior. Medical conditions should be explored as well.

Long-Term Outcomes for People with Paraphilic Disorders

The long-term prognosis for people with paraphilic disorders is largely unknown, partly because many are never identified or people drop out of treatment. Treatments for different paraphilic disorders remain in development, although cognitive behavioral therapies may be most useful for people with exhibitionism, fetishism, or masochism. Long-term outcome for many people with paraphilic disorders may simply improve, however, because of reduced sexual arousal with age and regular contact with a therapist (Craig & Bartels, 2021). Tom's extended therapy and the humiliation of being arrested resulted in successful abstinence from exhibitionistic exposures.

Much of the long-term outcome data for paraphilic disorders has centered on people with pedophilic disorder or those who have committed sexual offenses against children. *Recidivism rates*, or number of people arrested a second time, are typically examined. Recidivism rates for sexual offenses are about 20 percent but may be greater (33 percent) for high-risk individuals (Thornton et al., 2021). Those who recidivate or show limited treatment response are more likely to display strong sexual arousal to children, violence in their sexual offenses, poor mood and anger regulation, less cooperation with supervision, and more paraphilic interests and antisocial personality traits (Bazinet et al., 2022; Seto, 2022).

Table 11.24 Screening Questions for Paraphilic Disorder

Do you know someone whose sexual behavior constantly surrounds unusual urges or possibly illegal activities?
Do you know someone who has trouble concentrating or completing daily tasks because of their sexual desires and urges?
Do you know someone attracted sexually to children?
Do you know someone who has been arrested for unusual sexual activity?

Section Summary

- Interviews with people with paraphilic disorder often focus on paraphilic thoughts and behaviors as well as personality characteristics and comorbid problems.
- Self-report questionnaires may be used to assess sexual history and unusual interests, hypersexuality, and sexually aggressive and pedophilic behavior.
- Physiological assessment for paraphilic disorders includes penile plethysmograph, vaginal blood volume, and measuring how long a person views erotic material.
- Drug treatment for paraphilic disorders aims to reduce testosterone and sex drive and to improve depression and compulsive behaviors.
- Psychological treatments for paraphilic disorders include procedures to reorient arousal to more appropriate stimuli and cognitive therapy to change unrealistic thoughts.
- People with paraphilic disorders can respond positively to treatment and tend not to be rearrested, though this may be due in part to reduced sex drive with age.

Review Questions

1. What topics might a clinician cover when interviewing someone with a paraphilic disorder?
2. What self-report questionnaires and physiological procedures might be useful for assessing someone with a paraphilic disorder?
3. What medications are used to treat paraphilic disorders?
4. What psychological interventions are used to treat paraphilic disorders?
5. What long-term outcomes apply to people with paraphilic disorders?

Gender Dysphoria: Features and Epidemiology

LO 11.12 Discuss the diagnostic criteria for and epidemiology of gender dysphoria.

Other problems have less to do with sex and more to do with gender. **Gender dysphoria** involves a strong desire to be of an alternative gender that is different than one's assigned gender. An important diagnostic requirement that such desire *must cause considerable distress or problems in daily life functioning* (refer to **Table 11.25**; APA, 2022). Gender dysphoria can include various types of attire and gender roles as well as a strong desire to be treated as another gender. People with gender dysphoria often experience anxiety and depression. Gender dysphoria is a controversial diagnosis because gender diversity itself is not a mental health problem. A diagnosis of gender dysphoria and accompanying distress are often required for health care services, however (Cooper et al., 2020). Gender dysphoria occurs in less than 1 in 1000 persons (APA, 2022). Prevalence rates are often based on referrals for treatment and not the general population.

Gender Dysphoria: Causes and Prevention

LO 11.13 Describe the risk factors for gender dysphoria.

Data are scarce regarding risk factors for gender dysphoria. Prenatal exposure to sex hormones has been investigated but biological risk factors for gender dysphoria are not well established (Perrotta, 2020). Psychological risk factors also remain unclear, and researchers have focused more on what impacts distress for youth with gender dysphoria. Gender dysphoria is often linked to emotional problems, suicidality, and self-harm. Psychological functioning can be affected substantially by level of family and peer support. Many youths with gender dysphoria experience family conflict, parent mental disorder, separation from important figures, and bullying (Kozlowska et al., 2021; Sievert et al., 2021).

Gender dysphoria is a formal diagnostic condition, but changes in gender are commonplace in many

Anchorage Daily News/Tribune News Service/Getty Images

In Polynesia, boys are sometimes raised as girls, even into adulthood, if a family has too many male children. Here, Tafi Toleafa, who was assigned male at birth and raised as a girl, helps serve food at a family party.

Table 11.25 DSM-5-TR

Gender Dysphoria
Gender Dysphoria in Children
A. A marked incongruence between one's experienced/expressed gender and assigned gender, of at least six months' duration, as manifested by at least six of the following (one of which must be Criterion A1): 1. A strong desire to be of the other gender or an insistence that one is the other gender (or some alternative gender different from one's assigned gender). 2. In boys (assigned gender), a strong preference for cross-dressing or simulating female attire; or in girls (assigned gender), a strong preference for wearing only typical masculine clothing and a strong resistance to the wearing of typical feminine clothing. 3. A strong preference for cross-gender roles in make-believe play or fantasy play. 4. A strong preference for the toys, games, or activities stereotypically used or engaged in by the other gender. 5. A strong preference for playmates of the other gender. 6. In boys (assigned gender), a strong rejection of typically masculine toys, games, and activities and a strong avoidance of rough-and-tumble play; or in girls (assigned gender), a strong rejection of typically feminine toys, games, and activities. 7. A strong dislike of one's sexual anatomy. 8. A strong desire for the primary and/or secondary sex characteristics that match one's experienced gender.
B. The condition is associated with clinically significant distress or impairment in social, school, or other important areas of functioning.
Gender Dysphoria in Adolescents and Adults
A. A marked incongruence between one's experienced/expressed gender and assigned gender, of at least six months' duration, as manifested by at least two of the following: 1. A marked incongruence between one's experienced/expressed gender and primary and/or secondary sex characteristics (or in young adolescents, the anticipated secondary sex characteristics). 2. A strong desire to be rid of one's primary and/or secondary sex characteristics because of a marked incongruence with one's experienced/expressed gender (or in young adolescents, a desire to prevent the development of the anticipated secondary sex characteristics). 3. A strong desire for the primary and/or secondary sex characteristics of the other gender. 4. A strong desire to be of the other gender (or some alternative gender different from one's assigned gender). 5. A strong desire to be treated as the other gender (or some alternative gender different from one's assigned gender). 6. A strong conviction that one has the typical feelings and reactions of the other gender (or some alternative gender different from one's assigned gender). Specify with a disorder of sex development and/or posttransition to desired gender.

American Psychiatric Association. (2022). *Diagnostic and statistical manual of mental disorders* (5th ed., text rev.). Arlington, VA: American Psychiatric Association.

parts of the world. A *fa'afafine* is a Polynesian boy voluntarily raised as a girl in a family with too many male children. Many of these boys continue to view themselves, and are viewed by others, as female even into adulthood. A *fakaletti* is a boy from Tonga who dresses and lives as a girl to help with chores and who may choose to continue to live as a woman in adulthood. Men adopt characteristics of women in androgynous and socially acceptable ways in many other cultures as well. Examples include *kathoey* male-to-female dancers in Thailand, *mukhannathun* Islamic men who adopt female appearance and other characteristics, and *evening people* of India who purposely assume colorful, effeminate clothing. These examples represent culturally accepted practices, which calls into question the universal validity of a diagnosis of gender dysphoria.

Gender Dysphoria: Assessment and Treatment

LO 11.14 Characterize the assessment of and interventions with youth and adults with gender dysphoria.

The assessment of youths with gender dysphoria includes interviews, observations of cross-gender behavior, and drawings of oneself and others. Important interview topics include current and future beliefs about one's gender, positive and negative beliefs about different genders, fantasies about different genders, and distress about one's assigned gender. Observations of cross-gender behavior are also important, including preference for various toys and attire and statements about other genders. Adults with gender dysphoria, especially those

Personal Narrative

Sam

Sam Bullington

I'm Sam, and there's nothing abnormal about me. There is, however, something incredibly disturbing and sick about a society that wants to hurt and annihilate me simply because I don't fit into its rigid gender binary. I am a transsexual, and I am in the process of being fired from my current job. This is the third job that I have lost due to the discomfort people feel about my gender presentation and my particular embodied journey through life. I have had men in pickup trucks pull up alongside me and shout "Freak!" and follow me home, making threatening gestures. I have had people walking by me shout that I'm going to burn in hell. In this, I am actually one of the lucky ones. Last night I attended the Transgender Day of Remembrance vigil on my campus to light candles and hear the stories of the transgender people who were murdered in the last year. There is, on average, one transgender person per month who is killed somewhere in the United States, and this statistic drastically underrepresents the staggering violence against transgender people, because it only documents those individuals whose murders were reported as transgender murders. This does not account for those bodies that were never recovered, nor does it count those transgender people who end up taking their own lives because they could no longer stand to face the kind of scorn and contempt that is part of living as transgender. These murders are not just clean and simple killings. The transgender women spoken about at the vigil last night were shot in the chest 10 times each. This is typical of such murders—multiple stab wounds, dismemberment. They are crimes of intense hatred and frenzy—signs of a very insecure and disturbed society. And yet it is transgender people who are labeled as mentally disordered.

Transgender people do not possess authority over our own bodies. We are not treated as trustworthy informants about our own experience. For instance, when I decided that I wanted to go on male hormones to effect particular changes in my body—after living as openly transgendered for 13 years, completing a Ph.D. in Gender Studies, and doing extensive research both abroad and within the United States on transgender issues/communities—I was required to obtain a letter from a therapist before I could schedule my appointment with the endocrinologist. This therapist knew far less about transgender issues than I did and I had only been seeing him for a couple of months, but his credentials were required before I could pursue changes to my body. When I met with the endocrinologist, he consulted with his young intern, not with me, about whether he would consent to writing me a prescription for testosterone. His ultimate decision was determined by asking my partner whether *she* thought it was a good idea. I was 40 years old at the time and was treated as though I were five—though without the lollypop afterward. This is extremely insulting to transgender people—folks who usually have done extensive personal research and often know more about the relevant medical interventions than the doctors themselves (especially those of us, like myself, who live in small towns). This is especially outrageous given the fact that "gender-normative" people can seek body modifications to

considering gender-affirming surgery (next paragraph), may be evaluated along various psychological tests to ensure a person is truly ready for such a life-changing experience. Information may also be obtained about history of gender dysphoria, peer relationships, medical status, family functioning, and sexual interests.

The primary biological treatment for adults with gender dysphoria is **gender-affirming surgery**. Adolescents with gender dysphoria may receive hormone treatments to halt the further development of secondary sex characteristics until the person can consent, as an adult, to a gender transition (Skordis et al., 2020). Children with gender dysphoria may be referred to specialist centers with multidisciplinary and family support that allow the developmental trajectory of the child to continue without pursuing a specific or irreversible outcome (Kyriakou et al., 2020).

What If I or Someone I Know Has Questions About Gender Dysphoria?

You or someone you know may have questions about the play, dress, and gender-related behavior of a child or concerns that a child may have gender dysphoria. If you feel a child has strong gender distress, then consulting a clinical psychologist or other mental health professional who understands these issues is important. Keep in mind, however, that cross-gender behavior is common and that gender dysphoria is rare.

enhance their gender performance (for instance, breast implants or penile enhancements) without needing permission from a therapist or being diagnosed with a mental disorder.

Society feels compelled to study and try to understand transgender experience because it seems to be so different from the "normal" experience of gender. However, there is nothing remotely normal about gender development in the contemporary United States. Gender socialization is entirely compulsory and usually begins before we are even born. We are given gendered names and pronouns, directed toward certain colors, toys, and hobbies while discouraged away from others, encouraged to express certain aspects of our personalities but warned against expressing others. My students constantly remind me of the often severe penalties of breaking these mandatory rules—being called names, getting beat up, being punished by parents and other authority figures, being a social outcast. It requires an awful lot of policing on the part of society to create something that is supposedly "natural" and inevitable.

Contrary to what we are taught, gender is a spectrum, not a binary—a rainbow of colors, not the limited choices of black and white. Even biologically, research has demonstrated that there is immense variation in our bodies and approximately one in every thousand of us (and this is a very conservative estimate) comes into the world with a body that doesn't neatly fit into the two available choices of "male" and "female." Our gender identities are even more complicated and individualized. Very few of us actually comfortably fit into the masculine men/feminine women poles—many have to commit considerable life energy to meet these expectations and such gender requirements harm all of us, not just transgender people. They inhibit our full range as human beings—from men who have health or family problems because the only emotion they were taught to express was anger, to women who can't access their full power, confidence, and potential because they were socialized to prioritize pleasing others and making their bodies attractive. Transgenderism is part of the beautiful diversity of human life. It is only pathological in a society whose resources are fundamentally allocated on the basis of what genitalia you were born with. If we did not live in a society in which there were so many social advantages to being male over female, it would not matter to which category you were assigned or whether you moved between them—or created your own new categories.

Again, my name is Sam, and there is nothing abnormal about me. I have a Ph.D., I'm an ordained minister, I've been in two 10-year relationships, and I'm currently married. Despite all of these social accomplishments, people constantly look down on me and regard me with suspicion because I am a transsexual. The only thing that is different about my journey is that I sought to look inwardly for my answers about myself, something that I continually recommend to my students. Despite living in a "free country" that prides itself on individualism, we are expected to conform most aspects of ourselves and our life journeys to extremely limited and proscribed paths and we are constantly bombarded with relentless media images telling us how we should look, what we should buy, how much we should weigh, what we should wear, what we should think, continually reinforced by admonitions from our families, religious organizations, educational institutions, and the state. I attempted for several decades to live in this manner and ended up miserable, as many others are currently. My path to happiness and ultimately freedom came from listening to my own heart above the din of all of the other voices trying to define my experience. I highly recommend it to anyone.

Section Summary

- Gender dysphoria involves a strong desire to be of an alternative gender that is different than one's assigned gender. An important diagnostic requirement that such desire must cause considerable distress or problems in daily life functioning.
- Risk factors for gender dysphoria remain unclear and researchers often focus on the distress associated with this condition.
- The assessment of gender dysphoria may involve asking questions about current and future beliefs about different genders, fantasies, and distress about one's assigned gender.
- The primary biological intervention for gender dysphoria in adults is gender-affirming surgery.

Review Questions

1. What are features of gender dysphoria?
2. What biological risk factors may relate to gender dysphoria?
3. What psychological risk factors may relate to gender dysphoria?
4. What methods are used to assess gender dysphoria?
5. What methods are used to treat gender dysphoria?

Final Comments

People with sexual dysfunctions, paraphilic disorders, or gender dysphoria experience enormous daily distress because sexual and gender-related behaviors are so central to human existence. Furthermore, these problems are much more common than previously thought, as evidenced by high demands for sexual therapy and related medications. Sexual problems are sometimes embarrassing to admit, but acknowledging a problem and addressing it appropriately can have an enormous positive impact on quality of life. Openly discussing problems with sexual response and unusual sexual desires with one's partner, and improving communication in general, is critical as well. Open communication and thought about a child's gender preferences is also important.

Thought Questions

1. Are there unusual sexual behaviors you feel should not be classified as a mental disorder, if any? Which unusual sexual behaviors do you feel should definitely be classified as a mental disorder, if any? Why or why not?
2. What is the impact of online activities on sexual fantasies and behaviors?
3. What guidelines would you recommend for defining pedophilic disorder? Would two young adolescents engaging in sexual activity qualify for the diagnosis?
4. How do you think Viagra and other drugs for sexual activity affect sexual practices in the United States and elsewhere?
5. What separates "normal" sexual activity from "unusual" sexual activity? Do you think sexuality has more to do with biological, family, or other factors? Why?
6. What cross-gender behaviors are common in children and adolescents?

Key Terms

sexual dysfunctions 314
male hypoactive sexual desire disorder 316
female sexual interest/arousal disorder 316
erectile disorder 316
female orgasmic disorder 316
delayed ejaculation 316
premature (early) ejaculation 318
genito-pelvic pain/penetration disorder 318
spectator role 322
stop–start procedure 326
sensate focus 326
masturbation training 326
paraphilias 328
paraphilic disorders 328
exhibitionistic disorder 329
fetishistic disorder 330
frotteuristic disorder 330
pedophilic disorder 331
sexual masochism 332
sexual sadism 332
transvestic disorder 333
voyeuristic disorder 333
orgasmic reconditioning 340
gender dysphoria 342
gender-affirming surgery 344

Schizophrenia and Other Psychotic Disorders 12

Learning Objectives

LO 12.1 Describe the continuum from unusual emotions, thoughts, and behaviors to psychotic disorders.

LO 12.2 Distinguish among the types of psychotic disorders based on their diagnostic criteria and clinical features.

LO 12.3 Summarize the epidemiology of psychotic disorders.

LO 12.4 Describe the stigma associated with schizophrenia and its impact on those with the disorder.

LO 12.5 Discuss the risk factors for psychotic disorders.

LO 12.6 Evaluate programs to prevent psychotic disorders.

LO 12.7 Characterize the assessment and treatment of individuals with psychotic disorders.

Case James

James was 29 years old when he was referred to an inpatient psychiatric unit at a city hospital. He was brought to the emergency room the night before by police, who initially found him trying to access a downtown Federal Bureau of Investigation (FBI) building. James fled down the street, yelling something, when first confronted by two police officers. He darted into traffic, nearly causing an accident, before entering a convenience store. The police officers eventually found James curled up in a corner of the store and sobbing.

James was taken to the hospital for evaluation. This was done because he engaged in self-destructive behavior by running into traffic and because he seemed intoxicated or greatly confused. A physician examined James's physical state in the emergency room. James seemed unhurt and had no signs of external injury. Toxicology tests later revealed James had been drinking alcohol, but not enough to justify his bizarre behavior. A psychiatrist from the inpatient unit was thus consulted.

The psychiatrist initially found James terrified of his immediate environment and others around him. After considerable discussion and some sedative medication, however, James became more receptive to the idea he would not be harmed. The psychiatrist asked James if he could remember his earlier behavior and piece together what happened that day. James did not recall his entire day but did convey some important bits of information.

James said he was overwhelmed lately with feelings of apprehension and fear that he and someone important were about to be harmed. He could not specify why he felt this way, but he was sure he had special information that the president of the United States was going to be harmed soon and that he, James, would also be harmed because he knew of the plot. These feelings eventually became so strong that James felt he had to leave his apartment and warn someone at the FBI office. James was still agitated and worried for his own life despite sedation. Nonetheless, he did provide the psychiatrist with names of people close to him.

James was transferred to the inpatient psychiatric unit and held for observation and medication. The psychiatrist spoke to James again the next morning and conveyed that his wife and parents were to visit him that day. Following their visit, the psychiatrist spoke to each family member to piece together James's personal history. They said James had always been an unusual child and adolescent and that things greatly worsened once he entered college in his early 20s. James would often become sullen, withdrawn, morbid, and focused on what might happen if he or family members or important people were harmed. These behaviors escalated whenever James was particularly stressed during college, and he barely completed requirements for his degree.

James worked intermittently as an assistant to a financial advisor the past four years but was hospitalized twice for severe depression and unusual behaviors. The last hospitalization occurred a year ago when James was reprimanded at work for trying to persuade an important client that their life was in danger. The reprimand triggered bizarre responses in James ranging from agitation to hiding in the basement of his house. James was placed on different medications that eased his agitation, but his wife said he "did not always take his pills." His wife said James was upset over a conversation he overheard at work, one in which a client was bragging about having met the president of the United States. Perhaps James misinterpreted this statement as one of threat toward the president, which triggered his current behavior. James remained in the inpatient unit for further assessment and treatment.

What Do You Think?

1. Why do you think James was so agitated and scared?
2. What external events and internal factors might be responsible for James's feelings?
3. What are you curious about regarding James and his family?
4. Does James remind you of a character you have seen in films or the media? How so?
5. How might James's behavior affect him in the future?

Unusual Emotions, Thoughts, and Behaviors and Psychotic Disorders: What Are They?

LO 12.1 Describe the continuum from unusual emotions, thoughts, and behaviors to psychotic disorders.

This textbook so far has covered mental disorders that affect *specific* areas of functioning. Anxiety-related and depressive disorders, for example, affect limited areas of functioning and are sometimes called neurotic disorders or *neuroses*. Someone with social anxiety disorder might have trouble functioning effectively in social situations but can function well in other tasks like caring for oneself or working independently.

Many people also experience odd emotions, thoughts, and behaviors during the course of obsessive-compulsive disorder, illness anxiety disorder, or schizotypal personality disorder. People with these disorders often have odd thoughts, but the thoughts are usually somewhat plausible or believable. A person with obsessive-compulsive disorder may obsess about bacteria growing on their hands, but this is something that could occur. People with illness anxiety disorder worry about having a serious disease, which may be a plausible though untrue explanation for their physical symptoms. Emotional states often associated with these conditions, such as anxiety and depression, are understandable as well. Behaviors associated with these thoughts and emotions, such as excessive hand washing and medical doctor visits, are also unusual but largely an extension of normal things that many people do.

Other mental disorders affect *many* areas of functioning and involve emotions, thoughts, and behaviors so bizarre a person cannot function in most areas of their life. Some of these disorders are **psychotic disorders** or *psychoses* (refer to **Continuum of Unusual Emotions, Cognitions, and Behaviors and Psychotic Disorder**). People with psychotic disorders may have unusual emotional states or affect. **Flat affect** refers to lack of emotion even in situations that call for great joy or sadness. **Inappropriate affect** refers to a mood that does not match the context of a given situation. A person may laugh as someone describes a sad story, become enraged for little reason, or cry after watching a reality television show. These kinds of emotional reactions can prevent a person from interacting well with others.

People with psychotic disorders also have extremely rigid or bizarre thoughts called **delusions**. James's unyielding belief that others wanted to harm him is an example of a delusion. People with psychotic disorders also have trouble organizing their thoughts to form clear sentences or communicate well with others.

People with psychotic disorders also show highly unusual behaviors. Some hear voices no one else does that tell them to do something. These voices are auditory examples of **hallucinations**, or sensory experiences without a real environmental stimulus. People with psychotic disorders can also display **catatonic** positions by remaining in a near immovable state for hours. Those with psychotic disorders often have trouble going to work or engaging in daily self-care. This is known as *avolition*.

Psychotic disorders affect a tiny minority of people, but their overall effect on those with the disorders is immense. People with psychoses, especially those in the active phase of the disorders, cannot work, communicate with others, think rationally, or care for themselves. James's symptoms progressed to the point where he was unable to work, was convinced others wanted to harm him, and was engaged in potentially severe self-destructive behavior.

Psychotic Disorders: Features and Epidemiology

LO 12.2 Distinguish among the types of psychotic disorders based on their diagnostic criteria and clinical features.

LO 12.3 Summarize the epidemiology of psychotic disorders.

The most well-known of the psychoses, and the one covered most in this chapter, is schizophrenia. Other psychotic disorders related to schizophrenia are also covered, including schizophreniform, schizoaffective, delusional, and brief psychotic disorders (refer to **Table 12.1**). Common to each disorder is a severe mental condition that impacts many aspects of daily life. Many people with psychotic disorders like James are affected every day by irrational fears, images, thoughts, and beliefs that do not seem like their own.

Schizophrenia

Schizophrenia generally consists of two main groups of symptoms: positive and negative. **Positive symptoms** of schizophrenia represent excessive or overt symptoms; **negative symptoms** of schizophrenia represent deficit or covert symptoms (refer to **Table 12.2**).

Table 12.1 Types of Psychotic Disorders

Disorder	Key features
Schizophrenia	Positive symptoms such as delusions and hallucinations and negative symptoms such as lack of speech or emotion and failure to care for oneself
Schizophreniform disorder	Features of schizophrenia for one to six months but not necessarily with great impairment in daily functioning
Schizoaffective disorder	Characteristic features of schizophrenia *and* a depressive or manic episode
Delusional disorder	No psychotic symptoms except for one or more delusions
Brief psychotic disorder	Several key features of schizophrenia for one day to one month

Table 12.2 Positive and Negative Symptoms of Schizophrenia

Positive symptoms	Negative symptoms
• Delusions (rigid, bizarre, irrational beliefs)	• Alogia (speaking very little to others)
• Hallucinations (sensory experiences in the absence of actual stimuli)	• Avolition (inability or unwillingness to engage in goal-directed activities)
• Disorganized speech (jumbled speech or speech conveys little information)	• Anhedonia (lack of pleasure or interest in life activities)
• Inappropriate affect (showing emotions that do not suit a given situation)	• Flat affect (showing little emotion in different situations)
• Catatonia (unusual symptoms marked partly by severe restriction of movement or extreme excitability)	• Lack of insight (limited awareness of one's mental condition)

Continuum of Unusual Emotions, Cognitions, and Behaviors and Psychotic Disorder

	Normal	Mild
Emotions	Laughing at a joke or crying at a funeral.	Slightly restricted range of emotions, such as not responding to a joke or sad story.
Cognitions	Ability to organize thoughts and sentences and communicate well.	Slight oddities of thinking, such as belief that a dead relative is in the room.
Behaviors	Working and interacting with others appropriately.	Slightly peculiar behaviors such as not washing or brushing one's teeth for a couple of days.

Positive symptoms of schizophrenia include delusions and hallucinations as well as disorganized speech and behavior. Negative symptoms of schizophrenia include lack of speech or emotion and failure to care for oneself (American Psychiatric Association [APA], 2022). Different positive and negative symptoms are described next in more detail.

Delusions

A key positive symptom of schizophrenia is a delusion. A delusion is an irrational belief involving a misperception of life experiences. Delusions are usually fixed beliefs, meaning they are highly resistant to others' attempts to persuade the person otherwise, and are often incomprehensible and simply untrue. James's strong but strange belief that the conversation he overheard at work meant the president of the United States was about to be harmed is a delusion. Delusions can come in several forms, including persecutory, control, grandiose, referential, and somatic, among others.

Persecutory delusions are the type of delusion most commonly seen in people with schizophrenia; these delusions represent irrational beliefs that one is being harmed or harassed in some way (De Rossi & Georgiades, 2022). A person with a persecutory delusion may believe secret government officials are following them and about to do something dire. Persecutory delusions may intersect with *control delusions*, in which a person may believe others are deliberately:

- Placing thoughts in their mind without permission (*thought insertion*)
- Transmitting their thoughts so everyone can know them (*thought broadcasting*)
- Stealing their thoughts and creating memory loss (*thought withdrawal*; López-Silva et al., 2022)

Grandiose delusions represent irrational beliefs that one is an especially powerful or important person, when actually this is not so (Isham et al., 2022). Delusions of grandiosity are more peculiar than simple beliefs about grandiosity in people with bipolar disorder or narcissistic personality disorder (Chapters 7 and 10). A person with bipolar disorder or narcissistic personality disorder may truly but wrongly believe they are a great writer, but a person with a grandiose delusion may truly but wrongly believe they are a top government official, a company's chief executive officer, or Napoleon! Charles Cullen, a nurse sentenced to 11 consecutive life terms for killing up to 40 patients, may have suffered from a grandiose delusion in claiming at one time he was an "angel of mercy."

Referential delusions (or delusions of reference) are irrational beliefs that events in everyday life have

Moderate	Psychotic Disorder—less severe	Psychotic Disorder—more severe
Greater restrictions in emotions or odd emotional content for a situation, such as getting upset for little reason.	Intense restrictions in mood or intense anger at a coworker for innocuous behaviors such as not responding immediately to an e-mail.	No mood changes whatsoever or extreme inappropriate affect such as laughing for no reason or sobbing during a happy story.
Greater oddities of thinking, such as a belief that one's life resembles segments on a television news program, or some difficulty forming clear thoughts.	Delusional or very odd beliefs that seem possible, such as belief that a coworker is deliberately poisoning one's lunch, or greater difficulty forming clear thoughts.	Delusional or extremely odd beliefs that seem impossible, such as a belief that one is being abducted by aliens, or complete inability to form clear thoughts.
Greater peculiarity of behavior, such avoiding all television shows because of possible resemblance to one's life or not washing for one to two weeks.	Intense peculiarity of behavior, such as refusing to go to work for several weeks due to fear of being harmed or great difficulty caring for oneself.	Extremely peculiar behavior such as hearing voices, running carelessly down a street, not moving at all for hours, or loss of interest in caring for oneself.

something special to do with oneself. A person may be watching local television news and believe each story is based on some aspect of their life from that day (Fuentes-Claramonte et al., 2022). *Somatic delusions* represent irrational beliefs that one's physical body is affected, usually in a negative way and often by an outside source (González-Rodríguez & Seeman, 2022). A person may believe an inability to sleep is caused by excessive microwave radiation outside the house.

Hallucinations

Hallucinations are sensory experiences a person believes to be true, when actually they are not. The most common hallucination in schizophrenia is *auditory*, in which a person may hear voices that repeat their thoughts, comment on their appearance or behavior, argue, or command them to do something (Tsang et al., 2021). Unlike many media portrayals, however, the voices the person hears are not always threatening or demanding of violent behavior. The voice or voices may be recognizable and comforting to the person, or it may be the person's own voice. The latter may relate to a thought broadcasting delusion, where a person hears their thoughts repeated aloud and assumes others can hear them as well. Imagine how distressing that can be!

Hallucinations can also be *visual* or *tactile*, as when a person sees images or visions not seen by others or feels bizarre sensations on their skin. Sometimes visual and tactile hallucinations are linked in an especially distressing way, as when a person "sees" and "feels" large bugs and snakes crawling up their arms (Noel et al., 2020). Hallucinations can even be *olfactory* as when a person smells different things in the same way. Hallucinations can obviously be extremely upsetting and interfere with ability to interact with others.

Disorganized Speech

Many people with schizophrenia also show **disorganized speech**. Speech patterns can be so disorganized a person cannot maintain a regular conversation. Verbalizations may be disconnected, jumbled, interrupted, forgotten in midsentence, or mixed in their phrasing (*loose association*). A person might say "store I go to the have to" instead of "I have to go to the store." A person may also simply make up words that do not make sense to anyone (*neologism*), repeat the same words over and over, say words together because they rhyme (*clang association*), or not speak at all (*alogia*; Tang et al., 2022). Other people with schizophrenia speak quite clearly, stop without warning, and then talk about a completely different topic. This phenomenon, known as *tangentiality*, requires the listener to constantly steer the speaker back to the original topic of conversation.

Amoret Tanner/Alamy Stock Photo

D. Bayes/Lebrecht Music & Arts/Lebrecht Music and Arts Photo Library/Alamy Stock Photo

Pictures drawn by artist Louis Wain. Cats were the subject matter of Wain's art even as he experienced intense periods of psychosis.

Disorganized or Catatonic Behavior

Many people with schizophrenia are disorganized not only in their speech but also in their behavior. A person may be unable to care for oneself and not engage in appropriate hygiene, dress, or even eating. The person may be highly agitated as well (like James) or show *inappropriate affect* or emotions in a given situation (Chan et al., 2020). The person may laugh during a sad story. Such behavior is often unpredictable and frightening to others, as was James's behavior when encountered by police.

Even more bizarre is **catatonic behavior**, which may include unusual motor symptoms (Mormando & Francis, 2020). A person with schizophrenia may not react to environmental events such as someone saying hello or may seem completely unaware of their surroundings (*catatonic stupor*). A person's body part, such as an arm, can be moved to a different posture and that posture is maintained for long periods. This is *waxy flexibility* or *catalepsy*. Other people with schizophrenia may:

- Show uncontrolled motor activity (*stereotypy or agitation*)
- Repeat others' words (*echolalia*) or actions (*echopraxia*)
- Adopt a rigid posture that is difficult to change

Negative Symptoms

Delusions, hallucinations, and disorganized speech and behavior are positive symptoms of schizophrenia. Negative symptoms of schizophrenia refer to pathological *deficits* in behavior, or showing too little of a certain behavior. Common negative symptoms in schizophrenia include:

- **Flat affect**, or showing very little emotion even in situations that seem to demand much emotion, such as a wedding or funeral. A person often speaks in monotone and shows few changes in their facial expression.
- **Alogia**, or speaking very little to other people and appearing withdrawn. Even when a person with schizophrenia does speak, their language is often very basic and brief.
- **Avolition**, or inability or unwillingness to engage in goal-directed activities such as caring for oneself, working, or speaking to others. A person with these negative symptoms may appear depressed.
- **Anhedonia**, or lack of pleasure or interest in life activities.

Lack of insight or limited awareness of one's mental condition, a common occurrence in schizophrenia, sometimes links to negative symptoms as well (Kim et al., 2021). Negative symptoms are not as dramatic or obvious as positive symptoms such as delusions and hallucinations but are nevertheless crucial aspects of schizophrenia and often more difficult to treat (Galderisi et al., 2021). Positive symptoms of schizophrenia may relate to neurochemical changes amenable to medication, but negative symptoms may relate to structural brain changes not largely affected by medication (this is discussed further in later sections).

Other Criteria

Other criteria must also be present for a diagnosis of schizophrenia. Symptoms of schizophrenia must interfere significantly with one's ability to function on an everyday basis. James became unable to work or appropriately interact with others. A person's symptoms must not be due to a substance or medical condition (refer to **Table 12.3**; APA, 2022). Schizophrenia must not be diagnosed with schizoaffective disorder (refer to later section), depressive or bipolar disorder with psychotic features (Chapter 7), or autism spectrum disorder (Chapter 13) unless prominent delusions and hallucinations are present.

Phases of Schizophrenia

People with schizophrenia often, but not always, progress through stages of symptoms (refer to **Figure 12.1**). Many begin with a **prodromal phase** that can last days,

Table 12.3 DSM-5-TR

Schizophrenia
A. Two (or more) of the following, each present for a significant portion of time during a one-month period (or less if successfully treated). At least one of these must be (1), (2), or (3): 1. Delusions. 2. Hallucinations. 3. Disorganized speech (e.g., frequent derailment or incoherence). 4. Grossly disorganized or catatonic behavior. 5. Negative symptoms (i.e., diminished emotional expression or avolition).
B. For a significant portion of the time since the onset of the disturbance, level of functioning in one or more major areas, such as work, interpersonal relations, or self-care, is markedly below the level achieved prior to the onset (or when the onset is in childhood or adolescence, there is failure to achieve expected level of interpersonal, academic, or occupational functioning).
C. Continuous signs of the disturbance persist for at least six months. This six-month period must include at least one month of symptoms (or less if successfully treated) that meet Criterion A (i.e., active-phase symptoms) and may include periods of prodromal or residual symptoms. During these prodromal or residual periods, the signs of the disturbance may be manifested by only negative symptoms or by two or more symptoms listed in Criterion A present in an attenuated form.
D. Schizoaffective disorder and depressive or bipolar disorder with psychotic features have been ruled out because either 1) no major depressive or manic episodes have occurred concurrently with the active-phase symptoms, or 2) if mood episodes have occurred during active-phase symptoms, they have been present for a minority of the total duration of the active and residual periods of the illness.
E. The disturbance is not attributable to the physiological effects of a substance or another medical condition.
F. If there is a history of autism spectrum disorder or a communication disorder of childhood onset, the additional diagnosis of schizophrenia is made only if prominent delusions or hallucinations, in addition to the other required symptoms of schizophrenia, are also present for at least one month (or less if successfully treated). Specify if first episode, multiple episodes, continuous, or unspecified; if with catatonia; and severity.

American Psychiatric Association. (2022). *Diagnostic and statistical manual of mental disorders* (5th ed., text rev.). Arlington, VA: American Psychiatric Association.

weeks, months, or even years. This phase is often marked by peculiar behaviors such as minor disturbances in speech and thought processes, odd or withdrawn social interactions, perceptual distortions, attention and memory problems, and symptoms of depression and anxiety (Wen et al., 2021). The prodromal phase is often marked by negative symptoms that make it difficult to determine exactly what problem a person has. This phase may resemble severe depression. Positive symptoms in attenuated or lesser form, such as unusual perceptual experiences or beliefs, may be present in the prodromal phase as well.

Grunnitus Studio/Science Source

People with catatonia may display bizarre motor movements and postures.

Following the prodromal phase, a person may enter a **psychotic prephase** marked by the first "full-blown" positive symptom of schizophrenia such as a hallucination. A particular stressor may trigger the psychotic prephase, such as James's overheard conversation, and the prephase often lasts less than two months. Positive symptoms usually increase at this point and a person may be admitted for treatment. Positive or negative symptoms must last at least six months for a diagnosis of schizophrenia, which may

Figure 12.1 Phases of Schizophrenia.

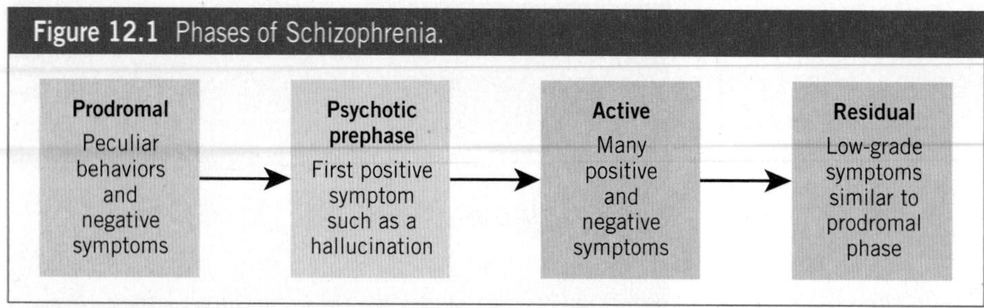

constitute the prodromal phase and psychotic prephase (Mei & McGorry, 2020).

This six-month (or longer) period must include a one-month phase in which the symptoms are especially acute, or an **active phase** (APA, 2022). A person in the active phase usually experiences many "full-blown" positive and negative symptoms, as James did, and needs hospitalization to protect himself and others. Following treatment, many people with schizophrenia advance to a **residual phase** that usually involves symptoms similar to the prodromal phase (Tsai et al., 2020). Many people with schizophrenia remain in this residual phase for much of their life.

Many people with schizophrenia show *heterogeneous* behavior, meaning their symptoms are present in different combinations and severity. The *Diagnostic and Statistical Manual of Mental Disorders* thus provides a rating scale for *dimensions* of schizophrenia that are fluid and that may apply better to people with mixed symptoms of schizophrenia (APA, 2022). These dimensions represent a continuum of different symptoms a person may have, ranging from not present and equivocal to mild, moderate, and severe. These dimensions include hallucinations, delusions, disorganized speech, unusual psychomotor behavior (e.g., catatonia), negative symptoms, impaired cognition, depression, and mania (refer to **Figure 12.2**).

Another possible dimension of schizophrenia relates to social disturbance (Blanchard et al., 2020). All of these dimensions allow a therapist to describe someone with a psychotic disorder more specifically. James showed a moderate to severe degree of delusions and milder degrees of disorganized speech and negative symptoms. Someone with schizophrenia could have any combination of these problems to any degree in this dimensional approach.

Schizophreniform Disorder

What about people who experience psychotic symptoms for less than six months? People who show features of schizophrenia for one to six months, and whose daily life functioning may not yet be greatly impaired, may have **schizophreniform disorder** (refer to **Table 12.4**; APA, 2022). This disorder is sometimes studied within the context of a *first-episode psychosis* (Pinho et al., 2022).

James experienced times in his life, as in college, when he had psychotic features for less than six months and was able to function at a basic level. If a person with schizophreniform disorder has psychotic symptoms that last longer than six months, then the diagnosis could be changed to schizophrenia. People with schizophreniform disorder may be those *with* or *without good prognostic features* (APA, 2022). Those with good prognostic features, like James, have adequate daily functioning before the onset of psychotic symptoms, confusion during the most active psychotic symptoms, no flat affect, and quick onset of psychotic symptoms after their behavior becomes noticeably different (Compton et al., 2014).

Figure 12.2 DSM-5-TR Dimensions of Schizophrenia.

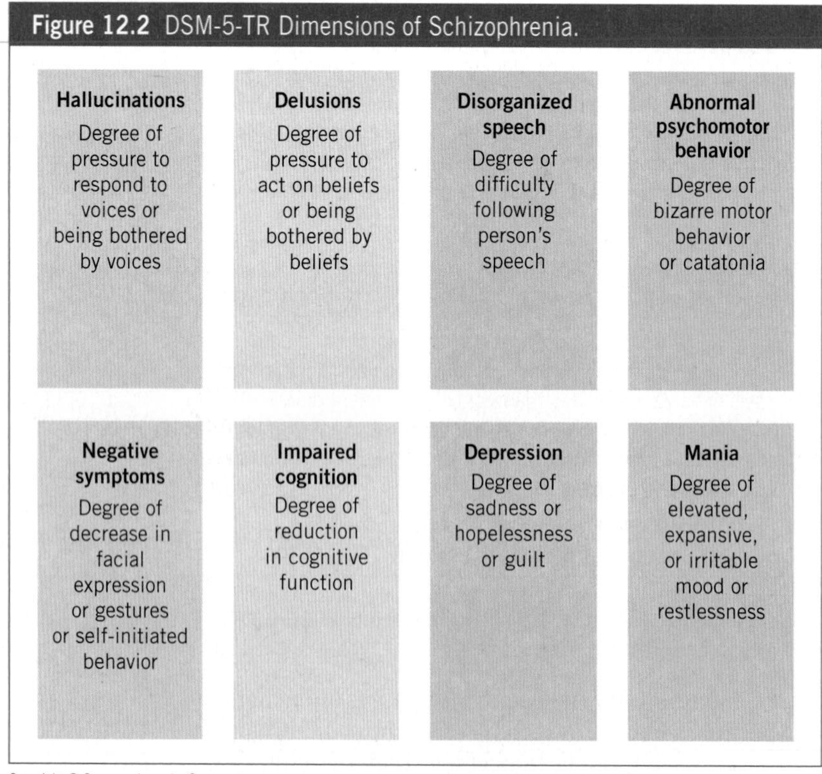

Hallucinations
Degree of pressure to respond to voices or being bothered by voices
Delusions
Degree of pressure to act on beliefs or being bothered by beliefs
Disorganized speech
Degree of difficulty following person's speech
Abnormal psychomotor behavior
Degree of bizarre motor behavior or catatonia
Negative symptoms
Degree of decrease in facial expression or gestures or self-initiated behavior
Impaired cognition
Degree of reduction in cognitive function
Depression
Degree of sadness or hopelessness or guilt
Mania
Degree of elevated, expansive, or irritable mood or restlessness

Table 12.4 DSM-5-TR

Schizophreniform Disorder
A. Two (or more) of the following, each present for a significant portion of time during a one-month period (or less if successfully treated). At least one of these must be (1), (2), or (3): 1. Delusions. 2. Hallucinations. 3. Disorganized speech (e.g., frequent derailment or incoherence). 4. Grossly disorganized or catatonic behavior. 5. Negative symptoms (i.e., diminished emotional expression or avolition).
B. An episode of the disorder lasts at least one month but less than six months. When the diagnosis must be made without waiting for recovery, it should be qualified as "provisional."
C. Schizoaffective disorder and depressive or bipolar disorder with psychotic features have been ruled out because either 1) no major depressive or manic episodes have occurred concurrently with the active-phase symptoms, or 2) if mood episodes have occurred during active-phase symptoms, they have been present for a minority of the total duration of the active and residual periods of the illness.
D. The disturbance is not attributable to the physiological effects of a substance (e.g., a drug of abuse, a medication) or another medical condition. Specify if with or without good prognostic features; if with catatonia; and severity.

American Psychiatric Association. (2022). *Diagnostic and statistical manual of mental disorders* (5th ed., text rev.). Arlington, VA: American Psychiatric Association.

Table 12.5 DSM-5-TR

Schizoaffective Disorder
A. An uninterrupted period of illness during which there is a major mood episode (major depressive or manic) concurrent with criterion A of schizophrenia. Note: The major depressive episode must include Criterion A1: Depressed mood.
B. Delusions or hallucinations for two or more weeks in the absence of a major mood episode (depressive or manic) during the lifetime duration of the illness.
C. Symptoms that meet criteria for a major mood episode are present for the majority of the total duration of the active residual portions of the illness.
D. The disturbance is not attributable to the effects of a substance (e.g., a drug of abuse, a medication) or another medical condition.

American Psychiatric Association. (2022). *Diagnostic and statistical manual of mental disorders* (5th ed., text rev.). Arlington, VA: American Psychiatric Association.

Schizoaffective Disorder

You may have noticed that people with schizophrenia often have symptoms that resemble depression, such as loss of interest in things and decreased movement and talking. A person who meets many of the diagnostic criteria for schizophrenia may *also* meet diagnostic criteria for depression. The person may thus qualify for a diagnosis of **schizoaffective disorder** (refer to **Table 12.5**; APA, 2022).

Schizoaffective disorder includes characteristic features of schizophrenia *and* a depressive or manic episode (Chapter 7). Symptoms of schizophrenia, however, are considered primary—delusions or hallucinations must last at least two weeks without prominent symptoms of a mood disorder. A person often develops schizophrenia and later develops depression, which may happen when they experience negative consequences such as a job loss due to odd behavior. Two subtypes of schizoaffective disorder include *depressive type* and *bipolar type,* the latter meaning the co-occurrence of main features of schizophrenia with manic episodes. Recall from Chapter 7 that people with depressive and bipolar disorders can also have psychotic symptoms, but in these cases, the depressive or bipolar disorder is most prominent (Yan et al., 2022).

Schizoaffective disorder is sometimes considered part of a schizophrenia spectrum that includes depression, bipolar disorder, and schizotypal personality disorder (Lynham et al., 2022). Clinicians often have a difficult task distinguishing symptoms of severe depressive or bipolar disorder from symptoms of schizophrenia. Imagine someone who is intensely withdrawn, who fails to move for hours at a time, and who has distorted thoughts—this could be someone with severe depression, symptoms of schizophrenia, or both.

Delusional Disorder

People with schizophrenia or schizophreniform or schizoaffective disorder have psychotic symptoms such as delusions, hallucinations, disorganized speech, disorganized or catatonic behavior, and negative symptoms. Other people with a psychotic disorder, such as those with **delusional disorder**, however, have no psychotic symptoms except for one or more

Personal Narrative

John Cadigan

John Cadigan described living with schizophrenia in a film he made for HBO/Cinemax called People Say I'm Crazy (www.peoplesayimcrazy.org). His woodcuts have been exhibited at museums and galleries nationwide.

John Cadigan

My worst symptom is paranoia. A lot of times my paranoia comes in the form of thinking people hate me, thinking people don't like me just because of the way they look at me or because of what they do with their hands or what they say or what they don't say. At my boarding house, I can tell whether they like me or they don't like me by the way they make my bed. If the sheets are not slick and they are old sheets, with little bumps on them—that means they're sending me a message that they don't like what I'm doing. They're trying to get rid of me, they don't like me. If the sheets are all new and slick—that means I'm doing OK.

My disorder hit when I was in college at Carnegie Mellon. I had my first psychotic break six months before graduating, and I've been struggling with a form of schizophrenia ever since. Growing up, sports and art were the most important things in my life. I sometimes fantasized about being a professional soccer player. When I was in fifth grade I was voted most popular, most athletic, and most artistic. My senior year I was voted most quiet, which was pretty much true. I was. I think that was the beginning of my symptoms.

The first three years of my disorder I was sick all the time. I tried every antipsychotic, mood stabilizer and antidepressant on the market. But nothing worked. I couldn't read for a few years. Schizophrenia affects logic and comprehension. I literally could not understand the words. It was even hard to watch television. Basically, what I did all day was pace and drink coffee. And I eventually turned to alcohol and was getting drunk every day.

Finally the new generation of medication became available—the first new drugs for schizophrenia in decades. And I began taking one of them. Very very slowly, it started working. And, I got a new doctor, who is wonderful.

When my family realized that my schizophrenia was not going to go away, my mother moved out to California (where I live) from Boston. My disorder brought everyone in my family together. Since my parents' divorce, my family had been very fractured. But they all united to try and help me.

I'm really close with my oldest sister Katie, who's a filmmaker. I usually go to Katie or my Mom when I'm having a bout of paranoia or depression. In the beginning of my disorder, when we really didn't know what was going on, Katie and her husband let me live with them. I was very sick then, so I wasn't the easiest person to live with. Now I hang out at Mom's house a lot and watch TV. There I can be alone. I can be safe. I'm lucky to have such a supportive family.

A lot of other families don't understand that schizophrenia is a mental disorder. One of my best friends, Ann, was disowned by her family. Her children don't talk to her because they think she's crazy and don't want anything to do with her. She doesn't get to see her grandchildren. My mom and I have adopted her into our family. She calls me her adopted son and calls my mom her sister.

Here's what some of my family said when I asked what the hardest part of my disorder was for them:

MY MOM: "The hardest part? To single out one I couldn't do it. There were a hundred hardest parts. Just to watch the amount of difficulty. . . . Once I understood how much having

delusions (refer to **Table 12.6**; APA, 2022). A delusion could be nonbizarre or bizarre, the latter meaning it is not plausible. Jody's belief that a coworker poisoned her lunch is plausible, though not true, and thus nonbizarre. People with delusional disorder do not experience significant impairments in daily functioning apart from the impact of the delusion but may be quite distressed.

A person with delusional disorder may have one or more of the following delusions:

- *Erotomanic,* such as the mistaken belief a special person, such as a celebrity, loves the person from a distance
- *Grandiose,* such as the mistaken belief one is an especially powerful, famous, or knowledgeable person
- *Jealous,* such as the mistaken belief a partner is having an affair
- *Persecutory,* such as Jody's mistaken belief another person aimed to harm her
- *Somatic,* or a mistaken belief about one's body, such as having some serious medical disease (Muñoz-Negro et al., 2020).

Some people develop a delusion because of their close relationship with another person who also has

this mental disorder was affecting you, how much you struggled with it and how much pain you were in—it felt unbearable to me and that I couldn't do anything, really, to help you."

MY BROTHER STEVE: "There was a time when we went to see you in the hospital and you couldn't speak. Your eyes had this look of entrapment—that you were trapped inside yourself. And there was just sheer terror in your eyes. That was hard. Really hard."

MY SISTER KATIE: "The very hardest part was when you started getting suicidal. It was about two years into your disorder. It was horrible. I didn't want you to die."

People think that schizophrenia means split personality or multiple personality, but they're making a big mistake. The "schizo-" prefix doesn't mean personality split—it means a break with reality. I don't know what reality is. I can't trust my own perceptions. The hardest struggle is to know what's real and what's not real. And that's a daily struggle for me.

I have a hard time being around people. Sometimes I feel restless and I feel like I've got to pace. I guess it's my constant fear that people are out to purposely drive me crazy or mess with my mind. Like there's a secret agenda. As if everybody is interconnected and they are slowly and subtly dropping clues. A glance here, and a glance there. It is evil and the evil is after me. It makes it really difficult to communicate to others and to get up the courage to reach out to others and make friends.

These thoughts—they just get in my head and fester in there. Then I tell myself, "It's not true. It's not true. It's not true. It's not true. It's not true. It's not true." And, I try to just say that over and over again. "It's not true. It's not true. It's not true."

My doctor helped me learn how to do reality checks. When I'm having a hard time with terrible thoughts, and I think it might be paranoia, I try to get up my courage to go to a safe person. It might be one of my sisters or my mom, or even my doctor. And I tell them what I'm thinking. And every single time, they tell me, "John, you're wrong. Your perceptions and your thoughts aren't based in reality." It doesn't take away the paranoia, but it helps lessen the intensity.

There are times when I can work and there are times when I can't work. When my thoughts are racing or when I'm incredibly paranoid, those are times when I can't work. It feels awful. It's just a terrible feeling. I don't have much hope. I don't. But I try to keep telling myself that it will pass. It will pass.

I've been volunteering at a food closet with my friend Patrick. He was signed up and it was his first time going and I just decided to go along and help. Clients are allowed two visits a week. They have a little computer there and Patrick checks them in. They move about a ton of food a week. So many people helped me and I get so much support from other people. I think it's good for my own soul to help others. It makes me feel good doing it. I enjoy it. I really enjoy doing it.

At the food closet, everything was fine for a while. Until the paranoia crept in. It all revolved around nametags. My friend Patrick had a nametag and this woman Shelly did and this guy Morris did and so did Gloria. They all had nametags and I didn't. And I thought it was a secret message telling me: "We hate you, John. We don't want you around, John. We think you are an awful person, John." It sounds so stupid when I say it but it really devastates me. This kind of thing happens to me all the time.

I wonder if I am ever going to get better. I know I've gotten better. But I wonder if I'm ever going to get a lot better. Totally better. I'm 30 years old now and have been struggling with this disorder for close to nine years. Nine years. I remember one thing my friend Ed said to me. He said something like, "when you get to around 50 the symptoms kind of ease up a bit." That's another 20 years for me.

a delusion. This is sometimes called *folie à deux*. The two people often share similar ideas with respect to the irrational belief. This process could explain why Wanda Barzee, the wife of the man who kidnapped Elizabeth Smart in Utah, consented to and participated in this terrible crime. She appeared to believe, as her husband Brian Mitchell did, that kidnapping Smart was a "revelation from God" and that polygamy (multiple spouses) was acceptable. This process is also sometimes evident in cases of child maltreatment in which both parents believe their maladaptive behavior benefits the child (Erickson, 2014). The delusion may weaken in the second person when they are separated from the more dominant, delusional partner.

Brief Psychotic Disorder

What happens when a person has psychotic symptoms for less than one month? A person with such symptoms may qualify for a diagnosis of **brief psychotic disorder**, which involves several key features of schizophrenia occurring for one day to one

Table 12.6 DSM-5-TR

Delusional Disorder
A. The presence of one (or more) delusions with a duration of one month or longer.
B. Criterion A for schizophrenia has never been met.
C. Apart from the impact of the delusion(s) or its ramifications, functioning is not markedly impaired, and behavior is not obviously bizarre or odd.
D. If manic or major depressive episodes have occurred, these have been brief relative to the duration of the delusional periods.
E. The disturbance is not attributable to the physiological effects of a substance or another medical condition and is not better explained by another mental disorder, such as body dysmorphic disorder or obsessive-compulsive disorder. Specify if erotomanic, grandiose, jealous, persecutory, somatic, mixed, or unspecified type; if first episode, multiple episodes, continuous, or unspecified; if with bizarre content; and severity.

American Psychiatric Association. (2022). *Diagnostic and statistical manual of mental disorders* (5th ed., text rev.). Arlington, VA: American Psychiatric Association.

month (refer to **Table 12.7**; APA, 2022). These features include delusions, hallucinations, disorganized speech, and disorganized or catatonic behavior. Symptoms of brief psychotic disorder often occur after an environmental stressor or traumatic event (Valdés-Florido et al., 2022).

Psychotic symptoms may occur in a parent after giving birth—**postpartum psychosis** (Perry et al., 2021). Recall from Chapter 7 that some parents have postpartum depression; some parents experience postpartum depression *and* psychosis. Andrea Yates, a woman from Texas who drowned her five children, appeared to have delusional and depressive symptoms following the birth of her most recent child and the death of her father. Her condition underscores the need for greater knowledge and prevention of postpartum psychosis and depression. Symptoms of brief psychotic disorder often dissipate as a person becomes better able to cope with the stressor, if one exists. In other cases, however, symptoms can persist and lead to harmful consequences or schizophreniform disorder or schizophrenia.

Epidemiology of Psychotic Disorders

Schizophrenia occurs in 0.3 to 0.7 percent of the general population. Median age of onset is 20.5 years (although the disorder could occur at any age), and schizophrenia

Case Jody

Jody was a 38-year-old office manager who worked for a large law firm. She interacted with lawyers and their administrative assistants to conduct financial and other business necessary for the firm to function efficiently. The firm was a competitive environment that involved substantial turnover and jockeying for better positions and offices. Jody was a competent manager, but she consistently wondered if her coworkers deliberately tried to sabotage her to gain her position.

Jody was involved in many discussions with the law partners over the years about these concerns, few of which were substantiated. Problems intensified recently, however, when one of the lawyers was promoted to partner, and his administrative assistant was appointed as Jody's assistant. Jody felt threatened by this organizational move and became suspicious of Rachel, her new assistant. These suspicions deepened when Rachel moved her desk near Jody's and when Rachel took initiative to help Jody with daily tasks.

Jody's suspicions became more unusual—she believed Rachel was deliberately poisoning her lunch in an effort to make her sick. Jody thought this was an effort on Rachel's part to eventually secure Jody's position. Jody accused Rachel on several occasions of stealing, inserting substances into, and spitting on her lunch. Rachel vehemently denied all of this, but Jody enlisted the help of others in the office to spy on Rachel and even asked one of the lawyers to represent her in a lawsuit against Rachel. The law partners eventually had to intervene and told Jody she would lose her job if she continued these accusations and that she needed professional help.

Table 12.7 DSM-5-TR

Brief Psychotic Disorder
A. Presence of one (or more) of the following symptoms. At least one of these must be (1), (2), or (3): 1. Delusions. 2. Hallucinations. 3. Disorganized speech (e.g., frequent derailment or incoherence). 4. Grossly disorganized or catatonic behavior.
B. Duration of an episode of the disturbance is at least one day but less than one month, with eventual full return to premorbid level of functioning.
C. The disturbance is not better explained by major depressive or bipolar disorder with psychotic features or another psychotic disorder such as schizophrenia or catatonia, and is not attributable to the physiological effects of a substance (e.g., a drug of abuse, a medication) or another medical condition.

American Psychiatric Association. (2022). *Diagnostic and statistical manual of mental disorders* (5th ed., text rev.). Arlington, VA: American Psychiatric Association.

Vera Livchak/Moment/Getty Images

Postpartum depression and psychosis are serious mental conditions that can occur after the birth of a child.

is somewhat more frequent among men than women (Charlson et al., 2018; Nuño et al., 2019; Solmi et al., 2022). Men with schizophrenia tend to have symptoms at a younger age than women with schizophrenia. This means men usually have more severe symptoms as well (Giordano et al., 2021).

One possible reason why men have more severe schizophrenia symptoms than women may be that women have certain biological factors, such as protective hormones or less severe brain changes, that help prevent the development of more serious symptoms. Another possibility is that women function better than men in work and social settings, which may enhance positive long-term outcome (Ayesa-Arriola et al., 2020). Ethnicity and income level may relate to schizophrenia as well (refer to **Focus On Diversity: Ethnicity and Income Level in Schizophrenia** and later section on cultural influences). Symptoms of psychotic disorders are also sometimes evident in college students (refer to **Focus On College Students: Psychotic Symptoms**).

Schizophrenia can be associated with many other mental disorders because of its complex symptoms. Recall that schizophrenia can be, for some people, the final phase of a psychotic spectrum that initially includes brief psychotic disorder (less than one month) and schizophreniform disorder (one to six months). The odd behaviors associated with schizophrenia, such as unusual perceptual experiences and persecutory thoughts, may also mean schizophrenia is part of a spectrum of disorders that includes schizotypal, schizoid, and paranoid personality disorders (Chapter 10; refer to **Figure 12.3**; Liu et al., 2020). These disorders generally involve bizarre and suspicious behaviors and thought-related problems that greatly interfere with many aspects of a person's life.

The most common mental disorders otherwise associated with schizophrenia are anxiety-related, depressive, bipolar, and substance use disorders (Strålin & Hetta, 2021). Depression could develop before schizophrenia and help trigger psychotic symptoms, or the development of psychotic symptoms could lead to a process involving difficult events such as job loss that causes someone to later become depressed (Etchecopar-Etchart et al., 2021).

Suicide is also much more common among people with schizophrenia (5–15 percent) than the general population. Suicide in people with schizophrenia closely relates to onset of the disorder, depression, excessive substance use, recent loss, agitation, and limited adherence to treatment. People with

Focus On Diversity

Ethnicity and Income Level in Schizophrenia

A controversial issue is whether ethnicity and income level have an impact on schizophrenia. An analysis of different countries generally indicates no large variation in prevalence rates for schizophrenia (Charlson et al., 2018). Certain groups of people may be at increased risk for psychotic disorder, however. Schizophrenia is more common in certain immigrant populations of ethnic minority status. People in urban settings may also be at higher risk for schizophrenia than those in rural settings (Abrahamyan Empson et al., 2020).

Possible reasons for these findings include exposure to more pollution and noise, higher rates of excessive substance use, increased risk of infectious diseases and malnutrition, chronic stress from poverty conditions and unemployment, racism, social isolation, less access to treatment services, and the interaction of these conditions with genetic predispositions for psychotic disorder (Lee et al., 2020). One single factor does not seem responsible, however, for possible ethnic differences in schizophrenia.

Schizophrenia also relates to lower income level. Knowing the direction of this relationship is not easy, however. Some people may develop schizophrenia following the chronic stressors of poverty, but some people may first develop schizophrenia and then drift into lower socioeconomic levels as their disorder progresses and their income declines, such as after job loss. People with more income may also have access to earlier treatment. Some people with less income may also believe their disorder will result in substantial discrimination from others (Balogun-Mwangi et al., 2022; Schneider et al., 2022).

Focus On College Students

Psychotic Symptoms

You might think that the disorders described in this chapter do not apply much to college students, but researchers have focused on what is called *attenuated psychotic symptoms*. Attenuated symptoms refer to mild or subtle signs of a psychotic episode to the point that they cause distress for a person. Examples include perceptual differences, delusional ideas, or a negative symptom. One group of researchers assessed college students for attenuated signs of psychosis. A large majority of the students (84 percent) endorsed one or more early psychotic symptoms, and 57 percent said at least one of the symptoms worried them or caused problems. Many of the students experienced self-stigma about the symptoms and thus did not seek support from friends about the symptoms (Denenny et al., 2015).

Others have looked at attenuated psychotic symptoms in college students in greater detail. A key finding is that these symptoms are often linked to a prior traumatic event in a person's life, which is a theme evident for other mental problems in college students. In particular, researchers have found that stress sensitivity relates closely to the association between traumatic life events and attenuated psychotic symptoms. Stress sensitivity refers to perceived threat to one's physical or psychological health (Muñoz-Samons et al., 2021). Attenuated psychotic symptoms in college students also relate to depression and suicidal ideation (Ma et al., 2021). These data indicate that, despite the substantial stigma often attached to the symptoms described in this chapter, seeking help must be a priority.

schizophrenia most at risk for suicide tend to be male, younger, and socially isolated (Bornheimer et al., 2020; De Sousa et al., 2020). Violence toward others is sometimes but not usually a feature of schizophrenia (refer to **Focus On Violence: Are People with Schizophrenia More Violent?**). Schizophreniform disorder is quite similar to schizophrenia, especially the prodromal phase of schizophrenia. Most people with the disorder have thus not yet presented for treatment, so prevalence rates for schizophreniform disorder are likely much lower than for schizophrenia. Only about one third of those with a first episode psychosis fully recover and many eventually receive a diagnosis of schizophrenia or schizoaffective disorder (Ajnakina et al., 2021).

Figure 12.3 Schizophrenia Spectrum Disorders.

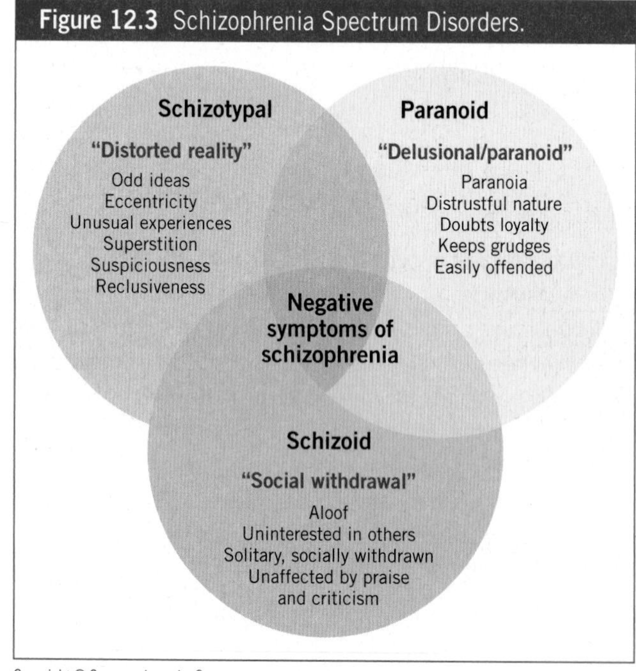

The prevalence of schizoaffective disorder is also likely lower than schizophrenia (0.3 percent). Those with schizophrenia and bipolar disorder tend to display symptoms at a younger age than those with schizophrenia and depression. Schizoaffective disorder tends to be more prevalent among women than men. This is likely due to frequent presence of depression in schizoaffective disorder (Miller & Black, 2019).

Unusual beliefs about people or events are common in the general population, but formal delusional disorder is rare. Many people with delusional disorder have persecutory (45.3 percent), somatic (12.6 percent), and grandiose (6.3 percent) delusions. Delusional disorder may be slightly more common in women than men, but men with the disorder may have more severe symptoms and worse functioning (Picardi et al., 2018).

Less is known about brief psychotic disorder because the problem is often limited in duration and scope and because many people recover quickly. Brief psychotic disorder is thus considered to be an *acute transient psychosis*. Acute transient psychoses differ from schizophrenia in that they involve more women, a later age of onset, greater anxiety and fluctuation of symptoms, and less social withdrawal (Malhotra et al., 2019). Postpartum psychosis occurs in about 1 to 2 of 1,000 births and can be linked to social isolation, confusion, disorganized behavior, sleep deprivation, and severe symptoms of depression and bipolar disorder (Forde et al., 2020). Suicide or harm to a newborn, as was the case with Andrea Yates, can occur in extreme cases as well.

Focus On Violence

Are People with Schizophrenia More Violent?

Media portrayals of people with psychotic disorders such as schizophrenia are often skewed toward images of voices commanding a person to commit violent acts. A serial killer in 1970s New York City was murdering women and young lovers with a .44 caliber handgun. The murderer claimed in a letter that "Papa Sam" was commanding him to go out and kill—the murderer was later dubbed the "Son of Sam." David Berkowitz, a man with psychotic delusions about demons telling him to hunt for blood, was eventually arrested for these terrible crimes. Newspaper headlines screamed almost daily about the hunt for Berkowitz and later about his mental state. The widespread and intensive coverage gave people the impression that those with psychoses must necessarily be dangerous. Many voices heard by people with schizophrenia do not command them to kill, but intense media coverage of certain cases such as Berkowitz's does raise the question about whether this population is particularly violent.

People with schizophrenia do have higher rates of violence perpetration than the general population (Whiting et al., 2022). Possible risk factors for violence in this population include history of child maltreatment, hostile behavior, limited impulse control, excessive substance use, and nonadherence with medication (Ranu et al., 2022). Furthermore, those imprisoned in various countries have a generally three times greater rate of psychotic disorder than the general population (Meinert et al., 2020).

Consider other evidence regarding violence and schizophrenia, however. First, the great majority of people in prison do not have psychotic disorders and more have depression than psychotic disorder (Butcher et al., 2021). Second, only about 4 to 6 percent of those arrested for a crime have a serious mental disorder (Hall et al., 2019). Third, after people with psychotic disorders begin treatment, rates of violence often decline (Hodgins, 2022). Fourth, people at risk for psychotic disorders are much more likely to be *victimized* by, rather than commit, a crime (van der Stouwe et al., 2021). Finally, people with a first episode of psychosis are much more likely to harm themselves than others (Moe et al., 2022). Some people with schizophrenia are at risk for committing violent crimes, but the vast majority do not do so and are more likely to be harmed themselves.

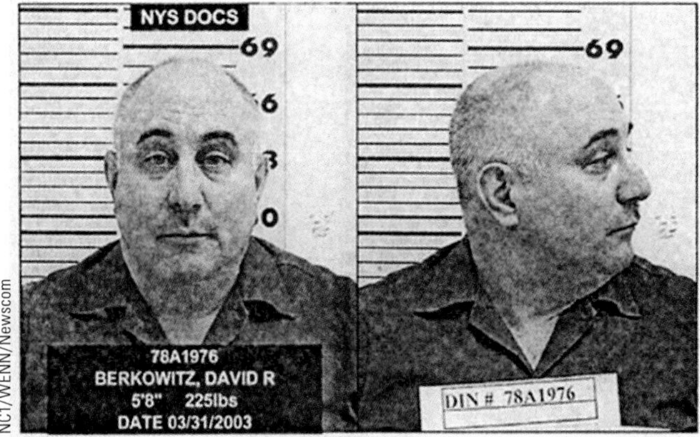

NC1/WENN/Newscom

The violent crimes of "Son of Sam" David Berkowitz were prominently displayed in newspaper headlines, which may have skewed the public's perception of people with schizophrenia as overly dangerous.

Stigma Associated with Psychotic Disorders

LO 12.4 Describe the stigma associated with schizophrenia and its impact on those with the disorder.

Schizophrenia is a severe disorder, so stigma associated with the problem is clearly a concern. One group of researchers surveyed hundreds of people with schizophrenia about their perceptions of discrimination and stigma. Almost three quarters (72 percent) said they felt the need to conceal their diagnosis because of difficulties they anticipated with family members or possible coworkers. In addition, 64 percent said they had stopped applying for work or educational opportunities, and 58 percent said they had stopped looking for a close relationship. The latter was especially true if those with schizophrenia felt disrespected by mental health staff members. Others reported ceasing travel, social activities, applying for mortgages, and having children, often due to perceived discrimination from others (Üçok et al., 2012). People with schizophrenia with more social support may experience less self-stigma, however. Stigma resistance, or one's capacity to counteract stigma, is associated with a social network that provides good support (Dihmes et al., 2020).

Stigma associated with schizophrenia and other psychotic disorders is important because it affects symptoms and treatment. Greater self-stigma relates to more depression and social anxiety and withdrawal, as well as worsened treatment outcome, among people with schizophrenia spectrum disorders (Dubreucq et al., 2021). Conversely, less self-stigma and more insight into one's symptoms are related to better alliance with one's therapist among people with psychotic disorder (Surmann et al., 2021). Helping people with schizophrenia actively resist stigma can also be an important component of treatment (Lysaker et al., 2022). Stigma can be a powerful force in the lives of people with psychotic disorders, so addressing the problem directly is important.

Section Summary

- People with psychotic disorders have bizarre emotions, thoughts, and behaviors that greatly interfere with many different areas of daily functioning.
- Positive or excessive symptoms of schizophrenia include delusions, hallucinations, and disorganized speech and behavior.
- Negative or deficit symptoms of schizophrenia include flat affect, alogia, avolition, and anhedonia.
- Schizophrenia may also be rated by severity across dimensions that include positive and negative symptoms as well as impaired cognition, depression, and mania.
- Schizophreniform disorder is similar to schizophrenia but lasts one to six months and may not involve serious impairment in daily functioning.
- Schizoaffective disorder applies to those who have features of schizophrenia and a depressive or manic episode.
- Delusional disorder involves one or more delusions that may or may not have bizarre content.
- Brief psychotic disorder involves features of schizophrenia that last one day to one month and can be triggered by a traumatic event.
- Schizophrenia is a rare disorder but is more commonly seen in men. The disorder is often viewed along a spectrum of disorders and is associated with depression and suicide and substance use.
- Stigma associated with schizophrenia can be severe and affects symptoms and treatment.

Review Questions

1. What are key positive and negative symptoms of schizophrenia?
2. Describe the main dimensions of schizophrenia.
3. Describe the main features of schizophreniform, schizoaffective, and brief psychotic disorder.
4. What types of delusions are common to people with psychotic disorders?
5. Who most commonly has schizophrenia and what conditions relate to the disorder?

Psychotic Disorders: Causes and Prevention

LO 12.5 Discuss the risk factors for psychotic disorders.

LO 12.6 Evaluate programs to prevent psychotic disorders.

Why would someone like James have such bizarre thoughts and behaviors? Recall that many mental disorders are thought to result from a combination of biological and environmental variables. Many people are born with a genetic or biological predisposition toward certain personality characteristics and mental conditions. These biological predispositions are sometimes stronger and sometimes weaker, but they appear to be quite strong in schizophrenia. The next sections thus concentrate mostly on biological risk factors for schizophrenia but cover environmental factors that may have some impact as well.

Biological Risk Factors for Psychotic Disorders

Biological predispositions in people with psychotic disorders may involve genetics, brain and neurochemical features, and cognitive deficits.

Genetics

Family, twin, and adoption studies indicate that schizophrenia has a strong genetic basis. **Figure 12.4** summarizes studies of the prevalence of schizophrenia in relatives of people with schizophrenia. Recall that schizophrenia is present in less than 1 percent of the general population. Children of people with schizophrenia, however, are about 12 times more likely than the general population to develop schizophrenia. The risk factor is high even among more distant relatives. Grandchildren of people with schizophrenia are about three times more likely than the general population to develop schizophrenia. Close relatives are also at increased risk for schizophreniform, schizoaffective, and aspects of schizotypal and avoidant personality disorders (Docherty et al., 2020; Perrotta, 2020; Poletti et al., 2020).

Twin studies also indicate that schizophrenia has a genetic component. Concordance rates for schizophrenia among identical twins (33 percent) are higher than for fraternal twins (7 percent; Hilker et al., 2018). Adoption studies reveal a similar finding. Children born to mothers with schizophrenia but raised by parents without schizophrenia still show a higher likelihood of

Dr. Allan F. Mirsky/National Institute of Mental Health

The Genain quadruplets were identical siblings, all women, who developed schizophrenia. Researchers at the National Institute for Mental Health studied them closely to learn more about genetic contributions to psychosis.

developing schizophrenia (5.6–9.1 percent) than control groups (0.9–1.1 percent). This appears to be especially true if parents have problems communicating with their adoptive children whose biological mothers had schizophrenia (Lawrence et al., 2015). Heritability for schizophrenia is estimated to be about 0.80 (Legge et al., 2021).

Researchers have found linkages to schizophrenia on different chromosomes but the data are not consistent because many people with schizophrenia show different genetic markers. Other genetic mechanisms may thus be evident. Researchers often focus on genetic mutations that could lead to schizophrenia (Tromp et al., 2021). Many people with schizophrenia may also have multiple genes that work together to help produce the disorder. This is known as a *polygenic* or *multilocus model* (Smeland et al., 2020). In addition, genetic predispositions may be stronger for some types of schizophrenia or specific behaviors related to the disorder, and other biological and environmental variables may contribute as well (Lemvigh et al., 2022).

Brain Features

Some people with schizophrenia have certain brain features that may help produce the disorder. One key feature is *enlarged ventricles,* or spaces or gaps in the brain (refer to **Figure 12.5**). This finding is not specific to schizophrenia because some people with neurocognitive disorders (Chapter 14) also have enlarged ventricles. This brain feature is a highly replicated biological finding in people with schizophrenia, however (Svancer & Spaniel, 2021).

How might enlarged ventricles lead to schizophrenia? One possibility is that enlarged ventricles mean changes in normal brain development or disruption of pathways from one area of the brain to another. An important disruption may involve neural connections between areas of the brain that influence cognition and language. Schizophrenia is increasingly seen as a disorder of cortical connectivity (Pokorny et al., 2021). Another possibility is that added space means critical brain areas are less well developed than they should be. This leads to the next major finding in this area: differences in lobes of the brain.

Schizophrenia researchers have paid particular attention to limited development of the temporal lobe of the brain, which is partially responsible for auditory processing and language (refer to **Figure 12.6**). People with schizophrenia often have key problems in auditory processing and language, so these problems may be due to differences in temporal lobe areas. The medial temporal lobe, especially the amygdala and hippocampus, is smaller in people with schizophrenia than in control participants (Bobilev et al., 2020). These areas are partially responsible for verbal and spatial memory processing and emotion, which are also problematic for people with schizophrenia. Reduced size in the superior and middle temporal gyri, which can affect auditory memory and language processing, has also been linked to schizophrenia (Bustillo et al., 2020).

Figure 12.4 Lifetime Prevalence of Schizophrenia by Degree of Relationship to a Person with Schizophrenia.

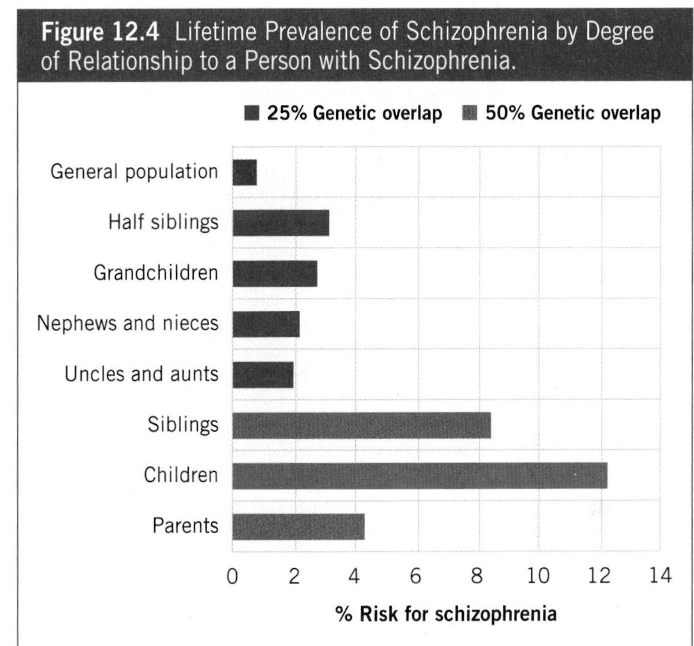

From Faraone, S.V., Tsuang, M.T., & Tsuang, D.W. (1999). Genetics of mental disorders: A guide for students, clinicians, and researchers. New York: Guilford. Copyright © 1999 by Guilford Publications, Inc. Reprinted by permission.

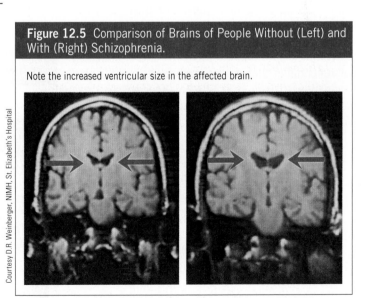

Figure 12.5 Comparison of Brains of People Without (Left) and With (Right) Schizophrenia.

Note the increased ventricular size in the affected brain.

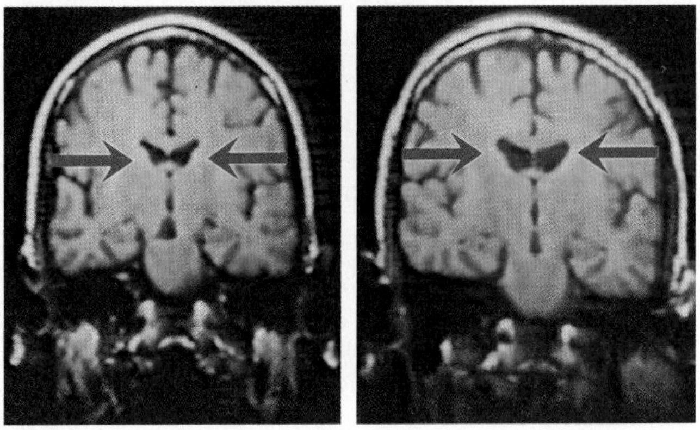

Courtesy D.R. Weinberger, NIMH, St. Elizabeth's Hospital

From "Regional deficits in brain volume in schizophrenia: A meta-analysis of voxel based morphometry studies," by R. Honea, T.J. Crow, D. Passingham, and C.E. Mackay, *American Journal of Psychiatry, 162,* 2005. Reprinted with permission from the American Journal of Psychiatry, Copyright (2005) American Psychiatric Association.

Figure 12.6 Brain Areas Most Implicated in Schizophrenia.

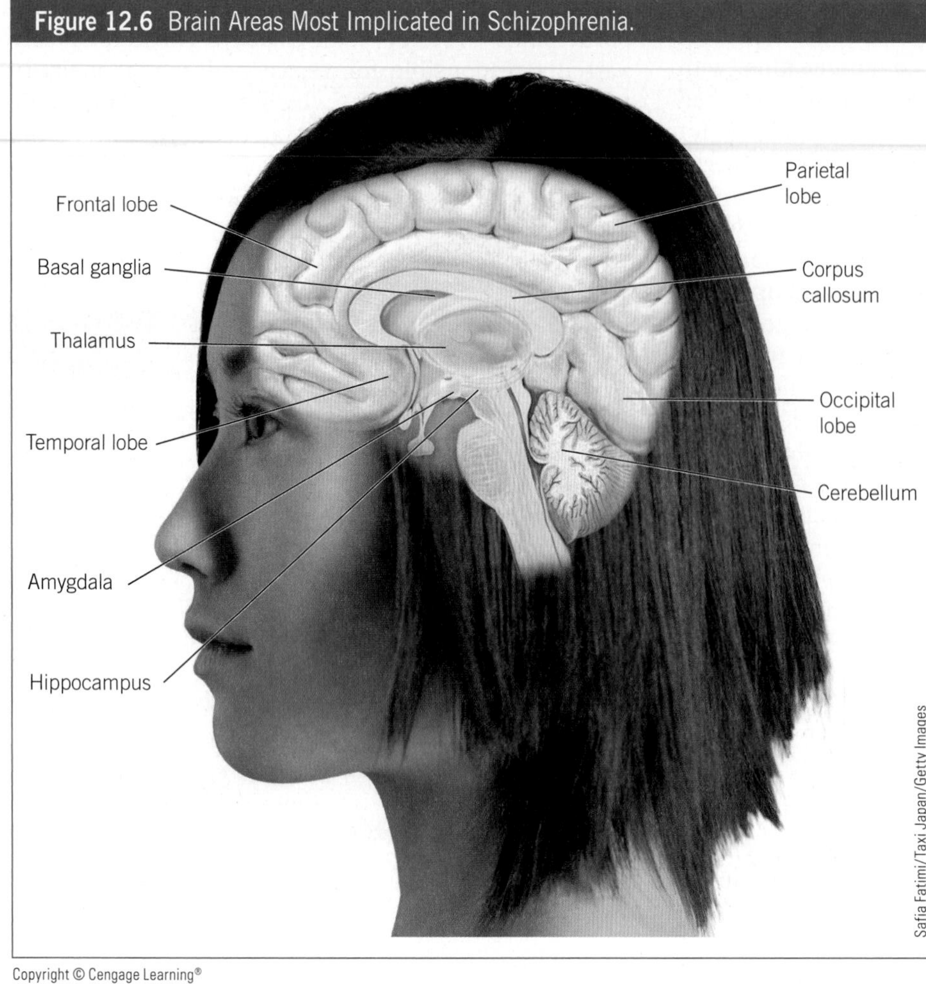

Other researchers have found reductions in total brain size and gray matter, which affect the size of different brain lobes and thus cognition (refer to **Figure 12.7**; Xu et al., 2022). Some have pointed to more specific deficits with respect to the frontal lobe, which is heavily involved in complex information processing and organization of functioning and may contribute to auditory hallucinations (Dixon et al., 2022). Other specific brain differences implicated in schizophrenia, which also often involve smaller size, include the following:

- *Thalamus and parietal/occipital lobes,* differences in which may affect the integration of sensory information and visual attention
- *Basal ganglia* and *cerebellum,* differences in which may affect motor behavior and output to higher-order brain areas
- *Corpus callosum,* differences in which may affect language and communication between the brain hemispheres

Enlarged ventricles and reduced brain size in certain areas such as the frontal lobe may help explain negative symptoms of schizophrenia (Hepdurgun et al., 2021). Differences in other areas, such as the temporal lobe, may help explain positive symptoms of schizophrenia. Loss of gray matter may start in the parietal lobe, perhaps even during adolescence, and later spread to the frontal and temporal lobes (Kraguljac et al., 2021). How this loss spreads and the degree to which it does may help determine a person's specific symptoms of schizophrenia.

Another major finding with respect to brain changes and schizophrenia is *lack of asymmetry* in certain areas. Some people with schizophrenia may have differences in the *heteromodal association cortex,* which includes two key brain areas for language processing: *Broca's area* and *planum temporale*. Lack of asymmetry in the planum temporale is a possible risk factor for learning disorder (Chapter 13), and a similar finding has been found for people with schizophrenia (Takayanagi et al., 2020). Lack of asymmetry in other brain areas has also been implicated in schizophrenia, including the *anterior cingulate cortex* (Roberts et al., 2020), which is partially responsible for types of decision making.

Figure 12.7 Comparison of Brains of People with Schizophrenia at an Earlier (Upper Row) and Later (Bottom Row) Stage.

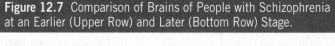

Note progressive loss of gray matter.

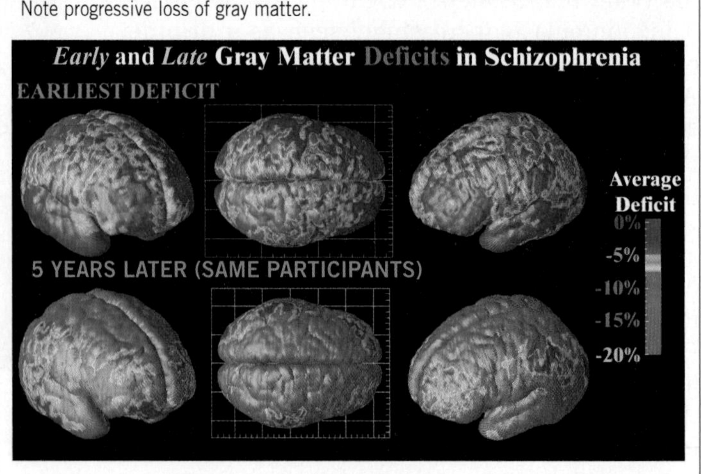

Courtesy, Dr. Arthur W. Toga and Dr Thompson, Laboratory of Neuro Imaging at UCLA

Studies of brain features represent fascinating advances in the field, but bear in mind that findings are often less than conclusive. How these brain changes might lead to specific symptoms of schizophrenia is not completely known either. These brain changes could be due to genetic predispositions, simple anatomical differences in the general population, degeneration in the brain over time, environmental factors, or other variables. Not everyone with schizophrenia shows measurable brain differences, which means that other causes, such as the neurochemical features discussed next, may be present.

Neurochemical Features

One of the most prominent theories of schizophrenia is that symptoms are caused by an excess of certain neurotransmitters in the brain, especially dopamine (refer to **Figure 12.8**). The *excess dopamine hypothesis* has been popular largely because:

- Many people with positive symptoms of schizophrenia are successfully treated with drugs that lower dopamine levels (discussed later in the treatment section).
- Antipsychotic drugs may actually produce very low levels of dopamine and create side effects similar to Parkinson's disease, which is related to deficient levels of dopamine (Chapter 14).
- Excess levels of dopamine, from methamphetamine intoxication for example, can lead to motor problems and psychotic symptoms.
- L-dopa, a drug that boosts levels of dopamine in people with Parkinson's disease, can produce psychotic symptoms if taken in excess and can aggravate symptoms of schizophrenia.
- Dopamine receptors, especially D2 receptors, may be denser in the brains of some people with schizophrenia (Howes & Shatalina, 2022; Plavén-Sigray et al., 2022).

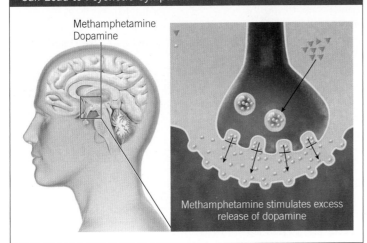

Figure 12.8 Methamphetamine Use, Which Increases Dopamine, Can Lead to Psychotic Symptoms.

Methamphetamine
Dopamine

Methamphetamine stimulates excess release of dopamine

A revised theory regarding dopamine is that the neurotransmitter itself is less important than its role in helping to control information processing in the cortex (Howes et al., 2020). Recall that changes in brain lobes have been implicated in schizophrenia and many of these areas involve large amounts of dopamine receptors. Areas of the brain that link to the cortex, such as the basal ganglia or amygdala, also have large amounts of dopamine receptors. Changes in dopamine and key areas of the brain may interact to help produce symptoms of schizophrenia, but the precise nature of this possibility remains under study.

Other neurotransmitters have been implicated in schizophrenia as well, including serotonin, gamma-aminobutyric acid, and glutamate (Cummings et al., 2022). Perhaps these other neurotransmitters, especially serotonin, interact with dopamine and deficits in key brain areas to help produce symptoms of schizophrenia. Less serotonin in the frontal cortex may lead to more activity in this brain area and thus more dopamine activity (Cieslik et al., 2021).

Cognitive Deficits

Brain changes and other biological factors may help explain why many people with schizophrenia have certain cognitive deficits. Key deficits include memory, attention, learning, language, and executive functions such as problem-solving and decision-making abilities. Memory and attention in particular are problematic for many people with schizophrenia. With respect to memory, many people with schizophrenia have great difficulty recalling information and retaining information over time (Kwok et al., 2021).

Many people with schizophrenia also experience sustained attention problems that begin in childhood or adolescence. Close relatives of people with schizophrenia often have attention problems as well (Feng et al., 2020). Also, many people with schizophrenia have problems processing rapid visual information, tracking objects with their eyes, and concentrating on one subject (Wolf et al., 2021). Difficulty processing information may lead to sensory overload, and this may help explain positive symptoms such as hallucinations and delusions. Negative symptoms might be the result of withdrawal from this sensory overload. Difficulty processing information may also be central to the disorganized speech found in many people with psychotic disorders (Tang et al., 2022).

Some researchers believe schizophrenia subtypes could be based on cognitive functioning. Some people with schizophrenia have little cognitive impairment, but others have severe and generalized impairment similar to dementia

(Chapter 14). Main cognitive clusters in people with schizophrenia may include the following:

- Less verbal fluency (ability to form and express words)
- Limited verbal memory and motor control
- Slower information processing
- Diminished intellectual functioning

Each of these clusters may be linked to a specific brain change (Green et al., 2020). Severity levels and symptoms of schizophrenia are quite diverse and not easily subject to such classification, however (Liu et al., 2021). Still, cognitive distinctions may be important for assessment and treatment.

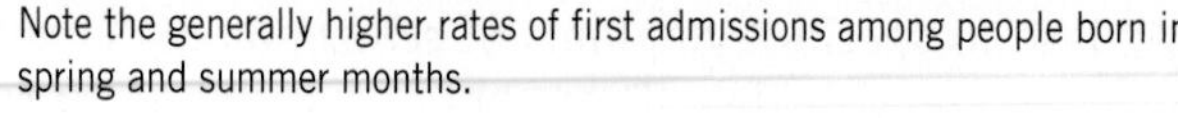

Figure 12.9 Rates of First Admissions and Readmissions of Schizophrenia by Birth Month.

Note the generally higher rates of first admissions among people born in spring and summer months.

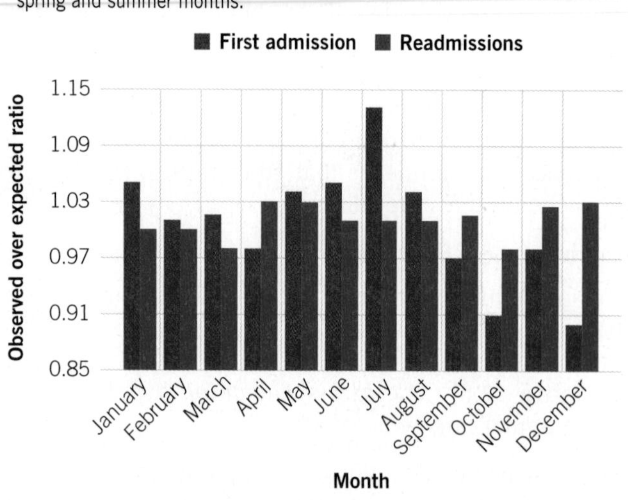

Source: Clarke, M., Moran, P., Keogh, F., Morris, M., Kinsella, A., Larkin, C., Walsh, D., & O'Callaghan, E. (1999). Seasonal influences on admissions for affective disorder and schizophrenia in Ireland: A comparison of first and readmissions. *European Psychiatry, 14,* 253.

Environmental Risk Factors for Psychotic Disorders

Early and later environmental factors also influence the development of psychotic disorders. These environmental factors include prenatal complications, adverse life events and excessive substance use, and cultural and evolutionary influences.

Prenatal Complications

People with schizophrenia, if they had some developmental delay, tend to have had more prenatal complications than the general population (Davies et al., 2020). One prenatal complication that seems closely involved in psychotic disorders is *hypoxic ischemia,* or low blood flow and oxygen to the brain. This can lead to enlarged ventricles (refer to the earlier brain features section). Lower birth weight and smaller head circumference are also common to this population (Wortinger et al., 2022).

Prenatal complications can also come in the form of viruses and infections. People with schizophrenia are born disproportionately in late winter or spring months; therefore, the fetus developed in times involving higher risk for influenza and other diseases (refer to **Figure 12.9**). This risk may be even more so if a child is born in a large urban setting or if their family recently migrated to another country. Schizophrenia may also be more frequent during times of famine (Davies et al., 2020). Exposure to rubella, viral encephalitis, or severe malnutrition could place a fetus at increased risk for schizophrenia and other disorders (Birnbaum & Weinberger, 2020).

Adverse Life Events and Excessive Substance Use

Maternal stress during the prenatal period may lead to important brain changes and later mental disorders, including schizophrenia (Paquin et al., 2021). Later environmental factors such as adverse life events and excessive substance use could also influence the development of psychotic disorders. Many people with schizophrenia experience stressful life events in weeks and months before the onset of psychotic symptoms, especially if they are emotionally reactive (Betz et al., 2020). Such was the case with James. Traumatic life events, such as physical maltreatment, are also common to people with schizophrenia (Kotowicz et al., 2021). What remains unclear, however, is whether stressful life events trigger psychotic symptoms or whether psychotic symptoms place people in vulnerable positions in which they may be exploited by others.

People with psychotic disorders are also much more likely to use marijuana excessively than the general population (Patel et al., 2020). Other drugs could lead to psychotic symptoms as well. Excessive substance use among people with schizophrenia symptoms is common (refer to **Table 12.8**). Whether stressful life events and excessive substance use trigger psychotic symptoms or whether they develop afterward is not clear. Some people may use alcohol or other drugs to cope with psychotic

Table 12.8 Comorbidity of Substance Use Disorder and Schizophrenia

Substance	Substance use disorder and schizophrenia
Cannabis	27.0%
Alcohol	20.6%
Cocaine	15–50%
Amphetamine	8.9%
Opioid	4.1%

Diagnostic distributions of people with a lifetime or cumulative prevalence of substance use disorder and schizophrenia. Some people may have had more than one substance use disorder.

From Kivimies et al. (2015) and Thoma & Daum (2013).

symptoms, but substance use disorder and schizophrenia also share common risk factors such as increased mesolimbic dopaminergic activity (Hernández-Huerta & Morillo-González, 2021).

Cultural and Evolutionary Influences

Other factors related to schizophrenia may include cultural and evolutionary influences. Schizophrenia does seem more common in people in developing countries and in immigrants and migrant workers than in people in developed countries and native populations (Dykxhoorn et al., 2020). Social isolation and lack of access to care among migrant workers may be key risk factors for schizophrenia (Terhune et al., 2022).

Sociocultural models of schizophrenia also focus on the issue of *labeling* or assigning someone with a diagnosis of severe mental disorder. The process of labeling someone with a diagnosis like schizophrenia may indeed predispose the person to display symptoms that could be construed as consistent with the disorder. A person just diagnosed with schizophrenia may withdraw from others to avoid discrimination, experience lowered self-esteem and quality of life, and become depressed (DeVylder et al., 2020).

Labeling can also affect how others view someone. One famous study involved people without mental disorder who went to various hospitals and falsely claimed to hear voices. All of these "pseudo-patients" were hospitalized and kept on an inpatient unit despite the fact that they purposefully displayed normal behavior on the unit. Hospital records indicated that staff members often judged normal behavior such as note-taking as pathological, simply on the basis that the person was admitted to an inpatient unit (Rosenhan, 1973). The study underscored the fact that stigma can be quite difficult to challenge once a diagnosis of severe mental disorder is given.

The issue of social functioning has also been raised with respect to evolutionary hypotheses about schizophrenia. One theory is that humans tolerate greater deviation from normal functioning the more they develop complex social lives further removed from the basic "hunter-gatherer" status of our distant ancestors. Early groups of humans could not tolerate people incapable of protecting and nourishing the group because of psychotic symptoms, but people with these symptoms today can more easily be assimilated into, and contribute to, society. Another evolutionary hypothesis is that a genetic mutation occurred in some humans as they split from other primates eons ago. This genetic mutation might affect areas of functioning that separate us from other primates—most notably language. Deficits in language, of course, are often central to psychotic disorders (Bhattacharyya et al., 2021).

Causes of Psychotic Disorders

How do all of these risk factors interact to produce a psychotic disorder? A popular integrative model for how schizophrenia and other psychotic disorders might develop is the **neurodevelopmental hypothesis**. Proponents of this model essentially state that a subtle disease process affects brain areas early in life, perhaps as early as the second trimester of the prenatal period, and progresses gradually to the point where full-blown symptoms are produced (refer to **Figure 12.10**; De Berardis et al., 2021). Early brain changes could come from disease, famine, and low birth weight, among other variables. Genetic predispositions could also affect fetal and child brain development that may contribute to later symptoms of schizophrenia.

Some theorists believe these early brain changes become especially pertinent when the adolescent brain goes through significant reorganization and increased use. One possibility is that neurons are insufficiently pruned at this time, which means old synaptic connections are not discarded as they are in most people.

Figure 12.10 Sample Developmental Pathway of Psychotic Disorder.

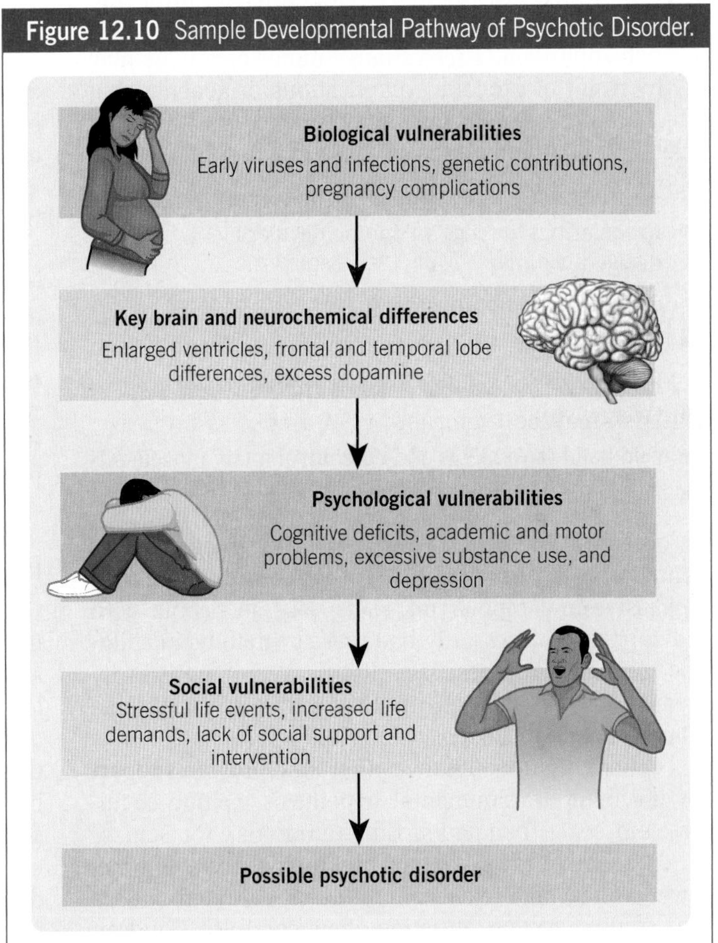

This can lead to a "packing" of useless neurons in key areas of the brain such as the hippocampus. Such differences can help lead to full-blown symptoms of schizophrenia (Haszto et al., 2020). Another possibility is that a less well-developed brain can no longer handle the increased complexities of life during adolescence and adulthood.

If the neurodevelopmental hypothesis is true, then one might expect signs of early problems and brain changes to emerge as a child develops. Some evidence indicates this to be so. People with schizophrenia often have other physical anomalies that probably developed about the same time as key brain changes, and some of these anomalies may be evident in children and adolescents. Physical anomalies may occur in the ears, head, face, tongue, palate, hands, and feet (Wang et al., 2022). Some anomalies have been linked to brain ventricle size in schizophrenia (Svancer & Spaniel, 2021). Many people with schizophrenia do not have these anomalies, however, and many people with these anomalies do not have schizophrenia.

Stronger evidence for the neurodevelopmental hypothesis comes from strange motor behaviors sometimes seen in children of parents with schizophrenia or children who eventually develop schizophrenia. Some of these strange motor behaviors have been identified in home movies and videotapes of children whose parents had schizophrenia. These strange motor behaviors may be the result of prenatal complications or genetics that affect brain development, or may have to do with excess levels of dopamine. Some of these children display the following characteristics:

- Irregularities or lags in motor development, such as delayed walking
- Slow head and body growth
- Limited fine and gross motor coordination and perception
- Overactivity
- Odd hand movements and other involuntary movements
- Twitching and grimacing

Keep in mind, however, that these odd motor behaviors sometimes predict other disorders such as depressive and bipolar disorders. Not all people with schizophrenia necessarily had these symptoms in childhood either, and these symptoms do not necessarily mean someone will go on to develop schizophrenia (Dickson et al., 2020).

Other childhood changes that may provide support for the neurodevelopmental hypothesis include cognitive and social behaviors. Children at risk for schizophrenia tend to show a decline in intelligence over time, lower tested intelligence, and more repeated grades and trouble paying attention than controls (Knudsen et al., 2022). Some children who eventually develop schizophrenia also show schizotypy (odd behavior and speech) and unusual perceptual experiences (Green et al., 2022). People with schizophrenia often develop limited social cognition and **theory of mind**, or an understanding of the thoughts and beliefs of others (van Neerven et al., 2021). James did not always fully appreciate or understand the perspectives of other people. These cognitive and social changes can be inconsistent and are not always predictive of schizophrenia, however.

As a child develops further, environmental events certainly have an impact on development and may speed or even prevent the onset of full-blown symptoms of a later psychotic disorder. Recall that stressful life events and excessive substance use have been linked to schizophrenia. A child who displays problematic behavior as a youngster may experience stress from loss of family members, academic demands, and peer conflicts. This may lead to various outcomes such as depression, excessive substance use to cope, or triggered psychotic symptoms. Conversely, environmental support from others and early intervention may help prevent serious symptoms from occurring. This is discussed further in the prevention section.

Once full-blown symptoms of schizophrenia begin, levels of functioning tend to remain stable. This provides even more support for the neurodevelopmental hypothesis, which predicts that early brain changes will outline a fairly consistent course of behavior for a person. Many people with schizophrenia eventually show remission or some improvement in their symptoms over time, meaning early and stable brain changes are more likely a cause for schizophrenia than ongoing brain deterioration (Krebs et al., 2021).

Whatever the actual cause of schizophrenia and other psychotic disorders, these problems are clearly among the most complex mental disorders. We may find over time that many different types of schizophrenia exist and that each has its own developmental pathway. Charting these pathways will require substantial research effort and collaboration among mental health professionals. In the meantime, efforts to prevent these disorders must be a priority.

Prevention of Psychotic Disorders

Given what we know about risk factors for psychotic disorders, what could be done to prevent them? Early symptoms of psychotic disorders may emerge in adolescence or early adulthood, so it makes sense to think of prevention in the childhood and adolescent years. Genetics play a large role in schizophrenia, so it might be useful to focus on children whose parents had schizophrenia and look for early signs of stressful life events and motor, cognitive, and social problems. Children identified as at risk could then be taught ways to improve their functioning and perhaps blunt the onset of schizophrenia symptoms.

Some researchers discuss a *two-hit model of schizophrenia* that may help guide prevention efforts (da Costa et al., 2021). A child is deemed to be at particular risk for schizophrenia if their close relatives had schizophrenia (the first hit) and if they experienced a severe environmental stressor such as prenatal complications, residence in an institution, or family conflict, among others (the second hit). A special kind of "second hit" involves problems in early child rearing. Children at risk for schizophrenia often experience negative life events, maltreatment, and loss of a parent (Setién-Suero et al., 2020).

This model may be useful for prevention efforts. At-risk children could be identified by evaluating family history, early environmental stressors, minor physical anomalies, and early problematic behaviors. "First hits" are difficult to prevent, but "second hits" could be targeted. Possible ideas to address second hits include the following:

- Use of foster care homes instead of institutions for residential placement
- Family therapy to address problem-solving and communication skills
- Academic skills training to boost sustained attention and verbal skills
- Social skills training to improve abilities to interact with others
- Motor skills training to improve coordination
- Instruction about psychotic disorders and recognizing their symptoms
- Psychosocial therapy to help a child cope with daily stressors
- Early use of neuroleptic medications (refer to treatment section)

Large-scale prevention studies focused on these ideas remain necessary. Some researchers, however, have provided intervention to adolescents and young adults at high risk of having a first psychotic episode. This often involves a supportive approach that focuses on helping participants address social, vocational, and family problems in addition to cognitive-behavioral therapy and medication (refer to treatment sections). These procedures can delay the onset of a full-blown psychotic disorder (Catalan et al., 2021).

Another target of prevention in general, and relapse prevention in particular, is *expressed emotion*. Recall from Chapter 7 that expressed emotion refers to emotional overinvolvement and hostility on the part of family members toward one another as well as inability to cope with a person's mental disorder, in this case schizophrenia. A person with schizophrenia is often blamed for their mental disorder and harshly criticized by families with high expressed emotion. High levels of expressed emotion produce greater relapse in people with schizophrenia and so expressed emotion may be a good target for relapse prevention (Izon et al., 2021).

Section Summary

- Biological risk factors for psychotic disorders include genetics, brain and neurochemical differences, and cognitive deficits.
- Environmental risk factors for psychotic disorders include prenatal complications, disease, famine, stressful life events, and excessive substance use.
- Biological and environmental risk factors can make a person vulnerable to having a psychotic disorder. These risk factors may produce early brain changes that, over time, do not allow a person to fully address life's stressful and complex tasks.
- One causal theory for psychosis is a neurodevelopmental model in which an early disease state leads to key brain changes and stable psychotic symptoms.
- Preventing psychosis may involve assessing for markers early in life, enhancing important cognitive and social skills, and reducing expressed emotion in families.

Review Questions

1. Describe data supporting a genetic contribution to psychotic disorders.
2. What key brain changes and environmental factors relate to psychotic disorders?
3. Explain the neurodevelopmental model of schizophrenia.
4. What factors might be important for a program to prevent psychotic disorders?
5. What is expressed emotion?

Psychotic Disorders: Assessment and Treatment

LO 12.7 Characterize the assessment and treatment of individuals with psychotic disorders.

Psychotic disorders often involve multiple and severe deficits, so assessment can be quite difficult. Information often comes from partners, children, family members, and friends to form a history of symptoms and behavior patterns. Such was true for James. Clinical observations by mental health professionals who have experience with this population are invaluable as well. These methods are discussed in the following sections.

A full medical examination should always precede a psychological assessment of schizophrenia because certain medical conditions could produce psychotic symptoms. Examples include epilepsy, brain trauma such as stroke, central nervous system infections such as AIDS, endocrine and metabolic disorders, vitamin deficiency, and autoimmune disorders. Substances such as amphetamines, marijuana, phencyclidine (PCP), and lysergic acid diethylamide (LSD) could produce psychotic symptoms as well. Alcohol and sedative withdrawal can also lead to psychotic-like symptoms (Martinotti et al., 2021).

Interviews

Interviews are difficult for many people with psychotic disorders because of delusions, hallucinations, suspicion, and disorganized thoughts and behaviors. Still, unstructured interviews may be conducted to get as much useful information as possible. Information about the following areas should be a priority:

- Current level of functioning and specific problem behaviors and cognitive deficits
- Recent life events and personal history
- Medication and treatment history and degree of compliance
- Comorbid medical and psychological conditions
- Financial resources and support from significant others

A semistructured interview often used for people with severe mental disorder is the *Schedule for Affective Disorders and Schizophrenia*. This interview concentrates on background and demographic characteristics as well as past and present symptoms of various disorders including psychoses. The interview, and other similar ones, can take a long time to administer, requires much expertise to give, and may not be useful for someone with highly disorganized thoughts. Other interviews thus focus more on current level of functioning, such as living independently, employment, friendships, and romantic partnerships (Seiler et al., 2020).

Brief rating scales used as semistructured interviews are thus sometimes used. These scales focus mainly on negative and positive symptoms of schizophrenia as well as impaired thinking. The scales are usually completed by mental health professionals who obtain information from chart reviews, observations, or discussions with a person with schizophrenia, significant others, and other professionals. An individual may also be asked to complete certain scales if possible. The *Psychotic Symptom Rating Scales*, for example, measures frequency of and distress associated with delusions and auditory hallucinations (Woodward et al., 2014). **Table 12.9** includes simulated items from a psychoticism subscale.

Behavioral Observations

Behavioral observations of people with psychotic disorders are useful to evaluate social and self-care skills. Important skills to observe include starting and maintaining a conversation, solving problems, managing stress and one's symptoms, taking medications, engaging in hygiene, working well with others, and maintaining appropriate facial expressions and affect, among others. Side effects of medications should also be observed closely. One could also evaluate "neurological soft signs" that may indicate some brain change (Viher et al., 2022). These signs could include poor balance and coordination, awkward movements and reflexes, tremors, and speech and sleep problems.

The most common method for evaluating these behaviors is to carefully monitor a person with a psychotic disorder and get information from family and friends. Behavioral observations are most useful if they occur in multiple settings, especially at home, work, and during recreational activities. Role-play or scales that measure social and self-care skills may be helpful with observations in these areas as well (Glenthøj et al., 2020).

Cognitive Assessment

Many people with schizophrenia and other psychotic disorders have difficulties with language and verbal ability, attention and concentration, memory, problem solving, decision making, and sensory-perceptual functioning. Tests to evaluate these areas of cognitive function in this population are thus often crucial.

Table 12.9 Simulated Items from a Psychoticism Subscale

How much were you distressed by:	Not at all (0)	A little bit (1)	Moderately (2)	Quite a bit (3)	Extremely (4)
The idea that someone else can control your thoughts					
Hearing voices that other people do not hear					
Other people being aware of your private thoughts					
Having thoughts that are not your own					
The idea that something is wrong with your mind					

Tests of language and verbal ability are often derived from certain subtests of intelligence and achievement tests. These include verbal subtests from the *Wechsler Adult Intelligence Test* (WAIS-IV) and reading subtests from the *Wide Range Achievement Test* (WRAT-5; Wechsler, 2008; Wilkinson & Robertson, 2017). Problems in language fluency, perception, production, and syntax as well as differences in scores on these tests are assessed. Reading scores on the WRAT-5 may not deteriorate even after development of a severe mental disorder or brain dysfunction, so these scores may be used as a premorbid (before disorder) level of functioning. These scores can then be compared with WAIS-IV verbal subtest scores, which indicate current functioning, to identify what changes have taken place. This assessment strategy may be less helpful, however, for someone with severely disorganized symptoms or intense reading problems. Attention or concentration deficits may be evaluated using the *Conners Continuous Performance Test*, which requires a person to react to a long series of stimuli presented at regular intervals (Conners, 2014).

Other neuropsychological tasks such as sorting objects into categories like color are also used to assess frontal cortex problems in schizophrenia, especially problems in decision making, problem solving, and verbal memory. People with psychotic disorders often have motor problems, so specific subtests of neuropsychological measures that evaluate finger tapping and grip strength in dominant and nondominant hands may be useful as well. Other subtests may be used to evaluate sensory perceptual problems in vision, hearing, or touch. An example is the Fingertip Number Writing subtest of the *Halstead-Reitan* test where a person closes their eyes and identifies what number is written on their fingertip by the examiner. This test can differentiate people with and without brain dysfunction. Other neuropsychological tests for people with schizophrenia measure concepts such as verbal learning and memory (Ruiz et al., 2020).

Physiological Assessment

People with psychotic disorders often have intense symptoms that may have a strong biological basis, so competing medical explanations should be ruled out first. Laboratory tests such as urine and blood analyses may also be done to examine levels of neurotransmitters and drug use. Such tests are often done as well to monitor a person's compliance with prescribed medication as well as potentially dangerous interactions with other drugs. These tests are not foolproof, however, so behavioral observations and rating scales may be used with laboratory testing. Magnetic resonance imaging is becoming increasingly common for people with psychotic conditions as well (Faria et al., 2021).

Biological Treatments of Psychotic Disorders

Someone like James with a severe psychotic disorder likely needs intense treatment for bizarre and complex symptoms. Schizophrenia and other psychotic disorders have a strong biological component, so treatment often begins with medication (refer to **Focus On Law and Ethics: Making the Choice of Antipsychotic Medication**). Medication for psychotic symptoms is sometimes called *antipsychotic* or *neuroleptic medication*. These medications are usually divided into **typical antipsychotics** and **atypical antipsychotics** (refer to **Table 12.10**).

Typical antipsychotics such as phenothiazines are traditionally used for this population and focus primarily on reducing excess levels of dopamine in the brain. These drugs led to a widespread decline in people hospitalized for severe mental disorders such as schizophrenia (refer to **Figure 12.11**).

Table 12.10 Common Antipsychotic Medications

Typical antipsychotics	Atypical antipsychotics
Chlorpromazine (Thorazine)	Aripiprazole (Abilify)
Fluphenazine (Prolixin)	Asenapine (Saphris)
Haloperidol (Haldol)	Clozapine (Clozaril)
Loxapine (Loxitane)	Iloperidone (Fanapt)
Perphenazine (Trilafon)	Lurasidone (Latuda)
Thioridazine (Mellaril)	Olanzapine (Zyprexa)
Thiothixene (Navane)	Paliperidone (Invega)
Trifluoperazine (Stelazine)	Quetiapine (Seroquel)
	Risperidone (Risperdal)
	Ziprasidone (Geodon)

Figure 12.11 The Population in State and County Hospitals.

The number of people hospitalized for severe mental disorders such as schizophrenia declined partly because of the introduction of antipsychotic drugs.

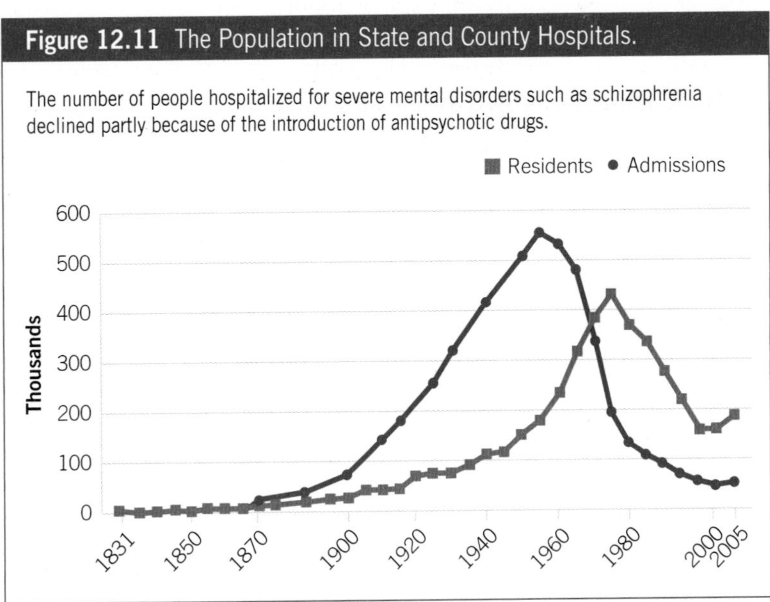

Source: Manderscheid, R. W., Atay, J. E., & Crider, R. A. (2009). Changing trends in state psychiatric hospital use from 2002 to 2005. *Psychiatric Services, 60*, 29–34. Reprinted by permission.

Typical antipsychotics are helpful but have several problems:

- Many people with psychotic disorders do not respond well to these drugs
- The drugs are useful for treating positive symptoms of psychotic disorders such as delusions and hallucinations but not negative symptoms
- Side effects may be extremely unpleasant or irreversible in some cases (discussed later)

Atypical antipsychotic drugs are newer (or second-generation) agents developed to treat more people with psychotic disorders, address depressive and negative symptoms, and minimize side effects. These newer drugs affect various dopamine receptors as well as other neurotransmitter systems such as serotonin (Fasciani et al., 2020).

Typical and atypical antipsychotic drugs do work better than no drug treatment. Typical and atypical antipsychotic drugs are similar in effectiveness with respect to rehospitalization rates, but atypical antipsychotics appear more effective for severe cases of schizophrenia. Other data indicate that the long-term effectiveness of atypical antipsychotics is better than typical antipsychotics (Agrawal & Rath, 2021).

Antipsychotic medication is useful for people with schizophrenia and is often necessary for someone to complete even self-care tasks. Still, key problems remain. First, the drugs are not effective for all people with psychotic disorders. Second, many people experience significant side effects from antipsychotic medication. Common side effects of typical antipsychotics include muscle spasms and rigidity, restlessness, pacing, fixed facial expression, sedation, and seizures. Involuntary movements of the body, or **extrapyramidal effects**, are also common. Another side effect of typical antipsychotics, *tardive dyskinesia,* is a potentially irreversible condition marked by involuntary tics of the face, mouth, tongue, and upper body (Levchenko et al., 2021). Side effects of atypical antipsychotics tend to be less severe but may include low blood pressure, diabetes, sedation, weight gain, concentration problems, and seizures, among others (Kaar et al., 2020).

Another problem with medication is that one must take the drug for it to work. Compliance rates for taking medication are not always strong for people with psychotic disorders (Mitchell et al., 2021). People often struggle with multiple medications, memory and thought difficulties, stressful life events, side effects, excessive substance use, and transportation to pharmacies and doctors' offices. The cost of antipsychotic drugs is also prohibitive for many people. A person with a psychotic disorder has a higher chance of relapse if they delay or stop taking prescribed medication (Özgüven & Yagmur, 2021). Methods of increasing compliance are part of the psychological treatment approach for psychotic disorders.

Psychological Treatments of Psychotic Disorders

Medications are a mainstay ingredient of many treatment plans for psychotic disorders, but they are typically supplemented with psychological approaches. Psychological approaches usually aim to improve medication compliance, social and self-care skills, employment duration, support from relevant others, mood, and cognitive abilities. Psychological approaches for this population are designed to enhance a person's quality of life and help prevent relapse.

Focus On Law and Ethics

Making the Choice of Antipsychotic Medication

Making the independent choice to take medication is a crucial step toward recovery for many people with mental disorders. Controversy arises, however, with respect to antipsychotic medication and what to do if a person is legally incapable of making choices about treatment. Imagine someone referred by police to an inpatient psychiatric unit who has acute delusions and hallucinations. If their ability to understand reality is impaired, and they cannot give consent about antipsychotic medication, then what?

Most jurisdictions allow physicians to administer antipsychotic medication without consent of the individual in situations that involve emergencies, obvious incompetence of the individual, and/or dangerousness to self or others (as with James). Even in these cases, however, every attempt should be made to include the person in the consent process as soon and as much as possible, to consult with family members about treatment options, and to provide only enough treatment to help the person make competent decisions about further treatment.

A more serious issue is *forced medication.* Should the government mandate that someone arrested for a crime and who is acutely psychotic receive antipsychotic medication against their will for the purpose of increasing legal competence and the possibility of imprisonment? This issue has been raised in several court cases and has deep ramifications for other practices. Could government agencies eventually mandate medications for children and adults with certain other mental disorders? How would the line be drawn for other kinds of treatments as well? For now, these questions are answered on a case-by-case basis by the courts.

Milieu Therapy and Token Economy

Two psychological techniques adopted on inpatient psychiatric units for people with acute psychotic symptoms are milieu therapy and token economy. **Milieu therapy** involves establishing an environment in which prosocial and self-care skills are encouraged. Mental health professionals, physicians, nurses, and other staff continually praise and encourage a person with psychotic symptoms to dress, eat, groom, attend therapy services, interact appropriately with others, and engage in other positive behaviors (Cooper et al., 2020).

Milieu therapy is sometimes linked to a **token economy** system in which prosocial and self-care skills are tangibly rewarded via points (or other items) later exchanged for privileges such as day trips outside the hospital (Paul et al., 2020). A token economy might involve rewards for teeth brushing and eating dinner with others. James was allowed more time outside the hospital as he attended inpatient group therapy sessions. These inpatient strategies can help reduce symptoms, improve social behavior, and facilitate earlier discharge.

KatarzynaBialasiewicz/iStock/iStockphoto.com

People with schizophrenia in an inpatient unit are often encouraged, via milieu therapy, to be together to build social skills and support and reduce isolation.

Cognitive-Behavioral and Supportive Psychotherapies

You might think psychotherapy for someone with strong psychotic symptoms would not be useful, but think again! Cognitive-behavioral and supportive psychotherapies do help prevent relapse (Bighelli et al., 2021). Cognitive-behavioral therapy is typically better than routine care for people with schizophrenia and aims to achieve the following:

- Create a strong therapeutic alliance with a client built on acceptance, support, and collaboration
- Educate a client about their psychosis and reduce stigma associated with symptoms
- Reduce stress associated with psychotic symptoms
- Decrease delusions and hallucinations and change erroneous expectancies and thoughts about them
- Address comorbid conditions such as substance use, anxiety, and depression
- Lower chances of relapse by identifying and eliminating triggers such as stress, family conflict, and forgotten medication

Recall that Jody had delusions about her coworkers harming her and that her employers asked her to seek professional help. Her therapist helped Jody separate more realistic from less realistic thoughts and reduce life stress to help prevent her suspiciousness. Jody learned to examine evidence for and against her thoughts, talk to others about her concerns in a socially appropriate way, and pursue enjoyable activities outside of work.

Medication Compliance

People with schizophrenia and other psychotic disorders often need to stay on medication to function better on a daily basis, so helping them comply with medication is important. Behavioral strategies to do so could include discussions about benefits of taking medication and disadvantages of not taking medication, education about medications and their main and side effects, pairing medication use with an essential part of a daily routine such as dinner, putting medication in obvious places so it is remembered, and rewarding appropriate medication use, perhaps using a token economy. Significant others or an electronic device may also monitor a person closely and even count pills, especially after hospitalization or during times of high stress (El Abdellati et al., 2020).

Social Skills Training

Many people with schizophrenia have great difficulty interacting with others, either because of their developmental history or current symptoms. They are thus at risk for social withdrawal, depression, and related problems. Social skills training has been used to enhance contact with others, decrease distress, and prevent relapse. Social skills training usually consists of repeated modeling and practice and feedback regarding small behaviors first. A person with schizophrenia could watch two people have a short conversation and then try the same task with their therapist. The therapist closely watches for key behaviors such as lack of eye contact, inaudible or incoherent speech, interruptions, limited emotional control, and other important problems.

Feedback to educate a client about these deficiencies is crucial, and a person should continue to practice until the skill is well developed. The person could practice their skills in natural settings with different people, be rewarded for their efforts, and later advance to more difficult tasks such as introducing themselves and participating in long conversations. Social skills training could be done individually but is quite effective when done with a group of people. Such training is useful in therapy settings, but good generalization of skills to more natural settings requires extensive and ongoing practice (Frawley et al., 2021).

Cognitive and Vocational Rehabilitation

Psychotherapy for people with psychotic disorders also involves rehabilitation of cognitive and vocational deficits. Many people with schizophrenia have great problems in attention, memory, and decision-making and problem-solving skills. The main goal of cognitive rehabilitation is to improve performance in these areas and integrate performance into social interactions. Examples of cognitive rehabilitation techniques include repeated instruction and practice on neuropsychological tests, computer exercises, use of self-instructions to maintain focus and guide performance in social situations, careful listening to others' statements, training in specific tasks that require attention and memory, and ongoing vigilance and encoding of important information. Reinforcement of these tasks is important as well. These techniques are generally effective for improving cognitive skills, but questions remain about whether they can lead to long-lasting and broad changes (Allott et al., 2020).

Vocational rehabilitation aims to reintegrate a person with a psychotic disorder into a productive occupational environment. Vocational rehabilitation concentrates mainly on job training, support, and employment in an area a person is motivated to work. Other areas of vocational rehabilitation include practicing language and cognitive skills in a work setting, receiving detailed work performance feedback, and resolving job-related difficulties. These efforts may help enhance job performance for this population (Singh et al., 2021).

Family Therapy

Recall that expressed emotion, or family hostility and criticism and overinvolvement, is a risk factor for psychotic disorders and relapse. Many people with schizophrenia also return to their partners or families for care. Family therapy is thus an important component of treatment for this population. Therapy usually concentrates on educating family members about a psychotic disorder, providing support, reducing highly emotional communications within the family, decreasing stress and depression, helping family members cope with caring for a relative with a psychotic disorder, managing crises, and improving problem-solving skills.

Family therapy may be conducted for a single family or done within a support group of many people. Family therapy may also be done in early or later stages of a person's psychotic disorder. Family therapy at any stage should be coordinated closely with other psychological and drug treatments. Family therapy may contribute to lower relapse rates for people with schizophrenia (McGlanaghy et al., 2021).

Community Care

A person with a psychotic disorder is often treated for acute symptoms in a hospital setting, but simple discharge afterward is not a suitable care strategy. This is especially true if families are initially overwhelmed with the task of caring for the person. Extensive support is thus offered to a person via community or residential treatment (refer to **Figure 12.12**). A person may live in a group home or another living arrangement for persons with severe mental disorder. This approach involves case managers who assist and supervise a person as well as mental health services, help with work and money management and self-care skills,

Figure 12.12 Alternatives to Psychiatric Hospitals.

Community-based alternatives to hospital care for people with psychotic disorders have been developed historically to help prevent relapse and rehospitalization.

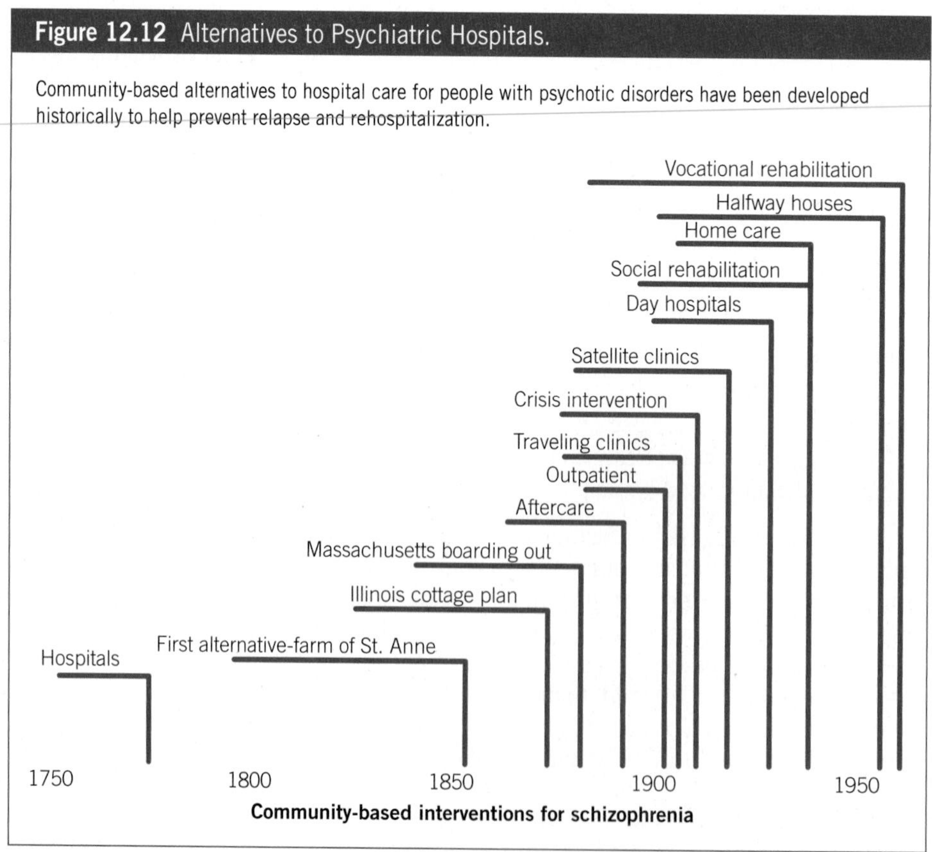

From A. Kales et al., Recent Advances in Schizophrenia, New York: Springer-Verlag, 1990, Figure 1. Reprinted by permission of Springer Science and Business Media.

efforts to improve social and verbal skills, and family therapy (Cooper et al., 2020). The eventual goal for the person is often to return to the care of family members or perhaps live more independently. James was eventually discharged from the hospital once his mental condition was stable. He was placed in a group home with five other individuals with severe mental disorder and staff members who served as case managers.

Another model of community care is *assertive community treatment*. A person with schizophrenia may live independently but receive frequent (assertive) contact from psychiatrists and other mental health professionals. Treatment often occurs at a person's home or nearby area such as a park. Emphasis is placed on community integration, family support, employment, and long-term physical and mental health services. Assertive community treatment can be effective for maintaining patient contact and for reducing hospitalizations and homelessness (Benrimoh et al., 2021).

What If I or Someone I Know Has a Psychotic Disorder?

Knowing if someone is developing a psychotic disorder can be difficult, but some telltale signs may suggest that further evaluation or treatment is warranted. Some screening questions are in **Table 12.11**. If you find the answer to most of these questions is yes, then you or the person you know may wish to consult a clinical psychologist, psychiatrist, or other mental health professional (Chapter 15). You may wish to contact mental health professionals affiliated with local inpatient psychiatric units and/or community care settings for people with severe mental disorder. Provide detailed information about the person's thought patterns, behaviors, and positive symptoms such as delusions and hallucinations. Signs of depression and excessive substance use should be monitored closely as well. Talk to family and friends about your concerns. Early symptom recognition and intervention is often the best approach to prevent potentially life-threatening behaviors. Additional professional information is available from the National Alliance for Research on Schizophrenia and Depression (www.narsad.org) and the National Institute of Mental Health (www.nimh.nih.gov).

Table 12.11 Screening Questions for Psychotic Disorder

Do you find that any of the psychotic symptoms described in this chapter apply to someone you know much more so than most people your age?
Does someone you know show very peculiar behaviors that impair their ability to function in daily life (e.g., go to work, do well in school)?
Does someone you know have great suspicions or paranoia about others?
Is someone you know greatly troubled by symptoms of impaired attention, concentration, or other higher-order thought processes?
Does someone you know have greater problems organizing and expressing thoughts?
Does someone you know seem very socially withdrawn for the first time?
Has someone you know recently experienced a traumatic event that seems to have triggered bizarre behaviors?
Does the person you are concerned about have a family history of serious mental disorders?

Long-Term Outcome for People with Psychotic Disorders

What is the long-term picture, or prognosis, for people like James and Jody with psychotic disorders? Evidence suggests a variable course. About 45 to 67 percent of people with schizophrenia show significant improvement over time, and 7 to 52 percent achieve complete remission (Lawrence et al., 2015). Factors that predict better outcome include less brain volume reduction and substance use, shorter length of untreated symptoms, preserved cognitive function, good social and work skills, supportive family, good response to antipsychotic medication, treatment adherence, and female gender (Cowman et al., 2021; Glenthøj et al., 2021; Montemagni et al., 2020).

James's long-term prognosis was thought to be fair because he did receive treatment soon after each of his episodes of strange behavior, because he had extensive social support, because his cognitive functioning was still relatively good (if bizarre), and because each of his episodes was triggered by a specific event such as an overheard conversation. Jody's long-term prognosis is good because she had intact cognitive functioning and pursued effective therapy. The best approach for addressing psychotic disorders at any age is early and complete treatment.

Section Summary

- Assessing people with psychotic disorders is important because of their complicated symptoms and is often based on family discussions and observations.
- Interviews have been created for people with psychotic disorders, although brief rating scales in the form of interviews are often used.
- Behavioral observations of people with psychotic disorders often focus on social and self-care skills.
- Cognitive assessment of people with psychotic disorders involves intelligence, neurological, and

attention-based tests that can be linked to physiological assessment.

- Treating psychotic disorders often involves a biological approach first, and many typical and atypical neuroleptic drugs are available. Side effects, compliance, and relapse are common problems, however.
- Psychological treatments for people with psychotic disorders aim to improve quality of life and focus on milieu therapy, token economy, cognitive-behavioral and supportive psychotherapies, compliance with medication, social skills training, cognitive and vocational rehabilitation, and family therapy.
- Long-term outcome for people with psychotic disorders is variable and often depends on age of onset, negative symptoms, cognitive abilities, family functioning, and medication adherence.

Review Questions

1. Outline major assessment techniques for psychotic disorders, including interviews, brief rating scales, observations, and cognitive and physiological measurements.
2. What biological methods may be used to manage symptoms of psychoses, and what are some problems associated with these methods?
3. What psychological strategies could a mental health professional use to help someone with a psychotic disorder on an inpatient unit?
4. What psychological strategies could a mental health professional use to help someone with a psychotic disorder in an outpatient clinical or residential setting?
5. What is the long-term outcome for people with psychotic disorders?

Final Comments

People with psychotic disorders experience substantial distress and impairment from their symptoms. Imagine hearing voices, believing others can hear your personal thoughts, having trouble forming sentences, and being unable to work or go to school. These problems are extremely disruptive for a person, so be as compassionate and helpful as possible when addressing someone with a psychotic disorder. Try to consider the person first and their disorder second—a person with schizophrenia, not a schizophrenic. Try also to get help for someone you may come across in your life who begins to have these symptoms.

Thought Questions

1. Think about shows or films with characters with psychotic symptoms in them. Do you think these characters display realistic or unrealistic symptoms of psychosis? Do you think the entertainment industry has skewed the public's view of psychotic disorders?
2. What symptoms of psychotic disorders do you think many people experience to a lesser degree at different times of their lives?
3. What would you now say to a friend who might be developing symptoms of a psychosis? Has what you have learned here helped you understand these symptoms and become more compassionate?
4. What separates "normal" thought patterns from "psychopathological" thought patterns? How can you tell if someone's thinking processes are affected?
5. What do you think could be done socially to reduce psychotic experiences in people?

Key Terms

psychotic disorders 351
flat affect 351
inappropriate affect 351
delusions 351
hallucinations 351
catatonic 351
schizophrenia 351
positive symptoms 351
negative symptoms 351
disorganized speech 353
catatonic behavior 354
alogia 354
avolition 354
anhedonia 354
prodromal phase 354
psychotic prephase 355
active phase 356
residual phase 356
schizophreniform disorder 356
schizoaffective disorder 357
delusional disorder 357
brief psychotic disorder 359
postpartum psychosis 360
neurodevelopmental hypothesis 369
theory of mind 370
typical antipsychotics 373
atypical antipsychotics 373
extrapyramidal effects 374
milieu therapy 375
token economy 375

Developmental and Disruptive Behavior Disorders

13

Learning Objectives

LO 13.1 Describe the continuum from typical development to developmental disorders.

LO 13.2 Distinguish between the developmental disorders using their diagnostic criteria and clinical characteristics.

LO 13.3 Summarize the epidemiology of developmental disorders.

LO 13.4 Describe the stigma associated with developmental disorders and its impact on those with the disorders and their families.

LO 13.5 Discuss the risk factors for and prevention of developmental disorders.

LO 13.6 Characterize the assessment and treatment of individuals with developmental disorders.

LO 13.7 Describe the continuum from typical rambunctious behavior to disruptive behavior disorders.

Learning Objectives (continued)

LO 13.8 Distinguish between the disruptive behavior disorders using their diagnostic criteria and clinical characteristics.

LO 13.9 Summarize the epidemiology of disruptive behavior disorders.

LO 13.10 Describe the stigma associated with disruptive behavior disorders and its impact on those with the disorders and their families.

LO 13.11 Discuss the risk factors for and prevention of disruptive behavior disorders.

LO 13.12 Characterize the assessment and treatment of individuals with disruptive behavior disorders.

Developmental and Disruptive Behavior Disorders

Many disorders discussed in this textbook apply largely to adults, such as somatic symptom, personality, and psychotic disorders. Other mental disorders, however, apply more to children and adolescents than adults, although the disorders often persist into adulthood. Examples include developmental disorders and disruptive behavior disorders. These disorders are the main focus of this chapter.

Developmental disorders involve delay in normal maturity, especially with respect to intellect, cognition, learning, and methods of self-care (refer to **Continuum of Normal Development and Developmental Disorder**). Examples of developmental disorders include intellectual developmental disorder, autism, and learning disorder. Disruptive behavior disorders involve *externalizing* or obvious behavior problems that include overactivity, impulsivity, inattention, aggression, noncompliance, and other disturbances. Examples of disruptive behavior disorders include

Continuum of Normal Development and Developmental Disorder

	Normal	Mild
Emotions	Good control of emotions and appropriate emotional experiences.	Mild delays in impulse, anger, or other emotional control.
Cognitions	Normal intelligence and thinking.	Below average intelligence but little interference in daily functioning.
Behaviors	Good self-care skills and academic achievement.	Low academic achievement and perhaps delay in some self-care skills.

attention-deficit/hyperactivity disorder (ADHD) and oppositional defiant and conduct disorders.

Developmental and disruptive behavior disorders may be comorbid, occurring together in a particular child. Consider, for example, Robert's case, which opened this chapter. Youths with autism are sometimes aggressive and impulsive and fail to pay close attention to others. Youths with ADHD commonly have learning problems such as difficulty reading. Researchers generally study these sets of disorders—developmental and disruptive—as separate entities, however, and they are described separately here.

Normal Development and Developmental Disorders: What Are They?

LO 13.1 Describe the continuum from typical development to developmental disorders.

We develop many skills during childhood necessary for us to become independent and function well in various situations. We learn how to speak clearly, dress and feed ourselves, interact with others, tell time, read, use complex arithmetic, drive a car, and balance a checking account. Many of these skills we now take for granted because we learned them at an early age and practiced them repeatedly during our life. Think about all the basic things you did this morning to get ready for the day. You generally do these things automatically or with little thought.

Some children, however, experience difficulty or delay in a particular area of development. These children may be slower than peers to learn to speak in a grammatically correct way or to read. These children may have **limited developmental disorders** because one area but not many areas of functioning are affected. A learning disorder is one example. A child with trouble learning to read is often of normal intelligence, has friends, and performs fine in other school subjects. People with limited developmental disorders can often function independently and care for themselves adequately as adults.

For other children, *many* areas of normal development are delayed. These areas include intellect and cognition, language, social interactions, and even physical growth. Skills may not develop or may develop much more slowly compared with peers. These delays are often so severe a youth cannot care for themself. Robert was unable to learn to read and his language development was quite slow for many years. His ability to interact with others was also severely impaired and he was sometimes aggressive to himself and others.

Robert had a **pervasive developmental disorder**. His delays were evident in many areas and interfered with his ability to communicate with, or function independently of, others. Robert was thus unable to live on his own. People with pervasive developmental disorders often have unique talents, but many have limited cognitive ability or intelligence. Examples of pervasive

Moderate	Developmental Disorder—less severe	Developmental Disorder—more severe
Moderate delays in impulse, anger, or other emotional control.	Substantial delays in emotional control that may lead to instances of aggression or self-injury.	Extremely poor emotional control that may lead to frequent aggression or self-injury.
Below average intelligence and some difficulty with language.	Severely impaired intelligence with considerable difficulty forming and expressing thoughts.	Profoundly impaired intelligence with extreme difficulty forming and expressing thoughts.
Failing subjects at school and greater difficulty caring for oneself.	Inability to function in a normal classroom and in need of considerable assistance in daily living.	Extreme delays in functioning and inability to eat, dress, and wash, requiring complete assistance in daily living.

Case Robert

Robert was a 17-year-old male recently transferred to a small residential facility (group home) for people with severe developmental disorders. He was transferred to the facility after several years of living with his family at home or with peers in a large developmental center. He was often placed in the developmental center when he was overly aggressive or emotional and when his parents feared he might hurt himself or others. His behavior generally improved over the past year, but Robert's parents said they were no longer able to physically care for their son. They approved his transfer to the group home where trained staff members could supervise and help him.

Robert had several developmental delays in language, social and motor skills, and cognitive ability during childhood. He rarely interacted with others and preferred to play by himself. He had enormous difficulty in school and was placed in special education after being diagnosed with autism. Robert assaulted other people as an adolescent and was on medication to control an explosive temper. His transfer to the smaller group home was designed to simulate family-type living but in an environment where his behavior toward others could be monitored frequently.

What Do You Think?

1. How are Robert's behaviors different from a typical child or young adult? Which of his behaviors might seem normal for a child or adolescent?
2. What external events and internal factors might be responsible for Robert's behaviors?
3. What are you curious about regarding Robert?
4. Does Robert remind you in any way of someone you know? How so?
5. How might Robert's behaviors affect his life in the future?

developmental disorders include severe forms of intellectual developmental disorder as well as autism. These pervasive and limited developmental disorders are discussed in the next section.

Developmental Disorders: Features and Epidemiology

LO 13.2 Distinguish between the developmental disorders using their diagnostic criteria and clinical characteristics.

LO 13.3 Summarize the epidemiology of developmental disorders.

This section summarizes the major features of the most commonly diagnosed developmental disorders. Symptoms of intellectual developmental disorder, autism, and learning disorder are discussed.

Intellectual Developmental Disorder

Have you ever known someone unable to attend regular classroom settings or who has difficulty learning fundamental skills? People with these problems are often diagnosed with a pervasive developmental disorder known as **intellectual developmental disorder**. Intellectual developmental disorder can be the sole diagnosis given to a child, although the disorder is often part of other pervasive developmental disorders such as autism. Major features of intellectual developmental disorder are thus covered first.

Intellectual developmental disorder consists of three main features (refer to **Table 13.1**; American Psychiatric Association [APA], 2022). The first main feature is limited cognitive (thinking) development, sometimes defined as a score of less than 70 on an intelligence test. Clinical judgment or alternative testing may be used to assess cognitive delay, however. The second main feature of intellectual developmental disorder is deficits in **adaptive functioning** that refer to the ability to complete everyday tasks that allow one to be independent. Consider these important areas of adaptive functioning and think how hard your life might be if you were unable to do them:

- *Language*: stating one's desires, understanding others, and asking for help
- *Social interaction*: conversing, initiating activities, and being assertive

Table 13.1 DSM-5-TR

Intellectual Developmental Disorder
Intellectual developmental disorder is a disorder with onset during the developmental period that includes both intellectual and adaptive functioning deficits in conceptual, social, and practical domains. The following three criteria must be met: **A.** Deficits in intellectual functions, such as reasoning, problem solving, planning, abstract thinking, judgment, academic learning and learning from experience, confirmed by both clinical assessment and individualized, standardized intelligence testing.
B. Deficits in adaptive functioning that result in failure to meet developmental and sociocultural standards for personal independence and social responsibility. Without ongoing support, the adaptive deficits limit functioning in one or more activities of daily life, such as communication, social participation, and independent living, across multiple environments, such as home, school, work, and community.
C. Onset of intellectual and adaptive deficits during the developmental period. Specify mild, moderate, severe, or profound severity.

American Psychiatric Association. (2022). *Diagnostic and statistical manual of mental disorders* (5th ed., text rev.). Arlington, VA: American Psychiatric Association.

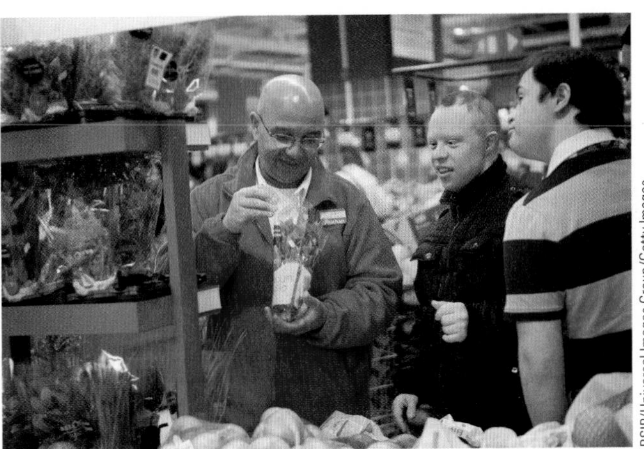

Many of us take for granted social and work skills that are often difficult for people with developmental disorders.

- *Academic*: studying, taking tests, reading, and using numbers
- *Self-care*: eating, washing, dressing, toileting, driving, and telling time
- *Home living*: paying bills, doing yard work, cleaning, and caring for a child
- *Community*: shopping, taking a bus, and using mail or money
- *Self-direction*: deciding on a career, marriage, or whether to have children
- *Leisure*: watching a movie or playing a sport, game, or musical instrument
- *Health*: knowing when to see a doctor, take medications, and apply first aid
- *Safety*: preventing fire and theft and knowing what to do in an emergency
- *Work*: filing an application, managing compensation, and delegating tasks

The third main feature of intellectual developmental disorder is that the disorder must begin during the developmental period, usually before age 18 years, which excludes certain people. A person who experiences a head injury at age 30 years and now has trouble thinking and dressing would not be diagnosed with intellectual developmental disorder. A 65-year-old with Alzheimer's disease (Chapter 14), who may have cognitive and adaptive functioning problems for the first time, also would not be diagnosed with intellectual developmental disorder.

Intellectual delay, deficits in adaptive functioning, and onset during the developmental period must occur *together* for a diagnosis of intellectual developmental disorder. This is important because a lower score on an intelligence test does not necessarily mean a person has intellectual developmental disorder. A person may score lower on an intelligence test but still be able to work independently and manage a place to live. A diagnosis of intellectual developmental disorder would thus not apply. Intellectual developmental disorder is a diagnosis that should be given only after a thorough assessment of cognitive *and* adaptive functioning.

Intellectual developmental disorder can be subtyped by mild, moderate, severe, and profound severity. These subtypes were previously based on intelligence test scores but such groupings are not always helpful; someone who scores a 52 on an intelligence test could have better adaptive functioning than someone who scores a 60. Grouping people with intellectual developmental disorder based on how much help they need in daily living is preferable to intelligence test scores; the following categories have been defined (APA, 2022):

- *Intermittent or mild*: support when needed, such as moving, shopping for groceries, or seeking a new job
- *Limited or moderate*: consistent support, such as transportation, employment training, or help paying bills
- *Extensive or severe*: regular, daily support, such as preparing food, getting dressed, or bathing
- *Pervasive or profound*: constant, intense support, such as ongoing medical attention or complete care

Autism Spectrum Disorder

Another pervasive developmental disorder associated with multiple cognitive and social deficits is **autism spectrum disorder** (sometimes called *autism*, *autistic disorder*, or *infantile autism*). People with autism often have intellectual developmental disorder, but autism is a distinctly different disorder in certain key ways.

Autism is marked by three main sets of symptoms (refer to **Table 13.2**; APA, 2022). The first set involves severe impairment in *social interaction*. People with autism often prefer to be by themselves (the prefix "auto" meaning "self"). Robert squirmed away from others and did not develop good relationships. This is an important difference between people with autism and people with intellectual developmental disorder—the latter often enjoy playful social interactions. People with autism often avoid eye contact, show limited facial expressions and bodily gestures, and have few friendships (Griffin et al., 2021). People with autism may not share their experiences with others or reciprocate emotions like joy. A child with autism would not typically show their parents a new finger-painting (as many children would) or react strongly to praise or criticism. Social interaction is a difficult process for many people with autism.

The second set of symptoms of autism is severe impairment in *communication* with others. This problem overlaps to some extent with intellectual developmental disorder, though language deficits are often more extreme and atypical in people with autism (Ketcheson et al., 2021). Many people with autism like Robert are nonverbal or show a long delay in language. Even if a person with autism does have some speech, the speech is often unusual. Some people with autism have *echolalia*, or repeating what one has just heard. Your author once worked with a child with autism named Hope who would get off the bus each day and be greeted with "Hi, Hope!" to which she replied "Hi, Hope!" This *immediate* echolalia occurred for several months despite daily efforts to correct her response. Echolalia can also be *delayed* as a person suddenly says something recalled from several days earlier. Other strange speech patterns include *pronoun reversal*, such as switching "I" for "you," and incoherent sentences such as jumbling words in a nonsensical way (Finnegan et al., 2021).

The third main set of symptoms of autism is *unusual behavior patterns.* Many children with autism do not engage in pretend play, and they often do not imitate others, as most young children do. Their play is instead marked by withdrawal and preoccupation with parts of objects, such as spinning a wheel on a toy truck. People with autism also tend to be routine-oriented, and disruptions in their routine can lead to tantrums or aggression. Many people with autism also show socially inappropriate *self-stimulatory* or *stereotypic behavior* such as excessive rocking, hand flapping, or walking on their toes (Negin et al., 2021). People with autism may also be aggressive toward themselves or others. Self-injurious behavior can include biting or hitting oneself, among other dangerous behaviors (Luiselli et al., 2021).

The severity of autism spectrum disorder depends on the level of deficits in social communication and restricted, repetitive behaviors (refer to **Table 13.3**; APA, 2022). About 35.2 percent of children with autism have below average intellectual ability (Maenner et al., 2021). However, autism is marked in some cases by special savant skills, such as superior memory, calendar, mathematical, or artistic abilities (Pennisi et al., 2021).

Learning Disorder

The developmental disorders discussed so far involve delays or problems in *multiple* areas of functioning. Developmental disorders can also be *limited* in scope,

Wallybird/Alamy Stock Photo

AP Images/ERIC SUCAR

Autism is a severe developmental disorder. Some people with autism engage in strange, repetitive motor behaviors known as self-stimulation. People with autism are also capable of working hard and offering heartwarming stories of accomplishment, like Jason McElwain (right), who scored six 3-pointers in his high school basketball game.

Table 13.2 DSM-5-TR

Autism Spectrum Disorder
A. Persistent deficits in social communication and social interaction across multiple contexts, as manifested by the following, currently or by history: 1. Deficits in social-emotional reciprocity. 2. Deficits in nonverbal communicative behaviors used for social interaction. 3. Deficits in developing, maintaining, and understanding relationships. Severity is based on social communication impairments and restricted, repetitive patterns of behavior.
B. Restricted, repetitive patterns of behavior, interests, or activities, as manifested by at least two of the following, currently or by history: 1. Stereotyped or repetitive motor movements, use of objects, or speech. 2. Insistence on sameness, inflexible adherence to routines, or ritualized patterns of verbal or nonverbal behavior. 3. Highly restricted, fixated interests that are abnormal in intensity or focus. 4. Hyper- or hyporeactivity to sensory input or unusual interest in sensory aspects of the environment. Severity is based on social communication impairments and restricted, repetitive patterns of behavior.
C. Symptoms must be present in the early developmental period.
D. Symptoms cause clinically significant impairment in social, occupational, or other important areas of current functioning.
E. These disturbances are not better explained by intellectual developmental disorder or global developmental delay. Specify if with intellectual impairment, language disturbance, catatonia, or medical factor or mental disorder.

American Psychiatric Association. (2022). *Diagnostic and statistical manual of mental disorders* (5th ed., text rev.). Arlington, VA: American Psychiatric Association.

Table 13.3 DSM-5-TR

Severity Levels for Autism Spectrum Disorder

Severity level	Social communication	Restricted, repetitive behaviors
Level 3 "Requiring very substantial support"	Severe deficits in verbal and nonverbal social communication skills cause severe impairments in functioning, very limited initiation of social interactions, and minimal response to social overtures from others. For example, a person with few words of intelligible speech who rarely initiates interaction and, when he or she does, makes unusual approaches to meet needs only and responds to only very direct social approaches.	Inflexibility of behavior, extreme difficulty coping with change, or other restricted/repetitive behaviors markedly interfere with functioning in all spheres. Great distress/difficulty changing focus or action.
Level 2 "Requiring substantial support"	Marked deficits in verbal and nonverbal social communication skills; social impairments apparent even with supports in place; limited initiation of social interactions; and reduced or abnormal responses to social overtures from others. For example, a person who speaks simple sentences, whose interaction is limited to narrow special interests, and who has markedly odd nonverbal communication.	Inflexibility of behavior, difficulty coping with change, or other restricted/repetitive behaviors appear frequently enough to be obvious to the casual observer and interfere with functioning in a variety of contexts. Distress and/or difficulty changing focus or action.
Level 1 "Requiring support"	Without supports in place, deficits in social communication cause noticeable impairments. Difficulty initiating social interactions, and clear examples of atypical or unsuccessful responses to social overtures of others. May appear to have decreased interest in social interactions. For example, a person who is able to speak in full sentences and engages in communication but whose to-and-fro conversation with others fails, and whose attempts to make friends are odd and typically unsuccessful.	Inflexibility of behavior causes significant interference with functioning in one or more contexts. Difficulty switching between activities. Problems of organization and planning hamper independence.

American Psychiatric Association. (2022). *Diagnostic and statistical manual of mental disorders* (5th ed., text rev.). Arlington, VA: American Psychiatric Association.

however, affecting just one or two areas of functioning. People with limited developmental disorders usually function much better than people with pervasive developmental disorders but still struggle in key areas. One type of limited developmental disorder is learning disorder.

A **learning disorder** (or *specific learning disorder*) is marked by difficulties in reading, spelling, math, or written expression, which could mean a student is failing that particular subject (refer to **Table 13.4**; APA, 2022). A learning disorder cannot be explained by intellectual problems, however, because the person's intelligence is usually normal. A large *discrepancy* may exist between the person's actual school achievement (below average) and their potential to learn (average or better). A learning disorder is not due to sensory problems such as visual or hearing impairments, although a child with these problems could still be diagnosed with learning disorder. Learning disorders are not a result of simple lack of motivation in school or environmental disadvantage such as poor teaching.

Dyslexia is a broader term used to refer to learning problems in reading and spelling. Some people with dyslexia reverse letters when viewing them, but not all do (Sanfilippo et al., 2020). *Dyscalculia* is used to refer to problems learning mathematics and can relate to dyslexia because a person may have trouble reading mathematical symbols or story problems (Agostini et al., 2022). Other terms related to learning disorder include the following:

- *Dysgraphia:* problems of written expression, such as writing very slowly or off a page
- *Dysnomia:* problems naming or recalling objects, such as saying "fork" when viewing a "spoon"
- *Dysphasia:* problems comprehending or expressing words in proper sequence, such as difficulty understanding what others say or trouble speaking logically to others
- *Dyspraxia:* problems of fine motor movements, such as trouble buttoning a shirt
- *Dyslalia:* problems of articulation or trouble saying words clearly and understandably

Case Alison

Alison was an eight-year-old girl experiencing great trouble in school. She consistently failed reading and spelling assignments despite enormous effort. Her teacher said Alison's work was barely legible and often contained basic errors of writing, such as misspelled words and incomplete letters. These errors were beginning to affect her arithmetic work as well because many of the math problems contained stories and symbols. Alison was still working at a first-grade level by the middle of third grade.

Alison regularly struggled when asked to read a story in a group setting. She read very slowly, paused often, and had trouble answering questions about the story afterward. Her teacher was particularly confused by Alison's performance because the girl seemed bright, capable, motivated, and alert. Alison performed well in other subjects such as science, music, art, and physical education. She also had no problem with self-care skills and showed no behavior problems in class. Alison's teacher did notice, however, that her student was becoming quite frustrated with her homework and was turning in fewer assignments on time.

Table 13.4 DSM-5-TR

Specific Learning Disorder
A. Difficulties learning and using academic skills, as indicated by the presence of at least one of the following symptoms that have persisted for at least six months, despite the provision of interventions that target those difficulties: 1. Inaccurate or slow and effortful word reading. 2. Difficulty understanding the meaning of what is read. 3. Difficulties with spelling. 4. Difficulties with written expression. 5. Difficulties mastering number sense, number facts, or calculation. 6. Difficulties with mathematical reasoning.
B. The affected academic skills are substantially and quantifiably below those expected for the individual's chronological age, and cause significant interference with academic or occupational performance, or with activities of daily living, as confirmed by individually administered standardized achievement measures and comprehensive clinical assessment. For individuals age 17 years and older, a documented history of impairing learning difficulties may be substituted for the standardized assessment.
C. The learning difficulties begin during school-age years but may not become fully manifest until the demands for those affected academic skills exceed the individual's limited capacities (e.g., as in timed tests, reading or writing lengthy complex reports for a tight deadline, excessively heavy academic loads).
D. The learning difficulties are not better accounted for by intellectual disabilities, uncorrected visual or auditory acuity, other mental or neurological disorders, psychosocial adversity, lack of proficiency in the language of academic instruction, or inadequate educational assessment. Specify if impairment in reading, written expression, or mathematics and severity as mild, moderate, or severe.

American Psychiatric Association. (2022). *Diagnostic and statistical manual of mental disorders* (5th ed., text rev.). Arlington, VA: American Psychiatric Association.

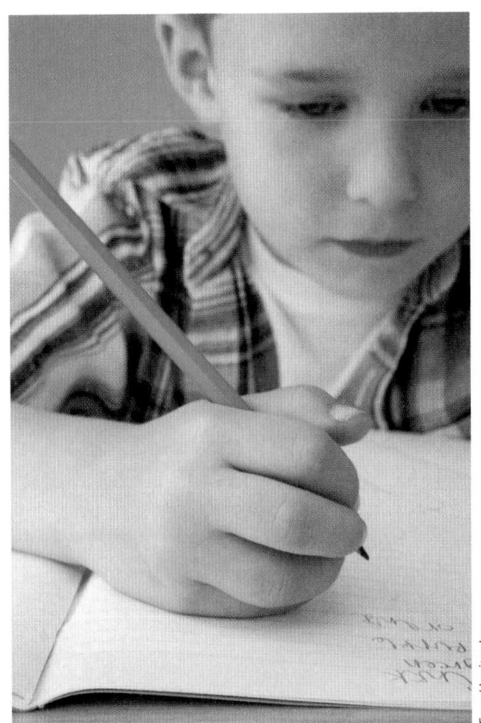

Dysgraphia refers to a learning problem involving writing.

Epidemiology of Developmental Disorders

Intellectual developmental disorder occurs in 1 to 2 percent of the population (Glasson et al., 2020). The disorder is much more common in boys than girls and is typically diagnosed in preschool and elementary school-age years when a child is compared academically with peers. Intellectual developmental disorder can be comorbid with autism and can be associated with anxiety, depression, dementia, and psychotic disorders (Reddihough et al., 2021). The onset of intellectual developmental disorder is usually gradual because early developmental delays are sometimes hard to spot or are confused with other possible problems such as hearing impairment.

Autism spectrum disorder occurs in 1 percent of children worldwide and is about four times more common in boys than girls (Zeidan et al., 2022). Boys with autism tend to show more repetitive and stereotypical behaviors than girls with autism, but no consistent gender differences have emerged with respect to social or communication problems (Calderoni, 2022). People with autism are not often diagnosed with comorbid psychiatric disorders, perhaps because of restricted emotions, but symptoms of anxiety and depression are common (Kirsch et al., 2020). Autism is associated with medical problems such as seizures and hearing and visual problems, however (Clark & Koutsogianni, 2022).

Learning disorder affects about 7 to 8 percent of students, although problems in specific areas, such as reading or math, may be more common (Zablotsky & Black, 2020). Learning disorder may be more common among boys than girls, especially if processing deficits are severe. Learning disorder may be comorbid with any other disorder but is linked in many cases (25–50 percent) with attention-deficit/hyperactivity disorder (refer to later section on disruptive behavior disorders). Problems with social skills, aggression, and substance use are also common to youths with learning disorder. Onset of learning disorder is gradual and often marked by early language delays and medical conditions (Grigorenko et al., 2020).

Stigma Associated with Developmental Disorders

LO 13.4 Describe the stigma associated with developmental disorders and its impact on those with the disorders and their families.

Children are especially susceptible to stigma because they are more vulnerable and powerless than adults. This applies especially to children with developmental disorders and their parents. Parents of children with autism often report feeling blamed for their child's behavior, isolated from family and friends, and distressed about others' anger and pity. Part of this may be because children with autism appear normal physically but can display severe behavior problems. Self-stigma can occur as well, as some parents blame themselves or their parenting style for their child's autism (Deguchi et al., 2021). Some teachers may also be less empathetic toward children with autism and their caregivers (Ebadi et al., 2021). Stigma may affect college students with autism as well (refer to **Focus On College Students: Autism**). These perceptions illustrate the importance of educating the public about pervasive developmental disorders.

Section Summary

- People with pervasive or limited developmental disorders experience delays in key areas of functioning and impaired cognitive ability or intelligence.
- Intellectual developmental disorder is a pervasive developmental disorder involving early deficits in cognitive ability and adaptive functioning.
- Autism is a pervasive developmental disorder involving severe impairments in social interaction and communication as well as unusual behavior patterns.
- Learning disorder is a limited developmental disorder involving deficits in a subject like reading, math, spelling, or writing.
- Stigma is an important part of developmental disorders and can affect others' view of a child.

Review Questions

1. What are major features and subtypes of intellectual developmental disorder?
2. What are major symptoms of autism?

3. Outline differences between pervasive and limited developmental disorders.
4. Describe major features of learning disorder and its related terms.
5. Describe the epidemiology of pervasive and limited developmental disorders.

Developmental Disorders: Causes and Prevention

LO 13.5 Discuss the risk factors for and prevention of developmental disorders.

Factors that cause developmental disorders, and how understanding these factors might help prevent developmental disorders, are covered next.

Biological Risk Factors for Developmental Disorders

Many mental disorders are caused by a combination of biological and environmental variables. This is also true for developmental disorders, although biological predispositions tend to be strong. These predispositions include genetic influences, chromosomal aberrations, and prenatal and perinatal problems that lead to brain changes.

Genetic Influences: Gene Damage

Genes represent individual units on a *chromosome* that contain important information about a person's traits and characteristics. Thousands of genes are part of each of the typically 46 chromosomes in a human. Genes predispose us to become whoever we are but may also become damaged and lead to developmental disorders. Many cases of severe intellectual problems relate to genetic and other organic defects.

Fragile X syndrome is a condition that results when the *FMR1* gene of the X chromosome narrows, breaks, or otherwise becomes mutated. Fragile X syndrome affects 1 in 7,000 males but is less common in females (1 in 11,000) because they have another X chromosome to help compensate for damage. Females may, however, experience effects of fragile X syndrome or be carriers of the problem—they may have the genetic mutation but not the full syndrome. The genetic mutation leads to certain brain changes (refer to brain changes section). People with fragile X syndrome often show hyperactivity, self-stimulatory and self-injurious behavior, aggression, limited social skills, perseveration (doing the same thing over and over), and language and intellectual problems (Salcedo-Arellano et al., 2020).

Another example of how genetics influence intellectual problems is **phenylketonuria (PKU)**. PKU is also caused by a genetic mutation, this time on chromosome 12. PKU

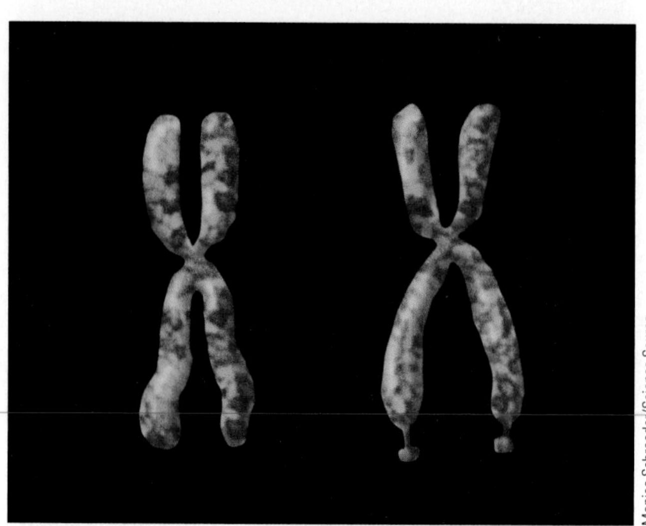

Monica Schroeder/Science Source

People with fragile X syndrome often experience narrowing or breakage in the X chromosome.

Focus On College Students

Autism

An increasing number of young adults with autism are entering college, but this population has been understudied. Adolescents with autism who do enroll in college often struggle with its less structured and more complicated learning environment and may be less likely to graduate as a result. College students with autism must often deal with fear and misunderstanding from others regarding their condition and even bullying and social exclusion by classmates. As such, college students with autism feel considerable stigma on campus (Gillespie-Lynch et al., 2021).

Some researchers have thus attempted to address conceptions of autism among college students. In one study, hundreds of college students watched an online presentation that introduced them to current research about autism at different stages of development. Participants were initially educated about the definition and prevalence of autism, autism as a spectrum disorder, and major causes of the disorder. Later components focused on the challenges faced by adults with autism, such as difficulties in relationships, mood, and independence, as well as impaired empathy. Results indicated that desire for social distance from people with autism decreased significantly following the presentation, although stigma related to having a romantic relationship with someone with autism remained high (Gillespie-Lynch et al., 2015). The findings support the point made several times in this textbook that proper education about a mental disorder often reduces stigma, which can be especially important for someone with as severe a disorder as autism.

is an *autosomal recessive disorder*, meaning the defective gene must be inherited from both parents for problems to occur. The defective gene leads to the body's inability to break down *phenylalanine*, an amino acid. Excess phenylalanine in the body can damage the liver and brain. Some food products carry a warning about containing phenylalanine. Untreated PKU may create physical problems such as awkward gait and spasms and cognitive problems such as severe language delay, learning disorder, and intellectual developmental disorder. Fortunately, early screening can detect newborns with PKU, and a special diet limiting phenylalanine intake can prevent many of these problems. PKU occurs in 1 in 10,000 births, although many more people may be carriers with no symptoms (van Spronsen et al., 2021).

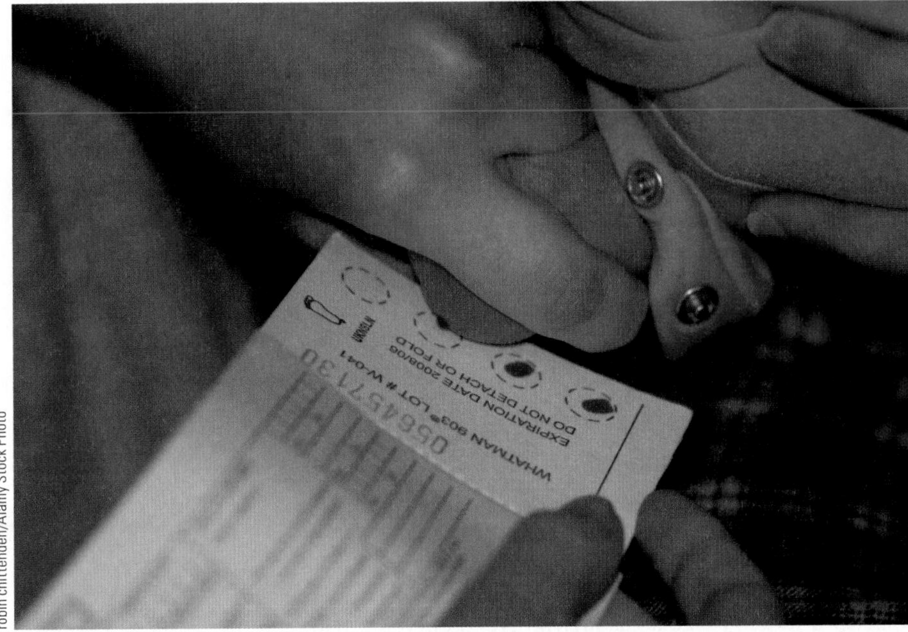

robin chittenden/Alamy Stock Photo

Newborns are tested for PKU by a heel-prick and given a special diet if they test positive.

Genetic influences can lead to intellectual problems in other ways as well. People with **sickle cell disease**, which affects 1 of 600 live births, especially African Americans, experience damaged red blood cells, slow blood movement, and less oxygenation to the body. The problem has been linked to a genetic mutation (HbS) and could lead to severe brain damage and intellectual developmental disorder, especially early in life (Brown et al., 2022). People with **Tay-Sachs disease**, which affects 1 in 300,000 births, especially Ashkenazi Jews, experience severe motor and sensory impairments, intellectual developmental disorder, and death at age two to four years. Several genetic mutations have been linked to this disorder as well (Vahhab et al., 2020) (refer to **Focus On Law and Ethics: Key Ethical Issues and Developmental Disorders**).

Genetic Influences: Concordance

A genetic component seems at least partially responsible for causing autism. Concordance rates for autism are up to 90 percent in identical twins but up to 30 percent in fraternal twins (van der Heijden et al., 2021). Siblings of a child with autism have a slightly increased chance of having autism themselves (Ejlskov et al., 2021). Parents of children with autism are not more likely than the general population to have autism themselves but sometimes show traits related to autism (Marriott et al., 2021). Because identical twin

Focus On Law and Ethics

Key Ethical Issues and Developmental Disorders

People with developmental disorders are often children or those who have trouble speaking for themselves, so many ethical dilemmas arise with this population. One dilemma that arises almost immediately is the question of what parents should do if they discover, through genetic testing, that their fetus has a severe and potentially fatal developmental disorder. A related question surrounds the decision to have children if a person knows a developmental disorder will likely be genetically transmitted. What would you do in these situations, and why?

Another key issue for this population surrounds quality of life and level of control and choice that should be made available to someone with a pervasive developmental disorder. How much choice should Robert have in his living environment, and could too much freedom lead to harm toward others or lack of progress toward his educational goals? All people have the right to available and effective treatment that causes the least amount of restriction on freedom (Chapter 15). For Robert, this meant placement in a group home that simulated family living as opposed to a more impersonal developmental center.

Ethical considerations for people with developmental disorders also concern medication and punishment, which are often used without a person's explicit consent (and usually with the consent of others). Is it fair to medicate, restrain, or severely punish someone for misbehavior when they have not given consent? What if a behavior such as head-banging is life-threatening? An ethical dilemma such as this involves juxtaposing an individual's right to expression with societal right to prevent harm. What might you do in this situation?

concordance rates for autism are not 100 percent, however, influences other than genetic must be contributing as well.

A genetic component also accounts for about 40 to 60 percent of the cause of learning disorder, especially reading problems (dyslexia) (Gialluisi et al., 2021). Twin studies of reading-related skills reveal higher concordance rates for monozygotic twins than for dizygotic twins (Andreola et al., 2021). In addition, about 45 percent of children with dyslexia may have a first-degree relative with dyslexia (Erbeli et al., 2021).

Chromosomal Aberrations

Changes in sections of a chromosome or an entire chromosome also influence about 20 percent of severe developmental problems (Hu et al., 2019). Almost all (95 percent) cases of **Down syndrome** are due to an extra chromosome 21. Most people with Down syndrome thus have 47 chromosomes in their cells. This "extra" genetic information leads to several discrete characteristics, especially physical ones such as a larger tongue, distinctive eye shape, short fingers, brittle hair, and visual, hearing, and cardiac problems (Heinke et al., 2021).

People with Down syndrome often develop symptoms of Alzheimer's disease after age 40 to 50 years (refer to Chapter 14). Down syndrome affects 1 in 600 live births, but the chances of having a child with the condition increase greatly with maternal age. A 25-year-old mother has a 1 in 1,350 chance of giving birth to a child with Down syndrome, but a 35-year-old mother has a 1 in 350 chance and a 44-year-old mother has a 1 in 40 chance. This is likely due to problems in chromosome separation at conception (Ward et al., 2016). Other syndromes and chromosomal aberrations linked to intellectual developmental disorder are in **Table 13.5**.

NDAB Creativity/Shutterstock.com

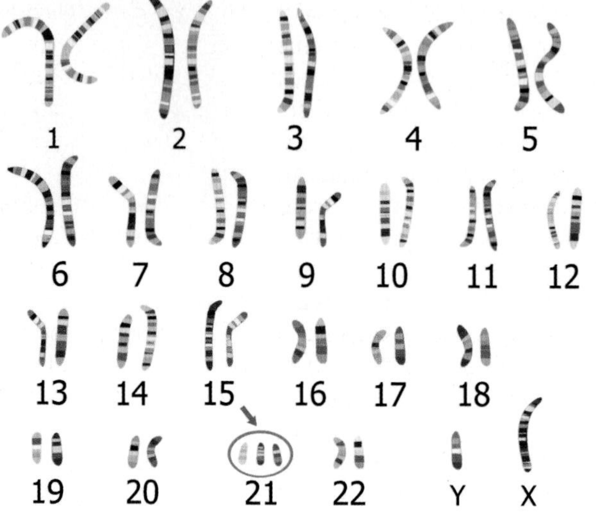

zuzanaa/Fotolia LLC

Children with Down syndrome often have an extra chromosome 21 and intellectual developmental disorder but can still participate in and enjoy many typical childhood activities.

Prenatal and Perinatal Problems

Genetic and chromosomal changes are obviously very important, but other biological phenomena can also lead to developmental disorders. **Teratogens** are conditions that negatively impact physical development of a child during prenatal (before birth) or perinatal (during birth) periods. Teratogens that occur early in pregnancy can lead to many structural changes because this is a key time for organ development. Teratogens that occur later

Table 13.5 Other Syndromes and Chromosomal Aberrations That May Lead to Intellectual Developmental Disorder

Syndrome	Possible cause	Prevalence
Prader–Willi syndrome	Deletion on chromosome 15	1/10,000–25,000 births
Klinefelter syndrome	Males with extra X chromosome(s)	1/500–1,000 male births
Turner syndrome	Females with one X chromosome	1/2,000–3,000 female births
Noonan syndrome	May be similar to Turner syndrome	1/1,000–2,500 births
Neurofibromatosis	Deletion on chromosomes 17 or 22	1/3,000 births
Williams syndrome	Deletion on chromosome 7	1/7,500–20,000 births
Smith–Magenis syndrome	Deletion on chromosome 17	1/25,000 births
Angelman syndrome	Deletion on chromosome 15	1/10,000–20,000 births
Rett's disorder	Mutation on MECP2 gene on X chromosome	1/10,000–15,000 births

Sources: Dulac, Lassonde, & Sarnat (2013); Kelly (2013); Nelson & Trussler (2016).

in pregnancy, or even during birth, can also affect brain development and may produce a developmental disorder in conjunction with genetic/chromosomal problems (Li et al., 2022).

A key teratogen is maternal use of alcohol and other drugs during pregnancy. A child exposed to alcohol prenatally may develop fetal alcohol syndrome (FAS; refer to Chapter 9) or broader *fetal alcohol effects* (Gutherz et al., 2022). Children with fetal alcohol effects tend to have a small head size, facial and heart defects, and lower intelligence, the latter of which may last for years. These children also show problems in learning, memory, hyperactivity, impulsivity, and communication and social skills (Coles et al., 2022). Maternal use of other drugs such as nicotine, narcotics, and stimulants can also lead to lower birth weight, premature birth, behavioral problems, inattention, and developmental disorders (Little et al., 2021). Other important teratogens include diseases such as HIV and toxins such as lead and mercury.

Excessive maternal stress can increase adrenaline and thus limit oxygen to a fetus. Malnourished fetuses are especially likely to perish or have malformations, low birth weight, or premature birth. Some children also experience a lack of oxygen, termed *anoxia* or *hypoxia*, during birth from delays in the birth canal or choking by the umbilical cord (Disdier & Stonestreet, 2020). All of these experiences could lead to brain damage and thus severe developmental delay. Specific brain areas affected by genetic, chromosomal, and teratogenic influences are discussed next.

Brain Features

Key brain changes with respect to intellectual problems include gross malformations and subtle markers of brain damage. Gross malformations include induction and migration defects. **Induction defects** are problems in closure of the neural tube (linking the spinal cord to the brain), proper development of the forebrain, and completion of the corpus callosum, the part of the brain linking left and right hemispheres (refer to **Figure 13.1**). **Migration defects** refer to problems in cell growth and distribution in the second to fifth month of pregnancy, which can lead to underdeveloped brain areas (Xie & Bankaitis, 2022).

Subtle markers of brain damage usually involve minor changes in size and shape of certain brain areas. A larger than normal cerebellum has been found in youth with developmental delays, and a smaller cerebellum has been found in adults with fragile X syndrome (van der Heijden et al., 2021). Developmental disorders have also been linked to *enlarged ventricles*, a phenomenon discussed for schizophrenia in Chapter 12 (Duy et al., 2022).

Other developmental disorders have even more specific types of brain changes. Autism seems associated in some cases with enlargement of the overall brain, especially with respect to the midsagittal area, limbic system, amygdala, and occipital, parietal, and temporal lobes. Increased brain size relates to less well-connected neurons (Lee et al., 2021). This may help explain unusual emotional and social behaviors observed in people like Robert.

People with autism tend to have a smaller corpus callosum, which may affect motor coordination and emotion regulation. Those with autism also may have fewer *Purkinje cells*, which relate to behavioral inhibition (Li et al., 2021). Autism has also been linked to high levels of serotonin, a neurotransmitter involved in motor activity (Zhao et al., 2022). These latter changes may be related to self-stimulatory behavior and perseveration. People with autism may have changes in the

Figure 13.1 Major Brain Areas Implicated in Developmental Disorders.

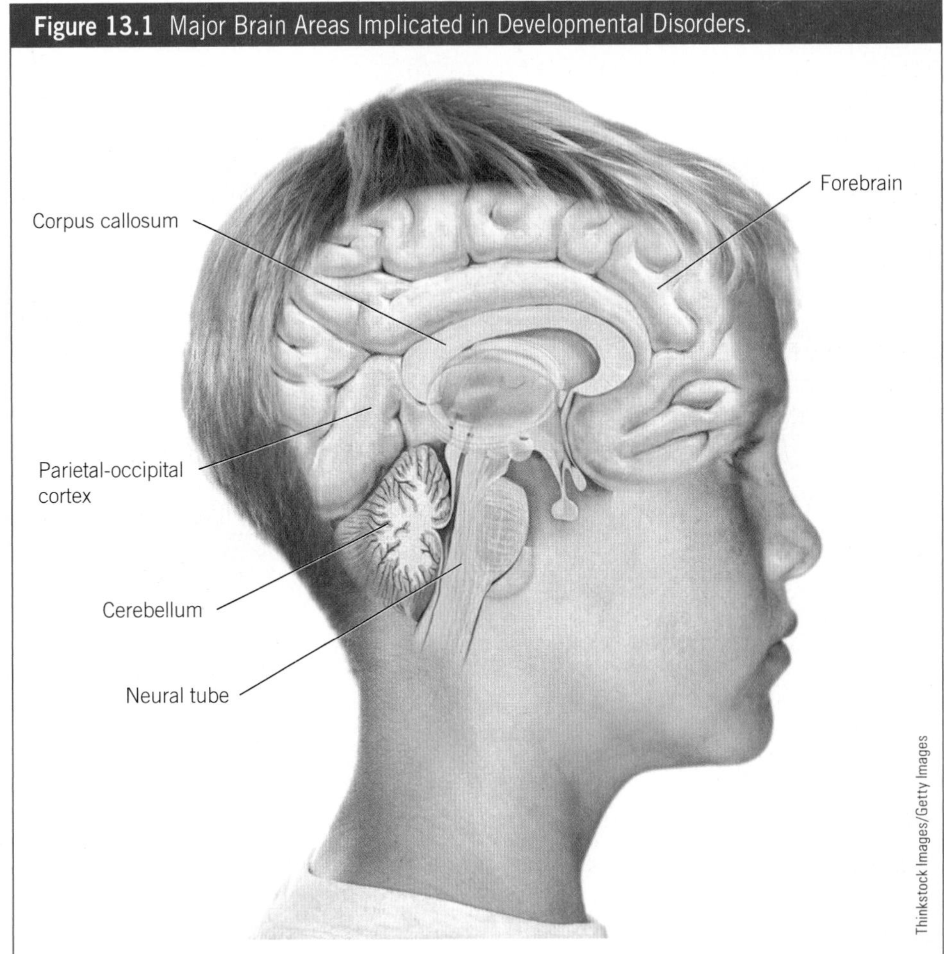

amygdala-prefrontal cortex pathway that affect facial expressions of emotion (Christian et al., 2022).

Children with learning disorder often show brain *symmetry*, in which opposing sides of a brain area are more equal in size. Most people have asymmetry, where one side is larger than the other. Brain areas most implicated in learning disorder, especially reading and language problems, are the *planum temporale* and *parietal lobe* (Kuhl et al., 2020). These areas may not be as well developed as they are for people without learning disorder. Disruptions of the posterior (rear) areas of the left hemisphere closely link to learning disorder (Banker et al., 2020).

Environmental Risk Factors for Developmental Disorders

Environmental factors can also be important for shaping developmental disorders. Many of these factors relate to the teratogens mentioned earlier and can also include exposure to heavy metals and other toxins (Cheroni et al., 2020). Some have noted a higher prevalence of autism among migrant populations (Morinaga et al., 2021). Recall this same kind of finding for people with schizophrenia (Chapter 12). Most of the research on autism has been conducted in high-income countries, however, which limits a full understanding of cultural factors for this population (de Leeuw et al., 2020).

Developmental disorders can also result from traumas that lead to brain damage. Shaken baby syndrome can lead to death or permanent brain damage (Cartocci et al., 2021). Many of those who shake babies are fathers, some of whom are frustrated by a child's crying or toileting problems (Feld et al., 2021). Other forms of physical child maltreatment could cause brain damage as well. Brain injury can also result from hitting one's head after a fall, a near-drowning experience, a car accident, poisoning from lead or cleaners, or being punched. Neurological damage could also come from diseases such as meningitis (Principi & Esposito, 2020). Most of these problems are preventable, and education about ways to protect children from brain injury is crucial.

Causes of Developmental Disorders

How do these risk factors interact to produce a developmental disorder? Strong biological factors clearly predispose certain people to have intellectual developmental disorder and/or autism. These biological factors lead to brain changes that cause problems or delays in thinking, reasoning, decision making, judgment, and other higher-order cognitive processes. These problems then lead to severe deficits in self-care, academic, communication, and other crucial skills. Environmental factors could also help cause critical brain changes or maintain a developmental disorder over time.

You may find it difficult to sort out all the biological influences related to developmental disorders. Consider a model called the *final common pathway* (Happé & Frith, 2020; refer to **Figure 13.2**). In this model, various biological factors conspire or interact in different ways for children with different disorders. One child may have a certain genetic predisposition in addition to a key neurotransmitter change, such as increased serotonin, that leads to autism. Another child may have a certain chromosomal aberration in addition to anoxia at birth that leads to moderate intellectual developmental disorder. Another child

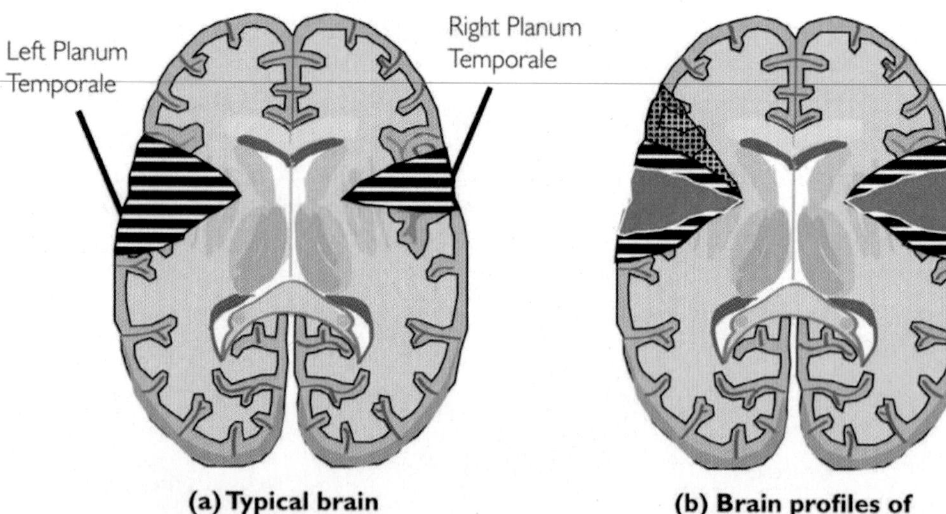

Profiles of individuals with dyslexia (b)

- Asymmetrical profile based on enlarged left planum temporale
- Symmetrical profile based on enlarged right planum temporale
- Exaggerated leftward asymmetry profile from enlarged left planum temporale

Children with reading problems sometimes show symmetry or other changes in a key brain area known as the planum temporale.

Source: *Essentials of Dyslexia Assessment and Intervention,* 1st Edition, Wendling/Mather. ©2012 Publisher, Wiley 978-0470927601, page 29.

may have been exposed to alcohol prenatally and was born prematurely, which may lead to learning disorder. In the final common pathway model, various combinations of biological factors could lead to certain key brain changes that then lead to a specific type of developmental disorder.

Prevention of Developmental Disorders

Developmental disorders begin early in life, so it makes sense to think of prevention before and immediately after birth. Prevention may thus involve genetic testing and counseling, fetal care, screening of newborns, and early medical care for babies. Preventing accidents and other factors that could lead to brain damage is also imperative. Delivering educational services to at-risk children may be helpful as well.

Prenatal genetic testing can occur in different ways, most commonly through *chorionic villus sampling* or *amniocentesis*. These methods involve DNA extraction as a fetus develops. DNA testing can be easily done after birth as well by examining hair, skin, or blood. These methods are done to check number of chromosomes or conduct a more thorough DNA assessment to find missing or defective genes. Genetic testing is often done for adolescent and older mothers, when a family history exists of a certain problem, or when a child shows signs of a genetically based disorder (Hodges et al., 2020). If a fetus has a genetic disorder or chromosomal aberration, then genetic counseling would follow to explore all options with the parents.

Prenatal care of the fetus is also crucial for prevention of developmental disorders, and this can involve proper diet, especially folic acid, regular visits to a medical doctor, and avoidance of drugs, high stress, toxins, and diseases. Proper diet includes limits on caffeine and plenty of grains, fruits, vegetables, water, and sources of protein. Vitamin supplements are also important. Pregnant women should also consult a physician before taking medications or exercising vigorously (Bertels et al., 2021).

Screening newborns is another important prevention technique, and not just for PKU. Many diseases potentially related to developmental disorders, such as HIV, can be identified after birth. Early medical care for babies and insurance coverage for minimum hospital stays after birth are also important. Adherence to immunization schedules, proper diet, and ongoing checkups are critical as well (Lipkin et al., 2020).

Accident prevention is also a large part of pediatric psychology. This includes preventing head injury, such as wearing helmets when bike riding, using proper car seats and cribs, and providing safe toys. Prevention must also include denying access to poisons, eliminating items that could choke a child, locking cabinets and toilets and pools, placing gates before stairs, and ensuring a small child cannot reach a stove, topple a television, enter a refrigerator, or place a finger in an electrical socket (Jullien, 2021).

Educating children at risk for developmental disorders may help prevent their onset or severity. Services include preschool interventions for children predisposed to learning and other developmental disorders. Parents can also learn about the importance of developing language in their children, monitoring early delays, and refraining from shaking or hitting a child. Early screening is critical as well. The earlier a child with a developmental disorder is identified, the earlier appropriate services can be provided and the better a child's long-term outcome may be (Fuller & Kaiser, 2020).

Figure 13.2 Sample Final Common Pathway of Pervasive Developmental Disorder.

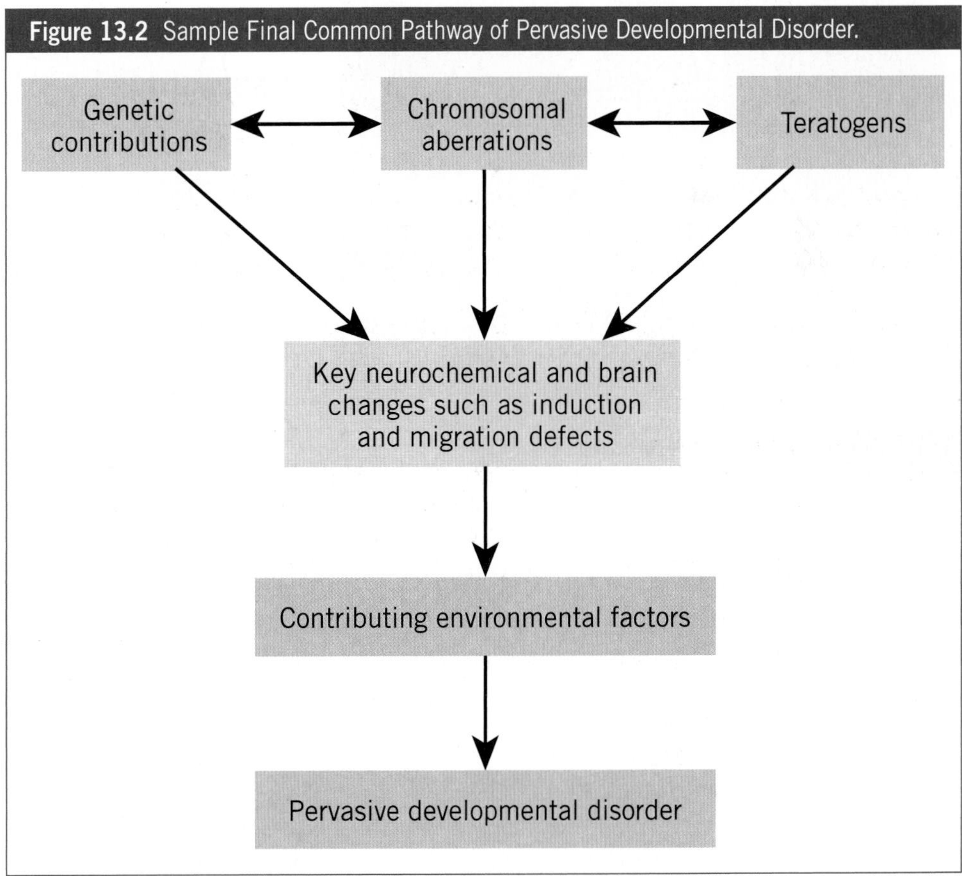

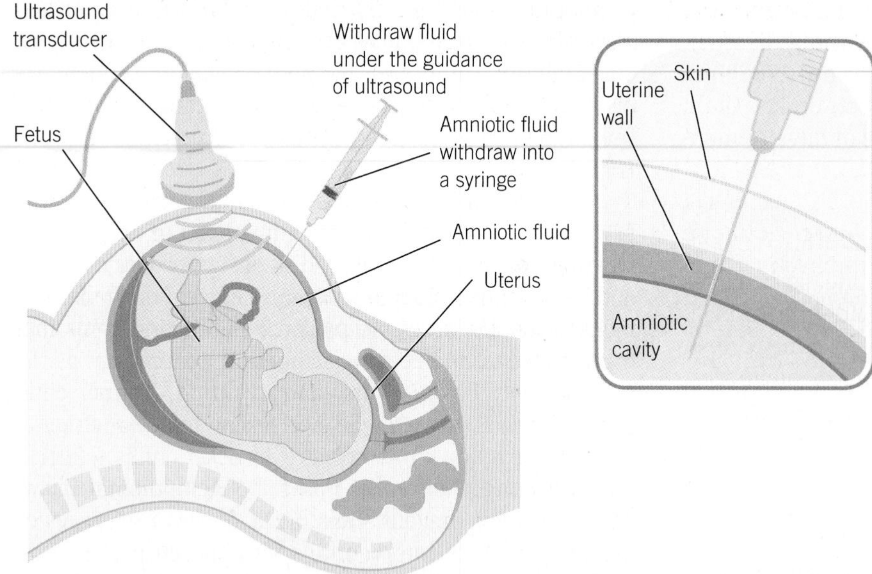

Reducing instances of developmental disorder include prenatal screening via amniocentesis, which involves obtaining a sample of amniotic fluid to detect possible genetic defects, and accident prevention that could lead to head and brain injury.

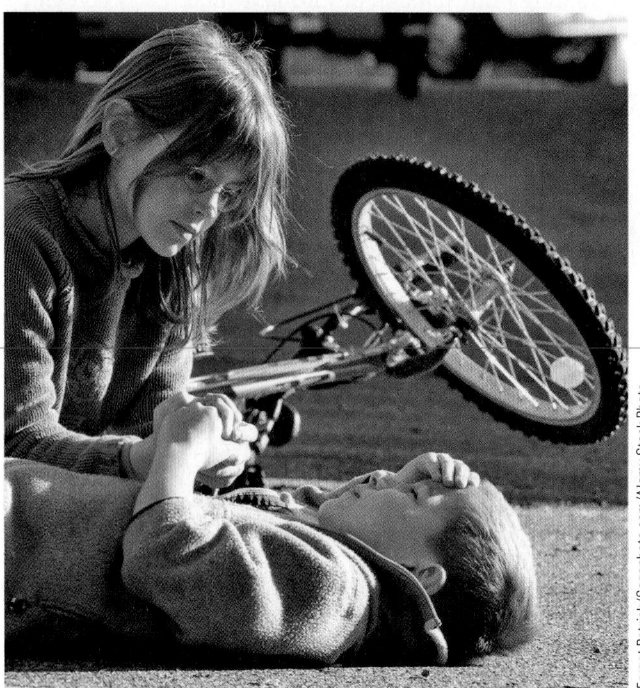

Section Summary

- Biological risk factors for developmental disorders include genetic contributions, chromosomal aberrations, prenatal teratogens, perinatal problems, and induction and migration brain defects.
- Environmental risk factors for developmental disorders include toxins and traumatic brain injury.
- Biological and environmental risk factors can create brain changes that impair cognition and ability to live an independent life.
- Preventing developmental disorders often involves genetic testing and counseling, prenatal care, newborn screening, early medical care for babies, accident prevention, and delivering educational services to at-risk children and parents.

Review Questions

1. Explain how genetic and chromosomal problems can lead to developmental disorder.
2. Define teratogens and indicate how they can lead to developmental disorder.
3. Outline brain changes associated with different developmental disorders.
4. What could happen in the environment to help create a developmental disorder?
5. How might biological predispositions and environmental factors work together to cause a developmental disorder?
6. How might developmental disorder be prevented?

Developmental Disorders: Assessment and Treatment

LO 13.6 Characterize the assessment and treatment of individuals with developmental disorders.

Mental health professionals use various methods to examine people with developmental disorders. These methods include cognitive, achievement, and other tests as well as interviews, rating scales, and behavioral observation.

Cognitive Tests

People with developmental disorders often experience severe cognitive and intellectual deficits, so a basic assessment strategy is to use tests that assess for overall intellectual and problem-solving functioning. Commonly used intelligence tests were described in Chapter 4. Intelligence tests generally assess two types of cognitive ability: *verbal* and *performance*. Verbal tasks that intelligence tests address include knowledge of general information and vocabulary, comprehension of verbal material, and drawing comparisons. Performance tasks include sequencing items, arranging designs, putting pieces together to form a whole, identifying missing parts, and recalling information. Collectively, these tasks are used to assess for attention, concentration, short-term and long-term memory, practical knowledge, social judgment, motivation and persistence, visual discrimination, mental processing speed, distractibility, visual association, conceptual thinking, ordering and planning ability, and perceptual and spatial ability.

Many intelligence tests are *norm-referenced,* which means test scores are compared with those from thousands of people who previously took the test. The norms are age-based, so Robert's performance could be compared with people his age. Most intelligence tests are based on a mean total score of 100 and a standard deviation of 15. Recall that intellectual developmental disorder may partly involve a score less than 70 (or 2 standard deviations below the mean) on a standardized intelligence test. Robert's early score on one of these tests was 55.

Intelligence tests are highly useful for gathering information about cognitive ability and potential for future scholastic achievement. They are not a measure of how "smart" one is, however. The tests measure global problem-solving ability, not what specific information a person knows (Sternberg, 2020). Intelligence tests must be used carefully (refer to **Focus On Diversity: Testing People with Developmental Disorders**). One should never diagnose a developmental disorder based *only* on an intelligence test score. Test results should be combined with other information (described below) to determine diagnosis and functioning level.

Neuropsychological testing may also be used if brain damage is suspected in a person with developmental disorder. These tests are more specific than intelligence tests and assess for sensation, motor speed and strength, perceptual ability, memory, language, attention, abstract and flexible thought processes, and orientation or knowledge of time, people, and places. Common neuropsychological tests were described in Chapter 4.

Some children may be too young to be formally tested. An examiner could thus rely on developmental tests such as the *Bayley Scales of Infant and Toddler Development—Fourth Edition* (Bayley & Aylward, 2019). The Bayley assesses youngsters aged 16 days to 42 months by comparing performance on certain tasks to normal developmental milestones. For example, children commonly recognize themselves at age 12 months (a cognitive ability) and can walk up stairs alone at age 21 to 25 months (a motor ability). The test covers cognitive, language, motor, adaptive, and social-emotional abilities.

Developmental tests are also available for newborns, such as the *Neonatal Intensive Care Unit Network Neurobehavioral Scale*; these tests assess muscle tone, motor activity, and stress (Parikh et al., 2022). Developmental test scores relate to intelligence test scores but are not exactly the same. Performance on these tests, however, may help identify developmental delay and predict how well a child may function over time.

Achievement Tests

Intelligence tests measure general problem-solving ability, but *achievement tests* measure more specific types of knowledge. Achievement tests are often *criterion-referenced*, meaning they measure a child against a level of performance. Children are assessed on reading, spelling, and arithmetic tasks to determine their grade level on the *Wide Range Achievement Test 5* (Wilkinson & Robertson, 2017). A fourth-grader who scores at the 2.5 grade level would thus be considered low achieving. Achievement tests are popular for assessing children with learning disorder, but scores do not always correspond well with school performance.

Interviews

Interviews are also used to assess people with developmental disorders, although the measures are obviously limited if communication problems are present.

Focus On Diversity

Testing for People with Developmental Disorders

Many cognitive, achievement, and other tests are available for assessing people with developmental disorders. These tests are standardized on thousands of people and have shown excellent reliability and validity. Still, questions remain about how applicable these tests are to minorities and people from disadvantaged backgrounds. Concerns have arisen that the tests unfairly predispose certain groups toward diagnoses of developmental disorder and placement in special education settings.

According to the American Educational Research Association and American Psychological Association testing and ethical guidelines, those who use tests must recognize situations in which assessment techniques may not apply to certain people based on their gender, age, ethnicity, religion, sexual orientation, disability, language, socioeconomic status, and other key distinctions. Examiners must always be aware that certain tests may not be the best method of gathering information about a particular child. Many children have parents who speak only Spanish at home, for example, and these children could be wrongly penalized on an intelligence test that may be biased toward good English-speaking ability.

The best approach to evaluating people with developmental disorders is to rely on a *multimethod, multisource assessment approach.* This means, in addition to testing, that one should rely on other assessment methods such as rating scales, interviews, and observation. One should also speak to parents, siblings, peers, teachers, and other sources who know a person well. A more complete picture can thus be gathered about a person's functioning in their environment and whether a diagnosis of developmental disorder is valid.

Some interviews have been designed specifically for people with developmental disorders using pictures and nonverbal tasks. Interviews specific to autism have also been designed, such as the *Autism Diagnostic Interview—Revised* (de Bildt et al., 2015). Questions when interviewing people with developmental disorders often surround mental status, concerns about one's environment, individual choice and quality of life, communication ability, relationships with others, anxiety and depression, and needed support.

Interviews can also shed light on a person's abilities to function independently and adaptively. A common instrument is the *Vineland Adaptive Behavior Scales, Third Edition* (Vineland-3; Sparrow et al., 2016). The Vineland-3 covers four primary domains of adaptive functioning: communication, daily living skills, socialization, and motor skills. Like intelligence tests, the measure is based on a mean total score of 100 and a standard deviation of 15. People who know a person well, such as caregivers and siblings, can also be interviewed regarding a person with a developmental disorder.

Rating Scales

Rating scales are also available to assess people with a developmental disorder and can be useful when testing and interviewing is not possible. Many scales focus on adaptive and problem behaviors and are completed by mental health professionals or caregivers. An example is the *Adaptive Behavior Assessment System, Third Edition* (Harrison & Oakland, 2015). Other rating scales are more specific to a certain disorder, like autism, to help diagnose the problem. A common example is the *Childhood Autism Rating Scale, Second Edition* (Schopler et al., 2010), sample items of which are in **Table 13.6**. Rating scales have the advantage of providing fast information but should generally be supplemented with behavioral observations.

Table 13.6 Sample Items from Childhood Autism Rating Scale, Second Edition (CARS2) Rating Sheet for "Relating to People"

Relating to people
1—No evidence of difficulty or abnormality in relating to people (The child's behavior is appropriate for their age. Some shyness, fussiness, or annoyance at being told what to do may be observed, but not to an atypical degree.)
1.5-2—Mildly abnormal relationships (The child may avoid looking the adult in the eye, avoid the adult or become fussy if interaction is forced, be excessively shy, not be as responsive to the adult as is typical, or cling to parents somewhat more than most children of the same age.)
2.5-3—Moderately abnormal relationships (The child shows aloofness [seems unaware of adult at times]. Persistent and forceful attempts are necessary to get the child's attention at times. Minimal contact is initiated by the child.)
3.5-4—Severely abnormal relationships (The child is consistently aloof or unaware of what the adult is doing. They almost never respond or initiate contact with the adult. Only the most persistent attempts to get the child's attention have any effect.)

Sample items from the CARS2-ST "Standard Version Rating Booklet" copyright © 2010 by Western Psychological Services.

Behavioral Observation

Direct behavioral observation of a person with a developmental disorder is important when examining specific behavior problems. Direct observation is often used to gauge the frequency and severity of self-injurious and self-stimulatory behaviors, aggression, and tantrums. One could also observe adaptive behaviors regarding social interactions and language (Thompson & Borrero, 2021).

For children with a learning disorder, direct observation is used to measure inattention, motivation, out-of-seat behavior, and actual schoolwork behaviors such as on-task and test-taking behavior and organization and study skills. Reviewing a child's schoolwork and home behavior is also important. Behavioral observations can be formally structured but more often involve a rater who simply watches a person and records the presence and severity of certain behaviors in short time intervals (Hyman et al., 2020).

Biological Treatment for Developmental Disorders

Medications may be used to treat specific aspects of developmental disorders. Seizures are quite common in people with autism, so anticonvulsant medications are often prescribed. Sedative and neuroleptic medications may be used to control agitation or dangerous behaviors such as aggression and self-injury. *Fenfluramine* leads to decreased serotonin levels and has been used with limited success to treat dangerous motor behaviors in people with autism (Zhou et al., 2021). Medications may also be used to ease comorbid symptoms of attention-deficit/hyperactivity, anxiety-related, depressive, bipolar, and sleep disorders (Feroe et al., 2021). Medication use in this population must be considered carefully because many who take the drugs cannot give consent or accurately report side effects.

Gene therapy may also be a key biological treatment in the future for people with developmental disorders (Chapter 14). Examples include replacing fragile X and other genetic mutations with healthy genes to reverse or stem developmental delay. Early work with rodents is promising, but gene therapy for humans remains a distant hope (Pena et al., 2020).

Psychological Treatments for Developmental Disorders

Psychological treatments for people with developmental disorders, like Robert, often target individual areas of functioning. Treatments to improve language, social relationships, self-care and academic skills, and problem behaviors are covered next. These treatments are based largely on behavioral principles and models of learning (Chapter 2) and have been found to be quite effective for people with developmental disorders.

Language Training

Many developmental disorders involve language problems, and language skills are an excellent predictor of long-term functioning in this population. A child must first pay attention, however, to learn language and other skills. This is especially important for children with autism, many of whom vigorously avoid social and eye contact with others. **Discrete-trial training** may be used to increase eye contact. A teacher issues a command ("Look at me") and rewards the child if they comply. If not, the teacher holds a desirable item such as a cookie near their own eye to entice the child to make eye contact. Such training must eventually eliminate use of the cookie, but the training successfully increases eye contact and attention (Bravo & Schwartz, 2022).

Language training can begin once good attention is established. Such training often focuses first on building *receptive labeling ability* for various objects. A child may be shown four pictures, one of which is a chair, and told to "Point to the chair." Rewards are given for correct answers; incorrect answers are met with prompts toward the correct response. Pictures usually include items commonly used by the child or that are important for daily functioning such as eating utensils, types of food or drink, the toilet, or clothing. A main goal is to enhance later expressive speech and give a child a way to communicate their wants. This is also important for reducing problem behaviors—a child pointing to a toilet to indicate a need to go is less likely to be aggressive in communicating that desire than a child with no language (Ghaemmaghami et al., 2021).

Language training then involves more *expressive speech*. Early expressive language programs often focus on *shaping*, or rewarding approximations of talking. A child might first be given a reward every time they make a vocalization, even babbling, yelling, or crying. As the child vocalizes more, these sounds are shaped into basic speech sounds. A child's lips could be pressed together to make the "m" sound. Easier sounds are trained first, then more difficult ones such as "j" and "q." These sounds may be shaped eventually into words and sentences. Unfortunately, such training can last years and is often incomplete (Yu et al., 2020).

Language training can also involve *speech imitation* in which a teacher places an object before a child, names it, and asks a child to repeat the name. The child may eventually be asked to name the object without help. The child will hopefully learn to make requests of different items independently and generalize their language to request other items. *Natural incidental training* is used as a person's language develops further. Extensive language is taught in a more natural way (Blackwell & Stockall, 2021). A teacher may look at a child and wait a few seconds for a request for an item. Appropriate requests are then rewarded with the item or the teacher prompts the request by telling the child they need to communicate what they want.

Language training is best if a child has some language before age five years, even echolalia, and if the intervention is intensive. If formal language training is not working, then *sign language* may be taught (Pezzuoli et al., 2020). Sign language is an especially desirable option for children with autism who often have excellent motor skills but who resist verbal language training. Robert learned signs for 15 objects. Sign language is valuable but has limitations because many other people do not recognize the signs. Technological assistance to help with communication may thus be useful (Lorah et al., 2021).

Socialization Training

Another key aspect of treating people with developmental disorders is *socialization training*. A person is taught to perform and use social skills such as making eye contact, conversing appropriately, and playing and cooperating with others. Basic socialization training consists of *imitation and observational learning*. A teacher will model certain social behaviors as a child watches, then prompt imitation on the child's part. Initial social behaviors often include basic play actions such as stacking blocks, group activities such as rolling a ball to others, and manipulating objects such as opening a door. Advanced training involves generalization to other settings and behaviors, use of language, and quicker imitation of others (Moody & Laugeson, 2020). Caregiver involvement is also important.

Another socialization training method involves *social playgroups* where children are rewarded for play

Olesia Bilkei/Shutterstock.com

A key treatment for children with developmental disorders, especially autism, is socialization training.

with peers instead of solitary play. Children may also be taught to act out different imaginary scenes to build pretend play, use appropriate facial expressions and verbalizations to express affection, and cooperate with others (Kent et al., 2020). Another socialization training method is *peer-mediated interventions* in which children without developmental disorders teach different social skills to children with developmental disorders (Aldabas, 2020). Peers or siblings could ask a child with autism to share an object, join a group activity, give a hug, carry on a short conversation, or make eye contact. Teaching children to initiate social contacts on their own and learn social cognitive abilities such as understanding others' emotions is also an important part of socialization training (Lee et al., 2022).

Self-Care Skills Training

For people with severe developmental disorders, improving self-care skills is often necessary. These skills lie at the heart of adaptive functioning and one's ability to be independent, so developing these skills is usually a priority. Self-care skills training programs are most effective for toileting, eating, dressing, and grooming.

Self-care skills training programs typically involve *task analysis, chaining,* and *feedback and reinforcement*. A skill is divided into steps in task analysis. If a person wants to put on a jacket, steps might include picking up the jacket, placing one arm in the correct sleeve, placing the other arm in the other sleeve, pulling the jacket over the shoulders, and zippering the jacket. In a *forward* chaining process like this one, a person is taught each step from beginning to end. Frequent feedback and rewards for completing the step correctly are given (Kobylarz et al., 2020).

In a *backward* chaining process, a person is taught each step from end to beginning. A teacher could help a person put on a jacket using all steps except final zippering, which the person would do themself. As that step was mastered, the teacher would work backward until each step was accomplished independently. Some adaptive behaviors can only be done in a forward way, of course—you cannot brush your teeth or apply deodorant backward!

Academic Skills Training

Academic skills training programs are most pertinent for children with learning disorder, though they can certainly apply to people with pervasive developmental disorders. Academic skills can include *readiness* skills such as holding a pencil, using scissors, staying in a seat, and raising a hand to talk. For people with a learning disorder, however, academic skills training must also include detailed educational programs that target and improve specific deficits in reading, spelling, writing, and mathematical ability (Grigorenko et al., 2020).

Abo Photography/Shutterstock.com

Children with learning disorder often benefit from individualized teaching.

Educational programs for reading generally center on helping children recognize and decode words that delay reading. This often involves a *phonetic* approach to reading that requires children to "break down" the sounds of difficult words. A teacher may present a child with a book passage and ask a child to note words that might be difficult. The child then sounds out a word, writes it several times, and perhaps looks it up in the dictionary. The teacher then reads the passage to the child as they follow along. The child is then asked to read the passage, with special attention to the difficult words. Reading programs for children with learning disorder focus on being aware of basic speech sounds, understanding the relationship between sounds and symbols, blending speech sounds together, and reading and writing certain texts (Denton et al., 2021).

Teachers who address writing problems focus on handling a pencil correctly, tracing and saying letters, writing from memory, and having a child describe what they are writing, such as a circle and tail for "Q." A focus is made as well on organizing writing tasks and producing coherent written products. Computers may also be used to increase writing efficiency (Roitsch et al., 2021).

Programs for spelling problems can include the *cover, copy, and compare method*, which involves asking a child to look at a written spelling word, cover and then copy the word, and then compare the word with the original and make corrections as needed (Lundberg et al., 2022). Teachers who address mathematical problems concentrate on a student's ability to read symbols, count efficiently without using fingers, recall basic arithmetic facts and words such as "divide," and follow logical steps to solve a problem (Nelson et al., 2022).

Addressing Problem Behaviors

Recall that people with developmental disorders often show problem behaviors such as self-stimulation, self-injury, aggression, tantrums, and noncompliance. Several behavioral procedures are thus used to reduce these misbehaviors:

- *Time-out*, or isolating a person to extinguish attention-seeking misbehavior.

SolStock/E+/Getty Images

Technology is often used to help children with learning disorder develop better reading, spelling, mathematical, and writing skills.

- *Token economy,* or establishing a set system of points or tokens for appropriate behavior later exchanged for rewards such as special food or playtime. This may also include *response cost,* or losing points for misbehavior.
- *Differential reinforcement of incompatible behavior,* or rewarding behaviors that cannot be done at the same time as the misbehavior. One could write on a piece of paper, a behavior incompatible with slapping someone. *Differential reinforcement of other behavior* involves rewarding the absence of a certain misbehavior after a time interval such as five minutes.
- *Restitution and practice positive overcorrection,* or requiring a person to practice appropriate behavior after some disruptive behavior, such as cleaning one's deliberate spill as well as others' messes.
- *Punishment,* or using restraint or other aversive procedures after misbehavior. Punishment is often used with other procedures because it may suppress but not eliminate misbehavior.

What If I Think Someone Has a Developmental Disorder?

Children are often screened for developmental disorders in school, especially learning disorder. If you feel a child you know is struggling in school or having difficulty with language or social skills, then you may wish to consult a clinical or school psychologist, special education teacher, or other mental health professional (Chapter 15).

Long-Term Outcome for People with Developmental Disorders

What is the long-term picture for people like Robert? Those with severe developmental disorders such as profound intellectual developmental disorder or autism generally have a poor prognosis. Nearly all of those with autism spectrum disorder continue to show at least several symptoms of the disorder into adulthood. Intelligence levels remain fairly stable or decrease over time, but improvements in daily living and communication skills are sometimes observed. Language skills may also improve, but social communication and socialization skills may remain limited. Even in less severe autism, social awkwardness, thought disturbance, and desire to be left alone are often present (Simonoff et al., 2020).

Other people with developmental disorders show substantial improvement and function fairly independently. People with Down syndrome often live and work independently with some assistance, although many experience later dementia (Fortea et al., 2021). Good prognosis for people with pervasive developmental disorders relates to language before age five years, early and intensive intervention, higher intelligence, better adaptive skills, attention to others, less delay in major developmental milestones, less neurological impairment, and fewer genetic/chromosomal problems (Mihaljevic, 2022; Styles et al., 2020).

Children with learning disorder continue to experience several difficulties into adolescence and adulthood. Children with reading problems often have continued trouble naming words quickly, recognizing

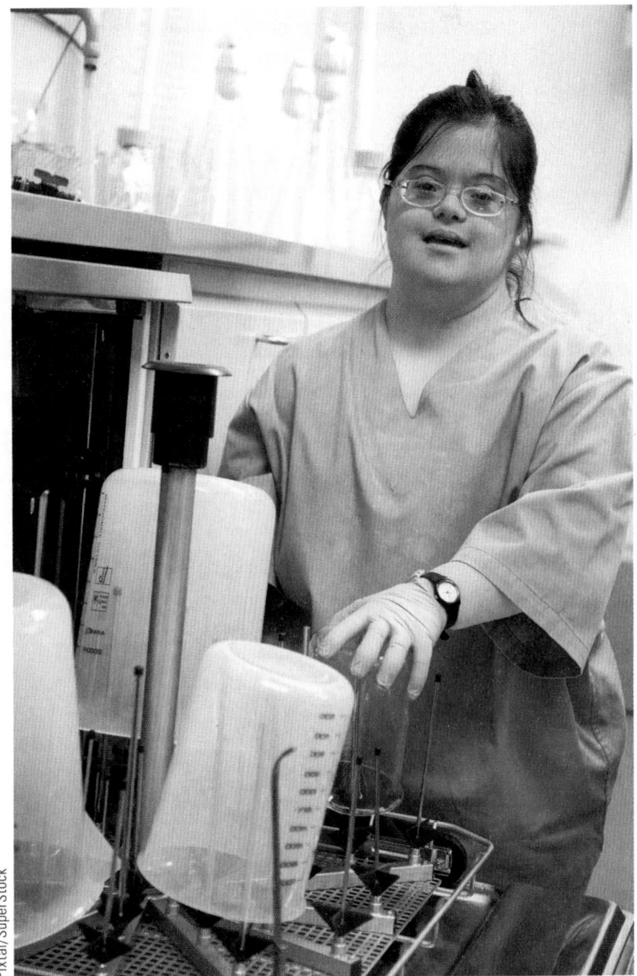

Pixtal/SuperStock

Many people with developmental disorders live productive lives.

basic speech sounds, spelling, and reading symbols. Many schools are better equipped now to assist students with learning disorder, however, often providing arrangements such as longer test-taking sessions and computer facilities for writing. Positive long-term outcome for this population generally relates to higher intelligence, early diagnosis and intervention, early language ability, fewer comorbid diagnoses such as ADHD, and less severe disorder (Boland & Verduin, 2023; Sanfilippo et al., 2020).

Section Summary

- Cognitive assessment for people with developmental disorders includes intelligence, neuropsychological, and achievement tests.
- Interviews and rating scales for people with developmental disorders cover current functioning as well as needs, support systems, and behavior problems.
- Direct observation is often used to assess frequency and severity of problem behaviors but can also be used to examine adaptive and academic behaviors.
- Medications for people with developmental disorders are sometimes used for agitation, seizures, and symptoms of comorbid problems.
- Psychological treatment for people with developmental disorders includes attention and language training, socialization training, self-care skills training, and academic tutoring.
- Treatments for problem behaviors in people with developmental disorders include time-out, token economy, differential reinforcement of incompatible or other behavior, restitution and practice positive overcorrection, and punishment.
- Long-term functioning of many people with developmental disorders is difficult, but good prognostic signs include early language and intervention, higher intelligence, and less severe disorder and neurological impairment.

Review Questions

1. Describe methods of cognitive assessment for people with developmental disorders.
2. What are primary aspects of achievement and other tests for people with developmental disorders?
3. Outline main features of attention, language, socialization, and self-care skills training for those with severe developmental disorders.
4. Describe strategies for treating youth with learning disorder.
5. Describe interventions to address problem behaviors in people with developmental disorders.
6. What is the long-term functioning for most people with developmental disorders?

Developmental disorders are not the only kind of mental disorders that occur mostly in children and adolescents. Recall that youth may also have disruptive behavior disorders involving inattention, impulsivity, overactivity, noncompliance, or aggression. These disorders are discussed next.

Continuum of Disruptive Behavior and Disruptive Behavior Disorder

	Normal	Mild
Emotions	Good control of emotions and appropriate emotional experiences.	Mild problems in impulse, anger, or other emotional control.
Cognitions	Rational thoughts about social situations and interactions with parents.	Occasional thoughts of noncompliance or aggression.
Behaviors	Good self-control of behavior and compliance toward authority figures.	Occasional rambunctiousness and noncompliance to authority figures.

Normal Rambunctious Behavior and Disruptive Behavior Disorders: What Are They?

LO 13.7 Describe the continuum from typical rambunctious behavior to disruptive behavior disorders.

Have you ever baby-sat a highly active preschooler? Or perhaps you have small children that constantly test your patience. Watching and raising young children can be an arduous and exhausting task, so much so that many caregivers look forward to work on Monday morning! Many children are naturally curious about their environment and are egocentric, meaning they have trouble understanding the needs of others. They focus on what they want and may interrupt, throw a tantrum, or even hit someone to get what they want. Young children eventually learn to better control emotions, delay impulses, and act in socially appropriate ways to get what they want. A child may learn that they first need to pick up some toys or eat dinner using good manners to watch a favorite program (refer to **Continuum of Disruptive Behavior and Disruptive Behavior Disorder**).

Other children take longer to control their emotions and impulses and might be described as rambunctious. They constantly test limits placed on them by parents and teachers. They may continue, even into the school-age years, to throw tantrums or become upset when something happens they do not like. Or they may continue to be very physically active, always climbing on the furniture or running about. Many of these children are difficult to control but can pay attention and comply with others when they absolutely have to, such as dinnertime or when at church. These children eventually learn appropriate ways to channel their excess energy, such as playing soccer or running as hard as possible during recess.

For other children like Will, severe problems of impulsivity, overactivity, and inattention continue for lengthy periods of time. These problems greatly interfere with their ability to function in daily situations that require behavior control and concentration. Many children are able to adjust their behavior from recess (wild horseplay) to a classroom (sitting at a desk quietly) within a few minutes. Other children such as Will, however, cannot do so and continue to be disruptive. They thus have trouble following class rules and concentrating on academic tasks. These children may have **attention-deficit/hyperactivity disorder (ADHD)**.

Other children continue to show noncompliance and aggression during and after elementary school. Severe problems of noncompliance comprise **oppositional defiant disorder**, and severe problems of aggression comprise **conduct disorder**. ADHD and oppositional defiant and conduct disorders are **disruptive behavior disorders**. The disorders can occur separately but sometimes occur together in a child like Will. Major features of disruptive behavior disorders are discussed next.

Moderate	Disruptive Behavior Disorder—less severe	Disruptive Behavior Disorder—more severe
Moderate problems in impulse, anger, or other emotional control.	Substantial problems regulating one's impulses and emotions that create trouble functioning in a classroom.	Extremely poor emotional control or lack of emotion that leads to aggression or explosiveness.
Frequent irritation toward others and thoughts of defiance or aggression.	Intense thoughts that others are actively hostile to the person, even in ambiguous situations.	Frequent thoughts of aggression, hostility toward others, and rule-breaking.
Significant rambunctiousness and noncompliance at home or school.	Highly disruptive behavior at home and school and/or property destruction and severe noncompliance.	Extreme disruptive behavior and/or aggression to people and animals.

Case Will

Will was an eight-year-old boy referred to a psychologist and psychiatrist for severe disruptive behavior. His behavior problems began in preschool and consisted of running about the classroom, failing to comply with parent and teacher requests, and being aggressive to other children. The problems became so difficult that Will was expelled from two preschools. Will's problems were stable during kindergarten, but his entry into first grade was highly problematic. He ran about his classroom, often disturbing his classmates, and was regularly sent to the principal's office. Will threw a metal object at a child's head on one occasion and was suspended for three school days. His teacher described him as a highly impulsive child who did not have control over his behavior. Will seemed to do as he pleased, rarely completed class assignments, and was disorganized. He had great trouble comprehending what others were saying to him, perhaps because he was not paying much attention.

Will's entry into second grade was marked by severe escalation of his disruptive behaviors. His teacher said Will was difficult to control, especially because he was physically strong for his age. Repeated attempts by the teacher and principal to engage Will's parents to address their son's behavior were fruitless. Will's parents seemed unfazed by the school's complaints and attributed his behavior to lack of school discipline. They said they were "tired" of their son's misbehavior and learned it was best to just "give him what he wants."

Will's impulsive, hyperactive, and noncompliant behavior became so bad he was failing school at the end of second grade. He also became more brazen in his aggressiveness toward others, often using obscene language and bullying tactics to get what he wanted. The final straw came when Will was caught with a razor blade at school. He was suspended indefinitely and his parents were told he would be allowed to return to class only after they sought professional help for their son's misbehavior.

What Do You Think?

1. How do Will's behaviors differ from a typical child? Which of his behaviors might seem normal for a child?
2. What external events and internal factors might be responsible for Will's behaviors?
3. What are you curious about regarding Will?
4. Does Will remind you in any way of someone you know? How so?
5. How might Will's behaviors affect his life in the future?

Disruptive Behavior Disorders: Features and Epidemiology

LO 13.8 Distinguish between the disruptive behavior disorders using their diagnostic criteria and clinical characteristics.

LO 13.9 Summarize the epidemiology of disruptive behavior disorders.

Attention-Deficit/Hyperactivity Disorder

Children with attention-deficit/hyperactivity disorder (ADHD) have three key behavior problems: *inattention, overactivity,* and *impulsivity* (refer to **Table 13.7**; APA, 2022). Inattention means a child has ongoing problems listening to others, attending to details in schoolwork and other tasks such as chores, and organizing work. Such children are constantly distracted by irrelevant stimuli—they may suddenly run to a window to look outside as a teacher is speaking. Children with ADHD, especially those with inattention, are also forgetful, reluctant to complete schoolwork, sloppy, and somewhat absentminded, meaning they always seem to be losing things and unaware of what is happening around them. Such children may be diagnosed with ADHD that is predominantly *inattentive* (APA, 2022).

Children may also be diagnosed with ADHD that is predominantly *hyperactive-impulsive.* Hyperactive means a particular child always seems to be fidgeting, leaving their seat at school or the dinner table, climbing excessively on furniture or desks, and talking too much. These children are often described as "having no 'off' switch," meaning they are always moving from the time they wake up to the time they go to bed. They also have trouble playing quietly. Impulsive means a particular child often interrupts others, tries to answer questions before a questioner is finished, and has trouble waiting their turn, such as when playing a game.

Children with ADHD may have problems with all three symptoms—inattention, hyperactivity, and impulsivity; this is ADHD with a *combined presentation.* Will had all these characteristics. A diagnosis of ADHD is made only when a child's behaviors impair their abilities to function in at least two settings, such as home and school. This excludes children who act fine in school but not at home. To be diagnosed as such, symptoms of ADHD must also be present before age 12 years, as was true for Will (APA, 2022). The diagnosis of ADHD

Table 13.7 DSM-5-TR

Attention-Deficit/Hyperactivity Disorder
A. A persistent pattern of inattention and/or hyperactivity-impulsivity that interferes with functioning or development, as characterized by (1) and/or (2): 1. **Inattention:** Six (or more) of the following symptoms have persisted for at least six months to a degree that is inconsistent with developmental level and that negatively impacts directly on social and academic/occupational activities: Note: The symptoms are not solely a manifestation of oppositional behavior, defiance, hostility, or failure to understand tasks or instructions. For older adolescents and adults (age 17 and older), at least five symptoms are required. a. Often fails to give close attention to details or makes careless mistakes in schoolwork, at work, or during other activities. b. Often has difficulty sustaining attention in tasks or play activities. c. Often does not seem to listen when spoken to directly. d. Often does not follow through on instructions and fails to finish schoolwork, chores, or duties in the workplace. e. Often has difficulty organizing tasks and activities. f. Often avoids, dislikes, or is reluctant to engage in tasks that require sustained mental effort. g. Often loses things necessary for tasks or activities. h. Is often easily distracted by extraneous stimuli. i. Is often forgetful in daily activities. 2. **Hyperactivity and impulsivity:** Six (or more) of the following symptoms have persisted for at least six months to a degree that is inconsistent with developmental level and that negatively impacts directly on social and academic/occupational activities: Note: The symptoms are not solely a manifestation of oppositional behavior, defiance, hostility, or failure to understand tasks or instructions. For older adolescents and adults (age 17 and older), at least five symptoms are required. a. Often fidgets with or taps hands or feet or squirms in seat. b. Often leaves seat in situations when remaining seated is expected. c. Often runs about or climbs in situations where it is inappropriate. d. Often unable to play or engage in leisure activities quietly. e. Is often "on the go," acting as if "driven by a motor." f. Often talks excessively. g. Often blurts out an answer before a question has been completed. h. Often has difficulty waiting his or her turn. i. Often interrupts or intrudes on others.
B. Several inattentive or hyperactive-impulsive symptoms were present prior to age 12 years.
C. Several inattentive or hyperactive-impulsive symptoms are present in two or more settings.
D. There is clear evidence that the symptoms interfere with, or reduce the quality of, social, academic, or occupational functioning.
E. The symptoms do not occur exclusively during the course of schizophrenia or another psychotic disorder and are not better explained by another mental disorder. Specify if combined, predominantly inattentive, or predominantly hyperactive/impulsive presentation; if in partial remission; severity as mild, moderate, or severe.

American Psychiatric Association. (2022). *Diagnostic and statistical manual of mental disorders* (5th ed., text rev.). Arlington, VA: American Psychiatric Association.

is somewhat controversial because many children with true ADHD are often misdiagnosed with oppositional defiant or conduct disorder. At the same time, however, medications for ADHD may be overprescribed. ADHD may thus be both an underdiagnosed *and* an overdiagnosed disorder (Gascon et al., 2022).

Oppositional Defiant Disorder and Conduct Disorder

Children with oppositional defiant disorder often refuse to comply with others' commands (refer to **Table 13.8**; APA, 2022). They can be hostile and angry toward

Table 13.8 DSM-5-TR

Oppositional Defiant Disorder

A. A pattern of angry/irritable mood, argumentative/defiant behavior, or vindictiveness lasting at least six months as evidenced by at least four symptoms from any of the following categories, and exhibited during interaction with at least one individual who is not a sibling.

Angry/Irritable Mood

1. Often loses temper.
2. Is often touchy or easily annoyed.
3. Is often angry and resentful.

Argumentative/Defiant Behavior

4. Often argues with authority figures or, for children and adolescents, with adults.
5. Often actively defies or refuses to comply with requests from authority figures or with rules.
6. Often deliberately annoys others.
7. Often blames others for his or her mistakes or misbehavior.

Vindictiveness

8. Has been spiteful or vindictive at least twice within the past six months.

B. The disturbance in behavior is associated with distress in the individual or others in his or her immediate social context, or it impacts negatively on social, educational, occupational, or other important areas of functioning.

C. The behaviors do not occur exclusively during the course of a psychotic, substance use, depressive, or bipolar disorder. Also, the criteria are not met for disruptive mood dysregulation disorder.

Specify if mild (symptoms in one setting), moderate (symptoms in two settings), or severe (symptoms in three or more settings).

American Psychiatric Association. (2022). *Diagnostic and statistical manual of mental disorders* (5th ed., text rev.). Arlington, VA: American Psychiatric Association.

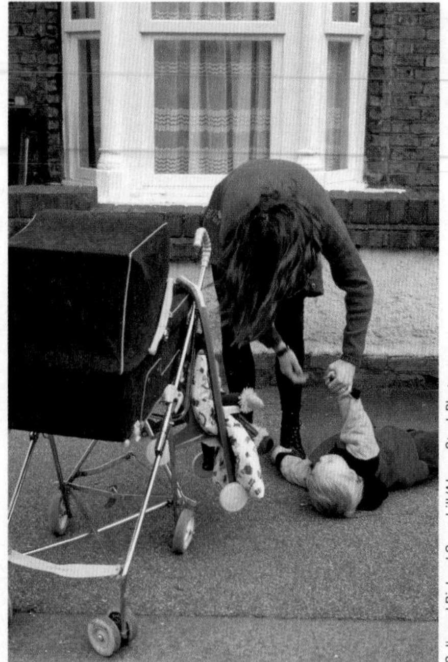
Sally and Richard Greenhill/Alamy Stock Photo

Many children are occasionally disruptive in public, but some show such frequent and intense misbehaviors that they have a disruptive behavior disorder.

others, argumentative, bullying, spiteful, and overly sensitive. They lose their tempers easily, and these behaviors cause substantial impairment in daily functioning. Will's mean-spirited attitude toward others meant few children wanted to be near him, much less play with him.

Oppositional defiant disorder may continue over time and eventually evolve into a more severe condition: conduct disorder. Conduct disorder, sometimes equated with *juvenile delinquency*, involves a consistent pattern of violating the rights of others (refer to **Table 13.9**; APA, 2022). Symptoms of conduct disorder may be divided into four main categories. First, these youths may be aggressive toward other people or animals, displaying cruel behavior such as using a weapon or torturing someone (or an animal), assaulting and stealing from someone, or engaging in sexual assault. Second, these youths may destroy property, such as setting fires or vandalizing a school building. Third, many youths with conduct disorder lie to others to get something or to avoid punishment. They may also steal from others in a secretive way, such as shoplifting, or forcibly break into someone's home or car. Finally, many youths with conduct disorder violate laws or rules for their age group, such as missing school or curfew or running away from home. Collectively, these behaviors must cause serious impairment in functioning, such as being expelled from school or being arrested for a crime (Frick & Kemp, 2021). Conduct disorder may begin in childhood or adolescence and its symptoms can range from mild to moderate to severe (APA, 2022).

Epidemiology of Disruptive Behavior Disorders

ADHD affects about 7.2 percent of youth and 2.6 percent of adults, including college students (refer to **Focus On College Students: ADHD**). Many general problems are associated with ADHD, including academic and social skill deficits, school failure, low self-esteem, and excessive substance use. Specific mental disorders associated with ADHD include oppositional defiant and conduct disorder, anxiety-related and depressive disorders, and learning disorder. ADHD is much more prevalent among boys than girls. Girls with ADHD tend to have less disruptive behavior problems but greater internalizing problems such as depression than boys with ADHD. ADHD appears to

Table 13.9 DSM-5-TR

Conduct Disorder

A. A repetitive and persistent pattern of behavior in which the basic rights of others or major age-appropriate societal norms or rules are violated, as manifested by the presence of at least three of the following 15 criteria in the past 12 months from any of the categories below, with at least one criterion present in the past six months:

Aggression to People and Animals

1. Often bullies, threatens, or intimidates others.
2. Often initiates physical fights.
3. Has used a weapon that can cause serious physical harm to others (e.g., a bat, brick, broken bottle, knife, gun).
4. Has been physically cruel to people.
5. Has been physically cruel to animals.
6. Has stolen while confronting a victim.
7. Has forced someone into sexual activity.

Destruction of Property

8. Has deliberately engaged in fire setting with the intention of causing serious damage.
9. Has deliberately destroyed others' property (other than by fire setting).

Deceitfulness or Theft

10. Has broken into someone else's house, building, or car.
11. Often lies to obtain goods or favors or to avoid obligations.
12. Has stolen items of nontrivial value without confronting a victim.

Serious Violations of Rules

13. Often stays out at night despite parental prohibitions, beginning before age 13 years.
14. Has run away from home overnight at least twice while living in the parental or parental surrogate home, or once without returning for a lengthy period.
15. Is often truant from school, beginning before age 13 years.

B. The disturbance in behavior causes clinically significant impairment in social, academic, or occupational functioning.

C. If the individual is age 18 years or older, criteria are not met for antisocial personality disorder.

Specify if childhood, adolescent, or unspecified onset; if with limited prosocial emotions, lack of remorse or guilt, callous, lack of empathy, unconcerned about performance, shallow or deficient affect; mild, moderate, or severe.

American Psychiatric Association. (2022). *Diagnostic and statistical manual of mental disorders* (5th ed., text rev.). Arlington, VA: American Psychiatric Association.

be a worldwide phenomenon (Cabral et al., 2020; De Rossi et al., 2022; Kanarik et al., 2022; Massuti et al., 2021; Song et al., 2021).

Oppositional defiant disorder affects about 3.6 percent of youth and is observed more in boys than girls. The disorder is commonly associated with other disruptive behavior and learning problems. Oppositional defiant disorder can evolve into conduct disorder, especially when a child shows severe disruptive behavior and callous unemotional traits (refer to later section on personality factors) at an early age. This tends to be the case more so for boys than girls (Burke et al., 2021; Dachew et al., 2021; Ezpeleta et al., 2022).

Photobac/Shutterstock.com

Children with conduct disorder are often aggressive and bullying toward others.

Conduct disorder affects about 2.1 percent of youth, though many more show symptoms without the full disorder, and is much more common in boys than girls. Girls with conduct disorder usually show more covert and less aggressive behaviors than boys with conduct disorder and are often diagnosed later in adolescence. Conduct disorder is often comorbid with other mental conditions, especially anxiety-related, depressive, learning, and substance use disorders (Konrad et al., 2022; Nujić et al., 2021).

Stigma Associated with Disruptive Behavior Disorders

LO 13.10 Describe the stigma associated with disruptive behavior disorders and its impact on those with the disorders and their families.

Stigma can affect children with disruptive behavior disorders. Studies indicate that adults often have negative views of children with ADHD. Childhood ADHD symptoms are often labeled by adults as serious, less likely to constitute a mental disorder, and less likely to be viewed as a condition that requires treatment. In addition, the symptoms are sometimes viewed as dangerous, violent, and harmful. Other studies indicate that some adults favor coercive measures to force a child with ADHD symptoms to see a clinician, take medication, or be hospitalized. A substantial number of parents say they do not want a child

Focus On College Students

ADHD

Many adolescents with ADHD enter college, and approximately 2 to 5 percent of college students report ADHD or significant ADHD symptoms. In addition, about 25 percent of students who receive disability services on college campuses do so for ADHD symptoms. On average, college students with ADHD or significant ADHD symptoms tend to have lower grade point averages, are more likely to be on academic probation, and are less likely to graduate than their classmates without ADHD. College students with ADHD also report more difficulties with respect to social skills and adjustment, self-esteem, mood symptoms, substance use, and relationships with parents and peers (DuPaul et al., 2021; Weyandt et al., 2013).

Some have examined these problems in greater depth. College students with ADHD have been found to report more obsessive-compulsive behaviors, depression, anxiety, and hostility compared with controls. College students with ADHD also reported lower grades on specific course assignments, less well-developed organizational skills, and more problems related to social adjustment as students. Finally, those with ADHD reported specific cognitive problems related to emotional control, working memory, and task management more so than control participants. Students with ADHD should thus be assessed for impairment as well as symptoms and treatment should be broad in scope and include problems in academic, cognitive, and social functioning (Weyandt et al., 2013).

with ADHD to live next door, have their child befriend a child with ADHD, spend an evening with a child with ADHD or their family, or have a child with ADHD in their child's classroom. Teachers also tend to perceive children with ADHD as less successful academically (Metzger & Hamilton, 2021; Nguyen & Hinshaw, 2020)).

Stigma can also apply to youths with conduct disorder, especially those with a juvenile record. Youths given a label as "delinquent" often face restricted academic and vocational opportunities (Smith et al., 2022). In addition, many juveniles feel stigmatized after involvement with the justice system and shun mental health treatment. This may be especially so for youths who experienced traumatic experiences before or during detention (Aguirre Velasco et al., 2020). Some thus contend that legal and other professionals should move away from viewing status offenses as criminal and toward an understanding that many juveniles have unaddressed mental disorders (Quinn et al., 2022).

Section Summary

- Many children may be described as rambunctious, but some have disruptive behavior disorders involving inattention, impulsivity, overactivity, aggression, and noncompliance.
- Attention-deficit hyperactivity/disorder refers to intense problems of inattention, impulsivity, and/or overactivity.
- Oppositional defiant disorder refers to noncompliance, hostility and anger toward others, argumentativeness, and bullying behavior, among other symptoms.
- Conduct disorder refers to intense problems of aggression, property destruction, lying and stealing, and status violations.
- Disruptive behavior disorders are common and observed more in boys than girls. The problems seem universal and are often comorbid with one another.
- Stigma is an important part of disruptive behavior disorders and can affect others' view of a child.

Review Questions

1. How do disruptive behavior disorders differ from normal rambunctious behavior?
2. Define major symptoms and subtypes of attention-deficit/hyperactivity disorder.
3. Outline main symptoms of oppositional defiant disorder.
4. What are main categories of symptoms of conduct disorder?
5. Describe the epidemiology of the disruptive behavior disorders.

Disruptive Behavior Disorders: Causes and Prevention

LO 13.11 Discuss the risk factors for and prevention of disruptive behavior disorders.

Disruptive behavior disorders involve biological and environmental risk factors. ADHD relates especially to biological risk factors and oppositional and conduct disorders relate to many environmental risk factors.

Biological Risk Factors for Disruptive Behavior Disorders

Genetic Influences

Strong evidence supports a genetic basis for ADHD. First, the disorder runs in families: siblings of children with ADHD are nine times more likely than to have ADHD themselves. Second, twin studies worldwide indicate that genetic factors account for about 75 to 80 percent of the variance when explaining ADHD onset. Third, findings from adoption studies reveal biological relatives of children with ADHD to have an elevated rate of ADHD compared with the general population (Faraone & Larsson, 2019; Grimm et al., 2020).

Studies of the biology of conduct disorder indicate that the problem has moderate to strong genetic influences. Much of the explanation for this, however, may be due to genetic overlap with ADHD and oppositional defiant disorder (Tistarelli et al., 2020). In addition, some genetic basis may be more pertinent to certain aspects of conduct disorder, such as aggression, emotionality, and impulsivity. Proactive aggression in children tends to have a stronger genetic basis than reactive aggression (Romero-Martínez et al., 2022). In addition, callous-unemotional traits (refer to later section on personality factors), which are often part of severe conduct disorder, appear to have a strong genetic basis (Takahashi et al., 2021). Negative emotionality refers to persistent experiences of nervousness, sadness, and anger and is often associated with conduct disorder. Negative emotionality also has some genetic basis (Shewark et al., 2021). Impulsive antisocial behavior and the neurochemical features associated with this (refer to next section) are influenced by genetics as well (da Cunha-Bang & Knudsen, 2021).

Neurochemical Features

Neurochemical changes implicated for children with ADHD include deficiencies or imbalances in dopamine and norepinephrine, especially in prefrontal brain areas. Such changes may help explain problems of motor control, behavior inhibition, and cognition. ADHD may be an inability to regulate one's own behavior, so medications to help improve symptoms of ADHD focus on increasing these neurotransmitter levels (Mamiya et al., 2021).

Serotonin levels have been found to be low among youths with aggression and conduct disorder. Lower levels of cortisol and higher levels of testosterone also appear among youths with disruptive behavior disorders, which is consistent with findings that these youths have lower heart rates and less physiological arousal. Some of these youths may thus lack anxious inhibition to engage in aggressive or other antisocial acts (Erjavec et al., 2022; Junewicz & Billick, 2020).

Brain Features

Children with disruptive behavior disorders have characteristic brain changes, some of which may relate to genetic predispositions and that may interact with neurochemical changes. Youths with ADHD have smaller or different volumes of key brain areas, especially the prefrontal cortex, anterior cingulate cortex, basal ganglia, caudate, putamen, pallidum, corpus callosum, and cerebellum. Less blood flow and poor connectivity in some neural pathways involving these brain areas have been observed as well. Such changes help explain problems of inattention, overactivity, and impulsivity in this population (Chang et al., 2021; Yadav et al., 2021).

Neuroimaging studies of youths with oppositional defiant or conduct disorder are less common, though some work has focused on aggression and antisocial behavior. The most reliable finding is less volume in the prefrontal cortex, a result that overlaps with ADHD (refer to **Figure 13.3**). Others have implicated changes in the amygdala, basal ganglia, and brain stem. Deficits in these brain areas may help explain trouble controlling excess emotions and aggressive behaviors (Cupaioli et al., 2021; Göttlich et al., 2022).

Figure 13.3 Major Brain Areas Implicated in Disruptive Behavior Disorders.

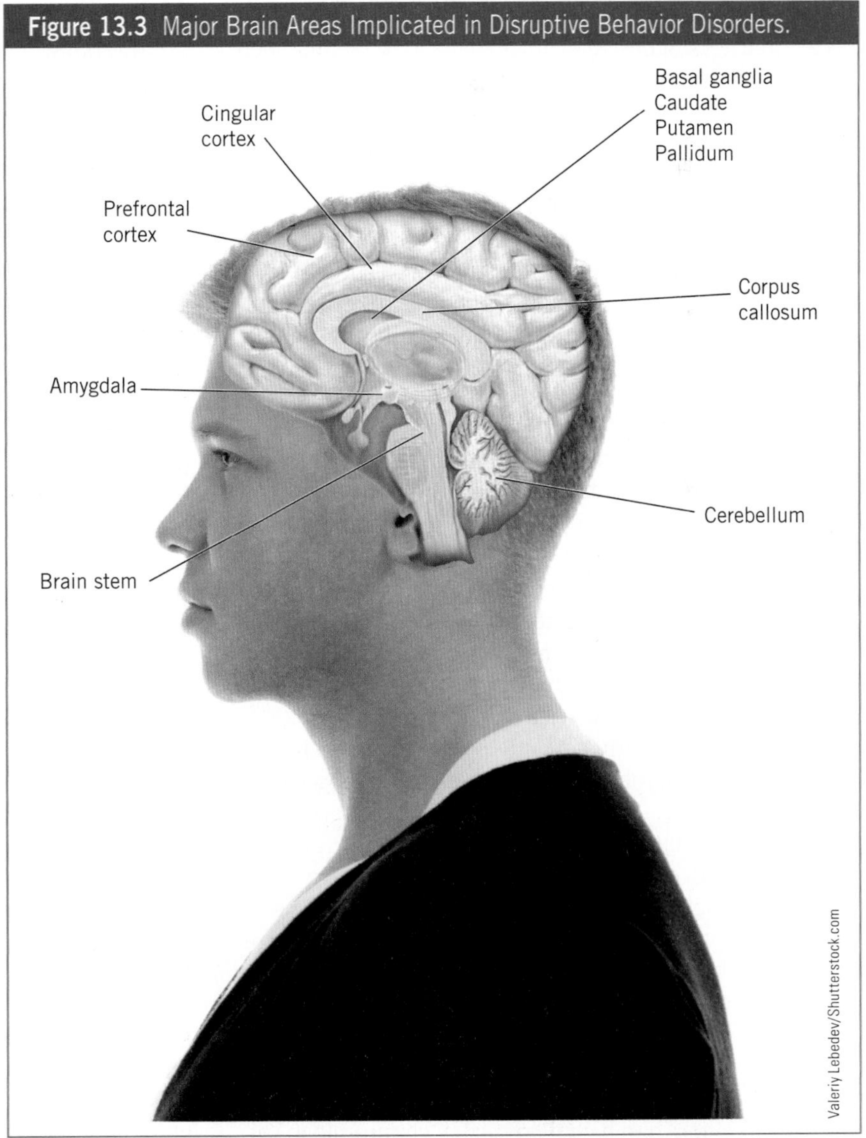

Personality Factors

Personality factors also impact disruptive behavior disorders, particularly oppositional defiant or conduct disorder. These personality factors could relate to temperament issues raised earlier and involve *callous-unemotional traits*. Youths with these traits often lack guilt or remorse for their hurtful acts toward others, show little emotion, are unempathetic to others, and manipulate others for their own gratification. A teenager with this personality pattern might resemble someone with antisocial personality disorder (Chapter 10). They will use others for personal gratification, such as sexually or to obtain goods or services, and do so with little regard for others. This personality pattern seems particularly relevant to youths with severe conduct disorder (Craig et al., 2021).

Marital conflict is a key risk factor for children with behavior problems.

Environmental Risk Factors for Disruptive Behavior Disorders

Teratogens

Recall that teratogens refer to prenatal risk factors such as maternal drug use and exposure to toxins. Youths with disruptive behavior disorders may have been exposed to various prenatal teratogens more so than the general population. Key teratogens related to later disruptive behavior disorders, especially ADHD, include maternal smoking and alcohol use, which closely relate to problems of attention, cognition, and learning. Increased stress during pregnancy, pregnancy and delivery complications, premature birth, and lower birth weight are significant risk factors as well (Alamolhoda et al., 2021; Kian et al., 2022).

Family Conflict and Parenting Practices

Conflict in a marriage and among family members closely relates to disruptive behavior problems in youth. Distress associated with watching parents fight may cause attachment problems and contribute to a child's inability to control their emotions. Youngsters could also model parental aggression as a way to solve problems. Other youths may be rewarded for aggression or overactivity by a parent's unwillingness to address the behavior (Van Dijk et al., 2020; van Eldik et al., 2020).

Ineffective parenting practices closely relate to disruptive behavior problems. Examples include rewarding child misbehavior by providing positive consequences or removing negative ones. A child could become aggressive and overactive so parents will entice them to stop the behaviors. Or a child could misbehave in response to parent commands to avoid a chore. Patterns of *coercion* begin early in life, can escalate to extreme forms of misbehavior, and can be accelerated by ineffective parent discipline (Yan et al., 2021).

Other parenting problems associated with disruptive behavior disorders include less monitoring of a child's behavior, harsh and uncaring communications, overcontrol, excessive physical punishment, and use of unclear commands. Some parents phrase commands in the form of a question ("Will you please just go to school?"), interrupt or lecture their children when giving a command, or issue vague commands that are open to interpretation ("Go clean your room"). This can lead to child noncompliance or defiance. Parent commands are often a focus of treatment (Kohlhoff et al., 2021).

Deviant Peers

Youths with disruptive behavior disorders, especially those with conduct disorder, associate more with deviant peers, are rejected by nondeviant peers, and have hostile interpersonal relationships. Many of these youths also have limited social and verbal skills, which contribute to their inability to form positive friendships. Oftentimes such rejection from others leads a child to associate with others who have also been rejected because of aggression. Hostile and aggressive behavior may thus be rewarded by peers (Lin et al., 2022).

Association with deviant peers is sometimes linked to bullying behavior. Bullying refers to victimizing someone through aggression and other hostile behavior such as yelling or verbal threats. Bullying appears to be a stable behavior—many children who bully continue to do so during adolescence. Factors associated with ongoing bullying, especially for boys, include disruptive behavior problems and limited social competence (Gao et al., 2022; Mandira & Stoltz, 2021).

Cognitive Factors

Older children and adolescents with disruptive behavior disorders, particularly those with conduct disorder, have key information-processing differences. Many of these youth misinterpret actions of others as hostile or threatening when little threat exists. A teenager may be accidentally bumped by someone in a school hallway and immediately assume the person committed the act intentionally and with intent to harm. Such assumptions could help trigger thoughts and behaviors of vengeance or spitefulness. Youths with conduct disorder also favor aggressive solutions for problems, fail to fully understand the negative consequences of aggression, define problems in hostile ways, and perceive their self-worth as low (Revill et al., 2020).

Maltreatment

Early sexual and physical maltreatment toward a child also relates to disruptive behavior problems. If a child is maltreated during the infancy, toddler, or preschool phases of life, various externalizing behavior problems during later childhood and adolescence are much more likely to occur than if the child was not maltreated. Of course, maltreatment may also occur in response to a child's misbehavior. Why might maltreatment help produce disruptive behaviors? Possibilities include poor attachment to parents, difficulty controlling emotions, and development of cognitive distortions and low self-esteem (Chong et al., 2022).

Cultural Factors

Race and ethnicity do play some role in disruptive behavior disorders. European American children are more likely to receive a diagnosis of ADHD than children who are African American, Hispanic, or Asian (Cénat et al., 2022). At the same time, however, cultural, racial, and language biases may lead to the overidentification of ethnic minority children as disabled and to more severe ratings of ADHD symptoms (Slobodin & Masalha, 2020). In addition, ethnic minority children are sometimes less likely to receive needed medication for ADHD (Glasofer & Dingley, 2022). Parents and teachers also rate children with ADHD differently, perhaps due to implicit bias. Losing items and running about are rated higher for African American children, whereas inattentiveness and excessive talking are rated higher for European American children (DuPaul et al., 2020).

The relationship between race/ethnicity and conduct disorder is also complex. European American youth account for a larger proportion of aggravated assaults and are more likely to be diagnosed with conduct disorder, but youths of color are more likely to be arrested overall and have deeper contact with the juvenile justice system (Office of Juvenile Justice and Delinquency Prevention, 2022; Puzzanchera, 2022; Yockey et al., 2021). Many youths of color live in neighborhoods with concentrated violence and poverty, which can help lead to behavior problems in part due to trauma and because many of these areas lack access to quality education and health care (White et al., 2020). Risk of conduct problems also increases among youth exposed to racial discrimination (Blakey et al., 2021).

Causes of Disruptive Behavior Disorders

Researchers have focused on *multifactorial* or *biopsychosocial* models of disruptive behavior disorders that combine many risk factors. A multifactorial model of ADHD includes biological and environmental factors that interact to help produce the disorder. Many risk factors have been suggested and multiple pathways to ADHD likely exist. Some of these pathways could be largely genetic, some largely due to stress and teratogens, and some largely due to a combination of these factors. The latter pathway is the most likely early scenario. These pathways may then lead to key brain and neurochemical changes, especially changes that affect ability to self-regulate behavior. When combined with certain environmental factors such as ineffective parenting, these brain changes help trigger symptoms of inattention, impulsivity, and overactivity (Martel et al., 2022; and refer to **Figure 13.4**).

A multifactorial approach may also apply to oppositional defiant disorder and conduct disorder, although the pathways to these disorders may rely more heavily on environmental factors. General biological predispositions can set the stage for certain difficult and hostile temperaments as well as tendencies toward aggression and impulsivity. Irritable temperaments and tendencies toward antisocial behavior could set the stage for poor attachment with parents, ineffective parenting, and social and academic problems. Later factors can aggravate conduct problems as well, such as harsh parenting, family conflict, peer rejection, school failure, and excessive substance use or depression (Frick & Kemp, 2021; also refer to **Figure 13.5**).

Figure 13.4 Sample Multifactorial Model of Attention-Deficit/Hyperactivity Disorder.

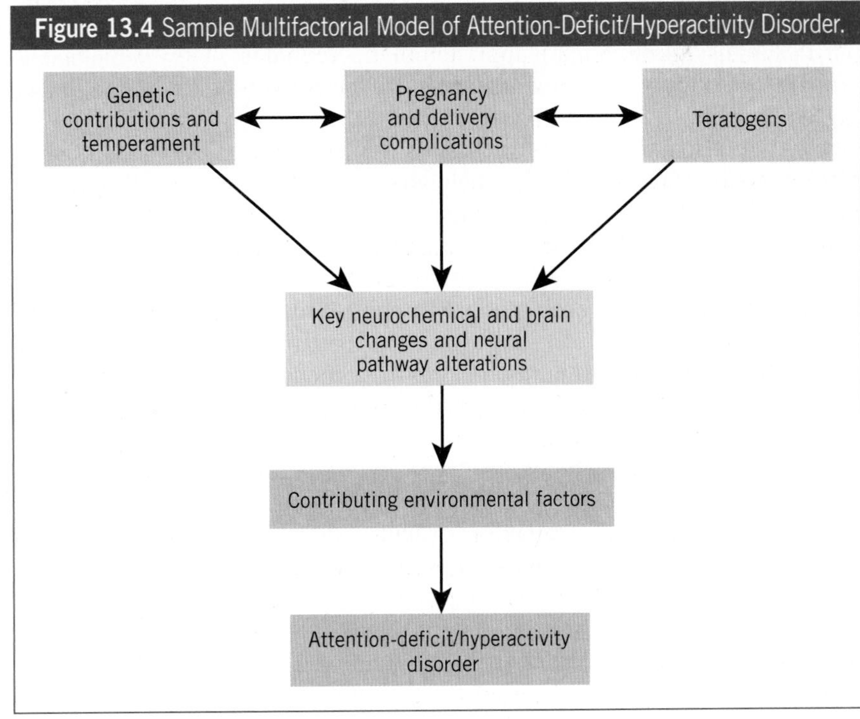

Figure 13.5 Sample Multifactorial Model of Oppositional Defiant Disorder and Conduct Disorder.

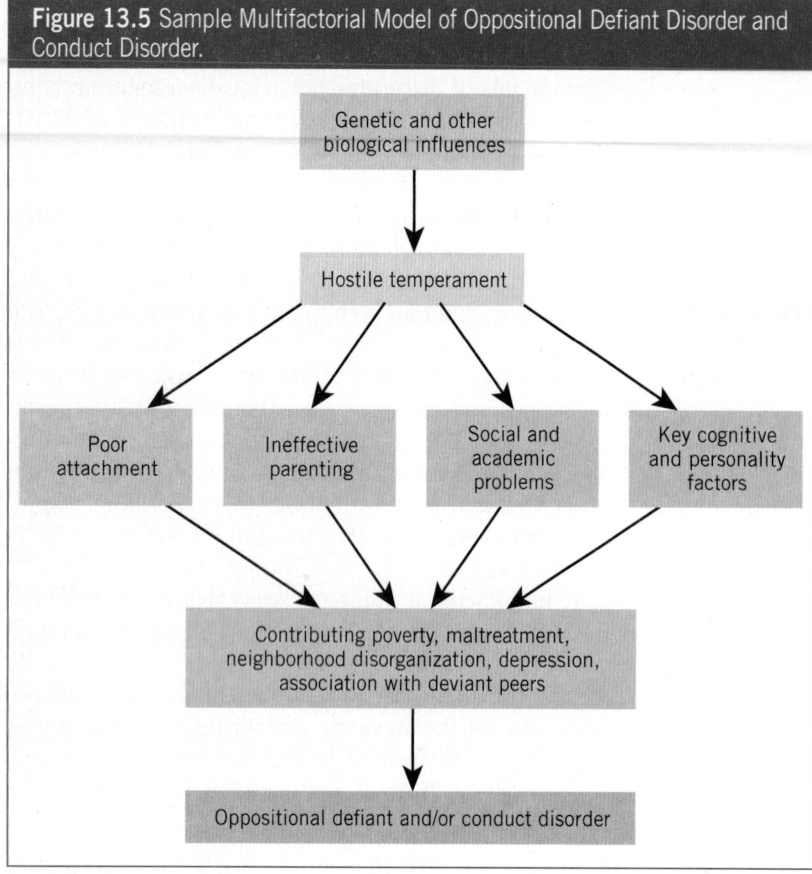

Prevention of Disruptive Behavior Disorders

Prevention programs for disruptive behavior disorders are often school-based to help youths improve social and academic competence and to reduce unfair disparities in discipline. A main approach in this regard is effective classroom behavior management by providing feedback and a supportive learning environment, developing effective teaching practices and routines, setting clear expectations for behavior, and minimizing exclusionary discipline such as suspensions (Bradshaw et al., 2021). These approaches have been effective at reducing long-term negative outcomes such as behavior problems and school dropout (Sinclair et al., 2021).

Other prevention programs in this area focus on effective parenting skills and adaptive family functioning (Thongseiratch et al., 2020). Many of these programs focus on enhancing positive caregiver-child relationships, reducing coercive processes, helping caregivers understand principles of child development, using more effective behavior management and disciplinary strategies, and helping caregivers improve their mental approach toward parenting as well as their own emotional well-being (Gubbels et al., 2019). Parenting programs are generally effective at reducing behavior problems though less effective at preventing related issues such as emotional regulation problems (Kjøbli et al., 2022).

Section Summary

- Evidence strongly supports a genetic basis for ADHD but less so for conduct disorder.
- Imbalances of dopamine and norepinephrine have been noted in ADHD and low serotonin has been noted in conduct disorder.
- Youth with disruptive behavior disorders may have smaller brain areas as well as key differences in the prefrontal cortex and other areas.
- Prenatal teratogens implicated in disruptive behavior disorders include maternal drug use.
- Family conflict, ineffective parenting practices, and association with deviant peers seem especially related to conduct disorder but may also apply to cases of ADHD.
- Youth with disruptive behavior disorders often interpret actions of others as hostile, have other social-cognitive deficits, and have callous-unemotional personality traits.
- Causal theories for disruptive behavior disorders focus on multifactorial models that include biological predispositions and environmental risk factors as well as various pathways that can lead to ADHD or conduct disorder.
- Preventing disruptive behavior disorders often involves classroom behavior management and parenting programs.

Review Questions

1. What genetic predispositions exist for disruptive behavior disorders?
2. What other biological risk factors exist for disruptive behavior disorders?
3. Describe child-based, parent-based, and community-based factors that may cause disruptive behavior disorders.
4. Outline a multifactorial model for the cause of ADHD and conduct disorder.
5. What methods have been used to prevent disruptive behavior disorders?

Disruptive Behavior Disorders: Assessment and Treatment

LO 13.12 Characterize the assessment and treatment of individuals with disruptive behavior disorders.

Mental health professionals use various methods to examine children with disruptive behavior disorders. These methods primarily include interviews, rating scales, and behavioral observation.

Interviews

Interviews of a child and their parents and school officials are essential when assessing a child with a possible disruptive behavior disorder. Questions should surround various aspects of a child's cognitive, emotional, and social development. The presence of risk factors mentioned in this chapter should also be determined. Ongoing risk factors in a child's daily environment should be assessed as well, including parent-child interactions, parenting style and discipline, marital and family interactions, and school-based interactions with peers and teachers. Medical conditions and school performance should also be evaluated.

A thorough history of a child's symptoms must also be obtained, especially the frequency, intensity, and duration of overactivity, impulsivity, inattention, noncompliance, and aggression. Interviews to assess these problems can be unstructured or structured. Commonly used structured interviews for youths with disruptive behavior disorders include the *National Institute of Mental Health Diagnostic Interview Schedule for Children* and *Structured Clinical Interview for Childhood Diagnoses* (Roelofs et al., 2015).

Rating Scales

Parent and teacher rating scales are also available for assessing disruptive behavior in youths. Scales commonly used to assess global levels of disruptive behavior include the *Child Behavior Checklist, Teacher Report Form, Conners Rating Scales (Conners 3),* and *Behavior Assessment System for Children, Third Edition* (Achenbach & Rescorla, 2001; Conners, 2008; Reynolds & Kamphaus, 2015). For youth with ADHD, a common measure is the *ADHD Rating Scale—5* (DuPaul et al., 2016). For conduct disorder, a common rating scale is the *Home and School Situations Questionnaire* (Barkley, 2013). Sample items from this questionnaire are in **Table 13.10**.

Table 13.10 Sample Items from the Home and School Situations Questionnaire

Does your child present any problems with compliance to instructions, commands, or rules for you in any of these situations?
Playing with other children
Mealtimes
When you are on the telephone
In public places
While in the car

Note. Items are scored as yes/no and then on a 1 to 9 scale where 1 = mild and 9 = severe.

Behavioral Observation

Observing the behavior of children with disruptive behavior in their natural environments, such as school and home, is an essential part of assessment. Behavioral observations help add information and clarify discrepancies from interview and rating scale data and are useful for examining specific aspects of behavior. Behavioral observations are also conducted to determine reasons for misbehavior. Examples include getting attention from parents, escaping situations such as classrooms, or obtaining tangible rewards such as toys. Therapists sometimes link behavioral observations to specific tests for ADHD symptoms. The *Continuous Performance Test* measures a child's ability to sustain attention and limit impulsivity on various tasks (Conners, 2014).

Biological Treatments for Disruptive Behavior Disorders

The primary biological treatment for youths with disruptive behavior disorders is *stimulant medication*. This might seem odd when considering ADHD and excessive aggressive behavior—why stimulate those symptoms? Recall, however, that a major problem in disruptive behavior disorders is trouble regulating one's behavior. Self-regulation deficits may be due to low levels of neurotransmitters such as dopamine and norepinephrine in key brain areas such as the prefrontal and cingulate cortexes (Pozzi et al., 2020). Stimulating inhibitory centers of the brain may actually help children regulate their behavior and become less overactive and impulsive.

The main stimulant medication for ADHD is *methylphenidate* (Ritalin or Concerta). About 55 to 75 percent of youths with ADHD benefit from the drug, as do many adults. The drugs help reduce overactivity, impulsivity, and inattentiveness, although less strong effects are evident for related issues such as academic learning (Boland et al., 2020; Pelham et al., 2022). One problem with stimulant medication is side effects that include headaches, stomachaches, tics, restlessness, weight loss, reduced appetite, and insomnia. For those with severe side effects, who do not respond to stimulant medication, or who have tic disorders, a nonstimulant medication, *atomoxetine* (Strattera), is also helpful for increasing norepinephrine levels and improving ADHD symptoms (Gul et al., 2022). Another problem with respect to stimulant medications is illicit use by college students to improve concentration, stay awake, control appetite, or change mood (Edinoff et al., 2022).

Stimulant medications have also been used for youths with conduct disorder, but the drugs tend to be more effective if a youth has comorbid ADHD symptoms. These medications help reduce classroom disruption, aggression, property destruction, and other conduct problems. Other drugs such as antianxiety, mood stabilizing, and antipsychotic medications are sometimes used as well to help control irritability or intense anger outbursts. Psychological treatments for oppositional defiant and conduct disorders are typically recommended as a first resort, however (Pisano & Masi, 2020).

Psychological Treatments for Disruptive Behavior Disorders

Psychological treatments for disruptive behavior disorders primarily focus on home-, school-, and community-based programs to reduce problematic symptoms and develop academic, social, and self-regulation skills. These treatments are described next.

Parent Training

Ineffective parenting is a key risk factor for disruptive behavior disorders, and home-based misbehaviors likely have to be addressed by parents. Parent training programs are thus a key treatment element for this population. Many parent training programs have been proposed, and their effectiveness with youth with disruptive behavior disorders is well documented. Parent training programs typically include the following components:

- Educate parents about a child's behavior problems and how best to address them.
- Teach parents to identify and specifically define problem behaviors, such as "My son will not wash the dishes when told," and establish clear rules for behavior.
- Provide appropriate attention and tangible rewards when a child engages in prosocial behaviors such as completing homework, finishing chores, and eating dinner quietly.
- Ignore minor inappropriate behaviors such as whining.
- Provide appropriate and consistent disciplinary procedures such as time-out or loss of privileges when a child engages in serious misbehaviors.
- Give effective commands that are clear, short, and linked to consequences.
- Use a token economy for prosocial and antisocial behaviors.
- Increase daily monitoring and supervision of a child.
- Teach parents to solve problems effectively and refrain from conflict.
- Increase daily contact with school officials to coordinate treatment and consequences for behavior, such as asking teachers to send home a daily behavior report card (Barkley & Robin, 2014; Dedousis-Wallace et al., 2021).

School-Based Behavior Management

Children with disruptive behavior disorders pose a challenge to teachers trying to maintain classroom order, so school-based behavior management is also a key treatment for this population. School-based treatment does overlap with parent-based training and the two procedures are often coordinated so a child always faces clear guidelines and consequences regarding their behavior. Will's transgressions at school should have been met with school- and home-based consequences such as loss of privileges. School-based strategies for children with ADHD can also include rotating rewards to maintain novelty and interest in them, providing frequent feedback about rules and self-regulation, developing social skills, and encouraging peers to help a child modify their behavior (Van der Oord & Tripp, 2020).

Social and Academic Skills Training

Children with disruptive behavior disorders have social and academic problems that can lead to further aggression and other misbehaviors, so training programs to enhance skills in these key areas are important and effective. These programs focus on helping youth control impulses and anger, develop social and problem-solving skills, cooperate better with others, and enhance academic competence. This may be done by challenging and modifying unrealistic thoughts, recognizing and addressing early warning signs of anger and impulsivity such as muscle tension, considering alternative explanations for another's behavior, rewarding appropriate participation in prosocial group activities, and receiving extra tutoring and educational support for academic deficits (Smith et al., 2020).

Katherine Frey/The Washington Post/Getty Images

The Freestate Challenge Academy is a residential program for at-risk high school students who have past issues with disruptive behavior.

Residential Treatment

A teenager may have to temporarily leave their family and be placed in residential or community-based treatment if disruptive behavior is severe. Such programs include camps, group homes, or other facilities where adolescents live until they can be reintegrated to their regular home. Residential treatment can consist of group therapy to develop social and self-care skills, anger management, family therapy to reduce conflict and build problem-solving strategies, supervised chores and other work, and systematic consequences for prosocial and inappropriate behavior. Residential treatment programs have been shown to produce short-term improvements in disruptive behavior, but their long-term effectiveness is less strong (Yeheskel et al., 2020).

Multisystemic Treatment

Another way to address severe disruptive behavior in children and adolescents is to provide extensive family services that include many psychological treatments. **Multisystemic treatment** is a family based approach that includes procedures described here as well as the following: therapy for parent psychopathology and substance use problems, involvement with appropriate peers, social support, school and vocational achievement, and linkage to agencies that can provide financial, housing, and employment support. This approach is effective in the long-term for reducing aggressive criminal activity, although ongoing access to treatment is likely necessary. This approach is sometimes used as a diversion program for adolescents arrested for a crime (refer to **Focus On Violence: Juvenile Arrests and Diversion**; Henggeler, 2015).

Table 13.11 Screening Questions for Disruptive Behavior Disorders

Does a particular child always seem to be in trouble both at home and school?
Does a particular child always seem to be "on the go" even at mealtime and bedtime?
Does a particular child seem much more inattentive, hyperactive, or impulsive than most kids his age?
Can the child in question concentrate well on her homework or chores?
Is a particular child often noncompliant with adult requests, much more so than most kids his age?
Does a particular child frequently engage in aggression, theft, deceitfulness, and rule-breaking behavior much more so than most kids her age?
Has the child in question been arrested?
Does a particular child often seem hostile, argumentative, and overly sensitive?

What If I Think a Child Has a Disruptive Behavior Disorder?

If you suspect your child or someone you know has ADHD or another disruptive behavior disorder, consider the screening questions in **Table 13.11**. If the answer to most of these questions is yes, a good idea would be to consult a clinical child psychologist and a psychiatrist who specialize in these issues. Consulting both professionals is especially important for ADHD because medication in conjunction with behavior management may be the best treatment approach. Many adults with ADHD symptoms may be helped with these therapies as well. If the answers to these questions are mostly no but you still believe considerable family conflict is resulting from a child's misbehavior, then seeking the help of a family therapist is a good idea.

Focus On Violence

Juvenile Arrests and Diversion

Adolescents with disruptive behavior disorders sometimes display aggression toward others as well as antisocial behavior such as property destruction or stealing. The issue of juvenile violence and other antisocial behavior has been widely debated, and many states lowered the age at which juveniles could be arrested and tried as adults for various crimes. Many youth have been incarcerated with adult prisoners and are at risk for severe exploitation because of their youth and inexperience.

Some states have reevaluated this practice and instituted "diversion" programs allowing first-time offenders to avoid incarceration (Sandøy, 2020). Examples include wilderness and boot camps, court-based mediation and conflict resolution, and referral to counseling services or group homes. Diversion programs typically focus on detailed assessment of a particular youth, expunging arrest and conviction records, family-based treatment, and linkage to community-based agencies.

A prominent example is the Miami-Dade Juvenile Assessment Center Post-Arrest Diversion Program. This program evaluates and addresses first-time youth offenders by providing treatment services as an alternative to incarceration. Charges against a youth may be dismissed after intense supervision and completion of treatment, often for substance use and family-related problems. This practice helps reduce stigma associated with "delinquency" and allows youths to experience a second chance at entering adulthood without the detriment of an arrest record.

Personal Narrative

Toni Wood

Toni Wood

As I sat among piles of unfolded laundry, sorted through junk mail and unpaid bills, and walked through the clutter in the house, my newly received diagnosis of ADHD did not surprise me. What *did* surprise me was not being diagnosed until I was 38 years old. My two boys had already been diagnosed years earlier, the oldest with ADHD inattentive and the youngest with ADHD combined. Both were diagnosed by first seeing a developmental pediatrician and ruling out physical ailments that could mimic symptoms of ADHD. From there they went to a health care practitioner for psychoeducational testing through the local children's hospital. They received comprehensive evaluations, but as an adult I could not utilize the same resources they used.

I started talking to other adults about this once-thought childhood disorder to gauge their reactions and seek referrals. I was mostly met with cynicism and doubt. Adult ADHD was just coming onto the scene as a plausible occurrence. Surprisingly, my search led to a friend who had recently been diagnosed. I say surprisingly because at the time, ADHD was not something people talked about openly. In a lot of ways, it still isn't.

Formally receiving the diagnosis did a number of things for me. It lifted a big weight off my shoulders by providing an answer to so many "why's?" in my past. But then it opened a bigger chasm by asking another question: "If I'm not who I thought I was, then who am I . . . really?" The diagnosis threw me into confusion as I tried to deal with these questions.

I soon found myself at the door of a therapist's office, certain I would be deemed "crazy." I wasn't. I *was* diagnosed as depressed, though: a common occurrence among adults diagnosed with ADHD. My treatment now included an antidepressant with the stimulant medication for ADHD while in therapy to learn how to integrate this new "person" into my view of myself.

During a period of four years or so, I rode the rollercoaster of depression. It took me in and out of valleys, through tunnels, up over mountains where things looked stunning only to plunge back to the valley by way of a long, dark tunnel. I withdrew from life, not trusting what it had to offer. I recall times when my children would walk past and see the glazed look in the general direction of the television, and hear them announce that "Mom's depressed again."

I can't recall that last journey out of the valley, how it was different from the others. I just knew it was. Life began

Long-Term Outcome for Children with Disruptive Behavior Disorders

Children with disruptive behavior disorders are at serious risk for later aggression and other mental disorders. Severe symptoms of hyperactivity and impulsivity in young children often predict later onset of oppositional defiant disorder. Oppositional defiant disorder is also an excellent predictor of later conduct disorder. The eventual comorbidity of all three disorders is especially likely if strong genetic contributions exist (Kanarik et al., 2022).

Children with ADHD generally experience stable symptoms over time, although these symptoms can change. Preschoolers with ADHD sometimes have sleep disturbances and can be difficult to control, overactive, inattentive, and noncompliant. Full-blown symptoms of inattention, overactivity, and impulsivity are observed as these children enter elementary school. Many children with ADHD then experience social and academic problems such as rejection by others, limited social skill development, and school failure. Will was having many of these problems (Nigg et al., 2020).

Severe levels of overactivity and impulsivity improve somewhat as children with ADHD reach adolescence. Still, about two-thirds continue to experience inattention, restlessness, and difficulty with impulse control. These adolescents are also at serious risk for conduct disorder, excessive substance use, depression, and school dropout. Parental inattention, family history of ADHD, intense family conflict, and social disadvantage often predict persistence of symptoms. Approximately 15 to 20 percent of those with ADHD in adolescence continue to have the full disorder in adulthood (Shaw & Sudre, 2021). For most adults, however, ADHD symptoms such as inattention and impulsivity often remain in the form of poor concentration or underachievement at work, forgetfulness and working memory problems, low frustration tolerance, loss of temper, and difficulty completing a college degree (Cherkasova et al., 2021; Di Lorenzo et al., 2021).

again. The piles seemed to have taken on a life of their own and the bills were all merged into one heap, as the phone rang off the hook with bill collectors on the other end. Taking the medication and armed with knowledge about myself, I started on the trek out of the abyss, tackling one issue at a time and creating systems that worked with my processing styles. My family looked on with guarded optimism wondering if they could trust what they were seeing.

The biggest change that came about was my desire to help others. Since my youngest son was diagnosed, I advocated for him at his school, getting accommodations, trying to keep his playing field level. I learned what his challenges were, found his strengths, and then went to work getting approval for him to use those strengths to overcome the challenges. I had learned a lot about myself and what I could do for others. The medication allowed me to focus and follow through on projects. I wanted to put those new skills to work helping others go through their difficult times.

Although I wanted to get to work instantly, I was able to recognize I needed further education. As I looked back, I saw that school had not been easy for me, despite the embossed gold sticker on the diploma. I remembered the long hours reading texts, and then rereading them, taking copious notes in class, feeling like every teacher talked too fast and I wrote too slow, then copying the notes later using different colors to set things apart. Remembering the anxiety around tests brought about its own anxiety; how was I going to survive another go-round? (It had been so long, I thought, since I had been to school.)

And the house—how would I be able to keep up with the bills, feed the kids, do the laundry . . . all the "normal" things others seemed to do so naturally? I didn't have answers to those questions; I just had the answer to how I was going to use my experience. I had determined it was not going to control me; I was going to control it. Once I made that determination, my life changed.

I learned what I believe to be one of the critical concepts that everyone needs to learn: experiences don't make or mold the person . . . it's what the person does with the experiences that defines who they are. I went back to college, using general education credits from my first degree to apply toward my second Bachelor of Science degree. With the help of the Disabilities Services office at the university, I graduated 18 months later, feeling much more successful than my first time through college. From there I went on to another challenge, taking an 11-month tele-class to become a coach to fulfill my goal of helping others. There was no Disabilities Services office but I knew enough that I managed just fine, and today I am now a certified coach working out of my home . . . helping others with ADHD.

Three developmental pathways may mark youths with oppositional defiant or conduct disorder. Two pathways begin in childhood and one in adolescence. The first childhood pathway is largely associated with symptoms of ADHD, especially impulsivity and severe family dysfunction. Such a pathway might apply best to Will. The second childhood pathway is associated with a callous-unemotional personality and difficult temperament. About half of youth whose conduct problems begin with these early pathways show enduring antisocial behavior into adolescence and adulthood. Finally, an adolescent-onset pattern is marked by general rebelliousness and association with deviant peers normally associated with adolescence, and usually does not lead to severe adjustment problems in adulthood (Dugré & Potvin, 2022; Junewicz & Billick, 2020).

Persistent ADHD and oppositional defiant/conduct symptoms seem best predicted by severity and complexity. This means that particularly severe symptoms, greater impairment, and substantial comorbidity predict problems throughout adolescence and adulthood. Other high-risk factors include early age of onset and aggression, depression, behavior problems in multiple settings, excessive substance use, and parental psychopathology (Bonham et al., 2021; Retz et al., 2021).

Section Summary

- Methods to assess youths with disruptive behavior disorders include interviews, rating scales, and behavioral observations.
- Biological treatment of disruptive behavior disorders includes stimulant medication to address imbalances in dopamine and norepinephrine.
- Parent training for treating disruptive behavior disorders involves defining behavior problems, providing appropriate consequences for child behavior, giving effective commands, and increasing supervision of a child and contact with school officials.

- School-based behavior management of disruptive behavior problems is often done in coordination with parent training and focuses on methods of helping children enhance control over their behavior.
- Social and academic skills training is used to help youth control impulses and anger and develop better social and academic skills.
- Residential treatment is sometimes used for severe cases of adolescent disruptive behavior disorder and includes placement in community-based settings with an eventual goal of returning a child to their home.
- Multisystemic treatment is a strategy for addressing severe disruptive behavior problems by providing treatment at different levels: family, school, and agency.
- Children with disruptive behavior disorders often have stable symptoms, especially in cases involving greater symptom severity and complexity.

Review Questions

1. What are the primary methods of assessing youths with disruptive behavior?
2. What are the main medications for children with ADHD, and what are their side effects?
3. Outline major goals of parent training and school-based behavior management for youths with disruptive behavior.
4. Describe social and academic skills training and residential and multisystemic treatments. How might these strategies be combined to address a child with severe disruptive behavior?
5. What is the long-term outcome for youths with ADHD and/or oppositional defiant and conduct disorder?

Final Comments

People with developmental disorders experience many problems functioning on a daily basis. They often rely on others for help and are frustrated with their inability to be fully independent. This is important to remember the next time you observe someone struggle with a seemingly simple task or have difficulty reading quickly. Of course, many of us need help from other people in our daily lives. If you know someone who seems to need a lot of extra help, then talking to someone about it or contacting a qualified mental health professional is a good idea.

Think about a child who acts up in a supermarket, movie theater, or airplane. Your first response is likely annoyance, and your second response might be to wonder what is wrong with the parents. Why don't they control their child? Many kids who act up can be managed better by parents, but consider the possibility that a parent is trying to address a child with a severe disruptive behavior disorder. Children with ADHD, oppositional defiant disorder, or conduct disorder can be challenging, both at home and out in public. When you next observe a child being disruptive, consider many possibilities.

Thought Questions

1. When you notice people with developmental disorders portrayed in television shows and films, what strikes you most? How realistic are the portrayals, given what you have learned here?
2. Who should make decisions for adults with developmental disorders? If you had a relative with mild intellectual developmental disorder, how much supervision would you want to provide?
3. If a friend of yours was pregnant with a child who had a major chromosomal aberration, what would you tell them?
4. What are the challenges of teaching children with learning disorders or ADHD or conduct problems in classrooms?
5. How might parents and teachers deal differently with boys and girls with disruptive behavior disorders?
6. What is the difference between normal adolescent rebelliousness and conduct disorder?
7. What are risks of medicating youths with ADHD?

Key Terms

developmental disorders 382
limited developmental disorders 383
pervasive developmental disorder 383
intellectual developmental disorder 384
adaptive functioning 384
autism spectrum disorder 385
learning disorder 388
fragile X syndrome 390
phenylketonuria (PKU) 390
sickle cell disease 391
Tay-Sachs disease 391
Down syndrome 392
teratogens 392
induction defects 393
migration defects 393
gene therapy 398
discrete-trial training 399
attention-deficit/hyperactivity disorder (ADHD) 403
oppositional defiant disorder 403
conduct disorder 403
disruptive behavior disorders 403
multisystemic treatment 415

Neurocognitive Disorders 14

Learning Objectives

LO 14.1 Describe the continuum from healthy cognitive functioning to neurocognitive disorders.

LO 14.2 Distinguish between the neurocognitive disorders using their diagnostic criteria and clinical characteristics.

LO 14.3 Summarize the epidemiology of neurocognitive disorders.

LO 14.4 Describe the stigma associated with neurocognitive disorders and its impact on those with the disorders and their caregivers.

LO 14.5 Discuss the risk factors for and prevention of neurocognitive disorders.

LO 14.6 Characterize the assessment and treatment of individuals with neurocognitive disorders.

Case William and Laura

William Ponder and his wife, Laura, were both 83 years old. They had been married 58 years and lived in a rural area much of their lives. The Ponders were arrested after an incident in which their checking account was grossly overdrawn. The bank manager said the couple had written more than $22,000 worth of bad checks during the previous several months. Detectives sought help from the Ponders' two grown sons and discovered that Mr. Ponder simply added zeroes to his checkbook balance whenever he needed to pay bills—he would change a $100 balance to $1,000 as necessary. No actual funds had been placed into the checking account for some time, however.

Detectives found the couple to be agitated, argumentative, and confused. The Ponders insisted no problem existed with their checking account and that they should not be hassled because "we're old and you just want our money." They could not recall their address at times, but other times seemed lucid. Mr. Ponder's memory of events was worse than his wife's memory, and he could no longer drive because of poor motor skills and forgetfulness about where he was. The couple thus depended on Mrs. Ponder's driving and on their two sons, who would check on their parents from time to time.

The presiding judge at a court hearing about the bad checks asked the couple to submit to a neuropsychological examination. The examination was to determine the extent to which Mr. and Mrs. Ponder were impaired and could no longer care for each other or manage their finances. Mrs. Ponder had moderate memory problems and seemed somewhat withdrawn and occasionally confused, and her scores on the test were in the low normal range. Mr. Ponder, however, struggled mightily on many of the items, especially those related to sensory-motor functioning and memory. He struggled to such an extent he began yelling at the examiner and refused to finish the examination.

The neuropsychologist also interviewed the couple's two sons, who said they were stunned at the recent turn of events. They did reveal their parents were not as "sharp" as in years past and that their parents had become more withdrawn from others. Both sons were particularly concerned about their father, who displayed major personality changes over the past two years. They described their father as typically mellow and easygoing who was transforming into a belligerent, short-tempered, and tense man. The sons once approached their parents about the possibility of living in an assisted care facility, but their father verbally threatened them for even mentioning the subject.

Mr. Ponder refused a second interview with the neuropsychologist, but Mrs. Ponder agreed. She confirmed her sons' reports and admitted she was sometimes afraid to live with her husband. He was becoming more aggressive and even struck her on two occasions, although he had never done so earlier in their marriage. He spent much of his day consuming alcohol, watching television, and sleeping. She also worried he might wander about and get lost.

Normal Changes During Aging and Neurocognitive Disorders: What Are They?

LO 14.1 Describe the continuum from healthy cognitive functioning to neurocognitive disorders.

Most of us experience subtle changes in memory and other thinking processes as we age. As we enter middle age, slightly greater problems start to occur with respect to *short-term memory*. Some may start to wonder more why they went upstairs (what was I looking for?), where they misplaced something (what did I do with those keys?), or the name of someone they met last night (who was that guy?). Other people experience changes in *long-term memory*, such as forgetting who won the World Series five years ago. Still others experience more problems with *episodic memory*, or ability to recall personal experiences from further in the past, such as the name of their fifth-grade teacher (Madore & Wagner, 2022).

These normal changes may relate to alterations in brain areas most responsible for memory. The *hippocampus* and *frontal lobes* may lose brain cells or be affected by neurochemical changes such as loss of dopamine over time (Ruíz-Salinas et al., 2020). These alterations, however, are often slow to develop, only mildly annoying, and do not significantly interfere with daily functioning. Once a person is reminded of something (you went upstairs to look for keys), the sought-after memory is usually retrieved quickly. Still, one can usually tell they are not as "quick" to remember things as in the past. They may experience more of what is known as the *tip-of-the-tongue phenomenon*, or feeling they know something they cannot immediately remember.

Normal changes occur in the frontal lobe and other brain areas over time, so one might also experience subtle difficulties in other cognitive areas. Such difficulties often involve processing and reasoning speed, decision-making, planning for events, paying attention, and exercising good judgment (Armstrong et al., 2020). A person may find it takes more time than usual to decide which car to buy, has trouble keeping straight

Mrs. Ponder conceded she was feeling overwhelmed by having to care for her husband as well as the house. She continued to allow Mr. Ponder to control the couple's finances and worried that "something awful" was going to happen to their retirement account. Mrs. Ponder was reportedly becoming more depressed and confused and was having trouble eating and sleeping. Her mood was somber as she realized her husband was changing, that he was not the same loving man he used to be, and that they could be in serious legal trouble or be forced to sell their home. Mrs. Ponder knew her future must involve enormous change. She worried about where she would live and how much money was left, but mostly she worried about her husband's fading physical and mental health.

Darryl Brooks/Shutterstock.com

The neuropsychologist concluded that Mr. Ponder was likely in middle stages of a neurocognitive disorder, perhaps due to Alzheimer's disease. Mrs. Ponder displayed normal memory changes for someone her age, but she was also depressed and occasionally confused, which may have led to mild thought and memory problems. The neuropsychologist reported to the court her findings and the Ponders were allowed to make proper restitution to various businesses without additional legal trouble. The state department of aging was notified, however, and the Ponders' life as they had known it for decades was about to change dramatically.

What Do You Think?

1. Which of Mr. and Mrs. Ponder's symptoms seem typical of someone in later stages of life and which seem very different?
2. What external events and internal factors might be responsible for Mr. Ponder's dramatic changes in thoughts and behaviors?
3. What are you curious about regarding Mr. and Mrs. Ponder?
4. Do the Ponders remind you in any way of someone you know? How so?
5. How might the Ponders' memory problems affect their lives in the future?

all the details of organizing a wedding or concentrating on a long lecture, or cannot navigate a complex driving trip in a strange city. Subtle changes may also occur with respect to computing mathematical problems, sorting objects, and discriminating patterns. What makes all of these changes normal, however, is the fact that most everyone experiences them to some extent and that these experiences do not interfere significantly with daily functioning.

General memory, learning, or concentration problems do increase over time. The percentage of people experiencing mild cognitive impairment is 10.9 percent at age 50 to 59 years, 11.5 percent at age 60 to 69 years, 15.8 percent at age 70 to 79 years, and 21.3 percent at age 80 years or older (Bai et al., 2022). These figures are significant but also tell us that the large majority of older people *do not* have substantial cognitive problems. People aged 65 years and older tend to be married, living in a household, and owners of their own home (U.S. Department of Health and Human Services, 2021). These facts dispel the notion that most older people must depend on others for their livelihood.

For some people, however, memory and thinking changes do become much more severe under *certain circumstances* (refer to **Continuum of Thinking and Memory Problems and Neurocognitive Disorder**). Someone's ability to remember information and pay close attention to others is likely impaired when they

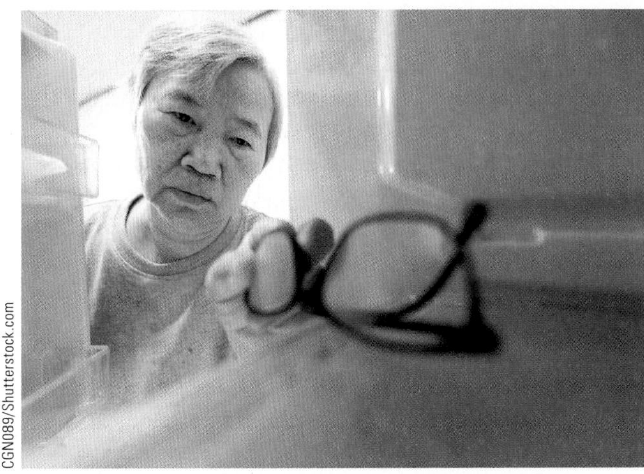
CGN089/Shutterstock.com

For some older people, memory and thinking changes can be severe.

Continuum of Thinking and Memory Problems and Neurocognitive Disorder

	Normal	Mild
Emotions	Stable emotions during thinking and recall.	Mild frustration and concern following memory lapses.
Cognitions	Good thinking and memory processes.	Occasional lapses of attention or memory or tip-of-the-tongue phenomenon.
Behaviors	Engaging in good work and social behavior.	Slight delays in work or requests to repeat something someone has said.

have been drinking heavily, have just come out of surgery under general anesthesia, or have a high fever. People in these states are often confused and have trouble staying awake. Such impairments in cognition, which are usually temporary and reversible, are often referred to as **delirium**.

For other people, memory and thinking changes become much more severe as they age. Someone's ability to recall information may still be impaired even after a reminder is given, or a person's forgetfulness may become very frequent. A person may start to forget how to do simple things like tying a shoelace or using a microwave oven. They may also have trouble learning new tasks, especially complicated ones, and struggle to have conversations with others. Other problems might include the need to repeat oneself or to constantly ask the same question to get information and remember it. A person in this situation, like Mr. Ponder, might also experience personality changes, loss of social skills or interest in daily activities, and psychological issues such as worry and sadness about cognitive changes. These cognitive changes are massive, often irreversible, and *do* significantly interfere with daily functioning. People undergoing such dramatic changes in memory and cognition experience **dementia**. The following sections review features of these two major sets of **neurocognitive disorders**: delirium and dementia.

Ian Shaw/Alamy Stock Photo

People with delirium often have trouble understanding time and location.

Moderate	Neurocognitive Disorder—less severe	Neurocognitive Disorder—more severe
Increasing frustration at loss of attention and memory or irritability with others.	Intense anxiety and concern about attention and memory loss.	Dramatically decreased emotional behavior, including apathy about one's condition.
Ongoing and regular lapses of attention or memory, especially short-term memory.	Intense decreases in attention, memory, processing speed, planning ability, and judgment.	Extreme loss of attention and memory, such that long-term memories become lost.
Greater difficulties organizing and completing work and engaging in conversations.	Ongoing inability to converse well with others; getting lost frequently and wandering.	Dramatically decreased physical behavior; little verbal activity and sleeping much.

Neurocognitive Disorders: Features and Epidemiology

LO 14.2 Distinguish between the neurocognitive disorders using their diagnostic criteria and clinical characteristics.

LO 14.3 Summarize the epidemiology of neurocognitive disorders.

Delirium

Have you ever been in a state of mind where things around you seemed fuzzy or confusing? Perhaps you were just coming out of surgery with general anesthesia, were extremely tired, or stayed a little too long at happy hour. Your ability to think clearly or even to stay awake may have been affected. Delirium exists when someone's normal state of thinking or consciousness is impaired (refer to **Table 14.1**; American Psychiatric Association [APA], 2022). Impairment due to delirium is typically short-lived, and a person usually recovers fully. Examples include fading of general anesthesia or another drug, becoming rehydrated, recovering from a high fever, or reducing stress or exhaustion.

A person in a state of delirium often has trouble interacting with others and is not clearly aware of surrounding events. They may have great trouble maintaining attention in a conversation or moving attention from one person to another. Focused attention

Table 14.1 DSM-5-TR

Delirium
A. A disturbance in attention and awareness (reduced orientation to the environment).
B. The disturbance develops over a short period of time (usually hours to a few days), represents a change from baseline attention and awareness, and tends to fluctuate in severity during the course of a day.
C. An additional disturbance in cognition.
D. The disturbances in Criteria A and C are not better explained by another preexisting, established, or evolving neurocognitive disorder and do not occur in the context of a severely reduced level of arousal, such as coma.
E. There is evidence from the history, physical examination, or laboratory findings that the disturbance is a direct physiological consequence of another medical condition, substance intoxication or withdrawal, or exposure to a toxin, or is due to multiple etiologies. Specify if due to substance intoxication, substance withdrawal, medication, another medical condition, or multiple etiologies; if acute or persistent; if hyperactive, hypoactive, or mixed level of activity.

American Psychiatric Association. (2022). *Diagnostic and statistical manual of mental disorders* (5th ed., text rev.). Arlington, VA: American Psychiatric Association.

or concentration is difficult in these situations as well. Other higher-order cognitive processes are also impaired, including ability to remember information, speak clearly, or integrate information such as assembling a puzzle. Delirium is sometimes associated with *disorientation*, meaning a person has difficulty remembering personal information, where they are, or even what time it is (Stollings et al., 2021). A person may have been in a car accident that caused temporary inability to identify oneself, realize they are in a hospital, or recognize day or night. Mrs. Ponder sometimes showed symptoms of delirium when she appeared confused or unsure around others. These symptoms may have been due to sleep deprivation or stress.

Another key aspect of delirium is fluctuation of the problem over hours and days. A person may be lucid and can maintain a conversation at times but seem confused and sleepy at other times (Cortés-Beringola et al., 2021). Many people in a state of delirium slip in and out of sleep or conscious awareness. A person's mood may also shift quickly, perhaps from anger to apathy to giddiness within a short time. Motor behavior can change quickly as well, as when someone becomes agitated and then slows down considerably or sleeps (Ramirez-Bermudez et al., 2022). Psychotic-like symptoms of delusions and hallucinations can also occur, which make states of delirium potentially dangerous. Someone in this state should never drive a car or be left unsupervised.

Delirium is usually caused by general medical conditions or substance intoxication or withdrawal, but many other factors can lead to the problem as well (refer to **Table 14.2**). Specific medical evidence is usually necessary to assign a diagnosis of delirium, but direct observation can sometimes be enough. If delirium might be due to an electrolyte imbalance, then a medical assessment is likely necessary. If delirium might be due to recent alcohol intake, however, then simply observing the person or interviewing significant others may be sufficient. States of delirium should not be assumed when a person may actually be in a state of dementia, aspects of which are discussed next.

Table 14.2 Possible Causes of Delirium

Possible Causes of Delirium
Substance intoxication
Substance withdrawal
Metabolic/endocrine disturbance
Traumatic brain injury
Seizures
Neoplastic disease
Intracranial infection
Systemic infection
Cerebrovascular disorder
Organ insufficiency
Other central nervous system etiologies
Other systemic etiologies:
Heat stroke
Hypothermia
Radiation
Electrocution
Postoperative state
Immunosuppression
Fractures

Innovated Captures/Fotolia LLC

Delirium is often induced by alcohol or other drug use.

Dementia and Major and Mild Neurocognitive Disorder

Delirium involves cognitive deficits that are acute, develop quickly, fluctuate, and are typically reversible. Dementia, on the other hand, involves cognitive deficits that:

- are *chronic*, meaning the deficits last for long periods
- develop *slowly*, meaning gradual onset of the deficits
- show a *progressive* course, meaning little fluctuation in the deficits
- are usually *irreversible*, meaning the deficits do not improve with time

Cognitive deficits in dementia also involve problems with learning, memory, attention, language, recognition, planning, decision making, problem solving, concentration, judgment, and perceptual-motor ability (such as driving). Mr. Ponder had many problems with mathematical ability, memory, and focused attention. Delirium and dementia often occur together and share common etiologies such as general medical conditions, substance use, or some combination of these, and symptoms of each also commonly resemble those of depression and schizophrenia (refer to **Table 14.3**; Utsumi et al., 2021). Delirium is usually reversible, however, so this chapter concentrates on dementia or delirium with dementia.

Dementias may be characterized as a neurocognitive disorder that can differ in severity (refer to **Table 14.4**; APA, 2022). A **major neurocognitive disorder** involves significant cognitive decline and interference with daily activities such as paying bills. This was the case for Mr. Ponder. A **mild neurocognitive disorder** involves modest cognitive decline but without interference in daily activities. This was the case for Mrs. Ponder. A mild neurocognitive disorder may eventually progress to a major neurocognitive disorder. The terms dementia and major neurocognitive disorder remain generally synonymous, although dementia sometimes specifically refers to older persons with multiple cognitive problems.

Dementias can also be characterized as presenile or senile. You may have heard the term "senile" sometimes applied to older people. This term is not a clinical one but refers only to some loss of mental ability with age. *Presenile dementia*, however, commonly refers to onset of dementia symptoms before age 65 years, whereas *senile dementia* is a term that commonly refers to onset of dementia symptoms after age 65 years (van de Veen et al., 2021). People with presenile (or early onset) dementias typically show more severe symptoms and often die from the disorders much sooner than people with senile dementias. Presenile dementias may have a more aggressive course due to stronger genetic or other biological links (Bezine, 2022).

The most common types of neurocognitive disorder are described in this chapter. Many *other* types exist, however. Examples include neurocognitive disorder brought on by HIV disease, Prion disease, Huntington's disease, brain tumor, thyroid problems, malnutrition, blood that collects on the surface of the brain (subdural hematoma), infections, metabolic disorders, and advanced stages of multiple sclerosis (APA, 2022). Creutzfeldt-Jakob disease, a condition that leads to rapid neurological impairment, can also produce neurocognitive disorder and death (Hermann et al., 2021). Various substances or toxins can also lead to neurocognitive disorder if ingested for prolonged periods. Examples include carbon monoxide, inhalants, lead, and mercury (Cha et al., 2022).

Alzheimer's Disease

One of the most severe mental problems discussed in this textbook is **Alzheimer's disease** (refer to **Table 14.5**; APA, 2022). Some of you may already be familiar with this disorder by reading about famous people who had the disorder or by knowing older family members with the disorder. Alzheimer's disease involves slow and irreversible progression of dementia. Alzheimer's disease necessarily involves multiple cognitive deficits, but especially those related to memory. The disorder accounts for about 60 to 70 percent of all cases of dementia (World Health Organization [WHO], 2021).

Table 14.3 Differential Diagnosis of Delirium, Dementia, Depression, and Schizophrenia

	Delirium	Dementia	Depression	Schizophrenia
Onset	Acute	Insidious[a]	Variable	Variable
Course	Fluctuating	Often progressive	Diurnal variation	Variable
Reversibility	Usually[b]	Not usually	Usually but can be recurrent	No, but has exacerbations
Level of consciousness	Impaired	Unimpaired until late stages	Generally unimpaired	Unimpaired (perplexity in acute stage)
Attention and memory	Inattention is primary with poor memory	Poor memory without marked inattention	Mild attention problems, inconsistent pattern, memory intact	Poor attention, memory intact
Hallucinations	Usually visual; can be auditory, tactile, gustatory, olfactory	Can be visual or auditory	Usually auditory	Usually auditory
Delusions	Fleeting, fragmented, usually persecutory	Paranoid, often fixed	Complex and mood congruent	Frequent, complex, systematized, often paranoid

[a]Except for large strokes.
[b]Can be chronic (paraneoplastic syndrome, central nervous system adverse events of medications, severe brain damage).
From *Essentials of Neuropsychiatry and Behavioral Neurosciences* (2nd ed.), by Stuart C. Yudofsky, M.D, and Robert E. Hales, M.D., M.B.A., Table 5.3 p. 154.

The following cognitive deficits are likely to occur in someone with Alzheimer's disease:

- *Aphasia*, or impaired ability to use or comprehend spoken language, as when a person has difficulty speaking or cannot understand what is being said to them
- *Apraxia*, or impaired voluntary movement despite adequate sensory and muscle functioning, as when a person can no longer tie their shoes
- *Agnosia*, or impaired ability to recognize people or common objects, as when a person fails to recognize loved ones or basic items such as a spoon
- *Executive functioning deficits*, which include impaired ability to plan or organize daily activities, engage in abstract thinking, or understand the sequence of events, such as maneuvering driving turns to get to and from a grocery store

Table 14.4 DSM-5-TR

Major Neurocognitive Disorder
A. Evidence of significant cognitive decline from a previous level of performance in one or more cognitive domains based on: 1. Concern of the individual, a knowledgeable informant, or the clinician that there has been a significant decline in cognitive function; and 2. A substantial impairment in cognitive performance, preferably documented by standardized neuropsychological testing or, in its absence, another quantified clinical assessment.
B. The cognitive deficits interfere with independence in everyday activities.
C. The cognitive deficits do not occur exclusively in the context of a delirium.
D. The cognitive deficits are not better explained by another mental disorder. Specify if due to Alzheimer's disease, frontotemporal lobar degeneration, Lewy body disease, vascular disease, traumatic brain injury, substance/medication use, HIV infection, Prion disease, Parkinson's disease, Huntington's disease, another medical condition, multiple etiologies, or unspecified.
Mild Neurocognitive Disorder
A. Evidence of modest cognitive decline from a previous level of performance in one or more cognitive domains based on: 1. Concern of the individual, a knowledgeable informant, or the clinician that there has been a mild decline in cognitive function; and 2. A modest impairment in cognitive performance, preferably documented by standardized neuropsychological testing or, in its absence, another quantified clinical assessment.
B. The cognitive deficits do not interfere with capacity for independence in everyday activities.
C. The cognitive deficits do not occur exclusively in the context of a delirium.
D. The cognitive deficits are not better explained by another mental disorder.

American Psychiatric Association. (2022). *Diagnostic and statistical manual of mental disorders* (5th ed., text rev.). Arlington, VA: American Psychiatric Association.

Table 14.5 DSM-5-TR

Major or Mild Neurocognitive Disorder Due to Alzheimer's Disease
A. The criteria are met for major or mild neurocognitive disorder.
B. There is insidious onset and gradual progression of impairment in one or more cognitive domains.
C. Criteria are met for either probable or possible Alzheimer's disease as follows: **For major neurocognitive disorder:** **Probable Alzheimer's disease** is diagnosed if either of the following is present; otherwise, **possible Alzheimer's disease** should be diagnosed. 1. Evidence of a causative Alzheimer's disease genetic mutation from family history or genetic testing. 2. All three of the following are present: a. Clear evidence of decline in memory and learning and at least one other cognitive domain. b. Steadily progressive, gradual decline in cognition, without extended plateaus. c. No evidence of mixed etiology. **For mild neurocognitive disorder:** **Probable Alzheimer's disease** is diagnosed if there is evidence of a causative Alzheimer's disease genetic mutation from either genetic testing or family history. **Possible Alzheimer's disease** is diagnosed if there is no evidence of a causative Alzheimer's disease genetic mutation from either genetic testing or family history, and all three of the following are present: 1. Clear evidence of decline in memory and learning. 2. Steadily progressive, gradual decline in cognition, without extended plateaus. 3. No evidence of mixed etiology.
D. The disturbance is not better explained by cerebrovascular disease, another neurodegenerative disease, the effects of a substance, or another mental, neurological, or systemic disorder.

American Psychiatric Association. (2022). *Diagnostic and statistical manual of mental disorders* (5th ed., text rev.). Arlington, VA: American Psychiatric Association.

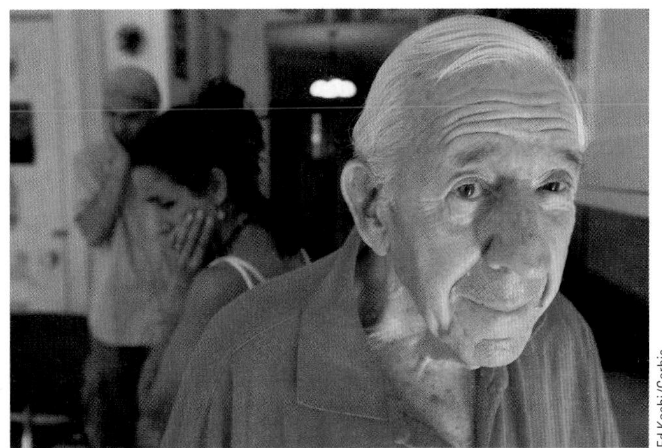

Ed Kashi/Corbis

Herb Winokur has dementia and Parkinson's disease. His daughter must decide how to provide the best care for him because his condition makes it virtually impossible for him to complete sentences and maintain his independent lifestyle.

These cognitive problems develop slowly and worsen over a period of five to nine years. People with Alzheimer's disease in early stages of the disorder may appear simply forgetful or distracted when speaking to others. They may become confused about where they are, take less initiative in daily activities, and have trouble with logical thought. These subtle impairments eventually worsen, however, as people with Alzheimer's disease will often take longer time to complete simple tasks such as making a sandwich or will have greater difficulty with more complicated tasks (Vik-Mo et al., 2020). Mr. Ponder could no longer drive himself places or compute complex mathematical problems.

As Alzheimer's disease progresses further, personality changes are observed, and problems start to develop with skills practiced for many years, such as reading and writing (Strikwerda-Brown, 2022). Mr. Ponder was becoming more belligerent and tense and clearly had trouble with his checking account. People with Alzheimer's disease also begin to have enormous problems interacting with others and completing basic motor tasks such as tying shoelaces. Long-term memory and other cognitive areas of functioning eventually become much more impaired, even to the point where a person cannot recognize others or care for themself (McDonough et al., 2020). Mr. Ponder needed assistance doing everyday activities such as getting dressed and may get to the point where he will not recognize his wife of nearly 60 years. Basic abilities such as speech, walking, feeding, and toileting are severely impaired in final stages of Alzheimer's disease. Someone with the disorder is often placed under supervised care and usually dies from pneumonia or other diseases (Wong, 2020).

Lewy Bodies

Another neurocognitive disorder that is similar to Alzheimer's disease involves **Lewy bodies** (refer to **Table 14.6**; APA, 2022). This disorder, sometimes called *Lewy body disease*, includes most of the key features of Alzheimer's disease, but may also include visual hallucinations, muscle tremors, and a more fluctuating course of symptoms (Borghammer et al., 2021). A person with advanced Lewy body disease may speak normally at one time of day and later experience great difficulty interacting with others. The problem is linked mostly to *Lewy bodies* in the cortex, substantia nigra, and other brain areas (Silva-Rodriguez et al., 2022). Lewy bodies are accumulations of certain proteins in neurons that lead to cell damage. Lewy body disease may account for about 3 to 7 percent of cases of dementia, although significant overlap with Alzheimer's disease is often found (Milán-Tomás et al., 2021).

Table 14.6 DSM-5-TR

Major or Mild Neurocognitive Disorder with Lewy Bodies
A. The criteria are met for major or mild neurocognitive disorder.
B. The disorder has an insidious onset and gradual progression.
C. The disorder meets a combination of core diagnostic features and suggestive diagnostic features for either probable or possible neurocognitive disorder with Lewy bodies. **For probable major or mild neurocognitive disorder with Lewy bodies**, the individual has two core features, or one suggestive feature, with one or more core features. **For possible major or mild neurocognitive disorder with Lewy bodies**, the individual has only one core feature, or one or more suggestive features. 1. Core diagnostic features: a. Fluctuating cognition with pronounced variations in attention and alertness. b. Recurrent visual hallucinations that are well formed and detailed. c. Spontaneous features of parkinsonism, with onset subsequent to the development of cognitive decline. 2. Suggestive diagnostic features: a. Meets criteria for rapid eye movement sleep behavior disorder. b. Severe neuroleptic sensitivity.
D. The disturbance is not better explained by cerebrovascular disease, another neurodegenerative disease, the effects of a substance, or another mental, neurological, or systemic disorder.

American Psychiatric Association. (2022). *Diagnostic and statistical manual of mental disorders* (5th ed., text rev.). Arlington, VA: American Psychiatric Association.

Vascular Disease

Vascular disease, sometimes also referred to as *cerebrovascular disease*, is another common form of neurocognitive disorder but one caused by problems with blood vessels that supply the brain with oxygen and other nutrients (refer to **Table 14.7**; APA, 2022). The most common blood vessel problem that leads to vascular-based neurocognitive disorder, sometimes called *vascular dementia*, is a *stroke*. A stroke occurs when a blood vessel is blocked or bursts, which denies oxygen to parts of the brain; various areas of the brain, especially the *cortex*, can suffer potentially severe damage. Vascular disease that results in vascular dementia could also affect only *subcortical* areas of the brain. This can occur from hypertension, diabetes, or heart disease (Bir et al., 2021).

A stroke is most often caused by blood clots that block a key artery to the brain—an *ischemic* stroke. More unusually, a stroke may be caused by a ruptured blood vessel—a *hemorrhagic* or bleeding stroke. Damage from strokes may be limited, as when a person is treated quickly and perhaps only suffers moderate memory problems. Damage from a stroke can also be severe and lead to paralysis and dementia that resemble symptoms of Alzheimer's disease (Papanastasiou et al., 2021). Severe damage is often the result of multiple strokes.

What is the difference between neurocognitive disorder due to vascular disease versus Alzheimer's disease? The general symptoms of each disorder are quite similar, but people with vascular-based neurocognitive disorder more often experience:

- *a history of stroke*
- *faster, even abrupt, onset of dementia symptoms*, such as after a stroke
- *better retention of overall cognitive functioning*, especially memory
- *stepwise deterioration*, meaning dementia symptoms can fluctuate
- *focal neurological signs*, meaning certain deficits such as difficulty writing can indicate what areas of the brain, such as the parietal lobe, were most affected
- *patchy distribution of deficits*, meaning some areas of cognitive functioning are left intact and others are greatly impaired (Arena et al., 2020)

Vascular dementia accounts for about 15 percent of all dementias, although many people with vascular-based neurocognitive disorder also have Alzheimer's disease (Wolters & Ikram, 2019). This is *mixed dementia*. People with vascular-based neurocognitive disorder, like those with Alzheimer's disease, usually deteriorate with respect to mental and physical health, but death may come sooner for people with vascular problems (Wu et al., 2021).

Table 14.7 DSM-5-TR

Major or Mild Vascular Neurocognitive Disorder
A. The criteria are met for major or mild neurocognitive disorder.
B. The clinical features are consistent with a vascular etiology, as suggested by either of the following: 1. Onset of the cognitive deficits is temporally related to one or more cerebrovascular events. 2. Evidence for decline is prominent in complex attention (including processing speed) and frontal-executive function.
C. There is evidence of the presence of cerebrovascular disease from history, physical examination, and/or neuroimaging considered sufficient to account for the neurocognitive deficits.
D. The symptoms are not better explained by another brain disease or systemic disorder. **Probable vascular neurocognitive disorder** is diagnosed if one of the following is present; otherwise **possible vascular neurocognitive disorder** should be diagnosed: 1. Clinical criteria are supported by neuroimaging evidence of significant parenchymal injury attributed to cerebrovascular disease. 2. The neurocognitive syndrome is temporally related to one or more documented cerebrovascular events. 3. Both clinical and genetic evidence of cerebrovascular disease is present. **Possible vascular neurocognitive disorder** is diagnosed if the clinical criteria are met but neuroimaging is not available and the temporal relationship of the neurocognitive syndrome with one or more cerebrovascular events is not established.

American Psychiatric Association. (2022). *Diagnostic and statistical manual of mental disorders* (5th ed., text rev.). Arlington, VA: American Psychiatric Association.

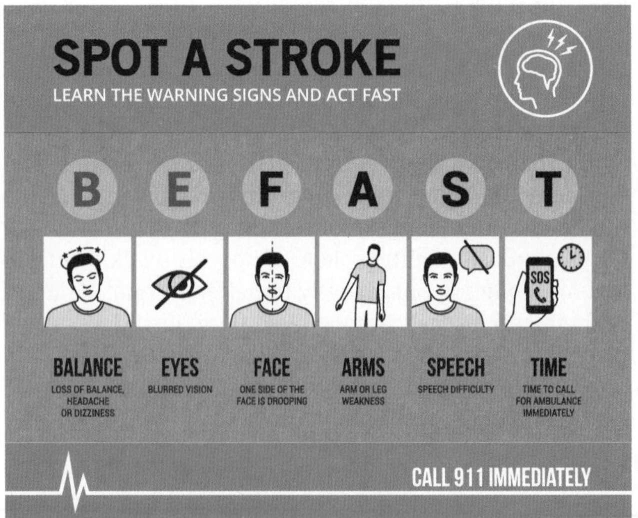

Elenabsl/Shutterstock.com

Vascular dementia and partial paralysis are often caused by stroke. Knowing the warning signs of stroke and acting fast can be important for prevention.

Parkinson's Disease

Parkinson's disease is a progressive neurological disorder marked by unusual movements that may lead to a neurocognitive disorder (refer to **Table 14.8**; APA, 2022). Unusual movements include *resting tremors* in which a person has uncontrollable hand shaking or "pill-rolling" behavior with the fingers. The tremors are called resting ones because shaking tends to be worse when the person is idle. Other unusual movements also characterize this population, including the following:

- *rigidity*, or difficulty moving muscles and feeling stiff
- *bradykinesia*, or very slow movement or trouble initiating movement, such as trying to walk again after stopping
- *hypokinesia* and *akinesia*, or poor quality of movement and lack of movement
- *postural instability*, or difficulty standing after sitting, staying in one position, maintaining balance, or standing erect
- *hypomimia*, or lack of facial expression
- *other unusual actions* such as inability to blink eyes, maintain appropriate eye movements, swing arms, or walk without shuffling

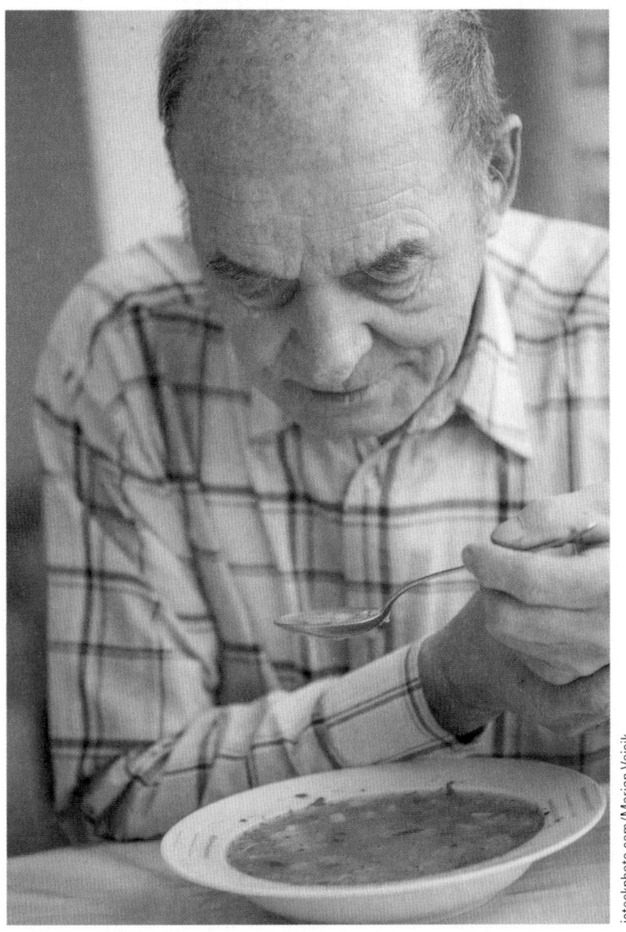
istockphoto.com/Marian Vejcik

People with Parkinson's disease typically have motor difficulties and may develop dementia in advanced stages of the disorder.

Dementia occurs in about 25 to 30 percent of those with Parkinson's disease, especially in later stages (Scheffels et al., 2020). People with Parkinson's disease show less of the classic characteristics of *cortical* dementia found in people with Alzheimer's disease. Instead, they often display *subcortical* dementia, meaning their primary cognitive problems include slowed thinking and difficulty using newly acquired knowledge and retrieving information from memory (Saini et al., 2020). A person with advanced Parkinson's disease may have trouble processing what others say, thinking abstractly to understand something new, and integrating visual information for tasks like driving. Language is also problematic for people with Parkinson's disease—many have monotone, slurred, and repetitive speech. Depression and apathy are common in people with subcortical dementias due to Parkinson's disease (Giannouli & Tsolaki, 2021). Parkinson's disease has a chronic, progressive course that can lead to severe motor problems and death (Weintraub et al., 2022).

Pick's Disease

Pick's disease is characterized mainly by deterioration in the *frontal* and *temporal* brain lobes. Pick's disease is thus perhaps the most well-known of what is called *frontotemporal dementias*. People with Pick's disease demonstrate many of the major characteristics of people with Alzheimer's disease but generally experience earlier age of onset of dementia and personality and

Table 14.8 DSM-5-TR

Major or Mild Neurocognitive Disorder Due to Parkinson's Disease
A. The criteria are met for major or mild neurocognitive disorder.
B. The disturbance occurs in the setting of established Parkinson's disease.
C. There is insidious onset and gradual progression of impairment.
D. The neurocognitive disorder is not attributable to another medical condition and is not better explained by another mental disorder. **Major or mild neurocognitive disorder probably due to Parkinson's disease** should be diagnosed if 1 and 2 are both met. **Major or mild neurocognitive disorder possibly due to Parkinson's disease** should be diagnosed if 1 or 2 is met: 1. There is no evidence of mixed etiology. 2. The Parkinson's disease clearly precedes the onset of the neurocognitive disorder.

American Psychiatric Association. (2022). *Diagnostic and statistical manual of mental disorders* (5th ed., text rev.). Arlington, VA: American Psychiatric Association.

behavioral changes. Frontotemporal dementias account for about 10 to 20 percent of all dementia cases, especially early-onset cases. These dementias are marked by severe personality changes that can lead to disinhibition, poor social skills, and lack of insight into one's behavior (Guger et al., 2021). Major features of neurocognitive disorder due to frontotemporal problems are in **Table 14.9**. Outward symptoms of Pick's disease and Alzheimer's disease are difficult to distinguish, and many times an accurate diagnosis can be made only at autopsy.

Table 14.9 DSM-5-TR

Major or Mild Frontotemporal Neurocognitive Disorder
A. The criteria are met for major or mild neurocognitive disorder.
B. The disturbance has insidious onset and gradual progression.
C. Either (1) or (2): 1. Behavioral variant: a. Three or more of the following behavioral symptoms: i. Behavioral disinhibition. ii. Apathy or inertia. iii. Loss of sympathy or empathy. iv. Perseverative, stereotyped or compulsive/ritualistic behavior. v. Hyperorality and dietary changes. b. Prominent decline in social cognition and/or executive abilities. 2. Language variant: a. Prominent decline in language ability, in the form of speech production, word finding, object naming, grammar, or word comprehension.
D. Relative sparing of learning and memory and perceptual-motor function.
E. The disturbance is not better explained by cerebrovascular disease, another neurodegenerative disease, the effects of a substance, or another mental, neurological, or systemic disorder. **Probable frontotemporal neurocognitive disorder** is diagnosed if either of the following is present; otherwise, **possible frontotemporal neurocognitive disorder** should be diagnosed: 1. Evidence of a causative frontotemporal neurocognitive disorder genetic mutation, from either family history or genetic testing. 2. Evidence of disproportionate frontal and/or temporal lobe involvement from neuroimaging. **Possible frontotemporal neurocognitive disorder** is diagnosed if there is no evidence of a genetic mutation, and neuroimaging has not been performed.

American Psychiatric Association. (2022). *Diagnostic and statistical manual of mental disorders* (5th ed., text rev.). Arlington, VA: American Psychiatric Association.

Other Problems

Neurocognitive disorders can also arise from other problems such as traumatic brain injury (APA, 2022). In addition, severe memory problems are sometimes observed in people with chronic and excessive substance use. Memory problems may be *anterograde*, meaning a person has trouble forming new memories, or *retrograde*, meaning memories of past events and experiences are affected (Fang et al., 2022). People with chronic, excessive substance use may have trouble learning others' names and remembering events that recently happened, such as what they had for dinner last night. *Spontaneous recall*, in which a person is asked to remember something on the spot, such as their address, can be impaired as well. The problem may be so severe a person is continually lost, unable to communicate effectively, or has difficulty holding a job.

Korsakoff's syndrome is a problem associated with chronic alcohol use. Ongoing memory problems of people with this syndrome can be severe and linked to confusion and disorientation. Many people with Korsakoff's syndrome engage in *confabulation*, or the creation of fables or stories to fill memory gaps and hide memory problems. Korsakoff's syndrome is caused by lack of *thiamine* because a person drinks alcohol instead of eating a balanced diet. Blood vessel hemorrhages and damage to neurons can thus occur (Segobin & Pitel, 2021). Some but not complete improvement in symptoms may result when a person withdraws from alcohol use and resumes appropriate nutrition (Popa et al., 2021).

Epidemiology of Neurocognitive Disorders

The U.S. Department of Health and Human Services reports that people aged 65 years and older represent 16.0 percent of the total American population, but this percentage is expected to rise to 21.6 percent by 2040. The percentage of people aged 85 years and older will more than double by 2040 and include 14.4 million people. This oldest age group will be one of the fastest growing age groups in the country! This trend in aging occurs in many other countries as well. The prevalence of neurocognitive disorders increases with age, so we can expect many more people to experience problems of delirium and dementia over the next decades.

Delirium is a disorder that can affect anyone because the problem can result from various medical conditions, substances, and other variables (refer to **Focus On College Students: Delirium**). The prevalence of delirium does increase with age, however: 1 to 2 percent for people aged 65+ years and 10 percent for people aged 85+ years (de Lange et al., 2013). Medication is a common variable that results in delirium. Patients medicated for a stroke-related condition often experience delirium (Rhee et al., 2022). About 9 to 32 percent of people in inpatient settings, especially those leaving surgery, have delirium (Koirala et al., 2020). People living in geriatric hospitals and nursing homes also have relatively high rates of delirium (Komici et al., 2022).

The rate of dementia also increases with age, especially after age 80 years (refer to **Figure 14.1**). Most older persons are still *unaffected*, however—only about 5 to 8.5 percent of people older than 60 years have dementia (Kreisl & Reitz, 2018). Rates of dementia increase sharply among persons in long-term care facilities such as hospices and nursing homes (44.5 to 47.7 percent; Centers for Disease Control and Prevention, 2022). Rates of Alzheimer's disease closely follow rates of general dementia because Alzheimer's disease comprises most cases of dementia. Approximately two thirds of people with Alzheimer's disease are women (Rosende-Roca et al., 2021) and most are age 75 years and older (refer to **Figure 14.2**).

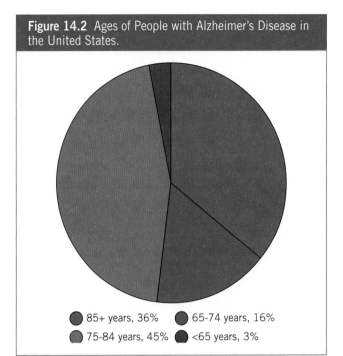

Figure 14.2 Ages of People with Alzheimer's Disease in the United States.

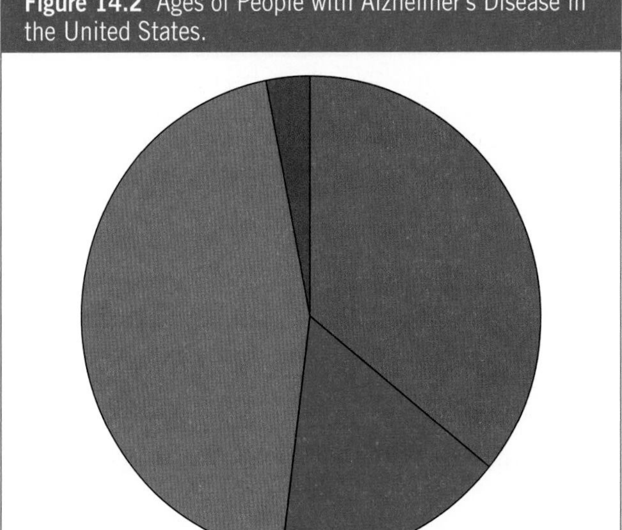

Source: Alzheimer's Association (2019). 2019 Alzheimer's disease facts and figures. *Alzheimer's and Dementia, 15,* 321–387, Figure 1.

The prevalence of dementia, especially Alzheimer's disease, does vary somewhat across cultures. Dementia tends to be diagnosed more in developed countries, where about 60 percent of all cases occur. This trend is expected to change with time to include more cases in less developed countries. Rates of dementia are generally highest in the Americas and Europe and lower in Africa, the Middle East, and Asia. Less developed countries tend to have higher rates of vascular dementia, however (Bir et al., 2021; Li et al., 2021). This discrepancy may be due to genetic, diagnostic, or cultural differences. People in certain cultures may find it more acceptable to have an obvious physical problem account for a mental disorder. In the United States, risk for Alzheimer's disease is higher for African Americans and Hispanics than European Americans and Asian Americans (Rubin et al., 2021).

Figure 14.1 Prevalence of all Dementia by Gender and Age.

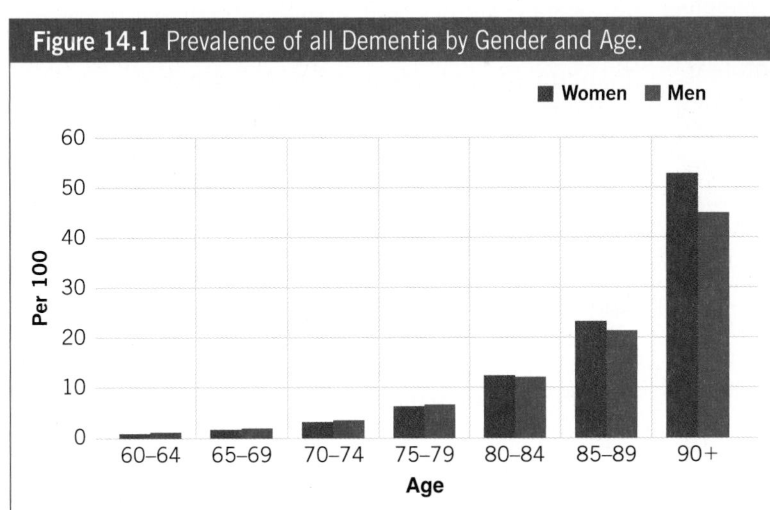

Source: Prince, M., Bryce, R., Albanese, E., Wimo, A., Ribeiro, W., & Ferri, C. P. (2013). The global prevalence of dementia: A systematic review and metaanalysis. *Alzheimer's and Dementia, 9,* 63–75, Table 2.

Vascular dementia also increases with age, but men generally display vascular dementia more than women. The general prevalence of vascular dementia is about 1.5 percent, and rates are higher for people aged 85+ years (4.8 percent) and those who experience a stroke (9.0–30.0 percent) (Bir et al., 2021; Kim et al., 2020). African Americans tend to have higher rates of vascular dementia than European Americans. Reasons for this difference are unclear but could include genetic factors, cardiovascular disease, perceptions about what is normal aging and what is not, and less access to medical care (Simpkins, 2020).

The prevalence of dementia due to Parkinson's disease is 0.3 to 0.5 percent in people older than age 65 years (Aarsland & Bernadotte, 2015). Men and women show equal rates of *dementia* due to Parkinson's disease, but prevalence of the disease itself is more common among men than women. This difference may be partly due to genetic or educational factors, but this remains

Focus On College Students

Delirium

One neurocognitive problem that has been investigated in college students is delirium, including some of the factors that are associated with this change in consciousness. Of course, substance-related issues discussed in Chapter 9 can create problems of delirium in college students. Other areas of focus have included stimulant medication use and sleep deprivation, which are common to those with demanding academic schedules and frequent projects, papers, and exams. Rate of stimulant medication misuse among college students is 17 percent, and commonly used medications include Adderall, Ritalin, Concerta, Dexedrine, Desoxyn, Metadate, Cylert, and Focalin. Students most likely to misuse stimulant medication include those with attention-deficit/hyperactivity disorder (Chapter 13), problematic alcohol use, marijuana use, and membership in fraternities or sororities. Reasons for using these medications generally surround the need for better concentration, study skills, and to stay awake. Ironically, however, nonusers appear to be more successful in academics than those misusing stimulant medication (Benson et al., 2015).

Sleep deprivation is another common element of college life. Estimates are that 50 percent of college students have daytime sleepiness (compared to 36 percent in the general population) and that 70 percent do not get enough sleep. Consequences of excessive sleepiness include lower grade point averages, increased risk of academic failure and motor vehicle accidents, learning problems, and mood changes such as depression. Factors that most affect lack of sleep in college students include (1) alcohol use, which creates fragmented sleep; (2) caffeine and energy drinks, the effects of which can last five to eight hours; (3) stimulant medication; and (4) technology use. With respect to the latter, about 57 percent of young adults leave their phone on during sleep, but light exposure from devices can lower melatonin and delay sleep onset. Sleep deprivation impairs learning and academic outcomes, but high academic performers are more likely to take a nap during the day than low academic performers (Hershner & Chervin, 2014). Stimulant medications and staying up all night may seem on the surface like good academic strategies, but the data suggest otherwise.

unclear (Reekes et al., 2020). Racial differences for Parkinson's disease have been noted as well, with rates somewhat higher for Hispanics and European Americans than African Americans. Parkinson's disease is generally less observed in Asia and Africa than Europe and North America (Ben-Joseph et al., 2020).

Frontotemporal dementias, which include Pick's disease, are presenile problems that generally occur at earlier ages than other dementias, and especially in cases involving traumatic brain injury (Pugh & Van Cott, 2021). Men may display the disorders more so than women, but other studies indicate no gender difference. The prevalence of frontotemporal dementia is 15 to 22 cases per 100,000 people. Data are scarce regarding cultural differences, but frontotemporal dementia has been reported in many countries (Onyike et al., 2021).

The neurocognitive disorders described here are highly comorbid with one another, and a conclusive diagnosis is often difficult to determine. Many people with major neurocognitive disorder also have comorbid problems such as apathy, psychosis, agitation, aggression, depression, and anxiety (Cummings, 2021). Changes in eating and sleeping patterns, wandering, and problems communicating with others are also common. Family members and clinicians often have difficulty distinguishing someone with severe emotional problems from someone with a major neurocognitive disorder. Maltreatment of this population is often a concern as well (refer to **Focus On Violence: Maltreatment of Older People**).

Stigma Associated with Neurocognitive Disorders

LO 14.4 Describe the stigma associated with neurocognitive disorders and its impact on those with the disorders and their caregivers.

Stigma often affects those who care for people with neurocognitive disorders such as Alzheimer's disease. One group of researchers noted that family stigma associated with Alzheimer's disease includes caregiver, lay public, and structural stigma. Caregiver stigma includes the caregiver's concerns about the inability of the person with Alzheimer's disease to remember information or to engage in self-care such as toileting. Shame, embarrassment, and disgust were also commonly reported by caregivers. Lay public stigma includes family concerns about how others stigmatize a person with Alzheimer's disease such as focusing only on a person's confusion or messy appearance, worrying about contagion, or fearing the disease. Structural stigma includes family concerns about social configurations such as health care services. Participants reported that physicians often had insufficient knowledge about Alzheimer's disease and that inadequate services were available for people with dementia. Stigma, including shame and declining involvement in caregiving, accounted for a significant percentage of caregiver burden (Werner et al., 2020).

Focus On Violence

Maltreatment of Older People

Substantial media and research attention has focused on maltreatment toward children and domestic violence. One form of cruelty that receives less attention, however, is *maltreatment of older people.* Maltreatment of older people involves psychological or physical harm, neglect, or exploitation of an older person. Examples include physical and sexual aggression, neglect of basic needs, and theft of assets (van den Bruele & Crandall, 2022). About 2 to 10 percent of older people are maltreated in some way. Some of this maltreatment occurs in nursing homes and related settings, but much is done by family members at home. The most significant risk factors for such maltreatment are disability, shared living situations, social isolation of families, and abuser psychopathology (Corbi et al., 2015).

Maltreatment of an older person is also much more likely if a person has dementia (Henderson et al., 2021). Part of the reason for this may be the older person's agitation or aggression toward a caregiver or a caregiver's exhaustion or lack of patience. Maltreatment of older people with dementia may also be due to their problems communicating needs or pain to others, inability to make decisions about living arrangements, and depression and stress (Chao et al., 2020).

Some researchers have advocated strategies for caregivers to combat maltreatment of people with dementia. These strategies include helping caregivers identify stressful situations and their own behaviors that set the stage for maltreatment as well as seeking assistance from others when needed. Others have focused on coping skills to reduce caregiver anxiety and depression (Sperling et al., 2020). Caring for someone with dementia can be difficult, so providing extensive support and respite is crucial to prevent maltreatment.

Stigma can obviously affect people with Parkinson's disease as well, given their sometimes extensive and visible physical symptoms. Conversely, some people with Parkinson's disease show facial masking, or less expressive facial movement, that may give the appearance of apathy or social disengagement. People with high facial masking, especially women, may be viewed by others as more depressed, less sociable, and less cognitively competent than those with low facial masking (Henry et al., 2021). Such negative judgments may cause some people with Parkinson's disease to withdraw from others or to seek less treatment.

Section Summary

- Normal memory and cognitive changes occur with age and do not interfere with daily functioning. These changes may progress to more serious sets of neurocognitive disorders such as delirium and dementia.
- Delirium is an often temporary and reversible condition where a person is disoriented and has trouble with attention, concentration, and memory. Delirium may result from substance intoxication or medical situations such as anesthesia.
- Dementia is a more serious type of neurocognitive disorder that includes chronic and irreversible declines in memory and other cognitive processes. Neurocognitive disorders can be mild or major.
- The most common form of neurocognitive disorder is Alzheimer's disease, a progressive condition marked by cognitive deficits such as aphasia, apraxia, and agnosia and deficits in executive functioning.
- Neurocognitive disorder due to Lewy bodies occurs when masses of proteins create neuron damage.
- Vascular dementia is a neurocognitive disorder caused by a blood vessel problem, especially a stroke. People with vascular dementia often face a more abrupt and acute onset of symptoms but less cognitive impairment than people with Alzheimer's disease.
- Neurocognitive disorder may be due to Parkinson's disease, a progressive neurological disorder involving severe problems in motor functioning.
- Neurocognitive disorder due to Pick's disease is the most well-known of the frontotemporal dementias, meaning deterioration occurs in the frontal and temporal brain lobes.
- Neurocognitive disorders can also be caused by substances or medical conditions. Korsakoff's syndrome involves intense memory problems resulting from long-term alcohol use and thiamine deficiency.
- Dementia occurs in about 5 to 8.5 percent of older persons, and many people with one form of dementia also have another form of dementia.
- Caregiver, public, and structural stigma are often associated with neurocognitive disorders.

Review Questions

1. What normal changes in memory and general cognitive functioning occur with age?
2. Define and contrast delirium and dementia.
3. What problems commonly lead to dementia or neurocognitive disorder?
4. What is mixed dementia?
5. How common are different neurocognitive disorders in the general population?

Neurocognitive Disorders: Causes and Prevention

LO 14.5 Discuss the risk factors for and prevention of neurocognitive disorders.

Most disorders covered in this textbook generally involve a complex combination of biological and environmental risk factors. With neurocognitive disorders, however, biological changes play a dominant role. This section thus concentrates on genetics, neurochemical changes, and major brain changes related to neurocognitive disorders. Evidence for environmental risk factors does exist, however, and awareness of these factors may help with prevention efforts regarding neurocognitive disorders.

Biological Risk Factors for Neurocognitive Disorders

Genetics

A genetic link to neurocognitive disorders appears to be clearer in early-onset cases. Late-onset Alzheimer's disease has an estimated heritability rate of 58 to 79 percent, but early-onset Alzheimer's disease has an estimated heritability rate of over 90 percent (Sims et al., 2020). Late-onset Alzheimer's disease may have several environmental components but early-onset Alzheimer's disease may be more a biological problem. Family and twin studies also reveal increased risk and thus a genetic basis for Alzheimer's disease (Wightman et al., 2021).

Four main genetic factors seem related to Alzheimer's disease:

- Amyloid precursor protein and chromosome 21
- Apolipoprotein E and chromosome 19
- Presenilin 1 and chromosome 14
- Presenilin 2 and chromosome 1

Amyloid precursor protein is a normal brain substance related to a specific gene on chromosome 21. This gene undergoes changes, or *mutations*, in some people (Abondio et al., 2021). As these gene mutations occur, severe brain changes can result because large amounts of this protein are produced. Alzheimer's disease is found in a high percentage of people with Down syndrome (Chapter 13). People with Down syndrome usually have three #21 chromosomes and thus substantial overproduction of this protein (Bram et al., 2021).

Apolipoprotein E (APOE) is a protein related to a specific gene on chromosome 19. APOE, and especially one type of allele (gene part), APOE-4, are highly predictive of Alzheimer's disease in general and declines in episodic memory in particular (Emrani et al., 2020). People without APOE-4 have an estimated risk of 9 to 20 percent for developing Alzheimer's disease, but people with one copy of the gene have a 25 to 60 percent risk and people with two copies of the gene have a 50 to 90 percent risk (Fuller et al., 2015). Like the amyloid precursor protein, APOE-4 causes severe brain changes, and the two substances likely interact in some way (van der Kant et al., 2020).

Other key influences on Alzheimer's disease include the presenilin 1 gene on chromosome 14 and the presenilin 2 gene on chromosome 1 (Tarkowska et al., 2021). These genes also mutate in some people and lead to massive brain changes. Scores of mutations have been charted on the presenilin 1 gene alone. Mutations of presenilin genes may be associated with earlier onset and more familial types of Alzheimer's disease (Deaton & Johnson, 2021). Dozens of other genes also relate to Alzheimer's disease, and the true cause of the disorder likely involves the interaction of these many different genes (Zhou et al., 2021).

What about other forms of dementia? Many single-gene disorders such as sickle cell disease predispose people toward stroke, a major cause of vascular dementia. Researchers have also identified genes that predispose people specifically toward strokes (Abraham et al., 2021). Family history and twin studies suggest a genetic link for stroke as well (Osler et al., 2022). Others believe genetic factors implicated in Alzheimer's disease, including APOE-4, are also present in vascular dementia. This may help explain mixed dementia, or the presence of Alzheimer's disease and vascular dementia in a person (Li et al., 2020).

Other neurocognitive disorders have some genetic basis as well. Early forms of Parkinson's disease may relate to mutations in certain genes, called *parkin genes*, which cause neuron loss as well as harmful accumulation of proteins in the brain's substantia nigra region (van der Vlag et al., 2020). Frontotemporal dementias such as Pick's disease may relate to problems of the *tau gene* on chromosome 17. This gene is responsible for a protein that helps keep neurons from breaking apart, so mutations of the gene can lead to neuron disintegration (Gallo et al., 2022). Problems such as Korsakoff's syndrome may have some genetic basis as well (O'Brien et al., 2022).

Neurochemical Features

Neurochemical changes also influence the development of different neurocognitive disorders. Dementias are often marked by low levels of neurotransmitters, especially *acetylcholine*, *serotonin*, and *norepinephrine*. These neurotransmitter deficits may be especially pertinent to key brain areas such as the limbic system, as well as connections between the frontal cortex and other brain areas (Holland et al., 2021). This may help explain some key features of dementia, including problems of memory and other cognitive functioning, motor behavior, and emotional and personality changes. Low levels of these neurotransmitters would also help explain symptoms that commonly occur with dementia, including apathy and depression (Miller et al., 2021).

Another neurotransmitter lower among people with dementias, especially those with Parkinson's disease and dementia with Lewy bodies, is *dopamine.* People with Parkinson's disease show progressively lower levels of dopamine in the substantia nigra and other areas of the brain (Bae et al., 2021). Lowered dopamine clearly relates to motor symptoms of Parkinson's disease and may influence Parkinson's-related dementia (Yang et al., 2021). People with Lewy body dementia also have lowered dopamine levels, though some overlap with Parkinson's disease is likely (Yoo et al., 2022).

Other neurochemicals may occur in *excess* in people with dementia. One such substance is *L-glutamate,* which is an excitatory neurotransmitter in the brain. High levels of L-glutamate activity are present in people with Alzheimer's disease and may be high after an ischemic stroke, which could lead to vascular dementia (Li et al., 2020). L-glutamate activity is important for normal learning and memory, but excessively high levels have been linked to neuron damage (Al-Nassar et al., 2022).

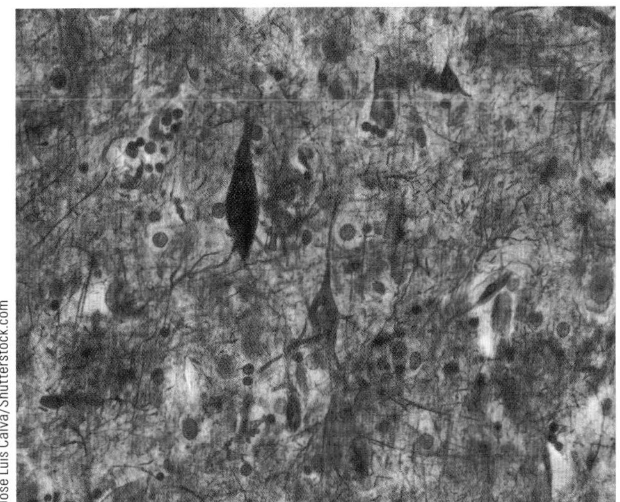

Jose Luis Calva/Shutterstock.com

Neurofibrillary tangles, implicated in neurocognitive disorder in general and Alzheimer's disease in particular, impair various brain functions.

Brain Features

Genetic predispositions and neurochemical changes likely lead to massive brain changes in people with dementia, especially the following:

- *neurofibrillary tangles,* or twisted fibers inside nerve cells of the brain
- *senile* or *neuritic plaques,* or clusters of dead nerve cells and accumulations of amyloid proteins in the brain
- *Lewy bodies,* or deposits of alpha-synuclein proteins inside nerve cells of the brain
- *atrophy,* or gradual deterioration of different brain areas
- *oxidative stress* and *free radicals,* or damage to brain cells via oxygen exposure

Neurofibrillary tangles are a key aspect of dementia in general and Alzheimer's disease in particular. Neurons consist of a *microtubule,* or skeleton structure held together by a protein substance called *tau.* Think of the neuron microtubule as the rails of a train track and the tau proteins as the railroad ties that hold the tracks together. The tau protein may become changed chemically and so the individual "railroad ties" become twisted around each other and eventually collapse (Horie et al., 2021). The "tracks" of the neuron thus also collapse, and all of these pieces eventually snarl to form neurofibrillary tangles. The neurons in the brain begin to fall apart and these fragments eventually collect in spheres and other shapes.

As neurofibrillary tangles occur more frequently and affect multiple areas, the brain's ability to coordinate behavior and communicate with the body becomes severely impaired. A person with neurofibrillary tangles will have enormous problems with higher-order behaviors such as thinking and memory because the cortex and hippocampus of the brain are quite susceptible to this process (Taddei et al., 2022). Lower-order behaviors such as motor skills and, eventually, life-support functions, become impaired as well. This process is a slow and gradual but irreversible one and helps explain much of the progressive deterioration of functioning in people with dementia like Mr. Ponder.

Another common brain change in people with dementia is **senile or neuritic plaques.** These plaques

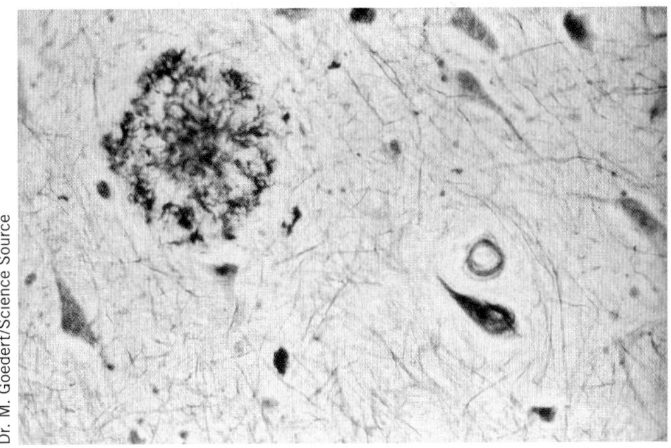

Dr. M. Goedert/Science Source

Neuritic plaques are a key aspect of Alzheimer's disease.

are made of certain proteins—*beta-amyloid proteins*—that accumulate in spaces between neurons in the brain (Hamilton et al., 2021). Many proteins in the brain are *soluble*, meaning they can be dissolved or broken down by enzymes in the brain, but beta-amyloid proteins become *insoluble.* The proteins thus gradually accumulate into globs that eventually thicken by combining with other immune and support cells in the brain. This process eventually causes massive damage and an inability to process information or even resist minor infections.

Beta-amyloid proteins are formed from a larger protein called amyloid precursor protein, or APP. Recall that large amounts of APP relate to mutations of chromosome 21. Senile or neuritic plaques are most common to the temporal and occipital brain lobes and somewhat common to the parietal lobe (Chen et al., 2021). Another plaque often found in the brains of people with Alzheimer's disease is *diffuse plaque*, which is marked less by amyloid protein accumulations and is common to many older people and those with Down syndrome. Diffuse plaques may be a precursor to senile/neuritic plaques (Malpas et al., 2021).

Lewy bodies also represent collections of proteins in the brain that cause damage and are found in many people with dementia. Lewy bodies are not beta-amyloid proteins but rather *alpha-synuclein proteins* (Manzanza et al., 2021). Alpha-synuclein proteins can also become insoluble, accumulate on the synapses of neurons, and block effective transmission of information. Lewy body accumulation is likely due to genetic changes (Chia et al., 2021). Such accumulation may occur most in people with Alzheimer's disease, Parkinson's disease, and, of course, dementia with Lewy bodies (Orad & Shiner, 2022).

Other brain changes in people with dementia involve gradual **atrophy**, or deterioration, of key areas related to thinking, memory, personality, and other important functions. A gradual withering of the frontal and temporal lobes is observed in people with frontotemporal dementia such as Pick's disease. This atrophy is likely the result of key genetic changes, especially on chromosome 17, and involves intense deterioration of the neurons in these areas (Shafiei et al., 2022). *Pick bodies* may infest these areas as well and comprise various tau fibrils similar to what happens in neurofibrillary tangles (Younes & Miller, 2020).

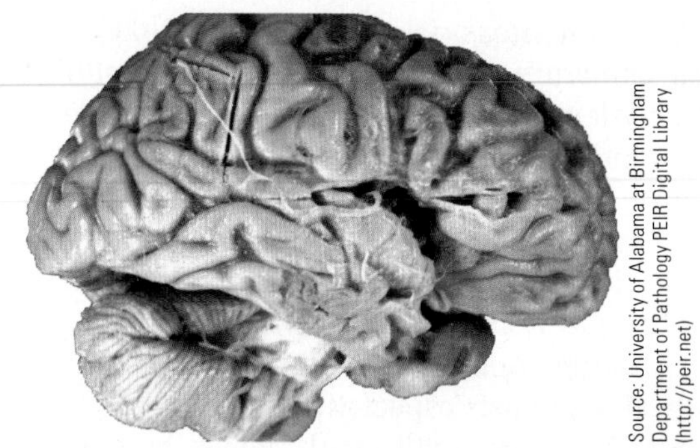
Source: University of Alabama at Birmingham Department of Pathology PEIR Digital Library (http://peir.net)

Atrophy of the frontotemporal regions of the brain occurs in people with Pick's disease. A healthy brain would not have the large gaps shown in this photo.

Brain atrophy also affects the substantia nigra in people with Parkinson's disease, which is a main dopamine pathway controlling motor behavior (Poston et al., 2020). Fewer neurons appear over time. Recall that Lewy bodies may also be found in people with Parkinson's disease. Atrophy in Parkinson's disease likely relates to the specific chromosomal changes mentioned earlier.

Effects of a stroke or other cerebrovascular disease can vary tremendously in people with vascular dementia. These effects may include cortical as well as subcortical areas of the brain. Key brain areas that can be affected, other than the cortex, include the

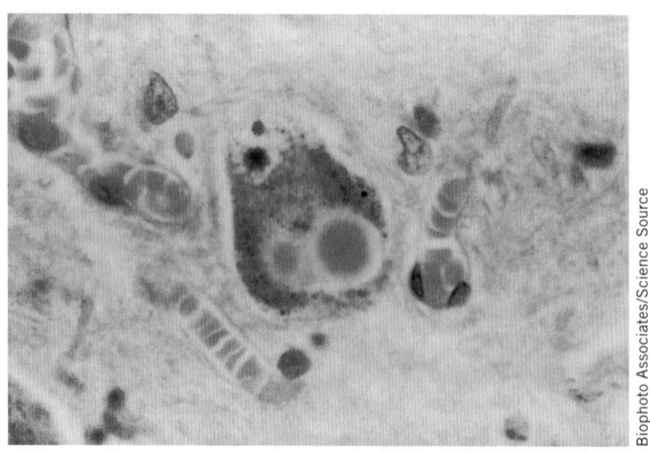
Biophoto Associates/Science Source

Many cases of neurocognitive disorder involve Lewy bodies, proteins that accumulate in the brain.

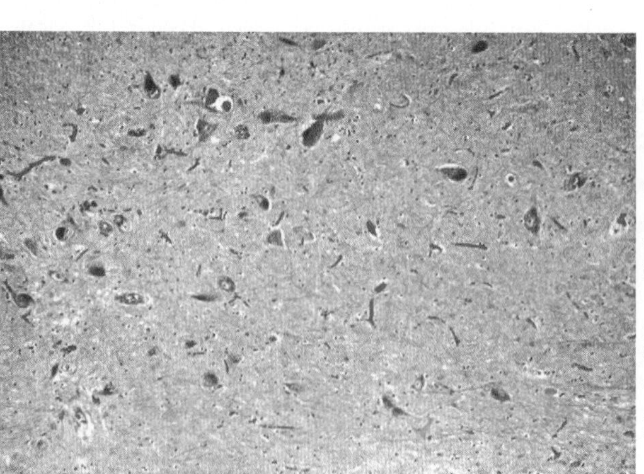
Source: University of Alabama at Birmingham Department of Pathology PEIR Digital Library (http://peir.net)

Loss of neurons in the substantia nigra is a main feature of Parkinson's disease.

angular gyrus, caudate nucleus, thalamus, basal ganglia, and white matter (Razek & Elsebaie, 2021). These areas are especially important for coordinating visual and auditory information, language comprehension, and motor behavior.

Other brain changes in people with dementia involve **oxidative stress** and **free radicals**. Brain cells are normally exposed to oxygen, which can damage the cells, but antioxidants in vitamins and other substances help prevent major damage. Oxidative stress involves general cell or tissue damage and brain inflammation that can occur when antioxidants are insufficient. Oxidative stress relates closely to release of free radicals in the brain; free radicals are aggressive substances possibly produced to fight viruses and bacteria. Oxidative stress from very high amounts of free radicals can be caused by many things, including stroke, brain injury, pollution, smoking, or excessive alcohol use (Akbari et al., 2022). Oxidative stress with resulting brain injury appears to be a significant risk factor in people with dementia (Jurcau & Simion, 2020). For the major brain areas implicated in dementia, refer to **Figure 14.3**.

Figure 14.3 Major Brain Areas Implicated in Neurocognitive Disorders.

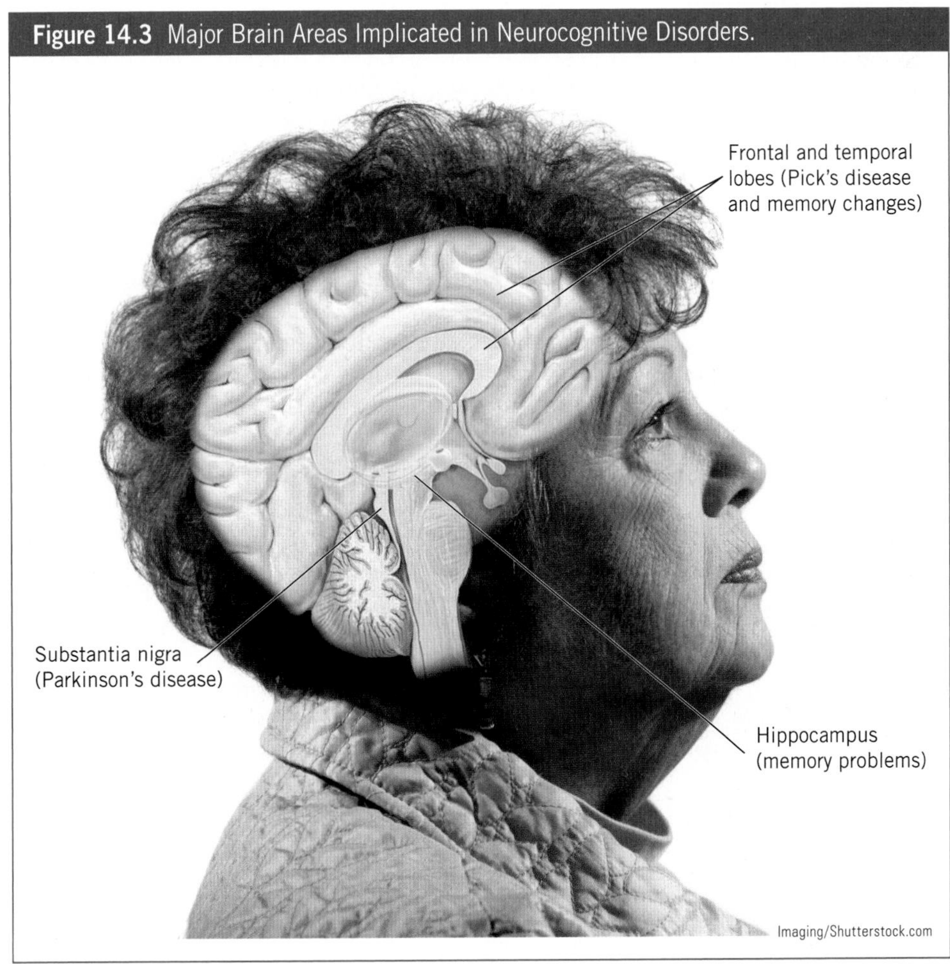

Environmental Risk Factors for Neurocognitive Disorders

Diet

Diet may be a risk factor for certain cases of Alzheimer's disease or other dementias. Dementia is probably not connected to one type of nutrient but perhaps to different food substances (Samieri et al., 2022). Medications or vitamins rich in *antioxidants* may help slow the progression of dementia. We are exposed daily to various oxidants, such as ozone (O_3), but over time these can lead to beta-amyloid protein accumulation and neuron cell damage in the brain (Ton et al., 2020). Ingesting antioxidants from yellow-orange fruits such as cantaloupe and green vegetables (for beta-carotene), and taking vitamins C and E, which have antioxidant qualities, are thus especially important.

High levels of antioxidants may slow (although not stop) the progression of Alzheimer's disease, perhaps lower the risk for developing dementia, or protect against cognitive decline, though data remain mixed (Wichansawakun et al., 2022). In addition, supplements of vitamin E and C may provide some protection from vascular and other dementia (Sinha et al., 2020). Other researchers have examined effects of other nutrients on cognitive functioning, especially vitamins B_6, B_{12}, and folic acid. Data are mixed, however, as to whether levels of these substances relate to the presence of Alzheimer's disease and whether supplements of these nutrients help improve symptoms of dementia (Gil Martínez et al., 2022). Vitamin B_{12} and folic acid help reduce *homocysteine*, high levels of which can cause artery damage (Wang et al., 2021).

Increased saturated fat and cholesterol intake has sometimes been found related to cognitive decline, although not always (Muth & Park, 2021). Increased fish or seafood intake seems related to lower risk of dementia as well in some studies (Zhang et al., 2021). A healthy diet heavy in fruits, vegetables, and fish will also help prevent cardiovascular conditions that could produce vascular dementia. These conditions include diabetes, hypertension, obesity, stroke,

A diet including ample amounts of fish, fruit, and vegetables, known as the "Mediterranean diet," may reduce risk for neurocognitive disorder.

and coronary artery disease (Limongi et al., 2020). A heart-healthy diet also seems useful as a brain-healthy diet.

Alcohol and Tobacco Use

People who drink *moderate* amounts of alcohol are less likely to experience dementia compared to people who abstain from alcohol (Visontay et al., 2021). People who drink *large* amounts of alcohol are clearly at risk for memory and cognitive deficits, however. Moderate alcohol use may protect some people from vascular damage, reduce stress, enhance acetylcholine release from the hippocampus to improve memory, and increase social interaction among older adults (Mewton et al., 2022). A key element of alcohol—flavonoids—has excellent antioxidant properties as well (Zhang et al., 2022). Flavonoids are common to certain kinds of alcohol such as red wine. Tobacco use, on the other hand, is a substantial risk factor for dementia (Otuyama et al., 2020).

Aluminum

Another possible environmental risk factor for dementia is exposure to various toxins. Some researchers have focused on *aluminum*, a common metal ingested from air, food, or water. Aluminum toxicity, which produces oxidation effects and increased beta-amyloid proteins and free radicals, could result in brain tissue damage and onset of age-related cognitive decline (Antoniadou et al., 2020). Aluminum can come from diet as well as drinking water, medications, and antacids. Aluminum is also present in neurofibrillary tangles (Kabir et al., 2021). Some recommend ingesting curry to mitigate possible effects of aluminum, but others claim no conclusive link can yet be made between aluminum exposure and Alzheimer's disease (Ogunsuyi et al., 2022).

Flavonoids such as those in red wine may serve a protective function against neurocognitive disorder.

Cultural Factors

Recall that Alzheimer's disease may be more prevalent among Western nations and vascular dementia may be more prevalent among Asian and other non-Western nations. This may be partly explained by how dementia is considered within a cultural context and whether shame and stigma are associated with severe cognitive dysfunction. Native Americans may view dementia as a normal part of aging and as an expected part of one's transition to the next world (Ekoh et al., 2020). Asians often emphasize more socially acceptable physical factors to explain dementia, possibly resulting in more reported cases of vascular dementia than Alzheimer's disease. Dementia among Nigerians is viewed as a debilitating condition that prevents one from completing prayer and work that requires higher-level cognition. Rates of reported dementia are thus quite low (Oyinlola & Olusa, 2020). Stigma may thus be a key reason for differences in reported dementia. Genetic and dietary differences across the world can also be fairly large and help explain cultural differences in dementia (Rosselli et al., 2022).

Cultural factors may also apply to caregivers of those with dementia. Minority caregivers often report more unmet service needs for family members with dementia. This may be due to lack of information about available diagnostic and treatment services, inaccurate diagnosis, poor feedback from physicians, and less membership in support groups (Dilworth-Anderson et al., 2020). Other reasons may include insensitivity of assessments (as discussed later in the chapter) to cultural differences in cognition, reluctance to use medical and social services perceived as not culturally competent, and language barriers (James et al., 2022).

Other Factors

Many other environmental risk factors could lead to dementia, including viral infections such as HIV and accidents leading to brain injury. Other significant risk factors could include poverty, malnutrition, poor parental education, and low socioeconomic status. Family history of dementia appears to be a better predictor of whether someone will acquire dementia than these variables, however (Koriath et al., 2021).

Stronger educational background is often linked to less dementia, possibly because cognitive decline is harder to identify. Highly educated people may have more *cognitive reserve*, or better problem-solving strategies when taking neuropsychological tests (Nelson et al., 2021). Some propose that *long-term potentiation*, or strengthening and development of new neuronal connections, can result from enhanced education and perhaps help reduce dementia onset (Bayat et al., 2020). So, study hard!

Causes of Neurocognitive Disorders

Many risk factors are involved for neurocognitive disorders in general and for severe dementia in particular. Organizing these risk factors into one general causal theory has been a difficult task for researchers. One theory of cognitive disorders—the **amyloid cascade hypothesis**—has received great research attention, especially for Alzheimer's disease. This hypothesis focuses on key brain changes that can cascade or result from various genetic and environmental factors and which, in the end, help produce a state of dementia (Wu et al., 2022). **Figure 14.4** illustrates a version of the amyloid cascade hypothesis.

A central aspect of the amyloid cascade hypothesis is that progressive dementias are at least partly caused by a toxic buildup of beta-amyloid proteins that lead to neuron damage and senile plaques. Amyloid precursor protein is a normal protein that the body regularly splices into shorter pieces. This splicing process is done by different enzymes called *secretases* and, in particular, *alpha-secretase*, *beta-secretase*, and *gamma-secretase* (Michelon et al., 2020). This is a normal process for all of us.

For reasons still unclear, beta-secretase and gamma-secretase often combine to produce the protein A-beta, or beta-amyloid. Again, this process is normal and not usually harmful because beta-amyloid is often soluble and dissolves quickly. Beta-amyloid becomes insoluble, or fails to dissolve, in some people, however. Large deposits of beta-amyloid thus collect and form senile plaques, contribute to the development of neurofibrillary tangles and neurotransmitter changes, and perhaps force the overproduction of free radicals (Kim et al., 2020). These toxic effects help lead to the brain damage central to dementia.

A key question in this model is what factors lead initially to changes in amyloid precursor protein splicing and toxic buildup of beta-amyloid. The answer, although still not definitive, may involve a combination of genetic and dietary or other environmental factors. Recall that changes in chromosome 21 and presenilin genes may lead to overproduction of amyloid precursor protein, such that huge amounts of beta-amyloid are also produced. The APOE-4 gene has also been closely linked to amyloid buildup and neurofibrillary tangles (van der Kant et al., 2020).

Diet likely intersects with genetic factors to act as a contributor to neurocognitive disorders via toxic amyloid buildup but also as a protective factor via high antioxidants. The interaction of diet and genes may help explain why people of some cultures experience less Alzheimer's disease and other neurocognitive disorders. Those whose diets are rich in fish, fruits, and vegetables may experience fewer cognitive problems than those whose diets are rich in fat, cholesterol, and possibly aluminum, although studies vary (Charisis et al., 2021).

The amyloid cascade hypothesis was largely designed as an explanation for Alzheimer's disease. Still, genetic changes that lead to certain body and brain alterations are likely main characteristics of other neurocognitive disorders as well. Many people are genetically predisposed to hypertension, diabetes, obesity, and stroke and possible vascular dementia (Zhang et al., 2021). Genetic changes are also important for aggressive neurocognitive disorders such as Pick's disease as well as alcoholism that can lead to Korsakoff's syndrome (Gallo et al., 2022). Some cases of Parkinson's disease are likely related to mutations in parkin genes that help create neuron damage and atrophy to brain areas such as the substantia nigra (Senkevich et al., 2022).

Figure 14.4 Sample Schematic of the Amyloid Cascade Hypothesis.

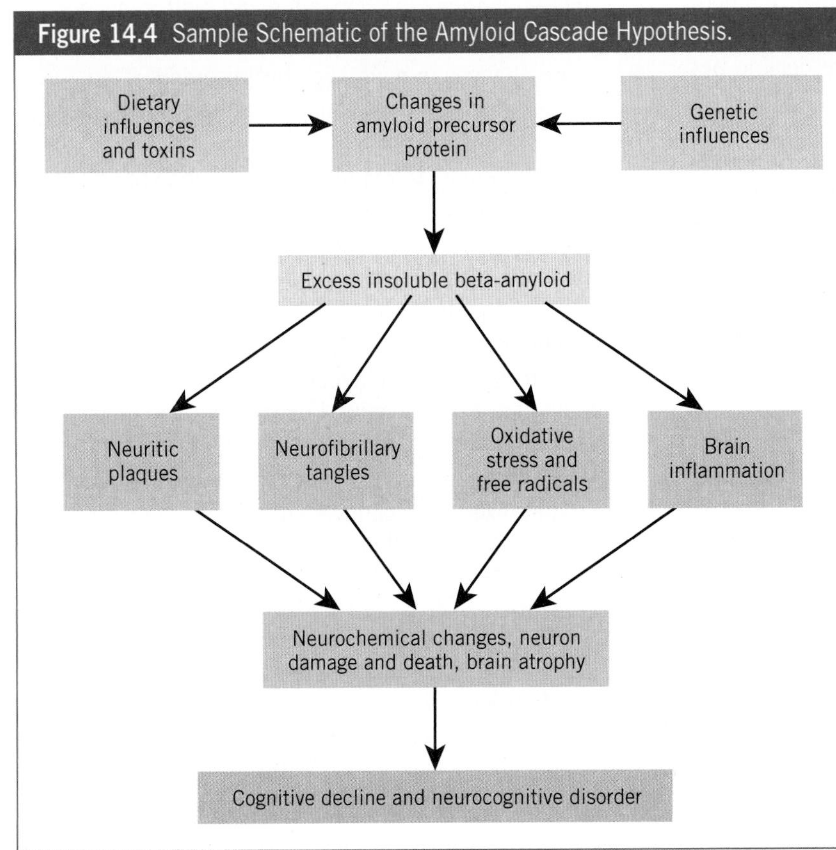

Discovering the true cause of neurocognitive disorders will likely be a high priority for future researchers given the substantially greater number of people who will be living lengthy lives. The debilitating nature of neurocognitive disorders also means a high priority for prevention, a topic discussed next.

Prevention of Neurocognitive Disorders

Recall one factor likely important for preventing Alzheimer's disease and other neurocognitive disorders: *diet*. People whose diets are healthy will be at less risk for cerebrovascular problems that could lead to dementia. General recommendations include diets that restrict calories and are rich in antioxidants, folic acid, fish oils, and *moderate* amounts of red wine—the so-called Mediterranean diet. Diet may reduce risk of dementia but not necessarily its course in people strongly genetically predisposed to neurocognitive disorder, however (Andreu-Reinón et al., 2021).

People with high-cholesterol diets or whose cholesterol is set genetically to a high level may benefit from a class of drugs called *statins*. These drugs help lower cholesterol levels. Statin drugs have not prevented onset of Alzheimer's disease or other forms of dementia, however (Olmastroni et al., 2022). People with high cholesterol will benefit from *exercise* as well. Some data indicate that exercise can increase a protective substance known as *brain-derived neurotrophic factor* that may enhance hippocampus activity and memory (Ruiz-Gonzalez et al., 2021). Physical activity may help prevent cognitive decline but not necessarily prevent dementia (Law et al., 2020).

Another focus of prevention involves *cognitively stimulating environments*, which include surroundings that constantly challenge the brain and help develop new neuronal connections. Social interactions with others and new intellectual stimulation seem particularly important for preventing cognitive decline (Fratiglioni et al., 2020). To help prevent cognitive decline:

- Continue to stay as socially active as possible and meet new people.
- Continue reading and writing, but try new publications such as detective novels.
- Take a class to learn a new skill such as carpentry or mechanics.
- Learn to play a musical instrument or speak a foreign language.
- Play mentally challenging games such as chess, and assemble puzzles.
- Travel and learn about new cultures.
- Seek treatment for stress and psychological and medical problems.
- Keep regular lists of things to do as well as a detailed daily calendar.
- Challenge your memory by recalling recent events on a regular basis, such as what you had for dinner three nights ago or the name of a new person you met yesterday.

Various drugs may also help reduce beta-amyloid buildup and prevent the cascade of problems that lead to dementia. One such drug, *crenezumab*, may be effective in this regard but only at very high doses (Guthrie et al., 2020). Lack of tobacco use as well as drugs to reduce the chance of stroke, such as antihypertension and anticlotting medications, are important as well. *Gene therapy* will likely be the approach to revolutionize the prevention of Alzheimer's disease and other dementias, and this is discussed more in the later treatment section (Iqubal et al., 2020).

Section Summary

- Biological risk factors for neurocognitive disorders include genetics, which may be most important for early-onset cases.
- Genetic changes in neurocognitive disorders include chromosome 21 and amyloid precursor protein, chromosome 19 and apolipoprotein E, and chromosomes 14 and 1 and presenilin 1 and 2.
- Neurochemical changes in neurocognitive disorders include low levels of acetylcholine, serotonin, norepinephrine, and dopamine and high levels of L-glutamate.
- Brain changes in neurocognitive disorders often include neurofibrillary tangles, senile plaques, Lewy bodies, atrophy, and oxidative stress and free radicals.
- Environmental factors may also influence neurocognitive disorders, especially diets high in antioxidants and fish and low in fat and cholesterol.
- Moderate alcohol use may be related to less dementia, and aluminum intake may relate to more dementia.
- The amyloid cascade hypothesis refers to various brain changes cascading from genetic and environmental factors to produce neurocognitive disorder.
- Prevention of neurocognitive disorder will likely hinge on diet, exercise, cognitive stimulation, medications, and perhaps gene therapy.

Review Questions

1. Describe genetic mutations associated with neurocognitive disorders.
2. What neurochemical and brain changes are central to dementia?
3. What dietary factors might relate closely to dementia?
4. Describe the amyloid cascade hypothesis.
5. Outline a strategy for preventing dementia.

Neurocognitive Disorders: Assessment and Treatment

LO 14.6 Characterize the assessment and treatment of individuals with neurocognitive disorders.

The previous sections covered some of the major features and causes of neurocognitive disorders, so the next sections turn to different strategies to assess and treat these problems.

Assessment of Neurocognitive Disorders

Interviews

Interviews to gather information about someone with possible neurocognitive disorder could include the person themself but will likely also include close family members and friends. This is especially so in cases involving severe cognitive or memory problems. Interviews of significant others can be especially useful if a person is currently in a state of delirium. Interviews for people with possible dementia are often designed to determine whether a problem is the result of normal aging or an early form of severe neurocognitive disorder.

Interviews for people with possible Alzheimer's disease or other dementia often cover some key topics (refer to **Table 14.10**; Grothe et al., 2021). An assessor will search for recent changes in behavior, thinking, and memory as well as changes in long-term skills such as language or ability to recognize others. Mr. and Mrs. Ponder's interview led the neuropsychologist to initially conclude that some form of neurocognitive disorder was likely occurring given their confusion and memory problems. Interviews are also commonly used in this population to assess for comorbid problems such as depression, anxiety, and psychosis.

Interviews with people with possible neurocognitive disorder are generally done to conduct a **mental status examination**. A mental status examination involves detailed questioning and observation of key areas of functioning such as appearance, mood, orientation, and odd behaviors, speech, or thoughts (Arevalo-Rodriguez et al., 2021). A clinician may pay close attention to disorganized attire, incoherent speech, agitation, bizarre thought patterns, aphasic speech, motor problems, and flat affect. A person's ability to be oriented to person, place, and time is also assessed. A clinician may ask someone to state their name, where they are, and current day and year. Failure to answer these basic questions appropriately may indicate a neurocognitive disorder.

Table 14.10 Possible Early Signs and Symptoms of Dementia

Sign	Symptoms
Forgetfulness	Commonly manifested as short-term memory loss for recently learned names, appointments, purpose of activities, points of conversation, and completed tasks or errands. An individual may repeat questions or requests. The degree of forgetfulness begins to interfere with daily activities and responsibilities.
Disorientation	Episodic confusion regarding the exact day, date, or location.
Impaired performance on daily tasks	Difficulty performing everyday tasks, such as preparing meals, running household appliances, cleaning, and hygiene (e.g., bathing, toileting, brushing teeth).
Impaired language	Increasing difficulty with selecting and using words. Sentences may become simpler or fragmented.
Impaired recognition	Diminished ability to remember or identify familiar faces, objects, sounds, and locations.
Impaired abstract thinking	Diminished ability to think clearly about issues, to discuss complex issues and to make logical connections between them, or to comprehend fully things that were previously understood.
Impaired judgment	Impairment in the ability to organize and plan and to make appropriate decisions or selections among several possibilities. A person may act in ways that were previously deemed uncharacteristic or inappropriate.
Changes in mood or behavior	Change in mood and behavior that may take many forms, including increased irritability, loss of emotional control (e.g., intense anger, frustration, tearfulness), abusive or inappropriate language, loss of pleasure in particular activities, and apathetic attitudes.
Changes in personality	The person may seem less sociable or more self-centered and may act out in disruptive or disinhibited ways. They may also seem more suspicious, fearful, or bothered by others, and reactions to everyday stress may be out of proportion.

From Agronin, M.E. (2014). *Alzheimer's disease and other dementias: A practical guide* (3rd ed.). New York: Routledge.

Interviewing caregivers of people with neurocognitive disorder is also an extremely important assessment area. Key topics to be covered here include family history of neurocognitive disorder, a person's need for help in various areas such as dressing, financial and other resources for care, knowledge about dementia, physical and emotional health of the caregiver, social support, and quality of life of the family (Hazzan et al., 2022). Recall that Mrs. Ponder said her quality of life was diminishing because her health was dwindling and she could no longer fully care for her husband.

Questionnaires

Mental status examinations and assessment of cognitive functioning can also be done via questionnaires, which may be administered in interview format. A commonly used measure to screen for neurocognitive disorder is the *Mini-Mental State Examination* (MMSE-2), a 30-item questionnaire that covers orientation, verbal and written comprehension, concentration, learning, writing and copying, and memory (refer to **Figure 14.5**; Folstein, & Folstein, 2010). The MMSE-2 takes only 10 to 15 minutes to administer and can distinguish people with or without dementia. Other commonly used screening tests include the *Mini-Cog* (Fage et al., 2015), *Dementia Severity Rating Scale* (Moelter et al., 2015), *Delirium Rating Scale—Revised* (Thurber et al., 2015), and *Confusion Assessment Method*, the latter of which can evaluate delirium even with difficult-to-assess patients (DiLibero et al., 2016).

Screening tests for dementia can also be very brief and include asking a person to draw a clock face for a given time (refer to **Figure 14.6**), tell time, make change for a dollar, and spell various words backward (Chan et al., 2021). Many questionnaires are also available to assess conditions related to delirium and dementia that were covered in previous chapters. Particularly important conditions include anxiety, depression, and adaptive behavior.

Cognitive Assessment

More formal tests can also be used to assess symptoms of neurocognitive disorders, especially if a screening questionnaire indicates delirium or dementia or if memory problems are clearly evident. A common example is the *Wechsler Memory Scale* (WMS-IV; Wechsler, 2009). The WMS consists of various subtests that measure immediate and delayed memory for visual and auditory stimuli as well as working memory. A person may be asked to immediately recall different words (*tree, table, dime*) and then, later in the test, be asked to recall them again. The WMS is often used in research and clinical settings to assess Alzheimer's disease and other

Figure 14.5 The Mini-Mental State Examination (MMSE) Sample Items.

Orientation to time

"What is the date?"

Registration

"Listen carefully. I am going to say three words. You say them back after I stop.

Ready? Here they are...

APPLE (pause), PENNY (pause), TABLE (pause). Now repeat those words back to me." [Repeat up to 5 times, but score only the first trial.]

Naming

"What is this?" [Point to a pencil or pen.]

Reading

"Please read this and do what it says." [Show examinee the words on the stimulus form.]

CLOSE YOUR EYES

Figure 14.6 Clock Drawing Test for a 75-Year-Old Male with Probable Alzheimer's Disease.

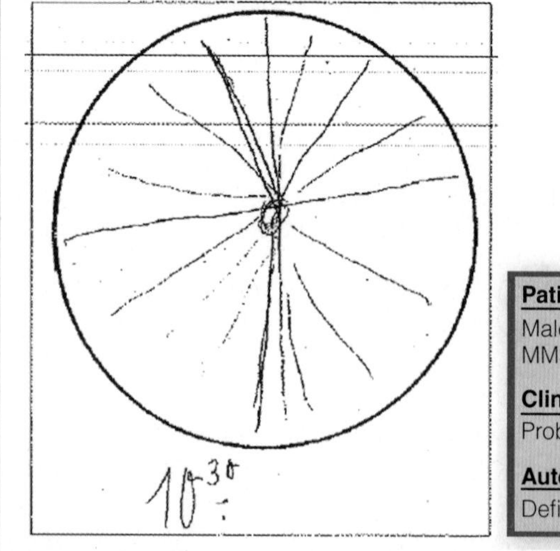

Patient
Male, 75 years old
MMSE = 28 points
Clinical diagnosis:
Probable AD
Autopsy 4 yrs later:
Definite AD

From Taylor, K.I., & Monsch, A.U. (2004). The neuropsychology of Alzheimer's disease. In R.W. Richter & B.Z. Richter (Eds.), *Alzheimer's disease: A physician's guide to practical management* (p. 119). Reprinted by permission of Springer/Humana Press.

dementias and was used for Mr. Ponder (Chun et al., 2020).

Other formal tests of cognitive functioning were covered in previous chapters. These primarily include intelligence tests such as the *Wechsler Adult Intelligence Scale* and neuropsychological tests such as the *Halstead-Reitan* (Chapters 12 and 13). These tests are useful for charting changes in cognitive ability over time to determine whether these changes are normal or an early form of neurocognitive disorder. Certain subtests of these scales are also useful for determining the extent of damage after a stroke. A clinician can examine certain "hold" tests such as vocabulary that tend to remain stable even after brain damage. Other methods include examining a specific profile of scores that seem predictive of people with Alzheimer's disease (Chung et al., 2020).

Figure 14.7 PET Scans of Brains of a Normal Older Person, Left; a Person with Alzheimer's Disease, Middle; and a Person with Frontotemporal Degeneration, Right.

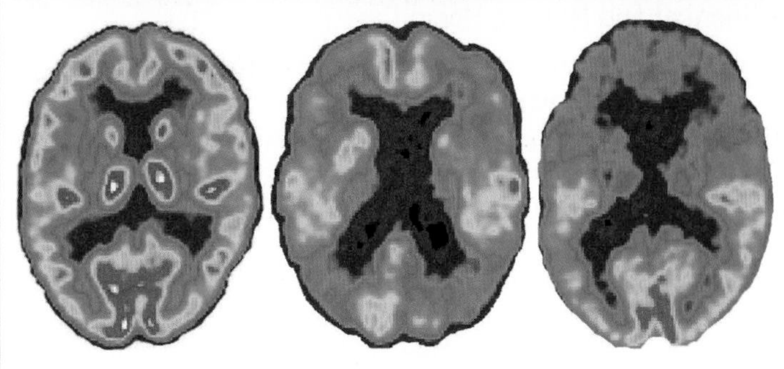

Source: Courtesy, Dr. Arthur W. Toga, Laboratory of Neuro Imaging at UCLA.

Medical and Laboratory Assessment

People who may have a neurocognitive disorder are often referred first to a physician for evaluation. A medical examination will likely include tests for cardiovascular and thyroid problems, substance intoxication, HIV and other infections, dehydration, and other basic factors that could explain delirium or dementia (Miled et al., 2020). A medical examination could also include more extensive laboratory procedures discussed in Chapters 4 and 12: *computerized axial tomography* (CAT scan), *magnetic resonance imaging* (MRI scan), *positron emission tomography* (PET scan), and *single photon emission computed tomography* (SPECT). MRI and PET scans are usually recommended as more definitive ways of determining Alzheimer's disease and other dementias (Oldan et al., 2021; refer to **Figure 14.7**).

Biological Treatments of Neurocognitive Disorders

Medication

Neurocognitive disorders are clearly affected by many biological variables and will certainly become more common given the rapidly aging population around the globe. The search for medical cures for neurocognitive disorder thus remains a high priority for researchers. Many drugs for people with other mental disorders that are described in this textbook are given to people with dementia. These drugs include antidepressants and mood stabilizers (Chapter 7) and antipsychotics (Chapter 12). These medications are useful for easing behavioral problems (such as delusions/hallucinations) associated with dementia, or depression or delirium, but are not too useful for changing severe cognitive and memory deficits brought on by Alzheimer's disease and other dementias (Tournier et al., 2022).

Researchers have thus focused on **cholinesterase inhibitors**. These drugs enhance the neurotransmitter acetylcholine, which is deficient in people with dementia and memory problems. These drugs inhibit enzymes in the brain from breaking down acetylcholine so more of the neurotransmitter is available. The primary cholinesterase inhibitors that have been studied include *physostigmine*, *tacrine*, *metrifonate*, *donepezil*, *rivastigmine*, and *galantamine*, and especially the latter three (Giocobini et al., 2022). These drugs produce only a modest increase in functioning for people with mild to moderate neurocognitive disorder, however, and work better if given sooner in the disease process (Marucci et al., 2021).

Another drug, *memantine*, helps control excess L-glutamate activity. Memantine has some beneficial cognitive effect for people with moderate to severe neurocognitive disorder (Parson et al., 2021). People with Parkinson's disease, a disorder that could lead to dementia, often take the drug *levodopa* (*L-dopa*) to increase dopamine levels in the brain, sometimes in concert with surgical strategies (Müller, 2020). Overall, a combination of medications is often used to treat dementia. Over time, however, the steady progression of dementia eventually overwhelms drug effectiveness.

Gene Therapy

A revolutionary approach to future treatment of neurocognitive disorder will likely include **gene therapy**, or introduction of genes to a person to help increase neuron growth and regeneration. Healthy genes are generally introduced not to replace but to compensate for dysfunctions from problematic genes. Gene therapy is experimental now but has the potential to address some of the most severe mental and physical disorders in humans. Some success has been shown in animal studies, but the approach requires pinpoint accuracy to prevent adverse effects (Predecki et al., 2020).

Residential and Nursing Home Care

Many biological treatments for people with dementia are given in hospitals, residential hospices, and nursing homes. Psychiatric care in these settings often consists of managing behavior problems such as hypersexuality, easing emotional issues such as depression, and reducing infections and pain (Lindsey et al., 2021). Hospice care is especially beneficial to people experiencing later, end-of-life stages of dementia. A family's decision to place a loved one in hospice or nursing home care can be excruciating, however, as it was for the Ponder family. Some questions for family members in this difficult position include the following (adapted from Mittelman et al., 2003):

- What would the person with dementia have wanted?
- What is the recommendation of the person's medical doctor?
- Will entry into a hospice or nursing home help reduce a person's suffering?
- What are the financial and emotional burdens of home care versus hospice/nursing home care?
- Do most family members feel a certain way in this decision?
- Do family members feel comfortable giving control of a person's care to others?
- What services are offered at the hospice or nursing home?
- What provisions are in place at the hospice or nursing home to maximize safety?

Psychological Treatments of Neurocognitive Disorders

Biological approaches to neurocognitive disorders are a popular area of research but their limited effectiveness at this stage means psychological approaches to improve a person's quality of life remain extremely important. Psychological treatments may be divided into two groups: those that target the person with neurocognitive disorder and those that focus on the person's caregivers.

Psychological Approaches for People with Neurocognitive Disorders

Psychological approaches targeted toward people with neurocognitive disorders are generally conducted in earlier stages of the disorder when confusion and disorientation are not yet severe. These approaches are designed to improve a person's quality of life and enhance cognitive functioning to delay onset of more severe symptoms. Some of these approaches were described previously in this textbook, including *reminiscence therapy* (Chapter 7). Reminiscence therapy involves a thorough review of a person's life to impart a sense of meaning and resolve remaining interpersonal conflicts or regrets. A person with dementia will likely lose the ability to interact with others, so such reflection will hopefully enhance present well-being and provide a positive sense of closure to one's life (Justo-Henriques et al., 2021).

Another popular psychological therapy for people with neurocognitive disorder is **reality orientation**. This is a technique to reduce confusion in people with dementia and often involves constant feedback about time, place, person, and recent events (Nishiura et al., 2021). A person may be consistently reminded about their daily events, settings, and identity. Often this consists of placing clocks and calendars around the living environment, directional arrows to places such as the refrigerator, and pictures to remind a person of loved ones. Reality orientation could be done by staff members at a nursing home or by family members at home. Reality orientation may have some initial benefits on cognitive functioning and may even delay nursing home placement, but these benefits are likely best for people in early and intermediate stages of neurocognitive disorder (Gibbor et al., 2021).

Memory training is used for people with neurocognitive disorders as well. A person is taught to enhance memory performance by repeatedly practicing various skills such as using a microwave oven, relying on external cues and mnemonic strategies to jog memory, increasing social interaction, and simplifying their living environment so less needs to be remembered. Common strategies include a "memory wallet" that contains written reminders and pictures of loved ones a person can refer to when faced with loss of memory and painting various rooms in bright, different colors and cues for

David Hancock/Alamy Stock Photo

Reality orientation kits are often used to help guide people with moderate Alzheimer's disease. The reality orientation clock this woman is holding, which includes the time and days, is frequently pointed out and used in conversations with her.

easy identification (e.g., "blue" for bedroom with a picture of a bed). Obstacles that interfere with memory, such as depression, apathy, or cognitive distortions, are addressed as well (Irozoki et al., 2020). Memory training is likely best for people in the early stages of a neurocognitive disorder.

Behavior therapy is another common form of treatment for people with neurocognitive disorder but one that focuses on reducing behavior problems and increasing frequency of self-care skills. Behavior problems typically addressed in this population include wandering alone, hypersexuality, depression, verbal and physical aggression, and agitation. Self-care skills typically addressed in this population include feeding, dressing, toileting, and grooming. Family members are taught to positively reward appropriate behaviors and redirect or ignore (if possible) inappropriate behaviors. This approach is often used in combination with reality orientation and memory training as well as music, art, and movement therapies to increase cognitive stimulation (Pinto et al., 2020).

Psychological Approaches for Caregivers of People with Neurocognitive Disorders

Other psychological approaches for people with neurocognitive disorder focus more on caregivers such as partners and other family members. A critical first step is to provide *information* about the nature of dementia and provide extensive social support and other resources (Xu et al., 2021). Information about dementia should include its major symptoms, cause, and course over time. Caregivers should know what to expect of a person in coming weeks and months, such as serious cognitive decline, and begin to plan accordingly. This often involves creating living wills and power of attorney documents, as well as resolving current or past conflicts (Jox, 2020; refer to **Focus On Gender: Grief in the Partner Caregiver**).

Resources should also be established so caregivers are relieved of the everyday burden of caring for someone with dementia. Arrangements can be made to rotate or add family members to daily care, provide expert respite care, and consider when placement in a nursing home or hospice might be most appropriate (van den Kieboom et al., 2020). Partners and caregivers of people with dementia are particularly prone to stress, burnout, and other psychological and physical problems, so easing the burden of care is crucial for their long-term health (Chan et al., 2021).

Support groups for caregivers of people with neurocognitive disorders are crucial as well. These groups allow members to share information about daily care and express frustrations and sadness about their current situation. Online support groups are also available and might be particularly important for caregivers largely confined to their home (Cheng & Zhang, 2020). If a caregiver has substantial depression or other psychological problems, then referral to a psychiatrist and psychologist for more formal intervention may be best.

Living with a person with Alzheimer's disease or other form of severe neurocognitive disorder can be extremely difficult. The Mayo Clinic has some practical tips for caregivers in this situation (refer to **Table 14.11**). These tips focus on assessing the independence of a person with dementia, creating a safe environment, adjusting expectations, limiting distractions, and promoting communication. A key aspect of this day-to-day strategy is to frequently rethink what a person with dementia can still do and what they can no longer do. Incorporating psychological interventions for people with dementia mentioned earlier would also be important in this process.

Focus On Gender

Grief in the Partner Caregiver

Treatment for people with dementia often falls to partners who care for their loved one—most people with dementia live at home. Much has been written about the burden of such treatment and how support and respite care are so important, but little has been written about the general grief partners go through when encountering this difficult situation. Such grief often includes thoughts about gradual isolation from one's life partner, increasing realization of the shortness of life, and sense of meaninglessness and hopelessness about the current situation. Grief of this nature usually accompanies strong feelings of anxiety, anger, sadness, and guilt (Dehpour & Koffman, 2022).

Partner and child caregivers differ in their approach to grief. Children who care for a parent with dementia tend to deny the presence of dementia and focus on how a parent's dementia affects them. Partner caregivers, however, tend to be more open about accepting their partner's dementia and the burdens of care to come. Partner caregivers also tend to focus on how a person's dementia affects that person and not themselves. They worry and are sad about their partner's loss of cognitive and memory abilities and grieve over the eventual loss of companionship. Child caregivers respond to nursing home placement of their parent with dementia with a sense of relief, but partner caregivers feel extensive sadness, anger, and frustration. In either case, attention to a caregiver's grief before a person's death is likely an important aspect of intervention in this population (Ashwill et al., 2015; Reed et al., 2014).

Table 14.11 Practical Tips for Caregivers of Those with Alzheimer's Disease

Assess independence	Involve loved one in tasks as much as possible. *Give your mother two choices for an outfit rather than asking her to choose from a closet full.* Reassess the level of assistance that is required daily. *Can your husband shave by himself if you set out the supplies? Or can he shave by himself if you turn on an electric razor and put it in his hand? Or does he need you to provide assistance with the entire task?*
Create a safe environment	Remove throw rugs, extension cords, and any clutter. Avoid rearranging furniture. Install locks on cabinets. Make sure there is a first-aid kit, a fire extinguisher, and working smoke alarms. *If your partner is a smoker, don't allow them to smoke alone.* Remove plug-in appliances. Set the temperature on the water heater no higher than 120° F to prevent burns.
Adjust your expectations	Allow more time to accomplish everyday tasks. Try not to worry about the way things should be done. *If no danger results from your father's actions, refrain from correcting him.* Try to stay flexible. *If your partner refuses to do something, back off and try again later using a different approach.*
Limit distractions	Shut off the television and limit background noise. Encourage visitors to call before they come.
Promote communication	To understand a behavior, consider what your loved one may be feeling. *If your partner is pacing, it may mean they are tired, feel hungry, or need to use the bathroom.*

Source: Adapted from the © 2013 Mayo Foundation for Medical Education and Research.

What If Someone I Know Has a Neurocognitive Disorder?

If you suspect someone you know might be experiencing symptoms of a neurocognitive disorder, then referring them for a full medical and neuropsychological examination is important. Catching these symptoms early on may be helpful to reverse delirium or slow the progression of dementia and improve someone's quality of life as long as possible. If someone you know does have Alzheimer's disease or another severe neurocognitive disorder, then sharing and enjoying what time that person has left is essential. Resolve conflicts with the person while you can and try to fully understand what they would like you to do in later stages of their disorder (refer to **Focus On Law and Ethics: Ethical Issues and Dementia**). Neurocognitive disorders are among the most vicious disorders discussed in this textbook. Pursuing what precious quality of life remains is imperative.

Long-Term Outcome for People with Neurocognitive Disorders

You may have guessed from the tone of this chapter that the long-term outcome for people with Alzheimer's disease and other major neurocognitive disorders is not optimistic. A person's life span averages 7.6 years after the onset of Alzheimer's disease and is usually less for people with vascular, Lewy body, Parkinson's, or frontotemporal dementia (Liang et al., 2021). Predictors of earlier mortality in people with dementia include more severe cognitive problems or disability, presence of Lewy bodies, older age, male gender, depression, and cardiovascular disease (Armstrong et al., 2022; Haaksma et al., 2020).

Some people (5–15 percent) with mild cognitive impairment progress to dementia, often Alzheimer's disease, each year (Dunne et al., 2021). Researchers have tried to identify exactly which cognitive impairments are most likely to predict Alzheimer's disease and other major neurocognitive disorders. Initial problems related to episodic memory (memory of recent personal events) and auditory verbal learning are possibly related to later onset of dementia (Boenniger et al., 2021). People with problems with attention, naming, and psychomotor and visuospatial tasks also seem at risk for later onset of dementia (Chehrehnegar et al., 2020).

Others note that strong predictors of the onset of major neurocognitive disorder, especially Alzheimer's disease, include age, less education, depression, stroke, poor health, presence of APOE-4, and poor cerebral blood flow (Battista et al., 2020; Kim et al., 2020). The presence of delirium is also a risk factor for older people to develop dementia (Fong & Inouye, 2022). People who

Focus On Law and Ethics

Ethical Issues and Dementia

As you might guess, serious ethical issues arise when addressing people with cognitive decline and dementia. One key question is whether people who qualify for a diagnosis of major neurocognitive disorder should be told of this diagnosis. Arguments in favor of doing so include respect for the person, their participation in care decisions while still able, and acceptance of limitations. Arguments against doing so include the fact that treatment options are few, the person may not understand the diagnosis, knowledge of the diagnosis could lead to depression and other psychological problems, and insurance may be lost (Sousa & D'Souza, 2021). Would you want to know?

Another set of ethical issues in this population arises when conducting research. Key questions include use of stem cells, ability of a person to give informed consent, genetic testing for risk factors for dementia such as APOE-4, and treatment and feeding of a person with dementia who refuses such help (Beetstra-Hill, 2021). Would you want to know that you have the APOE-4 gene even though this does not necessarily mean you would develop Alzheimer's disease? Should the general population be tested for this gene?

The eventual incapacitation of people with dementia has thrown new light onto the area of *advance directives* such as living wills. In these directives, a person states ahead of time under what conditions nourishment and medical treatment should be given. For example, the person may direct that if they were to eventually decline to a profoundly ill state, they would no longer want extensive lifesaving practices such as ventilators to be used. The creation of a living will may also reduce the stress of family members who may be otherwise burdened with such decisions.

have had a stroke and eventually progress to vascular dementia are generally those who have had less cognitive and memory ability, greater depression, and several cardiovascular risk factors such as hypertension and diabetes (van Sloten et al., 2020). Predictors of eventual dementia in people with Parkinson's disease include age, severe postural and gait problems, mild cognitive impairment, and visual hallucinations (Phongpreecha et al., 2020).

Section Summary

- Interviews are commonly used to assess people with neurocognitive disorders and their caregivers, and topics often include recent changes in behavior, thinking, memory, and long-term skills such as language or ability to recognize others.
- Questionnaires are also used to screen for delirium and dementia and typically cover orientation, verbal and written comprehension, concentration, learning, writing and copying, and memory.
- Cognitive tests such as neuropsychological and intelligence tests also evaluate strengths and limitations of people with neurocognitive disorders.
- Medical and laboratory tests, including neuroimaging techniques, can often be used to assess the development of neurocognitive disorders.
- Biological treatments for people with neurocognitive disorders include cholinesterase inhibitors to increase acetylcholine in the brain, memantine to control L-glutamate activity, and L-dopa to quell symptoms of Parkinson's disease.
- Gene therapy may be a key future way of treating people with neurocognitive disorders.
- Many biological treatments for people with neurocognitive disorders are conducted in hospice or nursing home settings.
- Psychological treatments for people with neurocognitive disorders include reminiscence therapy, reality orientation, memory training, and behavior therapy.
- Psychological treatments for caregivers of people with neurocognitive disorders include education about dementia and providing support and respite care to prevent caregiver burnout and improve quality of life.
- The long-term outcome for people with major neurocognitive disorders is not optimistic; many die a few years after onset of the disorder.

Review Questions

1. Describe various methods of assessing a person with neurocognitive disorder and devise an assessment strategy you think might be most helpful.
2. What medications might be best for people with neurocognitive disorders?
3. What questions might family members ask themselves when considering whether to admit a loved one to a nursing home?
4. Describe psychological treatments commonly used for people with neurocognitive disorders and their caregivers.
5. Outline the long-term outcome for people with neurocognitive disorders.

Final Comments

No cure exists for many major neurocognitive disorders, so preventing these problems and improving quality of life seems most important. You may find it easy to wait to worry about such problems until much later in life, but consider ways you can live a healthy lifestyle now that will allow you substantial independence and ability to function later in life. In the meantime, enjoy every day you have and make the most of it. *Carpe diem*: Seize the day!

Thought Questions

1. Think about famous people or even your own family members who have had Alzheimer's disease—what about their condition seems most concerning?
2. What do you think the future will bring with respect to treating people with major neurocognitive disorders?
3. What would you say to a friend who told you a parent or grandparent seems to be developing symptoms of a neurocognitive disorder?
4. What separates "normal aging" from dementia? At what point does one "cross the line" from regular changes in thinking and memory to more serious problems?
5. What do you think can be done to reduce the prevalence of neurocognitive disorder in the general population?

Key Terms

Audrey C '21

Consumer Guide to Psychopathology

15

Learning Objectives

LO 15.1 Discuss the occupational opportunities for mental health professionals, including their activities and educational and credentialing requirements.

LO 15.2 Outline important considerations when considering mental health treatment.

LO 15.3 Explain the active and process variables associated with successful individual-level treatment.

LO 15.4 Describe community-level treatments, including their purposes, processes, and effectiveness.

LO 15.5 Summarize the strengths and limitations of and caveats about mental health treatment.

LO 15.6 Discuss the ethical considerations of the mental health professions.

Introduction to the Consumer Guide

Many unusual, harmful, and distressing behaviors have been covered in this textbook. Various treatment strategies for people with different types of mental disorder have also been discussed. You might be wondering more, though, about people who conduct therapy and what it is about treatment that helps people change their behavior. You may also have questions about providing or seeking therapy services yourself.

This chapter focuses even more on the treatment process, with special emphasis on information most relevant to you, the consumer. Initial sections cover different types of mental health professionals and what to consider if you want to become a mental health professional or a client. Later sections cover important components of treatment at individual and community levels, caveats about treatment, and ethics.

Clinical and counseling psychologists often work in private practice settings.

Becoming a Mental Health Professional

LO 15.1 Discuss the occupational opportunities for mental health professionals, including their activities and educational and credentialing requirements.

Perhaps you have been so intrigued by the material in this textbook that you are thinking of becoming a mental health professional. Good for you! This section discusses different types of therapists and their qualifications as well as suggestions for preparing yourself to become a mental health professional.

Types of Therapists and Qualifications

Professionals who assess and treat people with mental disorders include psychologists, psychiatrists, psychiatric nurses, marriage and family therapists, social workers, and special education teachers, among others. Various kinds of psychologists (e.g., clinical, counseling, educational, and school) address people with mental disorders (refer to **Table 15.1**). **Clinical psychologists** often have a doctoral degree (Ph.D.) that allows them to serve both as *scientists*, or someone who conducts research on psychopathology, and as *practitioners*, or someone who conducts a wide range of psychological testing and provides diagnoses and treatment to people with mental disorders. Some clinical psychologists attend Psy.D. graduate programs that may focus less on research and more on developing clinical skills. A state licensing board must certify clinical psychologists to practice independently.

Clinical psychologists obtain an undergraduate degree, usually in psychology, and then attend graduate school for at least four years (usually five) in addition to a one-year internship. Many clinical psychologists also work in postdoctoral research positions after internship to further specialize in a given area, such as neuropsychology or substance use disorder. Many psychologists also become professors.

Clinical psychologists are often trained to work with people with severe behavior problems, and often do so using a *change-oriented* approach in which behavior change is the primary goal (Norcross et al., 2021). Clinical psychologists often rely on verbal treatment strategies to change problematic emotions, thoughts, and behaviors. They do not currently prescribe medication in most areas, but do in some states, and other jurisdictions are considering whether to give prescription privileges to clinical psychologists (Brown et al., 2021).

Counseling psychologists tend to focus on people with less severe problems, such as those needing vocational counseling or marriage and family therapy (Norcross et al., 2021). Counseling psychologists usually have a doctoral degree and are licensed as well. Many counseling psychologists adopt a *choice-oriented* approach in which the primary goal is to help a client make the right choices in their life. A client may need help deciding what career to pursue, for example, or whether to get a divorce.

Educational and school psychologists focus on children and learning-based issues. These psychologists often have a master's or doctoral degree. **Educational psychologists** tend to be more research-based and focus on developing effective strategies to teach children (and adults) different concepts like reading or arithmetic. **School psychologists** are usually affiliated with elementary, middle, and high schools and often assess children at risk for learning, developmental, and other mental disorders that could interfere with academic achievement.

Table 15.1 **Common Types of Psychologists**

Type	Description
Clinical psychologists	assess and treat mental, emotional, and behavioral disorders. These range from short-term crises, such as difficulties resulting from adolescent rebellion, to more severe, chronic conditions such as schizophrenia. Some clinical psychologists treat specific problems exclusively, such as phobias or depression. Others focus on specific populations: young people, ethnic minority groups, and older people, for instance. They also consult with physicians on physical problems that have underlying psychological causes.
Cognitive and perceptual psychologists	study human perception, thinking, and memory. Cognitive psychologists are interested in questions such as: How does the mind represent reality? How do people learn? How do people understand and produce language? Cognitive psychologists also study reasoning, judgment, and decision making. Cognitive and perceptual psychologists frequently collaborate with behavioral neuroscientists to understand the biological bases of perception or cognition or with researchers in other areas of psychology to better understand the cognitive biases in the thinking of people with depression, for example.
Counseling psychologists	help people recognize their strengths and resources to cope with their problems. Counseling psychologists do counseling/psychotherapy, teaching, and scientific research with individuals of all ages, families, and organizations (e.g., schools, hospitals, businesses). Counseling psychologists help people understand and take action on career and work problems. They pay attention to how problems and people differ across life stages. Counseling psychologists have great respect for the influence of differences among people (such as race, gender, sexual orientation, religion, disability status) on psychological well-being. They believe that behavior is affected by many things, including qualities of the individual (e.g., psychological, physical, or spiritual factors) and factors in the person's environment (e.g., family, society, and cultural groups).
Developmental psychologists	study the psychological development of the human being that takes place throughout life. Until recently, the primary focus was on childhood and adolescence, the most formative years. But as life expectancy in this country approaches 80 years, developmental psychologists are becoming increasingly interested in aging, especially in researching and developing ways to help older people stay as independent as possible.
Educational psychologists	concentrate on how effective teaching and learning take place. They consider a variety of factors, such as human abilities, student motivation, and the effect on the classroom of the diversity of race, ethnicity, and culture that makes up various countries.
Engineering psychologists	conduct research on how people work best with machines. For example, How can a computer be designed to prevent fatigue and eye strain? What arrangement of an assembly line makes production most efficient? What is a reasonable workload? Most engineering psychologists work in industry, but some are employed by the government. They are often known as human factors specialists.
Evolutionary psychologists	study how evolutionary principles such as mutation, adaptation, and selective fitness influence human thought, feeling, and behavior. Because of their focus on genetically shaped behaviors that influence an organism's chances of survival, evolutionary psychologists study mating, aggression, helping behavior, and communication. Evolutionary psychologists are particularly interested in paradoxes and problems of evolution. For example, some behaviors that were highly adaptive in our evolutionary past may no longer be adaptive in the modern world.
Experimental psychologists	are interested in a wide range of psychological phenomena, including cognitive processes, comparative psychology (cross-species comparisons), learning and conditioning, and psychophysics (the relationship between the physical brightness of a light and how bright the light is perceived to be, for example). Experimental psychologists study both human and nonhuman animals with respect to their abilities to detect what is happening in a particular environment and to acquire and maintain responses to what is happening. Experimental psychologists work with the empirical method (collecting data) and the manipulation of variables within the laboratory as a way of understanding certain phenomena and advancing scientific knowledge. In addition to working in academic settings, experimental psychologists work in places as diverse as manufacturing settings and engineering firms.
Forensic psychologists	apply psychological principles to legal issues. Their expertise is often essential in court. They can, for example, help a judge decide which parent should have custody of a child or evaluate a defendant's mental competence to stand trial. Forensic psychologists also conduct research on jury behavior or eyewitness testimony. Some forensic psychologists are trained in both psychology and the law.
Health psychologists	specialize in how biological, psychological, and social factors affect health and illness. They study how patients handle illness; why some people do not follow medical advice; and the most effective ways to control pain or to change poor health habits. They also develop health care strategies that foster emotional and physical well-being. Health psychologists team up with medical personnel in private practice and in hospitals to provide patients with complete health care.
Industrial/organizational psychologists	apply psychological principles and research methods to the workplace in the interest of improving productivity and the quality of work life. Many serve as human resources specialists, helping organizations with staffing, training, and employee development. Others work as management consultants in such areas as strategic planning, quality management, and coping with organizational change.

continued

Table 15.1 Common Types of Psychologists—cont'd

Neuropsychologists (and behavioral neuropsychologists) explore the relationships between brain systems and behavior. For example, behavioral neuropsychologists may study the way the brain creates and stores memories, or how various diseases and injuries of the brain affect emotion, perception, and behavior. They design tasks to study normal brain functions with imaging techniques such as positron emission tomography (PET), single photon emission computed tomography (SPECT), and functional magnetic resonance imaging (fMRI). Clinical neuropsychologists also assess and treat people; and many work with health teams to help brain-injured people resume productive lives.
Quantitative and measurement psychologists focus on methods and techniques for designing experiments and analyzing psychological data. Some develop new methods for performing analysis; others create research strategies to assess the effect of social and educational programs and psychological treatment. They develop and evaluate mathematical models for psychological tests. They also propose methods for evaluating the quality and fairness of the tests.
Rehabilitation psychologists work with stroke and accident victims, people with intellectual developmental disorder and autism, and those with developmental disorders caused by such conditions as cerebral palsy. They help clients adapt to their situation, frequently working with other health care professionals. They address issues of personal adjustment, interpersonal relations, the work world, and pain management. Rehabilitation psychologists are also involved in public health programs to prevent disabilities, including those caused by violence and excessive substance use. They also testify in court as expert witnesses about the causes and effects of a disability and a person's rehabilitation needs.
School psychologists work directly with public and private schools. They assess and counsel students, consult with parents and school staff, and conduct behavioral interventions when appropriate. Most school districts employ psychologists full time.
Social psychologists study how a person's mental life and behavior are shaped by interactions with other people. They are interested in all aspects of interpersonal relationships, including individual and group influences, and seek ways to improve such interactions. For example, their research helps us understand how people form attitudes toward others, and when these are harmful—as in the case of prejudice—suggests ways to change them. Social psychologists are found in a variety of settings, from academic institutions (where they teach and conduct research), to advertising agencies (where they study consumer attitudes and preferences), to businesses and government agencies (where they help with a variety of problems in organization and management).
Sports psychologists help athletes refine their focus on competition goals, become more motivated, and learn to deal with the anxiety and fear of failure that often accompany competition. The field is growing as sports of all kinds become more competitive and increasingly draw children at a young age.

Source: American Psychological Association (www.apa.org/topics/psychologycareer.html#aparesources).

Psychiatrists are physicians who can prescribe medication for people with mental disorders. Their training and background is typically from a biological perspective, so psychiatrists often rely on finding the right medication or other somatic treatment, such as electroconvulsive therapy (Chapter 7), to address mental health problems. Psychiatrists are usually trained in premedical, medical, and residency programs for many years. Psychologists and psychiatrists often work together so that different aspects of mental disorder, especially severe mental disorders like schizophrenia or depression, can be treated. A combination of psychological treatment and medication is best for many people. A psychologist or psychiatrist with specialized training in Freudian-based psychoanalysis may be referred to as a **psychoanalyst**.

Psychiatric nurses (R.N.s) are those who receive specialized training in addressing the needs of people with severe mental disorders like schizophrenia. These professionals often work in hospital-based, inpatient psychiatric units and are usually responsible for daily management of the unit as well as administering medications.

Marriage and family therapists can be licensed as a separate entity in several states (check yours) and often have a master's degree in clinical or counseling psychology. These therapists concentrate on couples with marital or relationship problems as well as families with communication or problem-solving difficulties. **Social workers** usually have a master's degree (M.S.W.) and are licensed as well. The traditional role of this profession has been to focus on social and cultural factors of psychopathology and link disadvantaged persons with mental disorders to community resources, such as residential programs or unemployment benefits, which could improve quality of life. Many social workers can thus be found working in prisons, hospitals, schools, and social service agencies.

Marmaduke St. John/Alamy Stock Photo

School psychologists often assess youth with learning problems.

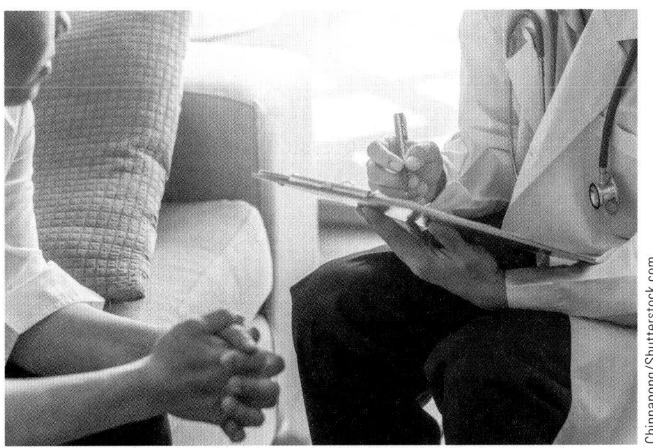
Chinnapong/Shutterstock.com

Psychiatrists are physicians who usually adopt a biological approach to mental disorder.

The role of social workers has expanded, and many work closely with psychologists and psychiatrists and/or practice therapy independently (Parker, 2020).

Special education teachers usually have a master's degree and often work closely with persons with developmental disorders, such as severe intellectual developmental disorder or autism. These teachers are responsible for designing and implementing specialized educational plans for these children and are often found in unique schools or segregated units of regular schools.

Many people also work with those with mental disorders in other ways. **Paraprofessionals** are those without advanced degrees who conduct assessments and interventions with people with mental disorders under the supervision of a mental health professional. Your textbook author has an on-campus research-based clinic staffed by undergraduate and graduate students who assist with assessment and treatment sessions. Students with a bachelor's degree in psychology may also work as paraprofessionals in hospitals and other community-based organizations for people with mental disorders. In addition, **psychotherapist** is a term sometimes used for a mental health professional who practices therapy under supervision but who is not yet licensed.

Preparing to Be a Mental Health Professional

What should you do if you want to become a mental health professional? A good first strategy is to talk to professors in different departments on campus, such as psychology, counseling, and social work. *Do not be afraid to do this!* A professor's job includes advising students about career options and helping them determine which options fit best for them. Talk to the instructor of the course about their background and ask what advice they have. Think about areas you might be most interested in, such as children or depression, and discuss with the professor what kinds of courses you might wish to take in the future to further develop your interests.

Next, examine different courses in these areas and decide which ones appeal most to you. Take these varied courses and decide if the content matches what you think you might like to do. Talk to the instructors of each course about their background, training, and advice for future work. As you do, you might find yourself drawn to a particular area of interest. If not, that is fine. Keep searching!

Also, check for which professors in different departments are actively engaged in clinical research. Your current instructor may be a good person to ask first. One usually needs diverse clinical and research experience or internships to enter graduate school to become a mental health professional. Engage in this kind of research with different people as early as possible in your undergraduate career—do not wait until your senior year! In addition to gaining valuable clinical and research experience, you will find people who might be willing to write future letters of recommendation for you. Remember, good grades and standardized test scores are only part of the equation for getting accepted into graduate school. Some other recommendations:

- Get involved in Psi Chi, the national honor society for psychology students.
- Develop contacts with on-campus social groups for certain majors, such as a psychology club.
- Talk with directors of community mental health agencies about openings for volunteers and paraprofessionals. Donate your time conducting assessments, observing treatment sessions, and engaging in telephone work, perhaps at a suicide hotline.
- Get ongoing advice from one or more faculty mentors about deciding on career options, writing a letter of intent, and choosing graduate schools of interest.
- Engage in some clinical research and, if possible, present a paper at a psychology conference.
- Find out which schools might best fit your interests, and tailor your application toward a specific faculty member or two who would best match your interests.
- Review information provided for students by the American Psychological Association (Washington, DC), such as the book *Graduate Study in Psychology* and the "Careers in Psychology" brochure (www.apa.org/topics/psychologycareer.html#aparesources).
- Read the books *What Can You Do with a Major in Psychology: Real People, Real Jobs, Real Rewards* (New York: Wiley) by Shelley O'Hara, and *Insider's Guide to Graduate Programs in Clinical and Counseling Psychology* by Tracy Mayne, John Norcross, and Michael Sayette (New York: Guilford).
- Above all, ask questions and get as much information as possible!

Becoming a mental health professional is exhausting but exciting work. Think carefully about the commitment

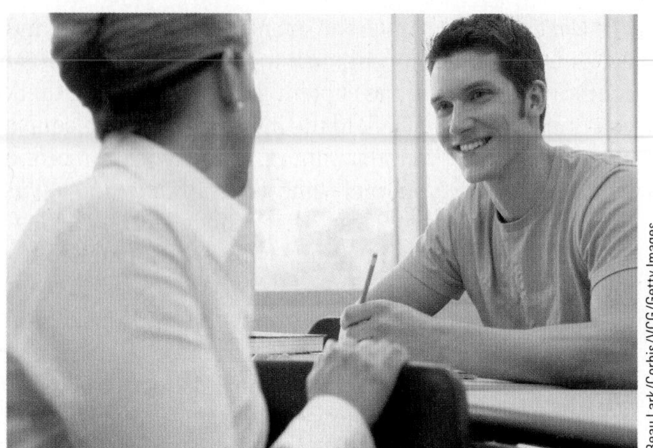
Beau Lark/Corbis/VCG/Getty Images

If you are interested in a career in psychology, a discussion with your instructor might be a good place to start gathering information.

you will make and how this will affect your life. But above all, do not get discouraged if the work seems challenging at times! Being a mental health professional is among the most rewarding professions available.

Becoming a Client

LO 15.2 Outline important considerations when considering mental health treatment.

Perhaps you are more interested in *consuming* mental health services than providing such services. What should you or someone you know do if seeking treatment for a psychological problem? An important idea to consider when seeking treatment is what goal you wish to accomplish in therapy. Are you going through a crisis that needs immediate attention? Are you entering an important life transition and need some direction? Do you have troublesome thoughts or behaviors that need change? Do you have a problem that seems to occur for no reason and might be responsive to medication? The answers to these questions might help you decide what type of mental health professional to choose, such as a crisis intervention counselor, counseling or clinical psychologist, or psychiatrist.

When seeking treatment, one should also get referrals from knowledgeable people, such as psychologists in the community. Most mental health professionals focus their practice in key areas, such as anxiety disorders or marital therapy, so find out who in your community specializes in a given area. Find out which agencies offer low-cost services if that is what you desire. Many universities offer community-based, sliding-scale cost treatment. Following this process, ask the mental health professional that you are considering several questions before scheduling the first appointment:

- What is your fee, and does my insurance cover this fee or some portion of it and for how many sessions?
- Do you offer sliding-scale fees (based on one's ability to pay) for those with limited financial resources or multiple dependents?
- What should I expect during the first session, and what type of assessment procedures do you use?
- What is the nature of the type of therapy you do, and what are its limits?
- What are your procedures regarding informed consent and confidentiality? (discussed later in this chapter)
- What types of problems do you specialize in addressing?
- What is your theoretical orientation and educational background?
- What is your status as a provider? Are you, for example, a licensed clinical psychologist, board-certified psychiatrist, or graduate student?

Focus On Gender

Graduate School and Mentors

Graduate programs in psychology have experienced a strong surge in applications from women, but a lower percentage of faculty members in clinical doctoral programs are female (Bichsel et al., 2019). This disparity raises the question of whether female graduate students receive sufficient or effective mentoring during their education process. This is important because well-mentored students tend to have more productive careers compared with those who have less mentoring.

One researcher surveyed women in graduate school to determine if they had a mentor and what those experiences were like. Several examples of effective mentoring practices were provided. Effective mentors provided advancement opportunities, such as networking with other professionals and inviting a mentee to participate in a special project. Good mentors also provided support and helped the mentee develop self-assurance, especially during times of stress or transition. Mentors help mentees focus on goals and a vision for the future and give constructive feedback about a student's development and progress. Mentors help facilitate independent thinking and help mentees experiment with different professional roles (e.g., as a therapist or researcher). Good mentors are also positive role models, especially with respect to maintaining balance in life (i.e., family and work) and engaging in proper self-care. Mentors help students realize their potential and allow them a good amount of autonomy to challenge the ideas of the mentor (Williams-Nickelson, 2009). If you are considering graduate school, talk to professors in your discipline who can help mentor you. Once you are in graduate school, look for mentors who have the characteristics mentioned here.

- Where are you located, and what are your hours?
- What is your policy for speaking with clients after regular business hours?

Remember, you are a *consumer* of treatment services and therefore entitled to specific answers to these and other relevant questions. Do not be afraid to ask these questions and find a good fit with a therapist.

Treatment at the Individual Level

LO 15.3 Explain the active and process variables associated with successful individual-level treatment.

Whether you want to provide or consume mental health services, you could find yourself in one of many settings. Some of these settings involve treatment at the individual level, as many mental health professionals conduct therapy one-on-one in private practices. Other settings involve therapy within larger community-based institutions, such as group homes, hospitals, prisons, or schools. The next sections cover important factors related to one-on-one therapy as well as practices in community-based settings. This includes discussions of common factors that enhance successful outcome regarding treatment as well as whether therapy itself is effective for people.

Active Ingredients of Treatment

Different kinds of treatment for mental disorders have been covered in this textbook, but what is it about treatment that makes it work? You have seen that mental disorders consist of three components: unsettling physical feelings or emotions, troublesome thoughts, and maladaptive behaviors. Effective treatment strategies must therefore affect these areas in positive ways. One active treatment ingredient is enhancing **self-control**. People with mental disorders learn in therapy to control their own maladaptive (1) physical responses, such as in relaxation training for panic symptoms (Chapter 5); (2) thoughts, such as in cognitive therapy for depression (Chapter 7); and (3) behaviors, such as in the stop–start procedure for premature ejaculation (Chapter 11). Self-control will lead to **mastery** of certain symptoms and less distress from them (Bilet et al., 2020).

Effective therapies and therapists also require clients to continually *practice* new skills. Examples include a child with learning disorder practicing reading and writing or a person with social anxiety disorder practicing conversations at a party. Practicing new skills may also mean a client has to *take risks*, perhaps by abandoning safety-seeking behaviors or doing things not previously done. A therapist will often encourage a client to boldly attempt different ways of behaving and continue to work toward treatment goals by practicing in real life what was learned in session (Caselli et al., 2021).

Klavdiya V./Shutterstock.com

A warm, supportive therapist–client relationship is essential for successful treatment.

As a client works in therapy, a key goal is to help them gain greater **insight** into why they continue to behave in a maladaptive way (Raftery et al., 2020). This is especially important when personality traits interfere with success in different areas of life. A client should gain greater knowledge about themself and how their behavior affects other people. A client should also gain greater knowledge about how to control their behavior or what to do if their behavior seems problematic. If a person finds themself becoming depressed, they may wish to consult friends, become more socially active, and practice cognitive skills to reduce maladaptive thoughts.

A client should also engage in constant *self-exploration* or *introspection* to challenge internal assumptions and enjoy positive life experiences. A therapist will also help a client *work through* hypothetical and real-life problems using more adaptive strategies (McPherson et al., 2020). For example, a therapist might help someone with schizotypal personality disorder interact with others in more socially acceptable ways and solve problems more effectively.

As a client improves in therapy, *ongoing successes* will hopefully and naturally lead to other positive, self-reinforcing events. A person who learns new interviewing skills may land a great job. Or a child who learns social skills and how to follow rules may be better able to make new friends and achieve in school. Ongoing *feedback* from the therapist and significant others will be helpful as well (Janse et al., 2020). Success in therapy and life in general often comes from one's ability to behave effectively in life situations, to resolve or come to terms with past negative experiences, to have realistic expectations for change, to control extremes of emotion and behavior, to seek advice from others about appropriate life choices, and to make good choices.

Process Variables in Treatment

Process variables, also known as *nonspecific factors*, are those common to all treatments that also contribute to treatment success. One powerful process variable is the **placebo effect**, which refers to improvement in treatment due to a client's expectation of help (Kern et al., 2020). Many clients, once they know a therapist has diagnosed their problem and has a potential solution, become much more motivated in therapy and expect good progress. This enhances treatment effectiveness. The placebo effect can be quite stable; placebo control group improvement is sometimes greater than no-treatment conditions (Wampold, 2021).

Other process variables involve the therapist specifically. Such variables include *experience of the therapist* as well as their ability to make the therapy session a *warm and respectful* place. Experienced therapists do not necessarily provide better treatment than less experienced therapists, but therapists who specialize in a given area such as substance use disorders tend to have much knowledge about how to best treat clients with that particular problem. More experienced therapists also tend to be more effective with clients with more severe symptoms (Frank et al., 2020).

John Slater/Digital Vision (RF)/Jupiter Images

One's ability to self-examine thoughts and behaviors is a key aspect of therapy.

A client will also feel free to communicate private thoughts without fear of rejection or ridicule if their therapist establishes an environment based on respect,

Personal Narrative

Julia Martinez, Graduate Student in Clinical Psychology

Courtesy of Julia Martinez

Julia Martinez

I was the first in my family to go to college, so I have always thought of graduate school as a very special challenge and opportunity. On the general academic level, I view it as a place where there are no limits to learning or thought. It becomes your job to think critically about everything, and to formulate research and ideas that have the potential to move us all forward. With respect to clinical psychology, it seems to be a relatively new field, with a lot of work to be done. I find this fact both inspiring and daunting. Lastly, I would never deny that graduate school is very difficult. You make a lot of emotional investments, both in your work and in your own personal development. Frustrations and victories are part of everyday life. Balance, tenacity, and maybe a sense of humor are all important.

Before I started graduate school, I thought a lot about what I might expect. Actually, I expected a lot of awful things that have not come to pass, perhaps because I made some preparations. For example, I knew that graduate school would be a lot of hard work, but I was dead set against pulling all-nighters and then feeling terrible (a familiar experience from my undergraduate years). I thought about how I could improve my work style so I could get a decent night's sleep. Also, a wise person, Dr. Karen Gillock, told me that graduate school would be filled with wonderful opportunities—but that if you did not prioritize well, you could easily find yourself overwhelmed, with the result of getting fewer things done (really important things, like your master's thesis). This advice turned out to be completely true, and it was helpful to expect this at the start. I guess the biggest thing that I did not expect was learning all the great things that I have learned. Going in, I had no idea what exactly I would learn. For instance, I was afraid of statistics, but I have learned to love them. I did not expect to grow and change so much.

And I have changed. I used to be really sensitive about psychology being called a "pseudo-science" or a "soft science," but I did not have enough knowledge about the field to dispute this claim. Over time, I have learned a lot about the impact that well-executed research in psychology can have on the public good, which is clearly of importance. I have also changed personally. I wanted graduate school to be a well-rounded and scholarly experience. Although I spend a great deal of time in

empathy, and *full acceptance* of their expressions (Watson et al., 2020). Another important therapist variable is *reassurance*, or regularly indicating to a client that solutions to problems can be solved if they put forward the work to do so. Providing a *rationale* to a client about why a certain treatment is important, and how it should work, is often crucial as well. People with anxiety disorders who must "face their fears" should be given a full explanation as to why, for example (Raeder et al., 2020).

Other process variables involve the therapist–client relationship. An important one is interactions of the therapist and client, or **therapeutic alliance**, which should be productive, free flowing, and honest. The relationship should be a positive one built on trust, full disclosure from the client, and hard work toward treatment goals. In other cases, the mere fact a client comes to treatment and interacts with someone is important. For these clients, who may be alone or feel rejected during the week, therapy is often an excellent means of unburdening themselves or relieving the stress of isolation. Therapeutic alliance is a good predictor of treatment outcome (Baier et al., 2020).

Therapeutic alignment is also an important process variable in marital and family therapy. This can refer to how a therapist supports certain members of a marriage or family to "balance out" differences in power. A therapist might align themself slightly more with a dependent spouse or an intimidated child to ease communication or problem solving. This must be done carefully, however, so as not to alienate someone in therapy (Holyoak et al., 2021).

Some process variables involve the client as well. Many clients report progress in therapy when they experience a release of emotions, or **catharsis** (Ilchenko et al., 2021). For some clients, this may involve a strong grief or anger reaction, and for others it may represent admissions of things long kept secret, such as child maltreatment or a previous sexual assault. Certain personality characteristics of clients may be important as well. Dependent and less defensive clients may do better in group therapy situations when more structure

the lab, I also have sought other ways to broaden my horizons. I have read a lot of classic novels, taken a fencing class, practiced foreign languages with friends, traveled to Spain, recorded my own music, taken up the banjo, and learned to Irish jig and flamenco dance. To me, these are not unessential things; they have helped me to better understand and to love my work.

I would like to share four tips for those preparing for graduate school:

1. *Know what you want going in.* More specifically, some people want a lot of guidance from their advisors; others want to be left alone until they really need their advisors. Also, some advisors enjoy closely mentoring their students, while others prefer giving students more independence. It saves a lot of time and energy to identify what type of learner you are, what type of advisor would be best suited to your working style, and how you want to carry out your graduate school experience.
2. *Make your cultural differences known (in a constructive way).* Sometimes we differ culturally, which is fine. It is particularly important to understand and to be sensitive to cultural differences in psychology. Yet lines of thinking, work habits, and interpersonal exchanges can sometimes be misunderstood, regarded negatively, or not appreciated as being related to cultural differences. If you ever feel that this is the case, never be afraid to tactfully and constructively share your thoughts about relevant cultural differences. This will help everyone involved to be more informed and to be a better psychologist.
3. *Know about "shining star" syndrome.* That is, a lot of students come into graduate school having been the shining star in their high school and college. All of a sudden, graduate school seems horrible because everyone is smart and outstanding. Some people get really depressed, thinking they have lost their identity as the "smart one." This is not so. We all build from each other's abilities. It really is a time to learn about everyone's individual skills, and how we can all work together to make the world a better place. With this in mind, please also remember the next point:
4. *You are not an imposter.* I definitely have felt intimidated, feeling as if my peers had a better feel for how to do things, or how to go about life in graduate school. The truth is that everyone has a lot to learn. Never be afraid to clarify things you do not completely understand. You will learn and grow as long as you do not give too much importance to your doubts.

Source: Used with permission.

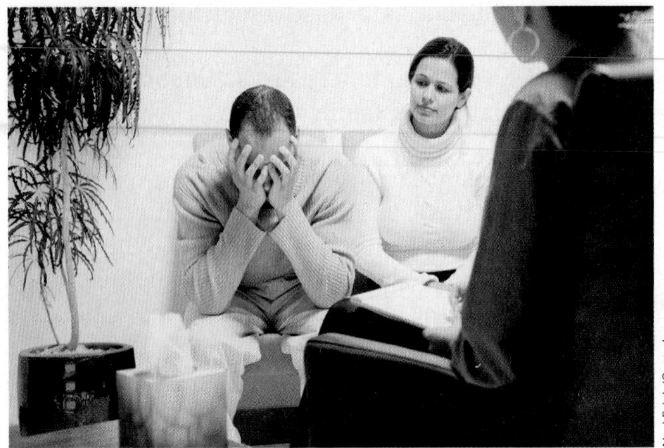
Ned Frisk/Getty Images

Appropriate expression of strong emotions is sometimes a part of successful treatment.

is provided by a therapist, but independent-minded people may benefit more from less therapist direction. The degree to which group members are cohesive, or how much they like one another and are committed to the group goals, also seems to be a key outcome factor in group therapy (Kivlighan et al., 2020).

Does Treatment Work?

Does treatment actually work for clients? The overall answer is yes—many types of psychotherapy seem effective and better than no treatment at all. One type of therapy has not been shown to be consistently and significantly better than another type of therapy (Gold, 2015). A trend in determining whether treatment works, however, is to examine specific types of treatment for specific types of disorders. Recall that cognitive-behavioral treatments are effective for people with many types of problems, including anxiety, depression, eating disturbances, sexual dysfunction, and schizophrenia. Other therapies are especially useful for other disorders if matched well. Examples include dialectical behavior therapy for borderline personality disorder, behavior modification for autism, and medication for bipolar disorder.

Another trend in evaluating treatment is the development of *manuals* for clinicians. Manuals provide detailed instructions for addressing clients with a certain problem and what techniques should be used. Researchers usually design manualized treatments for people with a certain type of mental disorder, such as obsessive-compulsive disorder, though transdiagnostic treatment manuals have also been developed for people with various mental disorders (Barlow & Eustis, 2022).

Manualized treatments have several advantages, including empirical basis, good validity and effectiveness, and specific recommendations for session-by-session assessment and treatment procedures. Manuals are usually brief, such as four to eight sessions, which is preferred by many clients and insurance companies. Manualized treatments may not apply to all people with a certain disorder, however, because they cannot account for all individual differences in clients. Also, some clients have multiple mental disorders, which could affect how a treatment manual for one disorder is implemented (Dalgleish et al., 2020).

Prescriptive Treatment

Another approach to clinical work is to find which treatments are best for certain groups of people with a mental disorder. Researchers evaluate different subtypes of a clinical population and provide a specific treatment to best fit the needs of that subtype. This is sometimes referred to as **prescriptive treatment** or personalized treatment (Lenze et al., 2020). One person with depression may feel sad because of a negative environmental event, such as death of a loved one or bankruptcy. Another person may become depressed for little reason, or "out of the blue," because of a neurochemical imbalance. A good prescriptive treatment for the first person might be grief counseling or cognitive-behavioral therapy. A good prescriptive treatment for the second person might be medication. The idea behind prescriptive treatment is that one must consider intricate individual differences when designing the best treatment for a particular client.

Prescriptive treatment is important when seeking therapy. Clients should expect a therapist to conduct a thorough assessment of their problem to determine the best treatment. A client should also be open with the therapist when providing important personal information and should ask many questions of the therapist about potential treatments. The therapist and client can thus design an effective and efficient treatment plan together. More specific suggestions for seeking treatment are discussed next.

Section Summary

- Professionals who work with people with mental disorders include psychologists, psychiatrists, psychiatric nurses, marriage and family therapists, social workers, and special education teachers. Paraprofessionals without advanced degrees may also work with special populations under supervision.
- Becoming a mental health professional involves gathering different types of experiences, speaking to different people, and taking varied courses.
- Finding the right therapist involves asking many important questions and identifying someone that best fits your personal needs.
- Active treatment ingredients improve outcome for clients; these include enhancing self-control, gaining mastery of symptoms, practicing new skills, exploring and gaining insight into problems, experiencing ongoing and reinforcing successes, and receiving therapist feedback.

- Process variables are general treatment ingredients that improve outcome for clients; these include placebo effect, therapist experience, warm and respectful therapy environment, reassurance, effective therapist–client interactions, and catharsis.
- Clinical manuals have been developed to provide treatment procedures for clients with specific or various problems. Prescriptive or personalized treatment refers to specific therapies that match best with certain types of mental problems.

Review Questions

1. What are different types of psychologists, and how do they focus their work?
2. How might one go about becoming a mental health professional or client?
3. What active treatment ingredients seem to contribute most to therapy success?
4. What nonspecific treatment factors also contribute to therapy success?
5. Does therapy work, and what are advantages and disadvantages of manualized treatments? What is prescriptive or personalized treatment?

Treatment at the Community Level

LO 15.4 Describe community-level treatments, including their purposes, processes, and effectiveness.

Treatment for mental disorders often involves one-on-one interactions between a therapist and client. Treatment can also occur, however, at a larger, community-based level. Various forms of such treatment are sometimes included under the rubric of **community psychology**, which focuses on enhancing quality of life for people and concentrating on their relationships with different social structures. Examples of such structures include family, work, school, church, neighborhood, and culture (Kagan et al., 2022). The next sections focus on areas of intervention that often involve groups of people and community structures.

Self-help Groups

A **self-help group** is an association of people who share a common problem or mental disorder the group tries to address. Examples include Alcoholics Anonymous and Narcotics Anonymous, in which the goal is to reduce maladaptive behavior such as excessive substance use among the membership. Self-help groups can also be simple neighborhood or church or online meetings for people in grief or isolation, those with a disability, or those who know others with a certain problem, such as depression. Groups may also form to protect the cultural, religious, or political values of the membership or advocate for resources. An example of the latter is the National Alliance for the Mentally Ill (nami.org).

A main advantage of self-help groups is that large numbers of people with problems can be helped. Such help often comes from emotional support and feedback from members, role models for successful recovery, information about a problem, new ideas regarding coping, opportunities for emotional expression, financial aid, self-empowerment, enhanced spirituality, sense of belonging to a group, and realizing one's problems are not unique (Marcovitz et al., 2020). People often find help by listening to others "who have been there" or who can empathize and have experience with the problem in question. Participation in self-help groups enhances treatment outcome for different groups, including those with substance use problems (Chapter 9).

A criticism of self-help groups is that not all have (or wish to have) mental health professionals present. Misinformation about ways to treat or cope with a problem could thus be circulated. Other potential problems with self-help groups include high dropout rates and inadequate help for complicated issues. Still, many people report significant improvements in quality of life from self-help group membership. Membership in self-help groups in addition to professional, individual intervention is an accepted treatment strategy (Marcovitz et al., 2020).

Aftercare Services for People with Severe Mental Disorders

Recall that various treatment procedures for people with severe mental disorders are used in inpatient settings. Examples include electroconvulsive therapy for depression, detoxification for substance use disorder, and antipsychotic medication for schizophrenia. Historically, many people with these disorders were treated in hospital settings and then released on their own recognizance once their symptoms subsided. Unfortunately, this led

Branislav Nenin/Shutterstock.com

Self-help groups offer support and guidance for people with similar problems.

to a situation in which many people eventually relapsed and returned to the hospital—a phenomenon known as the "revolving door" (Lamb & Weinberger, 2020).

Aftercare services have thus been established in many communities to help people with severe mental disorders make the transition between an inpatient setting and independent living. You may have heard the term "halfway house," which refers to an intervention provided "halfway" between a (1) restrictive hospital or rehabilitation setting and (2) a completely independent

Personal Narrative

Tiffany S. Borst, M.A., L.P.C.

I can't remember a time when I did not want to be a psychologist. From as early as middle school, I dreamed of having my own practice to provide therapy to people in their time of need. I was fascinated with the human mind; the interaction of our behaviors, emotions, and thoughts was always intriguing. I read everything on the subject that I could find and even subscribed to *Psychology Today*, a popular psychology magazine. I remember sitting in the chairs of my childhood living room imagining what it would be like to have my own office, my own clients.

Courtesy of Tiffany Borst

Tiffany S. Borst, M.A., L.P.C.

Being sure of my career path from the beginning of my undergraduate program, I sought any information I could get to help me achieve my goal. Repeatedly, I was told I must get a Ph.D., "You can't do anything in the field of psychology without a Ph.D." I did everything that was recommended to me, including research, publishing articles, and volunteering at local mental health agencies. I made sure that my grade point average was high and worked to get the highest GRE I could get. I knew that getting into a psychology doctoral program was very competitive, but I was willing to do whatever it took to realize my dream. I was devastated when I was an alternate to two programs. Although I was accepted into a master's level program in counseling psychology, I worried what options I would have and planned to eventually get the Ph.D. I was convinced I would need. I never did seek to complete that doctorate. As it turned out, my graduate program provided me with solid basic counseling skills and I soon found I was able to realize my dream of being a therapist without further formal education.

To my surprise, there were plenty of opportunities as a master's level counselor in the field of psychology. I was fortunate enough to experience a variety of these mental health positions, each further preparing me for the work I do now. First, while still in graduate school, I worked as an intake counselor at a local psychiatric hospital. In this position, I answered crisis calls for a hotline, did initial assessments, and recommended levels of treatment for people seeking psychiatric help. I also worked closely with the business office learning how to bill insurance, check benefits, and justify treatment to receive authorization. This experience proved to be invaluable. The business side of a practice was something I did not learn in graduate school and is something I use in my current job every day.

Upon completion of my master's program, as a new and developing therapist, I worked in group settings. I first worked as a therapist at a residential drug and alcohol treatment center for women. I provided individual, family, and group therapy to the women in the center, and play therapy to their children. I later worked in a group private practice, providing play therapy to kids in foster care, as well as seeing adults and adolescents for traditional outpatient therapy. In both settings, I received supervision, participated in staff meetings regarding clients, and consulted with peers frequently. I found it essential to process the work I was doing, to check my conceptualization of clients, and to share ideas with more experienced therapists. If I could give an aspiring therapist only one piece of advice, it would be to seek good supervision and peer consultation throughout your career.

Today I am a licensed professional counselor (L.P.C.), with a master's degree in counseling psychology. I have my own private practice, where my clients and I sit in those very same chairs from my childhood dreams. I treat people of all ages with a variety of mental health problems including depression, obsessive-compulsive disorder, generalized anxiety, panic attacks, post-traumatic stress disorder, and grief. While the majority of my time is spent providing individual or family therapy, I have also run a variety of groups, including expressive arts groups, educational groups, and support groups. As an L.P.C. in the state of Missouri, I am able to practice independently and bill insurance. This allows me flexibility and freedom I might not otherwise have to set my own schedule and to choose the cases I take.

Through the years I have built a successful practice, receiving referrals from physicians, school counselors, clergy, and former clients. I continue to be fascinated by the people I help and am amazed at their strength as they strive for personal healing. While my path was not what I initially thought it would be, I am now doing exactly what I always dreamed of doing and the work is just as rewarding as I imagined.

Source: Used with permission.

living environment. A person lives in a supervised setting, often a small home with others with severe mental disorders. Staff at the home provide support and therapy services but residents can enjoy greater personal space, choice, and independence than at a hospital. Aftercare services also include day hospitals where patients live with family members in the evening, as well as supervised work and occupational training centers (Caldwell et al., 2020).

Aftercare services are somewhat but not highly effective for people with severe mental disorders such as depression, substance use, and schizophrenia. Little effectiveness has been shown among youth. Much of this may be due to the severity and complexity of symptoms, medication refusal, unmet needs, and family dysfunction. Controversy also remains about how many people use or have access to aftercare services. Concern always exists as well about whether neighborhood residents will accept an aftercare home in their area. Many people with a chronic mental disorder discharged from a hospital thus relapse (recidivism) or become incarcerated or homeless (De Andrade et al., 2018).

Residential Facilities for People with Developmental Disorders

Another area of community-based intervention involves people with pervasive developmental disorders such as severe intellectual developmental disorder. People with pervasive developmental disorders were traditionally housed in large residential facilities, such as developmental centers, but many have moved to community-oriented and usually smaller facilities that more closely resemble normal life. These smaller facilities, usually group homes or foster-care placements, often involve more daily choice in one's routine, such as what to wear. Job training and work-oriented settings are usually associated with smaller living facilities as well.

Movement to smaller, community-based facilities is based on **normalization**, or the belief that people living in more normal circumstances will behave less unusually and be more valued by others. Such movement has led to substantial improvements in self-care skills and general adaptive behavior (Björne, 2020). Some attribute these improvements to better material well-being, staff attention, integration with others and the community, and contact with family members. Personal choice about daily activities can be generally higher as well (Devi et al., 2020). Some group homes are just as restrictive as larger residential facilities, however, which may hinder certain skills. One should thus assess level of available choice in a living environment for someone with a pervasive developmental disorder.

Criminal Justice System

Other community-based interventions occur in criminal justice settings. **Forensic psychology** is an exciting area involving the interaction of psychological and legal principles. Forensic psychologists are typically involved in many aspects of evaluation and treatment that intersect with the courts and criminal justice system. Many forensic psychologists work in prisons to treat people with severe mental disorders who have been incarcerated (Davis, 2021).

Other forensic psychologists conduct assessment, treatment, or research regarding child custody cases, criminal profiling, eyewitness testimony, police interrogations, interpersonal violence, sexual harassment, and jury selection. Forensic psychologists often serve as expert witnesses for specific cases or as general consultants for a court. Forensic work is often based on assessment of individuals, but large groups of people are also studied to identify important patterns of behavior. Examples include prisoners, sexual assault and maltreatment victims, and juvenile offenders. Other key aspects of forensic work include accurately determining whether someone is dangerous to others and whether to commit someone to a hospital (Chapter 2).

Public Policy and Mental Health

Community-based interventions can also include public health policy regarding people with mental disorders. This policy often comes in the form of government legislation to improve the quality of life for individuals. Examples include legislation regarding free education for all youth, services for people with severe mental disorders, health promotion and education, prenatal care, child and partner protective services, discrimination against people with mental disorder, and liability of mental health professionals, among other areas. Public policy can also be affected by individual or groups of mental health professionals who lobby politicians, testify as expert witnesses, or file briefs to inform judges

Olesia Bilkei/Shutterstock.com

Residential facilities for people with developmental disorders can involve smaller settings such as group homes.

Focus On Law and Ethics

Rights of Those Hospitalized for Mental Disorder

A key aspect of public mental health policy involves rights for people hospitalized for mental disorder or severely dangerous behavior. One basic right is the **right to treatment** itself, which mandates that people in mental health settings receive appropriate care that provides a meaningful chance at some improvement. A person also has the **right to refuse treatment**, meaning they do not have to be subjected to risky psychological or medical procedures such as surgery without proper consent. These rights often conflict with one another, as in the case of someone who wishes to continue hurting themself, or with society's right to be protected from a dangerous person.

Intervention for people with mental disorders is also based on the legal principle of **least restrictive treatment**, meaning a person should be effectively treated in a manner as least restrictive to their freedom as possible. Someone with a pervasive developmental disorder may be effectively treated in a large restrictive developmental center and in a group home. The latter is less restrictive, however, and should thus be chosen. Some people may have a severe mental disorder that requires hospitalization, but this does not mean they have lost basic rights to be treated with respect and dignity.

What do these rights mean for you? If you or someone you know is hospitalized for a mental condition, then ask what the treatment options are, how long a stay is required, and what conditions allow for discharge. If you or someone you know is hospitalized, ask as well about side effects of procedures, such as medication and electroconvulsive therapy. If you or someone you know is considering residential care for someone with a chronic mental condition, then explore different options that consider the person's freedom, choice, and quality of life.

---

about mental health issues (Ruggeri, 2021). Public policy regarding mental health has a long history in the United States and has shaped key legal rights for people hospitalized with mental disorders (refer to **Focus On Law and Ethics: Rights of Those Hospitalized for Mental Disorder**).

Section Summary

- Community psychology treatments focus on enhancing quality of life for people and their relationships with different social structures.
- Self-help groups involve people who share a common problem the group tries to address. Advantages include reaching large numbers of people, having people who can empathize with a certain problem, and facilitating therapist–client treatment. Disadvantages include high dropout rate and risk of inadequate information.
- Aftercare services represent transitional help for people with severe mental disorders before they pursue independent living.
- People with pervasive developmental disorders have gradually moved to community-oriented and usually smaller facilities that more closely resemble normal life.
- Forensic psychologists address issues that intersect psychology and the legal system, including prisoner treatment, child custody evaluations, criminal profiling, jury selection, and assessment of dangerousness.
- Treatment at the community level intertwines with social change and public health policy toward people with mental disorders, including rights for those hospitalized.

Review Questions

1. What are major advantages and disadvantages of self-help groups?
2. Describe aftercare services and problems potentially associated with them.
3. Outline key concepts related to residential treatment of people with pervasive developmental disorders.
4. What areas comprise forensic psychology?
5. What areas of public health policy have been targeted toward people with mental disorders? What are key rights for people hospitalized with mental disorders?

Limitations and Caveats About Treatment

LO 15.5 Summarize the strengths and limitations of and caveats about mental health treatment.

Treatment at individual and community levels works for many people with mental disorders, but not everyone. Why not? One possibility is that the most effective treatment was not chosen for a particular client. This relates to the issue of prescriptive treatment raised earlier, or the idea that treatment should be tailored to meet a client's individual needs. If a therapist uses a general treatment approach for all clients with depression, then some people with broader problems like an additional personality disorder or family conflict may not respond. Inappropriate application of treatment by a therapist can delay progress as well. Therapy may not work for some people because of changes in factors noted earlier. In addition, some clients may have little expectation for change, another factor that jeopardizes treatment success.

Another limitation on the therapy process is *treatment noncompliance*, when a client fails to put into action the plan developed with the therapist (Windle et al., 2020). A therapist may instruct a family to design a written contract to solve problems or show a couple how to develop good communication but, if these skills are not practiced during the week, then progress will be more difficult. Therapists often have to explore reasons for noncompliance and eliminate obstacles that interfere with treatment. Some specific obstacles to treatment are described next.

Client–Therapist Differences

One obstacle to treatment success occurs when significant personal differences exist between a client and therapist. If a client has very different *values* than their therapist, then therapy may be less productive (Abargil & Tishby, 2021). Imagine a client who enters therapy with very set ideas about politics, child rearing, partner treatment, or abortion and meets a therapist with completely opposite views on these subjects. A psychologist is expected to refrain from projecting their value system onto a client, but some cases involve too much friction to be fruitful. Severe personality conflicts can also exist between a therapist and client. Referral to another therapist is recommended if the therapy process cannot progress because of these conflicts.

Cultural Differences

Another important difference that affects therapy is *culture*. A therapist may not fully understand, properly empathize, or adjust to changes in a client's perspective of the world. Differences in language and communication style, beliefs about mental disorder and expression of symptoms, religion, and acculturation can also complicate treatment (Ramos et al., 2020). Therapists and clients often differ as well with respect to geographical and educational background and income level. These differences are not necessarily related to treatment outcome, but can affect how long a person stays in therapy or whether treatment is sought. A therapist should thus acknowledge differences with a client at the start of therapy and ask them if they have concerns about the differences. Special efforts to understand the client at multiple levels will also promote therapy progress (refer to **Focus On Diversity: Lack of Diversity in Research**).

Managed Care

Managed care is a system of health care delivery that influences the use and cost of medical and psychological procedures. Use of managed care can limit services clients receive under certain coverage plans because insurance companies often indicate what type of assessment and therapy a client can receive. Many insurance plans allow a client to visit a therapist for only a certain number of sessions. This forces therapists to use brief therapies when working with clients, a practice that may not be helpful when the problem is severe or complicated (Wander, 2020). A therapist may also urge a client to implement treatment plans quickly—perhaps too quickly.

Other insurance plans only cover costs associated with seeing a psychiatrist or other physician, not another mental health professional. This may lead a client toward drug or inpatient treatment for a problem when psychosocial or family treatment may have been a better long-term alternative (Sadock et al., 2015). Therapists may also be reluctant to treat a problem that is not a formal diagnosis, such as social withdrawal, because a diagnosis is often required by insurance companies for reimbursement.

Focus On Diversity

Lack of Diversity in Research

Ethnicity is extremely relevant to the therapy process, but research remains sparse with respect to some mental disorders. One group of researchers examined hundreds of articles in first-tier psychology journals and found that only 2 percent addressed cross-cultural issues and that only 4 percent addressed ethnic minority issues. In addition, journals that most featured these issues tended to have low readership (Hartmann et al., 2013). This may be due to difficulties accessing diverse samples for research, hesitancy of researchers to focus on sensitive issues, and bias on the part of researchers to focus more on the general population and less on individual differences that may be important in the therapy process.

Researchers must make more effort to examine ethnic, racial, and gender issues in their work. What does this mean for you? As a possible future mental health professional, and one who may be conducting research now, think about how individual differences can affect assessment and treatment procedures. Ask about how your research can include questions about diversity, think about designing a study that specifically focuses on individual differences, and review research in your area of interest that has examined cultural differences. Such practices will allow you to be better prepared to assess and treat people with mental disorders from different backgrounds.

Another possible consequence of managed care is that some clients may end therapy once their insurance company stops payments. This could lead to incomplete progress, more referrals to low-cost agencies, more use of support groups and related community services, or greater acceptance of "quick fixes" (refer to later section). Insurance companies prefer lower costs from treatment providers, so more emphasis may be placed on therapists not trained at the doctoral level, such as master's-level therapists or paraprofessionals (Thompson, 2020).

The focus on managed care raises other ethical questions as well. How much information should a therapist give an insurance company when seeking third-party payments (Martinez-Martin et al., 2020)? Information, such as a client's name and diagnosis, are often needed, and a client must give permission for this information to be released (refer to later ethics sections). Very personal information, including therapist–client dialogue, should not be revealed.

Differences Between Clinicians and Researchers

Another limitation to treatment is differences between clinicians in private practice and researchers in specialized clinics. Private practitioners are often *eclectic* or *generalist*, which means they use various techniques for various clients, depending on which seems most effective at the time. Researchers, however, often focus on very specific procedures for very specific types of clients to enhance internal validity of their studies. The problem is that many clinicians do not use research-based techniques even though the techniques are quite effective (Purtle et al., 2020). Why?

Part of the problem is that researchers often exclude the very cases clinicians have in their practice. A researcher may exclude clients with multiple or severe diagnoses, lack of English-speaking skills, limited intelligence, medication prescriptions, or treatment compliance problems to boost internal validity of their experiment. Clients with one specific problem, such as obsessive-compulsive disorder only, are thus examined. Private practitioners, however, usually have clients with multiple behavior problems and other complicated issues—they say many published research studies have little to do with their everyday situations. This is a common complaint about treatment manuals as well. Researchers have thus begun to focus on more diverse populations to determine whether their procedures are effective in general community settings.

Quick Fixes

Managed care and other constraints on therapy have led some people to seek solutions to problems that involve less time or effort. Many people are drawn to the allure of quick but ineffective fixes for a given problem. A once popular method of treating a youth with attention-deficit/hyperactivity disorder (ADHD) was to change their diet to include less sugar or additive intake. Subsequent studies found diet changes to be ineffective for treating this disorder (Uldall Torp & Thomsen, 2020).

Quick fixes for various behavior problems remain with us today. These include drug therapies for obesity, St. John's wort for depression, and facilitated communication for autism. Facilitated communication involves typists who supposedly translate what a nonverbal child with autism wants to communicate to parents and others. Controlled research studies, however, revealed that the so-called communications failed to emerge without biased input of the typist (Simmons et al., 2021). This false treatment crushes the hopes of parents who want desperately to converse with their child.

Misuse of Research

Related to the idea of "quick fixes" is misuse of legitimate research for less than honorable purposes. This refers to twisting the meaning of research findings or perhaps citing an isolated result out of context. Media descriptions of limited and controversial findings regarding intelligence in racial groups, immunization and potential links to developmental disorders, and vitamins and diet with respect to mental health, for example, can be overblown and have serious consequences for consumers. Use of selective statistics and a focus on certain studies over others can produce skewed conclusions as well (Andrade, 2021). You are a consumer of information from the media and other sources, so always consider the entire context of an original writing and do not assume someone's description of it is necessarily accurate.

Weak Research and How to Judge a Research Article

Another problem with some research, and therefore clinicians' ability to apply it to their own practice, is weak quality. Research articles on treatment procedures could be flawed in many ways, which limits how clinicians use the results to help their clients. A research study may have included clients from particular age, gender, or racial groups, which limits generalizability to the overall population (Chapter 4). Or the study may have involved unusual, expensive, or experimental procedures to which most clinicians do not have access.

What should you look for when judging the quality of a research article on treatment? Consider these questions:

- Is the sample in the study diverse and representative of the general population?
- Were there enough participants in the study to obtain a meaningful effect?

- Are dependent measures in the study varied and of good reliability and validity?
- Did the researchers rely on information gained from different sources, such as clients, parents, teachers, partners, children, and peers?
- Are treatment procedures defined well, are they understandable, and can they be applied to different clinical settings?
- What was the training of the therapists, and were different therapists used?
- How did the clients respond to treatment, and did they find the treatment acceptable?
- What was the long-term functioning of the clients?

Negative Therapist Characteristics

Another limitation of treatment may come from negative therapist characteristics. Some therapists, as with some people in any profession, are ill-tempered or abrasive and may not be suitable for certain clients. A client may leave therapy if uncomfortable. A therapist who engages in unethical behavior should also be avoided, especially one who solicits physical contact with a client. Therapists who are evasive about issues, such as fees or therapy procedures, who constantly disagree with a client about treatment goals, and who seem uninterested in a client should also be avoided.

Lack of Access to Treatment

Another reason some people do not benefit from therapy is lack of access to treatment services. Many people cannot afford therapy, do not have insurance to pay for therapy, cannot transport themselves to therapy, or have difficulty finding low-cost services that are right for them or that are culturally sensitive. People who are members of racial or ethnic minorities or those in low-income countries have less access to mental health care (Carbonell et al., 2020).

Finding a therapist in rural settings can also be difficult, and seeking a therapist in a small town can risk one's privacy. Some people may also wait until a particular problem is very severe before seeking help, and treatment at an advanced stage of mental disorder can be quite difficult. A person may be so debilitated in very advanced cases that they cannot contact someone for help. Examples include psychosis, chronic substance use disorder, and severe depression. These scenarios outline the importance of not only developing good treatment strategies but also making sure people have access to them. Establishing home visits, marketing low-cost and self-help services, providing transportation, developing prevention efforts and online-based therapies, and integrating community, psychotherapy, and pharmacological services will likely be an increasingly important part of treatment (Esponda et al., 2020).

Ethics

LO 15.6 Discuss the ethical considerations of the mental health professions.

All practitioners in the mental health profession are expected to follow highly stringent ethical guidelines. This section covers general ethical principles that guide work with clients and that you should be aware of when interacting with a therapist.

General Principles

Psychologists who conduct therapy are expected to follow the American Psychological Association's Ethical Principles of Psychologists and Code of Conduct (American Psychological Association, 2017). These guidelines represent behaviors psychologists should aspire to in their practice, though some states incorporate these guidelines into legal requirements for psychologists. The Ethical Principles are based on several general themes:

- *Beneficence* and *nonmaleficence*, or protecting the welfare of others
- *Fidelity* and *responsibility*, or acting professionally toward others
- *Integrity*, or employing high moral standards in one's work
- *Justice*, or exercising fairness and reasonable judgment
- *Respect for people's rights and dignity*, or valuing others and minimizing conflicts

The next sections discuss how these themes are specifically implemented with respect to assessment, treatment, and other variables. These sections each relate to a specific area within the Ethical Principles of Psychologists and Code of Conduct.

Assessment

When assessing clients, psychologists should act in appropriate ways that enhance knowledge about a certain client but at the same time protect the client's privacy. Psychologists using tests to assess clients must be competent in giving a particular test and interpreting test results for clients. These tests should also be kept secure and given only to clients in a professional relationship. Giving a personality test to people at a party, for example, would be unethical. Psychologists should also be familiar with data that support the reliability, validity, and cultural applicability of a given test and should design tests that have good strength in these areas. Psychologists must not use obsolete tests or outdated testing information to make clinical decisions about clients. One should be very careful about examining test information about a child from several years ago because the child may have changed dramatically since then.

Personal Narrative

Christopher A. Kearney, Ph.D.

Christopher A. Kearney, Ph.D.

I knew I wanted to be a clinical child psychologist the day a former mentor of mine gave a lecture to my undergraduate developmental psychology class. He worked with children with autism in a special on-campus school and told us of one child who threw a huge temper tantrum and ran around the room screaming when a person simply turned a block on its side in the boy's large playroom. When the block was returned to its original position, the boy immediately stopped his tantrum and resumed playing in his own world as if nothing happened. I spent much of the next two years working in that school for children with autism.

I also spent a great deal of time learning about graduate school, and I encourage you to do the same. The most important thing I learned was to talk to many people and be persistent. Consider different areas of psychology and what kinds of people you would like to work with. Get involved with different research labs and make sure people know you are reliable and trustworthy around clients. Get help if you need it on the GRE and retake courses you did not do well in. It's far better to take extra time to develop a strong resume before graduation than to rush toward graduation and have trouble getting into graduate school.

I was excited to enter graduate school and figured I would learn all I could about people with developmental disorders (Chapter 13). I found in graduate school, however, that many different paths and populations were available, and I eventually extended my clinical and research work to children with anxiety disorders (Chapter 5). Many of the anxious children who came to the clinic I worked at also had difficulty attending school. No one seemed to know what to do with these kids, so I took them on and developed my dissertation around them. I've been studying kids with school attendance problems and anxiety disorders ever since!

Today I live a full life as a college professor. I have undergraduate and graduate students who help me in different phases of research. Some have worked in my on-campus clinic for children with school attendance problems and anxiety disorders, some in a local child protective services unit, some in a hospital setting, and some in school settings. My students work on many diverse topics for their theses and dissertations, including posttraumatic stress disorder, selective mutism (difficulty speaking in public situations), school attendance problems, and ethnic variables in clinical child psychology.

I also teach, have seen clients with different psychological problems, publish journal articles and books, and consult across the country and worldwide with school districts and mental health professionals. I supervise graduate students who see clients with various mental disorders and review articles submitted for publication to clinical journals. I serve on various committees and mentor students as they try to enter graduate programs and full-fledged careers. I think the best job in the world is a college professor!

My main goal in preparing this book was to say many of the things I say to my own students—mental conditions are extraordinary problems that ordinary people have and we all share aspects of the disorders discussed in this textbook. I wanted to convey that we all feel anxious, sad, worried, and even disoriented from time to time. I teach my students to respect people with mental disorder and not refer to them as schizophrenics or bulimics, but people with schizophrenia or people with bulimia. I hope you enjoyed reading the many true stories in this textbook and come away with a greater appreciation of psychopathology and its part in life.

When explaining assessment results to others, psychologists are expected to state limitations to their conclusions based on testing. A person with Alzheimer's disease may have had great trouble paying attention to items given during an intelligence test, so the examiner should make this clear in their report. Psychologists must also base their statements or conclusions only on information they have received. This applies especially to child custody evaluations where parents are assessed for their capability to raise a child. If one parent refuses to participate in the evaluation and a second parent consents, then the psychologist could only make conclusions about the fitness of the person who was evaluated. Refusal to take part in an assessment does not necessarily mean a person is unfit or has a mental disorder. Psychologists should also make clear what their role is before an assessment so all those being tested know what is happening.

Treatment

One of the most delicate areas of psychological endeavor is treatment, which often involves discussing sensitive and personal issues with clients and interacting with other professionals, such as physicians and educators. Important ethical guidelines impact the therapy process.

Informed Consent and Confidentiality

Some of the most important ethical guidelines involve informed consent and confidentiality. **Informed consent** involves educating potential clients about therapy, especially variables that might influence their decision to seek therapy. Important variables to know include the nature of therapy, cost, status of a provider, risks, and confidentiality (discussed next). If a person cannot give consent, then psychologists must still provide an explanation of what is to happen, seek the person's verbal agreement or *assent* if possible, consider the person's best interests, and obtain consent from a legally authorized person (Stoll et al., 2020). Parents can give consent for children, but many psychologists also have children verbally agree to assessment and treatment procedures. Informed consent should be documented and is appropriate as well for participants entering a research project or most testing situations.

Confidentiality is based on *privileged communication*, which means discussions between a therapist and client should not be divulged to others unless consent is given. Many relationships enjoy such privilege, including husband–wife, physician–patient, lawyer–client, and clergy–parishioner relationships. Psychologists are expected to maintain the privacy of their clients, even going as far as to not admit a person is in therapy. Psychologists usually obtain a release of information consent form from a client to speak with others about a particular case. This release permits them to contact teachers, medical professionals, or relevant others (Stoll et al., 2020).

PeopleImages.com—Yuri A./Shutterstock.com

Spousal communications are considered privileged in our society, as are communications between a therapist and client.

Confidentiality is not absolute, however. Psychologists are ethically and legally allowed to break confidentiality under certain conditions. Psychologists are expected to take steps necessary to protect lives when a client is a clear threat to themself or others; this can even include contacting the police and/or someone else who is threatened. Confidentiality does not extend to child or older person maltreatment, which a psychologist is legally bound to report to a child protective agency or department of aging. Confidentiality may also be broken when a judge issues a court order for notes or testimony, when a client sues for malpractice, when a client tries to enlist a therapist's help to commit a crime, or when a psychologist seeks reimbursement for services. Even in these cases, however, a psychologist gives the minimum amount of information necessary about a client and should consult a legal representative. Clients should be informed at the start of therapy about limitations on confidentiality.

Who Is the Client?

An important question that often arises in couple and family therapy is "Who is the client?" In marital cases, one spouse may have initiated therapy for the couple and is paying for it. In family cases, parents usually refer themselves for therapy and pay for it, though a teenager may be the one having behavior problems and visiting the therapist. Who is the client in these situations? Is a spouse or are parents entitled to know what the other party said? Ethically, psychologists should clarify at the outset of therapy their relationship with each person.

A psychologist might say the couple is the client and they will try to be as fair as possible and not allow secrets between a therapist and one partner. A psychologist working with a family might say all information given privately by a child will be kept confidential unless the child is a threat to themself or others or if they allow the therapist to communicate certain information to the parents. If clients disagree with these conditions, then a referral to another therapist may be necessary. Psychologists should also not reveal more information than is needed for third-party payers such as insurance companies.

Sexual Intimacy

Sexual intimacy with clients is another important ethical issue for psychologists, and the ethics code and legal statutes make clear that such intimacy with current clients is unacceptable. Psychologists should also not accept into therapy anyone with whom they have had a sexual relationship in the past. Psychologists are expected to avoid **dual relationships**, meaning they should not act as a psychologist *and* friend, lover, significant other, or business partner. A psychologist should be unbiased and objective when helping a client, which is difficult to do when emotional feelings are involved.

What about sexual intimacies with *former* clients? The ethics code stipulates that psychologists must wait at least two years after the end of therapy before such intimacy can take place. Even if this does happen, a psychologist must show the client has not been exploited. Psychologists should generally avoid sexual and even social contact with former clients. Most cases of malpractice involve inappropriate sexual contact, and such contact is rife with potential for conflicts of interest and harm to a client (refer to **Focus On Law and Ethics: Sexual Intimacy and the Therapeutic Relationship**).

Ending Therapy

Important ethical guidelines still apply when a client nears the end of therapy. Psychologists should assist a client when they can no longer pay for services. A psychologist could make arrangements to lower the fee, engage the client for fewer sessions, refer them to a low-cost provider, or make alternative payment arrangements. Therapists are also expected to end treatment when a client is clearly no longer benefiting from, or is being harmed by, the process. Psychologists should not end therapy abruptly but rather prepare clients for termination by discussing the issue with them in previous sessions.

Public Statements

Psychologists often make public statements through advertisements, printed materials, interviews, lectures, legal proceedings, and interactions with media. Psychologists must ensure that public statements are honest and not deceptive. This includes information about their training, credentials, services, and other public knowledge. Psychologists who provide advice through the media, such as through a radio program, are expected to base their statements on available scientific literature and practice and perhaps remind listeners that their advice does not necessarily substitute for formal therapy. These principles are important to remember when you hear public figures speak and give advice. Pay close attention to how often they refer to scientific literature to support their statements.

Research

Ethical guidelines such as informed consent apply to research as well as clinical practice. Psychologists are expected to refrain from deceptive research unless the study is justified from a scientific perspective *and* if participants know about important and harmful aspects of the study that might influence their decision to participate. Psychologists engaging in research must also humanely care for animals, honestly report results, and give proper credit for sources of information and authorship of publications.

Resolving Ethical Issues

What should a psychologist do if they become aware of an ethical violation by a colleague? The psychologist should first speak with the colleague to informally address the issue. This might apply to a situation, for example, in which a colleague accidentally left a client's file on a receptionist's desk. If the problem is very serious, however, or cannot be addressed satisfactorily by informal means, then the psychologist should refer the matter to a state licensing board or national ethics committee. Client confidentiality must still be protected in these cases, however. If a client reveals a serious ethical violation by a previous therapist but insists on confidentiality, then the client's request must generally be honored. Psychologists are also expected to fully cooperate in ethics proceedings involving themselves or others.

Focus On Law and Ethics

Sexual Intimacy and the Therapeutic Relationship

Psychologists are expected to follow a strict ethics code in their professional practice. Almost all psychologists do so, but you might wonder what types of ethical violations are referred to the American Psychological Association (APA). Each year, the APA publishes an account of what ethical violations were reported. In one particular year, 10 cases were opened before the APA ethics committee. Most cases were allegedly due to sexual misconduct ($n = 4$) and nonsexual dual relationship ($n = 1$).

An overwhelming percentage of psychologists clearly comply with the ethics code. Some mental health professionals, however, inexplicably cross the line into severe misconduct. Most ethicists agree that touching a client—including hugs, touches of the hand, and two-handed handshakes—can be misunderstood. The professional relationship can be undermined if clients become confused about what message is being sent—is a therapist a professional or a friend? Such practice is also a "slippery slope" that can lead to even more dangerous practices, such as meeting outside of one's office or sending personal messages. Psychologists empathize with clients and their concerns but usually refrain from physical contact.

Section Summary

- Treatment for mental disorders is generally but not always effective. Ineffectiveness may be due to issues involving the therapist–client relationship, choice of treatment, treatment noncompliance, and therapist–client differences.
- Increased use of managed care means mental health services and confidentiality are often limited.
- Clinicians and researchers often differ in type of clients seen and treatments used, which has led to a gap in clinical practice between the two.
- Managed care and other constraints on therapy have led some people to seek quick fixes to problems.
- Misuse of research sometimes occurs, so one should always consult original sources of information when making clinical decisions.
- Published research articles are sometimes flawed, so one should always judge a study according to its methodological strength and applicability to the general population.
- Limitations on treatment may come in the form of negative therapist characteristics and lack of access to treatment.
- Psychologists are expected to adhere to a strict code of ethics in their clinical practice, and this code is based on several key themes surrounding fairness and respect.
- Psychologists are expected to use assessment devices properly and explain limitations regarding their evaluation results.
- Psychologists are expected to provide informed consent to potential clients and research participants and keep information confidential. Confidentiality may be breached with the client's permission or under certain conditions.
- An important ethical question in marital and family therapy is "Who is the client?" A therapist's relationship with each party should be clarified at the outset of therapy.
- Sexual intimacy with clients is unethical, and psychologists are advised to avoid dual relationships.
- Important ethical guidelines also apply to termination of therapy, public statements made by psychologists, research practices, and resolution of ethical issues.

Review Questions

1. Outline major limitations on treatment and caveats one should be aware of when conducting therapy.
2. What questions apply when judging the content of a research article on treatment?
3. What general ethical principles are psychologists expected to follow?
4. What ethical principles regarding assessment are psychologists expected to follow?
5. What ethical principles regarding treatment are psychologists expected to follow?

Final Comments

This textbook has covered many issues related to mental disorders, clients, and therapists. The symptoms and disorders and problems clients face are many, but there remain basic ways in which people with mental disorders should be viewed. People with mental disorders are often ordinary people with extraordinary problems, so remember that anyone can develop a mental disorder. A person should always be viewed first and their disorder second. Individuals with a particular mental disorder are always quite different, and these differences must be honored and respected. Try to avoid terms like "schizophrenic" and favor terms like "a person with schizophrenia." People with mental disorders, especially youth, often need advocates who can work hard and ethically on their behalf. As a possible future mental health professional, keep in mind you hold enormous responsibility for the welfare of your clients.

Thought Questions

1. Think about shows or films that involve therapists and their relationships with their clients. What strikes you as realistic or not realistic about these relationships? Why?
2. If you were to visit a therapist, what questions would you want to ask and what do you think the process would be like? If you have been in therapy or are currently seeing a therapist, what aspects of treatment have you appreciated most and least?
3. What are advantages and disadvantages of self-help groups, especially in contrast to seeing a mental health professional?

4. When should people be institutionalized for mental problems? What kinds of restrictions, if any, would you place on people with severe mental disorders?
5. Would you add or change anything to the ethics code that psychologists are asked to follow? Why?

Key Terms

clinical psychologists 454
counseling psychologists 454
educational psychologists 454
school psychologists 454
psychiatrists 456
psychoanalyst 456
psychiatric nurses 456
marriage and family therapists 456
social workers 456
special education teachers 457
paraprofessionals 457
psychotherapist 457
self-control 459
mastery 459
insight 459
process variables 459
placebo effect 460
therapeutic alliance 461
therapeutic alignment 461
catharsis 461
prescriptive treatment 462
community psychology 463
self-help group 463
aftercare services 464
normalization 465
forensic psychology 465
right to treatment 466
right to refuse treatment 466
least restrictive treatment 466
informed consent 471
confidentiality 471
dual relationships 471

Appendix: Stress-Related Problems

Case Ben

Ben is a 47-year-old man who is employed as a middle manager at a large corporation. He has experienced considerable stress at his job during the past two years, having endured downsizing of his staff, pay cuts, mandatory furloughs, and reduced benefits. Ben has thus been forced to take on additional responsibilities, and new rumors are swirling that his position may be cut soon. His work-related stress is beginning to cause problems at home. Ben is forced to work extended hours and thus has less time to spend with his family. His relationships with his wife and children have become strained in recent months.

Ben was able to expertly balance his responsibilities and adjust to a new pay scale initially, but the ongoing stress of his situation has begun to take a physical toll. He visited his primary physician recently and complained of trouble sleeping, abdominal pain, and headaches. Ben has gained considerable weight during the past few months because of a poor diet and little exercise. His blood pressure has risen since his last visit to the physician, which is a concern given Ben's family history of heart disease. After several tests, Ben was told that he appears to be in the early stages of developing a stomach ulcer and that he must reduce his stress or face potentially more serious physical symptoms.

Normal Stress and Unhealthy Stress-Related Problems: What Are They?

Stress is a construct that means different things. Stress can be *external*, meaning events in our daily lives that are taxing for us. Examples include relationship problems, financial worries, and academic pressures. Stress can also be *internal*, meaning we perceive events as demanding and thus experience bodily changes such as muscle tension, trouble sleeping, and headaches. Ben was clearly experiencing external and internal aspects of stress. Everyone experiences stress at some level, so stress is normal and even adaptive. Stress can make us more alert and can help motivate us to prepare for upcoming tasks.

Stress can obviously become excessive, however. We have all been through times when stress was intense, such as taking final exams, planning a wedding, or losing someone. In most cases, intense stress eventually dissipates as time passes, and we readjust to everyday living. In other cases, however, stress continues for lengthy periods and can become physically and otherwise harmful. Ben's ongoing and intense stress at work was clearly leading to several maladaptive physical symptoms and a lower quality of life.

A popular model for understanding acute and chronic stress and its effects on us was proposed by Hans Selye, who referred to the *general adaptation syndrome*. This model of stress consists of three stages (refer to **Figure A.1**). The first stage is *alarm*, which refers to the body's initial reaction to something stressful. This reaction may be in the form of higher adrenaline and cortisol, substances that allow the body to become energized and fight or flee a stressful stimulus. You may have noticed during final exams that you become quite energized by the stress of having to work so hard to study and concentrate and to balance many demands in your life. As final exams pass and your intense stress level declines, so too do your body's physical reactions.

In some periods of our life, however, intense stress continues past this initial point. Some intense stressors can be chronic, such as worries about job status or a child's severe illness. The body tries to increase *resistance* to stress in stage 2 but, over time, physical resources to do so become depleted. Over a longer period of time, a person enters the *exhaustion* phase, the third level of Selye's model, where physical resources and resistance to stress decline dramatically. This can set the stage for various stress-related physical problems that are discussed here. Ben's chronic stress and new physical problems perhaps meant he was near the end of the resistance stage or entering the exhaustion stage.

Stress-related physical problems have been traditionally referred to as **psychophysiological disorders**. Psychophysiological disorders specifically refer to organ dysfunction or physical symptoms that may be at least partly caused by psychological factors such as stress. Dysfunction often occurs in gastrointestinal, cardiovascular, immune, or respiratory systems, although other areas could be affected as well. The modern terminology for

Figure A.1 Hans Selye's General Adaptation Syndrome.

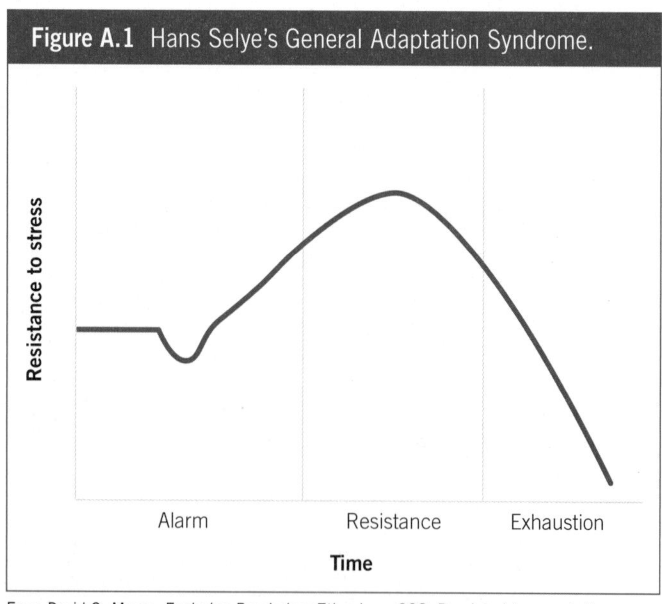

From David G. Myers, *Exploring Psychology* 7th ed., p. 398. Reprinted by permission.

these problems is *psychological factors affecting other medical conditions* (refer to **Table A.1**; American Psychiatric Association, 2022). This refers to a true medical condition that is influenced to some extent by a psychological factor such as anxiety, stress, or depression. The psychological factor can affect the course or treatment of the medical condition. A person may experience such intense stress that stomach problems develop very quickly, or depression in another person may cause them to delay visiting a physician for medical symptoms, which then worsen. Psychological factors can also pose additional health risks, as when a fear of needles prevents someone from taking a needed medication. Finally, stress-related physical responses, such as those noted in Selye's model, could help cause or worsen a medical problem such as breathing difficulties.

Stress-related physical problems are often studied by **health psychologists** who specialize in examining the interaction of biological, psychological, and social variables on traditional medical disorders. Health psychologists are often employed in health and human service agencies, medical settings, or universities affiliated with a hospital. Health psychologists may intersect with the area of **behavioral medicine**, which refers to a larger multidisciplinary approach to understanding the treatment and prevention of medical problems that may include a psychological approach. Health psychology and behavioral medicine may also overlap with the area of *psychoneuroimmunology*, which refers to the study of the interaction of psychological variables such as stress on the nervous and immune systems of the body.

Table A.1 DSM-5-TR

Psychological Factors Affecting Other Medical Conditions
A. A medical symptom or condition (other than a mental disorder) is present.
B. Psychological or behavioral factors adversely affect the medical condition in one of the following ways: 1. The factors have influenced the course of the medical condition as shown by a close temporal association between the psychological factors and the development or exacerbation of, or delayed recovery from, the medical condition. 2. The factors interfere with the treatment of the medical condition (e.g., poor adherence). 3. The factors constitute additional well-established health risks for the individual. 4. The factors influence the underlying pathophysiology, precipitating or exacerbating symptoms or necessitating medical attention.
C. The psychological and behavioral factors in Criterion B are not better explained by another mental disorder (e.g., panic disorder, major depressive disorder, posttraumatic stress disorder). Specify current severity: **Mild:** Increases medical risk (e.g., inconsistent adherence with antihypertension treatment). **Moderate:** Aggravates underlying medical condition (e.g., anxiety aggravating asthma). **Severe:** Results in medical hospitalization or emergency room visit. **Extreme:** Results in severe, life-threatening risk (e.g., ignoring heart attack symptoms).

American Psychiatric Association. (2022). *Diagnostic and statistical manual of mental disorders* (5th ed., text rev.). Arlington, VA: American Psychiatric Association.

Stress-Related Problems: Features and Epidemiology

The next sections cover various physical problems that may be partly caused or affected by psychological factors such as stress. Keep in mind that many physical problems can be affected by psychological factors, such as HIV/AIDS, cancer, and chronic fatigue syndrome. The next sections concentrate on medical problems that tend to be more common and that have a strong research base regarding contributing psychological factors. These medical problems include ulcers, irritable bowel syndrome, headache, asthma, sleep disorders, hypertension, and coronary heart disease.

Ulcers and Irritable Bowel Syndrome

Stress-related problems often affect the gastrointestinal area of the body. **Ulcers** refer to inflammation or erosion of a part of the body, and often occur in gastrointestinal areas such as the esophagus, stomach, or duodenum (part of the small intestine). A *peptic ulcer* refers to an ulcer in the stomach or intestine that can create severe abdominal pain. Recall that Ben appeared to be in the early stages of developing a stomach (gastric) ulcer, perhaps from his ongoing stress. The prevalence of gastric ulcers is 8.3 percent, and the problem is more frequent among older and obese persons, African Americans, tobacco users, and those with lung and cardiovascular diseases. Mortality for those with perforated (split open) ulcers is up to 30 percent (Chen et al., 2021; Kumar et al., 2020; Zhu et al., 2021).

Irritable bowel syndrome (IBS) refers to a chronic gastrointestinal disorder involving alternating and recurrent constipation and diarrhea as well as abdominal pain. The prevalence of IBS in the general population is difficult to determine but is likely about 7 to 18 percent. In addition, many people who visit a physician for gastrointestinal complaints appear to have the disorder. IBS is more common in women than men and is comorbid with anxiety, depression, and insomnia. Symptoms of IBS may be more common worldwide among those in industrialized and urbanized settings (Black & Ford, 2020; Pisipati et al., 2020).

Headache

Stress-related problems can also result in headaches, as they did for Ben. *Tension headaches* are most common and refer to short-term mild to moderate head pain that may feel as if muscles are contracting, although the actual cause of tension headaches remains unclear. Chronic tension headaches are unusual in the general population (2–3 percent), but most people experience a tension headache at least occasionally. Tension headaches are generally more common in women than men (Fuensalida-Novo et al., 2020; Kotb et al., 2020).

Migraine headaches refer to chronic and severe headaches that can last hours to days. Migraine headaches are often concentrated in one area, such as one side of the head or around the eye, and many people with a migraine headache are extremely sensitive to light and crave total darkness. Migraines are sometimes preceded by an *aura*, or early warning signs such as light flashes or tingling in the limbs. Migraines can be quite debilitating and may be associated with nausea and vomiting. About 9.7 percent of men and 20.7 percent of women experience migraines, and 5.4 percent of those with migraines experience 15 or more headache days per month (Rossi et al., 2022; Seddik et al., 2020). Migraine headaches appear to be more common among persons with lower income, which can be associated with greater stress (Langenbahn et al., 2021). *Cluster headaches* refer to a cyclical pattern of very severe head pain that can last weeks to months at a time. The prevalence of cluster headaches is about 1 in 500–1000 persons (Russell, 2020).

Asthma

Asthma refers to a chronic respiratory disease involving inflamed or constricted airways, tightening of the bronchial walls, and excess mucus, all of which hinders breathing. Asthma can involve regular or occasional attacks of wheezing, coughing, shortness of breath, and tightness in the chest. Asthma attacks can begin suddenly and can lead to decreased oxygen intake, lowered alertness, chest pain, and even death. Asthma attacks can last for minutes or much longer and can be triggered by allergens such as dust, animals, cold air, exercise, pollen, and tobacco smoke as well as stress (Anderson et al., 2020). The prevalence of asthma in the general population is 7.9 percent. Asthma rates are generally higher for children, women, and Puerto Rican Hispanics and African Americans compared with the general population (Lee et al., 2020; Stern et al., 2020).

Sleep Disorders

Sleep disorders include dyssomnias and parasomnias. **Dyssomnias** refer to problems in the amount, quality, or timing of sleep. Dyssomnias include difficulty initiating or maintaining sleep or excessive sleepiness. One of the most common dyssomnias is *insomnia*, which refers to difficulties falling asleep and staying asleep during the night as well as poor quality of sleep. Insomnia may or may not be related to a medical condition and is often the result of substantial stress or depression. Chronic insomnia can result in excessive sleepiness during the day, irritability or moodiness, difficulty concentrating, and limited alertness. Insomnia can be irregular, occurring some nights but not others, or could last for several weeks to months at a time. Insomnia affects 22 percent of adults and 30 percent of college students, and occurs in women at twice the rate for men (Gardani et al., 2022; Zeng et al., 2020).

Another dyssomnia is *hypersomnia* that refers to excessive sleepiness. Episodes of sleep may last 8 to 12 hours or longer with difficulty rising from bed in the morning. Frequent napping is common as well. The disorder must interfere with work and social relationships. Hypersomnia occurs in 10.3 of 100,000 persons and is associated with many different medical conditions (Acquavella et al., 2020).

Narcolepsy refers to a neurological disorder involving an irresistible desire to sleep during the daytime, especially during times of low activity and often after a strong emotion. People with narcolepsy often have "sleep attacks" that happen suddenly and involve quick entry into REM sleep with sleep-related hallucinations or vivid dreams. Narcolepsy may occur with *cataplexy*, or sudden loss of muscle tone, and a person may experience inability to move upon wakening. Narcolepsy occurs in 44.3 of 100,000 persons (Acquavella et al., 2020).

Circadian rhythm sleep–wake disorders refer to a collection of sleep problems that affect the timing of sleep and a person's sleep–wake system. As such, a person has difficulty sleeping, which could interfere with normal functioning at work or in other areas. These disorders could be influenced by environmental factors such as shift work or jet lag (Steele et al., 2021). Prevalence rates vary widely but the problem may be more common in certain populations such as people with visual problems (Tamura et al., 2021). *Breathing-related sleep disorder* refers to sleep disruption caused by ventilation problems, such as *sleep apnea* in which a person repeatedly stops breathing for a few seconds or more during sleep. Sleep apnea occurs in 6 percent of people and is more common among men than women (Fietze et al., 2019).

Parasomnias refer to unusual behavioral or physiological events that occur throughout sleep and include nightmare disorder, sleep terrors, and sleepwalking. *Nightmare disorder* refers to repeated awakenings following frightening dreams. Nightmares are common in problems such as posttraumatic stress disorder (Chapter 5). About 2.9 percent of men and 4.4 percent of women report frequent nightmares (Stefani & Högl, 2021). Repeated nightmares alone, without a concurrent mental disorder, that cause significant interference in daily functioning are uncommon, however. *Sleep terrors* refer to behavioral events during sleep involving screams, fear, and panicked behavior. A person, usually a child, with sleep terrors is difficult to awaken and has little recollection of the event. *Sleepwalking* refers to rising from bed and walking about during sleep. A person who is sleepwalking is difficult to awaken and has little recollection of the event. The prevalence of sleep terrors and sleepwalking in adults is 2 to 4 percent (Idir et al., 2022).

Hypertension

Hypertension refers to high blood pressure and is commonly identified if *systolic pressure* inside the blood vessels (created when the heart beats) is greater than 140 millimeters of mercury and/or if *diastolic pressure* inside the blood vessels (when the heart is at rest) is greater than 90 millimeters of mercury (i.e., a reading of 140 over 90, or 140/90, or greater). Pressures below 120/80 are preferred (although not too low). Hypertension has few outward symptoms but is a serious risk factor for problems affecting the heart, brain, and kidneys such as heart attack, stroke, and renal failure. *Essential hypertension* refers to high blood pressure caused by physical and psychological factors. Hypertension affects people of different cultures quite differently and tends to occur more in low- and middle-income countries (Mills et al., 2020). Approximately 45.4 percent of Americans have hypertension, with rates higher for men (51.0 percent), African Americans (57.1 percent) and those aged 60 years and older (74.5 percent) (Ostchega et al., 2020).

Coronary Heart Disease

Coronary heart disease refers to a narrowing of the small blood vessels that supply blood and oxygen to the heart. Coronary heart disease may be manifested by *angina* (chest pain or discomfort) or *myocardial infarction/heart attack* (blockage of blood vessels to the heart) when advanced. Blood vessels may become blocked when plaque and other material clog the arteries and slow or prevent blood flow. Coronary heart disease is the leading cause of death in the United States. Prevalence rates of coronary heart disease in the United States (5.5 percent) are higher for men (7.0 percent), those with less than a high school education (9.4 percent), and people aged 75 years or older (24.2 percent). Prevalence rates differ little by race and ethnicity, but deaths due to heart disease are much more prevalent among African Americans (National Center for Health Statistics, 2022).

Stress-Related Problems: Causes and Prevention

The stress-related problems described here all have biological factors that help cause the damaging symptoms. Stomach ulcers, for example, often involve a bacterial infection from *Helicobacter pylori* that requires treatment with antibiotics and anti-inflammatory medication. In addition, genetics, poor diet, smoking, allergens, plaque accumulation, and medical problems that affect sleep are common factors that help cause stress-related problems. The following sections concentrate on psychosocial factors that often affect these medical conditions.

Sociocultural Variables

Stress-related problems appear to manifest differently and for different reasons among people of varying ages, gender, and race. A particularly strong risk factor for many stress-related problems is socioeconomic status, which includes economic resources, social standing, and education. People with lower socioeconomic status are at increased risk of stress-related problems, especially coronary heart disease (Hamad et al., 2020). People with lower socioeconomic status may have less access to medical care, experience poor nutrition and living conditions, engage in less physical activity and more alcohol and tobacco use, and have less control over decisions in the workplace (De Bacquer et al., 2021).

Emotional Difficulties

Several physical problems appear to be related to emotional difficulties such as worry, sadness, and low self-esteem. Ulcers, irritable bowel syndrome, and pain in the head, neck, and back have long been related to stress, anxiety, depression, and lower quality of life (Miaskowski et al., 2020). Pain can be impacted by trauma, passive coping, poor emotional well-being, less social support, and cognitive distortions about the negative consequences of pain (Meints & Edwards, 2018). Headaches in college students are closely related to level of emotional functioning and perception of stress (de Vitta et al., 2021).

Asthma is clearly related to stress in many cases, which exacerbates autonomic function and constriction of the bronchial tubes. Asthma is linked to anxiety, especially panic symptoms, and depression in children and adults. People with asthma may also assess and manage their asthma symptoms poorly in more severe cases (Palumbo et al., 2020).

Insomnia has been linked to mood disorders such as depression and, among college students, also with attention-deficit/hyperactivity disorder (ADHD) (Mbous et al., 2022). Insomnia also appears closely related to excessive worry (about daily events and about not being able to sleep), stress and life change, overarousal, and obesity (Riemann et al., 2020).

Psychosocial risk factors for hypertension include work-related stress (as with Ben), anger, social isolation, and symptoms of anxiety and depression (Vancheri et al., 2022). Depression also appears to be a significant risk factor for coronary heart disease (Wu et al., 2021).

People with depression may engage in more high-risk behavior, such as using substances excessively and exercising less, and may experience greater arterial thickening and less heart rate variability, which are associated with worse cardiac outcomes (Ellins et al., 2020). People with depression are also likely to experience higher levels of bereavement and anxiety, which may be risk factors for cardiac problems as well (Zhou et al., 2021).

Personality Type

Personality type may be a key psychosocial factor for some stress-related problems. The traditional focus with respect to personality type was *type A personality,* which refers to someone who is overachieving and hostile and who aggressively and impatiently tries to accomplish more tasks in less time. Researchers have since focused more on hostility as a key psychosocial risk factor for coronary heart disease, especially in men. Impatience and hostility have also been linked to hypertension (Lim et al., 2021).

Other work has focused on **type D personality**. Type D personality refers to a distressed personality pattern marked by negative affectivity and social inhibition. This means that some people experience increased distress across many different situations but do not disclose this distress in social interactions. People with type D personality tend to worry excessively, experience tension and unhappiness, feel irritable and pessimistic, and are uncomfortable around strangers. They experience little positive emotion, have few friends, and fear rejection and disapproval from others.

Type D personality has been linked to several stress-related problems such as fatigue, irritability, depression, and low self-esteem. More important, people with type D personality seem to be at greater risk for cardiac problems than people without type D personality. The specific reason for this link remains under study, but some evidence indicates that people with type D personality who are socially inhibited tend to have higher blood pressure reactivity to certain stressful events. Type D personality also appears related to lower quality of life and feelings of exhaustion following a medical procedure for a cardiac problem (Lodder, 2020; Mesa-Vieira et al., 2021).

Social Support

Social support, or one's access to friends and family members and others who can be of great comfort during times of trouble, is clearly linked to several stress-related problems. Low social and family support contribute to asthma, for example, whereas enhanced support improves asthma outcomes (Sloand et al., 2021). Social support may ease the ill effects of coronary problems because it helps promote medication use and compliance, positive coping with illness-related stress, and reduced overarousal and worry (Hu et al., 2021). In contrast, social isolation, being unmarried, or experiencing relationship distress or low levels of emotional support are risk factors for coronary heart disease. Good social support may help calm aspects of the autonomic nervous system and reduce activation of serotonin and fear/anxiety centers in the brain such as the hypothalamic-pituitary-adrenal axis (Chapter 5) that could help prevent hypertension and later coronary problems (Uchino et al., 2020).

Causes of Stress-Related Problems

The stress-related problems described here are largely the result of a combination of biological problems exacerbated by psychological and social factors. A *biopsychosocial model* reflects the idea that biological, psychological (emotions, thoughts, and behaviors), and social factors combine to cause and influence a medical condition. This model is similar to the diathesis-stress model discussed in several chapters of this textbook. A biopsychosocial model is particularly relevant to psychophysiological disorders because of the unique combination of medical and nonmedical factors.

Consider coronary heart disease as an example. Several physiological factors predispose people to coronary heart disease, including genetics, inflammation, hormonal changes, elevated lipids, and restriction of arteries, among others. Several psychological factors can, however, combine with these predispositions to increase the likelihood of cardiac effects such as unstable electrical signals or blocked blood flow. These psychological factors include chronic anger, hostility, depression, and exhaustion as well as poor diet, little exercise, inadequate coping, and other unhealthy behaviors. Physiological and psychological factors can be worsened as well by social factors such as isolation from others, job stress, and low socioeconomic status. These factors increasingly interact over time to predispose a person to heart attack, angina, stroke, or death (Murray & DeBeard, 2022).

Other psychophysiological disorders can also be understood from a similar biopsychosocial perspective. Biological predispositions can interact with stress, anxiety, and depression as well as social variables to help produce ulcers and IBS, cause headaches or other pain, aggravate respiratory problems such as asthma or sleep problems such as insomnia, and raise blood pressure toward hypertension. Think about someone who has experienced an injury and develops chronic pain aggravated by depression, lack of social support, and trouble sleeping. Preventing these serious and chronic problems from developing requires a focus on several different variables, and this process is illustrated next.

Prevention of Stress-Related Problems

Prevention of stress-related problems focuses on wide-ranging programs to improve healthy practices and reduce the prevalence of these problems in the general population. Many of these programs focus on primary prevention of the leading cause of death in the United States: coronary heart disease. The American Heart Association published guidelines for preventing cardiovascular disease and stroke that involve behaviors that should begin at age 20 years. These guidelines include screening for potential risk factors such as family history and addressing smoking, alcohol use, diet, physical activity, blood pressure, waist circumference, cholesterol and blood glucose level, and diabetes.

Other primary prevention programs are tailored more specifically to an individual medical condition. Prevention of asthma attacks in children, for example, involves medication and stress management, early breast-feeding, and avoidance of exposure to dust, pets, tobacco smoke, and other allergens (von Mutius & Smits, 2020). Other psychophysiological disorders such as IBS, headache, and insomnia are usually treated after a person complains of symptoms or may be prevented by a program for another disorder. Prevention programs for depression and insomnia, for example, are often linked (Irwin et al., 2022).

Stress-Related Problems: Assessment and Treatment

Stress-related problems require a detailed medical assessment to determine the extent of biological causes for the conditions as well as a course of medical treatment. Mental health professionals who specialize in psychophysiological disorders have, however, developed assessment and treatment strategies that focus on the psychological factors that impact these problems. Some of these strategies overlap with those discussed in other chapters, but some are unique to psychophysiological disorders and are summarized next.

Psychological Assessment of Stress-Related Problems

Psychological assessment of stress-related problems often comes in the form of daily behavior records. People may be asked to record daily symptoms such as severity of pain and discomfort (for ulcer and headache), bowel function (for IBS), blood pressure (for hypertension), number of hours slept (for sleep disorders), and respiratory distress (for asthma). Health care professionals may also focus on intermittent records for variables such as weight, exercise, and cholesterol level (for coronary heart disease).

Questionnaires can be administered as well. Risk assessment questionnaires evaluate the degree to which a person is at risk for a certain psychophysiological disorder. A risk assessment questionnaire for ulcer, hypertension, or coronary heart disease might include screening questions about weight, diet, cholesterol level, blood pressure, exercise, stress, alcohol and tobacco use, and occupation. Other measures such as the *Health Assessment Questionnaire* focus on broader health-related issues such as pain and disability, quality of life, drug side effects, and medical costs. Questionnaires regarding anxiety, somatization, and depression are also helpful for people with psychophysiological disorders and were covered in Chapters 5, 6, and 7.

Other assessment procedures for stress-related problems involve more specific areas of focus. Assessment of pain, for example, involves not just how intense pain is but also how the pain interferes with a person's daily life and how a person thinks about a pain (e.g., "I can handle the pain"), feels about a pain (e.g., "I am really worried about my pain"), and behaves following a pain (e.g., complaining to others, using medication heavily). Pain quality may be assessed as well and refers to specific descriptors such as sharp, aching, hot, and cramping (Coninx, 2022).

Assessment measures can also target personality factors related to psychophysiological disorders. Measures are available to evaluate type A and type D personality, anger, and hostility. Another personality variable that has received substantial attention from researchers is *stress reactivity*, which refers to potentially increased physical responses to daily stressful events (Turner et al., 2020). Inventories that cover key personality variables associated with psychophysiological disorders were described in Chapter 4.

Stressful life events are also assessed by researchers because they have such an intense impact on physical problems. One group of researchers surveyed hundreds of university and community college students to identify exposure to stressful life events and traumatic experiences. Their results are in **Table A.2**. Note that the most common stressors often involve interpersonal relationships and events such as hurtful comments, bullying, lack of support, and exclusion. More serious traumatic events also included interpersonal events such as sudden and unexpected death or illness of someone close. Of course, other stressors in college can include academic, financial, sleep, and time management problems.

Psychological Treatment of Stress-Related Problems

As with assessment, psychological treatment for stress-related problems typically accompanies medical treatments such as medication or surgery. Psychological treatment for stress-related problems often consists of relaxation training, biofeedback, stress management, cognitive therapy, and support groups. Note that some of these treatments, such as relaxation training and biofeedback, are often used in combination.

Table A.2 Lifetime Event Exposure

Event	University students	Community college students
	%	%
Stressful life events		
1. Someone said hurtful things[a]	81	86
2. Broken an important promise[a]	67	70
3. Close other unsupportive[a]	66	69
4. Physically or verbally bullied[a]	62	67
5. Non-consensual end of relationship[a]	61	68
6. Witnessed the psychological mistreatment of a close other[b]	60	63
7. Someone excluded participant[a]	58	66
8. Emotional/psychological mistreatment[a]	54	74
9. Deceived about something important[a]	56	62
10. Lonely for extended periods of time[a]	55	61
11. Undesired relationship dissolution[a]	54	64
12. Social isolation for extended period[a]	49	56
13. Others' substance abuse[b]	47	58
14. Discriminated against[a]	43	51
15. Unrequited love[a]	41	53
16. Deliberately humiliated by others[a]	39	49
17. Emotional or physical neglect[a]	38	48
18. Cheated on by romantic partner[a]	33	50
19. Intense homesickness for extended period[a]	32	33
20. Uninvited/unwanted sexual attention[a]	30	35
21. Stalked[a]	14	22
22. Own substance abuse[a]	10	23
23. Self or partner abortion[c]	4	14
24. Self or partner miscarriage[c]	2	11
Traumatic experiences		
1. Sudden and unexpected death of close other[b]	46	53
2. Loved one serious accident/injury/illness[b]	39	42
3. Witnessed family violence[b]	27	39
4. Someone close attempted suicide[b]	28	33
5. Natural disaster[a]	20	20
6. Other type of accident[c]	16	18
7. Close other committed suicide[b]	13	18
8. Threatened[a]	11	20
9. Physically hurt by a romantic partner[a]	9	22
10. Motor vehicle accident[a]	11	13
11. Witnessed someone beaten[b]	9	17
12. 13–18 years of age, forced sexual contact[a]	8	16
13. Childhood physical abuse[a]	8	17
14. Sexual assault, after 18 years of age[a]	7	12

Table A.2 Lifetime Event Exposure—cont'd

Event	University students	Community college students
	%	%
Traumatic experiences		
15. Own life threatening illness[a]	8	8
16. Robbed, mugged, or held-up using threat of force[a]	6	12
17. Beaten up by a stranger[a]	5	15
18. Before 13 years of age, forced sexual contact with someone 5+ years older[a]	5	14
19. Before 13 years of age, forced sexual contact with someone close in age[a]	5	11
20. Lived or worked in a war zone[a]	3	5
Other events		
Other distressing events[c]	49	60
Other serious mental health problems[b]	39	44
Own suicidal ideation/attempt[a]	29	41
Own mental health problems[a]	18	21

[a]Direct event. [b]Indirect event.[c]Coded as direct or indirect.

Source: Anders, S.L., Frazier, P.A., & Shallcross, S.L. (2012). Prevalence and effects of life event exposure among undergraduate and community college students. *Journal of Counseling Psychology*, 59, 449–457.

Relaxation Training

Relaxation training was discussed in Chapter 5 as a key treatment for physical symptoms of anxiety-related disorders. *Relaxation training* often consists of tensing and releasing different muscle groups to achieve a sense of warmth and rest. Relaxation training may also consist of diaphragmatic breathing in which a person practices appropriate deep breathing to achieve a greater sense of ease and control over physical anxiety symptoms. *Meditation* and *hypnosis* are sometimes part of relaxation training as well. Meditation refers to practicing focused attention and minimizing distraction, and hypnosis refers to a state of focused attention with heightened suggestibility. Relaxation training has also been used to reduce stress in people with psychophysiological disorders such as IBS, hypertension, sleep problems, and headache and other pain (Belchamber, 2022).

Biofeedback

Biofeedback refers to a procedure that allows a person to monitor internal physiological responses and learn to control or modify these responses over time. A person is attached to one or more devices that provide feedback to the person about their brain wave patterns, respiration rate, muscle tension, blood pressure, heart rate, or skin temperature. The person can learn to control these responses by relaxing, using positive imagery, and thinking more flexibly. As the person does so, they can see on a monitor that their physiological responses such as heart rate are easing. With extended practice, the person learns to lower physiological arousal even without being attached to a biofeedback machine.

Biofeedback has been used most for people with migraine headaches and sleep problems. People with migraine headaches are encouraged to engage in *thermal biofeedback,* which involves feedback about skin temperature and warming the extremities (hands, feet) to improve blood flow and reduce throbbing head pain. People with tension headaches are encouraged to engage in *EMG (electromyography) feedback*, which involves feedback about muscle contraction and physically relaxing to ease tension and reduce head pain (Darling et al., 2020). Biofeedback has also been used to help people with insomnia, asthma, and hypertension (Fournié et al., 2021).

Stress Management

Stress management refers to a collection of techniques to help people reduce the chronic effects of stress on a daily basis as well as problematic physical symptoms. Stress management can involve using relaxation techniques, understanding stress better, managing workload effectively, incorporating spirituality and empathy, improving diet and exercise regimens, practicing good sleep hygiene, complying with a medication regimen, scheduling recreational activities, resolving interpersonal conflicts, and managing hostility and anger toward others. *Anger management* can consist of identifying

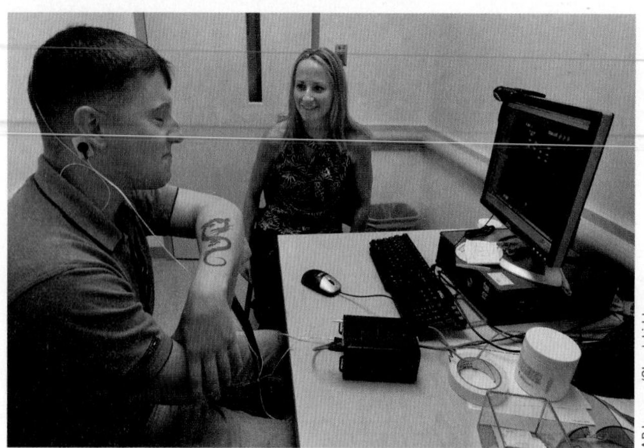
AP Images/Chuck Liddy

Biofeedback is an essential treatment component for stress-related problems.

triggers to anger, understanding what personal physical responses lead to anger, practicing techniques to lower physical arousal, managing social and work situations more effectively to reduce the chances of anger, and removing oneself from situations in which anger is rising (Toohey, 2021).

Another stress management technique is *mindfulness,* which has been discussed elsewhere in this textbook. Recall that mindfulness refers to greater daily awareness and acceptance of one's symptoms and how the symptoms can be experienced without severe avoidance or other impairment. A person is asked to engage in moment-by-moment awareness of their mental state including thoughts, emotions, imagery, and perceptions. Mindfulness may be especially useful for people with chronic pain as well as those with intense daily stress that can aggravate most physical disorders (Pardos-Gascón et al., 2021).

Cognitive Therapy

Cognitive therapy has been discussed throughout this textbook as an effective treatment for many different mental disorders. Cognitive therapy generally consists of helping people think more flexibly and realistically about their environment and interactions with others. Cognitive therapy may be useful for reducing anxiety and depression, which are key elements of many stress-related problems.

Cognitive therapy for people with psychophysiological disorders also involves correcting misperceptions about certain events. Cognitive therapy for insomnia may help correct misperceptions about sleep requirements, circadian rhythms, and sleep loss. This can be combined with a behavioral approach involving a standard wake-up time, rising from bed after a period of sleeplessness, avoiding behaviors incompatible with sleep in the bedroom, and eliminating napping during the day. Combined cognitive-behavioral treatment improves maintenance of sleep (Parsons et al., 2021).

Another type of cognitive therapy for this population is *self-instruction training*. Self-instruction training refers to identifying negative thoughts that may occur during a painful episode (e.g., "This pain is so awful") and replacing these thoughts with more adaptive coping ones (e.g., "I will allow my pain to escape my body and move forward"). Self-instruction training for pain can be accompanied by techniques to educate people about pain, distract oneself from pain, reduce anxiety, and have family members and others reinforce active and positive coping behaviors (Chaleat-Valayer et al., 2019).

Support Groups

Support groups are also a key aspect of treatment for people with psychophysiological disorders. Support groups were discussed in different chapters but most notably in Chapter 9 for substance-related disorders. Support groups refer to meetings of people who share a common problem, including a physical problem such as heart disease. Support groups are useful for sharing information and tips on coping, venting frustration, developing friendships, and practicing stress management and other techniques. Support groups for the stress-related problems discussed here are conducted by the Crohn's and Colitis Foundation of America (for ulcerative colitis), Irritable Bowel Syndrome Association, National Migraine Association, Asthma and Allergy Foundation of America, American Sleep Association (for sleep disorders), and American Heart Association (for cardiac problems).

What If I or Someone I Know Has a Stress-Related Problem?

If you suspect that you or someone you know has a physical problem that may be at least partly caused by stress or another psychological variable, then consultation with a physician and a psychologist who specializes in health issues may be best. In addition, many people do not share with their physician details about the stress of their lives, or the fact that they are depressed or lack social support. But these are important factors that may affect treatment, so share these details with your physician. You may also wish to explore support groups or begin daily stress management to ease physical symptoms and adhere to sound practices such as healthy diet, sleep and exercise regimens, periods of relaxation, and resolution of interpersonal conflicts.

Long-Term Outcome for People with Stress-Related Problems

Stress management is an effective strategy for reducing distress as well as cardiovascular risk factors such as low heart rate variability. Stress management also helps lower systolic and diastolic blood pressure among people with cardiovascular problems such as hypertension (Conversano et al., 2021). Stress management and relaxation training may be particularly useful for people with IBS and perhaps ulcer as well (Shorey et al., 2021; Xiao et al., 2021).

Other stress-related disorders appear responsive to psychological therapies. As noted earlier, relaxation training and biofeedback are especially useful for headache. Relaxation, family therapy, medication compliance, stress reduction, and education are particularly important for resolving asthma, especially in children (Guarnaccia et al., 2020). Insomnia is also commonly treated successfully using cognitive-behavioral approaches, relaxation, and sleep restriction (Alimoradi et al., 2022). In general, long-term outcome for stress-related problems is good as long as medication as well as stress, depression, and related psychological variables are appropriately managed.

Key Terms

stress 478
psychophysiological disorders 478
health psychologists 479
behavioral medicine 479
ulcers 479
irritable bowel syndrome (IBS) 479
asthma 480
sleep disorders 480
dyssomnias 480
parasomnias 480
hypertension 481
coronary heart disease 481
type D personality 482
biofeedback 485
stress management 485

Glossary

A

active phase A phase of schizophrenia marked by full-blown psychotic features such as delusions and hallucinations.

acute stress disorder A mental disorder marked by anxiety and dissociative symptoms following a traumatic experience.

adaptive functioning A person's ability to carry out daily tasks that allows them to be independent.

aftercare services Community-based services for people with severe mental disorders to ease the transition between hospital settings and independent living.

agonists Medications to treat substance-related disorders that have a similar chemical composition as an addictive drug.

agoraphobia A mental disorder marked by avoidance of places in which one might have an embarrassing or intense panic attack.

alogia Speaking very little to other people.

Alzheimer's disease A neurocognitive disorder often marked by severe decline in memory and other cognitive functioning.

amyloid cascade hypothesis A theory that genetic and environmental factors interact to produce substantial brain changes and dementia.

analogue experiment An alternative experimental design that involves simulating a real-life situation under controlled conditions.

anhedonia Lack of pleasure or interest in life activities.

anorexia nervosa An eating disorder marked by refusal to maintain a minimum, normal body weight, intense fear of gaining weight, and disturbance in perception of body shape and weight.

antagonists Medications to treat substance-related disorders that block pleasurable effects and cravings for an addictive drug.

antecedents Stimuli or events that precede a behavior.

antisocial personality disorder Personality disorder marked by extreme disregard for and violation of the rights of others and impulsive behavior.

anxiety An emotional state that occurs as a threatening event draws close and is marked by aversive physical feelings, troublesome thoughts, and avoidance and other maladaptive behaviors.

anxiety-related disorder A mental disorder involving overwhelming worry, anxiety, or fear that interferes with a person's daily functioning.

anxiety sensitivity A risk factor for anxiety-related disorders involving fear of the potential dangerousness of one's physical symptoms.

asthma A chronic respiratory disease involving inflamed or constricted airways, tightening of the bronchial walls, and excess mucus.

asylums Places reserved to exclusively treat people with mental disorder, usually separate from the general population.

atrophy Gradual deterioration or shrinkage of a brain area in people with dementia.

attention-deficit/hyperactivity disorder (ADHD) A mental disorder marked by severe problems of inattention, hyperactivity, and impulsivity.

atypical antipsychotics A newer class of drugs to treat schizophrenia and related psychotic disorders.

autism spectrum disorder A pervasive developmental disorder associated with multiple cognitive and social deficits.

automatic thoughts Cognitive distortions of the negative cognitive triad that are constantly repeated and often associated with depression.

aversive drugs Medications to treat substance-related disorders that make ingestion of an addictive drug quite uncomfortable.

avoidance conditioning A theory of fear development that combines classical and operant conditioning with internal states such as driving or motivating factors.

avoidant personality disorder Personality disorder marked by anxiousness and feelings of inadequacy and socially ineptness.

avolition An inability or unwillingness to engage in goal-directed activities.

B

basal ganglia Brain structures that control posture and motor activity.

behavior genetics A research specialty that evaluates genetic and environmental influences on development of behavior.

behavioral assessment An assessment approach that focuses on measuring overt behaviors or responses.

behavioral avoidance test An assessment technique for anxiety-related disorders that measures how close one can approach a feared object or situation.

behavioral inhibition A risk factor for anxiety-related disorders involving withdrawal from things that are unfamiliar or new.

behavioral medicine A multidisciplinary approach to understanding the treatment and prevention of medical problems that may include a psychological approach.

behavioral perspective A perspective of psychopathology that assumes that problematic symptoms develop because of the way we learn or observe others.

binge eating Eating an amount of food in a limited amount of time that is much larger than most people would eat in that circumstance.

binge-eating disorder An eating disorder marked by recurrent episodes of binge eating but no compensatory behavior.

biofeedback A procedure that allows a person to monitor internal physiological responses and learn to control or modify these responses over time.

biological model A perspective of mental disorder that assumes that mental states, emotions, and behaviors arise from brain function and processes.

bipolar disorder A mental disturbance sometimes characterized by depression and mania.

bipolar I disorder A mental disorder marked by one or more manic episodes.

bipolar II disorder A mental disorder marked by episodes of hypomania that alternate with episodes of major depression.

blood alcohol level Concentration of alcohol in the blood.

body dissatisfaction Negative self-evaluation of what one's body looks like.

body dysmorphic disorder A disorder marked by excessive preoccupation with some perceived body flaw.

borderline personality disorder Personality disorder marked by impulsivity, difficulty controlling emotions, and self-mutilation or suicidal behavior.

breathing retraining A treatment technique for physical anxiety symptoms that involves inhaling slowly and deeply through the nose and exhaling slowly though the mouth.

brief psychotic disorder A psychotic disorder marked by features of schizophrenia lasting one day to one month.

bulimia nervosa An eating disorder marked by binge eating, inappropriate methods to prevent weight gain, and self-evaluation greatly influenced by body shape and weight.

C

case study method In-depth examination and observation of one person over time.

catastrophizing A cognitive distortion involving the assumption that terrible but incorrect consequences will result from an event.

catatonic Tendency to remain in a fixed stuporous state for long periods.

catatonic behavior Unusual motor behaviors in people with schizophrenia.

category An approach to defining mental disorder by examining large classes of behavior.

catharsis A nonspecific factor in treatment that refers to venting emotions and release of tension in a client.

central nervous system The brain and spinal cord, which are necessary to process information from sensory organs and prompt the body into action if necessary.

cerebral cortex Gray matter of the brain that covers almost all of each hemisphere.

cholinesterase inhibitors A class of drugs to treat people with dementia that help increase levels of acetylcholine in the brain.

cirrhosis of the liver A severe medical condition in which scar tissue in the liver replaces functional tissue.

civil commitment Involuntary hospitalization of people at serious risk for harming themselves or others or who cannot care for themselves.

classical conditioning Pairing of an unconditioned stimulus so the future presentation of a conditioned stimulus results in a conditioned response.

classification Arranging mental disorders into broad categories or classes based on similar features.

client-centered therapy A humanistic therapy that relies heavily on unconditional positive regard and empathy.

clinical assessment Evaluating a person's strengths and weaknesses and formulating a problem to develop a treatment plan.

clinical psychologists Mental health professionals with a Ph.D. or Psy.D. who promote behavioral change usually via psychological interventions.

codependency Dysfunctional behaviors that significant others of a person with substance-related disorder engage in to care for and cope with the person.

cognitive-behavioral therapy A type of treatment that focuses on the connection between thinking patterns, emotions, and behavior and uses cognitive and behavioral techniques to change dysfunctional thinking patterns.

cognitive distortions Unrealistic, inaccurate thoughts that people have about environmental events.

cognitive perspective A perspective of psychopathology that assumes that problematic symptoms develop because of the way people perceive and think about present and past experiences.

cognitive restructuring Therapeutic technique that helps someone think more realistically in a given situation.

cognitive schema Set of beliefs or expectations that represent a network of already accumulated knowledge.

cognitive therapy A treatment technique for cognitive symptoms of anxiety that involves helping a person think more realistically and develop a sense of control over anxious situations.

cohort effects Significant differences in the expression of a disorder depending on age.

community psychology A branch of psychology that focuses on enhancing quality of life for people and concentrating on their relationships with different social structures.

community reinforcement approach Encouraging a person to change environmental conditions to make them more reinforcing than drug use.

comorbidity Two or more disorders in one person.

compensatory behaviors Inappropriate behaviors to prevent weight gain.

competency to stand trial Whether a person can participate meaningfully in their own defense and can understand and appreciate the legal process that is involved.

compulsions Ongoing and bizarre ritualistic acts performed after an obsession to reduce arousal.

computerized axial tomography (CAT scan) A neuroimaging technique that uses X-rays to identify structural differences.

concurrent validity Whether current test or interview results relate to an important feature or characteristic at the present time.

conditional positive regard An environment in which others set conditions or standards for one's life.

conduct disorder A childhood mental disorder marked by antisocial conduct in the form of aggression, property destruction, deceitfulness, theft, and serious rule violations.

confidentiality The idea that discussions between a therapist and a client should not be divulged to other people unless consent is given.

confounds Factors that may account for group differences on a dependent variable.

consequences Outcomes or events that follow a behavior.

construct validity Whether test or interview results relate to other measures or behaviors in a logical, theoretically expected fashion.

content validity Degree to which test or interview items actually cover aspects of the variable or diagnosis under study.

contingency management A behavioral treatment technique in which family members and friends reward appropriate behavior in an individual.

control group Those who do not receive the active independent variable in an experiment.

controlled observation A behavioral assessment technique that involves analogue tests or tasks to approximate situations people face in real life and that may elicit a certain problem behavior.

conversion disorder A somatic symptom disorder marked by odd pseudoneurological symptoms that have no discoverable medical cause.

coronary heart disease Narrowing of the small blood vessels that supply blood and oxygen to the heart.

correlational study A study that allows researchers to make some statements about the association or relationship between variables based on the extent to which they change together in a predictable way.

counseling psychologists Mental health professionals with an M.A. or Ph.D. who help clients make choices to improve quality of life.

criminal commitment Involuntary hospitalization of people charged with a crime, either for determination of competency to stand trial or after acquittal by reason of insanity.

cross-sectional study A developmental design examining different groups of people at one point in time.

cross-tolerance Tolerance for a drug one has never taken because of tolerance to another drug with a similar chemical composition.

cue exposure therapy Exposure of a person to drug cues to help them control urges to use the drug.

cultural syndrome A problem caused by culturally shared beliefs and ideas that lead to high levels of stress and mental disorder.

culture The unique behavior and lifestyle shared by a group of people.

cyclothymic disorder A mental disorder marked by fluctuating symptoms of hypomania and depression for at least two years.

D

defense mechanisms Strategies used by the ego to stave off threats from the id or superego.

delayed ejaculation Delay or absence of orgasm in males during sexual activity with a partner.

delirium A neurocognitive disorder marked by usually temporary and reversible problems in thinking and memory.

delusional disorder A psychotic disorder marked by one or more delusions without other features of schizophrenia.

delusions Irrational beliefs involving a misinterpretation of perceptions or life experiences.

dementia A neurocognitive problem marked by usually chronic, progressive, and irreversible problems in thinking and memory.

dependent personality disorder Personality disorder marked by extreme submissiveness and a strong need to be liked and be taken care of by others.

dependent variable Variables that measure a certain outcome that a researcher is trying to explain or predict.

depersonalization/derealization disorder A dissociative disorder marked by chronic episodes of detachment from one's body and feelings of derealization.

depressant A class of drugs that inhibit the central nervous system.

depressive disorder A mental disorder marked by substantial sadness and related characteristic symptoms.

detoxification Withdrawing a person from an addictive drug under medical supervision.

developmental disorder A mental disorder marked by delay in key areas of cognitive, adaptive, and academic functioning.

diagnosis A category of mental disorder defined by certain rules that outline how many and what features of a disorder must be present.

dialectical behavior therapy Cognitive-behavioral treatment for suicidal behavior and related features of borderline personality disorder.

diathesis A biological or psychological predisposition to disorder.

dieting Deliberate attempts to limit quantity of food intake or change types of foods that are eaten.

dimension An approach to defining mental disorder along a continuum.

diminished capacity A reduced mental state that may mitigate a charge or sentence for someone convicted of a crime.

discrete-trial training A structured and repetitive method of teaching various skills to a child.

disinhibition The state that occurs when alcohol inhibits key inhibitory systems of the brain.

disorganized speech Disconnected, fragmented, interrupted, jumbled, and/or tangential speech.

disruptive behavior disorders A class of childhood mental disorders that involves serious acting-out behavior problems and often includes attention-deficit/hyperactivity, oppositional defiant, and conduct disorders.

dissociation A feeling of detachment or separation from oneself.

dissociative amnesia A dissociative disorder marked by severe memory loss for past and/or recent events.

dissociative disorders A class of mental disorders marked by disintegration of memory, consciousness, or identity.

dissociative fugue A dissociative problem marked by severe memory loss and sudden travel away from home or work.

dissociative identity disorder A dissociative disorder marked by multiple personalities in a single individual.

distal factors Causal factors that indirectly affect a particular mental disorder.

double-blind design An experimental condition meaning that neither the experimenter nor the participants know who received a placebo or an active treatment.

Down syndrome A chromosomal condition often caused by an extra chromosome 21 and that leads to characteristic physical features and intellectual problems.

dream analysis A psychodynamic technique to access unconscious material thought to be symbolized in dreams.

dual relationships A client who is also a significant other in the therapist's life; ethics standards dictate that this practice is to be avoided.

dyssomnias Problems in the amount, quality, or timing of sleep.

E

eating disorder A class of mental disorder involving severe body dissatisfaction, weight concerns, and eating problems as well as significant distress, excessive limits on activities, or increased risk for medical problems.

eating problems Restricting eating/excessive dieting and lack of control of eating.

educational psychologists Psychologists typically with a Ph.D. who work in school settings or academia to study and improve learning strategies for youth and adults.

ego The organized, rational component of the personality.

electrocardiogram A psychophysiological measure that provides a graphical description of heart rate.

electroconvulsive therapy (ECT) A procedure in which an electrical current is introduced to the brain to produce a seizure to alleviate severe depression.

electroencephalogram (EEG) A psychophysiological measure of brain activity.

electronic diaries Electronic devices for self-monitoring.

emotional processing A person's ability to think about a past anxiety-provoking event without significant anxiety.

emotional reasoning A cognitive distortion involving the assumption that one's physical feelings reflect how things really are.

endogenous opioids Chemicals produced by the body that reduce pain, enhance positive mood, and suppress appetite.

epidemiologists Scientists who study the incidence, prevalence, and risk factors of disorders.

epidemiology The study of patterns of diseases, disorders, and other health-related behavior in a population of interest.

erectile disorder A sexual dysfunction involving difficulty obtaining and maintaining an erection during sexual relations.

ethnicity Clusters of individuals who share cultural traits that distinguish themselves from others.

etiology Cause of mental disorders.

exhibitionistic disorder A paraphilic disorder in which the predominant focus of sexual activity is exposure of one's genitals to others such as strangers.

exorcism An attempt to cast out a spirit possessing an individual.

experiment A research method that allows scientists to draw cause-and-effect conclusions.

experimental group A group that receives the active independent variable.

exposure-based practices Treatment techniques for behavioral symptoms of anxiety that involve reintroducing a person to situations she commonly avoids.

exposure treatment An element of systematic desensitization that involves directly confronting a feared stimulus.

expressed emotion Family interactions characterized by high levels of emotional overinvolvement, hostility, and criticism.

external validity Ability to generalize results from one investigation to the general population.

extrapyramidal effects A group of side effects from antipsychotic medication involving involuntary movements of different parts of the body.

F

factitious disorder A mental disorder marked by deliberate production of physical or psychological symptoms to assume the sick role.

family systems perspective The idea that each family has its own structure and rules that can affect the mental health of individual family members.

fear An immediate and negative reaction to imminent threat that involves fright, increased arousal, and an overwhelming urge to escape.

female orgasmic disorder A sexual dysfunction marked by delay or absence of orgasm during sexual activity.

female sexual interest/arousal disorder A sexual dysfunction marked by lack of interest in, or arousal during, sexual activity.

fetal alcohol syndrome A condition caused by prenatal alcohol use that results in distinctive facial features and learning problems in children.

fetishistic disorder A paraphilic disorder in which the predominant focus of sexual activity is a nonliving object or nongenital body part.

fixation Frustration and anxiety at a psychosexual stage that can cause a person to be arrested at that level of development.

flat affect Lack of variety in emotional expression and speech.

flooding An exposure-based therapy technique involving exposure to, and eventual extinction of, one's most intense fear.

forensic psychology A branch of psychology involving the interaction of psychological and legal principles.

fragile X syndrome A genetic condition that involves damage to the X chromosome and that often leads to intellectual problems, especially in men.

free association A psychodynamic technique in which a client speaks continuously without censorship.

free radicals Aggressive substances produced by the body possibly to fight viruses and bacteria but that, in excess, may lead to dementia.

frontal lobe An area in front of the brain that is responsible for movement, planning, organizing, inhibiting behavior, and decision making.

frotteuristic disorder A paraphilic disorder in which the predominant focus of sexual activity is physical contact with an unsuspecting person.

functional analysis A behavioral assessment strategy to understand antecedents and consequences of behavior.

functional MRI (fMRI) A neuroimaging technique that assesses brain structure and function as well as metabolic changes.

G

galvanic skin conductance A psychophysiological measure of the electrical conductance of skin.

gender-affirming surgery A treatment for people with gender dysphoria that involves physical transformation to another gender.

gender dysphoria A mental disorder marked by strong desire to be of another gender as well as clinically significant distress.

generalized anxiety disorder A mental disorder marked by constant worry about nondangerous situations and physical symptoms of tension.

gene therapy Insertion of genes into an individual's cells and tissues to treat a disorder.

genito-pelvic pain/penetration disorder A sexual dysfunction involving pain during vaginal penetration and/or fear of pain before penetration.

genotype The genetic composition of an individual that is fixed at birth and received from one's parents.

guilty but mentally ill A verdict that may mean a defendant is committed to a psychiatric facility for some period of time.

H

hallucinations Sensory experiences a person believes to be true when actually they are not.

hallucinogens A class of drugs that produce psychosis-like symptoms.

health psychologists Psychologists who specialize in examining the interaction of biological, psychological, and social variables on traditional medical disorders.

histrionic personality disorder Personality disorder marked by excessive need for attention, superficial and fleeting emotions, and impulsivity.

hopelessness A feeling of despair often related to severe depression and suicide.

hopelessness (attribution) theory A theory of depression that people are more likely to become depressed if they make global, internal, and stable attributions about negative life events.

humanistic model A model of psychopathology that emphasizes personal growth, free will, and responsibility.

hypertension High blood pressure commonly identified if systolic pressure is greater than 140 millimeters of mercury and/or if diastolic pressure is greater than 90 millimeters of mercury.

hypomanic episode A period during which a person experiences manic symptoms but without significant interference in daily functioning.

hypothalamus A region of the brain below the thalamus that influences body temperature, food intake, sleep, and sex drive.

hypothesis A statement about the cause of an event or about the relationship between two events.

I

id The deep, inaccessible portion of the personality that contains instinctual urges.

illness anxiety disorder A somatic symptom disorder marked by excessive preoccupation with fear of having a disease.

inappropriate affect Emotion not appropriate for a given situation.

incidence Rate of new cases of a disorder that occur or develop during a specific time period such as a month or year.

independent variable A variable manipulated by a researcher that is hypothesized to be the cause of the outcome.

indicated prevention Preventive intervention targeting individuals at high risk for developing extensive problems in the future.

induction defects Problems in closure of the neural tube, proper development of the forebrain, and completion of the corpus callosum, all of which may lead to developmental disorder.

informant report Assessment methodology in which individuals who know a person well complete ratings of their personality traits and behavior.

informed consent The practice of educating potential clients about the therapy process, especially variables that might influence their decision to seek therapy.

insanity A legal term that refers to mental incapacity at the time of the crime, perhaps because a person did not understand right from wrong or because they were unable to control personal actions at the time of the crime.

insight (1) An active treatment ingredient in which a client comes to understand reasons for their maladaptive behavior and how to address it. (2) Understanding the unconscious determinants of irrational feelings, thoughts, or behaviors that create problems or distress.

intellectual developmental disorder A pervasive developmental disorder marked by intelligence and adaptive behavior problems, and onset before age 18 years.

intelligence tests Measures of cognitive functioning that provide estimates of intellectual ability.

internal consistency reliability Extent to which test items appear to be measuring the same thing.

internal validity Extent to which a researcher can be confident that changes in the dependent variable are truly the result of manipulation of the independent variable.

interoceptive exposure A treatment technique involving exposure to, and eventual control of, physical symptoms of anxiety.

interpretation A method in which a psychodynamic theorist reveals unconscious meanings of a client's thoughts and behaviors to help the person achieve insight.

interrater reliability Extent to which two raters or observers agree about their ratings or judgments of a person's behavior.

irritable bowel syndrome (IBS) A chronic gastrointestinal disorder involving alternating and recurrent constipation and diarrhea as well as abdominal pain.

K

Korsakoff's syndrome A problem marked by confusion, memory loss, and coordination problems.

L

lack of control over eating A feeling of poor control when eating such that excessive quantities of food are consumed.

latent content The symbolic meaning of a dream's events.

learned helplessness A theory related to depression that people act in a helpless, passive fashion upon learning their actions have little effect on their overall environment.

learning disorder A limited developmental disorder marked by academic problems in reading, spelling, writing, arithmetic, or some other important area.

least restrictive treatment A principle according to which people with mental disorders should receive effective treatment that impinges least on their freedom.

lethal dose Dose of a substance that kills a certain percentage of test animals.

Lewy bodies Clusters of alpha-synuclein proteins that accumulate in the brain and may lead to dementia.

lifetime prevalence Proportion of those who exhibit symptoms of a disorder up to the point they were assessed.

limbic system An area of the brain in the forebrain that regulates emotions and impulses and is responsible for basic drives like thirst, sex, and aggression.

limited developmental disorders A developmental disorder in which one area but not many areas of functioning are affected.

longitudinal study A developmental design examining the same group of people over a long period of time.

M

magnetic resonance imaging (MRI) A neuroimaging technique that can produce high-resolution images of brain structure.

major depressive disorder A mental disorder often marked by multiple major depressive episodes.

major depressive episode A period of time, two weeks or longer, marked by sad or empty mood most of the day, nearly every day, and other symptoms.

major neurocognitive disorder A mental disorder marked by severe problems in thinking and memory.

maladaptive behavior A behavior that interferes with a person's life, including ability to care for oneself, have good relationships with others, and function well at school or at work.

male hypoactive sexual desire disorder A sexual dysfunction involving a lack of fantasies or desire to have sexual relations.

malingering Deliberate production of physical or psychological symptoms with some external motivation.

manic episode A period during which a person feels highly euphoric or irritable.

manifest content The literal meaning of a dream.

marijuana A drug produced from the hemp plant that contains tetrahydrocannabinol (THC).

marriage and family therapists Mental health professionals with an M.A. or Ph.D. who specialize in working with couples and families.

mass madness Groups of individuals afflicted at the same time with the same disorder or unusual behaviors.

mastery An active treatment ingredient involving strong control over one's symptoms to the point they are not problematic to the individual.

masturbation training A treatment for people with paraphilic disorder that involves practicing effective masturbation and stimulation to enhance orgasm.

memory training A psychological treatment to enhance a person's memory by repeatedly practicing skills relying on external cues and mnemonic strategies for jogging memory, increasing social interaction, and simplifying a living environment.

mental disorder A group of emotional (feelings), cognitive (thinking), or behavioral symptoms that cause distress or significant problems.

mental hygiene movement The science of promoting mental health and thwarting mental disorder through education, early treatment, and public health measures.

mental status examination An assessment strategy involving evaluation of appearance, mood, orientation, and odd behaviors, speech, or thoughts.

mesolimbic system A reward-based area in the brain implicated in substance-related disorders.

metabolites By-products of neurotransmitters that can be detected in urine, blood, and cerebral spinal fluid.

migration defects Problems in cell growth and distribution in the second to fifth month of pregnancy, which can lead to underdeveloped brain areas and developmental disorder.

mild neurocognitive disorder A mental disorder marked by emerging problems in thinking and memory.

milieu therapy An inpatient treatment approach involving professionals and staff members encouraging a person with a severe mental disorder to engage in prosocial and therapeutic activities.

mindfulness A therapy technique that emphasizes how a person can accept symptoms but still function in a given situation.

MMPI-3 clinical scales Subscales of the MMPI-3 used to identify various problematic behaviors and personality styles.

MMPI-3 validity scales Subscales of the MMPI-3 used to identify a person's defensiveness during testing and response sets.

model A systematic way of viewing and explaining what we observe.

modeling Learning a new skill or set of behaviors by observing another person perform the skill or behavior.

molecular genetics Analysis of deoxyribonucleic acid (DNA) to identify links between specific genetic material and mental disorders.

monoamine oxidase inhibitor (MAOI) A class of antidepressant drug that inhibits monoamine oxidase, which breaks down neurotransmitters, to increase levels of those neurotransmitters.

mood-stabilizing drugs Medications used to help people control rapid shifts in mood.

moral treatment The humane type of care emphasized during the reform movement period.

motivational interviewing A type of interview for substance-related disorders that focuses on obtaining information and propelling a person to change behavior.

multicultural psychology Examines the effect of culture on the way people think, feel, and act.

multidimensional family therapy A family based treatment approach that focuses on developing a strong parent–adolescent bond and correcting related problems.

multisystemic treatment An intensive family- and community-based treatment program designed to address conduct-related problems in children.

Munchausen syndrome A severe factitious disorder in which a person causes symptoms and claims they have a physical or mental disorder.

N

narcissistic personality disorder Personality disorder marked by grandiosity, arrogance, and a tendency to exploit others.

natural experiment An observational study in which nature itself helps assign groups.

naturalistic observation A behavioral assessment technique that involves observing a person in their natural environment.

negative cognitive triad Cognitive distortions involving the self, world, and the future.

negative correlation Two variables highly related to one another such that an increase in one variable is accompanied by a decrease in the other variable.

negative reinforcement Removing an aversive event following a behavior to increase frequency of the behavior.

negative symptoms Symptoms such as flat affect and alogia that represent significant deficits in behavior.

neurochemical assessment Biological assessment of dysfunctions in specific neurotransmitter systems.

neurocognitive disorder A mental disorder that involves mild to severe impairment in major cognitive functions.

neurodevelopmental hypothesis An etiological model for psychotic disorders that assumes early changes in key brain areas and gradual progression over the lifespan to full-blown symptoms.

neurofibrillary tangles Twisted fibers inside nerve cells of the brain that may lead to dementia.

neuron The basic unit of the nervous system that comprises a cell body, dendrites, axon, and terminal buttons.

neuropsychological assessment Indirect measures of brain and physical function by evaluating a person's performance on standardized tests and tasks that indicate brain–behavior relationships.

neurotransmitters Chemical messengers that allow a nerve impulse to cross the synapse.

normalization The idea that people with mental disorders in regular living environments will behave more appropriately than those in large institutions.

O

objective personality measures Measures of personality that involve administering a standard set of questions or statements to which a person responds using set options.

obsessions Ongoing and bizarre ideas, thoughts, impulses, or images that a person cannot control.

obsessive-compulsive disorder A mental disorder marked by ongoing obsessions and compulsions lasting more than one hour per day.

obsessive-compulsive personality disorder Personality disorder marked by rigidity, perfectionism, and strong need for control.

occipital lobe An area of the brain behind the parietal and temporal lobes and associated with vision.

operant conditioning A learning principle that behavior followed by positive or pleasurable consequences is likely to be repeated but behavior followed by negative consequences is not likely to be repeated.

opiates A class of drugs commonly used to relieve pain.

oppositional defiant disorder A childhood mental disorder marked by hostile and negative behavior that includes noncompliance and other problems.

organismic variables A person's physiological or cognitive characteristics important for understanding a problem and determining treatment.

orgasmic reconditioning A treatment for paraphilic disorders that involves initial masturbation to a paraphilic stimulus and later masturbation to more appropriate sexual stimuli.

oxidative stress Damage to the brain from extensive exposure to oxygen and related matter.

P

panic attack A brief episode of intense fear and physical symptoms that increases and decreases suddenly in intensity.

panic disorder A mental disorder marked by ongoing and uncued panic attacks, worry about the consequences of these attacks, and, sometimes, agoraphobia.

paranoid personality disorder Personality disorder marked by general distrust and suspiciousness of others.

paraphilias Preferential, intense, and/or persistent sexual interests that may be odd but are not a mental disorder.

paraphilic disorders A class of mental disorder involving problems arising from sexual behavior or fantasies of highly unusual activities.

paraprofessionals Persons without advanced degrees who often work in mental health settings and assist with assessment and treatment procedures.

parasomnias Problematic behavioral or physiological events that occur throughout sleep.

parietal lobe An area of the brain behind the frontal lobe that is associated with the sensation of touch.

Parkinson's disease A progressive neurological disorder marked by unusual movements that may lead to a neurocognitive disorder.

partial agonists Medications to treat substance-related disorders that may act as an agonist or antagonist depending on how much of a certain neurotransmitter is produced.

pedophilic disorder A paraphilic disorder in which the predominant focus of sexual activity is with children.

peripartum depression Symptoms of depression or a major depressive episode that occurs during pregnancy.

peripheral nervous system The somatic and autonomic nervous system that controls muscles and voluntary movement, impacts the cardiovascular and endocrine system, assists with digestion, and regulates body temperature.

persistent depressive disorder (dysthymia) A depressive disorder involving a chronic feeling of depression for at least two years.

personality assessment Instruments measuring different traits or aspects of character.

personality disorders Mental disorders involving dysfunctional personality traits and associated problems such as relationship disturbances and impulsive behavior.

personality trait A disposition or readiness to act in a certain way.

pervasive developmental disorders A developmental disorder in which many areas of functioning are affected.

phenomenological approach An assumption that one's behavior is determined by perceptions of herself and others.

phenotype Observable characteristics of an individual.

phenylketonuria (PKU) An autosomal recessive disorder that leads to buildup of phenylalanine and possible intellectual problems.

Pick's disease A neurocognitive disorder characterized mainly by deterioration in the frontal and temporal brain lobes.

placebo The improvement in treatment due to a client's expectation of help.

pleasure principle The rule of conduct by the id to seek pleasure and avoid pain.

positive correlation Two variables highly related to one another such that an increase in one variable is accompanied by an increase in the other variable.

positive reinforcement Presenting a pleasant event or consequence after a behavior to increase frequency of the behavior.

positive symptoms Symptoms such as delusions and hallucinations that are obvious and excessive.

positron emission tomography (PET scan) An invasive neuroimaging procedure to assess brain structure and functioning.

postpartum depression A major depressive episode during weeks following childbirth.

postpartum psychosis A mental condition marked by psychotic symptoms in a parent following the birth of their child.

posttraumatic stress disorder A mental disorder marked by a traumatic event and the reexperiencing of the event through unwanted memories, nightmares, flashbacks, and images.

predictive validity Whether test or interview results accurately predict some behavior or event in the future.

premature (early) ejaculation A sexual dysfunction in men marked by orgasm that occurs before the person wishes.

premenstrual dysphoric disorder A mental disorder marked by depressive symptoms during most menstrual periods.

prescriptive treatment Assigning a specific treatment to an individual with a specific mental health problem or subtype of a problem.

prevalence Rate of new and existing cases of a condition observed during a specific time period.

prevention Interventions intended to arrest the development of later problems.

primary prevention A type of prevention targeting large groups of people who have not yet developed a disorder.

primary process The irrational and impulsive type of thinking that characterizes the id.

process variables General ingredients common to most psychological treatments that promote mental health in a client.

prodromal phase An initial phase of schizophrenia marked by peculiar thoughts and behaviors but without active psychotic features.

projection A defense mechanism used when a person attributes their unconscious feelings to someone else.

projective hypothesis The assumption that, when faced with unstructured or ambiguous stimuli or tasks, individuals impose their own structure and reveal something of themselves.

projective tests Psychological testing techniques based on the assumption that people faced with an ambiguous stimulus such as an inkblot will project their own needs, personality, conflicts, and wishes.

protective factor A factor that buffers one against the development of a mental disorder.

proximal factors Causal factors that more directly affect a particular mental disorder.

pseudoseizures Seizure-like activity such as twitching or loss of consciousness without electrical disruptions in the brain.

psychiatric nurses Specialized nurses with an R.N. who often work on inpatient psychiatric units and have training specific to mental disorders.

psychiatrists Mental health professionals with an M.D. who often adopt a medical or biological model to treat people with mental disorders.

psychic determinism An assumption of psychodynamic theory that everything we do has meaning and purpose and is goal-directed.

psychoanalyst A mental health professional that specializes in Freudian psychoanalysis to treat people with mental disorders.

psychodynamic model A model of psychopathology that assumes all mental states, emotions, and behaviors arise from unconscious motives and intrapsychic conflicts.

psychoeducation A treatment technique that involves educating a person about the physical, cognitive, and behavioral components of anxiety or other problems and how these components occur in sequence for that person.

psychopathologists Professionals who study mental problems to see how disorders develop and continue and how they can be prevented or alleviated.

psychopathology The scientific study of problematic feelings, thoughts, and behaviors associated with mental disorders.

psychopathy Diagnostic construct related to antisocial personality disorder that focuses on problematic interpersonal styles such as arrogance, lack of empathy, and manipulativeness.

psychophysiological assessment Evaluating bodily changes possibly associated with certain mental conditions.

psychophysiological disorders Organ dysfunction or physical symptoms that may be at least partly caused by psychological factors such as stress.

psychosexual stages of development A series of developmental stages marked by a particular erogenous zone of the body.

psychotherapist A generic mental health professional, or one not currently licensed as a psychologist or psychiatrist.

psychotic disorders A class of mental disorder marked by schizophrenia and/ or related problems.

psychotic prephase A phase of schizophrenia between the prodromal and active phases involving the onset of the first positive symptom of schizophrenia.

public health model A model that focuses on promoting good health and good health practices to avert disease.

public stigma The general disgrace the public confers on people with mental disorder that can result in prejudice, stereotyping, and discrimination.

purging Ridding oneself of food or bodily fluids (and thus weight) by self-induced vomiting or misuse of laxatives or diuretics.

Q

quasi-experimental method A study in which an independent variable is manipulated but people are not randomly selected or assigned to groups.

R

race A socially constructed category typically based on physical characteristics.

randomization Selecting and assigning people to groups so each person has the same chance of being assigned to any one group.

reaction formation The process that occurs when an unconscious impulse is consciously expressed by its behavioral opposite.

reality orientation A psychological treatment to reduce confusion in people using constant feedback about time, place, person, and recent events.

reality principle The rule of conduct by the ego that defers gratification of instinctual urges until a suitable object and mode of satisfaction are discovered.

regression A defense mechanism that occurs when a person returns to a life stage that once provided substantial gratification.

rehabilitation Regarding substance-related disorders, treatment involving complete abstinence, education about drugs and consequences of their use, and relapse prevention.

relaxation training A treatment technique for physical anxiety symptoms that may involve having a person tense and release (relax) different muscle groups.

reliability Consistency of test scores or diagnoses.

reminiscence therapy A treatment procedure for older adults with depression involving a systematic review of one's life and resolution of regrets.

repetitive transcranial magnetic stimulation (rTMS) A procedure to treat depressive and bipolar disorders that involves rapidly changing magnetic fields.

repression A defense mechanism that involves keeping highly threatening sexual or aggressive material out of conscious awareness.

residual phase A phase of schizophrenia usually after the active phase involving peculiar thoughts and behaviors similar to the prodromal phase.

resilience Ability of an individual to withstand and rise above extreme adversity.

response (or ritual) prevention A treatment technique for obsessive-compulsive disorder involving exposure to an obsession such as thoughts of dirty hands without engaging in a related compulsion such as hand washing.

restricted eating Deliberate attempts to limit quantity of food intake or change types of foods that are eaten.

restricting behaviors Eating less overall, avoiding foods with high calories, and engaging in excessive exercise.

reuptake A feedback mechanism that informs a neuron about the amount of neurotransmitter needed to be released in the future.

reward deficiency syndrome The theory that some people may not be able to derive much reward from everyday events and so resort to excesses such as drug use.

right to refuse treatment A principle according to which clients have the right to refuse risky or unconventional or discomfiting treatments.

right to treatment A principle according to which clients have the right to receive treatment that provides a meaningful chance of improvement in their condition.

risk factor An individual, contextual, or environmental characteristic correlated with an outcome or condition such as a mental disorder that precedes the development of the disorder.

S

satiety Feeling of fullness from eating.

schizoaffective disorder A psychotic disorder marked by symptoms of schizophrenia and depression or mania.

schizoid personality disorder Personality disorder marked by social isolation and restricted emotional expression.

schizophrenia A psychotic disorder marked by positive symptoms such as delusions and hallucinations, negative symptoms such as flat affect and withdrawal, and disorganized behavior.

schizophreniform disorder A psychotic disorder marked by symptoms of schizophrenia that last one to six months.

schizotypal personality disorder Personality disorder marked by social anxiety, paranoid fears, and eccentric behavior, perceptions, and thoughts.

school psychologists Psychologists with an M.A. or Ph.D. who typically work in school settings to evaluate youth with learning and behavioral problems.

scientific method A set of agreed-upon rules for systematically gathering information that involves generating a hypothesis, developing a research design, and analyzing and interpreting data to test the hypothesis.

screening interview A type of assessment that helps clinicians obtain information about recent and lifetime use of alcohol and other drugs.

secondary prevention A type of prevention that addresses emerging problems while they are still manageable and before they become resistant to intervention.

secondary process The rational and self-preservative type of thinking that characterizes the ego.

selective prevention Preventive intervention targeting subgroups of people at risk for a particular problem.

selective serotonin reuptake inhibitor (SSRI) A class of antidepressant medication that specifically affects serotonin levels and has fewer side effects than other antidepressants.

self-actualization Striving to be the best one can be.

self-control An active treatment ingredient whereby a client learns to control wayward impulses or emotions to improve quality of life.

self-help group An association of people who share a common problem such as a mental disorder that the group tries to address.

self-monitoring A behavioral assessment technique in which individuals observe and record their own emotions, thoughts, and behaviors.

self-stigma The disgrace people assign themselves because of public stigma.

senile or neuritic plaques Clusters of dead nerve cells and accumulations of amyloid proteins in the brain that may lead to dementia.

sensate focus A treatment for sexual dysfunction that helps couples reestablish intimacy while gradually rebuilding pleasurable sexual behaviors.

separation anxiety disorder A mental disorder marked by extreme and developmentally inappropriate distress when separation from home or close family members occurs or is anticipated.

sequential design A developmental design involving aspects of longitudinal and cross-sectional studies.

sexual dysfunction A mental disorder involving disturbance of the normal sexual response cycle.

sexual masochism A paraphilic disorder in which the predominant focus of sexual activity is a desire to be humiliated or made to suffer.

sexual sadism A paraphilic disorder in which the predominant focus of sexual activity is a desire to humiliate or make suffer.

sickle cell disease A genetic condition that leads to damaged red blood cells, poor oxygenation of cells, and potential intellectual problems.

single-subject experimental design Experimental designs that involve one person or a small group of persons who are examined under certain conditions.

skills training A treatment for substance-related disorders involving skills to avoid or cope with high-risk situations.

sleep disorders Problems in the amount, quality, or timing of sleep or unusual behavioral or physiological events that occur throughout sleep.

social anxiety disorder A mental disorder marked by panic attacks in, and avoidance of, situations involving performance before others or possible negative evaluation.

social workers Mental health professionals with an M.A. or Ph.D. who work to improve quality of life for people with mental disorders.

sociocultural perspective A perspective of psychopathology that focuses on influences that other people, social institutions, and social forces exert on a person's mental health.

somatic control exercises Treatment techniques to help people with anxiety-related disorders decrease severity of their aversive physical feelings.

somatic symptom disorder A mental disorder in which a person experiences physical symptoms that may or may not have a discoverable physical cause, as well as distress.

somatization A tendency to communicate distress through physical symptoms and to pursue medical help for these symptoms.

special education teachers Specialized teachers with an M.A. or Ph.D. who work primarily with youth with developmental disorders in academic settings.

specific phobia A mental disorder marked by panic attacks surrounding, and avoidance of, objects and situations other than those involving social interaction and/or performance before others.

spectator role The process of attending more to, and worrying about, sexual behavior and performance than the enjoyment and pleasure of sexual activity.

standardization Administering or conducting clinical assessment measures in the same way for all examinees.

stigma A characterization by others of disgrace or reproach based on an individual characteristic.

stimulants A class of drugs that activate the central nervous system.

stop–start procedure A treatment for premature ejaculation that involves pinching the tip of the penis when sexual stimulation becomes intense.

stress External events in our daily lives that are taxing for us as well as internal events such as perceptions that external events are demanding as well as certain physical symptoms.

stress-induced relapse Relapse to excessive substance use following stress and a period of abstinence.

stress management A collection of techniques to help people reduce the chronic effects of stress on a daily basis as well as problematic physical symptoms.

structured interview A type of clinical interview that requires an interviewer to ask standardized questions in a specified sequence.

substance intoxication A usually reversible condition triggered by excessive alcohol or other drug use.

substance-related disorder A class of mental disorders characterized by substance use disorder as well as substance intoxication and withdrawal.

substance use A nonmaladaptive use of alcohol or other drug.

substance use disorder A mental disorder involving repeated use of substances to the point that recurring problems are evident.

substance withdrawal Maladaptive behavioral changes that result when a person stops using a particular drug.

suicide The act of killing oneself.

superego A component of the personality representing the ideals and values of society as conveyed by parents.

synapse A small gap between ends of neurons.

syndrome Symptoms that cluster or group together within individuals.

systematic desensitization An exposure-based treatment technique involving gradual exposure to feared objects or situations and relaxation/breathing training.

T

Tay-Sachs disease A genetic condition leading to severe motor and sensory disabilities as well as intellectual problems and early death.

temporal lobe A middle area of the brain associated with auditory discrimination.

teratogen A potentially harmful agent that affects fetuses during the prenatal stage and which may lead to developmental disorders.

tertiary prevention A type of prevention aimed to reduce the severity, duration, and negative effects of a mental disorder after it has occurred.

test–retest reliability Extent to which a person provides similar answers to the same test items across time.

thalamus A structure within the forebrain that relays sensory information to the cerebral cortex.

theory of mind An understanding of the thoughts and beliefs of others.

therapeutic alignment A nonspecific factor in treatment in which a therapist sides with a particular individual to balance communications or power.

therapeutic alliance A nonspecific factor in treatment that refers to the relationship between the therapist and a client.

thought-action fusion A risk factor for obsessive-compulsive disorder involving a belief that thinking something is the same as doing it.

token economy An operant conditioning system in which desired behaviors are promoted through reinforcements.

tolerance The need to ingest greater amounts of a drug to achieve the same effect.

transference A key phenomenon in psychodynamic therapy in which a client reacts to the therapist as if the latter represented an important figure from the client's past.

transvestic disorder A paraphilic disorder in which the predominant focus of sexual activity is cross-dressing.

trephination Ancient technique that involved cutting a hole in a person's skull to help release a harmful spirit.

tricyclic antidepressants A class of antidepressant medication that affects different neurotransmitter systems and often comes with many side effects.

triple-blind design Experiments in which participants, experimenters, independent raters of outcome, and data managers are unaware of who received a placebo or active treatment.

type D personality A distressed personality pattern marked by negative affectivity and social inhibition.

typical antipsychotics A class of older drugs to treat schizophrenia and related psychotic disorders primarily by reducing excess levels of dopamine in the brain.

U

ulcer Inflammation or erosion of a part of the body such as the esophagus, stomach, or duodenum.

unconditional positive regard An environment in which a person is fully accepted as they are and allowed to pursue their own desires and goals.

unconscious motivation Motivation that resides outside conscious awareness.

universal prevention Preventive intervention targeting large groups of people not afflicted by a particular problem.

unstructured interview A type of clinical interview in which clinicians ask any questions in any order.

V

validity Extent to which an assessment technique measures what it is supposed to measure.

vascular disease A contributing factor to vascular dementia or neurocognitive disorder caused by problems with blood vessels.

voyeuristic disorder A paraphilic disorder in which the predominant focus of sexual activity is secretly watching others undress or engage in sexual activity without being seen.

W

weight concerns A focus on, and often negative evaluation of, one's weight.

withdrawal Maladaptive behavioral changes when a person stops using a drug.

worry A largely cognitive construct that refers to concern about possible future threat.

worry exposure A treatment technique for generalized anxiety disorder involving extensive concentration on an anxious thought and alternatives to the worst-case scenario.

References

Aarsland, D., & Bernadotte, A. (2015). Epidemiology of dementia associated with Parkinson's disease. In M. Emre (Ed.), *Cognitive impairment and dementia in Parkinson's disease* (2nd ed., pp. 5–16). New York: Oxford.

Abargil, M., & Tishby, O. (2021). Countertransference as a reflection of the patient's inner relationship conflict. *Psychoanalytic Psychology, 38*, 68–78.

Abascal-Peiró, S., Barrigón, M. L., Baca-García, E., & Ovejero, S. (2022). Left anterior right temporal position and ultra-brief pulse stimulus in the management of ECT-induced mania. *Bipolar Disorders, 24*, 97–100.

Abdoli, N., Salari, N., Darvishi, N., Jafarpour, S., Solaymani, M., Mohammadi, M., & Shohaimi, S. (2021). The global prevalence of major depressive disorder (MDD) among the elderly: A systematic review and meta-analysis. *Neuroscience & Biobehavioral Reviews, 132*, 1067–1073.

Abdullah, M., Huang, L. C., Lin, S. H., & Yang, Y. K. (2022). Dopaminergic and glutamatergic biomarkers disruption in addiction and regulation by exercise: A mini review. *Biomarkers, 27*, 306–318.

Abdul-Rahman, H. (2019). Intra and inter-psyche conflicts and analysis of symptoms of jinn possession. *Malaysian Journal of Medicine and Health Sciences, 2019*, 110–113.

Abdurrachid, N., & Marques, J. G. (2022). Munchausen syndrome by proxy (MSBP): A review regarding perpetrators of factitious disorder imposed on another (FDIA). *CNS Spectrums, 27*, 16–26.

Abé, C., Adebahr, R., Liberg, B., Mannfolk, C., Lebedev, A., Eriksson, J., ... & Rahm, C. (2021). Brain structure and clinical profile point to neurodevelopmental factors involved in pedophilic disorder. *Acta Psychiatrica Scandinavica, 143*, 363–374.

Abondio, P., Sarno, S., Giuliani, C., Laganà, V., Maletta, R., Bernardi, L., ... & Bruni, A. (2021). Amyloid precursor protein A713T mutation in Calabrian patients with Alzheimer's disease: A population genomics approach to estimate inheritance from a common ancestor. *Biomedicines, 10*, 20.

Abraham, G., Rutten-Jacobs, L., & Inouye, M. (2021). Risk prediction using polygenic risk scores for prevention of stroke and other cardiovascular diseases. *Stroke, 52*, 2983–2991.

Abrahamyan Empson, L., Baumann, P. S., Söderström, O., Codeluppi, Z., Söderström, D., & Conus, P. (2020). Urbanicity: The need for new avenues to explore the link between urban living and psychosis. *Early Intervention in Psychiatry, 14*, 398–409.

Achenbach, T.M., & Rescorla, L.A. (2001). *Manual for the ASEBA school-age forms & profiles*. Burlington, VT: University of Vermont Research Center for Children, Youth, & Families.

Acle, A., Cook, B. J., Siegfried, N., & Beasley, T. (2021). Cultural considerations in the treatment of eating disorders among racial/ethnic minorities: A systematic review. *Journal of Cross-Cultural Psychology, 52*, 468–488.

Acquavella, J., Mehra, R., Bron, M., Suomi, J. M. H., & Hess, G. P. (2020). Prevalence of narcolepsy and other sleep disorders and frequency of diagnostic tests from 2013–2016 in insured patients actively seeking care. *Journal of Clinical Sleep Medicine, 16*, 1255–1263.

Afuseh, E., Pike, C. A., & Oruche, U. M. (2020). Individualized approach to primary prevention of substance use disorder: Age-related risks. *Substance Abuse Treatment, Prevention, and Policy, 15*, 1–8.

Agostini, F., Zoccolotti, P., & Casagrande, M. (2022). Domain-general cognitive skills in children with mathematical difficulties and dyscalculia: A systematic review of the literature. *Brain Sciences, 12*, 239.

Agrawal, R., & Rath, B. (2021). Effectiveness Study of Typical and atypical antipsychotics on patients with schizophrenia using WHO Disability Assessment Schedule (WHODAS 2.0). *Biomedical and Pharmacology Journal, 14*, 1143–1148.

Agüera, Z., Lozano-Madrid, M., Mallorquí-Bagué, N., Jiménez-Murcia, S., Menchón, J. M., & Fernández-Aranda, F. (2021). A review of binge eating disorder and obesity. *Neuropsychiatrie, 35*, 57–67.

Aguirre Velasco, A., Cruz, I. S. S., Billings, J., Jimenez, M., & Rowe, S. (2020). What are the barriers, facilitators and interventions targeting help-seeking behaviours for common mental health problems in adolescents? A systematic review. *BMC Psychiatry, 20*, 1–22.

Ajnakina, O., Stubbs, B., Francis, E., Gaughran, F., David, A. S., Murray, R. M., & Lally, J. (2021). Employment and relationship outcomes in first-episode psychosis: A systematic review and meta-analysis of longitudinal studies. *Schizophrenia Research, 231*, 122–133.

Akbari, B., Baghaei-Yazdi, N., Bahmaie, M., & Mahdavi Abhari, F. (2022). The role of plant-derived natural antioxidants in reduction of oxidative stress. *BioFactors, 48*, 611–633.

Akinhanmi, M. O., Biernacka, J. M., Strakowski, S. M., McElroy, S. L., Balls Berry, J. E., Merikangas, K. R., ... & Frye, M. A. (2018). Racial disparities in bipolar disorder treatment and research: A call to action. *Bipolar Disorders, 20*, 506–514.

Aktar, E., Nikolić, M., & Bögels, S. M. (2022). Environmental transmission of generalized anxiety disorder from parents to children: worries, experiential avoidance, and intolerance of uncertainty. *Dialogues in Clinical Neuroscience, 19*, 137–147.

Alamolhoda, S. H., Haghdoost, S., Shariatifar, N., Zare, E., & Ahmadi Doulabi, M. (2021). Risk of child ADHD and low birth weight: A systematic review study. *International Journal of Pediatrics, 9*, 14421–14434.

Alcañiz, M., Guillen, M., & Santolino, M. (2021). Differences in the risk profiles of drunk and drug drivers: Evidence from a mandatory roadside survey. *Accident Analysis & Prevention, 151*, 105947.

Aldabas, R. (2020). Effectiveness of peer-mediated interventions (PMIs) on children with autism spectrum disorder (ASD): A systematic review. *Early Child Development and Care, 190*, 1586–1603.

Alder, M. C., Dyer, W. J., Sandberg, J. G., Davis, S. Y., & Holt-Lunstad, J. (2018). Emotionally-focused therapy and treatment as usual comparison groups in decreasing depression: A clinical pilot study. *The American Journal of Family Therapy, 46*, 541–555.

Alegría, M., NeMoyer, A., Falgàs Bagué, I., Wang, Y., & Alvarez, K. (2018). Social determinants of mental health: Where we are and where we need to go. *Current Psychiatry Reports, 20*, 1–13.

Ali, A., Caplan, P.J., & Fagnant, R. (2010). Gender stereotypes in diagnostic criteria. In J. C. Chrisler & D. R. McCreary (Eds.), *Handbook of gender research in psychology* (pp. 91–109). New York: Springer.

Ali, K., Fassnacht, D. B., Farrer, L., Rieger, E., Feldhege, J., Moessner, M., ... & Bauer, S. (2020). What prevents young adults from seeking help? Barriers toward help-seeking for eating disorder symptomatology. *International Journal of Eating Disorders, 53*, 894–906.

Alimoradi, Z., Jafari, E., Broström, A., Ohayon, M. M., Lin, C. Y., Griffiths, M. D., ... & Pakpour, A. H. (2022). Effects of cognitive behavioral therapy for insomnia (CBT-I) on quality of life: A systematic review and meta-analysis. *Sleep Medicine Reviews*, 101646.

Alizadeh, A., & Farnam, F. (2021). Coping with dyspareunia, the importance of inter and intrapersonal context on women's sexual distress: A population-based study. *Reproductive Health, 18*, 1–11.

Allen, M. S., & Robson, D. A. (2020). Personality and body dissatisfaction: An updated systematic review with meta-analysis. *Body Image, 33*, 77–89.

Allen, T. A., Carey, B. E., Mcbride, C., Bagby, R. M., DeYoung, C. G., & Quilty, L. C. (2018). Big Five aspects of personality interact to predict depression. *Journal of Personality, 86*, 714–725.

Allison, S., Warin, M., Bastiampillai, T., Looi, J. C., & Strand, M. (2021). Recovery from anorexia nervosa: the influence of women's sociocultural milieux. *Australasian Psychiatry, 29*, 513–515.

Allott, K., van-der-EL, K., Bryce, S., Parrish, E. M., McGurk, S. R., Hetrick, S., ... & Velligan, D. (2020). Compensatory interventions for cognitive impairments in psychosis: A systematic review and meta-analysis. *Schizophrenia Bulletin, 46*, 869–883.

Almeida, F. B., Pinna, G., & Barros, H. M. T. (2021). The role of HPA axis and allopregnanolone on the neurobiology of major depressive disorders and PTSD. *International Journal of Molecular Sciences, 22*, 5495.

Al-Nasser, M. N., Mellor, I. R., & Carter, W. G. (2022). Is L-Glutamate toxic to neurons and thereby contributes to neuronal loss and neurodegeneration? A systematic review. *Brain Sciences, 12*, 577.

Alqarni, H., Alsaloum, M., & Alzaid, A. (2022). Prosthetic rehabilitation of meth mouth with implant-supported fixed dental prostheses: A clinical report. *The Journal of Prosthetic Dentistry, 128*, 1140–1144.

Altmann, U., Brümmel, M., Meier, J., & Strauss, B. (2021). Movement synchrony and facial synchrony as diagnostic features of depression: A pilot study. *Journal of Nervous and Mental Disease, 209*, 128–136.

Alvarez, K., Fillbrunn, M., Green, J. G., Jackson, J. S., Kessler, R. C., McLaughlin, K. A., ... & Alegría, M. (2019). Race/ethnicity, nativity, and lifetime risk of mental disorders in US adults. *Social Psychiatry and Psychiatric Epidemiology, 54*, 553–565.

Álvarez-Tomás, I., Ruiz, J., Guilera, G., & Bados, A. (2019). Long-term clinical and functional course of borderline personality disorder: A meta-analysis of prospective studies. *European Psychiatry, 56*, 75–83.

American Educational Research Association, American Psychological Association, National Council on Measurement in Education (2014). *Standards for educational and psychological testing*. Washington, DC: American Educational Research Association.

American Psychiatric Association. (2022). *Diagnostic and statistical manual of mental disorders (fifth edition, text revision)*. Washington, DC: Author.

American Psychological Association (2017). *Ethical principles and code of conduct*. Washington, DC: Author.

American Psychological Association. (2012). *5-year summary report: Commission on Accreditation*. Washington, DC: Author.

Amoroso, C. R., Hanna, E. K., LaBar, K. S., Schaich Borg, J., Sinnott-Armstrong, W., & Zucker, N. L. (2020). Disgust theory through the lens of psychiatric medicine. *Clinical Psychological Science, 8*, 3–24.

Amsalem, D., Markowitz, J. C., Jankowski, S. E., Yang, L. H., Valeri, L., Lieff, S. A., ... & Dixon, L. B. (2021). Sustained effect of a brief video in reducing public stigma toward individuals with psychosis: A randomized controlled trial of young adults. *American Journal of Psychiatry, 178*, 635-642.

Anderson, D., Laforge, J., Ross, M. M., Vanlangendonck, R., Hasoon, J., Viswanath, O., ... & Urits, I. (2022). Male sexual dysfunction. *Health Psychology Research, 10*, 37533.

Anderson, L. M., Smith, K. E., Nuñez, M. C., & Farrell, N. R. (2021). Family accommodation in eating disorders: a preliminary examination of correlates with familial burden and cognitive-behavioral treatment outcome. *Eating Disorders, 29*, 327–343.

Anderson, M. E., Zajac, L., Thanik, E., & Galvez, M. (2020). Home visits for pediatric asthma-A strategy for comprehensive asthma management through prevention and reduction of environmental asthma triggers in the home. *Current Problems in Pediatric and Adolescent Health Care, 50*, 100753.

Ando', A., Giromini, L., Ales, F., & Zennaro, A. (2020). A multimethod assessment to study the relationship between rumination and gender differences. *Scandinavian Journal of Psychology, 61*, 740–750.

Andrade, C. (2021). HARKing, cherry-picking, p-hacking, fishing expeditions, and data dredging and mining as questionable research practices. *Journal of Clinical Psychiatry, 82*, 25941.

Andreola, C., Mascheretti, S., Belotti, R., Ogliari, A., Marino, C., Battaglia, M., & Scaini, S. (2021). The heritability of reading and reading-related neurocognitive components: A multi-level meta-analysis. *Neuroscience & Biobehavioral Reviews, 121*, 175–200.

Andrés-Pepiñá, S., Plana, M. T., Flamarique, I., Romero, S., Borràs, R., Julià, L., ... & Castro-Fornieles, J. (2020). Long-term outcome and psychiatric comorbidity of adolescent-onset anorexia nervosa. *Clinical Child Psychology and Psychiatry, 25*, 33–44.

Andreu-Reinón, M. E., Chirlaque, M. D., Gavrila, D., Amiano, P., Mar, J., Tainta, M., ... & Huerta, J. M. (2021). Mediterranean diet and risk of dementia and Alzheimer's disease in the EPIC-Spain dementia cohort study. *Nutrients, 13*, 700.

Aneja, J., Grover, S., Avasthi, A., Mahajan, S., Pokhrel, P., & Triveni, D. (2015). Can masturbatory guilt lead to severe psychopathology: A case series. *Indian Journal of Psychological Medicine, 37*, 81–86.

Anglin, D.M., Polanco-Roman, L., & Lui, F. (2015). Ethnic variation in whether dissociation mediates the relation between traumatic life events and attenuated positive psychotic symptoms. *Journal of Trauma and Dissociation, 16*, 68–85.

Anmella, G., Gil-Badenes, J., Pacchiarotti, I., Verdolini, N., Aedo, A., Angst, J., ... & Murru, A. (2020). Do depressive and manic symptoms differentially impact on functioning in acute depression? Results from a large, cross-sectional study. *Journal of Affective Disorders, 261*, 30–39.

Anagha, K., Shihabudheen, P., & Uvais, N. A. (2021). Side effect profiles of selective serotonin reuptake inhibitors: A cross-sectional study in a naturalistic setting. *The Primary Care Companion for CNS Disorders, 23*, 35561.

Antoniadou, F., Papamitsou, T., Kavvadas, D., Kapoukranidou, D., Sioga, A., & Papaliagkas, V. (2020). Toxic environmental factors and their association with the development of dementia: A mini review on heavy metals and ambient particulate matter. *Materia Socio-medica, 32*, 299–306.

Aparcero, M., Picard, E. H., Nijdam-Jones, A., & Rosenfeld, B. (2022). Comparing the ability of MMPI-2 and MMPI-2-RF validity scales to detect feigning: A meta-analysis. *Assessment*, 10731911211067535.

Arab, J. P., Izzy, M., Leggio, L., Bataller, R., & Shah, V. H. (2022). Management of alcohol use disorder in patients with cirrhosis in the setting of liver transplantation. *Nature Reviews Gastroenterology & Hepatology, 19*, 45–59.

Archer, M., Harwood, H., Stevelink, S., Rafferty, L., & Greenberg, N. (2020). Community reinforcement and family training and rates of treatment entry: A systematic review. *Addiction, 115*, 1024–1037.

Arena, J. D., Johnson, V. E., Lee, E. B., Gibbons, G. S., Smith, D. H., Trojanowski, J. Q., & Stewart, W. (2020). Astroglial tau pathology alone preferentially concentrates at sulcal depths in chronic traumatic encephalopathy neuropathologic change. *Brain Communications, 2*, fcaa210.

Arevalo-Rodriguez, I., Smailagic, N., Roque-Figuls, M., Ciapponi, A., Sanchez-Perez, E., Giannakou, A., ... & Cullum, S. (2021). Mini-Mental State Examination (MMSE) for the early detection of dementia in people with mild cognitive impairment (MCI). *Cochrane Database of Systematic Reviews*, 7.

Ariss, T., & Fairbairn, C. E. (2020). The effect of significant other involvement in treatment for substance use disorders: A meta-analysis. *Journal of Consulting and Clinical Psychology, 88*, 526–540.

Armstrong, H.L. (Ed.) (2021). *Encyclopedia of sex and sexuality: Understanding biology, psychology, and culture*. Santa Barbara, CA: ABC-CLIO.

Armstrong, M. J., Song, S., Kurasz, A. M., & Li, Z. (2022). Predictors of mortality in individuals with dementia in the National Alzheimer's Coordinating Center. *Journal of Alzheimer's Disease*, 1–12.

Armstrong, N. M., An, Y., Shin, J. J., Williams, O. A., Doshi, J., Erus, G., ... & Resnick, S. M. (2020). Associations between cognitive and brain volume changes in cognitively normal older adults. *Neuroimage, 223*, 117289.

Arvilommi, P., Suominen, K., Mantere, O., Leppamaki, S., Valtonen, H., & Isometsa, E. (2014). Predictors of adherence to psychopharmacological and psychosocial treatment in bipolar I or II disorders: An 18-month prospective study. *Journal of Affective Disorders, 155*, 110–117.

Asher, M., & Aderka, I. M. (2018). Gender differences in social anxiety disorder. *Journal of Clinical Psychology, 74*, 1730–1741.

Ashwill, R., Mulhall, S., Johnson, D. K., & Galvin, J. E. (2015). Caregiving experience for people with Lewy body dementia: Spouse versus adult child. *Alzheimer's and Dementia, 11*, P601.

Asnaani, A., & Hall-Clark, B. (2017). Recent developments in understanding ethnocultural and race differences in trauma exposure and PTSD. *Current Opinion in Psychology, 14*, 96–101.

Asp, M., Lindqvist, D., Fernström, J., Ambrus, L., Tuninger, E., Reis, M., & Westrin, Å. (2020). Recognition of personality disorder and anxiety disorder comorbidity in patients treated for depression in secondary psychiatric care. *PLoS One, 15*, e0227364.

Atallah, S., Haydar, A., Jabbour, T., Kfoury, P., & Sader, G. (2021). The effectiveness of psychological interventions alone, or in combination with phosphodiesterase-5 inhibitors, for the treatment of erectile dysfunction: A systematic review. *Arab Journal of Urology, 19*, 310–322.

Atkin, A. L., Christophe, N. K., Stein, G. L., Gabriel, A. K., & Lee, R. M. (2022). Race terminology in the field of psychology: Acknowledging the growing multiracial population in the US. *American Psychologist, 77*, 81–93.

Attademo, L., Bernardini, F., & Verdolini, N. (2021). Neural correlates of schizotypal personality disorder: A systematic review of neuroimaging and EEG studies. *Current Medical Imaging, 17*, 1283–1298.

Atwood, M. E., & Friedman, A. (2020). A systematic review of enhanced cognitive behavioral therapy (CBT-E) for eating disorders. *International Journal of Eating Disorders, 53*, 311–330.

Auger, N., Potter, B. J., Ukah, U. V., Low, N., Israël, M., Steiger, H., ... & Paradis, G. (2021). Anorexia nervosa and the long-term risk of mortality in women. *World Psychiatry, 20*, 448.

Avenevoli, S., Swendsen, J., He, J. P., Burstein, M., & Merikangas, K. R. (2015). Major depression in the National Comorbidity Survey—Adolescent Supplement: prevalence, correlates, and treatment. *Journal of the American Academy of Child and Adolescent Psychiatry, 54*, 37–44.

Awad, G. H., Kashubeck-West, S., Bledman, R. A., Coker, A. D., Stinson, R. D., & Mintz, L. B. (2020). The role of enculturation, racial identity, and body mass index in the prediction of body dissatisfaction in African American women. *Journal of Black Psychology, 46*, 3–28.

Ayesa-Arriola, R., de la Foz, V. O. G., Setién-Suero, E., Ramírez-Bonilla, M. L., Suárez-Pinilla, P., Son, J. M. V., ... & Crespo-Facorro, B. (2020). Understanding sex differences in long-term outcomes after a first episode of psychosis. *NPJ Schizophrenia, 6*, 1–8.

Azevedo, J., Vieira-Coelho, M., Castelo-Branco, M., Coelho, R., & Figueiredo-Braga, M. (2020). Impulsive and premeditated aggression in male offenders with antisocial personality disorder. *PLoS One, 15*, e0229876.

Bae, Y. J., Kim, J. M., Sohn, C. H., Choi, J. H., Choi, B. S., Song, Y. S., ... & Kim, J. H. (2021). Imaging the substantia nigra in Parkinson disease and other Parkinsonian syndromes. *Radiology, 300*, 260–278.

Bai, W., Chen, P., Cai, H., Zhang, Q., Su, Z., Cheung, T., ... & Xiang, Y. T. (2022). Worldwide prevalence of mild cognitive impairment among community dwellers aged 50 years and older: A meta-analysis and systematic review of epidemiology studies. *Age and Ageing, 51*, afac173.

Baier, A. L., Kline, A. C., & Feeny, N. C. (2020). Therapeutic alliance as a mediator of change: A systematic review and evaluation of research. *Clinical Psychology Review, 82*, 101921.

Bakr, A. M., El-Sakka, A. A., & El-Sakka, A. I. (2022). Pharmaceutical management of sexual dysfunction in men on antidepressant therapy. *Expert Opinion on Pharmacotherapy*, 1–13.

Baldessarini, R. J. (2013). *Chemotherapy in psychiatry* (3rd ed.). New York: Springer.

Ballester, L., Valero, M., Orte, C., & Amer, J. (2020). An analysis of family dynamics: A selective substance abuse prevention programme for adolescents. *European Journal of Social Work, 23*, 93–105.

Balogh, L., Tanaka, M., Török, N., Vécsei, L., & Taguchi, S. (2021). Crosstalk between existential phenomenological psychotherapy and neurological sciences in mood and anxiety disorders. *Biomedicines, 9*, 340.

Balogun-Mwangi, O., DeTore, N. R., & Russinova, Z. (2022). "We don't get a chance to prove who we really are": A qualitative inquiry of workplace prejudice and discrimination among Black adults with serious mental illness. *Psychiatric Rehabilitation Journal*.

Baltodano-Calle, M. J., Onton-Díaz, M., & Gonzales, G. F. (2022). Androgens, brain and androgen deprivation therapy in paraphilic disorders: A narrative review. *Andrologia*, e14561.

Banaei, M., Kariman, N., Ozgoli, G., Nasiri, M., & Khiabani, A. (2021). Sexual penetration cognitions in women with genito-pelvic pain and penetration disorder: A systematic review and meta-analysis. *Sexual and Relationship Therapy*, 1–15.

Bandealy, S. S., Sheth, N. C., Matuella, S. K., Chaikind, J. R., Oliva, I. A., Philip, S. R., ... & Hoge, E. A. (2021). Mind-body interventions for anxiety disorders: A review of the evidence base for mental health practitioners. *Focus, 19*, 173–183.

Banjongrewadee, M., Wongpakaran, N., Wongpakaran, T., Pipanmekaporn, T., Punjasawadwong, Y., & Mueankwan, S. (2020). The role of perceived stress and cognitive function on the relationship between neuroticism and depression among the elderly: a structural equation model approach. *BMC Psychiatry, 20*, 1–8.

Banker, S. M., Ramphal, B., Pagliaccio, D., Thomas, L., Rosen, E., Sigel, A. N., ... & Margolis, A. E. (2020). Spatial network connectivity and spatial reasoning ability in children with nonverbal learning disability. *Scientific Reports, 10*, 1–10.

Baranyi, G., Di Marco, M. H., Russ, T. C., Dibben, C., & Pearce, J. (2021). The impact of neighbourhood crime on mental health: A systematic review and meta-analysis. *Social Science & Medicine, 282*, 114106.

Bardone-Cone, A. M., Thompson, K. A., & Miller, A. J. (2020). The self and eating disorders. *Journal of Personality, 88*, 59–75.

Barends, H., Claassen-van Dessel, N., van der Wouden, J. C., Twisk, J. W., Terluin, B., van der Horst, H. E., & Dekker, J. (2020). Impact of symptom focusing and somatosensory amplification on persistent physical symptoms: A three-year follow-up study. *Journal of Psychosomatic Research, 135*, 110131.

Barkley, R.A. (2013). *Defiant children: A clinician's manual for assessment and parent training* (3rd ed.). New York: Guilford.

Barkley, R.A., & Robin, A.L. (2014). *Defiant teens: A clinician's manual for assessment and family intervention* (2nd ed.). New York: Guilford.

Barlow, D. H., Curreri, A. J., & Woodard, L. S. (2021). Neuroticism and disorders of emotion: A new synthesis. *Current Directions in Psychological Science, 30*, 410–417.

Barlow, D. H., & Eustis, E. H. (2022). The importance of idiographic and functionally analytic strategies in the unified protocol for transdiagnostic treatment of emotional disorders. *Journal of Contextual Behavioral Science, 24*, 179–184.

Barnes, M., Abhyankar, P., Dimova, E., & Best, C. (2020). Associations between body dissatisfaction and self-reported anxiety and depression in otherwise healthy men: A systematic review and meta-analysis. *PLoS One, 15*, e0229268.

Barrett, P.M., Cooper, M., & Guajardo, J.G. (2014). Using the FRIENDS programs to promote resilience in cross-cultural populations. In S. Prince-Embury & D.H. Saklofske (Eds.), *Resilience interventions for youth in diverse populations* (pp. 85–108). New York: Springer.

Bartova, L., Dold, M., Kautzky, A., Fabbri, C., Spies, M., Serretti, A., ... & Kasper, S. (2019). Results of the European Group for the Study of Resistant Depression (GSRD)—basis for further research and clinical practice. *World Journal of Biological Psychiatry, 20*, 427–448.

Bartucz, M. B., David, D. O., & Matu, S. A. (2022). Cognitive vulnerabilities and depression: A culture-moderated meta-analysis. *Cognitive Therapy and Research*, 1–15.

Bas-Hoogendam, J. M., van Steenbergen, H., Tissier, R. L., Houwing-Duistermaat, J. J., Westenberg, P. M., & van der Wee, N. J. (2018). Subcortical brain volumes, cortical thickness and cortical surface area in families genetically enriched for social anxiety disorder–A multiplex multigenerational neuroimaging study. *EBioMedicine, 36*, 410–428.

Bass, C., & Wade, D. T. (2019). Malingering and factitious disorder. *Practical Neurology, 19*, 96–105.

Bateman, A. W. (2022). Mentalizing and group psychotherapy: a novel treatment for antisocial personality disorder. *American Journal of Psychotherapy, 75*, 32–37.

Battista, P., Salvatore, C., Berlingeri, M., Cerasa, A., & Castiglioni, I. (2020). Artificial intelligence and neuropsychological measures: The case of Alzheimer's disease. *Neuroscience & Biobehavioral Reviews, 114*, 211–228.

Baudinet, J., Eisler, I., Dawson, L., Simic, M., & Schmidt, U. (2021). Multi-family therapy for eating disorders: A systematic scoping review of the quantitative and qualitative findings. *International Journal of Eating Disorders, 54*, 2095–2120.

Baur, E., Forsman, M., Santtila, P., Johansson, A., Sandnabba, K., & Långström, N. (2016). Paraphilic sexual interests and sexually coercive behavior: A population-based twin study. *Archives of Sexual Behavior, 45*, 1163–1172.

Baxter, A.J., Scott, K.M., Vos, T., & Whiteford, H.A. (2013). Global prevalence of anxiety disorders: A systematic review and meta-regression. *Psychological Medicine, 43*, 897–910.

Bayat, M., Zabihi, S., Karbalaei, N., & Haghani, M. (2020). Time-dependent effects of platelet-rich plasma on the memory and hippocampal synaptic plasticity impairment in vascular dementia induced by chronic cerebral hypoperfusion. *Brain Research Bulletin, 164*, 299–306.

Bayes, A., Parker, G., & Paris, J. (2019). Differential diagnosis of bipolar II disorder and borderline personality disorder. *Current Psychiatry Reports, 21*, 1–11.

Bayley, N., & Aylward, G.P. (2019). *Bayley Scales of Infant and Toddler Development-Fourth Edition (Bayley-4)*. San Antonio, TX: Pearson.

Bazinet, A., Carniello, T. N., Abracen, J., Looman, J., & Valliant, P. M. (2022). The contribution of psychopathic traits and substance use in the prediction of recidivism of sexual offenders. *International Journal of Law and Psychiatry, 81*, 101779.

Beck, A.T., & Dozois, D.J.A. (2014). Cognitive theory and therapy: Past, present, and future. In S. Bloch, S.A. Green, & J. Holmes (Eds.), *Psychiatry: Past, present, and future* (pp. 366–382). New York: Oxford.

Beck, A. T., Finkel, M. R., & Beck, J. S. (2021). The theory of modes: Applications to schizophrenia and other psychological conditions. *Cognitive Therapy and Research, 45*, 391–400.

Beck, A. T., Himelstein, R., & Grant, P. M. (2019). In and out of schizophrenia: Activation and deactivation of the negative and positive schemas. *Schizophrenia Research, 203*, 55–61.

Becquet, C., Cogez, J., Dayan, J., Lebain, P., Viader, F., Eustache, F., & Quinette, P. (2021). Episodic autobiographical memory impairment and differences in pronoun use: Study of self-awareness in functional amnesia and transient global amnesia. *Frontiers in Psychology, 12*, 624010.

Bednarczuk, N., Milner, A., & Greenough, A. (2020). The role of maternal smoking in sudden fetal and infant death pathogenesis. *Frontiers in Neurology, 11*, 586068.

Beech, A. R., Miner, M. H., & Thornton, D. (2016). Paraphilias in the DSM-5. *Annual Review of Clinical Psychology, 12*, 13.1–13.24.

Beetstra-Hill, A. (2021). Alzheimer's disease and APOE: To test or not to test. *Journal of the Australasian College of Nutritional and Environmental Medicine, 40*, 6–10.

Behar, E., & Borkovec, T. D. (2020). The effects of verbal and imaginal worry on panic symptoms during an interoceptive exposure task. *Behaviour Research and Therapy, 135*, 103748.

Belchamber, C. (2022). *Payne's handbook of relaxation techniques: A practical guide for the health care professional*. New York: Elsevier.

Bellia, F., Vismara, M., Annunzi, E., Cifani, C., Benatti, B., Dell'Osso, B., & D'Addario, C. (2021). Genetic and epigenetic architecture of obsessive-compulsive disorder: In search of possible diagnostic and prognostic biomarkers. *Journal of Psychiatric Research, 137*, 554–571.

Ben-Joseph, A., Marshall, C. R., Lees, A. J., & Noyce, A. J. (2020). Ethnic variation in the manifestation of Parkinson's disease: A narrative review. *Journal of Parkinson's Disease, 10*, 31–45.

Ben-Porath, Y. S., Heilbrun, K., & Rizzo, M. (2022). Using the MMPI-3 in legal settings. *Journal of Personality Assessment, 104*, 162–178.

Ben-Porath, Y. S., & Tellegen, A. (2020). *Minnesota Multiphasic Personality Inventory-3*. San Antonio, TX: Pearson.

Benrimoh, D., Sheldon, A., Sibarium, E., & Powers, A. R. (2021). Computational mechanism for the effect of psychosis community treatment: a conceptual review from neurobiology to social interaction. *Frontiers in Psychiatry, 12*, 685390.

Benson, K., Flory, K., Humphreys, K. L., & Lee, S. S. (2015). Misuse of stimulant medication among college students: A comprehensive review and meta-analysis. *Clinical Child and Family Psychology Review, 18*, 50–76.

Bergman, H., Maayan, N., Kirkham, A.J., Adams, C.E., & Soares-Weiser, K. (2015). Schedule for Affective Disorders and Schizophrenia for School-Age Children (K-SADS) for diagnosing schizophrenia in children and adolescents with psychotic symptoms. *Cochrane Database of Systematic Reviews, 2015*, Issue 6.

Bergvall, L., & Himelein, M. J. (2014). Attitudes toward seeking help for sexual dysfunctions among US and Swedish college students. *Sexual and Relationship Therapy, 29*, 215–228.

Berlim, M.T., Van den Eynde, F., & Daskalakis, Z.J. (2012). A systematic review and meta-analysis on the efficacy and acceptability of bilateral repetitive transcranial magnetic stimulation (rTMS) for treating major depression. *Psychological Medicine, 2012*, 1–10.

Bertels, X., Mehuys, E., Boussery, K., & Lahousse, L. (2021). The implementation of risk minimization measures to prevent teratogenic pregnancy outcomes related to oral retinoid and valproate use in Belgium. *Acta Clinica Belgica, 77*, 815–822.

Berzoff, J., Flanagan, L. M., & Hertz, P. (Eds.) (2022). *Inside out and outside in: Psychodynamic clinical theory and psychopathology in contemporary multicultural contexts* (5th ed.). New York: Rowman & Littlefield.

Besnard, A., & Leroy, F. (2022). Top-down regulation of motivated behaviors via lateral septum sub-circuits. *Molecular Psychiatry*, 1–10.

Betz, L. T., Penzel, N., Kambeitz-Ilankovic, L., Rosen, M., Chisholm, K., Stainton, A., ... & Kambeitz, J. (2020). General psychopathology links burden of recent life events and psychotic symptoms in a network approach. *npj Schizophrenia, 6*, 1–8.

Bezine, M. (2022). Alzheimer's disease has a high rate of early onset. *Neurology and Neurorehabilitation, 4*, 3–4.

Bhattacharyya, U., Deshpande, S. N., Bhatia, T., & Thelma, B. K. (2021). Revisiting schizophrenia from an evolutionary perspective: An association study of recent evolutionary markers and schizophrenia. *Schizophrenia Bulletin, 47*, 827–836.

Bichsel, J., Christidis, P., Conroy, J., & Lin, L. (2019). *Datapoint: Diversity among psychology faculty*. Washington, DC: American Psychological Association.

Bickle, A., Cameron, C., Hassan, T., Safdar, H., & Khalifa, N. (2021). International overview of phallometric testing for sexual offending behaviour and sexual risk. *BJPsych International, 18*, E11.

Biernacka, J. M., Coombes, B. J., Batzler, A., Ho, A. M. C., Geske, J. R., Frank, J., ... & Karpyak, V. M. (2021). Genetic contributions to alcohol use disorder treatment outcomes: A genome-wide pharmacogenomics study. *Neuropsychopharmacology, 46*, 2132–2139.

Bighelli, I., Rodolico, A., García-Mieres, H., Pitschel-Walz, G., Hansen, W. P., Schneider-Thoma, J., ... & Leucht, S. (2021). Psychosocial and psychological interventions for relapse prevention in schizophrenia: a systematic review and network meta-analysis. *The Lancet Psychiatry, 8*, 969–980.

Bilet, T., Olsen, T., Andersen, J. R., & Martinsen, E. W. (2020). Cognitive behavioral group therapy for panic disorder in a general clinical setting: A prospective cohort study with 12 to 31-years follow-up. *BMC Psychiatry, 20*, 1–7.

Bir, S. C., Khan, M. W., Javalkar, V., Toledo, E. G., & Kelley, R. E. (2021). Emerging concepts in vascular dementia: A review. *Journal of Stroke and Cerebrovascular Diseases, 30*, 105864.

Bird, E. R., Piccirillo, M., Garcia, N., Blais, R., & Campbell, S. (2021). Relationship between posttraumatic stress disorder and sexual difficulties: A systematic review of veterans and military personnel. *The Journal of Sexual Medicine, 18*, 1398–1426.

Bird, M. D., Chow, G. M., & Yang, Y. (2020). College students' attitudes, stigma, and intentions toward seeking online and face-to-face counseling. *Journal of Clinical Psychology, 76*, 1775–1790.

Bird, T., Tarsia, M., & Schwannauer, M. (2018). Interpersonal styles in major and chronic depression: A systematic review and meta-analysis. *Journal of Affective Disorders, 239*, 93–101.

Birnbaum, R., & Weinberger, D. R. (2020). A genetics perspective on the role of the (neuro) immune system in schizophrenia. *Schizophrenia Research, 217*, 105–113.

Bittencourt, A. M. L., Bampi, V. F., Sommer, R. C., Schaker, V., Juruena, M. F. P., Soder, R. B., ... & Ferreira, P. E. M. S. (2021). Cortical thickness and subcortical volume abnormalities in male crack-cocaine users. *Psychiatry Research: Neuroimaging, 310*, 111232.

Björne, P. (2020). As if living like others: An idealisation of life in group homes for people with intellectual disability. *Journal of Intellectual & Developmental Disability, 45*, 337–343.

Black, C. J., & Ford, A. C. (2020). Global burden of irritable bowel syndrome: Trends, predictions and risk factors. *Nature Reviews Gastroenterology & Hepatology, 17*, 473–486.

Black, D. W., & Goldstein, R. B. (2022). Natural history and course of antisocial personality disorder. In D. W. Black & N. J. Kolla (Eds.), *Textbook of antisocial personality disorder* (pp. 99–111). Washington, DC: American *Psychiatric* Association.

Black, D. W., & Kolla, N. J. (Eds.) (2022). *Textbook of antisocial personality disorder*. Washington, DC: American Psychiatric Association.

Blackman, J. S., & Dring, K. (2016). *Sexual aggression against children: Pedophiles' and abusers' development, dynamics, treatability, and the law*. New York: Routledge.

Blackwell, W., & Stockall, N. (2021). Incidental teaching of conversational skills for students with autism spectrum disorder. *Teaching Exceptional Children, 54*, 116–123.

Blakey, R., Morgan, C., Gayer-Anderson, C., Davis, S., Beards, S., Harding, S., ... & Viding, E. (2021). Prevalence of conduct problems and social risk factors in ethnically diverse inner-city schools. *BMC Public Health, 21*, 1–13.

Blalock, J. R., & Bourke, M. L. (2022). A content analysis of pedophile manuals. *Aggression and Violent Behavior*, 101482.

Blanchard, J. J., Savage, C. L., Orth, R. D., Jacome, A. M., & Bennett, M. E. (2020). Sleep problems and social impairment in psychosis: A transdiagnostic study examining multiple social domains. *Frontiers in Psychiatry, 11*, 486.

Bland, A. M. (2022). A 15-year progress report on the presence of humanistic/existential psychology principles in mental health outcome measurement: Thematic discourse and summative content analyses. *Journal of Humanistic Psychology*, 00221678221077475.

Blondino, C. T., Gormley, M. A., Taylor, D. D., Lowery, E., Clifford, J. S., Burkart, B., ... & Prom-Wormley, E. C. (2020). The influence of co-occurring substance use on the effectiveness of opiate treatment programs according to intervention type. *Epidemiologic Reviews, 42*, 57–78.

Blosnich, J. R., Hilgeman, M. M., Cypel, Y. S., Akhtar, F. Z., Fried, D., Ishii, E. K., Schneiderman, A., & Davey, V. J. (2022).

Potentially traumatic events and health among lesbian, gay, bisexual and heterosexual Vietnam veterans: Results from the Vietnam Era Health Retrospective Observational study. *Psychological Trauma: Theory, Research, Practice, and Policy, 14,* 568–577

Blum, K., Baron, D., Jalali, R., Modestino, E. J., Steinberg, B., Elman, I., ... & Gold, M. S. (2020). Polygenic and multi locus heritability of alcoholism: Novel therapeutic targets to overcome psychological deficits. *Journal of Systems and Integrative Neuroscience, 7,* 10.15761.

Blum, K., Baron, D., McLaughlin, T., & Gold, M. S. (2020). Molecular neurological correlates of endorphinergic/dopaminergic mechanisms in reward circuitry linked to endorphinergic deficiency syndrome (EDS). *Journal of the Neurological Sciences, 411,* 116733.

Blum, K., Dennen, C. A., Elman, I., Bowirrat, A., Thanos, P. K., Badgaiyan, R. D., ... & Gold, M. S. (2022). Should reward deficiency syndrome (RDS) be considered an umbrella disorder for mental illness and associated genetic and epigenetic induced dysregulation of brain reward circuitry? *Journal of Personalized Medicine, 12,* 1719.

Blum, K., Steinberg, B., Gondre-Lewis, M. C., Baron, D., Modestino, E. J., Badgaiyan, R. D., ... & Gold, M. (2021). A review of DNA risk alleles to determine epigenetic repair of mRNA expression to prove therapeutic effectiveness in reward deficiency syndrome (RDS): Embracing "Precision Behavioral Management". *Psychology Research and Behavior Management, 14,* 2115.

Bobilev, A. M., Perez, J. M., & Tamminga, C. A. (2020). Molecular alterations in the medial temporal lobe in schizophrenia. *Schizophrenia Research, 217,* 71–85.

Bödicker, C., Reinckens, J., Höfler, M., & Hoyer, J. (2021). Is childhood maltreatment associated with body image disturbances in adulthood? A systematic review and meta-analysis. *Journal of Child & Adolescent Trauma, 15,* 523–538.

Bodnár, V., Nagy, K., Cziboly, Á., & Bárdos, G. (2021). Alcohol and placebo: The role of expectations and social influence. *International Journal of Mental Health and Addiction, 19,* 2292–2305.

Boenniger, M. M., Staerk, C., Coors, A., Huijbers, W., Ettinger, U., & Breteler, M. M. (2021). Ten German versions of Rey's auditory verbal learning test: Age and sex effects in 4,000 adults of the Rhineland Study. *Journal of Clinical and Experimental Neuropsychology, 43,* 637–653.

Boland, H., DiSalvo, M., Fried, R., Woodworth, K. Y., Wilens, T., Faraone, S. V., & Biederman, J. (2020). A literature review and meta-analysis on the effects of ADHD medications on functional outcomes. *Journal of Psychiatric Research, 123,* 21–30.

Boland, R., & Verduin, M. L. (2023). *Kaplan and Sadock's concise textbook of clinical psychiatry* (5th ed.). Philadelphia, PA: Wolters Kluwer.

Boness, C. L., Gatten, N., Treece, M. K., & Miller, M. B. (2022). A mixed-methods approach to improve the measurement of alcohol-induced blackouts: ABOM-2. *Alcoholism: Clinical and Experimental Research, 46,* 1497–1514.

Bonham, M. D., Shanley, D. C., Waters, A. M., & Elvin, O. M. (2021). Inhibitory control deficits in children with oppositional defiant disorder and conduct disorder compared to attention deficit/hyperactivity disorder: A systematic review and meta-analysis. *Research on Child and Adolescent Psychopathology, 49,* 39–62.

Bonilla-Jaime, H., Sánchez-Salcedo, J. A., Estevez-Cabrera, M. M., Molina-Jiménez, T., Cortes-Altamirano, J. L., & Alfaro-Rodríguez, A. (2022). Depression and pain: Use of antidepressants. *Current Neuropharmacology, 20,* 384–402.

Bonnaire, C., Liddle, H., Har, A., & Phan, O. (2020). Searching for change mechanisms in emotion-focused work with adolescents and parents: An example from multidimensional family therapy. *Couple and Family Psychology: Research and Practice, 9,* 100–121.

Booth, N., Saxton, J., & Rodda, S. N. (2020). Estimates of caffeine use disorder, caffeine withdrawal, harm and help-seeking in New Zealand: A cross-sectional survey. *Addictive Behaviors, 109,* 106470.

Bopp, L. L., Aparcero, M., & Rosenfeld, B. (2022). Detecting symptom exaggeration and minimization using translated versions of the MMPI-2 and MMPI-2-RF: A systematic review and preliminary meta-analysis. *Law and Human Behavior, 46,* 81–97.

Borghammer, P., Horsager, J., Andersen, K., Van Den Berge, N., Raunio, A., Murayama, S., ... & Myllykangas, L. (2021). Neuropathological evidence of body-first vs. brain-first Lewy body disease. *Neurobiology of Disease, 161,* 105557.

Bornheimer, L. A., Li, J., Im, V., Taylor, M., & Himle, J. A. (2020). The role of social isolation in the relationships between psychosis and suicidal ideation. *Clinical Social Work Journal, 48,* 54–62.

Borroto-Escuela, D. O., Ambrogini, P., Chruścicka, B., Lindskog, M., Crespo-Ramirez, M., Hernández-Mondragón, J. C., ... & Fuxe, K. (2021). The role of central serotonin neurons and 5-HT heteroreceptor complexes in the pathophysiology of depression: A historical perspective and future prospects. *International Journal of Molecular Sciences, 22,* 1927.

Boulet, C., Lopez-Castroman, J., Mouchabac, S., Olié, E., Courtet, P., Thouvenot, E., ... & Conejero, I. (2021). Stress response in dissociation and conversion disorders: A systematic review. *Neuroscience & Biobehavioral Reviews, 132,* 957–967.

Bouman, T.K. (2015). Somatic symptom and related disorders. In P.H. Blaney, R.F. Krueger, & T. Millon (Eds.), *Oxford textbook of psychopathology* (3rd ed.) (pp. 540–565). New York: Oxford.

Bountress, K. E., Gilmore, A. K., Metzger, I. W., Aggen, S. H., Tomko, R. L., Danielson, C. K., ... & Amstadter, A. B. (2020). Impact of disaster exposure severity: Cascading effects across parental distress, adolescent PTSD symptoms, as well as parent-child conflict and communication. *Social Science & Medicine, 264,* 113293.

Bouvard, M., Vuachet, M., & Marchand, C. (2011). Examination of the screening properties of the Personality Diagnostic Questionnaire-4 + (PDQ-4+) in a nonclinical sample. *Clinical Neuropsychiatry, 8,* 151–158.

Boyd, R.C., Joe, S., Michalopoulos, L., Davis, E., & Jackson, J.S. (2011). Prevalence of mood disorders and service use among US mothers by race and ethnicity: Results from the National Survey of American Life. *Journal of Clinical Psychiatry, 72,* 1538–1545.

Boysen, G., Ebersole, A., Casner, R., & Coston, N. (2014). Gendered mental disorders: Masculine and feminine stereotypes about mental disorders and their relation to stigma. *Journal of Social Psychology, 154,* 546–565.

Boysen, G.A., & VanBergen, A. (2013). A review of published research on adult dissociative identity disorder: 2000-2010. *Journal of Nervous and Mental Disease, 201,* 5–11.

Bozzatello, P., Bellino, S., Bosia, M., & Rocca, P. (2019). Early detection and outcome in borderline personality disorder. *Frontiers in Psychiatry, 10,* 710.

Bradshaw, C. P., Pas, E. T., Debnam, K. J., & Johnson, S. L. (2021). A randomized controlled trial of MTSS-B in high schools: Improving classroom management to prevent EBDs. *Remedial and Special Education, 42,* 44–59.

Bram, J. M. D. F., Cordeiro Sr, A. M. T., Talib, L. L., Carvalho, C. L., Gattaz, W. F., & Forlenza, O. V. (2021). Pattern of proteolytic processing of amyloid precursor protein in Down syndrome. *Alzheimer's & Dementia, 17,* e058713.

Brand, B.L., Lanius, R., Vermetten, E., Loewenstein, R.J., & Spiegel, D. (2012). Where are we going? An update on assessment, treatment, and neurobiological research in dissociative disorders as move toward the *DSM-5*. *Journal of Trauma and Dissociation, 13*, 9–31.

Brandt, L., Chao, T., Comer, S. D., & Levin, F. R. (2021). Pharmacotherapeutic strategies for treating cocaine use disorder—what do we have to offer? *Addiction, 116*, 694–710.

Branton, E., Thompson-Hodgetts, S., Johnston, D., Gross, D. P., & Pritchard, L. (2022). Motor skills and intelligence in children with fetal alcohol spectrum disorder. *Developmental Medicine & Child Neurology, 64*, 965–970.

Brauer, K., Sendatzki, R., & Proyer, R. T. (2022). Localizing gelotophobia, gelotophilia, and katagelasticism in domains and facets of maladaptive personality traits: A multi-study report using self-and informant ratings. *Journal of Research in Personality, 98*, 104224.

Bravo, A., & Schwartz, I. (2022). Teaching imitation to young children with autism spectrum disorder using discrete trial training and contingent imitation. *Journal of Developmental and Physical Disabilities, 34*, 655–672.

Breedvelt, J. J. F., Brouwer, M. E., Harrer, M., Semkovska, M., Ebert, D. D., Cuijpers, P., & Bockting, C. L. H. (2021). Psychological interventions as an alternative and add-on to antidepressant medication to prevent depressive relapse: Systematic review and meta-analysis. *The British Journal of Psychiatry, 219*, 538–545.

Brehl, A. K., Kohn, N., Schene, A. H., & Fernández, G. (2020). A mechanistic model for individualised treatment of anxiety disorders based on predictive neural biomarkers. *Psychological Medicine, 50*, 727–736.

Breiding, M.J. (2014). Prevalence and characteristics of sexual violence, stalking, and intimate partner violence victimization -National Intimate Partner and Sexual Violence Survey, United States, 2011. *MMWR Surveillance Summaries, 63*, 1–18.

Brenner, E., Tiwari, G. R., Kapoor, M., Liu, Y., Brock, A., & Mayfield, R. D. (2020). Single cell transcriptome profiling of the human alcohol-dependent brain. *Human Molecular Genetics, 29*, 1144–1153.

Brent, D.A., Brunwasser, S.M., Hollon, S.D., Weersing, V.R., Clarke, G.N., Dickerson, J.F., Beardslee, W.R., Gladstone, T.R.G., Porta, G., Lynch, F.L., Iyengar, S., & Garber, J. (2015). Effect of a cognitive-behavioral prevention program on depression 6 years after implementation among at-risk adolescents: A randomized clinical trial. *Journal of the American Medical Association, 72*, 1110–1118.

Brewster, G. S., Epps, F., Dye, C. E., Hepburn, K., Higgins, M. K., & Parker, M. L. (2020). The effect of the "Great Village" on psychological outcomes, burden, and mastery in African American caregivers of persons living with dementia. *Journal of Applied Gerontology, 39*, 1059–1068.

Briere, J. (2012). *TSCYC: Trauma symptom checklist for Young Children: Manual*. Hogrefe Psykologiförlaget.

Briken, P., Matthiesen, S., Pietras, L., Wiessner, C., Klein, V., Reed, G. M., & Dekker, A. (2020). Estimating the prevalence of sexual dysfunction using the new ICD-11 guidelines: Results of the first representative, population-based German health and sexuality survey (GeSiD). *Deutsches Ärzteblatt International, 117*, 653–658.

Brousse, G., Arnaud, B., Geneste, J., Pereira, B., De Chazeron, I., Teissedre, F., Perrier, C., Schwan, R., Malet, L., Schmidt, J., Llorca, P. M., & Cherpitel, C.J. (2014). How CAGE, RAPS4-QF, and AUDIT can help practitioners for patients admitted with acute alcohol intoxication in emergency departments? *Frontiers in Psychiatry, 5*, 72.

Brown, A., Barker, E. D., & Rahman, Q. (2022). Psychological and developmental correlates of paraphilic and normophilic sexual interests. *Sexual Abuse*, 10790632221120013.

Brown, C., Key, C., Agodoa, I., Olbertz, J., Duchin, K., Barth, A., & Lisbon, E. (2022). S268: safety, tolerability, and pharmacokinetic/pharmacodynamic results from phase 1 studies of GBT021601, a next-generation HbS polymerization inhibitor for treatment of sickle cell disease. *HemaSphere, 6*, 169–170.

Brown, R. T., Abrahamson, D. J., Baker, D. C., Bevins, R. A., Grus, C. L., Hoover, M., ... & Foster, E. O. (2021). The revised 2019 standards for psychopharmacological training: Model education and training program in psychopharmacology for prescriptive authority. *American Psychologist, 76*, 154–164.

Brown, T.A., & Barlow, D.H. (2013). *Anxiety and Related Disorders Interview Schedule for DSM-5® (ADIS-5)—Adult and Lifetime Version: Clinician Manual*. New York: Oxford.

Bruns, G.L., & Carter, M.M. (2015). Ethnic differences in the effects of media on body image: The effects of priming with ethnically different or similar models. *Eating Behaviors, 17*, 33–36.

Bryan, C. J., & Rudd, M. D. (2018). *Brief cognitive-behavioral therapy for suicide prevention*. New York: Guilford.

Buchnik-Daniely, Y., Vannikov-Lugassi, M., Shalev, H., & Soffer-Dudek, N. (2021). The path to dissociative experiences: A direct comparison of different etiological models. *Clinical Psychology & Psychotherapy, 28*, 1091–1102.

Bulik, C. M., Blake, L., & Austin, J. (2019). Genetics of eating disorders: what the clinician needs to know. *Psychiatric Clinics, 42*, 59–73.

Buoli, M., Cesana, B. M., Dell'Osso, B., Fagiolini, A., De Bartolomeis, A., Bondi, E., ... & Altamura, A. C. (2019). Gender-related differences in patients with bipolar disorder: A nationwide study. *CNS Spectrums, 24*, 589–596.

Burchfield, K., Sample, L. L., & Lytle, R. (2014). Public interest in sex offenders: A perpetual panic. *Criminology, Criminal Justice, Law and Society, 15*, 96–117.

Burdakov, D., & Peleg-Raibstein, D. (2020). The hypothalamus as a primary coordinator of memory updating. *Physiology & Behavior, 223*, 112988.

Burnett, L. B. (2021). Disaster and terrorism in emergency psychiatry. In L. S. Zun, K. Nordstrom, & M. P. Wilson (Eds.), *Behavioral emergencies for healthcare providers* (pp. 329–336). Cham: Springer.

Bush, N. R., Wakschlag, L. S., LeWinn, K. Z., Hertz-Picciotto, I., Nozadi, S. S., Pieper, S., ... & Posner, J. (2020). Family environment, neurodevelopmental risk, and the environmental influences on child health outcomes (ECHO) initiative: Looking back and moving forward. *Frontiers in Psychiatry, 11*: 547.

Busmann, M., Meyer, A. H., Wrege, J., Lang, U. E., Gaab, J., Walter, M., & Euler, S. (2021). Vulnerable narcissism as beneficial factor for the therapeutic alliance in borderline personality disorder. *Clinical Psychology & Psychotherapy, 28*, 1222–1229.

Bustillo, J. R., Upston, J., Mayer, E. G., Jones, T., Maudsley, A. A., Gasparovic, C., ... & Lenroot, R. (2020). Glutamatergic hypo-function in the left superior and middle temporal gyri in early schizophrenia: A data-driven three-dimensional proton spectroscopic imaging study. *Neuropsychopharmacology, 45*, 1851–1859.

Butcher, E., Packham, C., Williams, M., Miksza, J., Kaul, A., Khunti, K., & Morriss, R. (2021). Screening male prisoners for depression and anxiety with the PHQ-9 and GAD-7 at NHS Healthcheck: patterns of symptoms and caseness threshold. *BMC Psychiatry, 21*, 1–11.

Buzzell, G. A., Morales, S., Bowers, M. E., Troller-Renfree, S. V., Chronis-Tuscano, A., Pine, D. S., ... & Fox, N. A. (2021). Inhibitory control and set shifting describe different pathways from behavioral inhibition to socially anxious behavior. *Developmental Science, 24*, e13040.

Byrow, Y., Pajak, R., Specker, P., & Nickerson, A. (2020). Perceptions of mental health and perceived barriers to mental health help-seeking amongst refugees: A systematic review. *Clinical Psychology Review, 75*, 101812.

Bystritsky, A., Spivak, N. M., Dang, B. H., Becerra, S. A., Distler, M. G., Jordan, S. E., & Kuhn, T. P. (2021). Brain circuitry underlying the ABC model of anxiety. *Journal of Psychiatric Research, 138*, 3–14.

Cabral, M. D. I., Liu, S., & Soares, N. (2020). Attention-deficit/hyperactivity disorder: Diagnostic criteria, epidemiology, risk factors and evaluation in youth. *Translational Pediatrics, 9*, S104–S113.

Cai, H., Xie, X. M., Zhang, Q., Cui, X., Lin, J. X., Sim, K., ... & Xiang, Y. T. (2021). Prevalence of suicidality in major depressive disorder: A systematic review and meta-analysis of comparative studies. *Frontiers in Psychiatry*, 1347.

Cai, Z., Chen, M., Ye, P., & Yip, P. S. (2022). Socio-economic determinants of suicide rates in transforming China: A spatial-temporal analysis from 1990 to 2015. *The Lancet Regional Health-Western Pacific, 19*, 100341.

Calderoni, S. (2022). Sex/gender differences in children with autism spectrum disorder: A brief overview on epidemiology, symptom profile, and neuroanatomy. *Journal of Neuroscience Research.*

Caldwell, B., Lieberman, R.E., LeBel, J., & Blau, G.M. (Eds.) (2020). *Transforming residential interventions: Practical strategies and future directions.* New York: Routledge.

Campbell, C., & Craissati, J. (Eds.) (2018). *Managing personality disordered offenders: A pathways approach.* United Kingdom: Oxford.

Canna, M., & Seligman, R. (2020). Dealing with the unknown. Functional neurological disorder (FND) and the conversion of cultural meaning. *Social Science & Medicine, 246*, 112725.

Caplan, S., & Buyske, S. (2015). Depression, help-seeking and self-recognition of depression among Dominican, Ecuadorian and Colombian immigrant primary care patients in the northeastern United States. *International Journal of Environmental Research and Public Health, 12*, 10450–10474.

Capuzzi, D., & Stauffer, M.D. (Eds.) (2021). *Foundations of couples, marriage, and family counseling* (2nd ed.). Hoboken, NJ: Wiley.

Carbonell, A., Navarro-Pérez, J. J., & Mestre, M. V. (2020). Challenges and barriers in mental healthcare systems and their impact on the family: A systematic integrative review. *Health and Social Care in the Community, 28*, 1366–1379.

Carlucci, L., Saggino, A., & Balsamo, M. (2021). On the efficacy of the unified protocol for transdiagnostic treatment of emotional disorders: A systematic review and meta-analysis. *Clinical Psychology Review, 87*, 101999.

Carosa, E., Sansone, A., & Jannini, E. A. (2020). Management of endocrine disease: Female sexual dysfunction for the endocrinologist. *European Journal of Endocrinology, 182*, R101.

Carr, A. (2019). Couple therapy, family therapy and systemic interventions for adult-focused problems: The current evidence base. *Journal of Family Therapy, 41*, 492–536.

Carr, M. M., Wiedemann, A. A., Macdonald-Gagnon, G., & Potenza, M. N. (2021). Impulsivity and compulsivity in binge eating disorder: A systematic review of behavioral studies. *Progress in Neuro-Psychopharmacology and Biological Psychiatry, 110*, 110318.

Carrara, B. S., Fernandes, R. H. H., Bobbili, S. J., & Ventura, C. A. A. (2021). Health care providers and people with mental illness: An integrative review on anti-stigma interventions. *International Journal of Social Psychiatry, 67*, 840–853.

Cartocci, G., Fineschi, V., Padovano, M., Scopetti, M., Rossi-Espagnet, M. C., & Giannì, C. (2021). Shaken baby syndrome: Magnetic resonance imaging features in abusive head trauma. *Brain Sciences, 11*, 179.

Caselli, G., Ruggiero, G.M., & Sassaroli, S. (Eds.) (2021). *CBT case formulation as therapeutic process.* New York: Springer.

Catalan, A., Salazar de Pablo, G., Vaquerizo Serrano, J., Mosillo, P., Baldwin, H., Fernández-Rivas, A., ... & Fusar-Poli, P. (2021). Annual Research Review: Prevention of psychosis in adolescents–systematic review and meta-analysis of advances in detection, prognosis and intervention. *Journal of Child Psychology and Psychiatry, 62*, 657–673.

Cattarinussi, G., Aarabi, M. H., Moghaddam, H. S., Homayoun, M., Ashrafi, M., Soltanian-Zadeh, H., & Sambataro, F. (2021). Effect of parental depressive symptoms on offspring's brain structure and function: A systematic review of neuroimaging studies. *Neuroscience & Biobehavioral Reviews, 131*, 451–465.

Cénat, J. M., Kokou-Kpolou, C. K., Blais-Rochette, C., Morse, C., Vandette, M. P., Dalexis, R. D., ... & Kogan, C. S. (2022). Prevalence of ADHD among Black youth compared to White, Latino and Asian youth: A meta-analysis. *Journal of Clinical Child & Adolescent Psychology*, 1–16.

Centers for Disease Control and Prevention (2022). *Alzheimer disease*. Atlanta: Author.

Cha, Y. S., Chang, J. S., Kim, H., & Park, K. S. (2022). Application of mitochondrial and oxidative stress biomarkers in the evaluation of neurocognitive prognosis following acute carbon monoxide poisoning. *Metabolites, 12*, 201.

Chae, Y., Goodman, G.S., Eisen, M.L., & Qin, J. (2011). Event memory and suggestibility in abused and neglected children: Trauma-related psychopathology and cognitive functioning. *Journal of Experimental Child Psychology, 110*, 520–538.

Chakraborty, P., Sanchez, N. A., Kaddumukasa, M., Kajumba, M., Kakooza-Mwesige, A., Van Noord, M., ... & Koltai, D. C. (2021). Stigma reduction interventions for epilepsy: A systematized literature review. *Epilepsy & Behavior, 114*, 107381.

Chaleat-Valayer, E., Roumenoff, F., Bard-Pondarre, R., Ganne, C., Verdun, S., Lucet, A., & Bernard, J. C. (2019). Pain coping strategies in children with cerebral palsy. *Developmental Medicine & Child Neurology, 61*, 1329–1335.

Chaliy, M. E., Ohobotov, D. A., Sorokin, N. I., Kadrev, A. V., DI, L., Strigunov, A. A., ... & Kamalov, A. A. (2021). Normative parameters for monitoring of nocturnal penile tumescences: A systematic review and algorithm development. *Urologiia, 6*, 110–117.

Chan, C. Y., Cheung, G., Martinez-Ruiz, A., Chau, P. Y., Wang, K., Yeoh, E. K., & Wong, E. L. (2021). Caregiving burnout of community-dwelling people with dementia in Hong Kong and New Zealand: A cross-sectional study. *BMC Geriatrics, 21*, 1–15.

Chan, H. C. O. (2022). Paraphilic interests: The role of psychosocial factors in a sample of young adults in Hong Kong. *Sexuality Research and Social Policy, 19*, 159–178.

Chan, J. M. (2021). Current and future directions of supporting people with autism spectrum disorder to appropriately speak about preferred topics. *Evidence-Based Communication Assessment and Intervention, 15*, 214–217.

Chan, J. Y., Bat, B. K., Wong, A., Chan, T. K., Huo, Z., Yip, B. H., ... & Tsoi, K. K. (2021). Evaluation of digital drawing tests and paper-and-pencil drawing tests for the screening of mild cognitive impairment and dementia: A systematic review and meta-analysis of diagnostic studies. *Neuropsychology Review*, 1–11.

Chan, S. K. W., Chan, H. Y. V., Pang, H. H., Hui, C. L. M., Suen, Y. N., Chang, W. C., ... & Chen, E. Y. H. (2020). Ten-year trajectory and outcomes of negative symptoms of patients with first-episode schizophrenia spectrum disorders. *Schizophrenia Research, 220*, 85–91.

Chanen, A. M., & Nicol, K. (2021). Five failures and five challenges for prevention and early intervention for personality disorder. *Current Opinion in Psychology, 37*, 134–138.

Chanen, A. M., & Thompson, K. N. (2019). The development of personality disorders. In D. P. McAdams, R. L. Shiner, & J. L. Tackett (Eds.), *Handbook of personality development* (pp. 551–571). New York: Guilford.

Chanen, A. M., Nicol, K., Betts, J. K., & Thompson, K. N. (2020). Diagnosis and treatment of borderline personality disorder in young people. *Current Psychiatry Reports, 22*, 1–8.

Chang, J. C., Lin, H. Y., Lv, J., Tseng, W. Y. I., & Gau, S. S. F. (2021). Regional brain volume predicts response to methylphenidate treatment in individuals with ADHD. *BMC Psychiatry, 21*, 1–14.

Chao, Y. Y., Li, M., Lu, S. E., & Dong, X. (2020). Elder mistreatment and psychological distress among US Chinese older adults. *Journal of Elder Abuse & Neglect, 32*, 434–452.

Chapa, D. A., Johnson, S. N., Richson, B. N., Bjorlie, K., Won, Y. Q., Nelson, S. V., ... & Perko, V. L. Eating-disorder psychopathology in female athletes and non-athletes: A meta-analysis. *International Journal of Eating Disorders*, 55, 861–885.

Charlson, F. J., Ferrari, A. J., Santomauro, D. F., Diminic, S., Stockings, E., Scott, J. G., ... & Whiteford, H. A. (2018). Global epidemiology and burden of schizophrenia: Findings from the global burden of disease study 2016. *Schizophrenia Bulletin, 44*, 1195–1203.

Charisis, S., Ntanasi, E., Yannakoulia, M., Anastasiou, C. A., Kosmidis, M. H., Dardiotis, E., ... & Scarmeas, N. (2021). Mediterranean diet and risk for dementia and cognitive decline in a Mediterranean population. *Journal of the American Geriatrics Society, 69*, 1548–1559.

Charney, A., & Sklar, P. (2018). Genetics of schizophrenia and bipolar disorder. In D.S. Charney, J.D. Buxbaum, P. Sklar, & E.J. Nestler (Eds.), *Charney and Nestler's neurobiology of mental illness* (5th ed.) (pp. 161–176). New York: Oxford.

Chehrehnegar, N., Nejati, V., Shati, M., Rashedi, V., Lotfi, M., Adelirad, F., & Foroughan, M. (2020). Early detection of cognitive disturbances in mild cognitive impairment: A systematic review of observational studies. *Psychogeriatrics, 20*, 212–228.

Chekira, A., Bouchal, S., Tabril, T., El Amrani, R., Aarab, C., Aalouane, R., & Belahsen, M. F. (2020). Psychogenic pseudoptosis: Case report with review of literature. *Neurology, Psychiatry and Brain Research, 37*, 91–94.

Cheli, S. (2020). Assessment and treatment planning for schizotypal personality disorder: A metacognitively oriented point of view. *Psychiatric Rehabilitation Journal, 43*, 335–343

Chen, C. D., Joseph-Mathurin, N., Sinha, N., Zhou, A., Li, Y., Friedrichsen, K., ... & Benzinger, T. L. (2021). Comparing amyloid-β plaque burden with antemortem PiB PET in autosomal dominant and late-onset Alzheimer disease. *Acta Neuropathologica, 142*, 689–706.

Chen, T. H., Cheng, H. T., & Yeh, C. T. (2021). Epidemiology changes in peptic ulcer diseases 18 years apart explored from the genetic aspects of Helicobacter pylori. *Translational Research, 232*, 115–120.

Cheng, H-L., & Mallinckrodt, B. (2015). Racial/ethnic discrimination, posttraumatic stress symptoms, and alcohol problems in a longitudinal study of Hispanic/Latino college students. *Journal of Counseling Psychology, 62*, 38–49.

Cheng, S. T., & Zhang, F. (2020). A comprehensive meta-review of systematic reviews and meta-analyses on nonpharmacological interventions for informal dementia caregivers. *BMC Geriatrics, 20*, 1–24.

Cherkasova, M. V., Roy, A., Molina, B. S., Scott, G., Weiss, G., Barkley, R. A., ... & Hechtman, L. (2021). Adult outcome as seen through controlled prospective follow-up studies of children with attention-deficit/hyperactivity disorder followed into adulthood. *Journal of the American Academy of Child & Adolescent Psychiatry, 61*, 378–391.

Cheroni, C., Caporale, N., & Testa, G. (2020). Autism spectrum disorder at the crossroad between genes and environment: contributions, convergences, and interactions in ASD developmental pathophysiology. *Molecular Autism, 11*, 69.

Chesnut, M., Harati, S., Paredes, P., Khan, Y., Foudeh, A., Kim, J., ... & Williams, L. M. (2021). Stress markers for mental states and biotypes of depression and anxiety: A scoping review and preliminary illustrative analysis. *Chronic Stress, 5*, 24705470211000338.

Chia, R., Sabir, M. S., Bandres-Ciga, S., Saez-Atienzar, S., Reynolds, R. H., Gustavsson, E., ... & Chiò, A. (2021). Genome sequencing analysis identifies new loci associated with Lewy body dementia and provides insights into its genetic architecture. *Nature Genetics, 53*, 294–303.

Chiu, K., Clark, D. M., & Leigh, E. (2021). Prospective associations between peer functioning and social anxiety in adolescents: A systematic review and meta-analysis. *Journal of Affective Disorders, 279*, 650–661.

Choi, B., Kim, I., Lee, G. Y., Kim, S., Kim, S. H., Lee, J. G., & Lim, M. H. (2020). Estimated prevalence and impact of the experience of becoming a victim of exhibitionism and frotteurism in Korea: A general population based study. *Criminal Behaviour and Mental Health, 30*, 132–140.

Chong, L. S., Gordis, E., Hunter, L., Amoh, J., Strully, K., Appleton, A. A., & Tracy, M. (2022). Childhood violence exposure and externalizing behaviors: A systematic review of the role of physiological biomarkers. *Psychoneuroendocrinology*, 105898.

Choudhary, S., & Gupta, R. (2020). Culture and borderline personality disorder in India. *Frontiers in Psychology, 11*, 714.

Christensen, M. K., Lim, C. C. W., Saha, S., Plana-Ripoll, O., Cannon, D., Presley, F., ... & McGrath, J. J. (2020). The cost of mental disorders: A systematic review. *Epidemiology and Psychiatric Sciences, 29*, 1–8.

Christian, I. R., Liuzzi, M. T., Yu, Q., Kryza-Lacombe, M., Monk, C. S., Jarcho, J., & Wiggins, J. L. (2022). Context-dependent amygdala-prefrontal connectivity in youths with autism spectrum disorder. *Research in Autism Spectrum Disorders, 91*, 101913.

Chua, K. P., Dahlem, C. H. Y., Nguyen, T. D., Brummett, C. M., Conti, R. M., Bohnert, A. S., ... & Kocher, K. E. (2022). Naloxone and buprenorphine prescribing following US emergency department visits for suspected opioid overdose: August 2019 to April 2021. *Annals of Emergency Medicine, 79*, 225–236.

Chugani, C. D., Ghali, M. N., & Brunner, J. (2013). Effectiveness of short term dialectical behavior therapy skills training in college students with cluster B personality disorders. *Journal of College Student Psychotherapy, 27*, 323–336.

Chun, C. T., Seward, K., Patterson, A., Melton, A., & MacDonald-Wicks, L. (2021). Evaluation of Available cognitive tools used to measure mild cognitive decline: A scoping review. *Nutrients, 13*, 3974.

Chung, E., & Mulhall, J. (2021). Practical considerations in inflatable penile implant surgery. *Journal of Sexual Medicine, 18*, 1320–1327.

Chung, S. J., Lee, H. S., Kim, H. R., Yoo, H. S., Lee, Y. H., Jung, J. H., ... & Lee, P. H. (2020). Factor analysis–derived cognitive profile predicting early dementia conversion in PD. *Neurology, 95*, e1650–e1659.

Cieślik, P., Radulska, A., Burnat, G., Kalinowski, L., & Wieronska, J. M. (2021). Serotonergic–muscarinic interaction within the prefrontal cortex as a novel target to reverse schizophrenia-related cognitive symptoms. *International Journal of Molecular Sciences, 22*, 8612.

Cirone, C., Secci, I., Favole, I., Ricci, F., Amianto, F., Davico, C., & Vitiello, B. (2021). What do we know about the long-term course of early onset bipolar disorder? A review of the current evidence. *Brain Sciences, 11*, 341.

Clark, E., & Koutsogianni, M. (2022). Genetic investigations pathway for people with intellectual disability, autism and/or epilepsy. *BJPsych Advances*, 1–10.

Clark, G. I., Rock, A. J., Clark, L. H., & Murray-Lyon, K. (2020). Adult attachment, worry and reassurance seeking: Investigating the role of intolerance of uncertainty. *Clinical Psychologist, 24*, 294–305.

Cochrane, R. E., Laxton, K. L., Mulay, A. L., & Herbel, B. L. (2021). Guidelines for determining restorability of competency to stand trial and recommendations for involuntary treatment. *Journal of Forensic Sciences, 66*, 1201–1209.

Coelho, C. M., Gonçalves-Bradley, D., & Zsido, A. N. (2020). Who worries about specific phobias?–A population-based study of risk factors. *Journal of Psychiatric Research, 126*, 67–72.

Coles, C. D., Grant, T. M., Kable, J. A., Stoner, S. A., Perez, A., & Collaborative Initiative on Fetal Alcohol Spectrum Disorders. (2022). Prenatal alcohol exposure and mental health at midlife: A preliminary report on two longitudinal cohorts. *Alcoholism: Clinical and Experimental Research, 46*, 232–242.

Colonnello, E., Ciocca, G., Limoncin, E., Sansone, A., & Jannini, E. A. (2021). Redefining a sexual medicine paradigm: Subclinical premature ejaculation as a new taxonomic entity. *Nature Reviews Urology, 18*, 115–127.

Compton, M. T., Berez, C., & Walker, E. F. (2014). The relative importance of family history, gender, mode of onset, and age at onset in predicting clinical features of first-episode psychotic disorders. *Clinical Schizophrenia and Related Psychoses, 8*, 1–26.

Compton, W. M., Valentino, R. J., & DuPont, R. L. (2021). Polysubstance use in the US opioid crisis. *Molecular Psychiatry, 26*, 41–50.

Coninx, S. (2022). A multidimensional phenomenal space for pain: Structure, primitiveness, and utility. *Phenomenology and the Cognitive Sciences, 21*, 223–243.

Conners, C.K. (2008). *Conners Third Edition (Conners 3)*. Los Angeles: Western Psychological Services.

Conners, C.K. (2014). *Conners CPT 3(tm) Conners Continuous Performance Test, 3rd edition*. North Tonawanda, NY: MHS.

Consoloni, J. L., M'Bailara, K., Perchec, C., Aouizerate, B., Aubin, V., Azorin, J. M., ... & Groupe, F. B. (2021). Trajectories of medication adherence in patients with Bipolar Disorder along 2 years-follow-up. *Journal of Affective Disorders, 282*, 812–819.

Conversano, C., Orrù, G., Pozza, A., Miccoli, M., Ciacchini, R., Marchi, L., & Gemignani, A. (2021). Is mindfulness-based stress reduction effective for people with hypertension? A systematic review and meta-analysis of 30 years of evidence. *International Journal of Environmental Research and Public Health, 18*, 2882.

Conway, C. C., Latzman, R. D., & Krueger, R. F. (2020). A meta-structural model of common clinical disorder and personality disorder symptoms. *Journal of Personality Disorders, 34*, 88–106.

Cook, M. L., Zhang, Y., & Constantino, J. N. (2020). On the continuity between autistic and schizoid personality disorder trait burden: A prospective study in adolescence. *Journal of Nervous and Mental Disease, 208*, 94–100.

Cooper, K., Russell, A., Mandy, W., & Butler, C. (2020). The phenomenology of gender dysphoria in adults: A systematic review and meta-synthesis. *Clinical Psychology Review, 80*, 101875.

Cooper, R. E., Laxhman, N., Crellin, N., Moncrieff, J., & Priebe, S. (2020). Psychosocial interventions for people with schizophrenia or psychosis on minimal or no antipsychotic medication: A systematic review. *Schizophrenia Research, 225*, 15–30.

Corbi, G., Grattagliano, I., Ivshina, E., Ferrara, N., Cipriano, A. S., & Campobasso, C. P. (2015). Elderly abuse: Risk factors and nursing role. *Internal and Emergency Medicine, 10*, 297–303.

Corkrum, M., & Araque, A. (2021). Astrocyte-neuron signaling in the mesolimbic dopamine system: The hidden stars of dopamine signaling. *Neuropsychopharmacology, 46*, 1864–1872.

Cornejo, M., Agrawal, S., Chen, J., Yeung, A., & Trinh, N. H. (2020). Cultural risk and protective factors for depressive symptoms in Asian American college students. *Adolescent Research Review, 5*, 405–417.

Correll, D. N., Engle, K. M., Lin, S. S. H., Lac, A., & Samuelson, K. W. (2021). The effects of military status and gender on public stigma toward posttraumatic stress disorder. *Stigma and Health, 6*, 134–142.

Corrigan, P.W. (2015). Challenging the stigma of mental illness: Different agendas, different goals. *Psychiatric Services, 66*, 1347–1349.

Cortés-Beringola, A., Vicent, L., Martín-Asenjo, R., Puerto, E., Domínguez-Pérez, L., Maruri, R., ... & Bueno, H. (2021). Diagnosis, prevention, and management of delirium in the intensive cardiac care unit. *American Heart Journal, 232*, 164–176.

Cosci, F., & Guidi, J. (2021). The role of illness behavior in the COVID-19 pandemic. *Psychotherapy and Psychosomatics, 90*, 156–159.

Cowan, T., Masucci, M. D., Gupta, T., Haase, C. M., Strauss, G. P., & Cohen, A. S. (2022). Computerized analysis of facial expressions in serious mental illness. *Schizophrenia Research, 241*, 44–51.

Cowman, M., Holleran, L., Lonergan, E., O'Connor, K., Birchwood, M., & Donohoe, G. (2021). Cognitive predictors of social and occupational functioning in early psychosis: A systematic review and meta-analysis of cross-sectional and longitudinal data. *Schizophrenia Bulletin, 47*, 1243–1253.

Craig, L.A., & Bartels, R.M. (Eds.). (2021). *Sexual deviance: Understanding and managing deviant sexual interests and paraphilic disorders*. Hoboken, MJ: Wiley.

Craig, S. G., Goulter, N., & Moretti, M. M. (2021). A systematic review of primary and secondary callous-unemotional traits and psychopathy variants in youth. *Clinical Child and Family Psychology Review, 24*, 65–91.

Creed, F.H., Davies, I., Jackson, J., Littlewood, A., Chew-Graham, C., Tomenson, B., Macfarlane, G., Barsky, A., Katon, W., & McBeth, J. (2012). The epidemiology of multiple somatic symptoms. *Journal of Psychosomatic Research, 72*, 311–317.

Creswell, C., Waite, P., & Hudson, J. (2020). Practitioner Review: Anxiety disorders in children and young people–assessment and treatment. *Journal of Child Psychology and Psychiatry, 61*, 628–643.

Cretton, A., Brown, R. J., LaFrance Jr, W. C., & Aybek, S. (2020). What does neuroscience tell us about the conversion model of functional neurological disorders?. *The Journal of Neuropsychiatry and Clinical Neurosciences, 32*, 24–32.

Crocq, M. A. (2022). The history of generalized anxiety disorder as a diagnostic category. *Dialogues in Clinical Neuroscience, 19*, 107–116.

Cui, Y., Fang, H., Bao, C., Geng, W., Yu, F., & Li, X. (2021). Efficacy of transcranial magnetic stimulation for reducing suicidal ideation in depression: A meta-analysis. *Frontiers in Psychiatry, 12*, 764183.

Cuijpers, P., Cristea, I. A., Ebert, D. D., Koot, H. M., Auerbach, R. P., Bruffaerts, R., & Kessler, R. C. (2016). Psychological treatment of depression in college students: A metaanalysis. *Depression and Anxiety, 33*, 400–414.

Cummings, J. (2021). The role of neuropsychiatric symptoms in research diagnostic criteria for neurodegenerative diseases. *The American Journal of Geriatric Psychiatry, 29*, 375–383.

Cummings, J. L., Devanand, D. P., & Stahl, S. M. (2022). Dementia-related psychosis and the potential role for pimavanserin. *CNS Spectrums, 27*, 7–15.

Cupaioli, F. A., Zucca, F. A., Caporale, C., Lesch, K. P., Passamonti, L., & Zecca, L. (2021). The neurobiology of human aggressive behavior: Neuroimaging, genetic, and neurochemical aspects. *Progress in Neuro-psychopharmacology and Biological Psychiatry, 106*, 110059.

Curcio, C., & Corboy, D. (2020). Stigma and anxiety disorders: A systematic review. *Stigma and Health, 5*, 125–137.

da Costa, A. E. M., Gomes, N. S., Gadelha Filho, C. V. J., da Costa, R. O., Chaves Filho, A. J. M., Cordeiro, R. C., ... & Macêdo, D. S. (2021). Sex influences in the preventive effects of peripubertal supplementation with N-3 polyunsaturated fatty acids in mice exposed to the two-hit model of schizophrenia. *European Journal of Pharmacology, 897*, 173949.

da Costa Azevedo, J. N., Carvalho, C., Serrão, M. P., Coelho, R., Figueiredo-Braga, M., & Vieira-Coelho, M. A. (2022). Catechol-O-methyltransferase activity in individuals with substance use disorders: A case control study. *BMC Psychiatry, 22*, 1–9.

da Cunha-Bang, S., & Knudsen, G. M. (2021). The modulatory role of serotonin on human impulsive aggression. *Biological Psychiatry, 90*, 447–457.

Dachew, B. A., Scott, J. G., Heron, J. E., Ayano, G., & Alati, R. (2021). Association of maternal depressive symptoms during the perinatal period with oppositional defiant disorder in children and adolescents. *JAMA Network Open, 4*, e2125854–e2125854.

Dahlenburg, S. C., Gleaves, D. H., Hutchinson, A. D., & Coro, D. G. (2020). Body image disturbance and sexual orientation: An updated systematic review and meta-analysis. *Body Image, 35*, 126–141.

Dai, Y., Cook, O. Y., Yeganeh, L., Huang, C., Ding, J., & Johnson, C. E. (2020). Patient-reported barriers and facilitators to seeking and accessing support in gynecologic and breast cancer survivors with sexual problems: a systematic review of qualitative and quantitative studies. *The Journal of Sexual Medicine, 17*, 1326–1358.

Dalgleish, T., Black, M., Johnston, D., & Bevan, A. (2020). Transdiagnostic approaches to mental health problems: Current status and future directions. *Journal of Consulting and Clinical Psychology, 88*, 179–195.

Damborská, A., Honzírková, E., Barteček, R., Hořínková, J., Fedorová, S., Ondruš, Š., ... & Rubega, M. (2020). Altered directed functional connectivity of the right amygdala in depression: High-density EEG study. *Scientific Reports, 10*, 1–14.

Darling, K. E., Benore, E. R., & Webster, E. E. (2020). Biofeedback in pediatric populations: a systematic review and meta-analysis of treatment outcomes. *Translational Behavioral Medicine, 10*, 1436–1449.

Davies, C., Segre, G., Estradé, A., Radua, J., De Micheli, A., Provenzani, U., ... & Fusar-Poli, P. (2020). Prenatal and perinatal risk and protective factors for psychosis: a systematic review and meta-analysis. *The Lancet Psychiatry, 7*, 399–410.

Davies, P. T., Pearson, J. K., Coe, J. L., Hentges, R. F., & Sturge-Apple, M. L. (2021). Beyond destructive and constructive interparental conflict: Children's psychological vulnerability to interparental disorganization. *Developmental Psychology, 57*, 2192–2205.

Davis, T. (2021). *Forensic psychology: Fact and fiction*. Macmillan.

de Andrade, D., Elphinston, R. A., Quinn, C., Allan, J., & Hides, L. (2019). The effectiveness of residential treatment services for individuals with substance use disorders: A systematic review. *Drug and Alcohol Dependence, 201*, 227–235.

De Andrade, D., Ritchie, J., Rowlands, M., Mann, E., & Hides, L. (2018). Substance use and recidivism outcomes for prison-based drug and alcohol interventions. *Epidemiologic Reviews, 40*, 121–133.

Deak, J. D., & Johnson, E. C. (2021). Genetics of substance use disorders: a review. *Psychological Medicine*, 1–12.

Deaton, C. A., & Johnson, G. V. (2020). Presenilin 1 regulates membrane homeostatic pathways that are dysregulated in Alzheimer's disease. *Journal of Alzheimer's Disease, 77*, 961–977.

De Bacquer, D., van de Luitgaarden, I. A., De Smedt, D., Vynckier, P., Bruthans, J., Fras, Z., ... & De Backer, G. (2021). Socioeconomic characteristics of patients with coronary heart disease in relation to their cardiovascular risk profile. *Heart, 107*, 799–806.

De Berardis, D., De Filippis, S., Masi, G., Vicari, S., & Zuddas, A. (2021). A neurodevelopment approach for a transitional model of early onset schizophrenia. *Brain Sciences, 11*, 275.

de Bildt, A., Sytema, S., Zander, E., Bölte, S., Sturm, H., Yirmiya, N., Yaari, M., Charman, T., Salomone, E., LeCouteur, A., Green, J., Bedia, R. C., Primo, P. G., van Daalen, E., de Jonge, M. V., Guðmundsdottir, E., Johannsdottir, S., Raleva, M., Boskovska, M., Roge, B., Baduel, S., Moilanen, I., Yliherva, A., Buitelaar, J., & Oosterling, I. J. (2015). Autism Diagnostic Interview-Revised (ADI-R) algorithms for toddlers and young preschoolers: Application in a non-US sample of 1,104 children. *Journal of Autism and Developmental Disorders, 45*, 2076–2091.

Deblinger, E., Mannarino, A.P., Cohen, J.A., Runyon, M.K., & Heflin, A.H. (2015). *Child sexual abuse: A primer for treating children, adolescents, and their nonoffending parents* (2nd ed.). New York: Oxford.

De Brito, S. A., Forth, A. E., Baskin-Sommers, A. R., Brazil, I. A., Kimonis, E. R., Pardini, D., ... & Viding, E. (2021). Psychopathy. *Nature Reviews Disease Primers, 7*, 1–21.

Dedousis-Wallace, A., Drysdale, S. A., McAloon, J., & Ollendick, T. H. (2021). Parental and familial predictors and moderators of parent management treatment programs for conduct problems in youth. *Clinical Child and Family Psychology Review, 24*, 92–119.

Defeudis, G., Mazzilli, R., Tenuta, M., Rossini, G., Zamponi, V., Olana, S., ... & Gianfrilli, D. (2022). Erectile dysfunction and diabetes: A melting pot of circumstances and treatments. *Diabetes/Metabolism Research and Reviews, 38*, e3494.

Degli Esposti, M., Pereira, S. M. P., Humphreys, D. K., Sale, R. D., & Bowes, L. (2020). Child maltreatment and the risk of antisocial behaviour: A population-based cohort study spanning 50 years. *Child Abuse & Neglect, 99*, 104281.

Deguchi, N. K., Asakura, T., & Omiya, T. (2021). Self-stigma of families of persons with autism spectrum disorder: A scoping review. *Review Journal of Autism and Developmental Disorders, 8*, 373–388.

Dehpour, T., & Koffman, J. (2022). Assessment of anticipatory grief in informal caregivers of dependants with dementia: A systematic review. *Aging & Mental Health*, 1–14.

de Lange, E., Verhaak, P. F. M., & van der Meer, K. (2013). Prevalence, presentation and prognosis of delirium in older people in the population, at home and in long term care: review. *International Journal of Geriatric Psychiatry, 28*, 127–134.

de Leeuw, A., Happé, F., & Hoekstra, R. A. (2020). A conceptual framework for understanding the cultural and contextual factors on autism across the globe. *Autism Research, 13*, 1029–1050.

De Looff, P. C., Cornet, L. J., De Kogel, C. H., Fernández-Castilla, B., Embregts, P. J., Didden, R., & Nijman, H. L. (2021). Heart rate and skin conductance associations with physical aggression, psychopathy, antisocial personality disorder and conduct disorder: An updated meta-analysis. *Neuroscience & Biobehavioral Reviews, 132*, 553–582.

Del Popolo, G., Cito, G., Gemma, L., & Natali, A. (2020). Neurogenic sexual dysfunction treatment: A systematic review. *European Urology Focus, 6*, 868–876.

Delforterie, M.J., Larsen, J.K., Bardone-Cone, A.M., & Scholte, R.H.J. (2014). Effects of viewing a pro-ana website: An experimental study on body satisfaction, affect, and appearance self-efficacy. *Eating Disorders, 22*, 321–336.

Demartini, B., Nisticò, V., Edwards, M. J., Gambini, O., & Priori, A. (2021). The pathophysiology of functional movement disorders. *Neuroscience & Biobehavioral Reviews, 120*, 387–400.

deMello, R. A., Coimbra, B. M., Pedro, B. D., Benvenutti, I. M., Yeh, M. S., Mello, A. F., ... & Poyares, D. R. (2022). Peritraumatic dissociation and tonic immobility as severity predictors of posttraumatic stress disorder after rape. *Journal of Interpersonal Violence*, 08862605221114151.

Denis, C. M., Cacciola, J. S., & Alterman, A. I. (2013). Addiction Severity Index (ASI) summary scores: Comparison of the Recent Status Scores of the ASI-6 and the Composite Scores of the ASI-5. *Journal of Substance Abuse Treatment, 45*, 444–450.

Denenny, D., Thompson, E., Pitts, S. C., Dixon, L. B., & Schiffman, J. (2015). Subthreshold psychotic symptom distress, self-stigma, and peer social support among college students with mental health concerns. *Psychiatric Rehabilitation Journal, 38*, 164–170.

Denton, C. A., Montroy, J. J., Zucker, T. A., & Cannon, G. (2021). Designing an intervention in reading and self-regulation for students with significant reading difficulties, including dyslexia. *Learning Disability Quarterly, 44*, 170–182.

De Rossi, G., & Georgiades, A. (2022). Thinking biases and their role in persecutory delusions: A systematic review. *Early Intervention in Psychiatry, 16*, 1278–1296.

De Rossi, P., Pretelli, I., Menghini, D., D'Aiello, B., Di Vara, S., & Vicari, S. (2022). Gender-related clinical characteristics in children and adolescents with ADHD. *Journal of Clinical Medicine, 11*, 385.

De Sousa, A., Shah, B., & Shrivastava, A. (2020). Suicide and schizophrenia: an interplay of factors. *Current Psychiatry Reports, 22*, 1–5.

Desrosiers, L., Saint-Jean, M., Laporte, L., & Lord, M. M. (2020). Engagement complications of adolescents with borderline personality disorder: Navigating through a zone of turbulence. *Borderline Personality Disorder and Emotion Dysregulation, 7*, 1–15.

Devi, N., Prodinger, B., Pennycott, A., Sooben, R., & Bickenbach, J. (2020). Investigating supported decision-making for persons with mild to moderate intellectual disability using institutional ethnography. *Journal of Policy and Practice in Intellectual Disabilities, 17*, 143–156.

de Vitta, A., dal Bello Biancon, R., Cornélio, G. P., Bento, T. P. F., Maciel, N. M., & de Oliveira Perrucini, P. (2021). Primary headache and factors associated in university students: A cross sectional study. *ABCS Health Sciences, 46*, e021207–e021207.

de Vries, Y. A., Harris, M. G., Vigo, D., Chiu, W. T., Sampson, N. A., Al-Hamzawi, A., ... & de Jonge, P. (2021). Perceived helpfulness of treatment for specific phobia: Findings from the world mental health surveys. *Journal of Affective Disorders, 288*, 199–209.

DeVylder, J. E., Narita, Z., Horiguchi, S., Kodaka, M., Schiffman, J., Yang, L. H., & Koyanagi, A. (2020). Stigma associated with the labeling of schizophrenia, depression, and hikikomori in Japan. *Stigma and Health, 5*, 472–476.

Dewitte, M., Bettocchi, C., Carvalho, J., Corona, G., Flink, I., Limoncin, E., ... & Van Lankveld, J. (2021). A psychosocial approach to erectile dysfunction: Position statements from the European Society of Sexual Medicine (ESSM). *Sexual Medicine, 9*, 100434.

DeYoung, C. G., Chmielewski, M., Clark, L. A., Condon, D. M., Kotov, R., Krueger, R. F., ... & HiTOP Normal Personality Workgroup. (2022). The distinction between symptoms and traits in the Hierarchical Taxonomy of Psychopathology (HiTOP). *Journal of Personality, 90*, 20–33.

Diamond, D., & Hersh, R. G. (2020). Transference-focused psychotherapy for narcissistic personality disorder: An object relations approach. *Journal of Personality Disorders, 34*, 159–176.

Dickson, H., Roberts, R. E., To, M., Wild, K., Loh, M., & Laurens, K. R. (2020). Adolescent trajectories of fine motor and coordination skills and risk for schizophrenia. *Schizophrenia Research, 215*, 263–269.

Diez, I., Larson, A. G., Nakhate, V., Dunn, E. C., Fricchione, G. L., Nicholson, T. R., ... & Perez, D. L. (2021). Early-life trauma endophenotypes and brain circuit–gene expression relationships in functional neurological (conversion) disorder. *Molecular Psychiatry, 26*, 3817–3828.

di Giannantonio, M., Northoff, G., & Salone, A. (2020). The interface between psychoanalysis and neuroscience: The state of the art. *Frontiers in Human Neuroscience, 14*, 199.

Dihmes, S. E., Ahmed, A., Tucker, S., Mabe, A., & Buckley, P. (2020). Self-stigma, resilience, and recovery attitudes as predictors of functioning in people with serious mental illness. *Schizophrenia Bulletin, 46*, S219–S220.

Di Lorenzo, R., Balducci, J., Poppi, C., Arcolin, E., Cutino, A., Ferri, P., ... & Filippini, T. (2021). Children and adolescents with ADHD followed up to adulthood: A systematic review of long-term outcomes. *Acta Neuropsychiatrica*, 1–42.

Dilworth-Anderson, P., Moon, H., & Aranda, M. P. (2020). Dementia caregiving research: Expanding and reframing the lens of diversity, inclusivity, and intersectionality. *The Gerontologist, 60*, 797–805.

Disdier, C., & Stonestreet, B. S. (2020). Hypoxic-ischemic-related cerebrovascular changes and potential therapeutic strategies in the neonatal brain. *Journal of Neuroscience Research, 98*, 1468–1484.

Dixon, B. J., Kumar, J., & Danielmeier, C. (2022). Frontal neural metabolite changes in schizophrenia and their association with cognitive control: A systematic review. *Neuroscience & Biobehavioral Reviews, 132*, 224–247.

Dobbelstein, C.R. (2015). Somatic symptom and related disorders. In K.D. Ackerman & A.F. DiMartini (Eds.), *Psychosomatic medicine* (pp. 75–91). New York: Oxford.

Dobrescu, S. R., Dinkler, L., Gillberg, C., Råstam, M., Gillberg, C., & Wentz, E. (2020). Anorexia nervosa: 30-year outcome. *The British Journal of Psychiatry, 216*, 97–104.

Dobson, K.S., & Stuart, H. (Eds.) (2021). *The stigma of mental illness*. New York: Oxford.

Docherty, A. R., Shabalin, A. A., Adkins, D. E., Mann, F., Krueger, R. F., Bacanu, S. A., ... & Kendler, K. S. (2020). Molecular genetic risk for psychosis is associated with psychosis risk symptoms in a population-based UK cohort: Findings from generation Scotland. *Schizophrenia Bulletin, 46*, 1045–1052.

Dokucu, M. E., & Cloninger, C. R. (2019). Personality disorders and physical comorbidities: A complex relationship. *Current Opinion in Psychiatry, 32*, 435–441.

Donders, J. (2020). The incremental value of neuropsychological assessment: A critical review. *The Clinical Neuropsychologist, 34*, 56–87.

Dong, C., Shi, H., Liu, P., Si, G., & Yan, Z. (2022). A critical overview of systematic reviews and meta-analyses of light therapy for non-seasonal depression. *Psychiatry Research*, 114686.

Dong, H., Hayashi, K., Singer, J., Milloy, M. J., DeBeck, K., Wood, E., & Kerr, T. (2019). Trajectories of injection drug use among people who use drugs in Vancouver, Canada, 1996–2017: Growth mixture modeling using data from prospective cohort studies. *Addiction, 114*, 2173–2186.

Doria, N., & Numer, M. (2022). Dancing in a culture of disordered eating: A feminist poststructural analysis of body and body image among young girls in the world of dance. *PLoS One, 17*, e0247651.

Driessen, E., Dekker, J. J., Peen, J., Van, H. L., Maina, G., Rosso, G., ... & Cuijpers, P. (2020). The efficacy of adding short-term psychodynamic psychotherapy to antidepressants in the treatment of depression: A systematic review and meta-analysis of individual participant data. *Clinical Psychology Review, 80*, 101886.

Dubreucq, J., Plasse, J., & Franck, N. (2021). Self-stigma in serious mental illness: A systematic review of frequency, correlates, and consequences. *Schizophrenia Bulletin, 47*, 1261–1287.

Dugré, J. R., & Potvin, S. (2022). Multiple developmental pathways underlying conduct problems: A multitrajectory framework. *Development and Psychopathology, 34*, 1115–1124.

Duffy, A., Carlson, G., Dubicka, B., & Hillegers, M. H. J. (2020). Pre-pubertal bipolar disorder: Origins and current status of the controversy. *International Journal of Bipolar Disorders, 8*, 1–10.

Duffy, A., Saunders, K. E., Malhi, G. S., Patten, S., Cipriani, A., McNevin, S. H., ... & Geddes, J. (2019). Mental health care for university students: a way forward?. *The Lancet Psychiatry, 6*, 885–887.

Dunne, R. A., Aarsland, D., O'Brien, J. T., Ballard, C., Banerjee, S., Fox, N. C., ... & Burns, A. (2021). Mild cognitive impairment: The Manchester consensus. *Age and Ageing, 50*, 72–80.

Dunphy, L., Penna, M., & Jihene, E. K. (2019). Somatic symptom disorder: A diagnostic dilemma. *BMJ Case Reports CP, 12*, e231550.

DuPaul, G. J., Fu, Q., Anastopoulos, A. D., Reid, R., & Power, T. J. (2020). ADHD parent and teacher symptom ratings: Differential item functioning across gender, age, race, and ethnicity. *Journal of Abnormal Child Psychology, 48*, 679– 91.

DuPaul, G. J., Gormley, M. J., Anastopoulos, A. D., Weyandt, L. L., Labban, J., Sass, A. J., ... & Postler, K. B. (2021). Academic trajectories of college students with and without ADHD: Predictors of four-year outcomes. *Journal of Clinical Child & Adolescent Psychology, 50*, 828–843.

DuPaul, G.J., Power, T.J., Anastopoulos, A.D., & Reid, R. (2016). *ADHD Rating Scale—5 for Children and Adolescents: Checklists, norms, and clinical interpretation*. New York: Guilford.

Dusi, N., Bracco, L., Bressi, C., Delvecchio, G., & Brambilla, P. (2021). Imaging associations of self-injurious behaviours amongst patients with Borderline Personality Disorder: A mini-review. *Journal of Affective Disorders, 295*, 781–787.

Duy, P. Q., Rakic, P., Alper, S. L., Butler, W. E., Walsh, C. A., Sestan, N., ... & Kahle, K. T. (2022). Brain ventricles as windows into brain development and disease. *Neuron, 110*, 12–15.

Dvorak, R. D., Lamis, D. A., & Malone, P. S. (2013). Alcohol use, depressive symptoms, and impulsivity as risk factors for suicide proneness among college students. *Journal of Affective Disorders, 149*, 326–334.

Dykxhoorn, J., Lewis, G., Hollander, A. C., Kirkbride, J. B., & Dalman, C. (2020). Association of neighbourhood migrant density and risk of non-affective psychosis: a national, longitudinal cohort study. *The Lancet Psychiatry, 7*, 327–336.

Earnshaw, V. A. (2020). Stigma and substance use disorders: A clinical, research, and advocacy agenda. *American Psychologist, 75*, 1300–1311.

Eaton, W. W., Bienvenu, O. J., & Miloyan, B. (2018). Specific phobias. *The Lancet Psychiatry, 5*, 678–686.

Ebadi, M., Samadi, S. A., Mardani-Hamooleh, M., & Seyedfatemi, N. (2021). Living under psychosocial pressure: Perception of mothers of children with autism spectrum disorders. *Journal of Child and Adolescent Psychiatric Nursing, 34*, 212–218.

Ebenfeld, L., Stegemann, S. K., Lehr, D., Ebert, D. D., Funk, B., Riper, H., & Berking, M. (2020). A mobile application for panic disorder and agoraphobia: Insights from a multi-methods feasibility study. *Internet Interventions, 19*, 100296.

Ebesutani, C., McLeish, A.C., Luberto, C.M., Young, J., & Maack, D.J. (2014). A bifactor model of anxiety sensitivity: Analysis of the Anxiety Sensitivity Index-3. *Journal of Psychopathology and Behavioral Assessment, 36*, 452–464.

Ebneter, D.S., & Latner, J.D. (2013). Stigmatizing attitudes differ across mental health disorders: A comparison of stigma across eating disorders, obesity, and major depressive disorder. *Journal of Nervous and Mental Disease, 201*, 281–285.

Edershile, E. A., & Wright, A. G. (2021). Fluctuations in grandiose and vulnerable narcissistic states: A momentary perspective. *Journal of Personality and Social Psychology, 120*, 1386–1414.

Edinoff, A. N., Nix, C. A., McNeil, S. E., Wagner, S. E., Johnson, C. A., Williams, B. C., ... & Kaye, A. D. (2022). Prescription stimulants in college and medical students: A narrative review of misuse, cognitive impact, and adverse effects. *Psychiatry International, 3*, 221–235.

Efron, G., & Wootton, B. M. (2021). Remote cognitive behavioral therapy for panic disorder: A meta-analysis. *Journal of Anxiety Disorders, 79*, 102385.

Egbert, A. H., Hunt, R. A., Williams, K. L., Burke, N. L., & Mathis, K. J. (2022). Reporting racial and ethnic diversity in eating disorder research over the past 20 years. *International Journal of Eating Disorders, 55*, 455–462.

Ehlman, D. C., Yard, E., Stone, D. M., Jones, C. M., & Mack, K. A. (2022). Changes in suicide Rates—United States, 2019 and 2020. *Morbidity and Mortality Weekly Report, 71*, 306–312.

Eijsbouts, C., Zheng, T., Kennedy, N. A., Bonfiglio, F., Anderson, C. A., Moutsianas, L., ... & Parkes, M. (2021). Genome-wide analysis of 53,400 people with irritable bowel syndrome highlights shared genetic pathways with mood and anxiety disorders. *Nature Genetics, 53*, 1543–1552.

Eisenberg, D., Nicklett, E.J., Roeder, K., & Kirz, N.E. (2011). Eating disorder symptoms among college students: Prevalence, persistence, correlates, and treatment-seeking. *Journal of American College Health, 59*, 700–707.

Ejlskov, L., Wulff, J. N., Kalkbrenner, A., Ladd-Acosta, C., Fallin, M. D., Agerbo, E., ... & Schendel, D. (2021). Prediction of autism risk from family medical history data using machine learning: a national cohort study from Denmark. *Biological Psychiatry Global Open Science, 1*, 156–164.

Ekhtari, H., Verdejo-Garcia, A., Moeller, S.J., Baldacchino, A.M., & Paulus, M.P. (Eds.) (2021). *Brain and cognition for addiction medicine: From prevention to recovery*. Frontiers Media SA.

Ekoh, P. C., George, E. O., Ejimakaraonye, C., & Okoye, U. O. (2020). An appraisal of public understanding of dementia across cultures. *Journal of Social Work in Developing Societies, 2*, 54–67.

El Abdellati, K., De Picker, L., & Morrens, M. (2020). Antipsychotic treatment failure: A systematic review on risk factors and interventions for treatment adherence in psychosis. *Frontiers in Neuroscience, 14*, 531763.

Elling, C., Forstner, A. J., Seib-Pfeifer, L. E., Mücke, M., Stahl, J., Geiser, F., ... & Conrad, R. (2022). Social anxiety disorder with comorbid major depression–why fearful attachment style is relevant. *Journal of Psychiatric Research, 147*, 282–290.

Ellins, E. A., Shipley, M. J., Rees, D. A., Kemp, A., Deanfield, J. E., Brunner, E. J., & Halcox, J. P. (2020). Associations of depression-anxiety and dyslipidaemia with subclinical carotid arterial disease: Findings from the Whitehall II Study. *European Journal of Preventive Cardiology, 27*, 800–807.

Elliott, L., Thompson, K. A., & Fobian, A. D. (2020). A systematic review of somatic symptoms in children with a chronically ill family member. *Psychosomatic Medicine, 82*, 366–376.

Elliot, R., Watson, J., Timulak, L., & Sharbanee, J. (2021). Research on humanistic-experiential psychotherapies: Updated review. In M. Barkham, W. Lutz, & L. G. Castonguay (Eds.), *Bergin and Garfield's handbook of psychotherapy and behavior change* (pp. 421–464). Hoboken, NJ: Wiley.

Ellis, A.J., Portnoff, L.C., Axelson, D.A., Kowatch, R.A., Walshaw, P., & Miklowitz, D.J. (2014). Parental expressed emotion and suicidal ideation in adolescents with bipolar disorder. *Psychiatry Research, 216*, 213–216.

Emmelkamp, P. M., & Meyerbröker, K. (2021). Virtual reality therapy in mental health. *Annual Review of Clinical Psychology, 17*, 495–519.

Emrani, S., Arain, H. A., DeMarshall, C., & Nuriel, T. (2020). APOE4 is associated with cognitive and pathological heterogeneity in patients with Alzheimer's disease: A systematic review. *Alzheimer's Research & Therapy, 12*, 1–19.

Erbeli, F., Rice, M., & Paracchini, S. (2021). Insights into dyslexia genetics research from the last two decades. *Brain Sciences, 12*, 27.

Erjavec, G. N., Tudor, L., Perkovic, M. N., Podobnik, J., Curkovic, K. D., Curkovic, M., ... & Pivac, N. (2022). Serotonin 5-HT2A receptor polymorphisms are associated with irritability and aggression in conduct disorder. *Progress in Neuro-Psychopharmacology and Biological Psychiatry, 117*, 110542.

Erlenwein, J., Diers, M., Ernst, J., Schulz, F., & Petzke, F. (2021). Clinical updates on phantom limb pain. *Pain Reports, 6*, e888.

Erng, M. N., Smirnov, A., & Reid, N. (2020). Prevention of alcohol-exposed pregnancies and fetal alcohol spectrum disorder among pregnant and postpartum women: A systematic review. *Alcoholism: Clinical and Experimental Research, 44*, 2431–2448.

Eskander, N., Chakrapani, S., & Ghani, M. R. (2020). The risk of substance use among adolescents and adults with eating disorders. *Cureus, 12*: e10309.

Espada, N. C., Ortiz-Fune, C., Bersabe-Pérez, M., Delgado-Perales, S., Díaz-Trejo, S., González-Parra, D., & Roncero, C. (2021). Psychological profile of the bariatric surgery candidates in a spanish hospital in 2020: a descriptive study. *European Psychiatry, 64*, S653–S653.

Esponda, G. M., Hartman, S., Qureshi, O., Sadler, E., Cohen, A., & Kakuma, R. (2020). Barriers and facilitators of mental health programmes in primary care in low-income and middle-income countries. *The Lancet Psychiatry, 7*, 78–92.

Etchecopar-Etchart, D., Korchia, T., Loundou, A., Llorca, P. M., Auquier, P., Lançon, C., ... & Fond, G. (2021). Comorbid major depressive disorder in schizophrenia: A systematic review and meta-analysis. *Schizophrenia Bulletin, 47*, 298–308.

Ezpeleta, L., Penelo, E., Navarro, J. B., de la Osa, N., & Trepat, E. (2022). Co-developmental trajectories of defiant/headstrong, irritability, and prosocial emotions from preschool age to early adolescence. *Child Psychiatry & Human Development, 53*, 908–918.

Fahs, B., & Swank, E. (2021). Reciprocity, partner pressure, and emotional labor: Women discuss negotiations around oral and anal sex. *Sexuality & Culture, 25*, 217–234.

Fairburn, C.G., Bailey-Straebler, S., Basden, S., Doll, H.A., Jones, R., Murphy, R., O'Connor, M.E., & Cooper, Z. (2015). A transdiagnostic comparison of enhanced cognitive behavior therapy (CBT-E) and interpersonal psychotherapy in the treatment of eating disorders. *Behaviour Research and Therapy, 70*, 64–71.

Fanetti, M., O'Donohue, W., Happel, R. F., & Daly, K. (2015). *Forensic child psychology: Working in the courts and clinic.* New York: Wiley.

Fang, H., Tu, S., Sheng, J., & Shao, A. (2019). Depression in sleep disturbance: a review on a bidirectional relationship, mechanisms and treatment. *Journal of Cellular and Molecular Medicine, 23*, 2324–2332.

Fang, L., Lee, E., & Huang, F.Y. (2013). A child who sees ghosts every night: Manifestations of psychosocial and familial stress following immigration. *Culture, Medicine, and Psychiatry, 37*, 549–564.

Fang, X., Crumpler, R. F., Thomas, K. N., Mazique, J. N., Roman, R. J., & Fan, F. (2022). Contribution of cerebral microvascular mechanisms to age-related cognitive impairment and dementia. *Physiology International, 109*, 20–30.

Faraone, S. V., & Larsson, H. (2019). Genetics of attention deficit hyperactivity disorder. *Molecular Psychiatry, 24*, 562–575.

Faria, A. V., Zhao, Y., Ye, C., Hsu, J., Yang, K., Cifuentes, E., ... & Sawa, A. (2021). Multimodal MRI assessment for first episode psychosis: A major change in the thalamus and an efficient stratification of a subgroup. *Human Brain Mapping, 42*, 1034–1053.

Fasciani, I., Petragnano, F., Aloisi, G., Marampon, F., Carli, M., Scarselli, M., ... & Rossi, M. (2020). Allosteric modulators of g protein-coupled dopamine and serotonin receptors: A new class of atypical antipsychotics. *Pharmaceuticals, 13*, 388.

Favaro, A., Busetto, P., Collantoni, E., Santonastaso, P. (2019). The age of onset of eating disorders. In G. de Girolamo, P., McGorry, & N. Sartorius (Eds.), *Age of onset of mental disorders* (pp. 203–216). Cham: Springer.

Feld, K., Feld, D., Karger, B., Helmus, J., Schwimmer-Okike, N., Pfeiffer, H., ... & Wittschieber, D. (2021). Abusive head trauma in court: A multi-center study on criminal proceedings in Germany. *International Journal of Legal Medicine, 135*, 235–244.

Feng, Y., Wang, Z., Lin, G., Qian, H., Gao, Z., Wang, X., ... & Li, Y. (2020). Neurological soft signs and neurocognitive deficits in remitted patients with schizophrenia, their first-degree unaffected relatives, and healthy controls. *European Archives of Psychiatry and Clinical Neuroscience, 270*, 383–391.

Fernàndez-Castillo, N., Cabana-Domínguez, J., Corominas, R., & Cormand, B. (2022). Molecular genetics of cocaine use disorders in humans. *Molecular Psychiatry, 27*, 624–639.

Fernández-Teruel, A., & Tobeña, A. (2020). Revisiting the role of anxiety in the initial acquisition of two-way active avoidance: Pharmacological, behavioural and neuroanatomical convergence. *Neuroscience & Biobehavioral Reviews, 118*, 739–758.

Feroe, A. G., Uppal, N., Gutierrez-Sacristan, A., Mousavi, S., Greenspun, P., Surati, R., ... & Avillach, P. (2021). Medication use in the management of comorbidities among individuals with autism spectrum disorder from a large nationwide insurance database. *JAMA Pediatrics, 175*, 957–965.

Ferrari, M., Yap, K., Scott, N., Einstein, D. A., & Ciarrochi, J. (2018). Self-compassion moderates the perfectionism and depression link in both adolescence and adulthood. *PLoS One, 13*, e0192022.

Ferreira, I. M. S., Souza, A. P. L. D., Azevedo, L. D. S., Leonidas, C., Santos, M. A. D., & Pessa, R. P. (2021). The influence of mothers on the development of their daughter's eating disorders: An integrative review. *Archives of Clinical Psychiatry (São Paulo), 48*, 168–177.

Fietze, I., Laharnar, N., Obst, A., Ewert, R., Felix, S. B., Garcia, C., ... & Penzel, T. (2019). Prevalence and association analysis of obstructive sleep apnea with gender and age differences–Results of SHIP-Trend. *Journal of Sleep Research, 28*, e12770.

Fink, M., Kellner, C. H., & McCall, W. V. (2014). The role of ECT in suicide prevention. *Journal of ECT, 30*, 5–9.

Finnegan, E. G., Asaro-Saddler, K., & Zajic, M. C. (2021). Production and comprehension of pronouns in individuals with autism: A meta-analysis and systematic review. *Autism, 25*, 3–17.

First, M.B., Williams, J.B.W., Benjamin, L.S., & Spitzer, R.L. (2016). *Structured Clinical Interview for DSM-5® Personality Disorders (SCID-5-PD)*. Washington, DC: American Psychiatric Association Publishing.

First, M.B., Williams, J.B., Karg, R.S., & Spitzer, R.L. (2015). *Structured Clinical Interview for DSM-5 Disorders*. Washington, DC: American Psychiatric Publishing.

Fisher, J. S., Rezk, A., Nwefo, E., Masterson, J., & Ramasamy, R. (2020). Sexual health in the elderly population. *Current Sexual Health Reports, 12*, 381–388.

Fleming, C., Le Brocque, R., & Healy, K. (2021). How are families included in the treatment of adults affected by eating disorders? A scoping review. *International Journal of Eating Disorders, 54*, 244–279.

Flores, M. W., Moyer, M., Rodgers, C. R., & Lê Cook, B. (2021). Major depressive episode severity among adults from marginalized racial and ethnic backgrounds in the US. *JAMA Psychiatry, 78*, 1279–1280.

Fobian, A. D., & Elliott, L. (2019). A review of functional neurological symptom disorder etiology and the integrated etiological summary model. *Journal of Psychiatry and Neuroscience, 44*, 8–18.

Folmo, E. J., Stänicke, E., Johansen, M. S., Pedersen, G., & Kvarstein, E. H. (2021). Development of therapeutic alliance in mentalization-based treatment—Goals, Bonds, and Tasks in a specialized treatment for borderline personality disorder. *Psychotherapy Research, 31*, 604–618.

Fong, T. G., & Inouye, S. K. (2022). The inter-relationship between delirium and dementia: the importance of delirium prevention. *Nature Reviews Neurology*, 1–18.

Forde, R., Peters, S., & Wittkowski, A. (2020). Recovery from postpartum psychosis: a systematic review and metasynthesis of women's and families' experiences. *Archives of Women's Mental Health, 23*, 597–612.

Fortea, J., Zaman, S. H., Hartley, S., Rafii, M. S., Head, E., & Carmona-Iragui, M. (2021). Alzheimer's disease associated with Down syndrome: A genetic form of dementia. *The Lancet Neurology, 20*, 930–942.

Fountoulakis, K.N. (2015). *Bipolar disorder: An evidence-based guide to manic depression*. New York: Springer.

Fountoulakis, K. N., Tohen, M., & Zarate Jr, C. A. (2022). Lithium treatment of Bipolar disorder in adults: A systematic review of randomized trials and meta-analyses. *European Neuropsychopharmacology, 54*, 100–115.

Fournié, C., Chouchou, F., Dalleau, G., Caderby, T., Cabrera, Q., & Verkindt, C. (2021). Heart rate variability biofeedback in chronic disease management: A systematic review. *Complementary Therapies in Medicine, 60*, 102750.

Frank, G. K. (2020). Pharmacotherapeutic strategies for the treatment of anorexia nervosa–too much for one drug?. *Expert Opinion on Pharmacotherapy, 21*, 1045–1058.

Frank, H. E., Becker-Haimes, E. M., & Kendall, P. C. (2020). Therapist training in evidence-based interventions for mental health: a systematic review of training approaches and outcomes. *Clinical Psychology: Science and Practice, 27*, e12330.

Franko, D.L., Thompson-Brenner, H., Thompson, D.R., Boisseau, C.L., Davis, A., Forbush, K.T., Roehrig, J.P., Bryson, S.W., Bulik, C.M., Crow, S.J., Devlin, M.J., Gorin, A.A., Grilo, C.M., Kristeller, J.L., Masheb, R.M., Mitchell, J.E., Peterson, C.B., Safer, D.L., Striegel, R.H., Wilfley, D.E., & Wilson, G.T. (2012). Racial/ethnic differences in adults in randomized clinical trials of binge eating disorder. *Journal of Consulting and Clinical Psychology, 80*, 186–195.

Fratiglioni, L., Marseglia, A., & Dekhtyar, S. (2020). Ageing without dementia: can stimulating psychosocial and lifestyle experiences make a difference? *The Lancet Neurology, 19*, 533–543.

Frawley, E., Cowman, M., Lepage, M., & Donohoe, G. (2021). Social and occupational recovery in early psychosis: A systematic review and meta-analysis of psychosocial interventions. *Psychological Medicine*, 1–12.

Freels, T. G., Gabriel, D. B., Lester, D. B., & Simon, N. W. (2020). Risky decision-making predicts dopamine release dynamics in nucleus accumbens shell. *Neuropsychopharmacology, 45*, 266–275.

Frey, A. L., Frank, M. J., & McCabe, C. (2021). Social reinforcement learning as a predictor of real-life experiences in individuals with high and low depressive symptomatology. *Psychological Medicine, 51*, 408–415.

Frick, P. J., & Kemp, E. C. (2021). Conduct disorders and empathy development. *Annual Review of Clinical Psychology, 17*, 391–416.

Fronk, G. E., Sant'Ana, S. J., Kaye, J. T., & Curtin, J. J. (2020). Stress allostasis in substance use disorders: Promise, progress, and emerging priorities in clinical research. *Annual Review of Clinical Psychology, 16*, 401–430.

Frynta, D., Janovcová, M., Štolhoferová, I., Peléšková, Š., Vobrubová, B., Frýdlová, P., ... & Landová, E. (2021). Emotions triggered by live arthropods shed light on spider phobia. *Scientific Reports, 11*, 1–10.

Fuensalida-Novo, S., Parás-Bravo, P., Jiménez-Antona, C., Castaldo, M., Wang, K., Benito-González, E., ... & Fernández-De-Las-Peñas, C. (2020). Gender differences in clinical and psychological variables associated with the burden of headache in tension-type headache. *Women & Health, 60*, 652–663.

Fuentes-Claramonte, P., Salgado-Pineda, P., Argila-Plaza, I., García-León, M. Á., Ramiro, N., Soler-Vidal, J., ... & Pomarol-Clotet, E. (2022). Neural correlates of referential/persecutory delusions in schizophrenia: examination using fMRI and a virtual reality underground travel paradigm. *Psychological Medicine*, 1–8.

Fullana, M. A., Dunsmoor, J. E., Schruers, K. R. J., Savage, H. S., Bach, D. R., & Harrison, B. J. (2020). Human fear conditioning: From neuroscience to the clinic. *Behaviour Research and Therapy, 124*, 103528.

Fuller, E. A., & Kaiser, A. P. (2020). The effects of early intervention on social communication outcomes for children with autism spectrum disorder: A meta-analysis. *Journal of Autism and Developmental Disorders, 50*, 1683–1700.

Fuller, K. S., Demarch, E., & Winkler, P. A. (2015). Degenerative diseases of the central nervous system. In C.C. Goodman & K.S. Fuller (Eds.), *Pathology: Implications for the physical therapist* (4th ed.) (pp. 1455–1506). St. Louis: Elsevier.

Furnham, A., & Crump, J. (2015). A Big Five facet analysis of a paranoid personality disorder. *Journal of Individual Differences, 36*, 199–204.

Furukawa, T. A., Suganuma, A., Ostinelli, E. G., Andersson, G., Beevers, C. G., Shumake, J., ... & Cuijpers, P. (2021). Dismantling, optimising, and personalising internet cognitive behavioural therapy for depression: A systematic review and component network meta-analysis using individual participant data. *The Lancet Psychiatry, 8*, 500–511.

Fusar-Poli, P., de Pablo, G. S., De Micheli, A., Nieman, D. H., Correll, C. U., Kessing, L. V., ... & van Amelsvoort, T. (2020). What is good mental health? A scoping review. *European Neuropsychopharmacology, 31*, 33–46.

Galaj, E., & Ranaldi, R. (2021). Neurobiology of reward-related learning. *Neuroscience & Biobehavioral Reviews, 124*, 224–234.

Galderisi, S., Kaiser, S., Bitter, I., Nordentoft, M., Mucci, A., Sabé, M., ... & Gaebel, W. (2021). EPA guidance on treatment of negative symptoms in schizophrenia. *European Psychiatry, 64*, E21.

Gallo, D., Ruiz, A., & Sánchez-Juan, P. (2022). Genetic architecture of primary tauopathies. *Neuroscience.*

Galm, B. P., Qiao, N., Klibanski, A., Biller, B. M., & Tritos, N. A. (2020). Accuracy of laboratory tests for the diagnosis of Cushing syndrome. *The Journal of Clinical Endocrinology & Metabolism, 105*, 2081–2094.

Gao, L., Liu, J., Hua, S., Yang, J., & Wang, X. (2022). Teacher–student relationship and adolescents' bullying perpetration: A moderated mediation model of deviant peer affiliation and peer pressure. *Journal of Social and Personal Relationships*, 02654075221074393.

Garakani, A., Freire, R. C., & Murrough, J. W. (2021). Pharmacotherapy of anxiety disorders: Promises and pitfalls. *Frontiers in Psychiatry, 12*, 662963.

Garakani, A., Murrough, J. W., Freire, R. C., Thom, R. P., Larkin, K., Buono, F. D., & Iosifescu, D. V. (2020). Pharmacotherapy of anxiety disorders: Current and emerging treatment options. *Frontiers in Psychiatry*, 1412.

Garber, A. K., Cheng, J., Accurso, E. C., Adams, S. H., Buckelew, S. M., Kapphahn, C. J., ... & Golden, N. H. (2021). Short-term outcomes of the study of refeeding to optimize inpatient gains for patients with anorexia nervosa: a multicenter randomized clinical trial. *JAMA Pediatrics, 175*, 19–27.

Gardani, M., Bradford, D. R., Russell, K., Allan, S., Beattie, L., Ellis, J., & Akram, U. (2022). A systematic review and meta-analysis of poor sleep, insomnia symptoms and stress in undergraduate students. *Sleep Medicine Reviews, 61*, 101565.

Garey, L., Olofsson, H., Garza, T., Rogers, A. H., Kauffman, B. Y., & Zvolensky, M. J. (2020). Directional effects of anxiety and depressive disorders with substance use: A review of recent prospective research. *Current Addiction Reports, 7*, 344–355.

Garnett, M. F., Curtin, S. C., & Stone, D. M. (2022). *Suicide mortality in the United States, 2000-2020.* Washington, DC: US Department of Health and Human Services.

Gartlehner, G., Crotty, K., Kennedy, S., Edlund, M. J., Ali, R., Siddiqui, M., ... & Viswanathan, M. (2021). Pharmacological treatments for borderline personality disorder: A systematic review and meta-analysis. *CNS Drugs, 35*, 1053–1067.

Gascon, A., Gamache, D., St-Laurent, D., & Stipanicic, A. (2022). Do we over-diagnose ADHD in North America? A critical review and clinical recommendations. *Journal of Clinical Psychology, 78*, 2363–2380.

Geisner, I.M., Mallett, K., & Kilmer, J.R. (2012). An examination of depressive symptoms and drinking patterns in first year college students. *Issues in Mental Health Nursing, 33*, 280–287.

Geng, F., Lu, H., Zhang, Y., Zhan, N., Zhang, L., & Liu, M. (2022). Dissociative depression and its related clinical and psychological characteristics among Chinese prisoners: A latent class analysis. *Current Psychology*, 1–10.

Ghaemmaghami, M., Hanley, G. P., & Jessel, J. (2021). Functional communication training: From efficacy to effectiveness. *Journal of Applied Behavior Analysis, 54*, 122–143.

Ghosh, A., Singh, P., Das, N., Pandit, P. M., Das, S., & Sarkar, S. (2022). Efficacy of brief intervention for harmful and hazardous alcohol use: A systematic review and meta-analysis of studies from low middle-income countries. *Addiction, 117*, 545–558.

Giacobini, E., Cuello, A. C., & Fisher, A. (2022). Reimagining cholinergic therapy for Alzheimer's disease. *Brain, 145*, 2250–2275.

Giacolini, T., Conversi, D., & Alcaro, A. (2021). The brain emotional systems in addictions: From attachment to dominance/submission systems. *Frontiers in Human Neuroscience, 14*, 609467.

Gialluisi, A., Andlauer, T. F., Mirza-Schreiber, N., Moll, K., Becker, J., Hoffmann, P., ... & Schulte-Körne, G. (2021). Genome-wide association study reveals new insights into the heritability and genetic correlates of developmental dyslexia. *Molecular Psychiatry, 26*, 3004–3017.

Giannouli, V., & Tsolaki, M. (2021). Is depression or apathy playing a key role in predicting financial capacity in Parkinson's Disease with Dementia and Frontotemporal Dementia? *Brain Sciences, 11*, 785.

Gibbor, L., Yates, L., Volkmer, A., & Spector, A. (2021). Cognitive stimulation therapy (CST) for dementia: A systematic review of qualitative research. *Aging & Mental Health, 25*, 980–990.

Gibson, D., Benabe, J., Watters, A., Oakes, J., & Mehler, P. S. (2021). Personality characteristics and medical impact of stimulant laxative abuse in eating disorder patients—a pilot study. *Journal of Eating Disorders, 9*, 146.

Gilboa-Schechtman, E., Keshet, H., Peschard, V., & Azoulay, R. (2020). Self and identity in social anxiety disorder. *Journal of Personality, 88*, 106–121.

Gillespie-Lynch, K., Brooks, P. J., Someki, F., Obeid, R., Shane-Simpson, C., Kapp, S. K., Daou, N., & Smith, D. S. (2015). Changing college students' conceptions of autism: An online training to increase knowledge and decrease stigma. *Journal of Autism and Developmental Disorders, 45*, 2553–2566.

Gillespie-Lynch, K., Daou, N., Obeid, R., Reardon, S., Khan, S., & Goldknopf, E. J. (2021). What contributes to stigma towards autistic university students and students with other diagnoses?. *Journal of Autism and Developmental Disorders, 51*, 459–475.

Gil Martínez, V., Avedillo Salas, A., & Santander Ballestín, S. (2022). Vitamin supplementation and dementia: A systematic review. *Nutrients, 14*, 1033.

Ging, D., & Garvey, S. (2018). 'Written in these scars are the stories I can't explain': A content analysis of pro-ana and thinspiration image sharing on Instagram. *New Media & Society, 20*, 1181–1200.

Giordano, G. M., Bucci, P., Mucci, A., Pezzella, P., & Galderisi, S. (2021). Gender differences in clinical and psychosocial features among persons with schizophrenia: A mini review. *Frontiers in Psychiatry, 12*, 789179.

Gladstone, T.R.G., Forbes, P.W., Diehl, A., & Beardslee, W.R. (2015). Increasing understanding in children of depressed parents: Predictors and moderators of intervention response. *Depression Research and Treatment, 2015*, 1–9.

Glasofer, A., & Dingley, C. (2021). Diagnostic and medication treatment disparities in African American children with ADHD: A literature review. *Journal of Racial and Ethnic Health Disparities, 9*, 2027–2048.

Glasson, E. J., Buckley, N., Chen, W., Leonard, H., Epstein, A., Skoss, R., ... & Downs, J. (2020). Systematic review and meta-analysis: Mental health in children with neurogenetic disorders associated with intellectual disability. *Journal of the American Academy of Child & Adolescent Psychiatry, 59*, 1036–1048.

Glenthøj, L. B., Kristensen, T. D., Gibson, C. M., Jepsen, J. R. M., & Nordentoft, M. (2020). Assessing social skills in individuals at ultra-high risk for psychosis: validation of the High Risk Social Challenge task (HiSoC). *Schizophrenia Research, 215*, 365–370.

Glenthøj, L. B., Kristensen, T. D., Wenneberg, C., Hjorthøj, C., & Nordentoft, M. (2021). Predictors of remission from the ultra-high risk state for psychosis. *Early Intervention in Psychiatry, 15*, 104–112.

Goel, N. J., Thomas, B., Boutté, R. L., Kaur, B., & Mazzeo, S. E. (2021). Body image and eating disorders among South Asian American women: What are we missing? *Qualitative Health Research, 31*, 2512–2527.

Gold, A. K., Kredlow, M. A., Orr, S. P., Hartley, C. A., & Otto, M. W. (2022). Skin conductance levels and responses in Asian and White participants during fear conditioning. *Physiology & Behavior, 251*, 113802.

Goldfarb, M. R., & Trudel, G. (2019). Marital quality and depression: a review. *Marriage & Family Review, 55*, 737–763.

Gómez-Coronado, N., Walker, A. J., Berk, M., & Dodd, S. (2018). Current and emerging pharmacotherapies for cessation of tobacco smoking. Pharmacotherapy: *The Journal of Human Pharmacology and Drug Therapy, 38*, 235–258.

González-Rodríguez, A., & Seeman, M. V. (2022). Differences between delusional disorder and schizophrenia: A mini narrative review. *World Journal of Psychiatry, 12*, 683–692.

Gordovez, F. J. A., & McMahon, F. J. (2020). The genetics of bipolar disorder. *Molecular Psychiatry, 25*, 544–559.

Gosmann, N. P., Costa, M. D. A., Jaeger, M. D. B., Motta, L. S., Frozi, J., Spanemberg, L., ... & Salum, G. A. (2021). Selective serotonin reuptake inhibitors, and serotonin and norepinephrine reuptake inhibitors for anxiety, obsessive-compulsive, and stress disorders: A 3-level network meta-analysis. *PLoS Medicine, 18*, e1003664.

Göttlich, M., Buades-Rotger, M., Wiechert, J., Beyer, F., & Krämer, U. M. (2022). Structural covariance of amygdala subregions is associated with trait aggression and endogenous testosterone in healthy individuals. *Neuropsychologia, 165*, 108113.

Gottschalk, M. G., & Domschke, K. (2022). Genetics of generalized anxiety disorder and related traits. *Dialogues in Clinical Neuroscience, 19*, 159–168.

Gracy, S., & Patel, N. (2021). Short communication on paraphillia. *International Journal of Advances in Nursing Management, 9*, 225–229.

Grady, M. D., Yoder, J., & Brown, A. (2021). Childhood maltreatment experiences, attachment, sexual offending: Testing a theory. *Journal of Interpersonal Violence, 36*, NP6183–NP6217.

Grammer, A. C., Fitzsimmons-Craft, E. E., Laing, O., De Pietro, B., & Wilfley, D. E. (2020). Eating disorders on college campuses in the United States: Current insight on screening, prevention, and treatment. *Current Psychopharmacology, 9*, 91–102.

Grandgenett, H. M., Pittenger, S. L., Dworkin, E. R., & Hansen, D. J. (2021). Telling a trusted adult: Factors associated with the likelihood of disclosing child sexual abuse prior to and during a forensic interview. *Child Abuse & Neglect, 116*, 104193.

Grant, J. E., Dougherty, D. D., & Chamberlain, S. R. (2020). Prevalence, gender correlates, and co-morbidity of trichotillomania. *Psychiatry Research, 288*, 112948.

Graupensperger, S., Jaffe, A. E., Hultgren, B. A., Rhew, I. C., Lee, C. M., & Larimer, M. E. (2021). The dynamic nature of injunctive drinking norms and within-person associations with college student alcohol use. *Psychology of Addictive Behaviors, 35*, 867–876.

Grave, R.D., Sartirana, M., & Calugi, S. (2021). *Complex cases and comorbidity in eating disorders: Assessment and management*. New York: Springer.

Green, J. G., McLaughlin, K. A., Fillbrunn, M., Fukuda, M., Jackson, J. S., Kessler, R. C., ... & Alegría, M. (2020). Barriers to mental health service use and predictors of treatment drop out: Racial/ethnic variation in a population-based study. *Administration and Policy in Mental Health and Mental Health Services Research, 47*, 606–616.

Green, J. P., Lynn, S. J., Green, O. J., Bradford, V. R., & Rasekhy, R. (2020). Hypnotic responsiveness and dissociation: A multivariable analysis. *OBM Integrative and Complementary Medicine, 5*, 029.

Green, M. J., Girshkin, L., Kremerskothen, K., Watkeys, O., & Quidé, Y. (2020). A systematic review of studies reporting data-driven cognitive subtypes across the psychosis spectrum. *Neuropsychology Review, 30*, 446–460.

Green, M. J., O'Hare, K., Laurens, K. R., Tzoumakis, S., Dean, K., Badcock, J. C., ... & Carr, V. J. (2022). Developmental profiles of schizotypy in the general population: A record linkage study of Australian children aged 11–12 years. *British Journal of Clinical Psychology, 61*, 836–858.

Green, T., Flash, S., & Reiss, A. L. (2019). Sex differences in psychiatric disorders: What we can learn from sex chromosome aneuploidies. *Neuropsychopharmacology, 44*, 9–21.

Greenberg, D., Eagle, K., & Felthous, A.R. (2020). The insanity defense and psychopathic disorders in the United States and Australia. In A.R. Felthous & S. Henning (Eds.), *The Wiley international handbook on psychopathic disorders and the law* (2nd ed) (pp. 385–412). New York: Wiley.

Greene, A. L., & Eaton, N. R. (2016). Panic disorder and agoraphobia: A direct comparison of their multivariate comorbidity patterns. *Journal of Affective Disorders, 190*, 75–83.

Grella, C. E., Ostlie, E., Scott, C. K., Dennis, M. L., Carnevale, J., & Watson, D. P. (2021). A scoping review of factors that influence opioid overdose prevention for justice-involved populations. *Substance Abuse Treatment, Prevention, and Policy, 16*, 1–39.

Gregory, V.L. (2020). Psychological perspective: Psychodynamic, humanistic, and cognitive-behavioral theories. In R. Ow & A. W. C. Poon (eds.), *Mental health and social work* (pp. 47–65). Singapore: Springer.

Griffin, J. W., Bauer, R., & Scherf, K. S. (2021). A quantitative meta-analysis of face recognition deficits in autism: 40 years of research. *Psychological Bulletin, 147*, 268–292.

Griffiths, K.M., Carron-Arthur, B., Parsons, A., & Reid, R. (2014). Effectiveness of programs for reducing the stigma associated with mental disorders. A meta-analysis of randomized controlled trials. *World Psychiatry, 13*, 161–175.

Griffiths, S., Mond, J. M., Murray, S. B., & Touyz, S. (2015). The prevalence and adverse associations of stigmatization in people with eating disorders. *International Journal of Eating Disorders, 48*, 767–774.

Grigorenko, E. L., Compton, D. L., Fuchs, L. S., Wagner, R. K., Willcutt, E. G., & Fletcher, J. M. (2020). Understanding, educating, and supporting children with specific learning disabilities: 50 years of science and practice. *American Psychologist, 75*, 37–51.

Grimm, O., Kranz, T. M., & Reif, A. (2020). Genetics of ADHD: What should the clinician know?. *Current Psychiatry Reports, 22*, 1–8.

Grogan, K., MacGarry, D., Bramham, J., Scriven, M., Maher, C., & Fitzgerald, A. (2020). Family-related non-abuse adverse life experiences occurring for adults diagnosed with eating disorders: A systematic review. *Journal of Eating Disorders, 8*, 1–20.

Grothe, J., Schomerus, G., Dietzel, J., Riedel-Heller, S., & Roehr, S. (2021). Instruments to assess social functioning in individuals with dementia: A systematic review. *Journal of Alzheimer's Disease, 80*, 619–637.

Gruber, J., Prinstein, M. J., Clark, L. A., Rottenberg, J., Abramowitz, J. S., Albano, A. M., Aldao, A., Borelli, J. L., Chung, T., Davila, J., Forbes, E. E., Gee, D. G., Hall, G. C. N., Hallion, L. S., Hinshaw, S. P., Hofmann, S. G., Hollon, S. D., Joormann, J., Kazdin, A. E., . . . Weinstock, L. M. (2021). Mental health and clinical psychological science in the time of COVID-19: Challenges, opportunities, and a call to action. *American Psychologist, 76*, 409–426.

Gubbels, J., van der Put, C. E., & Assink, M. (2019). The effectiveness of parent training programs for child maltreatment and their components: A meta-analysis. *International Journal of Environmental Research and Public Health, 16*, 2404.

Guarnaccia, S., Quecchia, C., Festa, A., Magoni, M., Zanardini, E., Brivio, V., ... & Donato, F. (2020). Evaluation of a diagnostic therapeutic educational pathway for asthma management in children and adolescents. *Frontiers in Pediatrics, 8*, 39.

Guarneri, J. A., Oberleitner, D. E., & Connolly, S. (2019). Perceived stigma and self-stigma in college students: A literature review and implications for practice and research. *Basic and Applied Social Psychology, 41*, 48-62.

Guger, M., Raschbacher, S., Kellermair, L., Vosko, M. R., Eggers, C., Forstner, T., ... & Ransmayr, G. (2021). Caregiver burden in patients with behavioural variant frontotemporal dementia and non-fluent variant and semantic variant primary progressive aphasia. *Journal of Neural Transmission, 128*, 1623–1634.

Guglielmo, R., Kobylinska, L., & de Filippis, R. (2021). Topiramate, naltrexone, and acamprosate in the treatment of alcohol use disorders. In P. Riederer, G. Laux et al. (Eds.), *NeuroPsychopharmacotherapy* (pp. 1–16). Cham: Springer.

Gul, M., Bocu, K., & Serefoglu, E. C. (2022). Current and emerging treatment options for premature ejaculation. *Nature Reviews Urology, 19*, 659–680.

Gul, M. K., Sener, E. F., Onal, M. G., & Demirci, E. (2022). Role of the norepinephrine transporter polymorphisms in atomoxetine treatment: From response to side effects in children with ADHD. *Journal of Psychopharmacology, 36*, 715–722.

Gul, P., & Schuster, I. (2020). Judgments of marital rape as a function of honor culture, masculine reputation threat, and observer gender: A cross-cultural comparison between Turkey, Germany, and the UK. *Aggressive Behavior, 46*, 341–353.

Guliyev, C., İnce-Guliyev, E., & Ögel, K. (2021). Predictors of relapse to alcohol and substance use: Are there any differences between 3 and 12 months after inpatient treatment? *Journal of Psychoactive Drugs, 54*, 358–367.

Gutherz, O. R., Deyssenroth, M., Li, Q., Hao, K., Jacobson, J. L., Chen, J., ... & Carter, R. C. (2022). Potential roles of imprinted genes in the teratogenic effects of alcohol on the placenta, somatic growth, and the developing brain. *Experimental Neurology, 347*, 113919.

Guthrie, H., Honig, L. S., Lin, H., Sink, K. M., Blondeau, K., Quartino, A., ... & Ostrowitzki, S. (2020). Safety, tolerability, and pharmacokinetics of crenezumab in patients with mild-to-moderate Alzheimer's disease treated with escalating doses for up to 133 weeks. *Journal of Alzheimer's Disease, 76*, 967–979.

Haaksma, M. L., Eriksdotter, M., Rizzuto, D., Leoutsakos, J. M. S., Rikkert, M. G. O., Melis, R. J., & Garcia-Ptacek, S. (2020). Survival time tool to guide care planning in people with dementia. *Neurology, 94*, e538–e548.

Haber, S. N., Yendiki, A., & Jbabdi, S. (2021). Four deep brain stimulation targets for obsessive-compulsive disorder: Are they different?. *Biological Psychiatry, 90*, 667–677.

Hagan, K. E., & Walsh, B. T. (2021). State of the art: The therapeutic approaches to Bulimia Nervosa. *Clinical Therapeutics, 43*, 40–49.

Hakamata, Y., Mizukami, S., Izawa, S., Okamura, H., Mihara, K., Marusak, H., ... & Tagaya, H. (2022). Implicit and explicit emotional memory recall in anxiety and depression: Role of basolateral amygdala and cortisol-norepinephrine interaction. *Psychoneuroendocrinology, 136*, 105598.

Hall, D., Lee, L. W., Manseau, M. W., Pope, L., Watson, A. C., & Compton, M. T. (2019). Major mental illness as a risk factor for incarceration. *Psychiatric Services, 70*, 1088–1093.

Hallberg, J., Kaldo, V., Arver, S., Dhejne, C., Piwowar, M., Jokinen, J., & Öberg, K. G. (2020). Internet-administered cognitive behavioral therapy for hypersexual disorder, with or without paraphilia (s) or paraphilic disorder (s) in men: A pilot study. *The Journal of Sexual Medicine, 17*, 2039–2054.

Haller, H., Cramer, H., Lauche, R., & Dobos, G. (2015). Somatoform disorders and medically unexplained symptoms in primary care. *Deutsches Arzteblatt International, 112*, 279–287.

Hallion, L.S., Sockol, L.E., & Wilhelm, S. (2015). Obsessive-compulsive disorder. In D.J. Stein & B. Vythilingum (Eds.), *Anxiety disorders and gender* (pp. 69–87). New York: Springer.

Hamad, R., Penko, J., Kazi, D. S., Coxson, P., Guzman, D., Wei, P. C., ... & Bibbins-Domingo, K. (2020). Association of low socioeconomic status with premature coronary heart disease in US adults. *JAMA Cardiology, 5*, 899–908.

Hamilton, C. A., Matthews, F. E., Erskine, D., Attems, J., & Thomas, A. J. (2021). Neurodegenerative brain changes are associated with area deprivation in the United Kingdom: Findings from the Brains for Dementia Research study. *Acta Neuropathologica Communications, 9*, 1–10.

Hamm, A. O. (2020). Fear, anxiety, and their disorders from the perspective of psychophysiology. *Psychophysiology, 57*, e13474.

Hansen, N., Singh, A., Bartels, C., Brosseron, F., Buerger, K., Cetindag, A. C., ... & Goya-Maldonado, R. (2021). Hippocampal and hippocampal-subfield volumes from early-onset major depression and bipolar disorder to cognitive decline. *Frontiers in Aging Neuroscience, 13*, 626974.

Happé, F., & Frith, U. (2020). Annual Research Review: Looking back to look forward–changes in the concept of autism and implications for future research. *Journal of Child Psychology and Psychiatry, 61*, 218–232.

Hare, B. D., & Duman, R. S. (2020). Prefrontal cortex circuits in depression and anxiety: Contribution of discrete neuronal populations and target regions. *Molecular Psychiatry, 25*, 2742–2758.

Harrewijn, A., Vidal-Ribas, P., Clore-Gronenborn, K., Jackson, S. M., Pisano, S., Pine, D. S., & Stringaris, A. (2020). Associations between brain activity and endogenous and exogenous cortisol–A systematic review. *Psychoneuroendocrinology, 120*, 104775.

Harrison, M. A., & Murphy, B. E. (2022). Sexual fetishes: sensations, perceptions, and correlates. *Psychology & Sexuality, 13*, 704–716.

Hartmann, W.E., Kim, E.S., Kim, J.H.J., Nguyen, T.U., Wendt, D.C., Nagata, D.K., & Gone, J.P. (2013). In search of cultural diversity, revisited: Recent publication trends in cross-cultural and ethnic minority psychology. *Review of General Psychology, 17*, 243–254.

Hassen, C. B., Fayosse, A., Landré, B., Raggi, M., Bloomberg, M., Sabia, S., & Singh-Manoux, A. (2022). Association between age at onset of multimorbidity and incidence of dementia: 30 year follow-up in Whitehall II prospective cohort study. *BMJ*, 2022, 376.

Haszto, C. S., Stanley, J. A., Iyengar, S., & Prasad, K. M. (2020). Regionally distinct alterations in membrane phospholipid metabolism in schizophrenia: A meta-analysis of phosphorus magnetic resonance spectroscopy studies. *Biological Psychiatry: Cognitive Neuroscience and Neuroimaging, 5*, 264–280.

Häuser, W., Hausteiner-Wiehle, C., Henningsen, P., Brähler, E., Schmalbach, B., & Wolfe, F. (2020). Prevalence and overlap of somatic symptom disorder, bodily distress syndrome and fibromyalgia syndrome in the German general population: A cross sectional study. *Journal of Psychosomatic Research, 133*, 110111.

Hayashi, N., Igarashi, M., Imai, A., Yoshizawa, Y., Utsumi, K., Ishikawa, Y., Tokunaga, T., Ishimoto, K., Harima, H., Tatebayashi, Y., Kumagai, N., Nozu, M., Ishii, H., & Okazaki, Y. (2012). Post-hospitalization course and predictive signs of suicidal behavior of suicidal patients admitted to a psychiatric hospital: A 2-year prospective follow-up study. *BMC Psychiatry, 12*, 186.

Hazzan, A. A., Dauenhauer, J., Follansbee, P., Hazzan, J. O., Allen, K., & Omobepade, I. (2022). Family caregiver quality of life and the care provided to older people living with dementia: qualitative analyses of caregiver interviews. *BMC Geriatrics, 22*, 1–11.

Heapy, C., Emerson, L. M., & Carroll, D. (2022). Are failures to suppress obsessive-intrusive thoughts associated with working memory?. *Journal of Behavior Therapy and Experimental Psychiatry, 76*, 101724.

Hecht, M., Klob, A., & Bartsch, A. (2022). Stopping the stigma: How empathy and reflectiveness can help reduce mental health stigma. *Media Psychology, 25*, 367–386.

Heinke, D., Isenburg, J. L., Stallings, E. B., Short, T. D., Le, M., Fisher, S., ... & National Birth Defects Prevention Network. (2021). Prevalence of structural birth defects among infants with Down syndrome, 2013–2017: A US population-based study. *Birth Defects Research, 113*, 189–202.

Helps, S., & Le Coyte Grinney, M. (2021). Synchronous digital couple and family psychotherapy: A meta-narrative review. *Journal of Family Therapy, 43*, 185–214.

Henderson, C. R., Caccamise, P., Soares, J. J., Stankunas, M., & Lindert, J. (2021). Elder maltreatment in Europe and the United States: A transnational analysis of prevalence rates and regional factors. *Journal of Elder Abuse & Neglect, 33*, 249–269.

Hengartner, M. P., Amendola, S., Kaminski, J. A., Kindler, S., Bschor, T., & Plöderl, M. (2021). Suicide risk with selective serotonin reuptake inhibitors and other new-generation antidepressants in adults: a systematic review and meta-analysis of observational studies. *Journal of Epidemiology and Community Health, 75*, 523–530.

Henggeler, S.W. (2015). Preventing youth violence through therapeutic interventions for high-risk youth. In P.D. Donnelly & C.L. Ward (Eds.), *Oxford textbook of violence prevention: Epidemiology, evidence and policy* (pp. 161–168). New York: Oxford.

Henningsen, P., Gündel, H., Kop, W. J., Löwe, B., Martin, A., Rief, W., ... & Van den Bergh, O. (2018). Persistent physical symptoms as perceptual dysregulation: a neuropsychobehavioral model and its clinical implications. *Psychosomatic Medicine, 80*, 422–431.

Henry, R. S., Perrin, P. B., Lageman, S. K., Villaseñor, T., Cariello, A. N., Pugh, M., ... & Soto-Escageda, J. A. (2021). Parkinson's symptoms and caregiver affiliate stigma: A multinational study. *Current Alzheimer Research, 18*, 222–231.

Henssler, J., Alexander, D., Schwarzer, G., Bschor, T., & Baethge, C. (2022). Combining antidepressants vs antidepressant monotherapy for treatment of patients with acute depression: A systematic review and meta-analysis. *JAMA Psychiatry, 79*, 300–312.

Hepdurgun, C., Karakoc, G., Polat, I., Ozalay, O., Eroglu, S., Erdogan, Y., ... & Gonul, A. S. (2021). A longitudinal study of lateral ventricle volumes in deficit and non-deficit schizophrenia. *Psychiatry Research: Neuroimaging, 313*, 111311.

Herculano-Houzel, S. (2020). Remarkable, but not special: What human brains are made of. In J. H. Kaas (Ed.), *Evolutionary neuroscience* (pp. 803–813). New York: Academic.

Hermann, P., Appleby, B., Brandel, J. P., Caughey, B., Collins, S., Geschwind, M. D., ... & Zerr, I. (2021). Biomarkers and diagnostic guidelines for sporadic Creutzfeldt-Jakob disease. *The Lancet Neurology, 20*, 235–246.

Hernández-Huerta, D., & Morillo-González, J. (2021). Dopamine D3 partial agonists in the treatment of psychosis and substance use disorder comorbidity: A pharmacological alternative to consider? *CNS Spectrums, 26*, 444–445.

Hershner, S. D., & Chervin, R. D. (2014). Causes and consequences of sleepiness among college students. *Nature and Science of Sleep, 6*, 73–84.

Hilker, R., Helenius, D., Fagerlund, B., Skytthe, A., Christensen, K., Werge, T. M., ... & Glenthøj, B. (2018). Heritability of schizophrenia and schizophrenia spectrum based on the nationwide Danish twin register. *Biological Psychiatry, 83*, 492–498.

Himmerich, H., Kan, C., Au, K., & Treasure, J. (2021). Pharmacological treatment of eating disorders, comorbid mental health problems, malnutrition and physical health consequences. *Pharmacology & Therapeutics, 217*, 107667.

Hinton, D. E., Reis, R., & de Jong, J. (2020). Ghost encounters among traumatized Cambodian refugees: Severity, relationship to PTSD, and phenomenology. *Culture, Medicine, and Psychiatry, 44*, 333–359.

Hirschfeld, R. M., & Russell, J. M. (1997). Assessment and treatment of suicidal patients. *New England Journal of Medicine, 337*, 910-915.

Hlay, J. K., Johnson, B. N., & Levy, K. N. (2022). Attachment security predicts tend-and-befriend behaviors: A replication. *Evolutionary Behavioral Sciences*.

Hodges, H., Fealko, C., & Soares, N. (2020). Autism spectrum disorder: Definition, epidemiology, causes, and clinical evaluation. *Translational Pediatrics, 9*, S55–S65.

Hodgins, S. (2022). Could expanding and investing in first-episode psychosis services prevent aggressive behaviour and violent crime? *Frontiers in Psychiatry, 13*, 821760.

Hofmann, S.G., & Hinton, D.E. (2014). Cross-cultural aspects of anxiety disorders. *Current Psychiatry Reports, 16*, 450.

Hofstra, E., Van Nieuwenhuizen, C., Bakker, M., Özgül, D., Elfeddali, I., de Jong, S. J., & van der Feltz-Cornelis, C. M. (2020). Effectiveness of suicide prevention interventions: a systematic review and meta-analysis. *General Hospital Psychiatry, 63*, 127–140.

Holland, N., Robbins, T. W., & Rowe, J. B. (2021). The role of noradrenaline in cognition and cognitive disorders. *Brain, 144*, 2243–2256.

Holman, E.A., & Silver, R.C. (2011). Health status and health care utilization following collective trauma: A 3-year national study of the 9/11 terrorist attacks in the United States. *Social Science and Medicine, 73*, 483–490.

Holyoak, D. L., Fife, S. T., & Hertlein, K. M. (2021). Clients' perceptions of marriage and family therapists' way-of-being: A phenomenological analysis. *Journal of Marital and Family Therapy, 47*, 85–103.

Holzer, K. J., Vaughn, M. G., Loux, T. M., Mancini, M. A., Fearn, N. E., & Wallace, C. L. (2022). Prevalence and correlates of antisocial personality disorder in older adults. *Aging & Mental Health, 26*, 169–178.

Hone-Blanchet, A., Ciraulo, D. A., Pascual-Leone, A., & Fecteau, S. (2015). Noninvasive brain stimulation to suppress craving in substance use disorders: Review of human evidence and methodological considerations for future work. *Neuroscience and Biobehavioral Reviews, 59*, 184–200.

Hong, P. Y., & Lishner, D. A. (2016). General invalidation and trauma-specific invalidation as predictors of personality and subclinical psychopathology. *Personality and Individual Differences, 89,* 211–216.

Horie, K., Barthélemy, N. R., Sato, C., & Bateman, R. J. (2021). CSF tau microtubule binding region identifies tau tangle and clinical stages of Alzheimer's disease. *Brain, 144,* 515–527.

Horwitz, A.V. (2020). *Between sanity and madness: Mental illness from ancient Greece to the neuroscientific era.* New York: Oxford.

Hovenkamp-Hermelink, J. H., Jeronimus, B. F., Myroniuk, S., Riese, H., & Schoevers, R. A. (2021). Predictors of persistence of anxiety disorders across the lifespan: A systematic review. *The Lancet Psychiatry, 8,* 428–443.

Hovenkamp-Hermelink, J. H., Jeronimus, B. F., Spinhoven, P., Penninx, B. W., Schoevers, R. A., & Riese, H. (2019). Differential associations of locus of control with anxiety, depression and life-events: A five-wave, nine-year study to test stability and change. *Journal of Affective Disorders, 253,* 26–34.

Howard, R., & Duggan, C. (2022). *Antisocial personality: Theory, research, treatment.* Cambridge: Cambridge University Press.

Howe, L. K., Fisher, L. R., Atkinson, E. A., & Finn, P. R. (2021). Symptoms of anxiety, depression, and borderline personality in alcohol use disorder with and without comorbid substance use disorder. *Alcohol, 90,* 19–25.

Howes, O. D., Hird, E. J., Adams, R. A., Corlett, P. R., & McGuire, P. (2020). Aberrant salience, information processing, and dopaminergic signaling in people at clinical high risk for psychosis. *Biological Psychiatry, 88,* 304–314.

Howes, O. D., & Shatalina, E. (2022). Integrating the neurodevelopmental and dopamine hypotheses of schizophrenia and the role of cortical excitation-inhibition balance. *Biological Psychiatry, 92,* 501–513.

Hsu, C. W., Wang, L. J., Lin, P. Y., Hung, C. F., Yang, Y. H., Chen, Y. M., & Kao, H. Y. (2021). Differences in psychiatric comorbidities and gender distribution among three clusters of personality disorders: a nationwide population-based study. *Journal of Clinical Medicine, 10,* 3294.

Hu, J., Fitzgerald, S. M., Owen, A. J., Ryan, J., Joyce, J., Chowdhury, E., ... & Freak-Poli, R. (2021). Social isolation, social support, loneliness and cardiovascular disease risk factors: A cross-sectional study among older adults. *International Journal of Geriatric Psychiatry, 36,* 1795–1809.

Hu, T., Zhang, Z., Wang, J., Li, Q., Zhu, H., Lai, Y., ... & Liu, S. (2019). Chromosomal aberrations in pediatric patients with developmental delay/intellectual disability: A single-center clinical investigation. *BioMed Research International, 2019,* 9352581.

Hübel, C., Abdulkadir, M., Herle, M., Loos, R. J., Breen, G., Bulik, C. M., & Micali, N. (2021). One size does not fit all. Genomics differentiates among anorexia nervosa, bulimia nervosa, and binge-eating disorder. *International Journal of Eating Disorders, 54,* 785–793.

Huber, J., Jennissen, S., Nikendei, C., Schauenburg, H., & Dinger, U. (2021). Agency and alliance as change factors in psychotherapy. *Journal of Consulting and Clinical Psychology, 89,* 214–226.

Hugh-Jones, S., Beckett, S., Tumelty, E., & Mallikarjun, P. (2021). Indicated prevention interventions for anxiety in children and adolescents: A review and meta-analysis of school-based programs. *European Child & Adolescent Psychiatry, 30,* 849–860.

Hui, T. P., Kandola, A., Shen, L., Lewis, G., Osborn, D. P. J., Geddes, J. R., & Hayes, J. F. (2019). A systematic review and meta-analysis of clinical predictors of lithium response in bipolar disorder. *Acta Psychiatrica Scandinavica, 140,* 94–115.

Hulgaard, D., Dehlholm-Lambertsen, G., & Rask, C. U. (2019). Family-based interventions for children and adolescents with functional somatic symptoms: A systematic review. *Journal of Family Therapy, 41,* 4–28.

Hulvershorn, L., & Nurnberger, J. (2014). Bipolar disorder. In K.C. Koenen, S. Rudenstine, E. Susser, & S. Galea (Eds.), *A life course approach to mental disorders* (pp. 76–87). New York: Oxford.

Hummelen, B., Braeken, J., Buer Christensen, T., Nysaeter, T. E., Germans Selvik, S., Walther, K., ... & Paap, M. C. (2021). A psychometric analysis of the structured clinical interview for the DSM-5 alternative model for personality disorders module I (SCID-5-AMPD-I): Level of personality functioning scale. *Assessment, 28,* 1320–1333.

Hung, C. I., Liu, C. Y., Yang, C. H., & Gan, S. T. (2020). Comorbidity with more anxiety disorders associated with a poorer prognosis persisting at the 10-year follow-up among patients with major depressive disorder. *Journal of Affective Disorders, 260,* 97–104.

Hutsebaut, J., Weekers, L. C., Tuin, N., Apeldoorn, J. S., & Bulten, E. (2021). Assessment of ICD-11 personality disorder severity in forensic patients using the semi-structured interview for personality functioning DSM-5 (STiP-5.1): Preliminary findings. *Frontiers in Psychiatry, 12,* 617702.

Hyde, J. S., & Mezulis, A. H. (2020). Gender differences in depression: Biological, affective, cognitive, and sociocultural factors. *Harvard Review of Psychiatry, 28,* 4–13.

Hyman, S. L., Levy, S. E., Myers, S. M., Kuo, D. Z., Apkon, S., Davidson, L. F., ... & Bridgemohan, C. (2020). Identification, evaluation, and management of children with autism spectrum disorder. *Pediatrics, 145*: e20193447

Ibrahim, A.K., Kelly, S.J., Adams, C.E., & Glazebrook, C. (2013). A systematic review of studies of depression prevalence in university students. *Journal of Psychiatric Research, 47,* 391–400.

Idir, Y., Oudiette, D., & Arnulf, I. (2022). Sleepwalking, sleep terrors, sexsomnia and other disorders of arousal: The old and the new. *Journal of Sleep Research, 31,* e13596.

Ilchenko, E., Karavaeva, T., & Abritalin, E. (2021). Dynamics of clinical and psychological indicators of patients with anxiety neurotic disorders in the treatment of short-term individual analytic-cathartic therapy. *European Psychiatry, 64(S1),* S785–S786.

Iliakis, E. A., Ilagan, G. S., & Choi-Kain, L. W. (2021). Dropout rates from psychotherapy trials for borderline personality disorder: A meta-analysis. *Personality Disorders: Theory, Research, and Treatment, 12,* 193–206.

Imai, H., Ogawa, Y., Okumiya, K., & Matsubayashi, K. (2019). Amok: a mirror of time and people. A historical review of literature. *History of Psychiatry, 30,* 38–57.

Inkelis, S. M., Moore, E. M., Bischoff-Grethe, A., & Riley, E. P. (2020). Neurodevelopment in adolescents and adults with fetal alcohol spectrum disorders (FASD): A magnetic resonance region of interest analysis. *Brain Research, 1732,* 146654.

Iqubal, A., Iqubal, M. K., Khan, A., Ali, J., Baboota, S., & Haque, S. E. (2020). Gene therapy, a novel therapeutic tool for neurological disorders: Current progress, challenges and future prospective. *Current Gene Therapy, 20,* 184–194.

Irazoki, E., Contreras-Somoza, L. M., Toribio-Guzmán, J. M., Jenaro-Río, C., Van der Roest, H., & Franco-Martín, M. A. (2020). Technologies for cognitive training and cognitive rehabilitation for people with mild cognitive impairment and dementia. A systematic review. *Frontiers in Psychology, 11,* 648.

Irwin, M. R., Carrillo, C., Sadeghi, N., Bjurstrom, M. F., Breen, E. C., & Olmstead, R. (2022). Prevention of incident and recurrent major depression in older adults with insomnia: A randomized clinical trial. *JAMA Psychiatry, 79,* 33–41.

Isham, L., Loe, B. S., Hicks, A., Wilson, N., Bird, J. C., Bentall, R. P., & Freeman, D. (2022). The meaning in grandiose delusions: Measure development and cohort studies in clinical psychosis and non-clinical general population groups in the UK and Ireland. *The Lancet Psychiatry, 9*, 792–803.

Isometsa, E., Sund, R., & Pirkola, S. (2014). Post-discharge studies of inpatients with bipolar disorder in Finland. *Bipolar Disorders, 16*, 867–874.

Ivey-Stephenson, A.Z., Crosby, A.E., Hoenig, J.M., Gyawali, S., Park-Lee, E., & Hedden, S.L. (2022). Suicidal thoughts and behaviors among adults aged ≥18 years—United States, 2015–2019. *Surveillance Summaries, 71*, 1–19.

Izon, E., Berry, K., Wearden, A., Carter, L. A., Law, H., & French, P. (2021). Investigating expressed emotion in individuals at-risk of developing psychosis and their families over 12 months. *Clinical Psychology & Psychotherapy, 28*, 1285–1296.

Jadhakhan, F., Lindner, O. C., Blakemore, A., & Guthrie, E. (2019). Prevalence of medically unexplained symptoms in adults who are high users of health care services: A systematic review and meta-analysis protocol. *BMJ Open, 9*, e027922.

Jafferany, M., Khalid, Z., McDonald, K. A., & Shelley, A. J. (2018). Psychological aspects of factitious disorder. *The Primary Care Companion for CNS Disorders, 20*, 27174.

James, T., Mukadam, N., Sommerlad, A., Pour, H. R., Knowles, M., Azocar, I., & Livingston, G. (2022). Protection against discrimination in national dementia guideline recommendations: A systematic review. *PLoS Medicine, 19*, e1003860.

Jannini, T. B., Lorenzo, G. D., Bianciardi, E., Niolu, C., Toscano, M., Ciocca, G., ... & Siracusano, A. (2022). Off-label uses of selective serotonin reuptake inhibitors (SSRIs). *Current Neuropharmacology, 20*, 693–712.

Janse, P. D., de Jong, K., Veerkamp, C., van Dijk, M. K., Hutschemaekers, G. J., & Verbraak, M. J. (2020). The effect of feedback-informed cognitive behavioral therapy on treatment outcome: A randomized controlled trial. *Journal of Consulting and Clinical Psychology, 88*, 818–828.

Jansson-Fröjmark, M., & Jacobson, K. (2021). Cognitive behavioural therapy for insomnia for patients with co-morbid generalized anxiety disorder: an open trial on clinical outcomes and putative mechanisms. *Behavioural and Cognitive Psychotherapy, 49*, 540–555.

Jelovac, A., Kolshus, E., & McLoughlin, D. M. (2021). Relapse following bitemporal and high-dose right unilateral electroconvulsive therapy for major depression. *Acta Psychiatrica Scandinavica, 144*, 218–229.

Jiang, X., Wang, X., Jia, L., Sun, T., Kang, J., Zhou, Y., ... & Tang, Y. (2021). Structural and functional alterations in untreated patients with major depressive disorder and bipolar disorder experiencing first depressive episode: A magnetic resonance imaging study combined with follow-up. *Journal of Affective Disorders, 279*, 324–333.

Jiotsa, B., Naccache, B., Duval, M., Rocher, B., & Grall-Bronnec, M. (2021). Social media use and body image disorders: Association between frequency of comparing one's own physical appearance to that of people being followed on social media and body dissatisfaction and drive for thinness. *International Journal of Environmental Research and Public Health, 18*, 2880.

Johannsen, M., Nissen, E. R., Lundorff, M., & O'Toole, M. S. (2022). Mediators of acceptance and mindfulness-based therapies for anxiety and depression: A systematic review and meta-analysis. *Clinical Psychology Review, 94*, 102156.

Jones, M., Jacobi, C., & Taylor, C.B. (2015). Internet assisted family therapy and prevention for anorexia nervosa. In K.L. Loeb, D. Le Grange, & J. Lock (Eds.), *Family therapy for adolescent eating and weight disorders* (pp. 384–401). New York: Routledge.

Jox, R. J. (2020). Living will versus will to live? How to navigate through complex decisions for persons with Dementia. *The American Journal of Bioethics, 20*, 85–87.

Joyal, C. C., & Carpentier, J. (2016). The prevalence of paraphilic interests and behaviors in the general population: A provincial survey. *Journal of Sex Research, 2016*, 1–11.

Joyal, C. C., Cossette, A., & Lapierre, V. (2015). What exactly is an unusual sexual fantasy? *Journal of Sexual Medicine, 12*, 328–340.

Jullien, S. (2021). Prevention of unintentional injuries in children under five years. *BMC Pediatrics, 21*, 1–11.

Junewicz, A., & Billick, S. B. (2020). Conduct disorder: Biology and developmental trajectories. *Psychiatric Quarterly, 91*, 77–90.

Jung, S. H., Jin, M. J., Lee, J. K., Kim, H. S., Ji, H. K., Kim, K. P., ... & Hong, H. G. (2020). Improving the quality of sexual history disclosure on sex offenders: Emphasis on a polygraph examination. *PLoS One, 15*, e0239046.

Jurcau, A., & Simion, A. (2020). Oxidative stress in the pathogenesis of Alzheimer's disease and cerebrovascular disease with therapeutic implications. *CNS & Neurological Disorders-Drug Targets, 19*, 94–108.

Justo-Henriques, S. I., Pérez-Sáez, E., & Alves Apóstolo, J. L. (2021). Multicentre randomised controlled trial about the effect of individual reminiscence therapy in older adults with neurocognitive disorders. *International Journal of Geriatric Psychiatry, 36*, 704–712.

Kaar, S. J., Natesan, S., Mccutcheon, R., & Howes, O. D. (2020). Antipsychotics: mechanisms underlying clinical response and side-effects and novel treatment approaches based on pathophysiology. *Neuropharmacology, 172*, 107704.

Kabir, M., Uddin, M., Zaman, S., Begum, Y., Ashraf, G. M., Bin-Jumah, M. N., ... & Abdel-Daim, M. M. (2021). Molecular mechanisms of metal toxicity in the pathogenesis of Alzheimer's disease. *Molecular Neurobiology, 58*, 1–20.

Kagan, C., Akhurst, J., Alfaro, J., Lawthom, R., Richards, M., & Zambrano, A. (2022). *The Routledge international handbook of community psychology:*

Kahn, R. E., Jackson, K., Keiser, K., Ambroziak, G., & Levenson, J. S. (2021). Adverse childhood experiences among sexual offenders: Associations with sexual recidivism risk and psychopathology. *Sexual Abuse, 33*, 839–866.

Kalra, G., Gill, S., & Tang, T. S. (2020). Depression and diabetes distress in South Asian adults living in low-and middle-income countries: A scoping review. *Canadian Journal of Diabetes, 44*, 521–529.

Kan, F. P., Raoofi, S., Rafiei, S., Khani, S., Hosseinifard, H., Tajik, F., ... & Ghashghaee, A. (2021). A systematic review of the prevalence of anxiety among the general population during the COVID-19 pandemic. *Journal of Affective Disorders, 293*, 391–398.

Kanarik, M., Grimm, O., Mota, N. R., Reif, A., & Harro, J. (2022). ADHD co-morbidities: A review of implication of gene× environment effects with dopamine-related genes. *Neuroscience & Biobehavioral Reviews, 139*, 104757.

Kang, T., Ding, X., Zhao, J., Li, X., Xie, R., Jiang, H., ... & Huo, X. (2022). Influence of improved behavioral inhibition on decreased cue-induced craving in heroin use disorder: A preliminary intermittent theta burst stimulation study. *Journal of Psychiatric Research, 152*, 375–383.

Kar, S. K., Menon, V., Arafat, S. Y., Singh, A., Das, A., Shankar, A., ... & Perera, S. (2021). Dhat syndrome: Systematic review of epidemiology, nosology, clinical features, and management strategies. *Asian Journal of Psychiatry, 65*, 102863.

Karasewich, T. A., & Kuhlmeier, V. A. (2020). Trait social anxiety as a conditional adaptation: A developmental and evolutionary framework. *Developmental Review, 55*, 100886.

Karpel, M.G., & Jerram, M.W. (2015). Levels of dissociation and nonsuicidal self-injury: A quartile risk model. *Journal of Trauma and Dissociation, 16*, 303–321.

Karth, M. D., Baugher, B. J., Pellechia, S. A., Huq, S. N., Warner, A. K., Karth, M. M., & Sachs, B. D. (2022). Brain serotonin deficiency and fluoxetine lead to sex-specific effects on binge-like food consumption in mice. *Psychopharmacology, 239*, 2975–2984.

Kate, M. A., Hopwood, T., & Jamieson, G. (2020). The prevalence of dissociative disorders and dissociative experiences in college populations: A meta-analysis of 98 studies. *Journal of Trauma & Dissociation, 21*, 16–61.

Keefe, J. R., Kim, T. T., DeRubeis, R. J., Streiner, D. L., Links, P. S., & McMain, S. F. (2021). Treatment selection in borderline personality disorder between dialectical behavior therapy and psychodynamic psychiatric management. *Psychological Medicine, 51*, 1829–1837.

Keel, P.K., & Forney, K.J. (2015). Prevalence and incidence of eating disorders in Western societies. In L. Smolak & M.P. Levine (Eds.), *The Wiley handbook of eating disorders Volume 1: Basic concepts and foundational research* (pp. 53–63). New York: Wiley.

Keen, E., Kangas, M., & Gilchrist, P. T. (2022). A systematic review evaluating metacognitive beliefs in health anxiety and somatic distress. *British Journal of Health Psychology, 27*, 1398–1422.

Kelly, J. F., Abry, A., Ferri, M., & Humphreys, K. (2020). Alcoholics anonymous and 12-step facilitation treatments for alcohol use disorder: A distillation of a 2020 Cochrane review for clinicians and policy makers. *Alcohol and Alcoholism, 55*, 641–651.

Keltner, D., Sauter, D., Tracy, J., & Cowen, A. (2019). Emotional expression: Advances in basic emotion theory. *Journal of Nonverbal Behavior, 43*, 133–160.

Kemp, K. C., Bathery, A. J., Barrantes-Vidal, N., & Kwapil, T. R. (2021). Positive, negative, and disorganized schizotypy predict differential patterns of interview-rated schizophrenia-spectrum symptoms and impairment. *Assessment, 28*, 141–152.

Kendler, K. S., Aggen, S. H., Knudsen, G. P., Røysamb, E., Neale, M. C., & Reichborn-Kjennerud, T. (2011). The structure of genetic and environmental risk factors for syndromal and subsyndromal common DSM-IV axis I and all axis II disorders. *American Journal of Psychiatry, 168*, 29–39.

Kendler, K. S., Myers, J., & Reichborn-Kjennerud, T. (2011). Borderline personality disorder traits and their relationship with dimensions of normative personality: A web-based cohort and twin study. *Acta Psychiatrica Scandinavica, 123*, 349–359.

Kennedy, H. L., Dinkler, L., Kennedy, M. A., Bulik, C. M., & Jordan, J. (2022). How genetic analysis may contribute to the understanding of avoidant/restrictive food intake disorder (ARFID). *Journal of Eating Disorders, 10*, 1–13.

Kennedy, R. S. (2020). A meta-analysis of the outcomes of bullying prevention programs on subtypes of traditional bullying victimization: Verbal, relational, and physical. *Aggression and Violent Behavior, 55*, 101485.

Kent, C., Cordier, R., Joosten, A., Wilkes-Gillan, S., Bundy, A., & Speyer, R. (2020). A systematic review and meta-analysis of interventions to improve play skills in children with Autism Spectrum Disorder. *Review Journal of Autism and Developmental Disorders, 7*, 91–118.

Kenwood, M. M., Kalin, N. H., & Barbas, H. (2022). The prefrontal cortex, pathological anxiety, and anxiety disorders. *Neuropsychopharmacology, 47*, 260–275.

Keramatian, K., Chakrabarty, T., Saraf, G., Pinto, J. V., & Yatham, L. N. (2021). Grey matter abnormalities in first-episode mania: A systematic review and meta-analysis of voxel-based morphometry studies. *Bipolar Disorders, 23*, 228–240.

Kern, A., Kramm, C., Witt, C. M., & Barth, J. (2020). The influence of personality traits on the placebo/nocebo response: A systematic review. Journal of *Psychosomatic Research, 128*, 109866.

Kerr, L. K. (2014). Depersonalization, overview. In T. Teo (Ed.), *Encyclopedia of critical psychology* (pp. 384–386). New York: Springer.

Keski-Rahkonen, A. (2021). Epidemiology of binge eating disorder: prevalence, course, comorbidity, and risk factors. *Current Opinion in Psychiatry, 34*, 525–531.

Kessler, R.C., Avenevoli, S., Costello, E.J., Georgiades, K., Green, J.G., Gruber, M.J., He, J., Koretz, D., McLaughlin, K.A., Petukhova, M., Sampson, N.A., Zaslavsky, A.M., & Merikangas, K.R. (2012). Prevalence, persistence, and sociodemographic correlates of *DSM-IV* disorders in the National Comorbidity Survey Replication Adolescent Supplement. *Archives of General Psychiatry, 69*, 372–380.

Kessler, R.C., Berglund, P., Demler, O., Jin, R., Merikangas, K.R., & Walters, E.E. (2005). Lifetime prevalence and age-of-onset distributions of *DSM-IV* disorders in the National Comorbidity Survey Replication. *Archives of General Psychiatry, 62*, 593–602.

Kessler, R.C., & Bromet, E.J. (2013). The epidemiology of depression across cultures. *Annual Review of Public Health, 34*, 119–138.

Kessler, R.C., Calabrese, J.R., Farley, P.A., Gruber, M.J., Jewell, M.A., Katon, W., Keck, P.E., Nierenberg, A.A., Sampson, N.A., Shear, M.K., Shillington, A.C., Stein, M.B., Thase, M.E., & Wittchen, H.-U. (2013). Composite International Diagnostic Interview screening scales for *DSM-IV* anxiety and mood disorders. *Psychological Medicine, 43*, 1625–1637.

Kessler, R.C., Chiu, W.T., Demler, O., & Walters, E.E. (2005). Prevalence, severity, and comorbidity of 12-month *DSM-IV* disorders in the National Comorbidity Survey Replication. *Archives of General Psychiatry, 62*, 617–627.

Kessler, R.C., de Jonge, P., Shahly, V., van Loo, H.M., Wang, P.S-E., & Wilcox, M.A. (2014). Epidemiology of depression. In I.H. Gotlib & C.L. Hammen (Eds.), *Handbook of depression* (3rd ed., pp. 7–24). New York: Guilford.

Ketcheson, L. R., Pitchford, E. A., & Wentz, C. F. (2021). The relationship between developmental coordination disorder and concurrent deficits in social communication and repetitive behaviors among children with autism spectrum disorder. *Autism Research, 14*, 804–816.

Keyes, C. L. M., Eisenberg, D., Perry, G. S., Dube, S. R., Kroenke, K., & Dhingra, S. S. (2012). The relationship of level of positive mental health with current mental disorders in predicting suicidal behavior and academic impairment in college students. *Journal of American College Health, 60*, 126–133.

Khosravi, A., Riazi, H., Simbar, M., & Montazeri, A. (2022). Effectiveness of Kegel exercise and lubricant gel for improving sexual function in menopausal women: A randomized trial. *European Journal of Obstetrics & Gynecology and Reproductive Biology, 274*, 106–112.

Kian, N., Samieefar, N., & Rezaei, N. (2022). Prenatal risk factors and genetic causes of ADHD in children. *World Journal of Pediatrics, 18*, 308–319.

Kieseppä, T., Mäntylä, R., Luoma, K., Rikandi, E., Jylhä, P., & Isometsä, E. (2022). White matter hyperintensities after five-year follow-up and a cross-sectional FA decrease in bipolar I and major depressive patients. *Neuropsychobiology, 81*, 39–50.

Kihlstrom, J. F. (2022). Consciousness, the unconscious, and the self. *Psychology of Consciousness: Theory, Research, and Practice, 9*, 78–92.

Kim, J. H., Son, Y. D., Kim, H. K., & Kim, J. H. (2021). Association between lack of insight and prefrontal serotonin transporter availability in antipsychotic-free patients with schizophrenia: A high-resolution PET study with [11C] DASB. *Neuropsychiatric Disease and Treatment, 17*, 3195–3203.

Kim, J. O., Lee, S. J., & Pyo, J. S. (2020). Effect of acetylcholinesterase inhibitors on post-stroke cognitive impairment and vascular dementia: A meta-analysis. *PLoS One, 15*, e0227820.

Kim, K. W., Woo, S. Y., Kim, S., Jang, H., Kim, Y., Cho, S. H., ... & Seo, S. W. (2020). Disease progression modeling of Alzheimer's disease according to education level. *Scientific Reports, 10*, 16808.

Kim, M., Kang, J., Lee, M., Han, J., Nam, G., Tak, E., ... & Lim, M. H. (2020). Minimalistic principles for designing small molecules with multiple reactivities against pathological factors in dementia. *Journal of the American Chemical Society, 142*, 8183–8193.

King, C.A., Eisenberg, D., Zheng, K., Czyz, E., Kramer, A., Horwitz, A., & Chermack, S. (2015). Online suicide risk screening and intervention with college students: A pilot randomized controlled trial. *Journal of Consulting and Clinical Psychology, 83*, 630–636.

King, R. M., Grenyer, B. F., Gurtman, C. G., & Younan, R. (2020). A clinician's quick guide to evidence-based approaches: Narcissistic personality disorder. *Clinical Psychologist, 24*, 91–95.

Kirchner, S. K., Roeh, A., Nolden, J., & Hasan, A. (2018). Diagnosis and treatment of schizotypal personality disorder: Evidence from a systematic review. *NPJ Schizophrenia, 4*, 1–18.

Kirsch, A. C., Huebner, A. R., Mehta, S. Q., Howie, F. R., Weaver, A. L., Myers, S. M., ... & Katusic, S. K. (2020). Association of comorbid mood and anxiety disorders with autism spectrum disorder. *JAMA Pediatrics, 174*, 63–70.

Kishi, T., Ikuta, T., Matsuda, Y., Sakuma, K., Okuya, M., Mishima, K., & Iwata, N. (2021). Mood stabilizers and/or antipsychotics for bipolar disorder in the maintenance phase: A systematic review and network meta-analysis of randomized controlled trials. *Molecular Psychiatry, 26*, 4146–4157.

Kivlighan III, D. M., Aloe, A. M., Adams, M. C., Garrison, Y. L., Obrecht, A., Ho, Y. C. S., ... & Deng, K. (2020). Does the group in group psychotherapy matter? A meta-analysis of the intraclass correlation coefficient in group treatment research. *Journal of Consulting and Clinical Psychology, 88*, 322–337.

Kjøbli, J., Melendez-Torres, G. J., Gardner, F., Backhaus, S., Linnerud, S., & Leijten, P. (2022). Research review: Effects of parenting programs for children's conduct problems on children's emotional problems–a network meta-analysis. *Journal of Child Psychology and Psychiatry*.

Klanecky, A., McChargue, D.E., & Bruggeman, L. (2012). Desire to dissociate: Implications for problematic drinking in college students with childhood or adolescent sexual abuse exposure. *American Journal on Addictions, 21*, 250–256.

Klein, D.N. (2016). Can course help reduce the heterogeneity of depressive disorders? In E.J. Bromet (Eds.), *Long-term outcomes in psychopathology research: Rethinking the scientific agenda* (pp. 32–52). New York: Oxford.

Kluft, R.P. (2012). Hypnosis in the treatment of dissociative identity disorder and allied states: An overview and case study. *South African Journal of Psychology, 42*, 146–155.

Knight, M. J., & Baune, B. T. (2019). Social cognitive abilities predict psychosocial dysfunction in major depressive disorder. *Depression and Anxiety, 36*, 54–62.

Knudsen, C. B., Hemager, N., Greve, A. N., Lambek, R., Andreassen, A. K., Veddum, L., ... & Bliksted, V. F. (2022). Neurocognitive development in children at familial high risk of schizophrenia or bipolar disorder. *JAMA Psychiatry, 79*, 589–599.

Kobylarz, A. M., DeBar, R. M., Reeve, K. F., & Meyer, L. S. (2020). Evaluating backward chaining methods on vocational tasks by adults with developmental disabilities. *Behavioral Interventions, 35*, 263–280.

Koenders, M. A., Dodd, A. L., Karl, A., Green, M. J., Elzinga, B. M., & Wright, K. (2020). Understanding bipolar disorder within a biopsychosocial emotion dysregulation framework. *Journal of Affective Disorders Reports, 2*, 100031.

Kohlhoff, J., Morgan, S., Briggs, N., Egan, R., & Niec, L. (2021). Parent–Child interaction therapy with toddlers: A community-based randomized controlled trial with children aged 14–24 months. *Journal of Clinical Child & Adolescent Psychology, 50*, 411–426.

Koirala, B., Hansen, B. R., Hosie, A., Budhathoki, C., Seal, S., Beaman, A., & Davidson, P. M. (2020). Delirium point prevalence studies in inpatient settings: A systematic review and meta-analysis. *Journal of Clinical Nursing, 29*, 2083–2092.

Kolar, D. R., Meule, A., Naab, S., & Voderholzer, U. (2022). Early within-person weight gain and variability during inpatient treatment for anorexia nervosa: Age-dependent effects on treatment outcome. *European Eating Disorders Review, 30*, 328–340.

Kolla, N.J., & Brodie, J.D. (2012). Application of neuroimaging in relationship to competence to stand trial and insanity. In J.R. Simpson (Ed.), *Neuroimaging in forensic psychiatry: From the clinic to the courtroom* (pp. 147–162). New York: Wiley.

Komasi, S., Rezaei, F., Hemmati, A., Rahmani, K., Amianto, F., & Miettunen, J. (2022). Comprehensive meta-analysis of associations between temperament and character traits in Cloninger's psychobiological theory and mental disorders. *Journal of International Medical Research, 50*, 03000605211070766.

Komici, K., Guerra, G., Addona, F., & Fantini, C. (2022). Delirium in nursing home residents: A narrative review. *Healthcare, 10*, 1544.

König, H., König, H. H., & Konnopka, A. (2020). The excess costs of depression: a systematic review and meta-analysis. *Epidemiology and Psychiatric Sciences*, 29.

Konrad, K., Kohls, G., Baumann, S., Bernhard, A., Martinelli, A., Ackermann, K., ... & Freitag, C. M. (2022). Sex differences in psychiatric comorbidity and clinical presentation in youths with conduct disorder. *Journal of Child Psychology and Psychiatry, 63*, 218–228.

Korecki, J. R., Schwebel, F. J., Votaw, V. R., & Witkiewitz, K. (2020). Mindfulness-based programs for substance use disorders: A systematic review of manualized treatments. *Substance Abuse Treatment, Prevention, and Policy, 15*, 1–37.

Koriath, C. A., Kenny, J., Ryan, N. S., Rohrer, J. D., Schott, J. M., Houlden, H., ... & Mead, S. (2021). Genetic testing in dementia—Utility and clinical strategies. *Nature Reviews Neurology, 17*, 23–36.

Kornhuber, J., & Gulbins, E. (2021). New Molecular targets for antidepressant drugs. *Pharmaceuticals, 14*, 894.

Kotb, M. A., Kamal, A. M., Al-Malki, D., Abd El Fatah, A. S., & Ahmed, Y. M. (2020). Cognitive performance in patients with chronic tension-type headache and its relation to neuroendocrine hormones. *Egyptian Journal of Neurology, Psychiatry and Neurosurgery, 56*, 1–8.

Kotilahti, E., West, M., Isomaa, R., Karhunen, L., Rocks, T., & Ruusunen, A. (2020). Treatment interventions for severe and enduring eating disorders: systematic review. *International Journal of Eating Disorders, 53*, 1280–1302.

Kotowicz, K., Frydecka, D., Gawęda, Ł., Prochwicz, K., Kłosowska, J., Rymaszewska, J., ... & Misiak, B. (2021). Effects of traumatic life events, cognitive biases and variation in dopaminergic genes on psychosis proneness. *Early Intervention in Psychiatry, 15*, 248–255.

Kovacs, M. (2010). *CDI 2: Children's Depression Inventory 2nd edition*. North Tonawanda, NY: Multi-Health Systems.

Kozlowska, K., McClure, G., Chudleigh, C., Maguire, A. M., Gessler, D., Scher, S., & Ambler, G. R. (2021). Australian children and adolescents with gender dysphoria: Clinical presentations and challenges experienced by a multidisciplinary team and gender service. *Human Systems, 1*, 70–95.

Kraguljac, N. V., McDonald, W. M., Widge, A. S., Rodriguez, C. I., Tohen, M., & Nemeroff, C. B. (2021). Neuroimaging biomarkers in schizophrenia. *American Journal of Psychiatry, 178*, 509–521.

Kraus, C., Kadriu, B., Lanzenberger, R., Zarate Jr, C. A., & Kasper, S. (2019). Prognosis and improved outcomes in major depression: A review. *Translational Psychiatry, 9*, 1–17.

Krause-Utz, A., Frost, R., Chatzaki, E., Winter, D., Schmahl, C., & Elzinga, B. M. (2021). Dissociation in borderline personality disorder: recent experimental, neurobiological studies, and implications for future research and treatment. *Current Psychiatry Reports, 23*, 1–17.

Krebs, M. D., Themudo, G. E., Benros, M. E., Mors, O., Børglum, A. D., Hougaard, D., ... & Thompson, W. K. (2021). Associations between patterns in comorbid diagnostic trajectories of individuals with schizophrenia and etiological factors. *Nature Communications, 12*, 1–12.

Kreisl, W. C., & Reitz, C. (2018). Diagnosis and epidemiology of dementia. In D. S. Charney, J. D. Buxbaum, P. Sklar, & E. J. Nestler (Eds.), *Charney & Nestler's neurobiology of mental illness* (5th ed.) (pp. 673–684). New York: Oxford.

Krueger, R. F., & Hobbs, K. A. (2020). An overview of the DSM-5 alternative model of personality disorders. *Psychopathology, 53*, 126–132.

Kruithof, P., & Ban, S. (2021). A brief overview of fetal alcohol syndrome for health professionals. *British Journal of Nursing, 30*, 890–893.

Kuhl, U., Neef, N. E., Kraft, I., Schaadt, G., Dörr, L., Brauer, J., ... & Skeide, M. A. (2020). The emergence of dyslexia in the developing brain. *Neuroimage, 211*, 116633.

Kumar, S., Metz, D. C., Ellenberg, S., Kaplan, D. E., & Goldberg, D. S. (2020). Risk factors and incidence of gastric cancer after detection of Helicobacter pylori infection: A large cohort study. *Gastroenterology, 158*, 527–536.

Kunst, H., Lobbestael, J., Candel, I., & Batink, T. (2020). Early maladaptive schemas and their relation to personality disorders: A correlational examination in a clinical population. *Clinical Psychology & Psychotherapy, 27*, 837–846.

Kwok, S. C., Xu, X., Duan, W., Wang, X., Tang, Y., Allé, M. C., & Berna, F. (2021). Autobiographical and episodic memory deficits in schizophrenia: A narrative review and proposed agenda for research. *Clinical Psychology Review, 83*, 101956.

Kyriakou, A., Nicolaides, N. C., & Skordis, N. (2020). Current approach to the clinical care of adolescents with gender dysphoria. *Acta Bio Medica: Atenei Parmensis, 91*, 165–175.

LaFreniere, L. S., & Newman, M. G. (2020). Exposing worry's deceit: Percentage of untrue worries in generalized anxiety disorder treatment. *Behavior Therapy, 51*, 413–423.

Laksmidewi, A. A. A., & Soejitno, A. (2021). Endocannabinoid and dopaminergic system: The pas de deux underlying human motivation and behaviors. *Journal of Neural Transmission, 128*, 615–630.

Lamb, H. R., & Weinberger, L. E. (2020). Deinstitutionalization and other factors in the criminalization of persons with serious mental illness and how it is being addressed. *CNS Spectrums, 25*, 173–180.

Langenbahn, D., Matsuzawa, Y., Lee, Y. S. C., Fraser, F., Penzien, D. B., Simon, N. M., ... & Minen, M. T. (2021). Underuse of behavioral treatments for headache: a narrative review examining societal and cultural factors. *Journal of General Internal Medicine, 36*, 3103–3112.

Längle, A., & Klaassen, D. (2021). Phenomenology and depth in existential psychotherapy. *Journal of Humanistic Psychology, 61*, 745–756.

Långström, N., Babchishin, K. M., Fazel, S., Lichtenstein, P., & Frisell, T. (2015). Sexual offending runs in families: A 37-year nationwide study. *International Journal of Epidemiology, 44*, 713–720.

Lanius, R. A., Boyd, J. E., McKinnon, M. C., Nicholson, A. A., Frewen, P., Vermetten, E., ... & Spiegel, D. (2018). A review of the neurobiological basis of trauma-related dissociation and its relation to cannabinoid- and opioid-mediated stress response: A transdiagnostic, translational approach. *Current Psychiatry Reports, 20*, 1–14.

Lapidus, R. C., Puhl, M., Kuplicki, R., Stewart, J. L., Paulus, M. P., Rhudy, J. L., ... & Tulsa 1000 Investigators. (2020). Heightened affective response to perturbation of respiratory but not pain signals in eating, mood, and anxiety disorders. *PloS One, 15*, e0235346.

Lappan, S. N., Brown, A. W., & Hendricks, P. S. (2020). Dropout rates of in-person psychosocial substance use disorder treatments: A systematic review and meta-analysis. *Addiction, 115*, 201–217.

Large, M. M. (2022). The role of prediction in suicide prevention. *Dialogues in Clinical Neuroscience, 20*, 197–205.

Lasalvia, A., Zoppei, S., Van Bortel, T., Bonetto, C., Cristofalo, D., Wahlbeck, K., Bacle, S.V., Van Audenhove, C., van Weeghel, J., Reneses, B., Germanavicius, A., Economou, M., Lanfredi, M., Ando,S., Sartorius, N., Lopez-Ibor, J.J., & Thornicroft, G. (2013). Global pattern of experienced and anticipated discrimination reported by people with major depressive disorder: A cross-sectional survey. *Lancet, 381*, 55–62.

Latella, D., Maggio, M. G., Andaloro, A., Marchese, D., Manuli, A., & Calabrò, R. S. (2021). Hypersexuality in neurological diseases: Do we see only the tip of the iceberg? *Journal of Integrative Neuroscience, 20*, 477–487.

Law, C. K., Lam, F. M., Chung, R. C., & Pang, M. Y. (2020). Physical exercise attenuates cognitive decline and reduces behavioural problems in people with mild cognitive impairment and dementia: A systematic review. *Journal of Physiotherapy, 66*, 9–18.

Lawless, N. J., Karantzas, G. C., Mullins, E. R., & McCabe, M. P. (2022). Does it matter who you feel sexually aroused by? Associations between sexual arousal, relationship quality, and sexual satisfaction. *Sexual Medicine, 10*, 100523.

Lawrence, R. E., First, M. B., & Lieberman, J.A. (2015). Schizophrenia and other psychoses. In A. Tasman, J. Kay, J.A. Lieberman, M. B. First, & M. B. Riba (Eds.), *Psychiatry* (4th ed., pp. 791–857). New York: Wiley.

Le, T. T., Di Vincenzo, J. D., Teopiz, K. M., Lee, Y., Cha, D. S., Lui, L. M., ... & McIntyre, R. S. (2021). Ketamine for psychotic depression: An overview of the glutamatergic system and ketamine's mechanisms associated with antidepressant and psychotomimetic effects. *Psychiatry Research, 306*, 114231.

LeCloux, M. C., Aguinaldo, L. D., Lanzillo, E. C., & Horowitz, L. M. (2022). Provider opinions of the acceptability of Ask Suicide-Screening Questions (ASQ) Tool and the ASQ Brief Suicide Safety Assessment (BSSA) for universal suicide risk screening in community healthcare: Potential barriers and necessary elements for future implementation. *Journal of Behavioral Health Services & Research, 49*, 346-363.

Lee, D. S., Gross, E., Hotz, A., & Rastogi, D. (2020). Comparison of severity of asthma hospitalization between African American and Hispanic children in the Bronx. *Journal of Asthma, 57*, 736–742.

Lee, E. B., Barney, J. L., Twohig, M. P., Lensegrav-Benson, T., & Quakenbush, B. (2020). Obsessive compulsive disorder and thought action fusion: Relationships with eating disorder outcomes. *Eating Behaviors, 37*, 101386.

Lee, G. T., Tang, Y., & Xu, S. (2022). Improving eye contact and gaze following in children with autism spectrum disorder: Systematic withdrawal of stimulus prompts and tangible reinforcers. *Behavior Modification*, 01454455211073741.

Lee, J., Salloum, R. G., Lindstrom, K., & McHugh, R. K. (2021). Benzodiazepine misuse and cigarette smoking status in US adults: Results from the National Survey on Drug Use and Health, 2015–2018. *Addictive Behaviors, 123*, 107058.

Lee, J. K., Andrews, D. S., Ozonoff, S., Solomon, M., Rogers, S., Amaral, D. G., & Nordahl, C. W. (2021). Longitudinal evaluation of cerebral growth across childhood in boys and girls with autism spectrum disorder. *Biological Psychiatry, 90*, 286–294.

Lee, S., Creed, F.H., Ma, Y-L., & Leung, C.M.C. (2015). Somatic symptom burden and health anxiety in the population and their correlates. *Journal of Psychosomatic Research, 78*, 71–76.

Lee, S. C., DelPozo-Banos, M., Lloyd, K., Jones, I., Walters, J. T., Owen, M. J., ... & John, A. (2020). Area deprivation, urbanicity, severe mental illness and social drift—A population-based linkage study using routinely collected primary and secondary care data. *Schizophrenia Research, 220*, 130–140.

Lee, Y. T., Huang, Y. H., Tsai, F. J., Liu, H. C., Sun, F. J., Tsai, Y. J., & Liu, S. I. (2021). Prevalence and psychosocial risk factors associated with current cigarette smoking and hazardous alcohol drinking among adolescents in Taiwan. *Journal of the Formosan Medical Association, 120*, 265–274.

Legge, S. E., Santoro, M. L., Periyasamy, S., Okewole, A., Arsalan, A., & Kowalec, K. (2021). Genetic architecture of schizophrenia: A review of major advancements. *Psychological Medicine, 51*, 2168–2177.

Leiderman, L. M. (2020). Psychodynamic group therapy with Hispanic migrants: Interpersonal, relational constructs in treating complex trauma, dissociation, and enactments. *International Journal of Group Psychotherapy, 70*, 162–182.

Lemmens, L. H. J. M., Arntz, A., Peeters, F. P. M. L., Hollon, S. D., Roefs, A., & Huibers, M. J. H. (2015). Clinical effectiveness of cognitive therapy v. interpersonal psychotherapy for depression: Results of a randomized controlled trial. *Psychological Medicine, 45*, 2095–2110.

Lemmens, L. H., van Bronswijk, S. C., Peeters, F. P., Arntz, A., Roefs, A., Hollon, S. D., ... & Huibers, M. J. (2020). Interpersonal psychotherapy versus cognitive therapy for depression: How they work, how long, and for whom—key findings from an RCT. *American Journal of Psychotherapy, 73*, 8–14.

LeMoult, J., Humphreys, K. L., Tracy, A., Hoffmeister, J. A., Ip, E., & Gotlib, I. H. (2020). Meta-analysis: exposure to early life stress and risk for depression in childhood and adolescence. *Journal of the American Academy of Child & Adolescent Psychiatry, 59*, 842–855.

Lemvigh, C. K., Brouwer, R. M., Pantelis, C., Jensen, M. H., Hilker, R. W., Legind, C. S., ... & Fagerlund, B. (2022). Heritability of specific cognitive functions and associations with schizophrenia spectrum disorders using CANTAB: a nation-wide twin study. *Psychological Medicine, 52*, 1101–1114.

Lenze, E. J., Rodebaugh, T. L., & Nicol, G. E. (2020). A framework for advancing precision medicine in clinical trials for mental disorders. *JAMA Psychiatry, 77*, 663–664.

Levchenko, A., Kanapin, A., Samsonova, A., Fedorenko, O. Y., Kornetova, E. G., Nurgaliev, T., ... & Ivanova, S. A. (2021). A genome-wide association study identifies a gene network associated with paranoid schizophrenia and antipsychotics-induced tardive dyskinesia. *Progress in Neuro-Psychopharmacology and Biological Psychiatry, 105*, 110134.

Levinson, D.F., & Nichols, W.E. (2018). Genetics of depression. In D.S. Charney, J.D. Buxbaum, P. Sklar, & E.J. Nestler (Eds.), *Charney and Nestler's neurobiology of mental illness* (5th ed.) (pp. 301–314). New York: Oxford.

Levitan, R. D. (2022). The chronobiology and neurobiology of winter seasonal affective disorder. *Dialogues in Clinical Neuroscience.*

Li, F., Luo, S., Mu, W., Li, Y., Ye, L., Zheng, X., ... & Chen, X. (2021). Effects of sources of social support and resilience on the mental health of different age groups during the COVID-19 pandemic. *BMC Psychiatry, 21*, 1–14.

Li, F., Qin, W., Zhu, M., & Jia, J. (2021). Model-based projection of dementia prevalence in China and worldwide: 2020–2050. *Journal of Alzheimer's Disease, 82*, 1823–1831.

Li, L., Cavuoto, M., Biddiscombe, K., & Pike, K. E. (2020). Diabetes mellitus increases risk of incident dementia in APOE ε4 carriers: A meta-analysis. *Journal of Alzheimer's Disease, 74*, 1295–1308.

Li, M., Gong, J., Gao, L., Zou, T., Kang, J., & Xu, H. (2022). Advanced human developmental toxicity and teratogenicity assessment using human organoid models. *Ecotoxicology and Environmental Safety, 235*, 113429.

Li, M., Lyu, J. H., Zhang, Y., Gao, M. L., Li, R., Mao, P. X., ... & Ma, X. (2020). Efficacy of group reminiscence therapy on cognition, depression, neuropsychiatric symptoms, and activities of daily living for patients with Alzheimer disease. *Journal of Geriatric Psychiatry and Neurology, 33*, 272–281.

Li, W., Dorstyn, D. S., & Jarmon, E. (2020). Identifying suicide risk among college students: A systematic review. *Death Studies, 44*, 450–458.

Li, W., Kutas, M., Gray, J. A., Hagerman, R. H., & Olichney, J. M. (2020). The role of glutamate in language and language disorders-evidence from ERP and pharmacologic studies. *Neuroscience & Biobehavioral Reviews, 119*, 217–241.

Li, X., Zhang, K., He, X., Zhou, J., Jin, C., Shen, L., ... & Zhang, H. (2021). Structural, functional, and molecular imaging of autism spectrum disorder. *Neuroscience Bulletin, 37*, 1051–1071.

Li, Z. F., Chometton, S., Guèvremont, G., Timofeeva, E., & Timofeev, I. (2021). Compulsive eating in a rat model of binge eating disorder under conditionedfear and exploration of neural mechanisms with c-fos mRNA Expression. *Frontiers in Neuroscience, 15*, 777572.

Liang, C. S., Li, D. J., Yang, F. C., Tseng, P. T., Carvalho, A. F., Stubbs, B., ... & Chu, C. S. (2021). Mortality rates in Alzheimer's disease and non-Alzheimer's dementias: A systematic review and meta-analysis. *The Lancet Healthy Longevity, 2*, e479–e488.

Lichtman, J.H., Froelicher, E.S., Blumenthal, J.A., Carney, R.M., Doering, L.V., Frasure-Smith, N., Freedland, K.E., Jaffe, A.S., Leifheit-Limson, E.C., Sheps, D.S., Vaccarino, V., & Wulsin, L. (2014). Depression as a risk factor for poor prognosis among patients with acute coronary syndrome: Systematic review and recommendations. *Circulation, 129*, 1350–1369.

Lightman, S. L., Birnie, M. T., & Conway-Campbell, B. L. (2020). Dynamics of ACTH and cortisol secretion and implications for disease. *Endocrine Reviews, 41*, bnaa002.

Lillard, C. M., Cooper-Lehki, C., Fremouw, W. J., & DiSciullo, V. A. (2020). Differences in psychosexual development among child, peer, and mixed juvenile sex offenders. *Journal of Forensic Sciences, 65*, 526–534.

Lim, L. F., Solmi, M., & Cortese, S. (2021). Association between anxiety and hypertension in adults: A systematic review and meta-analysis. *Neuroscience & Biobehavioral Reviews, 131*, 96–119.

Limongi, F., Siviero, P., Bozanic, A., Noale, M., Veronese, N., & Maggi, S. (2020). The effect of adherence to the Mediterranean diet on late-life cognitive disorders: a systematic review. *Journal of the American Medical Directors Association, 21*, 1402–1409.

Lin, H. C., Yang, Y., Elliott, L., & Green, E. (2020). Individual differences in attachment anxiety shape the association between adverse childhood experiences and adult somatic symptoms. *Child Abuse & Neglect, 101*, 104325.

Lin, L. Y., Wang, K., Kishimoto, T., Rodriguez, M., Qian, M., Yang, Y., ... & Tian, C. (2020). An internet-based intervention for individuals with social anxiety and different levels of Taijin Kyofusho in China. *Journal of Cross-Cultural Psychology, 51*, 387–402.

Lin, S., Yu, C., Chen, J., Sheng, J., Hu, Y., Zhong, L., & Zhang, Y. (2022). Deviant peer affiliation mediates the influence of parental psychological control on adolescent aggressive behavior: The moderating effect of self-esteem. *Personality and Individual Differences, 186*, 111330.

Lindsey, J. M., Shelton, K. M., Beito, A. H., & Lapid, M. I. (2021). Palliative care: Critical concepts for the geropsychiatrist. *Focus, 19*, 311–319.

Linehan, M. M. (2020). *Dialectical behavior therapy in clinical practice*. New York: Guilford.

Linehan, M. M., & Kehrer, C. A. (1993). Borderline personality disorder. In D. H. Barlow (Ed.), *Clinical handbook of psychological disorders: A step-by-step treatment manual* (2nd ed., pp. 396–441). New York: Guilford.

Lipkin, P. H., Macias, M. M., Norwood, K. W., Brei, T. J., Davidson, L. F., Davis, B. E., ... & Voigt, R. G. (2020). Promoting optimal development: identifying infants and young children with developmental disorders through developmental surveillance and screening. *Pediatrics, 145*, e20193449.

Lipscomb, A., & Arkadie, N. (2020). It takes a community: Preventing child maltreatment of toddler-aged children in the US from an ecological systems perspective. *Journal of Social Work Education and Practice, 4*, 34–42.

Little, B., Sud, N., Nobile, Z., & Bhattacharya, D. (2021). Teratogenic effects of maternal drug abuse on developing brain and underlying neurotransmitter mechanisms. *Neurotoxicology, 86*, 172–179.

Liu, A., Zhang, E., Leroux, E. J., & Benassi, P. (2022). Sexual sadism disorder and coercive paraphilic disorder: A scoping review. *The Journal of Sexual Medicine, 19*, 496–506.

Liu, J., Chua, J. J. X., Chong, S. A., Subramaniam, M., & Mahendran, R. (2020). The impact of emotion dysregulation on positive and negative symptoms in schizophrenia spectrum disorders: A systematic review. *Journal of Clinical Psychology, 76*, 612–624.

Liu, J., Gill, N. S., Teodorczuk, A., Li, Z. J., & Sun, J. (2019). The efficacy of cognitive behavioural therapy in somatoform disorders and medically unexplained physical symptoms: A meta-analysis of randomized controlled trials. *Journal of Affective Disorders, 245*, 98–112.

Liu, S., Kang, W. J., Abrimian, A., Xu, J., Cartegni, L., Majumdar, S., ... & Pan, Y. X. (2021). Alternative pre-mRNA splicing of the mu opioid receptor gene, OPRM1: Insight into complex mu opioid actions. *Biomolecules, 11*, 1525.

Liu, S., Wang, S., Zhang, M., Xu, Y., Shao, Z., Chen, L., ... & Yuan, K. (2021). Brain responses to drug cues predict craving changes in abstinent heroin users: A preliminary study. *Neuroimage, 237*, 118169.

Liu, X., Wang, S., & Wang, G. (2021). Prevalence and risk factors of postpartum depression in women: A systematic review and meta-analysis. *Journal of Clinical Nursing, 31*, 2665–2677.

Liu, X. Q., Guo, Y. X., Zhang, W. J., & Gao, W. J. (2022). Influencing factors, prediction and prevention of depression in college students: A literature review. *World Journal of Psychiatry, 12*, 860–873.

Liu, Z., Palaniyappan, L., Wu, X., Zhang, K., Du, J., Zhao, Q., ... & Feng, J. (2021). Resolving heterogeneity in schizophrenia through a novel systems approach to brain structure: individualized structural covariance network analysis. *Molecular Psychiatry, 26*, 7719–7731.

Livesley, W.J., Dimaggio, G., & Clarkin, J.F. (Eds.). (2016). *Integrated treatment for personality disorder: A modular approach*. New York: Guilford.

Lodder, P. (2020). A re-evaluation of the Type D personality effect. *Personality and Individual Differences, 167*, 110254.

Long, J. S., & Ebert, R. S. (2022). Intellectual disability and the criminal justice system. In H. V. Hall & J. G. Poirier (Eds.), *Forensic psychology and neuropsychology for criminal and civil cases* (2nd ed.) (pp. 333–364). Boca Raton, FL: CRC Press.

Longobardi, C., Badenes-Ribera, L., & Fabris, M. A. (2020). Emotional intelligence in child molesters. *Journal of Forensic Psychology Research and Practice, 20*, 377–394.

López-Silva, P., Harrow, M., Jobe, T. H., Tufano, M., Harrow, H., & Rosen, C. (2022). 'Are these my thoughts?': A 20-year prospective study of thought insertion, thought withdrawal, thought broadcasting, and their relationship to auditory verbal hallucinations. *Schizophrenia Research*.

Lorah, E. R., Holyfield, C., Miller, J., Griffen, B., & Lindbloom, C. (2021). A systematic review of research comparing mobile technology speech-generating devices to other AAC modes with individuals with autism spectrum disorder. *Journal of Developmental and Physical Disabilities, 34*, 187–210.

Lorentzen, R., Kjaer, J. N., Østergaard, S. D., & Madsen, M. M. (2020). Thyroid hormone treatment in the management of treatment-resistant unipolar depression: A systematic review and meta-analysis. *Acta Psychiatrica Scandinavica, 141*, 316–326.

Lorusso, L., & Winther, R. G. (Eds.) (2022). *Remapping race in a global context*. New York: Routledge.

Loveless, J. (2014). *Criminal law: Text, cases, and materials* (4th ed.). New York: Oxford.

Löwe, B., Levenson, J., Depping, M., Hüsing, P., Kohlmann, S., Lehmann, M., ... & Weigel, A. (2021). Somatic symptom disorder: A scoping review on the empirical evidence of a new diagnosis. *Psychological Medicine*, 1–17.

Lowe, S. R., Ratanatharathorn, A., Lai, B. S., van der Mei, W., Barbano, A. C., Bryant, R. A., ... & Kessler, R. C. (2021). Posttraumatic stress disorder symptom trajectories within the first year following emergency department admissions: Pooled results from the International Consortium to predict PTSD. *Psychological Medicine, 51*, 1129–1139.

Luca, G., Parrettini, S., Sansone, A., Calafiore, R., & Jannini, E. A. (2021). The Inferto-Sex Syndrome (ISS): sexual dysfunction in fertility care setting and assisted reproduction. *Journal of Endocrinological Investigation, 44*, 2071–2102.

Luetke, M., Giroux, S., Herbenick, D., Ludema, C., & Rosenberg, M. (2021). High prevalence of sexual assault victimization experiences among university fraternity men. *Journal of Interpersonal Violence, 36*, 11755–11767.

Luiselli, J. K., Bird, F., & Wachtel, L. E. (2021). Electroconvulsive therapy (ECT) for autism spectrum disorder associated with catatonia and self-injury: a clinical review. *Advances in Neurodevelopmental Disorders, 5*, 117–125.

Luo, Q., & Sahakian, B. J. (2022). Brain sex differences: The androgynous brain is advantageous for mental health and well-being. *Neuropsychopharmacology, 47*, 407–408.

Luoma, J. B., Kulesza, M., Hayes, S. C., Kohlenberg, B., & Larimer, M. (2014). Stigma predicts residential treatment length for substance use disorder. *American Journal of Drug and Alcohol Abuse, 40*, 206–212.

Lundberg, A., Petersen-Brown, S., Houlihan, D. D., Panahon, C., & Wagner, D. (2022). Applying peer tutoring to spelling with elementary-aged students. *Journal of Applied School Psychology*, 1–23.

Luxton, D.D., June, J.D., & Comtois, K.A. (2013). Can postdischarge follow-up contacts prevent suicide and suicidal behavior? A review of the evidence. *Crisis, 34*, 32–41.

Lynham, A. J., Cleaver, S. L., Jones, I. R., & Walters, J. T. (2022). A meta-analysis comparing cognitive function across the mood/psychosis diagnostic spectrum. *Psychological Medicine, 52*, 323–331.

Lynn, S. J., Kirsch, I., Terhune, D. B., & Green, J. P. (2020). Myths and misconceptions about hypnosis and suggestion: Separating fact and fiction. *Applied Cognitive Psychology, 34*, 1253–1264.

Lynn, S. J., Maxwell, R., Merckelbach, H., Lilienfeld, S. O., van Heugten-van der Kloet, D., & Miskovic, V. (2019). Dissociation and its disorders: Competing models, future directions, and a way forward. *Clinical Psychology Review, 73*, 101755.

Lynn, S. J., Polizzi, C., Merckelbach, H., Chiu, C. D., Maxwell, R., van Heugten, D., & Lilienfeld, S. O. (2022). Dissociation and dissociative disorders reconsidered: Beyond sociocognitive and trauma models toward a transtheoretical framework. *Annual Review of Clinical Psychology, 18*, 259–289.

Lysaker, P. H., Wiesepape, C. N., Hamm, J. A., & Leonhardt, B. L. (2022). Recovery from psychosis: Emerging definitions, research and select clinical application. In B. Carpiniello, A. Vita, & C. Mencacci, (Eds.), *Recovery and major mental disorders* (pp. 99–116). Cham: Springer.

Lyssenko, L., Schmahl, C., Bockhacker, L., Vonderlin, R., Bohus, M., & Kleindienst, N. (2018). Dissociation in psychiatric disorders: A meta-analysis of studies using the dissociative experiences scale. *American Journal of Psychiatry, 175*, 37–46.

Lyu, W., & Wehby, G. L. (2020). Community use of face masks and COVID-19: Evidence from a natural experiment of state mandates in the US: Study examines impact on COVID-19 growth rates associated with state government mandates requiring face mask use in public. *Health Affairs, 39*, 1419–1425.

Ma, C. F., Chan, S. K. W., Chung, Y. L., Ng, S. M., Hui, C. L. M., Suen, Y. N., & Chen, E. Y. H. (2021). The predictive power of expressed emotion and its components in relapse of schizophrenia: A meta-analysis and meta-regression. *Psychological Medicine, 51*, 365–375.

Ma, H. X., Zhao, J., Lin, I. A., Zhang, X. J., Li, Z. J., Wang, C. Y., ... & Verma, S. (2022). Differential contributions between objective and subjective psychosis-like experiences to suicidal ideation in college students. *Early Intervention in Psychiatry, 16*, 1112–1120.

Ma, L., Zhang, Y., Huang, C., & Cui, Z. (2020). Resilience-oriented cognitive behavioral interventions for depressive symptoms in children and adolescents: A meta-analytic review. *Journal of Affective Disorders, 270*, 150–164.

Maccaferri, G. E., Dunker-Scheuner, D., De Roten, Y., Despland, J. N., Sachse, R., & Kramer, U. (2020). Psychotherapy of dependent personality disorder: The relationship of patient–therapist interactions to outcome. *Psychiatry, 83*, 179–194.

Macina, C., Bendel, R., Walter, M., & Wrege, J. S. (2021). Somatization and Somatic Symptom Disorder and its overlap with dimensionally measured personality pathology: A systematic review. *Journal of Psychosomatic Research, 151*, 110646.

Maenner, M. J., Shaw, K. A., Bakian, A. V., Bilder, D. A., Durkin, M. S., Esler, A., ... & Cogswell, M. E. (2021). Prevalence and characteristics of autism spectrum disorder among children aged 8 years—autism and developmental disabilities monitoring network, 11 sites, United States, 2018. *MMWR Surveillance Summaries, 70*, 1.

Maessen, G. C., Wijnhoven, A. M., Neijzen, R. L., Paulus, M. C., van Heel, D. A., Bomers, B. H., ... & van der Heyden, M. A. (2020). Nicotine intoxication by e-cigarette liquids: A study of case reports and pathophysiology. *Clinical Toxicology, 58*, 1–8.

Maddock, A., & Blair, C. (2021). How do mindfulness-based programmes improve anxiety, depression and psychological distress? A systematic review. *Current Psychology*, 1–23.

Madore, K. P., & Wagner, A. D. (2022). Readiness to remember: predicting variability in episodic memory. *Trends in Cognitive Sciences, 26*, 707–723.

Maffioletti, E., Minelli, A., Tardito, D., & Gennarelli, M. (2020). Blues in the brain and beyond: Molecular bases of major depressive disorder and relative pharmacological and non-pharmacological treatments. *Genes, 11*, 1089.

Mahdi, Y.S., & Moustafa, A.A. (2020). The benefits and limitations of methadone: A comparison to other opioid replacement treatments. In A.A. Moustafa (Ed.), *Cognitive, clinical, and neural aspects of drug addiction* (pp. 267–288). London: Academic.

Mahjani, B., Bey, K., Boberg, J., & Burton, C. (2021). Genetics of obsessive-compulsive disorder. *Psychological Medicine*, 1–13.

Maiti, T., Langan, L. (2021). Gender and crime. In S.P. Sahni & P. Bhadra (Eds.) *Criminal psychology and the criminal justice system in India and beyond* (pp. 119–131). Singapore: Springer.

Maldonado, R., Calvé, P., García-Blanco, A., Domingo-Rodriguez, L., Senabre, E., & Martín-García, E. (2021). Genomics and epigenomics of addiction. *American Journal of Medical Genetics Part B: Neuropsychiatric Genetics, 186*, 128–139.

Malhotra, S., Sahoo, S., & Balachander, S. (2019). Acute and transient psychotic disorders: newer understanding. *Current Psychiatry Reports, 21*, 1–11.

Malivoire, B. L. (2020). Exploring DBT skills training as a treatment avenue for generalized anxiety disorder. *Clinical Psychology: Science and Practice, 27*, e12339.

Malpas, C. B., Sharmin, S., & Kalincik, T. (2021). The histopathological staging of tau, but not amyloid, corresponds to antemortem cognitive status, dementia stage, functional abilities and neuropsychiatric symptoms. *International Journal of Neuroscience, 131*, 800–809.

Mamiya, P. C., Arnett, A. B., & Stein, M. A. (2021). Precision medicine care in ADHD: The case for neural excitation and inhibition. *Brain Sciences, 11*, 91.

Mandira, M. R., & Stoltz, T. (2021). Bullying risk and protective factors among elementary school students over time: A systematic review. *International Journal of Educational Research, 109*, 101838.

Manfredi, L., Accoto, A., Couyoumdjian, A., & Conversi, D. (2021). A systematic review of genetic polymorphisms associated with binge eating disorder. *Nutrients, 13*, 848.

Mangiulli, I., Otgaar, H., Jelicic, M., & Merckelbach, H. (2022). A critical review of case studies on dissociative amnesia. *Clinical Psychological Science, 10*, 191–211.

Manning, L., Ferris, M., Narvaez Rosario, C., Prues, M., & Bouchard, L. (2019). Spiritual resilience: understanding the protection and promotion of well-being in the later life. *Journal of Religion, Spirituality & Aging, 31*, 168–186.

Manzanza, N. D. O., Sedlackova, L., & Kalaria, R. N. (2021). Alpha-synuclein post-translational modifications: Implications for pathogenesis of lewy body disorders. *Frontiers in Aging Neuroscience, 13*, 690293.

Marchand, E. (2021). Psychological and behavioral treatment of female orgasmic disorder. *Sexual Medicine Reviews, 9*, 194–211.

Marcovitz, D. E., McHugh, R. K., Roos, C., West, J. J., & Kelly, J. (2020). Overlapping mechanisms of recovery between professional psychotherapies and Alcoholics Anonymous. *Journal of Addiction Medicine, 14*, 367–375.

Marek, R. J., Anderson, J. L., Tarescavage, A. M., Martin-Fernandez, K., Haugh, S., Block, A. R., ... & Ben-Porath, Y. S. (2020). Elucidating somatization in a dimensional model of psychopathology across medical settings. *Journal of Abnormal Psychology, 129*, 162–176.

Marhenke, T. (2022). *Sexual disorders: An introduction*. Wiesbaden: Springer.

Marincowitz, C., Lochner, C., & Stein, D. J. (2021). The neurobiology of obsessive-compulsive personality disorder: A systematic review. *CNS Spectrums*, 1–39.

Marriott, E., Stacey, J., Hewitt, O. M., & Verkuijl, N. E. (2022). Parenting an autistic child: Experiences of parents with significant autistic traits. *Journal of Autism and Developmental Disorders, 52*, 3182–3193.

Marsh, R. J., Dorahy, M. J., Butler, C., Middleton, W., de Jong, P. J., Kemp, S., & Huntjens, R. (2021). Inter-identity amnesia for neutral episodic self-referential and autobiographical memory in Dissociative Identity Disorder: An assessment of recall and recognition. *PLoS One, 16*, e0245849.

Martel, M. M., Elkins, A. R., Eng, A. G., Goh, P. K., Bansal, P. S., Smith-Thomas, T. E., ... & Nigg, J. T. (2022). Longitudinal temperament pathways to ADHD between childhood and adolescence. *Research on Child and Adolescent Psychopathology, 50*, 1055–1066.

Martinez-Martin, N., Dasgupta, I., Carter, A., Chandler, J. A., Kellmeyer, P., Kreitmair, K., ... & Cabrera, L. Y. (2020). Ethics of digital mental health during COVID-19: Crisis and opportunities. *JMIR Mental Health, 7*, e23776.

Martinotti, G., De Risio, L., Vannini, C., Schifano, F., Pettorruso, M., & Di Giannantonio, M. (2021). Substance-related exogenous psychosis: A postmodern syndrome. *CNS Spectrums, 26*, 84–91.

Martin-Tuite, P., & Shindel, A. W. (2020). Management options for premature ejaculation and delayed ejaculation in men. *Sexual Medicine Reviews, 8*, 473–485.

Martini, M. G., Barona-Martinez, M., & Micali, N. (2020). Eating disorders mothers and their children: A systematic review of the literature. *Archives of Women's Mental Health, 23*, 449–467.

Marucci, G., Buccioni, M., Dal Ben, D., Lambertucci, C., Volpini, R., & Amenta, F. (2021). Efficacy of acetylcholinesterase inhibitors in Alzheimer's disease. *Neuropharmacology, 190*, 108352.

Mascayano, F., Toso-Salman, J., Ho, Y. C. S., Dev, S., Tapia, T., Thornicroft, G., ... & Susser, E. (2020). Including culture in programs to reduce stigma toward people with mental disorders in low-and middle-income countries. *Transcultural Psychiatry, 57*, 140-160.

Masdrakis, V. G., & Baldwin, D. S. (2021). Anticonvulsant and antipsychotic medications in the pharmacotherapy of panic disorder: a structured review. *Therapeutic Advances in Psychopharmacology, 11*, 20451253211002320.

Mason, W. A., Stevens, A. L., & Fleming, C. B. (2020). A systematic review of research on adolescent solitary alcohol and marijuana use in the United States. *Addiction, 115*, 19–31.

Massuti, R., Moreira-Maia, C. R., Campani, F., Sônego, M., Amaro, J., Akutagava-Martins, G. C., ... & Rohde, L. A. (2021). Assessing undertreatment and overtreatment/misuse of ADHD medications in children and adolescents across continents: A systematic review and meta-analysis. *Neuroscience & Biobehavioral Reviews, 128*, 64–73.

Matherne, C. E., Watson, H., Fassnacht, D. B., Ali, K., Zerwas, S., Peat, C., ... & Bulik, C. M. (2022). An exploratory investigation of predictors of outcome in face-to-face and online cognitive-behavioural therapy for bulimia nervosa. *European Eating Disorders Review, 30*, 373–387.

Matsumoto, N., & Kawaguchi, J. (2020). Negative item memory and associative memory: Influences of working memory capacity, anxiety sensitivity, and looming cognition. *Journal of Behavior Therapy and Experimental Psychiatry, 68*, 101569.

Mbous, Y. P. V., Nili, M., Mohamed, R., & Dwibedi, N. (2022). Psychosocial correlates of insomnia among college students. *Preventing Chronic Disease, 19*, 220060.

McCartney, M., Nevitt, S., Lloyd, A., Hill, R., White, R., & Duarte, R. (2021). Mindfulness-based cognitive therapy for prevention and time to depressive relapse: Systematic review and network meta-analysis. *Acta Psychiatrica Scandinavica, 143*, 6–21.

McCloskey, K. D., Cox, D. W., Ogrodniczuk, J. S., Laverdière, O., Joyce, A. S., & Kealy, D. (2021). Interpersonal problems and social dysfunction: Examining patients with avoidant and borderline personality disorder symptoms. *Journal of Clinical Psychology, 77*, 329–339.

McDaid, D., Park, A. L., & Wahlbeck, K. (2019). The economic case for the prevention of mental illness. *Annual Review of Public Health, 40*, 373–389.

McDonough, I. M., Festini, S. B., & Wood, M. M. (2020). Risk for Alzheimer's disease: A review of long-term episodic memory encoding and retrieval fMRI studies. *Ageing Research Reviews, 62*, 101133.

Mc Glanaghy, E., Turner, D., Davis, G. A., Sharpe, H., Dougall, N., Morris, P., ... & Hutton, P. (2021). A network meta-analysis of psychological interventions for schizophrenia and psychosis: Impact on symptoms. *Schizophrenia Research, 228*, 447–459.

McIntyre, R. S., Berk, M., Brietzke, E., Goldstein, B. I., López-Jaramillo, C., Kessing, L. V., ... & Mansur, R. B. (2020). Bipolar disorders. *The Lancet, 396*, 1841–1856.

McKay, J. R. (2021). Impact of continuing care on recovery from substance use disorder. *Alcohol Research: Current Reviews, 41, 01*.

McMain, S. F., Chapman, A. L., Kuo, J. R., Dixon-Gordon, K. L., Guimond, T. H., Labrish, C., ... & Streiner, D. L. (2022). The effectiveness of 6 versus 12 months of dialectical behavior therapy for borderline personality disorder: A noninferiority randomized clinical trial. *Psychotherapy and Psychosomatics, 91*, 382–397.

McPhail, I. V., Olver, M. E., Nicholaichuk, T. P., & Haynes, A. (2021). Convergent and predictive associations of three measures of pedophilic interest. *Sexual Abuse, 33*, 816–838.

McPherson, S., Wicks, C., & Tercelli, I. (2020). Patient experiences of psychological therapy for depression: A qualitative metasynthesis. *BMC Psychiatry, 20*, 1–18.

McTeague, L. M., Rosenberg, B. M., Lopez, J. W., Carreon, D. M., Huemer, J., Jiang, Y., ... & Etkin, A. (2020). Identification of common neural circuit disruptions in emotional processing across psychiatric disorders. *American Journal of Psychiatry, 177*, 411–421.

Medeiros, G. C., Roy, D., Kontos, N., & Beach, S. R. (2020). Post-stroke depression: A 2020 updated review. *General Hospital Psychiatry, 66*, 70–80.

Mehanović, E., Vigna-Taglianti, F., Faggiano, F., & Galanti, M. R. (2022). Does parental permissiveness toward cigarette smoking and alcohol use influence illicit drug use among adolescents? A longitudinal study in seven European countries. *Social Psychiatry and Psychiatric Epidemiology, 57*, 173–181.

Mei, C., & McGorry, P. D. (2020). Historical perspectives on psychosis risk. In A.D. Thompson & M.R. Broome (Eds.), *Risk factors for psychosis: Paradigms, mechanisms, and prevention* (pp. 1–10). New York: Academic.

Meinert, P., Behr, J., Gauger, U., Krebs, J., Konrad, N., & Opitz-Welke, A. (2020). Psychosis in German prisoners: Comparison of the clinical appearance of psychotic disorder of an imprisoned population with a not detained community group. *Behavioral Sciences & the Law, 38*, 482–492.

Meints, S. M., & Edwards, R. R. (2018). Evaluating psychosocial contributions to chronic pain outcomes. *Progress in Neuro-Psychopharmacology and Biological Psychiatry, 87*, 168–182.

Meixner Jr, J. B. (2021). Modern sentencing mitigation. *Northwestern University Law Review, 116*, 1395–1480.

Melbye, S., Kessing, L. V., Bardram, J. E., & Faurholt-Jepsen, M. (2020). Smartphone-based self-monitoring, treatment, and automatically generated data in children, adolescents, and young adults with psychiatric disorders: Systematic review. *JMIR Mental Health, 7*, e17453.

Mele, G., Alfano, V., Cotugno, A., & Longarzo, M. (2020). A broad-spectrum review on multimodal neuroimaging in bulimia nervosa and binge eating disorder. *Appetite, 151*, 104712.

Memis, C. O., Dogan, B., Sevincok, D., Ashik, I., & Sevincok, L. (2020). Mediating role of childhood abuse for the relationship between schizotypal traits and obsessive-compulsive disorder. *Archives of Clinical Psychiatry, 47*, 40–44.

Mendelson, T., & Eaton, W. W. (2018). Recent advances in the prevention of mental disorders. *Social Psychiatry and Psychiatric Epidemiology, 53*, 325–339.

Mercan, N., Bulut, M., & Yüksel, Ç. (2021). Investigation of the relatedness of cognitive distortions with emotional expression, anxiety, and depression. *Current Psychology*, 1–10.

Mérelle, S., Van Bergen, D., Looijmans, M., Balt, E., Rasing, S., van Domburgh, L., ... & Popma, A. (2020). A multi-method psychological autopsy study on youth suicides in the Netherlands in 2017: Feasibility, main outcomes, and recommendations. *PLoS One, 15*, e0238031.

Merikangas, A. K., & Almasy, L. (2020). Using the tools of genetic epidemiology to understand sex differences in neuropsychiatric disorders. *Genes, Brain and Behavior, 19*, e12660.

Merikangas, K.R., Jameson, N., & Tohen, M. (2016). Course of bipolar disorder in adults and children. In E. J. Bromet (Eds.), *Long-term outcomes in psychopathology research: Rethinking the scientific agenda* (pp. 15–31). New York: Oxford.

Mersha, A. G., Gould, G. S., Bovill, M., & Eftekhari, P. (2020). Barriers and facilitators of adherence to nicotine replacement therapy: A systematic review and analysis using the capability, opportunity, motivation, and behaviour (COM-B) model. *International Journal of Environmental Research and Public Health, 17*, 8895.

Mesa-Vieira, C., Grolimund, J., von Känel, R., Franco, O. H., & Saner, H. (2021). Psychosocial risk factors in cardiac rehabilitation: Time to screen beyond anxiety and depression. *Global Heart, 16*: 16.

Messing, J.T., Campbell, J., Wilson, J.S., Brown, S., & Patchell, B. (2015). The Lethality Screen: Validity of an intimate partner violence risk assessment for use by first responders. *Journal of Interpersonal Violence*, 1–22.

Metzger, A. N., & Hamilton, L. T. (2021). The stigma of ADHD: Teacher ratings of labeled students. *Sociological Perspectives, 64*, 258–279.

Meulders, A. (2020). Fear in the context of pain: Lessons learned from 100 years of fear conditioning research. *Behaviour Research and Therapy, 131*, 103635.

Mewton, L., Visontay, R., Hoy, N., Lipnicki, D. M., Sunderland, M., Lipton, R. B., ... & Cohort Studies of Memory in an International Consortium. (2022). The relationship between alcohol use and dementia in adults aged over 60 years: A combined analysis of prospective, individual-participant data from 15 international studies. *Addiction.*

Meyer, N., Faulkner, S. M., McCutcheon, R. A., Pillinger, T., Dijk, D. J., & MacCabe, J. H. (2020). Sleep and circadian rhythm disturbance in remitted schizophrenia and bipolar disorder: a systematic review and meta-analysis. *Schizophrenia Bulletin, 46*, 1126–1143.

Meyer, T., & Morina, N. (2022). Social comparison modulates acute responses to traumatic footage and the development of intrusive memories. *Journal of Experimental Psychopathology, 13*, 20438087221075889.

Miaskowski, C., Blyth, F., Nicosia, F., Haan, M., Keefe, F., Smith, A., & Ritchie, C. (2020). A biopsychosocial model of chronic pain for older adults. *Pain Medicine, 21*, 1793–1805.

Michaels, T. I., Stone, E., Singal, S., Novakovic, V., Barkin, R. L., & Barkin, S. (2021). Brain reward circuitry: The overlapping neurobiology of trauma and substance use disorders. *World Journal of Psychiatry, 11*, 222–231.

Michelon, C., Michels, M., Abatti, M., Vieira, A., Borges, H., Dominguini, D., ... & Dal-Pizzol, F. (2020). The role of secretase pathway in long-term brain inflammation and cognitive impairment in an animal model of severe sepsis. *Molecular Neurobiology, 57*, 1159–1169.

Mihaljevic, M. (2022). Neuropsychiatric risk in children with intellectual disability: Knowns and unknowns. *The Lancet Psychiatry, 9*, 690–691.

Miklowitz, D. J., Efthimiou, O., Furukawa, T. A., Scott, J., McLaren, R., Geddes, J. R., & Cipriani, A. (2021). Adjunctive psychotherapy for bipolar disorder: A systematic review and component network meta-analysis. *JAMA Psychiatry, 78*, 141–150.

Milán-Tomás, Á., Fernández-Matarrubia, M., & Rodríguez-Oroz, M. C. (2021). Lewy body dementias: A coin with two sides? *Behavioral Sciences, 11*, 94.

Miled, Z. B., Haas, K., Black, C. M., Khandker, R. K., Chandrasekaran, V., Lipton, R., & Boustani, M. A. (2020). Predicting dementia with routine care EMR data. *Artificial Intelligence in Medicine, 102*, 101771.

Miller, D. S., Robert, P., Ereshefsky, L., Adler, L., Bateman, D., Cummings, J., ... & Lanctôt, K. L. (2021). Diagnostic criteria for apathy in neurocognitive disorders. *Alzheimer's & Dementia, 17*, 1892–1904.

Miller, J. N., & Black, D. W. (2019). Schizoaffective disorder: A review. *Annals of Clinical Psychiatry, 31*, 47–53.

Miller, J. N., & Black, D. W. (2020). Bipolar disorder and suicide: a review. *Current Psychiatry Reports, 22*, 1–10.

Miller, L., Archer, R. L., & Kapoor, N. (2020). Conversion disorder: early diagnosis and personalized therapy plan is the key. *Case Reports in Neurological Medicine, 2020*: 1967581.

Millman, L. M., Hunter, E. C., Orgs, G., David, A. S., & Terhune, D. B. (2022). Symptom variability in depersonalization–derealization disorder: A latent profile analysis. *Journal of Clinical Psychology, 78*, 637–655.

Mills, K. T., Stefanescu, A., & He, J. (2020). The global epidemiology of hypertension. *Nature Reviews Nephrology, 16*, 223–237.

Mina, S. (2019). Predictors of marriage in psychiatric illness: A review of literature. *Journal of Psychiatry and Psychiatric Disorders, 3*, 14–22.

Mital, S., Wolff, J., & Carroll, J. J. (2020). The relationship between incarceration history and overdose in North America: A scoping review of the evidence. *Drug and Alcohol Dependence, 213*, 108088.

Mitchell, K. J., Turner, H. A., Gewirtz-Meydan, A., & Jones, L. M. (2022). Relationships between caregiver substance use disorder and child maltreatment in the context of non-victimization life adversities: Findings from a nationally representative sample of youth. *International Journal on Child Maltreatment: Research, Policy and Practice, 5*, 197–214.

Mitchell, N., Sajjad, A., Grocholewska-Mhamdi, A., & McMain, C. (2021). Improving baseline and follow-up physical health monitoring when commencing oral antipsychotics. *BJPsych Open, 7*, S92–S92.

Mittelman, M.S., Epstein, C., & Pierzchala, A. (2003). *Counseling the Alzheimer's caregiver: A resource for health care professionals.* Chicago, IL: American Medical Association.

Modiano, Y. A., Webber, T., Cerbone, B., Haneef, Z., & Pastorek, N. J. (2021). Predictive utility of the Minnesota Multiphasic Personality Inventory-2-RF (MMPI-2-RF) in differentiating psychogenic nonepileptic seizures and epileptic seizures in male veterans. *Epilepsy & Behavior, 116*, 107731.

Moe, A. M., Llamocca, E., Wastler, H. M., Steelesmith, D. L., Brock, G., Bridge, J. A., & Fontanella, C. A. (2022). Risk factors for deliberate self-harm and suicide among adolescents and young adults with first-episode psychosis. *Schizophrenia Bulletin, 48*, 414–424.

Molen, L. V., Ronis, S. T., Benoit, A. A., & Walmark, S. (2021). Differential associations between paraphilic interests and sexual satisfaction. *Sexual Addiction & Compulsivity, 27*, 274–292.

Molen, L. V., Ronis, S. T., & Benoit, A. A. (2022). Paraphilic interests versus behaviors: Factors that distinguish individuals who act on paraphilic interests from individuals who refrain. *Sexual Abuse*, 10790632221108949.

Momen, N. C., Plana-Ripoll, O., Yilmaz, Z., Thornton, L. M., McGrath, J. J., Bulik, C. M., & Petersen, L. V. (2022). Comorbidity between eating disorders and psychiatric disorders. *International Journal of Eating Disorders, 55*, 505–517.

Mongelli, F., Georgakopoulos, P., & Pato, M. T. (2020). Challenges and opportunities to meet the mental health needs of underserved and disenfranchised populations in the United States. *Focus, 18*, 16–24.

Monteleone, A. M., Pellegrino, F., Croatto, G., Carfagno, M., Hilbert, A., Treasure, J., ... & Solmi, M. (2022). Treatment of eating disorders: A systematic meta-review of meta-analyses and network meta-analyses. *Neuroscience & Biobehavioral Reviews, 142*, 104857.

Montemagni, C., Bellino, S., Bracale, N., Bozzatello, P., & Rocca, P. (2020). Models predicting psychosis in patients with high clinical risk: A systematic review. *Frontiers in Psychiatry, 11*, 223.

Moody, C. T., & Laugeson, E. A. (2020). Social skills training in autism spectrum disorder across the lifespan. *Psychiatric Clinics, 43*, 687–699.

Moriarty, A. S., Coventry, P. A., Hudson, J. L., Cook, N., Fenton, O. J., Bower, P., ... & McMillan, D. (2020). The role of relapse prevention for depression in collaborative care: A systematic review. *Journal of Affective Disorders, 265*, 618–644.

Morinaga, M., Rai, D., Hollander, A. C., Petros, N., Dalman, C., & Magnusson, C. (2021). Migration or ethnic minority status and risk of autism spectrum disorders and intellectual disability: Systematic review. *European Journal of Public Health, 31*, 304–312.

Mormando, C., & Francis, A. (2020). Catatonia revived: A unique syndrome updated. *International Review of Psychiatry, 32*, 403–411.

Morriss, J., Zuj, D. V., & Mertens, G. (2021). The role of intolerance of uncertainty in classical threat conditioning: Recent developments and directions for future research. *International Journal of Psychophysiology, 166*, 116–126.

Mortier, P., Auerbach, R. P., Alonso, J., Bantjes, J., Benjet, C., Cuijpers, P., ... & Vives, M. (2018). Suicidal thoughts and behaviors among first-year college students: results from the WMH-ICS project. *Journal of the American Academy of Child & Adolescent Psychiatry, 57*, 263–273.

Morton, E., & Murray, G. (2020). Assessment and treatment of sleep problems in bipolar disorder—A guide for psychologists and clinically focused review. *Clinical Psychology & Psychotherapy, 27*, 364–377.

Mullarkey, M. C., & Schleider, J. L. (2020). Contributions of fixed mindsets and hopelessness to anxiety and depressive symptoms: A commonality analysis approach. *Journal of Affective Disorders, 261*, 245–252.

Müller, T. (2020). Pharmacokinetics and pharmacodynamics of levodopa/carbidopa cotherapies for Parkinson's disease. *Expert Opinion on Drug Metabolism & Toxicology, 16*, 403–414.

Mumper, E. E., Dyson, M. W., Finsaas, M. C., Olino, T. M., & Klein, D. N. (2020). Life stress moderates the effects of preschool behavioral inhibition on anxiety in early adolescence. *Journal of Child Psychology and Psychiatry, 61*, 167–174.

Mun, E. Y., Li, X., Lineberry, S., Tan, Z., Huh, D., Walters, S. T., ... & Project INTEGRATE Team. (2022). Do brief alcohol interventions reduce driving after drinking among college students? A two-step meta-analysis of individual participant data. *Alcohol and Alcoholism, 57*, 125–135.

Muncan, B., Walters, S. M., Ezell, J., & Ompad, D. C. (2020). "They look at us like junkies": influences of drug use stigma on the healthcare engagement of people who inject drugs in New York City. *Harm Reduction Journal, 17*, 1–9.

Muñoz-Negro, J. E., Gómez-Sierra, F. J., Peralta, V., González-Rodríguez, A., & Cervilla, J. A. (2020). A systematic review of studies with clinician-rated scales on the pharmacological treatment of delusional disorder. *International Clinical Psychopharmacology, 35*, 129–136.

Muñoz-Samons, D., Tor, J., Rodriguez-Pascual, M., Alvarez-Subiela, X., Sugranyes, G., de la Serna, E., ... & Baeza, I. (2021). Recent stressful life events and stress sensitivity in children and adolescents at clinical risk for psychosis. *Psychiatry Research, 303*, 114017.

Muratore, A. F., & Attia, E. (2022). Psychopharmacologic management of eating disorders. *Current Psychiatry Reports, 24*, 345–351.

Murphy, C. E., Wang, R. C., Montoy, J. C., Whittaker, E., & Raven, M. (2022). Effect of extended-release naltrexone on alcohol consumption: A systematic review and meta-analysis. *Addiction, 117*, 271–281.

Murray, A.M., Toussaint, A., Althaus, A., & Lowe, B. (2016). The challenge of diagnosing non-specific, functional, and somatoform disorders: A systematic review of barriers to diagnosis in primary care. *Journal of Psychosomatic Research, 80*, 1–10.

Murray, J., & DeBerard, S. (2022). *Biopsychosocial model and health*. New York: Routledge.

Musshoff, F., Schwarz, G., Sachs, H., Skopp, G., & Franz, T. (2020). Concentration distribution of more than 100 drugs and metabolites in forensic hair samples. *International Journal of Legal Medicine, 134*, 989–995.

Muth, A. K., & Park, S. Q. (2021). The impact of dietary macronutrient intake on cognitive function and the brain. *Clinical Nutrition, 40*, 3999–4010.

Nagl, M., Jacobi, C., Paul, M., Beesdo-Baum, K., Hofler, M., Lieb, R., & Wittchen, H-U. (2016). Prevalence, incidence, and natural course of anorexia and bulimia nervosa among adolescents and young adults. *European Child and Adolescent Psychiatry, 25*, 903–918.

Nappi, R. E., Cucinella, L., Martini, E., & Cassani, C. (2021). The role of hormone therapy in urogenital health after menopause. *Best Practice & Research Clinical Endocrinology & Metabolism, 35*, 101595.

National Center for Health Statistics (2022). *Heart disease prevalence*. Atlanta: Centers for Disease Control and Prevention.

National Institute on Alcohol Abuse and Alcoholism (2021). *College drinking*. https://www.niaaa.nih.gov/publications/brochures-and-fact-sheets/college-drinking

National Institute on Alcohol Abuse and Alcoholism. (2022). *College drinking*. Retrieved from http://www.niaaa.nih.gov/alcohol-health /special-populations-co-occurring-disorders /college-drinking

Nay, W., Brown, R., & Roberson-Nay, R. (2013). Longitudinal course of panic disorder with and without agoraphobia using the national epidemiologic survey on alcohol and related conditions (NESARC). *Psychiatry Research, 208*, 54–61.

Negin, F., Ozyer, B., Agahian, S., Kacdioglu, S., & Ozyer, G. T. (2021). Vision-assisted recognition of stereotype behaviors for early diagnosis of Autism Spectrum Disorders. *Neurocomputing, 446*, 145–155.

Nelson, G., Hunt, J. H., Martin, K., Patterson, B., & Khounmeuang, A. (2022). Current knowledge and future directions: proportional reasoning interventions for students with learning disabilities and mathematics difficulties. *Learning Disability Quarterly, 45*, 159–171.

Nelson, M. E., Jester, D. J., Petkus, A. J., & Andel, R. (2021). Cognitive reserve, Alzheimer's neuropathology, and risk of dementia: A systematic review and meta-analysis. *Neuropsychology Review, 31*, 233–250.

Nester, M. S., Schielke, H. J., Brand, B. L., & Loewenstein, R. J. (2022). Dissociative identity disorder: Diagnostic accuracy and DSM-5 criteria change implications. *Journal of Trauma & Dissociation, 23*, 451–463.

Newlands, R.T., Brito, J., Denning, D.M. (2020). Cultural considerations in the treatment of sexual dysfunction. In L. Benuto, F. Gonzalez, & J. Singer (Eds.), *Handbook of cultural factors in behavioral health* (pp. 345–361). Cham: Springer.

Nguyen, P. T., & Hinshaw, S. P. (2020). Understanding the stigma associated with ADHD: Hope for the future? *The ADHD Report, 28*, 1–10.

Nguyen, T. D., Hieronymus, F., Lorentzen, R., McGirr, A., & Østergaard, S. D. (2021). The efficacy of repetitive transcranial magnetic stimulation (rTMS) for bipolar depression: A systematic review and meta-analysis. *Journal of Affective Disorders, 279*, 250–255.

Nichita, E. C., & Buckley, P. F. (2020). Comorbidities of antisocial personality disorder: Prevalence and implications. In A.R. Felthous & S. Henning (Eds.), *The Wiley international handbook on psychopathic disorders and the law* (2nd ed) (pp. 645–670). New York: Wiley.

Nigg, J. T., Sibley, M. H., Thapar, A., & Karalunas, S. L. (2020). Development of ADHD: Etiology, heterogeneity, and early life course. *Annual Review of Developmental Psychology, 2*, 559–583.

Nikčević, A. V., Marino, C., Kolubinski, D. C., Leach, D., & Spada, M. M. (2021). Modelling the contribution of the Big Five personality traits, health anxiety, and COVID-19 psychological distress to generalised anxiety and depressive symptoms during the COVID-19 pandemic. *Journal of Affective Disorders, 279*, 578–584.

Nikolin, S., Tan, Y. Y., Schwaab, A., Moffa, A., Loo, C. K., & Martin, D. (2021). An investigation of working memory deficits in depression using the n-back task: A systematic review and meta-analysis. *Journal of Affective Disorders, 284*, 1–8.

Nishiura, Y., Nihei, M., Nakamura-Thomas, H., & Inoue, T. (2021). Effectiveness of using assistive technology for time orientation and memory, in older adults with or without dementia. *Disability and Rehabilitation: Assistive Technology, 16*, 472–478.

Noble, L. A., Firth, N., Delgadillo, J., & Kellett, S. (2021). An investigation of the competencies involved in the facilitation of CBT-based group psychoeducational interventions. *Behavioural and Cognitive Psychotherapy, 49*, 732–744.

Noel, J. P., Failla, M. D., Quinde-Zlibut, J. M., Williams, Z. J., Gerdes, M., Tracy, J. M., ... & Cascio, C. J. (2020). Visual-tactile spatial multisensory interaction in adults with autism and schizophrenia. *Frontiers in Psychiatry, 11*, 578401.

Norcross, J. C., Sayette, M. A., & Martin-Wagar, C. A. (2021). Doctoral training in counseling psychology: Analyses of 20-year trends, differences across the practice-research continuum, and comparisons with clinical psychology. *Training and Education in Professional Psychology, 15*, 167–175.

North, C. S., Kotamarti, V., & Pollio, D. E. (2022). Deconstructing childhood conduct and adult antisocial criteria for the diagnosis of antisocial personality disorder. *Annals of Clinical Psychiatry, 34*, 97–105.

Notaras, M., & van den Buuse, M. (2020). Neurobiology of BDNF in fear memory, sensitivity to stress, and stress-related disorders. *Molecular Psychiatry, 25*, 2251–2274.

Nujić, D., Musić Milanović, S., Milas, V., Miškulin, I., Ivić, V., & Milas, J. (2021). Association between child/adolescent overweight/obesity and conduct disorder: A systematic review and meta-analysis. *Pediatric Obesity, 16*, e12742.

Nuño, L., Guilera, G., Coenen, M., Rojo, E., Gómez-Benito, J., & Barrios, M. (2019). Functioning in schizophrenia from the perspective of psychologists: A worldwide study. *PloS One, 14*, e0217936.

O'Brien, N. L., Quadri, G., Lightley, I., Sharp, S. I., Guerrini, I., Smith, I., ... & McQuillin, A. (2022). SLC19A1 genetic variation leads to altered thiamine diphosphate transport: Implications for the risk of developing Wernicke–Korsakoff's Syndrome. *Alcohol and Alcoholism, 57*, 581–588.

O'Connor, E., Thomas, R., Senger, C. A., Perdue, L., Robalino, S., & Patnode, C. (2020). Interventions to prevent illicit and nonmedical drug use in children, adolescents, and young adults: Updated evidence report and systematic review for the US Preventive Services Task Force. *JAMA, 323*, 2067–2079.

O'Connor, E. E., Holly, L. E., Chevalier, L. L., Pincus, D. B., & Langer, D. A. (2020). Parent and child emotion and distress responses associated with parental accommodation of child anxiety symptoms. *Journal of Clinical Psychology, 76*, 1390–1407.

Office of Juvenile Justice and Delinquency Prevention (2022). *Racial and ethnic disparity in juvenile justice processing: Literature review: A product of the Model Programs Guide*. Washington, DC: Author.

Ogloff, J. R. P., & Davis, M. R. (2020). From predicting dangerousness to assessing and managing risk for violence: A journey across four generations. In J. S. Wormith, L. A. Craig, & T. E. Hogue (Eds.), *The Wiley handbook of what works in violence risk assessment: Theory, research, and practice* (pp. 81–98). Hoboken, NJ: Wiley.

Ogunsuyi, O. B., Aro, O. P., Oboh, G., & Olagoke, O. C. (2022). Curcumin improves the ability of donepezil to ameliorate memory impairment in Drosophila melanogaster: involvement of cholinergic and cnc/Nrf2-redox systems. *Drug and Chemical Toxicology*, 1–9.

Okur Güney, Z. E., Sattel, H., Witthöft, M., & Henningsen, P. (2019). Emotion regulation in patients with somatic symptom and related disorders: A systematic review. *PLoS One, 14*, e0217277.

Onyike, C.U., Shinagawa, S., & Ellajosyula, R. (2021). Frontotemporal dementia: A cross-cultural perspective. In B. Ghetti, E. Buratti, B. Boeve, & R. Rademakers (Eds.) *Frontotemporal dementias: Advances in experimental medicine and biology* (pp. 141–150). Cham: Springer.

Olatunji, B.O., Kauffman, B.Y., Meltzer, S., Davis, M.L., Smits, J.A.J., & Powers, M.B. (2014). Cognitive-behavioral therapy for hypochondriasis/health anxiety: A meta-analysis of treatment outcome and moderators. *Behaviour Research and Therapy, 58*, 65–74.

Oldan, J. D., Jewells, V. L., Pieper, B., & Wong, T. Z. (2021). Complete evaluation of dementia: PET and MRI Correlation and diagnosis for the neuroradiologist. *American Journal of Neuroradiology, 42*, 998–1007.

Olmastroni, E., Molari, G., De Beni, N., Colpani, O., Galimberti, F., Gazzotti, M., ... & Casula, M. (2022). Statin use and risk of dementia or Alzheimer's disease: A systematic review and meta-analysis of observational studies. *European Journal of Preventive Cardiology, 29*, 804–814.

Oltmanns, J. R., & Widiger, T. A. (2021). The self-and informant-personality inventories for ICD-11: Agreement, structure, and relations with health, social, and satisfaction variables in older adults. *Psychological Assessment, 33*, 300–310.

Orad, R. I., & Shiner, T. (2021). Differentiating dementia with Lewy bodies from Alzheimer's disease and Parkinson's disease dementia: An update on imaging modalities. *Journal of Neurology, 269*, 639–653.

Orsolini, L., Latini, R., Pompili, M., Serafini, G., Volpe, U., Vellante, F., ... & De Berardis, D. (2020). Understanding the complex of suicide in depression: from research to clinics. *Psychiatry Investigation, 17*, 207.

Orzechowska, A., Maruszewska, P., & Gałecki, P. (2021). Cognitive behavioral therapy of patients with somatic symptoms—Diagnostic and therapeutic difficulties. *Journal of Clinical Medicine, 10*, 3159.

Osler, M., Villumsen, M. D., Jørgensen, M. B., Hjelmborg, J. V., Christensen, K., & Wium-Andersen, M. K. (2022). Familial risk and heritability of ischemic heart disease and stroke in Danish twins. *Scandinavian Journal of Public Health, 50*, 199–204.

Ossola, P., Gerra, M. C., Gerra, M. L., Milano, G., Zatti, M., Zavan, V., ... & Di Gennaro, C. (2021). Alcohol use disorders among adult children of alcoholics (ACOAs): Gene-environment resilience factors. *Progress in Neuro-Psychopharmacology and Biological Psychiatry, 108*, 110167.

Ostchega, Y., Fryar, C.D., Nwankwo, T., & Nguyen, D.T. (2020). *Hypertension prevalence among adults aged 18 and over: United States, 2017–2018*. Atlanta: Centers for Disease Control and Prevention.

Oswalt, S. B., Lederer, A. M., Chestnut-Steich, K., Day, C., Halbritter, A., & Ortiz, D. (2020). Trends in college students' mental health diagnoses and utilization of services, 2009–2015. *Journal of American College Health, 68*, 41–51.

Otgaar, H., Howe, M. L., & Patihis, L. (2022). What science tells us about false and repressed memories. *Memory, 30*, 16–21.

Otte, C. (2022). Cognitive behavioral therapy in anxiety disorders: Current state of the evidence. *Dialogues in Clinical Neuroscience, 13*, 413–421.

Otuyama, L. J., Oliveira, D., Locatelli, D., Machado, D. D. A., Noto, A. R., Galduróz, J. C. F., ... & Ferri, C. P. (2020). Tobacco smoking and risk for dementia: Evidence from the 10/66 population-based longitudinal study. *Aging & Mental Health, 24*, 1796–1806.

Oyinlola, O., & Olusa, O. (2020). Social work with older persons living with dementia in Nigeria: COVID-19. *Journal of Gerontological Social Work, 63*, 638–641.

Ozdemir, O., Ozdemir, P.G., Boysan, M., & Yilmaz, E. (2015). The relationships between dissociation, attention, and memory dysfunction. *Archives of Neuropsychiatry, 52*, 36–41.

Özgüven, H. D., & Yağmur, K. I. R. (2021). Long acting injectable antipsychotics in the treatment of schizophrenia and bipolar disorder. *Archives of Neuropsychiatry, 58*, S47–S52.

Paetzold, R. L., & Rholes, W. S. (2021). The link from child abuse to dissociation: The roles of adult disorganized attachment, self-concept clarity, and reflective functioning. *Journal of Trauma & Dissociation, 22*, 615–635.

Pahng, A. R., & Edwards, S. (2021). The convergent neuroscience of affective pain and substance use disorder. *Alcohol Research: Current Reviews, 41*: 14.

Palavras, M. A., Hay, P., Mannan, H., da Luz, F. Q., Sainsbury, A., Touyz, S., & Claudino, A. M. (2021). Integrated weight loss and cognitive behavioural therapy (CBT) for the treatment of recurrent binge eating and high body mass index: a randomized controlled trial. *Eating and Weight Disorders-Studies on Anorexia, Bulimia and Obesity, 26*, 249–262.

Pallanti, S., Grassi, G., Antonini, S., Quercioli, L., Salvadori, E., & Hollander, E. (2014). rTMS in resistant mixed states: An exploratory study. *Journal of Affective Disorders, 157*, 66–71.

Palumbo, M. L., Prochnik, A., Wald, M. R., & Genaro, A. M. (2020). Chronic stress and glucocorticoid receptor resistance in asthma. *Clinical Therapeutics, 42*, 993–1006.

Pan, N., Wang, S., Qin, K., Li, L., Chen, Y., Zhang, X., ... & Gong, Q. (2022). Common and distinct neural patterns of attention-deficit/hyperactivity disorder and borderline personality disorder: A multimodal functional and structural meta-analysis. *Biological Psychiatry: Cognitive Neuroscience and Neuroimaging.*

Pandi-Perumal, S. R., Monti, J. M., Burman, D., Karthikeyan, R., BaHammam, A. S., Spence, D. W., ... & Narashimhan, M. (2020). Clarifying the role of sleep in depression: A narrative review. *Psychiatry Research, 291*, 113239.

Panksepp, J. (2022). Affective neuroscience of the emotional BrainMind: evolutionary perspectives and implications for understanding depression. *Dialogues in Clinical Neuroscience.*

Papanastasiou, C. A., Theochari, C. A., Zareifopoulos, N., Arfaras-Melainis, A., Giannakoulas, G., Karamitsos, T. D., ... & Kokkinidis, D. G. (2021). Atrial fibrillation is associated with cognitive impairment, all-cause dementia, vascular dementia, and Alzheimer's disease: A systematic review and meta-analysis. *Journal of General Internal Medicine, 36*, 3122–3135.

Paquin, V., Lapierre, M., Veru, F., & King, S. (2021). Early environmental upheaval and the risk for schizophrenia. *Annual Review of Clinical Psychology, 17*, 285–311.

Pardos-Gascón, E. M., Narambuena, L., Leal-Costa, C., & Van-der Hofstadt-Román, C. J. (2021). Differential efficacy between cognitive-behavioral therapy and mindfulness-based therapies for chronic pain: Systematic review. *International Journal of Clinical and Health Psychology, 21*, 100197.

Parikh, A. N., Triplett, R. L., Wu, T. J., Arora, J., Lukas, K., Smyser, T. A., ... & Smyser, C. D. Neonatal Intensive Care Unit Network Neurobehavioral Scale profiles in full-term infants: Associations with maternal adversity, medical risk, and neonatal outcomes. *Journal of Pediatrics, 246*, 71–79.

Paris, J. (2015). *A concise guide to personality disorders*. Washington, DC: American Psychological Association.

Paris, J. (2019). Dissociative identity disorder: Validity and use in the criminal justice system. *BJPsych Advances, 25*, 287–293.

Parish, S. J., Cottler-Casanova, S., Clayton, A. H., McCabe, M. P., Coleman, E., & Reed, G. M. (2021). The evolution of the female sexual disorder/dysfunction definitions, nomenclature, and classifications: A review of DSM, ICSM, ISSWSH, and ICD. *Sexual Medicine Reviews, 9*, 36–56.

Park, Y. M., Shekhtman, T., & Kelsoe, J. R. (2020). Effect of the type and number of adverse childhood experiences and the timing of adverse experiences on clinical outcomes in individuals with bipolar disorder. *Brain Sciences, 10*, 254.

Parker, J. (2020). *Social work practice: Assessment, planning, intervention and review*. Thousand Oaks, CA: Sage.

Parsons, C., Lim, W. Y., Loy, C., McGuinness, B., Passmore, P., Ward, S. A., & Hughes, C. (2021). Withdrawal or continuation of cholinesterase inhibitors or memantine or both, in people with dementia. *Cochrane Database of Systematic Reviews, 2.*

Parsons, C. E., Zachariae, R., Landberger, C., & Young, K. S. (2021). How does cognitive behavioural therapy for insomnia work? A systematic review and meta-analysis of mediators of change. *Clinical Psychology Review, 86*, 102027.

Patel, S., Akhtar, A., Malins, S., Wright, N., Rowley, E., Young, E., ... & Morriss, R. (2020). The acceptability and usability of digital health interventions for adults with depression, anxiety, and somatoform disorders: Qualitative systematic review and meta-synthesis. *Journal of Medical Internet Research, 22*, e16228.

Patel, S., Khan, S., Saipavankumar, M., & Hamid, P. (2020). The association between cannabis use and schizophrenia: Causative or curative? A systematic review. *Cureus, 12*, e9309.

Patrick, M. E., Schulenberg, J. E., Miech, R. A., Johnston, L. D., O'Malley, P. M., & Bachman, J. G. (2022). *Monitoring the Future Panel Study annual report: National data on substance use among adults ages 19 to 60, 1976–2021*. Ann Arbor, MI: Monitoring the Future Monograph Series. University of Michigan Institute for Social Research.

Paul, N. B., Maietta, J. E., & Allen, D. N. (2020). Cultural considerations for schizophrenia spectrum disorders II: Assessment and treatment. In L. Benuto, F. Gonzalez, & J. Singer (Eds.), *Handbook of cultural factors in behavioral health*. Cham: Springer.

Payne, N., Seenan, S., & van den Akker, O. (2021). Experiences of involuntary childlessness and treatment in the UK: What has changed in 20 years?. *Human Fertility, 24*, 333–340.

Pedersen, S. C., Maindal, H. T., & Ryom, K. (2021). "I Wanted to Be There as a Father, but I Couldn't": A qualitative study of fathers' experiences of postpartum depression and their help-seeking behavior. *American Journal of Men's Health, 15*, 15579883211024375.

Pedrotti, J. T., & Isom, D. A. (2021). *Multicultural psychology: Self, society, and social change*. Thousand Oaks, CA: Sage.

Peebles, R., Wilson, J. L., Litt, I. F., Hardy, K. K., Lock, J. D., Mann, J. R., & Borzekowski, D.L.G. (2012). Disordered eating in a digital age: Eating behaviors, health, and quality of life in users of websites with pro-eating disorder content. *Journal of Medical Internet Research, 14*, e148.

Pelham, W. E. III, Altszuler, A. R., Merrill, B. M., Raiker, J. S., Macphee, F. L., Ramos, M., Gnagy, E. M., Greiner, A. R., Coles, E. K., Connor, C. M., Lonigan, C. J., Burger, L., Morrow, A. S., Zhao, X., Swanson, J. M., Waxmonsky, J. G., & Pelham, W. E., Jr. (2022). The effect of stimulant medication on the learning of academic curricula in children with ADHD: A randomized crossover study. *Journal of Consulting and Clinical Psychology, 90*, 367–380.

Pena, S. A., Iyengar, R., Eshraghi, R. S., Bencie, N., Mittal, J., Aljohani, A., ... & Eshraghi, A. A. (2020). Gene therapy for neurological disorders: Challenges and recent advancements. *Journal of Drug Targeting, 28*, 111–128.

Pendergast, L. L., Youngstrom, E. A., Brown, C., Jensen, D., Abramson, L.Y., & Alloy, L.B. (2015). Structural invariance of General Behavior Inventory (GBI) scores in Black and White young adults. *Psychological Assessment, 27*, 21.

Pennisi, P., Giallongo, L., Milintenda, G., & Cannarozzo, M. (2021). Autism, autistic traits and creativity: a systematic review and meta-analysis. *Cognitive Processing, 22*, 1–36.

Perez, D. L., Barsky, A. J., Vago, D. R., Baslet, G., & Silbersweig, D. A. (2015). A neural circuit framework for somatosensory amplification in somatoform disorders. *Journal of Neuropsychiatry and Clinical Neuroscience, 27*, e40–e50.

Perez, J. A., Otowa, T., Roberson-Nay, R., & Hettema, J.M. (2013). Genetics of anxiety disorders. In D.S. Charney, P. Sklar, J.D. Buxbaum, & E.J. Nestler (Eds.), *Neurobiology of mental illness* (4th ed., pp. 537–548). New York: Oxford.

Pérez-López, F. R., Ornat, L., López-Baena, M. T., Pérez-Roncero, G. R., Tajada-Duaso, M. C., & Chedrau, P. (2020). Association of female genital mutilation and female sexual dysfunction: A systematic review and meta-analysis. *European Journal of Obstetrics & Gynecology and Reproductive Biology, 254*, 236–244.

Perich, T., Mitchell, P. B., & Vilus, B. (2022). Stigma in bipolar disorder: A current review of the literature. *Australian & New Zealand Journal of Psychiatry, 56*, 1060–1064.

Perrotta, G. (2020). Borderline personality disorder: Definition, differential diagnosis, clinical contexts, and therapeutic approaches. *Annals of Psychiatry and Treatment, 4*, 43–56.

Perrotta, G. (2020). Gender dysphoria: Definitions, classifications, neurobiological profiles and clinical treatments. *International Journal of Sexual and Reproductive Health Care, 3*, 42–50.

Perrotta, G. (2020). Pedophilia: Definition, classifications, criminological and neurobiological profiles, and clinical treatments. A complete review. *Open Journal of Pediatrics and Child Health, 5*, 19–26.

Perrotta, G. (2020). Psychotic spectrum disorders: definitions, classifications, neural correlates and clinical profiles. *Annals of Psychiatry and Treatment, 4*, 70–84.

Perrotta, G. (2021). Avoidant personality disorder: Definition, clinical and neurobiological profiles, differential diagnosis and therapeutic framework. *Journal of Neurology, Neurological Science and Disorders, 7*, 001–005.

Perugi, G., Hantouche, E., Vannucchi, G., & Pinto, O. (2015). Cyclothymia reloaded: A reappraisal of the most misconceived affective disorder. *Journal of Affective Disorders, 183*, 119–133.

Perry, A., Gordon-Smith, K., Jones, L., & Jones, I. (2021). Phenomenology, epidemiology and aetiology of postpartum psychosis: A review. *Brain Sciences, 11*, 47.

Peter, L. J., Schindler, S., Sander, C., Schmidt, S., Muehlan, H., McLaren, T., ... & Schomerus, G. (2021). Continuum beliefs and mental illness stigma: A systematic review and meta-analysis of correlation and intervention studies. *Psychological Medicine*, 1-11.

Pettorruso, M., d'Andrea, G., Martinotti, G., Cocciolillo, F., Miuli, A., Di Muzio, I., ... & Camardese, G. (2020). Hopelessness, dissociative symptoms, and suicide risk in major depressive disorder: Clinical and biological correlates. *Brain Sciences, 10*, 519.

Pezzuoli, F., Tafaro, D., Pane, M., Corona, D., & Corradini, M. L. (2020). Development of a new sign language translation system for people with autism spectrum disorder. *Advances in Neurodevelopmental Disorders, 4*, 439–446.

Pfund, R. A., Cook, J. E., McAfee, N. W., Huskinson, S. L., & Parker, J. D. (2021). Challenges to conducting contingency management treatment for substance use disorders: Practice recommendations for clinicians. *Professional Psychology: Research and Practice, 52*, 137–145.

Phillips, K. A. (2015). Body dysmorphic disorder. In K. A. Phillips & D. J. Stein (Eds.), *Handbook on obsessive-compulsive and related disorders*. Arlington, VA: American Psychiatric Association.

Phongpreecha, T., Cholerton, B., Mata, I. F., Zabetian, C. P., Poston, K. L., Aghaeepour, N., ... & Montine, T. J. (2020). Multivariate prediction of dementia in Parkinson's disease. *NPJ Parkinson's Disease, 6*, 20.

Piazza, C. C., Roane, H. S., & Fisher, W. W. (Eds.) (2021). *Handbook of applied behavior analysis* (2nd ed). New York: Guilford.

Picardi, A., Fonzi, L., Pallagrosi, M., Gigantesco, A., & Biondi, M. (2018). Delusional themes across affective and non-affective psychoses. *Frontiers in Psychiatry, 9*, 132.

Piccoli, E., Bergamaschini, I., Molteni, L., Vanzetto, S., Varinelli, A., Viganò, C., ... & Dell'Osso, B. (2021). Latency to selective serotonin reuptake inhibitor vs benzodiazepine treatment in patients with panic disorder: A naturalistic study. *CNS Spectrums*, 1–7.

Pick, S., Goldstein, L. H., Perez, D. L., & Nicholson, T. R. (2019). Emotional processing in functional neurological disorder: A review, biopsychosocial model and research agenda. *Journal of Neurology, Neurosurgery & Psychiatry, 90*, 704–711.

Pinheiro, P., Gonçalves, M. M., Nogueira, D., Pereira, R., Basto, I., Alves, D., & Salgado, J. (2022). Emotional processing during the therapy for complicated grief. *Psychotherapy Research, 32*, 678–693.

Pinho, M., Freitas, A., & Ribeiro, J. P. (2022). Schizophreniform disorder related hospitalizations–a Big Data analysis of a national hospitalization database. *European Psychiatry, 65*, S322–S323.

Pinto, J. O., Dores, A. R., Geraldo, A., Peixoto, B., & Barbosa, F. (2020). Sensory stimulation programs in dementia: A systematic review of methods and effectiveness. *Expert Review of Neurotherapeutics, 20*, 1229–1247.

Pisano, S., & Masi, G. (2020). Recommendations for the pharmacological management of irritability and aggression in conduct disorder patients. *Expert Opinion on Pharmacotherapy, 21*, 5–7.

Pisipati, S., Connor, B. A., & Riddle, M. S. (2020). Updates on the epidemiology, pathogenesis, diagnosis, and management of postinfectious irritable bowel syndrome. *Current Opinion in Infectious Diseases, 33*, 411–418.

Pistorello, J., Fruzzetti, A. E., MacLane, C., Gallop, R., & Iverson, K. M. (2012). Dialectical behavior therapy (DBT) applied to college students: a randomized clinical trial. *Journal of Consulting and Clinical Psychology, 80*, 982–994.

Plavén-Sigray, P., Ikonen Victorsson, P., Santillo, A., Matheson, G. J., Lee, M., Collste, K., ... & Cervenka, S. (2022). Thalamic dopamine D2-receptor availability in schizophrenia: a study on antipsychotic-naive patients with first-episode psychosis and a meta-analysis. *Molecular Psychiatry, 27*, 1233–1240.

Pokorny, V. J., Espensen-Sturges, T. D., Burton, P. C., Sponheim, S. R., & Olman, C. A. (2021). Aberrant cortical connectivity during ambiguous object recognition is associated with schizophrenia. *Biological Psychiatry: Cognitive Neuroscience and Neuroimaging, 6*, 1193–1201.

Polanco-Roman, L., Miranda, R., Hien, D., & Anglin, D. M. (2021). Racial/ethnic discrimination as race-based trauma and suicide-related risk in racial/ethnic minority young adults: The explanatory roles of stress sensitivity and dissociation. *Psychological Trauma: Theory, Research, Practice, and Policy, 13*, 759–767.

Poletti, M., Gebhardt, E., Pelizza, L., Preti, A., & Raballo, A. (2020). Looking at intergenerational risk factors in schizophrenia spectrum disorders: new frontiers for early vulnerability identification? *Frontiers in Psychiatry, 11*, 566683.

Pomeroy, E. (2015). *The clinical assessment workbook: Balancing strengths and differential diagnosis* (2nd ed.). Boston, MA: Cengage.

Popa, I., Rădulescu, I., Drăgoi, A. M., Trifu, S., & Cristea, M. B. (2021). Korsakoff syndrome: An overlook. *Experimental and Therapeutic Medicine, 22*, 1–5.

Pope, K.S., & Vasquez, M.J.T. (2011). *Ethics in psychotherapy and counseling: A practical guide* (4th ed.). New York: Wiley.

Porta-Casteràs, D., Cano, M., Camprodon, J. A., Loo, C., Palao, D., Soriano-Mas, C., & Cardoner, N. (2021). A multimetric systematic review of fMRI findings in patients with MDD receiving ECT. *Progress in Neuro-Psychopharmacology and Biological Psychiatry, 108*, 110178.

Posamentier, J., Seibel, K., & DyTang, N. (2022). Preventing youth suicide: A review of school-based practices and how social–emotional learning fits into comprehensive efforts. *Trauma, Violence, & Abuse*, 15248380211039475.

Post, R. M., Goldstein, B. I., Birmaher, B., Findling, R. L., Frey, B. N., DelBello, M. P., & Miklowitz, D. J. (2020). Toward prevention of bipolar disorder in at-risk children: Potential strategies ahead of the data. *Journal of Affective Disorders, 272*, 508–520.

Poston, K. L., Ua Cruadhlaoich, M. A., Santoso, L. F., Bernstein, J. D., Liu, T., Wang, Y., ... & Zeineh, M. M. (2020). Substantia nigra volume dissociates bradykinesia and rigidity from tremor in Parkinson's disease: A 7 Tesla imaging study. *Journal of Parkinson's Disease, 10*, 591–604.

Pozza, A., Starcevic, V., Ferretti, F., Pedani, C., Crispino, R., Governi, G., ... & Coluccia, A. (2021). Obsessive-compulsive personality disorder co-occurring in individuals with obsessive-compulsive disorder: A systematic review and meta-analysis. *Harvard Review of Psychiatry, 29*, 95–107.

Pozzi, M., Bertella, S., Gatti, E., Peeters, G. G., Carnovale, C., Zambrano, S., & Nobile, M. (2020). Emerging drugs for the treatment of attention-deficit hyperactivity disorder (ADHD). *Expert Opinion on Emerging Drugs, 25*, 395–407.

Prendecki, M., Kowalska, M., Toton, E., & Kozubski, W. (2020). Genetic editing and pharmacogenetics in current and future therapy of neurocognitive disorders. *Current Alzheimer Research, 17*, 238–258.

Priebe, K., Sorem, E. B., & Anderson, J. L. (2022). Perceived rejection in personality psychopathology: The role of attachment and gender. *Journal of Psychopathology and Behavioral Assessment, 44*, 713–724.

Principi, N., & Esposito, S. (2020). Bacterial meningitis: new treatment options to reduce the risk of brain damage. *Expert Opinion on Pharmacotherapy, 21*, 97–105.

Prochaska, J.O., & Norcross, J.C. (2013). *Systems of psychotherapy: A transtheoretical analysis* (8th ed.). Stamford, CT: Cengage.

Promodu, K., Nair, K.R., & Pushparajan, S. (2012). Koro syndrome: Mass epidemic in Kerala, India. *Indian Journal of Clinical Psychology, 39*, 152–156.

Pugh, M. J., & Van Cott, A. (2021). Risk for early onset dementia among veterans: The contributions of TBI and epilepsy. *Archives of Physical Medicine and Rehabilitation, 102*, e18.

Pulverman, C. S., & Meston, C. M. (2020). Sexual dysfunction in women with a history of childhood sexual abuse: The role of sexual shame. *Psychological Trauma: Theory, Research, Practice, and Policy, 12*, 291–299.

Purtle, J., Marzalik, J. S., Halfond, R. W., Bufka, L. F., Teachman, B. A., & Aarons, G. A. (2020). Toward the data-driven dissemination of findings from psychological science. *American Psychologist, 75*, 1052–1066.

Puzzanchera, C. (2022). *Trends in youth arrests for violent crimes*. Washington, DC: Office of Juvenile Justice and Delinquency Prevention.

Pyke, R. E. (2020). Sexual performance anxiety. *Sexual Medicine Reviews, 8*, 183–190.

Qian, J., Wu, Y., Liu, F., Zhu, Y., Jin, H., Zhang, H., ... & Yu, D. (2022). An update on the prevalence of eating disorders in the general population: a systematic review and meta-analysis. *Eating and Weight Disorders-Studies on Anorexia, Bulimia and Obesity*, 27, 415–428.

Quinn, M. C., Copeland, T., Hopkins, T., & Brody, M. (2022). A more grown-up response to ordinary adolescent behaviors: Repealing PINS laws to protect and empower DC youth. *University of the District of Columbia Law Review, 25*, 66.

Raccah, O., Block, N., & Fox, K. C. (2021). Does the prefrontal cortex play an essential role in consciousness? Insights from intracranial electrical stimulation of the human brain. *Journal of Neuroscience, 41*, 2076–2087.

Raeder, F., Merz, C. J., Margraf, J., & Zlomuzica, A. (2020). The association between fear extinction, the ability to accomplish exposure and exposure therapy outcome in specific phobia. *Scientific Reports, 10*, 1–11.

Raftery, D., Kelly, P. J., Deane, F. P., Baker, A. L., Ingram, I., Goh, M. C., ... & McKetin, R. (2020). Insight in substance use disorder: A systematic review of the literature. *Addictive Behaviors, 111*, 106549.

Raihani, N., Martinez-Gatell, D., Bell, V., & Foulkes, L. (2021). Social reward, punishment, and prosociality in paranoia. *Journal of Abnormal Psychology, 130*, 177–185.

Rajkumar, R. P. (2020). Contamination and infection: what the coronavirus pandemic could reveal about the evolutionary origins of obsessive-compulsive disorder. *Psychiatry Research, 289*, 113062.

Ramadas, E., Lima, M. P. D., Caetano, T., Lopes, J., & Dixe, M. D. A. (2021). Effectiveness of mindfulness-based relapse prevention in individuals with substance use disorders: A systematic review. *Behavioral Sciences, 11*, 133.

Ramchand, R., Gordon, J. A., & Pearson, J. L. (2021). Trends in suicide rates by race and ethnicity in the United States. *JAMA Network Open, 4*, e2111563-e2111563.

Ramirez, J. J., Rhew, I. C., Patrick, M. E., Larimer, M. E., & Lee, C. M. (2020). A daily-level analysis of moderators of the association between alcohol expectancies and alcohol use among college student drinkers. *Substance Use & Misuse, 55*, 973–982.

Ramirez-Bermudez, J., Medina-Gutierrez, A., Gomez-Cianca, H., Arias, P., Pérez-Gonzalez, A., Lebrija-Reyes, P. A., ... & Sachdev, P. S. (2022). Clinical significance of delirium with catatonic signs in patients with neurological disorders. *Journal of Neuropsychiatry and Clinical Neurosciences, 34*, 132–140.

Ramos, G., Brookman-Frazee, L., Kodish, T., Rodriguez, A., & Lau, A. S. (2020). Community providers' experiences with evidence-based practices: The role of therapist race/ethnicity. *Cultural Diversity and Ethnic Minority Psychology, 27*, 471–482.

Ramos, G. G., West, A. E., Begay, C., Telles, V. M., D'Isabella, J., Antony, V., & Soto, C. (2021). Substance use disorder and homelessness among American Indians and Alaska Natives in California. *Journal of Ethnicity in Substance Abuse*, 1–22.

Ramos-Lima, L. F., Waikamp, V., Antonelli-Salgado, T., Passos, I. C., & Freitas, L. H. M. (2020). The use of machine learning techniques in trauma-related disorders: A systematic review. *Journal of Psychiatric Research, 121*, 159–172.

Ramsay, L., Carter, A. J., & Walton, J. S. (2020). Contemporary programs designed for the tertiary prevention of recidivism by people convicted of a sexual offense: A review, and the UK perspective. In J. Proulx, F. Cortoni, L. A. Craig, & E. J. Letourneau (Eds.), *The Wiley handbook of what works with sexual offenders: Contemporary perspectives in theory, assessment, treatment, and prevention* (pp. 185–199). Hoboken, NJ: Wiley.

Rantala, M. J., Luoto, S., Borráz-León, J. I., & Krams, I. (2021). Bipolar disorder: An evolutionary psychoneuroimmunological approach. *Neuroscience & Biobehavioral Reviews, 122*, 28–37.

Rantala, M. J., Luoto, S., Krams, I., & Karlsson, H. (2018). Depression subtyping based on evolutionary psychiatry: Proximate mechanisms and ultimate functions. *Brain, Behavior, and Immunity, 69*, 603–617.

Ranu, J., Kalebic, N., Melendez-Torres, G. J., & Taylor, P. J. (2022). Association between adverse childhood experiences and a combination of psychosis and violence among adults: A systematic review and meta-analysis. *Trauma, Violence, & Abuse*, 15248380221122818.

Rashtbari, A., & Saed, O. (2020). Contrast avoidance model of worry and generalized anxiety disorder: A theoretical perspective. *Cogent Psychology, 7*, 1800262.

Raveendran, A. V., & Agarwal, A. (2021). Premature ejaculation-current concepts in the management: a narrative review. *International Journal of Reproductive BioMedicine, 19*, 5–22.

Razek, A. A. K. A., & Elsebaie, N. A. (2021). Imaging of vascular cognitive impairment. *Clinical Imaging, 74*, 45–54.

Reddihough, D., Leonard, H., Jacoby, P., Kim, R., Epstein, A., Murphy, N., ... & Downs, J. (2021). Comorbidities and quality of life in children with intellectual disability. *Child: Care, Health and Development, 47*, 654–666.

Reddy, A. G., Khoei, A. A., & Khera, M. (2022). The potential for pharmacological interventions for low sex drive in men. *Journal of Sexual Medicine, 19*, 165–169.

Redgrave, G. W., Schreyer, C. C., Coughlin, J. W., Fischer, L. K., Pletch, A., & Guarda, A. S. (2021). Discharge body mass index, not illness chronicity, predicts 6-month weight outcome in patients hospitalized with anorexia nervosa. *Frontiers in Psychiatry, 12*, 641861.

Reed, C., Belger, M., Dell'Agnello, G., Wimo, A., Argimon, J. M., Bruno, G., Dodel, R., Haro, J.M., Jones, R.W., & Vellas, B. (2014). Caregiver burden in Alzheimer's disease: Differential associations in adult-child and spousal caregivers in the GERAS observational study. *Dementia and Geriatric Cognitive Disorders Extra, 4*, 51–64.

Reekes, T. H., Higginson, C. I., Ledbetter, C. R., Sathivadivel, N., Zweig, R. M., & Disbrow, E. A. (2020). Sex specific cognitive differences in Parkinson disease. *Parkinson's Disease, 6*, 1–6.

Rehm, J., & Shield, K. D. (2019). Global burden of disease and the impact of mental and addictive disorders. *Current Psychiatry Reports, 21*, 1–7.

Reich, J., & Schatzberg, A. (2021). Prevalence, factor structure, and heritability of avoidant personality disorder. *Journal of Nervous and Mental Disease, 209*, 764–772.

Reichl, C., & Kaess, M. (2021). Self-harm in the context of borderline personality disorder. *Current Opinion in Psychology, 37*, 139–144.

Reid, J. E., Laws, K. R., Drummond, L., Vismara, M., Grancini, B., Mpavaenda, D., & Fineberg, N. A. (2021). Cognitive behavioural therapy with exposure and response prevention in the treatment of obsessive-compulsive disorder: A systematic review and meta-analysis of randomised controlled trials. *Comprehensive Psychiatry, 106*, 152223.

Reilly, T. J., Wallman, P., Clark, I., Knox, C. L., Craig, M. C., & Taylor, D. (2022). Intermittent selective serotonin reuptake inhibitors for premenstrual syndromes: A systematic review and meta-analysis of randomised trials. *Journal of Psychopharmacology*, 02698811221099645.

Reinders, A. A., Chalavi, S., Schlumpf, Y. R., Vissia, E. M., Nijenhuis, E. R., Jäncke, L., ... & Ecker, C. (2018). Neurodevelopmental origins of abnormal cortical morphology in dissociative identity disorder. *Acta Psychiatrica Scandinavica, 137*, 157–170.

Reinders, A. A., & Veltman, D. J. (2021). Dissociative identity disorder: Out of the shadows at last? *The British Journal of Psychiatry, 219*, 413–414.

Reisinger, B. A., & Gleaves, D. H. (2022). Comparing social stigma of dissociative identity disorder, schizophrenia, and depressive disorders. *Journal of Trauma and Dissociation*, 1–14.

Reivich, K., Gillham, J.E., Chaplin, T.M., & Seligman, M.E.P. (2013). From helplessness to optimism: The role of resilience in treating and preventing depression in youth. In S. Goldstein & R.B. Brooks (Eds.), *Handbook of resilience in children* (pp. 201–214). New York: Springer.

Retz, W., Ginsberg, Y., Turner, D., Barra, S., Retz-Junginger, P., Larsson, H., & Asherson, P. (2021). Attention-Deficit/Hyperactivity Disorder (ADHD), antisociality and delinquent behavior over the lifespan. *Neuroscience & Biobehavioral Reviews, 120*, 236–248.

Revill, A. S., Patton, K. A., Connor, J. P., Sheffield, J., Wood, A. P., Castellanos-Ryan, N., & Gullo, M. J. (2020). From impulse to action? Cognitive mechanisms of impulsivity-related risk for externalizing behavior. *Journal of Abnormal Child Psychology, 48*, 1023–1034.

Reynolds, C. F. (2020). Optimizing personalized management of depression: The importance of real-world contexts and the need for a new convergence paradigm in mental health. *World Psychiatry, 19*, 266–268

Reynolds, C. R., & Kamphaus, R. W. (2015). *Behavior Assessment System for Children-3*. San Antonio, TX: Pearson.

Rhee, J. Y., Colman, M. A., Mendu, M., Shah, S. J., Fox, M. D., Rost, N. S., & Kimchi, E. Y. (2022). Associations between stroke localization and delirium: A systematic review and meta-analysis. *Journal of Stroke and Cerebrovascular Diseases, 31*, 106270.

Ribeiro, P. R. D. S., & Schlindwein, A. D. (2021). Benzodiazepine deprescription strategies in chronic users: A systematic review. *Family Practice, 38*, 684–693.

Richardson, C., Robb, K. A., & O'Connor, R. C. (2021). A systematic review of suicidal behaviour in men: A narrative synthesis of risk factors. *Social Science & Medicine, 276*, 113831.

Richardson, K., & Barkham, M. (2020). Recovery from depression: A systematic review of perceptions and associated factors. *Journal of Mental Health, 29*, 103–115.

Ridley, M., Rao, G., Schilbach, F., & Patel, V. (2020). Poverty, depression, and anxiety: Causal evidence and mechanisms. *Science, 370*, eaay0214.

Riemann, D., Krone, L. B., Wulff, K., & Nissen, C. (2020). Sleep, insomnia, and depression. *Neuropsychopharmacology, 45*, 74–89.

Ringrose, J.L. (2012). *Understanding and treating dissociative identity disorder (or multiple personality disorder)*. London: Karnac.

Ritz, L., Laniepce, A., Cabé, N., Lannuzel, C., Boudehent, C., Urso, L., ... & Pitel, A. L. (2021). Early identification of alcohol use disorder patients at risk of developing Korsakoff's syndrome. *Alcoholism: Clinical and Experimental Research, 45*, 587–595.

Robbins, S.P. (2015). Working with clients who have recovered memories. In K. Corcoran & A.R. Roberts (Eds.), *Social workers' desk reference* (3rd ed., pp. 691–696). New York: Oxford.

Roberts, R. C., McCollum, L. A., Schoonover, K. E., Mabry, S. J., Roche, J. K., & Lahti, A. C. (2020). Ultrastructural evidence for glutamatergic dysregulation in schizophrenia. *Schizophrenia Research, 249*, 4-15.

Robinson, K., & Wade, T. D. (2021). Perfectionism interventions targeting disordered eating: A systematic review and meta-analysis. *International Journal of Eating Disorders, 54*, 473–487.

Rodante, D. E., Grendas, L. N., Puppo, S., Vidjen, P., Portela, A., Rojas, S. M., ... & Daray, F. M. (2019). Predictors of short-and long-term recurrence of suicidal behavior in borderline personality disorder. *Acta Psychiatrica Scandinavica, 140*, 158–168.

Rodríguez-Testal, J. F., Bendala-Rodríguez, P., Perona-Garcelán, S., & Senín-Calderón, C. (2019). Examining the structure of ideas of reference in clinical and community samples. *Comprehensive Psychiatry, 93*, 48–55.

Roelofs, J., Muris, P., Braet, C., Arntz, A., & Beelen, I. (2015). The structured clinical interview for *DSM-IV* childhood diagnoses (Kid-SCID): First psychometric evaluation in a Dutch sample of clinically referred youths. *Child Psychiatry and Human Development, 46*, 367–375.

Roitsch, J., Gumpert, M., Springle, A., & Raymer, A. M. (2021). Writing instruction for students with learning disabilities: quality appraisal of systematic reviews and meta-analyses. *Reading & Writing Quarterly, 37*, 32–44.

Rolls, G. (2015). *Classic case studies in psychology* (3rd ed.). New York: Routledge.

Romero-Martínez, Á., Sarrate-Costa, C., & Moya-Albiol, L. (2022). Reactive vs proactive aggression: a differential psychobiological profile? Conclusions derived from a systematic review. *Neuroscience & Biobehavioral Reviews*, 104626.

Ronningstam, E. F., Keng, S. L., Ridolfi, M. E., Arbabi, M., & Grenyer, B. F. (2018). Cultural aspects in symptomatology, assessment, and treatment of personality disorders. *Current Psychiatry Reports, 20*, 1–10.

Roos, C. R., Carroll, K. M., Nich, C., Frankforter, T., & Kiluk, B. D. (2020). Short-and long-term changes in substance-related coping as mediators of in-person and computerized CBT for alcohol and drug use disorders. *Drug and Alcohol Dependence, 212*, 108044.

Rosenberg, A., & Hamiel, D. (2021). Reducing test anxiety and related symptoms using a biofeedback respiratory practice device: A randomized control trial. *Applied Psychophysiology and Biofeedback, 46*, 69–82.

Rosende-Roca, M., Abdelnour, C., Esteban, E., Tartari, J. P., Alarcon, E., Martínez-Atienza, J., ... & Boada, M. (2021). The role of sex and gender in the selection of Alzheimer patients for clinical trial pre-screening. *Alzheimer's Research & Therapy, 13*, 1–13.

Ross, J., Armour, C., Kerig, P. K., Kidwell, M. C., & Kilshaw, R. E. (2020). A network analysis of posttraumatic stress disorder and dissociation in trauma-exposed adolescents. *Journal of Anxiety Disorders, 72*, 102222.

Ross, J. A., & Van Bockstaele, E. J. (2021). The locus coeruleus-norepinephrine system in stress and arousal: Unraveling historical, current, and future perspectives. *Frontiers in Psychiatry, 11*, 601519.

Rosselli, M., Uribe, I. V., Ahne, E., & Shihadeh, L. (2022). Culture, ethnicity, and level of education in Alzheimer's Disease. *Neurotherapeutics, 19*, 26–54.

Rossi, M. F., Tumminello, A., Marconi, M., Gualano, M. R., Santoro, P. E., Malorni, W., & Moscato, U. (2022). Sex and gender differences in migraines: A narrative review. *Neurological Sciences, 43*, 5729–5734.

Roughan, W. H., Campos, A. I., García-Marín, L. M., Cuéllar-Partida, G., Lupton, M. K., Hickie, I. B., ... & Rentería, M. E. (2021). Comorbid chronic pain and depression: Shared risk factors and differential antidepressant effectiveness. *Frontiers in Psychiatry, 12*, 643609.

Roydeva, M. I., & Reinders, A. A. (2021). Biomarkers of pathological dissociation: A systematic review. *Neuroscience & Biobehavioral Reviews, 123*, 120–202.

Rubin, L., Ingram, L. A., Resciniti, N. V., Ashford-Carroll, B., Leith, K. H., Rose, A., ... & Friedman, D. B. (2021). Genetic risk factors for Alzheimer's Disease in racial/ethnic minority populations in the US: A scoping review. *Frontiers in Public Health, 9*, 784958.

Rudolph, A. E., Upton, E., Young, A. M., & Havens, J. R. (2021). Social network predictors of recent and sustained injection drug use cessation: findings from a longitudinal cohort study. *Addiction, 116*, 856–864.

Ruggeri, K. (2021). *Psychology and behavioral economics: Applications for public policy*. Taylor and Francis.

Ruíz-Salinas, A. K., Vázquez-Roque, R. A., Díaz, A., Pulido, G., Treviño, S., Floran, B., & Flores, G. (2020). The treatment of Goji berry (Lycium barbarum) improves the neuroplasticity of the prefrontal cortex and hippocampus in aged rats. *Journal of Nutritional Biochemistry, 83*, 108416.

Rumschik, S. M., & Appel, J. M. (2019). Malingering in the psychiatric emergency department: Prevalence, predictors, and outcomes. *Psychiatric Services, 70*, 115–122.

Rusch, H. (2022). Heroic behavior: A review of the literature on high-stakes altruism in the wild. *Current Opinion in Psychology, 43*, 238–243.

Russell, L., Abbass, A., & Allder, S. (2022). A review of the treatment of functional neurological disorder with intensive short-term dynamic psychotherapy. *Epilepsy & Behavior, 130*, 108657.

Russell, M.B. (2020). Epidemiology of cluster headache. In M. Leone, & A. May (Eds.), *Cluster headache and other trigeminal autonomic cephalgias* (pp. 7–10). Cham: Springer.

Ruiz, I., Raugh, I. M., Bartolomeo, L. A., & Strauss, G. P. (2020). A meta-analysis of neuropsychological effort test performance in psychotic disorders. *Neuropsychology Review, 30*, 407–424.

Ruiz-Gonzalez, D., Hernandez-Martinez, A., Valenzuela, P. L., Morales, J. S., & Soriano-Maldonado, A. (2021). Effects of physical exercise on plasma brain-derived neurotrophic factor in neurodegenerative disorders: A systematic review and meta-analysis of randomized controlled trials. *Neuroscience & Biobehavioral Reviews, 128*, 394–405.

Russo, G. I., di Mauro, M., Cocci, A., Cacciamani, G., Cimino, S., Serefoglu, E. C., ... & Verze, P. (2020). Consulting "Dr Google" for sexual dysfunction: A contemporary worldwide trend analysis. *International Journal of Impotence Research, 32*, 455–461.

Ryan, D., Tornberg-Belanger, S. N., Perez, G., Maurer, S., Price, C., Rao, D., ... & Ornelas, I. J. (2021). Stress, social support and their relationship to depression and anxiety among Latina immigrant women. *Journal of Psychosomatic Research, 149*, 110588.

Rymarczyk, K. (2021). The role of personality traits, sociocultural factors, and body dissatisfaction in anorexia readiness syndrome in women. *Journal of Eating Disorders, 9*, 1–10.

Sabri, B., Campbell, J.C., & Dabby, F.C. (2016). Gender differences in intimate partner homicides among ethnic subgroups of Asians. *Violence Against Women, 22*, 432–453.

Sadock, B.J., Sadock, V.A., & Ruiz, P. (2015). *Kaplan and Sadock's synopsis of psychiatry: Behavioral sciences/clinical psychiatry* (11th ed.). Philadelphia, PA: Wolters Kluwer.

Saha, S., Lim, C. C., Cannon, D. L., Burton, L., Bremner, M., Cosgrove, P., ... & J McGrath, J. (2021). Co-morbidity between mood and anxiety disorders: A systematic review and meta-analysis. *Depression and Anxiety, 38*, 286–306.

Saini, D., Mukherjee, A., Roy, A., & Biswas, A. (2020). A comparative study of the behavioral profile of the behavioral variant of frontotemporal dementia and Parkinson's disease dementia. *Dementia and Geriatric Cognitive Disorders Extra, 10*, 182–194.

Salami, B., Salma, J., & Hegadoren, K. (2019). Access and utilization of mental health services for immigrants and refugees: Perspectives of immigrant service providers. *International Journal of Mental Health Nursing, 28*, 152–161.

Salcedo-Arellano, M. J., Dufour, B., McLennan, Y., Martinez-Cerdeno, V., & Hagerman, R. (2020). Fragile X syndrome and associated disorders: Clinical aspects and pathology. *Neurobiology of Disease, 136*, 104740.

Saleh, D. A., Oyakose, P. J., Talko, A. P., Balle, K. B., Job, J. J., & Dabit, J. (2021). Age and religious devotion as predisposing factors of female orgasmic disorder in a sample of Jos-North women. *International Journal of Religious and Cultural Practice, 6*, 33–40.

Saleh, F. M., Bradford, J. M., & Brodsky, D. J. (Eds.) (2021). *Sex offenders: Identification, risk assessment, treatment, and legal issues* (2nd ed.). New York: Oxford.

Saleh, R., Majzoub, A., & Abu El-Hamd, M. (2021). An update on the treatment of premature ejaculation: A systematic review. *Arab Journal of Urology, 19*, 281–302.

Samieri, C., Yassine, H. N., Melo van Lent, D., Lefèvre-Arbogast, S., van de Rest, O., Bowman, G. L., & Scarmeas, N. (2022). Personalized nutrition for dementia prevention. *Alzheimer's & Dementia, 18*, 1424-1437.

Sanchez-Roige, S., Palmer, A. A., & Clarke, T. K. (2020). Recent efforts to dissect the genetic basis of alcohol use and abuse. *Biological Psychiatry, 87*, 609–618.

Sandøy, T. A. (2020). Alternative (to) punishment: Assessing punishment experiences in youth diversion programmes. *The British Journal of Criminology, 60*, 911–929.

Sandstrom, A., Uher, R., & Pavlova, B. (2020). Prospective association between childhood behavioral inhibition and anxiety: A meta-analysis. *Research on Child and Adolescent Psychopathology, 48*, 57–66.

Sanfilippo, J., Ness, M., Petscher, Y., Rappaport, L., Zuckerman, B., & Gaab, N. (2020). Reintroducing dyslexia: Early identification and implications for pediatric practice. *Pediatrics, 146*: e20193046.

Sanmartin, M. X., Ali, M. M., Lynch, S., & Aktas, A. (2020). Association between state-level criminal justice–focused prenatal substance use policies in the US and substance use–related foster care admissions and family reunification. *JAMA Pediatrics, 174*, 782–788.

Santa Ana, E. J., LaRowe, S. D., Gebregziabher, M., Morgan-Lopez, A. A., Lamb, K., Beavis, K. A., ... & Martino, S. (2021). Randomized controlled trial of group motivational interviewing for veterans with substance use disorders. *Drug and Alcohol Dependence, 223*, 108716.

Sar, V. (2017). Dissociative disorders: Epidemiology. In A. Wenzel (Ed.), *The SAGE encyclopedia of abnormal and clinical psychology* (pp. 1141–1143). Thousand Oaks, CA: Sage.

Sato, A., Hashimoto, T., Kimura, A., Niitsu, T., & Iyo, M. (2018). Psychological distress symptoms associated with life events in patients with bipolar disorder: A cross-sectional study. *Frontiers in Psychiatry, 9*, 200.

Sato, K. (2021). Why is lithium effective in alleviating bipolar disorder? *Medical Hypotheses, 147*, 110484.

Satterfield, N. A., & Stutts, L. A. (2021). Pinning down the problems and influences: Disordered eating and body satisfaction in male wrestlers. *Psychology of Sport and Exercise, 54*, 101884.

Scarella, T. M., Boland, R. J., & Barsky, A. J. (2019). Illness anxiety disorder: Psychopathology, epidemiology, clinical characteristics, and treatment. *Psychosomatic Medicine, 81*, 398–407.

Schalkwijk, F., Luyten, P., Ingenhoven, T., & Dekker, J. (2021). Narcissistic personality disorder: Are psychodynamic theories and the alternative DSM-5 model for personality disorders finally going to meet?. *Frontiers in Psychology, 12*, 676733.

Schaumberg, K., Reilly, E. E., Gorrell, S., Levinson, C. A., Farrell, N. R., Brown, T. A., ... & Anderson, L. M. (2021). Conceptualizing eating disorder psychopathology using an anxiety disorders framework: Evidence and implications for exposure-based clinical research. *Clinical Psychology Review, 83*, 101952.

Scheer, V., Blanco, C., Olfson, M., Lemogne, C., Airagnes, G., Peyre, H., ... & Hoertel, N. (2020). A comprehensive model of predictors of suicide attempt in individuals with panic disorder: Results from a national 3-year prospective study. *General Hospital Psychiatry, 67*, 127–135.

Scheffels, J. F., Fröhlich, L., Kalbe, E., & Kessler, J. (2020). Concordance of Mini-Mental State Examination, Montreal Cognitive Assessment and Parkinson Neuropsychometric Dementia Assessment in the classification of cognitive performance in Parkinson's disease. *Journal of the Neurological Sciences, 412*, 116735.

Schilling, E.A., Lawless, M., Buchanan, L., & Aseltine, R.H. (2014). "Signs of Suicide" shows promise as a middle school suicide prevention program. *Suicide and Life- Threatening Behavior, 44*, 653–667.

Schneider, E., Higgs, S., & Dourish, C. T. (2021). Lisdexamfetamine and binge-eating disorder: A systematic review and meta-analysis of the preclinical and clinical data with a focus on mechanism of drug action in treating the disorder. *European Neuropsychopharmacology, 53*, 49–78.

Schneider, M., & Hirsch, J. S. (2020). Comprehensive sexuality education as a primary prevention strategy for sexual violence perpetration. *Trauma, Violence, & Abuse, 21*, 439–455.

Schneider, M., Müller, C. P., & Knies, A. K. (2022). Low income and schizophrenia risk: A narrative review. *Behavioural Brain Research, 435*, 114047.

Scholzman, S.C., & Nonacs, R.M. (2016). Dissociative disorders. In T.A. Stern, M. Fava, & J.F. Rosenbaum (Eds.), *Massachusetts General Hospital comprehensive clinical psychiatry* (2nd ed., pp. 395–401). New York: Elsevier.

Schopler, E., Van Bourgondien, M. E., Wellman, G.J., & Love, S. R. (2010). *Childhood Autism Rating Scale, Second Edition (CARS2)*. San Antonio, TX: Pearson.

Schramm, E., Klein, D. N., Elsaesser, M., Furukawa, T. A., & Domschke, K. (2020). Review of dysthymia and persistent depressive disorder: History, correlates, and clinical implications. *The Lancet Psychiatry, 7*, 801–812.

Schuckit, M. A., & Smith, T. L. (2021). Endorsement of specific alcohol use disorder criterion items changes with age in individuals with persistent alcohol use disorders in 2 generations of the San Diego Prospective Study. *Alcoholism: Clinical and Experimental Research, 45*, 2059–2068.

Schuckit, M. A., Smith, T. L., & Clarke, D. F. (2021). Cross-sectional and prospective associations of drinking characteristics with scores from the Self-Report of the Effects of Alcohol questionnaire and findings from alcohol challenges. *Alcoholism: Clinical and Experimental Research, 45*, 2282–2293.

Schulte Holthausen, B., & Habel, U. (2018). Sex differences in personality disorders. *Current Psychiatry Reports, 20*, 1–7.

Schwalm, F. D., Zandavalli, R. B., de Castro Filho, E. D., & Lucchetti, G. (2022). Is there a relationship between spirituality/religiosity and resilience? A systematic review and meta-analysis of observational studies. *Journal of Health Psychology, 27*, 1218–1232.

Scott, K. M., Hastings, J. A., & Temme, K. E. (2021). Sexual dysfunction and disability. In D. X. Cifu (Ed.), *Braddom's physical medicine and rehabilitation* (6th ed.) (pp. 431–446). New York: Elsevier.

Scott, T. M., Arnsten, J., Olsen, J. P., Arias, F., Cunningham, C. O., & Rivera Mindt, M. (2021). Neurocognitive, psychiatric, and substance use characteristics in a diverse sample of persons with OUD who are starting methadone or buprenorphine/naloxone in opioid treatment programs. *Addiction Science & Clinical Practice, 16*, 1–10.

Scott, W. K., & Ritchie, M. D. (Eds.) (2022). *Genetic analysis of complex diseases* (3rd ed.). Hoboken, NJ: Wiley.

Scott-Sheldon, L.A.J., Carey, K.B., Elliott, J.C., Garey, L., & Carey, M.P. (2014). Efficacy of alcohol interventions for first-year college students: A meta-analytic review of randomized controlled trials. *Journal of Consulting and Clinical Psychology, 82*, 177–188.

Seal, B. N., & Meston, C. M. (2020). The impact of body awareness on women's sexual health: A comprehensive review. *Sexual Medicine Reviews, 8*, 242–255.

Sealock, J. M., Lee, Y. H., Moscati, A., Venkatesh, S., Voloudakis, G., Straub, P., ... & Davis, L. K. (2021). Use of the PsycheMERGE network to investigate the association between depression polygenic scores and white blood cell count. *JAMA Psychiatry, 78*, 1365–1374.

Seddik, A. H., Branner, J. C., Ostwald, D. A., Schramm, S. H., Bierbaum, M., & Katsarava, Z. (2020). The socioeconomic burden of migraine: An evaluation of productivity losses due to migraine headaches based on a population study in Germany. *Cephalalgia, 40*, 1551–1560.

Segobin, S., & Pitel, A. L. (2021). The specificity of thalamic alterations in Korsakoff's syndrome: Implications for the study of amnesia. *Neuroscience & Biobehavioral Reviews, 130*, 292–300.

Sedlacek, D., Stevenson, S., Kray, C., Henson, T., Burrows, C., & Rosenboom, M.N. (2015). The impact of a history of childhood abuse on life as a college student. *Journal of Research on Christian Education, 24*, 169–184.

Seiler, N., Nguyen, T., Yung, A., & O'Donoghue, B. (2020). Terminology and assessment tools of psychosis: A systematic narrative review. *Psychiatry and Clinical Neurosciences, 74*, 226–246.

Sellbom, M., Flens, J., Gould, J., Ramnath, R., Tringone, R., & Grossman, S. (2022). The Millon Clinical Multiaxial Inventory-IV (MCMI-IV) and Millon Adolescent Clinical Inventory-II (MACI-II) in legal settings. *Journal of Personality Assessment, 104*, 203–220.

Senkevich, K., Rudakou, U., & Gan-Or, Z. (2022). New therapeutic approaches to Parkinson's disease targeting GBA, LRRK2 and Parkin. *Neuropharmacology, 202*, 108822.

Serrano-Ibáñez, E. R., Ruiz-Párraga, G. T., Gómez-Pérez, L., Ramírez-Maestre, C., Esteve, R., & López-Martínez, A. E. (2021). The relationship between experiential avoidance and posttraumatic stress symptoms: A moderated mediation model involving dissociation, guilt, and gender. *Journal of Trauma & Dissociation, 22*, 304–318.

Setién-Suero, E., Suárez-Pinilla, P., Ferro, A., Tabarés-Seisdedos, R., Crespo-Facorro, B., & Ayesa-Arriola, R. (2020). Childhood trauma and substance use underlying psychosis: A systematic review. *European Journal of Psychotraumatology, 11*, 1748342.

Seto, M. C. (2022). Clinical and conceptual problems with pedophilic disorder in the DSM-5-TR. *Archives of Sexual Behavior*, 1–5.

Seto, M. C., Curry, S., Dawson, S. J., Bradford, J. M., & Chivers, M. L. (2021). Concordance of paraphilic interests and behaviors. *The Journal of Sex Research, 58*, 424–437.

Shafiei, G., Bazinet, V., Dadar, M., Manera, A. L., Collins, D. L., Dagher, A., ... & GENetic Frontotemporal dementia Initiative. (2023). Network structure and transcriptomic vulnerability shape atrophy in frontotemporal dementia. *Brain, 146*, 321–336.

Shah, B. B., Nieweglowski, K., & Corrigan, P. W. (2022). Perceptions of difference and disdain on the self-stigma of mental illness. *Journal of Mental Health, 31*, 22-28.

Shahnaz, A., & Klonsky, E. D. (2021). Clarifying the association of eating disorder features to suicide ideation and attempts. *Journal of Clinical Psychology, 77*, 2965–2977.

Shaw, P., & Sudre, G. (2021). Adolescent attention-deficit/hyperactivity disorder: Understanding teenage symptom trajectories. *Biological Psychiatry, 89*, 152–161.

Shen, J., & Tomar, J. S. (2021). Elevated brain glutamate levels in bipolar disorder and pyruvate carboxylase-mediated anaplerosis. *Frontiers in Psychiatry, 12*, 640977.

Sher, L., Rutter, S. B., New, A. S., Siever, L. J., & Hazlett, E. A. (2019). Gender differences and similarities in aggression, suicidal behaviour, and psychiatric comorbidity in borderline personality disorder. *Acta Psychiatrica Scandinavica, 139*, 145–153.

Shewark, E. A., Ramos, A. M., Liu, C., Ganiban, J. M., Fosco, G., Shaw, D. S., ... & Neiderhiser, J. M. (2021). The role of child negative emotionality in parenting and child adjustment: Gene–environment interplay. *Journal of Child Psychology and Psychiatry, 62*, 1453–1461.

Shochet, I., Montague, R., Smith, C., & Dadds, M. (2014). A qualitative investigation of adolescents' perceived mechanisms of change from a universal school-based depression prevention program. *International Journal of Environmental Research and Public Health, 11*, 5541–5554.

Shorey, R. C., Stuart, G. L., Moore, T. M., & McNulty, J. K. (2014). The temporal relationship between alcohol, marijuana, angry affect, and dating violence perpetration: A daily diary study with female college students. *Psychology of Addictive Behaviors, 28*, 516–523.

Shorey, S., Chee, C. Y. I., Ng, E. D., Chan, Y. H., San Tam, W. W., & Chong, Y. S. (2018). Prevalence and incidence of postpartum depression among healthy mothers: a systematic review and meta-analysis. *Journal of Psychiatric Research, 104*, 235–248.

Shorey, S., Demutska, A., Chan, V., & Siah, K. T. H. (2021). Adults living with irritable bowel syndrome (IBS): A qualitative systematic review. *Journal of Psychosomatic Research, 140*, 110289.

Shrestha, K., Ojha, S. P., Dhungana, S., & Shrestha, S. (2020). Depression and its association with quality of life among elderly: An elderly home-cross sectional study. *Neurology, Psychiatry and Brain Research, 38*, 1–4.

Shorey, S., Ng, E. D., & Wong, C. H. (2022). Global prevalence of depression and elevated depressive symptoms among adolescents: A systematic review and meta-analysis. *British Journal of Clinical Psychology, 61*, 287–305.

Sibrava, N. J., Bjornsson, A. S., Pérez Benítez, A. C. I., Moitra, E., Weisberg, R. B., & Keller, M. B. (2019). Posttraumatic stress disorder in African American and Latinx adults: Clinical course and the role of racial and ethnic discrimination. *American Psychologist, 74*, 101–116.

Sicorello, M., & Schmahl, C. (2021). Emotion dysregulation in borderline personality disorder: A fronto–limbic imbalance?. *Current Opinion in Psychology, 37*, 114–120.

Sievert, E. D., Schweizer, K., Barkmann, C., Fahrenkrug, S., & Becker-Hebly, I. (2021). Not social transition status, but peer relations and family functioning predict psychological functioning in a German clinical sample of children with Gender Dysphoria. *Clinical Child Psychology and Psychiatry, 26*, 79–95.

Silva, S. A., Silva, S. U., Ronca, D. B., Gonçalves, V. S. S., Dutra, E. S., & Carvalho, K. M. B. (2020). Common mental disorders prevalence in adolescents: A systematic review and meta-analyses. *PLoS One, 15*, e0232007.

Silva-Rodriguez, J., Labrador-Espinosa, M. A., Moscoso, A., Scholl, M., Mir, P., & Grothe, M. (2022). Differential effects of tau stage, Lewy body pathology, and substantia nigra degeneration on FDG-PET patterns in clinical AD. *Journal of Nuclear Medicine*.

Simmel, E. C., & Fuller, J. L. (Eds.) (2021). *Behavior genetics: Principles and applications*. United Kingdom: Taylor & Francis.

Simmons, W. P., Boynton, J., & Landman, T. (2021). Facilitated communication, neurodiversity, and human rights. *Human Rights Quarterly, 43*, 138–167.

Simon, J. A., Clayton, A. H., Kim, N. N., & Patel, S. (2022). Clinically meaningful benefit in women with hypoactive sexual desire disorder treated with flibanserin. *Sexual Medicine, 10*, 100476.

Simonoff, E., Kent, R., Stringer, D., Lord, C., Briskman, J., Lukito, S., ... & Baird, G. (2020). Trajectories in symptoms of autism and cognitive ability in autism from childhood to adult life: Findings from a longitudinal epidemiological cohort. *Journal of the American Academy of Child & Adolescent Psychiatry, 59*, 1342–1352.

Simpkins, A. N. (2020). Impact of race-ethnic and economic disparities on rates of vascular dementia in the national inpatient sample database from 2006–2014. *Journal of Stroke and Cerebrovascular Diseases, 29*, 104731.

Sims, R., Hill, M., & Williams, J. (2020). The multiplex model of the genetics of Alzheimer's disease. *Nature Neuroscience, 23*, 311–322.

Sinclair, J., Herman, K. C., Reinke, W. M., Dong, N., & Stormont, M. (2021). Effects of a universal classroom management intervention on middle school students with or at risk of behavior problems. *Remedial and Special Education, 42*, 18–30.

Singh, S. P., Mohan, M., & Giacco, D. (2021). Psychosocial interventions for people with a first episode psychosis: between tradition and innovation. *Current Opinion in Psychiatry, 34*, 460–466.

Sinha, K., Sun, C., Kamari, R., & Bettermann, K. (2020). Current status and future prospects of pathophysiology-based neuroprotective drugs for the treatment of vascular dementia. *Drug Discovery Today, 25*, 793–799.

Sistad, R. E., Simons, R. M., Mojallal, M., & Simons, J. S. (2021). The indirect effect from childhood maltreatment to PTSD symptoms via thought suppression and cognitive reappraisal. *Child Abuse & Neglect, 114*, 104939.

Sisti, D., Mann, J. J., & Oquendo, M. A. (2020). Toward a distinct mental disorder—suicidal behavior. *JAMA Psychiatry, 77*, 661–662.

Skewes, M. C., & Blume, A. W. (2019). Understanding the link between racial trauma and substance use among American Indians. *American Psychologist, 74*, 88–100.

Skodol, A. E., & Oldham, J. M. (Eds.) (2021). *The American Psychiatric Association Publishing textbook of personality disorders* (3rd ed.). Washington, DC: American Psychiatric Association.

Skordis, N., Kyriakou, A., Dror, S., Mushailov, A., & Nicolaides, N. C. (2020). Gender dysphoria in children and adolescents: An overview. *Hormones, 19*, 267–276.

Sloand, E., Butz, A., Rhee, H., Walters, L., Breuninger, K., Pozzo, R. A., ... & Tumiel-Berhalter, L. (2021). Influence of social support on asthma self-management in adolescents. *Journal of Asthma, 58*, 386–394.

Slobodin, O., & Masalha, R. (2020). Challenges in ADHD care for ethnic minority children: A review of the current literature. *Transcultural Psychiatry, 57*, 468–483.

Smaniotto, B., Réveillaud, M., Dumet, N., & Guenoun, T. (2021). Clinical analysis of an exhibitionist patient in a psychoanalytic psychodrama group. *Contemporary Psychoanalysis, 57*, 564–595.

Smeland, O. B., Frei, O., Dale, A. M., & Andreassen, O. A. (2020). The polygenic architecture of schizophrenia—rethinking pathogenesis and nosology. *Nature Reviews Neurology, 16*, 366–379.

Smith, L. E., Weinman, J., Yiend, J., & Rubin, J. (2020). Psychosocial factors affecting parental report of symptoms in children: A systematic review. *Psychosomatic Medicine, 82*, 187–196.

Smith, M. L., Hoven, C. W., Cheslack-Postava, K., Musa, G. J., Wicks, J., McReynolds, L., ... & Link, B. G. (2022). Arrest history, stigma, and self-esteem: a modified labeling theory approach to understanding how arrests impact lives. *Social Psychiatry and Psychiatric Epidemiology, 57*, 1849–1860.

Smith, N. S., Bauer, B. W., & Capron, D. W. (2022). Comparing symptom networks of daytime and nocturnal panic attacks in a community-based sample. *Journal of Anxiety Disorders, 85*, 102514.

Smith, T. E., Sheridan, S. M., Kim, E. M., Park, S., & Beretvas, S. N. (2020). The effects of family-school partnership interventions on academic and social-emotional functioning: A meta-analysis exploring what works for whom. *Educational Psychology Review, 32*, 511–544.

Smolak, L. & Levine, M.P. (Eds.). (2015). *The Wiley handbook of eating disorders Volume 1: Basic concepts and foundational research*. New York: Wiley.

Snyder, A. E., & Silberman, Y. (2021). Corticotropin releasing factor and norepinephrine related circuitry changes in the bed nucleus of the stria terminalis in stress and alcohol and substance use disorders. *Neuropharmacology, 201*, 108814.

Solmi, M., Radua, J., Olivola, M., Croce, E., Soardo, L., Salazar de Pablo, G., ... & Fusar-Poli, P. (2022). Age at onset of mental disorders worldwide: Large-scale meta-analysis of 192 epidemiological studies. *Molecular Psychiatry, 27*, 281–295.

Solmi, M., Wade, T. D., Byrne, S., Del Giovane, C., Fairburn, C. G., Ostinelli, E. G., ... & Cipriani, A. (2021). Comparative efficacy and acceptability of psychological interventions for the treatment of adult outpatients with anorexia nervosa: a systematic review and network meta-analysis. *The Lancet Psychiatry, 8*, 215–224.

Soloff, P.H., & Chiappetta, L. (2012). Prospective predictors of suicidal behavior in borderline personality disorder at 6-year follow-up. *American Journal of Psychiatry, 169*, 484–490.

Song, P., Zha, M., Yang, Q., Zhang, Y., Li, X., & Rudan, I. (2021). The prevalence of adult attention-deficit hyperactivity disorder: A global systematic review and meta-analysis. *Journal of Global Health, 11*: 04009.

Song, X., & Vilares, I. (2021). Assessing the relationship between the human learned helplessness depression model and anhedonia. *PLoS One, 16*, e0249056.

Sontate, K. V., Kamaluddin, M. R., Mohamed, I. N., Mohamed, R. M. P., Shaikh, M. F., Kamal, H., & Kumar, J. (2021). Alcohol, aggression, and violence: from public health to neuroscience. *Frontiers in Psychology, 12*, 699726.

Sørensen, K. D., Wilberg, T., Berthelsen, E., & Råbu, M. (2020). Subjective experience of the origin and development of avoidant personality disorder. *Journal of Clinical Psychology, 76*, 2232–2248.

Sousa, A. D., & D'Souza, R. (2021). Ethical issues in dementia—Global challenges. In M. K. Shankardass (Ed.), *Dementia care: Issues, responses and international perspectives* (pp. 283–300). Singapore: Springer.

South, M., & Palilla, J. (2021). Bender Visual-Motor Gestalt Test II. In F.R. Volkmar (Ed.), *Encyclopedia of autism spectrum disorders* (pp. 679–682). Cham: Springer International Publishing.

Sparrow, S.S., Cicchetti, D.V., & Saulnier, C.A. (2016). *Vineland Adaptive Behavior Scales Third Edition Vineland-3*. Hoboken, NJ: Pearson.

Sperling, S. A., Brown, D. S., Jensen, C., Inker, J., Mittelman, M. S., & Manning, C. A. (2020). FAMILIES: An effective healthcare intervention for caregivers of community dwelling people living with dementia. *Aging & Mental Health, 24*, 1700–1708.

Sperry, L. (2015). Personality disorders. In L. Sperry, J. Carlson, J.D. Sauerheber, & J. Sperry (Eds.), *Psychopathology and psychotherapy: DSM-5 diagnosis, case conceptualization, and treatment* (3rd ed., pp. 27–62). New York: Routledge.

Sperry, S.H., Walsh, M.A., & Kwapil, T.R. (2015). Measuring the validity and psychometric properties of a short form of the Hypomanic Personality Scale. *Personality and Individual Differences, 82*, 52–57.

Spokas, M., Wenzel, A., Brown, G.K., & Beck, A.T. (2012). Characteristics of individuals who make impulsive suicide attempts. *Journal of Affective Disorders, 136*, 1121–1125.

Spruit, A., Goos, L., Weenink, N., Rodenburg, R., Niemeyer, H., Stams, G. J., & Colonnesi, C. (2020). The relation between attachment and depression in children and adolescents: A multilevel meta-analysis. *Clinical Child and Family Psychology Review, 23*, 54–69.

Stapp, E. K., Mendelson, T., Merikangas, K. R., & Wilcox, H. C. (2020). Parental bipolar disorder, family environment, and offspring psychiatric disorders: a systematic review. *Journal of Affective Disorders, 268*, 69–81.

Steele, T. A., St Louis, E. K., Videnovic, A., & Auger, R. R. (2021). Circadian rhythm sleep–wake disorders: A contemporary review of neurobiology, treatment, and dysregulation in neurodegenerative disease. *Neurotherapeutics, 18*, 53–74.

Stefani, A., & Högl, B. (2021). Nightmare disorder and isolated sleep paralysis. *Neurotherapeutics, 18*, 100–106.

Steiger, H., & Booij, L. (2020). Eating disorders, heredity and environmental activation: Getting epigenetic concepts into practice. *Journal of Clinical Medicine, 9*, 1332.

Stein, A. T., Carl, E., Cuijpers, P., Karyotaki, E., & Smits, J. A. (2021). Looking beyond depression: A meta-analysis of the effect of behavioral activation on depression, anxiety, and activation. *Psychological Medicine, 51*, 1491–504.

Stein, M. B., Calderon, S., Ruchensky, J., Massey, C., Slavin-Mulford, J., Chung, W. J., ... & Blais, M. A. (2020). When's a story a story? Determining interpretability of Social Cognition and Object Relations Scale-Global ratings on Thematic Apperception Test narratives. *Clinical Psychology & Psychotherapy, 27*, 567–580.

Stern, J., Pier, J. & Litonjua, A. A. (2020). Asthma epidemiology and risk factors. *Seminars in Immunopathology, 42*, 5–15

Sternberg, R. J. (2020). *Human intelligence: An introduction*. Cambridge: Cambridge University Press.

Sternberg, R. J. (2020). Rethinking what we mean by intelligence. *Phi Delta Kappan, 102*, 36–41.

Stewart, C. S., Baudinet, J., Hall, R., Fiskå, M., Pretorius, N., Voulgari, S., ... & Simic, M. (2021). Multi-family therapy for bulimia nervosa in adolescence: a pilot study in a community eating disorder service. *Eating Disorders, 29*, 351–367.

Stice, E., Onipede, Z. A., & Marti, C. N. (2021). A meta-analytic review of trials that tested whether eating disorder prevention programs prevent eating disorder onset. *Clinical Psychology Review, 87*, 102046.

Stice, E., Rohde, P., Shaw, H., & Marti, C.N. (2012). Efficacy trial of a selective prevention program targeting both eating disorder symptoms and unhealthy weight gain among female college students. *Journal of Consulting and Clinical Psychology, 80*, 164–170.

Stinson, J. D., Puszkiewicz, K. L., & Lasher, M. P. (2022). Associations between self-regulation, experiences of childhood adversity, and problematic sexual and aggressive behaviors. *Sexual Abuse*, 10790632211058067.

Stockl, H., Devries, K., Rotstein, A., Abrahams, N., Campbell, J., Watts, C., & Moreno, C.G. (2013). The global prevalence of intimate partner homicide: A systematic review. *Lancet, 382*, 859–865.

Stoffers-Winterling, J., Völlm, B., & Lieb, K. (2021). Is pharmacotherapy useful for treating personality disorders? *Expert Opinion on Pharmacotherapy, 22*, 393–395.

Stoll, J., Müller, J. A., & Trachsel, M. (2020). Ethical issues in online psychotherapy: A narrative review. *Frontiers in Psychiatry, 10*, 993.

Stollings, J. L., Kotfis, K., Chanques, G., Pun, B. T., Pandharipande, P. P., & Ely, E. (2021). Delirium in critical illness: Clinical manifestations, outcomes, and management. *Intensive Care Medicine, 47*, 1089–1103.

Stortenbeker, I., Stommel, W., olde Hartman, T., van Dulmen, S., & Das, E. (2022). How general practitioners raise psychosocial concerns as a potential cause of medically unexplained symptoms: A conversation analysis. *Health Communication, 37*, 696–707.

Strakowski, S.M. (2014). *Bipolar disorder*. New York: Oxford.

Strålin, P., & Hetta, J. (2021). First episode psychosis: Register-based study of comorbid psychiatric disorders and medications before and after. *European Archives of Psychiatry and Clinical Neuroscience, 271*, 303–313.

Strawbridge, R., Kurana, S., Kerr-Gaffney, J., Jauhar, S., Kaufman, K. R., Yalin, N., & Young, A. H. (2022). A systematic review and meta-analysis of treatments for rapid cycling bipolar disorder. *Acta Psychiatrica Scandinavica, 146*, 290–311.

Strikwerda-Brown, C. (2022). Chicken or egg? Untangling the associations between personality traits and Alzheimer's Disease pathology. *Biological Psychiatry, 91*, e17–e19.

Strom, N. I., Soda, T., Mathews, C. A., & Davis, L. K. (2021). A dimensional perspective on the genetics of obsessive-compulsive disorder. *Translational Psychiatry, 11*, 1–11.

Styles, M., Alsharshani, D., Samara, M., Alsharshani, M., Khattab, A., Qoronfleh, M. W., & Al-Dewik, N. I. (2020). Risk factors, diagnosis, prognosis and treatment of autism. *Frontiers in Bioscience, 25*, 1682–1717.

Su, Q., Yu, M., Liu, F., Li, Y., Li, D., Deng, M., ... & Guo, W. (2020). Abnormal functional asymmetry in the salience and auditory networks in first-episode, drug-naive somatization disorder. *Neuroscience, 444*, 1–8.

Sudheer, N., & Banerjee, D. (2021). The Rohingya refugees: a conceptual framework of their psychosocial adversities, cultural idioms of distress and social suffering. *Global Mental Health, 8*, e46.

Surmann, M., Falke, S., von Gruchalla, L., Maisch, B., Uhlmann, C., Arolt, V., & Lencer, R. (2021). Understanding the multidimensional phenomenon of medication adherence attitudes in psychosis. *Psychiatry Research, 295*, 113601.

Sutar, R., & Sahu, S. (2019). Pharmacotherapy for dissociative disorders: A systematic review. *Psychiatry Research, 281*, 112529.

Svancer, P., & Spaniel, F. (2021). Brain ventricular volume changes in schizophrenia. A narrative review. *Neuroscience Letters, 759*, 136065.

Swift, J. K., Trusty, W. T., & Penix, E. A. (2021). The effectiveness of the collaborative assessment and management of suicidality (cams) compared to alternative treatment conditions: A meta-analysis. *Suicide and Life-Threatening Behavior, 51*, 882–896.

Taddei, R. N., Sanchez-Mico, M. V., Bonnar, O., Connors, T., Gaona, A., Denbow, D., ... & Gómez-Isla, T. (2022). Changes in glial cell phenotypes precede overt neurofibrillary tangle formation, correlate with markers of cortical cell damage, and predict cognitive status of individuals at Braak III-IV stages. *Acta Neuropathologica Communications, 10*, 1–20.

Takahashi, Y., Pease, C. R., Pingault, J. B., & Viding, E. (2021). Genetic and environmental influences on the developmental trajectory of callous-unemotional traits from childhood to adolescence. *Journal of Child Psychology and Psychiatry, 62*, 414–423.

Takayanagi, Y., Kulason, S., Sasabayashi, D., Takahashi, T., Katagiri, N., Sakuma, A., ... & Suzuki, M. (2020). Structural MRI study of the planum temporale in individuals with an at-risk mental state using labeled cortical distance mapping. *Frontiers in Psychiatry, 11*, 593952.

Tamura, N., Sasai-Sakuma, T., Morita, Y., Okawa, M., Inoue, S., & Inoue, Y. (2021). Prevalence and associated factors of circadian rhythm sleep-wake disorders and insomnia among visually impaired Japanese individuals. *BMC Public Health, 21*, 1–9.

Tang, A., Crawford, H., Morales, S., Degnan, K. A., Pine, D. S., & Fox, N. A. (2020). Infant behavioral inhibition predicts personality and social outcomes three decades later. *Proceedings of the National Academy of Sciences, 117*, 9800–9807.

Tang, S., Hänsel, K., Cong, Y., Berretta, S., Cho, S., Nikzad, A., ... & Liberman, M. (2022). Dimensions of speech and language disturbance in psychosis and computational linguistic markers. *Biological Psychiatry, 91*, S49–S50.

Tang, S. X., Cong, Y., Nikzad, A. H., Mehta, A., Cho, S., Hänsel, K., ... & Malhotra, A. K. (2022). Clinical and computational speech measures are associated with social cognition in schizophrenia spectrum disorders. *Schizophrenia Research.*

Tarkowska, A., Furmaga-Jabłońska, W., Bogucki, J., Kocki, J., & Pluta, R. (2021). Alzheimer's disease associated presenilin 1 and 2 genes dysregulation in neonatal lymphocytes following perinatal asphyxia. *International Journal of Molecular Sciences, 22*, 5140.

Tarugu, J., Pavithra, R., Vinothchandar, S., Basu, A., Chaudhuri, S., & John, K. R. (2019). Effectiveness of structured group reminiscence therapy in decreasing the feelings of loneliness, depressive symptoms and anxiety among inmates of a residential home for the elderly in Chittoor district. *International Journal of Community Medicine and Public Health, 6*, 847–854.

Tavares, I. M., Moura, C. V., & Nobre, P. J. (2020). The role of cognitive processing factors in sexual function and dysfunction in women and men: A systematic review. *Sexual Medicine Reviews, 8*, 403–430.

Taylor, J. L., Johnson, S., Cruz, R., Gray, J. R., Schiff, D., & Bagley, S. M. (2021). Integrating harm reduction into outpatient opioid use disorder treatment settings. *Journal of General Internal Medicine, 36*, 3810–3819.

Taylor, S., & Asmundson, G.J.G. (2012). Etiology of hypochondriasis: A preliminary behavioral-genetic investigation. *International Journal of Genetics and Gene Therapy, 2*, 1–5.

Taylor, S., Zvolensky, M. J., Cox, B. J., Deacon, B., Heimberg, R. G., Ledley, D. R., ... & Cardenas, S. J. (2007). Robust dimensions of anxiety sensitivity: Development and initial validation of the Anxiety Sensitivity Index-3. *Psychological Assessment, 19*, 176–188.

Temes, C. M., Frankenburg, F. R., Fitzmaurice, G. M., & Zanarini, M. C. (2019). Deaths by suicide and other causes among patients with borderline personality disorder and personality-disordered comparison subjects over 24 years of prospective follow-up. *Journal of Clinical Psychiatry, 80*, 18m12436.

Teodoro, T., & Afonso, P. (2020). Culture-bound syndromes and cultural concepts of distress in psychiatry. *Revista Portuguesa de Psiquiatria e Saúde Mental, 6*, 118–126.

Terhune, J., Dykxhoorn, J., Mackay, E., Hollander, A. C., Kirkbride, J. B., & Dalman, C. (2022). Migrant status and risk of compulsory admission at first diagnosis of psychotic disorder: A population-based cohort study in Sweden. *Psychological Medicine, 52*, 362–371.

Thege, B.K., Pilling, J., Cserhati, Z., & Kopp, M.S. (2012). Mediators between bereavement and somatic symptoms. *BMC Family Practice, 13*, 59.

Thibaut, F., Cosyns, P., Fedoroff, J. P., Briken, P., Goethals, K., Bradford, J. M., & WFSBP Task Force on Paraphilias. (2020). The World Federation of Societies of Biological Psychiatry (WFSBP) 2020 guidelines for the pharmacological treatment of paraphilic disorders. *The World Journal of Biological Psychiatry, 21*, 412–490.

Thompson, M. F. (2020). Subdoctoral practitioners in psychology: Implications for master's-level psychologists. *Practice Innovations, 5*, 105–113.

Thompson, R. H., & Borrero, J. C. (2021). Direct observation. In W. W. Fisher, C. C. Piazza, & H. S. Roane (Eds.), *Handbook of applied behavior analysis* (2nd ed.) (pp. 202–213). New York: Guilford.

Thomson, N. D., Kevorkian, S., & Verdugo-Thomson, A. A. (2022). Psychopathology and violence. In J.E. Vitale (Ed.), *The complexity of psychopathy* (pp. 85–106). Cham: Springer.

Thongseiratch, T., Leijten, P., & Melendez-Torres, G. J. (2020). Online parent programs for children's behavioral problems: A meta-analytic review. *European Child & Adolescent Psychiatry, 29*, 1555–1568.

Thornton, D., Hanson, R. K., Kelley, S. M., & Mundt, J. C. (2021). Estimating lifetime and residual risk for individuals who remain sexual offense free in the community: Practical applications. *Sexual Abuse, 33*, 3–33.

Timko, C., Moos, R.H., & Finney, J.W. (2016). The course of substance use disorders: Trajectories, endpoints, and predictors. In E.J. Bromet (Ed.), *Long-term outcomes in psychopathology research:*

Rethinking the scientific agenda (pp. 53–76). New York: Oxford.

Tistarelli, N., Fagnani, C., Troianiello, M., Stazi, M. A., & Adriani, W. (2020). The nature and nurture of ADHD and its comorbidities: A narrative review on twin studies. *Neuroscience & Biobehavioral Reviews, 109*, 63–77.

Titus, C. E., & DeShong, H. L. (2020). Thought control strategies as predictors of borderline personality disorder and suicide risk. *Journal of Affective Disorders, 266*, 349–355.

Todd, J., Downey, J., Grafton, B., & MacLeod, C. (2022). Attentional bias to alcohol information: A novel dual-probe task. *International Journal of Behavioral Medicine*, 29, 820–826.

Ton, A. M. M., Campagnaro, B. P., Alves, G. A., Aires, R., Côco, L. Z., Arpini, C. M., ... & Vasquez, E. C. (2020). Oxidative stress and dementia in Alzheimer's patients: Effects of synbiotic supplementation. *Oxidative Medicine and Cellular Longevity, 2020*, 2638503.

Toohey, M. J. (2021). Cognitive behavioral therapy for anger management. In A. Wenzel (Ed.), *Handbook of cognitive behavioral therapy: Applications* (pp. 331–359). Washington, DC: American Psychological Association.

Tost, M., Monreal, J. A., Armario, A., Barbero, J. D., Cobo, J., García-Rizo, C., ... & Labad, J. (2020). Targeting hormones for improving cognition in major mood disorders and schizophrenia: Thyroid hormones and prolactin. *Clinical Drug Investigation, 40*, 1–14.

Tournier, M., Pambrun, E., Maumus-Robert, S., Pariente, A., & Verdoux, H. (2022). The risk of dementia in patients using psychotropic drugs: Antidepressants, mood stabilizers or antipsychotics. *Acta Psychiatrica Scandinavica, 145*, 56–66.

Toussaint, A., Hüsing, P., Kohlmann, S., Brähler, E., & Löwe, B. (2021). Excessiveness in symptom-related thoughts, feelings, and behaviors: An investigation of somatic symptom disorders in the general population. *Psychosomatic Medicine, 83*, 164–170.

Tozdan, S., Briken, P. (2021). Paraphilias: Diagnostics, comorbidities, and treatment. In M. Lew-Starowicz, A. Giraldi, & T. Krüger (Eds.), *Psychiatry and sexual medicine* (pp. 407–416). Cham: Springer.

Trachsel, M., Biller-Andorno, N., Gaab, J., Sadler, J., & Tekin, S. (Eds.) (2021). *Oxford handbook of psychotherapy ethics*. New York: Oxford.

Trankner, A., Sander, C., & Schonknecht, P. (2013). A critical review of the recent literature and selected therapy guidelines since 2006 on the use of lamotrigine in bipolar disorder. *Neuropsychiatric Disease and Treatment, 9*, 101–111.

Tretiakov, A., Malakhova, A., Naumova, E., Rudko, O., & Klimov, E. (2020). Genetic Biomarkers of Panic Disorder: A Systematic Review. *Genes, 11*, 1310.

Trinchieri, M., Trinchieri, M., Perletti, G., Magri, V., Stamatiou, K., Cai, T., ... & Trinchieri, A. (2021). Erectile and ejaculatory dysfunction associated with use of psychotropic drugs: A systematic review. *The Journal of Sexual Medicine, 18*, 1354–1363.

Tromp, A., Mowry, B., & Giacomotto, J. (2021). Neurexins in autism and schizophrenia—a review of patient mutations, mouse models and potential future directions. *Molecular Psychiatry, 26*, 747–760.

Trucco, E. M. (2020). A review of psychosocial factors linked to adolescent substance use. *Pharmacology Biochemistry and Behavior, 196*, 172969.

Tsai, S. Y., Sajatovic, M., Hsu, J. L., Chung, K. H., Chen, P. H., & Huang, Y. J. (2020). Body mass index, residual psychotic symptoms, and inflammation associated with brain volume reduction in older patients with schizophrenia. *International Journal of Geriatric Psychiatry, 35*, 728–736.

Tsang, A., Bucci, S., Branitsky, A., Kaptan, S., Rafiq, S., Wong, S., ... & Varese, F. (2021). The relationship between appraisals of voices (auditory verbal hallucinations) and distress in voice-hearers with schizophrenia-spectrum diagnoses: A meta-analytic review. *Schizophrenia Research, 230*, 38–47.

Tsapekos, D., Seccomandi, B., Mantingh, T., Cella, M., Wykes, T., & Young, A. H. (2020). Cognitive enhancement interventions for people with bipolar disorder: A systematic review of methodological quality, treatment approaches, and outcomes. *Bipolar Disorders, 22*, 216–230.

Tseng, W-S. (2015). *Culture and psychotherapy: Theory and applications—A world perspective*. New York: Routledge.

Turchik, J. A., & Hassija, C. M. (2014). Female sexual victimization among college students: Assault severity, health risk behaviors, and sexual functioning. *Journal of Interpersonal Violence, 29*, 2439–2457.

Turecki, G., Brent, D. A., Gunnell, D., O'Connor, R. C., Oquendo, M. A., Pirkis, J., & Stanley, B. H. (2019). Suicide and suicide risk. *Nature Reviews Disease Primers, 5*, 1–22.

Turner, A. I., Smyth, N., Hall, S. J., Torres, S. J., Hussein, M., Jayasinghe, S. U., ... & Clow, A. J. (2020). Psychological stress reactivity and future health and disease outcomes: A systematic review of prospective evidence. *Psychoneuroendocrinology, 114*, 104599.

Turton, H., Berry, K., Danquah, A., & Pratt, D. (2021). The relationship between emotion dysregulation and suicide ideation and behaviour: A systematic review. *Journal of Affective Disorders Reports, 5*, 100136.

Tyler, K. A., Schmitz, R. M., & Adams, S. A. (2015). Alcohol expectancy, drinking behavior, and sexual victimization among female and male college students. *Journal of Interpersonal Violence, 31*, 1–25.

Tyrer, P. (2018). Recent advances in the understanding and treatment of health anxiety. *Current Psychiatry Reports, 20*, 1–8.

Uchino, B.N., Cronan, S., Scott, E., Landvattar, J., & Papadakis, M. (2020). Social support and stress, depression, and cardiovascular disease. In P.D. Chantler & K.T. Larkin (Eds.), *Cardiovascular implications of stress and depression* (pp. 211–223). New York: Academic.

Üçok, A., Brohan, E., Rose, D., Sartorius, N., Leese, M., Yoon, C. K., Plooy, A., Ertekin, B.A., Milev, R., & Thornicroft, G. (2012). Anticipated discrimination among people with schizophrenia. *Acta Psychiatrica Scandinavica, 125*, 77–83.

Uldall Torp, N. M., & Thomsen, P. H. (2020). The use of diet interventions to treat symptoms of ADHD in children and adolescents–a systematic review of randomized controlled trials. *Nordic Journal of Psychiatry, 74*, 558–568.

Ungar, M., & Theron, L. (2020). Resilience and mental health: How multisystemic processes contribute to positive outcomes. *The Lancet Psychiatry, 7*, 441–448.

Urrego-Parra, H. N., Rodriguez-Guerrero, L. A., Pastells-Peiró, R., Mateos-García, J. T., Gea-Sanchez, M., Escrig-Piñol, A., & Briones-Vozmediano, E. (2022). The health of migrant agricultural workers in Europe: A scoping review. *Journal of Immigrant and Minority Health, 24*, 1580–1589.

US Department of Health and Human Services (2021). *2020 profile of older Americans*. Washington, DC: Author.

US Department of Health and Human Services. (2022). *2020 NSDUH detailed tables*. Washington, DC: Author.

Utsumi, K., Fukatsu, R., Hara, Y., Takamaru, Y., & Yasumura, S. (2021). Psychotic features among patients in the prodromal stage of dementia with lewy bodies during longitudinal observation. *Journal of Alzheimer's Disease, 83*, 1917–1927.

Vahhab, N., Ebrahimi, N., Amirmahani, F., & Vallian, S. (2020). Analysis of polymorphic markers located in the HEXA gene region associated with Tay-Sachs disease. *Meta Gene, 26*, 100772.

Vaishnav, M., Saha, G., Mukherji, A., & Vaishnav, P. (2020). Principles of marital therapies and behavior therapy of sexual dysfunction. *Indian Journal of Psychiatry, 62*, S213–S222.

Valbrun, L. P., & Zvonarev, V. (2020). The opioid system and food intake: use of opiate antagonists in treatment of binge eating disorder and abnormal eating behavior. *Journal of Clinical Medicine Research, 12*, 41–63.

Valdés-Florido, M. J., López-Díaz, Á., Palermo-Zeballos, F. J., Garrido-Torres, N., Álvarez-Gil, P., Martínez-Molina, I., ... & Ruiz-Veguilla, M. (2022). Clinical characterization of brief psychotic disorders triggered by the COVID-19 pandemic: A multicenter observational study. *European Archives of Psychiatry and Clinical Neuroscience, 272*, 5–15.

Valentino, V., Centonze, A., Inchausti, F., MacBeth, A., Popolo, R., Ottavi, P., ... & Dimaggio, G. (2020). Addressing maladaptive interpersonal schemas, poor metacognition and maladaptive coping strategies in Avoidant Personality Disorder: The role of experiential techniques. *Psychology Hub, 37*, 19–28.

Van Boekel, L. C., Brouwers, E. P., Van Weeghel, J., & Garretsen, H. F. (2013). Stigma among health professionals towards patients with substance use disorders and its consequences for healthcare delivery: Systematic review. *Drug and Alcohol Dependence, 131*, 23–35.

Vancheri, F., Longo, G., Vancheri, E., & Henein, M. Y. (2022). Mental stress and cardiovascular health—Part I. *Journal of Clinical Medicine, 11*, 3353.

van de Veen, D., Bakker, C., Peetoom, K., Pijnenburg, Y., Papma, J. M., de Vugt, M., ... & PRECODE Study Group. (2021). An integrative literature review on the nomenclature and definition of dementia at a young age. *Journal of Alzheimer's Disease, 83*, 1891–1916.

van den Bruele, A. B., & Crandall, M. (2022). Violence in the elderly: A review of the literature. *Current Trauma Reports, 8*, 12–16.

van den Kieboom, R., Snaphaan, L., Mark, R., & Bongers, I. (2020). The trajectory of caregiver burden and risk factors in dementia progression: A systematic review. *Journal of Alzheimer's Disease, 77*, 1107–1115.

van der Heijden, M. E., Gill, J. S., & Sillitoe, R. V. (2021). Abnormal cerebellar development in autism spectrum disorders. *Developmental Neuroscience, 43*, 181–190.

van der Kant, R., Goldstein, L. S., & Ossenkoppele, R. (2020). Amyloid-β-independent regulators of tau pathology in Alzheimer disease. *Nature Reviews Neuroscience, 21*, 21–35.

Van der Oord, S., & Tripp, G. (2020). How to improve behavioral parent and teacher training for children with ADHD: Integrating empirical research on learning and motivation into treatment. *Clinical Child and Family Psychology Review, 23*, 577–604.

van der Stouwe, E. C. D., Steenhuis, L. A., Pijnenborg, G. H. M., de Vries, B., Bartels-Velthuis, A. A., Castelein, S., ... & van Busschbach, J. T. (2021). Gender differences in characteristics of violent and sexual victimization in patients with psychosis: a cross-sectional study. *BMC Psychiatry, 21*, 1–9.

van der Vlag, M., Havekes, R., & Heckman, P. R. (2020). The contribution of Parkin, PINK1 and DJ-1 genes to selective neuronal degeneration in Parkinson's disease. *European Journal of Neuroscience, 52*, 3256–3268.

Van Dijk, R., Van Der Valk, I. E., Deković, M., & Branje, S. (2020). A meta-analysis on interparental conflict, parenting, and child adjustment in divorced families: Examining mediation using meta-analytic structural equation models. *Clinical Psychology Review, 79*, 101861.

Van Dis, E. A., Van Veen, S. C., Hagenaars, M. A., Batelaan, N. M., Bockting, C. L., Van Den Heuvel, R. M., ... & Engelhard, I. M. (2020). Long-term outcomes of cognitive behavioral therapy for anxiety-related disorders: A systematic review and meta-analysis. *JAMA Psychiatry, 77*, 265–273.

Van Dongen, J. D. (2020). The empathic brain of psychopaths: From social science to neuroscience in empathy. *Frontiers in Psychology, 11*, 695.

van Eeden, A. E., van Hoeken, D., & Hoek, H. W. (2021). Incidence, prevalence and mortality of anorexia nervosa and bulimia nervosa. *Current Opinion in Psychiatry, 34*, 515–524.

van Eldik, W. M., de Haan, A. D., Parry, L. Q., Davies, P. T., Luijk, M. P., Arends, L. R., & Prinzie, P. (2020). The interparental relationship: Meta-analytic associations with children's maladjustment and responses to interparental conflict. *Psychological Bulletin, 146*, 553–594.

Van Houtem, C. M. H. H., Laine, M. L., Boomsma, D. I., Ligthart, L., van Wijk, A. J., & De Jongh, A. (2013). A review and meta-analysis of the heritability of specific phobia subtypes and corresponding fears. *Journal of Anxiety Disorders, 27*, 379–388.

Van Leeuwen, E., Driel, M. L., Horowitz, M. A., Kendrick, T., Donald, M., De Sutter, A. I., ... & Christiaens, T. (2021). Approaches for discontinuation versus continuation of long-term antidepressant use for depressive and anxiety disorders in adults. *Cochrane Database of Systematic Reviews, 4*.

Van Meter, A.R., Youngstrom, E.A., & Findling, R.L. (2012). Cyclothymic disorder: A critical review. *Clinical Psychology Review, 32*, 229–243.

van Neerven, T., Bos, D. J., & van Haren, N. E. (2021). Deficiencies in Theory of Mind in patients with schizophrenia, bipolar disorder, and major depressive disorder: A systematic review of secondary literature. *Neuroscience & Biobehavioral Reviews, 120*, 249–261.

van Sloten, T. T., Sedaghat, S., Carnethon, M. R., Launer, L. J., & Stehouwer, C. D. (2020). Cerebral microvascular complications of type 2 diabetes: stroke, cognitive dysfunction, and depression. *The Lancet Diabetes & Endocrinology, 8*, 325–336.

van Spronsen, F. J., Blau, N., Harding, C., Burlina, A., Longo, N., & Bosch, A. M. (2021). Phenylketonuria. *Nature Reviews Disease Primers, 7*, 1–19.

Vasileva, M., Graf, R. K., Reinelt, T., Petermann, U., & Petermann, F. (2021). Research review: A meta-analysis of the international prevalence and comorbidity of mental disorders in children between 1 and 7 years. *Journal of Child Psychology and Psychiatry, 62*, 372–381.

Vázquez, G. H., Bahji, A., Undurraga, J., Tondo, L., & Baldessarini, R. J. (2021). Efficacy and tolerability of combination treatments for major depression: Antidepressants plus second-generation antipsychotics vs. esketamine vs. lithium. *Journal of Psychopharmacology, 35*, 890–900.

Vegunta, S., Kling, J. M., & Kapoor, E. (2020). Androgen therapy in women. *Journal of Women's Health, 29*, 57–64.

Ventriglio, A., Bhugra, D., Sampogna, G., Luciano, M., De Berardis, D., Sani, G., & Fiorillo, A. (2020). From dysthymia to treatment-resistant depression: evolution of a psychopathological construct. *International Review of Psychiatry, 32*, 471–476.

Ventriglio, A., Bonfitto, I., Ricci, F., Cuoco, F., & Bhavsar, V. (2018). Delusion, possession and religion. *Nordic Journal of Psychiatry, 72*, S13–S15.

Ventura, L., Cano-Vindel, A., Muñoz-Navarro, R., Barrio-Martínez, S., Medrano, L. A., Moriana, J. A., ... & González-Blanch, C. (2021). The role of cognitive factors in differentiating individuals with somatoform disorders with and without depression. *Journal of Psychosomatic Research, 148*, 110573.

Vera, M., Obén, A., Juarbe, D., Hernández, N., & Pérez-Pedrogo, C. (2021). Randomized pilot trial of cognitive-behavioral therapy and acceptance-based behavioral therapy in the treatment of Spanish-speaking Latino primary care patients with generalized anxiety disorder. *Journal of Behavioral and Cognitive Therapy, 31*, 91–103.

Vialichko, I. M., Lelevich, S. V., Lelevich, V. V., Doroshenko, E. M., & Smirnov, V. Y. (2021). Neurotransmitter changes in the rat brain under combined intoxication induced by alcohol and morphine. *Biomeditsinskaia Khimiia, 67*, 323–330.

Vidal, L., Ortega, M. A., Alvarez-Mon, M. A., Álvarez-Mon, M., & Lahera, G. (2021). Volumetric Alterations of the Cerebral Cortex in Eating Disorders. *Journal of Clinical Medicine, 10*, 5480.

Viglione, D. J., de Ruiter, C., King, C. M., Meyer, G. J., Kivisto, A. J., Rubin, B. A., & Hunsley, J. (2022). Legal admissibility of the Rorschach and R-PAS: A review of research, practice, and case law. *Journal of Personality Assessment, 104*, 137–161.

Viher, P. V., Stegmayer, K., Bracht, T., Federspiel, A., Bohlhalter, S., Strik, W., ... & Walther, S. (2022). Neurological soft signs are associated with altered white matter in patients with schizophrenia. *Schizophrenia Bulletin, 48*, 220–230.

Vik-Mo, A. O., Giil, L. M., Borda, M. G., Ballard, C., & Aarsland, D. (2020). The individual course of neuropsychiatric symptoms in people with Alzheimer's and Lewy body dementia: 12-year longitudinal cohort study. *British Journal of Psychiatry, 216*, 43–48.

Vilsaint, C. L., NeMoyer, A., Fillbrunn, M., Sadikova, E., Kessler, R. C., Sampson, N. A., ... & Alegría, M. (2019). Racial/ethnic differences in 12-month prevalence and persistence of mood, anxiety, and substance use disorders: Variation by nativity and socioeconomic status. *Comprehensive Psychiatry, 89*, 52–60.

Vinci, C., Sawyer, L., & Yang, M. J. (2021). Minding the gap: Leveraging mindfulness to inform cue exposure treatment for substance use disorders. *Frontiers in Psychology, 12*, 649409.

Virtanen, S., Kuja-Halkola, R., Mataix-Cols, D., Jayaram-Lindström, N., D'Onofrio, B. M., Larsson, H., ... & Latvala, A. (2020). Comorbidity of substance misuse with anxiety-related and depressive disorders: A genetically informative population study of 3 million individuals in Sweden. *Psychological Medicine, 50*, 1706–1715.

Vismara, L., Sechi, C., & Lucarelli, L. (2019). Fathers' and mothers' depressive symptoms: Internalizing/externalizing problems and dissociative experiences in their adolescent offspring. *Current Psychology, 41*, 247–257.

Visontay, R., Rao, R. T., & Mewton, L. (2021). Alcohol use and dementia: New research directions. *Current Opinion in Psychiatry, 34*, 165–170.

Voineskos, D., Daskalakis, Z. J., & Blumberger, D. M. (2020). Management of treatment-resistant depression: Challenges and strategies. *Neuropsychiatric Disease and Treatment, 16*, 221.

Volpicelli, J. R., & Menzies, P. (2022). Rethinking unhealthy alcohol use in the United States: A structured review. *Substance Abuse: Research and Treatment, 16*, 11782218221111832.

von Mutius, E., & Smits, H. H. (2020). Primary prevention of asthma: From risk and protective factors to targeted strategies for prevention. *The Lancet, 396*, 854–866.

Waddell, J. T., Elam, K. K., & Chassin, L. (2022). Multidimensional impulsive personality traits mediate the effect of parent substance use disorder on adolescent alcohol and cannabis use. *Journal of Youth and Adolescence, 51*, 348–360.

Wagner, B., Steiner, M., Huber, D. F. X., & Crevenna, R. (2021). The effect of biofeedback interventions on pain, overall symptoms, quality of life and physiological parameters in patients with pelvic pain. *Wiener Klinische Wochenschrift, 134*, 11–48.

Waldron, K. A., Turrisi, R. J., Mallett, K. A., & Romano, E. (2021). Examining parental permissiveness toward drinking and perceived ethnic discrimination as risk factors for drinking outcomes among Latinx college students. *Addictive Behaviors, 118*, 106900.

Walker, W. H., Walton, J. C., DeVries, A. C., & Nelson, R. J. (2020). Circadian rhythm disruption and mental health. *Translational Psychiatry, 10*, 1–13.

Wambua, G. N., Kilian, S., Ntlantsana, V., & Chiliza, B. (2020). The association between resilience and psychosocial functioning in schizophrenia: A systematic review and meta-analysis. *Psychiatry Research, 293*, 113374.

Wampold, B. E. (2021). Healing in a social context: The importance of clinician and patient relationship. *Frontiers in Pain Research, 2*, 684768.

Wander, C. (2020). Schizophrenia: opportunities to improve outcomes and reduce economic burden through managed care. *American Journal of Managed Care, 26(3 Suppl)*, S62–S68.

Wang, G. A., Corsini-Munt, S., Dubé, J. P., McClung, E., & Rosen, N. O. (2022). Regulate and communicate: Associations between emotion regulation and sexual communication among men with hypoactive sexual desire disorder and their partners. *The Journal of Sex Research*, 1–11.

Wang, J., Zhao, H., & Girgenti, M. J. (2022). Posttraumatic stress disorder brain transcriptomics: Convergent genomic signatures across biological sex. *Biological Psychiatry, 91*, 6–13.

Wang, P. S., Lane, M., Olfson, M., Pincus, H. A., Wells, K. B., & Kessler, R. C. (2005). Twelve-month use of mental health services in the United States: Results from the National Comorbidity Survey Replication. *Archives of General Psychiatry, 62*, 629–640.

Wang, Q., Zhao, J., Chang, H., Liu, X., & Zhu, R. (2021). Homocysteine and folic acid: Risk factors for Alzheimer's Disease—An updated meta-analysis. *Frontiers in Aging Neuroscience, 13*, 665114.

Wang, S., & Blazer, D. G. (2015). Depression and cognition in the elderly. *Annual Review of Clinical Psychology, 11*, 331–360.

Wang, S. M., Han, C., Bahk, W. M., Lee, S. J., Patkar, A. A., Masand, P. S., & Pae, C. U. (2018). Addressing the side effects of contemporary antidepressant drugs: A comprehensive review. *Chonnam Medical Journal, 54*, 101–112.

Wang, X. Y., Lin, J. J., Lu, M. K., Jang, F. L., Tseng, H. H., Chen, P. S., ... & Lin, S. H. (2022). Development and validation of a web-based prediction tool on minor physical anomalies for schizophrenia. *Schizophrenia, 8*, 1–7.

Wang, Y., Tian, L., Guo, L., & Huebner, E. S. (2020). Family dysfunction and adolescents' anxiety and depression: A multiple mediation model. *Journal of Applied Developmental Psychology, 66*, 101090.

Waqas, A., Malik, S., Fida, A., Abbas, N., Mian, N., Miryala, S., ... & Naveed, S. (2020). Interventions to reduce stigma related to mental illnesses in educational institutes: A systematic review. *Psychiatric Quarterly, 91*, 887-903.

Ward, S. L., Hisley, S. M., & Kennedy, A. M. (2016). *Maternal-child nursing care: Optimizing outcomes for mothers, children, and families* (2nd ed.). Philadelphia, PA: F.A. Davis.

Warlick, C. A., Poquiz, J., Huffman, J. M., DeLong, L., Moffitt-Carney, K., Leonard, J., Schellenger, B., & Nelson, J. (2022). Effectiveness of a brief dialectical behavior therapy intensive-outpatient community health program. *Psychotherapy, 59*, 125–132.

Wasil, A. R., Patel, R., Cho, J. Y., Shingleton, R. M., Weisz, J. R., & DeRubeis, R. J. (2021). Smartphone apps for eating disorders: A systematic review of evidence-based content and application of user-adjusted analyses. *International Journal of Eating Disorders, 54*, 690–700.

Waters, L., Algoe, S. B., Dutton, J., Emmons, R., Fredrickson, B. L., Heaphy, E., ... & Steger, M. (2022). Positive psychology in a pandemic: Buffering, bolstering, and building mental health. *The Journal of Positive Psychology, 17*, 303–323.

Watson, H. J., Palmos, A. B., Hunjan, A., Baker, J. H., Yilmaz, Z., & Davies, H. L. (2021). Genetics of eating disorders in the genome-wide era. *Psychological Medicine, 51*, 2287–2297.

Watson, J. C., McMullen, E. J., Rodrigues, A., & Prosser, M. C. (2020). Examining the role of therapists' empathy and clients' attachment styles on changes in clients' affect regulation and outcome in the treatment of depression. *Psychotherapy Research, 30*, 693–705.

Webb, C. A., Cohen, Z. D., Beard, C., Forgeard, M., Peckham, A. D., & Björgvinsson, T. (2020). Personalized prognostic prediction of treatment outcome for depressed patients in a naturalistic psychiatric hospital setting: A comparison of machine learning approaches. *Journal of Consulting and Clinical Psychology, 88*, 25–38.

Wechsler, D. (2008). *WAIS-IV: Wechsler Adult Intelligence Scale—Fourth Edition*. San Antonio, TX: Pearson.

Weck, F., Gropalis, M., Hiller, W., & Bleichhardt, G. (2015). Effectiveness of cognitive-behavioral group therapy for patients with hypochondriasis (health anxiety). *Journal of Anxiety Disorders, 30*, 1–7.

Wei, M., Liao, K. Y.-H., Chao, R. C.-L., Mallinckrodt, B., Tsai, P.-C., & Botello-Zamarron, R. (2010). Minority stress, perceived bicultural competence, and depressive symptoms among ethnic minority college students. *Journal of Counseling Psychology, 57*, 411–422.

Weinberg, I., & Ronningstam, E. (2020). Dos and don'ts in treatments of patients with narcissistic personality disorder. *Journal of Personality Disorders, 34*, 122–142.

Weinberger, J. M., Houman, J., Caron, A. T., & Anger, J. (2019). Female sexual dysfunction: A systematic review of outcomes across various treatment modalities. *Sexual Medicine Reviews, 7*, 223–250.

Weintraub, D., Aarsland, D., Chaudhuri, K. R., Dobkin, R. D., Leentjens, A. F., Rodriguez-Violante, M., & Schrag, A. (2022). The neuropsychiatry of Parkinson's disease: advances and challenges. *The Lancet Neurology, 21*, 89–102.

Weissman, M. M. (2020). Interpersonal psychotherapy: history and future. *American Journal of Psychotherapy, 73*, 3–7.

Welsh, B. C., Yohros, A., & Zane, S. N. (2020). Understanding iatrogenic effects for evidence-based policy: A review of crime and violence prevention programs. *Aggression and Violent Behavior, 55*, 101511.

Wen, D., Wang, J., Yao, G., Liu, S., Li, X., Li, J., ... & Xu, Y. (2021). Abnormality of subcortical volume and resting functional connectivity in adolescents with early-onset and prodromal schizophrenia. *Journal of Psychiatric Research, 140*, 282–288.

Wenzel, A. (Ed.) (2021). *Handbook of cognitive behavioral therapy*. Washington, DC: American Psychological Association.

Werner, P., Shpigelman, C. N., & Raviv Turgeman, L. (2020). Family caregivers' and professionals' stigmatic experiences with persons with early-onset dementia: A qualitative study. *Scandinavian Journal of Caring Sciences, 34*, 52–61.

Weyandt, L., DuPaul, G. J., Verdi, G., Rossi, J. S., Swentosky, A. J., Vilardo, B. S., O'Dell, S.M., & Carson, K. S. (2013). The performance of college students with and without ADHD: Neuropsychological, academic, and psychosocial functioning. *Journal of Psychopathology and Behavioral Assessment, 35*, 421–435.

Wheeler, L. J., & Guntupalli, S. R. (2020). Female sexual dysfunction: Pharmacologic and therapeutic interventions. *Obstetrics & Gynecology, 136*, 174–186.

White, A. M. (2020). Gender differences in the epidemiology of alcohol use and related harms in the United States. *Alcohol Research: Current Reviews, 40*: 01.

White, R. M., Pasco, M. C., Korous, K. M., & Causadias, J. M. (2020). A systematic review and meta-analysis of the association of neighborhood ethnic-racial concentrations and adolescent behaviour problems in the US. *Journal of Adolescence, 78*, 73–84.

Whiting, D., Gulati, G., Geddes, J. R., & Fazel, S. (2022). Association of schizophrenia spectrum disorders and violence perpetration in adults and adolescents from 15 countries: A systematic review and meta-analysis. *JAMA Psychiatry, 79*, 120–132.

Whiting, D., Lichtenstein, P., & Fazel, S. (2021). Violence and mental disorders: A structured review of associations by individual diagnoses, risk factors, and risk assessment. *The Lancet Psychiatry, 8*, 150–161.

Whitman, M. R., Tylicki, J. L., Mascioli, R., Pickle, J., & Ben-Porath, Y. S. (2021). Psychometric properties of the Minnesota Multiphasic Personality Inventory-3 (MMPI-3) in a clinical neuropsychology setting. *Psychological Assessment, 33*, 142–155.

Wichansawakun, S., Chupisanyarote, K., Wongpipathpong, W., Kaur, G., & Buttar, H. S. (2022). Antioxidant diets and functional foods attenuate dementia and cognition in elderly subjects. In R.B. Singh, S. Watanbe, & A.A. Isaza (Eds.), *Functional foods and nutraceuticals in metabolic and non-communicable diseases* (pp. 533–549). New York: Academic.

Wieder, L., Brown, R. J., Thompson, T., & Terhune, D. B. (2022). Hypnotic suggestibility in dissociative and related disorders: A meta-analysis. *Neuroscience & Biobehavioral Reviews*, 104751.

Wightman, D. P., Jansen, I. E., Savage, J. E., Shadrin, A. A., Bahrami, S., Holland, D., ... & Posthuma, D. (2021). A genome-wide association study with 1,126,563 individuals identifies new risk loci for Alzheimer's disease. *Nature Genetics, 53*, 1276–1282.

Wilfley, D.E., Agras, W.S., & Taylor, C.B. (2013). Reducing the burden of eating disorders: A model for population-based prevention and treatment for university and college campuses. *International Journal of Eating Disorders, 46*, 529–532.

Wilkinson, G. S., & Robertson, G. J. (2017). *Wide Range Achievement Test–Fifth Edition (WRAT5)*. San Antonio: Pearson.

Williams-Nickelson, C. (2009). Mentoring women graduate students: A model for professional psychology. *Professional Psychology: Research and Practice, 40*, 284–291.

Wincze, J. P., & Weisberg, R. B. (2015). *Sexual dysfunction: A guide for assessment and treatment* (3rd ed.). New York: Guilford.

Winder, B., Gough, B., & Seymour-Smith, S. (2015). Stumbling into sexual crime: The passive perpetrator in accounts by male internet sex offenders. *Archives of Sexual Behavior, 44*, 167–180.

Windle, E., Tee, H., Sabitova, A., Jovanovic, N., Priebe, S., & Carr, C. (2020). Association of patient treatment preference with dropout and clinical outcomes in adult psychosocial mental health interventions: A systematic review and meta-analysis. *JAMA Psychiatry, 77*, 294–302.

Winsper, C. (2021). Borderline personality disorder: course and outcomes across the lifespan. *Current Opinion in Psychology, 37*, 94–97.

Winsper, C., Bilgin, A., Thompson, A., Marwaha, S., Chanen, A. M., Singh, S. P., ... & Furtado, V. (2020). The prevalence of personality disorders in the community: a global systematic review and meta-analysis. *The British Journal of Psychiatry, 216*, 69–78.

Wirz-Justice, A., Ajdacic, V., Rössler, W., Steinhausen, H. C., & Angst, J. (2019). Prevalence of seasonal depression in a prospective cohort study. *European Archives of Psychiatry and Clinical Neuroscience, 269*, 833–839.

Withers, M., Jahangir, T., Kubasova, K., & Ran, M. S. (2021). Reducing stigma associated with mental health problems among university students in the Asia-Pacific: A video content analysis of student-driven proposals. *International Journal of Social Psychiatry, 68*, 827–835.

Wittchen, H. U., Mühlig, S., & Beesdo, K. (2022). Mental disorders in primary care. *Dialogues in Clinical Neuroscience, 5*, 115–128.

Wittenborn, A. K., Woods, S. B., Priest, J. B., Morgan, P. C., Tseng, C. F., Huerta, P., & Edwards, C. (2022). Couple and family interventions for depressive and bipolar disorders: Evidence base update (2010–2019). *Journal of Marital and Family Therapy, 48*, 129–153.

Witthöft, M., Bräscher, A. K., Jungmann, S. M., & Köteles, F. (2020). Somatic symptom perception and interoception: A latent-variable approach. *Zeitschrift für Psychologie, 228*, 100–109.

Wittström, F., Långström, N., Landgren, V., & Rahm, C. (2020). Risk factors for sexual offending in self-referred men with pedophilic disorder: A Swedish case-control study. *Frontiers in Psychology, 11*, 571775.

Wogen, J., & Restrepo, M. T. (2020). Human rights, stigma, and substance use. *Health and Human Rights, 22*, 51–60.

Wojnarowski, C., Firth, N., Finegan, M., & Delgadillo, J. (2019). Predictors of depression relapse and recurrence after cognitive behavioural therapy: a systematic review and meta-analysis. *Behavioural and Cognitive Psychotherapy, 47*, 514–529.

Wolf, A., Ueda, K., & Hirano, Y. (2021). Recent updates of eye movement abnormalities in patients with schizophrenia: A scoping review. *Psychiatry and Clinical Neurosciences, 75*, 82–100.

Wolters, F. J., & Ikram, M. A. (2019). Epidemiology of vascular dementia: Nosology in a time of epiomics. *Arteriosclerosis, Thrombosis, and Vascular Biology, 39*, 1542–1549.

Wong, W. (2020). Economic burden of Alzheimer disease and managed care considerations. *American Journal of Managed Care, 26*, S177–S183.

Woods, A., Solomonov, N., Liles, B., Guillod, A., Kales, H. C., & Sirey, J. A. (2021). Perceived social support and interpersonal functioning as predictors of treatment response among depressed older adults. *The American Journal of Geriatric Psychiatry, 29*, 843–852.

Woods, S. W., Choi, J., & Mamah, D. (2021). Full speed ahead on indicated prevention of psychosis. *World Psychiatry, 20*, 223–224.

Woodward, T. S., Jung, K., Hwang, H., Yin, J., Taylor, L., Menon, M., Peters, E., Kuipers, E., Waters, F., Lecomte, T., Sommer, I.E., Daalman, K., van Lutterfeld, R., Hubl, D., Kindler, J., Homan, P., Badcock, J.C., Chhabra, S., Cella, M., Keedy, S., Allen, P., Mechelli, A., Preti, A., Siddi, S., & Erickson, D. (2014). Symptom dimensions of the psychotic symptom rating scales in psychosis: A multisite study. *Schizophrenia Bulletin, 40*(Suppl. 4), S265–S274.

World Health Organization (2021). *Dementia*. New York: Author.

World Health Organization. (2021). *Depression*. Geneva: Author.

World Health Organization (2021). *Suicide*. Switzerland: Author.

Wortinger, L. A., Engen, K., Barth, C., Andreassen, O. A., Jørgensen, K. N., & Agartz, I. (2022). Asphyxia at birth affects brain structure in patients on the schizophrenia-bipolar disorder spectrum and healthy participants. *Psychological Medicine, 52*, 1050–1059.

Wu, H., Le Couteur, D. G., & Hilmer, S. N. (2021). Mortality trends of stroke and dementia: Changing landscapes and new challenges. *Journal of the American Geriatrics Society, 69*, 2888–2898.

Wu, T., Lin, D., Cheng, Y., Jiang, S., Riaz, M. W., Fu, N., ... & Zheng, Y. (2022). Amyloid cascade hypothesis for the treatment of Alzheimer's Disease: Progress and challenges. *Aging and Disease.*

Wu, Y., Zhu, B., Chen, Z., Duan, J., Luo, A., Yang, L., & Yang, C. (2021). New insights into the comorbidity of coronary heart disease and depression. *Current Problems in Cardiology, 46*, 100413.

Xi, Z. X., & Jordan, C. (2022). Identification of the risk genes associated with vulnerability to addiction: Major findings from transgenic animals. *Frontiers in Neuroscience, 15*, 811192.

Xiao, H., Zhao, Z., Zhang, C., & Wang, J. (2021). Influence of standardized nursing intervention combined with mindfulness stress reduction training on the curative effect, negative emotion, and quality of life in patients with chronic gastritis and gastric ulcer. *Evidence-Based Complementary and Alternative Medicine, 2021*, 2131405.

Xie, Z., & Bankaitis, V. A. (2022). Phosphatidylinositol transfer protein/planar cell polarity axis regulates neocortical morphogenesis by supporting interkinetic nuclear migration. *Cell Reports, 39*, 110869.

Xu, L., Liu, Y., He, H., Fields, N. L., Ivey, D. L., & Kan, C. (2021). Caregiving intensity and caregiver burden among caregivers of people with dementia: The moderating roles of social support. *Archives of Gerontology and Geriatrics, 94*, 104334.

Xu, X., Li, Q., Qian, Y., Cai, H., Zhang, C., Zhao, W., ... & Yu, Y. (2022). Genetic mechanisms underlying gray matter volume changes in patients with drug-naive first-episode schizophrenia. *Cerebral Cortex, 2022,* bhac211.

Yadav, S. K., Bhat, A. A., Hashem, S., Nisar, S., Kamal, M., Syed, N., ... & Haris, M. (2021). Genetic variations influence brain changes in patients with attention-deficit hyperactivity disorder. *Translational Psychiatry, 11*, 1–24.

Yamashita, A., Yoshioka, S. I., & Yajima, Y. (2021). Resilience and related factors as predictors of relapse risk in patients with substance use disorder: A cross-sectional study. *Substance Abuse Treatment, Prevention, and Policy, 16*, 1–9.

Yan, N., Ansari, A., & Peng, P. (2021). Reconsidering the relation between parental functioning and child externalizing behaviors: A meta-analysis on child-driven effects. *Journal of Family Psychology, 35*, 225–235.

Yan, W., Zhao, M., Fu, Z., Pearlson, G. D., Sui, J., & Calhoun, V. D. (2022). Mapping relationships among schizophrenia, bipolar and schizoaffective disorders: A deep classification and clustering framework using fMRI time series. *Schizophrenia Research, 245*, 141–150.

Yan, W. S., Chen, R. T., Liu, M. M., & Zheng, D. H. (2021). Monetary reward discounting, inhibitory control, and trait impulsivity in young adults with internet gaming disorder and nicotine dependence. *Frontiers in Psychiatry, 12*, 628933.

Yang, P., Knight, W. C., Li, H., Guo, Y., Perlmutter, J. S., Benzinger, T. L., ... & Xu, J. (2021). Dopamine D1 + D3 receptor density may correlate with parkinson disease clinical features. *Annals of Clinical and Translational Neurology, 8*, 224–237.

Yang, Y., Li, X., Cui, Y., Liu, K., Qu, H., Lu, Y., ... & Lv, L. (2022). Reduced gray matter volume in orbitofrontal cortex across schizophrenia, major depressive disorder, and bipolar disorder: A comparative imaging study. *Frontiers in Neuroscience, 16*, 919272.

Yatham, L. N., Chakrabarty, T., Bond, D. J., Schaffer, A., Beaulieu, S., Parikh, S. V., ... & Post, R. (2021). Canadian Network for Mood and Anxiety Treatments (CANMAT) and International Society for Bipolar Disorders (ISBD) recommendations for the management of patients with bipolar disorder with mixed presentations. *Bipolar Disorders, 23*, 767–788.

Yeheskel, A., Jekielek, A., & Sandor, P. (2020). Taking up residence: A review of outcome studies examining residential treatment for youth with serious emotional and behavioural disorders. *Children and Youth Services Review, 111*, 104842.

Yesilyaprak, N., Batmaz, S., Yildiz, M., Songur, E., & Akpinar Aslan, E. (2019). Automatic thoughts, cognitive distortions, dysfunctional attitudes, core beliefs, and ruminative response styles in unipolar major depressive disorder and bipolar disorder: A comparative study. *Psychiatry and Clinical Psychopharmacology, 29*, 854–863.

Yockey, R. A., King, K. A., & Vidourek, R. A. (2021). Family factors and parental correlates to adolescent conduct disorder. *Journal of Family Studies, 27*, 356–365.

Yokoyama, A., Yokoyama, T., Kimura, M., Matsushita, S., & Yokoyama, M. (2021). Combinations of alcohol-induced flushing with genetic polymorphisms of alcohol and aldehyde dehydrogenases and the risk of alcohol dependence in Japanese men and women. *PLoS One, 16*, e0255276.

Yoo, H. S., Jeong, S. H., Oh, K. T., Lee, S., Sohn, Y. H., Ye, B. S., ... & Lee, P. H. (2022). Interrelation of striatal dopamine, brain metabolism and cognition in dementia with Lewy bodies. *Brain, 2022*, awac084.

Younes, K., & Miller, B. L. (2020). Frontotemporal dementia: Neuropathology, genetics, neuroimaging, and treatments. *Psychiatric Clinics, 43*, 331–344.

Yu, Q., Li, E., Li, L., & Liang, W. (2020). Efficacy of interventions based on applied behavior analysis for autism spectrum disorder: A meta-analysis. *Psychiatry Investigation, 17*, 432–443.

Zablotsky, B., & Black, L. I. (2020). Prevalence of children aged 3–17 years with developmental disabilities, by urbanicity: United States, 2015–2018. *National Health Statistics Reports, 139*.

Zahler, L., Sommer, K., Reinecke, A., Wilhelm, F. H., Margraf, J., & Woud, M. L. (2020). Cognitive vulnerability in the context of panic: Assessment of panic-related associations and interpretations in individuals with varying levels of anxiety sensitivity. *Cognitive Therapy and Research, 44*, 858–873.

Zargar, F., Rahafrouz, L., & Tarrahi, M. J. (2021). Effect of mindfulness-based stress reduction program on psychological symptoms, quality of life, and symptom severity in patients with somatic symptom disorder. *Advanced Biomedical Research, 10*: 9.

Zeidan, J., Fombonne, E., Scorah, J., Ibrahim, A., Durkin, M. S., Saxena, S., ... & Elsabbagh, M. (2022). Global prevalence of autism: A systematic review update. *Autism Research, 15*, 778–790.

Zeng, L. N., Zong, Q. Q., Yang, Y., Zhang, L., Xiang, Y. F., Ng, C. H., ... & Xiang, Y. T. (2020). Gender difference in the prevalence of insomnia: A meta-analysis of observational studies. *Frontiers in Psychiatry, 11*, 577429.

Zgoba, K. M., & Mitchell, M. M. (2021). The effectiveness of Sex Offender Registration and Notification: A meta-analysis of 25 years of findings. *Journal of Experimental Criminology*, 1–26.

Zgourides, G. D. (2020). Disposition and treatment of paraphilia in non-western cultures. In D. Rowland & E. Jannini (Eds.) *Cultural differences and the practice of sexual medicine: A guide for sexual health practitioners* (pp. 253–272). Cham: Springer.

Zhang, F., Baranova, A., Zhou, C., Cao, H., Chen, J., Zhang, X., & Xu, M. (2021). Causal influences of neuroticism on mental health and cardiovascular disease. *Human Genetics, 140*, 1267–1281.

Zhang, H., Greenwood, D. C., Risch, H. A., Bunce, D., Hardie, L. J., & Cade, J. E. (2021). Meat consumption and risk of incident dementia: cohort study of 493,888 UK Biobank participants. *The American Journal of Clinical Nutrition, 114*, 175–184.

Zhang, H., Lee, Z. X., White, T., & Qiu, A. (2020). Parental and social factors in relation to child psychopathology, behavior, and cognitive function. *Translational Psychiatry, 10*, 1–9.

Zhang, Y., Cheng, L., Liu, Y., Zhan, S., Wu, Z., Luo, S., & Zhang, X. (2023). Dietary flavonoids: a novel strategy for the amelioration of cognitive impairment through intestinal microbiota. *Journal of the Science of Food and Agriculture, 103*, 488–495.

Zhang, Y., Jin, X., Lutz, M. W., Ju, S. Y., Liu, K., Guo, G., ... & Yao, Y. (2021). Interaction between APOE ϵ4 and dietary protein intake on cognitive decline: A longitudinal cohort study. *Clinical Nutrition, 40*, 2716–2725.

Zhang, Z., Zhang, L., Zhang, G., Jin, J., & Zheng, Z. (2018). The effect of CBT and its modifications for relapse prevention in major depressive disorder: A systematic review and meta-analysis. *BMC Psychiatry, 18*, 1–14.

Zheng, B. X., Yin, Y., Xiao, H., Lui, S., Wen, C. B., Dai, Y. E., ... & Gong, Q. (2021). Altered cortical reorganization and brain functional connectivity in phantom limb pain: A functional MRI study. *Pain Practice, 21*, 394–403.

Zheng, J., Skiba, M. A., Bell, R. J., Islam, R. M., & Davis, S. R. (2020). The prevalence of sexual dysfunctions and sexually related distress in young women: A cross-sectional survey. *Fertility and Sterility, 113*, 426–434.

Zhao, F., Zhang, H., Wang, P., Cui, W., Xu, K., Chen, D., ... & Wei, S. (2022). Oxytocin and serotonin in the modulation of neural function: Neurobiological underpinnings of autism-related behavior. *Frontiers in Neuroscience, 16*: 919890.

Zhao, X., Prandstetter, K., Jansen, E., Hahlweg, K., Schulz, W., & Foran, H. M. (2021). Interparental relationship adjustment, parenting, and offspring's cigarette smoking at the 10-Year follow-up. *Family Process, 60*, 523–537.

Zhao, Y., Sallie, S. N., Cui, H., Zeng, N., Du, J., Yuan, T., ... & Zhang, C. (2021). Anterior cingulate cortex in addiction: New insights for neuromodulation. Neuromodulation: *Technology at the Neural Interface, 24*, 187–196.

Zhou, M. S., Nasir, M., Farhat, L. C., Kook, M., Artukoglu, B. B., & Bloch, M. H. (2021). Meta-analysis: pharmacologic treatment of restricted and repetitive behaviors in autism spectrum disorders. *Journal of the American Academy of Child & Adolescent Psychiatry, 60*, 35–45.

Zhou, X., Guo, J., Lu, G., Chen, C., Xie, Z., Liu, J., & Zhang, C. (2020). Effects of mindfulness-based stress reduction on anxiety symptoms in young people: A systematic review and meta-analysis. *Psychiatry Research, 289*, 113002.

Zhou, X., Li, Y. Y., Fu, A. K., & Ip, N. Y. (2021). Polygenic score models for Alzheimer's disease: from research to clinical applications. *Frontiers in Neuroscience, 15*, 650220.

Zhou, Y., Zhu, X. P., Shi, J. J., Yuan, G. Z., Yao, Z. A., Chu, Y. G., ... & Hu, Y. H. (2021). Coronary heart disease and depression or anxiety: A bibliometric analysis. *Frontiers in Psychology, 12*, 669000.

Zhu, C., Badach, J., Lin, A., Mathur, N., McHugh, S., Saracco, B., ... & Hong, Y. K. (2021). Omental patch versus gastric resection for perforated gastric ulcer: Systematic review and meta-analysis for an unresolved debate. *The American Journal of Surgery, 221*, 935–941.

Zhu, Y., Owens, S. J., Murphy, C. E., Ajulu, K., Rothmond, D., Purves-Tyson, T., ... & Weickert, C. S. (2022). Inflammation-related transcripts define "high" and "low" subgroups of individuals with schizophrenia and bipolar disorder in the midbrain. *Brain, Behavior, and Immunity, 105*, 149–159.

Zielinski, M. J., & Veilleux, J. C. (2014). Examining the relation between borderline personality features and social support: The mediating role of rejection sensitivity. *Personality and Individual Differences, 70*, 235–238.

Zimmermann, M., Chong, A. K., Vechiu, C., & Papa, A. (2020). Modifiable risk and protective factors for anxiety disorders among adults: A systematic review. *Psychiatry Research, 285*, 112705.

Zsigo, C., Sfärlea, A., Lingl, C., Piechaczek, C., Schulte-Körne, G., Feldmann, L., &

Greimel, E. (2022). Emotion regulation deficits in adolescent girls with major depression, anorexia nervosa and comorbid major depression and anorexia nervosa. *Child Psychiatry & Human Development*, 1–13.

Zunhammer, M., Eberle, H., Eichhammer, P., & Busch, V. (2013). Somatic symptoms evoked by exam stress in university students: The role of alexithymia, neuroticism, anxiety and depression. *PLoS One, 8*, e84911.

Zuo, B., Zhang, X., Wen, F. F., & Zhao, Y. (2020). The influence of stressful life events on depression among Chinese university students: Multiple mediating roles of fatalism and core self-evaluations. *Journal of Affective Disorders, 260*, 84–90.

Name Index

A

B

F

G

H

L

M

N

O

P

Q

R

S

T

X

Y

Z

Subject Index

Note: Page numbers followed by "f" and "t" indicate figures and tables respectively.

B

C

D

E

Q

R

DSM-5-TR Classifications

Neurodevelopmental Disorders

Intellectual Developmental Disorders

Intellectual Developmental Disorder (Intellectual Disability)/Global Developmental Delay/Unspecified Intellectual Developmental Disorder (Intellectual Disability)

Communication Disorders

Language Disorder/Speech Sound Disorder/Childhood-Onset Fluency Disorder (Stuttering)/Social (Pragmatic) Communication Disorder/Unspecified Communication Disorder

Autism Spectrum Disorder

Autism Spectrum Disorder

Attention-Deficit/Hyperactivity Disorder

Attention-Deficit/Hyperactivity Disorder/Other Specified Attention-Deficit/Hyperactivity Disorder/Unspecified Attention-Deficit/Hyperactivity Disorder

Specific Learning Disorder

Motor Disorders

Developmental Coordination Disorder/Stereotypic Movement Disorder

Tic Disorders

Tourette's Disorder/Persistent (Chronic) Motor or Vocal Tic Disorder/Provisional Tic Disorder/Other Specified Tic Disorder/Unspecific Tic Disorder

Other Neurodevelopmental Disorders

Other Specified Neurodevelopmental Disorder/Unspecified Neurodevelopmental Disorder

Schizophrenia Spectrum and other Psychotic Disorders

Schizotypal (Personality) Disorder
Delusional Disorder
Brief Psychotic Disorder
Schizophreniform Disorder
Schizophrenia
Schizoaffective Disorder
Substance/Medication-Induced Psychotic Disorder
Psychotic Disorder Due to Another Medical Condition
Catatonia Associated with Another Mental Disorder
Catatonic Disorder Due to Another Medical Condition
Unspecified Catatonia
Other Specified Schizophrenia Spectrum and Other Psychotic Disorder
Unspecified Schizophrenia Spectrum and Other Psychotic Disorder

Bipolar and Related Disorders

Bipolar I Disorder/Bipolar II Disorder/Cyclothymic Disorder/Substance/Medication-Induced Bipolar and Related Disorder/Bipolar and Related Disorder Due to Another Medical Condition/Other Specified Bipolar and Related Disorder/Unspecified Bipolar and Related Disorder/Unspecified Mood Disorder

Depressive Disorders

Disruptive Mood Dysregulation Disorder/Major Depressive Disorder/Persistent Depressive Disorder/Premenstrual Dysphoric Disorder/Substance/Medication-Induced Depressive Disorder/Depressive Disorder Due to Another Medical Condition/Other Specified Depressive Disorder/Unspecified Depressive Disorder/Unspecified Mood Disorder

Anxiety Disorders

Separation Anxiety Disorder/Selective Mutism/Specific Phobia/Social Anxiety Disorder/Panic Disorder/Panic Attack Specifier/Agoraphobia/Generalized Anxiety Disorder/Substance/Medication-Induced Anxiety Disorder/Anxiety Disorder Due to Another Medical Condition/Other Specified Anxiety Disorder/Unspecified Anxiety Disorder

Obsessive-Compulsive and Related Disorders

Obsessive-Compulsive Disorder/Body Dysmorphic Disorder/Hoarding Disorder/Trichotillomania (Hair-Pulling Disorder)/Excoriation (Skin-Picking) Disorder/Substance/Medication-Induced Obsessive-Compulsive and Related Disorder/Obsessive-Compulsive and Related Disorder Due to Another Medical Condition/Other Specified Obsessive-Compulsive and Related Disorder/Unspecified Obsessive-Compulsive and Related Disorder

Trauma- and Stressor-Related Disorders

Reactive Attachment Disorder/Disinhibited Social Engagement Disorder/Posttraumatic Stress Disorder/Acute Stress Disorder/Adjustment Disorders/Prolonged Grief Disorder/Other Specified Trauma- and Stressor-Related Disorder/Unspecified Trauma- and Stressor-Related Disorder

Dissociative Disorders

Dissociative Identity Disorder/Dissociative Amnesia/Depersonalization/Derealization Disorder/Other Specified Dissociative Disorder/Unspecified Dissociative Disorder

Somatic Symptom and Related Disorders

Somatic Symptom Disorder/Illness Anxiety Disorder/Functional Neurological Symptom Disorder (Conversion Disorder)/Psychological Factors Affecting Other Medical Conditions/Factitious Disorder/Other Specified Somatic Symptom and Related

Disorder/Unspecified Somatic Symptom and Related Disorder

Feeding and Eating Disorders

Pica/Rumination Disorder/Avoidant/Restrictive Food Intake Disorder/Anorexia Nervosa/Bulimia Nervosa/Binge-Eating Disorder/Other Specified Feeding or Eating Disorder/Unspecified Feeding or Eating Disorder

Elimination Disorders

Enuresis/Encopresis/Other Specified Elimination Disorder/Unspecified Elimination Disorder

Sleep-Wake Disorders

Insomnia Disorder/Hypersomnolence Disorder/Narcolepsy

Breathing-Related Sleep Disorders

Obstructive Sleep Apnea Hypopnea/Central Sleep Apnea/Sleep-Related Hypoventilation/Circadian Rhythm Sleep-Wake Disorders

Parasomnias

Non-Rapid Eye Movement Sleep Arousal Disorders/Nightmare Disorder/Rapid Eye Movement Sleep Behavior Disorder/Restless Legs Syndrome/Substance/Medication-Induced Sleep Disorder/Other Specified Insomnia Disorder/Unspecified Insomnia Disorder/Other Specified Hypersomnolence Disorder/Unspecified Hypersomnolence Disorder/Other Specified Sleep-Wake Disorder/Unspecified Sleep-Wake Disorder

Sexual Dysfunctions

Delayed Ejaculation/Erectile Disorder/Female Orgasmic Disorder/Female Sexual Interest/Arousal Disorder/Genito-Pelvic Pain/Penetration Disorder/Male Hypoactive Sexual Desire Disorder/Premature (Early) Ejaculation/Substance/Medication-Induced Sexual Dysfunction/Other Specified Sexual Dysfunction/Unspecified Sexual Dysfunction

Gender Dysphoria

Gender Dysphoria/Other Specified Gender Dysphoria/Unspecified Gender Dysphoria

Disruptive, Impulse-Control, and Conduct Disorders

Oppositional Defiant Disorder/Intermittent Explosive Disorder/Conduct Disorder/Antisocial Personality Disorder/Pyromania/Kleptomania/Other Specified Disruptive, Impulse-Control, and Conduct Disorder/Unspecified Disruptive, Impulse-Control, and Conduct Disorder

Substance-Related and Addictive Disorders

Substance-Related Disorders

Alcohol-Related Disorders: Alcohol Use Disorder/Alcohol Intoxication/Alcohol Withdrawal/Alcohol-Induced Mental Disorders/Unspecified Alcohol-Related Disorder

Caffeine-Related Disorders: Caffeine Intoxication/Caffeine Withdrawal/Caffeine-Induced Mental Disorders/Unspecified Caffeine-Related Disorder

Cannabis-Related Disorders: Cannabis Use Disorder/Cannabis Intoxication/Cannabis Withdrawal/Cannabis-Induced Mental Disorders/Unspecified Cannabis-Related Disorder

Hallucinogen-Related Disorders: Phencyclidine Use Disorders/Other Hallucinogen Use Disorder/Phencyclidine Intoxication/Other Hallucinogen Intoxication/Hallucinogen Persisting Perception Disorder/Phencyclidine-Induced Mental Disorders/Hallucinogen-Induced Mental Disorders/Unspecified Phencyclidine-Related Disorder/Unspecified Hallucinogen-Related Disorder

Inhalant-Related Disorders: Inhalant Use Disorder/Inhalant Intoxication/Inhalant-Induced Mental Disorders/Unspecified Inhalant-Related Disorder

Opioid-Related Disorders: Opioid Use Disorder/Opioid Intoxication/Opioid Withdrawal/Opioid-Induced Mental Disorders/Unspecified Opioid-Related Disorder

Sedative-, Hypnotic-, or Anxiolytic-Related Disorders: Sedative, Hypnotic, or Anxiolytic Use Disorder/Sedative, Hypnotic, or Anxiolytic Intoxication/Sedative, Hypnotic, or Anxiolytic Withdrawal/Sedative-, Hypnotic-, or Anxiolytic-Induced Mental Disorders/Unspecified Sedative-, Hypnotic-, or Anxiolytic-Related Disorder

Stimulant-Related Disorders: Stimulant Use Disorder/Stimulant Intoxication/Stimulant Withdrawal/Stimulant-Induced Mental Disorders/Unspecified Stimulant-Related Disorder

Tobacco-Related Disorders: Tobacco Use Disorder/Tobacco Withdrawal/Tobacco-Induced Mental Disorders/Unspecified Tobacco-Related Disorder

Other (or Unknown) Substance-Related Disorders: Other (or Unknown) Substance Use Disorder/Other (or Unknown) Substance Intoxication/Other (or Unknown) Substance Withdrawal/Other (or Unknown) Substance-Induced Mental Disorders/Unspecified Other (or Unknown) Substance-Related Disorder

Non-Substance-Related Disorders

Gambling Disorder

Neurocognitive Disorders

Delirium

Major and Mild Neurocognitive Disorders

Major or Mild Neurocognitive Disorder Due to Alzheimer's Disease

Major or Mild Frontotemporal Neurocognitive Disorder

Major or Mild Neurocognitive Disorder with Lewy Bodies

Major or Mild Vascular Neurocognitive Disorder

Major or Mild Neurocognitive Disorder Due to Traumatic Brain Injury

Substance/Medication-Induced Major or Mild Neurocognitive Disorder

Major or Mild Neurocognitive Disorder Due to HIV Infection

Major or Mild Neurocognitive Disorder Due to Prion Disease

Major or Mild Neurocognitive Disorder Due to Parkinson's Disease

Major or Mild Neurocognitive Disorder Due to Huntington's Disease

Major or Mild Neurocognitive Disorder Due to Another Medical Condition
Major and Mild Neurocognitive Disorders Due to Multiple Etiologies
Unspecified Neurocognitive Disorder

Personality Disorders

Cluster A Personality Disorders

Paranoid Personality Disorder/Schizoid Personality Disorder/Schizotypal Personality Disorder

Cluster B Personality Disorders

Antisocial Personality Disorder/Borderline Personality Disorder/Histrionic Personality Disorder/Narcissistic Personality Disorder

Cluster C Personality Disorders

Avoidant Personality Disorder/Dependent Personality Disorder/Obsessive-Compulsive Personality Disorder

Other Personality Disorders

Personality Change Due to Another Medical Condition/Other Specified Personality Disorder/Unspecified Personality Disorder

Paraphilic Disorders

Voyeuristic Disorder/Exhibitionist Disorder/Frotteuristic Disorder/Sexual Masochism Disorder/Sexual Sadism Disorder/Pedophilic Disorder/Fetishistic Disorder/Transvestic Disorder/Other Specified Paraphilic Disorder/Unspecified Paraphilic Disorder

Other Mental Disorders and Additional Codes

Other Specified Mental Disorder Due to Another Medical Condition/Unspecified Mental Disorder Due to Another Medical Condition/Other Specified Mental Disorder/Unspecified Mental Disorder/No diagnosis or condition

Medication-Induced Movement Disorders and Other Adverse Effects of Medication

Neuroleptic-Induced Parkinsonism/Neuroleptic Malignant Syndrome/Medication-Induced Acute Dystonia/Medication-Induced Acute Akathisia/Tardive Dyskinesia/Tardive Dystonia/Tardive Akathisia/Medication-Induced Postural Tremor/Other Medication-Induced Movement Disorder/Antidepressant Discontinuation Syndrome/Other Adverse Effect of Medication

Other Conditions That May Be a Focus of Clinical Attention

Suicidal Behavior and Nonsuicidal Self-Injury

Abuse and Neglect

Child Physical Abuse/Child Sexual Abuse/Child Neglect/Child Psychological Abuse/Spouse or Partner Violence, Physical/Spouse or Partner Violence, Sexual/Spouse or Partner Neglect/Spouse or Partner Abuse, Psychological/Adult Abuse by Nonspouse or Nonpartner

Relational Problems

Educational Problems

Occupational Problems

Housing Problems

Economic Problems

Problems Related to the Social Environment

Problems Related to Interaction with the Legal System

Problems Related to Other Psychosocial, Personal, and Environmental Circumstances

Problems Related to Access to Medical and Other Health Care

Circumstances of Personal History

Other Health Service Encounters for Counseling and Medical Advice

Additional Conditions or Problems That May Be a Focus of Clinical Attention